THE ESSENTIAL CROSSWORD DICTIONARY

THE ESSENTIAL CROSSWORD DICTIONARY

COMPILED AND EDITED BY KATHLEEN RAFFERTY
REVISED AND UPDATED BY MARGARET S. DOHERTY
EDITORIAL CONSULTANT, ROSALIND MOORE

Originally titled *The Dell Crossword Dictionary*

WINGS BOOKS
New York • Avenel, New Jersey

Originally titled *The Dell Crossword Dictionary*

This 1995 edition is published by Wings Books,
distributed by Random House Value Publishing, Inc.,
40 Engelhard Avenue, Avenel, New Jersey 07001,
by arrangement with Dell Publishing, a division of
Bantam Doubleday Dell Publishing Group, Inc.

Random House
New York • Toronto • London • Sydney • Auckland

Printed and bound in the United States of America

Library of Congress Cataloging–in–Publication Data
Rafferty, Kathleen.
[Dell crossword dictionary]
The essential crossword dictionary / compiled and edited by Kathleen Rafferty ; editorial consultant, Rosalind Moore. -- Rev. and updated / by Margaret S. Doherty.
p. cm.
Originally published: The Dell crossword dictionary. New York : Dell Pub. Co., c1984. With new introd.
ISBN 0-517-12437-8
1. Crossword puzzles--Glossaries, vocabularies, etc. I. Doherty, Margaret S. II. Title.
GV1507.C7R27 1995
793.73'2'03--dc20 94-46604
CIP

8 7 6 5 4 3 2 1

ABOUT THIS BOOK . . .

Looking for an "Assam silkworm"? Can't find a "Brazilian coin"? Don't know a "candlenut tree"? They're easily found —with the aid of this book.

The purpose of this dictionary is to give puzzlers the pleasure of COMPLETING, down to the last two-letter word, every crossword that they begin. It is meant to eliminate the frustration of filling in "all but a few" of those final puzzle squares. Here, in a handy, easy-to-use format, is a complete 432-page reference book, including the exclusive cross-referenced Word-Finder, where puzzle solvers can find all those little-known, but much-used, crossword words.

We believe this book is the most useful book ever published for crossword solvers. It is the outgrowth of many years of exhaustive research and was prepared by Kathleen Rafferty who was, for many years, editor-in-chief of the Dell crossword magazines and books.

ABOUT THIS EDITION

Many of the words and definitions used in crosswords remain the same today as when this dictionary was first compiled. However, new words have come into our language since that time, and today's crosswords utilize these words. Since such words, in the main, are in specialized areas, this edition has been expanded by adding to the Special Section, instead of including additional words and definitions in the general section. This arrangement of the new information will make it easier for you to find the words you need to complete your puzzles!

In this edition, the Special Section now includes such listings as Computer Terminology, Aerospace, and Acronyms and Abbreviations. Though not new to the language, sections on Music and Sports, among others, have also been added. Both the Gazetteer and the First and Last Names sections have been completely revised and updated. You will undoubtedly find the all-new Celebrities' Original Names section entertaining, as well as a handy reference.

These new additions have been compiled from material I have gathered, both as solver and editor, over the past twelve years. The lists are in no way meant to be all-inclusive; they are not intended as exhaustive reference works, but as invaluable puzzle-solving aids.

Margaret S. Doherty

TABLE OF CONTENTS

DEFINITIONS SECTION 5

All the important crossword puzzle words are listed alphabetically by definition.

Look under group headings for these special word listings:

SPECIAL SECTION
READY REFERENCE WORD LISTS

Every essential two-, three-, and four-letter word in the English language. Cross-referenced to the Definitions section for utmost aid to solving. You can complete unfinished puzzle words with this section.

ABBREVIATIONS USED IN THIS BOOK

abbr.	abbreviation
Abyssin.	Abyssinia(n)
Afgh.	Afghanistan
Afr.	Africa(n)
Am.	American
Arab.	Arabia(n)
Arch.	Architecture
A.-S.	Anglo-Saxon
Austr.	Austria(n)
Austral.	Australia(n)
Babyl.	Babylonian
Bibl.	Biblical
biol.	biology
bot.	botany; botanical
Braz.	Brazil(ian)
Cent. Am.	Central America(n)
Chin.	Chinese
comb. form	combining form
Dan.	Danish
Du.	Dutch
Du. E. Ind.	Dutch East Indies
E.	East
Egyp.	Egypt(ian)
E. Ind.	East Indies
Eng.	England; English
Eur., Europ.	Europe(an)
fort.	fortification
Fr.	France; French
geol.	geology; geological
geom.	geometry
Ger.	German(y)
Goth.	Gothic
govt.	government
Gr.	Greek
Hebr.	Hebrew
Her.	heraldry
Himal.	Himalayan
Holl.	Holland
Ind.	India(n)
Indo-Chin.	Indo-Chinese
Ir.	Ireland; Irish
Is.	Island
Ital.	Italian; Italy
Jap.	Japan(ese)
Lat.	Latin
math.	mathematics
med.	medical
Medit.	Mediterranean
Mex.	Mexican; Mexico
milit.	military
Min.	Minor
mus.	music; musical
myth.	mythological; mythology
N., No.	North
naut.	nautical
N. Hebr.	New Hebrides
N. T.	New Testament
N. Z.	New Zealand
Nor.	Norway; Norwegian
O. Eng.	Old English
P. I.	Philippine Islands
P. R.	Puerto Rico
Pacif.	Pacific
Pers.	Persian
pert.	pertaining
pharm.	pharmacy
philos.	philosophical
poet.	poetry
Polyn.	Polynesia(n)
Port.	Portugal; Portuguese
Pruss.	Prussian
R. C.	Roman Catholic
Rom.	Roman
Russ.	Russian
S.	South
S. Afr.	South Africa(n)
Scot.	Scottish
Sp.	Spanish
Teut.	Teutonic
Turk.	Turkey; Turkish
W.	West
W. Ind.	West Indian
WW	World War
zool.	zoology

DEFINITIONS SECTION

CROSSWORD DEFINITIONS AND ANSWERS

HOW TO USE THIS SECTION:

Here are crossword DEFINITIONS, arranged alphabetically.

Look up the DEFINITION of a crossword word, and you will find, in bold-face type, the word you want.

There are two kinds of crossword definitions. One is the almost unvarying definition: "Bitter vetch" or "Vetch" is used to define ERS. If you look in this dictionary under "B" for "bitter vetch" or under "V" for "vetch" you will find it there.

The other kind of definition, far more common, is the more varied definition where the puzzle-maker can choose from among many descriptive words when he defines a puzzle word: "India nurse," "Oriental nurse," "Oriental maid," "Oriental nursemaid" are all used in crossword puzzles as definitions for AMAH. For efficiency's sake, crossword words with varying definitions are listed here under the ESSENTIAL definition word. In the case of AMAH, the listing is under "nurse," "maid," and "nursemaid".

So, if you don't find your wanted word under the first word of the definition given, look for it under the other words of the definition.

The length of a word is important to crossword solvers, and so, when a definition fits two or more words the words are arranged according to length. For example: adage **.... SAW, MAXIM, PROVERB.**

Remember to use also the efficiently-arranged reference word lists in the SPECIAL SECTION, beginning on page 187.

A

a Aaron's brother .... **MOSES**
Aaron's sister .... **MIRIAM**
Aaron's miracle worker ... **ROD**
Aaron's son, oldest .... **NADAB**
abaca .... **LINAGA**
abaca, top-quality ..... **LUPIS**
Abadan's land .... **IRAN**
abalone shell money **ULLO, UHLLO**
abandon **MAROON, DISCARD**
abandoned .... **DERELICT**
abate .... **EBB, LESSEN**
abatement .... **LETUP**
abbess .... **AMMA**
abbey: Sp. .... **ABADIA**
abbot: Lat. .... **ABBAS**
abbreviations **PTA, SRO, NATO** (1949 pact)
abdominal .... **VENTRAL**
Abel's brother .... **CAIN**
abhor **HATE, DETEST, LOATHE**
Abie's girl .... **ROSE**
Abijah's son .... **ASA**
ability ...... **POWER, TALENT**
abject .... **BASE**
b abode, blissful .... **EDEN**
abode of dead .. **HADES, SHEOL**
abode of dead: Egypt. **AALU, AARU**
abound .... **TEEM**
abounding .... **RIFE**
about .. **OF, RE, ANENT, CIRCA**
about: Lat. .... **CIRCITER**
above ..... **O'ER, OVER, UPON**
abrade .... **RUB, CHAFE**
Abraham's birthplace ..... **UR**
Abraham's brother **HARAN, NAHOR**
Abraham's father ..... **TERAH**
Abraham's nephew .... **LOT**
Abraham's son **ISAAC, ISHMAEL**
Abraham's wife . **SARAH, SARAI**
abrasive .... **EMERY**
abrogate .... **ANNUL**
abrupt flexure .... **GENU**
Absalom's cousin ..... **AMASA**
Absalom's sister ...... **TAMAR**
abscond ...... **ELOPE, LEVANT**
absence, license for .... **EXEAT**
absent ..... **OFF, OUT, AWAY, GONE**
absolute .... **UTTER, PLENARY**
absolve sins .... **SHRIVE**

c absorbed .... **RAPT**
abstruse .... **ESOTERIC**
abundance, in .... **GALORE**
abundant .... **RIFE, AMPLE**
abuse: India .... **GALI, GALEE**
abuse ... **VIOLATE, MISTREAT**
abusive, be .... **REVILE**
abusive charges .... **MUD**
abut .... **ADJOIN, BORDER**
abyss .... **GULF, HOLE, CHASM**
Abyssinian ..... **KAFA, KAFFA**
Abyssin. fly .... **ZIMB**
Abyssin. grain .... **TEFF**
Abyssin. Hamite . **AFAR, AGAO, BEJA, AFARA**
Abyssin. language ...... **SAHO**
Abyssin. mountain wolf **KABERU**
Abyssin. ruler's title ... **NEGUS**
Abyssin. ox .. **GALLA, SANGA, SANGU**
Abyssin. Semitic dialect **GEEZ, GHESE**
Abyssin. tree ....**KOSO**
Abyssin. tribesman ..... **SHOA**
Abyssin. vizier .... **RAS**
accent .... **TONE**
accent, Irish .. **BLAS, BROGUE**
d access .... **ENTREE**
accommodate .... **LEND**
"— accompli" .... **FAIT**
according to . **ALA, AUX, ALLA**
accost .... **HAIL, GREET**
account entry ...**ITEM, DEBIT, CREDIT**
accumulate .... **AMASS, HOARD, ACCRUE**
accumulation .... **FUND**
accustomed ..... **USED, WONT, ENURED**
acetic acid ester .... **ACETATE**
acetone derivative ... **ACETOL**
acetylene .... **ETHIN, ETHINE**
Achilles' adviser ...... **NESTOR**
Achilles' father .... **PELEUS**
Achilles' mother ...... **THETIS**
Achilles' slayer .... **PARIS**
acid, kind of .. **AMINO, BORIC**
acid radical .... **ACYL, ACETYL**
acidity .... **ACOR**
acknowledge .... **OWN**
acknowledge frankly .. **AVOW**
acorns, dried .... **CAMATA**
acoustics apparatus ... **SIRENE**
acquainted .... **VERSANT**
acquiesce .... **ASSENT**

a acquiesce, fully ..... **ACCEDE**
acquire .... **WIN, GAIN, REAP**
acrobat of India .... **NAT**
Acropolis of Thebes .. **CADMEA**
across: comb. form **TRAN, TRANS**
acrostic, Hebrew .... **AGLA**
act ...... **DEED, FEAT, EMOTE**
act: Lat. ...... **ACTU, ACTUS**
action, put into .... **ACTUATE**
action word .... **VERB**
active ... **SPRY, AGILE, BRISK, LIVELY, NIMBLE**
actor .... **HISTRIO, HISTRION**
actor's group .... **TROUPE**
actor's hint .... **CUE**
actor's valet .... **DRESSER**
actual .... **REAL, TRUE**
actual being .... **ESSE**
actuality .... **FACT**
adage .... **SAW, MAXIM, PROVERB**
Adam's ale .... **WATER**
Adam's 1st mate: legend **LILITH**
Adam's grandson .... **ENOS**
Adam's son . **ABEL, CAIN, SETH**
adapt .... **FIT**
adept .... **ACE**
add on .... **AFFIX, ANNEX,**
b **ATTACH**
adder, common .... **ASP**
additions .... **ADDENDA**
addition, bill's .... **RIDER**
adequate .... **DUE, FULL, AMPLE, EQUAL**
adhere .... **CLING, STICK, CLEAVE**
adherent .... **IST**
adhesive .. **GUM, GLUE, PASTE**
ADJECTIVE ENDING, see SUFFIX, ADJECTIVE
adjust ...... **FIX, SET, ADAPT, ATTUNE, ORIENT**
adjutant ....**AIDE**
adjutant bird .... **ARGALA, HURGILA, MARABOU**
admonish .... **WARN, EXHORT, REPROVE**
admonisher .... **MONITOR**
adolescence .... **TEENS, YOUTH, NONAGE**
adopted son of Mohammed . **ALI**
Adriana's servant ...... **LUCE**
adroit ...... **READY, HABILE, SKILLFUL**
adulterate .. **DEBASE, DEFILE, DENATURE**
advance guard .... **VAN**
advantage .... **USE, GAIN, PROFIT, BENEFIT**

c adventitious lung sound .. **RALE**
adventure ...... **GEST, GESTE**
adviser, woman ...... **EGERIA**
Aeëtes' daughter ..... **MEDEA**
Aegir's wife .... **RAN**
Aeneas' wife .... **CREUSA**
Aeneid author **VERGIL, VIRGIL**
Aesir ... **TIU, TYR, ULL, FREY, LOKE, LOKI, ODIN, THOR, VALE, VALI, DONAR, FREYA, BRAGI, WODEN, BALDER**
affectionate ... **FOND, WARM, LOVING, TENDER**
affirm .. **AVER, POSIT, ASSERT**
affirmative .... **AY, AYE, YEA, YES**
affirmative vote .... **AY, AYE, YEA, YES**
afflict ...... **TRY, VEX, PAIN, DISTRESS**
affluence ...... **EASE, RICHES, WEALTH**
affray .... **BRAWL, FIGHT, MELEE**
Afghan prince .. **AMIR, AMEER**
Afghan title .... **KHAN**
afresh .... **ANEW**
d afraid: obsolete .... **REDDE**
AFRICAN .... see also SOUTH AFRICAN and AFRICAN in SPECIAL SECTION
AFRICAN ANTELOPE see ANTELOPE
Afr. bass .... **IYO**
Afr. bustard .... **KORI**
Afr. cotton garment .... **TOBE**
Afr. disease .... **NENTA**
Afr. worm .... **LOA**
Afr. grass, millet-like .. **FUNDI**
Afr. hornbill .... **TOCK**
Afr. plant .... **ALOE**
Afr. scrub .... **BITO**
Afr. soldier .... **ASKARI**
Afr. squirrel .... **XERUS**
Afr. stockade .... **BOMA**
Afr. tableland .... **KAROO**
Afrikaans ...... **TAAL, BOERS**
aft .... **ABAFT, ASTERN**
after awhile .... **ANON**
aftermath .... **ROWEN**
afterpart of ship's keel **SKAG, SKEG**
afterpiece, comic ..... **EXODE**
aftersong .... **EPODE**
again .... **ENCORE**
against .... **CON, ANTI, CONTRA, VERSUS**
agalloch wood .. **AGAR, ALOE, GAROO**
Agamemnon's son .... **ORESTES**

a agate stone .... **ACHATE**
age .... **EON, ERA, AERA, RIPEN, PERIOD**
aged .... **OLD, ANILE, SENILE**
agave fiber .... **ISTLE**
agency, depression-era .. **N R A**
agency, govt. ... **E C A, F H A**
agency, wage, price .... **E S A**
agency, ration-book .... **O P A**
agency, World-War II .. **O P A**
agent .... **DOER, FACTOR, FACIENT**
agents acted through .. **MEDIA**
aggregate . **SUM, MASS, TOTAL**
agitate .... **STIR**
agitation ...... **STIR, DITHER, TUMULT**
agitation, be in state of **SEETHE**
agnomen .... **NAME**
agree ..... **GIBE, JIBE, TALLY, ASSENT, CONCUR**
agreeable: old Eng. ... **AMENE**
agreeableness of letters **EUTONY**
agreement ...... **MISE, PACT, CONCORD, ENTENTE**
agriculture goddess .... **CERES, VACUNA, DEMETER**
Agrippina's son .... **NERO**
Ahasuerus' minister .. **HAMAN**
b ahead . **ON, BEFORE, FORWARD**
Ahiam's father .... **SACAR**
aid ... **ABET, ASSIST, SUCCOR, FURTHER**
aim ...... **END, GOAL, ASPIRE**
aims, with the same ... **AKIN**
air .. **AER, ARIA, MIEN, TUNE**
air apparatus ...... **AERATOR**
air current, ascending **THERMAL**
air, fill with .... **AERATE**
air, fresh .... **OZONE**
air passage ...... **FLUE, VENT**
air spirit .... **SYLPH**
air, upper .... **ETHER, AETHER**
aircraft, motorless .... **GLIDER**
airplane .... **JET, AERO**
airplane: Fr. .... **AVION**
airport marker .... **PYLON**
airport, Paris .... **ORLY**
airship . **AERO, BLIMP, PLANE**
airy .... **LIGHT, ETHEREAL**
ait .... **ISLE**
Ajax, tale about ...... **MYTH**
Ajax's father ...... **TELAMON**
akin .... **SIB**
alang grass .... **LALANG**
alarm . **SCARE, SIREN, AROUSE**
alas! .. **ACH, HEU, OCH, OIME**
alas: Irish .. **OHONE, OCHONE**
alas: poetic .... **AY**
Alaska glacier .... **MUIR**

c **ALBANIAN** see COINS, TRIBES, GAZETTEER in SPECIAL SECTION
Albanian dialect .. **GEG, CHAM, GHEG, TOSK**
albatross, sooty ...... **NELLY**
alchitran .... **TAR, PITCH**
alcohol radical .... **AL**
alcohol, solid . **STERIN, STEROL**
alcoholic drink .... **GIN, RUM, RHUM**
Alcott heroine ...... **JO, AMY, MEG, BETH**
alcove .... **BOWER, RECESS**
alder tree: Scot .... **ARN**
ale mug .... **TOBY**
ale, sour .... **ALEGAR**
alewife fish .... **POMPANO**
ALEUTIAN see TRIBES, GAZETTEER in SPECIAL SECTION
Alexandrian theologian . **ARIUS**
Alexander victory **ISSUS, ARBELA**
alfalfa .... **LUCERN, LUCERNE**
Alfonso's queen .... **ENA**
alga .... **NORI**
alga, one-cell .... **DIATOM**
algae genus, fan-shaped **PADINA**
algarroba tree ...... **CALDEN**
d Algerian governor .... **DEY**
ALGERIA—see SPECIAL SECTION
ALGONQUIN .... see Page 192
Ali Baba's word ...... **SESAME**
Ali, caliph descendants **ALIDS**
Alien in Hebrew territory .. **GER**
alienate ... **WEAN, ESTRANGE**
align ... **TRUE, ALINE, RANGE**
alkali ..... **LYE, REH, USAR**
alkaline solution .... **LYE**
alkaloid .. **CAFFEIN, CAFFEINE**
alkaloid, calabar bean **ESERINE**
all: Lat. .... **TOTO**
all religions, believer in **OMNIST**
all right .... **OKAY, OKEH**
allanite .... **CERINE**
allay .... **CALM, ASSUAGE, RELIEVE**
alleged force .... **OD**
allegory, religious ... **PARABLE**
Allepo native .... **SYRIAN**
alleviate .... **EASE, ALLAY, LESSEN**
alley .... **MIB, MIG**
alliance ..... **UNION, LEAGUE**
alliance, Western ...... **NATO**
alligator .... **LAGARTO**

a alligator pear ..... **AVOCADO**
alligator, S.A. ...... **CAIMAN, CAYMAN**
allot .... **METE, GRANT, ASSIGN, PORTION**
allotment .... **QUOTA, RATION**
allow .... **LET**
allowance **TARE, TRET, RATION**
alloy .... **MOKUM, OROIDE**
alloy, aluminum ...... **DURAL**
alloy, copper .... **BRASS**
alloy, copper-tin ..... **BRONZE**
alloy, gold-silver: Egyp. . **ASEM**
alloy, lead-tin .. **CALIN, TERNE**
alloy, non-ferrous ...... **TULA**
alloy, yellow .... **AICH**
allspice .... **PIMENTO**
allure .... **TICE, TOLE, TEMPT, ENTICE**
allusion .... **HINT**
almond emulsion ..... **ORGEAT**
almost .... **ANEAR**
alms box or chest ...... **ARCA**
aloe .... **AGAVE**
aloe derivative .... **ALOIN**
aloes product .... **ALOIN**
alone, on stage .. **SOLA, SOLUS**
along .... **ON, BESIDE**
alp .... **PEAK**
b alpaca .... **PACO**
alphabet letter, old .... **RUNE**
Alps, Austro-It. **TIROL, TYROL, TIROLO**
Alps, one of .... **BLANC**
Alps pass .... **CENIS**
Alps, river rising in .. **RHONE**
Altar constellation ...... **ARA**
altar end of church .... **APSE**
altar screen .... **REREDOS**
altar shelf . **GRADIN, RETABLE**
altar side curtain .... **RIDDEL**
altar top .... **MENSA**
alternate .... **ROTATE**
alternative ...... **OR, EITHER**
alumni .... **GRADS**
always ... **AY, AYE, EER, EVER**
amadou .... **PUNK**
amass ...... **HOARD, GATHER**
amateur **TIRO, TYRO, NOVICE**
Amazon cetacean ...... **INIA**
Amazon tributary .. **APA, ICA**
ambary .... **DA**
ambary hemp ...... **NALITA**
ambassador .. **ENVOY, LEGATE**
amber fish **RUNNER, MEDREGAL**
Amen-Ra's wife .... **MUT**
amend **ALTER, EMEND, REVISE**
amendment, document . **RIDER**
amends, make .... **ATONE**
ament .... **CHAT**

c Am. artist ..... **WEST, HICKS, HOMER, MARIN, PEALE, BENTON, COPLEY, INNESS, CORBINO, ALBRIGHT**
AMERICAN INDIAN ...... see INDIANS, Page 192
Am. aloe fiber .... **PITA, PITO**
Am. author . **ADE, POE. AMES, BAUM, HARTE, WYLIE, YERBY, CORWIN, FERBER, HERSEY, KANTOR, MORLEY**
Am. author, illustrator ... **PYLE**
Am. capitalist .... **ASTOR**
Am. caricaturist .. **REA, NAST**
Am. dramatist . **AKINS, BARRY, ODETS, CROUSE**
Am. editor .... **BOK**
Am. educator .... **MANN**
Am. explorer . **BYRD, FREMONT**
Am. general **LEE, OTIS, GREENE**
Am. humorist ...... **ADE, NYE, COBB, NASH, ROGERS**
Am. jurist .... **TANEY**
Am. inventor ... **IVES, MORSE, TESLA, EDISON**
American: Mex. ..... **GRINGO**
Am. nature writer **BEEBE, SETON**
Am. nighthawk .... **PISK**
AM. PAINTER see AM. ARTIST
d Am. patriot ...... **HALE, OTIS, ALLEN, REVERE**
Am. philanthropist ...... **RIIS**
Am. philosopher ..... **EDMAN**
Am. pianist **ARRAU, DUCHIN, LEVANT**
Am. poet . **POE, AUDEN, BENET, FROST, GUEST, RILEY, STEIN, MILLAY**
Am. poetess ... **STEIN, LOWELL**
Am. sculptor .... **CALDER**
AM. SINGER ... see SOPRANO
Am. statesman **CLAY, BARUCH, DULLES**
Am. suffragist .... **CATT**
Am. surgeon .... **PARRAN**
AM. WRITER see AM. AUTHOR
AMERIND (means any American Indian) See pages 192, 193
amide, pert. to .... **AMIC**
a mine: Corn. .... **BAL**
ammonia compound .. **AMIN, AMIDE, AMINE**
ammoniac plant ...... **OSHAC**
ammunition . **SHOT, SHRAPNEL**
ammunition, short for: . **AMMO, AMMU**
ammunition wagon ... **CAISSON**
among ...... **IN, MID, AMID**
amorously, stare .. **LEER, OGLE**
amount assessed ...... **RATAL**

a amount staked in gambling **MISE**
amuse .... **DIVERT**
ampere................ **WEBER**
amphibian .... **FROG, TOAD, ANURAN**
amphibian, order **HYLA, ANURA**
amphitheater .... **ARENA**
amphitheater, natural ... **CIRQUE**
amplification factor......... **MU**
amulet ..... **CHARM, PERIAPT**
analyze...... **ASSAY, DISSECT**
analyze grammatically ... **PARSE**
ancestor of Irish .. **IR, ITH, MIL, MILED**
ancestor of man, Hindu .. **MANU**
ancestral spirit, P. I....... **ANITO**
ancestral .... **AVITAL**
ancestral spirits **LARES, MANES**
anchor **FIX, TIE, MOOR, KEDGE**
anchor part............. **FLUKE**
anchor, small, light ..... **KEDGE**
anchor tackle .... **CAT**
ancient Asiatic .... **MEDE**
ancient Briton............ **CELT**
ancient Chinese......... **SERES**
anchovy sauce........... **ALEC**
ancient city, Asia Minor .. **MYRA, NICAEA**
ancient country .... **GAUL**
Ancient Egyp. kingdom **SENNAR**
ancient flute .... **TIBIA**
ancient Greece division **AETOLIA**
ancient invader, India .... **SAKA, SACAE**
b ancient people of Gaul .... **REMI**
ancient Persian .... **MEDE**
ancient Persian money... **DARIC**
ancient philosophy ...... **YOGA**
ancient race .... **MEDES**
ancient Slav ..... **VEND, WEND, VENED**
ancient times ...... **ELD, YORE**
ancient tribe of Britons ... **ICENI**
ancient weight .... **MINA**
and .. **TOO, ALSO, PLUS, WITH**
and: Lat.................... **ET**
and not .... **NOR**
and so on: abbr........... **ETC.**
Andes cold higher region . **PUNA**
Andes grass .... **ICHU**
Andes mountain....... **SORATA**
andiron.................. **DOG**
"Andronicus,—"......... **TITUS**
anecdotage or anecdotes . **ANA, TALES**
anent .... **RE, ABOUT, BESIDE**
anent, close— .... **TO**
anesthetic .... **GAS, ETHER**
Angel of Death........ **AZRAEL**
angel, Pers................ **MAH**

c anger .... **IRE, RAGE, RILE, CHOLER**
anger, fit of... **PIQUE, TEMPER**
angle, 57 degrees..... **RADIAN**
angle of leaf and axis...... **AXIL**
angle of leafstalk.......... **AXIL**
angle of stem, pert. to... **AXILE**
Anglo-Saxon "G" ... **YOK, YOGH**
A.–S. god of peace .... **ING**
A.–S. lord's man **THANE, THEGN**
A.–S. king .... **INE**
A.–S. money (coin) .... **ORA**
A.–S. slave .... **ESNE**
A.–S. warrior... **THANE, THEGN**
Angora goat .... **CHAMAL**
angry .... **HOT, MAD, SORE, IRATE**
animal, Afr..... **CIVET, GENET, POTTO, ZEBRA, GENETTE**
animal, ant-eating .... **ECHIDNA**
animal, aquatic.. **SEAL, OTTER, WHALE, DUGONG, WALRUS, MANATEE**
animal, arboreal...... **TARSIER**
animal, Austral....... **ECHIDNA**
animal, badgerlike, Java **TELEDU**
animal body .... **SOMA**
animal, draft........ **OX, OXEN**
d animal, fabulous...... **DRAGON**
animal, giraffelike .... **OKAPI**
animal, India .... **DHOLE**
animal, Madagascar .... **FOSSA, FOUSSA**
animals of area .... **FAUNA**
animal-plant life .... **BIOTA**
animal, Peru .... **ALPACA**
animal, sea ..... **SEAL, CORAL, WHALE, WALRUS, DUGONG, MANATEE**
animal, S. Afr. .... **ZORIL**
animal, S. Am. . **APARA, COATI**
animal trail . **RUN, SLOT, SPUR, SPOOR**
animating principle .... **SOUL**
ankle.. **TALUS, TARSI, TARSUS**
ankle, pert. to......... **TARSAL**
Annamese measure .... **TAO**
Annapolis student **PLEB, PLEBE**
annatto seeds: Sp. ... **ACHIOTE**
anneal ... **TEMPER, TOUGHEN**
annex .... **ADD, ELL, WING, ATTACH**
annihilate........... **DESTROY, DISCREATE**
ANNIVERSARY .. see WEDDING
announce............ **HERALD**
annoy ... **IRK, TRY, VEX, RILE, PEEVE, TEASE, BOTHER, MOLEST, PESTER, DISTURB**

a annual, as winds .... **ETESIAN**
annuity, form of .... **TONTINE**
annul .... **UNDO, VOID, CANCEL, REVOKE**
annular die .... **DOD**
annulet: Her. .... **VIRE**
anoint ... **OIL, ANELE, ENELE**
another ... **NEW, ADDITIONAL**
ant .... **EMMET, PISMIRE**
antarctic bird ...... **PENGUIN**
antarctic icebreaker .... **ATKA**
antecedent . **PRIOR, ANCESTOR**
antelope, Afr. .... **GNU, KOB, BISA, GUIB, KOBA, KUDU, ORYX, POKU, PUKU, TORA, ADDAX, ELAND, ORIBI, RHEBOK**
antelope, Afr., large .. **IMPALA**
antelope, Afr., small .. **DUIKER**
antelope, Ind. **SASIN, NILGAI, NILGAU**
antelope, Siberian ..... **SAIGA**
antelope, tawny .... **ORIBI**
antenna **HORN, PALP, AERIAL FEELER**
antenna, with nodose **NODICORN**
anthracite, inferior ..... **CULM**
anti-aircraft shells ..... **FLAK**
anti-tank gun .... **PIAT**
b antic ... **DIDO, CAPER, PRANK**
antique red color .. **CHAUDRON**
antiseptic .... **EUPAD, EUSOL, IODIN, SALOL, CRESOL, IODINE**
antiseptic, mercury **EGOL, METAPHEN**
antitoxin ...... **SERA, SERUM**
antler point .... **SNAG, TINE, PRONG**
antler, unbranched ...... **DAG**
antlers, stag's .... **ATTIRE**
"Anthony and Cleopatra" character .... **IRAS**
anvil .... **INCUS, TEEST**
anxiety .... **CARE**
any: dialect .... **ONI**
any one .... **AN**
aoudad .... **ARUI**
apathy ... **ENNUI, DOLDRUMS**
ape .... **ORANG**
ape, long-tailed, India ... **KRA**
appelation ..... **NAME, TITLE**
APERTURE . see also OPENING
aperture .... **GAP, HOLE, SLOT, VENT, ORIFICE**
apex, at the .... **APICAL**
aphasia, motor .... **ALALIA**
aphorism .. **SAW, RULE, SUTRA**
Aphrodite .... **VENUS**
c Aphrodite, got apple from **PARIS**
Aphrodite, love of ... **ADONIS**
Aphrodite's mother .... **DIONE**
Aphrodite's son .... **EROS**
apocopate .... **ELIDE**
Apocrypha, book from . **ESDRAS**
Apollo's instrument ..... **BOW, LUTE, LYRE**
Apollo's mother **LETO, LATONA**
Apollo's sister **DIANA, ARTEMIS**
Apollo's son .... **ION**
Apollo's twin .... **ARTEMIS**
Apollo's vale, sacred ... **TEMPE**
apoplexy, plant .... **ESCA**
Apostle (12) .... **JOHN, JUDE (THADDEUS), JAMES, JUDAS, PETER (SIMON PETER), SIMON, ANDREW, PHILIP, THOMAS (DIDYMUS), MATTHEW (LEVI), MATTHIAS, BARTHOLOMEW**
Apostle, Capernaum **MATTHEW**
Apostles, teaching of . **DIDACHE**
apparent ..... **OVERT, PLAIN, EVIDENT**
apparition .. **SPECTER, SPECTRE**
appear .... **LOOK, LOOM, SEEM**
appearance . **AIR, MIEN, GUISE**
d appease ...... **CALM, ALLAY PLACATE**
appellation ..... **NAME, TITLE**
append .... **ADD, AFFIX, ATTACH**
appendage, caudal ... ...**TAIL**
appetizer . **CANAPE, APERITIF**
apple ... **POME, TREE, FRUIT, PIPPIN**
apple acid .... **MALIC**
apple seed .... **PIP**
apple tree .... **SORB**
apple tree genus ...... **MALUS**
apple, winter .... **ESOPUS**
apples, crushed .... **POMACE**
apple-like fruit .... **POME**
appoint .. **SET, NAME, CHOOSE**
apportion **DEAL, METE, ALLOT**
appraise **RATE, VALUE, ASSESS**
apprise ...... **ADVISE, NOTIFY**
approach ...... **NEAR, ANEAR, ACCESS**
appropriate, ... **APT, FIT, MEET**
appropriate, not **INAPT, UNFIT**
apricot, Jap. .... **UME**
apricot, Korean . **ANSU, ANZU**
apricots .... **MEBOS**
apropos .... **PAT, FITTING**
apteryx .... **KIWI**
aptitude ..... **FLAIR, ABILITY**

a aptitude, natural **FLAIR, TALENT**
aquamarine .... **BERYL**
AQUATIC . see SEA or MARINE
Arab ....**GAMIN, SEMITE**
Arab cloak, sleeveless .... **ABA**
Arab drink ...... **BOSA, BOZA, BOZAH**
Arab name .... **ALI**
Arab's state of bliss ..... **KEF**
Arabia, people of ..... **OMANI**
ARABIAN . see ARAB, ARABIA, SPECIAL SECTION
Arabian chief . **SAYID, SAYYID**
Arabian chieftain **AMIR, EMIR, AMEER, EMEER**
Arabian chieftain's domain **EMIRATE**
Arabian cloth .... **ABA**
Arabian district .... **TEMA**
Arabian garment .... **ABA**
Arabian jasmine .... **BELA**
Arabian judge .... **CADI**
"Arabian Nights" dervish . **AGIB**
Arabian noble .. **AMIR, EMIR, AMEER, EMEER**
Arabian nomadic tribesman **SLEB**
Arabian sailboat .. see VESSEL, ARAB
Arabian sleeveless garment **ABA**
b Arabian tambourine **TAAR, DAIRA, DAIRE**
Arabic jinni, evil **AFRIT, AFREET, AFRITE**
Arabic letter . **GAF, KAF, MIM, WAW, ALIF, DHAL**
Arabic script .... **NESKI**
Arabic surname .... **SAAD**
arachnid . **MITE, TICK, SPIDER**
Arawakan language .... **TAINO**
arbitrator ... **UMPIRE, REFEREE**
arboreal .... **DENDRAL**
arc .... **LINE, CURVE**
arch of heaven .... **COPE**
arch, pointed .... **OGIVE**
archaeology, mound ..... **TERP**
archangel .... **URIEL**
archbishop .... **PRIMATE**
archbishop, Canterbury **BECKET**
archer in Eng. ballad **CLIM, CLYM**
archetype ... **MODEL, PATTERN**
archfiend .... **SATAN**
architect's drawing ..... **EPURE**
architecture, school of **BAUHAUS**
architecture, type **DORIC, IONIC**
ARCTIC ..... see GAZETTEER
Arctic . **NORTH, POLAR, FRIGID**

c arctic air force base .... **THULE**
arctic dog .... **SAMOYED**
arctic gull genus ...... **XEMA**
arctic plain .... **TUNDRA**
Arden .... **FOREST**
ardor ... **ELAN, ZEAL, FERVOR**
area measure .. **RADII, RADIUS**
area, small .... **AREOLA**
areca .... **BETEL**
arena .... **FIELD**
Ares' mother .... **ENYO**
Ares' sister .... **ERIS**
ares, 10 .... **DECARE**
Argonaut ... **JASON, ACASTUS**
Argonauts' leader ...... **JASON**
Argonauts' ship .... **ARGO**
argument .... **AGON, DEBATE, HASSLE**
arhat .... **LOHAN**
aria ...... **AIR, SOLO, SONG, TUNE, MELODY**
arias .... **SOLI**
aridity, having .... **XERIC**
arikara .... **REE**
arise .... **REBEL, ACCRUE, APPEAR**
arista .... **AWN**
Arizona aborigine ...... **HOPI**
ARIZONA INDIAN see page 192
d **ARIZONA** ... see also SPECIAL SECTION
Ark, porter of: Bible ..... **BEN**
Ark's landing place .. **ARARAT**
arm .... **LIMB, TENTACLE**
arm, movable with verniers **ALIDADE**
arm of sea . **BAY, FIRTH, FRITH**
armadillo ...... **APAR, APARA**
armadillo, Braz. . **TATU, TATOU**
armadillo, giant . **TATU, TATOU**
armadillo, large 12-banded **TATOUAY**
armadillo, 6-banded .. **PELUDO**
armadillo, small .. **PEBA, PEVA**
armadillo, 3-banded .... **APAR, APARA, MATACO, MATICO**
armed band .... **POSSE**
armed galley of old Northmen **AESC**
ARMOR .... see also SPECIAL SECTION, page 194
armor bearer .... **ARMIGER**
armor, body .... **CUIRASS**
armor, chain .... **MAIL**
armor, horse .. **BARD, BARDE**
armor, leg .... **JAMB, JAMBE**
armor, leg below knee **GREAVE**
armor, lower body ..... **CULET**

a armor part .... LORICA
armor part, throat ... GORGET
armor, skirt .... TACE, TASSE, TASSET
armor, thigh ... CUISH, TUILE, CUISSE, TUILLE
armpit .... ALA
army .... HOST, TROOPS
army group .... CADRE
army provisioner ...... SUTLER
aroid, an .... ARAD, ARUM
aromatic herb DILL, MINT, SAGE
aromatic herb, carrot genus CARUM
aromatic herb-plant .... NARD
aromatic seed CUMIN, CUMMIN
aromatic seed, plant ... ANISE
aromatic substance ... BALSAM
aromatic weed .... TANSY
around .... CIRCA
arouse .... FIRE, STIR, PIQUE
arpeggio .... ROULADE
arquebus support ...... CROC
arraign ..... ACCUSE, INDICT
arrange ...... FIX, SET, FILE, DISPOSE
arrangement: comb. form . TAX, TAXI, TAXO, TAXEO, TAXIS
b arrangement, pert. to. .TACTIC
array .. DECK, ORDER, ATTIRE
arrest .... NAB, HALT
arrest writ .... CAPIAS
arris .... PIEN
arrow .... BOLT, DART
arrow, body of .... STELE
arrow, fit string to ..... NOCK
arrow, spinning .... VIRE
arrow wood .... WAHOO
arrowroot .... PIA, ARARU
arroyo .... HONDO
art: Lat. .... ARS
art style .... DADA, GENRE
Artemis . UPIS, DELIA, PHOEBE
Artemis' twin .... APOLLO
Artemis' victim ...... ORION
artery, largest .... AORTA
artery of neck ...... CAROTID
artful .... SLY, WILY
arthritis aid ACTH, CORTISONE
Arthur's foster brother ... KAY
Arthurian lady ENID, ELAIN, ELAINE
article .... AN, THE, ITEM
article, Fr. .... LA, LE, DES, LES, UNE
article, Ger. .... DAS, DER
article, Sp. .. EL, LA, LAS, LOS
articulated joint ...... HINGE
artifice ... RUSE, WILE, TRICK
c artificial language .... RO, IDO
ARTIST .... see also PAINTER and under Country of each artist
artist, primitive .... MOSES
artless .... NAIVE
arum family plant TARO, CALLA
arum plant ..... ARAD, AROID
Aryan .... MEDE, SLAV
as .. QUA, LIKE, SINCE, WHILE
as far as .... TO
as it stands: mus. .... STA
as written: mus. .... STA
asafetida .... HING
asbestos .... ABISTON
ascent .... UPGO, CLIMB
ascetic, ancient .... ESSENE
asceticism, Hindu ...... YOGA
ash, fruit, seed ..... SAMARA
ash key .... SAMARA
ashy pale .... LIVID
ASIA .. see also SPECIAL SECTION
Asia Minor district, old IONIA
Asia Minor region, pert. to EOLIC, AEOLIC
Asia native, S.E. ...... SHAN
Asiatic ancient people .. SERES
d Asiatic country .. see page 210
Asiatic cow .... ZO, ZOH
Asiatic evergreen ...... BAGO
Asiatic fowl .... SAT
Asiatic gangster .... DACOIT
Asiatic sardine .... LOUR
Asiatic shrub .... TEA, TCHE
Asiatic tree .... ACLE, ASAK, ASOK, ASOKA
"— asinorum" .... PONS
askew .... WRY, AGEE, ALOP, AWRY
aspect ... SIDE, FACET, PHASE
asperse .... SLANDER
aspire .... HOPE
ass, wild KULAN, ONAGER, QUAGGA
assail .... BESET, ATTACK
ASSAM ..... see also SPECIAL SECTION, Page 191
Assam hill tribe .... AKA
Assam mongol .... NAGA
Assam silkworm .... ERI, ERIA
Assam tribe, Naga Hills AO, NAGA
assault .... ONSET, STORM
assault, prolonged ...... SIEGE
assayer .... TESTER
assaying cup .... CUPEL
assemble .... MEET, MUSTER, COLLECT

a assembly .... **DIET, SYNOD SESSION, GATHERING**
assembly, A.-S. **GEMOT, GEMOTE**
assembly, China, Hawaii .. **HUI**
assembly, Dutch .... **RAAD**
assent, solemn .... **AMEN**
assert .... **AVER, POSIT, STATE**
assert formally .... **ALLEGATE**
assess ..... **TAX, LEVY, VALUE**
assessment **RATE, SCOT, RATAL**
asseverate .... **AVER**
assignor of property ... **CEDENT**
assimilate .. **ABSORB, DIGEST**
assistance **AID, HELP, SUPPORT**
assistant .... **AIDE**
associate .. **ALLY, COLLEAGUE**
association, trade **GILD, GUILD**
assuage .... **MITIGATE**
ASSYRIAN .. see also SPECIAL SECTION, Page 198
Assyrian king .... **PUL**
Assyrian queen, myth. **SEMIRAMIS**
asterisk .... **STAR**
astern ..... **AFT, BAFT, ABAFT**
astringent .... **ALUM, STYPTIC**
astringent, black ...... **KATH**
astringent fruit .... **SLOE**
astrologer of India .... **JOSHI**
b astronomical .... **URANIC**
astron. luminous "cloud" **NEBULA**
Aswan, ancient .... **SYENE**
asylum ...... **HAVEN, REFUGE**
at all .... **ANY**
at any time .... **EVER**
at odds .... **OUT**
at the home of: Fr. ..... **CHEZ**
Atahualpa, king ... ... **INCA**
atap palm .... **NIPA**
atelier .... **STUDIO**
Athamas' wife .... **INO**
Athena ... **PALLAS, MINERVA**
Athena, appellation, title . **ALEA**
Athena, possession of ... **EGIS**
Athenian .... **ATTIC**
Athenian bronze coin **CHALCUS**
Athenian demagogue ... **CLEON**
Athens, last king of .. **CODRUS**
athlete, famous ...... **THORPE**
a-tiptoe .... **ATIP**
atmospheric pressure, of **BARIC**
at no time: poet. ...... **NEER**
atoll's pool .... **LAGOON**
atom part .... **PROTON**
atomic machine **BETATRON, RHEOTRON**
atomic physicist .. **BOHR, RABI, UREY, FERMI, PAULI, COMPTON, MEITNER MILLIKAN**

c atomic submarine .... **SKATE, SARGO, TRITON, NAUTILUS**
atone for .... **REDEEM**
attach .... **ADD, FIX, TIE, APPEND**
attack .... **BESET, ONSET**
attack, mock .... **FEINT**
attar .... **OTTO**
attempt .... **TRY, STAB, ESSAY**
attendant, hunter's **GILLY, GILLIE**
attention ... **EAR, CARE, HEED**
attest ..... **VOUCH, CERTIFY**
attic .... **LOFT, GARRET**
Attica resident .... **METIC**
Attila .... **ATLI, ETZEL**
attitudinize .... **POSE**
attribute .. **IMPUTE, ASCRIBE**
attune .... **KEY, ACCORD**
auction .... **SALE**
audience ...... **EAR, HEARING**
auditory .... **OTIC, AURAL**
auger .... **BORE, BORER**
augment .... **EKE**
augur .... **BODE, PORTEND**
augury ...... **OMEN, PORTENT**
auk genus .. **ALCA, ALLE, URIA**
auk, little ... **ROTCH, ROTCHE**
aura, pert. to .... **AURIC**
d aureola .... **HALO**
auric acid salt ...... **AURATE**
auricle .... **EAR**
auricular ...... **OTIC, EARED**
aurochs .. **TUR, URUS, AURUS**
aurora .... **EOS, DAWN**
auspices .... **EGIS, AEGIS**
Australasian harrier-hawk **KAHU**
Australasian shrub genus **HOYA**
AUSTRALIA . see also SPECIAL SECTION
Australian boomerang .. **KILEY**
Austral. food .... **KAI**
Austral. gum tree **KARI, TUART**
Austral. hut .... **MIAM, MIMI**
Austral. marsupial **TAIT, KOALA**
Austral. scaly-finned fish **MADO**
Austral. tree, timber .. **PENDA**
Austrian folk dance .. **DREHER**
Austr. violinist .... **MORINI**
author .... **PARENT**
author, boys' .. **ALGER, HENTY**
author, nature stories .. **SETON**
authoritative .... **MAGISTRAL**
author unknown: abbr. .. **ANON**

a authority, name as **CITE, QUOTE**
auto, old .. **JALOPY, JALOPPY**
automaton .... **ROBOT**
automaton: Jew. legend **GOLEM**
automobile "shoe" . **TIRE, TYRE**
ave .... **HAIL**
avena .... **OAT**
avenger: Hebr. .... **GOEL**
average .... **PAR, MEAN, NORM, USUAL, MEDIAL**
averse .... **LOTH, LOATH**
Avesta division **YASNA, GATHAS, YASHTS**
avid .... **KEEN, EAGER**
avifauna .... **ORNIS**
avocado, Mex. .... **COYO**
avoid .... **SHUN, ESCHEW**

c avouch .... **AVER, ASSERT**
away .... **OFF, GONE, ABSENT**
aweather, opposed to .... **ALEE**
aweto .... **WERI**
awkward .... **INEPT**
awkward fellow .... **LOUT**
awn .... **ARISTA**
awned .... **ARISTATE**
awry .... **AGEE, AJEE, AGLEY**
axilla .... **ALA**
axilla, pert. to .... **ALAR**
axillary .... **ALAR**
axis deer .... **CHITAL**
Aztec god, sowing ...... **XIPE**
Aztec "Noah" (hero) ... **NATA**
Aztec "Noah's" wife .. **NANA**
Aztec spear .... **ATLATL**

B

babbler: Scot. ...... **HAVEREL**
Babism, founder .... **BAB**
babul tree pods .... **GARAD**
baby animal: Fr. .... **TOTO**
baby carriage .... **PRAM**
b **BABYLONIAN GODS, DEITY,** see also GODS and also SPECIAL SECTION on page 198
Babylonian abode of dead **ARALU**
Babylonian city .... **IS**
Babylonian chief gods ... **EA, ANU, BEL, HEA, ENKI**
Babylonian chief goddess **ISTAR, ISHTAR**
Babylonian chief priest of shrine .... **EN**
Babylonian division .... **SUMER**
Babylonian hero ...... **ETANA**
Babylonian lunar cycle **SAROS**
Babylonian neighbor **ELAMITE**
Babylonian numeral .... **SAROS**
Babylonian priestess .. **ENTUM**
Babylonian purgatory .. **ARALU**
Bacchanals' cry .... **EVOE**
bacchante .... **MAENAD**
Bacchus' follower ...... **SATYR**
Bacchus' son .... **COMUS**
back .. **AID, AFT, FRO, ABET, HIND, REAR, SPONSOR**
back, call .... **REVOKE**
back door .... **POSTERN**
back, flow ...... **EBB, RECEDE**
back, lying on ...... **SUPINE**
back of neck .... **NAPE**
back, pert. to ...... **DORSAL**

back, take .... **RETRACT**
back, thrust .... **REPEL**
back, toward .... **RETRAL**
back: Zool. **NOTA, NOTUM**
d backbone ...... **CHINE, SPINE**
bacteria-free .... **ASEPTIC**
bacteriologist's wire ..... **OESE**
bacteriostatic subst. . **CITRININ**
badge, Jap. .... **MON**
badger .... **DAS, BAIT**
badgerlike animal **PAHMI, RATEL**
badgers, Old World .... **MELES**
baffle .... **FOIL, POSE, ELUDE**
bag .... **SAC**
bag net .... **FYKE**
bagatelle .... **TRIFLE**
bagpipe, hole in .... **LILL**
bagpipe sound .... **SKIRL**
bailiff, old Eng. .... **REEVE**
baize fabric .... **DOMETT**
baker bird .... **HORNERO**
baking chamber ... **OST, KILN, OAST, OVEN**
baking pit .... **IMU**
balance .. **REST, POISE, SCALE**
balance, sentence ... **PARISON**
Balance, The .... **LIBRA**
balancing weight ... **BALLAST**
Balder's killer **LOK, LOKE, LOKI**
Balder's wife .... **NANNA**
baldness .... **ACOMIA**
Balkan .... **SERB**
ball, low .... **LINER**
ball, to hit **LOB, BUNT, SWAT**

a ball, yarn thread ...... **CLEW**
ballad .... **LAY, DERRY**
ballet jump .... **JETE**
ballet skirt .... **TUTU**
ballet turn .... **FOUETTE**
balloon basket **CAR, NACELLE**
ball-rope missile **BOLA, BOLAS**
balm of Gilead ..... **BALSAM**
balsalike wood .... **BONGO**
balsam .... **FIR, TOLU, RESIN**
Balt .... **ESTH**
BALTIC ... see also SPECIAL SECTION
Baltic Finn .... **VOD**
Baltimore stove .... **LATROBE**
Balto-Slav .... **LETT**
Baluchistan tribe .... **REKI**
Baluchistan tribesman .. **MARI**
"Bambi" author ...... **SALTEN**
bamboo .... **REED**
bamboo shoots, pickled **ACHAR**
Bana's daughter: Hindu **USHA**
banal .... **STALE, TRITE**
banana genus .... **MUSA**
banana, kind of .. **PLANTAIN**
banana, Polyn. .... **FEI**
band .... **BELT, TAPE, STRIP, FILLET**
band: Arch. .. **FACIA, FASCIA**
band, muscle, nerve .. **TAENIA**
band, narrow .. **STRIA, STRIAE**
bandage ...... **STUPE, TAENIA**
bandicoot .... **RAT**
b bandmaster, Am. .... **SOUSA**
banish ..... **EXILE, RELEGATE**
bank .... **RELY, DEPEND**
bank, of a river ... **RIPARIAN**
bank, river .... **RIPA**
banker, India .. **SARAF, SHROFF**
banner .... **FLAG, ENSIGN, BANDEROLE**
banter ... **CHAFF, PERSIFLAGE**
BANTU see also TRIBES in SPECIAL SECTION, Page 191
Bantu .... **KAFIR, KAFFIR**
Bantu, Congo ... **RUA, WARUA**
Bantu language .... **ILA**
Bantu nation .... **GOGO**
Bantu-speaking tribe **RAVI, RORI, PONDO**
Bantu tribesman ..... **DUALA**
baobab, dried .... **LALO**
baobab leaves, powdered . **LALO**
baptism font .... **LAVER**
baptismal basin .... **FONT**
bar .... **RAIL, INGOT, HINDER, STRIPE**
bar legally .... **ESTOP**
bar, supporting .... **FID**
barb, feather .... **HARL, HERL**

c Barbados native .... **BIM**
barbarian .... **HUN, GOTH**
Barbary ape .... **MAGOT**
barber ..... **SHAVER, TONSOR**
bard, Goth. .... **RUNER**
bare ..... **BALD, MERE, NUDE**
bargain .... **DEAL, PALTER**
bargain: Dutch .... **KOOP**
barge .... **HOY**
bark .... **BAY, YAP, YIP**
bark, bitter .. **NIEPA, NIOTA**
bark, inner .... **CORTEX**
bark, lime tree .. **BAST, BASTE**
bark, medicinal .... **COTO**
bark, paper mulberry .. **TAPA**
bark, pert. to ..... **CORTICAL**
bark remover .... **ROSSER**
bark, rough exterior .... **ROSS**
barking .... **LATRANT**
barn owl genus .... **TYTO**
barometric line ...... **ISOBAR**
barony, Jap. .... **HAN**
barracuda, small **SPET, SENNET**
barrelmaker .... **COOPER**
barrel slat .... **STAVE**
barren land .... **USAR**
Barrie character ...... **ALICE**
barrow, Russ. .... **KURGAN**
base .... **LOW, VILE**
base, architectural **SOCLE, PLINTH**
d base, attached by .... **SESSILE**
baseball position: abbr. .... **LF, RF, SS**
Bashan, king of .... **OG**
bashful .... **COY, SHY, TIMID**
basilica, Rome ..... **LATERAN**
basin: Geol. .... **TALA**
basis of argument ... **PREMISE**
basket .... **KISH, CABAS, PANIER, PANNIER**
basket, coarse .... **SKEP**
basket, Eng. ...... **PED, CAUL**
basket, fish ... **WEEL, CRAIL, CREEL, WICKER**
basket grass, Mex. ..... **OTATE**
basket, large .... **HAMPER**
basket strip .... **RAND**
basketball player ..... **CAGER**
basketry rod .... **OSIER**
Basra native .... **IRAQI**
bass, Europ. .... **BRASSE**
basswood .... **LINDEN**
bast fiber .... **RAMIE**
bat .... **RACKET**
batfish .... **DIABLO**
bathe .... **LAVE**
bathing-suit .... **MAILLOT**
baths, Roman ..... **THERMAE**
Bathsheba's husband **URIA, URIAH**

a baton .... **ROD**
batrachian ...... **FROG, TOAD**
batter .... **RAM**
battering machine ...... **RAM**
battery plate .... **GRID**
battle, Am. Rev. ... **CONCORD**
battle area .... **SECTOR**
battle, Arthur's last .. **CAMLAN**
battle ax ... **TWIBIL, TWIBILL**
battle, Civil War, Tenn. **SHILOH**
battle cry, Irish .. **ABU, ABOO**
battle, Eng.-Fr. **CRECY, CRESSY**
battle formation ...... **HERSE**
battle, Franco-Pruss. .. **SEDAN**
battle, 100 Years War **CRECY, CRESSY**
"Battle Hymn of Republic" author .... **HOWE**
battle, WWI .. **MARNE, SOMME, YPRES, VERDUN**
battlefield .... **ARENA**
bauble .... **BEAD**
bay .... **COVE, BIGHT, INLET**
bay, Orkney, Shetland ... **VOE**
bay tree .... **LAUREL**
bay window .... **ORIEL**
bazaar .... **FAIR**
be foolishly overfond ... **DOAT, DOTE**
be silent: music ...... **TACET**
b be still .... **SH, HUSH, QUIET**
beach .... **SHORE, STRAND**
beach cabin .... **CABANA**
beads, prayer .... **ROSARY**
beak .... **NEB, NIB, BILL**
beam, supporting **TEMPLET, TEMPLATE**
bean .... **SOY, URD, LIMA**
bean, E. Ind. .... **URD**
bean, field .... **PINTO**
bean, green .... **HARICOT**
bean, poisonous ... **CALABAR**
bean, S. Am. .... **TONKA**
bean tree .... **CAROB**
bear .. **STAND, YIELD, ENDURE**
Bear constellation ...... **URSA**
bear, nymph changed to **CALLISTO**
bear, Austral. .... **KOALA**
bear witness .. **VOUCH, ATTEST**
beard of grain .. **AWN, ARISTA**
bearded seal .... **MAKLUK**
bearer, Ind. .... **SINDAR**
bearing .... **MIEN, ORLE**
bearing plate .... **GIB**
bear's-ear .... **ARICULA**
beast of burden .... **ASS, BURRO, LLAMA**
beat .... **WIN, CANE, DRUB, FLAP, POMMEL, PULSE**
beat about: naut. ...... **BUSK**
c beater, mortar .... **RAB**
beauty, goddess of: Hindu **SRI, SHRI, SHREE, LAKSHMI**
beauty, Greek .... **LAIS**
beaver .... **CASTOR**
beaver skin .... **PLEW**
beche-de-mer ...... **TREPANG**
beckon .... **NOD**
bed .... **KIP, PALLET**
bed of dry stream .... **DONGA**
bed of press, handle .. **ROUNCE**
bed: slang .... **DOSS**
Bedouin headband cord .. **AGAL**
bee, honey, genus .... **APIS**
bee house ..... **APIARY, HIVE**
bee, male .... **DRONE**
bee tree .... **LINDEN**
bees, pert. to .... **APIAN**
bee's pollen brush ..... **SCOPA**
beech tree genus ...... **FAGUS**
beechnuts .... **MAST**
beefwood: Polyn. ...... **TOA, TOOA, BELAH**
beehive, straw .... **SKEP**
Beehive State .. see page 209
beer ...... **ALE, BOCK, LAGER**
beer, Afr. millet ..... **POMBE**
beer ingredient .. **HOPS, MALT**
beer mug .... **STEIN**
beer, P. I. rice ..... **PANGASI**
d beet variety .... **CHARD**
Beethoven's birthplace . **BONN**
beetle .... **DOR, ELATER**
beetle, burrowing ...... **BORER**
beetle, click .... **ELATER**
beetle, fruit-loving .... **BORER**
beetle genus, ground .. **AMARA**
beetle, ground .... **CARAB**
beetle, sacred Egyp. .. **SCARAB**
beetle, wood .... **SAWYER**
befall .... **HAP**
before .... **ERE, PRE, ANTERIOR**
before: obs. .... **ERER**
before: naut. .... **AFORE**
beget .... **EAN, SIRE**
"Beggar's Opera" dramatist **GAY**
beginner .... **TIRO, TYRO, NOVICE, NEOPHYTE**
beginning .... **GERM, ONSET, ORIGIN, INITIAL**
beginning .... **NASCENCY**
behave toward .... **TREAT**
behind .... **AFT, AREAR, ASTERN**
behold ..... **LO, ECCE, VOILA**
behoove .... **DOW**
beige .... **ECRU**
being .... **ENS, ENTITY**

a being, abstract **ENS, ESSE, ENTIA**
being, essential .... **ENS**
Bela, son of .... **IRI**
beleaguerment .... **SIEGE**
Belem .... **PARA**
belief .... **CREED, FAITH, TENET**
believe .... **TROW, CREDO, CREDIT**
believer in god of reason **DEIST**
bell, alarm .... **TOCSIN**
bell, sacring .... **SQUILLA**
bell tower .... **BELFRY, CAMPANILE**
bell's tongue ...... **CLAPPER**
bellbird, N.Z. .... **MAKO**
bellowing .... **AROAR**
below: nautical .... **ALOW**
belt .... **CEST, SASH**
belt, sword .... **BALDRIC, BAWDRIC, BALDRICK**
ben .... **BENE**
bench ...... **EXEDRA, SETTLE**
bench, judge's .. see JUDGE'S BENCH
bench in a galley ..... **BANK**
bend .... **SNY, FLEX, GENU, STOOP, FLEXURE**
benediction .... **BENISON**
benefactor .... **PATRON**
beneficiary: Law ...... **USES**
b benefit .... **BOON, AVAIL**
Bengal native .... **KOL**
Bengal singer .... **BAUL**
Benjamin's first born .. **BELA**
bent .... **PRONATE**
bequeath .... **WILL**
bequest .... **DOWER**
Berber .... **RIFF**
Bermuda arrowroot **ARARU, ARARAO**
Bermuda grass .. **DOOB, DOUB**
berserk .... **AMOK, AMUCK**
beseech .... **PRAY, OBTEST, ENTREAT**
beside .... **BY**
besides .. **TOO, YET, ALSO, ELSE**
bestow .... **AWARD, CONFER, IMPART**
bets, fail to pay **WELCH, WELSH**
betel leaf ...... **BUYO, PAUN**
betel nut .... **SERI, SIRI, BONGA, SIRIH**
betel palm .. **ARECA, PINANG**
betel pepper ..... **IKMO, ITMO**
Bethuel's son .... **LABAN**
betoken .... **DENOTE**
betroth .... **AFFY**
between: prefix .... **INTER**
Bevan's nickname .... **NYE**

c bevel .... **BEZEL, SLANT**
bevel out .... **REAM**
bevel ship timber ..... **SNAPE**
bevel to join .. **MITER, MITRE**
BEVERAGE ... see also DRINK
beverage .... **ADE, ALE, TEA, BEER**
beverage, curdled .... **POSSET**
beverage, hot wine .... **NEGUS**
beverage, Polyn. **KAVA, KAWA**
beverage, S. Am. .... **MATE**
bewitch .... **HEX, SPELL**
beyond: comb. form .. **ULTRA**
Bhutan pine .... **KAIL**
biased person .... **BIGOT**
BIBLICAL .. see also SPECIAL SECTION
Biblical city .... **DAN, BABEL, EKRON**
Biblical character .. **ARA, IRA, ERI, ARAN, ATER, ONAN**
Biblical country . **EDOM, ENON SEBA, SHEBA**
Biblical driver .... **JEHU**
Biblical judge .... **ELI, ELON, GIDEON, SAMSON**
Biblical king **OG, ASA, AGAG, AHAB, ELAH, OMRI, SAUL, HEROD, NADAB**
d Biblical kingdom ...... **ELAM, MOAB, SAMARIA**
Biblical land .... **NOD**
Biblical lion .... **ARI**
BIBLICAL MEASURE ...... see HEBREW MEASURE
BIBLICAL MOUNT see Page 197
Biblical name .... **ED, ER, IRI, ONO, REI, TOI, ABIA, ADER, ANER, ANIM, ASOM, DARA, ENOS, IRAD, IVAH, REBA, ABIAM, AHIRA, AMASA, ASEAS**
Biblical name for part of Arabia **SHEBA**
Biblical ornaments ..... **URIM**
Biblical priest, high ...... **ELI, AARON, ANNAS**
Biblical region .. **ARAM, EDAR**
Biblical ruler .... **IRA**
Biblical sacred objects .. **URIM**
Biblical serpent .. **NEHUSHTAN**
Biblical son .... **HAM**
Biblical spy .... **CALEB**
Biblical tower .... **EDAR**
Biblical town in Samaria **ENON**
BIBLICAL TRIBE .... see Page 197
Biblical weed .... **TARE**
Biblical well; spring . **AIN, ESEK**
Biblical wild ox .... **REEM**

a Biblical witch's home .. **ENDOR**

Biblical woman **RAHAB, LEAH**

Biblical word .. **SELAH, MENE**

Biblical word of reproach **RACA**

bicarbonate .... **SODA**

bice blue .... **AZURITE**

bicker .... **CAVIL**

bicycle for two ...... **TANDEM**

biddy .... **HEN**

"— bien" .... **TRES**

big casino .... **TEN**

bile .... **GALL**

bill .... **DUN, NEB, BEAK**

bill of fare ..... **MENU, CARTE**

bill, part of .... **CERE**

billiard shot .. **CAROM, MASSE**

billow .... **SEA, WAVE**

bind .... **TAPE, SWATH**

biography ..... **LIFE, MEMOIR**

biological .. **BIOTIC, BIOTICAL**

biological reproductive body **GAMETE**

biotic community ..... **BIOME**

bird .... **CLEE, COCK, CROW, DOVE, FINK, GLED, HUIA, IIWI, JACU, KALA, KIWI, KOEL, KORA, KUKU, KYAH, LARK, LOON, LORO, LORY, LOUN, LOWA, LULU, LUPE, MAKO, MAMO, MIRO, MOHO, MORO, MYNA,**
b **NENE, PAPE, PEHO, PISK, RAIL, RAYA, ROOK, RUFF, RURU, RYPE, SKUA, SMEE, SMEW, SORA, STIB, SWAN, TEAL, TERN, TOCK, TOCO, TODY, UTUM, WAEG, WREN, YENI, YUTU, DRAKE, ROBIN, SERIN, ELANET, SHRIKE, SISKIN,**

bird, Am. .... **TOWHEE**

bird, Arctic .. **BRANT, FULMAR**

bird, Austral. .... **EMU, KOEL, COOEE, COOEY**

bird, black **ANI, ROOK, RAVEN**

bird, blue .... **JAY**

bird, C. & S. Am. ...... **COIN, CONDOR, CONDORES**

bird cry .... **CAW, COO**

bird, diving ...... **AUK, LOON, LOUN, SMEW**

bird, ducklike .... **COOT**

bird, extinct .... **MOA, DODO, MAMO**

bird, Europ. .... **GLEDE, TEREK**

bird genus ...... **CRAX, RHEA**

bird, gull-like .... **TERN**

BIRD, HAWAIIAN .... see HAWAIIAN BIRD

bird house .... **COTE**

bird, hunting .... **FALCON**

c bird, India .... **SARUS, SHAMA, ARGALA**

bird, laughing .... **LOON**

bird life .... **ORNIS**

bird, long-legged **AGAMI, STILT**

bird, marsh .... **RAIL, SORA, BITTERN**

bird, mythical .... **ROC**

bird, national .... **EAGLE**

bird nest collector .. **OOLOGIST**

bird of prey ...... **ERN, ERNE, HAWK, KITE, EAGLE, CORMORANT**

bird, orange .... **ORIOLE**

bird order ..... **PICI, RASORES**

bird, oscine .. **CHAT, ORIOLE**

BIRD, OSTRICHLIKE ...... see OSTRICHLIKE BIRD

bird, Persian .... **BULBUL**

BIRD, SEA ..... see SEA BIRD

bird, shore **RAIL, SORA, SNIPE, WADER, AVOCET, PLOVER**

bird, small .... **TIT, PIPIT**

bird, small brown ...... **WREN**

BIRD, S. AM. .... see S. AMER. BIRD

bird, swimming .. **LOON, GREBE**

bird, talking .. **MYNA, MYNAH**

d bird, tropical ..... **ANI, ANO, TROGON, JACAMAR**

bird, U. S. **COLIN, VEERY, TANAGER**

BIRD, WADING .... see ..WADING BIRD

bird, wading, Afr. **UMBER, UMBRETTE**

bird, water see WADING BIRD

BIRD, WEB-FOOTED .... see WEB-FOOTED BIRD

bird, W. Ind. .... **TODY**

bird, white-plumed .... **EGRET**

bird, white-tailed .. **ERN, ERNE**

birds .... **AVES**

bird's beak .... **NEB, NIB**

bird's cry .... **CAW, WEET**

birds of region .... **ORNIS**

birds' route .... **FLYWAY**

biretta .... **CAP**

birth, by .... **NEE**

birth, of one's .... **NATAL**

birthmark **MOLE, NEVUS, NAEVUS**

birthplace, Apollo, Diana **DELOS**

birthplace, Constantine's **NIS, NISH**

birthplace, Mohammed's **MECCA**

birthplace, Muses, Orpheus **PIERIA**

a birthstone .... Jan., **GARNET**; Feb., **AMETHYST**; March, **JASPER, AQUAMARINE, BLOODSTONE**; April, **DIAMOND**; May, **AGATE, EMERALD**; June, **PEARL, MOONSTONE**; July, **ONYX, RUBY**; Aug., **CARNELIAN, SARDONYX, PERIDOT**; Sept., **SAPPHIRE**; Oct., **OPAL**; Nov., **TOPAZ**; Dec., **TURQUOISE, ZIRCON**
birthwort, Europ. .. **CLEMATITE**
bishop .... **PRELATE**
bishop of Rome .... **POPE**
bishopric .... **SEE**
bishop's attendant ... **VERGER**
bishop's hat
HURA, MITER, MITRE
bishop's office .... **LAWN**
bishop's seat ...... **SEE, APSE**
bishop's title, East ..... **ABBA**
bite .... **CHAM, MORSEL**
bite upon .... **GNAW**
biting .... **ACERB, ACRID**
bitter .... **ACERB, ACRID**
bitter almonds compound
AMARINE
bitter drug .... **ALOE**
bitter vetch .... **ERS**
b bittern .... **HERON**
bivalve .... **CLAM, MUSSEL**
bivalve genus .... **PINNA**
bizarre .... **OUTRE**
black .... **JET, EBON, INKY, RAVEN, SABLE, TARRY, NIGRINE**
black and blue .... **LIVID**
black buck .... **SASIN**
black gum tree genus **NYSSA**
black haw .... **SLOE**
black kelpie .... **BARB**
black nightshade .... **DUSCLE**
Black Sea arm ... **AZOF, AZOV**
blackbird
ANI, MERL, MERLE, RAVEN
blackbird, Europ.
OSSEL, OUSEL, OUZEL
blackbird: variant ...... **ANO**
blacken .... **INK, SOOT**
black-fin snapper .... **SESI**
blackfish .... **TAUTOG**
Blackmore heroine .... **LORNA**
blacksnake .... **RACER**
blacksmith's block .... **ANVIL**
blackthorn fruit .... **SLOE**
blackwood, India .... **BITI**
blade .... **OAR**
Blake's symbolic figure .. **ZOA**
Blake's symbolic figures **ZOAS**
blanch .... **ETIOLATE**
c blanket, cloak-like .. **PONCHO**
blanket, coarse wool .. **COTTA**
blanket, horse ...... **MANTA**
blanket, Sp.-Am. ..... **SERAPE**
blast furnace, stone in .. **TYMP**
blaubok, S. Afr. ...... **ETAAC**
blaze star .... **NOVA**
bleach .... **CHLORE**
bleaching vat .... **KEIR, KIER**
bleak .... **RAW**
blesbok .... **NUNNI**
bless .... **SAIN**
bless: Yiddish .... **BENSH**
blessing
BOON, GRACE, BENEFICE
blight .... **NIP**
blight of drought, India **SOKA**
blind, as hawks .... **SEEL**
blind dolphin .... **SUSU**
blind god, Teut. **HOTH, HODER**
blind impulse to ruin ... **ATE**
blindness .... **CECITY**
blister .. **BLEB, BULLA, BULLAE**
block, small arch
DENTEL, DENTIL
block, wood .... **NOG**
blockhead .... **ASS, DOLT**
blood factor .... **RH**
blood, lack of red
ANEMIA, ANAEMIA
d blood of gods .... **ICHOR**
blood, part of .... **SERUM**
blood, pert. to ...... **HEMAL, HEMIC, HAEMAL, HAEMIC**
blood vessel .... **VEIN**
blood vessel, main .... **AORTA**
blood, watery part of
SERA, SERUM
blood sucker .... **LEECH**
blood-sucking parasite .. **TICK**
blouse, long .... **TUNIC**
blow..... **COUP, CRIG, ONER, SWAT, WAFT**
blubber, piece of ..... **LIPPER**
blubber, to strip ..... **FLENSE**
blue .... **CADET, PERSE, SMALT, COBALT**
blue-dye yielding herb **WOAD**
blue dyestuff .... **WOAD**
"Blue Eagle" .... **NRA**
blue-footed petrel ...... **TITI**
blue grass (genus) ...... **POA**
blue grape anthocyanin
ENIN, OENIN
blue gray
CHING, MERLE, SLATE
blue, greenish .... **BICE, SAXE, TEAL, EMAIL**
blue mineral .... **IOLITE**
blue-pencil .... **EDIT**
blue pointer shark ..... **MAKO**

a blue pine .... LIM
Bluebeard's wife ..... FATIMA
bluebonnet .... LUPINE
bluff .... CRUSTY
bluish-white metal ...... ZINC
blunder .... ERR
blunt .... DULL
blushing .... ROSY
boa, ringed .... ABOMA
boast .... BRAG, VAUNT
boastful air .... PARADO
BOAT . see also SHIP, CANOE, GALLEY, VESSEL,
boat .... ARK, TUB, PUNT
boat, assault .... LST
boat, Ceylon, India
DONI, DHONI
boat, collapsible
FALTBOAT, FOLDBOAT
boat, dispatch .... AVISO
boat, E. Ind. .... DONI, DHONI
boat, Egypt .... BARIS
boat, Eskimo .. BIDAR, CAYAK, KAYAK, UMIAK, OOMIAC, OOMIAK, UMIACK
boat, fishing
TROW, DOGGER, CORACLE
boat, fishing, North Sea COBLE
boat, flat-bottomed
SCOW, BARGE
b boat, freight .... LIGHTER
boat front ...... BOW, PROW
boat, Ind. landing .. MASOOLA
boat, landing .... LCI, LST
boat, Levantine .... BUM
boat, light .... WHERRY
boat, mail .... PACKET
boat, Malay .... PAHI, PRAH, PRAO, PRAU, PROA, PRAHU, PRAHO
boat, Manila Harbor .. BILALO
boat, military ..... PONTOON
boat, Nile 2-masted .. SANDAL
boat, P. I. .. BANCA, BANKA
boat, racing .. SCULL, SHELL
boat, river
BARGE, FERRY, PACKET
boat, river, Chin. ... SAMPAN
boat, small .... DORY
boat, 3-oar .... RANDAN
boat, used on Tigris
GUFA, KUFA
boat, with decks cut
RASEE, RAZEE
bob bait for fish .... DIB
bobbin .. PIRN, REEL, SPOOL
bobbins, frame for .... CREEL
bobwhite .... COLIN
Boche .... HUN
bodice, India .... CHOLI
bodily motion, pert. to GESTIC

c body .... SOMA, LICHAM
body, heavenly . STAR, COMET
body of laws .... CODE
body of men .... FORCE
body of persons ...... CORPS
body of retainers .... RETINUE
body of writing .... TEXT
body, part of
THORAX, THORACES
body, pert. to SOMAL, SOMATIC
body, trunk of .. TORSE, TORSO
body: zool. .... SOMA
Boer general .... BOTHA
bog. FEN, MIRE, QUAG, MARSH
boggy .... FENNY
boil .... STEW, SEETHE
boil down .... DECOCT
boiled rice without salt: P. I.
CANIN
boiler, disk for hole in .. SPUT
"Bolero" composer .... RAVEL
boll weevil .... PICUDO
Bolshevik leader ...... LENIN
bolt .... SCREEN
bomb, defective .... DUD
bombardment, short, intense
RAFALE
bombast .... ELA
bombastic TURGID, OROTUND
Bombyx .... ERI
d bond .... NEXUS
bond-stone .... PERPEND
bondman ...... SERF, VASSAL
bonds, chem. with 2 double
DIENE
bone .... OS
bone, ankle TALUS, ASTRAGAL
bone, arm .... ULNA
bone, arm, pert. to ... ULNAR
bone, breast
STERNA, STERNAL, STERNUM
bone, ear ..... ANVIL, INCUS
bone: Greek .... OSTE
bone, leg .... FEMUR, TIBIA, FIBULA, TIBIAE
bone, pelvic, hip ...... ILIUM
bone, pert. to .... OSTEAL
bone scraper .... XYSTER
bone, skull .... VOMER
bones .... OSSA
bones, dorsal .... ILIA
bones, end of spine .. SACRA
bones, hip .... ILIA
bonnet monkey ZATI, MUNGA
bonnyclabber .... SKYR
bony .... OSTEAL
book .... MO, TOME, PRIMER
book, case for FOREL, FORREL
book, largest .... FOLIO
book, manuscript
CODEX, CODICES

a book, map .... **ATLAS**
book, Bible .. see SPECIAL SECTION, Page 196
book of devotions .... **MISSAL**
book of feasts, Catholic **ORDO**
book of hours .. **HORA, HORAE**
book palm, tree .... **TARA**
book, The .... **BIBLE**
books, Bible .... **GOSPEL**
bookbinding style ...... **YAPP**
bookkeeping entry **DEBIT, CREDIT**
booklet .... **BROCHURE**
boor **OAF, CLOD, LOUT, CHURL**
boot, Eskimo .... **KAMIK**
booth .... **STALL**
booth, Oriental market **SUQ, SOOK, SOUK**
bootlace .... **LACET**
booty ..... **LOOT, PELF, SWAG**
booty, take .... **REAVE**
borax, crude .... **TINCAL**
border ...... **HEM, RIM, EDGE, RAND, SIDE, MARGE**
border on .... **ABUT**
bore .... **TIRE, EAGRE, WEARY, CALIBER**
borecole .... **KAIL, KALE**
boredom .... **ENNUI**
boric acid salts ...... **BORATE**
b born ....**NEE**
born, being .... **NASCENT**
born: old Eng. .... **NATE**
Bornean squirrel shrew **PENTAIL**
Borneo native .. **DYAK, DAYAK**
boron, pert. to .... **BORIC**
borough .... **BURG**
borrowed stock: Irish law **DAER**
bosh .... **ROT, POOH**
boss .... **STUD**
boss on shield .... **UMBO**
Bostonian .... **HUBBITE**
botanical suffix ...... **ACEAE**
botanist .... **MENDEL**
botch .... **FLUB, MESS**
both ears, involving use of **BINAURAL**
bother ... **ADO, FUSS, TODO, TEASE, MOLEST, PESTER**
bo-tree .... **PIPAL**
bottle, glass water .. **CARAFE**
bottle, oil, vinegar **CRUET, FLASK**
bottomless pit .... **ABADDON**
boundary ...... **LINE, MERE, METE, LIMIT**
boundaries, mark off **DEMARCATE**
bounder .... **CAD**
bounding line .... **SIDE**

c bounds .... **AMBIT**
bouquet .... **AROMA**
bovine .... **OX, COW**
bovine, male .... **STEER**
bow of ship .... **PROW**
bow, low Oriental **SALAM, SALAAM**
bow-shaped .... **ARCATE**
bower .... **ARBOR**
bowfin .... **AMIA**
bowl: cricket .... **YARK**
bowling term .... **SPARE**
bowstring hemp **IFE, PANGANE**
box .... **BIN, BINN, CASE, CIST, SPAR, CHEST**
box, ecclesiastic .... **ARCA**
box canyon: Sp. ...... **CAJON**
box, metal .... **CANISTER**
box opener .... **PANDORA**
box, papyrus rolls, Rom. **CAPSA**
box, sacred, ancient Rom. **CIST**
box sleigh .... **PUNG**
boxing glove, Rom. .... **CESTUS**
boxing term .... **KO, TKO**
BOY'S NAME .. see MAN'S NAME
boy ... **BUB, BUD, LAD, TAD**
boys in blue .... **ELI'S**
B.P.O.E. member .... **ELK**
d brace .... **PAIR, TRUSS**
braced aback: nautical **ABOX**
bracing .... **TONIC**
brag .... **BOAST, VAUNT**
Brahman rule .. **SUTRA, SUTTA**
Brahmany bull .... **ZEBU**
braid ... **PLAT, PLAIT, QUEUE**
braid, kind of .... **LACET**
brain canal-passage .... **ITER**
brain, layer in .... **OBEX**
brain opening .... **LURA, PYLA**
brain part .... **PIA**
brain: P. I. .... **UTAC**
brain ridges .... **GYRI**
brain tissue .... **TELA**
brain ventricle opening **PYLA**
branch .... **ARM, LIMB, RAMI, RAME, RAMUS, SPRIG**
branch-like **RAMOSE, RAMOUS**
branchia .... **GILL**
branch of learning ...... **ART**
brass, man of .. **TALOS, TALUS**
brassart .... **BRACER**
"Brave Bulls" author .... **LEA**
brawl .... **MELEE, FRACAS**
BRAZIL ..... see also SPECIAL SECTION
Brazil drink .... **ASSAI**
Brazil red .... **ROSET**
Brazil dance .... **SAMBA**
Brazil heron .... **SOCO**

a Brazil Negro .... **MINA**
Brazil plant ..... **YAGE, YAJE**
Brazil rubber tree **ULE, HULE**
Brazil tree ...... **APA, ANDA**
Brazil capital .... **RIO**
breach .... **GAP**
bread, hard-baked ...... **RUSK**
bread crumbs, dish with **PANADA**
breadfruit: P. I. .... **RIMA**
breadfruit: P. R. ... **CASTANA**
bread-tree seeds .... **DIKA**
break .... **SNAP**
break in .... **STAVE**
breakers .... **SURF**
breakwater ...... **MOLE, PIER**
breastbone, of ...... **STERNAL**
breastplate .... **URIM**
breastwork .... **PARAPET**
breastplate, Gr. **THORAX, THORACES**
breath of life .... **PRANA**
breathed .... **SPIRATE**
breathing, harsh **RALE, STRIDOR**
breech-cloth, Polyn. .. **MALO**
breeches: Scot. .... **TREWS**
breed .... **REAR, RAISE**
Bremen's river .... **WESER**
breviary .. **PORTAS, PORTASS**
b brewer's ferment .. **LOB, LOBB**
brewer's vat .... **TUN**
brewing .... **MALTING**
brewing, one **GAAL, GAIL, GYLE**
bribe .... **SOP**
brick carrier .... **HOD**
brick, sun-dried ...... **ADOBE**
bricklayer .... **MASON**
bricklayer's helper ...... **CAD**
bridal wreath .... **SPIREA**
bridge .... **SPAN**
bridge, floating .... **PONTOON**
bridge, maneuver .... **FINESSE**
bridge, Mississippi ...... **EADS**
bridge part **TRESSEL, TRESTLE**
brief .... **SHORT, TERSE**
brigand .... **LATRON**
Brigham Young U. site **PROVO**
bright .... **APT, NITID**
bright colored fish **BOCE, OPAH, WRASSE**
bright: music .... **ANIME**
brilliance .... **ECLAT, ORIENCY**
brilliant group .... **PLEIAD**
bring forth .... **EAN**
bring on oneself ...... **INCUR**
bring together ...... **COMPILE**
bring up .... **REAR, RAISE**
brisk: music .... **ALLEGRO**
bristle .... **SETA**

c bristles .... **SETAE**
bristle, pert. to .... **SETAL**
bristly .... **SETOSE**
Britain's ancient inhabitant **PICT**
BRITISH .. also see ENGLISH
British conservative ..... **TORY**
British king, legendary .. **LUD, BELI, BRAN, BRUT, LUDD, NUDD**
Britisher, early .... **PICT**
Brittany; city, ancient ...... **IS**
broach .... **RIMER**
broad band: Her. .... **FESS**
broadbill, E. Ind. .... **RAYA**
broadbill duck .... **SCAUP**
broken glass to remelt .. **CALX**
broken seed coats ...... **BRAN**
broken spike of grain .. **CHOB**
broken stone, etc. ... **RUBBLE**
Bronte heroine .... **EYRE**
bronze, Rom. money ..... **AES**
brood ...... **SET, NIDE, COVEY**
brook, small ...... **RUN, RILL**
broom of twigs .... **BESOM**
broom-corn millet **HIRSE, KADIKANE**
brother .. **FRA, FRIAR, FRATER**
brought up .... **BRED**
brow of hill; Scot. ...... **SNAB**
d brown ..... **TAN, SEAR, SEPIA, UMBER, BISTER, RUSSET, SIENNA, SORREL**
brown kiwi .... **ROA**
brown, pale .... **ECRU**
brown, red-yellow ..... **PABLO**
brown, yellowish dull ... **DRAB**
brown-skinned race ... **MALAY**
brown sugar .... **PANELA**
browned .... **RISSOLE**
brownie ..... **NIS, NIX, NISSE**
Browning poem, girl in **PIPPA**
browse .... **GRAZE**
Brünnhilde's mother .... **ERDA**
brushwood .... **TINET, TINNET**
brusque ...... **BLUNT, TERSE**
Brythonic .... **CORNISH**
Brythonic sea god ...... **LER**
bubble .... **BLEB**
buck, 4th year .... **SORE**
Buddha .... **FO**
Buddha, Jap. **AMIDA, AMITA**
Buddha's foe .... **MARA**
Buddha's mother ...... **MAYA**
Buddha's tree .... **PIPAL**
Buddhist angel .... **DEVA**
Buddhist language ...... **PALI**
Buddhist church in Jap. .. **TERA**
Buddhist monastery, Jap. **TERA**
Buddhist Mongol ...... **ELEUT**
Buddhist monk .... **BO, LAMA**

a Buddhist pillar .... **LAT**
Buddhist monument .. **STUPA**
Buddhist novice ...... **GOYIN**
Buddhist priest .... **LAMA**
Buddhist relic .... **STUPA**
Buddhist sacred city .. **LASSA**
Buddhist sacred dialect **PALI**
Buddhist sacred mountain **OMEI**
Buddhist saint **LOHAN, ARHAT**
Buddhist scripture **SUTRA, SUTTA**
Buddhist sect, Jap. ..... **ZEN**
Buddhist shrine **TOPE, STUPA, DAGABA, DAGOBA, DAGHOBA, DHAGOBA**
Buddhist spirit of evil .. **MARA**
buds, pickled .... **CAPERS**
buffalo, India **ARNA, ARNI, ARNEE**
buffalo pea .... **VETCH**
buffalo, water, P. I. **CARABAO**
buffet .... **SLAP, SMITE, TOSS**
buffoon .. **FOOL, MIME, ZANY, CLOWN, MUMMER, JESTER**
bug .... **BEETLE**
bugaboo: S. Afr. **GOGA, GOGO**
bugle call **TATOO, TATTOO, TANTARA**
bugle note .... **TIRALEE**
build .... **REAR, ERECT**
builder .... **ERECTOR**
b builder, jetty-dam ...... **EADS**
building site .... **LOT**
building wing .... **ELL, ANNEX**
bulb, edible .... **SEGO**
bulb, Indian food **CAMAS, CAMASS, CAMMAS**
bulb-like stem .... **CORM**
BULGARIAN .. see also SPECIAL SECTION
Bulgarian czar .... **BORIS**
bulge, as eyes .... **BUG**
bulk .... **MASS**
bull, girl carried off on **EUROPA**
bull, sacred Egyp. .... **APIS**
bullet, size of **CALIBER, CALIBRE**
bullet sound ...... **ZIP, PHIT, PHUT, PIFF**
bullfight .... **CORRIDA**
bullfight cry .... **OLE**
bullfighter on foot .. **TORERO**
bullfighter's queue .... **COLETA**
bullfinch, Eng. .... **ALP**
bully .... **HECTOR**
bulrush .... **TULE**
Bulwer-Lytton heroine .. **IONE**
bumblebee .... **DOR**
bumpkin .... **LOUT**
bunch .... **TUFT, WISP**
bunch grass .... **STIPA**
bundle .... **BALE, PACK**

c bundle, small .... **PACKET**
bundle, twig, stick .... **FAGOT**
bundling machine ...... **BALER**
bungle .... **BOTCH**
bunting .. **ESTAMIN, ETAMINE, ORTOLAN, ESTAMENE**
bunting bird .... **CIRL**
buoy, Eng. .... **DAN**
buoy, kind of. **CAN, NUN, NUT, BELL, SPAR, WHISTLING**
buoyancy .... **FLOTAGE**
burbot .... **LING**
burbot genus .... **LOTA, LOTE**
Burchell's zebra .... **DAUW**
burden ... **LADE, LOAD, ONUS**
burden bearer .... **ATLAS**
burglar .... **YEGG**
burial place, Polyn. ..... **AHU**
BURMA .. see also SPECIAL SECTION
Burma Buddhist (native) **MON**
Burma chief .... **BO, BOH**
Burmese capital, ancient **AVA**
Burmese demon (devil) .. **NAT**
Burmese gibbon .... **LAR**
Burmese governor **WUN, WOON**
Burmese hill-dweller ..... **LAI**
Burmese hills .... **NAGA**
Burmese knife .. **DAH, DHAO**
Burmese language .. **WA, PEGU**
Burmese mongoloid ...... **LAI**
d Burmese native (s) **WA, LAI, WAS**
Burmese premier .... **UNU**
Burmese 3-string viol .. **TURR**
Burmese wood sprite .... **NAT**
burn incense .... **CENSE**
burn .... **ASH, CHAR, SERE**
Burnett, Frances, heroine **SARA**
burning bush .... **WAHOO**
burning, malicious .... **ARSON**
burnish .... **RUB**
burrowing animal **MOLE, RATEL**
burst asunder .... **SPLIT**
burst forth .... **ERUPT**
bury .... **INTER, INHUME**
bush or bushy clump .... **TOD**
bushel, fourth of .... **PECK**
Bushmen .... **SAN, SAAN**
bushy .... **DUMOSE**
business .... **TRADE**
business cartel .... **TRUST**
"Bus Stop" author ..... **INGE**
bustard genus .... **OTIS**
bustle .... **ADO, TODO**
bustle about .... **FISK**
busy, to be .... **HUM**
but .... **YET, ONLY, STILL**
butcher's hook .... **GAMBREL**
butter, illipe .... **MAHUA**
butter, India ..... **GHI, GHEE**
butter, liquid ..... **GHI, GHEE**

a butter tree .... **SHEA**
butter tub .... **FIRKIN**
butterbur .... **OXWORT**
butterfly .... **IO, SATYR**
butterfly, large .... **IDALIA**
butterfly-lily .... **SEGO**
button .... **STUD**
button, part of ...... **SHANK**
buyer .... **VENDEE**
buyer: Law .... **EMPTOR**

c buzzard .... **BUTEO**
buzzing sound .. **WHIR, WHIZ**
by .... **AT, PER, PAST, ALONG, BESIDE**
by birth .... **NEE**
by hand, bred .... **CADE**
by means of .... **PER**
bygone .... **AGO**
Byron poem .... **LARA**
Byzantine capital .... **NICAEA**

C

C, mark under ...... **CEDILLA**
caama .... **ASSE**
cab, Near East .... **ARABA**
cabal .... **PLOT**
cabbage .... **COLE, KAIL, KALE, KEAL**
cabbage type .... **SAVOY**
cabin, main .... **SALOON**
cabinet, open, bric-a-brac **ETAGERE**
cactus fruit, edible ... **COCHAL**
cactus, genus .... **CEREUS**
cactus-like .... **CACTOID**
caddis fly worm ..... **CADEW**
Caddoan Indian .... **REE**
b cadet .... **LAD**
Cadmus' daughter .... **INO**
Caen's river .... **ORNE**
Caesar's conspirator-slayer **CASCA, BRUTUS, CASSIUS**
cafe .... **CABARET**
caffein in tea **THEIN, THEINA, THEINE**
caffein-rich nut .. **COLA, KOLA**
cage .... **MEW**
Cain's brother .... **ABEL**
Cain's land .... **NOD**
Cain's son .... **ENOCH**
Cain's wife, Byron poem **ADAH**
cake, rich ... **TORTE, TORTEN**
cake, small ..... **BUN, BUNN**
calabar bean alkaloid **ESERIN, ESERINE**
calamity ..... **WOE, DISASTER**
calcium oxide .... **LIME**
calf of leg, pert. to ... **SURAL**
calf's cry .... **BLAT**
caliber .... **BORE, DIAMETER**
calico colors, mix ..... **TEER**
calico horse .. **PINTO, PIEBALD**
calico-printing method .. **LAPIS**
California army base .... **ORD**
Calif. fish ...... **RENA, REINA**
Calif. fort .... **ORD**

Calif. herb .... **AMOLE**
Calif. motto .... **EUREKA**
Calif. shrub, berry ..... **SALAL**
Calif. wine valley .... **NAPA**
Caliph .... **ALI, IMAM**
call .. **CRY, DUB, DIAL, NAME, ROUSE, WAKEN, MUSTER**
call for hogs .... **SOOK**
call forth .. **EVOKE, SUMMON, ELICIT, EVOCATE**
call, to attract attention **HEY, PST, HIST, PIST**
calling ... **METIER, VOCATION**
Calliope's sister .... **ERATO**
calm .... **LAY, COOL, LULL,**
d **QUIET, STILL, PLACID, SERENE, SMOOTH, SOOTHE**
calorie ..... **THERM, THERME**
calumniate .... **MALIGN**
calumny .... **SLANDER**
Calvinists, Scotch .. **BEREANS**
calyx leaf .... **SEPAL**
cam .... **TAPPET**
cambric .... **PERCALE**
cambric grass .... **RAMIE**
CAME ....see COME
camel: Anglo-Ind. ...... **OONT**
camel hair cloth .... **ABA**
camel hair robe .... **ABA**
camel-like animal ..... **LLAMA**
Camelot lady .... **ENID**
cameo stone .... **ONYX**
camera platform ..... **DOLLY**
Cameroons tribe .... **ABO**
"Camille" author .... **DUMAS**
camlet .... **PONCHO**
camp, fortified ...... **TABOR**
camp, pert. to ...... **CASTRAL**
camphor, kind of ..... **ALANT**
campus, restrict. to Eng. **GATED**
Canaanite month .... **BUL**
Canada goose ...... **OUTARDE**
canal bank .... **BERM, BERME**
canal betw. N. and Balt. Seas **KIEL**

a canary yellow ...... **MELINE**
canasta play .... **MELD**
cancel .. **DELE, ANNUL, ERASE**
candid .... **OPEN, FRANK**
candidates list .. **LEET, SLATE**
candle ..... **DIP, TEST, TAPER**
candle holder
SCONCE, GIRANDOLE
candle wick .. **SNAST, SNASTE**
candlenut tree .... **AMA**
candlenut tree fiber ..... **AEA**
cane ... **RATTAN, MALACCA**
Canio's wife "I Pagliacci"
NEDDA
canister, tea, alloy for .. **CALIN**
canna plant .... **ACHIRA**
cannabis .... **HEMP**
cannon .... **MORTAR**
cannon, old
MOYENNE, ROBINET
CANOE .. see also BOAT
canoe, Afr. .. **BONGO, BUNGO**
canoe, Hawaii ...... **WAAPA**
canoe, Malabar ...... **TONEE**
canoe, Malay (South Seas) outrigger ..... **PAHI, PRAH, PRAO, PRAU, PROA, PRAHO, PRAHU**
canoe, Maori .... **WAKA**
b canoe, P. I. .. **BANCA, BANKA**
canon .... **LAW, RULE**
canonical hour .. **SEXT** (noon), **LAUDS, NONES, PRIME, MATINS, TIERCE**
canopy **COPE, SHADE, TESTER**
cant **TIP, TILT, SLANG, CAREEN**
cant-hook .... **PEAVY, PEEVY, PEAVEY, PEEVEY**
cantankerous command. . **SCAT**
cantata, pastoral .. **SERENATA**
canticle, Scripture ...... **ODE**
"Cantique de Noel" composer
ADAM
CANTON .. see the country in SPECIAL SECTION
canvas .. **DUCK, TUKE, SAILS**
canvas, piece of .... **TARP**
canvas shelter .... **TENT**
canyon mouth .... **ABRA**
canyon, small .... **CANADA**
CAP .. see HEADGEAR
capable .... **ABLE**
cape .... **NES, RAS, NASE, NAZE, NESS**
cape, early .... **COPE**
cape, fur .... **PALATINE**
Cape Horn native .... **ONA**
cape, Pope's .. **FANON, ORALE**
Cape Verde native ..... **SERER**
Capek creature .... **ROBOT**

c caper .... **DIDO, LEAP, ANTIC**
CAPITAL .. see SPECIAL SECTION
caprice **WHIM, FANCY, VAGARY**
captain, fiction .... **AHAB**
captain, Nile ...... **RAIS, REIS**
capture **BAG, NAB, NET, SEIZE**
car .... **SEDAN**
car, last **CABOOSE, CAMBOOSE**
car, old make .... **REO**
caracal .... **LYNX**
Caradoc .... **BALA**
caravan .... **CAFILA**
caravansary
CHAN, KHAN, SERAI
caravel, Columbus **NINA, PINTA**
carbolic acid .... **PHENOL**
carbon, powdery .... **SOOT**
CARD .. see also GAME, CARD
card .. **ACE, PAM, SIX, TEN, TWO, FOUR, JACK, KING, NINE, TREY, KNAVE, POSTAL**
card game like bridge .. **VINT**
card game, 3-handed ... **SKAT**
card game, old ...... **TAROT**
card game, Sp. ...... **OMBER, OMBRE**
card holding .... **TENACE**
card in euchre .... **BOWER**
card, playing
TAROC, TAROT, TAROCCO
d card wool ...... **TUM, TEASE**
cards, highest ...... **HONORS**
care for .... **RECK, TEND**
care, heavy .... **CARK**
careen ...... **TIP, LIST, TILT**
caress .... **PET**
cargo .... **LOAD, PORTAGE**
cargo, put on .... **LADE, LOAD**
"Carmen" composer .... **BIZET**
carnation .... **PINK**
carnelian .... **SARD**
carnivore, Afr. .... **RATEL**
carol .... **NOEL, SING**
carol singer .... **WAIT**
carom .... **RICOCHET**
carousal **ORGY, BINGE, SPREE**
carouse .... **REVEL**
carp .... **ID, CAVIL**
carp, Jap. .... **KOI**
carp, red-eyed .... **RUD, RUDD**
carpet, Afgh.. .**HERAT, HERATI**
carpet, Caucasian **BAKU, KUBA**
carpet, India .... **AGRA**
carpet, Pers. ... **KALI, SENNA**
carriage .. **GIG, MIEN, POISE, CALASH, LANDAU, CARIOLE**
carriage: Fr. .... **FIACRE**
carriage, India .... **EKKA**
carriage, Java, Oriental **SADO**

a carried away .... **RAPT**
carrier, of Orient .... **HAMAL**
Carroll heroine .... **ALICE**
carrot-family plant .... **ANISE**
carrot-like herb genus .. **MEUM**
carrot ridges .... **JUGA**
carry ...... **LUG, BEAR, TOTE**
carry across water .... **FERRY**
carry on (a war) ...... **WAGE**
cart, heavy .... **DRAY**
carte .... **MENU**
Carthage, of .... **PUNIC**
Carthage queen .... **DIDO**
cartograph .... **MAP**
cartoonist
ARNO, CAPP, NAST, KIRBY
carve in itaglio ...... **INCISE**
case, grammatical .... **DATIVE**
case of explosives .... **PETARD**
case, toilet, small
ETUI, ETWEE
casing, bore-hole ...... **LINER**
cask .. **KEG, TUB, TUN, BUTT, CADE, TIERCE, PUNCHEON**
cassava .. **AIPI, JUCA, YUCA**
cassia leaves .... **SENNA**
cast, founded .. **FUSIL, FUSILE**
cast metal mass .. **PIG, INGOT**
cast off **MOLT, SHED, MOULT**
b caste **AHIR, BICE, GOLA, JATI**
caste, agricultural ...... **MEO**
caste, gardener .... **MALI**
caste, low **KOLI, KULI, PARIAH**
caste, Tamil merchant
CHETTY
caster ...... **CRUET, ROLLER**
casting mold ....**DIE**
castor-oil bean poison **RICIN**
castor-oil plant .... **KIKI**
Castor's killer .... **IDAS**
Castor's mother .... **LEDA**
cat .... **ANGORA**
cat, Afr.
CIVET, GENET, GENETTE
cat, Am.
PUMA, COUGAR, OCELET
cat cry .. **MEW, MIAU, MIAW, MIAOU, MIAOW, MIAUL**
cat genus .... **FELIS**
cat-headed goddess, Egypt **BAST**
cat, spotted
PARD, MARGAY, OCELET
cat, tailless .... **MANX**
catalogue ..... **LIST, RECORD**
catamaran ...... **BOAT, RAFT**
catapult .... **ONAGER**
cataract .... **FALLS**
catch .... **NAB, HAUL, HOOK, SNAG, TRAP, DETENT**
catchword ..... **CUE, SLOGAN**
c catechu-like resin ...... **KINO**
category .... **GENRE, SPECIES**
cater ...... **PANDER, PURVEY**
caterpillar .... **LARVA**
caterpillar hair .... **SETA**
caterpillar, N. Z. .... **WERI**
catfish, Egypt ...... **DOCMAC**
catfish, S. Am. .... **DORAD**
cathedral .... **MINSTER**
cathedral city, Eng. ..... **ELY**
cathedral, famous .. **CHARTRES**
cathedral passage ..... **SLYPE**
cathedral, Russian .... **SOBOR**
Catholic, Greek **UNIAT, UNIATA**
Catholic tribunal ...... **ROTA**
catkin ..... **AMENT, AMENTA**
catnip .... **NEP**
catspaw **DUPE, TOOL, STOOGE**
cattail ...... **TULE, MATREED**
cattail India, narrow .. **REREE**
cattail, N. Z. .... **RAUPO**
cattle, breed of .... **DEVON**
cattle dealer .... **DROVER**
cattle genus .... **BOS**
cattle stealing, crime of
ABIGEAT
CAUCASIAN .... see CAUCASUS NATIVE
Caucasian bharal ...... **TUR**
Caucasian goat .... **TUR, TEHR**
Caucasian ibex .... **ZAC**
d Caucasian language
ANDI, AVAR
Caucasion Moslem
LAZ, LAZZI
Caucasian race in China
LOLO, NOSU
Caucasus native
SVAN, SVANE, OSSET
caucho tree .... **ULE**
caudal appendage ...... **TAIL**
caulk lightly .... **CHINSE**
cause ...... **CAUSA, REASON**
caustic ... **LYE, LIME, ACRID, ERODENT, MORDANT**
caustic poison ...... **PHENOL**
cauterize .... **SEAR**
cautery plant .... **MOXA**
cautious **WARE, WARY, CHARY**
"Cavalleria Rusticana" heroine
LOLA
cavalryman .... **ULAN, UHLAN**
cavalryman, Turk., Alg.
SPAHI, SPAHEE
cave: archaic .... **ANTRE**
cave explorer .... **SPELUNKER**
cave: poet. .... **GROT**
cavern .. **CAVE, GROT, GROTTO**
caviar .... **ROE, IKRA**
caviar fish .... **SHAD, STERLET**
cavil .... **CARP, OBJECT**

a cavity .... **ATRIA, ANTRA, SINUS, ANTRUM**
cavity, ear, nose .... **ANTRUM**
cavity, in a rock .. **VUG, VOOG, VUGG, VUGH, GEODE**
cavy .... **APEREA**
cease! .... **HALT, AVAST**
Cecrops' daughter ...... **HERSE**
cedar, E. Ind. ...... **DEODAR**
Celebes ox .... **ANOA**
celebrated .... **EMINENT**
celery-like plant .... **UDO**
cella .... **NAOS**
cellulose acetate .... **ACETOSE**
cellulose: comb. form .. **CELLO**
Celt .... **ERSE, GAEL**
Celt, legendary **IR, ITH, MILED**
Celtic ... **ERSE, MANX, WELSH**
Celtic church early center **IONA**
Celtic dart .... **COLP**
Celtic god .... **TARANIS**
Celtic goddess **ANA, ANU, DANA, DANU**
Celtic mother of gods **ANA, ANU, DANA, DANU**
Celtic name meaning black **DHU**
Celtic Neptune .... **LER**
b Celtic paradise ..... **AVALON**
Celtic sea god .... **LER**
Celtic sun god .... **LUG, LUGH**
cement..**LUTE, PUTTY, SOLDER**
cement well lining .... **STEEN**
cenobite .... **MONK**
censure.**BLAME, CHIDE, SLATE**
center .... **HUB, CORE, FOCI, FOCUS, HEART**
center, away from .... **DISTAL**
center, toward ...... **ENTAD**
centerpiece .... **EPERGNE**
centesimal unit..**GRAD, GRADE**
centesimi, 100 .... **LIRA**
centipede: Tahiti .... **VERI**
central .... **MID, FOCAL**
Cent. Am. gum tree **TUNO, TUNU**
Cent. Am. tree .... **EBO, EBOE**
central line .... **AXIS**
central points .... **FOCI**
century plant .... **AGAVE**
century plant fiber..**PITA, PITO**
cere .... **WAX**
cereal .... **FARINA**
cereal grain .... **OAT, RYE**
cereal grass ...... **OAT, RYE, WHEAT, MILLET**
cereal grass, E. Ind. ... **MAND, RAGI, RAGGI, RAGGEE**
c cereal grass genus ... **SECALE**
cereal plant: obs. ...... **RIE**
cereal spike ...... **COB, EAR**
ceremonial chamber .... **KIVA**
Ceres' mother .... **OPS**
certificate, money ..... **SCRIP**
cerulean blue **COELIN, COELINE**
cervine animal .... **DEER**
cesspool .... **SUMP**
cetacean . **ORC, WHALE, NARWAL, NARWHAL, PORPOISE**
cetacean, dolphinlike, genus **INIA**
Ceylon ape .... **MAHA**
Ceylon foot soldier ..... **PEON**
Ceylon governor .... **DISAWA**
Ceylon moss .... **AGAR**
Ceylon native **VEDDA, VEDDAH, WEDDAH**
Ceylon sandstone ...... **PAAR**
Ceylon trading vessel .. **DONI**
chafe **RUB, FRET, FROT, GALL**
chaff .... **BANTER**
chaffinch ..... **CHINK, SPINK**
chain .... **CATENA**
chain, nautical .... **TYE**
chainlike .... **CATENATE**
chair .... **SEDAN**
chair part ...... **RUNG, SPLAT**
d chaise .... **GIG**
chalcedony .... **ONYX, AGATE**
chalcedony, red .... **SARD**
Chaldean astron. cycle .. **SAROS**
Chaldean city .... **UR**
chalice **AMA, AMULA, CALIX, GRAIL**
chalice veil .... **AER**
chalky silicate .... **TALC**
challenge .. **DARE, DEFY, CAGE**
chamber .... **ROOM, CAMERA**
chamber, pert. to ... **CAMERAL**
champagne, Marne .... **AY**
chance .... **HAP, LOT, LUCK**
chances, excess of ..... **ODDS**
chanced upon .... **MET**
chancel part .... **BEMA**
chancel screen .... **JUBE**
chancel seat .. **SEDILE, SEDILIA**
change .... **FLUX, VARY, ALTER, AMEND**
change appearance .. **OBVERT**
change direction **CANT, KANT, TACK, TURN, VEER**
change: music .... **MUTA**
channel .... **GAT, MEDIA, STRIA, MEDIUM, STRIAL**
Channel Island .... **SARK**
channel marker .... **BUOY**
channels .... **MEDIA**

a chant .... **INTONE**
chanticleer .... **COCK**
chantry .... **CHAPEL**
chaos .... **NU, NUN**
chaos, Babyl. .... **APSU**
chaos, Egypt. ...... **NU, NUN**
chaos, Maori myth .... **KORE**
Chaos' son .... **EREBUS**
chap: S. Afr. .... **KEREL**
chapel, private .... **ORATORY**
chapel, sailor's ...... **BETHEL**
chaperon: Sp. **DUENA, DUENNA**
chaplain .... **PADRE**
chaplet .. **ANADEM, WREATH**
chapped .... **KIBY**
character .... **NATURE**
characteristic .... **TRAIT**
charcoal: Pharm. ...... **CARBO**
charge .... **FEE, COST, DEBIT, INDICT**
charge solemnly ..... **ADJURE**
charged particle .... **ION**
charger .... **STEED**
chariot, ancient Briton **ESSED, ESSEDA, ESSEDE**
chariot race site ...... **CIRCUS**
chariot, religious **RATH, RATHA**
charity .... **ALMS**
Charlemagne, race subdued by **AVARS**

b Charlemagne's father ... **PEPIN**
Charlotte —, dessert .. **RUSSE**
charm .... **JUJU, SPELL, AMULET, GRIGRI**
Charon, payment for .. **OBOL**
Charon, river of .... **STYX**
chart .... **MAP**
Charybdis, rock opp. .. **SCYLLA**
chasm **GAP, ABYSS, CANYON**
chaste .... **PURE, VESTAL**
chat, friendly .... **COSE, COZE**
Chateaubriand heroine, novel **ATALA**
chatelaine bag .... **ETUI**
chatter **GAB, GAS, YAP, PRATE**
chatterbox .... **PIET**
cheat .... **RENIG, RENEGE**
cheat .... **BAM, CON, FOB, FUB, GIP, GYP, BILK, MUMP, COZEN, SHARP**
cheaters: slang ..... **GLASSES**
check ...... **NIP, TAB, REIN, STEM, BRAKE, STUNT**
checking block .... **SPRAG**
cheek .... **GENA, JOLE, JOWL**
"cheek" . **GALL, BRASS, NERVE**
cheek, pert. to ...... **MALAR**
cheek-bone .... **MALAR**
cheer .... **OLE, RAH, BRAVO, ELATE, ENCORE**
cheer pine .... **CHIR**

c cheer up .... **LIVEN**
cheerless .... **SAD, DRAB**
cheese ...... **EDAM, STILTON**
cheese, Dutch .... **EDAM**
cheese, hard brown .. **MYSOST**
cheese, soft .... **BRIE**
cheesy .... **CASEOUS**
cheetah, Ind. . **YOUSE, YOUZE**
chela .... **CLAW**
Chemical compound ... **IMID, AMIDE, AMINE, IMIDE, IMINE, ESTER**
CHEMICAL ELEMENT .... see SPECIAL SECTION
chemical ending **OL, INE, ENOL**
chemical prefix .... **ACI, OXA, AMIDO, AMINO**
chemical salt .... **SAL, ESTER, NITRE, BORATE**
CHEMICAL SUFFIX .. see SUFFIX, CHEMICAL
chemical unit .... **TITER**
chemist's pot .... **ALUDEL**
cherish ... **FOSTER, TREASURE**
cherry .... **GEAN**
cherry red .... **CERISE**
chess piece .... **MAN**
chess term,—passant ..... **EN**
chessman ..... **KING, PAWN, ROOK, QUEEN, BISHOP, CASTLE, KNIGHT**

d chest, acacia wood ...... **ARK**
chest, antique .... **CIST, KIST**
chest, sacred **ARK, ARCA, CIST**
chest sound .... **RALE**
chestnut, Eur. ...... **MARRON**
chestnut, Polyn. ...... **RATA**
chevrotain . **NAPU, MEMINNA**
chew .... **BITE, CHAM, GNAW**
chew, leaf to .... **COCA**
chewink .... **TOWHEE**
Chibcha chief's title .... **ZIPA**
chick-pea .... **GRAM**
chicken snake .... **BOBA**
chide **SCOLD, BERATE, REPROVE**
chief ... **ARCH, HEAD, MAIN**
chief, Afr. tribe .... **KAID**
chief, Am. Ind. ...... **SACHEM**
chief: Chinook .... **TYEE**
chief deity, Panopolis .... **MIN**
chief in Italy .... **DUCE**
chief, India .... **SIRDAR**
Chief Justice 1921-30 ... **TAFT**
Chief Justice 1941-46 .. **STONE**
chief, Moslem .... **RAIS, REIS**
chief officer, India .. **DEWAN, DIWAN**
chief Norse god ...... **ODIN, WODAN, WODEN, WOTAN**
chief, Pres. .... **MIR**
child .... **TIKE, TYKE**

a child of streets. . **ARAB, GAMIN**
"Child of the Sun" ..... **INCA**
child, pert. to .... **FILIAL**
child: Scot. .... **BAIRN**
child: Tagalog, P. I. .... **BATA**
Chilean proletariat ..... **ROTO**
Chilean timber tree ..... **PELU**
Chilean volcano ..... **ANTUCO**
chill .... **ICE, AGUE**
chills and fever **AGUE, MALARIA**
chimney: dialect .... **LUM**
chimney pipe .... **FLUE**
chin .... **MENTA, MENTUM**
China .... **CATHAY**
China blue .... **NIKKO**
China grass .... **BON**
Chinese .. **SERES, SERIC, SINIC**
Chinese aborigine . **YAO, MANS**
Chin. aboriginal population division .... **MIAO**
Chin. are .... **MU**
Chin. boat .... **JUNK**
Chin. brick bed .... **K'ANG**
Chin. Causasian tribesman **LOLO**
Chin. characters in Jap. . **MANA**
Chin. club .... **TONG**
CHIN. COIN .. see also COINS Page 190
Chin., coin, bronze .... **LI**
b Chin., coin, early .... **PU**
Chin. Communist .. **MAO, CHOU**
Chin. cult .... **JOSS**
Chin. department .... **FU**
Chin. dialect .... **WU**
Chin. division .... **MIAO**
Chin. dynasty . **HAN, KIN, SUI, WEI, YIN, CH'IN, CHOU, HSIA, T'ANG, MING, SUNG, TS'IN, YUAN**
Chin. factory .... **HONG**
Chin. feudal state .... **WEI**
Chin. flute .... **TCHE**
Chin. god .... **GHOS, JOSS**
Chin. govt. section **HIEN, HSIEN**
Chin. guild .... **HUI**
Chin. idol .... **GHOS, JOSS**
Chin. instrument, stringed . **KIN**
Chin. kingdom, old **WU, SHU, WEI**
CHIN. MEASURE .see also pages 188, 189
Chin. measure of length . **TSUN**
Chin. mile .... **LI**
Chin. monetary unit .... **YUAN**
CHIN, MONEY see also page 190
Chin. negative principle ... **YIN**
Chin. noodles .... **MEIN**
Chin. official .. **KUAN, KWAN**
Chin. philos. principle. **LI, YANG**

c Chin. plant .... **UDO**
Chin. pottery .... **CHUN, KUAN, MING, TING**
Chin. ruler .. **YAO, YAU, YAOU**
Chin. secret society ..... **TONG**
Chin. shop: Du. E. Ind. .. **TOKO**
Chin. silk .... **PONGEE**
Chin. wax, wax insect .. **PELA**
Chin. wormwood ...... **MOXA**
Chin. yellow .... **SIL**
chinin .... **COYO**
chink ...... **RIFT, RIMA, RIME**
chink-like .. **RIMAL, RIMATE**
chinky ...... **RIMAL, RIMOSE, RIMOUS**
chip .... **NICK**
chip of stone .. **SPALL, GALLET**
chipmunk .... **HACKEE**
chirp **CHEEP, TWEET, TWITTER**
chisel, primitive .... **CELT**
chisel, very broad .... **TOOLER**
chocolate powder ..... **PINOLE**
chocolate source ...... **CACAO**
choice .... **CREAM, ELITE, PRIME, SELECT**
choke up .... **DAM, CLOG**
choler .... **IRE, BILE, RAGE**
choose .... **OPT, ELECT**
chop ... **AXE, CUT, HEW, LOP**
chop fine .... **MINCE**
d chopped .... **HEWN**
choral music **MOTET, CANTATA**
chord, 3 tones .... **TRINE**
chore .... **JOB, CHARE**
Chosen ...... **COREA, KOREA**
Christ's thorn .. **NABK, NUBK**
Christmas .... **NOEL, YULE**
Christmas crib ...... **CRECHE**
chromosome .... **IDANT**
chronicle .... **ANNAL, ANNALS**
chrysalis .... **PUPA**
chrysanthemum .. **MUM, KIKU**
chub, Europ. .... **CHEVIN**
chunk .... **GOBBET**
church .... **FANE**
church bench .... **PEW**
church, body of .... **NAVE**
church calendar .... **ORDO**
church contribution .... **TITHE**
church council .... **SYNOD**
church court .... **ROTA**
church dignitary. **POPE, BISHOP, PRELATE, CARDINAL**
church dish .... **PATEN**
church, India .... **SAMAJ**
church living .... **BENEFICE**
church maintenance, canon's **PREBEND**
church officer .... **ELDER**

a church official
SEXTON, VERGER
church part ..... APSE, BEMA, NAVE, ALTAR
church, Pope's ..... LATERAN
church porch .... PARVIS
church property .... GLEBE
church reader .... LECTOR
church recess .... APSE
church, Scot. .... KIRK, KURK
church vessel .. AMA, PIX, PYX
churchman .... PRELATE
churl. CEORL, VILLAIN, VILLEIN
churl: var. .... CARLE
churn plunger .... DASHER
cibol .... ONION
cicatrix .... SCAR
cigar .... CLARO, SMOKE, CORONA, CHEROOT
cigar, cheap ... STOGY, STOGIE
cigarette, medicinal ... CUBEB
cigarfish .... SCAD
cincture .... BELT
cinnamon, kind of .... CASSIA
cion .... GRAFT
cipher .... ZERO, OUGHT
cipher system .... CODE
Circe's home .... AEAEA
circle .... CIRC, CIRQUE, RONDURE
b circle of light ... HALO, NIMB
circle, part of .... ARC
circle segment .... SECTOR
circuit .... LAP, TOUR, AMBIT, ORBIT
circuit judge, court ...... EYRE
circular motion .... GYRE
circular plate ...... DISC, DISK
circular turn .... LOOP
circular saw .... EDGER
cirque, geol. .... CWM
cistern .... BAC, VAT
citation .... CITAL
cite .... QUOTE, ADDUCE
citron ...... ETROG, CEDRAT, ETHROG
citrus fruit ....LIME, LEMON, ORANGE, SHADOCK, SHADDOCK
CITY .. see also TOWN and GAZETTEER
city, ancient, Asia Min. . MYRA, TYRE, SARDES, SARDIS
city, ancient Thessalian
LARISSA
city: Gr. .... POLIS
City of a Hundred Towers PAVIA
City of Bridges ...... BRUGES
City of God .... HEAVEN
City of Kings .... LIMA
City of Lights .... PARIS
c City of Luxury ...... SYBARIS
City of Masts .... LONDON
City of Rams .... CANTON
City of Refuge ...... MEDINA
City of Saints .... MONTREAL
City of the Prophet .. MEDINA
City of the Seven Hills .. ROME
City of the Violet Crown
ATHENS
City of Victory .... CAIRO
city, pert. to .. CIVIC, URBAN
city, Philistines' ...... EKRON
city political division ... WARD
civet, Chinese .... RASSE
civet, Indian .... ZIBET
civet, Java .... DEDES
civet, Madagascar .... FOSSA, FOUSSA
civetlike cat . GENET, GENETTE
civic goddess, Gr. ..... ALEA
Civil War commander ..... LEE, POPE, GRANT, EWELL, MEADE, SCOTT, SYKES, HOOKER, CUSTER, FORREST, JACKSON
civil wrong or injury .... TORT
claim ...... ASSERT, DEMAND
clam genus .... MYA
clam, giant .... CHAMA
clam, razor .... SOLEN
clamor .... DIN, NOISE
d clamp .... VICE, VISE
clan .... GEN, SEPT, TRIBE
clan chieftain successor. TANIST
clan division: Gr. .... OBE
clan, Gr. .... GENOS
clan, head of .... ALDER
clarinet socket .... BIRN
clash .... JAR, COLLIDE
clasp . HASP, ENFOLD, INFOLD
clasp for a cope ..... MORSE
class .... ILK, CASTE, GENUS, GENERA, SPECIES
class leader, Eng. .... DUX
class, lowest Jap. .... HEIMIN
class, scientific
GENUS, GENERA
classic tongue .... LATIN
classification .... RATING
classification method . SYSTEM
classify .. RANK, RATE, SORT, TYPE, GRADE
claw .... NAIL, TALON, UNGUIS, UNGUES
claw, crustacean's
CHELA, CHELAE
claw ornament .... GRIFF
claw: zool. .... UNCI, UNCUS
clay ..... BOLE, ARGIL, LOESS
clay, baked .... TILE

a clay bed .... GAULT
clay, building: Sp. ADOBE, TAPIA
clay-covered .... LUTOSE
clay, friable .... BOLE
clay layer ..... SLOAM, SLOOM
clay, melting pot ..... TASCO
clay mineral .... NACRITE
clay molding plate .... DOD
clay pigeon shooting ... SKEET
clay pipe .... TD
clay plug .... BOTT
clay, porcelain ...... KAOLIN
clay, potter's .... ARGIL
clayey .... BOLAR
clayey soil . BOLE, MALM, MARL
cleansing agent ...... BORAX
clear . NET, RID, LUCID, LIMPID, AUDIBLE, TRANSPARENT
clear, as anchor .... AWEIGH
clear of charges ..... ACQUIT
clearing of land, Eng. ... SART
cleave ... REND, RIVE, CLING
cleaving tool .... FROE
cleft ...... REFT, RIFT, RIMA
Clemenceau's nickname . TIGRE
clement .... MILD
Cleopatra's attendant ... IRAS
Cleopatra's handmaid ... IRAS
b Cleopatra's needle ... OBELISK
Cleopatra's serpent .... ASP
clergyman .... ABBE, CANON, VICAR, CURATE, PRIEST, RECTOR
cleric, Fr. .... ABBE
clerical cap .... BIRETTA
clerical, not .... LAIC, LAICAL
clever .... APT, HABILE
click beetle ...... DOR, DORR, ELATER
climb .... GRIMP, SCALE
climbing plant ..... IVY, VINE, LIANA, LIANE
cling .... STICK, ADHERE
clingfish .... TESTAR
clinging, for .... TENENT
Clio, sister of .... ERATO
clip . CUT, MOW, SNIP, SHEAR
clique .... SET
CLOAK .... see also GARMENT
cloak ... ABA, WRAP, CAPOT, CAPOTE, MANTLE
cloak, Ind. .... CHOGA
cloak, Rom. . SAGUM, ABOLLA, ABOLLAE
cloak, woman's ..... DOLMAN
clock, ship-form .... NEF
clog-like shoe .... PATTEN
cloister .... MONASTERY
"Cloister-Hearth" author . READE

c close eyes of .... SEEL
close, keep .... HUG
close: musical .... CODA
close to . AT, BY, NEAR, ANEAR
close, to fit ..... FAY, FADGE
closed, as wings .... PLIE
closing measure, music .. CODA
CLOTH .... see also SILK, COTTON, FABRIC
cloth, bark .... TAPA
cloth, figured old ..... TAPET
cloth measure .... ELL
cloth, old wool ..... CHEYNEY
cloth, stout .... BRIN
cloth strip, India .... PATA
cloth used in mourning . CRAPE
cloth, wrapping .... TILLOT
clothe .... GIRD, VEST, ENDUE
clothes moth .... TINEA
clothespress, old Dutch ... KAS
clothing .. DUDS, GARB, GEAR, TOGS, RAIMENT
cloud .... SMUR, CIRRI, NUBIA, CIRRUS
cloud dragon, Vedic ...... AHI
cloud, luminous ..... NIMBUS
clouds, broken .... RACK
clouds, wind-driven . RACK, SCUD
cloudberry .... MOLKA
cloudy .... DULL, LOWERY
d clout .... HIT, SWAT
cloven-footed ...... FISSIPED
clover .... HUBAM, ALSIKE, MELILOT
clown .... APER, GOFF, ZANY
clown, Shakesperean . LAVACHE
cloy .... PALL, SATE, ACCLOY
club member, Gr. .... ERANIST
club, women's .... ZONTA
clubfoot ... TALIPED, TALIPES
clumsily, handle . PAW, BOTCH
clumsy .... INEPT, OAFISH
cluster .... NEP, TUFT
cluster, grape .... RACEME
cluster pine .... PINASTER
coach dog ...... DALMATIAN
coach, Eastern .... ARABA
coagulate .... GEL, CLOT
coal dust ...... COOM, SMUT
coal, heat-treated ...... COKE
coal, live .... EMBER
coal, size of .. EGG, NUT, PEA
coal refuse .... CULM
coal scuttle .... HOD
coalfish .... CUDDY
coalition .... UNION, MERGER
coarse .... GROSS
coarse sugar, E. Ind. .... RAAB
coast bird .... GULL, TERN
coast dweller ...... ORARIAN
coastal range, India .... GHAT

a **COAT** ..... see also GARMENT
coat .... **LAYER**
coat, animal .... **PELAGE**
coat, Arab .... **ABA**
coat, soldier's .... **TUNIC**
coat with alloy .... **TERNE**
cob .... **SWAN**
cobbler .... **SUTOR**
cobra ... **HAJE, NAGA, MAMBA**
cobra genus ..... **NAIA, NAJA**
cocaine source ... **COCA, CUCA**
cockatoo, Austral. .... **GALAH**
cockatoo, palm .. **ARA, ARARA**
cockboat .... **COG**
cockpit .... **ARENA**
coconut, dried .... **COPRA**
coconut fiber .... **COIR, KOIR, KYAR, COIRE**
coconut, Ind. .... **NARGIL**
coconut palm, P. I. ..... **NIOG**
cocoon insect .... **PUPA**
cocoon, silkworm .... **CLEW**
cod genus .... **GADUS**
cod, pert. to .... **GADOID**
cod, young ... . **SCROD**
code .... **LAW, CIPHER**
codfish, Eur. .... **POOR**
coffee ... **RIO, JAVA, MOCHA**
coffee-chocolate flavor. **MOCHA**
coffer-dam, Egypt ...... **SADD**
b coffin stand .... **BIER**
cognizant .... **AWARE**
cognomen ... **NAME, EPITHET**
cohere .... **BIND**
coil .... **WIND, TWINE TWIST, WREATHE**
COIN ...... see also SPECIAL SECTION, Page 190
coin .... **RIN, YEN, SPECIE**
coin, cut edges of .... **NIG**
coin, edging .... **REEDING**
coin, gold .... **LEV**
coin, mill .... **NURL**
coin money .... **MINT**
coin, pewter .... **TRA**
coin, reverse side ...... **VERSO**
coin, silver .... **SCEAT**
coin tester, Orient **SARAF, SHROFF**
coin, tin .... **TRA**
coincide .... **JIBE, AGREE**
colander .... **SIEVE**
cold .... **ALGID, GELID**
cold, producing ...... **ALGIFIC**
cold tableland, Andes ... **PUNA**
collar .. **ETON, FICHU, GORGET**
collar, clerical ...... **RABAT, RABATO, REBATO**
collar, deep .... **BERTHA**
collar, wheel-shaped .... **RUFF**
collect ...... **AMASS, GARNER**

c collection .... **ANA, SET**
collection .... **SORTITE**
collection, motley ...... **RAFT**
collection of facts .... **ANA**
collection of sayings .... **ANA**
COLLEGE DEGREE . see DEGREE
college, Iowa .... **COE**
college, N.J., East Orange **UPSALA**
college official .... **DEAN**
college quadrangle ..... **QUAD**
colloquialism .... **IDIOM**
colonists greeting to Ind. **NETOP**
colonize .... **SETTLE**
colonizer .... **OECIST**
colonnade .... **STOA**
colony, Eng. ...... **CAROLINA**
colony, Fr. .... **ALGERIA**
color .... **DYE, HUE, TINT**
color .. **ASH, BAY, RED, TAN, BLUE, FAON, FAWN, GRAY, GREY, HOPI, JADE, LIME, NAVY, NILE, PINK, PUCE, ROSE, SAXE, AMBER, BEIGE, CORAL, CREAM, EBONY, HENNA, IVORY, MAUVE, MOCHA, SEPIA, UMBER, CERISE, CITRON, COBALT, MAROON, RESEDA, SEVRES, SIENNA, SORREL, CARMINE, CELESTE, CITRINE, MAGENTA**
d color brown sugar ... **CARAIBE**
color changer, photo ... **TONER**
color, neutral .. **GREGE, GREIGE**
color, purplish-brown ... **PUCE**
color, slightly .... **TINT, TINGE**
color, stripe of .... **PLAGA**
color, terrapin .... **FEUILLE**
Colorado park .... **ESTES**
coloring agent .... **RUDDLE**
coloring matter in fustic. **MORIN**
colorless .... **DRAB**
colorless alkaloid ...... **ESERIN**
colorless oil .... **CETANE**
columbite, variety of. **DIANITE**
Columbus' birthplace .. **GENOA**
Columbus' city sailed from **PALOS**
Columbus' ship .. **NINA, PINTA**
column, Buddhist-Hindu, building **LAT**
column, Gr. .... **DORIC, IONIC**
column, memorial .... **LAT**
column, twisted . **TORSE, TORSO**
columns, arranged in **TABULAR**
coma .... **TRANCE**
comb horse .... **CURRY**
comb wool ..... **CARD, TEASE**
combat, field, place of . **ARENA**
combat, knight's ...... **JOUST**

a combat, scene of ..... ARENA
combination .. UNION, CARTEL
combination, card .... TENACE
COMBINING FORMS:
above .... SUR
air ...... AER, AERI, AERO
all .... PAN, OMNI
ass .... ONO
bad .... MAL
bee .... API
beyond .... SUR
black .... MELA
blood .... HEMO
body ...... SOMA, SOMATO
bone .... OSTEO
both .... AMBI
boundary .... ORI
bread .... ARTO
bristle .... SETI
cetacean .... CETO
Chinese .... SINO
communications .... TEL
contemporary .... NEO
daybreak .... EO
dry .... XER
ear .... OTO, AURI
earth .... GEO
egg .... OO, OVI
eight .... OCT, OCTO
equal .... ISO, PARI
b eye .... OCULO
far .... TEL, TELE
fat ... SEBI, STEAT, STEATO
fearful .... DINO
feast day .... MAS
female .... GYNE
firm .... STEREO
five .... PENTA
follower .... IST
food .... SITO
foot ...... PED, PEDI, PEDO
four-parted .... TETRA
fruit .... CARPO
gas .... AER, AERO
gate .... PYLE
glade .... NEMO
gland .... ADEN
gray .... POLIO
great .... MEGA
gums .... ULO
hair .... PIL, PILI
half .... DEMI, SEMI
heat ..... THERM, THERMO
hundred ..... CENTI, HECTO
idea .... IDEO
ill .... MAL
individual .... IDIO
inner .... ENTO
in zoology .... EAE
late, latest .... NEO
line .... STICH
c many .... POLY
medicine .... IATRO
middle .... MEDI
milk .... LACT, LACTO
monster .... TERAT
mountain .... ORO
mouth ...... STOM, STOMO
moving .... KINO
narrow .... STENO
neck types .... DERA
needle .... ACU
nerve .... NEURO
new .... NEO
nine .... ENNE, ENNEA
nose .... NASI
not .... UN, NON
numerical .... UNI
numerous .... MULTI
oil .... OLEO
one .... UNI, MONO
on this side .... CIS
other .... HETER
outside .... ECTO
peculiar .... IDIO
power .... DYNA
powerful .... MEGA
quality .... ACY
recent .... NEO, CENE
reversal .... ALLO
d ribbon .... TENE
round .... GYRO
sad .... TRAGI
seeds .... CARPO
seizure of illness .... AGRA
self .... AUT, AUTO
shoulder .... OMO
small .... STENO
solid .... STEREO
speak .... LALO
star .... ASTRO
stone .... LITH
strange .... XENO
sun .... HELIO
ten .... DECA
thin .... SERO
third .... TRIT
thread .... NEMA
threefold, thrice .... TER
tooth .... ODONT
touch .... TAC
thought .... IDEO
thousand .... MILLE
up .... ANO
vapor .... ATMO
various .... VARI, VARIO
watery .... SERO
white .... ALBO
whole .... TOTO
wind .... ANEMO
within .... ENT, ESO,
ENDO, ENSO, ENTO

a without .... **ECT**
wood .... **XYLO**
worker .... **ERGATE**
come. **ENSUE, ACCRUE, ARRIVE**
come back .... **RECUR**
come forth .... **ISSUE, EMERGE, EMERSE**
come forth from .. **JET, GUSH, SPEW, EMANATE**
comedian's foil .... **STOOGE**
comedy .... **FARCE**
"Comedy of Errors" servant **LUCE**
comfort .... **EASE, SOLACE**
comfortable .... **COSH, SNUG**
comforter .... **SCARF**
command .... **BID, FIAT, ORDER, DICTATE**
command: archaic ..... **HEST**
command to horse **GEE, HAW, HUP**
commander, Egypt .... **SIRDAR**
commander, Moslem **AGA, AGHA**
commander, fortress **CAID, QAID**
commentary: Hebrew .... **BIUR**
commission, milit. .... **BREVET**
commodity .... **WARE, STAPLE**
common ... **VULGAR, GENERAL**
common brant .... **QUINK**
b common: Hawaiian ..... **NOA**
common man .... **PLEB**
commonplace .. **BANAL, TRITE**
commotion . **ADO, STIR, TO-DO**
commune, Dutch, Holland **EDE**
COMMUNE see its country in GAZETTEER
communion cup .... **AMA**
communion dish ...... **PATEN**
communion service ..... **MASS**
communion table ...... **ALTAR**
compact ...... **DENSE, SOLID**
companion .... **PAL, MATE**
comparative conjunction . **THAN**
comparative suffix ending . **ER**
compass point .... **NE, SE, SW, ENE, ESE, NNE, NNW, SSE, SSW, WNW, WSW**
compass point, mariner's **RHUMB**
compassion ...... **PITY, RUTH**
compel .... **MAKE, FORCE, COERCE**
compendium .... **SYLLABUS**
compensate .... **PAY**
compensation, N. Z. ...... **UTU**
competent .... **ABLE**
complain .... **FRET, FUSS, GRIPE, REPINE**
complainant .... **RELATOR**
complete ...... **TOTAL, UTTER, ENTIRE, PLENARY**

c completely .... **ALL, QUITE**
completely occupy ... **ENGROSS**
complication ..... **NODE, NODI**
comply .... **OBEY, YIELD**
composer, Am. . **NEVIN, SOUSA, FOSTER, COPLAND**
composer, Eng. .... **ARNE, ELGAR, COATES**
composer, Fr. .. **LALO, AUBER BIZET, IBERT, RAVEL**
composer, Ger. .... **ABT, BACH, WEBER**
composer, Roum. ..... **ENESCO**
COMPOSITION . see also MUSIC
composition ... **ESSAY, THEME**
composition, mus. ...... **OPUS, ETUDE, MOTET, RONDO, SUITE, SONATA, CONCERTO, FANTASIA**
composition of selections. **CENTO**
composition, operatic .. **SCENA**
composition, sacred ... **MOTET**
compositor .... **TYPO**
compound, organic .... **AMIDE**
compound with oxygen . **OXIDE**
comrade-in-arms .... **ALLY**
concave .... **DISHED**
conceal: law .... **ELOIN**
concealed ..... **INNER, PERDU**
concealed obstacle ...... **SNAG**
concede .... **ADMIT, GRANT, YIELD**
d conceive .... **IDEATE**
concern .... **CARE**
concerning .... **RE, INRE, ABOUT, ANENT**
conch .... **SHELL**
conciliate .... **ATONE**
conciliatory gift .... **SOP**
concise .. **BRIEF, SHORT, TERSE**
concluding passage music **CODA**
concoct .... **BREW**
concrete mixer .... **PAVER**
concur .. **JIBE, AGREE, ASSENT**
condescend .... **DEIGN, STOOP**
condiment .... **SALT, CURRY, SPICE**
condition .. **IF, STATE, STATUS**
condition in agreement **PROVISO**
conduct ...... **LEAD, GUIDE**
conductor .... **MAESTRO**
conductor's stick ..... **BATON**
conduit . **MAIN, DRAIN, SEWER**
cone ..... **STROBIL, STROBILE**
cone of silver .... **PINA**
confection .... **COMFIT**
confection, nut ...... **PRALINE**
confederate .... **ALLY**
Confederate soldier ...... **REB**
confederation .... **LEAGUE**
conference .... **PALAVER**

a confess .... **AVOW, ADMIT**
confession of faith .... **CREDO**
confidence .... **FAITH, TRUST**
confidences .... **SECRETS**
confident .... **RELIANT**
confidential .... **ESOTERIC**
confine ...... **BOX, HEM, PEN, CAGE, CRAMP**
confined .... **PENT**
confront .... **MEET**
confused, make .... **ADDLE**
confusion .... **BABEL**
congealed dew .... **RIME**
conger .... **EEL**
congregate .. **MEET, GATHER**
conical mass of thread ... **COP**
coniferous tree ..... **FIR, YEW, PINE, CEDAR, SPRUCE**
conjunction .... **OR, AND, BUT, NOR**
connect ... **JOIN, LINK, UNITE**
connecting strip of land **ISTHMUS**
connection **NEXUS, CORRELATION**
connective .... **AND, NOR**
connective tissue ..... **FASCIA**
connubial .... **MARITAL**
conquer .... **MASTER**
conqueror, Mex.
b **CORTES, CORTEZ**
Conrad's "Victory" heroine **LENA**
conscript .... **DRAFT**
consecrate .... **BLESS**
consecrated .... **OBLATE**
consequence .... **OUTCOME**
conservative .... **TORY**
consider .... **DEEM, RATE, TREAT, REGARD**
consonant, hard ...... **FORTIS**
consonant, unaspirated .. **LENE**
conspire .... **PLOT**
Constantine VIII's daughter . **ZOE**
constellation ...... **ARA, LEO, APUS, ARGO, LYNX, LYRA, PAVO, URSA, VELA, ARIES, CANIS, CETUS, DRACO, LIBRA, MENSA, ORION, VIRGO, AQUILA, GEMINI, PISCES, TAURUS**
constellation, Altar ...... **ARA**
constellation, Aquila ... **EAGLE**
constellation, Ara ..... **ALTAR**
constellation, Aries ..... **RAM**
constellation, Balance .. **LIBRA**
constellation, Bear ...... **URSA**
constellation, Bull .... **TAURUS**
constellation, Crab ... **CANCER**
constellation, Crane ..... **GRUS**
constellation, Crow ... **CORVUS**

c constellation, Dog .... **CANIS**
constellation, Dragon .. **DRACO**
constellation, Hunter ... **ORION**
constellation, Lion .... **LEO**
constellation near South Pole **APUS**
constellation, northern .... **LEO**
constellation, Peacock ... **PAVO**
constellation, Ram ..... **ARIES**
constellation, Southern ... **ARA, APUS, ARGO, GRUS, PAVO, VELA, INDUS**
constellation's main star .. **COR**
constitution supporter . **CARTIST**
constrictor ..... **BOA, ABOMA**
constructor .... **ERECTOR**
consume: obs. .... **ETE**
container .... **BOX, CAN, TIN, TUB, VAT, URN, CASE**
containing ore .... **ORY**
contempt, exclamation of . **PISH**
contempt, look of ..... **SNEER**
contend .... **VIE, COPE, DEAL, COMPETE**
contest .... **AGON, BOUT**
continent: abbr. ..... **NA, SA, AFR, EUR**
continue .... **LAST, ENDURE, RESUME**
contort . **WARP, GNARL, TWIST**
d contradict ..... **DENY, REBUT, NEGATE**
contrition .... **REMORSE**
contrive .... **MAKE, DEVISE**
control .... **STEER**
controversial .... **ERISTIC**
controversy .... **DEBATE**
conundrum .. **ENIGMA, RIDDLE**
convert to Judaism ...... **GER**
conveyance of estate .. **DEMISE**
convoy .... **ESCORT**
cony .. **DAS, DAMAN, GANAM**
cook in cream .... **SHIR, SHIRR**
cooking odor .... **NIDOR**
cooking pot .... **OLLA**
cooky .... **SNAP**
cool .... **ICE**
coolie woman ...... **CHANGAR**
Cooper novel .... **PILOT**
copal .... **ANIME**
copper .... **CENT**
Copperfield, Mrs. .... **DORA**
copse .... **HOLT, COPPICE**
Coptic bishop .... **ANBA**
copy .... **APE, MODEL, ECTYPE**
copy, court record ... **ESTREAT**
coral .... **POLYP**
cord .... **LINE, RAIP, ROPE, WELT**
cord, hat of Bedouin .... **AGAL**
cord, Hawaii .... **AEA**

a cordage fiber . DA, COIR, ERUC, FERU, HEMP, IMBE, JUTE, RHEA, ABACA, SISAL
cordage tree .... SIDA
Cordelia's father .... LEAR
"Cordiale, —" .... ENTENTE
core ...... AME, PITH, HEART
core, casting mold ..... NOWEL
core material of earth ..... NIFE
core to fashion metal ...... AME
core, wooden .... AME
cork .... SPILE
Cork County port .... COBH
cork, extract of .... CERIN
cork, flat .... SHIVE
cork helmet ...... TOPI, TOPEE
corkwood .... BALSA
corm .... BULB
corn crake bird .... RAIL
corn crake genus .... CREX
corn, hulled .... HOMINY
corn, India .... RAGEE, RAGGEE
corn lily .... IXIA
corn meal .... MASA
cornbread .... PONE
corner ... NOOK, TREE, ANGLE
cornerstone ..... COIN, COYN, COIGN, QUOIN, COIGNE
cornice support .... ANCON
b Cornish prefix: town .... TRE
Cornish prefix in names .... LAN, ROS
cornu .... HORN
Cornwall mine .... BAL
corolla part .... PETAL
corona .. AUREOLA, AUREOLE
coronach, Scot. .... DIRGE
coronation stone .... SCONE
corpulent .... OBESE
corral: Sp. .... ATAJO
correct . OKEH, TRUE, AMEND, EMEND, REVISE
correct behaviour, Chin. LI
correlative .... OR, NOR
correspond JIBE, AGREE, TALLY
corridor .... HALL
corrie .... CWM
corrode ... EAT, RUST, ERODE
corrupt .... TAINT, VENAL, VITIATE
corrupt with money ..... BRIBE
corsair .... PIRATE
corset bone .... BUSK
cortege .... RETINUE
corundum .... EMERY
cos lettuce .... ROMAINE
Cos, pert. to .... COAN
cosmic cycle .... EON
cosmic order: Vedic .... RITA
Cossack .... TATAR
Cossack chief .... ATAMAN

c Cossack headman .... HETMAN
Cossack regiment . POLK, PULK
cosset .... PET
costa .... RIB
coterie .... SET
cottage, Ind. .... BARI
cotton batting .... BATT
cotton, Bengal .... ADATI
cotton, Egypt ...... SAK, PIMA, SAKEL
cotton fabric ..... JEAN, LAWN, LENO, DENIM, SURAT, MADRAS
cotton fabric, corded CANTOON
cotton machine .... GIN
cotton, matted .... BATT
cotton tree .... SIMAL
cottonwood, Texas ..... ALAMO
couch .... LAIR
cougar ...... PUMA, PANTHER
council .... SOVIET
council, ecclesiastical ... SYNOD
council, king's .... WITAN
"Council of —" .... TRENT
counsel .... REDE
counselor .... MENTOR
count .... ENUMERATE
count, Ger. .... GRAF
counter .... BAR
counter, in cards .... MILLE
d countercurrent .... EDDY
countermand .... REVOKE
counterpart .... LIKE
countersink .... REAM
counting frame .... ABACUS
COUNTRY see also GAZETTEER, SPECIAL SECTION
country, ancient .... ELAM
country, ancient, Asia Min., Gr. EOLIS, AEOLIA, AEOLIS
country, ancient, Bib. .... SHEBA
country, ancient Greek ..... ELIS
country bumpkin .... RUBE, YOKEL, RUSTIC
country: law .... PAIS
COUNTY see also GAZETTEER, SPECIAL SECTION
county: Dan. .... AMT
county: Eng. .... SHIRE
county: Nor. ...... AMT, FYLKE
county: Swed. .... LAN
couple .... TWO, PAIR
courage .... METTLE
courier .... ESTAFET, ESTAFETTE
course .... WAY, ROAD, TACK, ROUTE
course, complete .... CYCLE
course, meal .. SALAD, ENTREE
course, part of .... LAP, LEG
court .... AREA

a court action .... **SUIT**
court, A.-S. .. **GEMOT, GEMOTE**
court, church .... **ROTA**
court cry .... **OYES, OYEZ**
court hearing .... **OYER**
court, inner .... **PATIO**
court, Jap. ..... **DARI, DAIRO**
court, old English .... **LEET**
court order .... **ARRET**
court panel .... **JURY**
court, pert. to church .. **ROTAL**
court proceeding ...... **TRIAL**
courtly .... **AULIC**
courtship strut, grouse's .. **LAK**
courtway .... **AREA**
courtyard .... **PATIO**
Covenant, — of the .... **ARK**
cover inner surface ..... **LINE**
covering .. **TEGMEN, TEGUMEN**
covey .... **BEVY, BROOD**
cow .... **BOSSY, BOVINE**
cow house .... **BYRE**
cows .... **KINE, BOSSIES**
coward .... **CRAVEN**
cowboy garment ...... **CHAPS**
cowboy, S. Am. ..... **GAUCHO**
cowfish .... **RAY, TORO**
cowl .... **HOOD**
cowlike .... **COUS**
coxcomb .... **FOP**
b coy .... **ARCH**
coyotillo .... **MARGARITA**
coypu .... **NUTRIA**
cozy .... **HOMY, SNUG**
cozy place .... **DEN, NEST**
crab-eating mongoose .. **URVA**
crab, front of .... **METOPE**
crack . **SNAP, CHINK, CREVICE**
crackling .... **CREPITANT**
crackpot .... **NUT**
craft .... **ART, TRADE**
craftsman .... **ARTISAN**
crafty ..... **SLY, FOXY, WILY**
craggy hill .... **TOR**
cramp .... **KINK**
crane arm .... **GIB, JIB**
crane genus .... **GRUS**
crane, India .... **SARUS**
crane, pert. to .... **GRUINE**
crane, ship's .... **DAVIT**
cranelike bird ...... **CHUNGA**
cranelike bird, S. Amer. **SERIEMA**
cranial nerve ... **VAGI, VAGUS**
cravat .... **TIE**
crave . **ASK, BEG, LONG, DESIRE**
craw .... **MAW, CROP**
crayon .... **CHALK, PASTEL**
craze .... **FAD, MANIA**
crazy .... **LOCO, LUNY, WILD**

c cream .... **ELITE**
credit transfer system .. **GIRO**
creed .... **CREDO, NICENE**
creek .... **RIA, KILL**
creek: N.Y. .... **VLEI**
creeper .... **IVY**
creeping .. **REPENT, REPTANT**
Cremona .... **AMATI**
crescent moon's point ... **CUSP**
crescent-shaped ..... **LUNATE**
crescent-shaped figure .. **LUNE**
crescent-shaped mark . **LUNULA**
crest . **TOP, COMB, PEAK, TUFT**
crest, sharp rugged mountain **ARETE**
crested as birds ..... **PILEATE**
Cretan princess .... **ARIADNE**
Cretan spikenard .... **PHU**
CRETE . see SPECIAL SECTION
crevice ... **CREVAS, CREVASSE**
crew .... **MEN, GANG, TEAM, EIGHT**
cribbage pin or score ..... **PEG**
cribbage term .... **NOB, NOBS**
cricket .... **GRIG**
cricket, ball in .... **EDGER**
cricket, field parts **ONS, OFFS**
cricket, run in .... **BYE**
cricket term **OVER, TICE, YORK**
d crime, Eccl. .... **SIMONY**
Crimean river .... **ALMA**
criminal .... **FELON**
crimp .... **CURL, GOFFER**
crimson ..... **RED, CARMINE**
crippled .... **HALT, LAME**
criticize .... **SLATE**
criticize in a small way **CARP, CAVIL**
crocodile, India ...... **GAVIAL**
crocodile-head god, Egyp. **SOBK, SEBEK**
crocus .... **IRID**
crocus bulb .... **CORM**
Croesus' land .... **LYDIA**
crony .... **PAL, CHUM, BUDDY**
crony: old Eng. .... **EME**
crooked .... **AGEE, AWRY**
crooner, early .... **VALLEE**
crop .... **MAW, CRAW**
crop, spring, India ...... **RABI**
cross ...... **IRATE, TRAVERSE**
cross, church .... **ROOD**
cross-examine .... **GRILL**
cross of life, Egypt .... **ANKH**
cross oneself .... **SAIN**
cross out .... **DELETE**
cross-stroke .... **SERIF**
cross timber, ship ...... **SPALE**
crossbeam ..... **TRAVE, TREVE**
crossbill genus .... **LOXIA**
crossbow .... **RODD**

a crossing, fence .... **STILE**
crosspiece . **BAR, RUNG, CLEAT**
crosspiece, vehicle ... **EVENER**
crossthreads ..... **WEFT, WOOF**
crosswise .... **THWART**
crossword champion, former **COOPER**
crow .. **ROOK, CRAKE, CORVUS**
crow: Eng. .... **BRAN**
crow, Guam .... **AGA**
crow, kind of .... **DAW**
crowd, common ... **MOB, RUCK**
crowd together .. **HERD, SERRY**
crowded .... **SERRIED**
crown .... **CAP, PATE, TIARA, DIADEM**
crown colony, Brit. **ADEN, BAHAMAS**
crown of Osiris or Egypt .. **ATEF**
crown: poetic .... **TIAR**
crown, Pope's triple **TIAR, TIARA**
crucial point .... **CRUX, PIVOT**
crucible .... **CRUSET**
crucifix .... **ROOD**
crude . **RAW, ROUGH, COARSE**
crude metal .... **ORE**
crude sugar-molasses **MELADA**
cruel person .... **SADIST**
cruet .... **AMA, CASTER**
b cruising .... **ASEA**
crumbled easily ..... **FRIABLE**
Crusader's foe ...... **SARACEN**
Crusader's headquarters . **ACRE**
crush .... **MASH, SUBDUE**
crustacean .... **CRAB, ISOPOD, SHRIMP, LOBSTER**
crustacean order, one of **DECAPOD**
cry .... **HO, HOA, SOB, HOWL, WAIL, WEEP, LAMENT**
cry, Austral. ... **COOEE, COOEY**
cry for silence, court **OYES, OYEZ**
crystal-clear .... **PELLUCID**
ctenophores, no tentacle . **NUDA**
Cuban dance .... **CONGA**
Cuban rodent .... **PILORI**
Cuban secret police ... **PORRA**
Cuban timber tree ..... **CUYA**
cubic decimeter .... **LITER**
cubic measure .. **CORD, STERE**
cubic meter .... **STERE**
cubicle .... **CELL**
cubitus .... **ULNA**
Cuchulain's wife . **EMER, EIMER**
cuckoo, black, keel-billed **ANI**
cuckoo, Oriental .. **COEL, KOEL**
cuckoopint .... **ARUM**
cucumber .... **CUKE, PEPO**
cud .... **QUID, RUMEN**

c cudgel .... **BAT, CLUB, DRUB, BASTE, STAVE, STICK**
cue .... **HINT**
cue, music .... **PRESA**
cuff fastener .... **TAB**
cuirass .... **LORICA**
cull .... **SORT**
culmination ..... **ACME, APEX**
cultivate land .... **HOE, PLOW, TILL, HARROW**
cultivation method, Bengal **JUM, JOOM**
cultivation, soil .... **TILTH**
culture medium .... **AGAR**
cunning ... **ART, CUTE, FOXY, WILY, DEDAL, CALLID, DAEDAL**
cup .... **CRUSE**
cup, assaying .... **CUPEL**
cup, ceremonial .... **AMA**
cup, gem cutting .... **DOP**
cup stand of metal .... **ZARF**
cup to hold gem .... **DOP**
cupbearer .... **SAKI**
cupbearer of gods ...... **HEBE**
cupboard .... **AMBRY, CLOSET**
Cupid .... **AMOR, EROS**
Cupid's title .... **DAN**
cupola .... **DOME**
cur .... **MUT, MUTT**
d curare ...... **URALI, OORALI**
curassow .... **MITU**
curassow genus .... **CRAX**
curdling powder ..... **RENNET**
cure-all .... **ELIXIR, PANACEA**
cure by salting .... **CORN**
cure with salt grass ..... **DUN**
curfew .... **BELL**
curios .... **VIRTU**
curl **COIL, FRIZ, WIND, FRIZZ**
curl of hair ...... **FEAK, TRESS, RINGLET**
curling, mark aimed at ... **TEE**
currant genus .... **RIBES**
current .... **AC, DC, EDDY, RIFE, TIDE, STREAM**
curt ...... **BRUSK, BRUSQUE**
curve .... **ARC, BOW, ESS, ARCH, BEND, SINUS**
curve in a stream . **HOEK, HOOK**
curve, plane .... **ELLIPSE, PARABOLA**
curve, sigmoid or double .. **ESS**
curved handle .... **BOOL**
curved in .. **ADUNC, CONCAVE**
curved out .... **CONVEX**
curved plank, vessel's .... **SNY**
Cush, son of .... **SEBA**
cushion ...... **PAD, HASSOCK**
custard .... **FLAN**
custard apple ...... **ANNONA**

a

custard cake .... **ECLAIR**
custard dish .... **FLAN**
custody .... **CHARGE**
custom .... **LAW, WONT, HABIT, USAGE**
custom, India .... **DASTUR**
custom: Lat. .... **RITUS**
custom: obs. .... **URE**
customer .... **PATRON**
customs .... **MORES**
cut **HEW, LOP, MOW, DOCK, GASH, HACK, KERF, REAP, SLIT, SNEE, SNIP, TRIM, SEVER, SHEAR, SLIVE, CLEAVE, TREPAN**
cut down .... **FELL**
cut edges of coins .... **NIG**
cut of meat .... **LOIN**
cut off ... **DOCK, SNIP, ELIDE**
cut off, as mane ..... **ROACH**
cut out .... **EXCISE**
cut: Shakespeare ...... **SLISH**
cut vertically **SCARP, ESCARP, ESCARPE**
cutter .... **SLED**
cutting .... **SECANT, INCISAL**

c

cutting tool .. **AX, ADZ, AXE, HOB, SAW, SAX, SYE, ADZE**
cuttlefish ...... **SEPIA, SQUID**
cuttlefish fluid .... **INK**
Cyclades, one of, see GAZETTEER
cycle, astronomical ..... **SAROS**
cyclorama .... **CYKE**
cylinder, moving ...... **PISTON**
cylindrical .... **TERETE**
cyma .... **GOLA**
cyma recta or reversa ... **OGEE**
cymbal, Orient .... **ZEL**
cymbals, India .... **TAL**
Cymbeline's daughter . **IMOGEN**
Cymric deity **GWYN, LLEU, LLEW**
Cymry .... **WELSH**
cypher system .... **CODE**
cyprinoid fish .... **ID, IDE, CARP, CHUB**
Cyrus' daughter ..... **ATOSSA**
cyst .... **WEN**
Czar .... **IVAN, FEDOR**
Czech .... **SLAV**
Czech, Eastern .... **ZIPS**

D

b

Dadaist .... **ERNST**
dado, pedestal ...... **SOLIDUM**
Daedalus' son .... **ICARUS**
dagger .. **DIRK, SNEE, BODKIN**
dagger, ancient . **SKEAN, SKENE**
dagger, Ir. **DHU, SKENE, SKEAN**
dagger, Malay .... **CRIS, KRIS, CREES, KREES, CREESE, KREESE**
dagger: obs. .... **SNEE**
dagger, thin .... **STILETTO**
Dahomey Negro .. **FON, FONG**
daily .... **DIURNAL**
dais .... **ESTRADE**
daisy . **MOON, OXEYE, SHASTA**
Dallas school .... **SMU**
dam .... **WAER, WEIR**
dam, Egypt ...... **SADD, SUDD**
dam site .... **ASWAN**
damage . **MAR, HARM, IMPAIR**
Damascus river ...... **ABANA**
damp .... **DANK**
damselfish .... **PINTANO**
dance .... **HOP, JIG, REEL, GALOP, GAVOT, POLKA, TANGO, RUMBA, REDOWA, RHUMBA, GAVOTTA, GAVOTTE**
dance, country . **REEL, ALTHEA**
dance, Gr. .... **HORMOS**
dance, Israeli .... **HORA**

d

dance, lively ..... **JIG, REEL, GALOP, POLKA, BOLERO**
dance, old Eng. ...... **MORRIS**
dance, Sp. ... **TANGO, BOLERO**
dance, stately, old **PAVAN, MINUET, PAVANE**
dance step ..... **PAS, CHASSE, GLISSADE**
dancer .... **KELLY, SHAWN, BOLGER, ZORINA, ASTAIRE**
dancing girl, Egypt .... **ALMA, ALME, ALMEH**
dancing girl, Jap. ..... **GEISHA**
dandy **FOP, DUDE, JAKE, TOFF**
DANISH ... see also DENMARK in SPECIAL SECTION
Danish astronomer .... **BRAHE**
Dan. borough (in Eng.) .. **BORG**
Dan. chieftain .... **JARL, YARL**
Dan. division, territorial . **AMT**
Dan. fjord .... **ISE**
Dan. king ..... **CNUT, KNUT, CANUTE**
Dan. measure .... **ALEN**
Dan. money ..... **ORA, ORAS**
Dan. physicist .... **BOHR**
Dan. speech sound ...... **STOD**
dank .... **WET**
Dante's patron .... **SCALA**
Danube city ..... **ULM, LINZ**
Danube, old name of ... **ISTER**

a Danube tributary
INN, OLT, ISAR, PRUT
daring .... **BOLD, NERVE**
dark .... **MIRKY, MURKY**
dark horse .... **ZAIN**
dark rock .... **CHERT**
dark wood ...... **TEAK, EBONY**
darkness .... **MIRK, MURK**
darling: Ir. . **ROON, ACUSHLA, ASTHORE**
darnel .... **TARE**
dart along .... **FLIT**
"Das Rheingold" role ... **ERDA**
dash .... **ELAN**
date, pert. to .... **DATAL**
date plum .... **SAPOTE**
date, Roman .... **IDES, NONES**
"David Copperfield" character
DORA, HEEP, DARTLE
David's captain .... **JOAB**
David's commander ... **AMASA**
David's daughter ..... **TAMAR**
David's father .... **JESSE**
David's nephew ...... **AMASA**
David's ruler, one of ..... **IRA**
David's son .... **SOLOMON**
David's wife .... **MICHAL**
dawn .... **DEW, EOS, AURORA**
dawn, pert. to .... **EOAN**
day, Hebr. .... **YOM**
b day, Rom. ...... **IDES, NONES**
day-breeze, It. .... **ORA**
days: Lat. .... **DIES**
day's march .... **ETAPE**
daybreak .... **DAWN**
dazing larks, device for **DARE**
deacon's stole ...... **ORARION**
dead ... **FLAT, AMORT, INERT**
dead, abode of . **HADES, SHEOL**
dead, region of: Egypt **AMENTI**
dead trees .... **DRIKI**
deadly ...... **FATAL, LETHAL**
deadly carrot .... **DRIAS**
deadly sins, 7 **ENVY, LUST, ANGER, PRIDE, SLOTH, GLUTTONY, COVETOUSNESS**
dealer .... **MONGER**
dealer, cloth
DRAPER, MERCER
dean ...... **DOYEN, DOYENNE**
dearth .... **WANT**
death .... **MORT, DEMISE**
death deity: Rom. ...... **MORS**
death note on hunter's horn
MORT
death notice .... **OBIT**
death rattle .... **RALE**
debate—debatable
AGON, MOOT
debauchee ...... **RAKE, ROUE**
debris, rocky .... **SCREE**

c decade .... **TEN**
decamp ...... **ELOPE, LEVANT**
decay, dental .... **CARIES**
decay tree ...... **CONK, KONK**
deceit .... **SHAM, WILE, FRAUD, GUILE**
deceive .. **BILK, DUPE, FOOL, GULL, TRICK, ILLUDE**
decelerate .... **RETARD**
deception **HOAX, STRATAGEM**
decide: Rom. law .... **CERN**
decimal unit .... **TEN**
deck, ship's .... **POOP**
decks, cut away . **RASEE, RAZEE**
declaim .... **RANT, RAVE, ORATE, RECITE**
declaration in whist ... **MISERE**
declare .... **AVER, AVOW, STATE, AVOUCH**
declare, in cards .... **MELD**
decline .... **EBB, SINK, WANE, REFUSE**
declivity ...... **SCARP, SLOPE**
declivity in menage .. **CALADE**
decorate .... **DECK, ADORN**
decorated letter .... **FAC**
decorated wall part ..... **DADO**
decorous ..... **STAID, DEMURE**
decoy .... **LURE, PLANT**
decrease .... **EBB, WANE, LESSEN, RECEDE**
d decree .... **ACT, FIAT, CANON, EDICT, ORDAIN**
decree, Fr. law .... **ARRET**
decree, Moslem .... **IRADE**
decree, Rom. law .... **DECRETE**
decree, Russian .... **UKASE**
deduce .... **INFER**
deed .... **GEST, GESTE**
deeds .... **ACTA**
deer, Asia ...... **AHU, KAKAR, SAMBAR, SAMBUR, SAMBHAR, SAMBHUR**
deer, barking .... **KAKAR**
deer, Chile, Andes ..... **PUDU**
deer, female . **DOE, ROE, HIND**
deer genus, E. Ind. ..... **RUSA**
deer, India .... **AXIS**
deer, Jap. .... **SIKA**
deer, Kashmir ...... **HANGUL**
deer, red .... **ROE, HART**
deer, S. Am. .... **GEMUL, GUEMAL, GUEMUL**
deer, spotted .... **CHITAL**
deer, Tibet .... **SHOU**
deer track .... **SLOT**
deerlet .... **NAPUS**
deerlike .... **CERVINE**
defamation .... **LIBEL**
defeat, chess .... **MATE**
defeat utterly ... **BEST, ROUT**

a defect, weaving .... **SCOB**
defendant's plea .... **NOLO**
deference .... **RESPECT**
defraud .... **GYP, BILK, GULL, CHEAT**
defy .... **DARE**
degrade ...... **ABASE, LOWER, DEBASE**
degrading .... **MENIAL**
degree .... **GRADE, STAGE**
degree .. **(dental) DDS, DDSC; (engineer) CE, EE; (divinity) DD; (science) BSC; (arts) BA, MA, MFA; (law) LLB, LLD**
degree, extreme .... **NTH**
degree taken, Cambridge **INCEPTOR**
degrees, angle of 57.30 . **RADIAN**
deified sky, Rom. ...... **CAELUS**
DEITY . see also GOD, GODDESS and SPECIAL SECTION
deity .... **GOD**
deity, Buddhist ... **DEV, DEVA**
deity, Hindu ...... **DEV, DEVA**
deity, Jap. .. **AMIDA, AMITA**
deity, primeval .... **TITAN**
deity, Sumerian .... **ABU**
deity, Syrian .... **EL**
b delay . **WAIT, DETAIN, LINGER**
delay, law .... **MORA, MORAE**
delicacy .... **FINESSE**
delight .... **REVEL**
delusion: Buddhism .... **MOHA**
demand . **NEED, CLAIM, INSIST**
demeanor .... **AIR**
Demeter's daughter **CORA, KORE**
demigod .... **HERO**
demolish .... **RASE, RAZE**
demon ... **IMP, DEVIL, FIEND**
demon, Arab, Moslem, Oriental **JIN, JINN, GENIE, GENII, JINNI, JINNEE**
demon, Hindu . **ASURA, DAITYA**
demon, sun-swallowing, Hindu myth .... **RAHU**
demon, Zoroastrian **DEV, DIV, DEVA**
demonstrative pronoun **THAT, THIS, WHOM**
den ...... **DIVE, LAIR, HAUNT**
denary .... **TEN**
denial .... **NO, NAY**
DENMARK .. see also DANISH and SPECIAL SECTION
denomination .... **SECT**
denote .... **MEAN, SHOW, INDICATE**
denoting unfit ships in Lloyd's registry .... **AE**

c dense . **CRASS, THICK, STUPID**
density .... **DORD**
dental tool .... **SCALER**
deny .... **NEGATE**
depart ..... **BEGONE, DECAMP**
depart fast **VAMOSE, VAMOOSE**
depart: Lat. .... **VADE**
departed ... **GONE, LEFT, WENT**
department, Chin. .. **FU, FOO**
departure .... **EXODUS**
dependent .... **MINION**
depict .... **DRAW, PAINT, DESCRIBE**
deplore .... **LAMENT**
deposit, alluvial **DELTA, GEEST**
deposit, clayey .... **MARL**
deposit, geyser .... **SINTER**
deposit, mineral .... **LODE**
deposit, river **ALLUVIA, ALLUVIUM**
deposit, wine cask ... **TARTAR**
depressed .... **SAD**
depression ...... **DENT, FOVEA**
deprivation .... **LOSS**
deprived .... **REFT**
depute .... **SEND**
deputy .... **AGENT, VICAR**
derby .... **BOWLER**
deride .... **GIBE, JIBE**
derrick .... **CRANE, STEEVE**
d dervish, "Arab. Nights" . **AGIB**
dervish, Moslem ...... **SADITE**
descendant .... **SON, CION**
descendant, Fatima's **SAID, SEID, SAYID**
descendants, male line .. **GENS**
descent, deep .... **SCARP**
descriptive term ..... **EPITHET**
desert dweller .... **EREMITE**
desert, Mongolia .... **GOBI**
desert plant .... **AGAVE**
deserter .... **RAT**
deserve .... **EARN, MERIT**
design .... **AIM**
desire .... **YEN, URGE, WANT, WISH**
desire eagerly .... **ASPIRE**
desirous .... **FAIN**
desolate .... **LORN, BLEAK**
despoil .... **RUIN**
despot .. **CZAR, TSAR, TZAR, TYRANT, DICTATOR**
dessert .... **ICE, PIE, MOUSSE, TRIFLE**
destiny . **DOOM, FATE, KARMA**
destroy .... **RASE, RAZE, DECIMATE**
destruction .... **RUIN**
detach .... **WEAN**
detachable button ...... **STUD**
detail .... **ITEM**

a detain **CHECK, DELAY, ARREST**
detecting device ...... **SONAR**
detective .... **TEC, DICK**
detent .... **PAWL**
determination .... **WILL**
determine .... **FIX, DECIDE, RESOLVE**
detest .... **HATE, LOATHE**
dethrone .... **DEPOSE**
detonator .... **CAP**
"— deum" .... **TE**
devaluate .... **DEBASE**
developed compound animal **ZOON**
Devi .... **UMA**
deviate ... **ERR, YAW, DIVERGE**
deviation .... **LAPSE**
deviation from course .... **YAW**
devil .. **DEMON, DEUCE, SATAN**
devil: Gypsy .... **BENG**
devil, Moslem **SHAITAN, SHEITAN**
devil, Russian folklore .. **CHORT**
devil worship ...... **SATANISM**
devilfish .... **MANTA**
Devon river .... **EXE**
devotee .... **FAN, IST**
devotion, nine-day .. **NOVENA**
devoutness .... **PIETY**
dewberry .... **MAYES**
b dewy .... **RORAL, RORIC**
dexterity .... **ART**
dexterous .... **CLEVER**
diadem .... **TIARA**
diagonal .... **BIAS**
DIALECT . see also LANGUAGE
dialect . **IDIOM, LINGO, PATOIS**
dialect, Chin. .... **CANTON**
dialect, Ethiopic .... **TIGRE**
dialect, Gr. .... **DORIC, IONIC**
diamond corner .... **BASE**
diamond fragments ..... **BORT**
diamond holder .... **DOP**
diamond, impure industrial **BORT**
diamond, perfect ... **PARAGON**
diamonds, low quality ... **BORT**
Diana .... **ARTEMIS**
Diana's grove .... **NEMUS**
Diana's mother ...... **LATONA**
diaphanous ..... **THIN, SHEER**
diaphragm, pert. to .. **PHRENIC**
diatonic note .... **MI**
diatribe .. **SCREED, HARANGUE**
dibble .... **DAP, DIB**
Dickens character .. **PIP, TIM, DORA, GAMP, HEEP, FAGIN, DORRIT**
Dickens' pseudonym ...... **BOZ**
"Die Fledermaus" girl .. **ADELE**
die for making drain pipe . **DOD**
die, gambling .. **TAT, TESSERA**

c "Dies —," "Day of Wrath" **IRAE**
diet .... **BANT, FARE**
differ ...... **VARY, DISAGREE**
difference between solar and lunar year .... **EPACT**
different ..... **OTHER, DIVERS**
difficulty .... **RUB, KNOT**
dig ...... **GRUB, PION, DELVE**
digest .... **PANDECT**
digit, foot .... **TOE**
digraph **AE, EA, OA, OE, SH, TH**
dike .... **LEVEE**
dilation .... **ECTASIA**
dilatory ...... **SLOW, TARDY, REMISS**
dilemma .... **FIX**
dill herb .... **ANET**
dilute .... **THIN, WATER**
dim, become .. **BLEAR, DARKLE**
diminish ... **EBB, BATE, SINK, WANE, ABATE, TAPER**
diminish front: military **PLOY**
dingle ..... **DALE, DELL, GLEN**
dining room, ancient ... **OECUS**
diocese center .... **SEE**
Dioscuri .... **ANAX**
dip .... **DAP, DIB, DOPP, DUNK, LADE**
dip out .... **BAIL**
diplomacy .... **TACT**
d diplomat .... **ENVOY, CONSUL, ATTACHE**
diphthong ..... **AE, IA, OA, UO**
Dipper constellation ..... **URSA**
direct .... **AIM, LEAD**
direct attention .... **REFER**
direct steering of boat .. **CONN**
dirge .... **LINOS, LINUS**
dirigible .... **BLIMP**
dirk ....**SNY, SNEE**
dirty lock .... **FRIB**
disable .... **LAME, MAIM**
disagreeable .... **ILL**
disappear gradually . **EVANESCE**
disavow ...... **DENY, RECANT**
disbeliever .... **ATHEIST**
disburse ...... **SPEND, EXPEND**
discard . **DROP, SCRAP, REJECT**
discernment .... **TACT**
discharge .... **EMIT, FIRE, SACK, SHOOT**
discharged .... **SHOT**
disciple .... **APOSTLE**
disciple: India .... **CHELA**
disciplinarian ..... **MARTINET**
disclaim .... **DENY**
disclose .... **BARE, REVEAL**
discolored ...... **DOTY, LIVID**
disconcert ..... **FAZE, ABASH**
discourse .. **HOMILY, DESCANT**
discourse, art of ... **RHETORIC**

a discover . **SEE, SPY, ESPY, FIND**
discriminate .... **SECERN**
discuss ...... **TREAT, DEBATE**
discussion group ...... **FORUM**
disease ..... **MAL, POX, HIVES**
disease, Afr. .... **NENTA**
disease cause .... **VIRUS**
disease, diver's .... **BENDS**
disease, fowl ...... **PIP, ROUP, PEROSIS**
disease, fungus .... **ERGOT**
disease, grape-vine **ESCA, ERINOSE**
disease, plant ... **SMUT, SCALD**
disease, skin .... **ECZEMA**
disease spreader **VECTOR, CARRIER**
disease, tropical .... **SPRUE**
disembark .... **LAND**
disembodied spirit: Chin. **KUEI, KWEI**
disencumber .... **RID**
disengage .... **FREE**
disfigure .... **MAR, DEFACE**
disgrace .... **SCANDAL**
disguise .... **MASK**
disgust, word of .... **AW**
DISH .... also see VESSEL
dish .... **PLATE**
dish, Hawaiian .... **POI**
b dish, highly seasoned **OLIO, OLLA**
dish, hominy .... **POSOLE**
dish, Hungarian .... **GOULASH**
dish, It. .... **RAVIOLI**
dish, main .... **ENTREE**
dish, meat .... **STEW, RAGOUT**
dish, Mex. .. **TAMAL, TAMALE, TAMALI**
dish, stemmed ..... **COMPOTE**
dishearten .... **DAUNT, DETER**
dishonor .... **SHAME, VIOLATE**
dishonorable .... **BASE**
disinclined .... **AVERSE**
disinfectant . **CRESOL, PHENOL, CRESSOL, CRESSYL**
disk, ice hockey ...... **PUCK**
disk, like a .. **DISCAL, DISCOID**
disk, metal .... **PATEN**
dislocate .... **LUXATE**
dismal .... **DREAR**
dismantle .... **STRIP**
dismay .... **APPAL, DAUNT**
dismiss .... **DEMIT, FIRE**
dismounted .... **ALIT**
disorder .... **MESS, DERAY, CLUTTER**
disorderly flight .... **ROUT**
disparaging .... **SNIDE**
disparaging remark ..... **SLUR**
dispatch .... **SEND, HASTE**

c dispatch boat .... **AVISO**
dispelled .... **GONE**
display .... **AIR, SHEW, SHOW, ARRAY, EVINCE**
display proudly **VAUNT, OSTENT**
displease .... **VEX, MIFF, ANGER, ANNOY**
disposed .... **PRONE**
disposition .... **MOOD, TEMPER**
dispossess .... **OUST, EVICT**
disprove .... **REFUTE**
disputable .... **MOOT**
dissertation ... **THESES, THESIS**
dissolute person .. **RAKE, ROUE**
dissonant .... **ATONAL**
distance, at-from a . **OFF, AFAR**
distant ... **FAR, YON, REMOTE**
distilling vessel .... **MATRASS**
distinctive air ... **AURA, MIEN, CACHET**
distracted .... **DISTRAIT**
distraint: old Eng. law .. **NAAM**
distribute .. **DEAL, DOLE, METE**
DISTRICT .... see also REGION
district .... **AREA, ZONE**
district, old Eng. court **SOC, SOKE**
disturb .... **ROIL, MOLEST**
disturbance ...... **ROW, RIOT**
d ditch .... **FOSS, RINE, FOSSE, TRENCH**
ditch, castle .... **MOAT**
ditch, fort. .... **RELAIS**
ditch millet .... **HUREEK**
ditto .... **SAME**
divan .... **SOFA**
dive .... **DEN, HEADER**
dive bomber .... **STUKA**
diverge .... **DEVIATE**
divers .... **SEVERAL**
divest .... **STRIP, DEPRIVE**
divide .... **PART, SHARE**
divide for study ..... **DISSECT**
divided .... **REFT, SPLIT**
divider .... **MERIST**
dividing wall, membrance, partition ..... **SEPTA, SEPTUM**
divination by lots: Lat. **SORS, SORTES**
"Divine Comedy" author **DANTE**
divine favor .... **GRACE**
divine law: Rom. .... **FAS**
divine revelation **TORA, TORAH**
divine utterance ..... **ORACLE**
divinity .... **DEITY**
divorce bill, Jewish law **GET, GETT**
divorce, Moslem ...... **TALAK**
"— dixit" .... **IPSE**
dizziness, pert. to ..... **DINIC**

a docile .... **TAME**
dockyard barge .... **LUMP**
doctor ..... **INTERN, INTERNE**
Dr. Brown's dog hero .... **RAB**
Dr. Jekyll's other self .. **HYDE**
doctrinaire .... **ISMY**
doctrine .. **ISM, DOGMA, TENET**
documents, box for .. **HANAPER**
dodder .... **AMIL**
dodo genus .... **DIDUS**
doe .... **HIND**
doe, young .... **TAG, TEG**
dog, ... **CANIS, CANINE**
dog ...... **POM, CHOW, PEKE, BASSET, POODLE, SPANIEL**
dog, chops of .... **FLEWS**
dog-faced ape .... **AANI**
dog-fisher .... **OTTER**
DOG, GUN see DOG, HUNTING
dog, Hungarian **PULI, KUVASZ**
dog, hunting (bird) ... **ALAN, ALAND, ALANT, BASSET, BEAGLE, SETTER, COURSER, HARRIER, POINTER**
dog, John Brown's ...... **RAB**
dog, large .... **ALAN**
dog, "Odyssey" .... **ARGOS**
dog salmon .... **KETA**
dog, small-toy ..... **POM, PUG, PEKE**
b dog snapper, fish ...... **JOCU**
dog, Sputnik's .... **LAIKA**
dog star .... **SEPT, SOPT, SEPTI, SIRIUS**
dog, tropical .... **ALCO**
dog, Welsh .... **CORGI**
dog, wild, Austral. ..... **DINGO**
dog, wild, India ...... **DHOLE**
doge, office of ...... **DOGATE**
dogfish .... **SHARK**
dogma .... **TENET**
dogwood ..... **OSIER, CORNEL**
dole .... **METE**
dolphin fish .... **DORADO**
dolphin genus .... **INIA**
dolphin-like cetacean .... **INIA**
dolt .... **ASS, OAF, CLOD, LOUT, DUNCE**
domain ..... **BOURN, REALM, BOURNE, DEMENE, ESTATE, DEMESNE**
dome .... **CUPOLA**
dome-shaped .... **DOMOID**
Domesday Book money ... **ORA**
domestic .... **MAID, LOCAL**
domestic animal .... **ASS, CAT, COW, DOG, HOG, PIG, RAM, SOW, MULE**
domestic slave .... **ESNE**
domesticated .... **TAME**
dominion .... **REALM, EMPERY**

c domino .... **MASK**
Don Juan's mother ...... **INEZ**
donkey .... **ASS, MOKE, BURRO, NEDDY**
doom .... **CONDEMN, DESTINE**
doom palm, Afr. .... **DUM**
door .... **PORTAL**
door: Lat. .... **JANUA**
door part ...... **JAMB, SASH, SILL, LINTEL**
door section .... **PANEL**
doorkeeper, Masonic .... **TILER**
dorado, color .... **CUIR**
Doric frieze slab ..... **METOPE**
dormant ..... **ASLEEP, LATENT**
dormouse .... **LOIR**
dormouse, garden ...... **LEROT**
dormouse genus .... **GLIS**
dorsal .... **NOTAL**
dote .... **DRIVEL**
dots, paint with ...... **STIPPLE**
dotted with figures ...... **SEME**
double . **DUAL, TWIN, BINATE**
double cocoon ...... **DUPION**
double dagger .... **DIESIS**
double, Egypt .... **KA**
double salt .... **ALUM**
double tooth .... **MOLAR**
doubletree .... **EVENER**
d dovkie ...... **ROTCH, ROTGE, ROTCHE**
Dovyalis .... **ABERIA**
dowel ...... **PIN, COAG, COAK**
dower, pert. to .... **DOTAL**
dower property .... **DOS**
down ...... **FUZZ, PILE, EIDER**
down, facing. **PRONE, PRONATE**
down quilt .... **DUVET**
"downunder" native clan .. **ATI**
downward, curve ...... **DEFLEX**
dowry .... **DOS, DOT**
drag ... **LUG, TUG, HAUL, SNIG**
dragnet .... **TRAWL**
dragon, like a ... **DRACONTINE**
dragon of darkness, Bibl. **RAHAB**
drain . **SAP, DEPLETE, VITIATE**
drain .... **SUMP, SEWER**
dram, small .... **NIP**
DRAMA .... see also PLAY
Dravidian **KOTA, MALE, NAIR, TODA, TULU, TAMIL**
draw ...... **TIE, TOW, LIMN, PULL, DEPICT**
draw forth .... **EDUCE**
draw from .... **DERIVE**
draw out . **EDUCE, ATTENUATE**
draw tight: naut. .... **FRAP**
drawing curve .... **SPLINE**
drawing room .... **SALON**
dreadful .... **DIRE**
dream, day .... **REVERIE**

a "Dream Girl" playwright . **RICE**
dregs .... **FAEX, LEES, DROSS, SEDIMENT**
drench .... **SOUSE, TOUSE**
drenched .... **WET, DEWED**
DRESS .... see also GARMENT
dress .... **GARB, CLOTHE, ACCOUTER**
dress, as stone ...... **DAB, NIG**
dress feathers .... **PREEN**
dress leather ...... **DUB, TAN**
dress up .... **TOG, PREEN**
dressed .... **CLAD**
dressing wounds, material for **LINT, LINTS**
dried berry: Sp. .... **PASA**
dried up .... **SERE**
drift .... **TREND**
drill .... **BORE, TRAIN**
drilling rod .... **BAR, BIT**
DRINK .... see also BEVERAGE
drink .... **GULP, SWIG, QUAFF, IMBIBE**
drink, Christmas **NOG, WASSAIL**
drink, fermented ...... **MEAD**
drink, honey .... **MEAD**
drink, hot .... **TODDY**
drink, hot milk .... **POSSET**
drink of gods .... **NECTAR**
drink of liquor .. **NIP, BRACER**
b drink, old honey ...... **MORAT**
drink, palm .... **NIPA**
drink, rum-gin .... **BUMBO**
drink slowly .... **SIP, SUP**
drink, small .... **NIP, PEG, DRAM, SLUG**
drink to excess .. **TOPE, BOUSE**
drink, whiskey .... **STINGER**
drinking bowl .... **MAZER**
drinking cup, Gr. .... **HOLMOS**
drinking vessel .... **CUP, MUG, TIG, TYG, JORUM, STEIN, TANKARD**
drive ..... **RIDE, URGE, IMPEL**
drive away ..... **SHOO, DISPEL**
drive back **ROUT, REPEL, REPULSE**
drive in .... **TAMP**
drivel .... **DROOL, SLAVER**
driver, fast reckless ..... **JEHU**
drizzle .. **MIST, SMUR, SMURR**
droll .... **ODD**
dromedary, female .... **DELUL**
dromedary, swift .... **MEHARI**
drone .... **BEE, DOR, HUM**
droop .... **LOP, SAG, WILT**
drooping .... **ALOP**
drop ...... **DRIB, FALL, SINK, GUTTA, GLOBULE**
drop a fish line or bait .. **DAP**
drop, one .... **MINIM**
c drop: Prov. Eng. ..... **SIE, SYE**
dropsy .... **EDEMA**
dross .. **SLAG, SPRUE, SCORIA**
drought-tolerant plant .. **GUAR**
drove .... **HERD, RODE**
drove of horses .... **ATAJO**
drowse .... **NOD**
drudge ... **MOIL, TOIL, LABOR**
drug ..... **DOPE, SINA, ALOES, OPIATE, DILANTIN**
drug, Hippocrates' .... **MECON**
drugged bliss .... **KEF**
drum-call to arms .... **RAPPEL**
drum roll, reveille .... **DIAN**
drum, small . **TABOR, TABOUR, TABRET**
drum, W. Ind. .... **GUMBY**
drumbeat .... **DUB, TATOO, TATTOO**
drunkard .... **SOT, SOAK, SOUSE, TOPER**
dry .... **SEC, ARID, SERE**
dry, as wine .... **SEC**
dry bed of river .... **WADI**
dry goods dealer ..... **DRAPER**
dub .... **NAME, KNIGHT**
duck .... **ANAS, SMEE, TEAL, PEKIN**
duck, Arctic .... **EIDER**
d duck, breed of .... **ROUEN**
duck, diving .... **SMEW**
duck eggs, Chin. ...... **PIDAN**
duck, fresh water .... **TEAL**
duck genus .. **AEX, AIX, ANAS**
duck, like a .... **ANATINE**
duck lure .... **DECOY**
duck, male .... **DRAKE**
duck, Muscovy .... **PATO**
duck, pintail .... **SMEE**
duck, ring-necked ...... **DOGY**
duck, river ..... **TEAL, EIDER, SHOVELER**
duck, sea ...... **COOT, SCAUP**
duck, sea, northern ... **SCOTER**
duck-shooting boat ..... **SKAG**
duck to cook: Fr. ... **CANETON**
duct: anat. .... **VAS, VASA**
dude .... **FOP, DANDY**
due, India .... **HAK, HAKH**
duet .... **DUI, DUO**
dugout canoe **BANCA, PIROGUE**
dugout, India . **DONGA, DUNGA**
duke's dominion ...... **DUCHY**
dulcimer .... **CITOLE**
dulcimer, Oriental ..... **SANTIR**
dull . **DRY, DUN, DRAB, LOGY, BLUNT, PROSY, BORING**
dull color .. **DUN, MAT, DRAB, MATTE, TERNE**
dull in finish .... **MAT, MATTE**

a dull silk fabric .... **GROS**
dullard .... **BOOR**
Dumas hero
ATHOS, ARAMIS, PORTHOS
dummy whist .... **MORT**
dung beetle .... **DOR**
dunlin bird .... **STIB**
dupe .... **USE, FOOL**
duration measure .... **TIME**
dusk .... **EVE**
dusky .... **DIM, DARK, SWART**
dusty: Scot. .... **MOTTY**
DUTCH see also NETHERLANDS, SPECIAL SECTION
Dutch: bit ....**DOIT**
cupboard .... **KAS**
donkey .... **EZEL**
"mister" .... **HEER**
out .... **UIT**
woman .... **FROW**
Dutch cheese .... **EDAM**
Dutch commune .... **EDE**
Dutch early geographer .. **AA**
Dutch fishing boat .. **DOGGER**
Dutch measure, old ..... **AAM**
Dutch meter .... **EL**
Dutch minor coin .... **DOIT**
Dutch news agency, old **ANETA**
Dutch painter
LIS, HALS, LELY, STEEN
Dutch two-masted vessel **KOFF**
duty .... **CHORE, TARIFF**
dwarf .. **RUNT, STUNT, TROLL**

c dwarf cattle, S. Am.
NATA, NIATA
dwell ...... **BIDE, LIVE, ABIDE**
dwelling .... **ABODE**
dwindle .... **PETER**
Dyak knife .... **PARANG**
Dyak, sea .... **IBAN**
dye base .... **ANILINE**
dye, blue .... **WOAD**
dye, blue-red ...... **ORSELLE**
dye gum .... **KINO**
dye, indigo .... **ANIL**
dye, lichen
ARCHIL, ORCHAL, ORCHIL
dye plant .... **ANIL**
dye, red **AAL, ANATO, AURIN, EOSIN, ANATTA, ANATTO, AURINE, EOSINE, ANNATTA, ANNATTO, ANNOTTO, ARNATTO**
dye, red, poisonous
AURIN, AURINE
dye stuff .. **EOSINE, MADDER**
dye, yellow .... **WELD, WOLD, WOALD**
dyeing apparatus ...... **AGER**
dyeing reagent .... **ALTERANT**
dyestuff from lichens .. **LITMUS**
dyewood tree .... **TUI**
dynamite inventor .... **NOBEL**
DYNASTY see CHIN. DYNASTY
dynasty, first Chin. ..... **HSIA**
dynasty, It. .... **SAVOY**

E

b eager .. **AGOG, AVID, ARDENT**
eagle .... **ERN, ERNE**
eagle, Bible .... **GIER**
eagle, tried to mount to heaven on .... **ETANA**
eagle, sea .... **ERN, ERNE**
eagle's nest
AERY, EYRY, AERIE, EYRIE
eaglestone ... **ETITE, AETITES**
ear .... **LUG, HANDLE**
ear canal .... **SCALA**
ear cavity .... **UTRICLE**
ear doctor .... **AURIST**
ear inflamation .... **OTITIS**
ear of wheat: archeol.
SPICA, SPICAE
ear, pert. to .... **OTIC, AURAL**
ear, prominence **TRAGI, TRAGUS**
ear shell .. **ORMER, ABALONE**
ear stone .. **OTOLITE, OTOLITH**
earache ... **OTALGY, OTALGIA**
eared seal .... **OTARY**

d early Britisher .... **PICT**
early Christian priest ... **ARIUS**
earnest
ARDENT, INTENT, SINCERE
earnest money: law .... **ARRA, ARLES, ARRHA**
earth .... **GEO**
earth deposit in rocks .. **GUHR**
earth: dial. .... **ERD**
earth god, Egypt. **GEB, KEB, SEB**
earth goddess ..... **GE, ERDA, GAEA, GAIA**
earth goddess, Khonds' .. **TARI**
earth goddess, Rom.
CERES, TERRA
earth, kind of .... **LOAM**
earth, pert. to .... **GEAL**
earth's surface, made on
EPIGENE
earthenware maker ... **POTTER**
earthly .... **TERRENE**
earthquake .. **SEISM, TEMBLOR**

a earthquake, pert. to .. **SEISMIC**
earthquake, shock of. **TREMOR**
earthwork, Rom. ...... **AGGER**
East .. **ASIA, LEVANT, ORIENT**
E. African native ... **SOMALI**
E. Afr. spiritual power .. **NGAI**
E. Indian animal .... **TARSIER**
E. Ind. dye tree .... **DHAK**
E. Ind. fruit **DURIAN, DURION**
E. Ind. grass .... **KASA**
E. Ind. herb .... **PIA, SESAME**
E. Ind. herb root **CHAY, CHOY**
E. Ind. palm .... **NIPA**
E. Ind. plant .. **JUTE, SESAME**
E. Ind. shrubby herb .... **SOLA**
E. Ind. tanning tree .. **AMLA, AMLI**
E. Ind. term of address **SAHIB**
E. Ind. timber tree. .**ACH, SAJ, SAL, SAIN, SAUL, TEAK**
E. Ind. tree, large ..... **SIRIS**
E. Ind. vine ..... **AMIL, GILO, ODAL, ODEL, SOMA**
E. Ind. vine, milky ..... **SOMA**
E. Ind. weight .... **TOLA**
E. Ind. wood, strong, heavy **ENG**
E. Ind. woody vine **ODAL, GILO**
East Indies .... **INDONESIA**
east wind .... **EURUS**
east wind's opposite .... **AFER**
Easter ...... **PASCH, PASCHA**
b Eastern .... **ORTIVE**
Eastern Catholic ...... **UNIAT**
Eastern Church doxology **DOXA**
Eastern European ...... **SLAV**
Eastern garment .... **SARI**
Eastern name ..... **ALI, ABOU**
Eastern title ...... **AGA, RAS**
Eastern Turkey tribesman **KURD**
easy .... **SOFT**
easy gait .... **LOPE**
easy job **SNAP,CINCH,SINECURE**
eat away .... **ERODE**
eat voraciously **RAVEN, RAVIN, RAVINE**
eaten away .... **EROSE**
eating away **CAUSTIC, ERODENT**
eccentric person .... **GINK**
eccentric piece, rotating .. **CAM**
ecclesiastic .... **PRELATE**
ECCLESIASTICAL see CHURCH
eclipse .... **DIM**
eclipse demon, Hindu **KETU, RAHU**
ecru .... **BEIGE**
Ecuadorian extinct Indians **CARA**
edentate genus .... **MANIS**
edge .... **HEM, LIP, RIM, ARRIS, BRINK, MARGE**
edged unevenly .... **EROSE**
edging .... **PICOT**

c edging, make .... **TAT**
edible fungus .... **CEPE**
edible root ...... **OCA, YAM, TARO, CASAVA, CASSAVA**
edible shoot, Jap. .... **UDO**
edict .... **LAW, FIAT, DECREE**
Edinburgh: poet ...... **EDINA**
edit .... **REVISE, REDACT**
editorial "I" .... **WE**
Edom district .... **TEMAN**
Edomite .... **OMAR**
Edomite city .... **PAU**
Edomite duke **UZ, ARAN, IRAM**
Edomite king, ruler ..... **BELA**
educated .... **BRED, LETTERED**
educator, Am. .... **MANN**
educe .... **EVOKE, ELICIT**
Edward Bradley's pseudo. **BEDE**
eel, marine .... **CONGER**
eel: old Eng. .... **ELE**
eel-shaped amphibian ... **OLM**
eel, S. Am. .... **CARAPO**
eel, young .... **ELVER**
eelworm .... **NEMA**
Eghbal's land .... **IRAN**
effervescent, to make . **AERATE**
effigy .... **IDOL**
effluvium ... **MIASM, MIASMA**
effort .... **DINT, ASSAY, NISUS, TRIAL**
d effusive .... **GUSHING**
eft .... **EVET, NEWT**
egg .... **OVUM**
egg dish .. **OMELET, OMELETTE**
egg drink .... **NOG, NOGG**
egg, insect .... **NIT**
egg-shaped **OOID, OVAL, OVATE, OVOID**
egg-shaped ornaments ... **OVA**
egg white, raw .... **GLAIR**
eggs .... **OVA, ROE**
ego .... **SELF**
Egypt, pert. to ...... **COPTIC**
Egyptian bird .... **IBIS**
Egyp. Christian .... **COPT**
Egyp. city, ancient **SAIS, THEBES**
Egyp. cobra .... **HAJE**
Egyp. crown .... **ATEF**
Egyp. dog-headed ape, deity **AANI**
Egyp. gateway .... **PYLON**
Egyp. god of creation ... **PTAH**
EGYPTIAN GODS — GODDESSES —DEITY see also GODS and SPECIAL SECTION
Egyp. guard .... **GHAFIR**
Egyp. heaven **AALU, AARU, IALU, YARU**
Egyp. immortal heart **AB, HATI**
Egyp. king .. **MENES, RAMESES**
Egyp. lute .... **NABLA**

a Egyp. nationalist party . **WAFD**
Egyp. precious alloy .... **ASEM**
Egyp. primeval chaos ..... **NU**
Egyp. queen of gods .... **SATI**
Egyp. sacred bird .. **BENU, IBIS**
Egyp. sacred bull .... **APIS**
Egyp. season .... **AHET**
Egyp. tambourine ...... **RIKK**
Egyp. thorn .... **KIKAR**
Egyp. writing surfaces **PAPYRI**
eh?: obs. ....**ANAN**
eight days after feast .. **UTAS**
eight, group of **OCTAD, OCTET, OCTAVE**
eight, set of .... **OGDOAD**
eighth day of feast .... **UTAS**
eighth day, on ...... **OCTAN**
eighth note .... **UNCA**
Eire legislature .... **DAIL**
ejaculation, mystic ...... **OM**
eject ...... **EMIT, OUST, SPEW**
elaborate .... **ORNATE**
Elam, capital of .... **SUSA**
eland .... **IMPOFO**
elanet .... **KITE**
elasmobranch fish **RAY, SHARK**
Elbe, river to ...... **EGER, ISER**
Elbe tributary .... **EGER, ISER**
elbow .... **ANCON**
elder .... **SENIOR**
b elder son of Zeus ...... **ARES**
elder statesmen, Jap. .. **GENRO**
eldest: law ...... **AINE, EIGNE**
electric catfish .... **RAAD**
electric force .... **ELOD**
electric force unit ...... **VOLT**
electric reluctance unit .. **REL**
electric unit .. **ES, AMP, MHO, OHM, REL, PERM, FARAD, HENRY, AMPERE**
electrified particle ...... **ION**
electrode .. **ANODE, CATHODE**
electromagnet .... **RELAY**
electron tube **TRIODE, KLYSTRON**
elegance .... **GRACE**
elegant .... **FINE, POSH**
elegist .... **POET**
elegy .... **NENIA**
ELEMENT, non-metallic and metallic, gaseous on page 195
elemi .... **ANIME**
element, radioactive of **URANIC**
elephant goad .... **ANKUS**
elephant: India .... **HATHI**
elephant's cry .... **BARR**
elephant's ear .... **TARO**
elevated ground **MESA, RIDEAU**
elevation of mind .. **ANAGOGE**
elevator: Brit. .... **LIFT**

c elf .... **SPRITE**
elf, Egypt. .... **OUPHE**
elfin .... **FEY**
Elia .... **LAMB**
elicit .... **EDUCE**
elide .... **DELE, OMIT**
Elija .... **ELIAS**
eliminate ... **DELETE, REMOVE**
Elizabeth I, name for **ORIANA**
elk, Am. .... **WAPITI**
elk, Europ. .... **MOOSE**
elk, Europ. genus ...... **ALCES**
elliptical ...... **OVAL, OVOID**
elm .... **ULM, ULME**
elm fruit seed ...... **SAMARA**
elongated .... **PROLATE**
else .... **OTHER**
elude .... **DODGE, EVADE**
elver .... **EEL**
emaciation .... **TABES, MACIES**
emanation .... **AURA**
emanation, star .... **BLAS**
embankment ... **DAM, BUND, DIKE, DYKE, DIGUE, LEVEE**
embellish **GILD, ADORN, DECORATE**
embellished .... **ORNATE**
ember .... **ASH, COAL**
emblem ... **INSIGNE, INSIGNIA**
d emblem of authority .... **MACE**
emblem of U.S. .... **EAGLE**
embrace **HUG, CLASP, ENARM, INARM**
embrocation ...... **LINIMENT**
embroidery frame **TABORET, TABOURET**
emend .... **EDIT**
emerald .... **BERYL, SMARAGD**
emerge **RISE, ISSUE, EMANATE**
emetic .... **IPECAC**
eminent .... **NOTED**
emit .... **REEK, EXUDE**
emmer .... **SPELT**
emmet .... **ANT**
Emperor of Russia **CZAR, TSAR, TZAR**
emphasis .... **ACCENT, STRESS**
empire .... **REALM**
employ .... **USE, HIRE, PLACE**
employed for wine, meas. **AAM**
employees .... **PERSONNEL**
employer .... **BOSS, USER**
employment .... **PLACE**
emporium ...... **MART, STORE**
Empress, Byzant. ...... **IRENE**
Empress, Russian ... **CZARINA, TSARINA, TZARINA**
empty ...... **VOID, INANE, DEPLETE**
emulate .... **RIVAL**
enamel ware .... **LIMOGES**

a enchantress .... **CIRCE, MEDEA**
encircle .... **ORB, GIRD, GIRT, RING, EMBAY**
encircled **GIRT, RINGED, SURROUNDED**
encircling band .... **ZONE**
enclose .... **MEW**
enclosure .... **MEW, PEN, REE, STY, CORRAL**
enclosure, cattle ..... **ATAJO**
enclosure: Sp. Am. ... **CANCHA**
encomium .... **ELOGE**
encompass .. **GIRD, GIRT, RING**
encompassed by .... **AMID**
encore .... **BIS**
encounter .... **MEET**
encourage .... **ABET**
end **TIP, FINIS, LIMIT, OMEGA**
end: music .... **FINE**
end result .... **PRODUCT**
end, tending to an ..... **TELIC**
endeavor .. **TRY, ESSAY, NISUS**
ENDING ... see also SUFFIX or type of ending
ending, comparative . **IER, IOR**
ENDING, NOUN see SUFFIX, NOUN ENDING
ending, plural .... **EN, ES**
ending, superlative ...... **EST**
endow ...... **DOWER, INVEST**
b endue .... **ENDOW**
endure .... **BEAR, LAST, WEAR**
endure: dial. .... **BIDE**
energy .... **PEP, VIM, ZIP, POWER, VIGOR, VIGOUR**
energy, potential ...... **ERGAL**
energy unit **ERG, RAD, ERGON**
enfeeble **WEAKEN, DEBILITATE**
engage **HIRE, ENTER, CHARTER**
engender .... **BEGET, BREED, PROMOTE, GENERATE**
engine, donkey ...... **YARDER**
engine of war .... **RAM**
engine part .... **STATOR**
engine, rotary ...... **TURBINE**
engineer, Am. .... **EADS**
engineer, military .... **SAPPER**
English actor .... **EVANS**
Eng. actress .... (Nell) **GWYN, TERRY, NEAGLE**
Eng. architect .... **WREN**
Eng. author .... **MORE, WEST, ARLEN, BACON, CAINE, DEFOE, DORAN, ELIOT, HARDY, READE, SHUTE, WAUGH, WELLS, AMBLER, AUSTEN, BARRIE, BELLOC, BRONTE, ORWELL, STERNE**
Eng. car .... **ROVER**
Eng. cathedral city **ELY, YORK**
Eng. city, historic **COVENTRY**
c Eng. college ... **ETON, BALIOL**
ENG. COMPOSER see COMPOSER, ENG.
Eng. country festival .... **ALE**
Eng. dramatist **SHAW, PEELE, DRYDEN**
Eng. emblem .... **ROSE**
Eng. essayist .... **SALA, STEELE**
Eng. explorer ... **ROSS, CABOT**
Eng. historian .... **BEDE**
Eng. king **BRAN, CNUT, KNUT, CANUTE**
Eng. monk ..... **BEDE, BAEDA**
Eng. murderer .... **ARAM**
Eng. musician .... **ARNE**
ENG. NOVELIST .... see ENG. AUTHOR
Eng. painter .... **OPIE, ORPEN**
Eng. philosopher ...... **HUME, JOAD, BACON, SPENCER**
Eng. playwright .... **SHAW**
Eng. poet ..... **GRAY, AUDEN, BLAKE, BYRON, CAREW, DONNE, ELIOT**
Eng. queen ..... **ANNE, MARY**
Eng. rebel leader, 1450 .. **CADE**
Eng. royal house **YORK, TUDOR**
Eng. scholar, schoolmaster **ARAM**
Eng. school, boys' ...... **ETON**
Eng. sculptor .... **EPSTEIN**
d Eng. spa .... **BATH, MARGATE**
Eng. spy .... **ANDRE**
Eng. statesman ... **EDEN, PITT**
Eng. theologian ..... **ALCUIN**
Eng. woman politician .. **ASTOR**
ENG. WRITER ..... see ENG. AUTHOR and ENG. ESSAYIST
engraver ... **CHASER, ETCHER, GRAVER**
engraver, famous .. **PYE, DORE**
engraver's tool .... **BURIN**
engrossed .... **RAPT**
enigma .... **RIDDLE**
enlarge **DILATE, EXPAND, INCREASE**
enlarge a hole .... **REAM**
enlarging, as chimneys .. **EVASE**
enmity .... **ANIMUS**
Enoch's father .... **CAIN**
enough .... **ENOW**
enrol .... **ENTER, ENLIST**
ensign .... **FLAG**
ensnare .... **NET, WEB**
entangle .... **MAT, MESH**
enter .... **ENROL**
entertain **AMUSE, DIVERT, REGALE**
enthusiasm **ELAN, ARDOR, VERVE, SPIRIT**
enthusiastic .... **RABID**

a entice .... **BAIT, LURE, TOLE, TEMPT, ALLURE**
enticement .... **TICE**
entire man .... **EGO**
entity .... **ENS, ENTIA**
entomb .... **INURN**
entrance **ADIT, DOOR, GATE, PORTAL**
entrance halls .... **ATRIA**
entreat .... **PRAY, PLEAD**
entreaty .... **PLEA**
entry, separate .... **ITEM**
entwine **WEAVE, ENLACE, WREATHE**
enumerate .... **COUNT**
envelop **WRAP, ENFOLD, INFOLD**
environment .... **MILIEU**
envoy .... **LEGATE**
envy .... **COVET**
enzyme .... **ASE, LOTASE, RENNIN, MALTASE**
eon .... **OLAM**
ephah, 1/10 .... **OMER**
epic poetry .... **EPOS, EPOPEE**
epoch .... **ERA**
epochal .... **ERAL**
epode .... **POEM**
eponymous ancestor .... **EBER**
equal **IS, ARE, TIE, EVEN, PEER**
equality .... **PAR, PARITY**
b equally .... **AS**
equilibrium .... **POISE**
equine .... **HORSE**
equip .... **FIT, RIG**
equitable ... **JUST, IMPARTIAL**
equivalence .... **PAR**
equivocate .... **EVADE**
era .... **EPOCH**
eradicate .... **ERASE, UPROOT**
eral .... **EPOCHAL**
erase .... **DELE, DELETE**
erect .... **REAR, RAISE**
ergo .... **HENCE**
Eris' brother .... **ARES**
ermine, summer .... **STOAT**
Eros .... **CUPID**
errand boy .... **PAGE**
error, publication ...... **TYPO, ERRATA, ERRATE, ERRATUM**
Esau .... **EDOM**
Esau's brother .... **JACOB**
Esau's father-in-law ... **ELON**
Esau's grandson ...... **OMAR**
Esau's home .... **SEIR**
Esau's wife .... **ADAH**
escape .. **LAM, ELUDE, EVADE**
eschew .... **SHUN**
escutcheon band .... **FESS**
Esdra's angel .... **URIEL**
eskers .... **OSAR**
Eskimo .... **ITA**
c Eskimo boat **KIAK, KYAK, KAYAK**
Eskimo boot .... **MUKLUK**
Eskimo coat **PARKA, NETCHA, TEMIAK**
Eskimo curlew .... **FUTE**
Eskimo house **IGLU, IGLOE, IGLOO, IGLOU**
Eskimo settlement ..... **ETAH**
Eskimo summer hut .... **TOPEK**
Eskimos of Asia **YUIT, INNUIT**
esoteric .... **INNER**
espy .... **SEE, SPY**
esquire .... **ARMIGER**
essay ... **TRY, TEST, ATTEMPT**
essay, scholarly **THESIS, TREATISE**
essence: Hindu religion .. **RASA**
essence, rose .... **ATTAR**
essential oils fluid ..... **NEROL**
essential part .... **CORE, PITH**
"— est" (that is) .... **ID**
establish .... **BASE, FOUND**
established value .... **PAR**
estate, landed, large .. **MANOR**
estate manager .... **STEWARD**
estate, not held by feudal tenure **ALOD, ALLOD, ALODIUM**
esteem .... **HONOR, PRIZE, ADMIRE, HONOUR**
d ester, hydriodic acid ... **IODIDE**
ester, liquid .... **ACETIN**
ester, oleic acid ..... **OLEATE**
estimate .... **RATE, APPRAISE**
Estonian .... **ESTH**
estuary .... **RIA**
estuary, Brazil .... **PARA**
estuary, S. Am. .... **PLATA**
Eternal City .... **ROME**
eternity ..... **AGE, EON, OLAM**
ether compound .... **ESTER**
ethereal .... **AERY, AERIAL**
ETHIOPIA see also ABYSSINIA
Ethiopia .... **CUSH**
Ethiopian title .... **RAS**
Ethiopic .... **GEEZ**
ethos, opposed to .... **PATHOS**
Etruscan god .... **LAR**
Etruscan Juno .... **UNI**
Etruscan Minerva ... **MENFRA**
Etruscan title, peer **LAR, LARS**
eucalyptus secretion **LAAP, LARP, LERP**
eucalyptus tree .... **YATE**
Eucharist case ...... **PIX, PYX**
Eucharist cloth **FANO, FANON, FANUM**
Eucharist spoon .... **LABIS**
Eucharist wafer .... **HOST**
eulogy .... **ELOGE**
euphorbia .... **SPURGE**

a Eurasian dock plant .. **PARELLE**
eureka red .... **PUCE**
Euripides heroine ..... **MEDEA**
EUROPEAN see also specific word, as FISH, ANIMAL, etc.
European .... **POLE, SLAV**
Eur. colorful fish ...... **BOCE**
EUROP. FISH .. see FISH, EUR.
European, in Moslem East **FRANGI**
Europ. iris .... **ORRIS**
Europ. kite ..... **GLED, GLEDE**
Europ. porgy .... **PARGO**
Eurytus' daughter ...... **IOLE**
evade **SHUN, DODGE, ELUDE, SHIRK**
evaluate .... **RATE, ASSESS**
Evangelist ...... **LUKE, MARK**
Evans, Mary Ann ...... **ELIOT**
Eve's grandson .... **ENOS**
even ..... **EEN, LEVEL, PLANE**
even if .... **THO**
evening party .... **SOIREE**
evening prayer .... **VESPER**
eventual lot .... **FATE**
ever .... **EER**
evergreen .... **FIR, YEW, PINE, CAROB, CEDAR, OLIVE, SAVIN, LAUREL, SABINE,**
b **SAVINE, SPRUCE**
evergreen, bean ...... **CAROB**
evergreen genus **OLAX, ABIES, CATHA**
evergreen, red-berry **YEW, WHORT**
evergreen, tropical .. **CALABA**
everlasting ... **ETERN, ETERNE**
evict .... **OUST**
evident **CLEAR, PLAIN, PATENT**
evil .... **MAL**
evil god, Egypt. ... **SET, SETH**
evil intent: law .... **DOLUS**
evil spirit, Haiti **BAKA, BOKO**
evil spirit, Hindu ..... **ASURA**
evolve .... **EDUCE**
ewe, old .... **CRONE**
exact **BLEED, DEMAND, EXTORT**
exacerbate .... **IRE**
exact point .... **TEE**
examine ..... **PRY, SPY, SCAN**
excavate .. **DIG, PION, DREDGE**
excavation for extracting ore **STOPE**
excavation, mine .. **PIT, STOPE**
exceed .... **TOP**
exceedingly: music .....**TRES**
excellence .... **VIRTU**
excellent .... **AONE**
except .... **BUT, SAVE**
excess ...... **LUXUS, NIMIETY**

c excess, fill to ... **GLUT, SATE**
excess of solar year ... **EPACT**
exchange medium, Chin. **SYCEE**
exchange premium, discount **AGIO**
exchequer .... **FISC, FISK**
excite .... **ELATE, ROUSE**
excited .... **AGOG, MANIC**
excitement, public **FUROR, FURORE**
exclamation .. **AH, EH, HA, HI, MY, OH, OW, UM, ACH, AHA, AUH, BAH, BAW, FIE, FOH, GRR, HAH, HAW, HAY, HEM, HEP, HEU, HEY, HIC, HIP, HOI, HOY, HUH, OHO, OUF, PAH, PEW, POH, PUE, SOH, TCH, TCK, TUT, UGH, WEE, WHY, WOW, YAH, YOI, YOW, ALAS, PHEW, ALACK**
exclamation, Fr. .... **HEIN**
exclamation, Ger. ..... **HOCH**
exclamation, Ir. ...... **ADAD, AHEY, ARAH, ARRA, ARRO, BOOH, EHEU, OCHONE**
exclude ... **BAR, OMIT, DEBAR**
exclusive .... **SOLE**
exclusive set .... **ELECT, ELITE**
exclusively .... **ONLY**
d excoriate .... **ABRADE**
excrete from skin ...... **EGEST**
excuse .. **PLEA, ALIBI, REMIT**
excuse, court **ESSOIN, ESSOINE**
execrated ..... **CURST, SWORE**
exemplar ... **MODEL, PATTERN**
exhaust **SAP, TIRE, SPEND, DEPLETE**
exhausted .... **EFFETE**
exhibits leaping ..... **SALTATE**
exigency .... **NEED**
exist .... **LIVE**
exist .. **all forms of verb "BE"**
exist, beginning to .. **NASCENT**
existence .... **ENS, ESSE**
existentialist leader ... **SARTRE**
existing **ALIVE, BEING, EXTANT**
exit .. **LEAVE, DEPART, EGRESS**
expand ..... **DILATE, DISTEND**
expanse .... **SEA**
expatriate .... **EXILE**
expectation .... **HOPE**
expedite .... **HURRY, HASTEN**
expedition .. **SAFARI, SUFFARI**
expert ... **ACE, ONER, ADEPT**
expiate .... **ATONE**
explain .... **DEFINE**
explode **POP, DETONATE, FULMINATE**
exploit **DEED, FEAT, GEST, GESTE**

a explosive
CAP, TNT, GAINE, TONITE
explosive sound ... POP, CHUG
expose .... AIR, DISPLAY
expression, elegant . ATTICISM
expression, local .... IDIOM
expressionless ..... WOODEN
expunge DELE, ERASE, DELETE
extend
JUT, LIE, REACH, BEETLE
extend the front ..... DEPLOY
extensive .... AMPLE
extent .... AREA
external .... EXOTERIC
external covering . HIDE, HUSK, PEEL, PELT, RIND, SKIN
extinct wild ox .... URUS
extirpate .. ROOT, ERADICATE
extort .... BLEED, EXACT
extra .... ODD, SPARE
extra leaf .... INSERT
extra, theatrical .... SUPE
extract DRAW, ELICIT, EVULSE
extraneous .... EXOTIC
extraordinary person, thing
ONER

c extravagance .... ELA
extreme .... ULTRA
extreme unction, give
ANELE, ENELE
exudate, plant
GUM, LAC, RESIN
exude ..... EMIT, OOZE, REEK
exult .... ELATE
eye .... ORB, SEE, OGLE
eye cosmetic ... KOHL, KUHL
eye inflammation STY, IRITIS
eye, inner coat ...... RETINA
eye, layer .... UVEA
eye of bean .... HILA, HILUM
eye of insect .... STEMMA
eye, part of the .... IRIS, UVEA, CORNEA, RETINA
eye, pert. to .... OPTIC
eye socket .... ORBIT
eye, symbolic .... UTA
eye-worm, Afr. .... LOA
eyelash .... CILIA, CILIUM
eyes: old Eng. .... NIE
eyestalk .... STIPE
eyewink ...... LOOK, GLANCE
eyot .... ISLE, ISLET

F

b Fabian .... SHAW
fable .... APOLOG, APOLOGUE
fable writer .... ESOP, AESOP
fabled bird .... ROC, RUKH
"Fables in Slang" author ADE
fabric .... REP, ACCA, BAFT, DRAB, DUCK, IKAT, LAWN, LENO, MOFF, REPP, SILK, SUSI, TAPA, TUKE, CRAPE, CREPE, MOIRE, NINON, ORLON, RAYON, CANVAS, COVERT, MANTUA, MOHAIR
farbic, Angora ..... CAMLET, MOHAIR
fabric, coarse cotton .. SURAT
fabric, coarse wool
TAMIN, TAMINE
fabric, corded REP, REPP, PIQUE
fabric, cotton ... LENO, MULL, DENIM, MANTA, SCRIM, CALICO, CRETON, NANKIN, PENANG, NANKEEN, CRETONNE
fabric, curtain ... NET, SCRIM
fabric, felt-like .... BAIZE
fabric, fig'd DAMASK, PAISLEY
fabric from remnants MUNGO
fabric, Ind. .. SHELA, SHELAH

d fabric, knitted .... TRICOT
fabric, light wool .... ALPACA
fabric, lustrous POPLIN, SATEEN
fabric, mourning ALMA, CRAPE
fabric, net .. TULLE, MALINE
fabric, plaid . MAUD, TARTAN
fabric, printed BATIK, BATTIK
FABRIC, RIBBED
see RIBBED FABRIC
fabric, satin .. PEKIN, ETOILE
fabric, satiny
SATINET, SATINETTE
fabric, sheer .... GAUZE, BEMBERG, ORGANZA
fabric, short nap .... RAS
fabric, silk .... SURAH, PONGEE, SAMITE, TOBINE
fabric, silk, gold, medieval ACCA
fabric, silk, thick ...... GROS
fabric, stiff .... WIGAN
fabric stretcher
TENTER, STENTER
fabric, striped .. SUSI, DOREA, DORIA, DOOREA, MADRAS
fabric, thick .... DRAB
fabric, twilled .... REP
fabric, upholstery .. BROCATEL, BROCATALL, BROCATELL BROCATELLE

a fabric, velvet-like .... **PANNE**
fabric, voile-like .... **ETAMINE**
fabric, wool .. **SERGE, TAMIN, TAMIS, MERINO, TAMINE, TAMINY, TAMISE, TAMMIN, ESTAMIN, ETAMINE, STAMMEL, ESTAMINE**
fabric, worsted ...... **ETAMINE**
fabricate .... **MAKE**
fabulist .... **ESOP, AESOP**
fabulous bird ..... **ROC, RUKH**
face **MAP, MUG, PHIZ, FACADE**
face with stone ...... **REVET**
facet of gem .. **BEZEL, BEZIL, CULET, COLLET**
facile .... **EASY**
facing glacier .... **STOSS**
fact .... **DATUM**
fact, by the: law ..... **FACTO**
facts .... **DATA**
faction .... **SECT, SIDE, CABAL**
factor .... **GENE**
factory .... **PLANT**
faculty .... **SENSE**
fade ...... **DIE, DIM, WITHER**
"Faerie Queene" iron man **TALUS**
"Faerie Queene" lady .... **UNA**
failure .... **DUD, FLOP**
fainting: med. ..... **SYNCOPE**
b fair . **BAZAR, FERIA, BAZAAR KERMIS, KIRMES**
fair **JUST, CLEAR, IMPARTIAL**
fair-haired .. **BLOND, BLONDE**
fair-lead, naut. .... **WAPP**
fairy .. **ELF, FAY, PERI, SPRITE**
fairy fort .... **LIS, LISS**
fairy king .... **OBERON**
fairy queen ... **MAB, TITANIA**
fairy, Serbo-Croat **VILA, VILY**
fairylike creature .... **PERI**
faith, article of ...... **TENET**
faith, pert. to .... **PISTIC**
faithful .... **LEAL, TRUE, STANCH, STAUNCH**
falcon .... **SACER, SAKER, LANNER, MERLIN, SAKERET**
falcon, Asia **LAGGAR, LUGGAR**
falcon genus .... **FALCO**
falcon-headed god **MENT, MENTU**
falcon, Ind. **SHAHIN, SHAHEEN**
falcon of sea ...... **ERN, ERNE**
falconer's bait .... **LURE**
fall **DROP, PLAP, PLOP, SPILL**
fall back .... **RETREAT**
fallacy ...... **IDOLA, IDOLUM**
fallow-deer, female ...... **TEG**
false excuse .... **SUBTERFUGE**
false friend .. **IAGO, TRAITOR**
false fruit of rose .... **HIP**

c false god .... **IDOL**
Falstaff's follower ...... **NYM**
fame .... **ECLAT, KUDOS, RENOWN, REPUTE**
famed .... **NOTED**
familiar .... **VERSANT**
familiar saying .... **SAW, TAG**
family, Florentine .... **MEDICI**
family, Genoese ...... **DORIA**
family: Scot. .... **ILK**
famous .... **NOTED**
fan .... **ROOTER**
fan palm genus ...... **INODES**
fan's stick .... **BRIN**
fanatical .... **RABID**
fancy ... **IDEA, WHIM, IDEATE**
fanfare .... **TANTARA, TANTARO, TANTARARA**
fanning device **PUNKA, PUNKAH**
fare .... **DIET**
farewell ... **AVE, VALE, ADIEU**
farinaceous .... **MEALY**
farinaceous food **SAGO, SALEP**
farm group .... **GRANGE**
farm, small, Sp. Am. **CHACRA**
farm, Sw. small leased .. **TORP**
farm: Swedish .... **TORP**
farm, tenant .... **CROFT**
farmer .... **KULAK, GRANGER**
d farmyard, S. Afr. ...... **WERF**
Faroe Is. wind .... **OE**
Faroe judge .... **FOUD**
Farouk's father .... **FUAD**
fashion .... **FORM, MODE, MOLD, MODEL, STYLE**
fasten ... **BOLT, LOCK, NAIL, SEAL, SNIB, TACK, RIVET**
fasten: naut **BELAY, BATTEN**
fastener .... **NUT, PIN, BRAD, CLIP, HASP, NAIL, SNAP, STUD, CLASP, RIVET, CLEVIS, COTTER**
fastener, wire .... **STAPLE**
fastener, naut. .... **BITT**
fastener, wood **FID, NOG, PEG, PIN**
fastening .... **LATCH**
fastidious .... **NICE**
fasting month .... **RAMADAN**
fasting period .... **LENT**
fat **LARD, LIPA, SUET, OBESE**
fat, animal .. **ADEPS, TALLOW**
fat: comb. form **STEAT, STEATO**
fat, liquid part ...... **ELAIN, OLEIN, ELAINE, OLEINE**
fat, natural .... **ESTER**
fat, of .... **SEBAIC**
fat, solid part **STEARIN, STEARINE**
fatal ...... **FUNEST, LETHAL**

a fate .... **LOT, DOOM, KISMET**
Fates, Gr. & Rom. .... **MOIRA, MORTA, PARCA, CLOTHO, DECUMA, MOIRAI, PARCAE, ATROPOS, LACHESIS**
fateful .... **DIRE**
father .... **SIRE, BEGET**
father: Arab. .... **ABU, ABOU**
father: Hebr. .... **ABBA**
father of modern engraving **PYE**
father's side, kinship on **AGNAT, AGNATE**
fathom .... **PROBE, SOUND**
fatigue .. **FAG, TIRE, WEARY**
Fatima's huband .... **ALI**
fatty .... **ADIPOSE**
fatty gland secretion **SEBUM**
fatuous .... **INANE**
faucet ... **TAP, COCK, SPIGOT**
fault find ...... **CARP, CAVIL**
faultfinder .. **MOMUS, CAVILER**
faulty .... **BAD**
faux pas ...... **ERROR, GAFFE**
favor .... **BOON**
favorable vote .. **AY, AYE, YES**
favorite .... **PET, IDOL**
fawn color .... **FAON**
fawning favorite .... **MINION**
fear .... **PHOBIA**
fearful .... **TREPID**
b feast .... **REGALE**
feast day: comb. form .... **MAS**
feather **PENNA, PINNA, PLUME**
feather grass .... **STIPA**
feather palms .... **EJOO, IROK**
feather: zool. .... **PLUMA**
feathers, cast .... **MEW**
feathers of o-o .... **HULU**
feathered scarf .... **BOA**
feeble .. **PUNY, WEAK, DEBILE**
feel .... **SENSE**
feel one's way .... **GROPE**
feeler **PALP, PALPI, ANTENNA**
feet, having .... **PEDATE**
feet, pert. to **PEDAL, PEDARY**
feign .... **ACT, SHAM**
feline .... **CAT, PUMA**
felis leo .... **LION**
fellow ..... **GUY, LAD, BOZO, CHAP, DICK, CHAPPY, CHAPPIE**
felt .... **GROPED, SENSATE**
female animal, parent **DAM, DOE**
female camel .... **NAGA**
female disciple at Joppa **DORCAS**
female insect .... **GYNE**
fence of shrubs .... **HEDGE**
fence of stakes .... **PALISADE**
fence step .... **STILE**
c fence, sunken, hidden **AHA, HAHA**
fence to restrain cattle .. **OXER**
fencer's cry .. **HAI, HAY, SASA**
fencing dummy .... **PEL**
fencing position **CARTE, SIXTE, QUARTE, QUINTE, TIERCE, SECONDE, SEPTIME**
fencing sword ...... **EPEE, FOIL**
fencing term .... **TOUCHE**
fencing thrust ...... **LUNGE, PUNTO, REMISE, RIPOST, RIPOSTE, REPRISE**
fend .... **WARD**
fennel: P. I. .... **ANIS**
"Ferdinand the Bull" author **LEAF**
feria, pert. to .... **FERIAL**
ferment .... **YEAST**
ferment: med. .... **ZYME**
fermented milk dessert **LACTO**
fern, climbing, P. I. .... **NITO**
fern, Polyn., edible .... **TARA**
fern root, N. Z. .... **ROI**
fern "seed" .... **SPORE**
fern species .... **WEKI**
fern spore ...... **SORI, SORUS**
Ferrara ducal family .... **ESTE**
ferrum .... **IRON**
ferryboat .... **BAC**
d ferryboat, Afr. .... **PONT**
fertilizer ..... **MARL, GUANO**
fervent .... **ARDENT**
fervor ... **ZEAL, ZEST, ARDOR**
fester .... **RANKLE**
festival .... **ALE, FAIR, FETE, GALA, FERIA, FIESTA, KERMIS, KIRMES**
festival, Creek Indian .. **BUSK**
festival, Gr. **AGON, DELIA, HALOA**
fetid .... **OLID, RANK**
fetish ...... **OBI, JUJU, OBIA, ZEME, ZEMI, CHARM, OBEAH, GRIGRI**
fetish, P. I. .... **ANITO**
fetter .... **GYVE, IRON**
feud, opposed to ...... **ALOD, ALLOD, ALODIUM, ALLODIUM**
feudal benefice .... **FEU**
feudal estate **FEOD, FEUD, FIEF**
feudal land .... **BENEFICE**
feudal service, form of **AVERA**
feudal tax **TAILAGE, TALLAGE, TAILLAGE**
feudal tenant .... **VASSAL**
fever, intermittent **AGUE, TERTIAN**
feverish .... **FEBRILE**
fez .... **TARBUSH, TARBOOSH, TARBOUCHE**

a fiber .... **JUTE, PITA, RAFFIA, STAPLE, THREAD**
fiber, bark **TAPA, OLONA, TERAP**
fiber, coarse .... **ADAD**
fiber, cordage .... **DA, COIR, FERU, HEMP, IMBE, JUTE, RHEA, ABACA, SISAL**
fiber from palm .... **ERUC**
fiber, hat or basket .... **DATIL**
fiber knot .... **NEP**
fiber plant **ISTLE, IXTLE, IXLE, RAMIE**
fiber plant, Brazil .... **CAROA**
fiber plant, E. Ind. **SANA, SUNN**
fiber, textile .... **SABA**
fiber, tropical **IXLE, ISTLE, IXTLE**
fiber, woody .... **BAST, BASTE**
fictional submarine character **NEMO**
fiddle, medieval .... **GIGA**
fiddler crab genus ...... **UCA**
field **LEA, ACRE, WONG, CROFT**
field deity ...... **PAN, FAUN**
field, enclosed: law ..... **AGER**
field, stubble .... **ROWEN**
fifth segment crustacean **CARPOS**
b fig marigold, Afr. ..... **SAMH**
figs, Smyrna .. **ELEME, ELEMI**
fight **CLEM, FRAY, MELEE, AFFRAY**
figurative use of word .. **TROPE**
figure .... **SOLID**
figure, equal angles **ISAGON, ISOGON**
figure, 4-sided .... **TETRAGON**
figure, geom. .... **SECTOR**
figure of speech **TROPE, SIMILE, METAPHOR**
figure, oval .... **ELLIPSE**
figure, 10-sided .... **DECAGON**
figwort .... **MULLEIN**
Fiji chestnut .... **RATA**
Fiji tree .... **BURI**
filament .... **FIBER, HAIR**
filament, flax ... **HARL, HARLE**
filament, plant **ELATER, THREAD**
filch .... **STEAL**
file .... **ROW**
file, coarse .... **RASP**
file, three-square single-cut **CARLET**
filled to capacity **SATED, REPLETE**
fillet, architectural **ORLE, ORLO**
fillet, narrow heraldic **ORLE, ORLO, LISTEL**
fillet, shaft's ..... **ORLE, ORLO**

c fillip .... **SNAP**
film, old green ..... **PATINA**
filthy .... **VILE**
filthy lucre .... **PELF**
finale: music .... **CODA**
finally: Fr. .... **ENFIN**
finback whale .... **GRASO**
finch .. **MORO, LINNET, SISKIN**
finch, Europ. **TARIN, TERIN, SERIN**
finch, S. Afr. .... **FINK**
find fault ...... **CARP, CAVIL**
fine, as a line .... **LEGER**
fine, punish by ...... **AMERCE**
fine, record of ...... **ESTREAT**
finesse .... **ART, SKILL**
Fingal's kingdom .... **MORVEN**
finger .... **DIGIT**
finger cymbals ... **CASTANETS**
finger, 5th **PINKIE, MINIMUS**
finger inflammation ... **FELON**
finger nail half-moon **LUNULA, LUNULE**
fingerless glove .... **MIT, MITT**
fingerprint pattern .... **WHORL**
finial ornament, slender .. **EPI**
finisher .... **EDGER, ENDER**
finishing tool .... **REAMER**
FINLAND, FINNISH see also SPECIAL SECTION
d Finland .... **SUOMI**
Finn in Ingria ..... **VOT, VOTE**
Finns .... **SUOMI**
Finnish god .... **JUMALA**
Finnish poetry .... **RUNES**
Finnish steam bath ... **SAUNA**
fire basket .... **CRESSET**
fire bullet .... **TRACER**
fire god .... **VULCAN**
fire god, Hindu .. **AGNI, AKAL, CIVA, DEVA, KAMA, SIVA**
fire in heart: Buddhism **RAGA**
fire opal: Fr. ...... **GIRASOL**
fire, sacrificial, Hindu .. **AGNI**
fire worshipper **PARSI, PARSEE**
firearm . **GUN, RIFLE, MAUSER, PISTOL, CARBINE, REVOLVER**
firecracker .... **PETARD**
fired clay .... **TILE**
firedog .... **ANDIRON**
fireplace **GRATE, INGLE, HEARTH**
fireplace side shelf .... **HOB**
firewood bundle **BARIN, FAGOT**
firewood, Tex. .... **LENA**
firework .... **GERB**
firm **FAST, STANCH, STAUNCH**
firm: Hawaii .... **HUI**
firmament .... **SKY**
firn .... **NEVE**
firs, true .... **ABIES**

a first **PRIME, INITIAL, ORIGINAL**
first American-born white child .... **DARE**
first appearance ...... **DEBUT**
first born: law .... **EIGNE**
first fruits of a benefice **ANNATES**
first miracle site ...... **CANA**
first mortal, Hindu ..... **YAMA**
first part in duet ..... **PRIMO**
first principles .... **ABCS**
first-rate .... **ACE**
firth: Scot. .... **KYLE**
fish .. **ANGLE, TRAWL, TROLL,**
fish ..... **ID, EEL, IDE, CARP, DACE, HAKE, HIKU, JOCU, LIJA, LING, MADO, MASU, OPAH, ORFE, PEGA, PETO, PIKE, POGY, ROUD, RUDD, SCAD, SCUP, SESI, SHAD, SIER, SKIL, SOLE, SPET, TOPE, TUNA, ULUA, PARGO, POWAN, POWEN, ROACH, SKATE, CONGER, MULLET, SABALO, TOMCOD**
fish, ancient .. **ELOPS, ELLOPS**
fish, Atlant. **TAUTOG, ESCOLAR**
fish, boneless .. **FILET, FILLET**
fish, bony .... **CARP, TELEOST**
fish, butterfly .... **PARU**
b fish by trolling .... **DRAIL**
fish, Calif. surf .... **SPRAT**
fish, carplike **RUD, DACE, ROUD, RUDD**
fish cleaner .... **SCALER**
fish, climbing ...... **ANABAS**
fish, cod-like **CUSK, HAKE, LING**
fish, colorful **BOCE, OPAH, WRASSE**
fish, Congo .... **LULU**
fish, Cuban .... **DIABLO**
fish, cyprinoid **ID, IDE, ORF, ORFE**
fish, edible .... **SPRAT**
fish eggs .... **ROE**
fish, Egypt. .... **SAIDE**
fish, elongated **EEL, GAR, PIKE**
fish, Europ. .. **ID, BOCE, DACE, BREAM, SPRAT, UMBER, BARBEL, BRASSE, PLAICE, SENNET, WRASSE**
fish, flat .. **DAB, RAY, SOLE, BRILL, FLUKE, FLOUNDER**
fish, Florida .... **TARPON**
fish, food .. **COD, CERO, HAAK, HAIK, HAKE, LING, SHAD, TUNA, TUNNY, SARDINE**
fish, food: Ind. .... **HILSA**
fish, fresh water **IDE, BASS, DACE, ESOX**
fish from boat .... **TROLL**

c fish, game .... **BASS, MARLIN, TARPON, TARPUN**
fish, gobeylike .... **DRAGONET**
fish, Gr. Lakes .. **CISCO, PERCH**
fish, Hawaiian .... **AKU**
fish, herringlike .... **SHAD**
fish, hook for **GIG, GAFF, DRAIL**
fish, lancet .... **SERRA**
fish line ...... **SNELL, TRAWL**
fish line cork .... **BOB**
fish, linglike .... **COD**
fish, long-nosed .... **GAR**
fish, mackerellike **CERO, TUNNY, TINKER**
fish, many .... **SHOAL**
fish, marine **BONITO, TARPON**
fish measure .... **MEASE**
fish, Medit. .... **NONNAT**
fish, nest-building .... **ACARA**
fish net **SEINE, TRAWL, SPILLER**
fish, N. Z. .... **IHI**
fish, No. Pacif. .... **INCONNU**
fish, parasitic .... **REMORA**
fish, perch-like ...... **DARTER**
fish, Pers. myth .... **MAH**
fish pickle .... **ALEC**
fish, piece of ... **FILET, FILLET**
fish, pikelike .... **GAR**
d fish-pitching prong . **PEW, GAFF**
fish-poison tree .... **BITO**
fish, predatory .... **GAR**
fish, river .... **BLAY**
fish, Russian ...... **STERLET**
fish sauce .... **ALEC, GARUM**
fish sign .... **PISCES**
fish, silvery .... **MULLET**
fish, small .. **ID, IDE, DARTER**
fish, snouted .... **SAURY**
fish, S. Am. ...... **ARAPAIMA**
fish, sparoid .... **SAR, SARGO**
fish, spiny ..... **GOBY, PERCH**
fish, sucking .... **REMORA**
fish, trap .... **WEEL, WEIR**
fish, tropical **SARGO, ROBALO, SALEMA**
fish, warm sea **GUASA, GROUPER**
fish, W. Ind. **BOGA, CERO, TESTAR**
fish whisker .... **BARBEL**
fish with moving line .. **TROLL**
fish with net .. **SEINE, TRAWL**
fish, young .... **FRY**
fisherman's hut, Orkney **SKEO, SKIO**
fishhook line-leader ... **SNELL**
fishhook part .... **BARB**
fishing expedition: Scot. **DRAVE**
fishing grounds, Shetlands **HAAF**

a fissure .... **RENT, RIFT, RIMA, RIME, CLEFT**
fissures, full of **RIMOSE, RIMOUS**
fist .... **NEAF**
fit .. **APT, RIPE, SUIT, ADAPT**
fit for cultivation .... **ARABLE**
fit for human consumption **POTABLE**
fit of sulks .... **HUFF**
five-dollar bill .... **VEE**
five-franc piece .... **ECU**
five, group of .... **PENTAD**
five in cards .... **PEDRO**
fix or fixed .... **SET**
fixed charge .... **FEE**
fixed income person .. **RENTIER**
fixed payment .... **KIST**
flaccid .... **LIMP**
flag **JACK, ENSIGN, BANDEROLE**
flag, flower, blue .... **IRIS**
flag, military .... **GUIDON**
flag, pirate .... **ROGER**
flag, small **BANNERET, BANNERETTE**
flagellants .... **ALBI**
flag's corner .... **CANTON**
flank .... **SIDE**
flank: dialect .... **LEER**
flannel .... **LANA**

b flap .... **TAB, LOMA**
flap, as sails .... **SLAT**
flare .... **FUSEE, FUZEE**
flaring edge.. .. **LIP, FLANGE**
flashed lightning ... **LEVINED**
flask, drinking ..... **CANTEEN**
flat .... **EVEN, LEVEL, PLANE**
flat-bottomed boat **ARK, DORY, PUNT, SCOW**
flat, music ...... **MOL, MOLLE**
flatfish ..... **DAB, RAY, SOLE, BRILL, FLUKE, FLOUNDER**
flatten out .... **CLAP**
flattened .. **OBLATE, PLANATE**
flatter .... **PALP**
flattery .... **PALAVER**
flavor .... **LACE, TANG, AROMA, SAPOR, SEASON**
flavoring plant .. **HERB, LEEK, MINT, ANISE, BASIL**
flavoring root ...... **LICORICE**
flax fiber .... **TOW**
flax, like .... **TOWY**
flax, prepare .... **RET**
flee .... **LAM, BOLT**
fleece .... **FELL, WOOL**
fleece, poorest .... **ABB**
fleet .... **NAVY**
fleet, esp. Span. **ARMADA, ARMADO, ARMATA**
fleet, merchant ...... **ARGOSY**
fleur-de-lis .... **LIS, LYS, LISS**

c fleur-de-lis, obs. ...... **LUCE**
flexible .... **LITHE**
flexible wood: dial. .... **EDDER**
flight ...... **HEGIRA, HEJIRA**
flight of ducks .... **SKEIN**
flight organ .... **WING**
flight, pert. to .... **AERO**
flightless bird **EMU, KIWI, WEKA, PENGUIN**
flip .... **SNAP**
flit .... **FLY, GAD**
float **BUOY, RAFT, SWIM, WAFT**
floating .... **NATANT**
floating vegetation on Nile **SADD, SUDD**
floating wreckage .. **FLOTSAM**
flock of quail .... **BEVY**
flock of swans .... **BANK**
flock, pert. to .... **GREGAL**
flock, small .... **COVEY**
flog **BEAT, LASH, WHIP, SWINGE**
flood .... **SEA, EAGRE, SPATE, FRESHET, TORRENT**
floodgate ..... **CLOW, SLUICE**
flora and fauna .... **BIOTA**
floral leaf ..... **BRACT, SEPAL**
Florentine family ..... **MEDICI**

d Florida tree .... **MABI**
flounder **DAB, SOLE, FLUKE, PLAICE**
flour sieve .... **BOLTER**
flour, unsorted Ind. **ATA, ATTA**
flourish, music ...... **ROULADE**
flourishing: dialect ..... **FRIM**
flow .... **RUN, FLUX**
flow out .... **EMIT, SPILL**
flow, to stop **STANCH, STAUNCH**
flower cluster **CYME, ANADEM, RACEME**
flower extract **ATAR, OTTO, ATTAR, OTTAR**
flower, fall **ASTER, COSMOS, SALVIA**
flower, field .... **GOWAN**
flower, genus of .... **ROSA**
flower-goddess, Norse **NANNA**
flower-goddess, Rom. .. **FLORA**
flower leaf ... **BRACT, SEPAL**
flower, Oriental ...... **LOTUS**
flower part .... **PETAL, SEPAL, CARPEL, SPADIX**
flower, showy .... **CALLA**
flower spike .... **AMENT**
flowering plant .... **ARUM**
fluctuate .... **WAVER**
fluent .... **GLIB**
fluff, yarn .... **LINT**

a fluid, aeriform .... GAS
fluid, medical ... SERA, SERUM
fluid, serous .... SERA, SERUM
fluidity unit .... RHE
flume .... SHUTE, SLUICE
flushed .... RED
flute, ancient Gr. .. HEMIOPE
flute, India ... BIN, MATALAN
flute, small .... FIFE
flutter .. FLAP, WAVE, HOVER
fly GNAT, SOAR, WING, AVIATE
fly agaric .... AMANITA
fly aloft .... SOAR
fly, artificial
HARL, HERL, CAHILL, CLARET
fly, kind of .... BOT
fly, small ...... GNAT, MIDGE
fly, S. Afr. .... TSETSE
flycatcher
TODY, ALDER, PEWEE, PHOEBE
flying .... VOLANT, VOLITANT
"Flying Dutchman" saver SENTA
flying fox .... KALONG
flying lemur .... COLUGO
flying, of .... AERO
flying saucer .... UFO
foam .... SUD, SUDS
focus .... CONCENTRATE
fodder pit .... SILO
fodder storage place .... SILO
b fodder, to store ...... ENSILE,
ENSILO, ENSILAGE, ENSILATE
fog .... MIST
fog horn .... SIRENE
fog: old Eng. .... RAG
foist .... FOB, PALM
fold .... LAP, PLY, PLIE,
RUGA, PLEAT, CREASE
fold of skin .... PLICA
folds, arrange in ...... DRAPE
folded .... PLICATE
folio .... PAGE
folk dance, Slavic ...... KOLO
folklore being .... TROLL
folkway .... MOS
folkways .... MORES
follow .... DOG, TAIL,
ENSUE, TRACE, SHADOW
follow suit, not RENIG, RENEGE
follower .. IST, ITE, ADHERENT
foment .... ABET
fondle .... PET, CARESS
fondness: Ir. .... GRA
font .... LAVER, STOUP
food .... FARE, MEAT,
MANNA, ALIMENT, PABULUM
food bit .... ORT
food, farinaceous ..... SAGO
food for animals .... FORAGE
food forbidden Israelites TEREFA

c food, Hawaii .... POI
food: Maori, N. Z. ...... KAI
food of gods
AMRITA, AMREETA, AMBROSIA
food: Polyn. .... KAI
food, provide .... CATER
food, soft invalid's ...... PAP
foods, choice .... CATES
fool. .ASS, DOLT, GABY, RACA,
SIMP, IDIOT, NINNY
fool's bauble ...... MAROTTE
fool's gold .... PYRITE
foolish .. DAFT, ZANY, INANE,
SILLY, HARISH, ASININE
foot, animal's ..... PAD, PAW
foot, Chin. .... CHEK
foot, Gr. poet. .... IONIC
foot, having .... PEDATE
foot part, horse's .. PASTERN
foot, poet. ... IAMB, IAMBIC,
IAMBUS, ANAPEST, ANAPAEST
foot soldier .... PEON
foot soldier, Ir. KERN, KERNE
foot, two-syllable
SPONDEE, TROCHEE
foot, verse .... IAMB,
DACTYL, ANAPEST, ANAPAEST
football position: abbr. ... FB,
HB, LE, LT, QB, RE, RT
d footless .... APOD, APODAL
footless animal APOD, APODE
footless animal genus .. APODA
footlike .... PEDATE
footlike part .... PES
footpad .... WHYO
footstalk, leaf .... STRIG
footstool HASSOCK, OTTOMAN
for .... PRO
for example .... EG
for fear that .... LEST
for shame .... FIE
forage plant .. GUAR, ALSIKE,
LUCERN, ALFALFA, LUCERNE
foramen .... PORE
foray .... RAID
forbidden
TABU, TABOO, BANNED
Forbidden City .... LASSA
forbidding .... STERN
force ..... VIS, DINT, DRIVE,
IMPEL, POWER, ENERGY,
VIOLENCE
force, alleged
OD, BIOD, ELOD, ODYL
force, hypothetical ...... OD
force, unit of .... DYNE
force, with .... AMAIN
foreboding .... OMEN
forefather .... SIRE
forefoot .... PUD
forefront .... VAN

a forehead, of the .... **METOPIC**
forehead strap .... **TUMP**
foreign in origin ...... **EXOTIC**
foreign trade discount .. **AGIO**
foreigner: Hawaii ..... **HAOLE**
foreigners' quarter, Constantinople .... **PERA**
foremost part
BOW, VAN, FRONT
foremost segment, insect's
ACRON
foreordain .... **DESTINE**
foreshadow .... **BODE**
forest: Brazil .... **MATTA**
forest clearing .... **GLADE**
forest: obsolete .... **WOLD**
forest ox .... **ANOA**
forest partly inundated **GAPO**
forest, pert. to
SILVAN, SYLVAN, NEMORAL
forest, P. I. .... **GUBAT**
forest warden .... **RANGER**
forestall .... **AVERT, PREVENT**
foretell .... **AUGUR, INSEE**
foreteller .... **SEER**
foretoken .... **OMEN**
forever .... **AY, AYE**
forever: Maori .... **AKE**
forever: poet. **ETERN, ETERNE**
forfeit .... **LOSE, LAPSE**
b forfeits, Jap. .... **KEN**
forgetfulness fruit .... **LOTUS**
forgetfulness water ... **LETHE**
forgive .... **REMIT**
forgiving .... **CLEMENT**
forgo .... **WAIVE**
form a network .... **PLEX**
form: Buddhism .... **RUPA**
form into line **ALIGN, ALINE**
form, pert. to .... **MODAL**
form, philos. .... **EIDOS**
formal choice .... **VOTE**
formation, military .. **ECHELON**
former .... **ERST**
former ruler **CZAR, TSAR, TZAR**
formerly .... **NEE, ERST, ONCE**
formerly: pref. .... **EX**
formic acid source ...... **ANT**
formicid .... **ANT**
formula .... **LAW**
forsaken .... **LORN**
fort .... **DIX, ORD, REDAN, CITADEL, REDOUBT, RAVELIN**
fort, N. Z. .... **PA, PAH**
forth .... **OUT**
forth, issuing ..... **EMANANT**
forthwith .... **NOW**
fortification
REDAN, RAVELIN, REDOUBT
c fortification, ditchside
SCARP, ESCARP, ESCARPE
fortification, felled trees
ABATIS
fortification, slope .... **TALUS**
fortified place ...... **LIS, LISS**
fortify .... **ARM, MAN**
fortunate (India) .... **SRI**
fortune: Gypsy .... **BAHI**
forty days fast ...... **CARENE**
forty: Gr. .... **MU**
forward .... **ON, AHEAD**
fossil, mollusk .... **DOLITE**
fossil resin .... **RETINITE**
fossil worm track ... **NEREITE**
foul smelling
OLID, FETID, REEKY
found .... **BASE**
found, thing .... **TROVE**
foundation .. **BED, BASE, BASIS**
fountain .... **FONS**
four, group of ...... **TETRAD**
four-inch measure ...... **HAND**
fourth calif (caliph) ..... **ALI**
fourth estate .... **PRESS**
fowl .... **HEN, CAPON, POULT**
fowl's gizzard, etc. .... **GIBLET**
fox .... **TOD**
fox, Afr. .... **FENNEC**
fox hunter's coat .... **PINK**
d fox, S. Afr. .... **ASSE, CAAMA**
"Fra Diavolo" composer **AUBER**
fraction ..... **PART, DECIMAL**
fragment, pottery
SHARD, SHERD, SHEARD
fragments .... **ANA, ORTS**
fragrant .... **OLENT**
frame, supporting
TRESSEL, TRESTLE
framework .... **TRUSS**
France .... **GAUL**
franchise .... **CHARTER**
Franciscan .... **MINORITE**
frank .... **OPEN, HONEST**
Franks, pert. to .... **SALIC**
frankincense ...... **OLIBANUM**
Frankish law .... **SALIC**
Frankish peasant .. **LITI, LITUS**
fraud .... **SHAM**
fraught .... **LADEN**
fray .... **MELEE**
free .... **RID, GRATIS**
free-for-all .... **FRAY, MELEE**
free from discount ..... **NET**
free from knots: obs. .. **ENODE**
freebooter .... **PIRATE**
freedman, Kentish law .. **LAET**
freehold land, Turkey .. **MULK**
freeman ...... **CEORL, THANE**
freight-boat .... **ARK**

a freight car .... **GONDOLA**
FRENCH WORDS: (accent marks omitted throughout)
according to ..... **ALA, AUX**
after .... **APRES**
again .... **ENCORE**
airplane .... **AVION**
alas .... **HELAS**
all .... **TOUT**
among .... **ENTRE**
and .... **ET**
angel .... **ANGE**
annuity .... **RENTE**
arm .... **BRAS**
article .... **LA, LE, DE,**
(plural) **DES, LAS, LES, UNE**
at the home of ..... **CHEZ**
aunt .... **TANTE**
baby .... **BEBE**
bacon .... **LARD**
back .... **DOS**
ball .... **BAL**
bang! .... **PAN**
bath .... **BAIN**
beach .... **PLAGE**
beast .... **BETE**
before .... **AVANT**
being .... **ETRE**
bench .... **BANC**
between .... **ENTRE**
b beware .... **GARE**
bitter .... **AMER**
black .... **NOIR, NOIRE**
blue .... **BLEU**
bread crumbs ...... **PANURE**
bridge .... **PONT**
business house .... **CIE**
but .... **MAIS**
cabbage .... **CHOU**
cake .... **GATEAU**
carefully groomed .. **SOIGNE**
carriage .... **FIACRE**
charmed .... **RAVI**
chicken .... **POULE**
child .... **ENFANT**
clear .... **NET**
climax, theatre .... **CLOY**
cloth .... **DRAP**
cloud .... **NUAGE**
coarse cloth .... **BURE**
connective .... **ET**
cowardly .... **LACHE**
cup .... **TASSE**
dance, formal .... **BAL**
dare .... **OSER**
daughter .... **FILLE**
deal .... **DONNE**
dear .... **CHER, CHERI**
deed .... **FAIT**
defy .... **DEFI**
c department .... see SPECIAL SECTION, GAZETTEER
depot .... **GARE**
detective force .... **SURETE**
devil .... **DIABLE**
dirty .... **SALE**
donkey .... **ANE**
down with .... **ABAS**
dream .... **REVE**
duck to cook .... **CANETON**
dugout .... **ABRI**
duke .... **DUC**
dungeon .... **CACHOT**
ear of grain .... **EPI**
east .... **EST**
egg .... **OEUF**
elegance .... **LUXE**
enamel .... **EMAIL**
equal .... **PAREIL**
evening .... **SOIR**
exaggerated .... **OUTRE**
exclamation .... **HEIN**
exist .... **ETRE**
fabric .... **RAS, DRAP**
father .... **PERE**
fear .... **PEUR**
finally .... **ENFIN**
fingering .... **DOIGTE**
fire .... **FEU**
d five .... **CINQ**
for .... **CAR**
friend .... **AMI, AMIE**
froth .... **BAVE**
full .... **PLEIN**
game .... **JEU, JEUX**
gift .... **CADEAU**
god .... **DIEU**
golden .... **DORE**
good .... **BON**
good-bye **ADIEU, AU REVOIR**
grain ear .... **EPI**
gray .... **GRIS**
gravy .... **JUS**
grimace .... **MOUE**
ground .... **TERRE**
half-mask .... **LOUP**
hall .... **SALLE**
handle .... **ANSE**
head .... **TETE**
health .... **SANTE**
here .... **ICI**
hill .... **PUY**
his .... **SES**
house .... **MAISON**
hunting match .... **TIR**
husband .... **MARI**
idea .... **IDEE**

(French words continued on pages 62 and 63)

French

a **FRENCH:**

impetuosity ... **ELAN**
in ... **DANS**
income, annual ... **RENTE**
is ... **EST**
island ... **ILE**
kind ... **SORTE**
king ... **ROI**
lamb ... **AGNEAU**
land ... **TERRE**
laugh ... **RIRE**
laughter ... **RISEE**
law ... **LOI, DROIT**
leather ... **CUIR**
lift ... **LEVE**
lily ... **LIS**
little ... **PEU**
lively ... **VIF**
lodging place ... **GITE**
low ... **BAS**
maid ... **BONNE**
mail ... **POSTE**
mask, half ... **LOUP**
material ... **DRAP**
May ... **MAI**
meat dish ... **SALMI**
milk ... **LAIT**
mine ... **AMOI**
mother ... **MERE**
b mountain ... **MONT**
museum ... **MUSEE**
nail ... **CLOU**
name ... **NOM**
near ... **PRES**
network ... **RESEAU**
night ... **NUIT**
no ... **NON**
nose ... **NEZ**
nothing ... **RIEN**
number, one ... **UNE**
nursemaid ... **BONNE**
of ... **DE**
one ... **UNE**
our ... **NOS, NOUS**
out ... **HORS**
outbreak ... **EMEUTE**
over ... **SUR**
oyster farm ... **PARC**
petticoat ... **JUPE, COTTE**
picnic spot ... **BOIS**
pinion ... **AILE**
poem ... **DIT**
pork ... **SALE**
pout ... **MOUE**
preposition ... **DES**
pretty ... **JOLI, JOLIE**
pronoun ... **CES, ILS, MES, TOI, UNE, ELLE**
queen ... **REINE**
quickly ... **VITE**
c rabbit ... **LAPIN**
railway station ... **GARE**
read ... **LIRE**
rear ... **ARRIERE**
reception ... **ACCUEIL**
rent ... **LOUER**
river ... **RIVIERE**
roast ... **ROTI**
royal edict ... **ARRET**
saint: abbr. ... **STE**
salt ... **SEL**
salted ... **SALE**
school ... **ECOLE, LYCEE**
scow ... **ACON**
sea ... **MER**
security ... **RENTE**
senior ... **AINE**
servant ... **BONNE**
she ... **ELLE**
sheath ... **ETUI**
sheep ... **MOUTON**
shelter ... **ABRI**
shine ... **LUSTRE**
shooting match ... **TIR**
sickness ... **MAL**
silk ... **SOIE**
situated ... **SISE**
small ... **PETIT**
smitten ... **EPRISE**
d soldier ... **POILU**
some ... **DES**
son ... **FILS**
soul ... **AME**
spirit ... **AME**
star ... **ETOILE**
state ... **ETAT**
stocking ... **BAS**
storm ... **ORAGE**
summer ... **ETE**
superior quality ... **LUXE**
superfluous ... **DETROP**
surnamed ... **DIT**
sweetmeat ... **DRAGEE**
that **CE, CET, QUE, QUI, CELA**
thee ... **TE**
there! ... **VOILA**
they ... **ILS**
thirty ... **TRENTE**
this ... **CE**
thou ... **TOI**
to be ... **ETRE**
to go ... **ALLER**
to love ... **AIMER**
too much ... **TROP**
under ... **SOUS**
upon ... **SUR**
us ... **NOUS**
verb ... **ETRE**
verse ... **RONDEL**

a **FRENCH:**
very .... **TRES**
vineyard .... **CRU**
wall .... **MUR**
water .... **EAU**
wave .... **ONDE**
weapon .... **ARME**
well .... **BIEN**
wine .... **VIN**
wine, delicacy of .... **SEVE**
wine-plant .... **CEP**
with .... **AVEC**
with the .... **AU**
without .... **SANS**
wing .... **AILE**
wood .... **BOIS**
yesterday .... **HIER**
you .... **TOI**
your .... **VOTRE**

Fr., annuity .... **RENTE**
Fr. art group .... **FAUVES**
Fr. artist .. **DORE, DUFY, GROS, COROT, DEGAS, MANET, MONET, BRAQUE, DERAIN, RENOIR, CHAGALL, CHIRICO, MATISSE, UTRILLO**
Fr. artist cult .... **DADA**
Fr. author .. **SUE, GIDE, HUGO, LOTI, ZOLA, CAMUS,**
b **DUMAS, RENAN, STAEL, VERNE, RACINE, SARTRE, COCTEAU**
Fr. Calvinist .... **CALAS**
Fr. chalk .... **TALC**
Fr. coin, old .... **SOU**
Fr. commercial company .. **CIE**
FR. COMPOSER see COMPOSER, FR.
Fr. dramatist .... **RACINE**
Fr. ecclesiastic city ...... **SENS**
Fr. explorer .... **CARTIER**
Fr. fort, battle of Verdun **VAUX**
Fr. general .... **FOCH, HOCHE GAMELIN**
Fr.-Ger. river basin ...... **SAAR**
Fr. guerillas .... **MAQUIS**
Fr. Guiana tribesman .... **BONI**
Fr. historical area ..... **ANJOU**
Fr. honeysuckle .... **SULLA**
Fr. illustrator .... **DORE**
Fr. island .... **ILE**
Fr. lace-making town **CLUNY**
Fr. marshal ..... **NEY, MURAT**
FR. NOVELIST see FR. AUTHOR
FR. PAINTER see FR. ARTIST
Fr. philosopher ...... **COMTE**
Fr. premier, former .... **LAVAL**
Fr. priest .... **ABBE, PERE**
Fr. protectorate ...... **TUNIS**
Fr. psychologist .... **BINET**

c Fr. Revolution month **NIVOSE, FLOREAL, PRAIRAL, VENTOSE, BRUMAIRE, FERVIDOR, FRIMAIRE, MESSIDOR, PLUVIOSE, THERMIDOR**
Fr. revolutionist ..... **MARAT**
Fr. sculptor .... **RODIN**
Fr. security .... **RENTE**
Fr. singer ..... **PIAF, SABLON**
Fr. soprano .... **PONS, CALVE**
Fr. statesman .... **COTY**
FR. WRITER .. see FR. AUTHOR
Frenchman .... **GAUL**
frenzied .... **AMOK**
frequently .... **OFT**
fresh .... **NEW, SPICK**
fresh supply .... **RELAY**
freshet .... **FLOOD, SPATE**
freshwater worm .. **NAID, NAIS**
fretted .... **EROSE**
Frey's wife .... **GERD**
friar .... **FRA, MONK**
friar, mendicant ..... **SERVITE**
friend: law .... **AMY**
friends .... **KITH**
Friendly Islands ...... **TONGA**
friendship .... **AMITY**
frigate bird, Hawaiian ... **IWA**
Frigg's brother-in-law ..... **VE**
Frigg's husband .... **ODIN**
d fright .... **FUNK, PANIC**
frighten **FLEY, ALARM, SCARE**
frill, neck ...... **RUFF, JABOT**
fringe of curls ...... **FRISETTE**
fringe: zool. .... **LOMA**
frisk .... **PLAY, ROMP**
frisky .... **PEART**
FROCK see GARMENT
frog .... **TOAD**
frog genus .... **RANA**
frogs, order of .... **ANURA**
frogs, pert. to .... **RANINE**
frolic ... **LARK, PLAY, ROMP, CAPER, SPORT, SPREE**
from head to foot . **CAP-A-PIE**
from: Lat. .... **DE**
from: prefix .... **AB**
front ... **VAN, FORE, FACADE**
front page weather box .. **EAR**
front, to extend ...... **DEPLOY**
frontier post .... **FORT**
frontiersman **BOONE, CARSON**
frost .... **ICE, HOAR, RIME**
frosty .... **RIMY**
froth .... **FOAM, SPUME**
frothlike .... **SPUMY, YEASTY**
frown .... **LOUR, GLOOM, LOWER, SCOWL, GLOWER**
frugal .... **CHARY**
fruit .... **BERRY, OLIVE**
fruit, Afr. .... **PECEGO**

a fruit, aggregate ..... **ETAERIO**
fruit decay .... **BLET**
fruit dish
COMPOTE, COMPOTIER
fruitdots, fern .... **SORI, SORUS**
fruit, dry .... **ACHENE**
fruit, fleshy ...... **PEAR, PEPO**
fruit, hard-shelled **NUT, GOURD**
fruit, India .... **BEL**
fruit-jelly .... **RHOB**
fruit, lemonlike ..... **CITRON**
fruit of maple ...... **SAMARA**
fruit pigeon, Polyn. ..... **LUPE**
fruit, plumlike .... **SLOE**
fruit, pulpy ..... **UVA, DRUPE**
fruit shrub, E. Ind. .... **CUBEB**
fruit, small, 1-seeded
AKENE, ACHENE, ACHENIUM
fruit, southern .... **PAPAW**
fruit squeezer ...... **REAMER**
fruit, tropical .. **DATE, MANGO**
fruit, vine .... **MELON**
fruit, yellow tropical
PAPAW, PAPAYA, PAWPAW
fruiting spike .... **EAR**
frustrate ... **SCOTCH, THWART**
fry lightly .... **SAUTE**
Fuegan Indian .... **ONA**
fuel **LOG, COAL, COKE, PEAT**
fuel ship .... **OILER, TANKER**
fuel, turf .... **PEAT, PEET**
fugue theme .... **DUX**
fulcrum, oar .... **THOLE**
full .... **PLENARY**
full and clear ..... **OROTUND**
fullness .... **PLENUM**
fulmar .... **NELLY, MALDUCK**
fume .... **REEK, SMOKE**

c fun .... **SPORT**
function ...... **GO, USE, WORK**
function, trig. ... **SINE, COSINE**
fundamental
BASIC, ELEMENTAL
funeral bell **KNELL, MORTBELL**
funeral music .... **DIRGE**
funeral notice .... **OBIT**
funeral oration .... **ELOGE**
funeral pile .... **PYRE**
funeral song .... **NENIA**
fungi, tissue in .... **TRAMA**
fungus .... **AGARIC**
fungus, edible
MOREL, MORIL, TRUFFLE
fungus, white-spored **AMANITA**
fur ...... **SEAL, VAIR, GENET**
MARTEN, NUTRIA, MINIVER
fur cape .... **PELERINE**
fur: Her. **PEAN, VAIR, VAIRE**
furbelow ...... **FRILL, RUFFLE**
Furies, Gr. .... **ERINYS**
ERINNYS, ERINYES, ERINNYES
Furies, one of
ALECTO, MEGAERA, TISIPHONE
Furies, Rom. .... **DIRAE**
furlongs, eight .... **MILE**
furnish crew .... **MAN**
furnish with .... **ENDOW**
furnishings, mode of .. **DECOR**
furrows, with **RIVOSE, RUTTED**
further .... **AID, YET**
furtive .... **SLY, SNEAKY**
fury .... **IRE**
furze .... **WHIN, WHUN,**
GORSE, GORST, GORSTE
fuse partly .... **FRIT**
fuss .... **ADO, TO-DO**

G

b gabi .... **TARO**
Gad, son of .... **ARELI**
gadget .... **GISMO**
Gael .... **SCOT**
Gaelic .. **ERSE, CELTIC, KELTIC**
Gaelic poem .... **DUAN**
Gaelic sea god .... **LER**
gaff .... **SPAR**
gain .... **GET, WIN, EARN**
gait .. **LOPE, CANTER, GALLOP**
gait, horse's ..... **PACE, RACK**
Galahad's mother ..... **ELAINE**
Galatea's beloved ..... **ACIS**
Galilee town .... **CANA**
galla ox ...... **SANGA, SANGU**
gallery, art .... **SALON**
gallery: hist. .... **ALURE**

d gallery, open .... **LOGGIA**
gallery protecting troops
ECOUTE
galley, armed, old Northmen's
AESC
galley, fast
DROMON, DROMOND
galley, 1 oar bank **UNIREME**
galley, 2 oar banks .. **BIREME**
galley, 3 oar banks **TRIREME**
gallop, rapid .... **TANTIVY**
gallop slowly .... **LOPE**
Galsworthy heroine .... **IRENE**
Galway Bay, isles in .... **ARAN**
gamble .... **GAME**
gambling place ...... **CASINO**

a gambol .... **DIDO, CAPER**
game ... **LOTO, BINGO, LOTTO**
game, Basque .... **PELOTA**
game, board ... **CHESS, HALMA**
game, card ..... **LU, LOO, NAP, PAM, PUT, FARO, CINCH, MACAO, MONTE, OMBER, OMBRE, STUSS, TAROT, WHIST, BASSET, CASINO, ECARTE, ROUNCE, CANASTA**
game, child's .... **TAG**
game, dice .... **LUDO**
game, follow .... **STALK**
game, gambling ... **FARO, PICO, STUSS**
game, Hawaii .... **HEI**
game, Ind. guessing ... **CANUTE**
game, It. guessing .... **MORA**
game of skill ..... **POOL, CHESS**
game piece ..... **MAN, DOMINO**
gamecock .... **STAG**
gamekeeper .... **RANGER**
gaming cube .... **DIE, DICE**
Ganges boat .... **PUTELI**
gangplank .... **RAMP**
gangster .. **MUG, THUG, WHYO**
gannet, common .... **SOLAN**
gannet genus .... **SULA**
gap .... **HIATUS, LACUNA**
gap in hedge
b **MUSE, MEUSE, MUSET**
gar fish .... **SNOOK**
garland .... **LEI, ANADEM**
GARMENT. see COAT, BLOUSE
garment .... **ROBE**
garment, Arab .... **ABA**
garment, bishop's .... **CHIMAR, CHIMER, CHIMERE**
garment, church .... **COTTA**
GARMENT, CLERICAL OR ECCLESIASTIC,.... see GARMENT, PRIESTLY
garment, fitted .... **REEFER**
garment, India, Hindu ..... **SARI, SAREE, BANIAN, BANYAN**
GARMENT, LITURGICAL .. see GARMENT, PRIESTLY
garment, loose **CAMIS, CAMUS, CYMAR, SIMAR, CAMISE**
garment, Malay .... **SARONG**
garment, Moslem .... **IZAR**
garment, N. Afr. .... **HAIK**
garment, Old Ir. .... **INAR**
garment, outer .... **CAPOTE, PALETOT**
garment, Polyn. .... **PAREU**
garment, priestly ... **ALB, COPE, AMICE, EPHOD, STOLE**
garment, rain .... **PONCHO**
garment, scarflike ...... **TIPPET**

c garment, Turk. .... **DOLMAN**
garment, woman's ..... **BODICE, MANTUA**
garnishment .... **LIEN**
garret .... **ATTIC**
garter snake genus ...... **ELAPS**
gas .... **FUEL, NEON**
gas apparatus ...... **AERATOR**
gas, charge with ...... **AERATE**
gas, colorless .... **OXAN**
gas, inert ..... **ARGON, XENON**
gas, radioactive .... **RADON, NITON**
GASEOUS ELEMENT...... see ELEMENTS, SPECIAL SECTION, Page 195
gaseous sky "cloud" .. **NEBULA**
GASTROPOD see also MOLLUSK
gastropod .... **WELK, WILK, WHELK, LIMPET**
gastropod, Haliotis .. **ABALONE**
gate .... **PORTAL**
gate, water .... **SLUICE**
gateway .... **PYLON**
gateway, Buddhist temple **TORAN, TORANA**
gateway, Pers. .... **DAR**
gateway, Shinto shrine .... **TORII**
gather .... **AMASS, GLEAN, GARNER, MUSTER**
gather, as grouse .... **LEK**
d gather in bundles ..... **SHEAVE**
gathers, put in .... **SHER, SHIR, SHIRR**
gaunt .... **SPARE**
Gawain's father .... **LOT**
gazelle .... **ARIEL**
gazelle, Afr. ...... **ADMI, DAMA, MOHR, KORIN, MHORR**
gazelle, Asia .... **AHU**
gazelle, black-tailed .... **GOA**
gazelle, Pers. .... **CORA**
gazelle, Sudan .... **DAMA**
gazelle, Tibetan .... **GOA**
gear .... **CAM**
gear tooth .... **COG**
gear wheel, smallest .... **PINION**
Geb's consort .... **NUT**
Gelderland city .... **EDE**
gelid .... **ICY, COLD**
GEM........... see also STONE
gem ..... **JADE, ONYX, OPAL, RUBY, SARD, AGATE, PEARL, STONE, GARNET, SPINEL, EMERALD, PERIDOT**
gem-bearing earth, Burma **BYON**
gem, carved .... **CAMEO**
gem facet ...... **BEZEL, BEZIL, CULET, COLLET**
gem weight .... **CARAT**
Gemini's mortal half ... **CASTOR**

a gender, a .... **NEUTER**
genealogy .... **TREE**
GENERAL, CIVIL WAR
see CIVIL WAR COMMANDER
general, Morocco .... **KAID**
general Sitting Bull defeated **CUSTER**
generation .... **AGE**
Genesis matriarch ...... **SARAI**
genie, Egypt. .... **HAPI**
genip tree .... **LANA**
genipap wood .... **LANA**
gentle . **MILD, TAME, TENDER**
gentle breeze .... **AURA**
gentle heat .... **TEPOR**
genuflect .... **KNEEL**
GENUS . see PLANT or ANIMAL named
genus of plants .... **ARUM**
geode **VUG, VOOG, VUGG, VUGH**
geological division . **LIAS, LYAS**
geol. epoch **BALA, ECCA, LIAS, MUAV, ERIAN, UINTA, PLIOCENE**
geol. formation ..... **TERRAIN, TERRANE, TERRENE**
geol. period .... **DYAS, EOCENE, MIOCENE**
geol. stage ...... **RISS, ACHEN**
geol. vein angle .... **HADE**
b geometric ratio .... **SINE**
geometric solid **CONE, CUBE, PRISM**
geometrical lines ...... **LOCI, LOCUS, SECANT**
geometry rule ...... **THEOREM**
geometry term .... **VERSOR**
geophagy .... **PICA**
George Sand novel ..... **LELIA**
Geraint's wife .... **ENID**
geranium lake color . **NACARAT**
germ .. **BUG, VIRUS, MICROBE**
germ-free **ASEPTIC, ANTISEPTIC**
germs, produced by ... **SEPTIC**
GERMAN . see also TEUTONIC
GERMAN WORDS: (umlauts omitted throughout)
"A" .... **EIN**
above .... **UBER**
again .... **UBER**
alas .... **ACH**
article ...... **DAS, DER, EIN**
ass .... **ESEL**
beer .... **BIER**
blood .... **BLUT**
conjunction .... **UND**
count .... **GRAF**
donkey .... **ESEL**
dumpling .... **KNODEL**
eat .... **ESSEN**
c eight .... **ACHT**
evening .... **ABEND**
everything .... **ALLES**
exclamation .... **HOCH**
four .... **VIER**
gentleman .. **HERR, HERREN**
hall .... **AULA, SAAL**
heaven .... **HIMMEL**
hunter .... **JAGER**
"I" .... **ICH**
ice .... **EIS**
iron .... **EISEN**
is .... **IST**
it .... **ES**
league (s) .... **BUND, BUNDE**
love .... **LIEBE**
mister .... **HERR**
nation .... **VOLK**
never .... **NIE**
new .... **NEUE**
no .... **NEIN**
noble .... **EDEL**
old .... **ALT**
one .... **EIN, EINE**
out of .... **AUS**
pronoun .... **ICH**
people .... **VOLK**
school hall .... **AULA**
softly .... **LEISE**
d song .... **LIED**
spirit .... **GEIST**
state .... **STAAT**
steel .... **STAHL**
temperament ...... **GEMUT**
than .... **ALS**
the .... **DAS, DER**
three .... **DREI**
thunder .... **DONNER**
title .... **VON, PRINZ**
town .... **STADT**
us .... **UNS**
very .... **SEHR**
with .... **MIT**
without .... **OHNE**
yes .... **JA**
you .... **SIE**
your ...... **IHR, DEIN, EUER**

German .... **BOCHE**
Ger. admiral .... **SPEE**
Ger. bacteriologist ...... **KOCH**
Ger. camp, war ...... **STALAG**
GER. COMPOSER
see COMPOSER, GER.
Ger.-Czech region ... **SUDETEN**
Ger. district, old .... **GAU**
Ger. dive bomber ...... **STUKA**
Ger. emperor .... **OTTO**
Ger. highway ..... **AUTOBAHN**
Ger. John .... **HANS**

a Ger. king .... OTTO
Ger. landscape painter .. ROOS
Ger. name prefix .... VON
Ger. philosopher . KANT, HEGEL
Ger. physicist .. OHM, ERMAN
Ger. president .... EBERT
Ger. princely family ..... WELF
Ger. theologian .... ARND
Ger. title .. VON, GRAF, PRINZ
Ger. tribal region
GAU, GAUE, GAUS
Germanic deity .... DONAR
Germanic letter .... RUNE
gesture dance, Samoa; Fiji SIVA
get out! . SCAT, SHOO, SCRAM
ghastly .... LURID
ghost .... HANT, SPOOK,
SPECTER, SPECTRE
ghost, India .... BHUT
ghost-town state: abbrev.: UT
giant .... TITAN
giant, frightful .... OGRE
giant, Hindu myth ..... BANA
giant, killed by Apollo .. OTUS
giant, Norse, Scand. myth YMER,
YMIR, JOTUM, MIMIR
giant, Rom. .... CACA
giant, 1000-armed, Hindu BANA
giants, Bibl. .... ANAK, EMIM
gibbon, Malay .... LAR
gift, receiver of .... DONEE
gig .... NAPPER
b gigantic person .... TITAN
"Gil —" LeSage novel .. BLAS
Gilead's descendant .... ULAM
Gilgit language, Kashmir SHINA
gills, four .... PINT
gilt .... DORE
gin .... TRAP
gingerbread tree .... DUM
ginkgo tree .... ICHO
GIPSY .... see GYPSY
giraffe-like animal .... OKAPI
girasol .... OPAL
girder .... TRUSS
girdle .... OBI, CEST, SASH
girl .... SIS, CHIT,
DAME, SKIRT
GIRL'S NAME
see WOMAN'S NAME
girth, saddle .... CINCH
gist .... NUB, PITH
give: law .... REMISE
give reluctantly ..... GRUDGE
give up .. CEDE, WAIVE, YIELD
give up wholly ...... DEVOTE
give way .... YIELD
glacial hill .... PAHA
glacial ice block, pinnacle SERAC
glacial ridge ... AS, OS, ASAR,
KAME, OSAR, ESCAR,
ESKAR, ESKER

c glacial snow field FIRN, NEVE
glacial stage .... WURM
glacier chasm
CREVAS, CREVASSE
glacier, facing a .... STOSS
gladiolus .... IRID
gladly .... FAIN
gland ..... PINEAL, THYROID
gland, edible .... NOIX
glass .... LENS
glass, blue .... SMALT
glass bubble .... BLEB
glass defect .... TEAR
glass, flatten .... PLATTEN
glass furnace mouth .. BOCCA
glass ingredient ...... SILICON
glass-like material .. .. PLASS
glass maker .... GLAZIER
glass, molten .... PARISON
glass, partly fused FRIT, FRITT
glass, transparent ..... UVIOL
glass vial .. AMPULE, AMPOULE
glassmaker's oven . LEER, LEHR
glasswort .... KALI
glassy .... HYALINE
glazier's tack .... BRAD
gleam .... GLINT
glide .... SKIM, SLIP,
SKATE, SLIDE
d glittering piece ..... SPANGLE
globe .... ORB, SPHERE
global .... ROUND, SPHERAL
gloom .... MIRK, MURK
gloomy .... DARK, DOUR,
DREAR, DREARY
"Gloomy Dean" .... INGE
glossy-surfaced .... GLACE
glottal stop: Dan. .... STOD
glove leather ..... KID, NAPA,
MOCHA, SUEDE
glove shape, unstitched TRANK
glowing .... CANDENT
glucoside, root .... GEIN
glut ... SATE, GORGE, SATIATE
gnarl ..... NUR, KNUR, NURR
gnat, small .... MIDGE
gnome .... NIS, GREMLIN
go .... WEND
go astray .... ABERRATE
go astray slightly .... ERR
go back .... REVERT
go forth .... FARE
go hence: Lat. .... VADE
go on! .... GARN, SCAT
go shufflingly .. MOSY, MOSEY
goad .... PROD, SPUR, INCITE
goal .... AIM, END
goat, Alpine mountain .. IBEX
goat antelope .... GORAL
goat, Asian .... JAGLA

a goat, genus .... **CAPRIA**
goat god .... **PAN**
goat, wild .. **TUR, IBEX, TAHR, TAIR, TEHR, THAR**
goatsucker .... **POTOO**
gob .... **TAR**
Gobi Desert .... **SHAMO**
goblet .... **HANAP**
goblin .... **POOK, PUCA, PUCK**
goblin, Egypt .... **OUPHE**
goblin, Norse **NIS,NISSE,KOBOLD**
goby, small .... **MAPO**
GOD . see also DEITY, and see also SPECIAL SECTION
god, Babyl. **EA, ABU, ANU, BEL**
GOD, CHIEF see CHIEF NORSE GOD, also BABYLONIAN CHIEF GOD
god: Chin. .... **SHEN**
god: Hebrew .... **EL**
god: Jap .... **KAMI**
god: Lat. .... **DEUS**
god of alcoholic drinks, **SIRIS**
god of Arcadia .... **PAN**
GOD OF CHAOS ... see CHAOS
god of darkness—evil, Egyp. **SET, SETH**
god of dead, Hindu .... **YAMA**
god of dead, Rom. .... **ORCUS**
b god of discord, Norse **LOK, LOKE, LOKI**
god of earth, Babyl. .. **DAGAN**
GOD OF EARTH, Egyptian see EARTH GOD
god of evil: Egyp. .. **SET, SETH**
god of evil, to ward off **BES,BESA**
god of fertility, Norse ... **FREY**
god of fields, flocks, forest **PAN, FAUN**
god of fire ... **AGNI, VULCAN**
god of Hades ..... **DIS, PLUTO**
god of harvests ...... **CRONUS**
god of light, Norse **BALDR, BALDER, BALDUR**
god of love, Gr. .... **EROS**
god of love, Rom. **AMOR, CUPID**
god of love, Vedic .... **BHAGA**
god of mirth .. **COMUS, KOMOS**
god (goddess) of mischief . **ATE**
god of michief, Norse **LOK, LOKE, LOKI**
GOD OF MOON see MOON GOD
god of music .... **APOLLO**
god of north wind ... **BOREAS**
god of pleasure ..... **BES, BESA**
god of procreation, Egyp. **MIN**
god of prosperity, Teutonic **FREY**
god of revelry, Gr. ... **COMUS, KOMOS**
god of ridicule .... **MOMUS**
GOD OF SEA .... see SEA GOD
GOD OF SKY .... see SKY GOD

c God of Southeast Wind: Gr. **EURUS**
GOD OF STORMS see STORM GOD
GOD OF SUN .... see SUN GOD
god of thunder **THOR, DONAR**
god of Tuesday **TIU, TIW, TYR**
GOD OF UNDERWORLD see UNDERWORLD GOD
god of war, Assyrian **ASUR, ASSUR**
god of war, Babyl. . **IRA, IRRA**
god of war, Gr. .... **ARES**
god of war, Norse **TY, TYR, TYRR**
god of war, Rom. .... **MARS**
god of war, Teut. .... **ER**
god of wind, Norse ... **VAYU**
god of wind, storm, Babylonian **ZU, ADAD, ADDA, ADDU**
god of winds, Gr. ..... **AEOLUS**
god of wisdom, Babyl. **NABU, NEBO**
god of wisdom, Norse .. **ODIN**
god of youth .... **APOLLO**
god skilled with bow, Norse **ULL**
god, Sumerian .... **ABU**
god, unknown, Hindu ..... **KA**
gods, Chief Teut., Norse **AESIR**
gods: Lat. .... **DI**
d gods, mother of .... **RHEA**
gods, mother of: Ir. **ANA, ANU**
GODS, QUEEN OF see QUEEN OF GODS
gods, the .... **DEI, DII**
GODDESS see also SPECIAL SECT.
GODDESS, CHIEF see BABYLONIAN CHIEF GODDESS
goddess, cow-headed ..... **ISIS**
goddess: Latin .... **DEA**
GODDESS, MOTHER see MOTHER GODDESS
goddess of agriculture **CERES, DEMETER**
goddess of art or science . **MUSE**
goddess of astronomy **URANIA**
goddess of beauty: Norse **FREYA**
goddess of betrothal, Norse **VOR**
goddess of chase .**DIAN, DIANA**
goddess of crops, Rom. **ANNONA**
goddess of dawn, Gr. ..... **EOS**
goddess of dawn, Rom. **AURORA**
goddess of dawn, Vedic .. **USAS**
goddess of dead ... **HEL, HELA**
goddess of deep, Babyl. . **NINA**
goddess of destiny, Norse **URD, URTH**
goddess of destruction ... **ARA**
goddess of discord .. **ATE, ERIS**
goddess of earth, Teut. . **ERDA**

a goddess of earth ... **GE, ERDA, GAEA, GAIA, TARI**
goddess of earth: Rom. **CERES, TERRA**
goddess of faith, Rom. . **FIDES**
goddess of fate, Rom. **NONA, PARCA**
goddess of fate, Teutonic **NORN**
goddess of fertility **ASTARTE**
goddess of fertility, Anatolian **MA**
goddess of field, Rom. . **FAUNA**
goddess of flowers, Gr. **CHLORIS**
goddess of flowers, Norse **NANNA**
goddess of flowers, Rom. **FLORA**
goddess of grain **CERES, DEMETER**
goddess of harvest ...... **OPS**
goddess of harvest, Attica **CARPO**
goddess of healing .... **EIR**
goddess of hearth ..... **VESTA**
goddess of heavens, Egyp. . **NUT**
goddess of hope .... **SPES**
goddess of hunt . **DIAN, DIANA**
goddess of infatuation .. **ATE**
goddess of justice . **MA, MAAT**
b goddess of love ...... **VENUS, ASTARTE, APHRODITE**
goddess of love, Babylonian **ISTAR, ISHTAR**
goddess of love, Norse **FREYA, FREYJA**
goddess of magic .... **HECATE**
GODDESS OF MATERNITY see MATERNITY GODDESS
goddess of mischief .... **ATE**
GODDESS OF MOON see MOON GODDESS
goddess of nature **CYBELE, ARTEMIS**
GODDESS OF NIGHT, NORSE see NIGHT, NORSE
goddess of night: Rom.**NOX,NYX**
goddess of peace **IRENE, EIRENE**
goddess of plenty .... **OPS**
goddess of prosperity: Rom. **SALUS**
goddess of retribution .... **ATE**
goddess of retribution, Gr. **ARA**
goddess of revenge .. **NEMESIS**
GODDESS OF SEA see SEA GODDESS
goddess of seasons .... **HORAE**
goddess of splendor, Hindu **UMA**
goddess of truth, Egypt **MA, MAAT**
GODDESS OF UNDERWORLD see UNDERWORLD GODDESS

c goddess of vegetation .. **CORA, KORE, CERES**
goddess of vengeance .... **ARA**
goddess of victory ...... **NIKE**
goddess of volcanoes, Hawaii **PELE**
goddess of war, Gr. .... **ENYO**
goddess of wisdom **ATHENA, PALLAS**
goddess of woods ...... **DIAN, DIANA, ARTEMIS**
goddess of youth .... **HEBE**
goddess, Queen .. **HERA, JUNO**
goddesses of destiny ... **FATES**
goddesses of fate, Gr. **MOERAE**
goddesses of fate, Norse **NORNS**
Goethe drama .... **FAUST**
Goethe heroine ...... **MIGNON**
golconda .... **MINE**
gold .... **AU, CYME, GILT**
gold alloy, ancient ..... **ASEM**
Gold Coast Negro .... **GA**
Gold Coast tong. **CHI, TWI, TSHI**
gold-colored metal . **ORMOLU**
gold, cover with .... **GILD**
gold deposit .... **PLACER**
gold district-field, Afr. .. **RAND**
gold: Her. .... **OR**
gold, mosaic .... **ORMOLU**
gold, pert. to .... **AURIC**
golden .... **AUREATE**
d Golden Fleece keeper .. **AEETES**
Golden Fleece seeker .. **JASON**
golden in color .. **DORE, DURRY**
golden oriole .... **PIROL**
golden oriole, Eur. .... **LORIOT**
golden-touch king ..... **MIDAS**
golf attendant .. **CADY, CADDY**
golf club ...... **IRON, CLEEK, MASHIE, PUTTER**
golf club, part .... **TOE**
golf club socket .... **HOSEL**
golf hole .... **CUP**
golf pro .... **SNEAD**
golf score .... **PAR**
golf stroke-shot .. **PUT, BAFF, CHIP, LOFT, PUTT, DRIVE, SCLAFF**
golf term ..... **LIE, PAR, TEE**
golfer .... **TEER**
gomuti .... **ARENGA**
gondolier's song **BARCAROLE, BARCAROLLE**
gone .... **OUT, AWAY**
gone by .... **AGO, PAST, YORE**
gonfalon .... **BANNER**
good-bye: Fr. **ADIEU,AU REVOIR**
good digestion ..... **EUPEPSIA**
good health, in .... **PEART**
"Good King" .... **HAL**
good news **EVANGEL, EVANGILE**

a "Good Queen Bess," name for ORIANA
good: Tagalog .... MABUTI
goods .... WARES
goods in sea .... JETSAM
goods sunk at sea LAGAN, LIGAN
goose barnacle genus .. LEPAS
goose cry ...... HONK, YANG
goose genus .... ANSER
goose, male .... GANDER
goose, sea .... SOLAN
goose, wild .... BRANT
gooseberry .... FABES
gopher tortoise ... MUNGOFA
gorge .... GLUT, CHASM, FLUME, RAVINE
Gorgons, one of .... MEDUSA
gorse ... WHIN, WHUN, FURZE
goshawk genus . ASTUR, BUTEO
gospel ... EVANGEL, EVANGILE
gossamer .... WEB
gossip .... EME
gossip: India .... GUP
Gottfried's sister .... ELSA
gourd fruit .... PEPO
gourd rattle .... MARACA
gourmet .... EPICURE
gout of knee ...... GONAGRA
government .... STATE
b government control .... REGIE STATISM
governor .... REGENT
governor, Mecca SHERIF, SHEREEF
governor, Persia ..... SATRAP
governor, Turkish .... BEY
GOWN .... see GARMENT
grace .... ADORN
Graces' mother .... AEGLE
Graces, The . AGLAIA, THALIA
graceful .... GAINLY
grackle .... DAW, MINA, MYNA, MYNAH
grade .... RANK, RATE, SORT, STEP
gradient .... SLOPE
Graf —, ship .... SPEE
graft .... CION, SCION
grafted: Her. .... ENTE
Grail, Holy, finder of .... BORS
grain .... OAT, RYE, SEED, WALE, SPELT, MILLET
grain beetle .... CADELLE
grain, chaff of .... BRAN
grain, coarse .... SAMP
grain given Romans . ANNONA
grain, sorghum, Ind., .. DARI, DORA, DURR, MILO, CHENA, DARRA, DARSO, DURRA, DHURRA, DOURAH, HEGARI

c grain, sorghum, U. S. FETERITA
grain, stalks of ...... HAULM
grain to grind .... GRIST
gram molecule .... MOL
grammatically, describe . PARSE
grampus .... ORC
granary, India GOLA, GUNJ, GUNGE
grandparental .... AVAL
grandson, Adam's, Eve's. . ENOS
grant .... CEDE, MISE, REMISE
grant, India, Hindu .... ENAM
grant of rights PATENT, CHARTER
granular snow .... FIRN, NEVE
grape .... UVA, MUSCAT, CATAWBA, CONCORD
grape conserve .... UVATE
grape disease .... ESCA
grape genus .... VITIS
grape jelly .... SAPA
grape juice DIBS, MUST, STUM
grape juice sirup .... SAPA
grape-like .. UVA, UVAL, UVIC
grape-like fruit .... UVA
grape refuse .... MARC
grape, white .... MALAGA
grapefruit .. POMELO, PUMELO
graphite .... KISH
grasp .... SEIZE
d grass .... POA, REED, DARNEL
grass, Andes .... ICHU
grass, blue .... POA
grass, coarse .... REED, SEDGE
grass genus ...... AIRA, COIX, AVENA, STIPA
grass, kind of .... RIE
grass, marsh .... REED SEDGE, FESCUE
grass, N. Afr. .... ALFA
grass, pasture .... GRAMA
grass rope: Sp. .... SOGA
grass, rope-making MUNG, MUNJ
grass, sour .... SORREL
grass stem .... CULM
grass tuft .... HASSOCK
grass, yard, wire .... POA
grasshopper .... GRIG
grassland SAVANNA, SAVANNAH
grassland, S. Afr. ..... VELDT
grasslands, Western ... RANGE
grate ...... JAR, RASP, GRIDE
gratify . SATE, ARRIDE, PLEASE
grating . GRID, GRILL, GRILLE
gratuitous .... FREE
gratuity .... FEE, TIP
gratuity, customer ..... PILON
grave .... SOBER

a gravestone, Gr. & Rom. **STELA, STELE, STELAE, STELAI**
graving tool .... **STYLET**
Gray, botanist .... **ASA**
gray .... **OLD, HOAR, ASHEN, SLATE**
gray kingbird .... **PIPIRI**
gray, mole .... **TAUPE**
gray parrot .... **JAKO**
gray plaid, gray shawl .. **MAUD**
grayish-brown ... **DUN, TAUPE**
graze .... **AGIST, BROWSE**
grease ... **OIL, LARD, AXUNGE**
great barracuda ..... **PICUDA**
Great Barrier Island, N. Z. **OTEA**
"Great Emancipator" .... **ABE**
great: Gypsy .... **BARO**
greater .... **MORE, MAJOR**
Greece, ancient name . **HELLAS**
Greece, modern .... **ELLAS**
greedy .... **AVID**

Greek Letters, Numbers:

Greek A, One .... **ALPHA**
Greek B, Two .... **BETA**
Greek D, Four .... **DELTA**
Greek E, Eight .... **ETA**
Greek I, Ten .... **IOTA**
Greek M, Forty .... **MU**
b Greek N, Fifty .... **NU**
Greek O, 800 .... **OMEGA**
Greek P, Eighty .... **PI**
Greek R, 100 .... **RHO**
Greek T, 300 .... **TAU**
Greek Z, Seven .... **ZETA**
Greek 90 .... **KOPPA**
Greek 900 .... **SAMPI**
Gr. ancient .... **ATTIC**
Gr. assembly .... **AGORA**
Gr. athletic contest ..... **AGON**
Gr. authors .... **ZENO, AESOP, HOMER, PLATO, TIMON, HESIOD, PINDAR, SAPPHO, STRABO, THALES, PLUTARCH**
Gr. city, ancient **ELIS, SPARTA**
Gr. city, word for ..... **POLIS**
Gr. colony, ancient .... **IONIA**
Gr. column ..... **DORIC, IONIC**
Gr. commonalty ...... **DEMOS**
Gr. community .... **DEME**
Gr. dialect ..... **EOLIC, AEOLIC**
Gr. district, ancient ... **ATTICA**
Gr. drama .... **MIME**
Gr. festival city .... **NEMEA**
Gr. galley **TRIREME, UNIREME**
Gr. garment .... **CHITON**
Gr. ghost .... **KER**
GREEK GODS, GODDESSES . see SPECIAL SECTION and see GODS, GODDESSES
Gr. hero ...... **AJAX, JASON**

c Gr. historian .... **CTESIAS**
Gr. January .... **GAMELION**
Gr. legendary hero ...... **IDAS**
Gr. market place ..... **AGORA**
Gr. meeting place of voters **PNYX**
Gr. musical term .. **MESE, NETE**
Gr. myth flier .... **ICARUS**
Gr. native .... **CRETAN**
Gr. patriarch .... **ARIUS**
Gr. philosopher **PLATO, THALES**
Gr. poet ..... **ARION, HOMER, PINDAR**
Gr. poetess ... **SAPHO, SAPPHO**
Gr. poetry, simple ..... **DORIC**
Gr. priest .... **MYST**
Gr. princess .... **IRENE**
Gr. province .... **NOME**
Gr. resistance group ..... **EDES**
Gr. rose .... **CAMPION**
Gr. sculptor .... **PHIDIAS**
Gr. shield .... **PELTA**
Gr. slave .... **PENEST**
Gr. statesman ..... **ARISTIDES**
Gr. temple .... **NAOS**
Gr. theologian .... **ARIUS**
Gr. township-commune .. **DEME**
Gr. underground .... **ELAS**
Gr. vase .... **PELIKE**
d Gr. weight, old .. **MNA, MINA**
green ..... **NILE, VERD, VERT, OLIVE, RESEDA**
green chalcedony ..... **JASPER**
green cheese .... **SAPSAGO**
green chrysolite ..... **PERIDOT**
green copper arsenate . **ERINITE**
green fly .... **APHID**
green: Her. .... **VERT**
Green Mountain hero ... **ALLEN**
green parrot: P. I. .... **CAGIT**
green stone ... **JADE, PERIDOT**
greenish yellow **OLIVE, RESEDA**
Greenland Eskimo .... **ITA**
Greenland geol. div. .... **KOME**
Greenland settlement, town, base .... **ETAH**
Greenland's colonizer ... **ERIC**
greeting .. **AVE, HAIL, SALUTE**
gridiron .... **GRILL**
grief .... **DOLOR, DOLOUR**
griffon genus .... **GYPS**
grimalkin .... **CAT**
grinding .... **MOLAR**
grindstone, Indian ..... **MANO**
grit .... **SAND**
grivet .... **WAAG**
grivet monkey .... **TOTA**
grommet, naut. ..... **BECKET**
groom, India . **SAIS, SICE, SYCE**
groove .... **RUT, SCARF**

a groove, pilaster STRIA, STRIAE
grooved ..... LIRATE, STRIATE
grope .... FEEL
gross .... CRASS
ground grain .... MEAL
ground wheat-husk ..... BRAN
groundhog .... MARMOT
group .... BAND, BODY, CREW, TEAM
group, animal ..... NID, NYE, HERD, NIDE, COVEY, DROVE, CLUTCH
grouper .... MERO
grouse .... PTARMIGAN
grouse, red: Scot. . MUIRFOWL
grove, small-tree ...... COPSE
grow .... WAX, RAISE
grow together ...... ACCRETE
growing out .... ENATE
growl .... YAR, GNAR, YARR, SNARL
growth, skin .... WEN
grub .... LARVA
grudge .... SPITE
gruel, maize .... ATOLE
gruesome .. GRISLY, MACABRE
guarantees .... SURETIES
b guard .... SENTRY
guard, as door .... TILE
guardhouse .... BRIG
guardian, alert ARGUS, CERBERUS
Guatemala fruit .... ANAY
guava .... ARACA
Gudrun's husband ATLI, SIGURD
Guenon monkey .... MONA
guest house .... INN
Guiana tree .... MORA
guide .... LEAD, PILOT, STEER
guiding .... POLAR
guiding rule .... MOTTO
Guido's note .... UT, ELA
guild, merchants' ..... HANSE
guillemot ...... COOT, MURR, MURRE
guilty .... NOCENT
guinea fowl's young ..... KEET
guinea pig .... CAVY
gulch: Sp. .... ARROYO
GULF, ... also see GAZETTEER
gulf, Ionia sea .... ARTA
gulf, Medit. .... TUNIS

c gull ..... MEW, SKUA, TERN, WAEG, XEMA
gull, fork-tailed .... XEMA
gull genus ...... LARI, XEMA
gulls, of, like .... LARINE
gullet .... MAW, CRAW
gullible person .. DUPE, GULL
"Gulliver's Travels," men YAHOOS
gully: Afr. .... DONGA
gulp .... SWIG
gum .... RESIN, BALATA
gum arabic ACACIA, ACACIN, ACACINE
gum, astringent .... KINO
gum resin .... ELEMI, LOBAN, MYRRH
gum resin, aromatic ... MYRRH
gum, Somaliland ..... MATTI
gums .... ULA
gumbo ... OCRA, OKRA, OKRO
gumbo limbo tree ... GOMART
gun .... GAT
gun, British .... STEN
gun fire, burst of ..... SALVO
gun, Ger. .... BERTHA
d gun, kind of .... BREN
gun lock catch .... SEAR
gun, P. I. .... BARIL
gun, slang ..... ROD, HEATER, ROSCOE
gun: S. Afr. ..... ROER, ROHR
gunny cloth .... TAT
gusto .... ZEST
gutta mixture .... SOH
gutta, Sumatra .... SIAK
guy-rope .. STAT, STAY, VANG
gym feat .... KIP
gymnast .... TURNER
gypsum, kind of . YESO, GESSO, YESSO, SELENITE
gypsy .... ROM, CALE, CALO, ROAMER, ROMANY
gypsy boy .... ROM
gypsy gentleman .... RYE
gypsy girl .... CHAI
gypsy husband .... ROM
gypsy lady .... RANI
gypsy married woman .. ROMI
gypsy: Sp. .... GITANO
gypsy tent, camp .... TAN
gypsy village .... GAV
gypsy word .... LAV
gypsy word for paper, book .LIL

H

a H .... **AITCH**
habit .... **RUT, WONT, USAGE**
habitat plant form ..... **ECAD**
habitation .... **ABODE**
habituate ..... **ENURE, INURE**
habituated .... **USED**
hackney coach, Fr. .... **FIACRE**
hackneyed ..... **STALE, TRITE**
Hades ... **DIS, ORCUS, PLUTO, SHEOL, TARTARUS**
Hades: Old Eng. .... **ADES**
Hades, place before .. **EREBUS**
Hades river **STYX, LETHE, ACHERON**
hag .... **CRONE**
haggard .... **DRAWN**
Haggard, H. Rider, novel .. **SHE**
hail .... **AVE, GREET**
hail: naut. .... **AVAST**
hair, arrange .... **COIF**
hair, caterpillar .... **SETA**
hair coat .... **MELOTE**
b hair-do, old .... **TETE**
hair dressing .... **POMADE**
hair, false . **RAT, WIG, TOUPEE**
hair, head of .... **CRINE**
hair, knot of .. **BUN, CHIGNON**
hair, lock of .... **CURL, TRESS**
hair net .... **SNOOD**
hair, remove .... **EPILATE**
hair, rigid .... **SETA**
hair, rough, matted .... **SHAG**
hair shirt .... **CILICE**
hair, standing .... **ROACH**
hair unguent .... **POMADE**
hairless: Sp. Am. ...... **PELON**
hairlike process **CILIA, CILIUM**
hairy . **PILAR, COMOSE, PILOSE**
Haiti bandit .... **CACO**
Halcyone's husband .... **CEYX**
half .... **MOIETY**
half-boot .... **PAC**
half-breed ... **MESTEE, MUSTEE**
half-caste .... **METIS**
half-moon figure .... **LUNE**
half-way .... **MID**
halfway house .... **INN**
halfpenny: Brit. .... **MAG**
hall: Ger. .... **AULA, SAAL**
hallow .... **BLESS**
halo .... **NIMB, CORONA, NIMBUS, AUREOLA, AUREOLE**
halt .... **LAME, STOP**
halting place, troops' .. **ETAPE**
Hamilton's party .... **FEDERAL**

c Hamite .... **SOMAL, BERBER, SOMALI**
Hamitic language **AGAO, AGAU**
hamlet ... **BURG, DORP, TOWN**
Hamlet's castle .... **ELSINORE**
hammer .... **KEVEL**
hammer head part ...... **PEEN**
hammer, heavy .... **MAUL**
hammer, large .... **SLEDGE**
hammer, lead .... **MADGE**
hammer, tilt .... **OLIVER**
hamper ..... **CRAMP, FETTER, TRAMMEL**
Ham's son .... **CUSH**
hand .... **PUD, NEAF, MANUS**
hand, pert. to .... **CHIRAL**
hand, whist .... **TENACE**
handbill .... **LEAF**
handcuff .... **MANACLE**
handle .... **EAR, LUG, PAW, ANSA, HILT, KNOB, HELVE, TREAT**
handle, bench plane .... **TOTE**
handle, having ...... **ANSATE**
handle roughly ... **PAW, MAUL**
handle, scythe .... **SNATH, SNEAD, SNEED, SNATHE**
d handstone for grinding . **MANO**
handwriting .... **SCRIPT**
handwriting on the wall . **MENE, MENE, TEKEL, UPHARSIN**
hang .... **DRAPE, DROOP, HOVER, IMPEND**
hank of twine .... **RAN**
Hannibal's defeat ...... **ZAMA**
Hannibal's victory .. **CANNAE**
happen ...... **OCCUR, BEFALL, BETIDE, CHANCE**
happening .... **EVENT**
happiness god, Jap. **EBISU, HOTEI**
harangue .... **ORATE, TIRADE, DIATRIBE**
Haran's son .... **LOT**
harass .... **NAG, BESET**
harbinger .... **HERALD**
harbor .... **BAY, COVE, PORT, HAVEN**
hard cash .... **SPECIE**
harden .... **GEL, SET ENURE, INURE, INDURATE**
hardship .... **TRIAL**
hardtack .... **PANTILE**
hardwood .... **ASH, OAK**
Hardy novel heroine ..... **TESS**
hare: dialect .... **WAT**

a hare, genus .... **LEPUS**
hare, young, 1 year .. **LEVERET**
harem ... **ZENANA, SERAGLIO**
harem room .... **ODA**
harlot of Jericho, Bibl. . **RAHAB**
harm . **BANE, DAMAGE, INJURE**
harm: old Eng. .... **DERE**
harm: poetic .... **BALE**
harmful .... **NOCENT**
harmonize .... **ATTUNE**
harmony .. **UNISON, CONCORD**
harp, ancient .... **TRIGON**
Harp constellation .... **LYRA**
harp guitar key .... **DITAL**
harp, kind of .... **EOLIC**
harp, Nubian .... **NANGA**
harpy, Gr. myth .... **AELLO**
harquebus projection .... **CROC**
harrow .... **DRAG**
harsh to taste .... **ACERB**
hartebeeste ..... **ASSE, TORA, CAAMA, KAAMA**
harvest .... **REAP**
harvest festival, Rom. . **OPALIA**
harvest goddess .... **OPS**
harvest, India ... **RABI, RABBI**
has not: Old Eng. .... **NAS**
hashish .... **BHANG**
hasty pudding .... **SEPON**
HAT .... see HEADGEAR

b hat: Anglo-Ir. ...... **CAUBEEN**
hat plant .... **SOLA**
hat, straw .. **MILAN, PANAMA**
hatchet, archeol. ...... **HACHE**
hatchet, stone .... **MOGO**
hatred .... **ODIUM, AVERSION**
hatred: Buddhism ...... **DOSA**
hatter's mallet .... **BEATER**
haul tight, naut. . **BOUSE, TRICE**
haunt, low .. **DEN, DIVE, NEST**
hautboy .... **OBOE**
haven .... **LEE**
having buttery account: Oxford .... **BATTEL**
having holes, as cheese **EYEY**
having true luster when uncut **NAIF**
haw!: P.I. .... **MANO**
haw, as cattle .... **HOI**
Hawaiian bird .. **IO, O-O, IIWI**
Hawaiian bird, extinct . **MAMO**
Hawaiian bird, red-tailed **KOAE**
Hawaiian blueberry ... **OHELO**
Hawaiian chant .... **MELE**
Hawaiian cloth .. **TAPA, KAPA**
Hawaiian cudweed ... **ENAENA**
Hawaiian dance .... **HULA**
Hawaiian farewell, greeting **ALOHA**
Hawaiian feather cloak . **MAMO**
Hawaiian fern .... **HEII**

c Hawaiian floral emblem **LEHUA**
Hawaiian food .... **POI**
Hawaiian food-game fish . **ULUA**
Hawaiian garland .... **LEI**
Hawaiian god .... **KANE**
Hawaiian goddess, fire .. **PELE**
Hawaiian goose .... **NENE**
Hawaiian gooseberry .... **POHA**
Hawaiian governor, 1st . **DOLE**
Hawaiian grass .... **HILO**
Hawaiian hawk .... **IO**
Hawaiian herb .... **HOLA**
Hawaiian loincloth .... **MALO**
Hawaiian musical instrument **PUA**
Hawaiian porch .... **LANAI**
Hawaiian president, 1st .. **DOLE**
Hawaiian royal chief ... **ALII**
Hawaiian shrub .... **AKIA**
Hawaiian staple .... **POI**
Hawaiian starch .... **APII**
Hawaiian timber tree ... **OHIA**
Hawaiian tree **KOA, AULU, ALANI, ILIAHI**
Hawaiian tree, dark .... **AALII**
Hawaiian tree fern ..... **PULU**
Hawaiian vine .... **IE**
Hawaiian volcano goddess. **PELE**
Hawaiian windstorm .... **KONA**
hawk .... **KITE**

d hawk, falconry .... **BATER**
hawk, fish .... **OSPREY**
hawk genus .... **BUTEO**
hawk-head god, Egypt . **HORUS**
hawk, India .... **SHIKRA**
hawk-like bird .... **KITE**
hawk, Scot. .... **ALLAN**
hawk, young ..... **BRANCHER**
hawks .... **IOS**
hawk's cage .... **MEW**
hawk's leash .... **LUNE**
hawthorn .... **MAY**
hawthorn berry .... **HAW**
hay, spread to dry .... **TED**
haystack .... **RICK**
hazard .... **DARE, RISK, PERIL**
hazardous .... **CHANCY**
haze: Old Eng. .... **HASE**
hazelnut .... **FILBERT**
hazy, make ..... **DIM, BEDIM**
"he remains": Lat. ... **MANET**
head ..... **NOB, LEAD, PATE, POLL, TETE, CAPUT, CHIEF, CAPITA, LEADER, NODDLE, NOODLE**
head covering .... **CAP, HAT, TAM, HOOD, VEIL, BERET**
head covering, fleecy .. **NUBIA**
head, crown of .... **PATE**
head, having round ... **RETUSE**
head, membrane covering **CAUL**

a head, Moslem .... **RAIS, REIS**
head of Benjamin's clan .. **IRI**
head, shaved .... **TONSURE**
head: slang .... **NOGGIN**
head wrap .... **NUBIA, SHAWL**
headband, Gr. .... **TAENIA**
HEADDRESS
see also HEADGEAR
headdress, bishop's
MITER, MITRE
headgear, brimless ..... **TOQUE**
headgear, clerical
BERETTA, BIRETTA
headgear, dervish .... **TAJ**
headgear, kind of ... **PANAMA**
headgear, military .... **SHAKO**
headgear, Moslem .. **TARBUSH, TARBOOCH, TARBOOSH, TARBOUCHE**
headgear, poetic .... **TIAR**
headgear, priest's
BERETTA, BIRETTA
headgear, tropics
TOPI, TERAI, TOPEE
headgear, Turk. .... **FEZ**
headland .. **RAS, CAPE, NASE, NESS, NOZE**
headless: Her. .... **ETETE**
headstrong .... **RASH**
healing goddess .... **EIR**
health, in good .... **FIT**
b health-drinking word
SALUD, PROSIT
health resort .... **SPA**
heap ...... **PILE, RAFF, RAFT**
hear ye! .... **OYES, OYEZ**
hearing: law .... **OYER**
hearken .. **HEAR, HEED, LIST, ATTEND, LISTEN**
heart .... **COR, CORE**
heart auricle . **ATRIA, ATRIUM**
heart contraction .... **SYSTOLE**
heart, immortal, Egyp. .... **AB**
heart trouble .... **ANGINA**
heartleaf .... **MEDIC**
heartless ... **CRUEL, SARDONIC**
heat .... **WARM, CALOR**
heated to whiteness .**CANDENT**
heath .... **MOOR**
heath genus .... **ERICA**
heathen .... **PAGAN**
heathen god .... **IDOL**
heather .... **LING, ERICA**
heating apparatus, vessel .**ETNA**
heave upward .... **SCEND**
heaven .. **SION, ZION, URANO**
heaven, eagle-borne flier to
ETANA
heaven personified: Babyl.. **ANU**
heavens, pert. to .... **URANIC**
heavenly .... **EDENIC**

c heavenly being .... **ANGEL SERAPH, SERAPHIM**
heavenly Jerusalem **SION, ZION**
heavy blow .... **ONER**
HEBREW see also JEWISH
and BIBLICAL
Hebr. Bible books .... **NEBIIM**
Hebr. Bible pronunciation aid
GRI, KRI, KERE, KERI, QERE, QERI, QUERI
Hebr. drum .... **TOPH**
Hebr. dry measure .. **CAB, KAB**
Hebr. lyre .... **ASOR**
Hebr. measure .... **KOR, EPHA, OMER, EPHAH**
Hebr. precept .... **TORA**
HEBREW PROPHETS . see
SPECIAL SECTION, Page 196
Hebr. proselyte .... **GER**
Hebr. reclaimer .... **GOEL**
Hebr. teacher ...... **RAB, REB**
Hebr. universe .... **OLAM**
Hebrews' ancestor, legend
EBER
Hector's mother ..... **HECUBA**
hedge plant .... **PRIVET**
hedgerow: Eng. .... **REW**
heed .... **HEAR, MIND, OBEY, RECK**
heel .... **CAD, CALX**
d height .... **STATURE**
heir .... **SON, SCION, HERITOR, LEGATEE**
held, able to be .... **TENABLE**
Helen: It. .... **ELENA**
Helen of Troy's mother . **LEDA**
Helen's lover .... **PARIS**
helical .... **SPIRAL**
Helios .... **SUN**
hell .... **HADES, SHEOL**
Hellespont swimmer . **LEANDER**
helm position .... **ALEE**
helmet, light .... **SALLET**
helmet, medieval
ARMET, HEAUME
helmet, Rom. .... **GALEA**
helmet-shaped ...... **GALEATE**
helmet-shaped part ... **GALEA**
helmsman .... **PILOT**
Heloise's husband ... **ABELARD**
help .. **AID, ABET, BACK, TIDE, ASSIST, SUCCOR, SUCCOUR**
helper .... **AIDE**
Helvetic .... **SWISS**
hem in .... **BESET**
hemp .... **TOW, RINE, RAMIE**
hemp, Afr. .... **IFE**
hemp, India ..... **KEF, BANG, KEEF, KEIF, KIEF, BHANG, DAGGA, RAMIE**
hemp, Manila .... **ABACA**

a hemp narcotic ...... **CHARAS**
hemp shrub, India **PUA, POOA, POOAH**
hen .... **LAYER**
hen harrier, Europ. .... **FALLER**
hence .... **SO, OFF, AWAY**
Hengist's brother ..... **HORSA**
Henry IV birthplace ...... **PAU**
"Henry IV" character ... **PETO**
"Henry V" knave ...... **NYM**
"Henry VI" character ... **IDEN**
hep .... **ONTO**
her: obs. .... **HIR**
Hera's son .... **ARES**
herald .... **USHER**
HERALDIC TERMS . see also SPECIAL SECTION, Page 194
herald's coat .... **TABARD**
heraldic bearing **ORLE, FILLET**
heraldic cross .... **PATEE**
heraldic wreath .... **ORLE**
herb ...... **RUE, LEEK, MINT, MOLY, WORT, ANISE, TANSY, YARROW, OREGANO**
herb, aromatic **BASIL, DITTANY**
herb, bitter .... **RUE, ALOE**
herb, carrot family .... **ANISE**
herb eve .... **IVA**
herb, fabulous **MOLY, PANACE**
herb, forage .... **SULLA**
b herb genus .... **ABFA GEUM, RUTA, ALETRIS**
herb, medicinal .. **ALOE, SENNA**
herb of grace .... **RUE**
herb, snake-charm ... **MUNGO**
herb with aromatic root .**NONDO**
herb, wooly .... **POLY**
Hercules' captive .... **IOLE**
Hercules, monster slain by **HYDRA**
Hercules' mother .. **ALCMENE**
herd .... **DROVE**
herd of horses .... **CAVIYA**
herd of whales .... **GAM, POD**
herdsman, Swiss .... **SENN**
hereditary right .... **UDAL**
hereditary factor .. **GEN, GENE**
heretic, 4th cent. **ARIAN, ARIUS**
heretofore .... **ERENOW**
Hermes' mother .... **MAIA**
Hermes' son .... **PAN**
hermit . **EREMITE, ANCHORITE**
hero, legendary .... **PALADIN**
Hero's love .... **LEANDER**
heroic .... **EPIC, EPICAL**
heroic poem **EPIC, EPOS, WORK**
heroic song .... **EDDA**
heron .... **EGRET**
heron brood, flock .... **SEDGE**
heron, kind of ...... **BITTERN**

c herring .... **ALEC, BRIT, SILL**
herring, grayback ..... **CISCO**
herring keg .... **CADE**
herring small Eur. ...... **SPRAT**
hesitate **DEMUR, FALTER, TEETER**
hesitation syllable .... **ER, UM**
Hesperides, one of .... **AEGLE**
Heyward, Du Bose, heroine. **BESS**
Hezekiah's mother .... **ABI**
hiatus .... **GAP, LACUNA**
hickory tree ...... **SHELLBARK**
hidden ..... **INNER, ARCANE, COVERT, LATENT**
hide .... **VEIL, CACHE**
hide of beast ..... **FELL, SKIN**
hide, thongs of .... **RIEM**
hide, undressed .... **KIP**
hides, Russian leather ... **JUFTI**
hiding in .... **PERDU**
high in pitch: mus. ...... **ALT**
high on scale .... **ELA**
high priest ...... **ELI, AARON, ANNAS**
highest note .... **ELA**
highest point .. **APEX, ZENITH**
highway .... **ITER, PIKE**
highway, Alaska-Canada **ALCAN**
highwayman .. **PAD, LADRONE**
hike .... **TRAMP**
d hill .... **TOR**
hill, broad .... **LOMA, LOMITA**
hill dweller, Ceylon .... **TODA**
hill dweller, India ..... **DOGRA**
hill, flat-topped .... **MESA**
hill fort: Ir. .... **RATH**
hill, isolated .... **BUTTE**
hill, pointed .... **TOR**
hill, Rome **CAELIAN, PALATINE**
hill, S. Afr. ...... **KOP, BULT**
hill: Turk. .... **DAGH**
hillock .... **TUMP**
hillside: Scot. .... **BRAE**
hilltop .... **KNAP**
hilt, sword .... **HAFT, HANDLE**
Himalayan animal .... **PANDA**
Himal. broadmouth ..... **RAYA**
Himal. ibex .... **KYL**
Himal. monkshood ...... **ATIS**
Himal. mountain .... **API**
Himal. wild goat . **KRAS, TAHR, TAIR, THAR**
hind ...... **ROE, BACK, REAR**
hinder by fear .... **DETER**
hindrance .... **BAR, LET**
Hindu age, cycle .... **YUGA**
Hindu ancestor .... **MANU**
Hindu ascetic .... **JOGI, YATI, YOGI, FAKIR, SADHU, FAKEER**

a Hindu bible .... **VEDA**
Hindu charitable gift ... **ENAM**
Hindu cymbal .... **TAL**
Hindu deity .... **DEVA, RAMA, SIVA, SHIVA**
HINDU DEITY . see also GOD and see SPECIAL SECTION
Hindu divorce law ..... **TALAK**
Hindu female slave ..... **DASI**
Hindu festival .... **HOLI**
Hindu festival, religious . **PUJA**
Hindu gentlemen **BABU, BABOO**
HINDU GODS .... see SPECIAL SECTION, Page 200, and also GOD
Hindu guitar .... **BINA, VINA, SITAR**
Hindu holy man .... **SADH**
Hindu laws, giver of ... **MANU**
Hindu legendary hero ... **NALA**
Hindu life energy .... **JIVA**
Hindu, low caste .... **KORI**
Hindu magic .... **MAYA**
Hindu mantra .... **OM**
Hindu mendicant ...... **NAGA**
Hindu monastery ...... **MATH**
Hindu "Olympus" ...... **MERU**
Hindu philosophy ...... **YOGA**
Hindu poet .... **TAGORE**
Hindu prince
RAJA, RANA, RAJAH
b Hindu progenitor, myth **MANU**
Hindu queen .... **RANI, RANEE**
Hindu religious adherent
JAIN, JAINA
Hindu rites .... **ACHARA**
Hindu sacred literature .. **VEDA**
Hindu sacred word .... **OM**
Hindu scripture ...... **AGAMA**
Hindu scriptures, pert. to **VEDIC**
Hindu sect, one of **SEIK, SIKH**
Hindu teacher .... **GURU**
Hindu temple .... **DEUL**
Hindu term of respect **SAHIB**
Hindu title .... **AYA, SRI**
Hindu trader
BANIAN, BANYAN
Hindu unknown god ...... **KA**
Hindu, unorthodox .... **JAINA**
Hindu widow, suicide .. **SUTTEE**
Hindu woman's garment
SARI, SAREE
Hindu word .... **OM**
Hindu writings .... **VEDA**
Hinduism, elixir
AMRITA, AMREETA
Hindustani .... **URDU**
hinge, kind of .... **BUTT**
hint .... **TIP, CLEW, POINTER**
hip .... **COXA, ILIA, ILIAC**
hipbone, of the .... **ILIAC**

c Hippocrates' birthplace ... **KOS**
Hippodrome .... **ARENA**
hire
LET, RENT, ENGAGE, CHARTER
hired carriage .... **HACK**
hired labor: S. Afr. ..... **TOGT**
history .... **LORE**
hitherto .... **YET**
Hittites ancestor .... **HETH**
hive for bees .... **SKEP**
hives .... **UREDO**
hoard .... **AMASS, STORE**
hoarder .... **MISER**
hoarfrost .... **RIME**
hoarfrost: Eng. .... **RAG**
hoary .... **OLD, GRAY**
hoax .... **RUSE, CANARD**
hobgoblin ..... **PUCK, SPRITE**
hock, horse's ...... **GAMBREL**
hockey ball .... **ORR**
hodgepodge ...... **MESS, OLIO**
hog cholera .... **ROUGET**
hog deer .... **AXIS**
hog, female .... **GILT**
hog plum, W. Ind. **AMRA, JOBO**
hog, wild .... **BOAR, PECCARY**
hog's heart, liver, etc. **HASLET**
Hogan, golfer .... **BEN**
hoist .... **HEAVE**
hold, as in war .... **INTERN**
d hold back .... **DETER**
hold fast: naut. ...... **BELAY**
holding .... **TENURE**
holding device .. **VISE, TONGS**
hole for molten metal .. **SPRUE**
hole in embankment .... **GIME**
hole in mold .... **GEAT**
hole-in-one .... **ACE**
holidays, Roman .... **FERIA**
HOLLAND see NETHERLANDS SPECIAL SECTION
hollow .... **DENT, HOWE**
holly .... **HOLM, ILEX**
holly, U. S. .... **ASSI, YAPON, YUPON, YAUPON**
holm oak .... **ILEX**
"Holy Hill," Gr. ...... **ATHOS**
Holy Land city .... **DAN**
holy orders, give .... **ORDAIN**
holy water font .... **STOUP**
homage .... **HONOR**
home .... **ABODE**
home of gods, Norse .. **ASGARD**
"Home Sweet Home" author
PAYNE
homeopath school-founder
HERING
Homer's epic .... **ODYSSEY**
hominy, Indian coarse .. **SAMP**
honey .... **MEL**
honey-badger .... **RATEL**

a honey buzzard .... **PERN**
honey drink .. **MEAD, MORAT**
honey eater bird
IAO, MOHO, MANUAO
honeybee .... **DESERET**
honeycomb, like a ... **FAVOSE**
honor .... **EXALT, REVERE**
honorarium .... **TIP**
honorary commission .. **BREVET**
Honshu bay .... **ISE**
Honshu port .... **KOBE**
hooded garment ...... **PARKA**
hoodoo .... **JINX, JYNX**
hoof .... **UNGUES, UNGUIS**
hook, bent into ..... **HAMATE**
hook, double curve .... **ESS**
hook, engine .... **GAB**
hook for pot .... **CLEEK**
hook money .... **LARI, LARIN**
hooks .... **HAMI**
hookah .... **NARGILE**
hooked .... **HAMUS, HAMATE, HAMOSE, FALCATE**
Hoover Dam lake ...... **MEAD**
hop-picker's basket ...... **BIN**
hope goddess, Rom. ..... **SPES**
hop plant .... **LUPULUS**
hopscotch stone ...... **PEEVER**
Horae, one of .... **DIKE, EIRENE, EUNOMIA**
Horeb .... **SINAI**
b horizontal stripe .... **BAR**
horizontal timber ..... **LINTEL**
horn .... **CORNU**
horn, crescent-moon ..... **CUSP**
horn, Hebr. **SHOFAR, SHOPHAR**
horn quicksilver ..... **CALOMEL**
horn-shaped structure .. **CORNU**
horn sounded for kill .. **MORT**
horn tissue, bit of ..... **SCUR**
horneblende .... **EDENITE**
hornless, Eng. dial. ...... **NOT**
hornless stag .... **POLLARD**
hors d'oeuvre .... **CANAPE**
horse .. **BAY, COB, NAG, ARAB, MARE, MERE, ROAN, MOUNT, STEED, EQUINE, JENNET**
horse, Austral. .... **WALER**
horse, Barbary native ... **BARB**
horse blanket .... **MANTA**
horse breed .... **MORGAN**
horse, brown
BAY, ROAN, SORREL
horse color **BAY, ROAN, SORREL**
horse dealer, Eng. .... **COPER**
horse, disease of .... **SPAVIN**
horse, draft .... **SHIRE**
horse genus .... **EQUUS**
horse: gypsy .. **GRI, GRY, GRAS**
horse-mackerel .... **SCAD**

c horse-man, myth ... **CENTAUR**
horse, piebald .... **PINTO**
horse, race .... **PACER**
horse-radish, fruit of ... **BEN**
horse, saddle .... **MOUNT**
horse, small .... **GENET, GENNET, JENNET, GENETTE**
horse, Sp. Am. ..... **CABALLO**
horse, swift .. **ARAB, COURSER**
horse, talking, Gr. .... **ARION**
horse, war .... **CHARGER**
horse, white-flecked ... **ROAN**
horse, wild Asiatic ... **TARPAN**
horse, young ..... **COLT, FOAL**
horses, goddess of ..... **EPONA**
horse's sideways tread ... **VOLT**
horsehair .... **SETON**
horsemanship, art of **MANEGE**
horseshoe gripper ...... **CALK**
horseshoeing stall
TRAVE, TREVE
Horus' mother .... **ISIS**
Hosea's wife .... **GOMER**
host .... **ARMY, HORDE**
hostelry .... **INN**
hot air chamber .... **OVEN**
hot iron to sear ..... **CAUTER**
hot spring, eruptive .. **GEYSER**
Hottentot .... **NAMA**
hourly .... **HORAL**
d house **ROOF, VILLA, COTTAGE**
house, like a .... **DOMAL**
house, mud, Afr. ..... **TEMBE**
house urn: Rom. ... **CAPANNA**
housefly genus ...... **MUSCA**
housefly genus, lesser **FANNIA**
household **MENAGE, MAINPOST**
household god .... **LAR, LARES**
howl .... **ULULATE**
howling monkey **MONO, ARABA**
hub .. **NAVE, BOSTON, CENTER**
hubbub .. **ADO, STIR, TUMULT**
hue .... **COLOR, TINGE**
huge .... **VAST, ENORM**
Huguenot leader ..... **ADRETS**
hull .... **POD, HUSK**
humble .... **ABASE**
hummingbird
AVA, TOPAZ, COLIBRI
humorist .... **WIT**
humpback salmon
HADDO, HOLIA
Humphreys, Mrs. (pseudo.)
RITA
hundred .... **CENTUM**
hundredweight ...... **CENTAL**
Hungarian dog .... **PULI**
Hungarian hero .... **NAGY**
Hungarian king .... **BELA**
Hungarian people ... **MAGYAR**
Hungarian pianist ... **SANDOR**

a Hungarian playwright MOLNAR
Hungarian violinist .... AUER
Huns, king of ATLI, ETZEL, ATTILA
hunt, Ind. .... SHIKAR
hunter ...... ORION, NIMROD
hunter, India .... SHIKARI
hunting cry .. HO, YOI, TOHO, HALLOO, YOICKS, TALLY-HO
hunting hat .... TERAI
hunting hound .... ALAN
huntress .... ATALANTA
huntsman .... JAGER
HUNTSMAN'S CRY see HUNTING CRY
hup: army .... ONE
hurdy-gurdy ..... LIRA, ROTA
hurry .... HIE, HASTEN
hurt .... MAR, ACHE, LESION
c hurt: old Eng. .... DERE
hurtful .... MALEFIC
husband's brother ...... LEVIR
hush .... SH, HSH
husk, cereal .... BRAN
hut, India .... BARI
hut, Mex. .... JACAL
hydrate, as lime ..... SLAKE
hydraulic pump .... RAM
hydrocarbon . TOLAN, ETHANE, OCTANE, RETENE, TERPENE
hydrogen compound ... IMINE
hydrogen isotope ... PROTIUM
hymn .... ODE
hymn of praise ..... ANTHEM
hypnotic state ...... TRANCE
hypothetical force OD, BIOD, ELOD, ODYL
hypothetical force of ... ODIC
hyson .... TEA

I

I .... EGO
"I have found it" .... EUREKA
"I love": Lat. .... AMO
Iago's wife .... EMILIA
Iberians .... IBERI, IBERES
b ibex .... KYL, TUR, KAIL
Ibsen character ... ASE, NORA
ice block, glacial ...... SERAC
ice mass .... BERG, FLOE
ice, slushy ...... SISH, LOLLY
iced .... GLACE
Iceland epic, literature, tales EDDA
Icelandic narrative ..... SAGA
icy .... GELID
"id —" (that is) .... EST
idea, Plato .... EIDOS
ideal .... UTOPIAN
ideal republic, imaginary OCEANA
ideal state .... UTOPIA
identical .... ONE, SAME
ideology .... ISM
idiocy .... ANOESIA
idiot .... AMENT, CRETIN
idle .... OTIANT, OTIOSE
idle, to be ...... LAZE, LOAF
idol: archaic .... PAGOD
idol: philos. .... EIDOLON
idolatrous .... PAGAN
ids, pert. to .... IDIC
Idumaea .... EDOM
if ever .... ONCE
if not .... ELSE
ignoble .... BASE
ignominy .... SHAME
ignorance, Hindu philos. TAMAS
ignorant .. STUPID, UNAWARE
ignore .... ELIDE
Igorot's neighbor tribesman ATA
ill .... EVIL
d ill-will .... SPITE, RANCOR
illumination unit .... LUX
illusion .... CHIMERA
illusory riches .... MINE
image .... IDOL, IDOLON, IDOLUM, EIDOLON
image, pert. to ...... ICONIC
image, religious .. ICON, IKON
imagine: arch. .... WIS
imbecile .... AMENT, ANILE, CRETIN
imbibe .... SIP, GULP, DRINK
imitate ... APE, MIME, MIMIC
imitation .... MIMESIS
imitation gems .... PASTE
immature seed .... OVULE
immature: zool. ..... NEANIC
immeasurable .... BOUNDLESS
immediately ..... NOW, ANON
immense .... VAST
immerse .. DIP, DUNK, DOUSE
immigrant, Greek ..... METIC
immunizing substance SERUM, HAPTEN, HAPTENE
imou pine .... RIMU
impair .. MAR, DAMAGE, SPOIL
impart .... GIVE, LEND
impartial .... EVEN
impede ...... ESTOP, HAMPER
impel .... URGE

a impertinent ..... **PERT, SAUCY**
IMPLEMENT ... see also TOOL
implement, pounding .. **PESTLE**
implement to skid logs .. **TODE**
implied .... **TACIT**
import .... **SENSE**
important, critically ... **VITAL**
importune .... **URGE**
impose .... **LAY**
impost .... **TAX**
imposture .... **SHAM**
impoverish .... **IMPOOR**
impressionist painter .. **DEGAS, MANET, MONET, RENOIR**
imprison .... **IMMURE**
improve .... **AMEND**
improvise music .... **VAMP**
impudence .... **LIP, BRASS, CHEEK, NERVE**
impure metal product .. **MATTE**
in addition .. **TOO, ALSO, YET**
in agreement .... **UNITED**
in disagreement .... **OUT**
in half, in — .... **TWO**
"in medias —" .... **RES**
in name only ...... **NOMINAL**
in same place .... **IBID**
in so far as .... **QUA**
in the know .... **AWARE**
in the matter of .... **INRE**
in the past .... **OVER**
b in the very near future..**ANON**
in unison .... **ONE**
in very truth .... **AMEN**
inability to hear ..... **ASONIA**
inactive .... **INERT**
inadequate .... **SCANT**
inborn .... **NATIVE**
incarnation, Hindu .... **RAMA, AVATAR**
incense ingredient **GUM, SPICE, STACTE**
incense receptacle, Rom.**ACERRA**
incense, Somali .... **MATTI**
incentive .... **GOAD, MOTIVE**
incessantly .... **EVER**
inch, .001 of .... **MIL**
incidentally .... **OBITER**
incinerate .... **CREMATE**
incite ..... **EGG, PROD, URGE, IMPEL, SET ON, SUBORN**
inciter .... **EGGER**
inclination .... **BENT**
incline .. **TEND, SLOPE, TREND**
inclined .... **APT, PRONE**
inclined way .... **RAMP**
income, annual, Fr. .... **RENTE**
incompletely .... **SEMI**
inconsiderable ..... **NOMINAL**
increase .... **WAX, RISE**
incrustation .... **SCAB**
c incursion, predatory .... **RAID**
indeed: Ir. ...... **ARU, AROO**
indentation **CRENA, CRENAE, CRENELET**
index mark .... **FIST**
INDIA, INDIAN ... see also SPECIAL SECTION and see also HINDU
India farmer .... **MEO**
India minstrel .... **BHAT**
India native chief .... **SIRDAR**
India native servant ... **MATY**
India: poet. .... **IND**
India, swamp belt of .. **TERAI**
INDIAN .. see also page 192
Indian .... **SAC**
INDIAN, ALGONQUIN .... see page 192
Indian, Arawak ...... **ARAUA**
Indian, Arikara .... **REE**
Indian, Athapasca ..... **TAKU**
Indian buzzard .... **TESA**
Indian corn .... **MAIZE**
Indian corn: N. Z. ... **KANGA**
Indian elk .... **SAMBAR**
Indian farmer, Fla. .. **CALUSA**
Indian in Chaco .... **TOBA**
Indian mahogany tree .. **TOON**
Indian mulberry **AL, AAL, ACH**
Indian of Jalisco ...... **CORA**
Indian of Keresan .... **SIA**
Indian of Mex., scattered **CORA**
d Indian ox .... **ZEBU**
Indian, Panamint .... **KOSO**
INDIAN, PLAINS . see page 193
Indian race .... **JAT**
Indian shell currency **ULO, UHLLO**
INDIAN, SIOUAN see page 193
Indian, S. Peru ..... **CHANCA**
INDIAN TREE.see TREE, INDIA
Indian, warlike ...... **APACHE**
Indian weight ..... **SER, TOLA**
Indian, whaler .... **HOH**
Indian yellow .... **PURI, PIURI, PURREE**
indicating succession **ORDINAL**
indict .... **ARRAIGN**
indifferent to pain **STOIC, STOICAL**
indigo plant .... **ANIL**
indistinct, make ...... **BEDIM**
indite .... **PEN, WRITE**
individual .... **ONE, SELF**
Indo-Chin. native **LAO,MRU,TAI**
Indo-Chin. tribe **TAI,LAOS,SHAN**
Indo-Chin. tribes .... **MOI**
Indo-European **ARYA, ARYAN**
Indo-Malayan animal .. **NAPU**
indolent ...... **OTIOSE, SUPINE**
Indonesian ..... **ATA, NESIOT**

a induce .... LEAD
Indus tribesman .... GOR
ineffectual .... VAIN
inelastic .... LIMP
inert .... SUPINE
infatuation .... ATE
infertile moor .... LANDE
infinity .... OLAM
infirm .... ANILE, SENILE
inflamed, be .... RANKLE
inflammable liquid .. ACETONE
inflammation: med. .. ANGINA
inflexible .... IRON, RIGID
inflict .... DEAL, IMPOSE
inflorescence RACEME, SPADIX
inflorescence, racemose AMENT
influence .... AFFECT
informer: slang .... NARK
infusion .... TEA
ingenuous .... NAIVE
inhabitant .... ITE
inhabitant of a town ..... CIT
inheritance .... ENTAIL
inheritor .... LEGATEE
initiate .. OPEN, BEGIN, START
initiate, Gr. ... EPOPT, EPOPTA
injure ... MAR, HARM, MAIM
injury ...... LESION, TRAUMA
inlaid .... MOSAIC
inlaid decoration .... BUHL
b inlet .. ARM, BAY, RIA, FIORD
inlet: Dutch .... ZEE
inlet, Orkneys .... VOE
inn .... KHAN, HOSTEL, POSADA, HOSPICE
inn, "Canterbury Tales" TABARD
inn, Oriental .... SERAI
inn, Turkish .... IMARET
inner .... ENTAL
inner meaning .. CORE, HEART
inner parlor: Scot. ...... BEN
innkeeper PADRONE, BONIFACE
insect ... ANT, BEE, BUG, DOR, FLY, FLEA, GNAT, MITE, APHID, CADEW, EMESA, BEETLE, CADDIS, CICADA, CICALA, MANTIS
insect, adult .... IMAGO
insect body THORAX, THORACES
insect, immature ...... PUPA, LARVA, INSTAR
insect mature .... IMAGO
insect order .... DIPTERA
insect, plant sucking .. APHID
insect, ruinous APHID, BORER
insertion mark .... CARET
inset .... PANEL
insidious .... SLY
insincere talk .... CANT
insipid, become .... PALL

c insist .... URGE, PRESS
inspire .... IMBUE
install .... INSTATE
instance .... CASE
instant .... MO, TRICE
instar .. PUPA, IMAGO, LARVA
instigate .. EGG, ABET, INCITE
instruct ..... BRIEF, EDUCATE
INSTRUMENT .. see also MUSICAL INSTRUMENT
instrument, Afr. reed GORA, GORAH, GOURA
instrument, Chin. ancient KIN
instrument, Hebr. ... TIMBREL
instrument, India ..... RUANA
instrument, Jap. .... SAMISEN
instrument, lutelike BANDORE
instrument, lyrelike ... KISSAR
instrument, math. .... SECTOR
instrument, medieval .. ROCTA
instrument, naut. PELORUS, SEXTANT
instrument, Sp. .... CASTANET
instrument, stringed ... LYRE, NABLA, REBAB, REBEC, SAROD, SITAR, VIOLA, CITHER, CITHARA, CITHERN, CITTERN, GITTERN
instrument, surveying TRANSIT
instrumentality MEDIA, MEDIUM
d insulate .... ISLE
insult .... CAG
insurgent .... REBEL
intact .... WHOLE
intellect .... MIND, NOUS, MAHAT, REASON
inter .... BURY, INHUME
intercharged ..... PERMUTED
interdict .... BAN
interferometer ...... ETALON
interior, ancient temple CELLA
interjection for silence .... TST
interlace .... WEAVE
interlock .... LINK
international language RO, IDO
inter. money unit .... BANCOR
international pact ... ENTENTE
interpret .... REDE
intersect .... MEET
interstice, small AREOLA, AREOLE
interstices, with .... AREOLAR
intervening: law ...... MESNE
interweave .. TWINE, RADDLE
intimidate AWE, COW, DAUNT
intone .... CHANT
intoxicant: India ...... SOMA
intoxicated .... SOSH
intricate .... DEDAL, DAEDAL, GORDIAN

a intrigue .... **CABAL**
introduce
BROACH, INSERT, PRESENT
introducer of jetties for deepening .... **EADS**
inundation .... **SPATE**
inveigle ...... **LURE, ENTICE**
inventor, claim of rights **PATENT**
inventor, elevator .... **OTIS**
inventor, sewing machine **HOWE**
inventor, steam engine **WATT**
invest ...... **ENDOW, ENDUE, INDUE, CLOTHE, ORDAIN**
invested .... **CLAD**
investigate .... **PROBE**
investigator .... **TRACER**
invite .... **ASK, BID**
involve **ENTAIL, ENTRAMMEL**
Io butterfly .... **KIHO**
iodine source .... **KELP**
ion, negative .... **ANION**
ion, positive .... **CATION**
Ionian city .... **TEOS**
iota .... **JOT, MITE**
Iowa college town ...... **AMES**
ipecac source .... **EVEA**
IRAN .. see also PERSIAN
Iran, former part of .... **ELAM**
Iranian .... **TAT, KURD**
b Iranian Turk .... **SART**
irascible .... **TESTY**
irate .... **MAD**
Ireland .... **EIRE, ERIN**
Ireland, old name ..... **IERNE**
Ireland personified .... **IRENA**
iridescent gem .... **OPAL**
iris .... **FLAG**
iris, Florentine, European **ORRIS**
iris, layer of .... **UVEA**
iris, of a layer .... **UVEAL**
iris root .... **ORRIS**
IRISH .. see also IRELAND
Irish .... **ERSE**
Ir. alphabet, early
OGAM, OGUM
Ir. ancestor **IR, MIL, ITH, MILED**
Ir. assembly .... **DAIL**
Ir. church .... **KIL**
Ir. city, ancient .... **TARA**
Ir. clan, ancient .... **SEPT**
Ir. competitive meet .... **FEIS**
Ir. crowning stone, — Fail **LIA**
Ir. dramatist .... **SYNGE**
Ir. exclamation .... **ARU, AROO, ARRA, WHIST, WURRA**
Ir. fairies .... **SHEE**
Ir. family .... **CINEL**
Ir. Free State .... **EIRE**
Irish-Gaelic .... **ERSE**
Ir. goddess, battle **BADB, BODB**
c **IR. GODS' MOTHER** see page 200
Ir. kings' home .... **TARA**
Ir. law, tribe .... **CINEL**
Ir. lower house parliament **DAIL**
Ir. nobleman .... **AIRE**
Ir. poet
AE, COLUM, MOORE, YEATS
Ir. rebel group .... **IRA**
Ir. tribe .... **SIOL**
Ir. writing .... **OGAM, OGHAM**
Irishman .. **AIRE, CELT, MICK**
iron disulfide .... **PYRITE**
iron, pert. to .... **FERRIC**
ironwood ...... **ACLE, COLIMA**
irony .... **SATIRE**
Iroquoian .... **ERIE**
Iroquois demon .... **OTKON**
irrational number ...... **SURD**
irregularity .... **JOG**
irrigation ditch **FLUME, SLUICE**
irritate .... **VEX, GALL, RILE, NETTLE, RANKLE**
Isaac's son **EDOM, ESAU, JACOB**
Ishmael .... **PARIAH**
Ishmael, son of ...... **DUMAH**
Ishmael's mother ..... **HAGAR**
isinglass .... **MICA**
Isis, husband of .... **OSIRIS**
ISLAM .... see MOSLEM
d island ... **OE, AIT, CAY, KAY, KEY, EYOT, HOLM, ILOT, ISLE, ATOLL, ISLET, ISLOT**
ISLAND, AEGEAN .... see GAZETTEER
island, Argyll .... **IONA**
island, coral .... **ATOLL**
island, Dodecanese . **COO, KOS, CASO, LERO, SIMI**
island, Great Barrier ... **OTEA**
island, Gr. (fine marble) **PAROS**
island, Gr., pert. to ... **CRETAN**
island, inhabiting an . **NESIOTE**
ISLAND, INNER HEBRIDES
see HEBRIDES GAZETTEER
island, Ionian .... **ZANTE**
island, Micronesia ... **PONAPE**
island near Ireland ..... **ARAN**
island, near Italy ...... **CAPRI**
island off Scotland .... **IONA, ARRAN**
island, Riga Gulf ...... **OESEL**
island, river **AIT, EYOT, HOLM**
island, South Seas ...... **ARU, TAITI, TAHITI, OTAHEITE**
island, west of Sumatra .. **NIAS**
islands, Gulf of Bothnia **ALAND**
islands, Irish .... **ARAN**
islands, off Timor ...... **LETI**
Isle of Man, pert. to ... **MANX**
islet .... **AIT, CAY, HOLM**
isolate .... **ENISLE**

a **Israel** .... **JACOB**
ISRAEL, KING OF ... see KING OF ISRAEL
ISRAELITE .. see also HEBREW and BIBLICAL
ISRAELITE JUDGE .... see BIBLICAL JUDGE
ISRAELITE KING .. see KING OF ISRAEL
Israelite tribe .... **DAN**
Israelites .... **SION, ZION**
issue. **EMIT, EMERGE, EMANATE**
isthmus .... **NECK**
istle fiber .... **PITA, PITO**
it proceeds: music .... **VA**
ITALIAN WORDS: (accent marks omitted throughout)
arts .... **ARTES**
article .... **LA**
canal (s) **CANALE, CANALI**
chest .... **CASSO**
custom house ..... **DOGANA**
day-breeze .... **ORA**
dear .... **CARA, CARO**
dough .... **PASTA**
drink .... **BEVERE**
enough .... **BASTA**
evening .... **SERA**
enthusiasm .... **ESTRO**
feast .... **FESTINO**
b field .... **CAMPO**
food .... **PASTO**
from beginning .... **DACAPO**
gentleman .... **SER**
goodby .... **ADDIO**
gondola cabin .... **FELZE**
hamlet .... **CASAL, CASALE**
hair .... **PELO**
hand .... **MANO**
harbor .... **PORTO**
harp .... **ARPA**
hatred .... **ODIO**
Helen .... **ELENA**
holiday .... **FESTA, FESTE**
host .... **OSTE**
Italy .... **ITALIA**
judge .... **PODESTA**
lady .... **DONNA, SIGNORA**
lake .... **LAGO**
little .... **POCO**
love .... **AMORE**
lover .... **AMOROSO**
mother .... **MADRE**
mountain peak ...... **CIMA**
nine .... **NOVE**
ninth .... **NONO**
c one .... **UNO**
paste .... **PASTA**
peak .... **CIMA**
pronoun .... **MIA**
right .... **DESTRO**
Rome .... **ROMA**
sign .... **SEGNO**
somebody .... **UNO**
street .... **CALLE**
three .... **TRE**
time .... **TEMPO**
tour .... **GIRO**
town ...... **CASAL, CASALE**
you .... **TU**
voice .... **VOCE**
well .... **BENE**
with .... **CON**

Italian actress .... **DUSE**
It., ancient **ITALI, OSCAN, SABINE**
It. astronomer ...... **GALILEO**
It. author .... **SILONE**
It. car .... **FIAT**
It. cathedral city .... **MILAN**
It. commune .... **ESTE**
It. composer .... **BOITO, GUIDO, VERDI, ROSSINI**
It. day breeze .... **ORA**
d It. family .... **ESTE, CENCI, DORIA, MEDICI**
It. family royal name ... **ESTE**
It. gambling game ..... **MORA**
It. gentleman .... **SER**
It. guessing game ...... **MORA**
It. lady ..... **DONA, SIGNORA**
It. millet ...... **BUDA, MOHA**
It. painter .... **RENI, LIPPI, VINCI, ANDREA, CRESPI, GIOTTO**
It. poet **DANTE, TASSO, ARIOSTO**
It. resort .... **LIDO**
It. rice dish .... **RISOTTO**
It.: Rome .... **ROMA**
It. sculptor .... **LEONI**
It. singer .... **AMATO**
It. title, early .... **SER**
It. university city **BARI, PADUA**
It. violin maker ...... **AMATI**
It. wine .... **ASTI**
Italy .... **ITALIA**
itch .... **PSORA**
itemize .... **LIST**
ivory nut ...... **ANTA, TAGUA**
ivy crowned .... **HEDERATED**
ivy thicket .... **TOD**

J

a jack in cribbage .... **NOB**
jack-in-the-pulpit **ARAD, AROID**
jack tree .... **JACA**
jackal, Afr. .... **THOS**
jackal, India .... **KOLA**
jackal, N. Afr. .... **DIEB**
jackdaw .... **DAW**
jackdaw: Scot. .... **KAE**
JACKET .. see also GARMENT
jacket .. **ETON, JUPE, BOLERO**
jacket, armor .... **ACTON**
jacket, Malay .... **BAJU**
Jackson heroine .. . **RAMONA**
Jacob's brother .. **EDOM, ESAU**
Jacob's son. . **DAN, GAD, ASER, LEVI, ASHER**
Jacob's twin brother .... **ESAU**
Jacob's wife .. **LEAH, RACHEL**
jaeger gull ..... **SKUA, ALLAN**
jagged line .... **ZAG, ZIG**
jai alai .... **PELOTA**
Jamashid .... **YIMA**
James II daughter ..... **ANNE**
Janizaries, Chief of ...... **DEY**
JAPANESE: . see also SPECIAL SECTION
Jap. aborigine ... **AINO, AINU**
Jap. admiral .... **ITO**
b Jap.-Am. .... **ISSEI, KIBEI, NISEI, SANSEI**
Jap. army reserve ..... **HOJU**
Jap. army second line ... **KOBI**
Jap. art of self-defense **JUDO**
Jap. badge, family ...... **MON**
Jap. badge, imperial **KIRIMON**
Jap. beer, rice .... **SAKE, SAKI**
Jap. beverage .... **SAKE**
Jap. box, girdle .... **INRO**
Jap. bush clover ...... **HAGI**
Jap. cedar .... **SUGI**
Jap. celery-like vegetable **UDO**
Jap. cherry .... **FUJI**
Jap. clogs .... **GETA**
Jap. deer .... **SIKA**
Jap. drama ..... **NO, KABUKI**
Jap. emperor's title ... **TENNO**
Jap. festival .... **BON**
Jap. fish .... **TAI, FUGU**
Jap. food, seaweed **KOBU, KOMBU**
Jap. gods .... **KAMI**
Jap. happiness god **EBISU, HOTEI**
Jap. harp .... **KOTO**
Jap. herb, stout .... **UDO**

c Jap. immigrant .... **ISSEI**
Jap. mile measure .... **RI**
Jap. monastery .... **TERA**
Jap. national park ..... **ASO**
Jap. naval station ..... **KURE**
Jap. news agency ... **DOMEI**
Jap. nobleman .... **KUGE**
Jap. outcast **ETA, YETA, RONIN**
Jap. outer garment **MINO, HAORI, KIMONO**
Jap. parliament .... **DIET**
Jap. perfecture .... **FU**
Jap. persimmon .... **KAKI**
Jap. plant .... **UDO**
Jap. plane .... **ZERO**
Jap. primitive ... **AINO, AINU**
Jap. province, old ... **ISE, KAI**
Jap. receptacle .... **INRO**
Jap. salad plant .... **UDO**
Jap. salmon .... **MASU**
Jap. sash, kimono .... **OBI**
Jap. school of painting **KANO**
Jap. ship name .... **MARU**
Jap. sock .... **TABI**
Jap. statesman .... **ITO**
Jap. straw cape .... **MINO**
Jap. sword .. **CATAN, CATTAN**
d Jap. vegetable ... **UDO, GOBO**
Jap. verse .... **UTA**
Jap. village .... **MURA**
Jap. volcano .... **FUJI**
Jap. writing .... **KANA**
Japheth, son of ...... **GOMER**
jar ...... **EWER, OLLA, CRUSE**
jar ring .... **LUTE**
jar, wide-mouthed ...... **OLLA**
jargon **CANT, ARGOT, PATOIS**
Jason's father .... **AESON**
Jason's 2d wife ..... **CREUSA**
Jason's ship .... **ARGO**
Jason's wife .... **MEDEA**
jaunty .... **PERK**
Java plum: P. I. ..... **DUHAT**
Javanese carriage ...... **SADO**
Javanese language **KAVI, KAWI**
Javanese poison tree ... **UPAS**
javelin, Afr. **ASSAGAI, ASSEGAI**
javelin game .. **JERID, JEREED**
javelin, Rom. .... **PILUM**
jeer .... **GIBE, SCOFF**
jeer at ...... **TAUNT, DERIDE**
Jehoshaphat, father of ... **ASA**
Jehovah .... **GOD**
Jehovah: Hebr. .... **JAH, JAVE, JAVEH, YAHWEH**

a jejune .. **DRY, ARID, BARREN**
jelly base .... **PECTIN**
jelly fruit .... **GUAVA**
jelly, meat .... **ASPIC**
jeopardize .... **ENDANGER**
Jericho, land opposite .. **MOAB**
jersey, woollen ..... **SINGLET**
Jerusalem, ancient name **SALEM**
Jerusalem: poet. ...... **ARIEL**
jest .... **JAPE**
jester .... **MIME, BUFFOON**
jet, U.S. .... **SABRE, SCORPION**
Jether, son of .... **ARA**
jetty .... **MOLE**
Jew .... **SEMITE**
JEWEL ...... see GEM, STONE
jewelry setting .... **PAVE**
jewels, adorn with ..... **BEGEM**
JEWISH .. see also HEBREW
Jewish ascetic ...... **ESSENE**
Jewish benediction ... **SHEMA**
Jewish bride .... **KALLAH**
Jewish ceremony **SEDAR, SEDER**
Jewish feast of tabernacles
SUCCOTH
Jewish festival **PURIM, SEDER**
Jewish law, body of .. **TALMUD**
Jewish marriage contract
KETUBA
Jewish offering ..... **CORBAN**
b Jewish prayer book . **MAHZOR**
Jewish scholar .... **RAB**
Jewish sect, ancient .. **ESSENES**
Jewish teacher ... **REB, RABBI**
Jewish title of honor
RAB, GAON
Jezebel's husband .... **AHAB**
Joan of Arc's victory **ORLEANS**
Job's-tears .... **COIX**
jog .... **TROT, NUDGE**
John: Gaelic, Scot. **IAN, EOAN**
John: Ir. .... **EOIN, SEAN**
John: Russ. .... **IVAN**
johnny-cake .... **PONE**
Johnson, Dr., hero .. **RASSELAS**
join ..... **LINK, PAIR, SEAM, WELD, YOKE, MERGE, UNITE, ATTACH**
join corners ... **MITER, MITRE**
join wood .... **RABBET**
joining bar .... **YOKE**
joint **HIP, KNEE, NODE, HINGE**
joint part **TENON, MORTISE**
joke with **KID, RIB, JAPE, JOSH**
joker .... **WAG, WIT**
Jordan city, ancient region
PETRA
Joseph's father .... **JACOB**
Joseph's nephew .... **TOLA**

c Joshua tree .... **YUCCA**
Joshua's father .... **NUN**
jostle .... **JOG, ELBOW**
jot .... **IOTA, TITTLE**
journey .... **ITER, RIDE, TOUR, TREK, TRIP, TRAVEL**
journey in circuit .... **EYRE**
joy ...... **DELIGHT, RAPTURE**
joyous .... **GLAD**
Judah, city in ... **ADAR, ENAM**
Judah's son .... **ER, ONAN**
Judaism scriptures
TORA, TORAH
judge .. **DEEM, RATE, ARBITER**
JUDGE, BIB. ... see BIBLICAL JUDGE
judge in Hades ...... **MINOS**
judge of dead, Egypt ... **OSIRIS**
judge's bench .... **BANC**
judge's chamber .... **CAMERA**
judges' rule, Israel **KRITARCHY**
judgment, Fr. law ..... **ARRET**
JUDICIAL see also LEGAL, LAW
judicial assembly ..... **COURT**
jug, large beer ..... **RANTER**
jug shaped like man ... **TOBY**
jug, wide-mouthed .... **EWER**
juice .... **SAP**
juice, thickened .... **RHOB**
jujitsu .... **JUDO**
jujube .... **BER, ELB**
Jules Verne character ... **NEMO**
d Juliet's betrothed ...... **PARIS**
Juliet's father, family **CAPULET**
jumble .... **PI, PIE, MESS**
jump: music .... **SALTO**
jumping disease, Malay **LATA**
jumping rodent ..... **JERBOA**
juncture, line of .... **SEAM**
June bug .... **DOR**
Jungfrau's site .... **ALPS**
jungle clearing .... **MILPA**
juniper .... **GORSE, SAVIN, SABINE, SAVINE**
juniper, Europ. .... **CADE**
juniper tree, Bibl. **EZEL, RETEM**
Jupiter .... **JOVE**
Jupiter's moon, inner ..... **IO**
Jupiter's wife .... **HERA, JUNO**
jurisdiction .... **VENUE**
jurisdiction, old Eng. **SOC, SOKE**
jurisprudence .... **LAW**
jury list .... **PANEL**
jury, writ summoning **VENIRE**
just .... **MORAL**
justice, goddess of . **MA, MAAT**
jute .... **DESI**
Jutlander .... **DANE**
jutting rock .... **TOR**
juxtaposition, place in **APPOSE**
jynx .... **SPELL**

K

a Kaffir language .... **XOSA**
Kaffir tribe .... **ZULU**
Kaffir war club .... **KIRI**
Kaffir warrior .... **IMPI**
Kalmuck ..... **ELEUT, ELEUTH**
Kandh language .... **KUI**
kangaroo, male ...... **BOOMER**
kangaroo, young .... **JOEY**
Katmandu's country ... **NEPAL**
kava .... **AVA**
kava bowl .... **TANOA**
Kaw .... **AKHA**
Keats poem-1820 .... **LAMIA**
keel .... **CAREEN**
keel, at right angle to **ABEAM**
keel block wedge ... **TEMPLET**
keel, having no ...... **RATITE**
keel, kind of .... **FIN**
keel, part of .... **SKEG**
keel-shaped part
CARINA, CARINAE
keen **ACUTE, SHARP, ASTUTE**
keep account of .... **TAB**
keepsake .... **TOKEN**
keeve .... **KIVER**
b Kentucky coffee tree . **CHICOT**
Kentucky college ..... **BEREA**
kerchief .... **MADRAS**
kernel .... **NUT**
ketch, Levant .... **SAIC**
ketone, liquid ...... **ACETONE**
ketone, oily .... **CARONE**
kettledrum .. **NAKER, ATABAL, ATTABAL, TIMPANI, TIMPANO, TYMPANO**
key .... **ISLE**
key fruit .... **SAMARA**
key notch .... **WARD**
key part .... **BIT**
key-shaped ...... **URDE, URDY**
keyed up .... **AGOG**
Khedive's estate ...... **DAIRA**
kid, undressed .... **SUEDE**
kidney .... **NEER**
kidney bean .... **BON**
kidneys, pert. to ..... **RENAL**
killer whale .... **ORCA**
kiln ...... **OST, OAST, OVEN**
kiloliter .... **STERE**
kind
ILK, SORT, GENRE, SPECIES
kind: Gr. .... **GENOS**
kindle: dialect .... **TIND**
kindly .... **BENIGN**
kindness .... **LENITY**
kindred .... **SIB**

c king .... **REX, REY, REGES**
king —, cartoon character
AROO
King Alfred's city: abbr. .. **LON**
king, Amalekite .... **AGAG**
King Arthur's abode
AVALON, AVALLON, CAMELOT
King Arthur's burial place
AVALON, AVALLON
King Arthur's court **CAMELOT**
King Arthur's father .. **UTHER**
King Arthur's fool .. **DAGONET**
King Arthur's lance ..... **RON**
King Arthur's mother **IGERNA, IGERNE, YGERNE, IGRAINE**
King Arthur's queen
GUINEVER, GUINEVERE
KING, BIBLICAL .... see BIBLICAL KING
King Ethelred "The —"
UNREADY
king, Gr. .... **MINOS**
King Gradlon's capital .... **IS**
king, Hebrew .... **HEROD**
king, Midianite .... **REBA**
king, mythical .... **MIDAS**
king of beasts .... **LION**
d King of Colchis' daughter
MEDEA
king of Crete .... **MINOS**
king of elves ...... **ERLKING**
king of gods, Egypt
AMEN, AMON, AMUN
king of Greece, ancient **MINOS**
king of Israel ... **AHAB, ELAH, OMRI, SAUL, NADAB**
king of Jews .... **HEROD**
king of Judah ... **ASA, AHAZ, AMON, UZZIAH**
king of Judea .... **HEROD**
king of Naples ...... **MURAT**
king of Persia .... **CYRUS**
king of Sodom .... **BERA**
king, pert. to .... **REGNAL**
king, Phrygian .... **MIDAS**
king, rich .... **CROESUS**
king, Spartan **AGIS, LEONIDAS**
king, Teut. Visigoth .. **ALARIC**
king's bodyguard ..... **THANE**
king's yellow ..... **ORPIMENT**
KINGDOM ..see also COUNTRY
kingdom, ancient ...... **MOAB**
KINGDOM, BIB. .. see page 197
kingfish .... **HAKU, OPAH**
kinkajou .... **POTTO**
kinship, Moslem law ... **NASAB**
Kipling hero .... **KIM**

a kismet .... **FATE**
kiss .... **BUSS, SMACK**
kitchen, ship's ...... **GALLEY**
kitchen tool
CORER, RICER, GRATER
kite, bird
GLED, GLEDE, ELANET
kittiwake gull, Shetlands **WAEG**
kitty, feed the .... **ANTE**
kiwi .... **ROA**
knave .... **ROGUE**
knave, in cribbage ..... **NOBS**
knave of clubs .... **PAM**
knead .... **ELT**
knead, in massage .... **PETRIE**
knee: Lat. .... **GENU**
kneecap ... **ROTULA, PATELLA**
KNIFE .. see also DAGGER
knife .... **CHIV, STAB, MACHETE, MACHETTE**
knife, Burmese .... **DAH, DOW**
knife dealer .... **CUTLER**
knife, Eskimo .... **ULU**
knife, large ...... **SNY, SNEE**
knife, loop-cutting
TREVAT, TRIVAT, TRIVET
knife, P. I. .... **BOLO**
knife, single-edge .... **BOWIE**
knife, surgical .... **SCALPEL**
knight **SIR, RITTER, TEMPLAR**
knight, heroic ...... **PALADIN**
knight, make .... **DUB**
knight, medieval ...... **BEVIS**
knight's mantel ..... **TABARD**

c knight's wife .... **DAME**
knitting stitch .... **PURL**
knob: anat. .... **CAPUT**
knobbed .... **TOROSE**
knoblike .... **NODAL**
knobkerrie .... **KIRI**
knockout .... **KO, KAYO**
knot ..... **MILE, NODE, NODI, SNAG, GNARL, KNURL, NODUS**
knot, fiber .... **NOIL, NOYL**
knot in wood .... **BURL, KNAR, KNOR, KNUR, NURL**
knot, insecure ..... **GRANNY**
knot lace .... **TAT, TATT**
knot, like a .... **NODAL**
knot of thread .... **BURL**
knots, fiber .... **NEP**
knots, having .... **NODED**
know .... **KEN, WIST**
knowledge .... **KEN, LORE**
knowledge, pert. to .. **GNOSTIC**
knowledge, pure ..... **NOESIS**
known as milo maize, grain
MILO
knucklebones, sheep ... **DOLOS**
kobold .... **NIS, NISSE**
Kol dialect .... **HO**
kopecks, 100 .... **RUBLE**
Koran chapter .... **SURA**
Koran interpreters .... **ULEMA**
Korea .... **CHOSEN**
Korean president ..... **RHEE**
Korean soldier .... **ROK**
Kronos' wife .... **RHEA**
kurrajong tree .... **CALOOL**

L

b "La Boheme" heroine ... **MIMI**
Laban, daughter of .... **LEAH**
label .... **TAG, PASTER**
LABOR GROUP ... see UNION
laborer, China . **COOLY, COOLIE**
laborer, India .... **TOTY**
Labrador tea .... **LEDUM**
labyrinth .... **MAZE**
lac .... **RESIN**
lace .... **BEAT, LASH**
lace, barred **GRILLE, GRILLEE**
lace, Fr. ... **CLUNY, ALENCON**
lace, gold, silver .... **ORRIS**
lace, metal tip of
AGLET, AIGLET
lace, square hole ...... **FILET**
lacerate .... **RIP, TEAR**
laceration .... **RIP, TEAR**
lack .... **NEED, WANT**
lack of power .... **ATONY**

d Laconian clan group ..... **OBE**
Laconian subdivision ..... **OBE**
ladder, scale fort wall with
SCALADE, SCALADO, ESCALADE, ESCALADO
ladderlike .... **SCALAR**
lady, India .... **BIBI**
"Lady of the Lake" outlaw **DHU**
ladylove, in poetry .... **DELIA**
lagoon .... **LIMAN**
lake .... **MERE**
lake, Afr. salt .. **SHAT, SHOTT**
lake, Blue Nile source .. **TANA**
Lake Erie battle officer **PERRY**
Lake, Great (5) **ERIE, HURON, ONTARIO, MICHIGAN, SUPERIOR**
lake, mountain .... **TARN**
lake near Galilee sea .. **MEROM**
lake, resort .... **TAHOE**

a lake: Scot. .... **LOCH**
Lake Tahoe trout ...... **POGY**
lake whitefish .... **POLLAN**
lama, head .... **DALAI**
lamb .... **EAN, EWE, YEAN**
lamb, holy .... **AGNUS**
lamb: Lat. .... **AGNI, AGNUS**
lamb, young .... **COSSET**
Lamb's pen name ...... **ELIA**
Lamech, ancestor of ... **CAIN**
Lamech's son **NOAH, JABAL, JUBAL**
lament .... **KEEN, WAIL, WEEP, GRIEVE, PLAINT**
lamentation .... **LINOS**
lamp black .... **SOOT**
lamprey .... **EEL**
lance head .... **MORNE**
lance, mythical .... **RON**
lance rest, breastplate **FAUCRE**
lance, short .... **DART**
Lancelot's beloved ... **ELAINE**
lancer, Ger. ... **ULAN, UHLAN**
lancewood .... **CIGUA**
land, absolute property **ALOD, ALLOD, ALODIUM, ALLODIUM**
land amid water .. **ISLE, ISLET**
land breeze .... **TERRAL**
land, church's .... **GLEBE**
b land held in fee simple **ODAL, UDAL**
land: law .... **SOLUM**
LAND MEASURE .. see also AREA in SPECIAL SECTION
land measure **AR, ARE, ROD, ACRE, ROOD**
land ownership, pert. to **ODAL**
land snail genus ..... **CERION**
land spring .... **LAVANT**
land, tilled, plowed: Sp. **ARADA, ARADO**
land under tenure: Scot. .. **FEU**
landing place ..... **KEY, PIER, QUAI, QUAY, LEVEE**
landing place, India **GAUT, GHAT**
landing ship .... **LST**
landmark .... **COPA**
landmark: Sp. .... **SENAL**
lands .... **ACRES**
language, Aramaic ... **SYRIAC**
language, Assam .... **AO, AKA**
language, dead .... **LATIN**
language, early It. .... **OSCAN**
language, Egypt. ..... **COPTIC**
language, Finnish ..... **UGRIC**
language form, peculiarity **IDIOM**
language, Gilgit ...... **SHINA**
language, Hittite ...... **PALA**
language, Indic .... **HINDI**
c language, Indo-Chin. .... **AO, WA, AKA, ANU, LAI, LAO, MRO, MRU, PWO, SAK, AHOM, AKHA, AMOY, BODO, GARO, KAMI, NAGA, RONG, SGAU, SHAN**
language, Ir. .. **CELTIC, KELTIC**
language, Kandh .... **KUI**
language, Kashmir .... **SHINA**
language, Mossi .... **MO, MOLE**
language, N. Afr. .... **BERBER**
language of Bible days **ARAMAIC**
language, P. I. **TAGAL, TAGALOG**
language, Scot. **CELTIC, KELTIC**
language, Semitic .... **ARABIC**
language, Siberian **ENISEI, YENISEI**
language, S. Afr. ...... **TAAL**
language, Sudanic **MO, MOLE**
language, synthetic .. **RO, IDO**
language, Welsh **CELTIC,KELTIC**
languages, E. Europ. ... **UGRIC**
languish .... **FLAG, PINE**
languor, drug-induced **KEF, KAIF, KIFF**
langur .... **MAHA**
lantern feast .... **BON**
d Laomedon's father ...... **ILUS**
Laomedon's son **PRIAM, TITHONUS**
Laos aborigine ... **KHA, YUN**
lapel .... **REVER**
lapidate .... **STONE**
Lapp's sledge ... **PULK, PULKA**
larboard .... **APORT**
larch **TAMARAC, TAMARACK**
large amount .... **SCAD**
lariat .... **LAZO, ROPE, LASSO, REATA, RIATA**
lariat, metal eye of **HONDA, HONDO, HONDOO**
larva .... **GRUB**
larva of fly ...... **BOT, BOTT**
lash .... **TIE, WHIP**
lasso **ROPE, REATA, RIATA, LARIAT**
last .... **FINAL, OMEGA**
last but one .... **PENULT**
"Last Days of Pompeii" character .... **IONE**
last Imam .... **MAHDI**
last section .... **FINALE**
Last Supper picture .... **CENA**
Last Supper room .. **CENACLE**
latching: naut. .... **LASKET**
late ... **NEW, TARDY, RECENT**
late, one at school ..... **SERO**
lateen-rigged boat ..... **DOW, DHOW, SETEE, MISTIC**

a latent .... **DORMANT**
lateral .... **SIDE**
lath .... **SLAT**
LATIN .... see also ROMAN
LATIN:
abbot .... **ABBAS**
above .... **SUPER, SUPRA**
about .... **CIRCITER**
across .... **TRANS**
act .... **ACTU, ACTUS**
after .... **POST**
aged .... **AET** (abbr.)
all .... **TOTO**
alone .... **SOLO, SOLUS**
and .... **ET**
and others .... **ETAL** (abbr.)
around .... **CIRCUM**
art .... **ARS**
backward .... **RETRO**
before .... **ANTE**
behold .... **ECCE**
being .... **ESSE**
believe, I .... **CREDO**
beneath .... **INERA**
bird .... **AVIS**
book .... **LIBER**
blessed .... **BEATA**
bronze .... **AES**
but .... **SED**
cattle .... **PECORA**
b country .... **RUS, RURIS**
cup .... **CALIX**
custom .... **RITUS**
day .... **DIEM**
days .... **DIES**
depart! .... **VADE**
divination by lots .... **SORS, SORTES**
door .... **JANUA**
earth .... **TERRA**
egg .... **OVUM**
eight .... **OCTO**
error .... **LAPSUS**
event .... **REI**
evil .... **MALA, MALUM**
fate .... **NONA**
field .... **AGER**
fields .... **AGRI**
fire .... **IGNIS**
first .... **PRIMUS**
fish .... **PISCES**
force .... **VIS**
from .... **DE**
go! .... **VADE**
god .... **DEUS**
goddess .... **DEA**
gods .... **DI**
gold .... **AURUM**
good .... **BONUM, BONUS**
grandfather .... **AVUS**
he .... **ILLE**
c he remains .... **MANET**
he was .... **ERAT**
head .... **CAPUT**
high .... **ALTA**
himself .... **IPSE**
I love .... **AMO**
in so far as .... **QUA**
is .... **EST**
itself .... **IPSO**
ivory .... **EBUR**
journey .... **ITER**
knee .... **GENU**
lamb .... **AGNI, AGNUS**
land .... **AGER**
learned .... **DOCTUS**
life .... **VITA, ANIMA**
lo .... **ECCE**
man .... **VIR**
mass .... **MISSA**
mine .... **MEUM**
more than .... **SUPER**
mountain .... **MONS**
name .... **NOMEN**
nose, of the .... **NAS**
not .... **NON**
observe .... **NOTA**
offense .... **MALA, MALUM**
d once .... **SEMEL**
or .... **AUT**
other .... **ALIA**
over .... **SUPER**
pardon .... **VENIA**
palm .... **VOLA**
part .... **PARS**
partly .... **PARTIM**
peace .... **PAX**
pin .... **ACUS**
pledge .... **VAS**
possessive .... **SUA**
power .... **VIS**
pronoun .... **SUA**
property .... **BONA**
quickly .... **CITO**
rate .... **RATA**
religious law .... **FAS**
right .... **DEXTER**
same .... **IDEM**
scarcely .... **VIX**
see .... **VIDE**
side .... **LATUS**
table .... **MENSA**
tail .... **CAUDA**
that is .... **"ID EST"**
that one .... **ILLE**
the same .... **IDEM**
thing .... **RES**

a **LATIN**(continued from page 89)
this one .... **HIC, HAEC**
thus .... **SIC**
throat .... **GULA**
to be .... **ESSE**
to use .... **UTOR**
tooth .... **DENS**
toward .... **AD**
twice .... **BIS**
under .... **SUB**
unless .... **NISI**
vein .... **VENA**
voice .... **VOX**
water .... **AQUA**
we .... **NOS**
well .... **BENE**
where .... **UBI**
within .... **INTRA**
without .... **SINE**
wool .... **LANA**
wrong ...... **MALA, MALUM**

Latvia, native of .... **LETT**
laugh .... **FLEER**
laugh, able to .... **RISIBLE**
laughing .... **RIANT**
laughing, pert. to .. **GELASTIC**
laurel .... **BAY, DAPHNE**
b laurel bark, medicinal .. **COTO**
lava .... **AA, LATITE, SCORIA**
lava, rough .... **AA**
lavender, Eur. .... **ASPIC**
lavish affection .... **DOTE**
law
JURE, RULE, CANON, EDICT
law, abstract .... **JUS**
law, D. E. Ind. .... **ADAT**
law excluding women from reign .... **SALIC**
law of Moses .. **TORA, TORAH**
law, Rom. .... **JUS, LEX**
lawful .... **LEGAL, LICIT**
lawgiver, Gr.
DRACO, MINOS, SOLON
lawgiver, Hebr. .... **MOSES**
lawmaker .... **SOLON**
lawyer .... **LEGIST**
lawyers' patron saint ... **IVES**
lay .... **PUT, DITTY**
layer .... **PLY,**
LAMINA, STRATA, STRATUM
layer of a plant ..... **PROVINE**
layer, wood .... **VENEER**
layman .... **LAIC**
lazar .... **LEPER**
lazy .... **OTIOSE**
lead-colored .... **LIVID**
lead: music **PRESA, PRECENT**
lead, ore .... **GALENA**

c lead, pellets of .... **SHOT**
lead, pencil ...... **GRAPHITE**
lead sulphide, native **GALENA**
lead telluride ...... **ALTAITE**
lead, white .... **CERUSE**
leaden color, having ... **LIVID**
leader, fishing .... **SNELL**
leader of movement .... **VAN**
leader, Rom. .... **DUX**
leaf appendage ...... **STIPEL**
leaf-cutting ant ...... **ATTA**
leaf division .... **LOBE**
leaf, fern .... **FROND**
leaf, flower .... **BRACT, SEPAL**
leaf-miner beetle ..... **HISPA**
leaf of book .... **FOLIO**
leaf vein .... **RIB**
league, Ger. .... **BUND**
league, trading .... **HANSE**
Leah's father .... **LABAN**
Leah's son .... **LEVI**
lean .. **CANT, GAUNT, SPARE**
lean-to .... **SHED**
Leander's love .... **HERO**
"Leaning Tower" city .... **PISA**
leap **LUNGE, VAULT, CURVET**
leap: music .... **SALTO**
leap: Scot. **LOUP, LOWP, STEND**
leaping .... **SALTANT**
learned .. **ERUDITE, LETTERED**
d learning .... **LORE**
learning, man of
SAGE, PEDANT, SAVANT
Lear's daughter ...... **REGAN**
Lear's faithful follower **KENT**
least bit .... **RAP**
leather bottle .... **MATARA**
leather flask, Gr. .... **OLPE**
leather, glove
KID, NAPA, MOCHA, SUEDE
leather, kind of ... **ELK, BOCK**
leather, prepare—make into
TAN, TAW
leather, soft
NAPA, ALUTA, SUEDE
leather thong, hawk's .. **BRAIL**
leatherfish .... **LIJA**
"leatherneck" .... **MARINE**
leave
GO, QUIT, EXEAT, DEPART
leave destitute ...... **STRAND**
leave of absence, school **EXEAT**
leave-taking .... **CONGE**
leaves, having: Her. .. **POINTE**
leaven .... **YEAST**
leaving .... **ORT**
leavings .... **DREGS, RESIDUE**
Lebanese port, old .... **TYRE**
ledge, fort .... **BERM, BERME**
ledger entry
ITEM, DEBIT, CREDIT

a lee, opposed to .... **STOSS**
leeangle .. **LEAWILL, LEEWILL**
leer .... **OGLE**
Leeward Island .... **NEVIS**
left: comb. form ...... **LEVO**
left-hand .... **LEVO**
left-hand page ... **VO, VERSO**
left, to turn .... **HAW**
leftover .... **ORT**
leg, covering, ancient **PEDULE**
leg, front of .... **SHIN**
leg joint, animal .... **HOCK**
leg-like part .... **CRUS**
leg of mutton, lamb .. **GIGOT**
leg, part of .... **SHIN, SHANK**
leg, pert. to calf of ... **SURAL**
legal action suit .. **RES, CASE**
legal claim .... **LIEN**
legal delays .... **MORAE**
legal injury .... **TORT**
legal job .... **CASE**
legal matter .... **RES**
legal offense .. **DELIT, DELICT**
legal order .... **WRIT**
legal paper .... **DEED**
legal profession ... **BAR, LAW**
legal prosecution .... **SUIT**
legend ... **MYTH, SAGA, TALE**
legion division, Rom. **COHORT**
legislate .... **ENACT**
b legislative assembly, Afr. **RAAS**
legislator ... **SOLON, SENATOR**
legislature ... **DIET, SENATE**
legislature: Sp. .... **CORTES**
legume ..... **PEA, POD, BEAN**
leisure .... **REST, OTIUM**
lemur .... **MAKI, INDRI, LORIS, AYE-AYE, SEMIAPE**
lemur, Afr. .... **GALAGO**
lemur, Asia, Ceylon **LORI, LORIS**
lemur, Ceylonese .... **LORI**
lemur, flying .... **COLUGO**
lemur, ruffed .... **VARI**
lemuroid .... **POTTO**
lengthily, address .. **PERORATE**
Leningrad's river .... **NEVA**
lens, hand .... **READER**
lentil .... **ERVUM**
leopard .... **PARD**
Leporidae, one of the ... **HARE**
leprosy .... **LEPRA**
Lepus genus, one of ..... **HARE**
lerp .... **LAAP**
Lesbos, poet of ...... **ARION**
"Les Etats —" .... **UNIS**
less .... **MINUS**
lessen **BATE, ABATE, MITIGATE**
let **HIRE, RENT, LEASE, PERMIT**
let bait drop .... **DAP**
let it stand! .... **STA, STET**

c let up .... **ABATE**
lethal .... **FATAL**
lethargy **COMA, STUPOR, TORPOR**
letter .. **AR (18), EF (6), EM (13), EN (14), EX (24), WY (25), BEE (2), CEE (3), DEE (4), ESS (19), GEE (7), JAY (10), PEE (16), TEE (20), VEE (22), WYE (25), ZED (26), ZEE (26), AITCH (8)**
letter, according to .. **LITERAL**
letter, Ang.-Sax. .. **EDH, ETH**
letter, early Gr. .... **SAN**
LETTER, GR. and NUMBER . see also GREEK LETTER
letter, Gr. .. **MU, NU, PI, XI, CHI, ETA, PHI, PSI, RHO, TAU, BETA, IOTA, ZETA, ALPHA, DELTA, GAMMA, KAPPA, OMEGA, SIGMA, THETA, LAMBDA, EPSILON, OMICRON, UPSILON**
letter, Hebr. **HE (5), PE (17), AIN (16), MEM (13), NUN (14), SIN (21), TAV (22), TAW (22), VAU (16), WAW (16), ALEF (11), AYIN (16), BETH (2), CAPH (11), ELEF (1),**
d **KAPH (11), KOPH (19), QOPH (19), RESH (20), SADE (18), SHIN (21), TETH (9), YODH, (10), ALEPH (13), GIMEL (3), LAMED (12), DALETH (4), LAMEDH (12)**
letter of resignation .. **DEMIT**
letters, sloping ...... **ITALICS**
lettuce, kind of **COS, ROMAINE**
Levantine ketch .... **SAIC**
levee .... **DIKE, DYKE**
level **EVEN, RASE, RAZE, PLANE**
leveling slip .... **SHIM**
lever .... **PRY, PEVY, PEAVY, PEEVY, PEAVEY, PEEVEY, TAPPET**
levy .... **TAX, CESS, IMPOST**
Lew Wallace hero .... **HUR**
Lhasa holy man .... **LAMA**
Lhasa's country .... **TIBET**
liability .... **DEBT**
liana .... **CIPO**
liang .... **TAEL**
liar .... **ANANIAS**
Liberian native ..... **VAI, VEI**
Liberian tribes .. **GI, KRA, KRU**
license: slang .... **READER**
lichen .... **MOSS**
lichen genus **USNEA, EVERNIA**

a lichen, kind **PARELLA, PARELLE**
lie in wait .... **LURK**
Liege, town near .... **ANS**
liegeman .... **VASSAL**
lieu .... **STEAD**
life .... **BIOS, BIOTA**
life: Lat. ...... **VITA, ANIMA**
life, of .... **VITAL**
life principle .... **PRANA**
life principle, Hindu .. **ATMAN**
life prolonger .... **ELIXIR**
life, relating to **BIOTIC, BIOTICAL**
life tenant .... **LIVIER**
lifeless **AMORT, AZOIC, INERT**
lifetime .... **AGE**
lifted with effort ...... **HOVE**
ligament .... **BOND**
light .... **LAMP, KLEIG, KLIEG, TAPER, ILLUME**
light and fine, as lines .. **LEGER**
light as a line .... **LEGER**
light bulb filler ...... **ARGON**
light, circle of **HALO, NIMB, NIMBUS**
light intensity unit ...... **PYR**
light, kind of .... **ARC**
light ring .... **CORONA**
light, science of ...... **OPTICS**
light, sun's **AUREOLA, AUREOLE**
b light unit **PYR, LUMEN, HEFNER**
lighter, lamp .... **SPILL**
lighter, make .... **LEAVEN**
lighthouse .... **PHAROS**
lightning: poet. .... **LEVIN**
ligulate .... **LORATE**
like .... **AS, AKIN**
likely .... **APT**
likeness .... **ICON, IMAGE**
likewise not .... **NOR**
lily .... **LIS, LYS, ALOE, ARUM, SEGO, CALLA**
lily family plant ..... **CAMAS CAMASS, CAMMAS**
lily genus .... **ALOE**
lily genus, plantain .... **HOSTA**
Lily Maid of Astolat **ELAIN, ELAINE**
lily, palm .... **TI**
limb ...... **ARM, LEG, MANUS**
limber .... **LITHE**
lime, to hydrate ..... **SLAKE**
lime tree .... **TEIL, TEYL**
limestone, grainy ..... **OOLITE**
limestone, Irish .... **CALP**
limestone, soft **MALM, CHALK**
limicoline bird **SNIPE, PLOVER**
limit .... **TERM, BOURN, STENT, STINT, BOURNE**
limn.......... **DRAW, PAINT**
Lindbergh's book .... **WE**

c linden .... **LIN, TEIL, TEYL**
line .... **ROW, RANK**
line, cutting .... **SECANT**
line, fine, on type letter **CERIF, SERIF, CERIPH**
line, fishing .... **SNELL**
line, in a .... **AROW**
line, intersecting ..... **SECANT**
line inside of .... **CEIL**
line, math. .... **VECTOR**
line, naut. . **EARING, MARLINE**
line not forming angle **AGONE**
line on a letter .... **SERIF**
line, pert. to .... **LINEAR**
line, thin ..... **STRIA, STRIAE**
line, waiting ..... **CUE, QUEUE**
line with stone **STEAN, STEENE**
lines, marked with **RULED, STRIATE, STRIATED**
lines, telescope-lens .. **RETICLE**
linen .... **CREA**
linen, fine ..... **LAWN, TOILE**
linen, household, table **NAPERY**
linen, one caring for royal **NAPERER**
linen tape, braid ...... **INKLE**
linger .... **WAIT, TARRY**
lingo .... **ARGOT**
lingua .... **GLOSSA**
liniment .... **ARNICA**
d link .... **YOKE, CATENATE**
links connected ..... **CATENAE**
linnet ...... **TWITE, LENARD**
lion .... **LEO, SIMBA**
lion group .... **PRIDE**
lion killed by Hercules **NEMEAN**
lion of God .... **ALI**
lionet .... **CUB**
lips, pert. to .... **LABIAL**
liqueur .... **CREME, NOYAU**
liqueur, sweet .... **GENEPI**
liquid element **BROMIN, BROMINE**
liquid, made ... **FUSIL, FUSILE**
liquid, without ..... **ANEROID**
liquor .. **GIN, RUM, RYE, GROG**
liquor, malt .... **ALE, PORTER**
liquor, oriental ..... **ARRACK**
liquor, P. I. .... **VINO**
liquor, Russian **VODKA, VODKI**
liquor, sugar-cane **TAFIA, TAFFIA**
Lisbon's river .... **TAGUS**
lissome .... **SVELTE**
list ....**ROTA, SLATE, ROSTER, CATALOG, CATALOGUE**
list of persons **ROTA, PANEL, ROSTER**
list, one of a .... **ITEM**
listen .... **HARK, HEAR**
listless, be .... **MOPE**

a listlessness ... **ENNUI, APATHY**
liter, Dutch ... **AAM, KAN**
literary collection ... **ANA**
literary extracts ... **ANALECTA, ANALECTS**
literary master ... **STYLIST**
literary scraps, bits ... **ANA, NOTES**
literate .. **LEARNED, LETTERED**
lithograph ... **CHROMO**
Lithuanian ... **BALT, LETT**
litter, E. Ind. ... **DOOLI, DOOLY, DOOLEE, DOOLEY, DOOLIE**
"Little Boy Blue" poet ... **FIELD**
little casino ... **TWO**
little chief hare ... **PIKA**
little: music ... **POCO**
liturgy ... **RITE**
live .... **all forms of verb "BE"**
live oak, Calif. ... **ENCINA**
lively .... **PERT, BRISK, PEART**
lively, make ... **PERK**
lively: music ... **VIVO, DESTO, ANIMATO**
lively person ... **GRIG**
lively song ... **LILT**
liver ... **HEPAR**
liver, pert. to ... **HEPATIC**
liverwort genus ... **RICCIA**
b livid ... **BLAE**
living in currents ... **LOTIC**
Livonian ... **LIV**
lixivium ... **LYE, LEACH**
lizard ... **GILA, GECKO, GUANA, SKINK, VARAN, IGUANA**
lizard, Am. ... **ANOLE, ANOLI**
lizard, beaded ... **GILA**
lizard, changeable **CHAMELEON**
lizard genus ... **UTA, AGAMA**
lizard, large ... **GILA, MONITOR**
lizard, old world ... **SEPS**
lizard, small ... **EFT, GECKO**
lizard, starred ... **AGAMA**
lizard, tropical ... **AGAMA**
lizardlike ... **SAURIAN**
llamalike animal ... **ALPACA**
load ... **LADE, ONUS**
loadstone ... **MAGNET**
loaf, small: dial. ... **BAP**
loam ... **LOESS**
loam, India ... **REGUR**
loath ... **AVERSE**
loathe ... **ABHOR**
lobster box ... **CAR**
local ... **TOPICAL**
locale ... **SITE**
locality ... **AREA, LOCUS, VENEW, VENUE**
location ... **SITE, SPOT, PLACE**
lock ... **CURL, TRESS**

c locks, Panama Canal ... **GATUN**
lockjaw ... **TETANUS, TRISMUS**
locust ... **ACACIA, CICADA, CICALA**
locust, N. Z. ... **WETA**
lodge, soldier's ... **BILLET**
lofty dwelling ... **AERIE**
log birling contest ... **ROLEO**
log drive, escape work on .. **SNIB**
log, spin floating ... **BIRL**
log splitter ... **WEDGE**
logarithmic unit ... **BEL**
loge ... **STALL**
logger's implement ... **PEAVY, PEAVEY**
logic, omission of step in proof **SALTUS**
logician ... **DIALECTOR**
Lohengrin's wife ... **ELSA**
Loire, city on ... **BLOIS**
loiter ... **LAG**
Loki's daughter ... **HEL, HELA**
Loki's son ... **NARE**
Loki's wife ... **SIGYN**
London district ... **SOHO**
long ... **YEN, PINE, CRAVE, YEARN, ASPIRE**
long ago ... **ELD, YORE**
long journey .. **TREK, ODYSSEY**
d long line (fishing) with hooks **TROT**
long live! ... **VIVA, VIVE**
long-suffering ... **MEEK**
look ... **LO, SEE**
look after ... **MIND, TEND**
look askance ... **LEER**
look at ... **EYE, SCAN, VIEW**
look here! ... **HIST**
look narrowly **PEEK, PEEP, PEER**
look slyly ... **LEER, OGLE**
loom, heddles of ... **CAAM**
loom, lever in ... **LAM**
loon, genus ... **GAVIA**
loon, kind of ... **DIVER**
loop, edging ... **PICOT**
loophole ... **MUSE, MEUSE**
looplike structure, anat. ... **ANSA**
loose ... **LAX**
loose coat **PALETOT, MANTEVIL**
loose robe ... **SIMAR**
loosen ... **UNDO, UNTIE**
lop .... **SNED, PRUNE, SNATHE**
lopsided ... **ALOP, ALIST**
loquat tree ... **BIWA**
Lord High Executioner in "Mikado" **KOKO**
Lord: Jacobite Church ... **MAR**
lord, Oriental ... **KHAN**
lord, Pers. ... **KAAN, KAUN, KAWN, KHAN**
lord, privileged ... **PALATINE**

a lord, Scot. .... **LAIRD**
lore, Norse .... **RUNE**
lorica .... **CUIRASS**
"Lorna Doone" character **RIDD**
lose .... **AMIT**
"Lost Chord" finale .... **AMEN**
lot .... **FATE**
Lotan's father .... **SEIR**
Lot's birthplace .... **UR**
Lot's father .... **HARAN**
Lot's son .... **MOAB**
lottery prize .... **TERN**
lotus enzyme .... **LOTASE**
Lotus: poet .... **LOTE**
lotus tree .... **SADR**
loud: music .... **FORTE**
loud-voiced one .... **STENTOR**
loudness, measurement unit **PHON**
loudspeaker for high sound **TWEETER**
loudspeaker for low sound **WOOFER**
Louis XVI's nickname .. **VETO**
Louisiana county ..... **PARISH**
b Louisiana native ..... **CREOLE**
lounge .... **LOAF, LOLL**
love . **JO, GRA, ADORE, AMOUR**
love: Anglo-Irish ...... **GRA**
love apple .... **TOMATO**
love feast .... **AGAPE**
love god
LOVE GOD . see GOD OF LOVE
LOVE GODDESS . see GODDESS OF LOVE
love, inflame with **ENAMOR, ENAMOUR**
love knot .... **AMORET**
love to excess ... **DOAT, DOTE**
lover .... **ROMEO**
"Love's Labour's Lost" constable **DULL**
loving **FOND, AMATIVE, AMATORY**
low .... **MOO, BASE**
low caste Hindu .. **PASI, TELI**
low caste Indian .... **DOM, MAL, GADDI**
Lowell, poetess .... **AMY**
lower **ABASE, DEBASE, NETHER**
lower: arch. .... **VAIL**
lower jaw, bird's .... **MALA**
lower world gods, Rom. **MANES**
lowest deck .... **ORLOP**
lowest part of base ... **PLINTH**

c lowest point .... **NADIR**
loyal .... **LEAL, TRUE, STANCH, STAUNCH**
loyalist .... **TORY**
lozenge ..... **PASTIL, ROTULA TROCHE, PASTILE, PASTILLE**
loyalty fulfilling religious obligations: Rom. . **PIETAS**
Lubeck, pert. to .... **LUBS**
lucerne .... **MEDIC, ALFALFA**
luck: Ir. .... **CESS**
luck, pert. to ..... **ALEATORY**
lucky stroke .... **FLUKE**
lugubrious .... **SAD**
lukewarm .... **TEPID**
lumber along ...... **LOB, LOBB**
Lumber State .... see page 223
lumberman .... **SAWYER**
lumberman's boot .... **PAC**
lumberman's boots **PACS, OVERS**
lumberman's hook ..... **PEVY, PEAVY, PEEVY, PEAVEY, PEEVEY**
luminaire .... **LAMP**
luminary .... **STAR**
d lump .... **NUB, WAD, CLOT, NODE, SWAD**
lunar crater .... **LINNE**
lunar god, Phrygian ..... **MEN**
luncheon .... **TIFFIN**
lurch .... **CAREEN**
lure .... **BAIT, DECOY**
luster .... **GLOSS, SHEEN**
lusterless .. **DIM, MAT, MATTE**
lustrous .... **NITID**
lute, Oriental .... **TAR**
luxuriant .... **LUSH, RANK**
luxuriate .... **BASK**
Luzon native .... **ATA, ITA, AETA, ATTA, TAGAL, TAGALA**
Luzon negrito .... **ATA, AETA, ITA, ATTA**
Luzon pagan .... **ITALON**
Lynette's knight .... **GARETH**
lynx, Afr. .... **SYAGUSH**
lynx, Pers. .... **CARACAL**
lyrebird genus ...... **MENURA**
lyric .... **ODE, MELIC**
lyric Muse .... **ERATO**
Lytton heroine .... **IONE**

M

a macaque Indian **BRUH, RHESUS**
macaw .... **ARA, ARARA**
macaw, Braz.
ARA, ARARA, MARACAN
mace-bearer .... **BEADLE**
macerate .... **RET, STEEP**
machine, finishing .... **EDGER**
machine, grain cleaner **AWNER**
machine gun .... **BREN, STEN**
machine, hummeling .. **AWNER**
machine, ore-dressing **VANNER**
machine part
CAM, PAWL, TAPPET
machine, rubber .. **EXTRUDER**
mackerel net .... **SPILLER**
mackerel, young .... **SPIKE**
Madagascar mammal .. **LEMUR**
Madagascar native .... **HOVA**
madam .... **MUM, MAAM**
madder ..... **RUBIA, MUNJEET**
madder, common Eu. **GARANCE**
madder shrub genus ... **EVEA**
madness .... **MANIA**
mafura tree .... **ROKA**
maggot .... **LARVA**
Magi, one of .... **GASPAR**
magic .... **RUNE**
magic: Hindustan **JADU, JADOO**
magic, pert. to .... **GOETIC**
b magic stone .... **AGATE**
magic: W. Ind. .... **OBEAH**
magician .... **MAGE,**
MAGI, MAGUS, MERLIN
magistrate, Athens **ARCHON**
magistrate, It. .... **DOGE**
magistrate, Rom. ...... **EDILE,**
AEDILE, CONSUL, PRETOR
magnate ... **MOGUL, TYCOON**
magnifying glass .... **LENS**
Magog, ruler of .... **GOG**
magpie .. **MAG, PIE, MAGG,**
PIET, PIOT, PYAT, PYET,
NINUT, PIANET
magpie genus .... **PICA**
mah-jongg piece .... **TILE**
mahatma
ARAHT, ARHAT, ARAHAT
mahogany pine ...... **TOTARA**
mahogany, Sp. .... **CAOBA**
mahogany streak .... **ROE**
mahogany tree, Ind. ... **TOON**
MAHOMET .. see MOHAMMED
MAHOMETAN ... see MOSLEM
maid .... **LASS, BONNE**
maid, lady's .... **ABIGAIL**
maid-of-all-work ..... **SLAVEY**
maid, Oriental
AMA, IYA, AMAH, EYAH
maiden .... **DAMSEL**

c maiden name, signifying..**NEE**
maiden of myth .... **IO**
mail .... **POST, SEND**
mail, coat of . **BRINIE, BYRNIE**
mail, India **DAK, DAUK, DAWK**
main point ... **NUB, GIST, PITH**
maintain.**AVER, HOLD, ASSERT**
maize .... **CORN**
maize bread .... **PIKI**
maize genus .... **ZEA**
major: music .... **DUR**
major third: Gr. mus. .. **DITONE**
make .... **RENDER**
make as one: obs. ...... **UNE**
make evident .... **EVINCE**
make fast: naut. ...... **BELAY**
make good by action . **REDEEM**
make happy .... **ELATE**
make public: Old Eng. **DELATE**
Makua .... **KUA**
malarial fever .... **AGUE**
malarial poison
MIASM, MIASMA
Malay apple .... **KAWIKA**
Malay canoe
PRAH, PRAO, PRAU, PROA
Malay chief or headman.**DATO,**
DATU, DATTO
d Malay dagger ... **CRIS, KRIS,**
CREES, KREES, CREESE, KREESE
Malay lanseh tree ..... **DUKU**
Malay law .... **ADAT**
Malay lugger .... **TOUP**
malay negrito ..... **ATA, ITA**
Malay nerve ailment ... **LATA**
MALAY OUTRIGGER see MALAY CANOE
Malay title of respect .. **TUAN**
Malay ungulate ...... **TAPIR**
Malay verse form ... **PANTUN**
Malay vessel
PRAH, PRAO, PRAU, PROA
Malay, word meaning dark **AETA**
Malayan ape .... **LAR**
male cat .... **GIB, TOM**
male figure, used as support
ATLAS, TELAMON
male swan .... **COB**
malefic .... **EVIL**
malic acid, fruit with
ATTA, APPLE, GRAPE
malign .... **REVILE**
malignant .... **EVIL**
malignant spirit ... **KER, KERES**
malleable ..... **SOFT, DUCTILE**
mallet .... **MALL, GAVEL**
malt drink, pert. to ..... **ALY**
malt infusion .... **WORT**
maltreat .... **ABUSE**

a MAMMAL .. see also ANIMAL
mammal, sea aquatic .. **SEAL, OTTER, WHALE, DUGONG, MANATEE**
mammoth .... **GIANT**
man-eating monster ... **LAMIA**
man, handsome ...... **ADONIS**
man, rich .... **CROESUS**
man's name .. **ELI, GUY, IAN, IRA, JOB, LEE, RAY, REX, ADAM, ALAN, AMOS, BRAM, CARL, DANA, DION, EBEN, EMIL, ENOS, ERIC, EVAN, EZRA, HANS, HUGH, HUGO, IVAN, JOEL, JOHN, JOSE, JUAN, JUDE, KARL, KNUT, LEON, LUKE, MARC, MARK, NEIL, NOEL, OTTO, OWEN, PAUL, SEAN, SETH, TEIG, BASIL, CALEB, CLARE, ENOCH, HIRAM, HOMER, SERGE, STEVE, TERRY, DEXTER, GASPAR, GEORGE, OLIVER, SAMSON, STEVEN, WARREN**
man's nickname. **AL, ABE, ALF, BEN, BOB, DON, GUS, JIM, JOE, KIT, LEW, LON, LOU, MAC, MAT, MAX, MOE, NED, PAT, ROB, SAM, SID,**
b **SIM, TED, TOM, ABIE, ALGY, ANDY, BART, BERT, BILL, BONY, DAVE, DAVY, DICK, DODE, FRED, GENE, JACK, JAKE, JOCK, JOEY, MART, MIKE, MOSE, NOLL, PETE, PHIL, RUBE, TOBY, TONY, WALT, ZACH, ZEKE**
manageable .... **YARE**
manager .... **GERENT**
Manasseh, city of ...... **ANER**
Manasseh, son of ..... **AMON**
mandarin's home **YAMEN, YAMUN**
manducate .... **EAT**
maned .... **JUBATE**
manger ...... **CRIB, CRECHE**
mangle .... **MAUL**
mango, P. I. ...... **CARABAO**
mania .... **CRAZE**
manifest .... **SHOW, OVERT, ATTEST, EVINCE**
manifestation .... **AURA**
manifestation of god of lower world .... **SERAPIS**
maniple **FANO, FANON, FANUM**
manner **AIR, WAY, MIEN, MODE**
manner of walking ..... **GAIT**
manners .... **MORES**
manor .... **DEMENE, DEMESNE**

c mantis crab .... **SQUILLA**
mantle .... **CAPE**
manual training, Swed. . **SLOID, SLOYD**
manuao .... **IAO**
Manxman .... **GAEL**
many .... **MAINT**
many-colored **PIED, PINTO, MOTLEY**
many-colored stone ... **AGATE**
Maori tattooing .... **MOKO**
Maori village ... **KAIK, KAIKA**
Maori wages .... **UTU**
Maori war club **MERE, MARREE**
Maori war-club wood ... **RATA**
map .... **PLAT**
map in a map .... **INSET**
maple fruit, seed .... **SAMARA**
maple genus .... **ACER**
maple tree tap .... **SPILE**
mar .... **DEFACE**
marabou .... **ARGALA**
marble **MIB, MIG, TAW, MIGG, AGATE, AGGIE, MARMOR, MEALIE, SHOOTER**
marble, Belgian **RANCE, RANSE**
marble, choice **ALAY, ALLEY**
marble, It. .... **CARRARA**
marble, Rom. .... **CIPOLIN**
d marble, white .... **DOLOMITE**
marbles, game at ...... **TAW**
March King .... **SOUSA**
mare: Gypsy .... **GRASNI**
margin .... **RIM, EDGE, MARGE**
marginal reading, Hebrew Bible .... **KRI**
margosa tree .... **NIM, NEEM**
Marie Wilson, character played by .... **IRMA**
MARINE .. see also SEA
marine annelid .... **LURG**
marine fish, E. Ind. ... **DORAB**
marine measure, Jap. ..... **RI**
marine snail **WELK, WILK, WHELK**
marine snail genus .. **NERITA**
marine turtle genus..**CARETTA**
marine worm .... **SYLLID**
marionette maker ...... **SARG**
mark .... **STIGMA, STIGMATA**
mark, diacritic **TILDE, MACRON**
mark of omission ..... **CARET**
mark, reference **OBELI, OBELUS, OBELISK**
mark, short vowel .... **BREVE**
marked with spots: bot. **NOTATE**
marker, Gr. & Rom. ... **STELA, STELE, STELAE, STELAI**

a market .... **MART, SELL, VEND, RIALTO**
market: India .... **PASAR**
market, Oriental **SUQ, SOOK, SOUK**
market place **BAZAR, BAZAAR**
market place, Gr. .... **AGORA**
marksman .... **AIMER**
marmalade tree **MAMEY, SAPOTE**
marmoset .... **MICO**
marmoset, S. Am. .. **TAMARIN**
"Marner, — " Eliot novel **SILAS**
marriage, absence of .. **AGAMY**
marriage notice **BAN, BANNS**
marriage portion, pert. to **DOTAL**
marriage portion: Scot. **DOS, DOTE**
marriage settlement **DOS, DOT, DOWRY, DOWERY**
marriage vows .... **TROTH**
marriageable .... **NUBILE**
marrow .... **PITH**
marry .... **WED, WIVE**
Mars .... **ARES**
Mars' outer satellite .. **DEIMOS**
Mars, pert. to .... **AREAN**
"Marseillaise" author ... **LISLE**
marsh .... **BOG, FEN,**
b **SLUE, LIMAN, SWALE**
marsh elder .... **IVA**
marsh fever .... **HELODES**
marsh gas .... **METHANE**
marsh hen .... **RAIL**
marsh mallow .... **ALTEA**
marsh marigold ...... **CAPER**
marsh plant **REED, SEDGE, FESCUE**
marshal, Waterloo .... **NEY**
marshy . **PALUDAL, PALUDINE**
marsupial, arboreal **COALA, KOALA, POSSUM**
marten .... **SOBOL**
martyr, 1st Christian . **STEPHEN**
marvel .... **MIRACLE**
Mascagni heroine .... **LOLA**
MASCULINE see also MALE, MAN'S
mashy .... **IRON**
masjid ...... **MOSK, MOSQUE**
mask, half .... **DOMINO**
mask topknot, Gr. ..... **ONKOS**
masons' pickax ...... **GURLET**
masquerade cloak ... **DOMINO**
mass ...... **GOB, WAD, BULK**
mass book .... **MISSAL**
mass meeting .... **RALLY**
mass, pert. to .... **MISSATICAL**
mass, rounded .... **BOLUS**
mast .... **SPAR**

c mast: obs. .... **SPIR**
mast, support .... **BIBB**
mast, wood for .... **POON**
master: archaic .... **DAN**
master, India **MIAN, SAHEB, SAHIB**
master, pert. to .... **HERILE**
master, S. Afr. .... **BAAS**
master-stroke .... **COUP**
mastic tree .... **ACOMA**
masticate ...... **CHAW, CHEW**
mat, ornamental ...... **DOILY**
match, friction . **FUSEE, FUZEE**
match, wax .... **VESTA**
matchmaker .... **EROS**
MATERIAL ... see also FABRIC
maternity goddess, Egypt . **APET**
matgrass .... **NARD**
math quantity . **SINE, OPERAND**
math ratio, quantity .. **PI, SINE**
math term, hyperbolic function **COSH, SECH, SINH, TANH**
matter: law .... **RES**
matter-of-fact ...... **LITERAL**
matter: philos. .... **HYLE**
mattress case .... **TICK**
mature ..... **AGE, RIPE, RIPEN**
mature reproductive cell **GAMETE**
d maul .... **MALLET**
Mau Mau territory .... **KENYA**
Mauna — .... **LOA**
mausoleum, at Agra ..... **TAJ**
maw: dialect .... **MAA**
maxilla .... **JAW, MALA**
maxim . **SAW, ADAGE, AXIOM, GNOME, MOTTO, SAYING**
maxwell per ampere turn . **PERM**
May 1, Celtic ...... **BELTANE**
May fly .... **DUN**
MAYAN . see MAYAN INDIAN, page 192
Mayan year .... **HAAB**
Mayan year-end days .. **UAYEB**
mayor, Sp. . **ALCADE, ALCALDE**
meadow .... **LEA, MEAD**
meadow barley .... **RIE**
meadow grass genus ..... **POA**
meadow mouse .... **VOLE**
meadow saxifrage ..... **SESELI**
meadowsweet **SPIREA, SPIRAEA**
meager .... **SCANT, LENTEN, SCANTY**
meal .... **REPAST**
meal, boiled .... **MUSH**
meal, fine .... **FARINA**
meal, grain .. **PINOLA, PINOLE**
meal, Indian, Hindu **ATA, ATTA**
meal, light .... **BEVER**

a meaning .... **SENSE, PURPORT**
meantime .... **INTERIM**
MEASURE ... Area, Liquid, Dry Length, Distance see SPECIAL SECTION
measure ...... **EM, EN, GAGE, METE, PACE, GAUGE**
MEASURE, BIB. .. see HEBREW MEASURE
measure, Chin. length .... **LI**
"Measure for Measure" character .... **ANGELO**
MEASURE, DRY, BIB. .... see HEBREW DRY MEASURE
measure, Jap. distance ... **RI**
measure of distance, Ang.-Ind. **COSS**
measure of spirits .... **PEG**
measure, old Arab ...... **SAA**
measure, old length ...... **ELL**
measure, poetry .... **SCAN**
measure, square .... **AR, ARE**
meat, cut of ...... **HAM, RIB, CHOP, LOIN, FILET, STEAK, FILLET**
meat on skewer ...... **CABOB, KABOB, KEBAB**
meat roll, fried ...... **RISSOLE**
Mecca pilgrim garb .... **IHRAM**
Mecca shrine .... **CAABA, KAABA, KAABEH**
b Mecca, trip to .... **HADJ**
mechanical man ...... **ROBOT**
mechanical part .... **CAM**
mechanics, branch of . **STATICS**
mechanics of motion **DYNAMICS**
meddle .... **PRY, TAMPER**
Medea's father .... **AEETES**
median line of valve ... **RAPHE**
medical .... **IATRIC**
medical fluid .... **SERUM**
medicinal capsule .... **CACHET**
medicinal fruit shrub ... **ALEM**
medicinal gum .... **KINO**
medicinal herb .... **ALOE, IPECAC, BONESET**
medicinal plant .... **ALOE**
medicinal plant, leaves **SENNA**
medicinal tablet ..... **TROCHE**
medicine man ...... **SHAMAN**
medicine man, S. Am. **PEAI, PIAY**
medieval lyric .... **ALBA**
medieval society **GILD, GUILD**
medieval tale, poem . **LAI, LAY**
Medina Arab .... **AUS**
MEDITERRANEAN .... see also GAZETTEER
Mediterranean, East of. **LEVANT**
Medit. grass .... **DISS**

c Medit. herb genus .... **AMMI**
Medit. island: It. .... **RODI**
Medit. resort .... **NICE**
medlar .... **MESPIL**
medley .... **OLIO**
Medusa's slayer ..... **PERSEUS**
meet .... **SIT**
meeting ..... **TRYST, SESSION**
meeting, political .... **CAUCUS**
megapode .... **MALEO**
melancholy . **SAD, BLUE, DREAR**
melancholy: poet. ..... **DOLOR**
mellow .... **AGE, RIPE**
melodic .... **ARIOSE**
melodious .... **ARIOSO**
melody .... **AIR, ARIA, TUNE, MELOS**
melon .... **PEPO, CASABA**
melt together ..... **FUSE, FUZE**
melted .... **MOLTEN**
membership .... **SEAT**
membrane .... **WEB, TELA, VELA, VELUM**
memento .... **RELIC**
memorabilia .... **ANA**
memorandum .... **CHIT, NOTE**
memorial post, Indian .. **TOTEM**
memory, pert. to **MNESIC, MNEMONIC**
Memphis chief god .... **PTAH**
d Memphis street, famous. **BEALE**
men .... **SONS**
mendacious person ...... **LIAR**
mender, chief .... **TINKER**
mendicant, Mos. **FAKIR, FAKEER**
Menelaus' wife .... **HELEN**
menhaden fish .... **POGY**
menhaden, young ... **SARDINE**
Mennonite .... **AMISH**
Menotti heroine ...... **AMELIA**
men's party .... **STAG**
mental .... **PHRENIC**
mental deficiency ... **AMENTIA**
mental deficient **IDIOT, MORON**
mention .... **CITE**
Mercator .... **MAP, CHART**
mercenary . **VENAL, HIRELING**
merchandise .... **WARES**
merchant .... **TRADER**
merchant: India .... **SETH**
"Merchant of Venice" heiress **PORTIA**
merchant ship .... **ARGOSY**
merchant vessel, Gr. . **HOLCAD**
Mercury, Gr. .... **HERMES**
Mercury's wand ... **CADUCEUS**
mercy, show .... **SPARE**
mere .... **SIMPLE**
merely .... **ONLY**

a merganser duck SMEW, GARBILL
merge .... MELD
merit .... EARN
merriment .... GLEE
merry-go-round ... CAROUSAL, CAROUSEL, CARROUSAL
"Merry Widow" composer LEHAR
"Merry Wives" character PISTOL
mesh .... NET, WEB
Mesopotamia ..... IRAK, IRAQ
Mesopotamian boat GUFA, KUFA
Mesopotamian city ..... URFA
mesquite bean flour ... PINOLE
mess, to make a ...... BOTCH
mestizo .... METIS
metal .... TIN, MONEL
metal alloy .... BRASS, MONEL, BRONZE
metal, bar of .... INGOT
metal bar on house door . RISP
metal casting .... PIG, INGOT
metal, coat with .PLATE, TERNE
metal-decorating art .. NIELLO
metal disk .... MEDAL
metal dross .... SLAG
metal filings .... LEMEL
metal fissure .... LODE
b metal leaf .... FOIL
metal mixture .... ALLOY
metal refuse .... SCORIA
metal spacer: print. ..... SLUG
metal suit .... MAIL
metal sulfide, impure . MATTE
metal, white .... TIN
metallic rock .... ORE
metalware, lacquered ... TOLE
metalwork, god of .. VULCAN
metarabic acid ..... CERASIN
meteor .... LEONID
meteor, exploding BOLIS, BOLIDE
meter, Dutch .... EL
meter, one-millionth .. MICRON
meters, 100 sq. ...... AR, ARE
metheglin .... MEAD
method .... PLAN, ORDER
Methuselah's grandson .. NOAH
methyl-phenol CRESOL, CRESSOL
metric measure ..... AR, ARE, GRAM, KILO, LITER, METER, STERE, DECARE, HECTARE
metric "quart" .... LITER
metrical beat .... ICTUS
metrical unit .... MORA
metropolitan .... URBAN
mew .... GULL
mew, cat's .... MIAU, MIAW, MIAOU, MIAUL

c Mexican dollar .... PESO
Mex. mush .... ATOLE
Mex. painter .... RIVERA
Mex. persimmon .... CHAPOTE
Mex. plant .... JALAP
Mex. president ...... ALEMAN, CALLES, MADERO
Mex. resin tree .... DRAGO
Mex. rodent .... TUCAN
Mex. slave .... PEON
Mex. spiny tree ...... RETAMA
Mex. timber tree ...... ABETO
Mex. wind instrument . CLARIN
mezzanine .... ENTRESOL
miasma .... MALARIA
mica, kind of .... BIOTITE
mica of muscovite ...... TALC
microbe .... GERM
microspores .... POLLEN
middle .... MESAL, MESNE, MEDIAN
middle, in the ...... ATWEEN
middle, toward .... MESAD
middling .... SOSO
Midgard Serpent slayer .. THOR
midge .... GNAT
midship, off .... ABEAM
d "Midsummer Night's Dream" character .. PUCK, SNUG
midwife: India .... DHAI
MID-EAST land .. IRAK, IRAQ
mien .... AIR
might .... POWER
mignonette ... GREEN, RESEDA
migrate .... TREK
migratory worker OKIE, ARKIE
Mikado's court . DAIRI, DAIRO
Milanion's wife ... ATALANTA
Milan's "Met" ..... LA SCALA
mild ...... SHY, MEEK, SOFT, BLAND, GENTLE
mildness .... LENITY
mile: naut. .... KNOT
mile, part of, Burma ... DHA
Miled, son of .... IR, ITH, EBER
milestone .... STELE
milfoil .... YARROW
military award .... DSO
military cap .... KEPI
military command ... AT EASE
military group . CADRE, CORPS
military maneuvers .. TACTICS
milk, coagulated ...... CURD
milk coagulator ..... RENNIN
milk, curdled .... CLABBER
milk, part of SERUM, LACTOSE
milk, pert. to .... LACTIC
milk: pharm. .... LAC
milk protein .... CASEINE

a milk, watery part of .... WHEY
milkfish .... AWA, SABALO
Milky Way .... GALAXY
mill .... QUERN
MILLET
see also GRAIN SORGHUM
millet, India JOAR,JUAR,CHENA
millimeter, 1000th part MICRON
millstone support ...... RYND
millwheel board .... LADE
millwheel bucket .... AWE
Milton, masque by .... COMUS
Milton rebel angel ..... ARIEL
mime .... APER
mimic ...... APE, APER, MIME
mimicking, practice of . APISM
mimosa .... ACACIA
minced oath .. GAD, GED, GEE, LUD, DRAT, EGAD, HECK, OONS, SWOW, MAFEY, MACKINS
mind .... CARE, TEND
mind, opposite of: Hindu ATTA, ATMAN
mind: philos. .... NOUS
Mindanao native, Indonesian ATA, AETA, MORO
mine ceiling .... ASTEL
mine entrance .... ADIT
mine narrow veins ..... RESUE
b mine passage .... STULM
mine roof support .... NOG
mine shaft drain pit .... SUMP
mine step .... LOB
mineral, alkaline ..... TRONA
mineral, blue .... IOLITE
mineral group ...... URANITE
mineral group, pert. to . SALIC
mineral, hard SPINEL, SPINELLE
mineral, lustrous .... SPAR
mineral, raw, native ..... ORE
mineral salt .... ALUM
mineral, soft .... TALC
mineral spring .... SPA
mineral tar .... BREA
mineral, transparent ... MICA
mineral used gun-powder NITER
Minerva .... ATHENA
minim .... DROP
mining refuse .... ATTLE
mining road .... BORD
mining tool ..... GAD, BEELE
minister, Moslem VIZIR, VIZIER
minister (to) .... CATER
mink, Amer. .... VISON
minority, legal ...... NONAGE
Minos' daughter .... ARIADNE
Minotaur's slayer .... THESEUS
minstrel .... RIMER
minstrel, medieval ... GOLIARD
minstrel, Norse . SCALD, SKALD

c mint .... COIN
mint, Europ. ... CLARE, CLARY, CLARRY, HYSSOP, DITTANY
mint genus .... MENTHA
mint herb .... SAGE
mints, the .... NEPETA
minus .... LESS
minute .... WEE, TINY, SMALL
mira .... STAR
miracle, scene of first .. CANA
mirage .... SERAB
miscellany .... ANA
mischief .... HOB
mischievous spirit ...... PUCK
misconceive .... ERR
Mishnah section . ABOT, ABOTH
Mishnah section festivals .MOED
misinterpret .... ERR
mislay .... LOSE
misplay .... ERROR
misrepresent .... BELIE
Miss Dombey's suitor .. TOOTS
missile .... DART, SNARK
missile, guided ... JUNO, NIKE, THOR, ATLAS, TITAN, BOMARC, JUPITER, PERSHING, REGULUS, REDSTONE, BOLD ORION,MINUTEMAN
mist .... HAZE, SMUR, MISLE
mist: Eng. .... RAG
d mistake, stupid .... BONER
mistakes .... ERRATA
mistakes, make .... ERR
mite .... ACARI, ATOMY, ACARID, ACARUS
mite genus .. ACARI, ACARUS
mite, tick, order of ACARIDA, ACARINA
mitigate . EASE, ABATE, ALLAY
mix .... STIR, ADDLE, KNEAD
mixture .... OLIO
mixture, mineral .... MAGMA
Moab city, chief .... UR
Moab king .... MESHA
Moabites, Bibl. .... EMIM
moat .... FOSS, FOSSE
"Moby Dick" pursuer .. AHAB
moccasin .... PAC
mock ..... GIBE, JIBE, FLEER, TAUNT, DERIDE
mock blow .... FEINT
mock orange ...... SYRINGA
mockingbird genus .... MIMUS
model, perfect ..... PARAGON
moderate .... BATE, ABATE, LESSEN
modernist .... NEO
modest .... SHY, DEMURE
modify .... VARY, ALTER, EMEND, TEMPER
Mogul emperor ...... AKBAR

a **MOHAMMEDAN** .. see MOSLEM
Mohammedanism ...... **ISLAM**
Mohammed's adopted son . **ALI**
Mohammed's birthplace . **MECCA**
Mohammed's daughter . **FATIMA**
Mohammed's descendant
SAID, SEID, SAYID
Mohammed's son-in-law .. **ALI**
Mohammed's supporters . **ANSAR**
Mohammed's title .... **ALI**
Mohammed's tomb city **MEDINA**
Mohammed's uncle .... **ABBAS**
Mohammed's wife ..... **AISHA**
Mohawk, city on .... **UTICA**
Mohicans, last of the .. **UNCAS**
moiety .... **HALF**
moist .... **WET, DAMP, DANK, DEWY, UVID, HUMID**
moist spot, rock-ledge .... **SIPE**
moisten ... **DAMPEN, IMBRUE**
moisture, having medium **MESIC**
mojarra fish .... **PATAO**
molasses .. **TREACLE, TRIACLE**
molasses, rum made from
TAFIA
mold .... **MUST**
mold, hole in casting . **GIT, GEAT**
molded clay .... **PUG**
molding .. **CYMA, GULA, OGEE,**
b **TORUS, REGLET, REEDING**
molding, concave
CONGE, SCOTIA
molding, convex
OVOLO, TORUS, ASTRAGAL
molding, curved . **CYMA, OGEE**
molding, edge of . **ARIS, ARRIS**
molding, flat .... **FILLET**
molding, rounded **TORI, TORUS**
molding, S-shaped ...... **OGEE**
molding, square ...... **LISTEL**
moldings, quarter-round . **OVOLI**
moldy .... **MUSTY**
mole .... **NEVUS, NAEVUS**
mole cricket, S. Am. . **CHANGA**
mole genus .... **TALPA**
molecule part .... **ION**
molelike mammal ... **DESMAN**
MOLLUSK . see also GASTROPOD
mollusk ...... **CLAM, CHITON, MUSSEL, ABALONE**
mollusk, bivalve ..... **SCALLOP**
mollusk, chamber-shelled
NAUTILUS
mollusk, gastropod
SNAIL, ABALONE
mollusk genus **ARCA, MUREX, OLIVA, ANOMIA**
mollusk, largest ...... **CHAMA**
mollusk's rasp organ .. **RADULA**
molt .... **MEW, SHED**

c molten rock ... **LÁVA, MAGMA**
moment ..... **MO, JIFF, TRICE**
Monaco, pert. to
MONACAN, MONEGASQUE
monad .... **ATOM, UNIT**
monastery .... **MANDRA**
monastery church .. **MINSTER**
MONEY . see also SPECIAL SECTION COINS
money ... **CASH, CUSH, GELT**
money, Amer. Ind. .. **WAMPUM**
money, bronze .... **AES**
money certificate . **BOND, SCRIP**
money, copper .... **AES**
money: dialect .... **SPENSE**
money, early Eng. .... **ORA**
money drawer .... **TILL**
money exchange fee .... **AGIO**
money, fishhook . **LARI, LARIN**
money, medieval .... **ORA**
money of account .... **ORA**
money, piece of .... **COIN**
money premium .... **AGIO**
money, put in .... **INVEST**
money reserve .... **FUND**
money, shell . **SEWAN, SEAWAN**
money, trade unit .... **UNITAS**
moneylender .... **USURER**
moneylender, Ind. .. **MAHAJAN**
Mongol ... **HU, ELEUT, TATAR,**
d **ELEUTH, TARTAR**
Mongol dynasty .... **YUAN**
Mongol warrior .... **TATAR**
Mongolian tent .... **YURT**
Mongoloid .... **TURK, DURBAN**
Mongoloid in Indo-China . **SHAN**
mongrel .... **CUR, MUTT**
monitor lizard .... **URAN**
monk .. **FRA, FRIAR, CENOBITE**
monk, Buddhist ...... **ARAHT, ARHAT, ARAHAT**
monk, Eng. ...... **BEDA, BEDE**
monk, Gr. Church ... **CALOYER**
monk, head .... **ABBOT**
monk settlement . **SCETE, SKETE**
monk's hood .... **COWL**
monk's title ..... **FRA, ABBOT**
monkey .... **APE, LAR, SAI, SIME, SIMIAN, MARMOSET**
monkey, Afr. .... **MONA, WAAG, GRIVET**
monkey, Asia ...... **LANGUR**
monkey, capuchin .... **SAI**
monkey, Chin. .... **DOUC**
monkey genus .... **CEBUS**
monkey, guenon ...... **NISNAS**
monkey, howling ...... **ARABA**
monkey, P. I. .... **MACHIN**
monkey puzzle .... **PINON**
monkey, red, Afr. ..... **PATAS**
monkey, small .... **LEMUR**

a monkey, S. Am. .. **SAKI, TITI, ACARI, ARABA, SAJOU, TETEE, PINCHE, SAGUIN, SAMIRI, SAIMIRI, SAPAJOU**
monkey, spider, genus . **QUATA, ATELES, COAITA**
monkshood .... **ATIS, ATEES, ACONITE**
monolith .... **MENHIR**
monopoly ..... **TRUST, CARTEL**
monosaccharide .... **OSE**
Mons, language of ...... **PEGU**
monster .. **GOUL, GOWL, OGRE**
monster, Gr. myth .. **CHIMERA**
monster, half-man-bull **MINOTAUR**
monster: med. ...... **TERAS**
monster, 100 eyes ..... **ARGUS**
monster slain by Hercules **HYDRA**
month, Egypt. .... **AHET, APAP, TYBI**
month, first day, Rom. **CALENDS, KALENDS**
month, Hindu .... **ASIN, JETH, KUAR, MAGH**
month, in last .... **ULTIMO**
month, Jewish ancient ..... **AB (11th), BUL (8th), ZIF (8th), ABIB (7th), ADAR**
b **(6th), ELUL (12th), IYAR, (8th), NISAN (7th), SEBAT (5th), SIVAN (9th), TEBET (4th), TIZRI (1st), TEBETH (4th), TISHRI (1st)**
month, Moslem .... **RABIA, RAJAB, SAFAR, SHABAN, RAMADAN**
month, Nisan .... **ABIB**
monument, stone . **LECH, CAIRN, DOLMEN, CROMLECH**
moon . **LUNA, DIANA, PHOEBE**
moon, age at beginning of calendar year ..... **EPACT**
moon angel .... **MAH**
moon flower .... **ACHETE**
moon god, Babyl. .. **SIN, ENZU**
moon goddess ...... **ASTARTE**
moon goddess, Gr. .... **SELENA, SELENE, ARTEMIS**
moon goddess, Rom. ... **LUNA, DIAN, DIANA**
moon nearest earth, point **PERIGEE**
moon valley ..... **RILL, RILLE**
moor grass .... **NARD**
moorhen .... **GORHEN**
Moorish .... **MORISCAN**
moose genus .... **ALCES**
mop .... **SWAB, SWOB**

c Moqui, one of .... **HOPI**
morals overseer ...... **CENSOR**
morass .... **QUAG, MARSH**
moray .... **EEL**
Mordecai, enemy of .. **HAMAN**
more .... **PLUS**
more! ...... **BIS, PIU, ENCORE**
more than enough ...... **TOO, EXTRA, EXCESS**
More's island .... **UTOPIA**
morepork, N. Z. .. **PEHO, RURU**
morindin dye .... **AL**
moringa seed .... **BEN**
morning glory .... **IPOMEA**
morning music ...... **AUBADE**
morning: P. I. .... **UMAGA**
morning prayer ...... **MATINS**
morning song .... **MATIN**
Moro .... **SULU, LANAO**
Moro chief **DATO, DATU, DATTO**
Moro mantle .... **JABUL**
Moroccan Berber .... **RIFF**
Moroccan land, public .. **GISH**
Moroccan native .... **MOOR**
moron .... **AMENT, IDIOT**
morose ... **BLUE, GLUM, GRUM**
morsel .... **ORT**
mortar implement .... **PESTLE**
d mortar ingredient ...... **LIME**
mortar mixer ... ... **RAB**
mortar tray .... **HOD**
mortise insert .... **TENON**
Mosaic law .... **TORA, TORAH**
mosaic piece .... **TESSERA**
Moselle, river to .... **SAAR**
Moses, law given to here **SINA, SINAI**
Moses' brother .... **AARON**
Moses' death mountain .. **NEBO**
Moses' father-in-law . **JETHRO**
Moses' spy in Canaan .. **CALEB**
MOSLEM ..... see also MECCA
Moslem .... **TURK**
Moslem ablution before prayer **WIDU, WUDU, WUZU**
Moslem, Afr. .... **MOOR**
Moslem beggar . **FAKIR, FAKEER**
Moslem bible .... **KORAN**
Moslem call to prayer **ADAN, AZAN**
Moslem chief .... **AGA, IMAM, DATTO**
Moslem chief gold coin . **DINAR**
Moslem converts ..... **ANSAR**
Moslem deity ... **JANN, ALLAH**
Moslem demon .. **JANN, EBLIS**
Moslem Easter .... **EED**
Moslem fast ...... **RAMADAN**
Moslem festival ...... **BAIRAM**

a Moslem fiat .... **IRADE**
Moslem fourth Caliph .... **ALI**
Moslem grant of property **WAKF, WAQF, WUKF**
Moslem guide .... **PIR**
Moslem holy city ..... **MECCA**
Moslem holy man **IMAM, IMAUM**
Moslem, hostile to Crusaders **SARACEN**
Moslem in Turkestan ... **SALAR**
Moslem judge .. **CADI, CAZI, CAZY, KADI, KAZI, KAZY**
Moslem leader . **IMAM, IMAUM**
Moslem marriage. **MOTA, MUTA**
Moslem marriage settlement **MAHR**
MOSLEM MORO ... see MORO CHIEF
Moslem mystic .... **SUFI**
Moslem name .... **ALI**
Moslem Negroids .... **MABA**
Moslem noble .... **AMIR, EMIR, AMEER, EMEER**
Moslem, N. W. India ... **SWAT**
Moslem official .... **AGA**
Moslem, orthodox ..... **HANIF**
Moslem, P.I. .... **MORO**
Moslem potentate .... **AGA**
Moslem prayer .... **SALAT**
Moslem prayer place ... **IDGAH**
Moslem priest . **IMAM, IMAUM**
b Moslem prince ... **AMIR, EMIR, AMEER, EMEER**
Moslem principle .... **IJMA**
Moslem pulpit ...... **MIMBAR**
Moslem reformer .... **WAHABI**
Moslem religion .... **ISLAM**
Moslem religious college **ULEMA**
Moslem ruler .... **HAKIM**
Moslem saber ...... **SCIMITAR**
Moslem saint .... **PIR**
Moslem school ..... **MADRASA**
Moslem spirit ... **JINN, JINNI**
Moslem spiritual guide ... **PIR**
Moslem teacher .. **ALIM, COJA**
Moslem temple. **MOSK, MOSQUE**
Moslem theologians ... **ULEMA**
Moslem title .... **AGA, RAIS, REIS, SEID, SIDI, SYED, SYUD, CALIF, SAYID, SEYID, CALIPH**
Moslem tunic .. **JAMA, JAMAH**
Moslem weight .... **ROTL**
Moslem woman's dress .. **IZAR**
Moslems, Sunnite .... **SART**
Moslemized Bulgarian . **POMAK**
mosque .... **MASJID**
mosque, central .... **JAMI**
mosque, Jerusalem .... **OMAR**
mosque student .... **SOFTA**

c mosquito, genus, yellow-fever **AEDES**
mossbunker fish .... **POGY**
moss of Ceylon .... **AGAR**
moth .... **IO, LUNA, EGGER, TINEA**
moth, clearwing, genus . **SESIA**
moth, clothes .... **TINEA**
moth, green .... **LUNA**
mother goddess; Baby. . **ERUA**
mother goddesses, Hindu **MATRIS**
mother of Arthur .... **IGRAINE**
mother of gods .... **RHEA**
MOTHER OF IRISH GODS .. see page 200
mother-of-pearl .... **NACRE**
mother-of-pearl shell. **ABALONE**
mother turned to stone . **NIOBE**
mother's side, related on **ENATE, ENATIC**
mother's side, relation on **ENATE, ENATION**
motherless calf .. **DOGY, DOGIE**
motion, producing .... **MOTILE**
motionless ..... **INERT, STILL**
motive ...... **CAUSE, REASON**
motmot, S. Am. ..... **HOUTOU**
motor part .... **ROTOR**
mottled .... **PIED, PINTO**
d mottled, as wood ...... **ROEY**
MOULDING .... see MOLDING
mound ...... **TUMP, BARROW**
mound, Polyn. .... **AHU**
Mount of Olives ...... **OLIVET**
mountain, Alps .... **BLANC**
mountain ash .. **SORB, ROWAN**
mountain, Asia Minor ..... **IDA**
mountain, Bibl. .. **HOR, NEBO, SEIR, SINA, HOREB, SINAI, ARARAT**
(see others on page 197)
mountain chain .... **SIERRA**
mountain climbing staff . **PITON**
mountain crest .... **ARETE**
mountain, Crete .... **IDA**
mountain, Edom .... **HOR**
mountain, fabled Hindu . **MERU**
mountain, famous .... **IDA**
mountain, Gr. ...... **HELICON**
mountain in Thessaly ... **OSSA**
mountain lion .... **PUMA**
mountain mint .... **BASIL**
mountain, Moab .... **NEBO**
mountain pass .... **COL**
mountain pass, Alps **CENIS**
mountain pass, India **GAUT, GHAT**
mountain peak .... **ALP**
mountain pool .... **TARN**
mountain recess .... **CWM**
mountain ridge .... **ARETE**

a mountain ridge, Port. .. **SERRA**
mountain, 2nd highest N.A. **LOGAN**
mountain sickness **PUNA, VETA**
mountain spinach ..... **ORACH**
mountain spur .... **ARETE**
mountains, Asia ...... **ALTAI**
mountains, myth ... **KAF, QAF**
mourn .... **WEEP, GRIEVE, LAMENT**
mournful .... **SAD, DIRE**
mourning band .... **CRAPE**
mouse .... **VOLE**
mouse, field .... **VOLE**
mouse genus .... **MUS**
mousebird ..... **COLY, SHRIKE**
mouth .... **OS, ORA**
mouth, away from .... **ABORAL**
mouth open .... **AGAPE**
mouth, river .... **DELTA**
mouth, tidal river ...... **FRITH**
mouth, toward .... **ORAD**
mouthful .... **SIP, SUP**
mouthlike orifice ...... **STOMA**
mouthpiece ..... **REED, BOCAL**
move .... **STIR, AFFECT**
move a camera .... **PAN**
move back ..... **EBB, RECEDE**
move to and fro **WAG, FLAP, SWAY**
b movement: biol. .... **TAXIS**
movement, capable of . **MOTILE**
movement: music ...... **MOTO**
movement,with:music **CONMOTO**
movie: Sp. .... **CINE**
moving part .... **ROTOR**
mow, barn's .... **LOFT**
mow of hay .... **GOAF**
mowed strip .... **SWATH**
Mowgli's bear friend ... **BALU, BALOO**
Mozambique native ...... **YAO**
muck .... **MIRE**
mud ...... **MIRE, MURGEON**
mud deposit .... **SILT**
mud, slimy .... **OOZE**
mud, stick in .... **MIRE**
mud, viscous .... **SLIME**
mud, volcano .... **SALSE**
muddle .... **MESS, ADDLE**
muddy .... **ROIL**
muffin .... **GEM**
mug .... **STEIN, NOGGIN**
mug, small .... **TOBY**
mugger .... **GOA**
mulatto .... **METIS**
mulberry bark cloth .... **TAPA**
mulberry genus ...... **MORUS**
mulberry, India ...... **AL, AAL**
mulct .... **FINE, AMERCE**
mullet, red .... **SUR**

c multiform .... **DIVERSE**
multiplicand: math. . **FACIEND**
multiplier: math. .... **FACIENT**
multitude ...... **HOST, HORDE**
mum .... **ALE**
munch .... **CHAMP**
mundane .... **TERRENE**
Munich's river .... **ISAR**
municipal officer, Sp. . **ALCADE, ALCAID, ALCAIDE, ALCAYDE**
muntjac deer . **KAKAR, RATWA**
murder by suffocation . **BURKE**
murder fine, Scot. .... **CRO**
murderer, first .... **CAIN**
murmuring sound **CURR, PURL, PURR**
Musci, plant of .... **MOSS**
muscle .... **THEW, SINEW**
muscle coordination, lack of **ATAXIA**
muscle, deep, pert. to **SCALENE**
muscle, kind of **ERECTOR, LEVATOR**
muscle, like .... **MYOID**
muscle, round, rolling .. **TERES**
muscle, stretching .... **TENSOR**
muscles .... **BRAWN**
muscular action, irregular **ATAXIA**
d muscular spasm .... **TIC**
Muse, chief .... **CALLIOPE**
muse in reverie .... **REVE**
Muse of astronomy ... **URANIA**
Muse of comedy ..... **THALIA**
Muse of dancing .**TERPSICHORE**
Muse of history .... **CLIO**
Muse of lyric poetry **CLIO, ERATO**
Muse of music ...... **EUTERPE**
Muse of poetry .... **ERATO**
Muse of sacred lyric **POLYMNIA**
Muse of tragedy . **MELPOMENE**
Muses, 9 .... **PIERIDES**
Muses' region .... **AONIA**
Muses, The .... **NINE**
musette .... **OBOE**
museum head ...... **CURATOR**
mush .... **ATOLE, SEPON**
mushroom .... **MOREL, MORIL**
mushroom cap .... **PILEUS**
music: as written .... **STA**
music character .... **DOT, CLEF, REST**
music drama .... **OPERA**
music for nine .... **NONET**
music for three .... **TRIO**
music for two .... **DUET**
music from the sign: abbr. . **DS**

a music hall .... **ODEA, ODEON, ODEUM**
music interval ...... **TRITONE**
music: it proceeds .... **VA**
music lines .... **STAFF**
music piece **SERENATA, SERENATE**
music, sacred **CHORAL, CHORALE**
music symbols, old ... **NEUME**
MUSICAL .... see also MUSIC
musical beat .... **TAKT**
musical composition, India **RAGA**
musical direction . **STA, TACET**
musical instrument ..... **ASOR, DRUM, FIFE, GIGA, HARP, HORN, LUTE, LYRE, OBOE, PIPE, REED, TCHE, TUBA, TURR, VINA, VIOL, CELLO, RAPPEL, SPINET, CLAVIER, HELICON, OCARINA**
musical sign .. **DOT, CLEF, REST**
musical study .... **ETUDE**
musical work .... **OPUS**
musician, 11th century . **GUIDO**

c musket ball, India ...... **GOLI**
Musketeer .... **ATHOS, ARAMIS, PORTHOS**
mussel, fresh-water ..... **UNIO**
must .... **STUM**
mustache monkey ... **MOUSTOC**
mustard family plant ... **CRESS**
musteline animal **OTTER, RATEL**
mustiness .... **FUST**
mutilate .... **MAIM**
muttonbird .... **OII**
muttonfish .... **SAMA**
"My Name is —" ..... **ARAM**
mysteries .... **ARCANA**
mysterious .... **OCCULT**
mystery .... **RUNE**
mystic word, Hindu ...... **OM**
mystic writing .... **RUNE**
mythical land ...... **LEMURIA**
mythical stream .... **STYX**
mythical submerged island **ATLANTIS**
mythical warrior .... **ARES**
MYTHOLOGY .... see SPECIAL SECTION, Page 198

N

b nab .... **GRAB, ARREST**
Nabal's wife: Bibl. ... **ABIGAIL**
NaCl .... **SALT**
nahoor sheep .... **SNA**
nail .... **CLAW, TALON, UNGUES, UNGUIS**
nail, hooked .... **TENTER**
nail, mining, surveying .. **SPAD**
nail, thin .... **BRAD**
nail with aperture ...... **SPAD**
nails, 100 lbs. .... **KEG**
namaycush .... **TOGUE**
NAME .... see also MAN'S NAME, WOMAN'S NAME
name .... **DUB, TERM, CLEPE, NOMEN, TITLE, ENTITLE**
name: Dan. .... **NAAM**
name plate, shop's .... **FACIA**
named ... **Y-CLEPT, Y-CLEPED**
namely .... **VIZ**
Naomi, name claimed by **MARA**
Naomi's daughter-in-law . **RUTH**
naos .... **CELLA**
nap, coarse, long .... **SHAG**
nap-raising device ... **TEASEL, TEASLE, TEAZEL, TEAZLE**
nap-raising machine ...... **GIG**
nap, to raise .... **TEASE**
napoleon, game like ..... **PAM**

d Napoleon's brother-in-law **MURAT**
Napoleon's isle .... **ELBA**
Napoleon's marshal general **NEY**
Napoleonic victory .**JENA, LODI**
Narcissus, nymph who loved **ECHO**
narcotic .... **DOPE, DRUG, HEROIN, OPIATE**
narcotic, India . **BANG, BHANG**
narcotic plant .... **DUTRA**
narcotic shrub **KAT, KAAT, KHAT**
narcotic shrub, S. Am. **COCA, CUCA**
narrate .... **TELL**
narrow ...... **LINEAL, STRAIT**
nasal .... **RHINAL**
Nata's wife: myth ..... **NANA**
nation: Ger. .... **VOLK**
nation, pert. to ...... **STATAL**
NATIVE .... see TRIBES in SPECIAL SECTION, Page 191
native .... **ITE, RAW, NATAL, ENDEMIC, INDIGENE**
natural luster, having ... **NAIF**
natural talent . **DOWER, FLAIR**
nature ...... **OUSIA, ESSENCE**
nature goddess ...... **CYBELE**

a nature principal: Hindu ... **GUNA**
nature spirit ... **NAT**
nature story writer ... **SETON**
nautical ... **MARINE**
nautical cry ... **AHOY, OHOY, AVAST**
Navaho hut ... **HOGAN**
naval hero ... **PERRY**
navy jail ... **BRIG**
near ... **AT, NIGH, ABOUT, CLOSE**
Near East native .. **ARAB, TURK**
Near East river valley ... **WADI**
near the ear ... **PAROTIC**
near to ... **BY, ON**
nearest ... **NEXT**
nearsighted person ... **MYOPE**
nearsightedness ... **MYOPIA**
neat ... **TIDY, TOSH, TRIG, TRIM, SPRUCE**
neat cattle ... **NOWT**
neatly ... **FEATLY**
necessitate ... **ENTAIL**
neck, nape of ... **NUCHA**
necklace ... **BEADS, RIVIERE**
neckline shape ... **VEE, BOAT, CREW**
neckpiece ... **ASCOT, STOLE**
neckpiece, feather ... **BOA**
neckpiece, woman's ... **FICHU**
NECKTIE ... see TIE
b need ... **WANT, REQUIRE**
needle ... **PROD, BODKIN**
needle bug ... **NEPA**
needle case ... **ETUI**
needle-shaped ... **ACUATE, ACERATE**
needlefish ... **GAR**
needlelike bristle ... **ACICULA**
negative ... **NE, NO, NAY, NON, NOT**
negative pole ... **CATHODE**
neglect ... **OMIT**
neglected school subject: abbr. **LAT.**
negligent ... **LAX**
negotiate ... **TREAT**
negrito ... **ATA, ATI, ITA, AETA, ATTA**
Negro dance ... **JUBA**
Negro: India ... **HUBSHI**
NEGRO TRIBE ... see SPECIAL SECTION, AFRICAN TRIBES
Nelson's victory site ... **NILE**
nematocyst ... **CNIDA**
nemesis ... **BANE**
Nepal Mongoloid ... **RAIS**
Nepal native ... **KHA**
Nepal people ... **RAIS**
nephew ... **NEPOTE**
c nephew, Fijian ... **VASU**
Neptune ... **LER**
Neptune's spear ... **TRIDENT**
nerve cell ... **NEURON**
nerve-cell process ... **AXON**
nerve layers, brain ... **ALVEI**
nervous ... **EDGY**
nervous disease ... **CHOREA**
nest .. **NID, NIDE, NIDI, NIDUS**
nest, eagle's ... **AERY, AERIE, EYRY, EYRIE**
nested boxes ... **INRO**
nestling ... **EYAS**
net ... **CLEAR**
net, fishing ... **SEINE, STENT, TRAWL**
net of hair-lines ... **RETICLE**
NETHERLANDS ... see SPECIAL SECTION
netlike ... **RETIARY**
nettle family ... **RAMIE, RAMEE**
network ... **WEB, MESH, RETE, RETIA**
neuroglia ... **GLIA**
neve ... **FIRN**
— Nevis, Gt. Brit. peak ... **BEN**
new ... **NOVEL, RECENT**
New Caledonia bird ... **KAGU**
New England state: abbr. ... **RI**
d New Guinea area ... **PAPUA**
New Guinea tribesman .. **KARON**
New Guinea victory ... **GONA**
New Guinea wild hog ... **BENE**
New Jerusalem foundation **JASPER**
new, lover of ... **NEO**
new star ... **NOVA**
new wine ... **MUST**
New York harbor isle ... **ELLIS**
New Zealand aborigine ... **ATI**
N.Z. bird ... **HUIA, KAKI, PEHO, RURU**
N.Z. clan ... **ATI**
N.Z. evergreen ... **TAWA**
N.Z. fruit pigeon ... **KUKU**
N.Z. laburnum ... **GOAI**
N.Z. mollusk ... **PIPI**
N.Z. native ... **MAORI**
N.Z. native fort ... **PA, PAH**
N.Z. parson bird ... **KOKO**
N.Z. plant ... **KARO**
N.Z. rail bird ... **WEKA**
N.Z. scabbard fish ... **HIKU**
N.Z. shrub ... **KARO**
N.Z. shrub, poisonous ... **TUTU**
N.Z. subtribe ... **HAPU**
N.Z. timber tree ... **GOAI, HINO, MIRO, PELU, RATA, RIMU, HINAU, HINOU, KAURI, KAURY, TOTARA**

a N.Z. tree..... **AKE, KOPI, NAIO, PUKA, TORO, WHAU**
N.Z. tribe.................. **ATI**
N.Z. wages.............. **UTU**
N.Z. wood hen.......... **WEKA**
news agency, Eng.... **REUTERS**
news agency, former Dutch **ANETA**
news agency, Jap........ **DOMEI**
news agency, Rus. Soviet. **TASS**
news paragraph.......... **ITEM**
newspaper service..... **AP, UP, INS, UPI, REUTERS**
newspapers............. **PRESS**
newt...... **EFT, EVET, TRITON**
nibble.... **GNAW, KNAB, KNAP**
niche................. **RECESS**
Nichols' hero............. **ABIE**
Nick Charles' dog........ **ASTA**
Nick Charles' wife....... **NORA**
nickel steel alloy........ **INVAR**
nicotine acid........... **NIACIN**
nictitate.................. **WINK**
Niger delta native.......... **IJO**
NIGERIA.......... see SPECIAL SECTION
Nigerian Negro....... **ARO, IBO**
Nigerian tribe............ **EDO**
NIGERIAN TRIBE OR PEOPLE see also SPECIAL SECTION page 191
b niggard................. **MISER**
nigh.................... **NEAR**
night, Norse...... **NATT, NOTT**
nightingale, Pers....... **BULBUL**
nightjar............... **POTOO**
nightmare demon, Teut.. **MARA**
nightmare, the....... **INCUBUS**
nightshade, black...... **MOREL, MORIL**
Nile, as god............. **HAPI**
Nile island............... **RODA**
Nile native.............. **NILOT**
Nile sailboat.......... **CANGIA**
Nile valley depression.... **KORE**
Nile, waste matter on.... **SADD, SUDD**
Nilotic Negro....... **JUR, LUO, LWO, SUK**
nimble.......... **SPRY, AGILE**
nimbus........... **HALO, NIMB**
nimrod.............. **HUNTER**
nine-angled polygon. **NONAGON**
nine, based on....... **NONARY**
nine, group of......... **ENNEAD**
nine inches............. **SPAN**
nine, music for......... **NONET**
Nineveh's founder....... **NINUS**
ninth day, every........ **NONAN**
ninth: mus............. **NONA**
niton................. **RADON**

c nitrogen.......... **AZO, AZOTE**
Noah, pert. to.......... **NOETIC**
Noah's landing........ **ARARAT**
Noah's 1st son.... **SEM, SHEM**
Noah's 2nd son.......... **HAM**
Nobel prize, literature '04 **MISTRAL**
Nobel prize, science...... **UREY**
noble, nobleman. **DUKE, EARL, LORD, PEER, BARON, COUNT**
noble: Ger...... **GRAF, RITTER**
NOBLEMAN....... see NOBLE
nobleman, Jap........... **KAMI**
nocturnal mammal **BAT, LEMUR**
nod.............. **BOW, BECK**
Nod, west of............ **EDEN**
nodding............. **NUTANT**
noddy tern: Hawaii....... **NOIO**
node............ **KNOB, KNOT, KNUR, NODUS**
"— noire".............. **BETE**
nomad....... **ARAB, SCENITE**
Nome in Greece........... **ELIS**
nomenclature........... **NAME**
nominal value............ **PAR**
nominate............... **NAME**
non-gypsy: Romany....... **GAJO**
non-Jew............ **GOI, GOY**
non-Moslem of Turkey or
d Ottoman Empire... **RAIA, RAYA**
non-professional.... **LAY, LAIC**
non-union worker......... **SCAB**
nonchalant............. **COOL**
none: dialect.............. **NIN**
nonsense. **PISH, POOH, HOOEY**
nonsense creature....... **GOOP**
noodles: Yiddish...... **FARFEL, FERFEL**
nook, sheltered.......... **COVE**
noose................... **LOOP**
Norn, one of **URD, URTH, WYRD**
Norse "Adam"........... **ASKR**
Norse bard.... **SCALD, SKALD**
Norse chieftain.... **JARL, YARL**
Norse epic.............. **EDDA**
Norse explorer...... **ERIC, LEIF**
NORSE GOD or GODDESSES see also GODS and GODDESSES and see also SPECIAL SECTION Page 200
Norse gods **VANS, AESIR, VANIR**
Norse letter............. **RUNE**
Norse myth. hero.. **EGIL, EGILL**
Norse myth. king.......... **ATLI**
Norse myth. "Life" force.... **LIF**
Norse myth. woman...... **IDUN**
Norse neighbor.......... **FINN**
Norse poetry........... **RUNES**
Norse prose............ **EDDA**
Norse sea goddess....... **RAN**
Norseman...... **DANE, SWEDE**

a North African .... **BERBER**
N. Afr. outer garment .. **HAIK**
North Carolina college .. **ELON**
North Carolinian .... **TARHEEL**
North Caucasian language **UDI, AVAR, UDIC, UDISH**
North, Mrs. of fiction . **PAMELA**
North Sea fishing boat . **COBLE**
North Sea, river into **ELBE, TEES**
North Star .... **POLARIS**
North Syrian deity .... **EL**
northern .... **BOREAL**
northern Scandinavian ... **LAPP**
northern tribe, China ..... **HU**
northernmost land ..... **THULE**
Northumberland river ... **TYNE**
Norway coin .... **ORE**
Norway territorial division . **AMT**
Norwegian author ... **HAMSUN**
Norwegian composer .... **GRIEG**
Norwegian county **AMT, FYLKE**
Norwegian saint .... **OLAF**
nose .... **CONK, NASI, NASUS, SNOOP**
nose, having large ... **NASUTE**
nose, having snub .... **SIMOUS**
nose openings .. **NARES, NARIS**
nose, snub .... **PUG**
nostrils .... **NARES, NARIS**
b nostrils, of .... **NARIC, NARIAL, NARINE**
"— Nostrum," Mediterranean **MARE**
not at home .... **OUT**
not ever: poet. .... **NEER**
not genuine .... **TIN**
not in style ...... **OUT, PASSE**
not long ago .... **LATELY**
not moving ... **INERT, STATIC**
not one .... **NARY, NONE**
not so great .... **LESS, FEWER, SMALLER**
notch ... **KERF, NICK, NOCK, CRENA, CRENAE**
notched .. **SERRATE, SERRATED**
note .... **CHIT, MEMO**
note, double, whole .... **BREVE**
note, Guido's .... **UT, ELA**
note, Guido's low ..... **GAMUT**
note, half .... **MINIM**
note, high, highest .... **ELA**
note, marginal **POSTIL, APOSTIL**
note: music .. **DI, DO, FA, FI, LA, LE, LI, ME, MI, RA, RE, RI, SE, SI, SO, TE, TI, SOL**
note, old Gr. musical .... **NETE**
note, old musical .... **ELA**
NOTE, SCALE ...... see NOTE: MUSIC
notes, furnish with . **ANNOTATE**
c notes in Guido's scale .. **ELAMI**
nothing . **NIL, NIX, NUL, NULL, ZERO, NIHIL**
notion .... **BEE, IDEA**
notion, capricious ..... **WHIM**
notional .... **IDEAL**
notorious .... **ARRANT**
Nott's son .... **DAG**
notwithstanding .... **YET**
nought .... **ZERO, NULL**
NOUN ENDING see SUFFIX, noun
noun form .... **CASE**
noun suffix of condition .. **ATE**
noun with only 2 cases . **DIPTOTE**
nourish .... **FEED, FOSTER**
nourishment ...... **PABULUM**
Nova Scotia .... **ACADIA**
novel, advocate of .... **NEO**
novel by A. France ..... **THAIS**
novelty .... **FAD**
novice .... **TIRO, TYRO**
now: dial. .... **NOO**
noxious .... **MIASMIC**
Nubian .... **NUBA**
nucha .... **NAPE**
nuclear element ...... **PROTON**
nudge .... **POKE**
nuisance .... **PEST**
nullify .... **NEGATE**
d nullify, legally .... **VOID**
number, describable by . **SCALAR**
number under 10 ...... **DIGIT**
number, whole ...... **INTEGER**
numbered: Bib. .... **MENE**
numerous .. **MANY, MULTIPLE**
nun, Franciscan .... **CLARE**
nun, head .... **ABBESS**
nun's dress .... **HABIT**
nunbird .... **MONASE**
nuque .... **NAPE**
nurse, Oriental, India .. **AMA, IYA, AMAH, AYAH, EYAH**
nurse, Slavic .... **BABA**
nursemaid: Fr. .... **BONNE**
nut ...... **COLA, KOLA, LICHI, ALMOND, CASHEW, LICHEE, LITCHI**
nut, beverage .... **COLA, KOLA**
nut, hickory .... **PECAN**
nut, pert. to .... **NUCAL**
nut, P. I. .... **PILI**
nut, pine .... **PINON**
nut, stimulating .... **BETEL**
nut tree, Afr. .... **COLA, KOLA**
nuts for food .... **MAST**
nuthatch genus .... **SITTA**
nutlike drupe .... **TRYMA**
nutmeg husk .... **MACE**
nutria .... **COYPU**

a nutriment ... FOOD, ALIMENT
nutritive .... ALIBLE
nymph .... MAIA, LARVA
nymph, fountain ...... EGERIA
nymph, laurel .... DAPHNE
nymph, Moslem .... HOURI

c nymph, mountain ..... OREAD
nymph, ocean ...... OCEANID
nymph, water . NAIAD, NEREID
nymph, wood . DRYAD, NAPEA, NAPAEA, HAMADRYAD
Nyx's daughter .... ERIS

O

O, plural .... OES
oaf .... LOUT
oak, Calif. .... ENCINA
oak, dried fruit of ... CAMATA
oak, evergreen .... HOLM
oak moss .... EVERNIA
oak, Turkey .... CERRIS
oakum, seal with .... CALK
oar .... ROW, BLADE, PROPEL
oar at stern .... SCULL
oasis, N. Afr. ... WADI, WADY
oat genus .... AVENA
oats as rent .... AVENAGE
oath, knight's .... EGAD
oath, old-fashioned . ODS, EGAD
oath, say under ...... DEPOSE
obeisance, Oriental BOW, SALAAM

b obey .... HEED, MIND
object ... AIM, CAVIL, DEMUR
object of art .... CURIO
objection, petty .... CAVIL
objective .... AIM, GOAL
obligation .... TIE, DEBT DUTY, ONUS
oblique .... CANT, BEVEL, SLANT, SLOPE
obliterate .... ERASE, EFFACE
obliteration .... RASURE
oblivion ..... LETHE, LIMBO
oblivion stream .... LETHE
obscure ..... DIM, FOG, DARK BEDIM, CLOUD
obscure, render ...... DARKLE
observe .. SEE, NOTE, BEHOLD, REMARK, CELEBRATE
obstinate .... SET, HARD
obstruction, petty .... CAVIL
obtain .... GET
obvious .... OPEN, PATENT
obvious, not . SUBTLE, SUBTILE
occasional .... ODD
Occident .... WEST
occipital protuberances ... INIA
occultism .... CABALA
occupant .... TENANT
occupation .... TRADE
occupy .... USE, FILL
occurrence .... EVENT

ocean's rise, fall ...... TIDE
oceanic .... PELAGIC
oceanic tunicate .... SALP
ocher, black ..... WAD, WADD
octave, designating high .. ALT
octave of church feast ... UTAS
octopus .... POULPE
octoroon METIS, MESTEE, MUSTEE
odd-job man .... JOEY
Odin. WODAN, WODEN, WOTAN
Odin's brother ...... VE, VILI
Odin's granddaughter . NANNA
Odin's son ... TY, TYR, THOR, TYRR, VALE, VALI
Odin's wife .... RIND
odor .... AROMA, SCENT
ODYSSEUS ... see also ULYSSES
Odysseus' companion . ELPENOR

d Odysseus' friend ..... MENTOR
Odyssey beggar .... IRUS
Odyssey singer .... SIREN
Oedipus' father .... LAIUS
Oedipus' mother .... JOCASTA
of speed of sound ...... SONIC
of the age: abbr. .... AET
off .... AWAY
offend .... CAG
offense .... CRIME
offense: law .. MALA, MALUM
offer .... BID, TENDER
offered up .... OBLATE
offhand .... CASUAL
office, ecclesiastic .. MATINS
office, priest's ...... MATINS
office, R. C. curia DATARY, DATARIA
officer, church ...... BEADLE
officer, court: Scot. ... MACER
officer, municipal: Scot. BAILIE
officer, Rom. .... LICTOR
officer, synagogue .... PARNAS
officer, university DEAN, BEADLE, BURSAR
official, Moslem .... HAJIB
official, Rom. EDILE, AEDILE, TRIBUNE
official, subordinate .. SATRAP
official, weights ...... SEALER
offspring .... SONS, HEIRS

a ogygian .... AGED
Ohio college town .... ADA
oil .... FAT, LARD, LUBE, ATTAR, OLEUM
oil beetle .... MELOE
oil bottle ..... CRUCE, CRUET, CRUSE, CRUIZE
oil, cruet .... AMPULLA
oil, edible .... ACEITE
oil, orange .... NEROLI
oil, pert. to .... OLEIC
oil, rub with .... ANOINT
oil-yielding Chinese tree . TUNG
oil-yielding tree ... EBO, EBOE
oilfish .... ESCOLAR
oilstone .... HONE
oily ketone .... IRONE
ointment .... BALM, NARD, SALVE, CERATE, POMADE
Ojibway secret order MEDA, MIDE
O.K. .... ROGER
okra .... GOMBO, GUMBO
old .... AGED, ANILE, SENILE
"Old Curiosity Shop" girl . NELL
old English army .... FYRD
old Eng. gold piece ..... RYAL
old Eng. rune .... WEN, WYN
old Greek coin .... OBOL
old Irish coin .... RAP
old Persian money .... DARIC
OLD TESTAMENT see BIBLICAL and SPECIAL SECTION
Old Testament objects ... URIM
b Old Test. people . PHUD, PHUT
old person .... DOTARD
old Sp. gold coin ...... DOBLA
old times .... ELD, YORE
old-womanish .... ANILE
oleaginous .... OILY
oleander genus ...... NERIUM
oleic acid salt ...... OLEATE
oleoresin .... ANIME, ELEMI, BALSAM
olive fly genus .... DACUS
olive genus .... OLEA
olive, inferior .... MORON
olive, stuffed .... PIMOLA
Oliver's nickname ...... NOLL
Olympian deity-god-goddess ARES, HERA, APOLLO, ATHENA, HERMES, ARTEMIS, DEMETER
Olympus, mountain near . OSSA
Olympus queen .... HERA
Olympus, region by .... PIERIA
omen .... BODE, PRESAGE
omission, vowel ...... ELISION
omit .... DELE, PASS, SKIP
omit in pronunciation .. ELIDE

c omitted, having part ELLIPTIC, ELLIPTICAL
onager .... ASS
once: dial. .... ANES
one .... AIN, UNIT
one-base hit .... SINGLE
one behind other .... TANDEM
one-eighth Troy ounce .. DRAM
one-eyed giant ..... CYCLOPS
one-horse carriage ..... SHAY
one hundred sq. meters AR, ARE
one hundred thousand rupees LAKH
one, music by .... SOLI, SOLO
one-spot .... ACE
one thousand .... MIL
one-year record ...... ANNAL
O'Neill heroine .... ANNA
onion .... CEPA
onion, Welsh .... CIBOL
onionlike plant .. CIVE, LEEK, CHIVE, SHALLOT, ESCHALOT
only .... MERE, SAVE, SOLE
onward .... AHEAD, FORTH
onyx, Mex. .... TECALI
oorial .... SHA
ooze .... LEAK, SEEP, SEIP, SIPE, SYPE, EXUDE
open .... AJAR, OVERT, BROACH, PATENT, UNWRAP
d open court .... AREA
open plain .... VEGA
opening .... GAP, HOLE, RIFT, SLOT, VENT, HIATUS
opening, long .... RIMA, SLOT
opening, mouthlike STOMA, STOMATA
opening, slit-like .... RIMA
opening, small .... PORE
opera ... AIDA, BORIS, ORFEO
opera, Beethoven .... FIDELIO
opera, Bizet .... CARMEN
opera composer, modern BRITTEN, MENOTTI
opera, Gounod .... FAUST
opera hat .... GIBUS
opera heroine ... AIDA, ELSA, MIMI, SENTA, ISOLDE
opera house, Milan .... SCALA
opera, Massenet MANON, THAIS
opera, Puccini .... TOSCA
opera scene .... SCENA
opera singer .... MELBA
opera soprano, star . ALDA, PONS BORI, RISE, RAISA, STEBER
opera star .... DIVA
opera, Verdi ... AIDA, ERNANI
opera, Wagner .... RIENZI
operate .... RUN, MANAGE
operetta composer ..... FRIML

a opium poppy seed ...... **MAW**
opossum, S. Am. ...... **QUICA**
opponent .. **FOE, ANTI, RIVAL**
opportune .... **TIMELY**
opportunity .... **CHANCE**
oppose .... **IMPUGN**
opposed, one .... **ANTI**
opposed to solo .... **TUTTI**
opposite extremities ... **POLES**
opposite .... **REVERSE**
Ops' daughter .... **CERES**
Ops' husband .... **SATURN**
optical glass .... **LENS**
optical illusion ...... **MIRAGE**
optical instrument lines **RETICLE**
optimistic .... **ROSY, ROSEATE**
oracle, Apollo's .... **DELOS**
oracle, Gr. .. **DELPHI, DELPHOI**
oral .... **PAROL**
orange-red stone .... **SARD**
orange tincture, Her. .. **TENNE**
orangutan, Malay ...... **MIAS**
orarion .... **STOLE**
orator .... **OTIS, RHETOR**
orb of day .... **SUN**
orbit point .... **APSIS, APOGEE**
orchid genus .... **DISA**
orchid leaves for tea
FAAM, FAHAM
orchid tuber .... **SALEP**
b ordain .... **DECREE**
order .... **BID, FIAT,**
ARRAY, EDICT, DECREE
order, one of Catholic. **MARIST**
order, put in .... **TIDY, SETTLE**
orderliness .... **SYSTEM**
ordinance .... **LAW**
ordnance piece ...... **MORTAR**
ore deposit ...... **LODE, MINE**
ore of iron .... **OCHER, OCHRE**
ore receptacle ...... **MORTAR**
organ .... **EAR, EYE**
organ of algae .... **PROCARP**
organ part .... **STOP**
organ pipe .... **REED**
organ pipe, displayed **MONTRE**
organ prelude .... **VERSET**
organ, seed-bearing .... **PISTIL**
organ stop **REED,SEXT,DOLCAN,**
CELESTE, MELODIA
organism, 1-cell
AMEBA, AMOEBA
organism, simple
MONAD, MONAS
organization .... **SETUP**
orgy .... **REVEL**
Orient .... **EAST**
Oriental ..... **ASIAN, TATAR**
Oriental dwelling .... **DAR**

c Oriental lute .... **TAR**
Oriental nursemaid .... **AMA,**
IYA, AMAH, AYAH, EYAH
Oriental plane tree .. **CHINAR**
Oriental porgy .... **TAI**
Oriental potentate ...... **AGA**
Oriental sailing ship ... **DHOW**
Oriental servant ..... **HAMAL**
Oriental ship captain .... **RAS**
Oriental weight .... **ROTL**
orifice. **PORE, STOMA, OSTIOLE**
orifices, sponge ...... **OSCULA**
origin .... **SEED**
original .... **NEW**
original sin .... **ADAM**
originate **ARISE, START, CREATE**
Orinoco tributary .... **ARO**
oriole, golden .... **LORIOT**
ornament .... **FRET**
ornament, curly ..... **SCROLL**
ornament in relief ... **EMBOSS**
ornament, spire .... **EPI**
ornamental border .... **DADO**
ornamental grass ... **EULALIA**
ornamental nailhead .... **STUD**
Orpheus' destination ... **HADES**
Orpheus' instrument ..... **LYRE**
orris .... **IRIS**
orris-root ketone, oil ... **IRONE**
oscillate .... **WAVE**
osier .... **WITHE**
d Osiris' brother .... **SET**
Osiris' wife, sister .... **ISIS**
ostentation .... **POMP**
ostracism ..... **TABU, TABOO**
ostrich, Am. .... **RHEA**
ostrich-like bird
EMU, EMEU, RATITE
Otaheite apple .... **HEVI**
Othello was one .... **MOOR**
Othello's lieutenant, foe **IAGO**
otherwise .... **ELSE**
otic .... **AURAL**
otologist .... **AURIST**
otter brown, color ... **LOUTRE**
otter genus .... **LUTRA**
Ottoman .... **TURK**
Ottoman court .... **PORTE**
Ottoman official ...... **PASHA**
"Our Mutual Friend," ballad-
seller in .... **WEGG**
oust .... **EJECT, EVICT**
out .... **AWAY, FORTH**
out-and-out .... **ARRANT**
out: Dutch .... **UIT**
out of style .... **PASSE**
out of the way .... **ASIDE**
outbreak, unruly .... **RIOT**
outburst, sudden ...... **SPATE**
outcast
LEPER, PARIAH, ISHMAEL

a outcome, final .... UPSHOT
outcry .... CLAMOR
outer .... ECTAL
outer portion of earth ... SIAL
outfit .. KIT, RIG, GEAR, SUIT
outfit, queer .... GETUP
outlet .... VENT
outline .... PERIMETER
outlook .... VISTA
outmoded .... PASSE
OUTRIGGER see MALAY CANOE
outward .... ECTAD
ova .... EGGS
oval ... ELLIPTIC, ELLIPTICAL
oven .... KILN, OAST
oven, annealing .. LEER, LEHR
oven, Polyn. native ...... UMU
over .... ATOP, ABOVE, AGAIN, ENDED, ACROSS
over-nice .... FINICAL
overnice person .... PRIG
over: poet. .... OER
over there ..... YON, YONDER
overact .... EMOTE
overcoat ... ULSTER, PALETOT
overdue payment ..... ARREAR
overflow .... DEBORD
overfond, be ..... DOAT, DOTE
overjoy .... ELATE
overlay .... CEIL
overripe grain .... BRITE
overseer, ranch: Sp. Am. CAPORAL
overshadow .... DOMINATE
overshoe GOLOE, GALOSH, GALOSHE
overskirt .. PANIER, PANNIER
overspreading mass ..... PALL

c overt .... OPEN, FRANK
overwhelm .... DELUGE
overwhelming amount .... SEA
Ovid's "— Amatoria" .... ARS
ovule .... SEED
ovum .... EGG
owala tree .... BOBO
owl, barn, Samoa ...... LULU
owl, eagle .. BUBO, KATOGLE
owl, horned .... BUBO
owl, S. Asia .... UTUM
owl's cry .... HOOT
own up to .... AVOW
ownership, of land, old law ODAL, UDAL
ox, extinct wild .... URUS
ox, forest .... ANOA
ox, long-haired .... YAK
ox of Caesar's time .... URUS
ox, wild .... ANOA
ox, wild: India .... GAUR, GOUR, ZEBU, GAYAL
oxalis, S. Amer. .... OCA
oxen .... KINE
oxhide strap ..... REIM, RIEM
oxide .... CALX
oxidize .... RUST
oxygen compound OXID, OXIDE
oxygen, form of ..... OZONE
oxygen radical .... OXYL
oyster bed material CULCH, CUTCH, CULTCH
oyster drill .... BORER
oyster farm: Fr. .... PARC
oyster, young .... SPAT
oysterfish .... TAUTOG
Ozarks, town west of in Okla. ADA
Oz books author ...... BAUM

P

b pace .... RATE, STEP
pachisi, kind of .... LUDO
pachyderm .... ELEPHANT
Pacific aroid food plant TARO
Pacific Island cloth ..... TAPA
Pacific pine .... HALA
Pacific shrub .... SALAL
pacify CALM, SOOTHE, PLACATE
pack .... WAD, STOW
pack animal .... ASS, BURRO, LLAMA, SUMPTER
pack horse .... SUMPTER
pack down .... RAM, TAMP
package, India ...... ROBBIN
package of spun silk .. MOCHE
pad .... TABLET

d padded jacket under armor ACTON
padnag .... TROT, AMBLE
Padua, town near ...... ESTE
pagan god .... IDOL
page, "Love's Labor Lost" MOTH
page number .... FOLIO
pageantry .... POMP
"Pagliacci" character .. CANIO
"Pagliacci" heroine ... NEDDA
pagoda, Chinese ..... TA, TAA
pagoda ornament ... EPI, TEE
paid notice .... AD
pail .... SKEEL
pain, dull .... ACHE
pain reliever OPIATE, ANODYNE
paint, face .... FARD, ROUGE

a pain-killer alkaloid source **COCA**
painted bunting: Creole .. **PAPE**
PAINTER .. see also ARTIST and country of each artist
painter, modernist **KLEE, MIRO, ERNST**
painting style .... **GENRE**
painting, wall .... **MURAL**
pair .... **DUO, DIAD, DUAD, DYAD, MATE**
pair of horses ... **SPAN, TEAM**
pairing .... **MATING**
palanquin .... **JAUN**
palanquin bearer ..... **HAMAL**
palanquin, Jap. .... **KAGO**
palatable, very .... **SAPID**
pale .... **WAN, ASHY, ASHEN, PASTY**
pale color .... **PASTEL**
pale-colored .... **MEALY**
Palestine in Jewish use **ERETS**
palisade: fort. .... **RIMER**
Pallas .... **ATHENA**
pallid .... **WAN, PALE**
palm ...... **TI, COCO, TALA, TALIPAT, TALIPOT, TALIPUT**
palm, Afr. .... **DUM**
palm, Asia .... **ARENG, BETEL**
palm, betel .... **ARECA**
palm, book .... **TARA**
b palm, Brazil .... **ASSAI**
palm, climbing ...... **RATTAN**
palm cockatoo .... **ARARA**
palm, dwarf genus ..... **SABAL**
palm fiber **DOH, TAL, RAFFIA**
palm fiber, S. Amer. **DATIL**
palm genus .... **ARECA**
palm genus, Asia ... **ARENGA**
palm juice, fermented .. **SURA**
palm leaf **OLA, OLE, OLAY, OLLA**
palm-leaf mat .... **YAPA**
palm lily .... **TI**
palm, liquor ..... **BENO, BINO**
palm, N. Z. .... **NIKAU**
palm, nipa ..... **ATAP, ATTAP**
palm off .... **FOB, FOIST**
palm, palmyra leaf ..... **OLA, OLE, OLLA, OLAY**
palm sago, Malay ... **GOMUTI**
palm sap .... **TODDY**
palm starch .... **SAGO**
palm, W. Ind. **GRIGRI, GRUGRU**
palmetto .... **SABAL**
palmyra leaf .... **OLA, OLE, OLAY, OLLA**
palmyra palm .... **BRAB**
palp .... **FEELER**
palpitation .... **PALMUS**

c pamper .... **COSHER, COSSET**
pamphlet .... **TRACT**
panacea .... **ELIXIR**
Panama gum tree **COPA, YAYA**
Panama, old name ... **DARIEN**
Panama tree, large .. **CATIVO**
Panay negrito .... **ATI**
panda .... **WAH, BEAR**
panel .... **PANE**
panel of jurors ...... **VENIRE**
pang .... **THROE**
pangolin .... **MANIS**
panic .... **FEAR, FUNK**
pannier .... **DOSSER**
Panopolis, chief god of .. **MIN, KHEM**
pant .... **GASP**
pantry .... **AMBRY, LARDER, SPENCE, BUTTERY**
— Paulo, Brazil .... **SAO**
papal cape ... **FANO, FANON, FANUM, ORALE, PHANO, FANNEL**
papal church .... **LATERAN**
papal collar .. **FANO, FANON, FANUM, ORALE, PHANO, FANNEL**
papal court ...... **SEE, CURIA**
papal fanon .... **ORALE**
papal letter .... **BULL, BULLA**
d papal scarf .... **ORALE**
papal veil .... **FANO, FANON, FANUM, ORALE, PHANO, FANNEL**
papal vestment .... **FANO, FANON, FANUM, ORALE, PHANO, FANNEL**
paper folded once ..... **FOLIO**
paper, imperfect, poor **CASSE, CASSIE, RETREE**
paper, lighting .... **SPILL**
paper measure .. **REAM, QUIRE**
paper mulberry .... **KOZO**
paper mulberry bark .... **TAPA**
paper size **DEMY, POTT, OCTAVO**
paper, thin crisp ...... **PELURE**
par, 2 under .... **EAGLE**
Para, Brazil, capital .. **BELEM**
parade .... **MARCH, STRUT**
paradise .... **EDEN**
paradise, Buddhist ...... **JODO**
paradise, like .... **EDENIC**
"Paradise Lost" angel .. **ARIEL**
paragraph .... **ITEM**
parallelogram .... **RHOMB**
paralysis .... **PARESIS**
parapet, solid portion of **MERLON**
parasite .... **LEECH**

parasite in blood .... TRYP
parasitic insect MITE, ACARID
parasitic plant MOSS, DODDER
paravane .... OTTER
Parcae .... FATES
Parcae, one of
NONA, MORTA, DECUMA
parcel of land .... LOT, PLAT
parchment, book
FOREL, FORREL
pardon .... REMIT, CONDONE
pardon, general .... AMNESTY
pare .... PEEL
Paris art exhibit ...... SALON
Paris, first bishop of
DENIS, DENYS
Paris section .... PASSY
Paris subway .... METRO
Paris thug .... APACHE
Paris' father .... PRIAM
Paris' wife .... OENONE
parish head .... RECTOR
parley .... PALAVER
Parliament report .. HANSARD
parol .... ORAL
paroxysm .... FIT, SPASM
parrot
KEA, LORY, VASA, VAZA
parrot, Brazil ... ARA, ARARA
parrot-fish
LORO, LAUIA, SCARID
parrot, hawk .... HIA
parrot, monk .... LORO
parrot, N. Z. large KEA, KAKA
parrot, P. I., green .... CAGIT
parrot, sheep-killing .... KEA
parrot's bill, part of .... CERE
parrotlike .... ARINE
parry .... FEND, EVADE
Parsi priest .... MOBED
Parsi scripture .... AVESTA
parsley camphor .... APIOL
parsley, plant kin to
ANISE, CELERY
parson bird
POE, TUE, TUI, KOKO
parsonage .... MANSE
part .... ROLE, SOME, PIECE, BREAK, SEVER, SHARE, CLEAVE, ELEMENT
part, Greek play
EXODE, EXODOS
part of church .... BEMA
NAVE, AISLE, ALTAR
part of horse's foot .. PASTERN
part of speech .. NOUN, VERB
parted .... PARTITE
participle ending .... ING
parti-colored .... PIED, PINTO
parti-colored horse
ROAN, CALICO
particle ...... ACE, BIT, ION, JOT, ATOM, IOTA, DROP, MITE, MOTE, GRAIN, SHRED, TITTLE
particle, electrically charged
ION
particle in cosmic rays MESON
particle of chaff ...... PALEA
particle, small
JOT, ATOM, IOTA, MOTE
particular .... ITEM
Partlet .... HEN, BIDDY
partnership: Hawaii HUI, HOEY
partridge call ... JUCK, JUKE
partridge, sand ...... SEESEE
partridge, snow ...... LERWA
party .... SECT
parvenu .... UPSTART
pasha .... DEY
pass .... HAND, ELAPSE
pass a rope through ... REEVE
pass between peaks ..... COL
pass by .... BYGO
pass on .... RELAY
pass over ... OMIT, SKIP, ELIDE
pass through .... REEVE
pass through mountains .. COL, DEFILE
passable .... SOSO
passage .... GUT, ITER, CANAL, TRANSIT
passage, bastion .... POSTERN
passage, covered .... ARCADE
passage: hist. .... ALURE
passage: music TUTTI, STRETTA
passage out .... EXIT, EGRESS
passageway ADIT, HALL, AISLE
Passover ..... PASCH, PASCHA
Passover meal SEDAR, SEDER
passport endorsement VISA,VISE
past AGO, GONE, OVER, AGONE
paste .... STRASS
pasteboard .... CARD
pasted-up art work .. COLLAGE
pastel .... TINT
pastoral .... IDYLLIC
pastoral place ...... ARCADIA
pastoral poem .. IDYL, IDYLL
pastoral staff .. PEDA, PEDUM
pastry
PIE, FLAN, TART, ECLAIR
pasture .... LEA
pasture: N. Eng. .... ING
pasture, to .... AGIST
pasty .... DOUGHY
pat .... DAB, TAP
pat, very .... APT
Patagonian cavy ...... MARA
patchwork, literary .... CENTO

a **patella** .... **ROTULA**
paten .... **ARCA, ARCAE**
patent from monarch .. **BERAT**
path: Anglo-Ir. ..... **CASAUN**
path: math. .... **LOCUS**
path of planet .... **ORBIT**
pathos, false .... **BATHOS**
patriarch Jacob ...... **ISRAEL**
patriarch's title .... **NASI**
patron .... **CLIENT**
patron saint of France
DENIS, DENYS
patronage ...... **EGIS, AEGIS**
pattern .... **NORM, TYPE, IDEAL, MODEL, PARAGON**
pattern, large square **DAMIER**
Paul, Apostle .... **SAUL**
Paul's birthplace ..... **TARSUS**
paulownia tree .... **KIRI**
pause .... **REST**
pause: poet. & music
SELAH, CESURA, CAESURA
paver .... **TUP**
paver's mallet .... **TUP**
pavilion .... **TENT**
paving stone .... **FLAG, SETT**
paw .... **PUD, FOOT**
pawl .... **DETENT**
b pawn .... **HOCK**
Pawnee Indian rite .... **HAKO**
Pawnee tribes .... **CHAUI**
pay .... **ANTE, WAGE, REMIT**
pay dirt .... **ORE**
pay, fixed .... **STIPEND**
pay for another ...... **TREAT**
pay homage: feudal law
ATTORN
pay one's part .... **ANTE**
pay out .... **SPEND**
payable .... **DUE**
paymaster, India ...... **BUXY**
payment back .... **REBATE**
payment for a bride, S. Afr.
LOBOLA
payment for death, feudal **CRO**
payment for homicide ... **ERIC**
payment, press for ...... **DUN**
payment to owner: Fr. law **CENS**
pea .... **LEGUME**
peace .... **PAX**
peace god, Anglo-Saxon .. **ING**
peace of mind .... **REST**
peaceful ... **IRENE, IRENICAL**
peach, clingstone ...... **PAVY**
peacock .... **MAO, PAVO**
peacock blue .... **PAON**
peacock butterfly .... **IO**
peacock fish .... **WRASSE**
peacock genus .... **PAVO**
peacock: Kipling .... **MAO**

c peak ...... **ALP, TOR, ACME, APEX, PITON, ZENITH**
peak: Scot. .... **BEN**
peanut ...... **MANI, GOOBER**
pear, autumn .... **BOSC**
pear cider .... **PERRY**
pearl blue color ...... **METAL**
Pearl Buck heroine ..... **OLAN**
pearl, imitation ...... **OLIVET**
pearl millet ... **BAJRA, BAJRI**
pearlweeds .... **SAGINA**
peasant. **CARL, CEORL, CHURL**
peasant, India .... **RYOT**
peasant, Scot.
COTTAR, COTTER
peat .... **TURF**
peat spade .... **SLADE**
pecan tree .... **NOGAL**
peccary, collared ..... **JAVALI**
peck .... **DAB, NIP, KNIP**
pedal .... **TREADLE**
peddle ... **HAWK, SELL, VEND**
peddle: Eng. .... **TRANT**
pedestal .... **GAINE**
pedestal part .. **DADO, PLINTH**
peduncle, plant .... **SCAPE**
peel . **BARK, PARE, RIND, SKIN**
peep-show .... **RAREE**
PEER .... see also NOBLE
peer .... **PEEK, PEEP**
d Peer Gynt's mother ...... **ASE**
peevish .... **PETULANT**
peg .... **KNAG**
peg, golf .... **TEE**
peg, wooden
NOG, TRENAIL, TREENAIL
Pegu ironwood .... **ACLE**
Peleg's son .... **REU**
pellucid ...... **CLEAR, LIMPID**
pelma .... **SOLE**
pelota court ...... **FRONTON**
pelt ...... **FELL, SKIN, STONE**
pelvic bone, pert. to .... **ILIAC**
pelvic bones .... **ILIA**
pen name, Dickens .... **BOZ**
pen name, G. Russell ...... **AE**
pen name, Lamb .... **ELIA**
pen point .... **NEB, NIB**
pen-text .... **RONDE**
penman, Yutang .... **LIN**
penalty .... **FINE**
pendulum weight .... **BOB**
Penelope's father .... **ICARIUS**
penetrate
GORE, ENTER, PERMEATE
penitential season ..... **LENT**
penmanship .... **HAND**
pennies .... **PENCE**
Pennsylvania sect ..... **AMISH**
Pentateuch .... **TORA, TORAH**

a **PEOPLE** .. see also TRIBES in SPECIAL SECTION
people .... **MEN, FOLK, ONES, RACE, DEMOS**
people, ancient Asian ... **SERES**
people: Ger. .... **VOLK**
people: Ir. .... **DAOINE**
people, Nigerian . **BENI, BENIN**
people: Sp. .... **GENTE**
people, spirit of ...... **ETHOS**
people, the .... **DEMOS**
pepper, climbing ...... **BETEL**
pepper, garden .... **PIMIENTO**
pepper plant, Borneo .... **ARA**
pepper shrub **AVA, CAVA, KAVA, KAWA**
pepper vine .... **BETEL**
Pequod's captain ...... **AHAB**
"per —" ..... **DIEM, ANNUM**
perceive .. **SEE, SENSE, DESCRY**
perception . **EAR, TACT, SENSE**
perch .... **SIT, ROOST**
perch genus .... **PERCA**
perchlike fish .... **DARTER**
percolate .. **OOZE, SEEP, LEACH**
peregrine .... **ALIEN**
perenially shifting sands region **AREG**
perfect .... **IDEAL, MODEL**
perforate ...... **BORE, DRILL, PUNCH, RIDDLE**
perform .... **RENDER**
performer
b **DOER, ACTOR, ARTISTE**
perfume **ATAR, OTTO, AROMA, ATTAR**
perfume base .... **MUSK**
perfume with incense .. **CENSE**
perfumed pad .... **SACHET**
Pericles' consort .... **ASPASIA**
periphery ... **RIM, PERIMETER**
period .... **DOT**
period, time **AGE, EON, ERA, STAGE**
periodic as Med. winds **ETESIAN**
permit .. **LET, ALLOW, LICENSE**
permission .... **LEAVE**
pernicious, something .... **PEST**
perplex **BAFFLE, CONFUSE, BEWILDER**
Persephone ..... **CORA, KORE**
Persephone's husband **HADES, PLUTO**
Persia .... **IRAN**
Persian .... **IRANI**
Persian coin, ancient .. **DARIC**
Pers. demigod .... **YIMA**
Pers. elf .... **PERI**
Pers. enameled tile ..... **KASI**
Pers. fairy .... **PERI**
Pers. governor, old ... **SATRAP**
Pers. headdress, ancient **TIARA**

c Pers. lord ..... **KAAN, KHAN**
Pers. mystic .... **SUFI**
Pers. native .... **LUR**
Pers. poet .... **OMAR**
Pers. potentate .... **SHAH**
Pers. priestly caste ..... **MAGI**
Pers. province, ancient .. **ELAM**
Pers. race, tribesman **LUR, KURD**
Pers. rug .. **SENNA, HAMADAN**
Pers. ruler .... **SHAH**
Pers. ruler of dead ..... **YIMA**
Pers. sect .... **BABI**
Pers. sprite .... **PERI**
PERS. TITLE .... see TITLE, PERSIAN
Pers. tribe member ..... **LUR**
Pers. weight .... **SER**
persimmon, E. Ind. **GAB, GAUB**
person of mixed blood **METIS, MESTIZO**
person, overnice .... **PRIG**
personage .... **NIBS**
personification of folly ... **ATE**
personification of light: Polyn. **AO**
personnel .... **STAFF**
perspiration .. **SUDOR, SWEAT**
perspire .... **EGEST, SWEAT**
pert girl .... **CHIT, MINX**
pertaining to the chin **MENTAL**
d pertinent .... **APT, PAT**
perturb .... **DERANGE, DISTURB, AGITATE, TROUBLE**
PERU INDIAN .. see page 193
peruse ..... **CON, READ, SCAN**
peruser .... **CONNER**
Peruvian fertility goddess **MAMA**
Peruvian plant .... **OCA**
pervade .... **PERMEATE**
pester .... **ANNOY, TEASE**
pestle .... **PILUM**
pestle vessel .... **MORTAR**
pet .... **CADE**
pet lamb ...... **CADE, COSSET**
"Peter Pan" dog ...... **NANA**
"Peter Pan" pirate ...... **SMEE**
petiole .... **STIPE**
Petrarch's love .... **LAURA**
petrol .... **GAS**
peyote .... **MESCAL**
phantoms .... **EIDOLA**
Pharaoh .... **RAMESES**
Pharaoh after Rameses I .. **SETI**
phase .... **FACET, STAGE**
pheasant brood **NID, NYE, NIDE**
pheasant, Himal. . **CHIR, CHEER**
pheasant, India ...... **MONAL**
Phidias statue .... **ATHENA**
philippic .... **TIRADE**
PHILIPPINE ISLANDS see also SPECIAL SECTION

a **Philippine Islands attendant** **ALILA**
P.I. bast fiber ...... **CASTULI**
P.I. cedar .... **CALANTAS**
P.I. chief **DATO, DATU, DATTO**
P.I. **DWARF** see P. I. NEGRITO
P.I. dyewood tree **TUI, IPIL, TUWI**
P.I. food .... **POI, SABA**
P.I. fort .... **COTA, KOTA**
P.I. grass ...... **BOHO, BOJO**
P.I. lighter .... **CASCO**
P.I. lizard .... **IBID, IBIT**
P.I. Moslem .... **MORO**
P.I. negrito, native, dwarf **ATA, ATI, ITA, AETA, ATTA**
P.I. palm wine ... **BENO, BINO**
P.I. peasant .... **TAO**
P.I. poisonous tree .... **LIGAS**
P.I. rice ...... **PAGA, MACAN**
P.I. sash .... **TAPIS**
P.I. servant .... **ALILA**
P.I. shrub, rope **NABO, ANABO**
P.I. skirt .... **SAYA**
P.I. tree .... **DAO, IBA, TUA, TUI, BOGO, DITA, IFIL, IPIL, YPIL**
P.I. warrior .... **MORO**
Philistine city .... **GATH, GAZA, EKRON**
b Philistine deity, principal **DAGON**
philosopher's stone .... **ELIXIR**
philosophical element ... **RECT**
philosophical theory **MONISM**
philosophy, pert. to Gr. **ELEATIC**
phloem .... **BAST**
phoebe .... **PEWEE, PEWIT**
Phoebus .... **SOL, SUN**
Phoenician city .... **TYRE**
Phoenician goddess .. **ASTARTE**
Phoenician port .... **SIDON**
Phoenician princess .. **EUROPA**
phonetic notation system **ROMIC**
phonetical sound .... **PALATAL**
phosphate of lime ... **APATITE**
photo-developing powder **METOL**
photography solution ... **HYPO**
Phrygian god .... **ATTIS**
Phrygian lunar god ..... **MEN**
physical ... **SOMAL, SOMATIC**
physician ..... **GALEN, MEDIC**
physician's group .... **AMA**
physician's symbol **CADUCEUS**
physicist, Am. .... **EINSTEIN**
physicist, Eng. .... **BOYLE**
physicist, Fr. .... **CURIE**
physicist, Nobel prize-winner 1944 .... **RABI**
physiological individual .. **BION**
c piano, upright ...... **CLAVIAL**
pick, miner's: Eng. **MANDREL, MANDRIL**
pick out .... **CULL, GLEAN**
picket .... **PALE**
pickled bamboo shoots **ACHAR**
pickled meat .... **SOUSE**
pickling fluid .... **BRINE**
pickling herb .... **DILL**
pickpocket .... **DIP**
"Picnic" author .... **INGE**
picture ... **DRAW, PORTRAIT**
picture border .... **MAT**
picture, composite .. **MONTAGE**
picturesque .... **SCENIC**
pie, meat, small .... **PASTY**
piebald .... **PINTO**
piebald pony ... **PIED, PINTO**
piece of eight .... **REALS**
piece out .... **EKE**
piece, thin .... **SLAT**
pier .... **KEY, DOCK, MOLE, QUAI, QUAY**
pier, architectural ..... **ANTA**
pier support .... **PILE, PILING**
pierce ... **GORE, STAB, SPEAR**
pig . **HOG, SOW, SHOAT, SHOTE**
pig, wild .... **BOAR**
pig, young .... **ELT, GRICE**
pigs .... **SUS**
d pigs' feet .... **PETTITOES**
pigs, litter of .... **FARROW**
pigs, red .... **DUROC**
pigeon ... **NUN, BARB, DOVE, POUTER, ROLLER**
pigeon hawk .... **MERLIN**
pigeon pea . **DAL, TUR, GANDUL**
piglike animal ..... **PECCARY**
pigment, blue-green ..... **BICE**
pigment, brown .... **SEPIA**
pigment, brown, from soot **BISTER, BISTRE**
pigment, deep blue .... **SMALT**
pigment, red .... **LAKE**
pigment test crystalline **DOPA**
pigment, without .... **ALBINO**
pigmentation, lack of **ACHROMA**
pigtail .... **CUE, QUEUE**
pike, full grown . **LUCE, LUCET**
pike, walleyed .... **DORE**
pilaster .... **ANTA**
pilchard .. **FUMADO, SARDINE**
pilchard-like fish ...... **SPRAT**
pile ...... **NAP, HEAP, SPILE**
pile driver .... **OLIVER**
pile driver ram .... **TUP**
pile of hay .... **RICK, STACK**
pilfer .... **STEAL**
pilgrim .... **PALMER**

a pilgrimage city .... **MECCA**
pilgrimage to Mecca .... **HADJ**
pill, large .... **BOLUS**
pillage .... **LOOT, SACK, STEAL**
pillage .... **RAPINE**
pillar, as of ore .... **JAMB**
pillar, Hindu .... **LAT**
pillar, resembling ..... **STELAR**
pillar, tapering ...... **OBELISK**
pillow .... **BOLSTER**
pilot .... **GUIDE, STEER**
pimento or —spice ..... **ALL**
pin .... **BROOCH**
pin, firing .... **TIGE**
pin, gunwale .... **THOLE**
pin, machine .... **COTTER**
pin, metal .... **RIVET**
pin, pivot .... **PINTLE**
pin, rifle firing .... **TIGE**
pin, Roman .... **ACUS**
pin, small, very .... **LILL**
pin, splicing .... **FID**
pin, wooden .. **FID, NOG, PEG, COAG, COAK, DOWEL**
pin wrench .... **SPANNER**
pinafore .... **TIER**
pincer claw .... **CHELA**
pinch .... **NIP**
pinched with cold ..... **URLED**
Pindar work .... **ODE**
b pine-cone, like a ...... **PINEAL**
pine, Mex. .... **OCOTE, PINON**
pine, Scot. .... **RIGA**
pine, textile screw **ARA, PANDAN**
pineapple **NANA, PINA, ANANA**
pineapple genus .... **PUYA**
pinfeather .... **PEN**
pinion .... **WING**
pink .... **DAMASK**
pinnacle .... **TOP, APEX**
pinnacle, ice .... **SERAC**
pinniped .... **SEAL**
pinochle score, term **DIX, MELD**
pint, half .... **CUP**
pintado fish .... **SIER**
pintail .... **SMEE**
pinworm .. **ASCARID, ASCARIS**
pious Biblical Jew ..... **TOBIT**
pipe .... **TUBE, RISER**
pipe, Irish .... **DUDEEN**
pipe joint, fitting .... **TEE**
pipe, pastoral .... **REED**
pipe, tobacco **BRIAR, BRIER, DUDEEN**
pipe, water. **HOOKAH, NARGILE**
pipe with socket ends **HUB, HUBB**
pipelike .... **TUBATE**
pique .... **PEEVE**

c pirate ...... **ROVER, CORSAIR**
pirate in War of 1812 **LAFITTE**
pismire .... **ANT, EMMET**
pistil part .... **CARPEL**
pistol .... **DAG, DAGG, MAUSER, SIDEARM**
pistol: slang .... **HEATER**
pit ..... **HOLE, ABYSS, STONE**
pit for roots, Maori ..... **RUA**
pit: medical .... **FOSSA**
pit, small .. **FOVEA, LACUNA**
pitch .... **KEY, TAR, TONE**
pitcher .... **JUG, EWER**
pitcher's false move .... **BALK**
pith .... **NUB, GIST**
pith helmet .... **TOPI, TOPEE**
pithy .... **TERSE**
pithy plant .... **SOLA**
pitiful quality ...... **PATHOS**
pittance .... **DOLE**
pitted .... **FOVEATE**
pity .... **RUTH**
placard .... **POSTER**
place .... **SET, LIEU, LOCI, SPOT, LOCUS, STEAD, LOCALE**
place before .... **APPOSE**
place, camping .... **ETAPE**
place case is tried .... **VENUE**
place in office again .. **RESEAT**
d place, in relation .... **POSIT**
place, market .... **FORUM**
place of shelter .. **GITE, HAVEN**
placid .... **CALM, SERENE**
plagiarize .... **STEAL**
plague .... **PEST, TEASE**
plain, arctic .... **TUNDRA**
plain, Argentine ...... **PAMPA**
plain, Asia .... **CHOL**
plain, Palestine .... **ONO**
plain, Russia .... **STEPPE**
plain, S. Am. .... **LLANO**
plain, treeless ..... **SAVANNA**
plain, treeless Arctic **TUNDRA**
plain, upland .. **WOLD, WEALD**
Plains Indian .... see page 193
plainly woven .... **UNI**
plait .... **PLY, BRAID**
plan .... **PLOT, INTEND**
plane, Fr. .... **SPAD**
plane, Ger. .... **STUKA**
plane, Jap. .... **ZERO**
plane part .... **FLAP, NOSE, TAIL, WING**
plane, Russ. fighter ...... **MIG**
planets (in order of distance from sun) **MERCURY (1), VENUS (2), EARTH (3), MARS (4), JUPITER (5), SATURN (6), URANUS (7), NEPTUNE (8), PLUTO (9)**

a planets in distance from Earth (closest first)
1—VENUS **5—SATURN**
2—MARS **6—URANUS**
3—MERCURY **7—NEPTUNE**
4—JUPITER **8—PLUTO**
planets in size (largest first)
1—JUPITER **6—VENUS**
2—SATURN **7—PLUTO**
3—NEPTUNE **8—MARS**
4—URANUS **9—MERCURY**
5—EARTH
planetarium .... **ORRERY**
planetary aspect **CUSP, TRINE**
plank's curve on ship ..... **SNY**
plant .... **SOW, SEED**
plant, bayonet .... **DATIL**
plant broom .... **SPART**
plant, bulb **CAMAS, CAMASS, CAMMAS**
plant cutter bird ...... **RARA**
plant cutting .. **SLIP, PHYTON**
plant disease .... **RUST, SMUT**
plant joined to another **GRAFT**
plant life .... **FLORA**
PLANT, LILY ...... see LILY
plant, lily-like **CAMAS, CAMASS, CAMMAS**
plant louse .... **APHID**
plant, male .... **MAS**
b plant, medicinal, S. Am. **ALOE, SENNA, IPECAC**
plant modified by environment to abnormal development **ECAD**
plant, mustard family **KALE, CRESS**
plant organ .... **LEAF**
plant pod .... **BOLL**
plant, poisonous .... **LOCO**
plant, sea-bottom ... **ENALID**
plant stem: bot. ..... **CAULIS**
plant stem tissue ...... **PITH**
plant used as soap ... **AMOLE**
plants of area .... **FLORA**
plantain lily genus ..... **HOSTA**
plantation, osier .... **HOLT**
planter .... **SEEDER**
plaster .... **SMEAR**
plaster, artist's painting . **GESSO**
plaster of Paris .... **GESSO**
plastic .... **LUCITE**
plate, battery .... **GRID**
plate, Eucharist .... **PATEN**
plate, reptile's .... **SCUTE**
plate to hurl .... **DISCUS**
plateau .... **MESA**
plateau, Andes .... **PUNA**
platform ...... **DAIS, STAGE**
platform, ancient ...... **BEMA**
c platform, mine shaft **SOLLAR, SOLLER**
platinum, of .... **OSMIC**
platinum wire loop ..... **OESE**
Plato's "Idea" ... **EIDE, EIDOS**
play .... **DRAMA**
play on words .... **PUN**
play, part of ..... **ACT, SCENE**
play unskillfully ...... **STRUM**
player .... **ACTOR**
playing card, old It. ... **TAROT**
playwright .... **INGE**
plea, to end: law .... **ABATER**
plead .... **SUE, ENTREAT**
pleading: law .... **OYER**
please .... **SUIT**
pleasing .... **NICE**
pleasure god, Egypt. . **BES, BESA**
pledge .... **VOW, GAGE, OATH, PAWN, TROTH, ENGAGE**
pledge, Rom. law .... **VAS**
plexus .... **RETE, RETIA**
pliable .... **WAXY**
pliant .... **LITHE**
plinth .... **ORLO, SOCLE**
plot .... **LOT, PLAT, CABAL, CONSPIRE**
plow, cutter **COLTER, COULTER**
d plow part .... **SHETH, SHEATH**
plow, sole of .... **SHARE**
plowed field .... **ERD, ARADA**
plug .... **BUNG, CORK, SPILE, STOPPER**
plum .... **GAGE, SLOE**
plume .. **EGRET, PREEN, AIGRET**
plummet .... **FATHOM**
plump child .... **FUB**
plunder .... **ROB, LOOT, PREY, SACK, BOOTY, RAVEN, RAVIN, REAVE, PILFER, RAPINE, RAVAGE, RAVINE**
plunder ruthlessly ... **MARAUD**
plunge .... **DIVE, DOUSE**
plural ending .... **EN, ES**
plus .... **AND**
Pluto .... **DIS, HADES, ORCUS**
Pluto's mother-in-law **DEMETER**
pneumonia, kind of .... **LOBAR**
Po tributary .... **ADDA**
pochard .... **SMEE**
pocket billiards .... **POOL**
pocket gopher, Mex. .... **TUZA**
pod, cotton .... **BOLL**
pods for tanning .... **PIPI**
Poe poem .... **RAVEN**
poem .... **ODE, ELEGY, EPODE**
poem division, or part . **CANTO**
poem, 8 line .... **TRIOLET**

a poem, long heroic .. **EPIC, EPOS**
poem, love .... **SONNET**
poem, lyric ...... **ODE, EPODE**
poem, mournful .... **ELEGY**
poem, of a .... **ODIC**
poem, old Fr. .... **DIT**
poem, sacred .... **PSALM**
poet .... **BARD, ODIST**
poet, A.-S. .... **SCOP**
poet, Bengal .... **TAGORE**
poet, blind, epic ..... **HOMER**
poet, lyric .... **ODIST**
poet, Norse ... **SCALD, SKALD**
poet, poor .... **RIMER**
poetry .... **EPOS, POESY**
poetry, early .... **RUNE**
poetry, Finnish .... **RUNES**
poetry, mournful, pert. to **ELEGIAC**
poetry, Norse god of **BRAGE, BRAGI**
poi, source of .... **TARO**
point **END, TIP, BARB, PUNTO**
point in moon's orbit nearest earth .... **PERIGEE**
point of curve .... **NODE**
point of land .... **SPIT**
point of moon .... **CUSP**
point of view .... **ANGLE**
b point on mariner's compass **RUMB**
point on tooth's crown .. **CUSP**
point, tennis or golf .... **ACE**
point won .... **GOAL**
pointed ..... **SHARP, ACUATE**
pointed arch .... **OGEE**
pointed end .... **CUSP**
pointed missile **DART, SPEAR**
pointed remark .... **BARB**
pointed staff .... **PIKE**
pointer .... **WAND**
pointless .... **INANE**
poison .... **BANE, TAINT**
poison, arrow ... **INEE, UPAS, URALI, URARE, URARI, CURARE, CURARI**
poison, hemlock ..... **CONINE**
poison, India **BISH, BISK, BIKH**
poisonous protein **RICIN, RICINE**
poisonous weed .... **LOCO**
poke ..... **JAB, PROD, NUDGE**
poker stake ...... **POT, ANTE**
pokeweed ..... **POCAN, SCOKE**
Polar explorer .... **BYRD**
pole .... **MAST**
pole, Gaelic games **CABER, CABIR**
Pole .... **SLAV**
pole, naut. .... **MAST, SPRIT**
pole to handle fish .... **PEW**
pole to pole, from **AXAL, AXIAL**

c polecat, Cape **ZORIL, ZORILLA**
police line .... **CORDON**
policeman ...... **COP, PEELER**
policeman, state .... **TROOPER**
policeman, S. Afr. ...... **ZARP**
polish .... **RUB, WAX, SHINE, LEVIGATE**
POLISH ... see also POLAND SPECIAL SECTION
Polish assembly ... **SEIM, SEJM**
Polish cake .... **BABA**
Polish general .. **BOR, ANDERS**
Polish title of address **PAN, PANI**
polished .... **SHINY, SLEEK, URBANE, ELEGANT**
polisher .... **EMERY**
polishing material **RABAT, ROUGE**
polite .... **CIVIL**
political booty .... **GRAFT**
pollack fish .... **SEY**
pollen brush .. **SCOPA, SCOPAE**
Pollux or Castor .... **ANAX**
Pollux' mother .... **LEDA**
Pollux' twin .... **CASTOR**
polo stick .... **MALLET**
Polynesian .... **MAORI**
Polyn. "Adam" .... **TIKI**
Polyn. chestnut .... **RATA**
d Polyn. cloth .... **TAPA**
Polyn. dance .... **SIVA**
Polyn. deity, demon **AKUA, ATUA**
Polyn. drink .... **AVA**
Polyn. for nature's power **MANA**
Polyn. god .... **ATEO**
Polyn. god of forest .... **TANE**
Polyn. herb .... **PIA**
Polyn. hero .... **MAUI**
Polyn. island group ... **SAMOA**
Polyn. languages **MAORI, MAHORI**
Polyn. lily .... **TI**
Polyn. stone heap .... **AHU**
pome .... **APPLE**
"Pomp and Circumstance" Composer .... **ELGAR**
pompous .... **TURGID**
pond .. **MERE, POOL, LOCHAN**
ponder .... **MUSE, PORE**
pontiff .... **POPE**
pony .... **CAVY**
pony, student's .... **CRIB**
pool .... **MERE, TARN, LAGOON, PUDDLE**
pool: Scot. .... **DIB, CARR, LINN, LLYN**
poon tree **DILO, DOMBA, KEENA**
poor .... **NEEDY**
poor joe .... **HERON**

a poor player .... **DUB**
poorly .... **ILL**
POPE .. see also PAPAL
Pope ... **JOHN, PIUS, ADRIAN**
Pope, English .... **ADRIAN**
Pope John XXIII first name **ANGELO**
Pope John XXIII last name **RONCALLI**
Pope Pius XI .... **RATTI**
Pope Pius XII .... **PACELLI**
POPE'S CAPE, COLLAR ... see PAPAL CAPE, COLLAR
Pope's triple crown **TIAR, TIARA**
poplar .... **ALAMO, ASPEN**
poplar, white ... **ABELE, ASPEN**
poppy red .... **GRANATE**
poppy seed .... **MAW**
populace, the .... **DEMOS**
popular girl .... **BELLE**
porcelain **CHINA, SEVRES, LIMOGES**
porcelain, ancient .... **MURRA**
porcelain, Chin. .... **JU, KO**
porcelain, Eng. .... **SPODE**
porch .... **ANTA, STOOP, VERANDA, VERANDAH**
porch, Gr. .... **STOA**
porch, Hawaiian ...... **LANAI**
b porch swing .... **GLIDER**
porcupine anteater .. **ECHIDNA**
porcupine, Canada .... **URSON**
pore .... **PORUS, STOMA, OSTIOLE, STOMATA**
porgy .... **SCUP**
porgy, Europ. .... **PARGO**
porgy genus .... **PAGRUS**
porgy, Jap. (Oriental) .... **TAI**
porkfish .... **SISI**
porous rock ..... **TUFA, TUFF**
porpoise .... **DOLPHIN**
porridge .... **POB, BROSE**
porridge, corn meal ..... **SAMP**
porridge: Sp. Am. ..... **ATOLE**
Porsena of Clusium ..... **LARS**
PORT .. see also SPECIAL SECTION — GAZETTEER
port .... **HAVEN**
port, banana, Hondurus .. **TELA**
port, Black Sea .... **ODESSA**
Port Moresby land ... **PAPUA**
port of Rome .... **OSTIA**
port opp. Gibraltar .... **CEUTA**
port, South Seas .... **APIA**
port, Suez .... **SAID**
port wine city .... **OPORTO**
portable chair .... **SEDAN**
portal .... **DOOR, GATE**
portend **BODE, AUGUR, PRESAGE**

c portent .... **OMEN, SIGN**
porter, Orient **HAMAL, HAMMAL**
Portia's waiting woman **NERISSA**
portico .... **STOA**
portion. **PART, SOME, SEGMENT**
portion out **DOLE, METE, ALLOT**
portray .... **DRAW, LIMN, DEPICT, DELINEATE**
Portuguese coin .... **REI**
Port. colony, India ...... **GOA**
Port. folk tune .... **FADO**
Port. lady .... **DONA**
Port. man .... **DOM**
Port. navigator .... **GAMA**
Port. title ..... **DOM, DONNA**
pose .... **SIT**
Poseidon .... **NEPTUNE**
Poseidon's son .... **TRITON**
posited .... **SET**
position ...... **SITUS, STATUS**
position without work **SINECURE**
positive .... **THETIC**
positive pole, terminal **ANODE**
possession, landed .... **ESTATE**
possum .... **COON**
possum, comic-strip ..... **POGO**
post .... **MAIL, SEND**
post-hole digger (slick) ... **LOY**
d postpone .... **DEFER**
postulate .... **POSIT**
posture .... **STANCE**
pot .... **OLLA**
pot, chem. .... **ALUDEL**
pot, earthen .... **CRUSE**
pot herb .... **WORT**
pot, India **LOTA, LOTO, LOTAH**
pot liquor .... **BREWIS**
pot metal .... **POTIN**
potassium .... **KALITE**
potassium chloride .. **MURIATE**
potassium nitrate **NITER, GROUGH**
potation, small .... **DRAM**
potato .... **SPUD**
potato, sweet .. **YAM, BATATA**
pother .... **ADO**
potpourri .... **OLIO**
potter's blade .... **PALLET**
pottery fragment .... **SHARD**
pottery, pert. to .... **CERAMIC**
pouch .... **SAC**
pouch-shaped ...... **SACCATE**
poultry .... **HENS, BIRDS**
poultry disease .... **PIP, ROUP**
pounce .... **SWOOP**
pound .... **TUND**
pound down ...... **RAM, TAMP**
pour .... **RAIN, TEEM**
pour off gently ...... **DECANT**

a pour out .... **LIBATE**
poverty .... **NEED, WANT**
powder, astringent .... **BORAL**
powder, mineral ingredient **TALC**
powder of aloes .... **PICRA**
powdered pumice .... **TALC**
power .. **DINT, MANA, FORCE**
practical joke .... **HOAX**
practice .... **HABIT**
practice exercise, musical **ETUDE**
praise **LAUD, EXTOL, EXTOLL**
prance .... **CAPER**
prank .... **DIDO, CAPER**
prate .... **GAB, YAP**
prate: India ..... **BUKH, BUKK**
pray: Yiddish .... **DAVEN**
prayer **AVE, BEAD, BENE, PLEA, CREDO, MATIN, ORISON**
prayer form .... **LITANY**
prayer, 9-day ...... **NOVENA**
prayer-rug, Hindu ..... **ASANA**
prayer stick, Am. Ind. **BAHO, PAHO, PAJO**
prayers, deacon's **ECTENE, EKTENE**
prayerbook **ORDO, PORTAS, PORTASS**
praying figure .... **ORANT**
preacher, Gospel .... **EVANGEL**
b precepts .... **DICTA**
precipice, Hawaii .... **PALI**
precipitous .... **STEEP**
preclude ...... **AVERT, DEBAR**
preconceive .... **IDEATE**
predicament .... **SCRAPE**
predicate **BASE, FOUND, AFFIRM**
predict **AUGUR, FORECAST, FORETELL**
predisposed .... **PRONE**
preen .... **PLUME, PRINK**
preface .... **PROEM**
prefecture, Jap. .... **KEN**
PREFIX:
about .... **PERI**
above .... **HYPER**
across .... **DIA, TRANS**
again .... **RE**
against .... **ANTI**
ahead .... **PRE**
an .... **AE**
apart .... **DIS**
away .... **DE, DI, APO**
back .... **ANA**
backward .... **RETRO**
bad .... **MAL**
badly .... **MIS**
beauty .... **CALLI**
before ..... **OB, PRE, ANTE**
blood .... **HAEM, HEMO**
c both .... **AMBI**
CHEMICALS .. see page 29
common .... **PRE**
distant .... **TEL, TELE**
double .... **DI**
down .... **DE, CATA**
eight ... **OCT, OCTA, OCTO**
equal .... **ISO**
far .... **TEL, TELE**
faulty .... **MIS**
fire .... **PYR**
former, formerly .... **EX**
four .... **TETRA**
from .... **EC**
half ..... **DEMI, HEMI, SEMI**
ill .... **MIS**
mountain .... **ORO**
negative .... **IR, NON**
new .... **NEO**
not ... **IL, IM, IR, UN, NON**
not fully .... **SEMI**
numerical .... **UNI**
of atmospheric pressure **BARO**
of the stars .... **ASTRO**
on this side .... **CIS**
one .... **UNI**
out of .... **EC, EX**
d outer ..... **ECT, EXO, ECTO**
outer skin .... **EPI**
outside .... **ECT, EXO**
over .... **EPI, SUPER, SUPRA, SUPERB**
partly .... **SEMI**
people .... **DEMO**
pray .... **ORA**
recent .... **NEO**
same .... **ISO, EQUI, HOMO**
separation .... **DIS**
single .... **MONO**
ten .... **DEC, DECA**
thousand .... **KILO**
three .... **TER, TRI**
thrice .... **TER, TRIS**
threefold .... **TRI**
through .... **DIA, PER**
to .... **AP**
together .... **COM**
town .... **TRE**
turning .... **ROTO**
twice .... **BI**
two .... **DI, DUA**
twofold .... **DI**
under .... **SUB**
upon .... **EPI**
upward .... **ANA, ANO**
with .... **SYN**
within .... **ENDO**
wrong .... **MIS**

a prehistoric implement ... CELT
prehistoric mound ...... TERP
prejudice .... BIAS
prelate, high .... PRIMATE
prelude .... PROEM
premium, exchange ..... AGIO
prepare .... FIT, GIRD, MAKE, ADAPT, EQUIP
prepare for publication .. EDIT
prepared opium CHANDU, CHANDOO
preposition ...... AT, IN, ON, UP, INTO
presage OMEN, HERALD, PORTEND
prescribed .... THETIC
prescribed quantity ..... DOSE
present .. GIFT, GIVE, DONATE
present, be .... ATTEND
present in brief .... SUM
presently. ANON, ENOW, SOON
preserve .... CAN, JAM, KEEP, SAVE, PROTECT, MAINTAIN
preserve in brine .. CORN, SALT
Presidential nickname ... ABE, CAL, IKE, TEDDY
press together .... SERRY
pressure .... DURESS
pressure unit .. BARAD, BARIE
pretend .. FAKE, SHAM, FEIGN
b pretense .... SHAM
pretensions .... AIRS
pretentious .... SIDY
prevail .... WIN
prevail on .... INDUCE
prevalent .... RIFE
prevent ... DETER, PRECLUDE
prevent by law .... ESTOP
prey .... RAVIN
prey upon RAVEN, RAVIN, RAVINE
Priam's son PARIS, HECTOR, HEKTOR
price .... RATE
price of transportation .. FARE
prickle .... SETA
prickles .... SETAE
prickly pear TUNA, NOPAL, CACTUS
prickly plant ... BRIAR, BRIER, NETTLE
prickly seed coat .. BUR, BURR
pride .... PLUME
PRIEST .. see also CLERGYMAN
priest FRA, ABBE, CURE, PADRE
priest, Celtic .... DRUID
priest, Gr. .... MYST

c PRIEST, HIGH, see HIGH PRIEST
priest in "Iliad" .... CALCHAS
priest, Mongol ...... SHAMAN
priest, Moro SARIP, PANDITA
priestess, Gr. .... AUGE
priestess, Rom. ...... VESTAL
priesthood, Rom. ...... SALII
priestly caste ... MAGI, MAGUS
prima donna .... DIVA
PRIMA DONNA ...... see also OPERA SOPRANO
prime minister: Brit. ... EDEN, PEEL
primeval .... OLD, EARLY, PRIMAL, PRISTINE
prince, Abyssin. .... RAS
prince, Arabian .. EMIR, SAYID, SAYYID, SHERIF, SHEREEF
prince, India RAJA, RANA, RAJAH
prince of Argos ...... DANAE
Prince of Darkness .... SATAN
prince, Oriental .... KHAN
prince, Persian .. AMIR, AMEER
prince, petty .... SATRAP
prince, Slavic .... KNEZ
Prince Val's father ... AGUAR
princeling .... SATRAP
princely .... ROYAL
princess, Gr. myth ...... IOLE
princess, India .. RANI, RANEE
d principal .... TOP, ARCH MAIN, CHIEF
principal commodity .. STAPLE
principle, accepted AXIOM, PRANA, TENET
print .... STAMP
print measure .... EM, EN
printer, 1st colonial .... DAYE
printer's direction ...... STET
printer's mark .... DELE
printer's mistake TYPO, ERRATUM
printer's mistakes .... ERRATA
printing plate .... STEREO
printing roller .... PLATEN
prison. JUG, GAOL, JAIL, QUOD
prison sentence .... RAP
prison spy .... MOUTON
privation .... LOSS
privilege, commercial .. OCTROI
prize .... PRY, AWARD
pro .... FOR
"— pro nobis" .... ORA
probe, medical .... STYLET
problem .... POSER
proboscis .... SNOUT
proboscis monkey ...... KAHA
proceed ... WEND, ADVANCE
proceedings .... ACTA

a procession .... **TRAIN, PARADE, MOTORCADE**
proclaim .... **CRY, VOICE, HERALD, DECLARE**
prod .... **URGE**
produce .... **BEGET, YIELD CREATE, INWORK, GENERATE**
produce as an effect ... **BEGET**
produced, quantity ..... **YIELD**
producing cold ...... **ALGIFIC**
production, artistic .. **FACTURE**
profane .... **VIOLATE**
profane, Hawaiian ...... **NOA**
profession **ART, CAREER, METIER**
professional, not **LAIC, LAICAL**
profit ... **GAIN, VAIL, AVAIL**
profit, to yield .... **NET**
profits, taker of: law . **PERNOR**
profitable ...... **FAT, USEFUL**
profound .... **DEEP**
"— profundis" .... **DE**
progenitor ..... **SIRE, PARENT**
progeny .... **ISSUE**
prohibit .... **BAN, BAR, VETO, DEBAR, ESTOP**
prohibition **BAN, VETO, EMBARGO**
Prohibition, against ...... **WET**
project ...... **JUT, IDEA, PLAN**
b projectile .... **MISSILE**
projecting edge **RIM, FLANGE**
projecting piece **ARM, RIM, TENON, FLANGE**
projecting rim .... **FLANGE**
projecting tooth .... **SNAG**
projection . **EAR, BARB, PRONG**
projection, fireplace . **HOB, HOBB**
projection, jagged **SNAG, TOOTH**
projection, studlike .... **KNOP**
promenade .... **MALL**
promise .... **WORD**
promise to pay .... **IOU, NOTE**
"Promised Land" fountain **AIN**
promontory ..... **CAPE, NASE, NAZE, NESS**
promontory, Orkneys .... **NOUP**
promontory, rocky ...... **TOR**
promote .... **FOSTER**
prompt .... **CUE, YARE**
prone .... **APT, FLAT**
prong .... **TINE, TOOTH**
pronghorn .... **CABREE, CABRET, CABRIE, CABRIT**
pronoun .. **IT, ME, US, WE, YE, HER, HIM, ONE, SHE, THAT, THIS, THEE, THEM, THEY, THOU, THESE, THOSE**

c pronoun, possessive . **MY, HER, HIS, ITS, OUR, HERS, MINE, OURS, YOUR**
pronounce indistinctly ... **SLUR**
pronounce strongly .... **STRESS**
pronouncement **DICTA, DICTUM**
proof, corrected ...... **REVISE**
proof, printer's .... **GALLEY**
proofreader's mark **DELE, STET, CARET**
prop .... **HOLD, STAY, BRACE, BOLSTER, SUSTAIN**
propeller .... **OAR**
proper .... **DUE, FIT**
properly .... **FEATLY**
property, hold on .... **LIEN**
property, India .... **DHAN**
property, item of **ASSET, CHATTEL**
property, landed ...... **ESTATE**
property owned absolutely **ALOD, ALLOD, ALODIUM, ALLODIUM**
property, receiver of .. **ALIENEE**
prophesy .... **FORETELL**
prophet .... **SEER, AUGUR, PREDICTOR, FORETELLER**
PROPHETS, BIBLICAL ..... see SPECIAL SECTION
prophets .... **VATES**
d prophetic ... **VATIC, VATICAL**
proportion .... **RATIO**
proportionally assess **PRORATE**
proposition **THESES, THESIS, PREMISE**
proposition, logic ..... **LEMMA**
proposition: math. .. **THEOREM**
prosecutor .... **SUER**
prosecutor: abbr. .... **DA**
proselyte to Judaism .... **GER**
"— prosequi," .... **NOLLE**
Proserpina ...... **CORA, KORE**
prospect .... **VISTA**
prosperity .... **WEAL**
prosperity god, Teut. .... **FREY**
Prospero's servant ..... **ARIEL**
prostrate .... **PRONE, REPENT**
protagonist .... **HERO**
protected .... **HOUSED**
protection .... **EGIS, AEGIS**
protection right, Old Eng. **MUND**
protective building .... **REDAN**
protective influence **EGIS, AEGIS**
Protestant denomination: abbr. **ME, PE, BAP, PRESB**
prototype .... **IDEAL**
protozoan order .... **LOBOSA**
protuberance .... **JAG, NUB, HUMP, KNOB, KNOT, NODE, WART, KNURL, TORUS**

a protuberant .... TOROSE
prove: law .... DERAIGN
proverb ...... SAW, ADAGE, AXIOM, MAXIM, SAYING
provide ...... ENDOW, ENDUE
provided .... IF
provided that .... SO
province, Rom. .... DACIA
provisional clause ... PROVISO
proviso .... CLAUSE
provoke............ IRE, RILE, ANGER, ANNOY
prow .... BOW, STEM
prune: prov. Eng. ...... SNED
pruning knife .... DHAW
Prussian spa, town ...... EMS
pry .... NOSE, LEVER, SNOOP
Psalm, 51st .... MISERERE
Psalmist .... DAVID
Psalms, selection of .. HALLEL
Psalms, word in .... SELAH
pseudonym ...... NOM, ALIAS
pseudonym of Louise Del La Ramee .... OUIDA
psyche .... SOUL
psychiatrist JUNG, ADLER, FREUD
Ptah, embodiment of ... APIS
ptarmigan .... RYPE
b pteropod genus ...... CLIONE
pua hemp .... POOA
public .... OPEN, OVERT
public: Chin. .... KUNG
public esteem .... REPUTE
public, make ... AIR, DELATE
public vehicle .... BUS, TAXI
publication, style of . FORMAT
publish .... ISSUE, PRINT
publish illegally ...... PIRATE
Puccini heroine .... MIMI
puck, hockey .... RUBBER
pudding......... DUFF, SAGO
pueblo dweller .... HOPI
Pueblo Indian ... HOPI, ZUNI, KERES, MOQUI, TANOA
Pueblo sacred chamber .. KIVA
Pueblo, Tanoan .... HANO
Puerto Rican plant ...... APIO
puff up .... ELATE
puffbird, Brazil .... DREAMER
puffbird genus ..... MONASA
puffer fish .... TAMBOR
Pulitzer poet .... FROST
pull .. TOW, TUG, DRAG, HALE
pull with nautical tackle BOUSE
pulley .... SHEAVE
pulp, fruit .... POMACE
pulpit .... AMBO, BEMA
pulpy mass left in cider POMACE
pulverize .... MICRONIZE
c pump handle .... SWIPE
pumpkin .... PEPO
punch .... JAB
"Punch and Judy" dog .. TOBY
punch, engraver's .. MATTOIR
punctuation mark DASH, COLON
pungent .. TEZ, SPICY, TANGY
punish by fine ...... AMERCE
punishment .... FERULE
punishment, of .... PENAL
punitive .... PENAL
Punjab native .... JAT
punk .... AMADOU
pupa .... INSTAR
pupil of eye .... GLENE
puppet .... DOLL
puppet, famous JUDY, PUNCH
puppeteer, famous ...... SARG
pure sirup .... CLAIRCE
pure thought .... NOESIS
purification, ancient Roman LUSTRUM
purloin .... STEAL
purple MAUVE, MODENA, TYRIAN
purple dye source .... MUREX
purple medic LUCERN, ALFALFA, LUCERNE
purple ragwort ...... JACOBY
purple seaweed . SION, LAVER
d purport, general ...... TENOR
purpose .... AIM, END, GOAL, SAKE, INTENT
purposive .... TELIC
purse net .... SEINE
pursy .... STOUT
push up .... BOOST
put aside .... DAFF
put away .... STORE
put back .... REPLACE
put forth .... EXERT
put in bank .... DEPOSIT
put off .... DEFER
put out .... OUST, EJECT
put up .... ANTE
puzzle .... POSER, REBUS, BAFFLE, ACROSTIC
puzzles .... CRUCES
Pygmalion's statue .. GALATEA
pygmy .... ATOMY
pygmy people, Congo AKKA, ACHUAS
pygmy people, Equatorial Africa BATWA, ABONGO, OBONGO
Pylos, kin of .... NESTOR
Pyramus, lover of .... THISBE
pyromaniac .... FIREBUG
Pythias' friend .... DAMON
python .... BOA

Q

a qua .... **AS**
"— qua non" .... **SINE**
quack **IMPOSTOR, CHARLATAN**
quack medicine .... **NOSTRUM**
quadrant .... **ARC**
quadrate .... **SQUARE**
"quae —" which see .... **VIDE**
quaff .... **DRINK**
quail .... **COLIN, COWER**
quake .... **SHAKE, SHIVER, TREMOR, TREMBLE**
Quaker .... **FRIEND**
Quaker Poet .... **WHITTIER**
quaking .... **TREPID**
qualify .... **FIT, ADAPT, EQUIP, PREPARE**
qualified .... **FIT, ABLE**
quality .... **CALIBER, CALIBRE**
quantity, indeterminate . **SOME**
quantity: math. **SCALER, VECTOR**

b quarrel .... **ROW, FEUD, SPAT, TIFF**
quarter of a year: Scot. **RAITH**
quartz .... **JASPER**
quartz, green .... **PRASE**
quartz, translucent ... **PRASE**
quash: law .... **CASSARE**
quaternion .... **TETRAD**
quay .... **LEVEE**
Quebec, district, town ... **LEVIS**
Quebec's patron saint .. **ANNE**
Queen .... **CLEO**
queen: Moslem **BEGUM, BEEGUM**
queen of gods, Egypt. ... **SATI**
queen of gods, Rom. ... **HERA, JUNO**
Queen of Italy .... **ELENA**
Queen of Ithaca ... **PENELOPE**
Queen of Roumania ... **MARIE**
Queen of Scots .... **MARY**
Queen of Spain, last ..... **ENA**
queen, "Romeo and Juliet" **MAB**

c queenly .... **REGAL, REGINAL**
Queensland hemp plant **SIDA**
Queensland tribe .... **GOA**
quell .... **CALM, CRUSH**
quench .... **SLAKE**
quench steel ..... **AUSTEMPER**
quern .... **MILL**
query .... **ASK**
queue .... **LINE**
question .... **ASK, GRILL**
question, hard .... **POSER**
quetzal .... **TROGON**
quibble .... **CAVIL, EVADE**
quick .... **FAST, AGILE, ALIVE, RAPID**
quick: music .... **TOSTO**
quicken ... **HASTEN, ENLIVEN**
quickly .... **CITO, APACE, PRESTO, PRONTO**
quickly, move **SCAT, SCUD, SKITE**
quicksilver ...... **HEAUTARIT**
quid .... **CUD**

d "quid — quo," equivalent . **PRO**
quiescent **LATENT, DORMANT**
quiet .... **CALM, LULL, STILL, SMOOTH**
quiet! .... **SH, PST, TST**
quilkin .... **FROG, TOAD**
quill .... **PEN, SPINE**
quill feathers **REMEX, REMIGES**
quill for winding silk ..... **COP**
quilt .... **EIDER, COVER**
quince, Bengal .... **BEL, BHEL**
quinine .... **KINA**
quintessence ... **PITH, ELIXIR**
quirt, cowboy's ...... **ROMAL**
quit .... **CEASE, LEAVE**
quite .... **ALL**
quivering ... **ASPEN, TREMOR**
"quod — demonstrandum" **ERAT**
"Quo Vadis" tyrant character **NERO**
quoits, mark of .... **MOT**
quote .... **CITE**

R

a Ra, consort of .... **MUT**
Ra, son of .... **SU, SHU**
rabbi, law-teaching ... **AMORA**
rabbit cage .... **HUTCH**
rabbit, Europ. . **CONY, CONEY**
rabbit, female .... **DOE**
rabbit fur .... **LAPIN**
rabbit home .... **WARREN**
rabbit, small swamp .. **TAPETI**
rabbit, So. Am. .... **TAPETI**
rabble .... **MOB**
rabies .... **LYSSA**
raccoon-like mammal .. **COATI**
RACE .. see also TRIBES in SPECIAL SECTION
race, boat .... **REGATTA**
race, kind of .... **RELAY**
race, short .... **SPRINT**
race-track .... **OVAL**
race-track circuit ...... **LAP**
race-track tipster ...... **TOUT**
races, pert. to ...... **ETHNIC**
Rachel's father ...... **LABAN**
racing boat .... **GIG**
racket, game .... **PELOTA**
radar screen .... **SCOPE**
radiate .... **EMANATE**
b radical .... **RED**
radicle .... **STEMLET**
radio advertiser .... **SPONSOR**
radio bulletin ..... **NEWSCAST**
radio-guided bomb ..... **AZON**
radio wave ..... **MICROWAVE**
radio wire .... **LITZ**
radio-TV awards ..... **EMMIES**
radioactive counter .. **GEIGER**
radioactive element ... **NITON**
radioactive ray ...... **GAMMA**
radium discoverer ...... **CURIE**
radium emanation .... **NITON**
radius, pert. to ...... **RADIAL**
radon .... **NITON**
raft, kind of ... **CATAMARAN**
raft, Maori .... **MOKI**
rag doll .... **MOPPET**
rage .... **RAMP, RANT, RESE, STORM**
ragged person: Sp. ...... **ROTO**
raging monster, Bibl. .. **RAHAB**
ragout, game .... **SALMI**
ragweed genus .... **IVA**
raid .... **FORAY, INROAD**
raid, soldier's .... **COMMANDO**
rail at .... **REVILE**
rail bird **SORA, WEKA, CRAKE**
railing .... **PARAPET**
c railroad bridge ...... **TRESSEL, TRESTLE**
railroad light .... **FLARE**
railroad signal **TRIMMER, SEMAPHORE**
railroad tie .... **SLEEPER**
railroad timber .... **TIE**
railway station: Fr. ..... **GARE**
rain after sunset ...... **SEREIN**
rain, fine .... **MISLE**
rain forest .... **SELVA**
rain gauge .... **UDOMETER**
rain serpent, Hindu .... **NAGA**
rain spout: Scot. ...... **RONE**
rain tree .... **SAMAN**
rainbow .... **ARC, IRIS**
rainbow goddess .... **IRIS**
rainbow, pert. to ..... **IRIDAL**
raincoat .... **PONCHO**
rainy .... **WET**
raise . **REAR, BREED, ELEVATE**
raised .... **BRED**
raisin: Sp. .... **PASA**
raising device .... **JACK**
Rajah's lady ... **RANI, RANEE**
rake ...... **ROUE, LOTHARIO**
d rake with gunfire .. **ENFILADE**
ram . **TUP, BUTT, TAMP, ARIES**
ram, male .... **TUP**
ram-headed god, Egypt **AMEN, AMON, AMUN**
Ramachandra, wife of .. **SITA**
ramble .... **GAD, ROVE**
Ramee, de la, penname . **OUIDA**
rammed earth building material **PISE**
rampart ..... **AGGER, VALLUM**
range .... **AREA, GAMUT, SCOPE, SIERRA**
Rangoon's state .... **PEGU**
rank .... **ROW, RATE, DEGREE**
ranks, press in .... **SERRY**
rankle .... **FESTER**
ransom .... **REDEEM**
rapeseed ..... **COLSA, COLZA**
rapid, more: music .. **STRETTA, STRETTE, STRETTI, STRETTO**
rapids, river .... **SOO**
rapidly .... **APACE**
rapier .... **BILBO**
rare earth element ... **ERBIUM**
rascal .... **IMP, ROGUE**
rase .... **INCISE**
rasorial .... **GNAWING**
rasp .... **FILE, GRATE**

a raspberry, variety . BLACKCAP
rasse .... CIVET
rat .... DESERTER
rat, Ceylon, India . BANDICOOT
rat hare .... PIKA
rate .... ESTIMATE
rate, relative .... AT
ratify .... SEAL
ratio .... RATE
RATIO: MATH see MATH, RATIO
rational .... SANE
rational integer .... NORM
rational principle ...... LOGOS
rationalize .... THOB
ratite bird ...... CASSOWARY
rattan .... CANE
rattlesnake
RATTLER, CROTALUS
rave .... RANT
"Raven" author .... POE
"Raven" character .... LENORE
ravine
GAP, DALE, VALE, GORGE
ravine, Afr. .... WADI, WADY
ravine, Arabia .. WADI, WADY
rawboned .... LEAN
rawboned animal ...... SCRAG
ray fish .... SKATE
rays, like .... RADIAL
rayon ... ACETATE, CELANESE
b raze .... DEVASTATE
razor-billed auk
ALCA, MURR, MURRE
reach across .... SPAN
react .... RESPOND
read, inability to ..... ALEXIA
read metrically .... SCAN
read publically ...... PRELECT
reader, first .... PRIMER
reading desk .... AMBO
reading substituted: Bibl.
KERE, KERI
ready: dialect .... YARE
ready-made tie .... TECK
real being, pert. to .... ONTAL
real thing .... MCCOY
reality .... FACT
realm .... DOMAIN
reamer .... BROACH
rear ... ERECT, RAISE, ARRIERE
rear, to the
AFT, ABAFT, ASTERN
rearhorse .... MANTIS
rearing of horse ...... PESADE
reason .... NOUS
reason, deprive of ... DEMENT
reasoning .... LOGIC
reasoning, deductive .. APRIORI
reata
LAZO, ROPE, LASSO, LARIAT

c rebec of India .... SAROD
Rebecca's hairy son ..... ESAU
rebound .. CAROM, RICOCHET
rebuff .... SLAP, SNUB
rebuke
CHIDE, SCOLD, REPROVE
recalcitrant .... RENITENT
recant .... RETRACT
recede .... EBB
recent
NEO, NEW, LATE, NEOTERIC
receptacle .... BIN, BOX,
TRAY, VESSEL
reception, a.m. .... LEVEE
reception: Fr. .... ACCUEIL
reception, India ..... DURBAR
recess .... APSE, ALCOVE
recess, wall .... NICHE
recipient .... DONEE
recite metrically .... SCAN
reckon .... ARET, COUNT
reckoning .... TALLY
reclaim .... REDEEM
recline .... LOLL
recluse .... ASCETIC, EREMITE,
ANCHORET, ANCHORITE
recoil .... SHY, RESILE
recommit .... REMAND
recompense .. PAY, FEES, MEED
reconnaissance RECCO, RECON
d reconnoiter .... SCOUT
reconstruct .... REMODEL
record .. TAB, NOTE, ENROL,
ENTER, ENTRY, REGISTER
record of investigation REPORT
record, ship's .... LOG
record, year's .... ANNAL
records .... ANNALS
recorded proceedings ... ACTA
recording device .... TAPE
records, one who ..... NOTER
recourse, have .... REFER
recover strength ...... RALLY
recovery, legal .... TROVER
recruit .... BOOT
rectifier, current ...... DIODE
rectify ...... AMEND, EMEND
recurring pattern ..... CYCLE
red .... CARMINE,
MAGENTA, NACARAT
red, Brazil .... ROSET
red cedar .... SAVIN, SAVINE
red circle: Her. .... GUZE
red currant .... RISSEL
red deer .... ELAPHINE
red dye root ... CHAY, CHOY
red garden flower .... CANNA
red: Her. .... GULES
red horse .... BAY, ROAN
red ocher .... KEEL, KIEL,
TIVER, RADDLE, RUDDLE

a red pigment .... ROSET, ASTACIN, ASTACENE
red pine .... RIMU
red planet .... MARS
red powder, India .... ABIR
red, painter's .... ROSET
Red River Rebellion leader RIEL
red: Sp. .... ROJO
red squirrel ...... CHICKAREE
red swine .... DUROC
red, Venetian .... SIENA
red-yellow color ...... ALOMA
redact .... EDIT
redbreast .... ROBIN
redcap .... PORTER
reddish yellow .... SUDAN
redeem .... RANSOM
redshank .... CLEE
reduce .... PARE, DEMOTE
reduce sail .... REEF
reduce taxes .... DERATE
reebok .... PEELE
reedbuck .... NAGOR
reek .... FUG, FUME
reef .... SHOAL
reel, fishing-rod .... PIRN
refer .... PERTAIN
refer to repeatedly ..... HARP
refined grace ...... ELEGANCE
b reflection .... GLARE
refracting device .... LENS
refractor, light .... PRISM
refrain .... FORBEAR
refrain in songs .. FALA, LALA, DERRY, LUDDEN
refrigerant .... FREON
refuge ...... HAVEN, SHELTER
refugee .... EMIGREE
refuse .... DENY
refuse .... ORT, DROSS, SCUM, OFFAL, TRASH
refuse, bit of .... SCRAP
refuse, flax .... POB
refuse: law .... RECUSE
refuse, metal . DROSS, SCORIA
refuse, wool .... COT
refute .... REBUT, DISPROVE
regale .... FETE
regard ...... ESTEEM, RESPECT
regarding .... RE, ANENT
regenerate .... RENEW
regiment's framework .. CADRE
REGION .... see also DISTRICT
region .... CLIME, SECTOR
region, Afr. .. CONGO, NUBIA
region, Boeotia ...... AONIA
region, Cent. Afr. SUDAN, SOUDAN
region, Fr. .... ALSACE
c region, Gr. .... DORIC
region, Indo-China ..... LAOS
region, pert. to .... AREAL
register .... ENROL, ENROLL, RECORD
reiterate .... REPEAT
regret .... RUE, DEPLORE
reign: India .... RAJ
reign, pert. to .... REGNAL
reigning .... REGNANT
reigning beauty .... BELLE
reimbursed .... PAID
reindeer .... CARIBOU
reindeer, Santa's .... DASHER, DONDER, BLITZEN, PRANCER
reinstate .... REVEST
reject .... SPURN, REPULSE
relate .... TELL, RECITE, NARRATE
related .... AKIN, TOLD, COGNATE, GERMANE
related by blood .... SIB
related on mother's side ENATE
relation .... SIB
relative. SIB, SIS, AUNT, NIECE
relative amount ...... RATION
relative pronoun .... WHO, THAT, WHAT
relative speed .... TEMPO
d relatives .... KIN
relatives, favoring .. NEPOTAL
relax .... EASE
relaxing of state tensions DETENTE
relay of horses ..... REMUDA
release .... LOOSE
release: law .... REMISE
release, phonetic .... DETENTE
relevant .... GERMANE
reliable .... HONEST
relief, — .... BAS
relief .... DOLE
relieve .... EASE, ALLAY
relieve: Scot. .... LISS
religieuse .... NUN
religion .... FAITH
religion, Jap. .... SHINTO
religious art, work of .. PIETA
religious brother .... FRA, MONK, FRIAR
religious festival ..... EASTER
religious festival, India .. MELA
religious law, Rom. ...... FAS
religious laywoman .. BEGUINE
religious opinion .... DOXY
religious order, one in . OBLATE
religious sayings ...... LOGIA
relinquish .... CEDE, WAIVE, YIELD

a reliquary .... **APSE, ARCA, ARCAE, CHEST**
relish .... **GUSTO**
reluctant ..... **LOATH, AVERSE**
rely .... **TRUST**
remain .... **BIDE, STAY**
remainder .... **REST**
remaining .... **OVER**
remark, witty .... **MOT, SALLY**
remiss .... **LAX**
remit .... **SEND**
remnant .... **END, SHRED**
remora fish . **PEGA, LOOTSMAN**
remove .. **DELE, DOFF, DELETE**
remove interior .... **GUT**
remove: law .... **ELOIN, ELOIGN, ELOIGNE**
remunerate .... **PAY**
rend ...... **RIP, TEAR, WREST**
render fat .... **TRY**
rendezvous .... **TRYST**
renegade .... **APOSTATE**
renounce .... **ABNEGATE**
renovated hat ..... **MOLOKER**
renown .... **FAME, NOTE, EMINENCE, PRESTIGE**
rent .... **LET, HIRE, TEAR, TORN, LEASE**
rent, old Eng. law .... **TAC**
renter .... **LESSEE**
b repair .... **DARN, MEND**
repartee .... **RIPOST, RIPOSTE**
repast .... **MEAL**
repay .... **REQUITE**
repay in kind .... **RETALIATE**
repeat .... **ECHO, ITERATE**
repeat: music .... **BIS**
repeat performance .. **ENCORE**
repeat sign: music .... **SEGNO**
repeat tiresomely .. **DIN, DING**
repeated phrase ..... **REPRISE**
repeatedly hit ...... **POMMEL**
repetition .... **ROTE**
replete .... **FULL**
report, small .... **POP**
repose .... **EASE, REST**
representation .... **IDOL**
representative .... **AGENT**
reproach ..... **BLAME, TAUNT**
reproach, old term ..... **RACA**
reproductive body .. **GAMETE**
reproductive cell ...... **SPORE**
reptile, pert. to ..... **SAURIAN**
repulse .... **REPEL**
reputation .... **NAME, REPUTE**
repute .... **CHARACTER**
request .... **PLEA**
rescind .... **REPEAL**
resentment .... **IRE**
reserve supply .... **STORE**

c residence ..... **HOME, ABODE**
residence, ecclesiastical. **MANSE**
resident of .... **ITE**
resign .... **QUIT, DEMIT**
resin ..... **GUM, LAC, ANIME, COPAL, ELEMI, JALAP, MYRRH, BALSAM, MASTIC**
resin, fossil . **AMBER, GLESSITE**
resin, fragrant .... **ELEMI**
resist .... **OPPOSE**
resist authority .... **REBEL**
resisting pressure ... **RENITENT**
resistor, current ... **RHEOSTAT**
resort .... **SPA**
resort, Fr. .... **PAU, NICE, CANNES**
resources .... **FUND, MEANS, ASSETS**
respect .... **ESTEEM**
respond .... **REACT**
rest .... **SIT, EASE, REPOSE**
rest, lay at .... **REPOSE**
restaurant, small ..... **BISTRO**
resthouse ...... **CHAN, KHAN**
resting .... **ABED**
restive .... **BALKY**
restore .... **RENEW**
restrain .. **CURB, REIN, DETER, STINT, TETHER**
d restrict .... **LIMIT**
retaliate .... **REPAY**
retain .... **HOLD, KEEP**
retaliation .... **TALION**
retinue .... **SUITE, TRAIN**
retort, quick . **RIPOST, RIPOSTE**
retract .... **RECANT**
retreat .... **RECEDE**
retreat, cosy . **DEN, NEST, NOOK**
retribution .... **NEMESIS**
retribution, get .... **VENGE**
retrograde .... **RECEDE**
return ...... **RECUR, RESTORE**
return a profit .... **PAY**
return blow .... **TIT**
return on investment .. **YIELD**
returning .... **REDIENT**
reunion, hold a .... **REUNE**
reveille, call to .... **DIAN**
revelry, cry of .... **EVOE**
revelry, drunken .... **ORGY**
revenue, church: Scot. **ANNAT**
reverberate .... **ECHO**
reverberating ...... **REBOANT**
revere ...... **HONOR, HONOUR**
reverence .... **AWE**
reversed in order .. **CONVERSE**
reversion to type .... **ATAVISM**

a **revert to state (land)** ESCHEAT
revise .... EDIT, AMEND
revive wine .... STUM
revoke legacy, grant .. ADEEM
Revolution hero . HALE, ALLEN
revolutions per minute .. REVS
revolve . SPIN, TURN, ROTATE
revolve: logging .... BIRL
revolver. GAT, GUN, ROD, COLT
reward .... MEED
rhebok .... PEELE
Rhine city .... MAINZ
Rhine tributary .... AAR
rhinoceros beetle ...... UANG
rhinoceros, black BORELE, NASICORN
rhinoceros: obs. ABADA, ABATH
Rhone tributary ...... SAONE
rhythm .... TIME, METER, METRE, CADENCE
rhythmical accent ...... BEAT
rhythmical swing .... LILT
rib .... COSTA
rib. pert. to .... COSTAL
rib, woman from .... EVE
ribs, with .... COSTATE
ribbed fabric ..... REP, CORD, REPP, PIQUE
b ribbon, badge ...... CORDON
ribbon: comb. form ..... TENE
ribbonfish .... GUAPENA
rice .... PADI, PADDY
rice dish ...... PILAU, PILAW
rice field, Java .... PADI
rice grass, P.I. .... BARIT
rice in husk .... PALAY
rice paste, Jap. .... AME
rice polishings .... DARAC
rich man .... MIDAS, NABOB, NAWAB
rich silk cloth .... CAFFA
riches .... PELF
rid .... FREE
riddle .... ENIGMA
ridge .... ARETE, SPINE, MOUNTAIN
ridge, camp's .... RIDEAU
ridge, glacial, sandy ...... OS, OSAR, ESKER, OESAR
ridge on cloth .... WALE
ridge on skin .... WELT
ridge, stony .... RAND
ridges, rounded .... GYRI
ridged area, Balkan ..... BILO
ridicule .... GUY, MOCK, RAZZ, DERIDE
ridicule personified, Gr. MOMUS

c riding academy ..... MANEGE
riding dress .... HABIT
rifle .... KRAG, MINIE, GARAND, CARBINE
rifle ball .... MINIE
rifleman, Ger. .... JAGER
right conduct, Buddhist ... TAO
right conduct: Taoism ..... TE
right hand: music .... DM
right-hand page .. RO, RECTO
right: law .... DROIT
right, pert. to .... DEXTER
right to speak .... SAY
right, turn .... GEE
rights, of ...... JURAL, UDAL
Rigoletto's daughter ... GILDA
rigorous ...... HARSH, STERN, STRICT, SEVERE, AUSTERE
rim ...... LIP, EDGE, FLANGE
rim of wheel .. FELLY, FELLOE
"Rime cold giant" . YMER, YMIR
ring ...... PEAL, TOLL, KNELL
ring, boxing .... ARENA
ring for reins . TERRET, TERRIT
ring, gun carriage ..... LUNET
ring, harness pad TERRET, TERRIT
ring, lamp condensing ... CRIC
ring, little .... ANNULET
ring, naut. .... GROMMET
d ring of light .... HALO, NIMB, NIMBUS, AUREOLA, AUREOLE
"Ring of the Nibelung" goddess ERDA
"Ring of the Nibelung" smith MIME
ring out .... PEAL
ring, part of .... CHATON
ring, rubber jar .... LUTE
ring, seal .... SIGNET
ring-shaped ...... CIRCINATE
ring-shaped piece ..... QUOIT
ring, stone of .... CHATON
ringlet .... CURL, TRESS
ringworm ..... TINEA, TETTER
ripening agent .... AGER
ripple ...... LAP, RIFF, WAVE
rise above .... TOWER
rise aloft .... TOWER
rise: old Eng. .... RIS
risible .... GELASTIC
rites, religious .... SACRA
ritual .... RITE
RIVER . see also GAZETTEER in SPECIAL SECTION
river .... RIO
river, Balmoral Castle's ... DEE
river bank .... RIPA
river bank, growing by RIPARIAN

a river-bank stair, Ind. **GAUT, GHAT**
river bed, dry, Afr. **WADI, WADY**
river between Europe and Asia **KARA**
river, Bremen's .... **WESER**
river Caesar crossed . **RUBICON**
river, Dutch Meuse ..... **MAAS**
river in Baltic .... **ODER**
river in Essex .... **CAM**
river in Orleans .... **LOIRE**
river in Petrograd ...... **NEVA**
river into Moselle ...... **SAAR**
river into Rhone ...... **SAONE**
river islet .... **AIT**
river, "Kubla Khan" .... **ALPH**
river, Munich's .... **ISAR**
river mouth ..... **LADE, DELTA**
river nymph .... **NAIS**
river to the Humber **OUSE, TRENT**
River of Woe ..... **ACHERON**
river, Southwest .... **PECOS**
river: Sp. .... **RIO**
river: Tagalog .... **ILOG**
river to Medit. .... **EBRO**
river valley .... **STRATH**
rivulet .... **RILL**
road .... **VIA, PATH, ITER, AGGER**
b road: Roman .... **ITER**
road: Gypsy .... **DRUN**
roadhouse .... **INN**
roam .... **GAD, ROVE**
roast .... **CALCINE**
roasted meat strip .... **CABOB**
roasting rod .... **SPIT**
rob .... **REAVE, DESPOIL**
Rob Roy .... **CANOE**
robber .... **THIEF**
ROBE ..... see also GARMENT
robe .... **MANTLE**
robe to ankles .... **TALAR**
"Roberta" composer .... **KERN**
robot drama .... **RUR**
rock aggregate .... **AUGE**
rock, basic igneous ..... **SIMA**
rock cavity ..... **VOOG, VUGG, VUGH, GEODE**
rock, dangerous ...... **SCYLLA**
rock, dark .... **BASALT**
rock, fine grained ...... **TRAP**
rock, flintlike .... **CHERT**
rock, granitoid **DUNITE, GNEISS**
rock, hard .... **WHIN**
rock, jutting .... **TOR**
rock, laminated ...... **SHALE SLATE, GNEISS**
rock, melted .... **LAVA**
rock, mica-bearing ... **DOMITE**
c rock, projecting ... **TOR, CRAG**
rock, rugged .... **CRAG**
rock snake .... **PYTHON**
rock whiting genus ..... **ODAX**
rock-wren .... **TURCO**
ROCKET .. see under MISSILE, GUIDED
rocket's goal .... **MOON**
rockfish ... **RASHER, TAMBOR**
rockfish, Calif. .. **RENA, REINA**
rockweed .... **FUCI, FUCUS**
Rocky Mt. peak .... **ESTES**
Rocky Mt. range **TETON, UINTA**
rocky peak, eminence, pinnacle .... **TOR**
rod ... **POLE, WAND, BATON, PERCH, STAFF**
rod, barbecue .... **SPIT**
rod, basketry .... **OSIER**
rod, billiard .... **CUE**
rod, chastening ...... **FERULE**
rodent .... **RAT, HARE**
rodent genus .... **MUS**
rodent, rabbit-like .... **PIKA**
rodent, S. Am. .. **CAVY, DEGU, PACA, COYPU, AGOUTI**
rodent, W. Ind. .... **HUTIA**
Rhoderick Dhu .... **SCOT**
rogue .... **PICARO**
roguish .... **SLY, ARCH**
d roister .... **REVEL**
Roland's destroyer ...... **GAN, GANO, GANELON**
roll and heave .... **TOSS**
roll of bread: dialect. .... **BAP**
roll of cloth .... **BOLT**
roll of paper .... **SCROLL**
roll up .... **FURL**
romaine .... **COS**
ROMAN GODS see SPECIAL SECTION
Rom. assembly ...... **COMITIA**
Rom. authors .... **CATO, LIVY, OVID, LUCAN, NEPOS, PLINY, CICERO, HORACE, SENECA, SILIUS, VERGIL, SALLUST**
Rom. barracks **CANABA, CANNABA**
Rom. box .... **CAPSA**
Rom. boxing glove ... **CESTUS**
Rom. bronze .... **AES**
Rom. brooch .... **FIBULA**
Rom. building .... **INSULA**
Rom. cap .... **PILEUS**
Rom. cavalry body **TURM, TURMA**
Rom. circus post .... **META**
Rom. clan ..... **GENS, GENTES**
Rom. cloak ... **TOGA, ABOLLA**

a Rom. coin, ancient **SEMIS, DINDER**
Rom. coins .... **AS, AES, ASSES, SOLIDUS**
Rom. Curia court ...... **ROTA**
Rom. date ...... **IDES, NONES**
Rom. dictator .... **SULLA**
Rom. dish .... **LANX**
Rom. emperor .... **NERO, OTHO, TITUS**
Rom. farce .... **EXODE**
Rom. galley **TRIREME, UNIREME**
Rom. gaming cube ..... **TALUS**
Rom. garment .. **TOGA, STOLA, TUNIC, PLANETA**
Rom. goal post in racing . **META**
Rom. highway ..... **VIA, ITER**
Rom. historian ... **LIVY, NEPOS**
Rom. judge .... **EDILE, AEDILE**
Rom. law control ..... **MANUS**
Rom. legendary king ... **NUMA**
Rom. liquid measure .... **URNA**
Rom. list ...... **ALBE, ALBUM**
Rom. magistrate or official **EDILE, AEDILE, ARCHON, CONSUL, PRETOR, TRIBUNE**
Rom. market ... **FORA, FORUM**
Rom. meal .... **CENA**
b Rom. money, copper ..... **AES**
Rom. numerals 1-**I**, 5-**V**, 10-**X**, 50-**L**, 100-**C**, 500-**D**, 1000-**M**
ROMAN OFFICIAL see ROMAN MAGISTRATE
Rom. patriot .... **CATO**
Rom. philosopher **CATO, SENECA**
Rom. platter .... **LANX**
Rom. pledge .... **VAS**
Rom. poet ..... **OVID, LUCAN, HORACE, VERGIL, VIRGIL**
Rom. pound .... **AS**
Rom. province .... **DACIA**
Rom. public games ...... **LUDI**
Rom. public lands ...... **AGER**
Rom. religious festivals . **VOTA**
Rom. road .... **VIA, ITER**
Rom. robe .... **TOGA**
Rom. room, principal **ATRIA, ATRIUM**
Rom. scroll .... **STEMMA**
Rom. statesman .... **CATO**
Rom. sword .... **FALX**
Rom. vessel .... **PATERA**
Rom. war garb .... **SAGUM**
Rom. weight .... **AS**
c Rom. well-curb ...... **PUTEAL**
Rom. writer .... **MACER**
romance, tale of . **GEST, GESTE**
ROMANIA .... see RUMANIA
Rome, a founder of ... **REMUS**
Rome's cathedral church **LATERAN**
Rome's conqueror ..... **ALARIC**
Rome's river .... **TIBER**
Romulus' twin .... **REMUS**
rood .... **CROSS**
roof .... **MANSARD**
roof edge .... **EAVE**
roof of mouth .... **PALATE**
roof of mouth, pert. to **PALATAL**
roof ornament .... **EPI**
roof, rounded . **DOME, CUPOLA**
roof, rounded like a ... **DOMAL**
roof, truncated .... **HIP**
roofing piece ...... **RAG, TILE**
roofing slate .... **TILE**
roofing timber .... **PURLIN**
rook's cry .... **CAWK**
room, Eng. college supply **BUTTERY**
room, snug .... **DEN**
room, rooms .... **SPACE, SUITE**
room, architecture ..... **OECUS**
room for household goods, linen, etc. . **EWRY, EWERY**
d room, main, Rom. **ATRIA, ATRIUM**
room, mineshaft . **PLAT, PLATT**
room, Rom. .... **ALA**
roomy .... **WIDE**
roost .... **PERCH**
rooster .... **COCK**
root .... **RADIX, RADICES**
root, drug-yielding ..... **JALAP**
root, edible ..... **OCA, TARO, CASSAVA**
root, tree used for sewing **WATAP**
root, word .... **ETYM**
rootlet .... **RADICEL, RADICLE**
rootstock, edible .... **TARO**
rootstock, fern (Maori) ... **ROI**
rootstock, fragrant .... **ORRIS**
rope ...... **JEFF, LAZO, LASSO, LONGE, REATA, RIATA, LARIAT, MARLINE**
rope, cringle **LEEFANG, LEEFANGE**
rope fiber .. **DA, COIR, FERU, HEMP, IMBE, JUTE, RHEA, ABACA, SISAL**
rope for animals ..... **TETHER**
rope guide: naut. ...... **WAPP**
rope loop .... **BIGHT**

a rope, naut. ... **FOX, TYE, STAY, VANG, HAWSER, RATLIN, LANIARD, LANYARD, RATLINE, SNOTTER**
rope to tie boat ..... **PAINTER**
rope, weave .... **REEVE**
rope, yardarm ..... **SNOTTER**
ropes, unite .... **SPLICE**
rosary bead .... **AVE**
rose: Byron .... **GUL**
rose fruit .... **HIP**
rose genus .... **ROSA, ACAENA**
rose-like plant .... **AVENS**
rose of Sharon **ALTHEA, ALTHAEA**
rose oil derivative ..... **ATAR, OTTO, ATTAR, OTTAR**
rose ornament ...... **ROSETTE**
rose, Pers. .... **GUL**
rosewood .... **MOLOMPI**
rosolic acid ... **AURIN, AURINE**
rostellum .... **ROSTEL**
roster .... **LIST, ROTA**
rotate .... **ROLL, GYRATE**
rotating muscle ..... **EVERTOR**
rotating part .... **CAM, ROTOR**
rotation producer .... **TORQUE**
rotten .... **PUTRID**
rouge ...... **RADDLE, RUDDLE**
b rough .... **RUDE, UNEVEN**
rough, as country ...... **HILLY**
rough copy .... **DRAFT**
rough in voice .... **GRUFF**
rough rock .... **KNAR**
roughness, sea .... **LIPPER**
roulette bet ...... **BAS, NOIR, MILIEU**
round, a ...... **ROTA, ROTULA**
round hand .... **RONDE**
round room .... **ROTUNDA**
Round Table Knight .... **KAY, BORS, BORT, BALAN, BALIN, BOHORT, GARETH, GAWAIN, GALAHAD, PELLEAS**
round-up .... **RODEO**
rounded projection ...... **LOBE**
rounder .... **RAKE, ROUE**
roundworm .... **NEMA, ASCARID, ASCARIS**
rouse . **WAKE, AWAKE, WAKEN**
Rousseau novel, hero ... **EMILE**
route .... **WAY, PATH**
route, plane's fixed ..... **LANE**
routine, fixed .... **ROTE**
row .... **LINE, SPAT, TIER**
rowan tree .... **ASH, SORB**
rowdy: slang .... **B'HOY**
rower .... **OAR**
rower's bench .... **ZYGA, ZYGON, THWART**

c royal authority ...... **SCEPTRE**
royal court, relating to . **AULIC**
royal edict: Fr. .... **ARRET**
royal family, Fr. ...... **VALOIS**
royal rights, having . **PALATINE**
royal rod .. **SCEPTER, SCEPTRE**
royal treasury ...... **FISC, FISK**
royalty, Hawaii .... **ALII**
rub harshly .... **GRATE**
rub off .... **ABRADE**
rub out .... **ERASE**
rub roughly .... **SCRAPE**
rub to polish .... **BUFF, SHINE**
rub to soreness .... **CHAFE**
rubber .... **PARA, LATEX, CAUCHO, ELASTIC**
rubber, black .... **EBONITE**
rubber source ..... **KOKSAGYZ**
rubber, S. Am. . **PARA, CEARA**
rubber tree ...... **ULE, HULE, SERINGA**
rubber, wild .... **CEARA**
rubbery substance **GUTTA, NOREPOL**
rubbish .... **ROT, JUNK, CULCH, RUBBLE**
rubble masonry ..... **MOELLON**
rubella .... **MEASLES**
ruby .... **RED**
ruby red quartz ..... **RUBASSE**
d ruby spinel ... **BALAS, BALASS**
rudder bushing .... **PINTLE**
rudder fish .... **CHOPA**
ruddle .... **KEEL, KIEL**
rudiment .... **GERM**
rudiments .... **ABC**
rue .... **REGRET**
rue herb genus .... **RUTA**
ruff, female ..... **REE, REEVE**
ruffed lemur .... **VARI**
ruffer .... **NAPPER**
ruffle .... **CRIMP**
ruffle, neck ... **JABOT, RUCHE**
RUG .... see also CARPET
rug, long narrow **KANARA, RUNNER**
ruin .... **DOOM**
rule .... **LAW, DOMINEER**
"Rule Britannia" composer **ARNE**
rules, dueling .... **DUELLO**
ruler .... **REGENT**
ruler, Afghanistan ...... **EMIR, AMEER, CALIF, EMEER, CALIPH, SULTAN**
ruler, Arabian .. **EMIR, AMEER, CALIF, EMEER, CALIPH, SULTAN**
RULER, BIBLICAL .... see SPECIAL SECTION

a **RULER IN EAST** ... see RULER, ARABIAN
ruler, India .... **NAWAB**
ruler, Morocco .... **SHERIF, SHEREEF**
ruler, Moslem ... **EMIR, AMEER, CALIF, EMEER, CALIPH, SULTAN**
ruler of gods............. **ZEUS**
ruler, Oriental .... **CALIF**
ruler, Tunis .... **DEY**
RUMANIA .... see also SPECIAL SECTION
Rumanian composer... **ENESCO**
Rumanian folk song ..... **DOINA**
Rumanian king's title .... **DOMN**
rumen.................... **CUD**
ruminant .... **DEER, GOAT, CAMEL, LLAMA, ANTELOPE**
ruminant genus .... **CAPRA**
ruminant, horned .... **DEER, GOAT**
ruminate ...... **MULL, PONDER**
Rumor personified....... **FAMA**
rumor, to ..... **BRUIT, NORATE, REPORT**
b rumple .... **MUSS**
run at top speed .... **SPRINT**
run before wind .... **SCUD**
run of the mill .... **PAR**
run out................. **PETER**
runner .... **SCARF, STOLO, STOLON**
runner, distance......... **MILER**
runner, plant.. **STOLO, STOLON**
rupees, 100,000.......... **LAC**
rural ..... **RUSTIC, PASTORAL**
rural deity ...... **PAN, FAUNUS**
rural poem........... **GEORGIC**
rush .... **HASTE, SPEED**
rush, marsh .... **SPART**
Russell's viper .... **DABOIA, DABOYA**
RUSSIA....... see also SOVIET and SPECIAL SECTION
Russia, most northern town **KOLA**
Russian .... **RED, RUSS, SLAV, KULAK, TATAR**
Russ. basso .... **KIPNIS**
Russ. author .... **BUNIN**
c Russ. beer....... **KVAS, QUAS, KVASS**
Russ. community........... **MIR**
Russ. convention......... **RADA**
Russ. cooperative society **ARTEL**
Russ. council .... **DUMA**
Russ. dress.......... **SARAFAN**
Russ. edict ... **UKASE, DECREE**
Russ. emperor .... **CZAR, TSAR, TZAR**
Russ. fiddle .... **GUDOK**
Russ. folk dance .... **KOLO**
Russ. girl's name......... **OLGA**
Russ. hemp............... **RINE**
Russ. labor union......... **ARTEL**
Russ. lagoon............ **LIMAN**
Russ. Lapland capital ..... **KOLA**
Russ. leather............. **YUFT**
Russ. liquid measure ..... **STOF, STOFF, STOOF**
Russ. log hut .... **ISBA**
Russ. marsh .... **LIMAN**
Russ. mile .... **VERST**
Russ. mountain range .... **ALAI, URAL**
d Russian mts., pert. to... **ALTAIC**
Russ. name, given.. **AKIM, IGOR**
Russ. news agency .... **TASS**
Russ. official........... **BERIYA**
Russ. opera.............. **BORIS**
Russ. peninsula .... **KOLA**
Russ. sea, inland .... **ARAL, AZOF, AZOV**
Russ. secret police .... **KGB, NKVD, OGPU**
Russ. tavern .... **CABACK**
Russ. tax, old .... **OBROK**
Russ. tea urn .... **SAMOVAR**
Russ. trade guild .... **ARTEL**
Russ. vehicle ... **ARBA, ARABA**
Russ. village .... **MIR**
Russ. whip............... **PLET**
Russ. writer.... **GORKI, GORKY**
Russ. "yes"................ **DA**
rust.............. **EAT, ERODE**
Rustam's father .... **ZAL**
rustic .... **BOOR, RUBE, CARL, CARLE, YOKEL, BUCOLIC, PEASANT**
Ruth's husband .... **BOAZ**
Ruth's son............... **OBED**
rye, disease of .... **ERGOT**

S

a sable .... SOBOL, MARTEN
sac .... BURSA
saccharine source .... TAR
sack fiber .... JUTE
sack, to .... LOOT
saclike cavity .... BURSA
sacred asp, symbol ... URAEUS
sacred bull, Egypt . APIS, HAPI
sacred chalice .... GRAIL
sacred city, India ... BENARES
sacred enclosure, Gr. .... SEKOS
sacred fig .... PIPAL
sacred Hindu word .... OM
sacred image .... ICON, IKON
sacred lily .... LOTUS
sacred object: Oceania .. ZOGO
sacred picture .... ICON, IKON
sacred place .... SHRINE
sacred place, Gr.
ABATON, HIERON
sacred tree, Hindu .. BO, PIPAL
sacrifice, place of ..... ALTAR
b sacrificial drink, Zoroaster's
SOMA
sacrificial offerings .... HIERA
sad: comb. form ...... TRAGI
sad cry .... ALAS, ALACK
sad: music .... MESTO
saddle horses, fresh . REMUDA
saddle knob .... POMMEL
saddle, rear of .... CANTLE
safe .... SECURE
safe place ...... PORT, HAVEN
safe: thief's slang ...... PETE
safety lamp .... DAVY
safflower .... KUSUM
saga .... EDDA
sage .... WISE
sagacious .... WISE,
ASTUTE, SAPIENT
sage genus .... SALVIA
sail fastener .... CLEW
sail-line .... EARING
sail nearer wind .... LUFF
sail, square .... LUG
sail, square, edge of ... LEECH
sail, triangular .... JIB
sail yard: Scot. .... RAE
sail's corner .... CLEW
"Sails" of constellation Argo
VELA
sailboat .... YAWL, KETCH
sailing race .... REGATTA
SAILING VESSEL .... see
VESSEL, SAILING
sailmaker's awl ..... STABBER

c sailor .GOB, TAR, SALT, SEADOG
sailor, India .... LASCAR
St. Anthony's cross ...... TAU
saint, British .... ALBAN
saint, Buddhist
ARAHT, ARHAT, ARAHAT
St. Catherine's home ... SIENA
saint, female: abbr. ...... STE
saint, 14th century ..... ROCH
St. Francis' birthplace .. ASSISI
St. John's-bread ..... CAROB
"St. Louis Blues" composer
HANDY
saint, Moslem .... PIR
St. Paul, deserter from . DEMAS
St. Vitus dance ...... CHOREA
sainte: abbr. .... STE
saint's relic box ...... CHASSE
salad green ...... UDO, CRESS,
KERSE, CRESSE, ENDIVE
salamander .. EFT, EVET, NEWT
salient angle .... CANT
Salientia, the .... ANURA
sally .... START, SORTIE
"Sally in Our Alley" composer
CAREY
salmon, female .... HEN
d salmon, male .... COCK
salmon net .... MAUD
salmon, silver .... COHO
salmon, third year ..... MORT
salmon, 2 yr. .. SMOLT, SPROD
salmon, young .. PARR, GRILSE
salt .... SAL, HALITE, SALINE
salt factory .... SALTERN
salt lake, Turkestan ..... SHOR
salt of tartaric acid .. TARTAR
salt pond or spring ... SALINA
salt, resembling ...... HALOID
salt, rock .... HALITE
salt, solution .. BRINE, SALINE
salt tax .... GABELLE
salt tree, Tamarisk ..... ATLE
salted .... ALAT
saltpeter ...... NITER, NITRE
saltwort .... KALI
saltworks .... SALINA
salty water .... BRINE
salutation .... AVE
salutation: Ir. ...... ACHARA
Salvation Army leader . BOOTH
salver .... TRAY
salvia .... CHIA
Sambal language .... TINO
sambar deer .... MAHA, RUSA
same .... ILK, DITTO

a same place: abbr. ...... **IBID**
samlet .... **PARR**
Samoan maiden ...... **TAUPO**
Samoan mollusk .... **ASI**
Samoan political council. **FONO**
Samuel, king killed by .. **AGAG**
Samuel, teacher of .... **ELI**
Samuel's son .... **ABIA**
samurai, straying ..... **RONIN**
sanction .... **AMEN, FIAT**
sanctuary ...... **BEMA, FANE, NAOS, CELLA**
sand .... **GRIT**
sand bar .... **REEF, SHOAL**
sand expanses .... **AREG**
sand hill .... **DENE, DUNE**
sand island .... **BAR**
sand, sea bottom .... **PAAR**
sand snake genus .... **ERYX**
sandal, Egypt .... **TATBEB**
sandal, Mex. **HUARACHE, HUARACHO**
sandalwood tree .... **MAIRE**
sandarac powder .... **POUNCE**
sandarac tree .... **ARAR**
sandbox tree genus ..... **HURA**
sandpiper .... **REE, RUFF, STIB, REEVE, STINT**
sandpiper, Europ. ...... **TEREK**
b sandpiper, red .... **KNOT**
sandpiper, small .... **KNOT, PUME, STINT**
sandstone .... **GRIT**
sandstorm .... **HABOOB**
sandwich .... **HERO**
Sandwich Island discoverer **COOK**
sandy .... **ARENOSE**
Sankhya philos. term ... **GUNA**
Sanskrit dialect .... **PALI**
Sanskrit precept **SUTRA, SUTTA**
Sanskrit school .... **TOL**
Sao —, Brazil .... **PAULO**
Sao Salvador .... **BAHIA**
sap spout .... **SPILE**
sapodilla ... **SAPOTA, SAPOTE**
sapota tree .... **ACANA**
Saracen ..... **MOOR, MOSLEM**
Sarah's slave .... **HAGAR**
sarcasm .... **IRONY**
Sardinia gold coin ... **CARLINE**
sargeant fish .... **SNOOK**
Sargon's capital ...... **ACCAD**
Sarmatia cave-dwellers . **TAURI**
sartor .... **TAILOR**
sash, C. Amer. .... **TOBE**
sash, Jap. kimono .... **OBI**
sassafras tree .... **AGUE**
Satan .... **DEVIL**
Satan: Arab .... **EBLIS**

c satellite .... **MOON, PLANET**
satellite .... **LUNIK, SPUTNIK, PIONEER, EXPLORER, VANGUARD, ATLAS-SCORE, DISCOVERER**
satellite, navigation . **TRANSIT**
satellite, television .... **TIROS**
satellite's path .... **ORBIT**
satiate .. **CLOY, GLUT, SATE**
satirical .... **DRY**
satisfaction Maori ...... **UTU**
satisfy ... **SATE, SUIT, PLEASE**
saturate . **SOAK, IMBUE, STEEP**
Saturn, satellite of ..... **DIONE**
Saturn's rings projection. **ANSA**
Saturn's wife .... **OPS**
Saturnalia .... **ORGY**
satyr .... **FAUN**
sauce .... **GRAVY**
sauce, Chinese, Oriental .. **SOY**
sauce, fish .... **ALEC**
sauce, peppery ..... **TABASCO**
sauce, tomato ...... **CATSUP, CATCHUP, KETCHUP**
saucy .... **PERT**
Saul's army leader .... **ABNER**
Saul's chief herdsman .. **DOEG**
Saul's father .... **KISH**
Saul's grandfather . **NER, ABIEL**
Saul's successor .... **DAVID**
Saul's uncle .... **NER**
Sault Ste. Marie .... **SOO**
saurel fish .... **SCAD**
d sausage, spiced ..... **SALAME, SALAMI**
savage .... **FERAL**
Savage Island language . **NIUE**
save .... **HOARD, STINT, REDEEM, CONSERVE**
saviour .... **REDEEMER**
savory .... **SAPID, TASTY**
saw .... **ADAGE, AXIOM, MAXIM, SAYING**
saw-leaved centaury **BEHN, BEHEN**
saw, notched like .... **SERRATE**
saw notching .... **REDAN**
saw, surgical **TREPAN,TREPHINE**
sawbill duck .... **SMEW**
sawlike organ, or part .. **SERRA**
sawlike parts . **SERRAS, SERRAE**
sawtooth ridge .... **SIERRA**
saxhorn .... **TUBA**
Saxon god .... **ER, EAR**
Saxon king ...... **INE, ALFRED**
Saxony natives .... **SORBS**
say .... **UTTER**
say again .... **ITERATE**
saying ... **MOT, SAW, ADAGE, AXIOM, MAXIM**
sayings .... **LOGIA**

a scabbard fish .... **HIKU**
scabbard, put into .. **SHEATHE**
scaffolding .... **STAGING**
scale .... **GAMUT**
scale, syllable of .. **DO, FA, LA, MI, RE, SO, TI, SOL**
scale under blossom **PALEA, PALET**
scales, having large . **SCUTATE**
scallop ..... **CRENA, CRENAE**
scallops, cut in small .... **PINK**
scalloped .... **CRENATE**
scalp disease .... **FAVI, FAVUS**
scamp ...... **ROGUE, RASCAL**
SCANDINAVIAN see also NORSE
SCANDINAVIAN . see also SWEDEN, NORWAY, in SPECIAL SECTION
Scandinavian ... **DANE, SWEDE**
Scand., ancient .... **NORSE**
Scand. countryman ..... **GEAT**
Scand. explorer .... **ERIC**
Scand. fertility god .... **NJORD**
Scand. legend .... **SAGA**
Scand. measure .... **ALEN**
Scand. nation .... **GEATAS**
Scandinavians in Russia **ROS, RUS**
b scanty .... **SPARSE**
scar, resembling a .... **ULOID**
scarce .... **RARE**
scarcely: Lat. .... **VIX**
scare away .... **SHOO**
scarf .... **BOA, TIE, ASCOT, ORALE**
scarf, long .... **STOLE**
scarf, Sp. Am. .... **TAPALO**
scarlet flower .... **SALVIA**
Scarlett O'Hara's home .. **TARA**
scatter ... **SOW, TED, STREW**
scatter: dial. .... **SCOAD**
scatter on .... **LITTER**
scattered: Her. .... **SEME**
scenario .... **SCRIPT**
scene .... **VIEW, TABLEAU**
scene of action. **ARENA, SPHERE**
scenic view .... **SCAPE**
scent .... **ODOR, AROMA**
scented .... **OLENT**
schedule .... **LIST**
scheme .... **PLAN, PLOT**
schism .... **RENT**
scholar .... **PEDANT**
scholars, Moslem .... **ULEMA**
scholarship .... **BURSE**
school, boy's .... **PREP**
school, Fr. ...... **ECOLE, LYCEE**
school grounds ...... **CAMPUS**

c **SCHOONER** ... see also BOAT, SHIP, VESSEL
schooner, 3-masted ..... **TERN**
sciences .... **ARTS**
scientific farmer . **AGRONOMIST**
scientific study: abbr. . **ANAT.**
scientist, Am. . **UREY, HOOTON, PARRAN, COMPTON, WAKSMAN, MILLIKAN**
scientist, Austr. .... **MEITNER**
scientist, Czech .... **CORI**
scientist, Dan. .... **BOHR**
scientist, Eng. .... **HOGBEN, FLEMING, HALDANE**
scientist, Ger. .. **BAADE, HABER**
scientist, Ital. .... **FERMI**
scissors .... **SHEARS**
scoff .... **GIBE, JEER, JIBE, RAIL, SNEER**
scold .... **JAW, NAG, RATE**
scold: dialect .... **FRAB**
scone: Scot. ..... **FARL, FARLE**
scoop .... **DIP**
scoot: Scot. ..... **SKYT, SKITE**
scope .. **AREA, AMBIT, RANGE**
scorch .... **CHAR, SEAR, SERE, SINGE**
score .... **TALLY**
scoria .... **SLAG, DROSS**
d scorpion fish .... **LAPON**
Scotch cake .... **SCONE**
scoter .... **COOT**
Scotland .... **SCOTIA**
Scott character .... **ELLEN**
Scott heroine .... **ELLEN**
Scott, poem by .... **MARMION**
SCOTTISH see Pages of SCOTTISH WORDS
Scot. alderman .... **BAILIE**
Scot. author .... **BARRIE**
Scot. chemist .... **URE, DEWAR**
Scot. chief landholder **THANE, THEGN**
Scot. cultural congress ... **MOD**
Scot. explorer .... **RAE**
Scot. highlander ...... **GAEL**
Scot. king .... **BRUCE**
Scot. lord ..... **THANE, THEGN**
Scot. pillory .... **JOUG**
Scot. playwright ...... **BARRIE**
Scot. poet .... **BURNS**
Scot. pottage .... **BROSE**
Scot. proprietor .... **LAIRD**
Scot. scholar .... **NICOLL**
Scot. singer .... **LAUDER**
SCOTTISH WORDS:
accept .... **TAE**
advise .... **REDE**
afraid .... **RAD, RADE**
age .... **EILD**

a against ... **GIN**
alder tree ... **ARN, ELLER**
an ... **AE**
animal, lean ... **RIBE**
any ... **ONY**
article ... **TA**
ashes ... **ASE**
ask ... **AX**
at all ... **AVA**
away ... **AWA**
awry ... **AJEE**
babbler ... **HAVEREL**
ball ... **BA**
bank ... **BRAE**
barter ... **TROKE**
beg ... **SORN**
bind ... **OOP**
biscuit ... **BAKE**
blockhead ... **CUIF, NOWT**
bloodhound ... **LYAM**
bone ... **BANE**
bound ... **STEND**
breeches ... **TREWS**
broth ... **BREE, BROO**
brow of hill ... **SNAB**
built ... **BAG**
burden ... **BIRN**
bushel ... **FOU**
calves ... **CAUR, CAURE**
b came ... **CAM**
catch ... **KEP**
chalk ... **CAUK**
check ... **WERE**
chest ... **KIST**
child ... **BAIRN**
church ... **KIRK, KURK**
comb ... **KAME**
contend ... **KEMP**
court, bring to ... **SIST**
cut ... **KNAP, SNEG**
dairymaid ... **DEY**
damage ... **TEEN**
damaged ... **LESED**
dare ... **DAUR**
devil ... **DEIL**
did not know ... **KENNA**
die ... **DEE**
dig ... **HOWK**
dining room ... **SPENCE**
do ... **DAE, DIV**
do not know ... **KENNA**
dread ... **DREE**
drip ... **SIE, SYE**
dusty ... **MOTTY**
earth ... **EARD**
elder ... **ELLER**
else ... **ENSE**
empty ... **TOOM**
endeavor ... **ETTLE**
endure ... **DREE**

c extra ... **ORRA**
eye ... **EE**
eyes ... **EEN, EES**
family ... **ILK**
fidget ... **FIKE**
firth ... **KYLE**
fishing expedition ... **DRAVE**
fit of sulks ... **GEE**
flax refuse ... **PAB, POB**
fog ... **DAG, HAR, HAAR**
foretell ... **SPAE**
give ... **GIE**
glimpse ... **STIME**
grandchild ... **OY, OYE**
grant as property . **DISPONE**
great-grandchild ... **IEROE**
grief ... **TEEN**
have ... **HAE**
hawk ... **ALLAN**
heavy ... **THARF**
hill . **BEN, DOD, BRAE, DODD**
hillside ... **BRAE**
howl ... **YOWT**
hurt ... **LESED**
injure ... **TEEN**
injured ... **LESED**
intent ... **ETTLE**
keg ... **KNAG**
d kinsman ... **SIB**
kiss ... **PREE**
knead ... **ELT**
knock ... **KNOIT**
lake ... **LOCH**
leap .. **LOUP, LOWP, STEND**
learning ... **LEAR**
list of candidates ... **LEET**
loaf ... **SORN**
lop ... **SNATHE**
lout ... **CUIF**
love ... **LOE**
loyal ... **LEAL**
marriage portion ... **DOTE**
millrace ... **LADE**
mire ... **GLAUR**
mist ... **URE**
mountain ... **BEN**
mouth, river ... **BEAL**
mouth ... **BEAL**
mud ... **GLAIR**
must ... **MAUN**
name ... **IAN**
near, nearest ... **NAR**
no ... **NAE**
none ... **NANE**
not matched ... **ORRA**
now ... **NOO**
nowhere ... **NAEGATE**
oak ... **AIK**

(Scottish words continued 140)

Scottish

a

oatmeal dish .... **BROSE**
odd .... **ORRA**
old age .... **EILD**
once .... **ANES**
one .... **AIN, ANE, YIN**
otherwise .... **ELS**
out .... **OOT**
own .... **AIN, ANE, AWN**
pantry .... **SPENCE**
parlor .... **BEN**
payment .... **MENSE**
paw ground .... **PAUT**
peat cutter .... **PINER**
pig .... **GRICE**
pike .... **GED, GEDD**
pillory .... **TRONE**
pipe .... **CUTTY**
pluck wool .... **ROO**
pool .... **DIB, CARR, LINN, LLYN**
present .... **GIE**
pretty .... **GEY**
prop .... **RANCE**
propriety .... **MENSE**
prune .... **SNED**
puddle .... **DUB**
pull .... **PU**
quagmire .... **HAG**
quarter of a year ...... **RAITH**
relieve .... **LISS**

b

revenue, church ...... **ANNAT**
ridge of a hill .... **SHIN**
river .... **DOON**
rowboat .... **COBLE**
sailyard .... **RAE**
same .... **ILK**
scone .... **FARL, FARLE**
scoot .... **SKYT, SKITE**
scratch .... **RIT**
seep .... **SIPE**
seize .... **VANG**
self .... **SEL**
serve .... **KAE**
severe blow .... **DEVEL**
sheepfold .... **REE**
sheep tick .... **KED**
sheep walk .... **SLAIT**
shelter .... **BIELD, SHEAL**
sift .... **SIE**
since .... **SIN, SYNE**
slope .... **BRAE**
slouch .... **LOUCH**
sly .... **SLEE**
small .... **SMA**
snow .... **SNA**
so .... **SAE**
son of .... **MAC**
song .... **STROUD**
sore .... **SAIR**
sorrow .... **TEEN**
sow .... **SOO**

c

steward .... **MORMAOR**
stipend .... **ANNAT**
stone **STANE, STEAN, STEEN**
stretch .... **STENT**
stupid one .... **CUIF**
suffer .... **DREE**
summit .... **DOD, DODD**
sweetheart .... **JO**
than .... **NA**
to .... **TAE**
toe .... **TAE**
tone .... **TEAN**
trench .... **GAW**
truant, play .... **TRONE**
try .... **ETTLE**
tune .... **PORT**
turnip .... **NEEP**
uncanny .... **UNCO**
uncle .... **EME**
urge .... **ERT**
very .... **VERA**
vex .... **FASH**
village .... **REW**
void, to render .... **CASS**
waterfall ..... **LIN, LYN, LINN**
wealthy .... **BIEN**
weep .... **ORP**
week .... **OUK**

d

weighing machine ..... **TRON, TRONE**
well .... **AWEEL**
wet .... **WAT**
whirlpool .... **WEEL, WIEL**
whiskey drink .... **ATHOL, ATHOLE**
widow's third .... **TERCE**
workhouse .... **AVER**
year, ¼ of .... **RAITH**
yell .... **GOWL**

scoundrel .... **ROGUE, VARLET**
scout unit . **DEN, PACK, TROOP**
scow .... **BARGE, LIGHTER**
scow: Fr. .... **ACON**
scrap, table .... **ORT**
scraps of literature .... **ANA**
scrape ... **RAKE, RASP, GRAZE**
scrape bottom .... **DREDGE**
scratch .... **MAR, RAKE**
scrawny animal .... **SCRAG**
screamer bird .... **CHAJA**
screed .... **TIRADE**
screen .... **SIFT, SHADE**
screen, altar .... **REREDOS**
screen, wind .... **PARAVENT**
script, modern Syriac .... **SERTA**
script, upright .... **RONDE**
scripture, early .... **ITALA**
scripture passage .... **TEXT**
scriptures, occult interpretation **CABALA**
scrutinize .... **EYE, SCAN**

a scuffle .... **MELEE**
sculptor of "Thinker" . **RODIN**
scum, metal .... **DROSS**
scup .... **BREAM, PORGY**
scuppernong ..... **MUSCADINE**
scuttle .... **HOD**
scuttle, coal .... **HOD**
scythe .... **SY, SYE**
scythe handle . **SNATH, SNEAD, SNEED, SNATHE**
sea anemone .. **POLYP, OPELET**
sea bird ... **ERN, ERNE, GULL, SKUA, SCAUP, TERN, FULMAR, GANNET, PETREL, SCOTER**
sea bird, north .... **PUFFIN**
sea cow . **DUGONG, MANATEE**
sea cucumber ...... **TREPANG**
sea demon, Teut. .... **WATE**
sea duck ...... **COOT, EIDER, SCAUP, SCOTER**
sea eagle .... **ERN, ERNE**
sea-ear .... **ABALONE**
sea: Fr. .... **MER**
sea girdles .... **CUVY**
sea god .... **LER, TRITON, NEPTUNE**
sea god, Gr. . **NEREUS, TRITON, POSEIDON**
sea god, Rom. ...... **NEPTUNE**
sea god, Teut. .. **HLER, AEGIR**
sea goddess, Norse ...... **RAN**
b sea green .... **CELADON**
sea gull, Eur. .... **MEW**
sea, kept bow on . **ATRY, ATRIE**
sea lettuce ..... **ALGA, LAVER**
sea lettuce genus **ULVA, ULUA**
sea marker .... **DAN**
sea pheasant .... **SMEE**
sea robber .... **PIRATE**
sea mile, Austral. .... **NAUT**
sea nymph .... **NEREID**
sea shell .... **TRITON**
(see also SHELL)
sea skeleton .... **CORAL**
sea slug genus . **DOTO, ELYSIA**
sea snail . **WELK, WILK, WHELK**
sea snake, Asia ...... **KERRIL**
sea soldier .... **MARINE**
sea worm . **SAO, LURG, NEREIS**
seal .... **SIGIL**
seal, eared .... **OTARY**
seal, fur .... **URSAL**
seal, letter .... **CACHET**
seal, official .... **SIGNET**
seal, papal .... **BULLA**
seal, young .... **PUP**
seals, group of .... **POD**
seamark .... **BEACON**
seamen: Brit. .... **RATINGS**
seamlike ridge .... **RAPHE**

c seams of boat, fill ..... **CALK**
SEAPORT .... see PORT
search .... **GROPE**
search for .... **HUNT, SEEK**
search for food ...... **FORAGE**
season ...... **AGE, FALL, SALT, TIDE, SPRING**
season, church . **LENT, ADVENT**
season, Fr. .... **ETE**
seasons, goddesses of .. **HORAE**
seasonal phenomenon .. **EPACT**
seasoning .... **SAGE, SALT**
seasoning herb .... **SAGE, BASIL, THYME**
seat, chancel .... **SEDILE**
seat, long .... **PEW, SETTEE**
seat of oracle of Zeus . **DODONA**
seat, Rom. .... **SELLA**
seaweed ... **ORE, AGAR, ALGA, KELP, ALGAE, LAVER, VAREC**
seaweed ashes .... **KELP**
seaweed, brown .... **KELP**
seaweed, edible .... **AGAR**
seaweed, edible Hawaiian . **LIMU**
seaweed, purple .... **LAVER**
seaweed, purple, Jap. ... **NORI**
seaweed, red .... **DULSE**
Seb, consort of .... **NUT**
d secluded .... **REMOTE**
second . **ABET, TRICE, MOMENT**
second brightest star ... **BETA**
second-growth crop ... **ROWEN**
Second Punic War's end, site of .... **ZAMA**
second team .... **SCRUB**
secondary .... **BYE, LESS**
secret .... **RUNE, ARCANE, COVERT, MYSTERY, ESOTERIC**
secret agent .... **SPY**
secret society, Afr. . **EGBO, PORO**
secret society in Sierra Leone **PORO**
secrets .... **ARCANA**
secrets, one learning ... **EPOPT**
secretion, sweet **LAAP, LERP, LAARP**
sect .... **CULT**
sect, Nepal . **ACHAR, ACHARA**
section of journey .... **LEG**
secular ... **LAY, LAIC, LAICAL**
secure .. **FIX, GET, PIN, FAST, NAIL, SAFE, FASTEN**
secure firmly . **MOOR, ANCHOR**
secure with rope .... **BELAY**
security .... **BOND**
Sec'y of State, 1933-44 .. **HULL**
sedate .... **STAID**
sedative .... **NEMBUTAL**

a sediment .... **LEES, SILT, DREGS, SILTAGE**
see .... **ESPY, LOOK**
see: Lat. .... **VIDE**
seed .... **PIP, PIT, GRAIN, SPORE, PYRENE**
seed coat or covering .. **ARIL, HULL, HUSK, TESTA, TEGMEN, TESTAE, TEGUMEN, TEGIMINA**
seed, edible ...... **PEA, BEAN, LENTIL, PINOLE**
seed, edible, Asia .... **SESAME**
seed, immature .... **OVULE**
seed, lens-shaped ..... **LENTIL**
seed, nutlike .... **PINON**
seed, opium poppy ..... **MAW**
seed plant .... **ENDOGEN**
seeds, remove .... **GIN**
seedless plant .... **FERN**
seek to attain .... **ASPIRE**
seem .... **LOOK**
seesaw .... **TEETER**
segment, last .... **TELSON**
segment of body ..... **SOMITE**
segment of circle .... **ARC**
segment, pert. to ...... **TORIC**
seine .... **NET**
seize .... **NAB, GRAB, GRASP, USURP, ARREST, COLLAR**
b seize: archaic .... **REAVE**
selections, literary **ANA, ANALECTA**
self .... **EGO**
self-assurance .... **APLOMB**
self-defense, art of ..... **JUDO**
self-denying .... **ASCETIC**
self-education doctrine **BIOSOPHY**
self-locking nut ..... **PALNUT**
self-reproach .... **REMORSE**
sell .... **VEND**
seller .... **COSTER, VENDER, VENDOR**
semblance .... **GUISE**
semester .... **TERM**
semi-precious stone **ONYX, SARD**
semicircular room ...... **APSE**
semidiameter .... **RADIUS**
semidiameters .... **RADII**
Seminole chief ..... **OSCEOLA**
Semitic deity .... **BAAL**
sen, tenth of .... **RIN**
senate house .... **CURIA**
senate houses .... **CURIAE**
Senator, former .... **BORAH**
send back ... **REMIT, REMAND**
send money .... **REMIT**
c send out .... **EMIT, ISSUE**
sending forth .... **EMISSIVE**
Senegambia gazelle .... **KORIN**
senility .... **DOTAGE**
senior .... **ELDER**
senior: Fr. .... **AINE**
senna, source of ...... **CASSIA**
sennet .... **SPET**
sense .... **FEEL**
senseless .... **INANE**
sensitive .... **SORE**
sentence, analyze ...... **PARSE**
sentence part .... **CLAUSE**
"Sentimental Journey" author **STERNE**
sentinel, mounted ... **VEDETTE**
separate . **SIFT, APART, SECERN**
separated .... **APART**
separation .... **SCHISM**
sequence, 3-card ..... **TIERCE**
sequester .... **ISOLATE**
Sequoia national park ... **MUIR**
seraglio .... **HAREM, SERAI**
serene .... **SERENO**
serf .... **ESNE**
serf, Rom. .... **COLONA**
serf, Spartan, ancient .. **HELOT**
sergeant fish .... **COBIA**
series .... **SET, GAMUT**
series, in a .... **SERIATIM**
d series of tones .... **SCALE**
serious ..... **GRAVE, EARNEST**
sermon .... **HOMILY**
serow .... **JAGLA**
SERPENT ..... see also SNAKE
serpent, Egypt. myth .... **APEPI**
serpent goddess, Egypt. . **BUTO**
serpent, Gr. .... **SEPS**
serpent, large .. **BOA, PYTHON**
serpent monster ...... **ELLOPS**
serpent, myth. .... **BASILISK**
serpent worship ...... **OPHISM**
serpentine .... **OPHITE**
servant........... **BOY, MAN, MAID, MENIAL**
servant, India .... **HAMAL, FERASH, HAMMAL**
servant, man's .... **VALET**
servant, P. I. .... **BATA**
servants, for .... **MENIAL**
serve soup .... **LADLE**
server .... **TRAY**
service, religious .... **MASS**
service tree .... **SORB**
servile .... **MENIAL**
serving boy .... **PAGE**
sesame .... **TIL, TEEL**
sesame oil ...... **BENI, BENNE**
sesame seed .... **GINGILI**
session, hold .... **SIT, MEET**

a set aside .... **DEFER**
set in type .... **PRINT**
set limits to .... **STINT**
set price .... **RATE**
set system .... **ROTE**
set thickly .... **STUD**
setback .... **REVERSE**
Seth's brother .... **CAIN**
Seth's mother .... **EVE**
Seth's son .... **ENOS**
setting .... **SCENE, MILIEU**
setting sun, Egyp. god of. **TEM, TUM, ATMU, ATUM**
settled .... **ALIT**
settler .... **BOOMER**
seven .... **SEPT**
Seven Dwarfs ... **DOC, DOPEY, HAPPY, GRUMPY, SLEEPY, SNEEZY, BASHFUL**
seven, group of .... **HEPTAD, PLEIAD, SEPTET, SEPTETTE**
"Seventh Heaven" heroine **DIANE**
seventh order, of ...... **SEPTIC**
seventh, pert. to ..... **SEPTAN**
sever .... **CUT, LOP, REND**
severe .... **STERN**
severely criticize ...... **PAN, SLATE, ROAST**

b sew hawk's eyelids ...... **SEEL**
"Seward's —," Alaska . **FOLLY**
sexes, common to both. **EPICENE**
shabby .... **WORN**
shabby woman .... **DOWD**
shackle .... **BOND, GYVE, IRON, FETTER**
shad .... **ALLIS, ALOSA, ALOSE, ALLICE**
shaddock .. **POMELO, PUMELO**
shade .... **HUE, SCREEN**
shade of difference .. **NUANCE**
shade of meaning ... **NUANCE**
shaded walk .... **MALL**
shadow .... **TAIL**
shadow, eclipse .... **UMBRA**
shaft .... **POLE, SPINDLE**
shaft column, feather .. **SCAPE**
shaft horse .... **THILLER**
shaft of column .... **FUST**
shaft, wooden .... **ARROW**
shafter .... **HORSE**
shake ..... **JAR, JOLT, NIDGE**
Shakespeare's elf ...... **PUCK**
Shakespeare's river .... **AVON**
Shakespeare's theatre .. **GLOBE**
Shakespeare's wife .... **ANNE**
Shakesperian clown .. **BOTTOM**
Shakesperian forest ... **ARDEN**
Shakesperian king ...... **LEAR**

c Shakesperian shrew ..... **KATE**
Shakesperian villain ..... **IAGO**
shallow receptacle ...... **TRAY**
sham .... **FAKE**
Shamash, wife of .... **AI, AYA**
"Shane," star of .... **LADD**
Shang dynasty .... **YIN**
shank .... **CRUS, SHIN**
shanks .... **CRURA**
shanty .... **HUT**
shape .... **FORM, MOLD**
shaped like a club .. **CLAVATE**
shaped like a needle **ACUATE, ACERATE**
shaping tool ... **LATHE, SWAGE**
share .... **LOT, RATION**
share .... **PARTAKE**
shark .... **TOPE**
shark, Eur. small .... **TOPE**
shark, long-nosed ..... **MAKO**
shark, nurse .... **GATA**
shark parasite fish ... **REMORA**
sharp .... **ACERB, ACUTE, ACUATE**
sharp .... **CHEAT**
sharp ridge .... **ARETE**
sharpen ... **EDGE, HONE, WHET**
sharpshooter .. **JAGER, SNIPER**
shavetail: abbr. .... **LT**
shawl ... . **MAUD, PAISLEY**

d shea tree .... **KARITE**
sheaf of grain: Her. .... **GERB**
shear .... **CLIP**
sheath, petiole .... **OCREA**
Sheba: Lat. .... **SABA**
shed, as feathers **MOLT, MOULT**
shed for sheep .... **COTE**
sheen .... **GLOSS**
sheep .... **EWE, RAM, MERINO**
sheep, Afr. domestic ... **ZENU**
sheep, Afr. wild **ARUI, UDAD, AOUDAD**
sheep, Asia wild .... **ARGALI**
sheep, Asia, wild, mountain **SHA, SNA, RASSE, URIAL, BHARAL, NAHOOR, OORIAL**
sheep cry .... **BAA, MAA**
sheep disease .. **COE, GID, ROT**
sheep dog .... **COLLIE**
sheep, Eng. black-faced **LONK**
sheep, female .... **EWE**
sheep genus .... **OVIS**
sheep in 2nd year **TEG, TEGG, BIDENT**
sheep, India, wild .. **SHA, SNA, URIAL, NAHOOR, OORIAL**
sheep, large-horned **AOUDAD, ARGALI**
sheep, Leicester ...... **DISHLEY**
sheep, male .... **RAM, TUP**

a sheep, N. Afr. wild
ARUI, UDAD, AOUDAD
sheep, of .... **OVINE**
sheep owner, Bibl. .... **NABAL**
sheep pasture, old Eng. .. **HEAF**
sheep, pert. to .... **OVINE**
sheep, Tibet .... **SHA, SNA, URIAL, BHARAL, NAHOOR, OORIAL**
sheep tick .... **KED, KADE**
sheep, unshorn .. **HOGG, HEDER**
sheep walk: Scot. .... **SLAIT**
sheep, wild .. **SHA, SNA, ARUI, UDAD, RASSE, BHARAL, NAHOOR, AOUDAD, ARGALI, OORIAL**
sheep, young ...... **TAG, TEG**
sheepfold .... **REE, COTE**
sheeplike .... **OVINE**
sheepskin leather ..... **BOCK, ROAN, SKIVER**
sheerly .... **SOLELY**
shekel, 1/4, Hebrew ...... **REBA**
shelf .... **LEDGE**
shelf above altar ... **RETABLE**
shell .... **BOMB**
shell .. **TEST, LORICA, TUNICA**
shell beads .... **PEAG**
shell, large .... **CONCH**
shell, marine .... **TRITON**
shell money .... **ULLO,**
b **COWRY, UHLLO, COWRIE**
shellfish, edible
CRAB, ABALONE, SCALLOP
shelter .... **LEE, COTE, SHED, HAVEN, SCREEN**
shelter, hillside .... **ABRI**
shelter: Scot. .. **BIELD, SHEAL**
shelter, to .... **ALEE**
sheltered .... **ALEE**
Shem descendant ..... **SEMITE**
Shem's brother .... **HAM**
Shem's son
LUD, ARAM, ELAM, ASSHUR
Sheol .... **HADES**
shepherd prophet ...... **AMOS**
shepherd's crook **PEDA, PEDUM**
shepherd's pipe .... **OAT, REED**
shepherd's song .. **MADRIGAL**
shepherdess, "Winter's Tale"
MOPSA
sheriff substitute ..... **ELISOR**
sheriff's men .... **POSSE**
Sherwood .... **FOREST**
Shetland court president **FOUD**
Shetland hill pasture ... **HOGA**
shield .... **ECU, EGIS, AEGIS, PAVIS, DEFEND, PROTECT**
shield, Athena's .... **AEGIS**
shield, Austral. .... **MULGA**
shield-bearing or border. **ORLE**
c shield, medieval .... **ECU**
shield, Rom.
SCUTA, SCUTUM, CLIPEUS
shield-shaped **PELTATE, SCUTATE**
shield, small .... **ECU**
shield strap .... **ENARME**
shield's corner: Her. **CANTON**
shift .... **VEER**
shift position. **GIBE, GYBE, JIBE**
shin .... **CNEMIS**
shine **GLOW, GLISTEN, ERADIATE**
shingle, wedge-shaped .. **SHIM**
shingles .... **ZONA**
shining .... **NITID**
Shinto deity .... **KAMI**
Shinto temple .... **SHA**
Shinto temple gate .... **TORII**
ship ..... **KEEL, SEND, LINER, TANKER, TENDER, VESSEL, CARAVEL**
ship, back part .... **STERN**
ship boat .... **GIG, DORY**
ship body or frame ..... **HULL**
ship bow, curve of ...... **LOOF**
ship canvas .... **SAIL**
ship clock .... **NEF**
d ship drainage hole .. **SCUPPER**
ship employee ...... **STEWARD**
ship, 1st Northwest Passage
GJOA
ship, forward part **BOW, PROW**
ship, fur-hunting ..... **SEALER**
ship, ironclad ...... **MONITOR**
ship: Jap. ...... **MARO, MARU**
ship keel, rear part ..... **SKEG**
ship, large .... **TONNER**
ship, lowest part ...... **BILGE**
ship, Medit. ... **SETEE, SETTEE**
ship, middle part ...... **WAIST**
ship mooring place
DOCK, BERTH
ship, oar-propelled ... **GALLEY**
ship, part of
RIB, DECK, HULL, KEEL
ship plank .... **STRAKE**
ship platform .... **DECK**
ship pole .... **MAST, SPAR**
ship shaped clock .... **NEF**
ship side, opp. middle **ABEAM**
ship timber, bevel ..... **SNAPE**
ship timber curve .... **SNY**
ship timber, extra ..... **RIDER**
ship wheel .... **HELM**
ship, wrecked .... **HULK**
ship, 1-masted .... **SLOOP**
ship, 2-masted ... **BRIG, SNOW**
ship's kitchen .... **GALLEY**
shipboard covering .... **CAPOT**

a shipbuilding curve ..... **SNY**
shipbuilding piece **SPALE, THWART**
shipworm .... **BORER, TEREDO**
shipwreck, causing **NAUFRAGEOUS**
shirk .... **GOLDBRICK**
SHIRT .... see also GARMENT
shirt .... **KAMIS, CAMISE**
shirt, Oriental .... **CAMISE**
shoal .... **REEF**
shoal water deposit .... **CULM**
shock .... **STUN, APPAL, APPALL, TRAUMA**
shock absorber ..... **SNUBBER**
shod, as monks ..... **CALCED**
shoe .... **GAITER, SANDAL**
shoe form .... **LAST**
shoe front .... **VAMP**
shoe gripper .... **CLEAT**
shoe, heavy. **BROGAN, BROGUE**
shoe latchet .... **TAB**
shoe, mule .... **PLANCH**
shoe part **LAST, RAND, WELT, INSOLE**
b shoe strip ...... **RAND, WELT**
shoe, wooden ... **GETA, SABOT**
shoe, wooden-soled ..... **CLOG**
shoes .... **SHOON**
shoes, Mercury's winged **TALARIA**
shoelace .... **LACET**
shoemakers' saint ... **CRISPIN**
shoemaker's tool .... **AWL**
shoot .... **BAG, POT**
shoot at from ambush **SNIPE**
shoot at, marble to ...... **MIG**
shoot, cotton .... **RATOON**
shoot, plant .... **BINE, CION, GEMMA, SPRIT, STOLO, STOLON**
shoot, small .... **SPRIG**
shoot, sugar cane ... **RATOON**
shooter, hidden ...... **SNIPER**
shooter marble .... **TAW, AGATE, AGGIE**
shooting match .... **TIR**
shooting match: Fr. ...... **TIR**
shooting star .... **LEONID**
shop .... **STORE**
shop, Rom. wine ... **TABERNA**
shops, Rom. wine .. **TABERNAE**
shop's name plate ..... **FACIA**
shore .... **COAST, STRAND**
SHORE BIRD . see BIRD, SHORE
short .... **CURT, BRIEF, TERSE, STUBBY**
c short-breathed .... **PURSY**
short comedy sketch .... **SKIT**
short-spoken ... **CURT, TERSE**
short tail .... **SCUT**
shorten .... **CUT, DELE, ELIDE**
shortly **ANON, SOON, PRESENTLY**
Shoshonean .... **UTE**
shoulder blade ..... **SCAPULA**
shoulder, of the **ALAR, SCAPULAR**
shoulder ornament **EPAULET, EPAULETTE**
shoulder, road .... **BERM**
shoulder wrap .... **SHAWL**
shout. **CRY, CALL, ROAR, YELL**
shove .... **PUSH**
shovel .... **SPADE**
show as false .... **BELIE**
show off .... **FLAUNT**
show place, Rom. .... **CIRCUS**
show, street .... **RAREE**
"Showboat" author .... **FERBER**
showy .... **LOUD**
shrew .... **ERD, TARTAR**
shrewd. **SAGE, CANNY, ASTUTE**
shrike genus .... **LANIUS**
d shrill .... **PIPY**
shrill, to .... **STRIDULATE**
shrimplike crustacean **PRAWN**
shrine .... **ALTAR**
shrink .... **CONTRACT**
shroud-stopper: naut. ... **WAPP**
SHRUB .... see also TREE
shrub and tree .... **ALDER**
shrub, Asia .... **CHE**
shrub, berry-bearing ... **ELDER**
shrub, berry, Pacific ... **SALAL**
shrub, Chin. .... **TEA**
shrub, Congo medical .. **BOCCA**
shrub, desert **RETEM, OCOTILLO**
shrub, Eng. .... **HEATH**
shrub, evergreen .. **BOX, YEW, TITI, ERICA, HEATH, SALAL, OLEANDER**
shrub, flowering **ITEA, AZALEA, PRIVET, SPIREA, SPIRAEA, SYRINGA**
shrub genus **BIXA, INGA, ITEA, ROSA, ALDER, IXORA, AZALEA**
shrub, Hawaiian ..... **OLONA**
shrub, low spiny .... **GORSE**
shrub, Medit. .... **CAPER**
shrub, poisonous **SUMAC, SUMACH**
shrub, prickly .... **CAPER**

a shrub, Rhus genus **SUMAC, SUMACH**
shrub, strong-scented .. **BATIS**
shrub with grapelike fruit **SALAL**
shrub, yellow flowers **OLEASTER**
shun .... **AVOID, DODGE**
shut up .... **IMMURE**
shy .... **JIB, BALK**
SIAM .. see also SPECIAL SECTION
Siamese .... **THAI**
Siam. coin .... **ATT**
Siam. garment ...... **PANUNG**
Siam. group .... **KUI, LAO**
Siam. monetary unit .... **BAHT**
Siamese twin ... **ENG, CHANG**
SIBERIAN .. see also RUSSIAN
Siberian .... **TATAR**
Siberian wild cat ..... **MANUL**
Siberian squirrel ..... **MINIVER**
sibilant sound .... **HISS**
Sicilian resort .... **ENNA**
sickle, curved like ... **FALCATE**
sickle: variant .... **SIVE**
side, jewel's .... **FACET**
side arm .... **GUN, SWORD, PISTOL, REVOLVER**
b side: Lat. .... **LATUS**
side of head ... **LORA, LORUM**
side, pert. to **COSTAL, LATERAL**
side-post, door's ...... **JAMB**
sidetrack .... **SHUNT**
side street, Chin. ... **HUTUNG**
side timber: naut. ..... **BIBB**
side, toward the .... **LATERAD**
sidereal .... **ASTRAL**
sidewalk .... **PAVEMENT**
sidewalk edge ... **CURB, KERB**
sidewinder .... **CROTALUS**
sidle .... **EDGE**
Siegfried's murderer ... **HAGEN**
siesta .... **NAP**
sieve .... **SIFT, PUREE, BOLTER**
sieve for clay .... **LAUN**
Sif, son of .... **ULL, ULLR**
sift .... **SCREEN**
sift: dialect .... **REE**
sift: old Eng. .... **LUE**
sift: Scot. .... **SIE**
sifter .... **SIEVE**
sigh .... **SOUF, SOUGH**
sight, come into .... **LOOM**
sight, dimness of ..... **CALIGO**
sight on gun .... **BEAD**
sight, pert. to .... **OCULAR**
sign ... **MARK, OMEN, TOKEN**

c sign, music .... **PRESA, SEGNO**
sign: old Eng. .... **SEIN**
sign, pert. to .... **SEMIC**
sign up ..... **ENROL, ENROLL**
signal for attention ...... **PST**
signal for parley ... **CHAMADE**
signal to act .... **CUE**
signal to begin .... **CUE**
signature, affix **SIGN, ENDORSE**
signet .... **SIGIL**
signify ...... **MEAN, DENOTE**
"Silas Marner" author .. **ELIOT**
silence .... **GAG, HUSH**
silence: music .... **TACET**
silent ... **MUM, MUTE, TACIT**
silica .... **SAND, SILEX**
silica, rich in .... **ACIOLIC**
silicate .... **MICA**
silk-cotton tree **CEIBA, KAPOK**
silk-cotton tree fiber **KAPOK, KUMBI**
silk fabric ..... **GROS, MOFF, PEKIN, SATIN, TULLE**
silk filament .... **BRIN**
silk, fine .... **CRIN, TULLE**
silk, heavy .... **GROS**
silk in cocoon .... **BAVE**
silk, India ... **ROMAL, RUMAL**
silk, old heavy ..... **CAMACA**
d silk, raw .... **GREGE**
silk substitute .... **NYLON, RAYON, ORLON, DACRON**
silk thread .... **FLOSS**
silk, twilled .... **ALMA**
silk, unravel .... **SLEAVE**
silken .... **SERIC**
silkworm, Assam ... **ERI, ERIA**
silkworm, China ...... **TASAR**
silkworm disease .... **UJI**
silly .... **INANE**
silver: Her. .... **ARGENT**
silver lactate .... **ACTOL**
silver ore .... **PACO**
silver, uncoined, in ingots **SYCEE**
silverfish .. **TARPON, TARPUN**
silverize .... **PLATE**
silvery .... **ARGENT**
silvery-white metal .. **COBALT**
simian .... **APE**
similar .... **LIKE, SUCH**
Simon .... **PETER**
simper .... **SMIRK**
simple .... **EASY, MERE**
simple sugar .... **OSE**
simpleton ... **ASS, DAW, OAF, BOOB, COOT, FOOL, GABY, GAWK, GOWK, SIMP, GOOSE**
simulate **APE, SHAM, FEIGN, PRETEND**

a sin ... **ERR, EVIL**
sin, grief for ... **ATTRITION**
Sinai ... **HOREB**
Sinbad's bird ... **ROC**
since ... **AGO**
since: Scot. ... **SIN, SYNE**
Sinclair Lewis character **CASS**
sine — non ... **QUA**
sine qua — ... **NON**
sinew ... **TENDON**
sinewy ... **WIRY**
sing ... **LILT, CAROL**
sing, as a round ... **TROLL**
sing softly ... **CROON**
sing, Swiss style **JODEL, YODEL, YODLE**
singer, synagogue ... **CANTOR**
singing bird ... **OSCINE**
singing girl, Egyptian .. **ALMA, ALME, ALMAH, ALMAI, ALMEH**
singing, suitable for ... **MELIC**
single ... **ONE, BILL, MONO, ONLY, UNAL**
single out ... **CHOOSE**
single: prefix ... **MONO**
single thing ... **ONE, UNIT**
singleton ... **ACE**
sink, as putt ... **HOLE**
sink: geol. ... **DOLINA**
b sinuous .. **WAVY, SERPENTINE**
sinus cavities ... **ANTRA**
Sioux, Siouan ... **OTO, OTOE**
sir: India ... **MIAN**
sir: Malay ... **TUAN**
siren, Rhine ... **LORELEI**
Sisera's killer ... **JAEL**
sister ... **NUN, SIB**
"Sistine Madonna" painter **RAPHAEL**
sitatunga, Afr. ... **NAKONG**
sitting **POSING, SEANCE, SESSION**
sitting on ... **ASTRIDE**
situation, difficult ... **STRAIT**
siva snake ... **COBRA**
Siva, wife of **DEVI, KALI, SATI**
six, group of **SENARY, SESTET, SEXTET**
six-line verse **SESTET, SESTINA**
six on a die .. **CISE, SICE, SISE**
six, series of ... **HEXAD**
six: Sp. ... **SEIS**
sixpence: slang ... **SICE**
sixteen annas ... **RUPEE**
sixth: music ... **SEXT**
sixth sense: abbr. ... **ESP**
size of shot ... **BB, FF, TT**
sizing ... **SEALER**
skate ... **RAY**
skate genus ... **RAIA**
c skating area ... **RINK**
skegger ... **PARR**
skein of yarn ... **RAP, HANK**
skeletal ... **BONY**
skeleton, sea animal **CORAL, SPONGE**
skeptic ... **AGNOSTIC**
sketch ... **DRAW, OUTLINE**
ski, heel spring ... **AMSTUTZ**
ski race ... **SLALOM**
ski run ... **SCHUSS, SLALOM**
ski wax ... **KLISTER**
skier, mark of ... **SITZMARK**
skiing position ... **VORLAGE**
skiing, zigzag ... **SLALOM**
skilled person ... **ADEPT**
skillful ... **ABLE, DEFT, ADEPT, HABILE**
skillfully ... **ABLY**
skim over ... **SKIP**
skin ... **FLAY, DERMA**
skin, deeper layer ... **CUTIS**
skin, design on **TATOO, TATTOO**
skin disease ... **ACNE, MANGE, PSORA, TETTER**
skin disease, horse's .. **CALORIS**
skin disease, Peru ... **UTA**
skin infection ... **LEPRA**
skin layer ... **DERM, CUTIS,**
d **DERMA, CORIUM, ENDERON**
skin of a beast ... **FELL**
skin, pert. to .. **DERIC, DERMIC**
skinflint ... **MISER**
skink, Egypt. ... **ADDA**
skip ... **OMIT**
skip a stone ... **DAP**
skip happily ... **CAPER**
skipjack ... **ELATER**
skirmish ... **MELEE**
skirt, ballet ... **TUTU**
skirt section ... **PANEL**
skittle ... **PIN**
skulk ... **LURK**
skull, pert. to .. **INIAL, INION**
skull protuberance ... **INION**
skullcap, Arab. ... **CHECHIA**
skunk .. **CHINCHA, CHINCHE**
sky ... **FIRMAMENT**
sky god, Assyrian ... **ANAT**
sky: Chin. ... **TIEN**
sky god, Babyl. ... **ABU, ANU**
sky god, Norse ... **TIU, TIW, TYR, ZIO, ZIU**
sky, highest part ... **ZENITH**
sky: Polyn. ... **LANGI**
sky serpent, Vedic ... **AHI**
slab, engraved ... **TABLET**
slab, flooring, decorative **DALLE**
slag ... **DROSS, SCORIA**

a slam .... BANG
slam in cards .... VOLE
slander ...... LIBEL, ASPERSE
slang .... ARGOT
slant .... BEVEL, SLOPE
slanted edge .... BEVEL
slanted: naut. .... ARAKE
slanting .... SKEW, ASKEW
slanting type .... ITALIC
slantingly, drive .... TOE
slap .... CUFF, SPANK
slash .... JAG, SLISH
slater's tool, same as slate-trimming tool
slate-trimming tool
SAX, ZAT, ZAX
Slav .... SERB
Slav, ancient
VEND, WEND, VENED
Slav, E. Ger. .... WEND
Slav in Saxony .... SORB
slave .... ESNE, SERF, THRALL
slave, fugitive ..... MAROON
slave, Spartan .... HELOT
sled, Swiss .... LUGE
sled to haul logs ...... TODE
sleep .... NAP, NOD, DOZE
sleep, deep .... SOPOR
sleep lightly .... DOZE
b sleeping .... DORMANT
sleeping place BED, COT, BERTH
sleeping sickness fly .. TSETSE
sleeve, large .... DOLMAN
sleigh .... PUNG
sleight-of-hand .... MAGIC
slender .... LANK, LEAN,
SLIM, THIN, REEDY
slender woman .... SYLPH
slice, bacon .... RASHER
slice of meat .... COLP
slice, thick .... SLAB
slick .... LOY
slide .... SKID, SLUE
sliding door, Jap. ... FUSUMA
sliding piece .... CAM
sliding valve .... PISTON
slight .... MERE, SLIM, FAINT
slight intentionally SLUR, SNUB
slimy .... OOZY
sling around .... SLUE
slip. ERR, BONER, GLIDE, LAPSE
slip by .... ELAPSE
slip out of course ...... SLUE
slip, plant .... CION, CUTTING
slipknot .... NOOSE
slipper .... MULE, MOYLE
slipper, P. I. .... CHINELA
slope ...... RAMP, GRADIENT
slope: fort. .... GLACIS

c slope of vein or lode ... HADE
slope: Scot .... BRAE
slope of land ...... VERSANT
slope, steep ... SCARP, ESCARP
sloping edge
BASIL, BEZEL, BEZIL
sloth, three-toed .... AI
sloth, two-toed .... UNAU
slouch: Scot. .... LOUCH
slow .... POKY
slow loris .... KOKAM
slow: music .. TARDO, LARGO
LENTO, ADAGIO, ANDANTE
slower: music .... RIT
sluggish .... DOPEY
sluice .... CLOW
slump .... RECESSION
slur over .... ELIDE
slushy mass .... POSH
sly look .... LEER, OGLE
sly: old Eng. .... SLEE, SLOAN
sly: Scot: .... SLEE
smack ...... BUSS, KISS, SLAP
small .... WEE, TINY,
PETIT, PETTY, PETITE
small amount .. DRAM, MINIM
small arachnid .... MITE
small bottle .... VIAL
small bunch .... WISP
d small case .... ETUI
small cluster .... SPRIG
small coin .... MITE
small creature MITE, MINIMUS
small dog .... POM, PUG,
PUP, PEKE, FEIST
small goby, Atlantic ... MAPO
small: law .... PETIT
small marine animal .... SALP
small monkey .... LEMUR
small pearl .... PEARLET
small poem .... ODELET
small: Scot. .... SMA
small stream RUN, RILL, RILLET
small: suffix .... ING
small weight ... GRAM, MITE
smallest .... LEAST
smallest integer .... ONE
smallpox .... VARIOLA
smaragd .... EMERALD
smart .... STING
smart CHIC, ASTUTE, CLEVER
smartly dressed ... CHIC, TRIG
smear on .... DAUB
smell, disagreeable
OLID, REEK, FETOR
smelting mixture ..... MATTE
smelting waste .. SLAG, DROSS
smirch .... SULLY
smith, aided Siegfried .. MIME

a smock .... **CAMISE**
smoke .... **FUME, REEK**
smoke-colored .... **FUMOUS**
smoke, wisp of .... **FLOC**
smoked beef ...... **PASTRAMI**
smokeless powder ..... **FILITE**
smoking .... **AREEK**
smoking pipe ... **BRIAR, BRIER**
smoking pipe, Oriental
HOOKAH, NARGILE
smoky .... **FUMID**
smooth
EVEN, IRON, LEVEL, PREEN
smooth-breathing ...... **LENE**
smooth, make ..... **LEVIGATE**
smooth: phonetics ...... **LENE**
smooth-spoken .... **GLIB**
smoothing tool .... **PLANE**
snail, large . **WHELK, ABALONE**
snail, marine .... **TRITON**
snake ..... **ASP, BOA, ADDER, VIPER, PYTHON, REPTILE**
snake, Amer. .. **ADDER, RACER**
snake-bite antidote
GUACO, CEDRON
snake, black .... **RACER**
snake charmer's clarinet **BEEN**
snake-haired woman **GORGON, MEDUSA, STHENO, EURYALE**
b snake, India .... **COBRA, KRAIT, DABOIA, DABOYA**
snake-like .... **SINUOUS**
snake, S. Amer. ...... **ABOMA**
snake, tree .... **LORA**
snake, venomous, Ind. . **BONGAR**
snakes, pert. to ..... **OPHIOID**
snakebird .... **DARTER**
snakeroot, white ...... **STEVIA**
snap up bargains ...... **SNUP**
snapper .... **SESI, PARGO**
snapper fish: Maori .. **TAMURE**
snapper: N. Z. ...... **TAMURE**
snare .. **GIN, NET, WEB, TRAP**
snarl .... **GNAR, GNARR**
snatch .... **GRAB, SEIZE**
sneer . **GIBE, JIBE, FLEER, SCOFF**
sniff .... **NOSE**
snipe, Europ. .... **BLEATER**
snipe's cry .... **SCAPE**
snoring .... **STERTOR**
snow field, Alpine . **FIRN, NEVE**
snow goose genus ...... **CHEN**
snow, ground down .... **LOLLY**
snow house
IGLU, IGLOE, IGLOO, IGLOU
snow leopard .... **OUNCE**
snow lily .... **VIOLET**
snow, living in .... **NIVAL**
snow mouse .... **VOLE**

c snow panther .... **OUNCE**
snow runner .... **SKI, SKEE**
snow: Scot. .... **SNA**
SNOW WHITE
see SEVEN DWARFS
snuff .... **RAPPEE**
snuffbox bean
CACOON, MACKAYBEAN
snug .... **COSY, COZY**
snuggery .... **NEST**
so .... **THUS, TRUE, VERY**
so be it! .... **AMEN**
so much: music ...... **TANTO**
so: Scot. .... **SAE**
soak .... **RET, SOG, SOP, WET**
soak flax .... **RET**
soap, fine .... **CASTILE**
soap-frame bar .... **SESS**
soap: pharm. .... **SAPO**
soap plant .... **AMOLE**
soap substitute ...... **AMOLE**
soap vine .... **GOGO**
soapstone .... **TALC**
soapy mineral .... **TALC**
sober .... **GRAVE, STAID**
social affair .... **TEA**
social division .... **CASTE**
social unit or group .... **SEPT**
society, entrance into .. **DEBUT**
d society swell .... **NOB**
sock, Jap. .... **TABI**
sock, Rom. .... **UDO**
sod .... **TURF**
sodium alum .... **MENDOZITE**
sodium carbonate .... **TRONA**
sodium chloride .... **SALT**
sodium chloride: pharm. .. **SAL**
sodium compound ..... **SODA**
sodium nitrate .. **NITER, NITRE**
sofa .... **DIVAN**
soft
LOW, EASY, WAXY, TENDER
soft area on bill .... **CERE**
soft drink
ADE, POP, COLA, SODA
soft feathers ... **DOWN, EIDER**
soft ice from floes ..... **LOLLY**
soft job ..... **SNAP, SINECURE**
soft mass .... **WAD**
soft palate .... **VELUM**
soft palate lobe ...... **UVULA**
soft palate, pert. to
VELAR, UVULAR
soft palates .... **VELA**
soft-spoken .... **MEALY**
soften in temper ..... **RELENT**
softly: music .... **SOAVE**
soil: comb. form .... **AGRO**
soil, organic part .... **HUMUS**

a soil, rich .... **LOAM**
soil, sticky .. **GOMBO, GUMBO**
soil, type of .... **PEDOCAL**
solar disc ...... **ATEN, ATON**
solar over lunar year, excess of .... **EPACT**
soldier: Am. Rev. .. **BUCKSKIN**
soldier, Austral., N. Z. **ANZAC**
soldier, Brit. .... **ATKINS**
soldier, former .... **LANCER**
soldier, Gr. .... **HOPLITE**
soldier, Indo-Brit. ...... **SEPOY**
soldier, native India ... **SEPOY**
soldier's shelter ..... **FOXHOLE**
sole .... **PELMA**
sole of foot .... **VOLA**
sole of plow .... **SLADE**
solemn declaration. **VOW, OATH**
solicit .... **BEG, URGE, COURT, CANVASS**
solicitor's chamber ...... **INN**
solicitude .... **CARE**
solid .... **CONE, CUBE, PRISM**
solid, become **GEL, SET, HARDEN**
solid: comb. form .... **STEREO**
solidify ... **GEL, SET, HARDEN**
solitary .... **LONE, ONLY, SOLE**
solo .... **ARIA**
Solomon's aid giver ... **HIRAM**
b Solomon's temple rebuilder **HIRAM**
solution .... **KEY**
solution, strength of **TITER, TITRE**
solvent .... **ACETONE**
solvent, treat with .. **SOLUTIZE**
some .... **ANY**
somite .... **MEROSOME**
son: Fr. .... **FILS**
son-in-law .... **GENER**
son: Ir. .... **MAC**
son of .... **MAC**
son of Agrippina .... **NERO**
son of Joktan .... **OPHIR**
son of Reuben .... **PALLU**
son of: Scot. .... **MAC**
song .... **LAY, ODE, DITE, DITTY, MELOS, TROLL**
song, Christmas **NOEL, CAROL, WASSAIL**
song for solo voices ..... **GLEE**
song: Ger. .... **LIED**
song, Hawaiian .... **MELE**
song, Jap. .... **UTA**
song, morning: poet. .. **MATIN**
song, of a .... **MELIC**
song of praise, joy **PEAN, PAEAN, ANTHEM**
"Song of the South" Uncle **REMUS**

c song, operatic .... **ARIA**
song, religious **HYMN, CHANT, ANTHEM**
song, sacred **HYMN, CHANT, ANTHEM**
song, sad .... **DIRGE**
song: Scot. .... **STROUD**
song, simple .... **DITTY**
song, Sp. .... **CANCION**
song thrush ... **MAVIE, MAVIS**
sonship .... **FILIETY**
soon .... **ANON**
sooner .... **ERE, ERER**
soot .... **COOM, SMUT**
soot: old Eng. .... **SOTE**
soothe .... **EASE, LULL**
soothing **ANODYNE, LENITIVE**
soothsayer .... **SEER**
Sophocles, play by ... **OEDIPUS**
soprano, prima donna .. **ALDA, BORI, PONS, RISE, RAISA, CALLAS, STEBER**
sora bird .... **RAIL**
sorceress .... **CIRCE**
sorceress, Hindu .... **USHA**
sorceress, myth. .... **LAMIA**
sorceress, "Odyssey," Greek **CIRCE**
d sorcery, W. Ind. **OBE, OBI, OBEAH**
sore, make .... **RANKLE**
sore: Scot. .... **SAIR**
sorghum variety .... **MILO**
sorrow ..... **DOLOR, REMORSE**
sorrow, feel **RUE, LAMENT, REPENT**
sorrowful . **SAD, BLUE, DOLENT**
sort .... **KIND, CLASS, GROUP, SPECIES**
sortie .... **SALLY**
sortilege .... **LOT**
sorting machine ..... **GRADER**
soul .... **ANIMA**
soul, Egyp. .... **BA, KA**
soul, Hindu .. **ATMA, ATMAN**
sound .. **TONE, NOISE, VALID**
sound, kind of ...... **PALATAL**
sound loudly .. **BLARE, LARUM**
sound, monotonous **HUM, DRONE**
sound perception .... **EAR**
sound, pert. to ...... **SONANT**
sound reasoning .... **LOGIC**
sound, resemblance of **ASSONANT**
sound, solid .... **KLOP**
sound the ocean **PLUMB, FATHOM**

a sound waves, of ...... **AUDIO**
sound, without ..... **ASONANT**
sounding .... **SONANT**
soundless .... **ASONANT**
soup, heavy .. **PUREE, POTAGE**
soup spoon .... **LADLE**
soup, thick .... **BISK, HOOSH, PUREE, BISQUE**
soup vessel .... **TUREEN**
soupfin shark .... **TOPE**
sour .... **ACID, ACERB, ACIDIC, ACETOSE**
sour curdled milk: Nor. .. **SKYR**
sour-leaved plant ..... **SORREL**
sour milk drink. **LEBAN, LEBEN**
source, mineral .... **ORE**
source, obsidian's ...... **LAVA**
soursop .... **ANNONA**
south: Sp. .... **SUR**
South African .... **BOER**
SOUTH AFRICA ..... see also SPECIAL SECTION
S. Afr. assembly .... **RAAD**
S. Afr. dialect .... **TAAL**
S. Afr. Dutch .... **BOER, TAAL**
S. Afr. garter snake .... **ELAPS**
S. Afr. grass country .... **VELD**
S. Afr. greenhorn ..... **IKONA**
S. Afr. gully .... **DONGA**
S. Afr. "out" .... **UIT**
b S. Afr. town .... **STAD**
S. Afr. village .... **KRAAL**
SOUTH AMERICA .... see also SPECIAL SECTION
South American animal . **TAPIR**
S. Amer. bird ... **GUAN, JACU, SYLPH, TURCO, SERIEMA**
S. Amer. game bird **TINAMOU**
S. Amer. Indian group .... **GES**
S. Amer. lizard .... **TEJU**
S. Amer. tree **VERA, CEBIL, FOTUI**
S. Amer. ungulate .... **TAPIR**
"South Pacific" hero .... **EMILE**
Southern Cross constellation **CRUX**
Southern France .... **MIDI**
Southern river .... **PEEDEE**
Southern state: abbr. .... **ALA**
Southwest river .... **RED**
sovereign (coin) .... **SKIV**
sovereignty .... **EMPERY**
SOVIET .... see also RUSSIAN
Soviet news agency ..... **TASS**
Soviet newspaper .... **PRAVDA**
sow .... **PIG, GILT**
sow .... **SEED, PLANT**
sow: Prov. Eng. .... **YELT**
sow: Scot. .... **SOO**
sower .... **SEEDER**
sown: her. .... **SEME**
soybean .... **SOJA, SOYA**

c spa, Bohemian .... **BILIN**
spa, Eng. .... **BATH**
spa, Ger. .... **EMS, BADEN**
space between bird's eye and bill ..... **LORA, LORE, LORUM**
space between triglyphs **METOPE**
space, small **AREOLA, AREOLE**
spaces on bird's face **LORAE, LORES**
spade .... **LOY, SHOVEL**
spade, narrow .... **LOY, SPUD**
spade-shaped .... **PALACEOUS**
spade, turf .... **SLANE**
Spain, ancient .... **IBERIA**
SPANISH see also SPAIN, SPECIAL SECTION
SP. ARTIST see SP. PAINTER
Sp. belle .... **MAJA**
Sp. cellist .... **CASALS**
Sp. coin, old .... **PISTOLE**
Sp. dance ..... **JOTA, BOLERO**
Sp. epic .... **CID**
Sp. explorer **CORTEZ, BALBOA, CORTES**
d Sp. fabric .... **CREA**
Sp. fortress commander .. **CAID**
Sp. game of ball .... **PELOTA**
Sp. general, duke. **ALBA, ALVA**
Sp. hero .... **CID**
Sp. kettle .... **OLLA**
Sp. lady ..... **DONA, SENORA**
Sp. length unit .... **VARA**
Sp. man .... **DON, SENOR**
Sp. nun .... **AVILA**
Sp. painter **GOYA, MIRO, SERT, PICASSO**
Sp. poet .... **ENCINA**
Sp. pot .... **OLLA**
Sp. title. **DON, SENOR, SENORA**

SPANISH WORDS:
(tilde omitted throughout)
abbey .... **ABADIA**
afternoon .... **TARDE**
annatto seeds ... **ACHIOTE**
another .... **OTRO**
article .... **EL, LA, LAS, LOS, UNO**
ass .... **ASNO**
aunt .... **TIA**
bay .... **BAHIA**
bean .... **HABA**
before .... **ANTES**
being .... **ENTE**
black .... **NEGRA**
blue .... **AZUL**
box canyon .... **CAJON**

Spanish

a boy .... NINO
bravo! .... OLE
bull .... TORO
but .... PERO
canal .... CANO
chaperon . DUENA, DUENNA
chest .... CAJETA
chief .... JEFE, ADALID
child .... NINO
church .... IGLESIA
city .... CIUDAD
clay building . ADOBE, TAPIA
cloak .... CAPA
clothes .... ROPA
corral .... ATAJO
cut .... TAJO
day .... DIA
dining hall .... SALA
dove .... PALOMA
drawing room .... SALA
estuary .... RIA
evening .... TARDE
evil .... MALO
first .... PRIMUS
for .... POR
friend .... AMIGO
funds .... CAJA
girl .... NINA
God .... DIOS
gold .... ORO
b good-bye .... ADIOS
grass fiber rope ...... SOGA
grille .... REJA
gulch .... ARROYO
gypsy .... GITANO
hall .... SALA
hamlet .... ALDA
harbor entrance ..... BOCA
health .... SANO
hello .... HOLLA
hill . ALTO, CERRO, MORRO
hillside .... FALDA
hotel .... POSADA
house .... CASA
Indian .... INDIO
inlet .... RIA, ESTERO
jail keeper .... CAID
judge .... JUEZ
king .... REY
lady .... DAMA
lake .... LAGO
landmark .... SENAL
latter .... ESTE
lawsuit .... ACTO
letter .... CARTA
lime .... LIMA
love .... AMOR
man .... HOMBRE
manservent .... MOZO
mayor .. ALCADE, ALCALDE

c mouth .... BOCA
movie house .... CINE
meadow .... VEGA
my .... MIO
of .... DE
open space .... COSO
other .... OTRA
parish priest .... CURA
peak .... PICO
people .... GENTE
pine .... PINO
pole .... PALO
pole, wooden .... PALO
porridge .... ATOLE
post office .... CORREO
pot .... OLLA
priest .... CURA, PADRE
queen .... REINA
ragged person .... ROTO
raisin .... PASA
red .... ROJO
river .... RIO
road .... CAMINO
room .... SALA
rum .... RON
saint, feminine .... SANTA
she .... ELLA
silver .... PLATA
six .... SEIS
snake .... CULEBRA
d song .... CANCION
south .... SUR
street ...... CALLE, CALLI
sweet potato ..... CAMOTE
tall .... ALTA
this .... ESTA, ESTE
three .... TRES
to be .... SER, ESTE
tomorrow .... MANANA
trench .... TAJO
uncle .... TIO
very .... MUY
water .... AGUA
wax .... CERA
wit .... SAL
with .... DE
work .... OBRA
yes .... SI
you .... TE

spar ...... BOX, BOOM, GAFF, MAST, YARD, SPRIT
spar for colors .... GAFF
spar, heavy .... BARITE
spar, loading .... STEEVE
spar, small .... SPRIT
spare .... LEAN, EXTRA, GAUNT, LENTEN
sparkle .... GLITTER
sparkling, as wine . MOUSSEUX
sparrow, hedge .... DONEY

a Sparta queen .... **LEDA**
Spartan army division .. **MORA**
Spartan magistrate ... **EPHOR**
spasm .... **FIT, TIC, JERK**
spawning place .... **REDD**
speak
UTTER, ORATE, DECLAIM
speak: comb. form ..... **LALO**
speak, inability to ... **ALALIA**
speak theatrically ..... **EMOTE**
speaker ... **ORATOR, LOCUTOR**
speaking tube, pilot's. **GOSPORT**
spear .... **DART, LANCE**
spear, Afr. **ASSAGAI, ASSEGAI**
spear, fish .... **GIG, GAFF**
spear-like weapon **PIKE, LANCE**
spear-shaped .... **HASTATE**
spear, 3-prong ..... **TRIDENT**
spear thrower, Austral.
WOMERA
special: Moslem law
KHAS, KHASS
species .... **KIND, SORT**
specific date .... **DAY**
specified time .... **DATE**
specimen .... **SAMPLE**
speck .... **DOT, MOTE, FLECK**
speckle .... **DOT, STIPPLE**
spectacle .... **PAGEANT**
specter .... **BOGY, BOGEY,**
b **GHOST, SHADE**
speech ... **LECTURE, ORATION**
speech, art of ..... **RHETORIC**
speech defect
LISP, ALOGIA, STAMMER
speech goddess, Hindu
VAC, DEVI, VACH
speech, local .... **PATOIS**
speech, long .... **SPIEL**
speech, loss of ...... **APHASIA**
speech peculiarity ..... **IDIOM**
speech, violent ...... **TIRADE**
speechless ...... **DUMB, MUTE**
speed ..... **HIE, RUN, PACE,**
RACE, HASTE, HASTEN,
RAPIDITY
speed, at full .... **AMAIN**
spelt .... **ADOR, EMMER**
Spenser heroine .... **UNA**
Spenser's name for Ireland
IRENA
sphere .... **ORB**
sphere of action ..... **ARENA**
spice .... **MACE**
spice ball .... **FAGOT, FAGGOT**
spicknel .... **MEU, MEW**
spicy .... **RACY**
spider crab genus **MAIA, MAJA**
spider fluid: Pharm. **ARANEIN**

c spider monkey
QUATA, ATELES, COAITA
spider nest .... **NIDUS**
spigot .... **TAP**
spike .... **EAR, GAD, BROB**
spikenard .... **NARD**
spin
BIRL, REEL, TWIRL, ROTATE
spinal column ... **AXIS, AXON**
spinal cord .... **MYELON**
spinal membrane ...... **DURA**
spindle .... **COP, AXLE**
spindle, yarn .... **HASP**
spine .... **AXIS, AXON**
spine bones .... **SACRA**
spine, slender .... **SETA**
spineless cactus ...... **CHAUTE**
spiniform .... **SPINATE**
spinning jenny .... **MULE**
spiny shrub genus ...... **ULEX**
spiral formation ..... **VOLUTE**
spire ornament .... **EPI**
spirit .... **ELAN, SOUL, METAL**
spirit: Egyp. myth ..... **BA, KA**
spirit: Ger. .... **GEIST**
spirit, Ir. . **BANSHEE, BANSHIE**
spirit lamp .... **ETNA**
spirit, Moslem ..... **JIN, JINN,**
GENIE, GENII, JINNI, JINNEE
spirit of air .... **ARIEL**
spirit of evil .. **DEMON, DEVIL**
d spirit of man: Egypt ..... **AKH**
spirit raiser .. **ELATER, ELATOR**
spirits and water ...... **GROG**
spirits of the dead .... **MANES**
spirited .... **EAGER, CONMOTO**
spirited horse .... **STEED**
spiritual body: Egypt. ... **SAHU**
spiritual struggle ..... **PENIEL**
spiritualist meeting ... **SEANCE**
splash .... **LAP**
spleen .... **MILT**
splendid .... **GRAND**
splendor .... **ECLAT**
splendor, goddess of: Hindu
UMA
split .... **RIT, RENT, RIVE,**
CLEFT, RIVEN, CLEAVE
split pulse .... **DAL**
spoil .... **ROT, BOTCH**
spoil, as eggs .... **ADDLE**
spoils of war .... **LOOT**
spoken .... **ORAL**
spoken word .... **AGRAPH**
spokes, having .... **RADIAL**
sponge, calcareous ... **LEUCON**
sponge gourd ... **LOOF, LOOFA**
sponge on ..... **MUMP, LEACH**
sponge spicule, bow-shaped
OXEA, TOXA, PINULUS
sponge, young .... **ASCON**

a spongewood .... **SOLA**
sponsor .... **PATRON**
sponsorship ...... **EGIS, AEGIS**
spool .... **REEL**
spore .... **SEED**
spore cluster .... **SORUS**
spore fruit of rust fungi **AECIA, TELIA, AECIUM, TELIUM**
spore sac, fungus **ASCI, ASCUS**
sport .... **RUX, GAME, GOLF, PLAY, POLO**
sports arena **STADIA, STADIUM**
sports center ... **RINK, ARENA**
sports hall .... **GYM**
spot in mineral ..... **MACLE**
spot on card .... **PIP**
spotted .... **PIED, PINTO, DAPPLED, MACULOSE**
spotted cavy .... **PACA**
spotted deer **KAKAR, CHITAL**
spotted moth ...... **FORESTER**
spotted sting-ray ..... **OBISPO**
spotted, to make **DAPPLE, STIPPLE**
spouse .... **MATE, WIFE**
spray .... **ATOMIZE**
spray, sea .... **LIPPER**
b spread .... **TED**
spread by peening .... **RIVET**
spread by report **BRUIT, NORATE**
spread out .... **FAN**
spread rumor .... **GOSSIP**
spread the word .... **TELL**
spread to dry, as hay .... **TED**
sprightly .... **PERT, PEART**
spring .... **SPA**
spring back .... **RESILE**
spring: Bible .... **AIN**
spring-like .... **VERNAL**
spring: old Eng. .... **KELD**
spring, mineral .... **SPA**
spring rice, India ...... **BORO**
spring, small .... **SEEP**
springs, warm ...... **THERMAE**
springboard .... **BATULE**
sprinkle **DEG, WATER, SPARGE**
sprinkling: her. .... **SEME**
sprint .... **RUN, RACE**
sprite .. **ELF, FAY, PIXY, PIXIE**
sprite, tricksy .... **ARIEL**
sprout ... **CION, GROW, SCION**
spruce ... **TRIG, TRIM, NATTY**
spruce, Jap. .... **YEDDO**
spruce, white ...... **EPINETTE**
spume .... **FOAM**
spun wool .... **YARN**
spur .... **GAD, GOAD, CALCAR**
spur of mountain ..... **ARETE**

c spur part .... **ROWEL**
spur wheel .... **ROWEL**
spurs, having .... **CALCARATE**
spurt .... **JET, GUSH**
spy, garment-trade slang **KEEK**
spy, British, Revolution **ANDRE**
squama .... **ALULA**
squander .... **SPEND**
square dance .... **REEL**
square-meshed net ..... **LACIS**
squash .... **PEPO, CRUSH, GOURD, FLATTEN**
squash bug .... **ANASA**
squaw .... **MAHALA**
squawfish .... **CHUB**
squid genus .... **LOLIGO**
squirrel fur, Siberian **CALABAR, CALABER**
squirrel, ground Europ. .. **SISEL**
squirrel-like animal **DORMOUSE**
squirrel skin .... **VAIR**
squirrel's nest ... **DRAY, DREY**
ST. .... **see** SAINT
stab .... **GORE**
stabilize .... **STEADY**
stable .... **FIRM, SOLID**
stable compartment ... **STALL**
stable-keeper, royal .. **AVENER**
stables, royal .... **MEWS**
stableman .... **OSTLER**
d stack of hay .... **RICK**
staff .... **ROD, MACE**
staff-bearer .... **MACER**
staff, bishop's ...... **CROSIER**
staff of office .... **MACE**
staff, royal **SCEPTER, SCEPTRE**
stag ..... **DEER, HART, MALE**
stage direction **MANET, SENET, EXEUNT**
stage equipment ...... **PROPS**
stage extra ..... **SUPE, SUPER**
stage horn signal .... **SENNET**
stage setting .... **SCENE**
stage whisper .... **ASIDE**
stagger .... **REEL**
stagger: Prov. Eng. ...... **STOT**
stagnation .... **STASIS**
stagnation, blood ..... **STASIS**
stain, **DYE, SOIL, SPOT, TASH**
stair part ...... **RISER, TREAD**
stair post .... **NEWEL**
staircase spindle .... **SPEEL**
stake .... **ANTE, WAGER**
stake, like a .... **PALAR**
stake, pointed ..... **PALISADE**
stake, poker .... **ANTE**
stakes .... **POT**
stakes, —, Epsom Downs Race **OAKS**
stale .... **TRITE**
stalk .... **STEM**

a stalk, flower . **SCAPE, PEDICEL**
stalk, frond .... **STIPE**
stalk, plant .... **CAULIS**
stalk, short .... **STIPE**
stalk, sugarcane....... **RATOON**
stall in mud.............. **STOG**
stammer .... **HAW, HEM**
stammering sound .... **ER**
stamp............ **MARK, SIGIL**
stamp battery block .... **VOL**
stamp of approval.......... **OK**
stamp-sheet part......... **PANE**
stamping device .... **DIE**
stamping machine...... **DATER**
stanch .... **STEM**
stand .... **RISE**
stand . **BEAR, ABIDE, ENDURE**
stand, cuplike............ **ZARF**
stand in awe of .... **FEAR**
stand, small .... **TABORET, TABOURET**
stand, 3-legged .... **TRIPOD, TRIVET**
standard . **PAR, FLAG, ENSIGN**
standard **NORM, TYPE, NORMA**
standard of chemical strength **TITER**
standard, Turk .... **ALEM**
standing............. **STATUS**
stannum................... **TIN**
stanza, last .... **ENVOY**
b stanza, Nor .... **STEV**
stanza, part of .... **STAVE**
star.................. **ASTRO**
star, blue................ **VEGA**
star, brightest............ **COR**
star cluster, distant... **NEBULA, NEBULAE**
star, day .... **SUN**
star, evening. **VENUS, HESPER, VESPER, HESPERUS**
star facet................ **PANE**
star, fixed .... **SUN, ALYA**
star: Fr. .... **ETOILE**
star in Aquarius.......... **SKAT**
star in Aquilla.......... **ALTAIR**
star in Argo.............. **NAOS**
star in Big Dipper .... **PHAD**
star in Bootes............. **IZAR**
star in Cetus............ **MIRA**
star in Cygenus . **SADR, DENEB**
star in Draco....... **ADIB, JUZA**
star in Eridanus .... **AZHA, BEID**
star in Leo... **DUHR, REGULUS**
star in Lyra ...... **VEGA, WEGA**
star in Orion .... **RIGEL**
star in Pegasus .. **ENIF, MATAR**
star in Pleiades .... **MAIA**
star in Perseus............ **ATIK**
star in Scorpio .... **ANTARES**

c star in Serpens .... **ALYA**
star in Taurus... **NATH, PLEIAD**
star in Virgo .... **SPICA**
star near Mizar......... **ALCOR**
star, new .... **NOVA**
star-shaped......... **STELLATE**
star-shaped spicule..... **ACTER, ACTINE**
star, temporary .... **NOVA**
stars, dotted with .... **SEME**
stars, pert. to .... **ASTRAL**
starch.......... **AMYL, ARUM, SAGO, FARINA, CASSAVA**
starchy rootstock .... **TARO**
starfish............ **ASTEROID**
starnose................ **MOLE**
— Starr, comic strip character **BRENDA**
starred lizard **AGAMA, HARDIM**
start ... **BEGIN, SALLY, ROUSE**
starvation .... **INEDIA**
starwort............... **ASTER**
state.................... **AVER**
STATE.... see also GAZETTEER
STATE FLOWERS. see SPECIAL SECTION
state, New England: abbr..... **RI**
state of affairs........... **PASS**
state, pert. to .... **CIVIL**
d state of: suffix .... **ERY**
state of being: suffix ...... **URE**
state precisely .... **SPECIFY**
stately home... **DOME, ESTATE**
statements, confused **RIGMAROLE**
statesman, Brit........... **PITT**
station . **POST, DEPOT, PLACE**
stationary ..... **FIXED, STATIC**
stationary motor part.. **STATOR**
statistician........... **STATIST**
statute .... **ACT, LAW**
stave, barrel .... **LAG**
stay............ **WAIT, TARRY**
stay rope .... **GUY**
stays................ **CORSET**
stead .... **LIEU, PLACE**
steal .... **COP, ROB, GLOM, SNITCH**
steal cattle .... **RUSTLE**
steal: Eng.............. **GLOM**
steal, Eng. dialect .... **NIM**
steel beam .... **GIRDER**
steel: Ger............. **STAHL**
steel splint, armor skirt .. **TACE, TASSE, TASSET**
steep .... **RET, SOP**
steep .... **SHEER**
steep in lime........... **BOWK**
steer wildly .... **YAW**
steer, young: Prov. Eng.... **STOT**

a steering, direct ship's
COND, CONN
steersman .... **COX**
stellar ...... **ASTRAL, STARRY**
stem
CION, CORM, SCAPE, STALK
stem, fungus .... **STIPE**
stem, hollow .... **CANE**
stem, jointed .... **CULM**
stem of hop .... **BINE**
stem, rudimentary .. **CAULICLE**
stem, ship's .... **PROW**
stench .... **ODOR, FETOR**
stentorian .... **LOUD**
step .... **GRADE, PHASE**
step ... **PACE, STAIR, TREAD**
step, dance ..... **PAS, CHASSE**
step up to mark .... **TOE**
step, upright part of .. **RISER**
steps, outdoor .... **PERRON**
steps over fence ...... **STILE**
steppes, storm on ..... **BURAN**
stern **GRIM, HARSH, AUSTERE**
steward: Scot. ..... **MORMAOR**
stick .. **BAR, BAT, ROD, CANE,**
WAND, BATON, MUNDLE
stick .... **GLUE,**
PASTE, ADHERE, CLEAVE
stick, conductor's ..... **BATON**
stick together ...... **COHERE**
stick used in hurling .. **CAMAN**
b sticks, bundle of ...... **FAGOT**
stickler for formality .. **TAPIST**
sticky substance ... **GOO, GUM**
stiffly nice .... **PRIM**
stigma .... **BRAND**
stigmatic point of mango **NAK**
still .... **BUT, YET**
stimulant, coffee
CAFFEIN, CAFFEINE
stimulant, tea **THEIN, THEINE**
stimulate .. **FAN, WHET, ELATE**
sting .... **BITE, SMART**
stinging ant .... **KELEP**
stinging herb .... **NETTLE**
stingy .... **MEAN**
stint .... **TASK**
stipend, church ..... **PREBEND**
stipend: Scot. .... **ANNAT**
stipulation .... **CLAUSE**
stir .. **ADO, MIX, TODO, ROUSE**
stir up .... **RILE, ROIL**
stitch .... **PUNTO**
stitchbird .... **IHI**
stitched fold .... **TUCK**
stithy .... **ANVIL**
stock .... **BREED**
stock .... **STORE**
stock exchange, membership in
SEAT
stock exchange, Paris **BOURSE**

c stock market crash .... **PANIC**
stockade: Russ. .... **ETAPE**
stocking run .... **LADDER**
stockings .... **HOSE**
stocky .... **STUB**
stolen goods .... **SWAG**
stomach .... **MAW, CRAW**
stomach division, ruminant's
OMASUM
stomach, first .... **RUMEN**
stomach, ruminant's ... **TRIPE**
stone .. **AGATE, LAPIS, SLATE**
Stone Age tool .... **CELT,**
EOLITH, NEOLITH
stone, aquamarine .... **BERYL**
stone, breastplate .... **JASPER**
stone chest .... **CIST**
stone chip .... **SPALL**
stone: comb. form ..... **LITH**
stone-cutter's chisel .... **DROVE**
stone fruit .... **DRUPE**
stone, green . **BERYL, OLIVINE**
stone hammer .... **MASH**
stone, hard .... **ADAMANT**
stone heap ..... **CARN, KARN,**
CAIRN, CARNE, CAIRNE
stone, hollow .... **GEODE**
stone implement ...... **CELT,**
EOLITH, NEOLITH
stone, like a .... **LITHOID**
stone, monument .... **MENHIR**
d stone paving block ..... **SETT**
stone pillar .... **STELE**
stone, red ...... **SARD, SPINEL**
stone roller fish ...... **TOTER**
stone, rough .... **RUBBLE**
stone: Scot. .... **STEAN, STEEN**
stone set .... **PAVER**
stone, squared ...... **ASHLAR**
stone to death .... **LAPIDATE**
stone, woman turned to **NIOBE**
stone worker .... **MASON**
stone, yellow **TOPAZ, CITRINE**
stonecrop
ORPIN, SEDUM, ORPINE
stonecutter **MASON, LAPICIDE**
stonecutter's chisel ... **DROVE**
stoneware: Fr. .... **GRES**
stool pigeon .... **NARK**
stop ..... **DAM, BALK, HALT,**
STEM, WHOA, DESIST
stop, as engine .. **CONK, STALL**
stop by accident ...... **STALL**
stop: naut. ... **AVAST, BELAY**
stop short .... **BALK**
stoppage .... **JAM**
stopper .... **BUNG, PLUG**
storage battery plate ... **GRID**
storage place **BIN, BARN, SILO**
store, army .... **CANTEEN**
store fodder .... **ENSILE**

a storehouse .... ETAPE
storehouse, army ..... DEPOT
storehouse, India .... GOLA
storehouse, public ..... ETAPE
stork .... MARABOU
storm FUME, FURY, RAGE, RAVE
storm, away from ...... ALEE
storm, dust .... SIMOON
storm: Fr. .... ORAGE
storm god, Babyl. ZU, ADAD, ADDA, ADDU
story, Norse .... SAGA
story, short .... CONTE
stoss, opposite of .... LEE
stout .... BURLY
stout, kind of .... PORTER
stove .... ETNA, RANGE
"Stowe" character EVA, TOM, TOPSY
straight .... DIRECT
straight-edge .... RULER
strain .... EXERT
strained .... TENSE
strainer .... SIEVE
strainer, wool cloth ... TAMIS
Straits Settlement region PENANG
strange .... ODD
strap on falcon's leg .... JESS
strap-shaped .... LORATE
b strass .... PASTE
stratagem .... RUSE, WILE
stratagem, sudden ...... COUP
stratum .... LAYER
straw hat ...... BAKU, MILAN
stray .... ERR
stray .... WAIF
stray animal .... CAVY
streak .... ROE, LINE, VEIN, STRIA, STRAKE, STRIAE
streaky .... LINY, ROWY
stream FLOW, RILL, BOURN, RIVER
streamlet ...... RILL, RUNNEL
street Arab .... GAMIN
street: It., Sp. .. CALLE, CALLI
street, narrow .... LANE
street roisterer .... MUN
street urchin .... ARAB
street, Venice water .. RIO, RII
strength .... POWER
strengthening .... ROBORANT
stress .... ICTUS
stressed beat, syllable .. ARSIS
stretch: Scot. .... STENT
stretched out ...... PROLATE
stretcher .... LITTER
stretching frame .... TENTER, STENTER
strewn with flowers: Her. SEME

c strife .... WAR
strife, civil .... STASIS
strike .. BAT, HIT, RAP, CONK, SLOG, SLUG, SOCK, SWAT, WHAM, SMITE
strikebreaker ..... FINK, SCAB
striking effect .... ECLAT
string of mules .... ATAJO
stringy .... ROPY
strip .. BARE, DIVEST, STRAKE
strip of land ... DOAB, DUAB
strip of wood .... LATH
strip off skin .... FLAY
strip, oxhide, S. Afr. ... RIEM
strip, wood, metal ... SPLINE
stripe .... BAR, BAND, WALE, WEAL, STREAK
stripe of color: zool. .. PLAGA
stripling .... BOY, LAD
strive .... AIM, VIE
strobile .... CONE
stroke .... FIT, ICTUS
stroke, brilliant .... COUP
stroll .... AMBLE
strong-arm man .... GOON
strong, as cigars .... MADURO
strong desire .... HUNGER
strong man .... SAMSON
strong man, Gr. .... ATLAS
strong point .... FORTE
d strong-scented ... OLID, RANK
strongbox .... SAFE
stronghold .. FORT, SION, ZION
struck with horror ... AGHAST
structure, tall .... TOWER
struggle .... COPE
struggle helplessly. FLOUNDER
struggled .... HOVE
stud .... BOSS
student in charge ... MONITOR
studio, art .... ATELIER
study ...... CON, PORE, READ
study group .... SEMINAR
stuff .... PAD, RAM, CRAM
stuffing .... KAPOK
stum .... MUST
stumble: prov. Eng. ..... STOT
stump of branch .... SKEG
stunted trees .... SCRUB
stupefied .... MAZED
stupefy .... DAZE, MAZE, STUN, BESOT
stupid .... CRASS, DENSE
stupid person ...... ASS, OAF CLOD, COOT, DOLT, LOON, LOUT, LOWN, MOKE
stupor .... COMA, SOPOR
sturgeon, small ..... STERLET
style .... MODE, NAME
style of art .... DADA, GENRE

a stylet, surgical ...... **TROCAR**
stymie .... **IMPEDE**
Styx ferryman ...... **CHARON**
subbase .... **PLINTH**
subdued shade .... **PASTEL**
subject ...... **TOPIC, VASSAL**
subject in grammar .... **NOUN**
subjoin .... **ADD**
sublime .... **NOBLE**
submarine **PIGBOAT, SNORKEL**
submit .... **BOW, YIELD**
subordinate
MINOR, DEPENDENT
subside
EBB, SINK, ABATE, RELAPSE
substance, lustrous .... **METAL**
substances, class of .... **LIPIN**
substantiate .... **VERIFY**
substantive word .... **NOUN**
substitute
VICE, PROXY, ERSATZ
substitute for: suffix .... **ETTE**
subtle emanation ...... **AURA**
subtle variation ..... **NUANCE**
subtract .... **DEDUCT**
subway, Eng. .... **TUBE**
subway entrance ...... **KIOSK**
subway, Fr. .... **METRO**
success .... **HIT, WOW**
b succession .... **LINE**
successively .... **AROW**
succinct .... **TERSE**
succor .... **AID**
succulent plant .. **ALOE, HERB**
such .... **SO**
sucking fish ... **PEGA, REMORA**
Sudan lake .... **CHAD**
Sudan native .... **FUL**
Sudan Negroid .... **SERE**
Sudan people .... **HAUSA**
sudden attack: Med. .. **ICTUS**
suet .... **TALLOW**
suffer .... **LET, BIDE**
suffer from hunger
CLEM, STARVE
suffer: Scot. .... **DREE**
sufficient: poet. .... **ENOW**

SUFFIXES:
act of .... **TION**
action .... **ANCE**
adjective .... **ENT, IAL, INE, ISH, IST, ITE, OUS**
agent .... **URE**
alcohol .... **OL**
carbohydrate .... **OSE**
chemical or chemistry . **ANE, ENE, IDE, INE, OLE, ONE, ENOL, ITOL, OLIC**
c common ending **ENT, INE, ING, ION**
common suffix ..... **ES, ESE, ESS, INE, IVE, ETTE, YNONE**
condition .... **ATE, ILE, ISE, ANCE, SION, STER**
comparative ...... **IER, IOR**
compound .... **ICAL, ILITY**
diminutive .... **ET, IE, ULA, ULE, ETTE**
feminine ... **INA, INE, ELLA**
feminine noun .... **ESS**
follower .... **IST, ITE**
forming nouns from verbs. **ER**
full of .... **OSE**
inflammation .... **ITIS**
inhabitant of .... **ITE**
into .... **EN**
like .... **OID**
little .... **ET**
made of .... **EN**
make .... **ISE**
medical .... **IA, OMA**
mineral .... **ITE, LITE**
native of .... **ITE**
noun ... **IA, OR, ATE, ENT, ERY, ESS, IER, ISE, IST, ITE, ANCY, ENCE, ENSE, STER**
d noun ending .... **STER**
noun forming diminutive. **CLE**
number .... **TEEN**
or ordinal number .... **ETH**
oil .... **OL, OLE**
one who .... **IST, STER**
one who does .... **IST**
order of animals .... **INI**
ordinal .... **ETH**
origin, denoting ...... **OTE**
participle .... **ING**
person .... **ER**
plural .... **(old EN), ES**
quality .... **ANCE, ILITY**
rocks, of .... **ITE, LITE**
science of .... **ICS**
skin .... **DERM**
small .... **ING**
state of .... **ERY, ANCE**
state of being .... **URE**
substitute for .... **ETTE**
superlative .... **EST**
sympathizer .... **ITE**
town .... **TON**
tumor .... **OMA**
verb .... **ISE, ESCE**
with mineral names ... **LITE**
zoological .... **ATA**
Sufi disciple .... **MURID**
sugar .... **OSE, SUCROSE**
sugar cane disease ..... **ILIAU**

a sugar cane residue .. **BAGASSE**
sugar, crude .... **GUR**
sugar, fruit .... **KETOSE**
sugar, raw ...... **CASSONADE**
sugar, simple .... **OSE**
sugar source .... **CANE**
suggestion .... **CUE, HINT**
suit of mail .... **ARMOR**
suitable. **APT, FIT, PAT, PROPER**
suitcase ... **BAG, GRIP, VALISE**
suitor .... **SWAIN**
sullen .. **DOUR, GLUM, MOROSE**
sullen, act .... **MOPE**
sullen, be ...... **POUT, SULK**
sully .... **SOIL, DIRTY**
sultan, Turkish .... **SELIM**
sultan's order .... **IRADE**
sultan's residence ...... **SERAI**
sultanate .... **OMAN**
sultry .... **HUMID**
Sulu Moslem .... **MORO**
"sum," infinitive following **ESSE**
sum paid as punishment .. **FINE**
sumac genus .... **RHUS**
sumac, P. I. .... **ANAM, ANAN**
Sumatra squirrel shrew .. **TANA**
Sumatra wildcat ...... **BALU**
Sumatran silk .... **IKAT**
b "summa — laude" ...... **CUM**
summary
DIGEST, PRECIS, EPITOME
summer: Fr. .... **ETE**
summer-house
ARBOR, PERGOLA
summer, pert. to ..... **ESTIVAL**
summit
APEX, KNAP, PEAK, SPIRE
summits .... **APICES**
summon .... **CALL, CITE, PAGE, CLEPE, EVOKE**
sun .... **SOL, HELIOS**
sun apartments ..... **SOLARIA**
sun bittern .... **CAURALE**
sun: comb. form ...... **HELIO**
sun disk .... **ATEN, ATON**
sun-dried brick
DOBE, DOBY, ADOBE, DOBIE
sun god, Babyl. .. **UTU, UTUG, BABBAR, SHAMASH**
sun god, Egypt. ..... **RA, TEM, TUM, AMON, AMEN, AMUN, ATMU, ATUM**
sun god, Gr., Rom. ...... **SOL, APOLLO, HELIOS**
sun god, Inca .... **INTI**
sun, halo around .... **CORONA**
sun, pert. to .... **SOLAR**
sun porches .... **SOLARIA**
sun tree, Jap. .... **HINOKI**

c sunbaked building
DOBE, DOBY, ADOBE, DOBIE
Sunday of Lent, 4th .. **LAETARE**
sunder
PART, REND, SPLIT, DIVIDE
sundial, style of ..... **GNOMON**
sunfish .... **BREAM**
sunfish genus .... **MOLA**
sunken fence .... **AHA, HAHA**
sunset, occurring at **ACRONICAL**
sunspot center
UMBRA, UMBRAE
supercilious person ..... **SNOB**
superfluous: Fr. ...... **DE TROP**
superintendent, office
MANAGER
superior, most .... **BEST, TOPS**
superior quality: Fr. .... **LUXE**
superiority, belief in .. **RACISM**
superlative, absolute .. **ELATIVE**
superlative ending ...... **EST**
supernatural .... **OCCULT**
supernatural being, Melanesia
ADARO
supernatural power, E. Afr. **NGAI**
supernatural power, Polyn.
MANA
superscribe .... **DIRECT**
superstition, object of
FETICH, FETISH
d supper .... **TEA**
supplication, make ..... **PRAY**
supply .... **STOCK, ENDUE**
supply, fresh .... **RELAY**
supply of horses ..... **REMUDA**
support ...... **LEG, RIB, ABET, BACK, PROP, BRACE**
support, one-legged .. **UNIPOD**
suppose ... **ASSUME, IMAGINE**
suppose: archaic .... **TROW**
suppress ...... **ELIDE, QUASH**
Supreme Being, Hebrew . **IHVH, JHVH, JHWH, YHVH, YHWH**
surety agreement ...... **BOND**
surf, roar of .... **ROTE**
surface, attractive ... **VENEER**
surface of gem .... **FACET**
surface of a tool .... **FACE**
surfeit .... **CLOY, GLUT, SATE**
surfeited .... **BLASE**
surge .... **TIDE, BILLOW**
surgeon's instrument .. **TREPAN, TROCAR, ABLATOR, LEVATOR, SCALPEL**
surgical thread .... **SETON**
Surinam toad .... **PIPA**
surly .... **GRUFF, SULLEN**
surmise .. **INFER, GUESS, OPINE**
surnamed: Fr. .... **DIT**

a surpass ...... CAP, TOP, BEST
surplice, chorister's .... COTTA
surplus .... EXTRA, EXCESS
surrender
CEDE, YIELD, DEDITION
surrender: law .... REMISE
surround GIRD, BESET, INARM
surrounding area ...... ZONE
surtout .... COAT
survey .... MAP, POLL
surveyor's assistant .. RODMAN
surveyor's instrument
ROD, ALIDADE
surveyor's rod, sight on TARGET
Susa inhabitant ..... ELAMITE
suspend .... HANG
suspenders .... BRACES
suture .... SEAM
svelte .... SLIM, TRIM
swab .... MOP
swain .... LOVER
swallow BOLT, GULP, MARTIN
swallow, sea .... TERN
swamp ..... BOG, FEN, MARSH,
MORASS, SLEW, SLOO, SLUE
swamp gas .. MIASM, MIASMA
swamp, S. Afr. ... VLEI, VLEY
swampy belt, India ..... TERAI
swan, female .... PEN
swan genus .... OLOR
b swan, male .... COB
swan, whistling .... OLOR
swap .... TRADE
sward .... SOD, TURF
swarm .... NEST, HORDE
swarthy .... DUN, DARK
swastika .... FYLFOT
sway .... ROCK, ROLL
swear .... AVER, CURSE
sweat ...... SUDOR, PERSPIRE
SWEDISH .... see also SPECIAL SECTION—SWEDEN
Swedish:
beer .... OL
tea .... TE
toe .... TA
you .... ER
Swedish coin .... ORE
Swedish county, district .. LAN
Swedish explorer ...... HEDIN
Swedish order of merit .. VASA
Swedish royal guard DRABANT
Swedish sculptor ..... MILLES
sweep, scythe's ...... SWATH
sweet flag .. SEDGE, CALAMUS
sweet gale .... GAGL
sweet liquid .... NECTAR
sweet potato
YAM, BATATA, OCARINA
sweet potato: Sp. .... CAMOTE

c sweet red wine .... ALICANTE
sweet-smelling
OLENT, REDOLENT
sweet spire .... ITEA
sweetfish .... AYU
sweetheart: Ir. .... GRA
sweetheart: Scot. .... JO
sweetmeat: Fr. .... DRAGEE
sweetsop .... ATA,
ATES, ATTA, ANNONA
swell .... DILATE
swell of water .... WAVE
swelling LUMP, NODE, EDEMA
swelling on plants ..... GALL
swerve .... SHY, SKEW
swift .... FAST, FLEET
swift, common ....CRAN
swift horse .. ARAB, PACOLET
swiftly, run ...... DART, SCUD
swimming .... NATANT
swimming bell .. NECTOPHORE
swindle GIP, GYP, DUPE, SWIZ
swindler .... COZENER
swine .. HOG, PIG, SOW, BOAR
swine, feeding of ... PANNAGE
swine fever .... ROUGET
swine genus .... SUS
swing music .... JIVE
swing musician ...... HEPCAT
d swinish .... PORCINE
swipe .... GLOM
swirl .... EDDY, GURGE
SWISS .. see also SPECIAL SECTION—SWITZERLAND
Swiss capital ... BERN, BERNE
Swiss card game .... JASS
Swiss critic .... AMIEL
Swiss patriot .... TELL
Swiss state .... CANTON
switch .... TOGGLE
swollen .... TURGID
swoon .... FAINT
swoon: old Eng. .... SWEB
sword ... PATA, EPEE, BLADE,
SABER, SABRE, RAPIER
sword, Arthur's
EXCALIBAR, EXCALIBUR
sword, curved .. SABER, SABRE
sword, fencing .... EPEE
sword, matador's ... ESTOQUE
sword, medieval .... ESTOC
sword, Norse myth. ... GRAM
sword, put away .... SHEATHE
sword, St. George's
ASCALON, ASKELON
sword-shaped .... ENSATE
sword, Siegfried's ..... GRAM
sword, slender .... RAPIER
swordsman's dummy stake PEL
syllable, last .... ULTIMA

a syllable, scale .... **DO, FA, LA, MI, RE, SO, TI, SOL**
syllable, short .. **MORA, MORAE**
sylvan deity **PAN, FAUN, SATYR**
SYMBOL, CHEMICAL .... see SPECIAL SECTION
symbol .... **TOKEN**
symbol of authority ... **MACE**
symbol of Crusaders ... **CROSS**
symbol of protection .... **EGIS**
sympathizer: suffix ...... **ITE**
synagogue .... **SHUL, TEMPLE**
syncopated music .... **RAG**
syncope ...... **FAINT, SWOON**
synod, Russian .... **SOBOR**
syntax, give the .... **PARSE**

c synthetic fabric or fiber **NYLON, ORLON, RAYON, DACRON**
synthetic rubber **BUNA, ELASTOMER**
Syria, ancient .... **ARAM**
Syrian, ancient port ... **SIDON**
Syrian bear .... **DUBB**
Syrian bishop's title .... **ABBA**
Syrian city, old ...... **ALEPPO**
system .... **ISM**
system of rule ...... **REGIME**
system of rules .... **CODE**
system of weights ..... **TROY**
system of worship ...... **CULT**
systematic regulation ... **CODE**

T

T-shaped .... **TAU**
tab .... **FLAP, LABEL**
tabard .... **CAPE**
table mountain, Abyssin. **AMBA**
tableland .... **MESA**
tablet .... **PAD, SLATE**
taboo, opposite of .... **NOA**
b tabor, Moorish **ATABAL, ATTABAL**
Tacoma's Sound ...... **PUGET**
tack: naut. .... **BUSK**
tact .... **FINESSE**
tackle, anchor .... **CAT**
tael, part of .... **LI**
tag .... **LABEL**
tag, metal .... **AGLET, AIGLET**
Tagalog for river .... **ILOG**
Tahitian national god ... **ORO**
Tai race branch .... **LAO**
tail, of ... **CAUDAL, CAUDATE**
tail of coin .... **VERSO**
tail, rabbit's .... **SCUT**
tail: zool. .... **CAUDA**
tailor .... **SARTOR**
Taino fetish ..... **ZEME, ZEMI**
Taj Mahal site .... **AGRA**
take away by force ... **REAVE**
take away: law .... **ADEEM**
take back .... **RECANT**
take effect again ..... **REVEST**
take off .... **DOFF**
take one's ease .... **REST**
take on cargo ... **LADE, LOAD**
take out **DELE, ELIDE, EXPUNGE**
take part .... **SIDE**
take up again ...... **RESUME**
take up weapons .... **ARM**
tale .... **SAGA, YARN, STORY**
tale, medieval Fr. .... **LAI**

tale, Norse .... **SAGA**
"Tale of Two Cities" girl **LUCIE**
"Tales of a Wayside —" .. **INN**
talent .... **FLAIR**
talented .... **SMART**
talisman .... **CHARM**
talisman, Afr. .... **GRIGRI**
talk .... **GAB, GAS, CHAT, PRATE, PALAVER**
d talk: slang .... **YAK**
talk freely .... **DESCANT**
talk pompously **ORATE, HARANGUE**
talk, rambling ... **RIGMAROLE**
talk wildly ..... **RANT, RAVE**
Tallinn .... **REVAL**
tallow tree .... **CERA**
tally .... **SCORE**
Talmud commentary .. **GEMARA**
talon .... **CLAW, NAIL**
tamarack .... **LARCH**
tamarisk .... **ATLE**
tame, as hawks .... **MAN**
tan .... **BUFF, BEIGE**
tan skins .... **TAW**
tanager ..... **YENI, REDBIRD**
tanager, S. Am. **HABIA, LINDO**
tanbark .... **ROSS**
tangle ...... **SNARL, SLEAVE**
tangled mass ..... **MAT, SHAG**
tanning gum .... **KINO**
tanning, plant for ..... **ALDER**
tanning shrub **SUMAC, SUMACH**
tanning tree, India **AMLA, AMLI**
tantalize .... **TEASE**
Tantalus' daughter .... **NIOBE**
tantra .... **AGAMA**
tantrum .... **RAGE**
tap **PAT, COCK, SPIGOT, FAUCET**

a tapering dagger .... **ANLACE**
tapering piece .... **SHIM**
tapestry .... **ARRAS, TAPIS, DOSSER**
tapestry center .... **ARRAS**
tapeworm .... **TAENIA**
tapeworm larva .... **MEASLE**
tapioca-like food .... **SALEP**
tapioca source .... **CASAVA, CASSAVA**
tapir, S. Amer. .... **DANTA**
Tapuyan .... **GE**
tarboosh .... **FEZ**
target .... **BUTT**
Tariff Act writer .... **SMOOT**
Tarkington character ...... **SAM**
tarnish .... **SPOT, SULLY**
taro .... **GABE, GABI, DASHEEN**
taro paste .... **POI**
taro root ... **EDO, EDDO, KALO**
tarpaulin .... **PAULIN**
tarpon .... **SABALO**
tarradiddle .... **FIB, LIE**
tarry .... **BIDE, WAIT, STAY, LINGER**
tarsus .... **ANKLE**
tarsus, insect .... **MANUS**
tart .... **ACID**
tartar, crude ... **ARGAL, ARGOL**
Tartini's B-flat .... **ZA**
b task .... **DUTY, CHORE, STENT, STINT**
task, punishing .... **PENSUM**
taste .... **SIP, SUP, SAPOR, SNACK, PALATE**
tasteful .... **ELEGANT**
tasty .... **SAPID**
Tatar .... **HU**
Tatar dynasty, China .... **WEI**
Tatar tribe, W. Siberia .... **SHOR**
tattle .... **BLAB**
tattler, idle .... **GOSSIP**
Tattler publisher .... **STEELE**
tau cross .... **ANKH**
taunt ...... **JEER, MOCK, TWIT**
taut .... **TENSE**
taut, pull .... **STRETCH**
tavern .... **INN**
tax .... **CESS, GELD, LEVY, SCOT, SESS, STENT, ASSESS, EXCISE, IMPOST**
tax, church .... **TITHE**
tea .... **CHA, CHAA**
tea, black .... **PECO, BOHEA, PEKOE**
tea bowl .... **CHAWAN**
tea box .... **CADDY, CALIN, CANISTER**
tea, China ... **BOHEA, CONGOU**
tea, Chin. green .... **HYSON**
c tea genus .... **THEA**
tea-growing region ..... **ASSAM**
tea, kind of . **OOPAK, OOLONG, OOPACK**
tea, Labrador .... **LEDUM**
tea, marsh .... **LEDUM**
tea, medicinal . **PTISAN, TISANE**
tea, Oriental .... **CHA**
tea, Paraguay ... **MATE, YERBA**
tea, rolled ... **CHA, TCHA, TSIA**
tea tree .... **TI**
teacake .... **SCON, SCONE**
teacher .... **DOCENT, MENTOR**
teacher, Hebrew .... **RABBI**
teacher, Islam religious ... **ALIM, MOLLA, MULLA**
teacher, Jewish ...... **RAB, REB**
teacher, Moslem .... **ALIM, MOLLA, MULLA**
teacher, Xenophon's **ISOCRATES**
teacher's association: abbr. **NEA**
team of horses .... **SPAN**
team, 3-horse .... **RANDEM**
teamster's command **GEE, HAW**
tear .... **RIP, REND, RENT**
tear apart ..... **REND, TATTER, DIVULSE**
tease .... **TWIT, BOTHER**
technical name: biol. ..... **ONYM**
technique .... **ART**
tedious writer .... **PROSER**
d teem .... **RAIN, POUR**
teeth, false .... **DENTURES**
teeth, incrustation ..... **TARTAR**
Telamon's son .... **AJAX**
telegraph inventor ...... **MORSE**
telegraph key .... **TAPPER**
telegraph signal .... **DOT, DASH**
telegraph, underwater ... **CABLE**
telegraphic speed unit .... **BAUD**
telephone exchange .. **CENTRAL**
telephone inventor .... **BELL**
telephone wire .... **LINE**
telescope part .... **LENS**
television .... **VIDEO**
television broadcast . **TELECAST**
television cable ...... **COAXIAL**
television recording **KINESCOPE**
television tube .. **MONOSCOPE, ICONSCOPE**
tell .... **IMPART, RELATE, NARRATE**
tell in detail .... **RECOUNT**
Tell, site of legend .... **URI**
telling blow .... **COUP, ONER**
temper .... **ANNEAL**
temper, fit of .... **PET**
temperament: Ger. ..... **GEMUT**
"Tempest" sprite .... **ARIEL**
"Tempest" slave ..... **CALIBAN**
temple .. **FANE, RATH, RATHA**
temple, Asian .... **PAGODA**

a temple chamber, Gr. .... **NAOS**
temple, inner part ..... **CELLA**
temple: Siam. .... **VAT, WAT**
temple tower, India .. **SHIKARA**
tempo: music .... **TAKT**
temporary decline ..... **SLUMP**
temporary fashion .... **FAD**
temporary relief ... **REPRIEVE**
tempt .... **LURE, TOLE**
temptation .... **ALLURE**
ten .... **DECAD**
ten ares .... **DECARE**
Ten Commandments
DECALOG, DECALOGUE
"Ten Days that Shook the World" author ..... **REED**
ten million ergs .... **JOULE**
tenant .... **LESSEE**
tenant, early Ir. .... **SAER**
tend .... **SERVE**
tender .... **SOFT, OFFER**
tending toward .... **FOR**
tendril: bot. .... **CAPREOL**
tennis score .... **LOVE, DEUCE**
tennis shoe .... **SNEAKER**
tennis stroke **ACE, LOB, LOBB**
tennis term .... **LET**
b Tennyson character .... **ENID, ARDEN**
Tennyson heroine
ELAIN, ELAINE
Tennyson sailor ...... **ENOCH**
tenon .... **COG**
tenonlike piece .. **COAG, COAK**
tenor, famous ..... **MELCHIOR**
tense .... **TAUT**
tent dweller
KEDAR, SCENITE
tent dwelling Arabs ... **KEDAR**
tent flap .... **FLY**
tentmaker, the .... **OMAR**
tents .... **CAMP**
tentacle .... **FEELER**
tenth part .... **DECI, TITHE**
tepid .... **WARM**
Tereus' son .... **ITYS**
term .... **NAME**
term .... **SESSION**
term: algebra .... **NOME**
TERM, GEOMETRY .... see GEOMETRY, GEOMETRIC
term in office .... **TENURE**
term, math. .... **SINE, COSINE**
term of address .... **SIR, SIRE, MADAM**
termagant .... **SHREW**
terminable .... **ENDABLE**
termite, P. I. .... **ANAI, ANAY**
tern .... **SKIRK**

c tern, black .... **DARR**
tern genus .... **STERNA**
tern, Hawaii .... **NOIO**
terpene alcohol .... **NEROL**
terpene compound . **TEREBENE**
terrapin .... **EMYD, POTTER, SLIDER**
terrapin, red-bellied
POTTER, SLIDER
terrestrial .... **GEAL**
terrible .... **DIRE**
terrier, kind of .. **SKYE, CAIRN**
terrier, Scottish breed of . **SKYE**
terrified .... **AFRAID**
territorial division .... **AMT**
territory .... **LAND, SOIL**
territory, additional
LEBENSRAUM
territory, enclosed .. **ENCLAVE**
terror .... **PANIC**
terrorist .... **GOON**
tessellated .... **MOSAIC**
tessera .... **TILE**
test .... **ASSAY, TEMPT, TRIAL, EXAMINE**
test ground .... **BOSE**
testament .... **WILL**
testifier .... **DEPONENT**
testify ...... **DEPONE, DEPOSE**
d tetrachord, upper tone of. **NETE**
Teutonic, ancient ...... **GOTH**
Teutonic barbarian ..... **GOTH**
Teutonic deity .... **ER**
Teut. Fate ...... **NORN, URTH**
TEUTONIC GODS, GODDESSES, DEITY see NORSE SPECIAL SECTION
Teut. legendary hero ... **OFFA**
Teut. letter of alphabet . **RUNE**
Teut. people .... **GEPIDAE**
Teut. sea goddess .... **RAN**
Teut. sky god .. **TY, TIU, TIW, TYR, ZIO, ZIU, TYRR**
Texas shrine .... **ALAMO**
textile screw pine
ARA, PANDAN
texture .... **WALE, WOOF, GRAIN**
Thailand .... **SIAM**
Thames estuary .... **NORE**
than: Ger. .... **ALS**
than: Scot. .... **NA**
thankless person .... **INGRATE**
that is: abbr. ...... **E.G., I.E.**
that not .... **LEST**
that one: Lat. .... **ILLE**

a that which follows .... **SEQUEL**
thatch, grass to .... **NETI**
thatching palm .... **NIPA**
the: Ger. .... **DAS, DER**
"The Ballad of Reading —"
GAOL
"The Jairite" .... **IRA**
"The Lion of God" .... **ALI**
"The Red" .... **ERIC**
the same: Lat. .... **IDEM**
the squint .... **SKEN**
theatre .... **ODEA, ODEON, ODEUM, STAGE**
theatre box seat .... **LOGE**
theatre district ...... **RIALTO**
theatre floor .... **PIT**
theatre, Grecian ...... **ODEA, ODEON, ODEUM**
theatre group .... **ANTA**
theatre, part of Greek . **SKENE, SCENA, SCENAE, SKENAI**
theatre sign .... **SRO**
"Theban Bard" ...... **PINDAR**
Thebes deity ... **AMEN, AMON, AMUN, MENT, AMENT, MENTU**
Thebes, king of
CREON, OEDIPUS
theme .... **MOTIF**
theme: music .... **TEMA**
then .... **ANON**
b then: music .... **POI**
theoretical .... **PLATONIC**
there: Fr. .... **VOILA**
therefore .... **ERGO**
theseli veil .... **TEMPE**
Theseus' father ..... **AEGEUS**
thesis, opp. of .... **ARSIS**
thespian .... **ACTOR**
Thessaly, king of .... **AEOLUS**
Thessaly mountain ...... **OSSA**
Thessaly valley .... **TEMPE**
they: Fr. .... **ILS**
thick-lipped .... **LABROSE**
thicket .. **BOSK, SHAW, COPSE, COPPICE, SPINNEY**
thicket: dialect .... **RONE**
thicket, game .... **COVERT**
thickness .... **PLY**
thief, gypsy .... **CHOR**
thief: Yiddish .... **GANEF, GANOF, GONOF**
thigh bone .... **FEMUR**
thigh, of the .... **FEMORAL**
thin ...... **LANK, LEAN, RARE, SHEER, DILUTE, PAPERY, SPARSE, TENUOUS**
thin cake .... **WAFER**
thin: comb. form .... **SERO**
thin disk .... **WAFER**
thin layer .... **FILM**

c "Thin Man" dog ...... **ASTA**
"Thin Man" wife .... **NORA**
thin-toned .... **REEDY**
thin out .... **ATTENUATE**
thing: law (Latin) .... **RES**
things added ...... **ADDENDA**
things done .... **ACTA**
things to be done
AGENDA, AGENDUM
think ... **DEEM, TROW, OPINE**
think: archaic .... **WIS**
think (over) .... **MULL, MUSE**
third: comb. form .... **TRIT**
third day, every .... **TERTIAN**
third king of Judah ...... **ASA**
third: music .... **TIERCE**
Third Reich special police: abbr.
SS
thirst-tortured king: Gr. myth
TANTALUS
thirsty .... **DRY, ADRY**
thirty: Fr. .... **TRENTE**
thirty, series of .... **TRENTAL**
this: Fr. .... **CE**
this: Sp. .... **ESTA, ESTE**
this one: Lat. ..... **HIC, HAEC**
thither .... **THERE**
Thomas Hardy heroine ... **TESS**
thong .... **STRAP**
thong, braided .... **ROMAL**
thong-shaped .... **LORATE**
d thong, S. Afr. .... **RIEM**
Thor's stepson ..... **ULL, ULLR**
Thor's wife .... **SIF**
thorax, crustacean's . **PEREION**
thorn ... **BRIAR, BRIER, SPINE**
thorn apple .... **METEL**
thorn, bearing a ..... **SPINATE**
thornback ray .. **DORN, ROKER**
Thorne Smith character. **TOPPER**
thorny plant ... **BRIAR, BRIER**
thorny shrub .... **NABK, NUBK**
thoroughfare .... **WAY, ROAD, AVENUE, STREET**
thoroughgoing ...... **ARRANT**
those .... **YON, YOND**
those in power or office ... **INS**
thou: Fr. .... **TU**
thought .... **IDEA**
thought: comb. form .... **IDEO**
thoughts, form .... **IDEATE**
thousand .... **MIL**
thousand: comb. form . **MILLE**
Thrace, ancient people of **EDONI**
thrall .... **ESNE, SLAVE**
thrash .... **LAM, BEAT**
thread: comb. form .... **NEMA**
thread, cotton .... **LISLE**
thread, guiding ball of .. **CLEW**
thread-like .... **NEMALINE**
thread-like process ..... **HAIR**

a thread-like structure ..... **FILUM**
thread, of a .... **FILAR**
threads, cross .... **RETICLE**
threads crossed by woof. **WARP**
threads crossing warp ... **WEFT, WOOF**
threads, lengthwise...... **WARP**
threaded fastener .... **NUT**
threaten.... **IMPEND, MENACE**
three........ **TER, TRIO, TRIAD**
three: Ger................ **DREI**
three: Ital................ **TRE**
three-legged stand .... **TRIPOD, TRIVET**
three-masted ship ...... **XEBEC, FRIGATE**
3 parts, divided into: Her. **TIERCE**
3.1416 .... **PI**
three: Sp................. **TRES**
three-spot .... **TREY**
threefold ..... **TRINE, TREBLE, TERNARY, TERNATE**
threefold: comb. form ..... **TER**
threshold .... **SILL**
threshold, psychology ... **LIMEN**
thrice: music............. **TER**
thrifty .... **FRUGAL, SAVING**
thrive ..... **BATTEN, PROSPER**
b throat .... **GORGE, GULLET**
throat: Lat.............. **GULA**
throat, pert. to .... **GULAR**
throb........... **BEAT, PULSE, PULSATE**
throe.................... **PANG**
throng .... **MOB, HORDE, SWARM**
through .... **PER**
through: prefix .... **DIA**
throw .... **CAST, PITCH**
throw aside............. **FLING**
throw back .... **REPEL**
thrush.......... **VEERY, MISSEL**
thrush, Hawaiian .... **OMAO**
thrush, India .... **SHAMA**
thrush, missel... **MAVIE, MAVIS**
thrust .... **LUNGE**
thrust back .... **REPEL**
thrust down .... **DETRUDE**
thunderfish .... **RAAD**
thurible............... **CENSER**
Thuringian city........... **JENA**
Thursday, source of name **THOR**
thus .... **SO, SIC**
thus far .... **YET**
thwart.................... **FOIL**
Tiber tributary .... **NERA**
Tibetan chief .... **POMBO**
Tibetan ox................ **YAK**
Tibetan priest........... **LAMA**
Tibetan tribe......... **CHAMPA**

c tibia.................. **CNEMIS**
Tichborne Claimant..... **ORTON**
tick .... **ACARID**
tick genus .... **ARGAS**
tick, S. Amer....... **CARAPATO**
tickets, sell illegally...... **SCALP**
tickle............... **TITILLATE**
Ticonderoga's commander **GATES**
tidal flood ...... **BORE, EAGRE**
tidal wave, flow or bore. **EAGRE**
tidbit.................... **CATE**
tide, lowest high .... **NEAP**
tidings .... **NEWS, WORD**
tidings, glad .... **GOSPEL, EVANGEL, EVANGILE**
tidy .... **NEAT, REDO, TRIM**
tie .... **BIND, BOND, LASH, TRUSS, CRAVAT**
tie, kind of............. **ASCOT**
tie-breaking game ..... **RUBBER**
tie off .... **LIGATE**
tie, railroad .... **SLEEPER**
tier .... **ROW**
tiger cat, S. Amer........ **CHATI**
tiger, Persian ...... **SHER, SHIR**
tight ..... **SNUG, TAUT, TENSE**
tight place.... **FIX, JAM, MESS**
tighten: naut............. **FRAP**
tightly stretched .... **TENSE**
til.................... **SESAME**
d tile, hexagonal .... **FAVI**
tile, roofing .... **PANTILE**
tilelike............... **TEGULAR**
till the earth ..... **FARM, PLOW**
tilled land..... **ARADA, ARADO**
tiller .... **HELM**
tilt........... **TIP, CANT, LIST**
tilt..................... **JOUST**
tilting: naut.............. **ALIST**
timber bend .... **SNY**
timber, flooring .... **BATTEN**
timber, nautical .... **KEVEL**
timber, pine: Asia ..... **MATSU**
timber rot .... **DOAT, DOTE**
timber truck .... **WYNN**
timber wolf .... **LOBO**
timbrel ...... **TABOR, TABOUR**
time ..... **ERA, TEMPI, TEMPO**
time before............... **EVE**
time being............. **NONCE**
time gone by .... **PAST**
time out.............. **RECESS**
time, space of .... **WHILE**
time value, equalling in **DIMORIC**
times, old .... **ELD, YORE**
timid............. **SHY, PAVID**
timorous .... **TREPID**
timothy .... **HAY**
Timothy's grandmother: Bib. **LOIS**

a tin .... **CAN, STANNUM**
tin, containing .... **STANNOUS**
tin foil .... **TAIN**
tin plate .... **TAIN**
tin roofing .... **TERNE**
tinamou .... **YUTU**
tincture: Her. .... **OR, GULES, VERT, AZURE, SABLE, ARGENT, PURPURE**
tinder .... **PUNK, AMADOU**
tine .... **PRONG**
tine of antler .... **SNAG**
tinge .... **TAINT**
tinge deeply .... **IMBUE**
tingle of feeling ...... **THRILL**
tinkle .... **TING**
tiny bird, W. Ind. ...... **TODY**
tip .... **END, FEE, APEX, KNAP**
tip .... **CANT, LEAN, TILT, CAREEN**
tipping .... **ALIST, ATILT**
tiptoe, on .... **ATIP**
tire .... **FAG, JADE**
tire casing .... **SHOE**
tire, face of .... **TREAD**
tire support .... **RIM**
tissue .... **TELA**
tissue, of a .... **TELAR**
tissue, pert. to .... **TELAR**
TITAN . see SPECIAL SECTION,
b GREEK MYTH page 200
Titania's husband .... **OBERON**
titanic iron-ore sand . **ISERENE**
titlark .... **PIPIT**
title ..... **EARL, NAME, TERM**
title, baronet's .... **SIR**
title, Benedictine .... **DOM**
title, church .... **PRIMATE**
title, East .... **COJA, HOJA**
title, Ethiopian .... **RAS**
title Hindu gives Moslem **MIAN**
title, India .... **AYA, NAWAB, SAHEB, SAHIB**
title, Jewish . **RAB, REB, RABBI**
title, knight's .... **SIR**
title, king's .... **SIRE**
title, lady's ... **DAME, MADAM**
title, Moslem ...... **AGA, ALI, MOLLA, MULLA, SHERIF, SHEREFF**
title of address .. **MME., MRS., SIR, MAAM, MADAM**
title of honor, Moslem . **SAYID, SAIYID, SAYYID**
title of kings of Edessa . **ABGAR**
title of respect ..... **SIR, SIRE, MADAME**
title of respect, Afr. ..... **SIDI**
c title of respect, India .... **SRI, SHRI, SAHIB, SHREE, HUZOOR**
title of respect, Malay .. **TUAN**
title, Oriental .... **BABA**
title, Persian **MIR, AZAM, KHAN**
title, Spanish **DOM, DON, SENOR**
title to property or land . **DEED**
title, Turkish .. **PACHA, PASHA**
titleholder .... **TITLIST**
titmice, genus of ...... **PARUS**
titmouse .... **MAG, PARUS**
tittle .... **JOT, IOTA, WHIT**
Titus Andronicus' daughter **LAVINIA**
Tiwaz .... **ER, TIU**
to .... **FOR, UNTO**
to: prefix .... **AP**
to: Scot. .... **TAE**
to be: Fr. .... **ETRE**
to be: Lat. .... **ESSE**
"to be," part of ...... **AM, IS, ARE, WAS**
to go: Fr. .... **ALLER**
to love: Fr. .... **AIMER**
to the point that ...... **UNTIL**
to use: Lat. .... **UTOR**
toad genus .... **BUFO**
toad, huge .... **AGUA**
toad, order of .... **ANURA**
d toad, tree genus .... **HYLA**
toadfish .... **SAPO**
toast, bit of .... **SIPPET**
toasting word .... **SALUD, SKOAL, PROSIT**
tobacco ash . **DOTTEL, DOTTLE**
tobacco, chewing .... **QUID**
tobacco, coarse **SHAG, CAPORAL**
tobacco, Cuban .... **CAPA**
tobacco, low grade ...... **SHAG**
tobacco, Peru .... **SANA**
tobacco, roll .... **CIGAR**
toddy palm juice ...... **SURA**
toe .... **DIGIT**
toe, fifth .... **MINIMUS**
toe: Scot. .... **TAE**
togs .... **DUDS**
toilet case .... **ETUI**
Tokyo Bay city .... **CHIBI**
Tokyo, old name ... **EDO, YEDO**
tolerable .... **SOSO**
toll .... **FEE, KNELL**
Tolstoi heroine .... **ANNA**
tomb, Moslem **TABUT, TABOOT**
tomboy .... **HOIDEN, HOYDEN**
tomcat .... **GIB**
tone down .... **SOFTEN**
tone, lack of .... **ATONY**
tone, of .... **TONAL**
tone quality .... **TIMBRE**

a tone: Scot. .... TEAN
tones, series of ...... OCTAVE
tongue, gypsy .... CHIB
tongue of Agni .... KALI
tongue, pert. to ..... GLOSSAL
tongue, using the ..... APICAL
tongue, wagon .... NEAP
tonic .... ROBORANT
tonic, dried India
CHIRATA, CHIRETTA
tonic herb ...... ALOE, TANSY
Tonkin native .... THO
too early .... PREMATURE
too much: Fr. .... TROP
tool, boring .... AWL, BIT, AUGER, GIMLET
tool, cutting .. AX, ADZ, AXE, HOB, SAW, SAX, SYE, ADZE
tool, engraver's
BURIN, MATTOIR
tool, enlarging ...... REAMER
tool, grass-cutting .... SITHE, SCYTHE, SICKLE
tool, machine .... LATHE
tool, molding .... DIE
tool, pointed .... BROACH
tool, post hole digging .... LOY
tool shaper .... SWAGER
tool, splitting .... FROE, FROW
b tool, stone, prehistoric
CELT, EOLITH
tool, threading ...... CHASER
tool's biting edge .... BIT
tooth ..... COG, TINE, MOLAR, CANINE, CUSPID, FANG
tooth-billed pigeon ... DODLET
tooth, canine .... CUSPID
tooth: comb. form .... ODONT
tooth, gear .... COG
tooth: Lat. .... DENS
tooth-like ornament .. DENTIL
tooth, long FANG, TUSH, TUSK
tooth pulp .... NERVE
toothed formation ..... SERRA
toothed margin, having
DENTATE
toothed wheel .... GEAR
toothless .... EDENTATE
toothless mammals . EDENTATA
top .... APEX, CAP, LID
top-notch .... AONE
top ornament ..... EPI, FINIAL
topaz humming bird ..... AVA
topee material .... SOLA
toper .... SOT, SOUSE
topic .... THEME
topmast crossbar support .. FID
topsail .... RAFFE
torment .... BAIT, ANNOY, DEVIL, HARRY, TEASE
torn: archaic .... REFT

c torn place .... RENT
torrid region or zone .. TROPIC
tortoise .... GALAPAGO
tortoise, fresh water .... EMYD
tortoise, marsh genus ... EMYS
tortoise, order of ... CHELONIA
torturer .... RACKER
"Tosca" villain ...... SCARPIA
toss ...... CAST, FLIP, HURL, FLING, PITCH
tosspot .... SOT
total ...... ADD, SUM, UTTER
total abstinence .. NEPHALISM
totalitarian ruler ... DICTATOR
totem pole .... XAT
toucan .... TOCO
toucan, S. Am. .... ARACARI
touch .... ABUT
touch lightly .... PAT
touch, organ of .... PALP
touch, pert. to HAPTIC, TACTIC, TACTILE, TACTUAL
touch sense, pert. to .. HAPTIC
touchwood .... PUNK
tough .... WIRY, HARDY, ROWDY, CHEWY
tour: It. .... GIRO
tourmaline, colorless
ACHROITE
d tow .... PULL, DRAW
towai .... KAMAHI
toward: Lat. .... AD
toward stern ..... AFT, ABAFF, ABAFT, ASTERN
towel .... WIPER
towel fabric .... HUCK, TERRY
tower, Bibl. .... BABEL
tower, India .... MINAR
tower, little .... TURRET
tower, mosque, slender
MINARET
towering .... STEEP
towhead .... BLOND, BLONDE
town, Arcadia ancient ... ALEA
town: Cornish prefix ..... TRE
town: Dutch .... STAD
town: Ger. .... STADT
town, India pilgrimage . SORON
town: It. .... CASAL, CASALE
town: Jap. .... MACHI
town: suffix .... TON
township, ancient Attica . DEME
townsman .... CIT
toxic protein .... ABRIN
toy with .... TRIFLE
trace .... TINGE, VESTIGE
track .... TRACE
track, animal ... RUN, SLOT, SPUR, SPOOR
track circuit .... LAP

a track of ship .... **WAKE**
track, deer's .... **SLOT**
track, otter's .... **SPUR, SPOOR**
track, put off .... **DERAIL**
track, put on another **SHUNT, SWITCH**
tracker, India .... **PUGGI**
tract .... **LOT, AREA**
tract of farm land ...... **FIELD**
trade .... **SWAP, SWOP BARTER, TRAFFIC**
trade .... **METIER**
trade agreement ..... **CARTEL**
trader ..... **DEALER, MONGER**
trader selling to soldiers **SUTLER**
trading exchange .... **PIT**
trading vessel of Ceylon **DONI, DHONI**
traditional story .... **SAGA**
traduce .... **SLUR, DEFAME**
traffic .... **TRADE**
trail .... **SLOT, SPOOR, TRACK**
train of attendants **SUITE, RETINUE**
train, overhead .... **EL**
train, slow, many-stops . **LOCAL**
tramp .... **BO, HOBO**
trample .... **TREAD**
tranquil or tranquilize
b **SERENE, SOOTHE**
transaction ...... **DEAL, SALE**
transfer .... **CEDE**
transfer, property **DEED, GRANT**
transfer, sovereignty .. **DEMISE**
transferer, property .. **ALIENOR**
transform .... **CONVERT**
transgress .... **ERR, SIN**
transit coach .... **BUS**
"— transit gloria mundi" . **SIC**
translator of Freud, Amer. **BRILL**
transmit .... **SEND**
transom .... **TRAVE**
transpire .... **OCCUR, HAPPEN, DEVELOP**
transverse pin .... **TOGGLE**
trap .... **SNARE, ENSNARE**
trap door .... **DROP**
trap, mouse: dial. .... **TIPE**
trap, rabbit: dial. .... **TIPE**
trappings .... **REGALIA**
travel .... **TREK**
traveler .... **PASSENGER**
tray .... **SALVER, SERVER**
tread softly ...... **PAD, SNEAK**
treasure .... **ROON, TROVE**
treasurer, college ..... **BURSAR**
treasury agents .... **TMEN**
treat .... **USE**

c treat with acid ..... **ACIDIZE**
treat with malice .... **SPITE**
treatment .... **USE**
tree (3 letters) **ASH, ELM, FIR, LIN, OAK, YEW**; (4 letters) **AKEE, AMLA, AMLI, ANAM, ANDA, ARAR, ASAK, AULU, AUSU, AUZU, BARU, BIJA, BITO, BIWA, BOBO, BOGO, DALI, DILO, DOON, DOUM, DUKU, EBOE, EJOO, GOAI, GUAO, HINO, IFIL, IPIL, KINO, KIRI, KOPI, KOZO, LIME, LINN, MAKO, MYXA, NAIO, NEEM, NIOG, NIPA, ODUM, OHIA, PALM, PELU, PINE, PUKA, RATA, RIMU, ROKA, SAUL, SHEA, SUPA, TALA, TARA, TAWA, TEAK, TEIL, TEYL, TOON, TORO, TUNG, TUNO, TUWI, UPAS, WHAU, YATE, YAYA, YPIL**; (5 letters) **ASPEN**; (6 letters) **LINDEN**
tree, African .... **AKEE, BAKU, COLA, KOLA, ROKA, SHEA, AEGLE, ARTAR**
d tree, Afr. & Asia .... **SIRIS**
tree, Afr. gum .... **BUMBO**
tree, Afr. tallow .... **ROKA**
TREE, AMER. TROPICAL...see TREE, TROPICAL AMER.
tree, Argentine timber ... **TALA**
TREE, ASIATIC .. see ASIATIC TREE
tree, arrow poison ...... **UPAS**
TREE, AUSTRAL. .... see AUSTRAL. TREE
tree, Bengal quince ...... **BEL**
tree, black gum ...... **TUPELO**
tree, body of .... **TRUNK**
tree, boxwood yielding . **SERON**
tree, buckwheat .... **TITI**
tree, butter .... **SHEA**
tree, caucho-yielding ..... **ULE**
tree, chicle .... **SAPOTA**
tree, Chin. ... **GINKO, GINKGO**
tree clump, prairie .... **MOTTE**
tree cobra .... **MAMBA**
tree, coniferous (cone) .. **FIR, YEW, PINE, LARCH**
TREE. E. IND. ... see E. IND. TREE and TREE, IND.
TREE, EVERGREEN .... see EVERGREEN
tree, flowering ..... **CATALPA**
tree genus .... **MABA**
tree genus, Afr. ...... **OCHNA**

a tree genus, elms ULMUS, CELTIS
tree genus, small ... **CATALPA**
tree, gum .... **ICICA**
tree, hardwood **ASH, OAK, IPIL**
tree, India .... **DAR, MEE, SAJ, SAL, AMLA, AMLI, DHAK, MYXA, NEEM, SHOQ, MAHUA, BANYAN**
tree knot .... **BURL**
tree, locust .... **ACACIA**
tree, maidenhair ..... **GINKGO**
tree, Malay .... **TERAP**
tree, Medit. .... **CAROB**
tree, mimosaceous ...... **SIRIS**
tree moss .... **USNEA**
tree, N. Am. **TAMARAC, TAMARACK**
TREE, N. Z. see NEW ZEALAND TREE
tree, oak .... **ENCINA**
tree of olive family ..... **ASH**
tree, Pacific .... **KOU**
tree, palm .. **GRIGRI, GRUGRU**
tree, palm, Asiatic .... **ARENG**
TREE, P.I. ..... see P. I. TREE
tree, pod .... **CAROB**
tree, resinous ...... **FIR, PINE, BALSAM**
tree, showy Asia .... **ASAK**
b tree-snake .... **LORA**
tree, sun, Jap. ...... **HINOKI**
tree, swamp .... **ALDER**
tree, tamarisk salt ...... **ATLE**
tree, tea .... **TI**
tree, thorny .... **ACACIA**
tree tiger .... **LEOPARD**
tree toad genus .... **HYLA**
tree, tropical .... **EBOE, PALM, BALSA, MANGO, COLIMA, SAPOTA, LEBBEK**
tree, tropical Amer. **CEBA, DALI, GUAO, CEIBA, COLIMA, GUAMA, CEDRON**
tree trunk .... **BOLE**
tree, W. Ind. .... **GENIP, SAPOTE, LIBIDIBI**
trees of a region .... **SILVA**
treeless plain .... **PAMPAS, TUNDRA, STEPPES**
tremble ...... **QUAKE, DIDDER**
trembling ..... **ASPEN, TREPID**
trench .... **SAP**
trench extension .... **SAP**
trench, rear wall of .. **PARADOS**
trend .... **TENOR**
trespass .. **INFRINGE, INTRUDE**

c trespass for game .... **POACH**
trespass to recover goods **TROVER**
triad .... **TRIO**
trial .... **TEST**
triangle .... **TRIGON, SCALENE**
triangle, side of .... **LEG**
triangular insert .... **GORE**
tribal symbol .... **TOTEM**
TRIBE see also SPECIAL SECTION
tribe ...... **CLAN, FOLK, RACE**
TRIBE, BIBLICAL .... see SPECIAL SECTION
tribe: Bib. tent-dwellers. **KEDAR**
tribe division, Rom. **CURIA, CURIAE**
TRIBE, ISRAELITE ...... see ISRAELITE TRIBE
TRIBESMAN .. see TRIBES in SPECIAL SECTION
tribulation .... **TRIAL**
tribunal .... **BAR, FORUM**
tribute .... **SCAT, SCATT**
tribute: Gaelic .... **CAIN**
trick **FLAM, GAWD, JEST, RUSE, WILE, DODGE, FICELLE, STRATAGEM**
tricks, game for no .... **NULLO**
tricks, win all .... **CAPOT**
d Trieste measure .. **ORNA, ORNE**
trifle ...... **TOY, DOIT, FICO, STRAW, NIGGLE, PALTER**
trifling ...... **SMALL, SLIGHT**
trig .... **NEAT, TRIM**
trigonometry function **SINE, COSINE**
trigonometry line ..... **SECANT**
trill, bird's .... **TIRALEE**
trim .... **NEAT, TRIG, ADORN, DECORATE**
trimmed .... **SNOD**
trimming, dress . **GIMP, RUCHE**
trimmings, overlapping . **FLOTS**
Trinidad tree .... **CYP**
trinket .... **GAUD**
triple .... **TRI, TREBLE**
triplet .... **TRIN**
tripletail, P. R. .... **SAMA**
tripod, 6-footed .... **CAT**
Tripoli: measure , see page 188
"Tristram Shandy" author **STERNE**
Tristram's beloved ..... **ISOLT, YSEUT, ISAUDE, ISAULT, ISEULT, ISOLDE, ISOLTA, ISOUDE, ISULTE**
trite .. **BANAL, CORNY, STALE**
triton ...... **EFT, EVET, NEWT**

a troche ...... **PASTIL, ROTULA, PASTILE, PASTILLE**
TROJAN .... see also TROY
Trojan hero .. **PARIS, ENEAS, AENEAS, AGENOR, DARDAN, HECTOR, HEKTOR, ACHILLES**
trolley .... **TRAM**
troop-carrying group: abbr. **ATS**
troop, division, Gr. .... **TAXIS**
troops .... **MEN**
troops, spread .... **DEPLOY**
trophy .... **CUP**
tropic .... **SOLAR**
tropical Am. bird genus **CACICUS**
tropical disease . **BUBA, BUBAS**
tropical fever .... **DENGUE**
TROPICAL FRUIT .... see FRUIT, TROPICAL
tropical plant .... **TARO**
tropical shrub genus **INGA, SIDA**
trot .... **JOG, AMBLE**
trouble ... **ADO, AIL, WORRY, EFFORT, MOLEST**
troubles .... **ILLS**
troublesome person **PEST, AGITATOR**
trough, inclined ...... **CHUTE**
trough, mining .... **SLUICE**
b trout, British .. **SEWEN, SEWIN**
trout, brook .... **CHAR**
trowel, plasterers' ..... **DARBY**
Troy .... **ILION, ILIUM**
Troy, founder of .... **ILUS**
Troy, land of .... **TROAS**
Troy, last king of ...... **PARIS, PRIAM, PRIAMOS**
Troy, of ancient **ILIAC, ILIAN**
Troy: poetic .... **ILIUM**
truant, play: Scot. .... **TRONE**
truck .... **LORRY, CAMION**
trudge .... **PACE, PLOD, SLOG**
true copy: law .... **ESTREAT**
true olives .... **OLEA**
trumpet ..... **HORN, CLARION**
trumpet call, reveille .... **DIAN**
trumpet, mouth of .... **CODON**
trumpet shell .... **TRITON**
trumpeter perch .... **MADO**
trumpeter, pigeon-like . **AGAMI**
trundle, as ore .... **RULL**
trunk of body .... **TORSO**
trunkfish .... **CHAPIN**
truss up .... **TIE**
trust .... **RELY, TROW, RELIANCE**
trustee of a wakf.**MUTAWALLI**
trusting .... **RELIANT**
truth: Chin. .... **TAO**

c truth drug ...... **PENTOTHAL**
Truth personified .... **UNA**
try .... **TEST, ESSAY, ATTEMPT**
try to equal ... **VIE, EMULATE**
tsetse fly .... **MAU, KIVU**
tsetse fly genus .... **GLOSSINA**
tub .... **VAT, KNAP, KNOP**
tub, brewer's .... **KEEVE**
tub, broad .... **KEELER**
tub, wooden: dialect ...... **SOE**
tube .... **DUCT**
tube, glass ... **PIPET, PIPETTE**
tube, plane's .... **PITOT**
tuber delicacy ...... **TRUFFLE**
tuber, edible **OCA, OKA, YAM, TARO, POTATO**
tuber, orchid .... **SALEP**
tuber, S. Amer. .... **OCA, OKA**
Tuesday, god who gave name to **TIU, TYR**
tuft .... **CREST**
tuft: bot. .... **COMA**
tufted plant .... **MOSS**
tulip tree .... **POPLAR**
TUMERIC ..... see TURMERIC
tumor .... **OMA, WEN**
tumor, skin .... **WEN**
tumult .... **RIOT**
tune .... **AIR, ARIA, SONG, MELODY**
tune, bagpipe .... **PORT**
d tune: Scot. .... **PORT**
tungstite ..... **OCHER, OCHRE**
tuning fork ...... **DIAPASON**
Tunis, ruler of ...... **BEY, DEY**
tunnel, train, Alps .... **CENIS**
tunny .... **AMIA, TUNA**
turban, Oriental .... **MANDIL**
turbid, make .... **ROIL**
turf .... **SOD**
turf, bit of: golf ...... **DIVOT**
Turkestan town dwellers . **SART**
turkey buzzard .... **AURA**
turkey red .... **MADDER**
turkeys, collection of .. **RAFTER**
Turkic person **TATAR, TARTAR**
Turkic person, 8th century **OGOR**
Turkish army corps ..... **ORDU**
Turkish army officer ..... **AGA**
Turkish caliph .... **ALI**
Turkish chamber .. **ODA, ODAH**
Turkish chieftain ...... **AMIR, ZAIM, AMEER**
Turkish commander . **AGA, ALI**
Turkish copper coin .... **PARA**
Turkish decree .... **IRADE**
Turkish flag .... **ALEM**
Turkish general .... **AGA**
Turkish gold coin ...... **LIRA, ALTUN, MAHBUB**

a Turkish government .... **PORTE**
Turkish govt. summer residence **YALI**
Turkish governor .. **VALI, WALI**
Turkish hostelry ..... **IMARET**
Turkish judge .... **CADI, KADI**
Turkish leader .... **AGA**
Turkish liquor .... **MASTIC**
Turkish magistrate. **CADI, KADI**
Turkish military district . **ORDO**
Turkish money of account **ASPER**
Turkish officer .. **AGA, AGHA**
Turkish oxcart . **ARBA, ARABA**
Turkish palace .... **SERAI**
Turkish pavilion .... **KIOSK**
Turkish president, former **INONU**
Turkish regiment .... **ALAI**
Turkish standard . **ALEM, TOUG**
Turkish sultan .... **SELIM**
Turkish title .... **AGA, AGHA, BABA, EMIR, EMEER, PASHA, BASHAW**
Turkish tribesman ..... **TATAR**
Turkish tribesman, Persia **GHUZ**
Turkoman tribesman **SEID, SHIK**
turmeric .... **REA, ANGO**
b turmoil .... **WELTER**
turn ..... **BEND, GYRE, VEER, ROTATE, SWERVE**
turn aside. **SKEW, VEER, SHUNT**
turn back to .... **REVERT**
turn direction .... **VERT**
turn inside out .... **EVERT**
turn over: mus. .... **VERTE**
turning point ... **CRISES, CRISIS**
turning: prefix .... **ROTO**
turnover .... **PIE**
turnip ... **BAGA, NEEP, SWEDE**
turnip: Scot. .... **NEEP**
turpentine derivative **ROSIN, PINENE**
turpentine distillate .... **ROSIN**
turpentine resin **ALK, GALLIPOT, GALIPOT**
turtle, Amazon .... **ARRAU**
turtle, edible **TERAPIN, TERRAPIN**
turtle, edible part of . **CALIPEE**
turtle enclosure ...... **CRAWL**
turtle genus .... **EMYS**
turtle, hawkbill .... **CARET**
turtle, order of .... **CHELONIA**
Tuscany art city .... **SIENA**
tusk, elephant .... **IVORY**
tutelary god ..... **LAR, LARES**
tutor .... **TUTE**

c TV advertiser ...... **SPONSOR**
"Twelfth Night" clown .. **FESTE**
"Twelfth Night" heroine **VIOLA**
twelve and one-half cents . **BIT**
twenty-fourth part **CARAT, KARAT**
twenty quires .... **REAM**
twice .... **BIS**
twice: prefix .... **BI**
twig, willow .. **WITHE, WITHY**
twilight .... **EVE, DUSK, GLOAM, EVENTIDE**
twilled coth .... **REP**
twilled wool fabric ..... **SERGE**
twin .... **GEMEL**
twin crystal .... **MACLE**
twin gods, Teut. .... **ALCIS**
twine .... **COIL, WIND, TWIST**
twining stem .... **BINE**
twist ..... **PLY, COIL, FEAK, KINK, SKEW, GNARL, WREATHE, CONTORT**
twist inwards .... **INTORT**
twist out of shape ..... **WARP**
twisted .... **AWRY, SKEW, TORTILE**
twisted roll of fibers .... **SLUB**
twisted spirally .... **TORSE**
twitch .... **TIC**
d twitching .... **TIC**
two .... **DUO, DUAD, PAIR**
two ears, affecting the **DIOTIC**
two elements, having . **BINARY**
two feet, verse of ..... **DIPODY**
two-footed ... **BIPED, BIPEDAL**
two-horse chariot .... **BIGA**
two-hulled boat . **CATAMARAN**
two-masted ship . **YAWL, ZULU**
two-month period .. **BIMESTER**
two, music for .... **DUET**
two notes, group of .... **DUOLE**
two-pronged, as sponges **DICELLATE**
two-pronged weapon .. **BIDENT**
two-spot .... **DEUCE**
two tenacles, having. **DICEROUS**
two-toed sloth .... **UNAU**
two-wheeled vehicle **GIG, CART**
two-year-old sheep **TEG, TEGG, BIDENT**
"Two Years Before the Mast" author .... **DANA**
twofold .. **DUAL, TWIN, BINAL**
twofold: prefix .... **DI**
tycoon .... **NABOB**
tymp arch of furnace ... **FAULD**
Tyndareus, wife of ..... **LEDA**
type collection .... **FONT**

Type

a type, conforming to ... TYPICAL
type face ... RUNIC, CASLON
type, 5½ point ... AGATE
type, jumbled ... PI, PIE
type, kind of ... ELITE
type measure ... EM, EN
type metal piece ... QUAD
type, mixed ... PI, PIE
type of script ... RONDE
type part ... KERN
type set ... FONT

c type size ... PICA, AGATE, BREVIER
type, slanting ... ITALIC
type square ... EM
type tray ... GALLEY
typewriter roller ... PLATEN
Tyr, Norse war god ... ER
tyrant ... DESPOT
tyrant of Rome ... NERO
Tyre, king of ... HIRAM
Tyre, princess of ... DIDO
tyro ... NOVICE

U

Uganda native ... KOPI
ukase ... EDICT
Ukraine legislature ... RADA
"Ulalume" author ... POE
ulexite ... TIZA
ultra-conservative ... TORY
ULYSSES ... see also ODYSSEUS
Ulysses' swineherd ... EUMAEUS
Ulysses' voyages ... ODYSSEY
umbrella ... GAMP
umbrella finial, Burma ... TEE
umbrella, India ... CHATTA
umbrella part ... RIB
b umpire ... REFEREE
unaccented vowel sound SCHWA
unadulterated ... PURE
unaffected .. SIMPLE, ARTLESS
Unalaskan ... ALEUT
unaspirate ... LENE
unassuming MODEST, NATURAL
unbeliever ... HERETIC
unbleached ... ECRU, BEIGE
unburnt brick .. DOBE, ADOBE
Uncas' beloved ... CORA
uncanny ... EERY, EERIE, WEIRD
unceasing ETERNAL, PERPETUAL
uncinate ... HAMATE
uncivil ... RUDE
uncle, dial. ... EME
uncle: Scot. ... EME
"Uncle Remus" author HARRIS
"Uncle Remus" rabbit ... BRER
unclean: Jewish law ... TREF
unclose ... OPE, OPEN
uncommon ... RARE, SPECIAL
unconcerned ... CALM, OPEN, SERENE
unconscious state ... COMA
unconstrained ... EASY

uncouth person ... CAD, BOOR, YAHOO, GALOOT
unction ... BALM
unctuous ... OILY, SUAVE
under ... INFRA, NEATH, SOTTO, NETHER
under: Fr. ... SOUS
under: naut. ... ALOW
under: prefix ... SUB
under side, pert. to .. VENTRAL
undergo: obs. ... DREE
underground bud ... BULB
d underground reservoir, natural water ... CENOTE
underground stream, S. Afr. AAR
underhand, throw ... LOB
undernsong ... TIERCE
undershirts ... SKIVVIES
undersized animal ... RUNT
understand ... GRASP
understanding ... KEN, SENSE, ENTENTE
underwater box ... CAISSON
underworld ... HADES, SHEOL
underworld, Egypt. DUAT, AMENTI
underworld god ... DIS, PLUTO
underworld god, Egypt. OSIRIS, SERAPIS
underworld goddess ... HEL
underwrite ... ENSURE, INSURE
undeveloped ... LATENT
undraped ... NUDE
undulant fever .. BRUCELLOSIS
undulating ... WAVY
undulation ... WAVE
unequal ... UNIQUE
unequal angled ... SCALENE
unequal conditions ... ODDS
uneven ... ODD, EROSE
unevenly shaped ... EROSE

a unfadable .... **FAST**
unfair move .... **FOUL**
unfair shove in marbles . **FULK**
unfasten ..... **UNTIE, LOOSEN**
unfavorable .... **BAD, ILL**
unfeeling ... **HARSH, CALLOUS**
unfermented grape juice **STUM**
unfit to eat, make . **DENATURE**
unfledged bird .... **EYAS**
unfold .... **EVOLVE**
unguent, Roman wrestlers' **CEROMA**
ungula .. **CLAW, HOOF, NAIL**
ungulate, S. Am. ...... **TAPIR**
unhappy .... **SAD, BLUE, MOROSE, RUEFUL**
unicorn fish ...... **LIJA, UNIE**
uniform .... **EVEN**
uniform in hue .. **FLAT, FLOT**
uninteresting .... **DULL**
union .... **MERGER**
union, labor ... **AFL, CIO, ILA, ITA, ILGWU**
union, political .... **BLOC**
union, Russ. workers' ... **ARTEL**
unique person .... **ONER**
unique thing: slang ..... **ONER**
unit .... **ACE, ONE**
b unit of capacity ...... **FARAD**
unit of conductance ..... **MHO**
unit of electrical intensity: abbr. .... **AMP**
unit of electrical resistance or reluctance .... **REL**
unit of electricity . **OHM, WATT, FARAD, WEBER**
unit of electromotive force **VOLT**
unit of energy .... **ERG, RAD, ERGON**
unit of fluidity .... **RHE**
unit of force .... **DYNE**
unit of heat .... **CALORIE**
unit of illumination ..... **PHOT**
unit of jet propulsion .... **JATO**
unit of light .... **PYR, LUMEN, HEFNER**
unit of power .... **DYNE**
unit of power, electric ... **OHM, WATT, FARAD, WEBER**
unit of pressure **BARAD, BARIE**
unit of reluctance .... **REL**
unit of resistance .... **OHM**
unit of weight .... **WEY**
unit of work ..... **ERG, ERGON**
unit, pert. to ...... **MONADIC**
unit, power ratio .... **BEL**

c unite .... **WED, ALLY, JOIN, KNIT, WELD, YOKE, MERGE, INTEGRATE**
unite edges .... **RABBET**
UNITED STATES see AMERICAN
unity .... **ONE**
univalent element .... **MONAD**
universal .. **WORLD, GENERAL**
universal language ... **RO, IDO**
universe .... **WORLD, COSMOS**
universe: Hindu .... **LOKA**
universe, pert. to ..... **COSMIC**
university degree-holder **LICENTIATE**
University in Conn. ..... **YALE**
unkeeled .... **RATITE**
unkind .... **ILL**
unknown Hindu god ...... **KA**
unless .... **BUT, SAVE**
unless: Lat. .... **NISI**
unlock .... **OPE, OPEN**
unmarried .... **CELIBATE**
unmatched .... **ODD**
unmixed .... **PURE, SHEER**
unmusical clang ...... **TONK**
unnecessary .... **NEEDLESS**
unplowed strip .... **HADE**
unpredictable .... **ERRATIC**
d unprincipled person .... **CAD, SCAMP, BOUNDER, REPROBATE**
unprofitable, as rents .... **SECK**
unrefined .... **EARTHY**
unrelenting . **IRON, ADAMANT**
unruffled .... **CALM, SERENE**
unruly outbreak .... **RIOT**
unruly person .... **RANTIPOLE**
unsophisticated .... **NAIVE**
unsorted flour .... **ATA, ATTA**
unspoken .... **TACIT**
unstable ... **ASTATIC, ERRATIC**
unsuitable ..... **INAPT, INEPT**
untamed .... **WILD, FERAL**
untidy person .... **SLOB**
untidiness .... **MESS, MUSS**
until .... **TILL**
untrained .... **RAW**
unusual .... **RARE, EXOTIC**
unusual person or thing . **ONER**
unwavering .... **SURE, STEADY**
unwholesome .... **ILL**
unwieldly thing .... **HULK**
unwilling .... **LOTH, LOATH, AVERSE**
unwilling, be: archaic ... **NILL**
unyielding .. **FIRM, ADAMANT**
unyielding: naut. .... **FAST**

a
up: comb. form .... ANO
Upanishad .... ISHA
upland plain .... WOLD
upbraid ...... CHIDE, SCOLD, REPROACH
upon ...... EPI, ATOP, ONTO
upon: law .... SUR
Upper Nile Negro ...... MADI
Upper Nile tribesman ... MADI
Upper Silurian .... ONTARIAN
uppermost part .... TOP
upright ...... ERECT, HONEST
upright column .... STELE
upright piece .... JAMB, STUD
uprising .... REVOLT
uproar .... DIN
upward, heave: naut. ... SCEND
uraeus .... ASP
Uranus' satellite .... ARIEL
urban office-holder ... MAYOR
urchin ..... IMP, TAD, GAMIN
Urfa, modern .... EDESSA
urge .... EGG, PLY, YEN, IMPEL, PRESS
urge: Scot. .... ERT

c
urial .... SHA
urticaria .... HIVES
urus .... TUR
us: Ger. .... UNS
usage .... WONT
use a divining rod ..... DOWSE
use, be of .... AVAIL
use exertions .... STRIVE
use one's efforts .... EXERT
used up ...... ATE, DEPLETED
useful ..... UTILE, PRACTICAL
useless .... IDLE, FUTILE, OTIOSE, INUTILE
usual .... NORMAL
Utah State flower .... SEGO
utmost .... LAST, FINAL, GREATEST
utmost hyperbole .... ELA
utter .... SAY, SHEER, SPEAK, STARK
utter, as greeting .... BID
utter loudly ..... VOCIFERATE
uttered ... ORAL, SAID, SPOKE
utterly .... STARK
Uz, brother of .... ARAN

V

b
V-shaped piece ...... WEDGE
vacant .... IDLE, EMPTY
vacuum .... VOID
vacuum, opposite of .. PLENUM
vacuum tube .... DIODE
vagabond . VAG, HOBO, TRAMP
vague .... HAZY, LOOSE
vainglory .... PRIDE
valance, short .... PELMET
vale ..... DALE, DELL, VALLEY
Vali, mother of .... RIND
valiant ... BRAVE, STALWART
Valkyrie .... DIS, NORN
valley ..... DALE, DELL, VAIL, VALE, GLADE
valley, deep .... COULEE
valley, Jordan .... GHOR
value .... RATE, PRIZE, WORTH, APPRAISE
value, thing of little ... TRIFLE
valve .... COCK
vampire .... LAMIA
van .... FORE
vandal .... HUN
vanish .... EVANESCE
vanity .... PRIDE
vanity case .... ETUI
vantage, place of ...... COIGN
vapid .... INANE, STALE

d
vapor .... STEAM
vapor: comb. form ..... ATMO
vapor: dialect.......... ROKE
vapor in air ...... HAZE, MIST
Varangians .... ROS
variable .... PROTEAN
variable, most ...... PROTEAN
variable star .... MIRA, NOVA
variation, small SHADE, NUANCE
variegated .... SHOT
variegated in color PIED, CALICO
variety .... KIND
variety of bean SOY, LIMA, PINTO
various: comb. form VARI, VARIO
varnish ingredient LAC, COPAL, RESIN
varnish, kind of SHELLAC, SHELLACK
varnish material .... ELEMI
vase .... URN
vat ...... BAC, TUB, CISTERN
vat, beer ... GAAL, GAIL, GYLE
vat, brewer's ... KIVE, KEEVE
vat, large .... KEIR, KIER
vault .... SAFE

a vault, church .... **CRYPT**
vaulted alcove .... **APSE**
vaunt .... **BRAG, BOAST**
vector, that which turns a **VERSOR**
Vedic dialect .... **PALI**
VEDIC GODS see SPECIAL SECTION
veer ..... **SHY, TURN, SHIFT**
veer off .... **SHEER**
vegetable ... **PEA, BEAN, BEET, KALE, OCRA, OKRA, OKRO, CHARD, ENDIVE, TOMATO, WOBBIE, CELTUCE**
vegetable fuel .... **PEAT**
vegetables, pod .... **PEASE**
vehicle .... **CAR, CART, CYCLE, HANSOM**
vehicle, Am. Ind. **TRAVOIS, TRAVOISE**
vehicle 4-wheeled .... **LANDAU**
vehicle, light, India ... **TONGA**
vehicle, Near East ..... **ARABA**
vehicle, Russ. .... **TROIKA**
vehicle, war .... **TANK**
veil, chalice .... **AER**
vein: Lat. .... **VENA**
b vein of body .... **CAVA**
vein, ore .... **LODE, SCRIN**
vein, ore: prov. Eng. .... **ROKE**
vein, ore beside .... **RIDER**
vein, throat .... **JUGULAR**
vellum .... **PARCHMENT**
velocity per second ..... **VELO**
velum .... **PALATE**
velvet .... **PANNE**
velvet grass .... **HOLCUS**
vend .... **SELL**
vendetta .... **FEUD**
venerable .... **OLD, HOARY**
"Venerable" monk ...... **BEDE**
venerate ..... **ESTEEM, REVERE**
veneration .... **AWE**
Venetian nobleman ..... **DOGE**
Venetian painter ..... **TITIAN**
Venetian red .... **SIENA**
Venetian resort .... **LIDO**
Venetian rose .... **SIENA**
Venetian traveler ...... **POLO**
Venezuela copper center **AROA**
Venezuela Ind. language **PUME**
vengeance goddess ...... **ARA**
Venice marble bridge ..**RIALTO**
Venice canals .... **RII**
Venice district .... **RIALTO**
ventral .... **HEMAD, HAEMAD**
venture .... **DARE**

c Venus, island of ..... **MELOS**
Venus' son .... **CUPID**
Venus, youth loved by **ADONIS**
veranda, Dutch, S. Afr. **STOEP**
veranda, Hawaii ...... **LANAI**
veranda, India .... **PYAL**
verb form .... **IS, AM, ARE, WAS, TENSE**
verbal .... **ORAL**
verbal ending .. **ED, ER, ES, ING**
verbal noun .... **GERUND**
verbal rhythm .... **METRE**
verbally .... **ALOUD**
Verdi heroine .... **AIDA**
verily .... **YEA, AMEN**
verity .... **TRUTH**
versatile .... **MOBILE**
verse .... **LINE, STICH**
verse, Fr. .... **RONDEL**
verse, Ir. .... **RANN**
verse, pert. to kind of **IAMBIC**
version, Bible .... **ITALA**
vertebral bones **SACRA, SACRUM**
verticle line, in a ..... **APEAK**
verticle timber: naut. ... **BITT**
vertigo .... **DINUS**
very .... **SO**
very abundant ... **LUXURIANT**
very: Fr. .... **TRES**
very: Scot. .... **VERA**
d very: Span. .... **MUY**
Ve's brother .... **ODIN**
vesicle, skin .... **BLISTER**
VESSEL .. see also BOAT, SHIP, GALLEY
vessel .... **ARK**
vessel, anat. ...... **VAS, VASA**
vessel, Arab .... **DOW, DHOW**
vessel, chemical .... **ETNA**
vessel, coasting, E. Ind. **PATAMAR**
vessel, cooking .... **PAN, POT**
vessel, drinking ...... **GOURD**
vessel for liquors .. **DECANTER**
vessel, glass .... **BOCAL**
vessel, Gr. **CADUS, AMPHORA**
vessel, heating .... **ETNA**
vessel, large .... **TANK**
vessel, liquor .... **FLAGON**
vessel, Medit. .. **SETEE, MISTIC**
vessel, Rom. .... **PATERA**
vessel, sacred ...... **PIX, PYX**
vessel, sailing .... **SAIC, SETEE, XEBEC**
vessel, shallow .... **BASIN**
vessel, supply .... **COALER**
vessel, 3-masted **XEBEC, FRIGATE**
vessel, 2-masted **YAWL, ZULU**

a vessel with two handles, Gr. .... **DIOTA**
vessel's curved planking .. **SNY**
vestal .... **CHASTE**
vestige .. **IOTA, RELIC, TRACE**
vestment .. **ALB, COPE, AMICE, EPHOD, STOLE**
vestment, white .. **ALB, AMICE**
vesuvianite, brown ... **EGERAN**
vetch .... **TARE**
vetch, bitter .... **ERS**
vetch, India .... **AKRA**
vetiver, grass .... **BENA**
vex **GALL, RILE, ROIL, HARRY**
vex persistently ...... **NETTLE**
vex: Scot. .... **FASH**
vexed .... **RILY**
via .... **PER**
viands .... **DIET**
viands, dainty .... **CATES**
Viaud's pseudonym ...... **LOTI**
vibrate .... **THRILL**
vibration: music .... **TREMOLO**
vice .... **SIN**
viceroy .... **VALI**
Vichy Premier .... **LAVAL**
vicious man .... **YAHOO**
victim .... **PREY**
victorfish .... **AKU**
victor's crown .... **LAUREL**
victory, Eng. .. **CRECY, CRESSY**
victory trophy .... **SCALP**
b victuals .... **FOOD**
"— victus," woe to the conquered .... **VAE**
"—vide," "which see" .. **QUAE**
vie with .... **EMULATE**
Viennese park .... **PRATER**
view .... **SCENE, VISTA**
vigilant .... **WARY, ALERT**
vigor .... **PEP, VIM, VIS, ZIP, FORCE**
Viking ... **ERIC, OLAF, ROLLO**
Viking explorer .... **ERIC**
vilify .... **REVILE**
village .. **DORP, VILL, HAMLET**
village, Afr. .... **KRAAL**
village, Java .... **DESSA**
village, Russ. .... **MIR**
village, Scot. .... **REW**
village, S. Afr. native ... **STAD**
villain .... **KNAVE**
villein .... **CEORL**
vindicate .... **AVENGE**
vindication .... **REVENGE**
vine .... **IVY, BINE**
vine: comb. form .... **VITI**
vine, N. Z. .... **AKA**
vine, P. I. .... **IYO**
c vine, woody .. **ABUTA, LIANA**
"vin du —," wine of the country .... **CRU**
vinegar of ale .... **ALEGAR**
vinegar, pert. to ...... **ACETIC**
vinegar worm .... **EEL, NEMA**
vinous .... **WINY**
viol, ancient type ...... **REBEC**
viol, bass .... **GAMBA**
viol, Shetlands .... **GUE**
viola .... **ALTO**
violent .... **HOT**
violet-odored ketone .. **IRONE**
violin, bass .... **CELLO**
violin, early .. **REBAB, REBEC**
violin, famous .... **STRAD**
violin, It. .. **AMATI, CREMONA**
violin, small .... **KIT**
violin, tenor ..... **ALTO, VIOLA**
violinist ...... **ELMAN, YSAYE**
viper .... **ASP, ADDER**
viper genus .... **ECHIS**
viper, horned .... **CERASTES**
Virgil's hero .. **ENEAS, AENEAS**
Virgin Mary pictured mourning **PIETA**
virus-fighting substance **ANTIVIRAL**
visage .... **FACE**
viscous
d **LIMY, ROPY, SIZY, SLIMY**
viscous substance .. **TAR, SLIME**
Vishnu, incarnation, 7th **RAMA**
Vishnu, soul of universe **VASU**
Vishnu's bow .... **SARAN**
Vishnu's serpent ...... **NAGA**
visible juncture .... **SEAM**
Visigoth king **ALARIC, ALARIK**
vision, defective ..... **ANOPIA**
vision, pert. to .... **OPTIC**
visionary ...... **AIRY, IDEAL, DREAMY, UNREAL, IDEALIST**
visit ...... **SEE, CALL, HAUNT**
visit at sea .... **GAM**
visit between whalers ... **GAM**
vison .... **MINK**
vital energy .... **HORME**
vital fluid .... **SAP**
vital principle .... **SOUL**
vitalize .... **ANIMATE**
vitamin ... **CITRIN, ADERMIN, ANEURIN, TORULIN**
vitamin B **NIACIN, THIAMINE**
vitamin B2 .... **FLAVIN**
vitamin H .... **BIOTIN**
vitiate .... **SPOIL, TAINT, POLLUTE, INVALIDATE**
vitriol-infused earth .... **SORY**
vituperate .... **SCOLD**

a vivacious ..... AIRY, BRIGHT
vivacity .... ELAN, LIFE
vocal flourish ...... ROULADE
vocation .... CAREER
"— voce" .... SOTTO
voice .... SAY
voice
ALTO, BASS, VOCE, TENOR
voice: It. .... VOCE
voice: Lat. .... VOX
voice, loss of ...... APHONIA
voiced .... SONANT
voiced, not .... ASONANT
voiceless .... SPIRATE
voiceless consonant ..... SURD
void .... NUL, NULL, ABYSS, SPACE, INVALID
void, to make. ANNUL, CANCEL
void, to render: Scot. ... CASS
voided escutcheon ...... ORLE
volcanic cinder .... SCORIA
volcanic islands, Atlantic
FAROE
volcanic rock
TUFA, TUFF, LATITE
volcanic scoria-matter
LAVA, SLAG
volcano .. ETNA, AETNA, PELEE
volcano crater .... MAAR
volcano hole .... CRATER

c volcano, Martinique Is. .. PELEE
volcano mouth ...... CRATER
volcano, P. I. .... APO
volcano pit .... CRATER
volcano, Sicily ETNA, AETNA
volcano, W. Indies .... PELEE
volition .... WILL
volt-ampere .... WATT
Voltaire .... AROUET
Voltaire play: Fr. ..... ZAIRE
voluble .... GLIB
volume .... MO, TOME
vomiting .... EMESIS
voodoo charm .... MOJO
voodoo snake deity .... ZOMBI
vote .... BALLOT
vote into office .... ELECT
vote, right to .... FRANCHISE
vote, take a .... POLL
votes ...... AYES, NOES, YEAS
vouch for .... SPONSOR
voucher .... CHIT, NOTE
"vous —": Fr., you are .. ETES
vowel, line over ..... MACRON
vowel suppression .... ELISION
voyaging .... ASEA
vulcanite .... EBONITE
Vulcan's wife .... MAIA
vulgar .... COARSE
vulture AURA, URUBU, CONDOR

W

b "W", old English .... WEN
wade across .... FORD
wading bird IBIS, RAIL, CRANE, EGRET, HERON, STILT, AVOCET, AVOSET, JACANA, FLAMINGO
wag .... WIT
wages .... PAY
Wagner heroine . ELSA, SENTA, ISOLDE
Wagnerian role .... ERDA
wagon .. CART, DRAY, WAIN
wagon pin .... CLEVIS
wagon, Russ. .... TELEGA
wagon shaft .... THILL
wagon tongue .... NEAP, POLE
wagtail .... LARK
wahoo, fish .... PETO
wail .... KEEN, LAMENT
waist ...... CAMISA, TAILLE
waistcoat VEST, GILET, JERKIN
wait .... BIDE
waken ...... ROUSE, AROUSE

d wale .... WELT
Wales emblem .... LEEK
walk ..... PACE, STEP, TREAD
walk affectedly ...... MINCE
walk heavily .... PLOD, SLOG
walk, inability to .... ABASIA
walk lamely .... LIMP
walk stiffly .... STALK
walk, tree-lined .... ALAMEDA
walking stick ... CANE, STILT
wall, arena .... SPINA
wall around fortified place
RAMPART
wall, divided by .... SEPTATE
wall: Fr. .... MUR
wall material .... COB
wall, of a .... MURAL
wall paneling .... WAINSCOT
wall piece TEMPLET, TEMPLATE
wall section .... DADO, PANEL
wall, squeeze against .. MURE
walls .... SEPTA
wallaba tree, Brazil ..... APA
walled city, Nigeria ..... KANO

a wallflower .... KEIRI
wallop .... LAM
wallow .... WELTER
walrus .... MORSE
wampum PEAG,SEWAN,SEAWAN
wan .... ASHY, PALE, ASHEN
wand .... BATON
wander .. ERR, HAAK, ROAM, ROVE, RAMBLE, DIGRESS
wander idly .... GAD
wanderer .... VAG, NOMAD
"Wandering Jew" author .. SUE
wane .... EBB
want .... LACK, NEED, DESIRE
wapiti .... ELK
war-club, medieval ..... MACE
war correspondent PYLE, BALDWIN
war cry, ancient Gr. ... ALALA
war god .... ARES, MARS
war god, Babyl. ... IRA, IRRA
war god, Norse TY, TYR, TYRR
war god, Teut. .... ER
war goddess, Gr. ...... ENYO
war horse .... CHARGER
war, religious ...... CRUSADE
war, Russ.-Eng. ...... CRIMEA
war vessel .... CRUISER
warble .. SING, TRILL, YODEL
b ward off ..... FEND, AVERT, PARRY, REPEL, STAVE
ward politician ...... HEELER
warden, fire .... RANGER
warehouse .... DEPOT
warehouse room .... LOFT
warm .... CALID, TEPID
warning of danger: biol. SEMATIC
warning signal .... SIREN
warning system, attack DEW, BMEWS
warp yarn .... ABB
warrant, from monarch BERAT
warrior, Samoa .... TOA
warship, sailing ..... FRIGATE
wary .... CAGY
was not: dialect .... NAS
wash .... LAVE
wash leather .... LOSH
wash out .... ELUTE
washings: chem. ..... ELUATE
Washington Irving character RIP
wasp .... HORNET
wasps, the .... VESPA
waste .... LOSS
waste allowance .... TRET
waste away GNAW, ATROPHY
waste fiber .... NOIL
waste land .... MOOR
waste matter .... DROSS
waste silk ..... KNUB, FRISON

c waste time .... IDLE
wastes, growing in .. RUDERAL
watch .... SEE, GLOM
watch chain .... FOB
watchdog, Hel's .... GARM
watchful .... ALERT
watchful guardian .... ARGUS
watchful, name meaning IRA
watchman, alert ...... ARGUS
watchman, night ..... SERENO
watchtower .... MIRADOR
water ... SPRINKLE, IRRIGATE
water arum .... CALLA
water chestnut, Chin. ... LING
water cock .... KORA
water, covered by .... AWASH
water: Fr. .... EAU, EAUX
water: Lat. .... AQUA
water lily .... LOTUS
water passage SLUICE, STRAIT
water pipe HOOKA, HOOKAH, NARGILE
water raising device TABUT, TABOOT
water reservoir, natural CENOTE
water scorpion genus ... NEPA
water, seek .... DOUSE
water, sound of ...... PLASH
water: Sp. .... AGUA
d water spirit ARIEL, SPRITE, UNDINE
water sprite ..... NIX, NIXIE
water sprite: Gaelic .. KELPIE
water surface .... RYME
water vessel, India LOTA, LOTO, LOTAH
water wheel NORIA, DANAIDE, TURBINE
water wheel, Persian .. NORIA
water's surface: naut. ... RYME
watercourse ... LADE, BROOK, CANAL, RIVER, STREAM
watered apearance .... MOIRE
watered silk .... MOIRE
waterfall, Scot. LIN, LYN, LINN
watering place .. SPA, BADEN
waterproof canvas ..... TARP
waterskin .... MATARA
watertight, make CALK, CAULK
waterway .... BAYOU, CANAL
waterway, narrow ..... STRAIT
watery .... SEROUS
watery: comb. form .... SERO
wattle tree .... BOREE
wattled honeyeater IAO, MANUAO
wave .... FLY, SEA
wave-crest comb. ...... COOM
wave: Fr. .... ONDE
wave, huge .... SEA

a waver ...... **FALTER, TEETER**
wavy: Her. **UNDE, UNDY, NEBULE**
wax .... **CERE**
wax ointment .... **CERATE**
wax, pert. to .... **CERAL**
wax: Sp. .... **CERA**
wax, yellow or white **CERESIN**
waxy chemical .... **CERIN**
waxy substance .... **CERIN**
way ...... **VIA, MODE, ROUTE**
way of walking .... **GAIT**
way out .... **EGRESS**
wayside — .... **INN**
wayside stop, India .. **PARAO**
we: Lat. .... **NOS**
weak .... **PUNY, FRAIL, DEBILE, EFFETE, FEEBLE**
weak cider .... **PERKIN**
weaken .... **SAP, LABEFY, VITIATE, ENERVATE, ENFEEBLE**
weakfish, S. Am. .... **ACOUPA**
weakness .... **ATONY**
weal .... **WALE**
wealth, man of .... **NABOB**
wealthy: Scot. .... **BIEN**
b weapon .... **LANCE, SPEAR, SWORD, MUSKET**
weapon, ancient .... **CELT**
weapon, dagger-like .. **BALAS**
weapon: Fr. .... **ARME**
weapon, gaucho's **BOLA, BOLAS**
weapon, Maori .... **PATU**
weapon, medieval ..... **ONCIN**
weapon, N. Z. .... **PATU**
weapon, P. I. .... **BOLO**
weapon, S. Am. .. **BOLA, BOLAS**
wear away **EAT, ERODE, ABRADE**
wear away slowly ... **CORRODE**
wear by friction .... **RUB**
wear off .... **ABRADE**
wearing down .... **ATTRITION**
weary .... **BORE, TIRE**
weasel **VARE, ERMINE, FERRET**
weasel: Eng. **STOT, STOAT, STOTE**
weather indicator **BAROMETER**
weathercock .... **VANE**
weaverbird ..... **BAYA, MAYA**
weaverbird, S. Afr. .... **TAHA**
weaver's bobbin on shuttle **PIRN**
weaver's reed .... **SLEY**
weaving frame .... **LOOM**
weaving term .... **LISSE**
weaving tool .... **EVENER**

c web .... **TELA**
web-footed bird . **DUCK, LOON, GOOSE**
web-like membrane ..... **TELA**
web-spinning **RETIARY, TELARIAN**
wed .... **MARRY**
wedding anniversaries .... **1st, PAPER; 2nd, COTTON; 3rd, CANDY OR LEATHER; 4th, SILK, FRUIT, FLOWERS, or LEATHER; 5th, WOODEN; 6th, IRON OR CANDY; 7th, WOOL, COPPER, OR FLORAL; 8th, WOOL, BRONZE, OR POTTERY; 9th, WILLOW OR POTTERY; 10th, TIN; 11th, STEEL; 12th, SILK OR LINEN; 13th, LACE; 14th, IVORY; 15th, CRYSTAL; 20th, CHINA; 25th, SILVER; 30th, PEARL; 35th, CORAL; 40th, RUBY OR EMERALD; 45th, RUBY OR SAPPHIRE; 50th, GOLDEN;**
d **55th, EMERALD; 75th, DIAMOND**
wedge, entering . **COIN, COIGN, QUOIN, COIGNE**
wedge-like piece ..... **QUOIN**
wedge-shaped ...... **CUNEATE**
wedge-shaped piece **GIB, SHIM**
wedge, steel .... **FROE**
Wednesday, source of name **WODEN**
weed .... **TARE, DARNEL**
weed, coarse .... **DOCK**
week ..... **SENNET, SENNIGHT**
week day .... **FERIA**
weep **CRY, SOB, BOHO, LAMENT**
weep, Scot. .... **ORP**
weeping statue .... **NIOBE**
weeping woman, Gr. myth **NIOBE**
weft .... **WOOF**
WEIGHT .. see also SPECIAL SECTION
weight .... **TON, HEFT**
weight allowance **TARE, TRET**
weight, ancient **MINA, TALENT**
weight, ancient: var. ... **MNA**
weight, Asiatic .... **TAEL**
weight, balance .... **RIDER**

a weight, Danish **ORT**
weight, India **SER, TOLA**
weight machine: Scot. **TRON, TRONE**
weight, metric unit of **GRAM**
weight of England **STONE**
weight of silk before degumming **PARI**
weight, pert. to **BARIC**
weight system **TROY**
weir **DAM**
weird **EERY, EERIE**
welcome **GREET**
well, Bib. **AIN**
well-bred people **GENTRY**
"well done" **EUGE, BRAVO**
well done: Eng. **EUGE**
well: Fr. **BIEN**
well: It. & Lat. **BENE**
well: Scot. **AWEEL**
Welsh dog **CORGI**
Welsh god of sea **DYLAN**
Welshman **CELT**
welt **WALE**
wen **TALPA**
Wend of Saxony **SORB**
wergeld **CRO**
W. Australia capital **PERTH**
W. Afr. timber tree **ODUM**
b W. Afr. tribe **IBO, BUBE, BUBI**
W. Ind. bayberry **AUSU, AUZU**
W. Ind. fish **BOGA, CERO, TESTAR**
W. Ind. idol **ZEME, ZEMI**
W. Ind. isle **CUBA, HAITI**
W. Ind. key **CAY**
W. Ind. scrapper **CAJI**
W. Ind. shrub plant **ANIL**
West Point mascot **MULE**
West Pointer **PLEB, CADET, PLEBE**
West Saxon king **INE**
Western division of Osset **DIGOR**
Western European **CELT, KELT**
Western Indian **UTE**
Western shrub **SAGE**
"Western Star" author **BENET**
Western state **UTAH**
Westphalian city **HERNE**
wet: Scot. **WAT**
wet **ASOP, MOIST**
whale **CET, ORC, ORK, CETE, BELUGA, GRAMPUS**
whale carcass **KRANG, KRENG**
whale hunter **AHAB**
whale oil cask **RIER**
whale-shark **MHOR**
whale tail part **FLUKE**
whale, white **BELUGA**

c whale, white Caspian **HUSE, HUSO**
whales, order of **CETE**
whales, herd of **GAM, POD**
whales, pert. to **CETIC**
whales, school of **GAM, POD**
whalebone **BALEEN**
wharf **KEY, PIER, QUAI, QUAY**
what is it? obs. **ANAN**
whatnot **ETAGERE**
wheal **WALE, WEAL**
wheat disease **BUNT**
wheat, German. **EMMER, SPELT**
wheat, India **SUJI, SUJEE**
wheat, kind of **EMMER, SPELT**
wheat middlings **SEMOLINA**
wheedle **COG, COAX**
wheedling **BUTTERY**
wheel **ROTA**
wheel band **STRAKE**
wheel center. **HOB, HUB, NAVE**
wheel, furniture **CASTER**
wheel, grooved **SHEAVE**
wheel horse **POLER**
wheel part **HUB, RIM, FELLY, SPOKE**
wheel projection **CAM**
wheel shaft **AXLE**
wheel-shaped **ROTATE**
wheel spindle **AXLE, ARBOR**
d wheel tread **TIRE**
wheels, pert. to **ROTAL**
where: Lat. **UBI**
whetstone, fine **BUHR, HONE**
whey of milk **SERA, SERUM**
which see: abbr. **QV**
whiff **PUFF**
while **AS, WHEN**
whimper **MEWL, PULE**
whin **GORSE**
whine **PULE**
whinny **NEIGH**
whip **CAT, BEAT, FLOG, LASH**
whip, cowboy **CHICOTE**
whip mark **WALE, WEAL**
whip, Russ. **KNOUT**
whipsocket **SNEAD**
whirl **REEL, SPIN**
whirlpool **EDDY, GURGE, VORTEX**
whirlpool: Scot. **WEEL, WIEL**
whirlwind in Atlantic **OE**
whirring sound **BIRR**
whiskers **BEARD, GOATEE**
whiskey: Ir. **POTEEN**
whiskey drink: Scot. **ATHOL, ATHOLE**
whist win **SLAM**
whistle **PIPE, SIREN**
whit **BIT, JOT, ATOM, DOIT, IOTA**

a white acid, pert. to .. **TROPIC**
white alkaline .... **SODA**
white ant, P. I. .. **ANAI, ANAY**
white, bitter compound **LININ**
white: comb. form ..... **ALBO**
"White Elephant" land .. **SIAM**
white ermine **LASSET, MINIVER**
white-flecked .... **ROAN**
White Friar ..... **CARMELITE**
white: Ir. .... **BAWN**
white man: P. I. ... **CACHILA**
white matter, brain .... **ALBA**
white oak .... **ROBLE**
white poplar .... **ABELE**
white spruce ...... **EPINETTE**
white with age .... **HOAR**
whitefish .... **CISCO**
whiten .... **ETIOLATE**
whitish .... **HOARY**
whitlow grass .... **DRABA**
Whittier heroine .... **MAUD**
whiz ..... **PIRR, WHIR, ZIZZ**
whoa .... **HOLLA**
whole amount .... **GROSS**
whole: comb. form ...... **TOTO**
wholesome .... **SALUTARY**
wholly .... **ALL**
wicked .... **EVIL**
wicker basket .... **CESTA, KIPSY, PANNIER**
b wicker basket, Guiana **PEGALL**
wickerwork .... **RATAN**
wickerwork hut .... **JACAL**
wicket, croquet .... **HOOP**
wide-mouthed vessel **EWER, OLLA**
widgeon .... **SMEE**
widgeon genus ...... **MARECA**
widow .... **RELICT**
widow in cards .... **SKAT**
widow monkey .... **TITI**
widow's bit or coin ..... **MITE**
widow's third: Scot. .... **TERCE**
wield .... **PLY, USE**
wife, Moroccan ruler's **SHERIFA**
wife ... **FEME, FRAU, FEMME**
wife's property .... **DOS**
wig .... **PERUKE**
wigwam .. **TIPI, TEPEE, TEEPEE**
wild .... **FERAL, SAVAGE**
wild animals, collection of **ZOO, MENAGERIE**
wild animal's trail **SLOT, SPUR, SPOOR**
wild apple .... **CRAB, DOUCIN**
wild ass, Afr. ...... **QUAGGA**
wild ass, Asia .... **ONAGER**
wild boar genus .... **SUS**
wild buffalo, India **ARNA, ARNI, ARNEE**

c wild buffalo, Malay ... **GAUR, SLADANG, SALADANG, SELADANG**
wild cat, Siberia, Tibet, steppes **MANUL**
wild cattle, India **GAUR, GOUR**
wild cry .... **EVOE**
wild dog .... **DHOLE**
wild dog genus .... **THOS**
wild dog, Japan ..... **TANATE**
"Wild Duck" author .... **IBSEN**
wild garlic .... **MOLY**
wild ginger .... **ASARUM**
wild hog .... **BOAR**
wild honeybee, E. Ind. **DINGAR**
wild horse of Tartary **TARPAN**
wild lime .... **COLIMA**
wild olive tree ..... **OLEASTER**
wild ox .... **ANOA**
wild ox, Malay. .... **BANTENG**
wild plum .... **SLOE**
wild plum, Calif. ...... **ISLAY**
wild sheep, Asia **RASSE, ARGALI**
wild sheep, horned . **MOUFLON**
wild sheep, India ... **SHA, SNA, URIAL, NAHOOR, OORIAL**
wild sheep, N. Afr. **ARUI, UDAD, AOUDAD**
wild sheep, Tibet .... **SHA**
d **SNA, BHARAL, NAHOOR**
wild turnip .... **NAVEW**
wild vanilla .... **LIATRIS**
wildcat .... **BALU, LYNX**
wildcat, Afr. & India .. **CHAUS**
wildcat, S. Am. .... **EYRA**
wildcat, Sumatra ...... **BALU**
wildebeest .... **GNU**
wile .... **ART**
will addition .... **CODICIL**
will, one inheriting from **DEVISEE**
will, one making .... **DEVISOR**
will power, loss of .... **ABULIA**
William: Ir. .... **LIAM**
William I, half brother of **ODO**
William the Conqueror's daughter .... **ADELA**
willingly .... **LIEF**
willow .... **ITEA, OSIER**
willow, Europ. .... **SALLOW**
willow genus, Virginia ... **ITEA**
Wilson's thrush .... **VEERY**
wilt .... **FADE, DROOP**
wily .... **FOXY**
wimple .... **GORGET**
win .... **GAIN**
winch .... **WHIN**
wind .... **GALE**
wind, Adriatic .... **BORA**

a wind, Andes ... **PUNA, PUNO**
wind, Austral. ...... **BUSTER**
wind, away from .... **ALEE**
wind, cold Malta .... **GREGALE**
wind, cold Medit. .... **MISTRAL**
wind, cold Swiss Alps **BISE, BIZE**
wind: comb. form .... **ANEMO**
wind-deposited loam ... **LOESS**
wind, dry, from Sahara .. **LESTE**
wind, east .... **EURUS**
wind god, Babyl. **ADAD, ADDA, ADDU**
wind god, Hindu ...... **VAYU**
wind god, pert. to **EOLIAN, AEOLIAN**
wind, hot, dry ...... **KAMSIN, SIMOOM, SIMOON, SIROCCO**
wind, hot, Medit. .... **SOLANO**
wind indicator .. **SOCK, VANE**
wind instrument **HORN, OBOE, PIPE, BUGLE**
wind, Levant .... **ETESIAN**
wind, Madeira .... **LESTE**
wind, Medit. .... **ETESIAN**
wind, Medit., poet. ..... **SIROC**
wind, Mesop. .... **SHAMAL**
wind, north .... **BOREAS**
wind off Faroe Islands .... **OE**
wind, Peru Andes **PUNA, PUNO**
wind, sand-laden **SAMIEL, SIMOOM, SIMOON**
b wind, Sahara .... **LESTE**
wind, South .. **NOTUS, AUSTER**
wind, southeast .... **EURUS**
wind, southwest .... **AFER**
wind, Trieste, cold ..... **BORA**
wind, warm dry **FOHN, FOEHN**
wind, west .... **AFER**
winds, south, Peru ..... **SURES**
windborne .... **AEOLIAN**
windflower .... **ANEMONE**
windlass .... **CAPSTAN**
windmill sail .... **AWE**
window lead .... **CAME**
window ledge .... **SILL**
window part .... **SASH**
window, semipolygonal .. **ORIEL**
window setter .... **GLAZIER**
windrow .... **SWATH**
windstorm **OE, BURAN, TORNADO**
windstorm, Asia **BURA, BURAN**
wine ...... **VIN, HOCK, PORT, SACK, VINO, MEDOC, TOKAY, CLARET, MALAGA, MUSCAT, SHERRY, MOSELLE**
wine, Am. .... **CATAWBA**
wine, ancient .... **MASSIC**
wine cask .... **TUN, BUTT**
wine city, It. .... **ASTI**

c wine cup .... **AMA**
wine, delicacy of: Fr. ... **SEVE**
wine disorder .... **CASSE**
wine district, Calif. .... **NAPA**
wine drink .... **NEGUS**
wine, dry .... **SEC, BRUT**
wine, golden .... **BUAL**
wine, heavy .... **TOKAY**
wine, honey and ...... **MULSE**
wine, Madeira .... **BUAL**
wine measure, Trieste **ORNA, ORNE**
wine merchant .... **VINTNER**
wine, new .... **MUST**
wine pitcher, Gr. .... **OLPE**
wine, red **PORT, TINTA, CLARET**
wine, sweet .... **MUSCAT**
wine, sweet: Fr. ..... **MASDEU**
wine, to make .... **VINT**
wine vessel ...... **AMA, OLPE, AMULA, CHALICE**
wine, white .... **HOCK, SHERRY, SAUTERNE**
wineberry, N. Z. ...... **MAKO**
wing .... **ALA, PENNA, PINNA, PINION**
wing, bastard .... **ALULA**
wing, beetle .... **TEGMAN, TEGMINA, TEGUMEN**
wing: Fr. .... **AILE**
d wing-footed animal .. **ALIPED**
winglike .... **ALAR**
wing-like part ..... **ALA, ALAE**
wing movement .... **FLAP**
wing tip, pert. to ... **ALULAR**
wings .... **ALAE**
wings, divested of **DEALATA, DEALATED**
wings, having .. **ALAR, ALATE**
wings: her. .... **VOL, AILE**
winged figure, Gr. **IDOLON, IDOLUM, EIDOLON**
winged fruit, indehiscent **SAMARA**
winged god ..... **EROS, CUPID**
winged seed .... **SAMARA**
winged victory .... **NIKE**
wingless .... **APTERAL**
wingless invertebrates **APTERA**
wink rapidly .... **BAT**
winning at bridge ...... **SLAM**
winnow .... **FAN**
winter, pert. to .... **BRUMAL, HIEMAL, HYEMAL, HIBERNAL**
winter squash ...... **CUSHAW**
wipe out .... **ERASE**
wire measure .... **MIL**
wire service .... **AP, UP, INS, UPI, REUTERS**

a wires, cross .... **RETICLE**
Wisconsin college ...... **RIPON**
wisdom ...... **LORE, GNOSIS**
wisdom god of: Babyl. **NABU, NEBO**
wisdom goddess of: Gr. **ATHENA, PALLAS**
wisdom, goddess of: Rom. **MINERVA**
wise .... **SAGE, SENSIBLE**
wise adviser .... **MENTOR**
wise man **SAGE, SOLON, NESTOR**
Wise Men .... **MAGI, GASPAR, MELCHIOR, BALTHASAR**
wise men, A-S .... **WITAN**
wisecrack .. **GAG, JOKE, QUIP**
wish for ..... **YEARN, DESIRE**
wish undone .... **RUE**
wisp of hair .... **TATE**
wit .... **WAG, HUMOR**
wit: Sp. .... **SAL**
witless chatter .... **GAB**
witch ... **HAG, HECAT, LAMIA, HECATE, HECCAT, HEKATE**
witch city .... **SALEM**
witch doctor .... **GOOFER**
witch in "Faerie Queene" **DUESSA**
witchcraft .... **OBEAH**
with: Fr. .... **AVEC**
b with: Ger. .... **MIT**
with joy .... **FAIN**
with: prefix .... **SYN**
withdraw .. **RECEDE, REMOVE, RETIRE, SECEDE, RETRACT**
wither .... **FADE**
withered .... **SERE**
within ...... **INTO, INTERIOR**
within: comb. form **ESO, ENDO, ENSO, ENTO**
within: prefix .... **ENDO**
without: comb. form ..... **ECT**
without energy .... **ATONY**
without: Fr. .... **SANS**
without: Ger. .... **OHNE**
without: Lat. .... **SINE**
without: poetic .... **SANS**
without teeth, claws, lion **MORNE**
without veins ...... **AVENOUS**
witness .... **SEE**
witness, law . **TESTE, DEPONENT**
witness, to bear ...... **ATTEST**
witty remark ..... **MOT, QUIP**
witty reply .... **REPARTEE**
wobble .... **TEETER**
Woden .... **ODIN**
woe .... **MISERY**
woe is me .... **ALAS**

c wolf, gray .... **LOBO**
wolf, Odin's ...... **GERE, GERI**
wolf, timber .... **LOBO**
wolfhound .... **ALAN**
wolfish .... **LUPINE**
wolframite .... **CAL**
wolverine genus .... **GULO**
woman diplomat, first U.S. **OWEN**
woman: Gr. .... **GYNE**
woman, ill-tempered **SHREW, VIRAGO**
woman personified, Ir. **EMER, EIMER**
woman's name (3 letters) **ADA, AMY, ANN, EVA, EVE, FAY, IDA, INA, MAE, MAY, NAN, RAE, UNA, ZOE,** (4 letters) **AFRA, ALIX, ALMA, ALYS, ANNA, ANNE, AVIS, BONA, CARA, CLOE, CORA, DORA, EDNA, ELLA, ELSA, EMMA, ENID, ERMA, ETTA, INEZ, JANE, JEAN, JOAN, JUNE, LEAH, LIDA, LILA, LOIS, LORA, LUCY, MARY, MAUD, MYRA, NONA, NORA, OLGA, RITA, ROSA, ROSE, RUTH, SARA, VERA, VIDA,** (5 letters) **ALICE, ANITA, CLARE, DELIA,**
d **DIANA, ELAIN, ELSIE, ERICA, FAITH, FLORA, GRACE, IRENE, SARAH, SELMA,** (6 letters) **ALTHEA, BERTHA, DAPHNE, EDWINA, ELAINE, EMILIA, PHOEBE,** (7 letters) **ABIGAIL, CELESTE, LAVINIA**
woman's nickname **CAT, DEB, HAT, KIT, LOU, MAB, MAG, MEG, SAL, SUE, ABBY, ADDY, BESS, BETH, CARO, DORA, GAIL, JILL, JOSY, JUDY, JULE, KATE, KATY, LINA, LISA, LULU, MART, MIMI, MINA, MOLL, NELL, NINA, ROXY, SUSY, TAVE, TAVY, TESS, TINA, XINA, SALLY, SALLIE**
Wonderland girl ...... **ALICE**
wont .... **HABIT**
wood .... **ALOE**
wood apple, Ind. .... **BEL**
wood, black .... **EBONY**
wood, flexible .... **EDDER**
wood, fragrant . **ALOES, CEDAR**
wood: comb, form ...... **XYLO**
wood: Fr. .... **BOIS**
wood gum .... **XYLAN**

a
wood, light .... **BALSA**
wood, long piece .... **POLE**
wood: obsolete .... **WOLD**
wood, piece of .... **SLAT, SPRAG, BILLET**
wood pussy .... **SKUNK**
wood robin, N. Z. ...... **MIRO**
wood sorrel .... **OCA, OKA**
wood, timber: P. I. ... **CAHUY**
woodchuck .... **MARMOT**
woodchuck: dialect **MOONACK**
wooden .... **TREEN**
wooden brick .... **DOOK**
wooden collar, convict's **CANG**
wooden pail .... **SOE**
wooden peg .... **SKEG**
wooden shoe **SABOT, PATTEN**
woodland deity **FAUN, SATYR**
woodland god .... **PAN**
woodpecker genus **JYNX, YUNX**
woodpecker, green **HICKWALL**
woodpecker group ...... **PICI**
woodpecker, red-bellied . **CHAB**
woodpecker, small ... **PICULE**
woodpeckers, of ...... **PICINE**
woodwind **OBOE, BASSOON, CLARINET**
woodworking tool ..... **SAPPER**
woodworm .... **TERMITE**
woody fiber .... **BAST**

b
woody hill .... **HOLT**
woody plant .... **TREE**
woof .... **WEFT**
wool ...... **ANGORA, MERINO**
wool cluster .... **NEP**
wool, coarse .... **GARE**
wool fat . **LANOLIN, LANOLINE**
wool: Lat. .... **LANA**
wool measure .... **HEER**
wool package .... **FADGE**
wool, reclaimed ...... **MUNGO**
woolen cloth .... **ETAMINE**
woolen cloth, coarse, twilled **KERSEY**
woolen fabric .... **FRISCA**
woolen thread .... **YARN**
woolly ...... **LANATE, LANOSE**
woolly pyrol .... **URD**
word by word .... **LITERAL**
word expressing action .. **VERB**
word meanings, pert. to **SEMANTIC**
word of affirmation .... **AMEN**
word of choice .... **OR**
word of God .... **LOGOS**
word of honor, promise **PAROL, PAROLE**
word of mouth, by **PAROL, PAROLE**
word of ratification .... **AMEN**
word, scrambled ... **ANAGRAM**

c
work **MOIL, TOIL, CHARE, LABOR**
WORK ..see also COMPOSITION
work aimlessly .... **POTTER**
work at steadily .... **PLY**
work hard **PEG, MOIL, TOIL, SLAVE**
work, in terms of heat **ERGON**
work, musical **OPUS, OPERA, ORATORIO**
work persistently .... **PEG**
work, piece of .... **JOB, STINT**
work: Sp. .... **OBRA**
work unit .... **ERG, ERGON**
workbasket .... **CABA, CABAS**
worker .... **HAND, OPERANT, OPERATOR**
worker ant .... **ERGATE**
worker: comb. form .. **ERGATE**
worker's group, worldwide .. **ILO**
worker's union, Soviet .. **ARTEL**
workhorse: Scot .... **AVER**
working boat, Chesapeake Bay **FLATTIE**
workman, mine .... **CAGER**
workman, S. Afr. .... **VOLK**
workshop .... **ATELIER**
world: Hindu myth ...... **LOKA**
world, holder of .... **ATLAS**
World War I battle site **MONS, MARNE**

d
World War I group . **AEF, AMEX**
World War II area ...... **ETO**
worm .. **ESS, TINEA, ANNELID**
worm, African .... **LOA**
worm, bait .... **LURG**
worm, eye-infesting ...... **LOA**
worm, S-shaped .... **ESS**
worm track, fossil .. **NEREITE**
worn, as rope .... **MAGGED**
worn by friction .... **ATTRITE**
worn out .... **EFFETE**
worn-out horse **NAG, HACK, PLUG**
worry .... **RUX, CARE, CARK, FRET, STEW**
worship .... **ADORE**
worship, form of ..... **RITUAL**
worship, house of .... **BETHEL**
worship, object of ...... **IDOL**
worship of saints ...... **DULIA**
worship, place of **ALTAR, TEMPLE**
worthless **BAD, RACA, TRASHY**
worthless bit from table .. **ORT**
worthless rock ...... **GANGUE**
wound: Her. .... **VULN**
wound mark .... **SCAR**
wrangle .... **HAGGLE**
wrap .... **SWATHE, SWADDLE**

a wrapping .... **PLIOFILM**
wrath .... **IRE**
wrathful .... **IRATE**
wreath .... **CHAPLET**
wreath: Her. .... **TORSE**
wreathe .... **COIL, WIND**
wrest .... **REND**
wrestle .... **TUSSLE**
wrestling throw ... **HIPE, HYPE**
wriggling .... **EELY**
wrinkle .... **RUCK, RUGA, SEAM, RUGAE, RIMPLE**
wrinkled ... **RUGATE, RUGOSE**
wrist .... **CARPUS**
wrists .... **CARPI**
wrist bone .... **CARPAL**
wrist guard .... **BRACER**
writ of execution ..... **ELEGIT**
writ, sheriff's .... **VENIRE**
writ to arrest .... **CAPIAS**

c write .... **PEN, SCRIVE**
write comments ...... **POSTIL**
write music .... **NOTATE**
writer .... **DITER, SCRIBE**
writer, Ger. .... **MANN**
writing instrument ...... **PEN**
writing on the wall **MENE, TEKEL**
writing paper size ...... **CAP**
writing table .... **ESCRITOIRE**
writing well, art of .. **RHETORIC**
wrong ...... **OUT, EVIL, AMISS**
wrong: Lat. ... **MALA, MALUM**
wrong, legal .... **TORT**
wrong: prefix .... **MIS**
wrongdoing .... **EVIL**
wrongdoing, serious .... **CRIME**
wryneck .... **LOXIA**
Wyoming peak, highest **GANNETT**

Y

Y, in Middle Eng. .. **YOK, YOGH**
Y's .... **WIES**
yacht .... **SAIL**
yacht pennant .... **BURGEE**
Yale .... **ELI**
b yam, Hawaii .... **HOI**
yam, white **UBE, UBI, UVE, UVI**
Yang, opposite of .... **YIN**
Yangtze tributary .... **HAN**
Yap Island stone money ... **FEI**
yarn ... **GARN, TALE, CREWEL**
yarn count .... **TYPP**
yarn for warp .... **ABB**
yarn measure ..... **LEA, HEER**
yarn projection **KNAP, KNOP**
yarn, quantity of ...... **SKEIN**
Yarura language .... **PUME**
yataghan .... **BALAS**
yaupon holly ...... **CASSENA**
yawn .... **GAPE**
yawn: obs. .... **GANE**
yearly .... **ETESIAN**
yearly church payment **ANNAT**
yearn .... **ACHE, LONG**
year's crops .... **ANNONA**
yeast .... **BEES**
yeast, brewer's .... **BARM**
yeast, Jap. .... **KOJI**
yeast, wild .... **ANAMITE**
yell: Scot. .... **GOWL**
yellow ...... **AMBER, OCHER, OCHRE, MELINE, CITRINE**
yellow-brown .... **TOPAZ**
yellow bugle .... **IVA**

yellow dye plant .... **AMIL**
yellow fish .... **ORF, ORFE**
yellow ide .... **ORF, ORFE**
yellow iris .... **SEDGE**
yellow ocher .... **SIL**
d yellow pigment .... **SIL**
yellow wood .... **AVODIRE**
yellowhammer, Eur. .. **AMMER**
yellowish .... **SALLOW**
yelp .... **KIYI, YOUP**
Yemenite .... **ARAB**
Yemen's capital .... **SANA**
yes: Sp. .... **SI**
yesterday: Fr. .... **HIER**
yesterday, pert. to **HESTERNAL**
yet .... **E'EN, STILL**
yew, pert. to .... **TAXINE**
yield **CEDE, ACCEDE, CONCEDE**
Yogi .... **SWAMI**
yoke bar, S. Afr. .... **SKEY**
yokel ...... **OAF, HICK, RUBE**
yolk of egg .... **VITELLUS**
yolky .... **EGGY**
yon .... **THERE**
yorker: cricket .... **TICE**
Yorkshire city .... **LEEDS**
Yorkshire river .... **URE, OUSE**
you: It. .... **TU**
you: Sp. .... **TE**
young animal **CUB, PUP, COLT, WHELP**
young female hog ...... **GILT**
young girl of Burma ... **MIMA**
young hog .... **SHOAT, SHOTE**
young kangaroo .... **JOEY**

a young man, handsome ADONIS
young ox: Eng. .... STOT
young plant .... SET
young rowdy ...... HOODLUM
youngest son .... CADET
youngster
KID, TAD, TOT, SHAVER
youth .... LAD
youth .... GOSSOON
youth shelter .... HOSTEL

c youthful: zool. ...... NEANIC
Yucatan Indian .... MAYA
yucca-like plant .... SOTOL
Yugoslav .... SERB, CROAT
Yugoslav leader .... TITO
Yum-Yum's friend
KOKO, NANKIPOO
Yutang .... LIN

Z

b zeal .... ELAN, ARDOR
zealot .... BIGOT
zealous .... AVID
Zebedee, son of JOHN, JAMES
zebra, young .... COLT
zebrawood .... ARAROBA
zebu-yak hybrid ZO, ZOH, ZOBO
zenith .... TOP, ACME, PEAK
zenith, opposite of .... NADIR
Zeno's follower .... STOIC
zeppelin .... BLIMP
Zeppelin .... GRAF
zero .... CIPHER
zest .... TANG
zetetic .... SEEKER
Zeus, epithet of ..... AMMON
Zeus, maiden loved by
IO, LEDA, EUROPA
Zeus, mother of .... RHEA
Zeus, old Doric name for ZAN
Zeus' daughter
ATE, HEBE, IRENE
Zeus' sister .... HERA

d Zeus' son ..... ARES, ARCAS, MINOS, APOLLO
Zeus' wife ..... HERA, METIS
Zilpah's son ..... GAD, ASHER
zinc in slabs .... SPELTER
zinc ingot .... SPELTER
Zionist group .... ITO
zipper .... TALON
zodiac sign ...... LEO, ARIES, LIBRA, VIRGO, CANCER, PISCES, TAURUS, SCORPIO
Zola novel .... NANA
zone .... AREA
zone: Lat. .... ZONA
zoophyte, marine ...... CORAL
Zophah, son of ...... BEERA
Zoroastrian .. PARSI, PARSEE
Zoroastrian bible .... AVESTA
zounds .... OONS
Zulu headman ..... INDUNA
Zulu language .... BANTU

SPECIAL SECTION

READY REFERENCE WORD LISTS

In one compact section, here are lists of the most useful and widely used word categories. Some of these words, having certain customary definitions, are also listed in the DEFINITIONS section of this book, but these word lists will be of greatest help when you are confronted with GENERALIZED definitions such as "Roman goddess," "South American Indian," "Heraldic term," "African tribe," "U.S. author," or "Ice hockey great."

In most cases, the words in each separate listing are placed according to the number of letters in the words. This is a tremendous advantage to puzzle solvers, who are more concerned with the length of a word than with its alphabetical placement. However, in some lists of people's names (U.S. Authors, Award-Winning Ice Hockey Players, and the like) you may be looking for either the first name or the last name, but it was impossible to list both ways, so they are listed alphabetically by the last name.

This section is intended as a handy reference for crossword puzzle solvers, and contains words and names often found in crosswords. Therefore, some of the lists are complete (such as Chemical Elements), but many are not (Some Names from the Baseball Hall of Fame, for example).

The listings for this Special Section are shown on the Table of Contents.

MEASURES

AREA MEASURES

AR, ARE, ACRE, DECARE (10 ARES), CENTIAR, CENTIARE

Annam .... **MAU, QUO, SAO**
Bengal .... **BEGA**
Czechoslovakia ... **LAN, MIRA**
Dutch E. Ind. .... **BOUW**
England, Old .... **HYDE**
Japan .... **BU, SE, TAN**
Norway .... **MAL, MAAL**
Paraguay .... **LINO**
Poland .... **MORG**
Rome, Ancient ...... **CLIMA, CLIMATA**
Serbia .... **RIF, RALO**
Shetlands, Orkney .... **URE**
Siam .... **RAI, NGAN**
Sweden .... **MORGEN**

DRY MEASURES

PECK, PINT, STERE

Algeria .... **TARRI**
Austria .... **MUTH**
Borneo .... **GANTANG**
Brazil .... **MOIO**
Burma .... **TENG**
Calcutta .... **KUNK, RAIK**
Channel Is. .... **CABOT**
China .... **HO, HU**
Dutch .... **KOP, ZAK**
Egypt .... **KADA, KILAH**
Hebrew .... **CAB, KAB, KOR, EPHA, OMER, SEAH, EPHAH**
Italy .... **SALM, SALMA**
Japan .... **SHO**
Morocco .... **SAHH**
Netherlands .... **KOP, ZAK**
Portugal .... **MEIO, PIPA**
Russia .... **LOF**
Tangier .... **MUDD**
Tunis ..... **SAA, SAAH, UEBA**

LENGTH, DISTANCE MEASURES

ELL, ROD, FOOT, HAND, INCH, MILE, YARD, METER, METRE, PERCH, MICRON, FURLONG

Annam .... **LY, GON, NGU**
Brazil .... **PE**
Calcutta .... **DHAN, JAOB**
China .... **HU, LI, PU, TU, CH'IH, TCHI, TSUN**
Czechoslovakia .. **SAH, LATRO**
Denmark **FOD, MIL, MUL, ALEN**
Domin. Repub. .... **ONA**
Dutch .... **DUIM, VOET**
D. E. Indies .... **DEPA**
Egypt .. **PIC, PIK, KHET, THEB**
Eritrea .... **CUBI**
Estonia .... **LIIN, SULD**
France .... **AUNE**
Greece .. **PIC, PIK, BEMA, PIKI POUS, ACAENA**
Hebrew .... **EZBA**
Iceland .... **FET, ALIN, LINA**
India .. **GAZ, GEZ, GUZ, JOW, KOS, JAOB, KOSS**
Italy .... **CANNA**
Japan .. **BU, JO, RI** (marine), **CHO, DJO, KEN, RIN, HIRO**
Java .... **PAAL**
Libya .... **DRA, PIK, DRAH**
Malabar .... **ADY**
Malacca .... **ASTA**
Netherlands .... **DUIM, VOET**
Norway .... **FOT, ALEN**
Persia ...... **GAZ, GEZ, GUZ, ZAR, ZER**
Poland .... **MILA, PRET**
Prussia .... **RUTE**
Rangoon . **LAN, DAIN, TAUN**
Rome, ancient .... **ACTUS, .. GRADUS, STADIA, STADIUM**
Russia .... **FUT, VERST**
Siam .... **WA, KUP, NIU, SEN, SOK, WAH, NIOU, SAWK**
Spain .... **BARA, CODO, DEDO, VARA**
Sweden ...... **FOT, REF, FAMN**
Switzerland .... **TOISE**
Tripoli .... **DRA, DRAA**
Turkey .... **PIC, PIK, KHAT, ZIRA**

(liquid measures on page 189)

WEIGHTS

KIP, TON, GRAM, KILO, CARAT, GRAIN, OUNCE, CENTRAL
Abyssinia .... **KASM, NATR, OKET, ALADA, NETER**
Annam .... **BINH**
Arabia .... **KELA**
Austria .... **UNZE**
Bavaria .... **GRAN**
Brazil .... **ONCA**
Bulgaria .... **OKA, OKE**
Burma ...... **VIS, KYAT, VISS**
Calcutta .. **PANK, PAWA, RAIK**
China .... **LI, FEN, HAO, KIN SSU, TAN, YIN, TAEL**
Columbia .... **SACO**
Denmark **ES, ORT, VOG, ESER, PUND**
Dutch .... **ONS, LOOD**
Dutch E. Ind ...... **TJI, HOEN, TALI, WANG**
Egypt ... **KAT, KET, OKA, OKE, HEML, KHAR, OHIA, OKIEH**
England .... **STONE**
Estonia .... **NAEL, PUUD**
Ethiopia .... See Abyssinia
France .... **GROS**
Germany .... **LOT, LOTE, LOTH, STEIN**
Greece .... **MNA, MINA, OBOLE, OBOLUS**
Guinea .... **AKEY, PISO, UZAN, SERON**
Hebrew .... **BEKA, REBA**
India .... **SER, BHAR, PALA, RATI, TOLA, VISS, RATTI**
Italian .... **SALM, SALMA**
Japan ...... **KIN, SHI, MORIN**
Malay .... **CHEE**
Malta .... **SALM, SALMA**
Mexico .... **LIBRA, ONZA**
Mongolia .... **LAN**
Morocco .... **ARTEL**
Moslem .... **ROTL**
Netherlands ...... **ONS, LOOD**
Norway .... **PUND**
ORIENT ...... **MANN, ROTL, TAEL, ARTAL**
Palestine ...... **ROTLA, ZUZA**
Persia .... **SER**
Poland .... **LUT**
Portugal **GRAO, ONCA, LIBRA**
Rangoon .... **RUAY**
Rome, Ancient ...... **AS, BES, LIBRA, SOLIDUS**
Russia .... **LAN, PUD, DOLA, POOD, POUD**
Siam .... **PAI, KLAM, KLOM, TICAL**
Shetland Island .. **URE** (ounce)
Spain .... **ONZA**
Sweden **ASS, ORT, STEN, UNTZ**
Turkey ..... **OCK, OKA, OKE, KILE, OCHA, KERAT**

LIQUID MEASURES

TUN, DRAM, GILL, PINT, MINIM
Abyssinia ...... **CUBA, KUBA**
Annam .... **TAO**
Arabia .... **SAA**
Austria .... **FASS**
Brazil .... **PIPA**
Burma .... **BYEE, SEIT**
China .... **KO, QUEI, SHIH**
Cyprus .... **CASS**
Dutch .. (old) **AAM, AUM, KAN**
Egypt .... **HIN**
England .... **PIN, CRAN**
Ethiopia .... see ABYSSINIA
Germany .... **AAM, EIMER**
Hebrew .... **HIN**
Hungary .... **AKO**
Japan .... **KOKU, SHO**
Malaya .... **PAU**
Netherlands . **AAM, AUM, KAN**
Portugal .... **BOTA, PIPA**
Rangoon .... **BYEE, SEIT**
Rome, Ancient .... **URNA**
Russia ... **STOF, STOFF, STOOF**
Somaliland .... **CABA**
Spain .... **COPA**
Sweden .... **AM, AMAR, KAPP**
Switzerland ..... **IMMI, SAUM**
Tangier .... **KULA**
Trieste .... **ORNA, ORNE**
Yugoslavia .... **AKOV**

COINS, MONEY

Abyssinia ..... **BESA, GIRSH, TALARI**
Afghanistan .... **AMANIA**
Albania .... **LEK**
Anglo-Saxon .... **ORA, SCEAT**
Annam .... **QUAN**
Austria .... **DUCAT**
Biblical .. **BEKA, MITE** (small), **SHEKEL, TALENT**
Brazil .... **REI**
Bulgaria ... **LEV, LEW, DINAR**
Chile .... **COLON**
China .. **LI, CASH, TAEL, TIAO, YUAN, PU** (early)
Colombia .... **REAL**
Costa Rica .... **COLON**
Czechslovakia ...... **DUCAT, KRONE** (plural, **KRONEN**)
Denmark ... **ORA, ORE, ORAS, KRONE** (plural, **KRONER**)
Dutch **OORD, DALER, GULDEN, STIVER**
D. E. Indies ..... **BONK, DUIT**
Egypt .... **GIRSH**
England ... **ORA, RIAL** (gold), **RYAL, RYEL, GROAT, PENCE, FLORIN, GUINEA**
Equador .... **SUCRE**
Ethiopia ..... see ABYSSINIA
Europe .... (old) **GROS, DUCAT**
France .. **ECU** (old), **SOL, SOU, AGNEL** (old), **FRANC, LIARD** (old), **LOUIS, OBOLE, BESANT** or **BEZANT** (old).
Genoa .... **JANE** (old)
Germany ..... **MARK, KRONE** (former), **TALER, THALER**
Ger. E. Africa .... **PESA**
Greece .. **OBOL** or **OBOLI** (old), **STATER** (old)
Hungary ...... **GARA, PENGO**
Iceland .... **AURAR, EYRIR, KRONA**
India. **LAC, PIE, ANNA, DAWM, FELS, HOON, LAKH, PICE** (small bronze), **TARA, MOHUR** (old), **RUPEE**
Iran .... see PERSIA
Iraq .... **DINAR**
Ireland .... **RAP** (old)
Italy .... **LIRA, LIRE, SOLDO, TESTER, TESTON, TESTONE, TESTOON**
Japan .... **BU, RIN, SEN, YEN, OBAN**
Latvia .... **LAT, LATU**
Lithuania .. **LIT, LITAI, LITAS**
Macao .... **AVO**
Malaya **TRA** (tin, pewter), **TRAH**
Mexico ...... **PESO, CENTAVO**
Montenegro .... **PARA**
Morocco .... **OKIA, RIAL**
Nepal .... **MOHAR**
Netherlands .... **DAALDER**
Norway .... **ORE, KRONE (KRONER)**
Oman .... **GAJ, GAZ, GOZ, GHAZI**
Persia. **PUL, KRAN, POUL, RIAL, DARIC, DINAR, MOHUR** (old), **TOMAN, STATER**
Peru .... **SOL, DINERO**
Poland .... **DUCAT**
Portugal ..... **JOE, REI, PECA, DOBRA** (former)
Rome, ancient . **SEMIS, DINDER**
Roman ...... **AS, AES, ASSES, SOLIDUS**
Rumania ..... **LEU, LEY, BANI**
Russia . **COPEC, KOPEK, RUBLE**
Siam .... **AT, ATT, BAHT, TICAL** or **TIKAL**
Sicily .... **TARI**
Somaliland .... **BESA**
South Africa ...... **DAALDER**
Spain ..... **COB, DURO, PESO, REAL, DOBLA** (old), **PESETA, PISTOLE** (old)
Sweden **ORE, KRONA (KRONOR), KRONE (KRONER)**
Switzerland .... **BATZ**
Thailand .... see SIAM
Timor .... **AVO**
Turkey .... **LIRA** (gold), **PARA, ALTUN** (gold), **ASPER, MAHBUB** (gold), **PIASTER**
United States .. **CENT, DIME, EAGLE**
Venice .... **BETSO** (old silver)
Yugoslavia .... **DINAR**

TRIBES (Including Peoples, Natives)

EUROPE:
Albania . . . . **GEG, CHAM, GHEG, TOSK**
Balto-Slav . . . . **LETT**
Celtic on Danube . . . . **BOII**
Finnish near Volga . . . . **VEPS, VEPSA**
Finnish, Ingria . . . . **VOT, VOTE, VOTH, WOTE**
Lithuania . . . . **BALT**
Syryenian . . . . **KOMI**
Teuton, ancient . . . . **UBII**

MIDDLE EAST:
Arab . . . . **AUS, IBAD**
Bedouin . . . . **ABSI, HARB**
Turkey . . . . **KURD**
East Turkey . . . . **KURD**
Persia . . . . see under **ASIA**

ASIA:
Afghanistan . . . . **SAFI**
Assam . . . . **AO, AKA; AHOM, GARO, NAGA**
Borneo . . . . **DYAK, IBAN; DAYAK**
Burma . . . . **WA, LAI, KAW, MON, WAS; AKHA, CHIN, KADU, KUKI, TSIN; KAREN**
Caucasus . . . . **IMER, KURI, LASI, LAZE, LAZI, SVAN; OSSET, SVANE**
Celebes, Malayan . . . . **BUGI**
China, Miao . . . . **HEH**
China, Nord . . . . **USUN, UZUN; USSUN**
China, Tatar . . . . **TOBA**
India . . . . **AWAN, BHIL, BHEEL, TURI**
Kolarian (India) . . . . **BHAR**
Japan, aborigine . . . . . **AINO, AINU**
Madagascar . . . . **HOVA**
Manchu . . . . **DAUR**
Mongol . . . . **CHUD**
Nepal . . . . **AOUL, KHAS**
Persia . . . . **LUR, KURD, FARSI, IRANIAN**
Tibet . . . . **CHAMPA**

AFRICA:
Abyssinian . . . . **SHOA**
Bantu . . . . **KUA; BANE, BAYA, BIHE, BULE, FANG, FUNG, GOGO, GOLO, GOMA, GUHA, HAKU, HEHE, JAGA, LUBA, MAKA, NAMA, SOGA, SUKU, VIRA, YAKA, ZULU (largest); KAFIR; KAFFIR**
Bedouin . . . . **ABSI**
Berber . **DAZA, RIFF, TEDA, TIBU**
Bushman . . . . . **SAN, SAAN, QUNG**
Congo . . . . **FIOT, SUSU**
Central Africa . . . . **ABO; BULO, DOMA, KALI, KURI, LURI, YAKO; LUREM**
Dahomey . . . . **FON, FONG**
East Africa . . . . . . **JUR, LUR, YAO; AKKA, ALUR, ASHA, BARI, BONI, GOLO, MADI, NUER, VITI**
Ethiopian . . . . **SHOA**
Gold Coast . . . . **AKAN, AKIM, AKRA**
Hamitic . . . . . **AFAR, BEJA, BENI, BOGO, GALA, HIMA**
Kaffir . . . . **XOSA, ZULU**
Kenya . . . . **BONI**
Lake Albert . . . . **ALUR, LURI**
Liberia . . . . **GI; KRA, KRU, VAI, VEI; KROO, TOMA**
Libya . . . . **FUL, FULA, MZAB**
Mozambique . . . . **YAO**
Nigeria . . . . . . **ARO, EDO, IBO, IJO; BENI, BINI, EBOE, EKOI, IDJO, IDYO, IDZO, NUPE; BENIN**
Nilotic . . . . **SUK, BARI**
Pygmy . . . . **AKKA, DOKO**
Slave Coast . . . . **EGBA**
Sudan . . . . . **FUL, FUR, VEI; FULA, GOLO, MABA, MEGE, NUBA, SUSU, TAMA**
West Africa . . . . . . **GA; AJA, EWE, IBO, KRU, KWA; AGNI, AKIM, APPA, BAGA, BINI, EFIK, EGBA, EKOI, GENG, GOLA, HABE, IKWE, JEBU, JOAT, JOLA, KETU, NALU, ONDO, REMO, SAPE, TCHI, TSHI, VACA, WARI**

ALASKA:
Aleutians . . . . **ATKA**

GREENLAND . . . . **ITA**

AUSTRALIA . . . . **KOKO**
NEW GUINEA . . . . **KARON**

SOUTH AMERICA:
Fr. Guiana . . . . **BONI**

INDIANS, INDIAN TRIBES

Alaska .... ALEUT, SITKA
Algonquin or Algonkian Indians ... FOX, SAC, WEA; CREE, SAUK; MIAMI; LENAPE, OTTAWA, PIEGAN; SHAWNEE
Amazon .... (lower) MURA, (upper) ANDOA
Apache .... LIPAN
Araucanian .... AUCA
Arawak ..... ARAUA, CAMPA, INERI
Arikara .... REE
Arizona .. HANO, HOPI, MOKI, PIMA, TEWA, YUMA; MOQUI; APACHE
Athapascan Indians ..... DENE, HUPA, TAKU; LIPAN, TINNE; APACHE, NAVAHO
Aymara .... COLLA
Bolivia ...... ITE, URO, URU; ITEN, LECA, MOJO, MOXO, URAN; CHOLO
Brazil ...... GE; YAO; CAME, DIAU, MAKU, MURA, PURI, PURU, TUPI; ACROA, ANDOA, ARAUA, CARIB, GUANA, SIUSI; ZAPARO
Caddoan Indians .. REE; ADAI; IONI, CADDO, BIDAI; PAWNEE
California ...... HUPA, KOSO, MONO, NOZI, POMO, SERI, TATU, YANA; MAIDU, YANAN; SALINA
Canada .... AHT, CREE, DENE, TAKU; NISKA, TINNE; SARCEE
Carib .... YAO, TRIO
Carolina .... CATAWBA
Chaco .... TOBA
Chile .... AUCA
Colorado .... UTE
Colombia .... BORO, DUIT, MUSO, MUZO, TAMA, TAPA; CHOCO; COLIMA
Costa Rica ...... BOTO VOTO
Cowichan Indians .. NANAIMO

Dakotas .. REE, SIOUX, TETON; MANDAN, SANTEE; ARIKARA
Delaware .... LENAPE
Ecuador: ..... CARA (extinct); ANDOA, ARDAN
Eskimo .... ATKA; ALEUT
Florida: .... CALUSA
Fuegan .... ONA
Great Lakes .... ERIE; HURON
Guatemala ...... MAM; CHOL, ITZA, IXIL, IXLI, MAYA, ULVA, VOTO; KICHE, PIPIL
Honduras .... PAYA
Iowa .... FOX, SAC; SAUK
Indiana .... WEA; MIAMI
Iroquoian Indians,
Iroquois: .... ERIE, HURON, CAYUGA, MOHAWK, ONEIDA, SENECA
Jalisco: .... CORA
Keresan Indians: . SIA; ACOMA
Kusan .... COOS
Lesser Antilles .... INERI
Mayan Indians: ... MAM, CHOL
Mexico ... MAM, CHOL, CORA, MAYA, MIXE, PIMA, PIME, SERI, TECA, TECO, WABI; AZTEC, OTOMI, SERIA; TOLTEC
Miami .... WEA
Mississippi ..... TIOU, BILOXI
Montana ...... CROW, HOHE
Muskohegan Indians: . CREEK, YAMASI, CHOCTAW, SEMINOLE
Nebraska .... KIOWA
Nevada .... PAIUTE
New Mexico . SIA, PIRO, TANO, TAOS, TEWA, ZUNI; ACOMA, KERES, PECOS
New York .... SENECA
Nicaragua . MIXE, RAMA, ULVA
Oklahoma .. KAW, OTO; LOUP, OTOE; CADDO, CREEK, KANSA, KIOWA, OSAGE, PONCA; PAWNEE
Oregon .... COOS, KUSAN, MODOC, CHINOOK

Panamint .... KOSO
Panama .... CUNA, CUEVA
Pawnee Indians .... LOUP
Payaguas .... AGAZ
Peru: .... ANDE, ANTI, BORO, CANA, INCA, INKA, LAMA, PEBA, PIBA, PIRO, YNCA; CAMPA, CHIMU, CHOLO, COLAN, YUNCA; CHANCA; QUICHU
Peru South .... CANA, COLLA, CHANCA
Piman Indians .. CORA, JOVA, MAYO, PIMA, XOVA, YAKI, YAQUI
Plains Indians ... CREE, CROW; KIOWA, OSAGE; PONCA, TETON, PAWNEE
Pueblo Indians .. HOPI, MOKI, TANO, TAOS, ZUNI; KERES, MOQUI
Rio Grande .... TANO
Sacramento Valley ..... YANA
Salishan Indians ..... ATNAH, LUMMI
Shoshonean Indians .... UTE; HOPI, KOSO, MOKI, MONO; MOQUI, PIUTE; UINTA, PAIUTE
Siouan Indians ... KAW, OTO; CROW, IOWA, OTOE; KANSA, OMAHA, OSAGE, PONCA; BILOXI, DAKOTA, MANDAN; CATAWBA
Sonora .... JOVA, PIMI, SERI
South America (widely distributed) .... GES, ONA, YAO; LULE, MOXO, PANO, PIRO, TOBA; CARIB, INERI; ARAWAK
South Carolina ..... CATAWBA
Tacanan Indians ..... CAVINA
Tanoan .... TEWA
Tapuyan Indians .... GE, GES, GHES, ACROA
Texas .... LIPAN
Tierra del Fuego: .... ONA
Tlingit: .... AUK, SITKA
Tupian .... ANTA
Utah: .... UTE
Washington .... HOH, LUMMI, MAKAH
Yucatan .... MAYA
Yukian .... TATU
Yukon .... TAKU
Yuncan .... CHIMU

ARMOR

Head .... **COIF, HELM; ARMET, VISOR; BEAVER, CAMAIL; BASINET, HAUBERK**
Neck .... **GORGET**
Shoulder .... **AILETTE, PAULDRON, EPAULIERE, PASSEGARDE**
Body .... **TACE; CULET, TASSE; CORIUM, GORGET, LORICA, TASSET; CUIRASS, HAUBERK, SURCOAT; BRAGUETTE**
Arm .... **BRASSARD, PALLETTE, VAMBRACE; CUBITIERE, REREBRACE**
Hand .... **GAUNTLET**
Thigh .... **CUISH, TASSE, TUILE; CUISSE, TASSET, TUILLE**
Leg, foot .... **JAMB, JAMBE; GREAVE; CHAUSSE, PEDIEUX; SOLLERET**
Complete suit .... **BARD, MAIL; BARDE**

HERALDRY—HERALDIC TERMS

Heraldic bearings: **BEND, ENTE, FESS, ORLE, FESSE, GIRON, GYRON, LAVER, PHEON; SALTIRE**
Heraldic tinctures:
gold, **OR**; fur, **PEAN, VAIR, VAIRE**; green, **VERT**; blue, **AZURE**; red, **GULES**; black, **SABLE**; orange, **TENNE**; silver, **ARGENT**; blood-red, **MURREY**; purple, **PURPURE**
attitude of animal
SEJANT, GARDANT, PASSANT, RAMPANT
ball .... **ROUNDEL**
band ..... **FESS, ORLE, FESSE**
barnacle .... **BREY**
bend .... **COTISE**
bird .... **MARTLET**
circle .... **BEZANT, ANNULET**
colter .... **LAVER**
creature .. **LION, PARD; BISSE, WYVER; CANNET, WYVERN; GRIFFON, MARTLET**
cross .. **CRUX, NOWY, PATY; FLORY, FORMY, PATEE, PATTE; CLECHE; SALTIRE**
curved in middle ...... **NOWY**
curves, made of ..... **NEBULE**
division .... **PALE, PALY**
dog, short-eared ...... **ALANT**
drops, seme of .... **GUTTE**
duck ..... **CANNET, CANETTE**
fillet .... **ORLE**
fish trap .... **WEEL**
flower strewn .... **SEME**
flying in air .... **FLOTANT**
fountain .... **SYKE**
grafted .... **ENTE**
headless .... **ETETE**
horizontal band ......see band
leaves, having .... **POINTE**
lines .... **UNDE, UNDY, URDY, NEBULY**
lozenge ..... **FUSIL, MASCLE**
manacle .... **TIRRET**
pointed .... **URDE**
powdered .... **SEME**
scattered .... **SEME**
sheaf of grain .. **GERB, GERBE**
shield .... **PAVIS**
shield division .... **ENTE**
shield's corner ...... **CANTON**
silver .... **ARGENT**
sitting .... **ASSIS**
snake .... **BISSE**
sown .... **SEME**
spangled .... **SEME**
star-strewn .... **SEME**
strewn .... **SEME**
three parts, divided into **TIERCE**
triangle ..... **GIRON, GYRON**
two-winged .... **VOL**
voided escutcheon ...... **ORLE**
walking .... **PASSANT**
wavy .... **ONDE, UNDE, UNDY, UNDEE, NEBULE**
winged .... **VOL, AILE**
wound .... **VULN**
wreath .... **ORLE, TORSE**

CHEMICAL ELEMENTS AND SYMBOLS

All elements are natural, metallic elements unless otherwise indicated. The chemical symbol of each element is indicated by the letter or letters in dark type that follow it. (Syn.) indicates synthetically produced.

3 letters
TIN **Sn**

4 letters
GOLD **Au**
IRON **Fe**
LEAD **Pb**
NEON **Ne** (gaseous)
ZINC **Zn**

5 letters
ARGON **Ar** (gaseous)
BORON **B** (nonmetallic)
RADON **Rn** (gaseous)
XENON **Xe** (gaseous)

6 letters
BARIUM **Ba**
CARBON **C** (nonmetallic)
CERIUM **Ce**
CESIUM **Cs**
COBALT **Co**
COPPER **Cu**
CURIUM **Cm** (syn.)
ERBIUM **Er**
HELIUM **He** (gaseous)
INDIUM **In**
IODINE **I** (nonmetallic)
NICKEL **Ni**
OSMIUM **Os**
OXYGEN **O** (gaseous)
RADIUM **Ra**
SILVER **Ag**
SODIUM **Na**
SULFUR **S** (nonmetallic)

7 letters
ARSENIC **As** (semimetallic)
BISMUTH **Bi**
BROMINE **Br** (nonmetallic)
CADMIUM **Cd**
CALCIUM **Ca**
FERMIUM **Fm** (syn.)
GALLIUM **Ga**
HAFNIUM **Hf**
HOLMIUM **Ho**
IRIDIUM **Ir**
KRYPTON **Kr** (gaseous)
LITHIUM **Li**
MERCURY **Hg**
NIOBIUM **Nb**
RHENIUM **Re**
RHODIUM **Rh**
SILICON **Si** (nonmetallic)
TERBIUM **Tb**
THORIUM **Th**
THULIUM **Tm**
URANIUM **U**
YTTRIUM **Y**

8 letters
ACTINIUM **Ac**
ALUMINUM **Al**
ANTIMONY **Sb**
ASTATINE **At** (semimetallic)
CHLORINE **Cl** (gaseous)
CHROMIUM **Cr**
EUROPIUM **Eu**
FLUORINE **F** (gaseous)
FRANCIUM **Fr**
HYDROGEN **H** (gaseous)
LUTETIUM **Lu**
NITROGEN **N** (gaseous)
NOBELIUM **No** (syn.)
PLATINUM **Pt**
POLONIUM **Po**
RUBIDIUM **Rb**
SAMARIUM **Sm**
SCANDIUM **Sc**
SELENIUM **Se** (nonmetallic)
TANTALUM **Ta**
THALLIUM **Ti**
TITANIUM **Ti**
TUNGSTEN **W**
VANADIUM **V**

9 letters
AMERICIUM **Am** (syn.)
BERKELIUM **Bk** (syn.)
BERYLLIUM **Be**
GERMANIUM **Ge**
LANTHANUM **La**
MAGNESIUM **Mg**
MANGANESE **Mn**
NEODYMIUM **Nd**
NEPTUNIUM **Np** (syn.)
PALLADIUM **Pd**
PLUTONIUM **Pu**
POTASSIUM **K**
RUTHENIUM **Ru**
STRONTIUM **Sr**
TELLURIUM **Te** (nonmetallic)
YTTERBIUM **Yb**
ZIRCONIUM **Zr**

10 letters
DYSPROSIUM **Dy**
GADOLINIUM **Gd**
LAWRENCIUM **Lr** (syn.)
MOLYBDENUM **Mo**
PHOSPHORUS **P** (nonmetallic)
PROMETHIUM **Pm**
TECHNETIUM **Tc**

11 letters
CALIFORNIUM **Cf** (syn.)
EINSTEINIUM **Es** (syn.)
MENDELEVIUM **Md** (syn.)

12 letters
PRASEODYMIUM **Pr**
PROTACTINIUM **Pa**

BIBLICAL REFERENCES

BOOKS OF THE BIBLE

Names and order of books of the:

OLD TESTAMENT

1 GENESIS
2 EXODUS
3 LEVITICUS
4 NUMBERS
5 DEUTERONOMY
6 JOSHUA
7 JUDGES
8 RUTH
9 SAMUEL 1
10 SAMUEL 2
11 KINGS 1
12 KINGS 2
13 CHRONICLES 1
14 CHRONICLES 2
15 EZRA
16 NEHEMIAH
17 ESTHER
18 JOB
19 PSALMS
20 PROVERBS
21 ECCLESIASTES
22 SONG OF SOLOMON
23 ISAIAH
24 JEREMIAH
25 LAMENTATIONS
26 EZEKIEL
27 DANIEL
28 HOSEA
29 JOEL
30 AMOS
31 OBADIAH
32 JONAH
33 MICAH
34 NAHUM
35 HABAKKUK
36 ZEPHANIAH
37 HAGGAI
38 ZECHARIAH
39 MALACHI

Names and order of books of the:

NEW TESTAMENT

1 MATTHEW
2 MARK
3 LUKE
4 JOHN
5 THE ACTS
6 ROMANS
7 CORINTHIANS 1
8 CORINTHIANS 2
9 GALATIANS
10 EPHESIANS
11 PHILIPPIANS
12 COLOSSIANS
13 THESSALONIANS 1
14 THESSALONIANS 2
15 TIMOTHY 1
16 TIMOTHY 2
17 TITUS
18 PHILEMON
19 HEBREWS
20 JAMES
21 PETER 1
22 PETER 2
23 JOHN 1
24 JOHN 2
25 JOHN 3
26 JUDE
27 REVELATION

BIBLICAL PROPHETS

AMOS (minor), ESAY, EZRA, JOEL (minor), HOSEA (minor), JONAH (minor), MICAH (minor), MOSES, DANIEL (major), NAHUM (minor), ELISHA, HAGGAI (minor), ISAIAH (major), EZEKIEL (major), JEREMIAH (major)

BIBLICAL PATRIARCHS

REU; ADAM, EBER, ENOS, NOAH, SETH, SHEM; ISAAC, JACOB, JARED, NAHOR, PELEG, SERUG, TERAH; LAMECH

BIBLICAL RULERS

OG; ASA (Judah), GOG, IRA; AGAG, AHAB, AHAZ, AMON, ELAH, JEHU, OMRI, SAUL; CYRUS, DAVID, DEBIR, HEROD, HIRAM, JORAM, NADAB, PEKAH, PIRAM, REZIN, SIHON, ZIMRI; ABIJAH, BAASHA. CAESAR, DARIUS, HEZION, HOSHEA, JAPHIA, JOSHUA, JOSIAH, JOTHAM, UZZIAH

BIBLICAL PEOPLES—TRIBES

DAN, GOG; ANAK, ARAD, CUSH, EMIM, MOAB, PHUD, PHUT (o.t.); ARKITE, HAMITE, HIVITE, KENITE, SEMITE, SHELAH, SINITE; EDOMITE, HITTITE, LEHABIM, MOABITE, REPHAIM

BIBLICAL PLACES

City . **DAN, GATH, GAZA, ZOAR; BABEL, EKRON, SODOM; HEBRON**
Country .... **EDOM, ENON, SEBA; SHEBA**
Hill, Jerusalem's .... **ZION**
Kingdom .... **ELAM, MOAB; SAMARIA**
Land .... **NOD**
Land of plenty .... **GOSHEN**
Mt. **HOR, EBAL, NAIN, NEBO, PEOR; HOREB, SEIR, SINA, SINAI, TABOR; ARARAT, GILEAD, HERMON**
Place .... **ENON, AENON; JORDAN, SHILOH**
Pool .... **SILOAM**
Region .. **ARAM, EDAR; BASHAN**
Town ...... **CANA (1st miracle), NAIN (miracle site); BETHEL**
River .... **ARNON, JORDAN**

BIBLICAL MEN

OG, UZ; ARA, DAN, ELI, GOG, HAM, IRA, LOT, NUN, URI; ABEL, AMOS, BOAZ, CAIN, CUSH, DOEG, EBAL, ENON, ENOS, ESAU, HETH, IRAD, JADA, JEHU, JOAB, KISH, LEVI, MASH, MOAB, OBAL, OBED. OMAR, OREB, OZEM, SETH, SODI, ULAM, UNNI, URIA; AARON (high priest), ABIAH, ABIEL, AHIRA, AMASA, ANNAS, CALEB, CHUZA, ENOCH, HAMAN, HARAN, HIRAM, HOHAM, IBZAN, ISAAC, JACOB, JAMES, JARED, MASSA, MOREH, NABAL, NAHBI, NAHOR, OPHIR, REZON, SACAR, TERAH, URIAH, ZAHAM; SAMSON; ANANIAS, ISHMAEL

BIBLICAL WOMEN

EVE; ADAH, JAEL, LEAH, MARY, RUTH; DINAH, EGLAH, HAGAR, JULIA, JUNIA, LYDIA, MERAB, NAOMI, PHEBE, RAHAB, SARAH, SARAI, SHUAH, TAMAR; ABITAL, BILHAH, DORCAS, ESTHER, HANNAH, HOGLAH, MAACAH, MAHLAH, MICHAL, MILCAH, MIRIAM, PERSIS, RACHEL, RIZPAH, SALOME, VASHTI, ZILLAH, ZILPAH; ABIGAIL, HAMUTAL

BIBLICAL NAMES

ED, ER; IRI, NER, ONO, REI, TOI; ABIA, ADER, ANER, ANIM, ASOM, DARA, ELON, ENOS, IRAD, IVAH, REBA; ABIAM, AHIRA, AMASA, ASEAS

GODS (DEITIES), GODDESSES AND MYTHOLOGY

ASSYRIAN GODS

ANAT (sky), ASUR or ASSUR (war)

BABYLONIAN GODS

Chief gods: EA, ABU or ANU, BEL

EA (chief), ZU (wind), ABU or ANU (chief, sky, sun), BEL (chief), HEA (see EA), IRA (war), SIN (moon), UTU (sun), ADAD or ADDA or ADDU (wind, storm), APSU (chaos), ENKI (see EA), ENZU (see SIN), IRRA (war), NABU or NEBO (wisdom), UTUG (sun), DAGAN (earth), ETANA (eagle rider), SIRIS (alcoholic drinks), BABBAR (sun), SHAMASH (sun)

BABYLONIAN GODDESSES

AI or AYA (consort of Shamash), ERUA (mother), NINA (watery deep), NANAI (daughter of Anu), ISTAR or ISHTAR (chief, love)

BRYTHONIC GODDESS

DON (ancestress of gods)

CELTIC GODS—GODDESS

ANA, ANU, DANA, DANU (mother, queen), LER (sea), LUG, LUGH (light, sun), DAGDA (chief)

CYMRIC GODS

GWYN, LLEU, LLEW (solar)

EGYPTIAN GODS

RA (sun), SU (solar deity), BES (evil, pleasure), GEB (earth), KEB (earth), MIN (procreation), SEB (earth), SET (evil), SHU (see SU), TEM or TUM (sun), AANI (dog-headed ape, sacred to Thoth), AMEN (king), AMON (sun and king), AMUN (king), ATMU or ATUM (sun), BESA (see BES), HAPI (the Nile as a god), KHEM (see MIN), MENT (falcon-headed), PTAH (Memphis god), SETH (evil), SOBK (crocodile-headed), AMMON (see AMEN), HORUS (hawk-headed), MENTU (see MENT), SEBEK (see SOBK), THOTH (wisdom, magic), OSIRIS (underworld), SERAPIS (see OSIRIS)

EGYPTIAN GODDESSES

MA (same as MAAT), MUT (Amen's wife), NUT (heavens), ANTA, APET (maternity), BAST (cat- or lion-headed), BUTO (serpent), ISIS (cow-headed, Horus' mother), MAAT (truth, justice), SATI (queen), ATHOR (see HATHOR), HATHOR (love, mirth, cow-headed)

EGYPTIAN MYTH

BA (soul of man), KA (body of man), NU (chaos), AKH (spirit of man), NUN (see NU), APIS (sacred bull), ATEN (solar disk), DUAT (see AMENTI), HAPI (Nile or Amenti's jinnee), AMENTI (underworld region)

GREEK GODS

DIS (underworld), PAN (field, flocks, forest), ZAN (old name for Zeus), ARES (war, Eris' brother), EROS (love), ZEUS (chief of Olympian gods), COMUS (mirth and revelry), EURUS (southeast wind), HADES (underworld), KOMOS (see COMUS), MOMUS (ridicule), PLUTO (underworld), AEOLUS (wind), APOLLO (sun, youth), AUSTER (south wind), BOREAS (north wind), CRONUS (a Titan, Rhea's spouse; harvest), HELIOS (sun), HERMES (herald), KRONOS (see CRONUS), NEREUS (sea), PLUTUS (wealth), TRITON (sea), BACCHUS (wine), POSEIDON (sea)

GREEK GODDESSES

GE (earth, mother of Titans), ARA (destruction, retribution, vengeance), ATE (discord, mischief, infatuation), EIR (healing), EOS (dawn), ALEA (ATHENA), CORA (see KORE), DICE or DIKE (one of Horae), ENYO (Ares' mother, war), ERIS (discord, sister of Ares), GAEA or GAIA (see GE), HEBE (youth), HERA (queen), HORA (one of Horae), KORE (vegetation), LEDA (Tyndareus' wife), NIKE (victory), RHEA (mother of gods, wife of Kronos), UPIS, ARTEMIS, HORAE (three goddesses of seasons), IRENE (peace), METIS (Zeus' first wife), MOIRA (fate or Fates), ATHENA (wisdom), CLOTHO (a Fate, thread spinner), CYBELE (nature), EIRENE (see IRENE), HECATE (moon, magic), MOERAE (see MOIRA), PALLAS (wisdom), SELENA and SELENE (moon), ARTEMIS (moon, woods, nature), ATROPOS (one of the Fates, thread cutter), DEMETER (grain, agriculture), CHLORIS (flowers), NEMESIS (revenge), LACHESIS (one of the Fates, thread length), APHRODITE (love)

GREEK MYTH

IO (Zeus' beloved changed to a heifer), INO (Cadmus' daughter), PAN (field, flocks, forest), ANAX (one of Dioscuri), AUGE (Arcadian princess), CEYX (Halcyone's husband turned into kingfisher), CLIO (Muse of History), FAUN (see PAN), IDAS (hero, killed Castor), IOLE (Hercules' captive), LETO (Apollo's mother), MAIA (Hermes' mother), OTUS (giant killed by Apollo), ALTIS (sacred grove, Olympic games), ATLAS (held up heavens), CREON (Oedipus' brother-in-law), DIONE (Aphrodite's mother), ENEAS (Troy's defender), ERATO (Clio's sister), HADES (underworld), HELLE (fell into Hellespont with golden fleece), HYDRA (9-headed monster), MINOS (king), NIOBE (weeping stone), SATYR (part-horse demigod), THEIA (Hyperion's sister, wife), ADONIS (beautiful youth), AENEAS (see ENEAS), AGENOR (Trojan warrior), ALECTO (a Fury), DAPHNE (Apollo's nymph turned into tree), EUROPA (carried off by Zeus in form of white bull), HECTOR (Trojan warrior), NEREID (sea nymph to Poseidon), NESTOR (wise king, fought Troy), THETIS (Achilles' mother), TITHON (see TITHONUS), TRITON (sea demigod,

Poseidon's son), URANIA (astronomy), ARIADNE (Theseus' love), ATHAMAS (Ino's husband), CENTAUR (half man, half horse), CYCLOPS (1-eyed giant), ERINYES, (avenging spirits), EUTERPE (Muse of Music), SILENUS (woodland deity, horse-goat-human), ATALANTA (picked up golden apples—lost the race), TARTARUS (infernal regions), TITHONUS (immortal king of Troy, Eos' favorite), TISIPHONE (one of Erinyes)
The Gorgons: MEDUSA, STHENO, EURYALE
The Graces: AGLAIA, THALIA
The Titans or Titanesses: primeval deities: GAEA or GE (mother of Titans). URANUS (father of Titans). Titans: RHEA, COEUS, CREUS, THEIA, CRONUS or KRONOS, PHOEBE, THEMIS

HINDU GODS

KA (unknown), AGNI (fire), AKAL (immortal), CIVA (see SIVA), DEVA or DEWA (divine being), KAMA (love), RAMA (incarnation of Vishnu), SIVA (supreme), VAYU (wind), YAMA (judge of dead), BHAGA (love), DYAUS (heaven, sky), VISHNU (supreme), KRISHNA (avatar of Vishnu)

HINDU GODDESSES

SRI (beauty, wealth, luck, Vishnu's wife), UMA (splendor), VAC (speech), DEVI (any divinity, Siva's consort), KALI (evil), SHRI (see SRI), USAS (dawn), VACH (see VAC), SHREE (see SRI), MATRIS (mothers), LAKSHMI (see SRI)

HINDU MYTH

BANA (1,000-arm giant), KALI (tongue of Agni), KETU (Rahu's tail), NAGA (Vishnu's serpent), RAHU (dragon, swallows sun), USHA (Bana's daughter)

INCA GOD

INTI (sun)

IRISH—see **CELTIC**

NORSE GODS

ER (war), TY (see TIU), VE (Odin's brother, slayed Ymir), EAR (see ER), LOK (see LOKI), TIU (sky, war, Tiwaz), TIW (see TIU), TYR (sky, war), ULL (bow skill), VAN (sea), ZIO (sky), ZIU (see ZIO), FREY (fertility), HLER (sea), HOTH (blind god), LOKE or LOKI (discord, mischief), ODIN chief god, war, wisdom, slayed Ymir), THOR (thunder), TYRR (war), ULLR (see ULL), VALE (see VALI), VALI (Odin's son), VANS (see VANIR), VILI (Odin's brother), AEGIR (sea), AESIR (chief), ALCIS (twin gods), BALDR (see BALDER), BRAGE or BRAGI (poetry), DONAR (see THOR), HODER or HOTHR (see HOTH), VANIR (early race of gods), WODAN or WODEN or WOTAN (see ODIN), BALDER or BALDUR (light)
The Aesir or chief gods: TIU, TYR, ULL, FREY, LOKI, ODIN, THOR, VALI, BRAGI, DONAR, WODEN, BALDER

NORSE GODDESSES

EIR (healing), HEL (Loki's daughter, underworld, dead), RAN (sea, death, wife of Aegir), SIF (Thor's wife), URD (destiny), VOR (betrothal), ERDA (earth), FREA or FRIA (see FRIGG), GERD (Frey's wife), HELA (see HEL), NORN (fate), RIND (Odin's wife, Vali's mother), SAGA (golden beaker), URTH (see URD), FREYA (love, beauty), FRIGG (Odin's wife), NANNA (flowers), NORNA or NORNS (see NORN), FREYJA (see FREYA)

NORSE MYTH

ASK (see ASKR), DIS (female spirit), ASKR (first man), ATLI (king), EGIL (story hero), GARM (Hel's watchdog, slays Tyr), GERI (Odin's wolf), IDUN (Bragi's wife), MARA (nightmare demon), NATT or NOTT (night), WATE (giant), YMIR or YMER ("rime-cold giant"), EGILL (see EGIL), MIMIR (giant), ASGARD (abode of gods)

PHOENICIAN GODDESS

ASTARTE (fertility, love)

ROMAN GODS

DIS (underworld), SOL (sun), AMOR (love), FAUN (field, herds, half goat), JOVE (chief god), MARS (war), MORS (death), COMUS (mirth, joy), CUPID (love), EURUS (southeast wind), KOMOS (see COMUS), MANES (spirits of dead, gods of underworld), ORCUS (dead), APOLLO (sun, music), AUSTER (south wind), BOREAS (north wind), FAUNUS (rural deity), VULCAN (fire), NEPTUNE (sea)

ROMAN GODDESSES

NOX or NYX (night), OPS (harvest, plenty), DIAN (moon, chase, woods), IRIS (rainbow, Zeus' messenger), JUNO (queen), LUNA (moon), MAIA (Vulcan's consort), NONA (Fate), SPES (hope), CERES (earth, grain, agriculture, vegetation), DIANA (see DIAN), EPONA (horses), FIDES (faith), FAUNA (field), FLORA (flowers), MORTA (a Fate), PARCA (a Fate), SALUS (prosperity), TERRA (earth), VENUS (love), VESTA (hearth), ANNONA (crops), AURORA (dawn), DECUMA (a Fate), PARCAE (the Fates), VACUNA (Sabine huntress)

The Fates or Parcae: NONA, MORTA, DECUMA

TEUTONIC GODS—see **NORSE GODS**

TEUTONIC GODDESSES—see **NORSE GODDESSES**

VEDIC GODS—see **HINDU GODS**

VEDIC GODDESSES—see **HINDU GODDESSES**

WELSH GOD

DYLAN

FIRST AND LAST NAMES COMMON TO CROSSWORD PUZZLES

You often find in crossword puzzles definitions like "Writer Aldous ——" or "—— Pavlova." The following list contains the most commonly used names, first names and last names. The part of the name which is usually given in the definition is here in light-face type, arranged alphabetically. The rest of the person's name follows in bold-face type.

Aaron . **BURR, HANK**
Abbot .... **BUD**
Abzug .... **BELLA**
Acheson....... **DEAN**
Adam .... **BEDE**
Adams .... **EDIE, MAUDE**
Addams .... **JANE**
Adoree .... **RENEE**
Agar .... **JOHN**
Alain .... **DELON**
Alan.... **ALDA, KING, LADD, ARKIN, BATES, PATON**
Albert .... **CAMUS**
Albertus ... **MAGNUS**
Albrecht..... **DURER**
Aldo............ **RAY**
Aldous ..... **HUXLEY**
Alejandro....... **REY**
Alexander .... **POPE, SEROV, CALDER, FLEMING**
Alexandre ... **DUMAS**
Alfred **LUNT, DRAKE**
Alfred B. .... **NOBEL**
Alighieri ..... **DANTE**
Allegra .... **KENT**
Allen .... **MEL, FRED, ETHAN, STEVE, WOODY**
Allison......... **FRAN**
Allyson .... **JUNE**
Alpert .... **HERB**
Ambler .... **ERIC**
Ambrose ... **BIERCE, FLEMING**
Amelia ... **BLOOMER**
Amundsen... **ROALD**
Anais............ **NIN**
Anatole..... **FRANCE**
Andersen...... **HANS**
Anderson....... **LONI**
Andersson...... **BIBI**
Andre .... **GIDE**
Andrea .... **DORIA**
Andrea del .. **SARTO**
Andress .... **URSULA**
Andrew...... **YOUNG**

Andrews...... **DANA, JULIE**
Andy .... **HARDY, DEVINE**
Aneurin Bevan.. **NYE**
Angelico........ **FRA**
Angelo ..... **MOSSO, PATRI, GIOTTO**
Anita .... **LOOS**
Anna ... **CASE, HELD, STEN, MOFFO, NEAGLE**
Anouk .... **AIMEE**
Anthony...... **EDEN, SUSAN, TUDOR**
Anton .... **DOLIN, SUSAN**
Antony .... **MARK**
Anya .... **SETON**
Arden .... **EVE, TONI, ENOCH**
Arlene......... **DAHL**
Arnaz .. **DESI, LUCIE**
Arnold.......... **HAP**
Arsene .... **LUPIN**
Artemus...... **WARD**
Arthur .... **BEA**
Arthur Conan **DOYLE**
Ataturk ..... **KEMAL**
Attlee .... **CLEMENT**
Auguste .... **COMTE, RODIN**
Autry.......... **GENE**
Ayres .... **LEW**
Baba .... **ALI**
Babe .... **RUTH**
Baer............ **MAX**
Bagnold .... **ENID**
Bailey .... **PEARL**
Bainter .... **FAY**
Baird .... **BIL**
Ballard .... **KAYE**
Balzac...... **HONORE**
Bambi .... **LINN**
Bara......... **THEDA**
Barbara ...... **EDEN, HALE, RUSH**
Barkley..... **ALBEN**
Barry... **GENE, JACK**

Barrymore.... **DREW, JOHN, ETHEL, LIONEL**
Bartok... **EVA, BELA**
Barton....... **CLARA**
Basie........ **COUNT**
Bates .... **ALAN**
Bayes .... **NORA**
Bea, Beatrice . **LILLIE**
Bean .. **ROY, ORSON**
Becky .... **SHARP**
Bede .... **ADAM**
Beerbohm ...... **MAX**
Beery .... **NOAH**
Begley .... **ED**
Beiderbecke ..... **BIX**
Ben **HOGAN, SHAHN**
Bennett ...... **CERF, JOAN, TONY**
Bergen ...... **EDGAR, POLLY**
Bernhardt ... **SARAH**
Berra.......... **YOGI**
Bert........... **LAHR**
Best........... **EDNA**
Bette **DAVIS, MIDLER**
Beverly........ **SILLS**
Bevin....... **ERNEST**
Billings .... **JOSH**
Billy .... **MAY, ROSE, SUNDAY**
Bing........ **CROSBY**
Bjorn.......... **BORG**
Blaise ...... **PASCAL**
Blake......... **EUBIE**
Blakeley..... **RONEE, SUSAN**
Blanc........... **MEL**
Blas............. **GIL**
Bloch........... **RAY**
Bloomer .... **AMELIA**
Blue........... **BEN**
Blum .... **LEON**
Blyth .... **ANN**
Bobby ... **ORR, HULL**
Bogarde....... **DIRK**
Bohan........ **MARC**
Bohr .... **NIELS**
Boleyn .... **ANNE**

Bolger.......... **RAY**
Bolivar .... **SIMON**
Bonheur....... **ROSA**
Boone. **PAT, DEBBY, DANIEL, RICHARD**
Bovary .... **EMMA**
Bradley....... **OMAR**
Brendan..... **BEHAN**
Bret......... **HARTE**
Brice .... **FANNY**
Bridges....... **BEAU, JEFF, LLOYD**
Brigham..... **YOUNG**
Brodie........ **STEVE**
Bronte .... **EMILY**
Brooke ..... **SHIELDS**
Brooks .... **HERB**
Brown........... **LES**
Broz............ **TITO**
Bruce **DERN, CABOT**
Brynner .... **YUL**
Buck .... **FRANK, HENRY, OWENS, PEARL, ROGERS**
Buddy. **RICH, HOLLY**
Buffalo Bill ... **CODY**
Bull .... **OLE**
Bunche...... **RALPH**
Burbank.... **LUTHER**
Burl .... **IVES**
Burr........ **AARON, RAYMOND**
Burrows........ **ABE**
Burstyn ...... **ELLEN**
Buttons .... **RED**
Byington .... **SPRING**
Cabeza de..... **VACA**
Caesar .... **SID**
Calloway .... **CAB**
Campbell...... **GLEN**
Canada.......... **LEE**
Cannon....... **DYAN**
Cantrell .... **LANA**
Capek....... **KAREL**
Carl .... **CORI, JUNG, FROST, SAGAN**
Carl Marie von **WEBER**
Carnegie ...... **DALE**
Carnera ...... **PRIMO**
Carney .... **ART**
Carpenter ... **KAREN, SCOTT**
Carrie Chapman **CATT**
Carrie Jacobs **BOND**
Carrillo .... **LEO**
Carroll **LEO, BAKER, LEWIS**
Carson .... **KIT**
Carter... **AMY, CHIP, JACK, JUNE, LYNDA**
Caruso ..... **ENRICO**
Cass .... **PEGGY**
Casals....... **PABLO**
Castle........ **IRENE, VERNON**
Cather .... **WILLA**
Catherine...... **PARR**
Cavalieri........ **LINA**
Celeste....... **HOLM**
Chagall....... **MARC**
Champion ... **GOWER**
Chaney......... **LON**
Channing.... **CAROL**
Chaplin. **LETA, OONA**
Chapman....... **CEIL**
Charisse........ **CYD**
Charles.. **RAY, NICK, NORA, DARWIN**
Charlie . **RICH, PRIDE**
Charlotte .. **BRONTE, CORDAY**
Chase. **ILKA, CHEVY**
Chekhov..... **ANTON**
Christian ...... **DIOR**
Christie..... **AGATHA**
Cid................ **EL**
Claire .... **INA**
Clapton......... **ERIC**
Clara **BOW, BARTON**
Clare Booth ... **LUCE**
Clarence ...... **DAY, DARROW**
Clark ... **ROY, DANE, DICK, KENT, MARK, GABLE**
Claude ..... **MONET, RAINS**
Clay......... **HENRY, CASSIUS**
Clemens...... **MARK TWAIN**
Clement.... **ATTLEE**
Cleveland... **AMORY, GROVER**
Cliburn .... **VAN**
Clifton........ **WEBB**
Cobb......... **TY, LEE**
Cole.. **NAT, PORTER**
Columbo ...... **RUSS**
Como .... **PERRY**
Conde......... **NAST**
Connelly...... **MARC**
Connery....... **SEAN**
Connie .... **MACK, FRANCIS**
Conway .. **TIM, TOM, SHIRL**
Cooper .... **GARY**
Copland ..... **AARON**
Cordell .... **HULL**
Cornel........ **WILDE**
Costello .... **LOU**
Cotton .... **MATHER**
Coty .... **RENE**
Count .... **BASIE**
Coward......... **NOEL**
Cox .... **WALLY**
Crane .... **HART**
Cregar .... **LAIRD**
Crockett...... **DAVY**
Cronyn .... **HUME**
Crosby . **BING, GARY**
Crystal ...... **GAYLE**
Curie ... **EVE, MARIE, PIERRE**
Curtis .... **TONY**
Dailey .... **DAN**
Dale.......... **EVANS**
Daniel .... **BOONE, DEFOE**
Daniels .... **BEBE**
Danny......... **KAYE**
Dantes .... **EDMOND**
David.. **SOUL, BOWIE**
Davis.... **MAC, JEFF, BETTE**
Dawber......... **PAM**
Day **DORIS, LARAINE**
De l'Enclos ... **NINON**
De Leon ..... **PONCE**
De Maupassant . **GUY**
De Valera.... **EAMON**
Dean .. **RUSK, DIZZY, JAMES, MARTIN**
Deborah....... **KERR**
Della **REESE, STREET**
Delmar .... **VINA**
Delon .... **ALAIN**
Dennis ... **DAY, KING**
Derek ..... **BO, JOHN**
Descartes ..... **RENE**
Devine .... **ANDY**
Dewey .. **TOM, JOHN**
DeLuise .... **DOM**
Diamond Jim **BRADY**
Diana... **DORS, ROSS**
Dickinson..... **EMILY**
Dionne ...... **MARIA, OLIVA, CECILE, EMELIE, YVONNE, ANNETTE**
Disney .... **WALT**
Dolin .... **ANTON**
Don .... **HO, ADAMS, KNOTTS**
Donahue **PHIL, TROY**
Donlevy ...... **BRIAN**
Donna........ **REED, SUMMER**

Doone....... **LORNA**
Dorfmann ..... **ANIA**
Doris.... **DAY, DUKE**
Dorothy ... **DIX, GISH**
Dors .... **DIANA**
Dostoevsky. **FEODOR**
Doubleday... **ABNER**
Downs .... **HUGH**
Drew......... **ELLEN**
Dreyfus .... **ALFRED**
Dufy .... **RAOUL**
Duke......... **DORIS**
Duke Astin .. **PATTY**
Dunaway ...... **FAYE**
Duncan. **SARA, TODD**
Dunne....... **IRENE**
Durocher .. **LEO, LIP, LIPPY**
Dvorak ...... **ANTON**
Dwight ...... **MOODY**
Eamon de .. **VALERA**
Earhart..... **AMELIA**
Eartha.......... **KITT**
Eastwood..... **CLINT**
Eddie.......... **FOY**
Edgar . **POE, DEGAS, GUEST**
Edith .... **PIAF**
Edmond .... **DANTES**
Edmund ..... **BURKE**
Edna **BEST, FERBER, MILLAY**
Edouard ..... **MANET**
Eduard **LALO, BENES**
Edvard .... **GRIEG**
Edward...... **ELGAR**
Edward Everett **HALE**
Edwards **GUS, VINCE**
Edwin .... **BOOTH, WEEKS**
Eisaku......... **SATO**
Ekberg .... **ANITA**
Ekland........ **BRITT**
Elaine .... **MAY**
Eleanora....... **DUSE**
Elia... **LAMB, KAZAN**
Elias.......... **HOWE**
Elihu ... **ROOT, YALE**
Ellen . **DREW, TERRY**
Ellington....... **DUKE**
Elliott........ **GOULD**
Ellsworth ..... **VINES**
Elmer .. **RICE, CRAIG**
Elmo .... **ROPER**
Emerson ..... **FAYE, RALPH WALDO**
Emile......... **ZOLA**
Emily **POST, BRONTE**
En-lai......... **CHOU**
Enoch **ARDEN, LIGHT**
Enrico .... **FERMI**
Erica .... **JONG**
Erik .... **SATIE**
Erikson......... **LIEF**
Ernest........ **BEVIN, BLOCK, SETON**
Ernie ... **FORD, PYLE**
Errol .. **LEON, FLYNN**
Estrada......... **ERIK**
Ethan **ALLEN, FROME**
Ethel .... **WATERS**
Ethelbert ..... **NEVIN**
Eugene. **DEBS, FIELD**
Eva .... **GABOR**
Eva Marie .... **SAINT**
Evans .... **DALE**
Everett .... **CHAD**
Evita .... **PERON**
Ewell .... **TOM**
Eydie........ **GORME**
Eyre........... **JANE**
Ezra. **POUND, STONE**
Fanny .... **BRICE**
Farrow .... **MIA**
Ferber......... **EDNA**
Ferde........ **GROFE**
Ferenc .... **MOLNAR**
Fermi ...... **ENRICO**
Fernand ...... **LEGER**
Fernando .... **LAMAS**
Ferrer .... **MEL, JOSE**
Field .... **SALLY**
Filippino .... **LIPPI**
Fisher ... **BUD, HAM, CARRIE, EDDIE**
Fitzgerald...... **ELLA, BARRY, F. SCOTT**
Flynn......... **ERROL**
Foch .... **NINA**
Fonda **JANE, HENRY, PETER**
Ford.. **EDSEL, ERNIE, HENRY**
Foscolo .... **UGO**
Fra Filippo..... **LIPPI**
Francesco ..... **NITTI**
Franchot ...... **TONE**
Francis ..... **BACON, DRAKE**
Francis Scott ... **KEY**
Franck .... **CESAR**
Francoise.... **SAGAN**
Frank.... **FAY, BUCK, CAPRA**
Frank Lloyd. **WRIGHT**
Frankie ...... **CARLE, LAINE**
Frans.......... **HALS**
Franz........ **KAFKA, LEHAR, LISZT**
Frederick .... **LOEWE**
Frobe .... **GERT**
Frome....... **ETHAN**
Gabor . **EVA, MAGDA, ZSA ZSA**
Gagarin .... **YURI**
Gale......... **STORM**
Gam .... **RITA**
Garbo .... **GRETA**
Gardner . **AVA, ERLE**
Garner ...... **JAMES, ERROLL**
Garson ...... **GREER**
Gavin........... **MUIR**
Gayle...... **CRYSTAL**
Gazzara .... **BEN**
Gehrig.......... **LOU**
Geller .... **URI**
Genghis ...... **KHAN**
George .. **ADE, OHM, BUSH, RAFT, SAND, BROWN, CLARK, DEWEY, GOBEL, LUCAS, SCOTT, SEGAL, CUSTER, PATTON**
George Bernard **SHAW**
George Frederick **HANDEL**
George Herman **RUTH**
Georges...... **BIZET, SEURAT**
Gerald......... **FORD**
Geraldine...... **PAGE**
Gershwin .... **IRA, GEORGE**
Gert.......... **FROBE**
Gertrude ..... **BERG, STEIN**
Getz........... **STAN**
Gibson .... **HOOT**
Gil .... **BLAS**
Gillespie...... **DIZZY**
Giuseppe ..... **BELLI, VERDI**
Gladys ..... **KNIGHT**
Glasgow...... **ELLEN**
Glenn . **FORD, JOHN, MILLER**
Gluck......... **ALMA**
Golda .... **MEIR**
Goldberg ...... **RUBE**
Goldie .... **HAWN**
Gordon **RUTH, FLASH**
Gorky .... **MAXIM**
Gorme .... **EYDIE**
Gould .... **JAY**
Grace .... **KELLY**
Graham ...... **BILLY, GREENE, MARTHA**
Grandma .... **MOSES**

Grant... **LEE, WOOD, TINKER**
Gray .... **ASA**
Greco ..... **EL, JOSE**
Greeley..... **HORACE**
Greene ...... **LORNE, GRAHAM**
Gregor ..... **MENDEL**
Gregory .... **PECK**
Grey ... **JANE, ZANE**
Griffith .... **ANDY**
Grissom **GUS, VIRGIL**
Grofe......... **FERDE**
Gueden....... **HILDE**
Guevara .... **CHE**
Guido .... **RENI**
Guitry .... **SACHA**
Gulager .... **CLU**
Gustav ..... **MAHLER**
Guthrie .... **ARLO, WOODY**
Guy .... **MOLLET**
Gypsy Rose ..... **LEE**
Hackett....... **JOAN, BUDDY**
Hackman ...... **GENE**
Hagen.......... **UTA**
Hal......... **MARCH, LINDEN, PRINCE**
Hale........... **ALAN**
Haley.......... **ALEX**
Hallstrom...... **IVAR**
Hals......... **FRANS**
Halsey......... **BULL**
Hammarskjold .. **DAG**
Hamsun .... **KNUT**
Hank **SNOW, AARON**
Hansson........ **OLA**
Harold. **ROME, TEEN, UREY**
Harriet Beecher **STOWE**
Harris ... **JOEL, PHIL, JULIE**
Harrison........ **REX, FORD, NOEL, GEORGE**
Hart......... **CRANE**
Harte.......... **BRET**
Haver .... **JUNE**
Havoc .... **JUNE**
Hawn........ **GOLDIE**
Hayward..... **SUSAN**
Hayworth....... **RITA**
Hazel........ **SCOTT**
Hefner .... **HUGH**
Heifetz ..... **JASCHA**
Heinrich ...... **HEINE**
Held.......... **ANNA**
Hemingway... **PAPA, ERNEST**
Hendrix......... **JIMI**
Henri...... **MATISSE, ROUSSEAU**
Henrik........ **IBSEN**
Henry . **CLAY, FORD, LUCE, FONDA, HUDSON**
Henry Cabot. **LODGE**
Herbert.... **HOOVER, VICTOR**
Herbert George **WELLS**
Herbie........ **MANN**
Herman ..... **HESSE, WOODY**
Hernando... **CORTES, DE SOTO**
Hernando de... **SOTO**
Hess .... **MYRA**
Heywood .... **BROUN**
Hieronymus . **BOSCH**
Hildegarde..... **NEFF**
Hirt .... **AL**
Ho Chi .... **MINH**
Hobson...... **LAURA**
Hogan.......... **BEN**
Hogg........... **IMA**
Holbein........ **HALS**
Holbrook .... **HAL**
Horace .... **MANN**
Horatio ...... **ALGER**
Horne .... **LENA**
Houdini...... **HARRY**
Houston .... **SAM**
Howard.. **RON, KEEL**
Howe......... **ELIAS**
Hubbell........ **CARL**
Hudson........ **ROCK**
Hugh .... **DOWNS**
Hume .... **DAVID**
Hunter .... **IAN, KIM, TAB, EVAN**
Hus .... **JAN**
Hyerdahl ...... **THOR**
Ian .... **HUNTER**
Ibn .... **SAUD**
Ilka.......... **CHASE**
Immanuel...... **KANT**
Imogene...... **COCA**
Imre.......... **NAGY**
Ina .... **CLAIRE**
Inonu......... **ISMET**
Irene . **RICH, DUNNE, CASTLE**
Irving........ **BERLIN**
Isaac......... **STERN**
Isadora .... **DUNCAN**
Ismet......... **INONU**
Italo........... **TAJO**
Iturbi .... **JOSE**
Ives .... **BURL**
J. Carrol ...... **NAISH**
Jack..... **SOO, LORD, PAAR, WEBB, OAKIE, LONDON**
Jacob .... **RIIS**
Jagger . **DEAN, MICK**
James. **AGEE, CAAN, COCO, DEAN, WATT, HARRY, HENRY, JESSE, JOYCE, BARRIE, GARNER**
Jamie .... **FARR**
Jan.... **HUS, SMUTS, STEEN, PEERCE, VERMEER**
Jan Van .... **EYCK**
Jane .. **EYRE, GREY, FONDA, AUSTEN**
Janet. **BLAIR, LEIGH, GAYNOR**
Janice......... **RULE**
Janis .... **IAN, PAIGE**
Jannings ...... **EMIL**
Janos .... **KADAR**
Jawaharlal... **NEHRU**
Jay.......... **GOULD**
Jean-Paul .... **MARAT**
Jeanmaire .... **RENEE**
Jeanne ...... **CRAIN, EAGELS**
Jefferson..... **DAVIS**
Jenny .... **LIND**
Jerome........ **KERN**
Jesse .... **JAMES**
Jessica ..... **TANDY**
Jim... **RYUN, CROCE**
Jimmy......... **SAVO**
Joan .... **RIVERS**
Joanne .... **DRU**
Joel Chandler **HARRIS**
Johan .... **SARS**
Johann Sebastian **BACH**
John ... **HAY, AGAR, DALY, DREW, ALDEN, KEATS, LOCKE, SAXON, CALVIN, LENNON**
John Foster **DULLES**
John Godfrey .. **SAXE**
John Jacob .. **ASTOR**
John Maynard **KEYNES**
John Philip .. **SOUSA**
John Singer **SARGENT**
John Stuart.... **MILL**
John Wilkes . **BOOTH**
Johnnie .... **RAY**

Johnny .... **CASH, MERCER**
Johnson .. **OSA, VAN, ARTE**
Jolson .... **AL**
Jonas .... **SALK**
Jonathan ..... **SWIFT**
Jones .. **TOM, DEAN, JACK**
Jong .... **ERICA**
Jonson .... **BEN**
Joplin **JANIS, SCOTT**
Jose **GRECO, MARTI**
Joseph ..... **COTTEN**
Josif .... **STALIN**
Josip Broz ...... **TITO**
Jubal .... **EARLY**
Jule .... **STYNE**
Jules .... **VERNE**
Julia Ward .... **HOWE**
Julie **ADAMS, HARRIS**
June **HAVER, HAVOC**
Kadar .... **JANOS**
Kafka .... **FRANZ**
Karel .... **CAPEK**
Karen .... **BLACK**
Karenina ..... **ANNA**
Karl .... **MARX**
Katherine ...... **ROSS**
Kay . **KYSER, STARR**
Kazan .... **ELIA**
Keach .... **STACY**
Keller .... **HELEN**
Kelly .. **GENE, WALT, GRACE, EMMET**
Kenton .... **STAN**
Khachaturian . **ARAM**
Khan . **AGA, ALI, ALY**
Khayyam ..... **OMAR**
Kibbee .... **GUY**
Kim **DARBY, NOVAK, HUNTER**
King. **ALAN, CAROLE**
Kingsley .... **BEN**
Kirkegaard .. **SOREN**
Klee .... **PAUL**
Knight. **TED, GLADYS**
Korbut .... **OLGA**
Koussevitzky . **SERGE**
Kovacs .... **ERNIE**
Kreisler .... **FRITZ**
Kristofferson ... **KRIS**
Kruger ...... **HARDY**
Krupa .... **GENE**
Kublai .... **KHAN**
Kurt .... **ADLER**
Kyser .... **KAY**
Ladd **ALAN, CHERYL**
Lagerlof ..... **SELMA**
Lahr .... **BERT**
Lancaster ..... **BURT**
Lanchester .... **ELSA**
Lange .... **HOPE**
Lanny .... **ROSS**
Lanza .... **MARIO**
Lardner .... **RING**
Laurel .... **STAN**
Laurence ... **OLIVIER**
Laurie .... **PIPER**
Lazarus .... **EMMA**
Learned ...... **HAND**
Lee .. **PEGGY, PINKY, GRANT, GYPSY, CANADA, HARPER, MAJORS**
Lehar .... **FRANZ**
Lehmann ..... **LOTTE**
Lehr .... **LEW**
Leinsdorf ..... **ERICH**
Lena .... **HORNE**
Lennon .... **JOHN**
Lenya .... **LOTTE**
Levant ...... **OSCAR**
Lew .. **CODY, AYRES**
Lewis ..... **ADA, TED, JOHN, LAWES, SHARI, STONE**
LeGallienne ..... **EVA**
Light .... **ENOCH**
Light-horse Harry **LEE**
Lillian ... **GISH, ROTH**
Lillie ..... **BEA, PEEL**
Linda .. **BLAIR, LAVIN**
Linkletter **ART, JACK**
Linn .... **BAMBI**
Liszt .... **FRANZ**
Little .... **RICH**
Lollobrigida .... **GINA**
Lombardo ...... **GUY CARMEN**
Long .... **HUEY**
Loos .... **ANITA**
Loren .... **SOPHIA**
Lorenz .... **HART**
Loretta **SWIT, YOUNG**
Lorna .... **DOONE**
Lorre .... **PETER**
Lotte .... **LENYA**
Louis .... **JOE**
Louise .. **TINA, ANITA**
Loy .... **MYRNA**
Lucretia ...... **MOTT**
Lucrezia .... **BORGIA**
Lucy .... **STONE**
Ludwig .... **EMIL**
Lugosi .... **BELA**
Luise .... **RAINER**
Lupino .... **IDA**
Lynn .... **BARI**
Lyon .... **SUE**
Mack .... **TED**
MacGraw .... **ALI**
Madame de ... **STAEL**
Magda .... **GABOR**
Maglie .... **SAL**
Magnani ...... **ANNA**
Mailer ..... **NORMAN**
Major .... **BOWES**
Majors .... **LEE**
Malbin .... **ELAINE**
Malden .... **KARL**
Malone ...... **MOLLY**
Mann .... **HERBIE, HORACE, THOMAS**
Manuel de .... **FALLA**
Marceau .... **MARCEL**
Marco .... **POLO**
Margaret ..... **MEAD**
Margaret Chase **SMITH**
Maria .... **CALLAS**
Marie .... **CURIE**
Mario .... **LANZA**
Mark .... **CLARK**
Marner .... **SILAS**
Marquette ..... **PERE**
Marquis .... **DON**
Marshall ..... **PENNY**
Martha . **HYER, RAYE**
Marti .... **JOSE**
Martin . **DEAN, MARY, ROSS, BUBER, STEVE, LUTHER**
Martin Luther .. **KING**
Marx . **KARL, CHICO, HARPO, ZEPPO, GROUCHO**
Mary ... **URE, ASTOR**
Mary Baker .... **EDDY**
Masaryk **JAN, TOMAS**
Mason .... **JAMES, MARSHA, PERRY**
Massey **CURT, ILONA**
Mata .... **HARI**
Mather ..... **COTTON**
Matisse ...... **HENRI**
Maude .... **ADAMS**
Maurice ..... **EVANS, RAVEL, UTRILLO**
Maurois ..... **ANDRE**
Maxim .... **GORKI, GORKY**
Maxwell .... **ELSA**
McDaniel .... **HATTIE**
McLeod ...... **GAVIN**
McPherson ... **AIMEE**
Mel ..... **OTT, ALLEN, BLANC, TORME, TILLIS**
Meriwether ... **LEWIS**
Merkel .... **UNA**
Merman ...... **ETHEL**
Merrill .... **DINA**

Meryl....... **STREEP**
Meyerson...... **BESS**
Mickey..... **MANTLE**
Midler........ **BETTE**
Miles. **VERA, SARAH, STANDISH**
Miller.. **ANN, GLENN, ROGER**
Mineo.......... **SAL**
Minnelli......... **LIZA**
Minnie........ **PEARL**
Minuit........ **PETER**
Mischa....... **AUER, ELMAN**
Mitchell. **GUY, JONI, BILLY**
Moffo........ **ANNA**
Mohandas.. **GANDHI**
Mollet.......... **GUY**
Mondrian....... **PIET**
Montand....... **YVES**
Montez **LOLA, MARIA**
Montgomery.... **WES**
Monty......... **HALL**
Moorhead... **AGNES**
Moreno......... **RITA**
Morgana **FATA, NINA**
Morley....... **SAFER**
Mostel......... **ZERO**
Mountbatten.. **EARL, LOUIS**
Mowbray...... **ALAN**
Muhammad...... **ALI**
Munson........ **ONA**
Murray... **DON, JAN, KEN, MAE, ANNE**
Musial......... **STAN**
Myra.......... **HESS**
Myrna.......... **LOY**
Nagy.......... **IMRE**
Nahum........ **TATE**
Nancy....... **HANKS**
Natalie....... **WOOD**
Nathan........ **HALE**
Nazimova...... **ALLA**
Ned........ **SPARKS**
Negri.......... **POLA**
Nelson **EDDY, GENE, MILES, RIDDLE**
Nero......... **PETER**
Newton....... **ISAAC**
Newton-John **OLIVIA**
Nicholas...... **AMATI**
Niels.......... **BOHR**
Nikola........ **TESLA**
Noel....... **COWARD**
Nora. **KAYE, BAYES**
Norman...... **LEAR, MAILER**
Normand.... **MABEL**
Novarro..... **RAMON**

Novello........ **IVOR**
O'Casey....... **SEAN**
O'Neal........ **RYAN, TATUM**
O'Neill........ **OONA**
O. Henry... **PORTER**
Ogden.. **NASH, REID**
Oley........ **SPEAKS**
Oliver **REED, HARDY, PERRY**
Oliver Wendell **HOLMES**
Olsen........... **OLE**
Omar....... **SHARIF, BRADLEY**
Onegin...... **EUGEN**
Opie........... **READ**
Orson........ **BEAN, WELLES**
Orville...... **WRIGHT**
Oscar....... **WILDE, LEVANT**
Ott............. **MEL**
Pablo....... **CASALS**
Pacino............ **AL**
Paderewski. **IGNACE**
Page......... **PATTI**
Paine.......... **TOM**
Palmer **ARNIE, LILLI, ARNOLD**
Pancho...... **SANZA, VILLA**
Parker......... **FESS**
Parton....... **DOLLY**
Pasternak.... **BORIS**
Pasteur....... **LOUIS**
Pastor......... **TONY**
Paton......... **ALAN**
Patti.......... **PAGE**
Paul... **ANKA, KLEE, MUNI**
Pauling....... **LINUS**
Pavlova...... **ANNA**
Pearl. **BUCK, WHITE, BAILEY, MINNIE**
Pearson..... **LESTER**
Peerce......... **JAN**
Peewee...... **REESE**
Peggy... **LEE, CASS, WOOD**
Peron... **EVA, JUAN, EVITA**
Perry **COMO, MASON**
Pete. **ROSE, SEEGER, FOUNTAIN**
Peter.. **ARNO, NERO, ROSE, LORRE**
Peter Paul.. **RUBENS**
Petula....... **CLARK**
Phileas........ **FOGG**
Philip.... **HALE, NERI**

Philo......... **VANCE**
Picasso...... **PABLO**
Pickens........ **SLIM**
Picon......... **MOLLY**
Pierre.. **LOTI, CURIE**
Pierre-Auguste **RENOIR**
Pinky............ **LEE**
Pinza........... **EZIO**
Pirandello...... **LUIGI**
Pola.......... **NEGRI**
Polo......... **MARCO**
Ponce de...... **LEON**
Pons........... **LILY**
Ponselle....... **ROSA**
Porter......... **COLE**
Pound......... **EZRA**
Preminger..... **OTTO**
Priscilla...... **ALDEN, MULLEN**
Prokofiev..... **SERGE**
Proust...... **MARCEL**
Pyle.......... **ERNIE**
Radner....... **GILDA**
Rainer....... **LUISE**
Rainer Maria.. **RILKE**
Raines......... **ELLA**
Rains....... **CLAUDE**
Ralph........ **NADER, BUNCHE**
Rand... **AYN, SALLY**
Rathbone..... **BASIL**
Ray.. **ALDO, BLOCH, NOBLE**
Rayburn........ **SAM**
Raymond..... **BURR, GENE**
Read.......... **OPIE**
Rebecca....... **WEST**
Red, the........ **ERIC**
Reed. **ALAN, DONNA**
Reese....... **DELLA, PEEWEE**
Rehan.......... **ADA**
Reiner... **ROB, CARL**
Rene.......... **COTY**
Rex.... **BELL, REED, STOUT**
Reynolds...... **BURT**
Rhodes....... **CECIL**
Richard.. **DIX, BYRD, LONG, ROWE, CONTE, STRAUSS**
Ringo....... **STARR**
Rip.. **TORN, TAYLOR**
Rita............ **GAM**
Ritter.... **TEX, JOHN, THELMA**
Rivera **CHITA, DIEGO**
Robb........... **INEZ**
Rockne...... **KNUTE**

Roger .... **BACON**
Rogers .. **ROY, CARL, WILL, KENNY, GINGER**
Romero ..... **CESAR**
Ronstadt ..... **LINDA**
Root .. **OREN, ELIHU**
Roper .... **ELMO**
Rose .... **PETE**
Rousseau..... **HENRI**
Rowlands...... **GENA**
Rubinstein .. **ANTON, ARTUR, ARTURO**
Ruby .... **DEE**
Rudolf. **BING, FRIML, DIESEL**
Runyon..... **DAMON**
Russell .... **SAGE**
Ruth **BABE, GORDON**
Saarinen....... **EERO**
Sagan .... **CARL**
Saint,—Marie ... **EVA**
Sally .. **RAND, FIELD**
Salmon P.... **CHASE**
Salvador........ **DALI**
Sam.......... **SNEAD, HOUSTON**
Samuel...... **MORSE**
Sand .... **GEORGE**
Sandra .... **DEE**
Sarah .... **MILES**
Saud .... **IBN**
Savalas....... **TELLY**
Schmeling...... **MAX**
Scholem....... **ASCH**
Schulberg ..... **BUDD**
Seegar .... **ALAN**
Seeger .... **PETE**
Seeley.... **BLOSSOM**
Segovia .... **ANDRES**
Selassie ...... **HAILE**
Serling .... **ROD**
Seton .... **ANYA**
Sevareid........ **ERIC**
Severinsen ..... **DOC**
Shahn.......... **BEN**
Shankar .... **RAVI**
Sharif .... **OMAR**
Sharp .... **BECKY**
Shaw......... **ARTIE**
Shawn .... **TED**
Shelley ...... **PERCY BYSSHE, WINTERS**
Shields ..... **BROOKE**
Shire .... **TALIA**
Shirley ...... **BOOTH**
Sidney ...... **LANIER**
Sigmund .... **FREUD**
Signe........ **HASSO**
Silvers .... **SID, PHIL**
Sinatra ...... **FRANK, NANCY**
Sinclair....... **LEWIS, UPTON**
Skelton.......... **RED**
Skinner......... **OTIS**
Smith .... **AL, ADAM, ALEXIS, ALFRED**
Snead.......... **SAM**
Sommer....... **ELKE**
Sonja......... **HENIE**
Sonny **BONO, TUFTS**
Sophia ...... **LOREN**
Sothern .... **ANN**
Spacek....... **SISSY**
Sparks .... **NED**
Speaker .... **TRIS**
Speaks .... **OLEY**
Spencer ..... **TRACY**
Spewack ..... **BELLA**
St. John **JILL, ADELA**
St. Vincent Millay **EDNA**
Stacy........ **KEACH**
Stalin.......... **JOSIF**
Standish...... **MILES**
Stanford...... **WHITE**
Starr ... **KAY, RINGO**
Steen .... **JAN**
Steiger .... **ROD**
Stengel...... **CASEY**
Stephen ..... **CRANE**
Stephen V. ... **BENET**
Sterling .... **JAN**
Stern......... **ISAAC**
Steve .... **ALLEN**
Stevens **CAT, MARK, RISE, STELLA**
Stevenson.... **ADLAI**
Stevie ..... **WONDER**
Stewart **ROD, JIMMY**
Stoker........ **BRAM**
Stone .. **LUCY, EZRA**
Storm .. **GALE, FIELD**
Stravinsky..... **IGOR**
Streep....... **MERYL**
Stuart .... **JEB**
Styne .... **JULE**
Sullivan .... **ED**
Sumac .... **YMA**
Summer..... **DONNA**
Sunday....... **BILLY**
Susan .... **DEY**
Susan B. . **ANTHONY**
Syngman ...... **RHEE**
Tab .... **HUNTER**
Tajo......... **ITALO**
Talia .... **SHIRE**
Tamiroff....... **AKIM**
Tanguay........ **EVA**
Tarbell .... **IDA**
Tarkington... **BOOTH**
Taylor . **LIZ, RIP, ROD**
Teasdale ...... **SARA**
Tebaldi ..... **RENATA**
Templar ...... **SIMON**
Templeton..... **ALEC**
Tennessee ... **ERNIE, WILLIAMS**
Terry......... **ELLEN**
Tex .... **RITTER**
Thatcher .... **BECKY**
Theda .... **BARA**
Thelma...... **RITTER**
Thelonious ... **MONK**
Thomas ...... **ARNE, GRAY, HOOD, MANN, NAST, DYLAN, HARDY, HICKS, DANNY, MARLO, MOORE, WOLFE, HOBBES**
Thompson..... **SADA**
Thornton ... **WILDER**
Tilden .... **BILL**
Tillis............ **MEL**
Tillstrom ...... **BURR**
Timothy .. **BOTTOMS**
Tito .... **BROZ**
Tolstoy......... **LEO**
Tom.... **MIX, EWELL, PAINE**
Tomlin .... **LILY**
Tony **SARG, CURTIS, PASTOR**
Toren .... **MARTA**
Torme.......... **MEL**
Torn .... **RIP**
Toscanini... **ARTURO**
Trotsky........ **LEON**
Truex .... **ERNIE**
Truman .... **BESS, HARRY, CAPOTE**
Trygve .... **LIE**
Tse-tung .... **MAO**
Tuesday...... **WELD**
Tunney........ **GENE**
Turner..... **IKE, NAT, LANA, TINA**
Turpin.......... **BEN**
Twain .... **MARK**
Ty............. **COBB**
Ulanova ..... **GALINA**
Ullmann .... **LIV**
Uriah.......... **HEEP**
Vallee .... **RUDY**
Vance .... **CYRUS, ETHEL, PHILO**
Vaughan..... **SARAH**
Velez.......... **LUPE**
Venerable, the . **BEDE**
Vera......... **MILES**

Verdon .... **GWEN**
Verdugo ...... **ELENA**
Vereen .... **BEN**
Vermeer........ **JAN**
Verne .... **JULES**
Vernon ..... **CASTLE**
Victor **HUGO, BORGE, BUONO**
Vigoda .... **ABE**
Vincent....... **PRICE**
Virginia....... **DARE, MAYO, WOOLF**
Virna .... **LISI**
Vivien .... **LEIGH**
Vladimir ...... **LENIN**
Voight.......... **JON**
W.C. **HANDY, FIELDS**
Wallace........ **LEW, HENRY, AGARD**
Wallach .... **ELI**
Waller .... **FATS**
Wally...... **COX, PIP**
Walter.. **ABEL, REED, BRUNO**
Walton .... **IZAAK**
Warburg....... **OTTO**
Warhol .... **ANDY**
Warren .... **EARL**
Washington.. **DINAH, BOOKER T.**
Waters .... **ETHEL**
Waugh .... **ALEC**
Webb... **ALAN, JACK**
Webster ...... **NOAH, DANIEL**
Weill .... **KURT**
Weld ..... **TUESDAY**
Welles....... **ORSON, SUMNER**
Wendell ..... **COREY, WILLKIE**
Werner Von . **BRAUN**
Wharton...... **EDITH**
White ...... **BYRON, PEARL, WILLIAM ALLEN**
Whiteman ..... **PAUL**
Whitman ..... **WALT**
Whitney .... **ELI**
Wilbur .... **CROSS, WRIGHT**
Wilde........ **OSCAR**
Wilder .. **GENE, BILLY**
Wiley.......... **POST**
Wilhelm von ... **OPEL**
Wilkins .... **ROY**
Willa .... **CATHER**
William **HART, HULL, INGE, PENN, PITT, BOOTH, HANDY, HOLDEN**
William Butler. **YEATS**
William Cullen **BRYANT**
William Randolph **HEARST**
William Rose. . **BENET**
William Sidney **PORTER**
Williams **TED, ROBIN, ROGER**
Wills .... **CHILL, HELEN**
Wilson.......... **FLIP**
Winding .... **KAI**
Winslow ..... **HOMER**
Winterhalter .. **HUGO**
Wolfgang Amadeus **MOZART**
Wood .... **GRANT**
Wray .... **FAY**
Wynn.... **ED, EARLY**
Wynter .... **DANA**
Xavier .... **CUGAT**
Yale.......... **ELIHU**
Yat-sen......... **SUN**
Yogi......... **BERRA**
Yoko .... **ONO**
Young...... **CY, GIG, ALAN, CHIC**
Youskevitch ... **IGOR**
Yutang .... **LIN**
Zasu .... **PITTS**
Zebulon .... **PIKE**
Zeppo .... **MARX**
Zetterling....... **MAI**
Zola .... **EMILE**
Zorina .... **VERA**
Zubin........ **MEHTA**

CELEBRITIES' ORIGINAL NAMES

Abbot, Bud....... **William Abbot**
Adams, Edie..... **Elizabeth Edith Enke**
Adoree, Renee .... **Jeanne de la Fonte**
Aimee, Anouk .. **Francoise Sorya**
Albert, Eddie ..... **Edward Albert Heimberger**
Alda, Robert **Alphonso d'Abruzzo**
Alexander, Jane ... **Jane Quigley**
Allen, Fred ...... **John F. Sullivan**
Allen, Woody .. **Allen Konigsberg**
Allyson, June...... **Ella Geisman**
Anderson, Dame Judith. **Frances Margaret Anderson**
Andrews, Dana.... **Carver Daniel Andrews**
Andrews, Julie........ **Julia Wells**
Angeli, Pier.......... **Anna Maria Pierangeli**
Ann-Margret **Ann-Margret Olsson**
Arden, Eve..... **Eunice Quedens**
Arlen, Harold..... **Hyman Arluck**
Arliss, George.. **George Andrews**
Arness, James .. **James Aurness**
Arthur, Jean...... **Gladys Greene**
Astaire, Fred .... **Frederick Austerlitz**
Astor, Mary . **Lucille Langehanke**
Auer, Mischa .... **Mischa Ounskowsky**
Aumont, Jean-Pierre. **Jean-Pierre Salomons**
Avalon, Frankie. **Francis Avallone**
Bacall, Lauren **Betty Joan Perske**
Ballard, Kaye.. **Catherine Balotta**
Bancroft, Anne...... **Anna Maria Italiano**
Bara, Theda **Theodosia Goodman**
Bardot, Brigitte.... **Camille Javal**
Bari, Lynn....... **Marjorie Fisher**
Barry, Gene .... **Eugene Klass**
Barrymore, John ... **John Blythe**
Barrymore, Lionel . **Lionel Blythe**
Bartholomew, Freddie . **Frederick Llewellyn**
Bayes, Nora...... **Dora Goldberg**
Bennett, Tony.......... **Anthony Benedetto**
Benny, Jack. **Benjamin Kubelsky**
Berg, Gertrude .... **Gertrude Edelstein**
Bergen, Polly...... **Nellie Burgin**
Berkeley, Busby......... **William Berkeley Enos**
Berle, Milton .. **Mendel Berlinger**
Berlin, Irving .... **Israel Baline**
Bishop, Joey .... **Joseph Gottlieb**
Black, Karen ...... **Karen Ziegler**
Blaine, Vivian **Vivienne Stapleton**
Blair, Janet........ **Martha Janet Lafferty**
Blake, Amanda .... **Beverly Neill**
Blake, Robert... **Michael Gubitosi**
Blue, Ben ... **Benjamin Bernstein**
Bogarde, Dirk ... **Derek Van Den Bogaerde**
Boone, Pat...... **Charles Eugene Boone**
Borgnine, Ernest **Ermes Borgnino**
Bowie, David **David Robert Jones**
Brice, Fanny...... **Fanny Borach**
Bridges, Beau ..... **Lloyd Vernet Bridges III**
Britt, May ..... **Maybritt Wilkens**
Brodie, Steve...... **John Stevens**
Bronson, Charles........ **Charles Buchinsky**
Brooks, Mel ... **Melvin Kaminsky**
Burns, George. **Nathan Birnbaum**
Burstyn, Ellen ... **Edna Gilhooley**
Burton, Richard. **Richard Jenkins**
Buttons, Red..... **Aaron Chwatt**
Byrnes, Edd (Kookie).... **Edward Breitenberger**
Caine, Michael.......... **Maurice Micklewhite**
Calhoun, Rory.... **Francis Durgin**
Callas, Maria .... **Maria Kalogeropoulos**
Cannon, Dyan..... **Samille Diane Friesen**
Cantor, Eddie... **Edward Iskowitz**
Capucine.... **Germaine Lefebvre**
Carroll, Diahann .. **Carol Diahann Johnson**
Castle, Irene .... **Irene Foote**
Castle, Vernon ... **Vernon Blythe**
Chandler, Jeff........ **Ira Grossel**
Charisse, Cyd **Tula Ellice Finklea**
Checker, Chubby.. **Ernest Evans**
Cher......... **Cherilyn Sarkisian**
Clark, Dane .... **Bernard Zanville**
Cobb, Lee J.......... **Leo Jacoby**
Colbert, Claudette **Lily Claudette Chauchoin**
Cole, Nat (King). **Nathaniel Coles**
Connery, Sean **Thomas Connery**
Connors, Michael......... **Kreker Ohanian**
Conrad, Robert... **Conrad Robert Falk**
Cooper, Alice.... **Vincent Furnier**
Cooper, Gary... **Frank J. Cooper**
Cord, Alex..... **Alexander Viespi**
Corday, Mara..... **Marilyn Watts**
Cosell, Howard... **Howard Cohen**
Costello, Elvis. **Declan McManus**
Costello, Lou...... **Louis Cristillo**
Crawford, Joan. **Lucille Le Sueur**

Crosby, Bing **Harry Lillis Crosby**
Curtis, Tony.. **Bernard Schwartz**
Damone, Vic .... **Vito Farinola**
Darby, Kim...... **Deborah Zerby**
Darren, James... **James Ercolani**
Davis, Bette...... **Ruth Elizabeth Davis**
Day, Dennis .... **Eugene McNulty**
Day, Doris. **Doris von Kappelhoff**
Day, Laraine.... **Laraine Johnson**
DaSilva, Howard.......... **Harold Silverblatt**
De Carlo, Yvonne. **Peggy Yvonne Middleton**
Dee, Ruby.... **Ruby Ann Wallace**
Dee, Sandra.... **Alexandra Zuck**
Deneuve, Catherine.... **Catherine Dorleac**
Denver, John........ **Henry John Deutschendorf Jr.**
Derek, John........ **Derek Harris**
Devine, Andy **Jeremiah Schwartz**
DeWolfe, Billy ..... **William Jones**
Dickinson, Angie **Angeline Brown**
Dietrich, Marlene .... **Maria von Losch**
Diller, Phyllis ...... **Phyllis Driver**
Donahue, Troy ... **Merle Johnson**
Dors, Diana .... **Diana Fluck**
Douglas, Kirk. **Issur Danielovitch**
Douglas, Melvyn......... **Melvyn Hesselberg**
Drake, Alfred... **Alfredo Capurro**
Dressler, Marie .... **Leila Koerber**
Drew, Ellen........... **Terry Ray**
Dylan, Bob .. **Robert Zimmerman**
Ebsen, Buddy ... **Christian Ebsen**
Eden, Barbara . **Barbara Huffman**
Ely, Ron.......... **Ronald Pierce**
Evans, Dale .... **Frances Octavia Smith**
Everett, Chad **Raymond Cramton**
Ewell, Tom .. **S. Yewell Tompkins**
Fabian . **Fabian Forte Bonaparte**
Fairbanks, Douglas ..... **Douglas Ullman**
Farrow, Mia .... **Maria Farrow**
Faye, Alice .... **Ann Leppert**
Fernandel ... **Fernand Contandin**
Fetchit, Stepin..... **Lincoln Perry**
Fields, Gracie .. **Grace Stansfield**
Fields, W. C...... **William Claude Dukinfield**
Finch, Peter .... **William Mitchell**
Fitzgerald, Barry. **William Shields**
Fleming, Rhonda .. **Marilyn Louis**
Fontaine, Joan **Joan de Havilland**
Ford, Glenn .... **Gwyllyn Ford**
Ford, John .... **Sean O'Fearna**
Forsythe, John ..... **John Freund**
Foxx, Redd.. **John Elroy Sanford**
Franciosa, Tony .... **Anthony Papaleo**
Francis, Arlene ... **Arlene Francis Kazanjian**
Francis, Connie....... **Constance Franconero**
Gabor, Zsa Zsa .... **Sari Gabor**
Garbo, Greta .. **Greta Gustafsson**
Gardenia, Vincent ...... **Vincente Scognamiglio**
Gardner, Ava...... **Lucy Johnson**
Garfield, John ... **Julius Garfinkle**
Garland, Beverly......... **Beverly Fessenden**
Garland, Judy ... **Frances Gumm**
Garner, James .... **James Baumgarner**
Gaynor, Janet ..... **Laura Gainer**
Gaynor, Mitzi... **Francesca Mitzi von Gerber**
Gentry, Bobbie **Roberta Streeter**
Gershwin, George .... **Jacob Gershowitz**
Gershwin, Ira.. **Israel Gershowitz**
Gilbert, John .... **John Pringle**
Gilford, Jack ..... **Jacob Gellman**
Gish, Dorothy **Dorothy de Guiche**
Gish, Lillian..... **Lillian de Guiche**
Goddard, Paulette .. **Marion Levy**
Goldwyn, Samuel........ **Samuel Goldfish**
Gordon, Gale .... **Gaylord Aldrich**
Gould, Elliott ... **Elliott Goldstein**
Goulet, Robert........... **Stanley Applebaum**
Granger, Stewart.......... **James Lablanche Stewart**
Grant, Cary .... **Archibald Leach**
Grant, Kathryn ... **Olive Kathryn Grandstaff**
Grant, Lee...... **Lyova Rosenthal**
Graves, Peter .... **Peter Aurness**
Grayson, Kathryn......... **Zelma Kathryn Hedrick**
Grey, Joel............. **Joel Katz**
Hackett, Buddy. **Leonard Hacker**
Harlow, Jean **Harlean Carpentier**
Harris, Barbara.......... **Sandra Markowitz**
Harvey, Laurence...... **Larushka Mischa Skikne**
Haver, June ..... **June Stovenour**
Hayden, Sterling.. **John Hamilton**
Hayes, Helen .... **Helen Hayes Brown**
Hayward, Louis... **Seafield Grant**
Hayward, Susan .... **Edythe Marrener**
Hayworth, Rita .... **Margarita Carmen Cansino**
Heflin, Van . **Emmett Evan Heflin**

Hepburn, Audrey .... **Audrey Hepburn-Ruston**
Heston, Charlton . **John Charlton Carter**
Holden, William.. **William Beedle**
Holliday, Judy ..... **Judith Tuvim**
Hope, Bob.. **Leslie Townes Hope**
Hopper, Hedda .... **Elda Furry**
Houdini, Harry..... **Ehrich Weiss**
Houseman, John .... **Jacques Haussmann**
Howard, Leslie .... **Leslie Stainer**
Hudson, Rock .. **Roy Scherer, Jr.**
Humperdinck, Engelbert .. **Arnold Dorsey**
Hunter, Jeffrey .... **Henry H. McKinnies**
Hunter, Kim .... **Janet Cole**
Hunter, Ross .... **Martin Fuss**
Hussey, Ruth......... **Ruth Carol O'Rourke**
Hutton, Betty........ **Betty Jane Thornburg**
Hutton, Lauren ..... **Mary Hutton**
Ives, Burl..... **Burle Icle Ivanhoe**
Jagger, Dean...... **Dean Jeffries**
Janssen, David ..... **David Meyer**
John, Elton..... **Reginald Dwight**
Johnson, Van....... **Charles Van Johnson**
Jolson, Al .... **Asa Yoelson**
Jones, Jennifer..... **Phyllis Isley**
Jones, Tom . **Thomas Woodward**
Jourdan, Louis..... **Louis Gendre**
Karloff, Boris...... **William Pratt**
Kaye, Danny .... **David Daniel Kaminsky**
Kazan, Elia .... **Elia Kazanjoglous**
Keel, Howard....... **Harold Leek**
Kerr, Deborah .... **Deborah Kerr-Trimmer**
King, Alan......... **Irwin Kinberg**
King, Carole........ **Carole Klein**
Knight, Ted .. **Tadeus Wladyslaw Konopka**
Ladd, Cheryl .... **Cheryl Stoppelmoor**
Lahr, Bert ...... **Irving Lahrheim**
Laine, Frankie .... **Frank Paul Lo Vecchio**
Lake, Veronica .... **Constance Ockleman**
Lamarr, Hedy.... **Hedwig Kiesler**
Lamour, Dorothy .... **Dorothy Kaumeyer**
Lanchester, Elsa....... **Elizabeth Sullivan**
Lanza, Mario ... **Alfredo Cocozza**
Laurel, Stan ..... **Arthur Stanley Jefferson**
Laurie, Piper .... **Rosetta Jacobs**
Lawrence, Gertrude... **Alexandra Dagmar Lawrence-Klasen**
Lawrence, Steve.......... **Sidney Leibowitz**
Lee, Canada.... **Lionel Canegata**
Lee, Gypsy Rose . **Louise Hovick**
Lee, Peggy..... **Norma Egstrom**
Leigh, Janet.. **Jeanette Morrison**
Leigh, Vivien ..... **Vivien Hartley**
Lenya, Lotte.. **Caroline Blamauer**
Lewis, Jerry..... **Joseph Levitch**
Liberace ..... **Wladziu Valentino Liberace**
Lillie, Beatrice........ **Constance Sylvia Munston**
Linden, Hal...... **Harold Lipshitz**
Lisi, Virna .... **Virna Pieralisi**
Lockwood, Gary...... **John Gary Yusolfsky**
Lombard, Carole...... **Jane Alice Peters**
London, Julie.......... **Julie Peck**
Lord, Jack.... **John Joseph Ryan**
Loren, Sophia .. **Sophia Scicoloni**
Lorre, Peter . **Laszlo Loewenstein**
Louise, Tina...... **Tina Blackmer**
Loy, Myrna...... **Myrna Williams**
Lynley, Carol .... **Carolyn Lee**
Lynn, Diana ...... **Dolores Loehr**
Maclaine, Shirley .... **Shirley Maclean Beaty**
Madison, Guy ... **Robert Moseley**
Main, Marjorie.. **Mary Tomlinson**
Malden, Karl. **Malden Sekulovich**
Mansfield, Jayne ..... **Vera Jane Palmer**
March, Frederic .... **Ernest Frederick McIntyre Bickel**
Martin, Dean . **Dino Paul Crocetti**
Martin, Ross . **Martin Rosenblatt**
Martin, Tony .... **Alvin Morris**
May, Elaine.......... **Elaine Berlin**
Mayo, Virginia.... **Virginia Jones**
McGee, Fibber.... **James Jordan**
McQueen, Butterfly...... **Thelma McQueen**
Meredith, Burgess....... **George Burgess**
Merman, Ethel **Ethel Zimmerman**
Merrill, Dina..... **Nedenia Hutton Rumbough**
Miles, Vera........ **Vera Ralston**
Milland, Ray.. **Reginald Truscott-Jones**
Miller, Ann ... **Lucille Ann Collier**
Miller, Marilyn .... **Mary Ellen Reynolds**
Monroe, Marilyn.... **Norma Jean Baker**
Montand, Yves .... **Ivo Levi**

Moore, Garry .. **Thomas Garrison Morfit**
Moreno, Rita ..... **Rosita Dolores Alverio**
Morgan, Dennis . **Stanley Morner**
Morgan, Harry .. **Harry Bratsburg**
Morgan, Helen ..... **Helen Riggins**
Mostel, Zero. **Samuel Joel Mostel**
Muni, Paul ... **Muni Weisenfreund**
Murray, Mae ..... **Marie Adrienne Koenig**
Naldi, Nita .. **Anita Donna Dooley**
Neagle, Anna **Marjorie Robertson**
Nelson, Barry .... **Robert Neilson**
Newmar, Julie .. **Julia Newmeyer**
Nichols, Mike .... **Michael Igor Peschkowsky**
North, Sheree ...... **Dawn Bethel**
Novak, Kim ...... **Marilyn Novak**
Novarro, Ramon .... **Ramon Samaniegos**
Nuyen, France ... **France Nguyen Vannga**
O'Brian, Hugh ..... **Hugh Krampe**
O'Brien, Margaret .... **Angela Maxine O'Brien**
O'Hara, Maureen .... **Maureen Fitzsimmons**
O'Keefe, Dennis .... **Edward Flanagan**
Oakie, Jack ..... **Lewis D. Offield**
Oberon, Merle ..... **Estelle Merle O'Brien Thompson**
Page, Patti .... **Clara Ann Fowler**
Paige, Janis .. **Donna Mae Jaden**
Palmer, Betsy .. **Patricia Brumek**
Palmer, Lilli .... **Lilli Peiser**
Papas, Irene .... **Irene Lelekou**
Parks, Bert .... **Bert Jacobson**
Pearl, Minnie ..... **Sarah Ophelia Cannon**
Peters, Bernadette .. **Bernadette Lazzaro**
Pickens, Slim. **Louis Bert Lindley**
Pickford, Mary ..... **Gladys Smith**
Pinza, Ezio ..... **Fortunato Pinza**
Powell, Jane ..... **Suzanne Burce**
Powers, Stefanie .... **Stefania Federkiewicz**
Prentiss, Paula .... **Paula Ragusa**
Preston, Robert .... **Robert Preston Meservey**
Raft, George ...... **George Ranft**
Raines, Ella .... **Ella Raubes**
Randall, Tony .... **Leonard Rosenberg**
Ray, Aldo .... **Aldo da Re**
Raye, Martha .. **Margaret O'Reed**
Reed, Donna .. **Donna Mullenger**
Reese, Della .... **Delloreese Patricia Early**
Reynolds, Debbie .. **Mary Frances Reynolds**
Rhue, Madlyn .. **Madeleine Roche**
Ritter, Tex .... **Woodward Ritter**
Rivera, Chita .. **Dolores Conchita Figueroa del Rivero**
Robinson, Edward G. . **Emmanuel Goldenberg**
Rogers, Ginger . **Virginia McMath**
Rogers, Roy .... **Leonard Slye**
Rooney, Mickey .... **Joe Yule, Jr.**
Roth, Lillian ..... **Lillian Rutstein**
Russell, Lillian ...... **Helen Louise Leonard**
Sales, Soupy .... **Milton Hines**
Savalas, Telly . **Aristotle Savalas**
Saxon, John ...... **Carmen Orrico**
Scala, Gia ..... **Giovanna Scoglio**
Schneider, Romy ..... **Rosemarie Albach-Retty**
Scott, Lizabeth .... **Emma Matzo**
Sharif, Omar ... **Michel Shalhoub**
Shearer, Moira ...... **Moira King**
Sheen, Martin ... **Ramon Estevez**
Shire, Talia .... **Talia Coppola**
Shore, Dinah ...... **Frances Rose Shore**
Signoret, Simone .... **Simone Kaminker**
Sills, Beverly .... **Belle Silverman**
Silverheels, Jay . **Harold J. Smith**
Singleton, Penny .... **Mariana McNulty**
Skelton, Red ... **Richard Skelton**
Smith, Alexis ...... **Gladys Smith**
Somers, Suzanne .... **Suzanne Mahoney**
Sommer, Elke ...... **Elke Schletz**
Soo, Jack .... **Gogo Suzuki**
Sothern, Ann ..... **Harriette Lake**
Sparks, Ned .. **Edward Sparkman**
St. James, Susan ... **Susan Miller**
St. John, Jill ..... **Jill Oppenheim**
Stack, Robert .... **Robert Modini**
Stanwyck, Barbara **Ruby Stevens**
Stapleton, Jean .. **Jeanne Murray**
Starr, Ringo .... **Richard Starkey**
Sterling, Jan ...... **Jane Sterling Adriance**
Sterling, Robert .... **William John Hart**
Stevens, Connie **Concetta Ingolia**
Stevens, Inger ... **Inger Stensland**
Storm, Gale ... **Josephine Cottle**
Streep, Meryl .... **Mary Louise Streep**
Summers, Donna .... **LaDonna Gaines**
Sweet, Blanche .. **Daphne Wayne**
Tati, Jacques .... **Jacques Tatischeff**

Taylor, Robert .... **Spangler Arlington Brugh**
Terry-Thomas .... **Thomas Terry Hoar-Stevens**
Thomas, Danny .. **Amos Muzyad Jacobs**
Thomas, Marlo .... **Margaret Thomas**
Tiffin, Pamela .... **Pamela Wonso**
Torn, Rip ...... **Elmore Rual Torn**
Tucker, Sophie .... **Sophia Kalish**
Turner, Lana .. **Julia Jean Turner**
Twiggy .... **Lesley Hornby**
Twitty, Conway ..... **Harold Lloyd Jenkins**
Vague, Vera ... **Barbara Jo Allen**
Vallee, Rudy .... **Hubert Prior Vallee**
Valli, Frankie . **Frank Castelluccio**
Van Devere, Trish .... **Patricia Dressel**
Van Doren, Mamie .. **Joan Lucille Olander**
Van, Bobby .... **Robert King**
Velez, Lupe ... **Maria Guadeloupe Velez de Villalobos**
Vera-Ellen . **Vera-Ellen Westmeyr Rohe**
Walker, Nancy ...... **Ann Swoyer Barto**
Wayne, John .... **Marion Michael Morrison**
Webb, Clifton .. **Webb Hollenbeck**
Welch, Raquel .... **Raquel Tejada**
Weld, Tuesday . **Susan Ker Weld**
Werner, Oskar ...... **Oskar Josef Schliessmayer**
West, Adam ... **William Anderson**
Wilder, Gene ... **Jerry Silberman**
Windsor, Marie ..... **Emily Marie Bertelson**
Winters, Shelley .. **Shirley Schrift**
Wonder, Stevie . **Stevland Morris**
Wong, Anna May ...... **Wong Liu Tsong**
Wood, Natalie ... **Natasha Gurdin**
Wynn, Ed. . **Isaiah Edwin Leopold**
Wynn, Keenan .... **Francis Xavier Aloysius Wynn**
Wynter, Dana . **Dagmar Spencer-Marcus**
York, Susannah .... **Susannah Yolande Fletcher**
Young, Gig . **Byron Elsworth Barr**
Young, Loretta .... **Gretchen Michaela Young**

SOME FAMOUS PEN NAMES

Boz .... **Charles Dickens**

Bell, Acton .... **Anne Bronte**
Bell, Carter .... **Charlotte Bronte**
Bell, Ellis .... **Emily Bronte**
Boyd, Nancy ... **Edna St. Vincent Millay**
Elia .... **Charles Lamb**
Loti, Pierre .... **Louis Viaud**
Saki .... **H. H. Munro**
Sand, George .. **Amandine Dupin Dudevant**
Ward, Artemus **Charles F. Browne**

Eliot, George ... **Mary Ann Evans**
Gorki, Maxim .... **Alexey Maximovich Peshkov**
Nasby, Petroleum ... **David Ross Locke**

Henry, O. **William Sydney Porter**
Ouida .... **Louise de la Ramee**
Twain, Mark .... **Samuel Clemens**

France, Anatole .... **Jacques Thibault**
Orwell, George . **Eric Arthur Blair**

Carroll, Lewis .. **Charles Dodgson**
Colette .... **Sidonie Gabrielle Claudine Colette**
LeCarre, John .... **David John Cornwell**

Stendhal .... **Henri Beyle**
Voltaire .. **Francois Marie Arouet**

Westmacott, Mary .... **Agatha Christie**

SOME U.S. AUTHORS

Abbot, George
Ade, George
Albee, Edward
Alcott, Louisa May
Alger, Horatio
Asimov, Isaac
Austen, Jane
Baldwin, James
Barth, John
Baum, L. Frank
Behrman, S.N.
Bellow, Saul
Benchley, Peter
Benchley, Robert
Benet, Stephen Vincent
Bierce, Ambrose
Bishop, Jim
Blume, Judy
Bradbury, Ray
Brand, Max
Brown, Dee
Buck, Pearl
Burroughs, Edgar Rice
Burrows, Abe
Caldwell, Erskine
Caldwell, Taylor
Capote, Truman
Cather, Willa
Chase, Mary
Chayefsky, Paddy
Cheever, John
Clavell, James
Connelly, Marc
Cooper, James Fennimore
Crane, Hart
Crane, Stephen
Crews, Harry
Crichton, Michael
cummings, e.e.
Dickinson, Emily
Didion, Joan
Dos Passos, John
Drury, Allen
Emerson, Ralph Waldo
Farrel, James T.
Faulkner, William
Ferber, Edna
Fitzgerald, F. Scott
Frost, Robert
Gardner, Erle Stanley
Grey, Zane
Guest, Edgar A.
Hailey, Arthur
Haley, Alex
Hammett, Dashiell
Harris, Joel Chandler
Hart, Moss
Harte, Bret
Heller, Joseph
Hellman, Lillian
Hemingway, Ernest
Henry, O.
Hersey, John
Holmes, Oliver Wendell
Hughes, Langston
Inge, William
Irving, John
Irving, Washington
James, Henry
Kazan, Elia
Kerr, Jean
Kesey, Ken
Kilmer, Joyce
Knowles, John
Lardner, Ring
Lee, Harper
Levin, Ira
Lewis, Sinclair
London, Jack
Longfellow, Henry Wadsworth
Loos, Anita
Lowell, Amy
Lowell, James Russell
Lowell, Robert
Ludlum, Robert
MacInnes, Helen
Mailer, Norman
Malamud, Bernard
Masters, Edgar Lee
Matthison, Peter
McCarthy, Mary
McCullers, Carson
Melville, Herman
Mencken, H.L.
Michener, James
Millay, Edna St. Vincent
Miller, Arthur
Moore, Clement C.
Moore, Marianne
Nash, Ogden
Oates, Joyce Carol
Odets, Clifford
O'Hara, John
O'Neill, Eugene
Parker, Dorothy
Poe, Edgar Allan
Porter, Katherine Ann
Potok, Chaim
Pound, Ezra
Puzo, Mario
Rice, Elmer
Riley, James Whitcomb
Rinehart, Mary Roberts
Roth, Philip
Runyon, Damon
Salinger, J.D.
Sandburg, Carl
Saroyan, William
Schary, Dore
Schulberg, Budd
Segal, Erich
Shaw, Irwin
Simon, Neil
Sinclair, Upton
Singer, Isaac Bashevis
Slaughter, Frank
Stein, Gertrude
Steinbeck, John
Stone, Irving
Stout, Rex
Stowe, Harriet Beecher
Styron, William
Tarkington, Booth
Teasdale, Sara
Thurber, James
Tryon, Thomas
Twain, Mark
Updike, John
Uris, Leon
Vidal, Gore
Vonnegut, Kurt Jr.
Wallace, Irving
Warren, Robert Penn
Welty, Eudora
West, Nathaniel
Wharton, Edith
White, Theodore H.
Whitman, Walt
Whittier, John Greenleaf
Wilder, Thornton
Williams, Tennessee
Wolfe, Thomas
Wouk, Herman
Wylie, Elinor
Yerby, Frank

NAMES FROM SHAKESPEARE

Listed by Plays

(Plays are listed alphabetically by the titles that are commonly used. The actual title, if different, follows in parentheses.)

ALL'S WELL THAT ENDS WELL

DIANA, LAFEU; HELENA; BERTRAM, LAVACHE, MARIANA; PAROLLES, VIOLENTA

ANTONY AND CLEOPATRA

EROS, IRAS; MENAS, PHILO; ALEXAS, CAESAR (OCTAVIUS), GALLUS, SCARUS, SEXTUS (POMPEIUS), SILIUS, TAURUS; AGRIPPA, LEPIDUS, MARDIAN, OCTAVIA, THYREUS, VARRIUS; CANIDIUS, CHARMIAN, DERCETAS, DIOMEDES, MAECENAS, SELEUCUS; DEMETRIUS, DOLABELLA, VENTIDIUS; EUPHRONIUS, MENECRATES, PROCULEIUS

AS YOU LIKE IT

ADAM; CELIA, CORIN, PHEBE; AMIENS, AUDREY, DENNIS, JAQUES, LE BEAU, OLIVER; CHARLES, ORLANDO, SILVIUS, WILLIAM; ROSALIND; FREDERICK; TOUCHSTONE

COMEDY OF ERRORS, THE

LUCE; PINCH; AEGEON, ANGELO, DROMIO; ADRIANA, AEMILIA, LUCIANA, SOLINUS; BALTHAZAR; ANTIPHOLUS

CORIOLANUS (The Tragedy of Coriolanus)

CAIUS, TITUS; BRUTUS, JUNIUS, TULLUS; AGRIPPA, LARTIUS, MARCIUS, VALERIA, VELUTUS; AUFIDIUS, COMINIUS, MENENIUS, SICINIUS, VIRGILIA, VOLUMNIA

CYMBELINE

CAIUS (LUCIUS), HELEN; CLOTEN, IMOGEN; IACHIMO, PISANIO; BELARIUS, LEONATUS, PHILARIO; ARVIRAGUS, CORNELIUS, GUIDERIUS, POSTHUMUS

HAMLET (The Tragedy of Hamlet, Prince of Denmark)

OSRIC; HORATIO, LAERTES, OPHELIA; BERNARDO, CLAUDIUS, GERTRUDE, POLONIUS, REYNALDO; CORNELIUS, FRANCISCO, MARCELLUS, VOLTIMAND; FORTINBRAS; ROSENCRANTZ; GUILDENSTERN

JULIUS CAESAR (The Tragedy of Julius Caesar)

CATO, LENA; CASCA, CINNA, VARRO; BRUTUS, CICERO, CLITUS, DECIUS, LUCIUS, MARCUS, PORTIA, STRATO; CASSIUS, FLAVIUS, LEPIDUS, MESSALA, PUBLIUS; CLAUDIUS, LIGARIUS, LUCILIUS, MARULLUS, METELLUS, OCTAVIUS, PINDARUS, POPILIUS, TITINIUS; CALPURNIA, DARDANIUS, TREBONIUS, VOLUMNIUS; ARTEMIDORUS

KING HENRY IV, PART I (The First Part of King Henry IV)

JOHN, PETO; BLUNT, HENRY, PERCY, POINS; MICHAEL, QUICKLY; BARDOLPH, FALSTAFF, GADSHILL; ARCHIBALD, GLENDOWER

KING HENRY IV, PART II (The Second Part of King Henry IV)

DAVY, FANG, JOHN, PETO, WART; BLUNT, GOWER, HENRY, POINS, SNARE; FEEBLE, MORTON, MOULDY, PISTOL, RUMOUR, SCROOP, SHADOW, THOMAS; MOWBRAY, QUICKLY, SHALLOW, SILENCE, TRAVERS; BARDOLPH, BULLCALF, FALSTAFF, HARCOURT, HASTINGS, HUMPHREY; DOLL TEARSHEET

KING HENRY V (The Life of King Henry V)

NYM; GREY, JAMY; ALICE, BATES, COURT, GOWER, LEWIS; ISABEL, PISTOL; SCROOP; CHARLES, MONTJOY, QUICKLY; BARDOLPH, FLUELLEN, GRANDPRE, RAMBURES, WILLIAMS; ERPINGHAM, KATHARINE, MACMORRIS

KING HENRY VI, PART I (The First Part of King Henry VI)

LUCY; BASSET, TALBOT, VERNON; CHARLES, RICHARD; BEAUFORT, FASTOLFE, GARGRAVE, MARGARET, REIGNIER, WOODVILE; GLANSDALE, LA PUCELLE (Joan of Arc), PLANTAGENET

KING HENRY VI, PART II (The Second Part of King Henry VI)

SAY; CADE, DICK, HUME, IDEN, VAUX; BEVIS, GOFFE, PETER, SMITH; EDMUND, EDWARD, HORNER, SCALES, THOMAS; ELEANOR, HOLLAND, MICHAEL, RICHARD, SIMPCOX, STANLEY; BEAUFORT, CLIFFORD, HUMPHREY, JOURDAIN, MARGARET, MORTIMER, STAFFORD; ALEXANDER, SOUTHWELL; BOLINGBROKE, PLANTAGENET

KING HENRY VI, PART III (The Third Part of King Henry VI)

BONA, GREY; HENRY, LEWIS; EDMUND, EDWARD, GEORGE, RIVERS; RICHARD, STANLEY, CLIFFORD, HASTINGS, MARGARET, MORTIMER, STAFFORD; SOMERVILLE; MONTGOMERY; PLANTAGENET

KING HENRY VIII (The Famous History of the Life of King Henry VIII)

VAUX; BUTTS, DENNY, SANDS; LOVELL, WOLSEY; BRANDON, CRANMER; CAMPEIUS, CAPUCIUS, CROMWELL, GARDINER, GRIFFITH, PATIENCE; GUILDFORD, KATHARINE; ANNE BULLEN; ABERGAVENNY

KING JOHN (The Life and Death of King John)

BIGOT, HENRY, JAMES, LEWIS, MELUN, PETER; ARTHUR, BLANCHE, ELINOR, GURNEY, HUBERT, PHILIP, ROBERT; DE BURGH, LYMOGES; PANDULPH; CONSTANCE, CHATILLON

KING LEAR (The Tragedy of King Lear)

CURAN, EDGAR, REGAN; EDMUND, OSWALD; GONERIL; CORDELIA

KING RICHARD II (The Tragedy of King Richard II)

ROSS; BAGOT, BUSHY, GREEN, HENRY, PERCY; EDMUND, PIERCE, SCROOP, THOMAS; AUMERLE, HOTSPUR, MOWBRAY; FITZWATER; WILLOUGHBY; BOLINGBROKE, JOHN OF GAUNT

KING RICHARD III (The Tragedy of King Richard III)

ANNE, GREY; HENRY, LOVEL; BLOUNT, EDWARD, GEORGE, MORTON, RIVERS, TYRREL; BRANDON, CATESBY, HERBERT, RICHARD, STANLEY, TRESSEL, URSWICK, VAUGHAN; BERKELEY, HASTINGS, MARGARET, RATCLIFF; BOURCHIER, ELIZABETH, ROTHERHAM; BRAKENBURY

MACBETH (The Tragedy of Macbeth)

ROSS; ANGUS; BANQUO, DUNCAN, HECATE, LENNOX, SEYTON, SIWARD; FLEANCE, MACDUFF, MALCOLM; MENTEITH; CAITHNESS, DONALBAIN

MEASURE FOR MEASURE

ELBOW, FROTH, LUCIO, PETER; ANGELO, JULIET, POMPEY, THOMAS; CLAUDIO, ESCALUS, MARIANA, VARRIUS; ABHORSON, ISABELLA, OVERDONE; FRANCISCA, VINCENTIO; BARNARDINE

MERCHANT OF VENICE, THE

GOBBO, TUBAL; PORTIA; ANTONIO, JESSICA, LORENZO, NERISSA, SALANIO, SALERIO, SHYLOCK; BASSANIO, GRATIANO, LEONARDO, SALARINO, STEPHANO; BALTHASAR

MERRY WIVES OF WINDSOR, THE

NYM; ANNE, FORD, PAGE; CAIUS, EVANS, ROBIN, RUGBY; FENTON, PISTOL, SIMPLE; QUICKLY, SHALLOW, SLENDER, WILLIAM; BARDOLPH, FALSTAFF

MIDSUMMER-NIGHT'S DREAM, A

MOTH, PUCK, SNUG; EGEUS, FLUTE, SNOUT; BOTTOM, COBWEB, HELENA, HERMIA, OBERON, QUINCE; THESEUS, TITANIA; LYSANDER; DEMETRIUS, HIPPOLYTA; STARVELING; PHILOSTRATE; PEASEBLOSSOM

MUCH ADO ABOUT NOTHING

HERO; URSULA, VERGES; ANTONIO, CLAUDIO, CONRADE, DON JOHN, FRANCIS, LEONATO; BEATRICE, BENEDICK, BORACHIO, DOGBERRY, DON PEDRO, MARGARET; BALTHASAR

OTHELLO (The Tragedy of Othello, The Moor of Venice)

IAGO; BIANCA, CASSIO, EMILIA; MONTANO; GRATIANO, LODOVICO, RODERIGO; BRABANTIO, DESDEMONA

PERICLES (Pericles, Prince of Tyre)

BOULT, CLEON, DIANA, GOWER; MARINA, THAISA; CERIMON, DIONYZA, ESCANES, LEONINE; PHILEMON, THALIARD; ANTIOCHUS, HELICANUS, LYCHORIDA, SIMONIDES; LYSIMACHUS

ROMEO AND JULIET (The Tragedy of Romeo and Juliet)

PARIS, PETER; TYBALT; ABRAHAM, CAPULET, ESCALUS, GREGORY, SAMPSON; BENVOLIO, LAURENCE, MERCUTIO, MONTAGUE; BALTHASAR

TAMING OF THE SHREW, THE

SLY; BIANCA, CURTIS, GREMIO, GRUMIO, TRANIO; BAPTISTA, LUCENTIO; BIONDELLO, HORTENSIO, KATHARINA, PETRUCHIO, VINCENTIO; CHRISTOPHER

TEMPEST, THE

IRIS, JUNO; ARIEL, CERES; ADRIAN, ALONSO; ANTONIO, CALIBAN; GONZALO, MIRANDA; PROSPERO, STEPHANO, TRINCULO; FERDINAND, FRANCISCO, SEBASTIAN

TIMON OF ATHENS (The Life of Timon of Athens)

CUPID, TITUS; CAPHIS, LUCIUS; FLAVIUS, PHRYNIA; LUCILIUS, LUCULLUS, PHILOTUS, TIMANDRA; APEMANTUS, FLAMINIUS, SERVILIUS, VENTIDIUS; ALCIBIADES, HORTENSIUS, SEMPRONIUS

TITUS ANDRONICUS (The Tragedy of Titus Andronicus)

AARON; CHIRON, LUCIUS, MARCUS, MUTIUS, TAMORA; ALARBUS, LAVINIA, MARTIUS, PUBLIUS, QUINTUS; AEMILIUS; BASSIANUS, DEMETRIUS; SATURNINUS

TROILUS AND CRESSIDA

AJAX; HELEN, PARIS, PRIAM; AENEAS, HECTOR, NESTOR; ANTENOR, CALCHAS, HELENUS, ULYSSES; ACHILLES, CRESSIDA, DIOMEDES, MENELAUS, PANDARUS; AGAMEMNON, ALEXANDER, CASSANDRA, DEIPHOBUS, PATROCLUS, THERSITES; ANDROMACHE, MARGARELON

TWELFTH NIGHT (Twelfth Night; or, What You Will)

BELCH, CURIO, FESTE, MARIA, VIOLA; FABIAN, OLIVIA, ORSINO; ANTONIO; MALVOLIO; AGUECHEEK, SEBASTIAN, VALENTINE

TWO GENTLEMEN OF VERONA, THE

JULIA, SPEED; LAUNCE, SILVIA, THURIO; ANTONIO, LUCETTA, PROTEUS; EGLAMOUR, PANTHINO; VALENTINE

WINTER'S TALE, THE

DION; MOPSA; DORCAS, EMILIA; CAMILLO, LEONTES, PAULINA, PERDITA; FLORIZEL, HERMIONE; ANTIGONUS, AUTOLYCUS, CLEOMENES, MAMILLIUS, POLIXENES; ARCHIDAMUS

U.S. PRESIDENTS INFORMATION

Note: State indicates state of birth. First Ladies' maiden or original names are given directly under each president's name.

	Name	Party	Vice-Pres.	State	Term
1.	WASHINGTON, George Martha Dandridge Custis	Fed.	Adams	VA	1789–1797
2.	ADAMS, John Abigal Smith	Fed.	Jefferson	MA	1797–1801
3.	JEFFERSON, Thomas Martha Wayles Skelton	Dem.-Rep.	Burr, Clinton	VA	1801–1809
4.	MADISON, James Dorothea Payne Todd "Dolley"	Dem.-Rep.	Clinton, Gerry	VA	1809–1817
5.	MONROE, James Elizabeth Kortright	Dem.-Rep.	Tompkins	VA	1817–1825
6.	ADAMS, John Quincy Louise Catherine Johnson	Dem.-Rep.	Calhoun	MA	1825–1829
7.	JACKSON, Andrew Rachel Donelson Robards	Dem.	Calhoun, Van Buren	SC	1829–1837
8.	VAN BUREN, Martin Hannah Hoes	Dem.	Johnson	NY	1837–1841
9.	HARRISON, William Henry Anna Symmes	Whig	Tyler	VA	1841
10.	TYLER, John Letitia Christian and Julia Gardiner	Dem.		VA	1841–1845
11.	POLK, James Knox Sarah Childress	Dem.	Dallas	NC	1845–1849
12.	TAYLOR, Zachary Margaret Smith	Whig	Fillmore	VA	1849–1850
13.	FILLMORE, Millard Abigail Powers and Caroline Carmichael McIntosh	Whig		NY	1850–1853
14.	PIERCE, Franklin Jane Mears Appleton	Dem.	King	NH	1853–1857
15.	BUCHANAN, James	Dem.	Breckenridge	PA	1857–1861
16.	LINCOLN, Abraham Mary Todd	Rep.	Hamlin, Johnson	KY	1861–1865
17.	JOHNSON, Andrew Eliza McCardle	Dem.		NC	1865–1869
18.	GRANT, Ulysses Simpson Julia Dent	Rep.	Colfax, Wilson	OH	1869–1877
19.	HAYES, Rutherford Birchard Lucy Ware Webb	Rep.	Wheeler	OH	1877–1881
20.	GARFIELD, James Abram Lucretia Rudolph	Rep.	Arthur	OH	1881
21.	ARTHUR, Chester Alan Ellen Lewis Herndon	Rep.		VT	1881–1885
22.	CLEVELAND, Stephen Grover Frances Folsom	Dem.	Hendricks	NJ	1885–1889
23.	HARRISON, Benjamin Caroline Lavinia Scott and Mary Scott Lord Dimmick	Rep.	Morton	OH	1889–1893

	Name	Party	Vice-Pres.	State	Term
24.	CLEVELAND, Stephen Grover Frances Folsom	Dem.	Stevenson	NJ	1893–1897
25.	MC KINLEY, William Ida Saxton	Rep.	Hobart, Roosevelt	OH	1897–1901
26.	ROOSEVELT, Theodore Alice Hathaway Lee and Edith Kermit Carow	Rep.	Fairbanks	NY	1901–1909
27.	TAFT, William Howard Helen Herron	Rep.	Sherman	OH	1909–1913
28.	WILSON, Thomas Woodrow Ellen Louise Axson and Edith Bolling Galt	Dem.	Marshall	VA	1913–1921
29.	HARDING, Warren Gamaliel Florence Kling De Wolfe	Rep.	Coolidge	OH	1921–1923
30.	COOLIDGE, John Calvin Grace Anna Goodhue	Rep.	Dawes	VT	1923–1929
31.	HOOVER, Herbert Clark Lou Henry	Rep.	Curtis	IA	1929–1933
32.	ROOSEVELT, Franklin Delano Anna Eleanor Roosevelt	Dem.	Garner, Wallace Truman	NY	1933–1945
33.	TRUMAN, Harry S Elizabeth (Bess) Wallace	Dem.	Barkley	MO	1945–1953
34.	EISENHOWER, Dwight David Mamie Geneva Doud	Rep.	Nixon	TX	1953–1961
35.	KENNEDY, John Fitzgerald Jacqueline Lee Bouvier	Dem.	Johnson	MA	1961–1963
36.	JOHNSON, Lyndon Baines Claudia Alta Taylor "Lady Bird"	Dem.	Humphrey	TX	1963–1968
37.	NIXON, Richard Milhous Thelma Catherine Patricia Ryan "Pat"	Rep.	Agnew, Ford	CA	1968–1974
38.	FORD, Gerald Rudolph Elizabeth Bloomer Warren "Betty"	Rep.	Rockefeller	NE	1974–1977
39.	CARTER, James Earl, Jr. Rosalynn Smith	Dem.	Mondale	GA	1977–1981
40.	REAGAN, Ronald Wilson Anne Frances Robbins Davis "Nancy"	Rep.	Bush	IL	1981–

U.S. STATES INFORMATION

STATE	ABBREVIATIONS (official P.O. abbr. appears first)	RANK BY AREA	RANK BY POPULATION
ALABAMA	AL, Ala.	29	22
ALASKA	AK, Alas., Alsk.	1	50
ARIZONA	AZ, Ariz.	6	29
ARKANSAS	AR, Ark.	27	33
CALIFORNIA	CA, Calif., Cal.	3	1
COLORADO	CO, Colo.	8	27
*CONNECTICUT	CT, Conn.	48	25
*DELAWARE	DE, Del., Dela.	49	47
†DISTRICT OF COLUMBIA	DC, D.C.		
FLORIDA	FL, Fla.	22	7
*GEORGIA	GA, Ga.	21	12
HAWAII	HI, H., Haw.	47	40
IDAHO	ID, Id., Ida.	13	41
ILLINOIS	IL, Ill.	24	5
INDIANA	IN, Ind.	38	13
IOWA	IA, Ia.	25	28
KANSAS	KS, Kan., Kans.	14	32
KENTUCKY	KY, Ky.	37	24
LOUISIANA	LA, La.	31	18
MAINE	ME, Me.	39	39
*MARYLAND	MD, Md.	42	19
*MASSACHUSETTS	MA, Mass.	45	11
MICHIGAN	MI, Mich.	23	8
MINNESOTA	MN, Minn.	12	21
MISSISSIPPI	MS, Miss.	32	31
MISSOURI	MO, Mo.	19	15
MONTANA	MT, Mont.	4	45
NEBRASKA	NE, Nebr.	15	36
NEVADA	NV, Nev.	7	44
*NEW HAMPSHIRE	NH, N.H.	44	43
*NEW JERSEY	NJ, N.J.	46	9
NEW MEXICO	NM, N.M.	5	38
*NEW YORK	NY, N.Y.	30	2
*NORTH CAROLINA	NC, N.C.	28	10
NORTH DAKOTA	ND, N.D.	17	46
OHIO	OH, O.	35	6
OKLAHOMA	OK, Okla.	18	26
OREGON	OR, Ore.	10	30
*PENNSYLVANIA	PA, Penna., Penn.	33	4
*RHODE ISLAND	RI, R.I.	50	41
*SOUTH CAROLINA	SC, S.C.	40	24
SOUTH DAKOTA	SD, S.D.	16	45
TENNESSEE	TN, Tenn.	34	17
TEXAS	TX, Tex.	2	3
UTAH	UT, Ut.	11	36
VERMONT	VT, Vt.	43	48
*VIRGINIA	VA, Va.	36	14
WASHINGTON	WA, Wash.	20	20
WEST VIRGINIA	WV, W. Va.	41	34
WISCONSIN	WI, Wisc., Wis.	26	16
WYOMING	WY, Wyo.	9	49

†District *One of the Thirteen Original States

STATE CAPITAL	STATE NICKNAME(S)	STATE FLOWER
Montgomery	Cotton, Heart of Dixie, Yellowhammer	Camellia
Juneau	The Last Frontier	Forget-Me-Not
Phoenix	Grand Canyon	Seguaro Cactus
Little Rock	Land of Opportunity	Apple Blossom
Sacramento	Golden, El Dorado	Golden Poppy
Denver	Centennial, Silver	Columbine
Hartford	Constitution, Nutmeg	Mountain Laurel
Dover	First, Diamond, Blue Hen	Peach Blossom
		American Beauty Rose
Tallahassee	Sunshine, Peninsular	Orange Blossom
Atlanta	Empire State of the South, Peach	Cherokee Rose
Honolulu	Aloha, Paradise of the Pacific	Hibiscus
Boise	Gem	Syringa
Springfield	Prairie, Sucker, The Inland Empire	Violet
Indianapolis	Hoosier	Peony
Des Moines	Hawkeye	Wild Rose
Topeka	Sunflower, Jayhawker	Sunflower
Frankfort	Bluegrass	Goldenrod
Baton Rouge	Pelican, Creole	Magnolia
Augusta	Pine Tree, Lumber	Pine Cone and Tassel
Annapolis	Old Line, Free, Cockade	Black-Eyed Susan
Boston	Bay, Old Colony	Mayflower
Lansing	Wolverine, Great Lake	Apple Blossom
St. Paul	North Star, Gopher	Lady's-Slipper
Jackson	Magnolia, Bayou	Magnolia
Jefferson City	Show Me, Bullion	Hawthorn
Helena	Treasure, Mountain	Bitterroot
Lincoln	Cornhusker, Blackwater	Goldenrod
Carson City	Sagebrush, Silver, Battle Born	Sagebrush
Concord	Granite	Purple Lilac
Trenton	Garden	Violet
Santa Fe	Sunshine, Land of Enchantment	Yucca
Albany	Empire, Excelsior	Rose
Raleigh	Tar Heel, Old North, Turpentine	Dogwood
Bismarck	Sioux, Flickertail	Wild Prairie Rose
Columbus	Buckeye	Scarlet Carnation
Oklahoma City	Sooner	Mistletoe
Salem	Beaver, Sunset, Valentine, Webfoot	Oregon Grape
Harrisburg	Keystone	Mountain Laurel
Providence	Little Rhody, Ocean	Violet
Columbia	Palmetto	Carolina Jessamine
Pierre	Coyote, Sunshine	Pasque Flower
Nashville	Volunteer	Iris
Austin	Lone Star	Bluebonnet
Salt Lake City	Beehive, Mormon	Sego Lily
Montpelier	Green Mountain	Red Clover
Richmond	Old Dominion, Mother of Presidents	Dogwood
Olympia	Evergreen, Chinook	Western Rhododendron
Charleston	Mountain	Big Rhododendron
Madison	Badger	Wood Violet
Cheyenne	Equality	Indian Paintbrush

GAZETTEER
OR
GEOGRAPHICAL DICTIONARY

Cities, States, Countries, Counties, Provinces, Towns, Rivers, Communes, Ports and Harbors, Regions, Lakes, Mountains, Islands, Volcanoes, Settlements, Kingdoms, Districts, Divisions, Peninsulas, Mountain Ranges, etc.

A

ABYSSINIA .... see ETHIOPIA

ADRIATIC ...... port and harbor, **FIUME**; peninsula, **ISTRIA**; resort, **LIDO**

AEGEAN..... gulf, **SAROS**; river, **STRUMA**; island, **IOS, KOS, KEOS, CHIOS, DELOS, KASOS, LEROS, MELOS, NAXOS, PAROS, SAMOS, SYROS, TELOS, TENOS, THIRA, ANDROS, PATMOS, RHODES, SKYROS**

AFGHANISTAN..... city, **HERAT**

AFRICA......... country, **CHAD, MALI, TOGO, BENIN, CONGO, EGYPT, GABON, GHANA, KENYA, LIBYA, NIGER, SUDAN, ZAIRE, ANGOLA,** (THE) **GAMBIA, GUINEA, MALAWI, RWANDA, UGANDA, ZAMBIA, ALGERIA, BURUNDI, LESOTHO, LIBERIA, NIGERIA, SENEGAL, SOMALIA, TUNISIA**; lake, **CHAD, TANA, NYASA**; mountains, **ATLAS**; river, **NILE, CONGO, NIGER, ORANGE**; canal, **SUEZ**

ALABAMA .... city, **SELMA, ANNISTON**

ALASKA.... city, **NOME, SITKA**; island, **ADAK, ATKA, ATTU, UNGA**; mountain, **ADA**; inlet, **COOK**; river, **YUKON**; highest peak in N. America, **MCKINLEY**; glacier, **MUIR**

ALBANIA ...... capital, **TIRANA**; river, **DRIN**

ALEUTIANS..... islands, **ADAK, ATKA, ATTU**

ALGERIA ... city, **ORAN, SETIF, ALGIERS**

ALPS... mountain, **ROSA, VISO, BLANC, LEONE, MATTERHORN**

ANGOLA .... city, **LOBITO, LUANDA**; mountain peak, **MOCO**

ANTARCTIC .... sea, **ROSS**

ARABIA ..... city, **ADEN, SANA**; district, **TEMA (TAIMA)**; nation, **OMAN, QATAR, YEMEN, KUWAIT**; gulf, **ADEN, OMAN**; old kingdom, **NEJD**; cape, **ASIR**

ARCTIC .... gulf, **OB**; sea, **KARA**

ARGENTINA .... city, **SALTA, CORDOBA, ROSARIO**; province, **CHACO**; volcano, **MAIPO**

ARIZONA .... city, **MESA, YUMA, TEMPE, TUCSON**; county, **GILA, PIMA, YUMA, PINAL, APACHE, MOHAVE, NAVAJO, COCHISE**; lake, **MEAD**; river, **SALT, GILA**

ARKANSAS .... city, **LITTLE ROCK**; county, **LEE, CLAY, DREW, PIKE, BOONE, CROSS, LOGAN, UNION**; river, **RED, WHITE**

ARMENIA. river, **ARAS (ARAKS)**

ARU ISLANDS....... port, **DOBO**

ASIA... mountains, **ALTAI**; lake, **ARAL**; sea, **ARAL**; river, **OB, ILI, AMUR, LENA, ONON, TIGRIS**; kingdom, **NEPAL**; old kingdom, **SIAM**; country, **IRAN, IRAQ (IRAK), BURMA, CHINA, KOREA, TIBET**; desert, **GOBI**

ASIA MINOR..... district, **IONIA**; mountains, **IDA**

ASIATIC.............. see ASIA

AUSTRALIA.... peninsula, **EYRE**; river, **SWAN**; city, **PERTH**

AUSTRIA..... city, **GRAZ, LINZ, VIENNA (WIEN)**; river, **MUR, ENNS, RABA (RAAB)**; spa, **BADEN**

AZORES........ port and harbor, **HORTA**; island, **PICO, FAYAL (FAIAL), FLORES**; volcano, **PICO (ALTO)**

B

BAHAMAS..... capital, **NASSAU**

BAHRAIN.... capital, **MANAMA**

BALEARIC ISLANDS .... port, **PALMA**; island, **MAJORCA**

BALTIC...... capital, **RIGA**; gulf, **RIGA**; river, **ODER**

BANGLADESH . capital, **DACCA**; river, **GANGES**

BAVARIA... river, **NAB (NAAB), ISAR**

BELGIUM. city, **GENT (GHENT), LIEGE**; commune or town, **ANS, ATH, HUY, SPA, MONS, NIEL, ROUX, NAMUR, MECHLIN (MALINES)**; river, **LYS, YSER, MEUSE, SENNE**; port and harbor, **OSTEND**; province, **LIEGE**

BENIN.......... city, **ABOMEY, COTONOU, PORTO-NOVO**; river, **VOLTA**

BOHEMIA.... river, **ELBE, ISER**;

BORNEO .. mountains, **KAPUAS, MULLER**; river, **BARITO, RAJANG**; state, **SABAH, SARAWAK**

BRAZIL...... city, **RIO, BELEM**; port and harbor, **PARA, NATAL, SANTOS, PELOTAS**; state, **PARA, BAHIA**; river, **APA, ICA, PARA**

BRITISH WEST INDIES.... island, **NEVIS**

BULGARIA....... capital, **SOFIA**

BURMA .. capital (former), **AVA**, (present), **RANGOON**; district, **PROME**

C

CALIFORNIA . city, **LODI, NAPA, POMONA, ALAMEDA, SALINAS**; town, **OJAI**; county, **NAPA, YOLO, MODOC, MADERA**; lake, **TAHOE**; mountain peak, **LASSEN, SHASTA**; valley, **NAPA**

CAMBODIA (KAMPUCHEA)...... capital, **PNOMPENH**; river, **MEKONG**

CAMEROON .... river, **SANAGA**

CANADA .... mountain, **LOGAN, ROBSON**; peninsula, **GASPE**; province, **ALBERTA (ALTA.), BRITISH COLUMBIA (B.C.), MANITOBA (MAN.), NEW BRUNSWICK (N.B.), NEWFOUNDLAND (NFLD.), NOVA SCOTIA (N.S.), ONTARIO (ONT.), PRINCE EDWARD ISLAND (P.E.I.), QUEBEC (QUE.), SASKATCHEWAN (SASK.)**; national park, **JASPER**

CAPE VERDE ..... island, **FOGO, MAIO (MAYO), BRAVA, SAL REI, BOA VISTA**

CARIBBEAN ...... island, **CUBA, ARUBA**

CAROLINES........ island, **YAP, TRUK, PALAU (PELEW), PONAPE**

CASPIAN .... seaport and harbor, **BAKU**

CENTRAL AMERICA .... river, **LEMPA**

CEYLON........ see SRI LANKA

CHAD ... town, **SARH, ABECHE**

CHANNEL ISLANDS ...... island, **SARK**

CHILE .. river, **LOA;** port, harbor, town, **ARICA**

CHINA (see also TAIWAN) ...... city, **AMOY, IPIN, CANTON;** port and harbor, **AMOY;** old kingdom, **SHU;** river, **SI, WU, HAN, HSI, ILI, KAN, PEI, WEI, AMUR, HUAI (HWAI);** province, **HONAN, HUNAN;** mountains, **OMEI (OMI)**

COLOMBIA river, **MAGDALENA;** city, **CALI**

COLORADO....... city, **LAMAR, OURAY, PUEBLO, DURANGO;** park, **ESTES;** range, **RATON;** mountain, **OSO, EOLUS;** peak, **OSO;** county, **OTERO, OURAY;** resort, **ASPEN**

CONNECTICUT.. town, **DARIEN, ANSONIA, MERIDEN;** city, **NEW HAVEN, HARTFORD, STAMFORD;** river, **THAMES**

CORSICA....... port and harbor, **BASTIA**

CRETE .... port and harbor, **CANDIA;** capital, **CANEA;** mountain, **IDA**

CRIMEA .... port and harbor, **KERCH;** river, **ALMA**

CUBA ...... town, **GUINES;** city, **HAVANA (HABANA)**

CYCLADES ... island, **IOS (NIO), SYRA (SYROS), DELOS, MELOS (MILO), TENOS, THIRA**

CYPRUS....... capital, **NICOSIA**

CZECHOSLOVAKIA .. city, **BRNO (BRUNN);** river, **GRAN, HRON, IPEL, ISER, ODER, OHRE (EGER), MOLDAU;** capital, **PRAGUE (PRAHA)**

D

DELAWARE .....capital, **DOVER;** county, **NEW CASTLE, KENT, SUSSEX**

DENMARK ...... island off, **ALS, AERO;** islands, **FAROE**

DOMINICAN REPUBLIC ..... city, **MOCA**

DUTCH...... see NETHERLANDS

DUTCH EAST INDIES .... see INDONESIA

E

EAST ASIA .... former kingdom, **KOREA**

EAST EUROPEAN .. river, **DRAU (DRAVA, DRAVE), TISA (TISZA, THEISS)**

EAST INDIES... island, **BORNEO**

ECUADOR ...... capital, **QUITO;** province, **EL ORO**

EGYPT ...... city, **GIZA, CAIRO;** ancient city, **SAIS, THEBES;** province, **GIZA;** river, **NILE**

ENGLAND .... city, **ELY, BATH, YORK, LEEDS, COVENTRY;** port and harbor, **HULL, DOVER, POOLE;** town, **ETON;** river, **ALN (ALNE), CAM, DEE, EXE, NEN (NENE), URE, AVON, OUSE, TEES, TYNE, TRENT;** county, **KENT, YORK, BERKS, BUCKS, DERBY, DEVON, ESSEX, HANTS, WILTS, DORSET, SURREY, SUSSEX**

ESTONIA ..... capital, **TALLINN;** former capital, **REVAL (REVEL);** town, **PARNU, TARTU;** river, **NARVA, PARNU, KASARI**

ETHIOPIA........ capital, **ADDIS ABABA;** lake, **TANA (TSANA), ABAYA;** province, **TIGRE;** river, **OMO, AWASH;** town, **HARER, GONDER**

EUROPE ...... river, **ISAR, OISE, URAL, DANUBE;** lake, **BALATON;** peninsula, **IBERIA;** resort, **LIDO**

F

FAROE ISLANDS island, **STROMO**

FIJI .... capital, **SUVA;** island, **KORO;** island group, **LAU**

FINLAND .... capital, **HELSINKI;** city, **OULU, ESPOO (ESBO), LAHTI, TURKU;** lake, **ENARE (INARI);** port and harbor, **ABO, PORI;** islands, **ALAND, KARLO;** town, northern, **ENARE (INARI);** province, **HAME, OULU, LAPPI, VASSA**

FLANDERS .... city, **LISLE**

FLORIDA .... county, **DADE, DUVAL;** resort, **DE LAND;** city, **MIAMI, OCALA, TAMPA, ORLANDO;** cape, **SABLE**

FRANCE....... city, **AIX, AGEN, ALBI, CAEN, LYON (LYONS), METZ, NICE, OPPY, SENS, VAUX, ARLES, ARRAS, BLOIS, DINAN, LILLE, NANCY, NESLE, PARIS, REIMS, SEDAN, TOURS, TULLE, CANNES, NANTES, SEVRES;** commune, **AY, EU, AIX, AUX, DAX, PAU, AUBY, BRON, ISSY, LAON, LOOS, MERU, ORLY, VIMY;** port and harbor, **CAEN, MEZE, SETE, BREST;** resort, **PAU, NICE, CANNES;** department, **VAR, GARD, JURA, NORD, OISE, ORNE, MEUSE, VENDEE;** river, **AIN, LOT, LYS, AIRE, AUDE, CHER, EURE, LOIR, OISE, ORNE, RHIN (RHINE), SAAR, YSER, AISNE, ISERE, LOIRE** (longest), **MARNE, MEUSE, RHONE, SAONE, SARRE, SEINE, SELLE, VESLE, MOSELLE;** Mount, **BLANC;** mountains, **ALPS, JURA;** region, **ANJOU, ALSACE**

G

GABON.... capital, **LIBREVILLE;** city, **PORT-GENTIL**

GAMBIA (THE) . capital, **BANJUL**

GASCONY .... capital, **AUCH**

GEORGIA .... city, **MACON, SPARTA, AUGUSTA;** county, **BIBB, COBB, DE KALB;** river, **FLINT, OCONEE, SAVANNAH**

GERMANY ... capital E. Germany, **E. BERLIN;** capital W. Germany, **BONN;** city, **AUE, EMS, ULM, GERA, JENA, LAHR, EMDEN, ESSEN, MAINZ, NEUSS;** spa, **AIX;** canal, **KIEL;** river, **EMS, ALLE, EDER, EGER, ELBE, ISAR, MAIN, ODER, REMS, RUHR, SAAR, LIPPE, MOSEL (MOSELLE), REGEN, RHINE (RHEIN), WESER;** mountain, **HARZ;** state, **HESSE;** district, **ALSACE;** former region, **SUDETEN**

GHANA.... capital, **ACCRA;** city, **KUMASI;** lake, **VOLTA;** region, **ASHANTI;** river, **VOLTA**

GREAT BARRIER ISLAND.. **OTEA**

GREECE...... ancient city, **ELIS;** ancient colony, **IONIA;** city, **SPARTA (SPARTI);** island, **COS (KOS), IOS, NIO, MILO (MELOS), SCIO (CHIOS), CRETE, DELOS, PAROS, SAMOS, IONIAN;** mountain, **OETA, OSSA, HELICON;** river, **ARTA;** peninsula, **MOREA;** region, **DORIS;** ancient district, **ATTICA**

GREENLAND .... base, town, settlement, **ETAH**

GUAM..... city, capital, **AGANA;** port and harbor, **APRA**

GUATEMALA ... volcano, **AGUA**

GUINEA .... capital, **CONAKRY;** island, **TOMBO;** island group, **LOS;** town, **BOKE, LABE**

H

HAWAII. city, **HILO, HONOLULU;** island, **MAUI, OAHU, KAUAI, LANAI;** district, **HANA;** islet, **KURE;** volcanoes, **MAUNA KEA, MAUNA LOA**

HEBRIDES, INNER . island, **IONA, SKYE**

HOLLAND ... see NETHERLANDS

HONDURAS......... port, **TELA**

HONSHU ..... bay, **ISE;** port and harbor, **KOBE**

HUNGARY ... city, **EGER, PECS;** river, **RAAB (RABA)**

I

IDAHO .... town, **ARCO**

ILLINOIS... city, **PANA, ALEDO, CAIRO, ELGIN, PEKIN, CANTON, MOLINE, PEORIA, SPARTA**

INDIA ..... capital, **NEW DELHI;** city, **AGRA, DELHI, POONA (PUNE), SIMLA, BOMBAY, KANPUR, MADRAS;** commune, town, **DHAR, ARCOT, SORON, SATARA;** mountains, **GHATS;** region, **GOA, JIND, BERAR, GWALIOR;** river, **SIND, INDUS, GANGES;** state, **ASSAM, BIHAR, MYSORE, PUNJAB**

INDIANA..... city, **GARY, PERU, MARION**

INDOCHINA........ see BURMA, CAMBODIA, LAOS, MALAYSIA, THAILAND, and VIETNAM

INDONESIA island, **AROE (ARU), BALI, JAVA, CELEBES, TERNATE;** island group, **ARU, KAI, OBI, ALOR, LETI;** gulf, **BONE (BONI);** capital, **DJAKARTA**

IOWA ..... city, **AMES** (college); county, **IDA**

IRAN .... capital, **TEHRAN;** city, **AHVAZ, RASHT, ABADAN, KERMAN, TABRIZ, MASHHAD**

IRAQ......... capital, **BAGDAD (BAGHDAD);** port and harbor, **BASRA;** ancient city, **KISH**

IRELAND (see also NORTHERN IRELAND)..... old capital, **TARA;** capital, **DUBLIN;** county, **CORK, MAYO, CLARE;** islands, **ARAN;** lake, **REE, ERNE;** port and harbor, **COBH, TRALEE;** river, **LEE, BANN, ERNE, NORE;** town, **TARA**

ISLE OF WIGHT ... port, **COWES**

ISRAEL......... port and harbor, **ACRE, HAIFA;** plain, **SHARON (SARON);** desert, **NEGEB (NEGEV)**

ISTRIAN PENINSULA ...... town, **PULA**

ITALY .. capital, **ROMA (ROME);** city, **BARI, COMO, PISA, ROMA (ROME), MILAN, PARMA, SIENA, TRENT, NAPLES, VENICE, CASERTA;** commune, town, **BRA, ALBA, ARCO, ASTI, ATRI, DEGO, ESTE, LARI, NOLA, ORIA, SAVA, TODI, ADRIA, ASOLA, ASOLO, PADUA, TURIN, EMPOLI;** resort, **LIDO;** port and harbor, **OSTIA, TRANI;** province, **ROMA, UDINE;** river, **PO, ADDA, ARNO, NERA, RENO, PIAVE, TIBER;** lake, **COMO, ISEO, NEMI;** strait, **OTRANTO;** gulf, **SALERNO;** isle, **CAPRI;** mountain, **VISO**

IVORY COAST ...... city, capital, **ABIDJAN;** Mount, **NIMBA;** town, **MAN, DALOA**

J

JAMAICA ... capital, **KINGSTON;** town, **MAY PEN**

JAPAN capital, **TOKYO (TOKIO,** old name, **EDO);** resort city, **HONSHU;** city, **KOBE, KOFU, NARA, CHIBA, OSAKA, OTARU, TOKYO (TOKIO);** harbor, port, or seaport, **OSAKA, OTARU;** island, **SADO, HONDO (HONSHU,** largest); volcano, **ASO, FUJI;** bay, **ISE;** province, old, **ISE, YAMATO;** mountain, **FUJI;** sea, **IYO**

JAVA .. stream, **SOLO;** mountain peak, **SEMERU**

JORDAN.. capital, **AMMAN;** city, **ZARQA;** gulf, **AQABA**

K

KAI ISLANDS ...... sea, **BANDA**

KANSAS .... city, **ARMA, IOLA, SALINA;** county, **OSAGE;** river, **SALINE**

KENTUCKY ...... county, **BATH, BELL, ADAIR, BOONE, LARUE, BUTLER**

KENYA....... capital, **NAIROBI;** river, **TANA, EWASO**

KIRIBATI ..... capital, **TARAWA**

KLONDIKE........ river, **YUKON**

KOREA, NORTH. city, **WONSAN**; river, **YALU**

KOREA, SOUTH......... capital, **SEOUL (KEIJO)**; city, **PUSAN, SUWON, INCHON**

L

LAOS ..... capital, **VIENTIANE**; river, **MEKONG**; town, **PAKSE**

LATVIA...... capital, port, **RIGA**; river, **AA**

LEBANON .... port, **SIDON**

LESOTHO .... capital, **MASERU**; river, **ORANGE**; town, **HOEK**

LIBERIA ... capital, **MONROVIA**; cape, **PALMAS**; river, **MANO, CESTOS**; town, **HARPER**

LIBYA.......... port and harbor, **DERNA**; capital, **TRIPOLI**; gulf, **SIDRA**; town, **TOBRUK**

LITHUANIA .... capital, **VILNIUS**

LITTLE AMERICA..... sea, **ROSS**

LOUISIANA .. parish, **ORLEANS**; river, **RED, PEARL, SABINE**

LUZON .... province, **ABRA**; mountain, **LABO**; river, **ABRA, AGNO**

M

MAINE ...... bay, **CASCO**; town, **BATH,** (university) **ORONO**; city, river, **SACO**

MALAWI.... town, **ZOMBA**; lake, **NYASA**; river, **SHIRE**

MALAY ARCHIPELAGO.... island, **JAVA, LARAT, LUZON, BORNEO, CELEBES**

MALAYSIA.......... city, **IPOH, KANGAR, PENANG, MALACCA**; state, **KEDAH, PERAK, SABAH, JOHORE, PERLIS, SARAWAK**

MALDIVES....... capital, **MALE**

MALI.... capital, **BAMAKO**; city, **KAYES, SEGOU**

MALTA........... island, **GOZO, COMINO**

MARTINIQUE.... volcano, **PELEE**

MARYLAND... city, **BOWIE, BEL AIR**; Mount, **BACKBONE**

MASSACHUSETTS .... city, **SALEM, NEWTON**; cape, **ANN, COD**; mountain, **TOM**; town, **LENOX**

MAURITANIA ...... town, **ATAR**

MEDITERRANEAN ... island, **IOS, GOZO, RODI (RHODES), CAPRI, CRETE, MALTA**; gulf, **TUNIS**; resort, **LIDO, NICE**

MESOPOTAMIA ... river, **TIGRIS**

MEXICO .. city, **LEON, PUEBLA**; lake, **CHAPALA**; state, **COLIMA, SONORA, TABASCO**; town, **TULA, LERDO**

MICHIGAN .... city, **ALMA, CLARE, FLINT, SPARTA**; county, **LUCE, EATON**

MINDANAO .. volcano, **APO**; gulf, **DAVAO**; town, **MATI**

MINNESOTA ..... city, **DULUTH**; Mount, **EAGLE**; river, **ST. CROIX**

MISSISSIPPI ...... city, **BILOXI**; county, **SCOTT**; river, **LEAF, YAZOO**

MISSOURI .... city, **AVA, LAMAR, LIBERTY, OSCEOLA, SEDALIA**

MONGOLIA .... desert, **GOBI**

MONTANA... city, **BUTTE**; peak, **KOCH**; river, **TETON**

MOROCCO .... capital, port, harbor, **RABAT**; city, **MEKNES, TANGIER**; mountains, **ATLAS**; region, **RIF (RIFF)**; river, **TENSIFT**; town, **FES (FEZ), IFNI**

MOZAMBIQUE capital, **MAPUTO;** port and harbor, **BEIRA;** river, **SAVE (SABI), LIMPOPO, LUGENDA**

N

NEBRASKA .... capital, **LINCOLN;** city, **ORD;** river, **LOUP, PLATTE;** county, **LOUP, OTOE**

NEPAL .... mountain, **API;** river, **KOSI**

NETHERLANDS .... city, **UTRECHT;** commune or town, **EDE, EPE, BEEK, ECHT, EDAM, ELST, OLST, UDEN, GEMERT;** port and harbor, **EDAM;** river, **EEM, LEK, MAAS** (Dutch Meuse), **RIJN** (Dutch Rhine), **WAAL**

NEVADA....... city, **ELY, ELKO, RENO;** county, **NYE, ELKO, WASHOE;** lake, **TAHOE**

NEW GUINEA ..... city, port, and harbor, **LAE;** island, **PAPUA**

NEW HAMPSHIRE .. city, **KEENE, NASHUA, LACONIA;** county, **COOS;** lake, **OSSIPEE**

NEW HEBRIDES .... capital, port, harbor, **VILA;** island, **EPI (API), TANA (TANNA), EFATE**

NEW JERSEY ... city, **NEWARK, TRENTON;** river, **RARITAN;** town, **LODI;** cape, **MAY**

NEW MEXICO ...... town, **TAOS;** river, **GILA;** resort, **TAOS;** county, **LEA, LUNA, TAOS**

NEW YORK ... city, town, **ROME, TROY, OLEAN, UTICA, ELMIRA, OSWEGO;** island, **STATEN;** county, **TIOGA;** village, **ILION, MALONE**

NEWFOUNDLAND .... peninsula, **AVALON**

NEW ZEALAND.... bay, **HAWKE;** lake, **TAUPO;** peninsula, **MAHIA;** island, **OTEA**

NICARAGUA .... city, **LEON**

NIGER.. capital, **NIAMEY;** region, **AIR;** town, **MARADI, ZINDER**

NIGERIA ... capital, **LAGOS;** city, **IWO, KANO, BENIN;** river, **NIGER, BENUE;** town, **ABA, KUMO**

NORMANDY ...... town, **ST.-LO**

NORTH CAROLINA .. river, **HAW, TAR, PEE DEE, YADKIN;** cape, **FEAR;** county, **ASHE**

NORTH DAKOTA .. city, **FARGO, MINOT;** river, **KNIFE**

NORTHERN IRELAND .... capital, **BELFAST;** city, **DERRY** (Londonderry), **NEWRY, ARMAGH;** county, **DOWN, TYRONE;** river, **BANN, FOYLE, LAGAN**

NORTHUMBERLAND .... river, **TYNE**

NORWAY ... capital, **OSLO;** river, **KLAR, TANA, LAGEN;** city, **HAMAR**

O

OHIO.. county, **ROSS;** city, **ADA** (college town Ohio Northern), **KENT, LIMA, AKRON, BEREA, NILES, XENIA, CANTON, FOSTORIA;** river, **MAD, MIAMI**

OKINAWA ...... port and harbor, **NAHA (NAFA, NAWA)**

OKLAHOMA ... city, **ADA, ENID, TULSA, SHAWNEE;** county, **MAJOR, MAYES;** river, **RED**

OMAN........ capital, **MUSCAT (MASQAT);** port, **MATRAH**

OREGON .... city, **SALEM, ASTORIA;** peak, **HOOD**

ORKNEYS .... island, **HOY**

P

PACIFIC ISLANDS .. island, **YAP, GUAM, TRUK, WAKE, LEYTE, TAHITI;** island group, **FIJI, SULU, PALAU (PELEW), SAMOA**

PAHANG .... capital, **KUANTAN**

PAKISTAN....... city **LAHORE, KARACHI**; province, **SIND, PUNJAB**; river, **SWAT, INDUS, KABUL, KUNDAR**; mountain pass, **BOLAN, GUMAL, KHYBER**

PANAMA......... city, **ANCON, COLON**; lake, **GATUN**

PARAGUAY...... city, **ITA**; river, **APA**

PENNSYLVANIA...... city, **ERIE, EASTON, CHESTER, TYRONE**; port, **ERIE**

PERSIA, Ancient..... city, **SUSA, NIRIZ**

PERU .... capital, **LIMA**; city, department, river, **ICA**; cold district, **PUNO**; port and harbor, **ILO, CALLAO**; town, **LAMAS**

PHILIPPINE ISLANDS (see also LUZON and MINDANAO)........ capital, (de facto) **MANILA**; city, **IBA, CEBU, LIPA, NAGA, ILOILO**; mountain or peak, **APO, IBA, LABO**; volcano, **APO**; port and harbor, **ILOILO, BATANGAS**; province, **DAPA**; island, **CEBU, BATAN, SAMAR, PANAY, LEYTE**; island group, **SULU**

POLAND... city, **LODZ, LUBAN, POSEN, SRODA**; commune, **KOLO, KONIN**; river, **SAN, BIALA, VISLA, STRYPA, VISTULA**; province, **KRAKOW (CRAKOW)**

PORTUGAL....... cape, **ROCA**; capital, **LISBON**; city, **OPORTO**; river, **LIS (LIZ), DOURO, MINHO, TAGUS**

PUERTO RICO..... capital, **SAN JUAN**; city, **PONCE**; town, **LAJAS, LARES**; highest point, **CERRO DE PUNTA**

Q

QATAR.......... capital, **DOHA**

QUEBEC... city, **HULL, MAGOG, LAVAL, VERDUN**; county, **LEVIS**; lake, **MINTO**; peninsula, **GASPE**

R

RHODE ISLAND .. city, **BRISTOL, NEWPORT, WARWICK**

ROMANIA (RUMANIA)...... city, **ARAD, CLUJ, IASI**; county, **ALBA**; river, **OLT**

RUSSIA .... city, **KEM, KIEV, LIDA, OMSK, OREL**; port and harbor, **OREL, ODESSA**; river, **OB, OM, DON (DUNA), ILI, KEM, OKA, UFA, LENA, NEVA, ONON, SEIM, STYR, URAL, TEREK**; lake, **ONEGA**; sea, **ARAL, AZOF (AZOV)**; mountains, **ALAI, URAL, ALTAI**; peninsula, **KOLA, KRYM (CRIMEA)**; lake in European Russia, **SEG**; region, **OMSK**

RWANDA....... capital, **KIGALI**

S

SAMOA .... capital, port, and harbor, **APIA**

SAUDI ARABIA.... city, **MECCA, MEDINA**

SAVAGE ISLAND... island, **NIUE**

SCOTLAND..... port and harbor, **OBAN**; seaport, **AYR**; former county, **AYR, BUTE, FIFE**; river, **DEE, TAY** (longest), **DOON, SPEY, TYNE, AFTON**; city, **AYR**; lake, **AWE, LOCH (LOCHY), LAGGAN**; district, **KYLE, ATHOLE (ATHOLL)**; island off, **ARRAN**

SENEGAL. capital, port, **DAKAR**; cape, **VERT**

SERBIA...... former capital, **NIS (NISH)**

SEYCHELLES ..... island, **MAHE**

SIAM............ see THAILAND

SIBERIA (see also RUSSIA)...... river, **OB, YENISEI (ENISEI)**

SICILY volcano, **ETNA (AETNA)**; commune, town, **RAGUSA**; city, province, resort, **ENNA**

SIERRA LEONE.......... capital, **FREETOWN**; city, **BO**

SOCIETY ISLANDS .... island, **TAHITI**

SOMALIA .... gulf, **ADEN**

SOUTH AFRICA .. city, **DURBAN** region, **RAND**; river, **VAAL**

SOUTH AMERICA ... river, **BENI, PLATA, JAPURA (YAPURA)**; district, **CHACO**; mountains, **ANDES**

SOUTH CAROLINA .... river, **SANTEE**; island, **PARRIS**

SOUTH DAKOTA .... capital, **PIERRE**; city, **LEMMON**

SOUTH PACIFIC .... isle, **FIJI, BALI, COOK, SAMOA**

SOUTHWEST ..... river, **PECOS**

SPAIN .... city, **JACA, JAEN, LEON, AVILA**; province, **JAEN, LEON, LUGO, AVILA, MALAGA**; port and harbor, **ADRA, NOYA, VIGO, MALAGA**; river, **EBRO, MINHO, TAGUS**; old kingdom, **LEON, CASTILE**; commune, **LALIN, LORCA**

SRI LANKA .... city, **KANDY**; province, **UVA**

SUDAN .... capital, **KHARTOUM**; desert region, **NUBIA**; river, **NILE**; town, **JUBA**

SUMATRA .... city, **MEDAN**; stream, **DELI**

SWEDEN .... city, **LUND, OREBRO**; river, **DAL, UME, KLAR, LULE, LAGAN**; island off, **ALAND**; port and harbor, **LULEA, MALMO**; strait, **ORESUND**

SWITZERLAND .... city, **BALE (BASEL, BASLE), BERN (BERNE), GENF (GENEVA)**; commune, town, **BEX, BIEL, CHUR, SION, AARAU, MORAT**; canton, **URI, ZUG (ZOUG), BERN (BERNE), VAUD, BASEL (BASLE)**; river, **AAR (AARE)**; lake, **ZUG, JOUX, LUCERNE**; mountain, **TODI, MATTERHORN**; resort, **DAVOS**; capital, **BERN (BERNE)**

SYRIA ..... capital, **DAMASCUS**; city, **ALEP (ALEPPO), HAMA, HOMS**; river, **EUPHRATES**

T

TAHITI ...... capital, **PAPEETE**; peak, **OROHENA**

TAIWAN (FORMOSA) .... capital, **TAIPEI**; city, **TAI-NAN**

TALAUD ISLANDS .... town, **BEO**

TANIMBAR ISLANDS ..... island, **LARAT**

TANZANIA .... capital, **DAR ES SALAAM**; city, **TANGA, MOSHI**; lake, **NYASA, RUKWA, VICTORIA, TANGANYIKA**; island, **MAFIA, PEMBA, ZANZIBAR**; region, **MARA**; town, **TABORA**

TAPUL ISLANDS .... island, **LAPAC, LUGUS, SIASI**

TASMANIA .... capital, **HOBART**

TENNESSEE .... city, **MEMPHIS**; county, **KNOX, MAURY, SHELBY**

TEXAS .... city, **WACO, LAREDO, ABILENE**; county, **CLAY, LAMB, CARSON, LOVING**; river, **LEON**

THAILAND .. capital, **BANGKOK**; gulf, **SIAM**; river, **PING, KLONG**; town, **TAK**

TIBET ... city, **LASSA (LHASA)**; mountain pass, **DANGLA**; river, **INDUS**

TOGO .... capital, **LOME**; Mount, **AGOU**; town, **PALIME**

TRINIDAD ...... port, **LA BREA**

TUNISIA .... capital, **TUNIS**

TURKEY ...... capital, **ANKARA (ANGORA)**; city, **ADANA, IZMIR**; lake, **MANYAS**; river, **ARAS (ARAKS), KURA**; town, city, **ORDU, URFA**; island, **TENEDOS**

TUSCANY .... river, **ARNO**

U

UGANDA . . . capital, **KAMPALA;** lake, **KYOGA, ALBERT, EDWARD, GEORGE, VICTORIA;** Mount, **ELGON;** river, **NILE;** town, **LIRA, ENTEBBE**

UNITED ARAB EMIRATES . . . city, **ABU DHABI**

URUGUAY . . . . capital, **MONTEVIDEO;** city, **MELO, MINAS, SALTO, RIVERA;** river, **RIO NEGRO**

U.S.S.R. . . . . see RUSSIA

UTAH . . . . city, **LEHI, HEBER, LOGAN, OGDEN, PROVO;** county, **CACHE, DAVIS;** mountains, **UINTA;** peak, **KINGS;** river, **GREEN, SEVIER**

V

VENEZUELA . capital, **CARACAS;** town, **CORO, MERIDA;** island off coast, **ARUBA;** river, **META, APURE, ARAUCA, ORINOCO**

VERMONT . . . . city, **BARRE, RUTLAND;** creek, **OTTER;** county, **ESSEX, ORANGE, ORLEANS, WINDSOR;** mountains, **GREEN;** river, **WHITE**

VIETNAM . . . . . . capital, **HANOI;** city, **HUE, DA NANG, SAIGON** (now **HO CHI MINH CITY);** region, **ANNAM;** river, **RED (HONG), MEKONG**

VIRGINIA . . . . city, **SALEM, NORTON, BRISTOL, EMPORIA, FAIRFAX, HAMPTON, RADFORD, NORFOLK, ROANOKE;** Mount, **ROGERS;** river, **DAN, JAMES, POTOMAC, RAPIDAN, ROANOKE**

VIRGIN ISLANDS . . . . capital, **CHARLOTTE AMALIE**

W

WALES . . . . capital, **CARDIFF;** city, **RHONDDA, SWANSEA;** county, **GWENT;** lake, **BALA;** mountains, **BERWYN, SNOWDON;** river, **DEE, LUG (LUGG), USK, TAFF**

WASHINGTON . . . . city, **LACEY, TACOMA, SEATTLE, SPOKANE;** Mount, **RAINIER;** river, **SNAKE, NACHES, YAKIMA, COLUMBIA**

WESTERN AUSTRALIA . . . capital, **PERTH**

WEST INDIES . . . . isle, island, **CUBA, HAITI, NEVIS**

WEST VIRGINIA . . . . city, **ELKINS, WHEELING;** river, **OHIO, POTOMAC, BIG SANDY**

WISCONSIN . . . . city, **ALMA, RIPON, RACINE, KENOSHA, MADISON, GREEN BAY, EAU CLAIRE;** river, **BLACK;** lake, **MENDOTA**

WYOMING . . . . city, **CASPER, LARAMIE;** highest mountain peak, **GANNETT;** range, **TETON;** river, **GREEN, SNAKE, POWDER, BIGHORN**

Y

YEMEN, NORTH . . . . capital, **SAN'A (SANAA);** city, **MOCHA;** ancient ruins, **MARIB**

YEMEN, SOUTH . . capital, **ADEN**

YORKSHIRE. . . . river, **OUSE;** city, **LEEDS**

YUGOSLAVIA . . . . island, **RAB (ARBE), SOLTA;** city, **NIS (NISH);** port, **KOPER;** river, **LIM, KUPA, SAVA, DRINA, NERETVA (NARENTA);** former district and province, **BANAT**

YUKON . . . . city, **DAWSON;** district, **KLONDIKE;** peak, **KEELE;** lake, **TAGISH;** river, **PEEL, TANANA;** creek, **HESS**

Z

ZAIRE . . . . . . capital, **KINSHASA;** province, **KIVU, SHABA;** river, **UELE, CONGO, KASAI, LINDI, LULUA, UBANGI**

ZAMBIA . . . . . . capital, **LUSAKA;** waterfall, **VICTORIA;** river, **KAFUE, ZAMBEZI**

AEROSPACE

SATELLITES, CAPSULES, SPACECRAFT

NOTES: Where the country of origin is other than the U.S., that information is given. Many of these names are from a series of launches. For example, there were hundreds of Soyuz launches. The year given is that of the first launch.

3 letters
AMS 1976
ANS .... Dutch, 1974
ATS 1966
BSE .... see YURI
CAT .... International, 1979
COS .... International, 1975
CTS .... Canadian, 1976
ETS .... see KIKU
FR-1 .... French, 1965
GRS .... W. German, 1963
IMP 1973
IUE .... International, 1976
LEM 1967
LES 1965
OAO 1966
OFO 1970
OGO 1964
OSO 1962
OTS .... International, 1977
SMS 1974
TIP 1975
TTS 1967
UME .... Japanese, 1976

4 letters
ANIK .... see TELESAT
ANNA 1962
AURA .... French, 1975
AZUR .... see GRS
BIOS 1966
DASH 1963
DIAL French & W. German, 1970
DMSP 1971
ECHO 1960
EOLE .... French, 1971
ERTS 1972
ESRO .... International, 1968
ESSA 1966
EXOS .... see KYOKKO
GEOS .... International, 1976
GOES 1975
HEAO 1977
HEOS .... International, 1968
IQSY .... International, 1978
IRIS .... International, 1968
ISEE .... International, 1977
ISIS .... Canadian, 1965
ITOS 1970
KIKU .... Japanese, 1975
LUNA .... Soviet, 1959
MARS .... Soviet, 1962
NATO ...... International, 1970
NOAA 1970
NOSS 1976
NOVA 1981
SAGE 1979
SERT 1964
SRET .... French, 1972
VELA 1963
YURI .... Japanese, 1978
ZOND .... Soviet, 1964

5 letters
AEROS ...... W. German, 1972
ARIEL .... British, 1962
ASTEX 1971
AYAME .... Japanese, 1979
CAMEO 1979
DENPA .... Japanese, 1972
DODGE 1967
DRIMS .... see TELESAT
EKRAN .... Soviet, 1976
FAITH 1963
IDCSP 1966
INJUN 1961
LOFTI 1961
MAGIC ..... see INTERCOSMOS
MIDAS 1960
OSCAR 1961
PEOLE .... French, 1970
RELAY 1962
SAMOS 1961
SIGMA 1962
SIGNE .... French, 1977
SIRIO .... Italian, 1977
SOYUZ .... Soviet, 1967
TAIYO .... Japanese, 1975
TIROS 1960
TRAAC 1961
TRIAD 1972
UOSAT 1981
VENUS 1961

6 letters
APOLLO 1965
ARIANE .... International, 1979
AURORA 1962
BOREAS .... International, 1969
CASTOR .... French, 1975
COMSAT 1969
COSMOS .... Soviet, 1962
GEMINI 1964
HELIOS ...... W. German, 1974
KYOKKO ..... Japanese, 1978

LAGEOS................ 1976
MAGION......... Czech, 1978
MAGSAT 1979
NIMBUS................ 1964
OHSUMI...... Japanese, 1970
PAGEOS................ 1966
PALAPA..... Indonesian, 1976
POLLUX......... French, 1975
POLYOT......... Soviet, 1963
PROTON......... Soviet, 1965
RADOSE................ 1963
RANGER................ 1961
ROHINI........... Indian, 1980
SAKURA...... Japanese, 1977
SALYUT......... Soviet, 1971
SATCOM 1975
SCATHA................ 1979
SEASAT 1978
SKYLAB 1973
SKYNET......... British, 1969
SOLRAD................ 1976
SYNCOM 1963
TANSEI....... Japanese, 1971
VIKING 1975
VOSTOK......... Soviet, 1961
WESTAR 1974
WRESAT ..... Australian, 1967

7 letters
ASTERIX .... French, 1965
AUREOLE........ French, 1971
AURORAE .... see ESRO
BHASKAR .... Indian, 1979
COMSTAR.............. 1976
COURIER.............. 1960
DIADEME........ French, 1967
DIAPSON .... French, 1966
ESA-GEOS .. International, 1977
FREEDOM 1961
HAKUCHO.... Japanese, 1979
HAWKEYE.............. 1974
INTASAT .... Spanish, 1974
JIKIKEN ...... Japanese, 1978
LANDSAT .... see ERTS
MARINER.............. 1962
MARISAT.............. 1976
MERCURY.............. 1960
MIRANDA .... British, 1974
MOLNIYA........ Soviet, 1965
NAVSTAR 1978
ORBITER . see LUNAR ORBITER
PEGASUS.............. 1965

PIONEER 1958
PROGNOZ .... Soviet, 1972
SHINSEI ...... Japanese, 1971
SOLWIND.............. 1979
SPUTNIK .... Soviet, 1957
STAR-RAD.............. 1962
TELESAT ...... Canadian, 1972
TELSTAR.............. 1962
TRANSAT 1977
TRANSIT 1960
VOSKHOD .... Soviet, 1964

8 letters
ALOUETTE .... Canadian, 1962
COLUMBIA 1981
ELEKTRON ...... Soviet, 1964
EXPLORER 1958
GORIZONT....... Soviet, 1978
HIMAWARI ... Japanese, 1977
INTELSAT .. International, 1965
LANI BIRD. . International, 1966
METEOSAT . International, 1977
PROGRESS ...... Soviet, 1978
PROSPERO ...... British, 1971
SAN MARCO ..... Italian, 1964
SURVEYOR............. 1966
VANGUARD 1958

9 letters
ARYABHATA ..... Indian, 1975
EARLY BIRD International, 1965
FLTSATCOM........... 1978
STARLETTE ..... French, 1975
SYMPHONIE......... French & W. German, 1974
TOURNESOL..... French, 1971
TRANSTAGE............ 1964

10 letters
CANNONBALL.... see LAGEOS
CHALLENGER 1983
COPERNICUS........... 1972
DISCOVERER........... 1959
DODECAPOLE 1965
FRIENDSHIP........... 1962

11 letters
INTERCOSMOS .. Soviet, 1969
LIBERTY BELL.......... 1961

12 letters
LUNAR ORBITER 1966

ASTRONAUTS

NOTES: The first Russian Cosmonaut was Yuri Gagarin. The others are not listed because you are not apt to find their names in crosswords. This listing includes all U.S. missions up to June 1983.

Aldrin, Edwin (Buzz)	Gemini-Titan 12, 1966; Apollo-Saturn 11, 1969
Allen, Joseph	Columbia, November, 1982
Anders, William	Apollo-Saturn 8, 1968
Armstrong, Neil	Gemini-Titan 8, 1966; Apollo-Saturn 11, 1969
Bean, Alan	Apollo-Saturn 12, 1969; Skylab 3, 1973
Bobko, Karol	Challenger, April, 1983
Borman, Frank	Gemini-Titan 7, 1965; Apollo-Saturn 8, 1968
Brand, Vance	Apollo 18, 1975; Columbia, November, 1982
Carpenter, M. Scott	Mercury-Atlas 7, 1962
Carr, Gerald	Skylab 4, 1973–1974
Cernan, Eugene	Apollo-Saturn 10, 1969; Apollo-Saturn 17, 1972
Collins, Michael	Gemini-Titan 10, 1966; Apollo-Saturn 11, 1969
Conrad, Charles	Gemini-Titan 5, 1965; Gemini-Titan 11, 1966; Apollo-Saturn 12, 1969; Skylab 2, 1973
Cooper, L. Gordon	Mercury-Atlas 9, 1963; Gemini-Titan 5, 1965
Crippen, Robert	Columbia, April, 1981; Challenger, June, 1983
Cunningham, R. Walter	Apollo-Saturn 7, 1968
Duke, Charles	Apollo-Saturn 16, 1972
Eisele, Donn	Apollo-Saturn 7, 1968
Engle, Joe	Columbia, November, 1981
Evans, Ronald	Apollo-Saturn 17, 1972
Fabian, John	Challenger, June, 1983
Fullerton, C. Gordon	Columbia, March, 1982
Garriott, Owen	Skylab 3, 1973
Gibson, Edward	Skylab 4, 1973–1974
Glenn, John	Mercury-Atlas 6, 1962
Gordon, Richard	Gemini-Titan 11, 1966; Apollo-Saturn 12, 1969
Grissom, Virgil (Gus)	Mercury-Redstone 4, 1961; Gemini-Titan 3, 1965
Haise, Fred	Apollo-Saturn 13, 1970
Hartsfield, Henry	Columbia, June–July, 1982
Hauck, Frederick (Rick)	Challenger, June, 1983
Irwin, James	Apollo-Saturn 15, 1971
Kerwin, Joseph	Skylab 2, 1973
Lenoir, William	Columbia, November, 1982
Lousma, Jack	Skylab 3, 1973; Columbia, March, 1982
Lovell, James	Gemini-Titan 7, 1965; Gemini-Titan 12, 1966; Apollo-Saturn 8, 1968; Apollo-Saturn 13, 1970
Mattingly, Thomas	Apollo-Saturn 16, 1972; Columbia, June–July, 1982
McDivitt, James	Gemini-Titan 4, 1965; Apollo-Saturn 9, 1969
Mitchell, Edgar	Apollo-Saturn 14, 1971

Musgrave, Story .... Challenger, April, 1983
Overmeyer, Robert .... Columbia, November, 1982
Peterson, Donald .... Challenger, April, 1983
Pogue, William .... Skylab 4, 1973–1974
Ride, Sally .... Challenger, June, 1983
Roosa, Stuart .... Apollo-Saturn 14, 1971
Schirra, Walter .... Mercury-Atlas 8, 1962; Gemini-Titan 6-A, 1965; Apollo-Saturn 7, 1968
Schmitt, Harrison .... Apollo-Saturn 17, 1972
Schweickart, Russell .... Apollo-Saturn 9, 1969
Scott, David .... Gemini-Titan 8, 1966; Apollo-Saturn 9, 1969; Apollo-Saturn 15, 1971
Shepard, Alan .... Mercury-Redstone 3, 1961; Apollo-Saturn 14, 1971
Slayton, Donald (Deke) .... Apollo 18, 1975
Stafford, Thomas .... Gemini-Titan 6-A, 1965; Apollo-Saturn 10, 1969; Apollo 18, 1975
Swigart, John .... Apollo-Saturn 13, 1970
Thagard, Norman .... Challenger, June, 1983
Truly, Richard .... Columbia, November, 1981
Weitz, Paul .... Skylab 2, 1973; Challenger, April, 1983
White, Edward .... Gemini-Titan 4, 1965
Worden, Alfred .... Apollo-Saturn 15, 1971
Young, John .... Gemini-Titan 3, 1965; Gemini-Titan 10, 1966; Apollo-Saturn 10, 1969; Apollo-Saturn 16, 1972; Columbia, April, 1981

ROCKETS, LAUNCH VEHICLES

4 letters
ABLE
ARGO
HAWK
JUNO
NIKE
TAID
THOR

5 letters
AGENA
ARCAS
ARCON
ARIES
ATLAS
CAJUN
DELTA
JASON
SCOUT
TITAN

6 letters
APACHE
BIG JOE
SATURN
THORAD

7 letters
AEROBEE
CENTAUR
JAVELIN
SHOTPUT
TERRIER

8 letters
ABLESTAR
ASTROBEE
BLUE SCOUT
MALEMUTE
REDSTONE
TOMAHAWK
VANGUARD

9 letters
LITTLE JOE

10 letters
BLACKBRANT
JOURNEYMAN

COMPUTER TERMINOLOGY

Note regarding computer languages: All computers actually work in machine language, which uses binary code. This is the "lowest" level of the languages. People don't think in binary codes, so "higher" level languages (symbolic languages), which are easier to understand, have been devised. The easier a language is to understand, the higher the level; hence the further it is from the computer's actual language.

3 letters

ADA........ High-level language
APL........ High-level language
BCD..... Binary Coded Decimal
BIT........ Binary digit (1 or 0)
BOX......... Flow-chart symbol
BUG Error, defect, or malfunction
BUS . Conductor for transmitting signals
CAD.... Computer Aided Design
CAI Computer Assisted Instruction
CAL Computer Assisted Learning
CAM........ Computer Assisted Manufacturing
CAT Computer Assisted Training
COM Computer Output Microfilm
CPS.... Characters Per Second
CPU.... Central Processing Unit
CRT......... Cathode Ray Tube
DMA.... Direct Memory Access
DOS.... Disk Operating System
EDP . Electronic Data Processing
HEX..... (hexadecimal notation) Number system using 16 as a base
HIT... The finding of a matching record
JCL...... Job Control Language
JOB Unit of work for the computer
LOG.......... Record events in chronological sequence
LPM.......... Lines Per Minute
MAC... Multi-Access Computing
MPU....... MicroProcessor Unit
PCM..... Pulse Code Modulation
PL-1........ High-level language
RAM... Random-Access Memory
ROM........ Read-Only Memory
RUN Begin execution of a program
ZAP........... Erase; wipe out

4 letters

ANSI........ American National Standards Institute
BAND Group of recording tracks on a magnetic disk or drum
BAUD Measurement unit of speed of data transmission
BEAD... Small unit of a program
BLIP.. Erratic signal on a screen
BOOT....... Protective housing
BYTE... Group of bits, usually 8 bits in length
CARD............ Circuit board
CHIP...... Tiny piece of silicon embedded with many electronic circuits
CODE.... Representation of data or instructions in symbolic form
COPY.... Reproduce data from one storage device onto another
DATA.. Information of any type; computer "food"; computer input
DISK . Magnetic storage medium
DOWN......... Not in operation
DRUM . Magnetic storage device
DUMP . Clear memory and store data elsewhere
ECOM.... Electronic Computer-Oriented Mail
EDIT........... Prepare data for subsequent processing
FIFO.......... First In, First Out
FILE.... Organized collection of related data
FLOW... Sequence of events in the solution of a problem
GATE......... Electronic switch
GIGO.. Garbage In, Garbage Out
HEAD...... Device used to read, record, or erase data on a magnetic storage medium
HOME... Starting position for a cursor on a screen (top left-hand corner, usually)
KILO....... Prefix denoting one thousand
LIFO.......... Last In, First Out
LISP........ High-level language
LOAD. Transfer information from a storage device into the computer
LOGO...... High-level language, primarily for children
LOOP...... Closed sequence of instructions performed repeatedly

MEGA Prefix denoting one million
MENU .. List of program options
MODE ..... Method of operation
NODE ..... One component in a network
PACK Compress data in order to save space in storage
PASS. Single execution of a loop
PEEK BASIC language command that displays the value of a specific memory location
POKE BASIC language command that puts a one-byte value into a given memory location
PORT...... Computer outlet for plugging in a peripheral
PROM Programmable Read-Only Memory
READ. Retrieve information from memory
SCAN...... Read; examine each part in sequence
SORT Put data in order according to the desired rule
TAPE Magnetic medium for data storage
TASK..... Single unit of work in multiprocessing
TEXT..... Information part of a message
USER.. Computer network client
WORD..... Group of characters representing a unit of data

5 letters
ALGOL ..... High-level language
ARRAY. Orderly arrangement of data in a list
ASCII....... Standard code that assigns values to numbers and letters; code which enables different computers to communicate
BASIC...... High-level language
BATCH.. Group of similar transactions collected for processing as a single unit
BLANK...... Character used to represent a space
BLOCK Group of records treated as a single unit of data
BOARD........ Sheet on which integrated circuits are mounted
BREAK............... Interrupt
CHART, FLOW... Diagrammatic representation of a data-processing problem
COBOL..... High-level language
CORAL..... High-level language
COUNT.. Total number of times an instruction is performed
CRASH... Hardware or software malfunction causing system breakdown
DEBUG.... Locate and eliminate errors
DRIVE. Device which causes the movement of a recording medium
ENTRY.... Item of data in a list
EPROM.... Electrically Programmable Read-Only Memory
FAULT.. Failure of any part of a system
FIELD Part of a record containing a specific unit of information
FORTH..... High-level language
FRAME Image in a display system
HERTZ....... Unit of frequency
INPUT Data that goes into a computer or its peripherals
LOG-ON . Sign onto a system or network
MERGE Combine two or more sets of records into a single file
MICRO............. Very small
MODEM... Device which allows computers to communicate over telephone lines
NEXUS Point in a system where interconnections occur
NOISE......... Spurious signals
OCTAL Number system using 8 as a base
PILOT. High-level language used in classrooms
PIXEL Division of a display screen
QUEUE Waiting list of programs to be run
RADIX Base of a number system
RERUN... Repeat the execution of a program
SLAVE.. Unit which is under the control of a larger unit
SPACE Empty unit of data storage
STACK........ Area of memory reserved for storage of data; LIFO area
STORE....... Memory medium
TABLE.. Set of data arranged as an array
TRACK.......... Channel on a magnetic medium
WRITE........ Record data on a storage medium

6 letters
ACCESS.... Retrieve data from a storage device or a peripheral

ANALOG Method of measurement that uses physical variables
ASSIGN Reserve part of a system for a specific purpose
BABBLE Cross-talk from several interfacing channels
BINARY . Notation system using only 1's and 0's to represent data
BUFFER .... Temporary storage space for data
CATENA.... Series of items in a chained list
CURSOR... Movable spot on the screen showing where the pointer is
DECADE.... Group of ten items
DUPLEX.. Communications line that allows simultaneous 2-way transmission
ENABLE.... Restore to ordinary operating conditions
ENCODE..... Represent data in digital form
FORMAT Specified arrangement of data; prepare (a diskette) for use
GLITCH.... Unwanted electronic pulse that causes errors
JITTER........ Signal instability
MASTER..... Unit that controls smaller (slave) units
MATRIX... Type of printer that forms letters by printing a pattern of dots
MEMORY The part of a computer that stores information
NIBBLE Four bit word; half a byte
ON-LINE. Under the control of a central processor
OUTPUT Information coming out of the computer; the end product of a program
PASCAL.... High-level language
PROMPT ..... Message from an operating system calling for action from the operator
RECORD. Set of information that contains all data about one item
SCREEN Surface of a CRT that is visible to the operator
SCROLL Move the contents of a screen up or down, one line at a time
SEARCH.... Look for a specific piece of data
SECTOR...... Defined area of a track or band
SERIAL Pertaining to transmission of data one bit at a time
SNOBOL.... High-level language
STRING..... Set of consecutive characters
SUBSET.. Group of items which belongs to a larger group
SYNTAX. Grammatical rules that specify how an instruction can be written
THREAD. Group of beads which form a complete program

7 letters
ADDRESS.... Particular number associated with each memory location
CIRCUIT.... Closed-loop electric current path
COMMAND..... Instruction to a computer
COMPILE... Translate symbolic language into machine language
COUNTER...... Device used to accumulate totals and maintain a count
DECODER. Device used to alter data from one coded format to another
DIGITAL Describing a method of measurement using precise quantities to represent variables
DISABLE... Inhibit or remove a hardware or software feature
DISPLAY. Output on the screen
EXECUTE....... Run a program
FLUTTER...... Recurring speed variation
FORTRAN.. High-level language
GARBAGE........ Meaningless, unwanted data
MEGABIT...... One million bits
MONITOR. High-resolution CRT
NESTING Writing a program that has loops within loops
NETWORK..... System of interconnecting components
OFF-LINE. Not under the control of a central processor
PLOTTER.... Special printer for graphics
PROGRAM... Set of instructions given a computer so it may perform a task
RAW DATA.. Information which has not been processed
READOUT Display of processed information on a screen
ROUTINE... Set of instructions; part of a program

SCANNER Device which samples the status of a file
SEGMENT . Division of a routine
STORAGE .. Place where data is held in the computer or its peripherals

8 letters
ALPHABET ...... Character set
ANNOTATE Add explanatory text to program instructions
ASSEMBLY .... Middle-level language
COMPILER . Program that translates symbolic language into machine language
COMPUTER .. Electronic device capable of accepting data, solving problems, and supplying results
CONSTANT. Item of data which does not vary in value
DATA BASE . Set of information available to the computer
DISCRETE ... Pertaining to data organized in distinct parts
DISKETTE .... Floppy disk
FUNCTION ...... The operation specified in an instruction
GRAPHICS. All non-alphanumeric displays generated by a computer
HARD COPY ... Output on paper
HARDWARE . The physical parts of a computer system
MEGABYTE... One million bytes
OPERATOR...... Person who is working the computer
PARALLEL.. Type of data transmission where all parts of an 8-bit word are sent simultaneously
REGISTER .. Specific location in memory
RESIDENT .... Any program permanently stored in the computer
RETRIEVE ... Search for, select, and extract data contained in a file
ROBOTICS..... Area of artificial intelligence pertaining to industrial use of robots
SIMULATE.. Represent physical problems by mathematical formulas
SOFTWARE... All programs that instruct the computer how to operate
TERMINAL ..... Peripheral of a computer system
VARIABLE. Symbol representing a quantity whose value can change

9 letters
ALGORITHM...... Step-by-step procedure for giving instructions to a computer
ASSEMBLER Code that converts symbolic language into machine language
CHARACTER ..... Single letter, number, symbol, or space
CONNECTOR Flow-chart symbol
DECREMENT Decrease a variable by a specified amount
HANDSHAKE . Acknowledgment between two computers of ability to communicate
INCREMENT Increase a variable by a specified amount
INTERFACE... Linkage between systems, programs, or between a person and a system
INTERRUPT Temporary break in the running of a program
MAIN FRAME....... Very large computer
PARAMETER Quantity which may be given variable values

10 letters
NANOSECOND.... Billionth of a second
PERIPHERAL ...... Any item of hardware that connects to a computer (printer, monitor, drive, etc.)
PHILOXENIC... Friendly to uninformed users; user-friendly
REPERTOIRE Set of instructions a given computer can execute

11 letters
CYBERNETICS The study of the theory of control systems

12 letters
ALPHANUMERIC . Pertaining to characters that represent numbers, letters, and/or symbols
INTELLIGENCE ..... Processing capability

13 letters
CONFIGURATION..... Specific makeup of the physical units of a computer system

MUSIC

MUSICAL TERMS

3 letters
AIR . . . . Tune or melody
BAR . . . . Vertical line dividing the staff
CON . . . . With
GAI . . . . Lively, brisk
PIU . . . . More

4 letters
ALLA . . . . In the style of
BEAT . . . . . Division of a measure
CHEF (D'ORCHESTRA) Conductor
CLEF . . . . Character on the staff
CODA . . . . Passage ending a movement
ECCO . . . . Echo
FINE . . . . End
FINO . . . . As far as; up to
FLAT . . . . Character on the staff
GLEE . . . English composition for 3 or more voices
HOLD . . . . Sign indicating prolongation of a note
IDYL . . . . . Romantic or pastoral composition
LENO . . . . Faint; quiet
LIED . . . . German song
LOCO . . . . Place
MANO . . . . Hand
POCO . . . . Little
POLO . . . . . . Syncopated Spanish dance
REEL . . . . Lively dance
REST Pause between two tones; character on the staff
SANS . . . . Without
SINO . . . . As far as; up to
TEMA . . . . Theme
VAMP . . . . Improvise an accompaniment
VIVO . . . . Lively; briskly
VOCE . . . . Voice

5 letters
A DEUX . . . . For two hands
ANCOR . . . . Again; also; yet
BALLO . . . . Dance
BATON . . . . . . Conductor's wand
BOCCA . . . . Mouth
CANTO . . . . Melody or chant
CHANT . . . . . . Short sacred song
CHORD . . . . . A harmony of 2 or more tones
CLOSE . . . . Cadenza ending a section or piece
DESTO . . . . Sprightly
DIRGE . . . . Funeral hymn
DOLCE . . . . Sweet; soft
ELEGY . . Melancholy composition
FLING . . . . Scottish dance
FOLIA . . . . Spanish dance
GALOP . . . . Lively French dance
JALEO . . . . Spanish dance
LARGO . . . . Slow and stately
LENTO . . Slow, but not dragging
MESTO . . . . Sad; melancholy
METER, METRE . . . Symmetrical grouping of musical rhythms
MEZZO . . . . Half
MINIM . . . . Half-note
MOLTO . . . . Very; much
PAUSA . . . . Rest; pause
PAVAN . . Stately Italian-Spanish dance
PEZZO . . . . Piece
PIANO . . . . Soft; softly
PIECE . . . . . Musical composition
PITCH . . . . . Position of a tone in the musical scale
POLKA . . . . Bohemian dance
SAMBA . . . . Brazilian dance
SCALE . . . . Series of tones which form any major or minor key
SEGNO . . . . A sign
SENZA . . . . Without
SHARP . . Character on the staff
SOAVE . . . . . . Suavely; flowingly
TANGO . . . . Argentine dance
TANTO . . . . . As much; so much
TARDO . . . . Slow; lingering
TEMPO . . . . Rate of speed
VALSE . . . . Waltz

6 letters
ADAGIO Slow; a slow movement
ANTHEM . . . . . . Piece of sacred vocal music
A TEMPO . . . . . At the preceding rate of speed
BOLERO . . . . Spanish dance
CHIARO . . . . Clear; pure
COMODO . . . . Leisurely
CON IRA . . . . Wrathfully
DA CAPO . . . From the beginning
DECISO . . . . With decision
DI GALA . . . . Gaily; merrily
EQUALE . . . Equal; even; smooth
FACILE . . . . Easy; fluent
FEBILE . . . . Feeble; weak
FEROCE . . . . Wildly
FINALE . . . . Last movement
FLORID . . Embellished with runs, passages, etc.
GIUSTO . . . . Proper

INFINO .... As far as; up to
INTIMO....... Heartfelt; fervent
JARABE........ Mexican dance
LEGATO... Slurred; played with no break between notes
LITANY.... Song of supplication
MINUET.... Early French dance form
PAVANA Stately Italian-Spanish dance
REDOWA..... Bohemian dance
SEMPRE.... Always; throughout
VELOCE................ Rapid
VIVACE....... Lively; animated

7 letters
AGILITA.............. Vivacity
AGILITE.............. Vivacity
AGITATO............. Agitated
ALLEGRO....... Lively or rapid
ALLONGE........... Prolonged
AMABILE.... Sweet and tender
ANDANDO.... Easy and flowing
ANDANTE... Moderately slowly
ANIMATO......... Vivaciously
ANIMOSO............. Spirited
BAROCCO......... Eccentric or whimsical
CADENCE............ Rhythm
CADENZA.... Elaborate ending passage
CALMATO............. Calmly
CAMPANA................ Bell
CANTATA..... Vocal work with instrumental accompaniment
CANTATO........... Singingly
CANZONE........ Folk song or part-song in madrigal style
CHANSON............... Song
CLAVIER............ Keyboard
COMPASS.... Range of a voice or instrument
CON BRIO........... Spiritedly
CON MOTO.. With an energetic movement
DECIBEL... Unit of loudness or intensity of sound
DI COLTA... Suddenly; at once
DI MOLTO..... Very; extremely
DOLENTE................. Sad
FERMATA.... A hold, pause, or interruption
FERVOSO... In an agitated style
GAVOTTE... Old French dance
GENTILE....... Gracefully; in a refined style
HANACCA..... Moravian dance
HAUTBOY.............. Oboe
INTRADA.... Short introduction or prelude
LEGGERO........... Light; airy
MAESTRO... Master; conductor
MARCATO.... With distinctness and emphasis
MAZURKA........ Polish dance
PARLATO............. Spoken
PASSAGE.... Portion or section of a composition
PENSOSO.. Pensive; thoughtful
PIETOSO.... Pitifully; movingly
PLACIDO....... Smooth; placid
REPLICA... A repeat or reprise
ROBUSTO.... Firmly and boldly
SCHERZO.. Vivacious movement in a symphony
SENTITO...... With expression
SERIOSO In a grave, impressive style

8 letters
A BALLATA.... In singing style
AFFABILE........ Sweetly and gracefully
BEL CANTO The art of beautiful song
BERCEUSE............ Lullaby
CALMANDO..... Growing calm
CANTICLE....... Sacred chant
CAVATINA.......... Short aria
CHACONNE.... Spanish dance
CON AMORE......... Lovingly
CON FURIA.... Furiously; wildly
CON GARBO........ Gracefully; elegantly
CON GIOCO.......... Playfully
CON GIOIA........... Joyously
CON TINTO...... With shading; expressively
CON UMORE...... With humor
DAL SEGNO..... From the sign
DELICATO... In a delicate style
DIAPASON............ Octave
DISCRETO...... Comparatively subdued
DOLCIATO....... Softer; calmer
ELEGANTE......... Gracefully
ENFATICO...... With emphasis
FANDANGO.... Lively Spanish dance
FANTASIA........... Free-form composition
FERVENTE.. Ardently; fervently
HABANERA............ Cuban contradance
LARGANDO... Growing broader
LENTANDO.... Growing slower
LIBRETTO.... The words of an opera, oratorio, etc.
MACHUCHA... Dance similar to the bolero
MADRIGAL.. Vocal setting of a short lyric poem

MODULATE..... Pass from one key or mode into another
NOCTURNE.. Dreamily romantic composition
RHAPSODY....... Instrumental fantasia on folk songs
RIGADOON Lively French dance
RIGOROSO .... In strict time
RISOLUTO... In a decided style
SARABAND.... Stately dance of Spanish or Oriental origin
SEMPLICE.... In a natural style
SERENADE...... Love song for the evening
SOGGETTO..... Subject; theme
VIGOROSO .... Vigorously

9 letters
A CAPPELLA .... Without instrumental accompaniment
ACOUSTICS Science of musical tones
AFTER NOTE...... Unaccented note of a pair
ALL' OTTAVA An octave higher
ANTIPHONY Responsive singing
BAGATELLE.. Short, fairly easy piece of music
BARCAROLE ... Venetian boat-song
BELLICOSO... In a warlike style
BERGAMASK.. Clownish dance
CANTABILE .. In a singing style
CAPRICCIO.......... Free-form instrumental piece
CHROMATIC.. Relating to tones foreign to a given key
CON AFFETO...... With feeling
CON CALORE..... Passionately
CON DOLORE.... Expressive of pain or grief
CON FRETTA........ Hurriedly
CON MAESTA ..... Majestically
CON RABBIA ...... With frenzy
CON RIPOSO ...... Calmly; in a tranquil manner
CON VIGORE .... Vigorously
FARANDOLA ..... Circle dance
GLISSANDO .... With a flowing, sliding move
IMPROMPTU ... Composition of extemporaneous form
MALAGUENA..... Spanish folk music
PIZZICATO ... Plucked with the fingers, as strings
POCO A POCO.... Little by little
POLONAISE ...... Polish dance

10 letters
ACCELERATO... Livelier; faster
ACCIDENTAL... Chromatic sign not in the key-signature
ALLA MARCIA.. In march style
ALLARGANDO. Growing slower
ALLEGRETTO...... Quite lively
BERGERETTE.... Pastoral song
CAMPANELLO....... Small bell
CLAVICHORD..... Precursor of the pianoforte
CON ANIMATO..... With spirit
CON AUDACIA .. With boldness
CON DELIRIO....... Deliriously
CON FERVORE ...... Ardently; fervently
CON GRAVITA Slowly; seriously
IMPRESARIO ... Manager of an opera or concert company
LARGAMENTE......... Broadly
LENTAMENTE.......... Slowly
NACHTMUSIK....... Serenade
RITARDANDO . Growing slower and slower
SEGUIDILLA.... Spanish dance
SEMIQUAVER 16th-note
TARANTELLA .... Italian dance

SOME NOTED COMPOSERS

3 letters
ABT .... Franz
BAX .... Arnold
CUI.......... Cesar

4 letters
ADAM ..... Adolphe
ARNE...... Thomas
BACH....... Johann Sebastian
BACH.......... Karl
BERG........ Alban
BULL .... John
BYRD....... William
CAGE......... John
FOSS .... Lukas
GADE......... Niels
IVES........ Charles
KERN....... Jerome
LALO ...... Edouard
PERI........ Jacopo
RAFF ...... Joachim
RIES...... Ferdinand
TOCH......... Ernst
WOLF......... Hugo

5 letters
AUBER ..... Daniel-Francois-Esprit
BALFE...... Michael
BIZET...... Georges
BLOCH ...... Ernest
BOITO .... Arrigo
BRUCH .... Max

CESTI. . Marc'Antonio
D'INDY ..... Vincent
DUFAY ... Guillaume
DUKAS .... Paul
ELGAR...... Edward
FALLA... Manuel de
FAURE...... Gabriel-Urbain
FOOTE....... Arthur
FRIML .... Rudolf
GLUCK ... Christoph
GRIEG ...... Edvard
HAYDN .... Franz Joseph
HOLST...... Gustav
IBERT ..... Jacques
ISAAK ..... Heinrich
LEHAR........ Franz
LISZT......... Franz
LOEWE .... Carl
LULLY Jean-Baptiste
MOORE.... Douglas
NEVIN .... Ethelbert
PAINE John Knowles
RAVEL..... Maurice
REGER......... Max
SATIE .... Erik
SOUSA .. John Philip
STILL. William Grant
SUPPE.... Franz von
VERDI .... Giuseppe
WEBER .. Carl Maria von
WEILL .... Kurt
WIDOR Charles-Marie

6 letters
BARBER.... Samuel
BARTOK....... Bela
BERLIN...... Irving
BOULEZ ..... Pierre
BRAHMS.. Johannes
CADMAN ... Charles
CARTER..... Elliott
CHAVEZ..... Carlos
CHOPIN ... Frederic
COWELL..... Henry
DELIUS ... Frederick
DUPARC...... Henri
DVORAK.... Antonin
ENESCO ... Georges
FLOTOW... Friedrich von
FOSTER ... Stephen
FRANCK..... Cesar
GLIERE .... Reinhold
GLINKA..... Mikhail
GOUNOD ... Charles
GRETRY ..... Andre
HALEVY ... Jacques
HANDEL.... George Frederick
HANSON.... Howard
HARRIS........ Roy
HILLER ... Ferdinand
JOPLIN .... Scott
KODALY..... Zoltan
KRENEK...... Ernst
KUHLAU... Friedrich
LASSUS . Roland de
LIADOV...... Anatol
MAHLER.... Gustav
MORLEY... Thomas
MOZART.. Wolfgang Amadeus
PIERNE Henri Gabriel
PISTON...... Walter
PLEYEL....... Ignaz
PORTER ...... Cole, Quincy
RAMEAU ..... Jean-Philippe
ROGERS..... James
SCHUTZ ... Heinrich
STRAUS ..... Oskar
TAYLOR.... Deems
THOMAS.. Ambroise
VECCHI...... Orazio
VITALI..... Giovanni
WAGNER ... Richard
WALTON ... William
WEBERN..... Anton

7 letters
ALBENIZ...... Isaac
ALLEGRI... Gregorio
ARENSKY ... Anton
BABBITT .... Milton
BELLINI... Vincenzo
BERLIOZ.... Hector
BORODIN Alexander
BRITTEN . Benjamin
CACCINI..... Giulio
CAVALLI. Francesco
COPLAND ... Aaron
CORELLI. Arcangelo
CRESTON...... Paul
DEBUSSY... Claude
DELIBES....... Leo
DES PREZ .. Josquin
DOWLAND.... John
GIBBONS .. Orlando
GRIFFES.... Charles
HASSLER..... Hans
HERBERT.... Victor
JANACEK..... Leos
LE JEUNE... Claude
MARTINU. Bohuslav
MENOTTI Gian Carlo
MILHAUD.... Darius
NICOLAI....... Otto
OBRECHT.... Jakob
OKEGHEM Johannes
POULENC... Francis
PUCCINI... Giacomo
PURCELL.... Henry
RIEGGER Wallingford
RODGERS... Richard
ROMBERG. Sigmund
ROSSINI Gioacchino
SCHUMAN.. William
SINDING.. Christian
SMETANA .. Bedrich
STRAUSS... Johann
STRAUSS... Richard
THOMSON.... Virgil
VIVALDI .... Antonio
WEELKES.. Thomas
YOUMANS.. Vincent

8 letters
ARCADELT .. Jacob
BRUCKNER.. Anton
CHAUSSON.. Ernest
CLEMENTI... Muzio
COUPERIN. Francois
DIABELLI .... Anton
GABRIELI... Andrea, Giovanni
GERSHWIN . George
GIORDANO Umberto
GOLDMARK.... Karl
GRANADOS. Enrique
HONEGGER.. Arthur
JOMMELLI.. Niccolo
LOEFFLER.. Charles
LORTZING... Albert
MACHAUT......... Guillaume de
MASCAGNI .. Pietro
MASSENET ... Jules
MESSIAEN... Oliver
PAGANINI ... Nicola
PALMGREN.. Selim
PICCINNI .... Nicola
PIZZETTI Ildebrando
RESPIGHI.. Ottorino
SCHUBERT ... Franz
SCHUMANN Robert
SCRIABIN Alexander
SESSIONS ... Roger
SIBELIUS ..... Jean
SPONTINI.. Gasparo
SULLIVAN ... Arthur
TELEMANN.. Georg Philipp
THOMPSON. Randall
VICTORIA... Tomas Luis de

SPORTS

KENTUCKY DERBY WINNERS

YEAR	HORSE	JOCKEY
1908	Stone Street	Pickens
1909	Wintergreen	Powers
1910	Donau	Herbert
1911	Meridian	Archibald
1912	Worth	Shilling
1913	Donerail	Goose
1914	Old Rosebud	McCabe
1915	Regret	Notter
1916	George Smith	Loftus
1917	Omar Khayyam	Borel
1918	Exterminator	Knapp
1919	Sir Barton	Loftus
1920	Paul Jones	Rice
1921	Behave Yourself	Thompson
1922	Morvich	Johnson
1923	Zev	Sande
1924	Black Gold	Mooney
1925	Flying Ebony	Sande
1926	Bubbling Over	Johnson
1927	Whiskery	McAtee
1928	Reigh Count	Lang
1929	Clyde Van Dusen	McAtee
1930	Gallant Fox	Sande
1931	Twenty Grand	Kurtsinger
1932	Burgoo King	James
1933	Brokers Tip	Meade
1934	Cavalcade	Garner
1935	Omaha	Saunders
1936	Bold Venture	Hanford
1937	War Admiral	Kurtsinger
1938	Lawrin	Arcaro
1939	Johnstown	Stout
1940	Gallahadion	Bierman
1941	Whirlaway	Arcaro
1942	Shut Out	Wright
1943	Count Fleet	Longden
1944	Pensive	McCreary
1945	Hoop, Jr.	Arcaro
1946	Assault	Mehrtens
1947	Jet Pilot	Guerin
1948	Citation	Arcaro
1949	Ponder	Brooks
1950	Middleground	Boland
1951	Count Turf	McCreary
1952	Hill Gail	Arcaro
1953	Dark Star	Moreno
1954	Determine	York
1955	Swaps	Shoemaker
1956	Needles	Erb
1957	Iron Liege	Hartack
1958	Tim Tam	Valenzuela
1959	Tomy Lee	Shoemaker
1960	Venetian Way	Hartack
1961	Carry Back	Sellers
1962	Decidedly	Hartack
1963	Chateaugay	Baeza
1964	Northern Dancer	Hartack
1965	Lucky Debonair	Shoemaker
1966	Kauai King	Brumfield
1967	Proud Clarion	Ussery
1968	Dancer's Image (or Forward Pass)	Ussery
1969	Majestic Prince	Hartack
1970	Dust Commander	Manganello
1971	Canonero II	Avila
1972	Riva Ridge	Turcotte
1973	Secretariat	Turcotte
1974	Cannonade	Cordero
1975	Foolish Pleasure	Vasquez
1976	Bold Forbes	Cordero
1977	Seattle Slew	Cruguet
1978	Affirmed	Cauthen
1979	Spectacular Bid	Franklin
1980	Genuine Risk	Vasquez
1981	Pleasant Colony	Velasquez
1982	Gato del Sol	Delahoussaye
1983	Sunny's Halo	Delahoussaye

TRIPLE CROWN WINNERS

YEAR	HORSE	JOCKEY
1919	Sir Barton	Loftus
1930	Gallant Fox	Sande
1935	Omaha	Saunders
1937	War Admiral	Kurtsinger
1941	Whirlaway	Arcaro
1943	Count Fleet	Longden
1946	Assault	Mehrtens
1948	Citation	Arcaro
1973	Secretariat	Turcotte
1977	Seattle Slew	Cruguet
1978	Affirmed	Cauthen

SOME NAMES FROM THE BASEBALL HALL OF FAME

Aaron, Hank
Alexander, Grover Cleveland
Anson, Cap
Appling, Luke
Baker, Home Run
Banks, Ernie
Bell, Cool Papa
Bender, Chief
Berra, Yogi
Boudreau, Lou
Brown, Mordecai
Campanella, Roy
Carey, Max
Chance, Frank
Chandler, Happy
Clarke, Fred
Clemente, Roberto
Cobb, Ty
Cochrane, Mickey
Combs, Earl
Conlan, Jocko
Connor, Roger
Cronin, Joe
Cummings, Candy
Cuyler, Kiki
Dean, Dizzy
Delahanty, Ed
Dickey, Bill
DiMaggio, Joe
Duffy, Hugh
Evers, John
Ewing, Buck
Faber, Urban
Feller, Bob
Flick, Elmer H.
Ford, Whitey
Foxx, Jimmy
Frick, Ford
Frisch, Frank
Gehrig, Lou
Giles, Warren
Gomez, Lefty
Goslin, Goose
Greenberg, Hank
Grove, Lefty
Hafey, Chick
Harridge, Will
Harris, Bucky
Hartnett, Gabby
Hooper, Harry
Hornsby, Rogers
Hoyt, Waite
Hubbard, Cal
Hubbell, Carl
Huggins, Miller
Irvin, Monte
Jackson, Travis
Johnson, Byron
Joss, Addie
Kaline, Al
Keefe, Timothy
Keeler, William
Kell, George
Kelley, Joe
Kelly, George
Kelly, King
Kiner, Ralph
Klein, Chuck
Klem, Bill
Koufax, Sandy
Lajoie, Napoleon
Landis, Kenesaw Mountain
Lemon, Bob
Lloyd, Pop
Lopez, Al
Mack, Connie
Mantle, Mickey
Manush, Henry
Marichal, Juan
Maranville, Rabbit
Marquard, Rube
Mays, Willie
McGinnity, Joe
McGraw, John
Medwick, Joe
Mize, Johnny
Musial, Stan
Nichols, Kid
Ott, Mel
Paige, Satchel
Plank, Ed
Rice, Sam
Rickey, Branch
Rixey, Eppa
Roberts, Robin
Robinson, Brooks
Robinson, Frank
Robinson, Jackie
Robinson, Wilbert
Roush, Edd
Ruffing, Red
Rusie, Amos
Ruth, Babe
Sisler, George
Snider, Duke
Spahn, Warren
Speaker, Tris
Stengel, Casey
Terry, Bill
Tinker, Joe
Traynor, Pie
Vance, Dazzy
Waddell, Rube
Wagner, Honus
Walsh, Ed
Waner, Lloyd
Waner, Paul
Ward, John
Weiss, George
Welch, Mickey
Wheat, Zach
Williams, Ted
Wilson, Hack
Wynn, Early
Yawkey, Tom
Young, Cy
Youngs, Ross

SOME NAMES FROM THE PRO FOOTBALL HALL OF FAME

Adderley, Herb
Alworth, Lance
Atkins, Doug
Badgro, Morris (Red)
Battles, Cliff
Baugh, Sammy
Bednarik, Chuck
Bell, Bert
Bell, Bobby
Berry, Raymond
Blanda, George
Brown, Jim
Brown, Paul E.
Brown, Roosevelt
Butkus, Dick
Canadeo, Tony
Carr, Joe
Chamberlin, Guy
Christiansen, Jack
Clark, Earl (Dutch)
Connor, George
Conzelman, Jimmy
Davis, Willie
Donovan, Art
Driscoll, John (Paddy)
Dudley, Bill
Edwards, Albert (Turk)
Ewbank, Weeb
Fears, Tom
Flaherty, Ray
Ford, Leonard (Len)
Fortmann, Daniel J.
George, Bill
Gifford, Frank
Gillman, Sid
Graham, Otto
Grange, Harold (Red)
Gregg, Forrest
Groza, Lou
Guyon, Joe
Halas, George
Healey, Ed
Hein, Mel
Henry, Wilbur (Pete)
Herber, Arnie
Hewitt, Bill
Hinkle, Clarke
Hirsch, Elroy (Crazy-legs)
Hubbard, Robert (Cal)
Huff, Sam
Hunt, Lamar
Hutson, Don
Jones, David (Deacon)
Jurgensen, Sonny
Kinard, Frank (Bruiser)
Lambeau, Earl (Curly)
Lane, Richard (Night Train)
Lary, Yale
Lavelli, Dante
Layne, Bobby
Leemans, Alphonse (Tuffy)
Lilly, Bob
Lombardi, Vince
Luckman, Sid
Lyman, William Roy (Link)
Marchetti, Gino
Matson, Ollie
McAfee, George
McElhenny, Hugh
McNally, John (Blood)
Michalski, August (Mike)
Millner, Wayne
Mitchell, Bobby
Mix, Ron
Moore, Leonard (Lenny)
Motley, Marion
Musso, George
Nagurski, Bronko
Neale, Earle (Greasy)
Nevers, Ernie
Nitschke, Ray
Nomellini, Leo
Olsen, Merlin
Otto, Jim
Owen, Steven
Parker, Jim
Perry, Fletcher (Joe)
Pihos, Pete
Ringo, Jim
Robustelli, Andy
Sayers, Gale
Schmidt, Joe
Starr, Bart
Stautner, Ernie
Strong, Ken
Taylor, Jim
Thorpe, Jim
Tittle, Y.A.
Trafton, George
Trippi, Charley
Tunnell, Emlen
Turner, Clyde (Bulldog)
Unitas, Johnny
Van Brocklin, Norm
Van Buren, Steve
Warfield, Paul
Waterfield, Bob
Willis, Bill
Wilson, Larry

SOME NAMES FROM THE BASKETBALL HALL OF FAME

Barlow, Thomas
Baylor, Elgin
Borgmann, Bennie
Bradley, Bill
Brennan, Joseph
Chamberlain, Wilt
Cooper, Charles (Tarzan)
Cousy, Robert
Davies, Robert
DeBernardi, Forrest
DeBusschere, Dave
Endacott, Paul
Foster, Harold (Bud)
Friedman, Max
Gale, Lauren (Laddie)
Gola, Thomas
Greer, Hal
Hagan, Clifford
Hanson, Victor
Holman, Nat
Krause, Edward
Kurland, Robert
Lapchick, Joe
Lucas, Jerry Ray
Luisetti, Angelo
McCracken, Branch
McCracken, Jack
Macauley, Edward
Martin, Slater
Mikan, George
Murphy, Charles
Pettit, Robert
Phillip, Andy
Pollard, James
Ramsey, Frank
Reed, Willis
Robertson, Oscar
Russell, John (Honey)
Russell, William
Schayes, Adolph
Schmidt, Ernest
Sedran, Barney
Sharman, William
Thompson, John
Twyman, Jack
Vandivier, Robert (Fuzzy)
West, Jerry Alan
Wooden, John

SOME AWARD-WINNING ICE HOCKEY PLAYERS

Beliveau, Jean
Bossy, Mike
Bourque, Ray
Bucyk, John
Clarke, Bobby
Cloutier, Real
Corlyle, Randy
Cournoyer, Yvan
Crozier, Roger
Devecchio, Alex
Dionne, Marcel
Dryden, Dave
Dryden, Ken
Esposito, Phil
Esposito, Tony
Ftorek, Robbie
Gainey, Bob
Giacomin, Ed
Goring, Butch
Goyette, Phil
Grant, Danny
Gretzky, Wayne
Hall, Glenn
Hawerchuk, Dale
Hodge, Charlie
Howe, Gordie
Howell, Harry
Hull, Bobby
Kasper, Steve
Kehoe, Rick
Keon, Dave
Lacroix, Andre
Lafleur, Guy
Laperriere, Jacques
Leach, Reg
Middleton, Rick
Mikita, Stan
Orr, Bobby
Parent, Bernie
Perreault, Gil
Pilote, Pierre
Plett, Willi
Potvin, Denis
Ratelle, Jean
Robinson, Larry
Sanderson, Derek
Savard, Serge
Selby, Brit
Smith, Billy
Stastny, Peter
Tardif, Marc
Trottier, Bryan
Vail, Eric
Vickers, Steve
Walton, Mike
Wharram, Ken
Wilson, Doug

ACRONYMS, INITIALS, ABBREVIATIONS

Acronyms (words or abbreviations formed by using key letters of the phrases they stand for) are seldom defined by those exact words. Hence, this special listing is arranged in sections to help you find the word you are looking for. For example, you may be given the definition "International pact" and you know it is a 4-letter word. Go to the INTERNATIONAL section and look at the 4-letter words (words are grouped by section, then word size, then alphabetically). Your answer will probably be NATO. You might also be given the definition "The 'A' in G.A.R."; you can then look for GAR in all the sections (it's in the MILITARY section) and find that A stands for ARMY. In each case, the letters from the acronym or initial-word have been capitalized, so you will know what the letters stand for. NOTE: Some of these organizations, acts, etc., no longer exist, but they have been included because they continue to appear in crossword puzzles.

Abbreviations Used in This Section

Admin.. Administration
Amer........ American
Assoc..... Association
Conf...... Conference
Corp...... Corporation
Dept...... Department
Fed........... Federal
Govt..... Government
Inc....... Incorporated
Inst.......... Institute
Internat'l.. International
Nat'l......... National
Org...... Organization

GOVERNMENTAL, POLITICAL

3 letters

AAA Agricultural Adjustment Act
AAA.... Agricultural Adjustment Admin.
AEC Atomic Energy Commission (now Nuclear Regulatory Commission)
ARA Area Redevelopment Admin.
BIA..... Bureau of Indian Affairs
BLM............ Bureau of Land Management
BLS.. Bureau of Labor Statistics
CAB.... Civil Aeronautics Board
CCA... Circuit Court of Appeals
CCC Civilian Conservation Corps
CIA. Central Intelligence Agency
CRC... Civil Rights Commission
CSA Community Services Admin.
CSA..... Confederate States of America
CSC.. Civil Service Commission
CWA....... Civil Works Admin.
DEA.. Drug Enforcement Admin.
DOE........... Dept. of Energy
EDA.... Economic Development Admin.
EOP..... Economic Opportunity Program
EPA... Environmental Protection Agency
ERA... Emergency Relief Admin.
ESA.... Employment Standards Admin.
FAA....... Fed. Aviation Admin.
FAC...... Fed. Advisory Council
FBI. Fed. Bureau of Investigation
FCC...... Fed. Communications Commission
FDA..... Food and Drug Admin.
FEC.. Fed. Election Commission
FET........... Fed. Excise Tax
FHA....... Fed. Housing Admin.
FRB........ Fed. Reserve Board
FRS...... Fed. Reserve System
FTC.... Fed. Trade Commission
GAO. General Accounting Office
GPO....... Gov't Printing Office
GSA... General Services Admin.
HRA... Health Resources Admin.
HUD........ Housing and Urban Development
IRS.... Internal Revenue Service
NBS.. Nat'l Bureau of Standards
NFS....... Nat'l Forest Service
NRA..... Nat'l Recovery Admin.
NRC........ Nuclear Regulatory Commission
NSA...... Nat'l Security Agency
NSC...... Nat'l Security Council
OEO........ Office of Economic Opportunity
OPA..... Office of Price Admin.
OSS......... Office of Strategic Services
PHA..... Public Housing Admin.
REA. Rural Electrification Admin.
RFC.... Reconstruction Finance Corp.

SBA ..... Small Business Admin.
SSA ..... Social Security Admin.
SSS... Selective Service System
TVA . Tennessee Valley Authority
WPA...... Works Project Admin.

4 letters
ADAP . Airport Development Aid Program
ADEA....... Age Discrimination Employment Act
AFDC...... Aid to Families with Dependent Children
ALRB......... Agriculture Labor Relations Board
BATF........ Bureau of Alcohol, Tobacco, and Firearms
BEOG.......... Basic Education Opportunity Grant
CETA.......... Comprehensive Employment and Training Act
CHAP . Child Health Assessment Program
CWPS .... Council on Wage and Price Stability
ECOA.. Equal Credit Opportunity Act
EEOC........ Equal Employment Opportunity Commission
FCRA.. Fair Credit Reporting Act
FDIC..... Fed. Deposit Insurance Corp.
FECA.......... Fed. Employees Compensation Act
FEPA Fair Employment Practices Act
FERA.... Fed. Emergency Relief Admin.
FERC... Fed. Energy Regulatory Commission
FHLA...... Farmers Home Loan Admin.
FICA............ Fed. Insurance Contributions Act
FLRB..... Farm Labor Relations Board
FNMA..... Fed. Nat'l Mortgage Assoc. (Fannie Mae)
FUTA.. Fed. Unemployment Tax Act
GNMA.... Gov't Nat'l Mortgage Assoc. (Ginnie Mae)
HHFA....... Housing and Home Finance Agency
HOAP........ Home Ownership Assistance Program
LMSA...... Labor-Management Services Admin.
MDTA . Manpower Development and Training Act
MGIC....... Mortgage Guaranty Insurance Corp. (Maggie Mae)
NASA..... Nat'l Aeronautics and Space Admin.
NDSL...... Nat'l Direct Student Loan
NEPA....... Nat'l Environmental Policy Act
NLRA.. Nat'l Labor Relations Act
NLRB...... Nat'l Labor Relations Board
NOAA....... Nat'l Oceanic and Atmospheric Admin.
NTSB...... Nat'l Transportation Safety Board
OSHA.... Occupation Safety and Health Admin.
SEOG... Supplemental Education Opportunity Grant
USBM.... U.S. Bureau of Mines
USCC......... U.S. Circuit Court
USDA.. U.S. Dept. of Agriculture
USDC.. U.S. Dept. of Commerce
USDE...... U.S. Dept. of Energy
USDI.. U.S. Dept. of the Interior
USDJ...... U.S. Dept. of Justice
USDL....... U.S. Dept. of Labor
USDT............. U.S. Dept. of Transportation
USIA.. U.S. Information Agency
USIS... U.S. Information Service

5 letters
FSLIC ... Fed. Savings and Loan Insurance Corp.
MORGA..... Municipal ORG. Act
NCPAC...... Nat'l Conservative Political Action Committee
NIOSH............ Nat'l Inst. for Occupational Safety and Health
VISTA . Volunteers In Service To America

6 letters
ADAMHA . Alcohol, Drug Abuse, and Mental Health Agency

MILITARY

3 letters
AAB............ Army Air Base
AAM........... Air-to-Air Missile
ABM........ AntiBallistic Missile
ADC..... Air Defense Command
AEF . Amer. Expeditionary Force
AGM....... Air-to-Ground Missile
AMM........ AntiMissile Missile
APO.......... Army Post Office
ARM.......... AntiRadar Missile
BAR.. Browning Automatic Rifle
CEO.... Chief Executive Officer
CIC........ Commander-In-Chief
CNO.. Chief of Naval Operations
DFC . Distinguished Flying Cross

DFM. Distinguished Flying Medal
DSC Distinguished Service Cross
DSM Distinguished Service Medal
DSO Distinguished Service Order
ETO .... European Theater of Operations
FPO .... Fleet Post Office
GAR Grand Army of the Republic
LCT .... Landing Craft Tank
LST.......... Landing Ship Tank
MAP Military Assistance Program
MIA .... Missing In Action
NCO. Non-Commissioned Officer
OCS ... Officer Candidate School
PFC .... Private First Class
RAF .... Royal Air Force
SAC .... Strategic Air Command
SAM...... Surface-to-Air Missile
SUM..... Surface-to-Underwater Missile
UAM .. Underwater-to-Air Missile
USN .... U.S. Navy
VAD .... Vice Admiral
WAC ..... Women's Army Corps
WAF.... Women in the Air Force

4 letters
AANS...... Advanced Automatic Navigation System
ADCC ..... Air Defense Control Center
ADIZ . Air Defense Identification Zone
AEAF... Allied Expeditionary Air Force
AWAC... Airborne Warning And Control
AWOL ... Absent WithOut Leave
ICBM.. InterContinental Ballistic Missile
ICCM.... InterContinental Cruise Missile
IRBM .... Intermediate Range Ballistic Missile
MASH .... Mobile Army Surgical Hospital
MATS .... Military Air Transport Service
RAAF. Royal Australian Air Force
RCAF. Royal Canadian Air Force
ROTC. Reserve Officers Training Corps
SLAM . Supersonic Low Altitude Missile
SLAR..... Side-Looking Airborne Radar
SLBM...... Submarine-Launched Ballistic Missile
STOL Short TakeOff and Landing
TCBM TransContinental Ballistic Missile

USAR....... U.S. Army Reserve
USMA ... U.S. Military Academy
USMC .... U.S. Marine Corps
USMM.... U.S. Merchant Marine
USNA...... U.S. Naval Academy
USNR....... U.S. Naval Reserve
WAAC. Women's Auxiliary Army Corps
WAAF ... Women's Auxiliary Air Force

5 letters
AICBM .... AntiInterContinental Ballistic Missile
CONAD CONtinental Air Defense
MIDAS... MIssile Defense Alarm System
NAVAR...... NAVigation radAR
NORAD....... NORth Amer. air Defense command
SHAPE . Supreme Headquarters, Allied Powers, Europe
USACE ..... U.S. Army Corps of Engineers
WAVES... Women Appointed for Volunteer Emergency Service (Naval Reserve)

6 letters
ACLANT....... Allied Command atLANTic
NAVAIR .... NAVal AIR
NAVCAD . NAVal aviation CADet

7 letters
CINCPAC. Commander-IN-Chief, PACific

INTERNATIONAL

3 letters
AID........ Agency for Internat'l Development
CMN .. Common Market Nations
EEC .... European Economic Community
FAO ...... Food and Agricultural Org. (U.N.)
IDA...... Internat'l Development Assoc.
ILA ... Internat'l Longshoreman's Assoc.
ILO .... Internat'l Labour Org.
ILU .... Internat'l Laborers Union
IOC......... Internat'l Olympics Committee
IRO...... Internat'l Refugee Org.
ITO........ Internat'l Trade Org.
MFN...... Most Favored Nation
OAS...... Org. of Amer. States
PAU.......... Pan Amer. Union

UAE ...... United Arab Emirates
UAR ...... United Arab Republic
WEU ..... Western Europe Union
WHO .... World Health Org.

4 letters
CARE .... Cooperative for Amer. Relief Everywhere
EFTA ..... European Free Trade Assoc.
METO .. Middle East Treaty Org.
NATO North Atlantic Treaty Org.
OPEC .... Org. of Petroleum Exporting Countries
SALT . Strategic Arms Limitation Treaty

5 letters
ASEAN ... Assoc. for SouthEast Asia Nations
ASPAC ...... ASian and PAcific Council
CENTO .... CENtral Treaty Org.
LAFTA ...... Latin America Free Trade Assoc.
ODECA .... *Organizacion De Estados CentroAmericanos* (Org. of Central Amer. States)
SEATO .. SouthEast Asia Treaty Org.
START .... STrategic Arms Reduction Talks
SWAPO ...... South West Africa People's Org.
UNRRA ... United Nations Relief and Rehabilitation Admin.
UNRWA .. United Nations Relief and Works Agency

6 letters
UNESCO .... United Nations Educational, Scientific and Cultural Org.
UNICEF .... United Nations Internat'l Children's Emergency Fund

7 letters
BENELUX BElgium, NEtherlands, LUXembourg

8 letters
INTERPOL .. INTERnat'l criminal POLice org.

ASSOCIATIONS

3 letters
AAA ... Amateur Athletic Assoc.
AAO .... Amer. Assoc. of Orthodontists
AAP . Assoc. of Amer. Publishers
AAU Assoc. of Amer. Universities
ABA .... Amer. Bar Assoc.
AEA ...... Actors' Equity Assoc.
AFM .... Amer. Federation of Musicians
AFT .... Amer. Federation of Teachers
AMA ..... Amer. Medical Assoc.
APA ... Amer. Psychiatric Assoc.
APA Amer. Psychological Assoc.
NEA ..... Nat'l Education Assoc.
SAG .... Screen Actors Guild

4 letters
AAMC . Amer. Assoc. of Medical Colleges
AAPS ... Amer. Assoc. of Plastic Surgeons
AARP ... Amer. Assoc. of Retired Persons
AAUP .... Amer. Assoc. of University Professors
AAUW .... Amer. Assoc. of University Women
ABLA ...... Amer. Business Law Assoc.
AGVA ... Amer. Guild of Variety Artists
ALPA ..... Air Line Pilots Assoc.
ASTA ... Amer. Society of Travel Agents
ATLA ...... Amer. Trial Lawyers Assoc.
SACM ...... Society of Authors and Composers of Music

5 letters
AFTRA .... Amer. Federation of Television and Radio Artists
ASCAP .... Amer. Society of Composers, Authors, and Publishers
PATCO . Professional Air Traffic Controllers Org.

SPORTS

3 letters
AAA ... Amateur Athletic Assoc.
AAU .... Amateur Athletic Union
ABA ... Amer. Basketball Assoc.
ABC ... Amer. Bowling Congress
AFC .... Amer. Football Conf.
AFL ..... Amer. Football League
ASL ...... Amer. Soccer League
ERA .... Earned Run Average
MVP ...... Most Valuable Player
NBA ..... Nat'l Basketball Assoc.
NFC .... Nat'l Football Conf.
NFL ...... Nat'l Football League
NHL .... Nat'l Hockey League

NIT Nat'l Invitational Tournament (basketball)
PBA Professional Bowlers Assoc.
PGA Professional Golfers' Assoc.
RBI .... Runs Batted In
WBA ...... World Boxing Assoc.

4 letters
LPGA .... Ladies Professional Golfers Assoc.
NCAA .. Nat'l Collegiate Athletic Assoc.
WPGA ... Women's Professional Golfers' Assoc.

MISCELLANEOUS

3 letters
AAA .. Amer. Automobile Assoc.
ABS .... Amer. Bible Society
ACA .... Arts Council of America
ACT ..... Amer. College Testing
ADA. Americans for Democratic Action
ADF . Automatic Direction Finder
ADL .... Anti-Defamation League
AHA .... Amer. Heart Assoc.
AKA .... Also Known As
AKC .... Amer. Kennel Club
ALP .... Amer. Labor Party
APB .... All Points Bulletin
ARC .... Amer. Red Cross
BBB .... Better Business Bureau
BBC . British Broadcasting Corp.
BMR ...... Basal Metabolic Rate
BTU .... British Thermal Unit
CAP .... Civil Air Patrol
CDC . Center for Disease Control
CEA .... Council of Economic Advisers
CED ... Committee for Economic Development
CID. Criminal Investigation Dept. (Scotland Yard)
CNS ... Central Nervous System
COD .... Cash On Delivery
CPI ...... Consumer Price Index
DAR .... Daughters of the Amer. Revolution
DAV ... Disabled Amer. Veterans
DBA .... Doing Business As
DNA ..... DeoxyriboNucleic Acid
EAB ..... Ethics Advisory Board
EBS ..... Emergency Broadcast System
EEG ..... ElectroEncephaloGram
EKG .... ElectroCardioGram
EMS Emergency Medical Service
EOE Equal Opportunity Employer
ERA .. Equal Rights Amendment
ESP ... ExtraSensory Perception
ETA .. Estimated Time of Arrival
ETV ..... Educational TeleVision
FAF .... Financial Aid Form
FCA .... Farm Credit Assoc.
FFA . Future Farmers of America
FOB .... Free On Board
FTA Future Teachers of America
GIM .... Gross Income Multiplier
GNI .... Gross Nat'l Income
GNP .... Gross Nat'l Product
GOP .... Grand Old Party (Republican)
ICU .... Intensive Care Unit
IFO ..... Identified Flying Object
IFR ..... Instrument Flight Rules
IRA .... Individual Retirement Account
JDL ..... Jewish Defense League
KGB . *Komitet Gosudarstvennoye Bezopastnosti* (Russian Security Police)
LCD Least Common Denominator
LCD ...... Liquid Crystal Display
LED .... Light Emitting Diode
MDR Minimum Daily Requirement
NAM .... Nat'l Assoc. of Manufacturers
NET Nat'l Educational Television
NHA. Nat'l Homebuilders Assoc.
NOW ..... Nat'l Org. for Women
NRA .... Nat'l Rifle Assoc.
OOB .... Off-Off Broadway
PAL ..... Police Athletic League
PBS Public Broadcasting Service
PLO ... Palestine Liberation Org.
POC .... Port Of Call
POE .... Port Of Entry
PSE .... Pacific Stock Exchange
PTA ... Parent-Teacher's Assoc.
RCA .... Radio Corp. of America
RDF ..... Radio Direction Finder
REM ...... Rapid Eye Movement
RFD .... Rural Free Delivery
RNA .... RiboNucleic Acid
ROI ...... Return On Investment
SAT ... Scholastic Aptitude Test
SEC .... Securities Exchange Commission
SIG ...... Special Interest Group
SOP .... Standard Operating Procedure
SRO .... Standing Room Only
SST ...... SuperSonic Transport
TLC .... Tender Loving Care
TWU .. Transport Workers Union
UFO .. Unidentified Flying Object
UFW ..... United Farm Workers
UHF ...... Ultra High Frequency
UPI ... United Press International
USO .... United Service Org.
UWA ... United Way of America
VAT .... Value-Added Tax
VCR ... Video Cassette Recorder

VFR .... Visual Flight Rules
VFW.. Veterans of Foreign Wars
VHF ...... Very High Frequency
WPI ..... Wholesale Price Index
ZIP ..... Zone Improvement Plan (post office)
ZPG .... Zero Population Growth

4 letters
AAAL... Amer. Academy of Arts and Letters
ACLU...... Amer. Civil Liberties Union
ALMA .... Adoptees Liberty Movement Assoc.
AMEX ... AMer. stock EXchange
ANRC ... Amer. Nat'l Red Cross
ANSI Amer. Nat'l Standards Inst.
ANTA . Amer. Nat'l Theatre and Academy
ASAP...... As Soon As Possible
BMOC ..... Big Man On Campus
BPOE.......... Benevolent and Protective Order of Elks
CATV...... Community Antenna TeleVision
CCTV.. Closed-Circuit TeleVision
CEEB......... College Entrance Examination Board
CLEP. College Level Examination Program
COLA. Cost Of Living Agreement
CORE....... Congress Of Racial Equality
CWSP ...... College Work-Study Program
FIFO.......... First In, First Out
GASP... Group Against Smoking Pollution
HOLC. Home Owners Loan Corp.
IOOF ..... Independent Order of Odd Fellows
KMPS ... KiloMeters Per Second
LEEP .... Law Enforcement Education Program
LIFO.......... Last In, First Out
LOOM ... Loyal Order Of Moose
MDAR ..... Minimum Daily Adult Requirement
MPAA . Motion Picture Assoc. of America
NCOA ... Nat'l Council On Aging
NIFO .... Next In, First Out
NYSE New York Stock Exchange
OCTV... Open-Circuit TeleVision
PSAT.... Preliminary Scholastic Aptitude Test
RADA .... Royal Academy of Dramatic Arts
RCMP . Royal Canadian Mounted Police
SASE.. Self-Addressed Stamped Envelope
SBLI......... Savings Bank Life Insurance
SCAN.. Senior Citizen Anticrime Network
SNCC....... Student Nonviolent Coordinating Committee
SPCA........... Society for the Prevention of Cruelty to Animals
SPCC........... Society for the Prevention of Cruelty to Children
SWAT .... Special Weapons And Tactics force
TASS. *Telegraphnoye Agentstvo Sovyetskovo Soyuza* (Soviet News Agency)
USOC.. U.S. Olympic Committee
USSR.. Union of Soviet Socialist Republics
WATS .... Wide Area Telephone Service
WCTU ...... Woman's Christian Temperance Union

5 letters
AMPAS..... Academy of Motion Picture Arts and Sciences
ASPCA ... Amer. Society for the Prevention of Cruelty to Animals
ATVAS .. Academy of TeleVision Arts and Sciences
ENDEX .... ENvironmental Data indEX
ILGWU........ Internat'l Ladies' Garment Workers' Union
LASER.... Light Amplification by Stimulated Emission of Radiation
LORAN . LOng-RAnge Navigation
MOPED... MOtor-assisted PEDal cycle
NAACP..... Nat'l Assoc. for the Advancement of Colored People
RADAR.... RAdio Detection And Ranging
SCORE .... Service Corps Of Retired Executives
SCUBA .... Self-Contained Underwater Breathing Apparatus
SONAR...... SOund NAvigation Ranging

6 letters
AFL-CIO ... Amer. Federation of Labor—Congress of Industrial Organizations
AMVETS....... AMer. VETeranS
ENCONA .... ENvironmental Coalition Of North America

THE WORD-FINDER
with cross-references

FOR THE SOLVER

You can complete any unfinished 2-, 3-, or 4-letter word in the crossword you are working by using this WORD-FINDER. Even though you are at first unable to locate it in the Definition section for some reason, if you have just two letters of your wanted word (just one if it's a 2-letter word) you can find it here.

The WORD-FINDER words are listed according to the following Letter-Combination system:

XX - -	(for cases when the first two letters are known)
- XX -	(when the second and third letters are known)
- - XX	(when the last two letters are known)
X - - X	(when the first and last letters are known)

Let us say that you need to complete a word that is four letters long.

STEP ONE: Find the Letter-Combination that is the same as the letters which you have written into the crossword puzzle. Have you, for example, found "ON" as the end of a 4-letter word? Then turn to the "- - ON" Letter-Combination. Of course, since the WORD-FINDER is thorough-going, a number of words, all containing the same letter combination, are listed under this Letter-Combination.

- - ON Acon, agon, Amon, anon, Avon, axon, azon, bion, boon, cion, coon, Dion, doon, ebon, Enon, Eton, faon, Gaon, hoon, icon, iron, Leon, lion, loon, moon, neon, etc.

STEP TWO: You may know, after looking through the words listed under your Letter-Combination, the word which is the only correct possibility. If not, you now begin to eliminate words in the list by working with the words in the crossword puzzle which CROSS your unfinished word. You do this by experimentally inserting words from the Letter-Combination list. When the experimental insert produces such impossible-looking combinations with the crossing word as "bv," "pv" etc. it can be discarded.

STEP THREE: After eliminating the words which make highly unlikely or "impossible" combinations with the crossing words, you still may not be sure how to complete your unfinished puzzle. Here you make use of the invaluable CROSS-REFERENCE listings following the words in the WORD-FINDER. Each number following a word is the number of the page of the Definitions Section on which the word and one of its definitions will be found. The alphabetical letters a, b, c, d indicate in exactly which section of the definition page you will be able to locate the word with its meaning.

Example: **adat** (90b,95d)

On page 90 of this Dictionary, in section b of the page, you will find the word ADAT in bold face type. The definition is "law, D. E. Ind". On page 95, section d, you will find another cross-reference to ADAT. The definition reads "Malay law."

STEP FOUR: Now re-examine the definition in your puzzle. Eliminate words in the WORD-FINDER by comparing definitions until you arrive at the "logical candidate" word for which you have been looking. Definitions in this dictionary and those in your puzzle will not always agree in exact wording. In that case, let the general meaning of the definitions be your guide. Everyday words are not always cross-referenced in this WORD-FINDER, nor are some words of exceptional terminology. Only some of the words listed in the Special Section are cross-referenced. If your definition calls for a word likely to be found in the Special Section, it is recommended that you look there first.

TWO-LETTER WORDS

A - **Aa** (47a), **aa** (90b), **Ab** (48d,75b,102a), **ab** (63d), **AC** (39d), **ad** (90a,112d,167d), **ae** (42b,43c,d,122b,139a), **Ae** (82c,115d), **ah** (52c), **ai** (143c,148c), **al** (8c,80c,102c,104b), **am** (166c,175c), **an** (11b, 13b), **Ao** (13d,88b,c,116c), **AP** (107a,182d), **ap** (122d,166c), **ar** (88b,91c,98a,99b,110c), **as** (51b,67b,92b,126a,133a,b,180d), **at** (25c,32c,106a,123a,128a), **au** (63a,69c), **aw** (44a), **ax** (40c,139a, 167a), **ay** (7c,8b,9b,28d,55a,60a)

- A **Aa** (47a), **aa** (90b), **BA** (42a), **Ba** (150d,153c), **ba** (139a), **da** (9b,37a, 56a,133d,135d), **DA** (124d), **ea** (43c), **EA** (15b,68a), **fa** (108b,138a, 161a), **Ga** (69c), **ha** (52c), **ia** (43d,158c), **ja** (66d), **ka** (45c), **Ka** (68c, 77b,150d,153c,173c), **la** (13b,61a,83a,108b,138a,151d,161a), **ma**, **MA** (42a), **Ma** (69a,b,85d), **na** (140c,163d), **NA** (36c), **oa** (43c,d), **pa** (60b,106d), **ra** (108b), **Ra** (159b), **SA** (36c), **ta** (112d,139a,160b), **VA** (83a), **va** (105a), **wa** (188), **Wa** (24c,d,88c), **ya**, **za** (162a)

B - **BA** (42a), **ba** (139a,150d,153c), **bb** (147b), **be**, **bi** (122d,171c), **bo** (23d,24c,136a,168a), **bu** (190), **by** (18b,32c,106a)

- B **ab** (63d,) **Ab** (48d,75b,102a), **bb** (147b), **FB** (59c), **HB** (59c), **ob** (122b), **QB** (59c)

C - **ce** (62d,164c), **CE** (42a)

- C **DC** (39d), **ec** (122c)

D - **da** (9b,37a,56a,133d,135d), **DA** (124d), **DC** (39d), **DD** (42a), **de** (63d,89b,122b,122c,124a,152c,d), **di** (68c,89b,108b,122b,122c, 122d,171d), **dm** (131c), **do** (108b,138a,161a)

- D **ad**, (90a,112d,167d), **DD** (42a), **ed** (175c), **Ed** (18d), **id** (26d, 40c,51c,57a,b,d), **od** (8d,59d,79c), **td** (32a)

E - **ea** (43c), **EA** (15b,68a), **ec** (122c), **ed** (175c), **Ed** (18d), **ee** (139c), **EE** (42a), **ef** (91c), **eg** (59d,163d), **eh** (52c), **el** (13b,42a,47a,99b, 151d,168a), **El** (68a,108a), **em** (91c,98a,123d,172a,c), **en** (15b, 29c,50a,91c,98a,119d,123d,158c,d,172a), **eo** (34a), **er** (35b,76c, 137d,155a,158c,d,160b,175c), **Er** (18d,68c,85c,163d,166c,172c, 178a), **es** (49b,50a,66c,119d,158c,d,175c), **et** (10b,61a,b,89a,158c), **ex** (60b,91c,122c)

- E **ae** (42b,43c,d,122b,139a), **Ae** (82c,115d), **be**, **CE** (42a), **Ce** (62d), **ce** (164c), **de** (63d,89b,122b,c,124a,152c,d), **ee** (139c), **EE** (42a), **Ge** (47d,69a), **he** (91c), **ie** (74c,158c,163d), **LE** (59c), **le** (13b,61a, 108b), **me** (108b,124b), **Me.** (124d), **ne** (35b,106b), **oe** (43c,54d, 82d,180d,182a,b), **pe** (91c), **Pe.** (124d), **re** (6b,10b,35d,108b,122b, 129b,138a,161a), **RE** (59c), **se** (35b,108b), **te** (43a,62d,108b,131c, 152d,160b,185d), **Ve** (63c,109c), **we** (48c,124b), **We** (92b), **ye** (124b)

F - **fa** (108b,138a,161a), **FB** (59c), **ff** (147b), **Fi** (108b), **Fo** (23d), **fu** (42c,84c), **Fu** (30b)

- F **ef** (91c), **ff** (147b), **if** (35d,125a), **LF** (16d), **of** (6b), **RF** 16d)

G - **Ga** (69c), **Ge** (47d,69a), **Gi** (91d), **go** (64c,90d)

- G **eg** (59d,163d), **Og** (16d,18c)

H - **ha** (52c), **HB** (59c), **he** (91c), **hi** (52c), **ho** (39b,79a), **Ho** (87c), **Hu** (101c,108a,162b)

- H **ah** (52c), **eh** (52c), **oh** (52c), **Rh** (20c), **sh** (17b,43c,79c,126d), **th** (43c)

I - **ia** (43d,158c), **id** (26d,40c,51c,57a,b,d), **ie** (74c,158c,163d), **if** (35d, 125a), **il** (122c), **im** (122c), **in** (9d,123a), **io** (74b,74c,103c,115b), **Io** (25a,85d,95c,186b), **ir** (9d,122c), **Ir** (10a,28a,82b), **is** (51a,166c, 175c), **Is** (15b,23c,86c), **it** (124b)

- I **ai** (143c,148c), **bi** (122d,171c), **di** (68c,89b,108b,122b,c,d,171d), **fi** (108b), **Gi** (91d), **hi** (52c), **li** (30a,b,37b,98a,108b,161b), **mi** (43b, 108b,138a,161a), **pi** (71b,85d,91c,165a,172a), **ri** (84c,96d,98a, 108b), **RI** (106c), **si** (108b,152d,185d), **ti** (92b,108b,113a,b,120d, 138a,161a,162c,169b), **xi** (91c)

J - **ja** (66d), **jo** (140c,160c), **Jo** (8c,94b), **ju** (121a)

K - **ka** (45c), **Ka** (68c,77b,150d,153c,173c), **ko** (22c,87c,121a)

- K **OK** (155a)

L - **la** (13b,61a,83a,108b,138a,151d,161a), **le** (13b,61a,108b), **LE** (59c), **Lf** (16d), **li** (30a,b,37b,98a,108b,161b), **Lt** (143c), **LT** (59c), **lu** (65a), **lo** (17d,93d)

- L **al** (8c,80c,102c,104b), **Al** (96b), **el** (13b,42a,47a,99b,151d,168a), **El** (68a,108a), **il** (122c), **ol** (29c,158b,d,160b)

M - **ma, Ma** (69a,b,85d), **MA** (42a), **me** (108b,124b), **Me.** (124d), **mi** (43b,108b,138a,161a), **mo** (21d,81c,101c), **Mo** (88c,177c), **mu** (10a, 30a,60c,71a,91c), **my** (52c,124c)

- M **am** (166c,175c), **em** (91c,98a,123d,172a,c), **dm** (131c), **im** (122c), **om** (49a,77a,77b,105c,136a), **um** (52c,76c)

N - **na** (140c,163d), **NA** (36c), **ne** (35b,106b), **no** (42b,106b), **No** (84b), **nu** (71b,91c), **Nu** (29a,49a)

- N **an** (11b,13b), **en** (15b,29c,50a,91c,98a,119d,123d,158c,d,172a), **in** (9d,123a), **on** (8b,9a,60c106a,123a), **un** (34c,122c)

O - **oa** (43c,d), **ob** (122b), **od** (8d,59d,79c), **oe** (43c,54d,82d,180d, 182a,b), **of** (6b), **Og** (16d,18c), **oh** (52c), **OK** (155a), **ol** (29c, 158b, d,160b), **om** (49a,77a,b,105c,136a), **on** (8b,9a,60c,106a,123a), **oo** (34a,74b), **or** (9b,36a,37b,69c,158c,166a,184b), **os** (21d,67b,104a, 131b), **ow** (52c), **ox** (10c,22c), **oy** (139c)

- O **Ao** (13d,88b,c,116c), **bo** (23d,24c,136a,168a), **do** (108b,138a 161a), **eo** (34a), **Fo** (23d), **go** (64c,90d), **ho** (39b,79a), **Ho** (87c), **io** (74b,c,103c,115b), **Io** (25a,85d,95c,186b), **jo** (140c,160c), **Jo** (8c, 94b), **ko** (22c,87c,121a), **lo** (17d,93d), **mo** (21d,81c,101c), **Mo** (88c, 177c), **no** (42b,106b), **No** (84b), **oo** (34a,74b), **Ro** (13c,81d,88c,131c, 173c), **so** (76a,108b,125a,138a,158b,161a,165b,175c), **to** (10b, 13c), **uo** (43d), **vo** (91a), **yo, zo** (13d,186b)

P - **pa** (60b,106d), **pe** (91c), **Pe.** (124d), **pi** (71b,85d,91c,165a,172a), **pu** (30b,140a)

- P **ap** (122d,166c), **AP** (107a,182d), **up** (123a), **UP** (107a,182d)

Q - **QB** (59c), **q.v.** (180d)

R - **ra** (108b), **Ra** (159b), **re** (6b,10b,35d,108b,122b,129b,138a,161a), **RE** (59c), **RF** (16d), **Rh** (20c), **ri** (84c,96d,98a,108b), **RI** (106c), **Ro** (13c,81d,88c,131c,173c), **RT** (59c)

- R **ar** (88b,91c,98a,99b,110c), **er** (35b,76c,137d,155a,158c,d,160b, 175c), **Er** (18d,68c,85c,163d,166c,172c,178a), **ir** (99d,122c), **Ir** (10a, 28a,82b), **or** (9b,36a,37b,69c158c,166a,184b), **Ur** (6b,28d,94a, 100d)

S - **SA** (36c), **se** (35b,108b), **Se, sh** (17b,43c,79c,126d), **si** (108b,152d, 185d), **so** (76a,108b,125a,138a,158b,161a,165b,175c), **SS** (16d, 164c), **Su** (127a), **Sw** (35b), **Sy** (141a)

- S **as** (51b,67b,92b,126a,133a,b,180d), **es** (49b,50a,66c,119d,158c, d,175c), **is** (51a,166c,175c), **Is** (15b,23c,86c), **os** (21d,67b,104a, 131b), **S.S.** (16d,164c), **us** (124b)

T - **ta** (112d,139a,160b), **td** (32a), **te** (43a,62d,108b,131c,152d,160b, 185d), **th** (43c), **ti** (92b,108b,113a,b,120d,138a,161a,162c,169b), **to** (10b,13c), **tt** (147b), **tu** (83c,164d,185d), **Ty** (68c,109c,163d, 178a)

- T **at** (25c,32c,106a,123a,128a), **et** (10b,61a,b,89a,158c), **it** (124b), **Lt** (143c), **LT** (59c), **RT** (59c), **tt** (147b), **ut** (72b,108b), **Ut** (67a)

U - **um** (52c,76c), **un** (34c,122c), **Uo** (43d), **up** (123a), **Ur** (6b,28d, 94a,100d), **UP** (107a,182d), **us** (124b), **ut** (72b,108b), **Ut** (67a), **Uz** (48c)

- U **au** (63a,69c), **bu** (190), **fu** (42c,84c), **Fu** (30b), **Hu** (101c,108a, 162b), **ju** (121a), **lu** (65a), **mu** (10a,30a,60c,71a,91c), **nu** (71b, 91c), **Nu** (29a,49a), **pu** (30b,140a), **Su** (127a), **tu** (83c, 164d, 185d), **Wu** (30b), **Zu** (68c,157a)

V - **va** (105a), **Va** (83a), **Ve** (63c,109c), **vo** (91a)

- V **q.v.** (180d)

W - **wa** (188), **Wa** (24c,d,88c), **we** (48c,124b), **We** (92b), **Wu** (30b), **wy** (91c)

- W **aw** (44a), **ow** (52c), **sw** (35b)

X - **xi** (91c)

- X **ax** (40c,139a,167a), **ex** (60b,91c,122c), **ox** (10c,22c)

Y - **ya, ye** (124b), **yo**

- Y **ay** (7c,8b,9b,28d,55a,60a), **by** (18b,32c,106a), **my** (52c,124c), **sy** (141a), **oy** (139c), **Ty** (68c,109c,163d,178a), **wy** (91c)

Z - **za** (162a), **zo** (13d,186b), **Zu** (68c,157a)

- Z **Uz** (48c)

THREE-LETTER WORDS

AA - **aal** (47c,80c,104b), **aam** (47a,49d,93a), **aar** (172d), **Aar** (131a)

A - A **aba** (12a,25d,32b,33a,65b), **Ada** (110a,112c,183c), **aea** (26a,36d), **aga** (35a,39a,48b,102d,103a,b,111c,166b,170d,171a), **aha** (52c,55c, 159c), **aka** (88b,c,176b), **Aka** (13d), **ala** (6d,13a,15c,61a,133d,

182c,d), **Ala** (151b), **ama** (26a,28d,31a,35b,39c,95b,108d,111c, 117b,182c), **ana** (10b,33c,60d,93a,98c,122b,d,140d,142b), **Ana** (28a,68d,100c), **apa** (23a,177d), **ara** (33a,114a,116a,118b,163d), **Ara** (9b,18c,36b,c,68d,69b,c,85a,95a,175b), **Asa** (6a,18c,71a,84d, 86d,164c), **ata** (58d,97d,158d,160c,173d), **Ata** (79c,80d,94d, 95d,100a,106b,117a,), **ava** (78d,86a,116a,120d,139a,167b), **Ava** (24c), **awa** (100a,139a), **aya** (77b,166b)

- AA **baa** (143d), **maa** (97d,143d), **saa** (98a), **taa** (112d)

AB - **aba** (12a,25d,32b,33a,65b), **abb** (58b,178b,185b), **ABC** (134d), **Abe** (71a,96a,123a), **Abi** (76c), **Abo** (25d), **Abt** (34c), **abu** (17a), **Abu** (15b,42a,55a,68a,c,147d)

A - B **abb** (58b,178b,185b), **alb** (65b,176a)

- AB **Bab** (15a), **cab** (75c), **dab** (46a,57b,58b,d,114d,115c), **gab** (29b, 78a,116c,122a,161c,183a), **jab** (120b,125c), **kab** (75c), **lab**, **Mab** (54b,126b,183d), **nab** (13b,26c,27b,142a), **pab** (139c), **rab** (17c,75c, 85b,102d,162c,166b), **Rab** (45a), **tab** (29b,39c,58b,86a,128d,145a)

AC - **ace** (7a,26c,52d,57a,77d,110c,114c,120b,147a,163a,173a), **ach** (8b, 48a,52c,66b,80c), **aci** (29c), **act** (41d,55b,119c,155d), **acu** (34c), **acy** (34c)

A - C **ABC** (134d), **arc** (31b,39d,92a,126a,127c,142a)

- AC **bac** (31b,55c,174d), **fac** (41c), **lac** (53c,99d,130c,135b,174d), **Mac** (96a,140b,150b), **pac** (73b,94c,100d), **sac** (15d,121d), **Sac** (80c), **tac** (34d,130a), **Vac** (153b), **zac** (27c)

AD - **Ada** (110a,112c,183c), **add** (10d,11d,14c,158a,167c), **ade** (18c, 149d), **Ade** (9c,53b), **ado** (22b,24d,35b,64c,78d,121d,156b,170a), **ady** (188), **adz** (40c,167a)

A - D **aid** (14a,15b,64c,75d,158b), **add** (10d,11d,14c,158a,167c), **and** (36a,119d)

- AD **bad** (55a,173a,184d), **cad** (22b,23b,75c,172c,173d), **dad**, **fad** (38b, 108c,163a), **gad** (58c,100a,b,127d,132b,153c,154b,178a), **Gad** (84a, 186d), **had**, **lad** (22c,25b,55b,157c,186a), **mad** (10c,82b), **pad** (39d, 59c,76c,157d,161a,168b), **rad** (50b,138d,173b), **sad** (29c,42c,94c, 98c,104a,150d,173a), **tad** (22c,174a,186a), **wad** (94d,97b,109c, 112b,149d)

AE - **aea** (26a,36d), **AEF** (184d), **aer** (8b,28d,34a,b,175a), **aes** (23c, 89a,101c,132d,133a,b), **aet** (89a,109d), **Aex** (46d)

A - E **Abe** (71a,96a,123a), **ace** (7a,26c,52d,57a,77d,110c,114c,120b, 147a,163a,173a), **ade** (18c,149d), **Ade** (9c,53b), **age** (51d,66a,92a, 97c,98c,116b,141c), **ake** (60a,107a), **ale** (17c,18c,50c,55d,92d, 104c), **ame** (37a,62d,131b), **ane** (61c,140a,158b), **ape** (36d,79d, 100a,101d,146d), **are** (51a,88b,98a,99b,110c,166c,175c), **ase** (51a, 139a), **Ase** (79b,115d), **ate** (81a,108c,158c,174c), **Ate** (20c,68b,d, 69a,b,116c,186b), **ave** (54c,71d,73a,122a,134a,136d), **awe** (81d, 100a,130d,175b,182b), **axe** (30c,40c,167a), **aye** (7c,9b,55a,60a)

- AE **dae** (139b), **eae** (34b), **hae** (139c), **kae** (84a,140b), **Mae** (183c), **nae** (139d), **rae** (136b,138d,140b), **Rae** (183c), **sae** (140b,149c), **tae** (138d,140c,166c,d), **vae** (176b)

AF - **AFL** (173a), **Afr.** (36c), **aft** (14a,15b,17d,128b,167d)

A - F **AEF** (184d), **Alf** (96a)

- AF **gaf** (12b), **kaf** (12b), **Kaf** (104a), **oaf** (22a,45b,146d,157d,185d), **Qaf** (104a)

AG - **aga** (35a,39a,48b,102d,103a,b,111c,166b,170d,171a), **age** (51d, 66a,92a,97c,98c,116b,141c), **ago** (25a,69d,114d,147a)

- AG **bag** (26c,139a,145b,159a), **cag** (81d,109d), **dag** (11b,118c,139c), **Dag** (108c), **fag** (55a,166a), **gag** (146c,183a), **hag** (140a,183a), **jag** (124d,148a), **lag** (93c,155d), **mag** (73b,95b,166c), **Mag** (183d), **nag** (73d,78b,138c,184d), **rag** (59b,77c,100c,133c,161a), **sag** (46b), **tag** (45a,54c,65a,87b,144a), **vag** (174b,178a), **wag** (85b,104a,183a), **zag** (84a)

AH - **aha** (52c,55c,159c), **Ahi** (32c,147d), **ahu** (24c,41d,65d,103d,120d)

A - H **ach** (8b,48a,52c,66b,80c), **akh** (153d), **ash** (24d,33c,49c,73d,134b, 168c,169a), **auh** (52c)

- AH **bah** (52c), **dah** (24c,87a), **hah** (52c), **Jah** (84d), **Mah** (10b,57c, 102b), **pah** (52c,60b,106d), **rah** (29b), **sah** (188), **wah** (113c), **yah** (52c)

AI - **aid** (14a,15b,64c,75d,158b), **aik** (139d), **ail** (170a), **aim** (42d,43d, 67d,109b,125d,157c), **ain** (18d,91c,110c,124b,140a,154b,180a), **air** (11c,12c,42b,44c,53a,96b,98c,99d,125b,170c), **ait** (82d,132a), **Aix** (46d)

A - I **Abi** (76c), **aci** (29c), **Ahi** (32c,147d), **Ali** (7b,12a,25c,48b,55a,60c, 92d,101a,103a,164a,166b,170d), **ami** (61d), **ani** (19b,d,20b,39b), **api** (34a,76d), **Ari** (18d), **asi** (137a), **ati** (106d,107a), **Ati** (45d,106b, 113c,117a)

- AI **hai** (55c), **kai** (59c), **Kai** (14d,84c), **lai** (98b,161b), **Lai** (24c,d,88c), **mai** (62a), **rai** (188), **sai** (101d), **tai** (84b,111c,121b), **Tai** (80d), **Vai** (91d)

- AJ **gaj** (190), **raj** (129c), **saj** (48a,169a), **taj** (75a,97d)

AK - **aka** (176b), **Aka** (13d,88b,c), **ake** (60a,170a), **akh** (153d), **ako** (189), aku (57c,176a)

A - K **aik** (139d), **alk** (171b), **ark** (21a,29d,38a,58b,60d,175d), **ask** (38b, 82a,126c), **auk** (19b)

- AK **dak** (95c), **hak** (46d), **lak** (38a), **nak** (156b), **oak** (73d,168c,169a), **sak** (37c), **Sak** (88c), **yak** (112c,161d,165b), **zak** (188)

AL - **ala** (6d,13a,15c,61a,133d,182c,d), **Ala.** (151b), **alb** (65b,176a), **ale** (17c,18c,50c,55d,92d,104c), **Alf** (96a), **Ali** (7b,12a,25c,48b,55a,60c, 92d,101a,103a,164a,166b,170d), **alk** (171b), **all** (35c,118a,126d, 181a), **alp** (24b,103d,115c), **als** (66d,163d), **alt** (66c,76c,109c), **aly** (95d)

A - L **aal** (47c,80c,104b), **AFL** (173a), **ail** (170a), **all** (35c,118a,126d,181a), **awl** (145b,167a)

- AL **aal** (47c,80c,104b), **bal** (9d,37b,61a,61b), **cal** (183c), **Cal** (123a), **dal** (117d,153d), **gal**, **Hal** (69d), **ial** (158b), **mal** (34a,b,44a,52b,62c, 122b), **Mal** (94b), **pal** (35b,38d), **sal** (29c,48a,136d,149d,152d, 169a,183a), **Sal** (183d), **tal** (40c,77a,113b), **Zal** (135d)

AM - **ama** (26a,28d,31a,35b,39c,95b,108d,111c,117b,182c), **ame** (37a, 62d,131b), **ami** (61d), **amo** (79a,89c), **amp** (49b,173b), **amt** (37d, 40d,108a,163c), **amy** (63c), **Amy** (8c,94b,183c)

A - M **aam** (47a,49d,93a), **aim** (42d,43d,67d,109b,125d,157c), **arm** (22d, 60c,81b,92b,124b,161b), **aum** (189)

- AM **aam** (47a,49d,93a), **bam** (29b), **cam** (48b,65d,95a,98b,134a,139b, 148b,180c), **dam** (30c,49c,55b,156d,180a), **gam** (76b,176d,180c), **ham** (98a,144b), **Ham** (18d,107c), **jam** (123a,156d,165c), **lam** (51b, 58b,93d,164d,178a), **Mam** (192), **pam** (26c,65a,87a,105b), **Ram** (36b), **ram** (17a,45b,50b,79c,112b,121d,143d,157d), **Sam** (96a, 162a), **tam** (74d), **yam** (48c,121d,160b,170c)

AN - **ana** (10b,33c,60d,93a,98c,122b,d,140d,142b), **Ana** (28a,68d,100c), **and** (36a,119d), **ane** (61c,140a,158b), **ani** (19b,d,20b,39b), **Ann** (183c), **ano** (19d,20b,34d,122d,174a), **Ans** (92a), **ant** (49d,60b,81b, 118c), **Anu** (15b,28a,68a,d,75b,88c,147d), **any** (14b,150b)

A - N **ain** (18d,91c,110c,124b,140a,154b,180a), **Ann** (183c), **arn** (8c, 139a), **awn** (12c,17b,140a)

- AN **ban** (81d,97a,124a), **can** (24c,36c,123a,166a), **dan** (24c,97c), **Dan** (18c,39c,77d,83a,84a,141b), **ean** (17d,23b,88a), **fan** (43a,154b), 156b,182d), **Gan** (132d), **Han** (16c,30b,185b), **Ian** (85b,96a,139d), **kan** (93a), **lan** (37b,37d,160b), **man** (29c,60c,64c,65a,142d,161d), **Nan** (183c), **pan** (34a,61a,104a,175d), **Pan** (56a,68a,68b,76b,120c, 135b,161a,184a), **ran** (73d), **Ran** (7c,107d,141a,163d), **san** (91c, **San** (24d), **tan** (23d,33c,46a,72d,90d), **van** (7b,59d,60a,63d,90c), **wan** (113a), **Zan** (186b)

A - O **Abo** (25d), **ado** (22b,24d,35b,64c,78d,121d,156b,170a), **ago** (25a, 69d,114d,147a), **ako** (189), **amo** (79a,89c), **ano** (19d,20b,34d, 122d,174a), **Apo** (122b,177c), **Aro** (107a,111c), **Aso** (84c), **azo** (107c)

- AO **dao** (117a), **hao** (189), **iao** (78a,96c,178d), **Lao** (80d,88c,146a, 161b), **mao** (115b), **Mao** (30b), **sao** (141b), **Sao** (113c), **tao** (10d, 131c,170b), **Tao** (117a), **Yao** (30a,c,104b)

AP - **apa** (23a,177d), **ape** (36d,79d,100a,101d,146d), **api** (34a,76d), **apo** (122b), **Apo** (177c), **apt** (11d,23b,32b,58a,80b,92b,114d,116d, 124b,159a)

A - P **alp** (24b,103d,115c), **amp** (49b,173b), **asp** (7b,32b,149a,174a, 176c)

- AP **bap** (93b,132d), **Bap** (124d), **cap** (19d,39a,43a,53a,74d,160a,167b, 185c), **dap** (43b,c,46b,91b,147d), **gap** (11b,23a,29b,76c,110d,128a), **hap** (17d,28d), **Jap,** **lap** (31b,37d,59b,127a,131d,153d,167d), **map** (27a,29b,54a,98d,160a), **nap** (65a,117d,146b,148a), **pap** (59c), **rap** (90d,110a,147c,157c), **sap** (45d,52d,85c,169b,176d,179a), **tap** (55a,114d,153c), **yap** (16c,29b,122a)

AR - **ara** (33a,114a,116a,118b,163d), **Ara** (8c,9b,36b,c,68d,69b,c, 85a,95a,175b), **arc** (31b,39d,92a,126a,127c,142a), **are** (51a,88b, 98a,99b,110c,166c,175c), **Ari** (18d), **ark** (21a,29d,38a,58b,60d, 175d), **arm** (22d,60c,81b,92b,124b,161b), **arn** (8c,139a), **Aro** (107a, 111c), **ars** (13b,89a), **Ars** (112c), **art** (22d,38b,39c,43b,56c,124a, 162c,181d), **aru** (80c,82b), **Aru** (82d)

A - R **aar** (172d), **Aar** (131a), **aer** (8b,28d,34a,b,175a), **Afr.** (36c), **air** (11c,12c,42b,44c,53a,96b,98c,99d,125b,170c)

- AR **aar** (172d), **Aar** (131a), **bar** (37c,39a,46a,52c,76d,78b,91a,124a,

137a,156a,157c,169c), **car** (16a,61d,93b,175a) **dar,** (65c,111b, 169a), **ear** (14c,d,28c,63d,64a,73c,111b,116a,124b,137d,150d, 153c), **far** (44c), **gar** (57b,c,d,106b), **har** (139c), **jar** (31d,70d,143b), **lar** (24c,51d,67a,78d,95d,101d,171b), **mar** (40b,44a,79a,d,81a, 140d), **Mar** (93d), **nar** (139d), **oar** (20b,124c,134b), **par** (15a,51a, 51b,c,69d,107c,135b,155a) **sar** (57d), **tar** (8c,68a,94d,111c,118c, 136a,c,176d), **war** (157c), **yar** (72a), **zar** (188)

AS - **Asa** (6a,18c,71a,84d,86d,164c), **ase** (51a,139a), **Ase** (79b,115d), **ash** (24d,33c,49c,73d,134b,168c,169a), **asi** (137a), **ask** (38b,82a, 126c) **Aso,** (84c), **asp** (7b,32b,149a,174a,176c), **ass** (17b,20c,45b, c,59c,110c,112b,146d,157d)

A - S **aes** (23c,89a,101c,132d,133a,b), **als** (66d,163d), **Ans** (92a), **ars** (13b,89a), **Ars** (112c), **ass** (17b,20c,45b,c,59c,110c,112b,146d, 157d), **aus** (66c), **Aus** (98b)

- AS **bas** (62a,d,129d,134b), **das** (13b,15d,36d,66b,d,164a), **fas** (44d,89d, 129d), **gas** (10b,29b,59a,116d,161c), **has, kas** (32c,47a), **las** (13b, (151d), **mas** (34b,55b,119a) **nas** (74a,89c,178b), **pas** (40d, 156a), **ras** (6c,26b,48b,51d,53d,61c,75a,111c,123c,166b), **vas** (46d, 89d,119c,133b,175d), **was** (166c,175c), **Was** (24d)

AT - **ata** (58d,97d,158d,160c,173d), **Ata** (79c,80d,94d,95d,100a, 106b,117a), **ate** (81a,108c,158c,174c), **Ate** (20c,68b,d,69a,b, 116c,186b), **ati** (106d,107a), **Ati** (45d,106b,113c,117a), **att** (146a)

A - T **Abt** (35c), **act** (41d,55b,119c,155d), **aet** (89a,109d), **aft** (14a,15b, 17d,128b,167d), **ait** (82d,132a), **alt** (66c,76c,109c), **amt** (37d,40d, 108a,163c), **ant** (49d,60b,81b,118c), **apt** (11d,23b,32b,58a,80b,92b, 114d,116d,124b,159a), **art** (22d,38b,39c,43b,56c,124a,162c,181d), **att** (146a), **aut** (34d,89d)

- AT **bat** (39c,107c,156a,157c,182d), **cat** (10a,45b,55b,71d,161b,169d, 180d,183d), **eat** (37b,96b,135d,179b), **fat** (110a,124a), **gat** (28d, 72c,131a), **hat** (74d), **Hat** (183d), **Jat** (80d,125c), **kat** (105d), **lat** (24a,33d,106b,118a), **mat** (46d,50d,94d,117c,161d), **Mat** (96a), **nat** (7a,24c,24d,106a), **oat** (15a,28b,70b,144b), **pat** (11d,116d, 159a,161d,167c), **Pat** (96a), **rat** 16a,42d,73b,132c), **sat** (13d), **tat** (48c,72d,87c), **Tat** (82a), **vat** (31b,36c,163a,170c), **wat** (73d,140d, 163a,180b), **xat** (167c), **zat** (148a)

AU - **auh** (52c), **auk** (19b), **aum** (189), **aus** (66c), **Aus** (98b), **aut** (34d, 89d), **aux** (6d,61a)

A - U **abu** (17a), **Abu** (15b,42a,55a,68a,c,147d), **acu** (34c), **ahu** (24c,41d, 65d,103d,120d), **aku** (57c,176a), **Anu** (15b,28a,68a,d,75b,88c, 147d), **aru** (80c,82b), **Aru** (82d), **ayu** (160c)

- AU **eau** (63a,178c), **gau** (66d,67a), **mau** (170c,188), **pau** (130c), **Pau** (48c,76a), **tau** (71b,91c,136c,161a), **vau** (91c), **Yau** (30c)

AV - **ava** (78d,86a,116a,120d,139a,167b), **Ava** (24c), **ave** (54c,71d,73a, 122a,134a,136d)

- AV **gav** (72d), **lav** (72d), **tav** (91c)

AW - **awa** (100a,139a), **awe** (81d,100a,130d,175b,182b), **awl** (145b,167a), **awn** (12c,17b,140a)

- AW **baw** (52c), **caw** (19b,d), **daw** (39a,70b,84a,146d), **gaw** (140c), **haw** (35a,52c,74d,91a,155a,162c), **jaw** (97d,138c), **law** (26b,33a,40a,

48c,60b,85d,91a,111b,134d,155d), **maw** (38b,d,72c,111a,121a, 142a,156c), **paw** (32d,59c,73c), **raw** (20c,39a,105d,173d), **saw** (7a, 11b,40c,54c,97d,125a,137d,167a), **taw** (90d,91c,96c,d,145b,161d), **waw** (12b,91c), **yaw** (43a,155d)

AX - **axe** (30c,40c,167a)

A - X **Aex** (46d), **Aix** (46d), **aux** (6d,61a)

- AX **lax** (93d,130a), **Max** (96a), **pax** (89d,115b), **sax** (40c,148a,167a), **tax** (13a,14a,80a,91d), **wax** (28b,72a,80b,120c), **zax** (148a)

AY - **aya** (77b,143c,166b), **aye** (7c,9b,55a,60a), **ayu** (160c)

A - Y **acy** (34c), **ady** (188), **aly** (95d), **amy** (63c), **Amy** (8c,94b,183c), **any** (14b,150b)

- AY **bay** (12d,16c,33c,73d,78b,81b,90a,128d), **cay** (82d,180b), **day** (153a), **fay** (32c,54b,154b), **Fay** (183c), **gay, Gay** (17d), **hay** (52c, 55c,165d), **jay** (19b,91c), **kay** (82d), **Kay** (13b,134b), **lay** (16a,25c,80a,98b,107d,141d,150b), **may** (74d), **May** (183c), **nay** (42b,106b), **pay** (35b,128c,130a,d,177b), **ray** (38a,49a,57b, 58b,147b), **Ray** (96a), **say** (131c,174c,177a), **way** (37d,96b,134b, 164d)

AZ - **azo** (107c)

A - Z **adz** (40c,167a)

- AZ **gaz** (188,190), **Laz** (27d)

BA - **baa** (143d), **Bab** (15a), **bac** (31b,55c,174d), **bad** (55a,173a,184d), **bag** (26c,139a,145b,159a), **bah** (52c), **bal** (9d,37b,61a,b), **bam** (29b), **ban** (81d,97a,124a), **bap** (93b,132d), **Bap.** (124d), **bar** (37c, 39a,46a,52c,76d,78b,91a,124a,137a,156a,157c,169c), **bas** (62a,d, 129d,134b), **bat** (39c,107c,156a,157c,182d), **baw** (52c), **bay** (12d, 16c,33c,73d,78b,81b,90a,128d)

B - A **baa** (143d) **boa** (36c,55b,106a,125d,138b,142d,149a)

- BA **aba** (12a,25d,32b,33a,65b), **iba** (117a)

B - B **Bab** (15a), **bib, bob** (57c,115d), **Bob** (96a), **bub** (22c)

- BB **abb** (58b,178b,185b), **ebb** (6a,15b,41c,43c,104a,128c,158a,178a)

B - C **bac** (31b,55c,174d), **BSC** (42a)

- BC **ABC** (134d)

B - D **bad** (55a,173a,184d), **bed** (60c,148b), **bid** (35a,82a,109d,111b, 174c), **bud** (22c)

BE - **bed** (60c, 148b), **bee** (46b,81b,91c,108c), **beg** (38b,150a), **bel** (64a, 93c,168d,173b,183d), **Bel** (15b,68a,126d), **ben** (78c,81b,102c,115c), **Ben** (12d,77c,96a,106c,139d,140a), **ber** (85c), **Bes** (68b,119c), **bet, bey** (70b,170d)

B - E **bee** (46b,81b,91c), **bye** (38c,141d)

- BE **Abe** 71a,96a,123a), **obe** (31d,87d,150d), **ube** (185b)

B - G **bag** (26c,139a,145b,159a), **beg** (38b,150a), **big, bog** (97a,160a), **bug** (24b,66b,81b)

B - H **bah** (52c), **boh** (24c)

BI - **bib, bid** (35a,82a,109d,111b,174c), **big, Bim** (16c), **bin** (22c,59a, 78a,128c,156d), **bis** (50a,90a,102c,130b,171c), **bit** (46a,86b,114c, 167a,b,171c,180d), **biz**

- BI **Abi** (76c), **obi** (55d,67b,84c,137b,150d), **ubi** (90a,180d,185b)

B - K **Bok** (9c)

B - L **bal** (9d,37b,61a,61b), **bel** (64a,93c,168d,173b,183d), **Bel** (15b,68a, 126d), **Bul** (25d,102a)

B - M **bam** (29b), **Bim** (16c), **bum** (21b)

B - N **ban** (81d,97a,124a), **ben** (78c,81b,102c,115c,139d,140a), **Ben** (12d, 77c,96a,106c), **bin** (22a,59a,78a,128c,156d), **bon** (30a,61d,86b,88c), **Bon** (84b), **bun** (25b,73b)

BO - **boa** (36c,55b,106a,125d,138b,142d,149a), **bob** (57c,115d), **Bob** (96a), **bog** (97a,160a), **boh** (24c), **Bok** (9c), **bon** (30a,61d,86b,88c), **Bon** (84b), **boo**, **Bor** (120c), **Bos** (27c), **bot** (59a,88d), **bow** (11c,21b, 39d,60a,107c,109a,125a,144d,158a), **box** (36a,128c,145d,152d), **boy** (142d,157c), **Boz** (43b,115d)

B - O **boo**

- BO **Abo** (25d), **ebo** (28b,110a), **Ibo** (107a,180a)

B - P **Bap.** (124d), **bap** (93b,132d)

B - R **bar** (37c,39a,46a,52c,76d,78b,91a,124a,137a,156a,157c,169c), **ber** (85c), **Bor** (120c), **bur** (123b)

BS - **BSC** (42a)

B - S **bas** (62a,d,129d,134b), **Bes** (68b,119c), **bis** (50a,90a,102c,130b, 171c), **Bos** (27c), **bus** (125b,168b)

B - T **bat** (39c,107c,156a,157c,182d), **bet**, **bit** (46a,86b,114c,167a,b, 171c,180d), **bot** (59a,88d), **but** (36a,52b,156b,173c)

- BT **Abt** (35c)

BU - **bub** (22c), **bud** (22c), **bug** (24b,66b,81b), **Bul** (25d,102a), **bum** (21b), **bun** (25b,73b), **bur** (123b), **bus** (125b,168b), **but** (36a,52b, 156b,173c), **buy**

- BU **abu** (17a), **Abu** (15b,42a,55a,68a,c,147d)

B - W **baw** (52c), **bow** (11c,21b,39d,60a,107c,109a,125a,144d,158a)

B - X **box** (36a,c,128c,145d,152d)

BY - **bye** (38c,141d)

B - Y **bay** (12d,16c,33c,73d,78b,81b,90a,128d), **bey** (70b,170d), **boy** (142d,157c), **buy**

B - Z **biz**, **Boz** (43b,115d)

CA - **cab** (75c), **cad** (22b,23b,75c,172c,173d), **cag** (81d,109d), **cal** (183c), **Cal** (123a), **cam** (48b,65d,95a,98b,134a,139b,148b,180c), **can** (24c, 36c,123a,166a), **cap** (19d,39a,43a,53a,74d,160a,167b,185c), **car** (16a,61d,93b,175a), **cat** (10a,45b,55b,71d,161b,169d,180d), **Cat** (183d), **caw** (19b,d) **cay** (82d, 180b)

C - A **cha** (162b,c)

- CA **ECA** (8a), **oca** (48c,112c,116d,133d,170c,184a), **Uca** (56a)

C - B **cab** (75c), **cob** (28c,78b,95d,160b,177d), **cub** (92d,185d)

C - D **cad** (22b,23b,75c,172c,173d), **Cid** (151c,d), **cod** (57b,c), **cud** (126c, 135a)

CE - **cee** (91c), **cep** (63a), **ces** (62b), **cet** (62d,180b)

C - E **cee** (91c), **che** (145d), **cie** (61b,63b), **cle** (158d), **coe** (143d),

Coe (33c), **cue** (7a,27b,92c,117d,124b,132c,146c,159a)

- CE **ace** (7a,26c,52d,57a,77d,110c,114c,120b,147a,163a,173a), **ice** (30a, 36d,42d,63d)

C - G **cag** (81d,109d), **cig,** **cog** (33a,65d,163b,167b,180c)

CH - **cha** (162b,c), **che** (145d), **chi** (91c), **Chi** (69c), **cho** (188)

- CH **ach** (8b,48a,52c,66b,80c), **ich** (66c), **och** (8b), **tch** (52c)

CI - **Cid** (151c,d), **cie** (61b,63b), **cig,** **CIO** (173a), **cis** (34c,122c), **cit** (81a,167d)

C - I **chi** (91c), **Chi** (69c)

- CI **aci** (29c), **ici** (61d), **Ici** (9b), **LCI** (21b)

- CK **ock** (189), **tck** (52c)

CL - **cle** (158d)

C - L **cal** (183c), **Cal** (123a), **col** (103d,114c)

C - M **cam** (48b,65d,95a,98b,134a,139b,148b,180c), **com** (122d), **cum** (159b), **cwm** (31b,37b,103d)

C - N **can** (24c,36c,123a,166a), **con** (7d,29b,83c,116d,157d)

CO - **cob** (28c,78b,95d,160b,177d), **cod** (57b,c), **coe** (143d), **Coe** (33c), **cog** (33a,65d,163b,167b,180c), **col** (103d,114c), **com** (122d), **con** (7d,29b,83c,116d,157d), **coo** (19b), **Coo** (82d), **cop** (36a,120c, 126d,153c,155d), **cor** (36c,75b,155b), **cos** (91d,132d), **cot** (129b, 148b), **cow** (22c,45b,81d), **cox** (156a), **coy** (16d), **coz**

C - O **cho** (188), **CIO** (173a), **coo** (19b), **Coo** (82d), **cro** (104c,115b,180a)

C - P **cap** (19d,39a,43a,53a,74d,160a,167b,185c), **cep** (63a), **cop** (36a, 120c,126d,153c,155d), **cup** (46b,69d,118b,170a), **cyp** (169d)

CR - **cro** (104c,115b,180a), **cru** (63a,176c), **cry** (25c,124a,145c,179d)

C - R **car** (16a,61d,93b,175a), **cor** (36c,75b,155b), **cur** (101d)

C - S **ces** (62b), **cis** (34c,122c), **cos** (91d,132d)

- CS **ics** (158d)

C - T **cat** (10a,45b,55b,71d,161b,169d,180d,183d), **cet** (62d,180b), **cit** (81a,167d), **cot** (148b), **cut** (30c,32b,145c)

- CT **act** (41d,55b,119c,155d), **ect** (35a,122d,183b), **oct** (34a,122c)

CU - **cub** (92d,185d), **cud** (126c,135a), **cue** (7a,27b,92c,117d,124b,132c, 146c,159a), **cum** (159b), **cup** (46b,69d,118b,170a), **cur** (101d), **cut** (30c,32b,145c)

C - U **cru** (63a,176c)

- CU **acu** (34c), **ecu** (58a,144b,c)

CW - **cwm** (31b,37b,103d)

C - W **caw** (19b,d), **cow** (22c,45b,81d)

C - X **cox** (156a)

CY - **cyp** (169d)

C - Y **cay** (82d,180b), **coy** (16d), **cry** (25c,124a,145c,179d)

- CY **acy** (34c), **icy** (65d)

C - Z **coz**

DA - **dab** (46a,57b,58b,d,114d,115c), **dad,** **dae** (139b), **dag** (11b,118c, 139c), **Dag** (108c), **dah** (24c,87a), **dak** (95c), **dal** (117d,153d), **dam**

(30c,49c,55b,156d,180a), **dan** (24c,97c), **Dan** (18c,39c,77d,83a, 84a,141b), **dao** (117a), **dap** (43b,c,46b,91b,147d), **dar** (65c,111b, 169a), **das** (13b,15d,36d,66b,d,164a), **daw** (39a,70b,84a,146d), **day** (153a)

D - A **dea** (68d,89b), **dha** (99d), **dia** (122b,d,152a,165b), **dra** (188), **dua** (122d)

- DA **Ada** (110a,112c,183c), **Ida** (103d,183c), **oda** (74a,170d)

D - B **dab** (46a,57b,58b,114d,115c), **deb, Deb** (183d), **dib** (21b,43b,c, 120d,140a), **dub** (25c,46a,c,87a,105b,121a,140a)

D - C **dec** (122d), **doc** (143a), **duc** (61c)

DD - **DDS** (42a)

D - D **dad, did, dod** (11a,32a,43b,140c), **dud** (21c,54a)

- DD **add** (10d,11d,14c,158a,167c), **odd** (46b,53a,109b,157a,172d,173c)

DE - **dea** (68d,89b), **deb, Deb** (183d), **dec** (122d), **dee** (91c), **Dee** (131d, 139b), **deg** (154b), **dei** (68d), **den** (38b,44d,74b,130d,133c,140d), **der** (13b,66b,d,164a), **des** (13b,61a,62b,d), **dev** (42a,b), **dew** (41a), **dey** (8d,84a,114c,135a,139b,170d)

D - E **dae** (139b), **dee** (91c), **Dee** (131d,139b), **die** (27b,54a,65a,155a, 167a), **doe** (41d,55b,127a), **due** (7b,115b,124c), **dye** (33c,154d)

- DE **ade** (18c,149d), **Ade** (9c,53b), **Ede** (35b,65d), **ide** (40c,57a,b,d, 158b), **ode** (26b,79c,94d,118a,119d,120a,150b)

D - G **dag** (11b,118c), **Dag** (108c,139c), **deg** (154b), **dig** (52b), **dog** (10b, 45b,59b), **dug**

DH - **dha** (99d), **dhu** (40b), **Dhu** (28a,87d)

D - H **dah** (24c,87a), **doh** (113b)

- DH **edh** (91c)

DI - **dia** (122b,d,152a,165b), **dib** (21b,43b,c,120d,140a), **did, die** (27b, 54a,65a,155a,167a), **dig** (52b), **dii** (68d), **dim** (47a,48b,54a,74d, 94d,109b), **din** (31c,130b,174a), **dip** (26a,79d,117c,138c), **dis** (122b,d), **Dis** (68b,73a,119d,172d,174b), **dit** (62b,d,120a,159d), **div** (42b,139b), **dix** (118b), **Dix** (60b)

D - I **dei** (68d) **dii** (68d), **dui** (46d)

- DI **Udi** (108a)

DJ - **djo** (188)

D - K **dak** (95c)

D - L **dal** (117d,153d)

D - M **dam** (30c,49c,55b,156d,180a), **dim** (47a,48b,54a,74d,94d,109b), **dom** (121c,166b,c), **Dom** (94b), **dum** (45c,67b,113a)

D - N **dan** (24c,97c), **Dan** (18c,39c,77d,83a,84a,141b), **den** (38b,44d,74b, 130d,133c,140d), **din** (130b,174a), **don** (151d,166c), **Don** (96a), **dun** (19a,39d,46d,71a,97d,115b,160b)

DO - **Doc** (143a), **dod** (11a,32a,43b,140c), **doe** (41d,55b,127a), **dog** (10b, 45b,59b), **doh** (113b), **dom** (121c,166b,c), **Dom** (94b), **don** (151d, 166c), **Don** (96a), **dop** (39c,43b), **dor** (17d,24b,32b,46b,47a,81b, 85d), **dos** (45d,61a,97a,181b), **dot** (45d,97a,104d,105a,116b,153a, 162d), **dow** (17d,87a,88d,175d)

D - O **dao** (117a) **djo** (188), **DSO** (99d), **duo** (46d,113a,171d)

- DO **ado** (22b,24d,35b,64c,121d,156b,170a), **edo** (162a), **Edo** (107a, 166d), **Ido** (13c,81d,88c,173c), **Odo** (181d), **udo** (28a,30c,48c,84b, c,d,136c,149d)

D - P **dap** (43b,c,46b,91b,147d), **dip** (26a,79d,117c,138c), **dop** (39c,43b)

DR - **dra** (188), **dry** (46d,85a,137c,164c)

D - R **dar** (111b,169a), **der** (13b,66b,d,164a), **dor** (17d,24b,32b,46b,47a, 81b,85d), **dur** (95c)

DS - **DSO** (99d)

D - S **das** (13b,15d,36d,66b,d,164a), **DDS** (42a), **des** (13b,61a,62b,d), **dis** (122b,d), **Dis** (68b,73a,119d,172d,174b), **dos** (45d,61a,97a,181b)

- DS **DDS** (42a), **ods** (109a)

D - T **dit** (62b,d,120a,159d), **dot** (45d,97a,104d,105a,116b,153a,162d)

DU - **dua** (122d), **dub** (25c,46a,c,87a,105b,121a,140a), **duc** (61c), **dud** (21c,54a), **due** (7b,115b,124c), **dug, dui** (46d), **dum** (45c,67b,113a), **dun** (19a,39d,46d,71a,97d,115b,160b), **duo** (46d,113a,171d), **dur** (95c), **dux** (31d,64a,90c)

D - U **dhu** (40b), **Dhu** (28a,87d)

D - V **dev** (42a,b), **div** (42b,139b)

D - W **daw** (39a,70b,84a), **dew** (41a), **dow** (17d,87a,88d,175d)

D - X **dix** (118b), **Dix** (60b), **dux** (31d,64a,90c)

DY - **dye** (33c,154d)

D - Y **day** (153a), **dey** (8d,84a,114c,135a,139b,170d), **dry** (46d,85a,137c, 164c)

- DY **ady** (188)

- DZ **adz** (40c,167a)

EA - **eae** (34b), **ean** (17d,23b,88a), **ear** (14c,d,28c,63d,64a,73c,111b, 116a,124b,137d,150d,153c), **eat** (37b,96b,135d,179b), **eau** (63a, 178c)

E - A **ECA** (8a), **ela** (21c,53c,72b,76c,108b,174c), **Ena** (8c,126b), **era** (8a, 51a,116b,165d), **ESA** (8a), **eta** (71a,84c,91c), **Eva** (157a,183c)

- EA **aea** (26a,36d), **dea** (68d,89b), **Hea** (15b), **kea** (114a,b), **lea** (56a, 97d,114d,185b), **Lea** (22d), **N.E.A.** (162c), **pea** (32d,91b,142a,175a), **rea** (9c,171a), **sea** (19a,52d,58c,112c,178d), **tea** (13d,18c,79c,81a, 145d,149c,159d), **Wea** (192), **yea** (7c,175c), **zea** (95c)

EB - **ebb** (6a,15b,41c,43c,104a,128c,158a,178a), **ebo** (28b,110a)

E - B **ebb** (6a,15b,41c,43c,104a,128c,158a,178a), **elb** (85c)

- EB **deb, Deb** (183d), **Geb** (47d), **Keb** (47d), **neb** (17b,19a,d,115d), **reb** (35d,75c,85b,162c,166b), **Seb** (47d), **web** (50d,70a,98c,99a,106c, 149b)

EC - **ECA** (8a), **ect** (35a,122d,183b), **ecu** (58a,144b,c)

E - C **etc** (10b)

- EC **dec** (122d), **sec** (46c,182c), **tec** (43a)

ED - **Ede** (35b,65d), **edh** (91c), **edo** (162a), **Edo** (107a,166d)

E - D **Eed** (102d), **eld** (10b,93c,110b,165d), **end** (8b,67d,120a,125d,130a, 166a), **erd** (47d,119d,145c)

- ED **bed** (60c,148b), **Eed** (102d), **fed**, **ged** (100a,140a), **ked** (140b,144a), **led**, **Ned** (96a), **ped** (16d,34b), **red** (33c,38d,59a,127b,134c,135b), **Red** (151b), **sed** (89a), **ted** (74d,138b,154b), **Ted** (96b), **wed** (97a, 173c), **zed** (91c)

EE - **Eed** (102d), **eel** (36a,49c,57a,b,88a,102c,176c), **een** (52a,139c, 185d), **eer** (9b,52a), **ees** (139c)

E - E **eae** (34b), **Ede** (35b,65d), **eke** (14c,117c), **ele** (48c), **eme** (38d,70a, 140c,172b), **ene** (35b,158b,c), **ere** (17d,150c), **ese** (35b,158c), **ete** (36c,62d,141c,159b), **eve** (47a,131a,143a,165d,171c), **Eve** (183c), **ewe** (88a,143d), **Exe** (43a), **eye** (93d,111b,140d)

- EE **bee** (46b,81b,91c,108c), **cee** (91c), **dee** (91c), **Dee** (131d,139b), **fee** (29a,58a,70d,166a,d), **gee** (35a,91c,100a,131c,139c,162c), **lee** (74b, 144b), **Lee** (9c,31c,96a), **mee** (169a), **nee** (19d,22b,25c,60b,95c), **pee** (91c), **ree** (12c,50a,80c,134d,137a,140b,144a,146b), **Ree** (25a), **see** (20a,43c,44a,51c,53c,93d,109b,113c,116a,176d,178c,183b), **tee** (39d,52b,69d,91c,112d,115d,118b,172a), **vee** (58a,91c,106a), **wee** (52c,100c,148c), **zee** (81b,91c)

EF - **eft** (93b,107a,136c,169d)

E - F **elf** (54b,154b)

- EF **AEF** (184d), **kef** (12a,46c,75d,88c), **nef** (32b,144c,d), **ref**

EG - **egg** (32d,80b,81c,112c,174a), **ego** (51a,79a,142b)

E - G **egg** (32d,80b,81c,112c,174a), **eng** (48a,146a), **erg** (50b,173b, 184c)

- EG **beg** (38b,150a), **deg** (154b), **Geg** (8c), **keg** (27a,105b), **leg** (37d, 92b,141d,159d,169c), **Meg** (8c,183d), **peg** (38c,46b,54d,98a,118a, 184c), **teg** (45a,54b,171d)

E - H **edh** (91c), **eth** (91c,158d)

- EH **Heh** (191), **reh** (8d)

EI - **ein** (66b,c), **Eir** (69a,75a), **eis** (66c)

E - I **Eli** (18c,d,76c,96a,137a,185a), **epi** (56c,61c,d,111c,112d,122d, 133c,153c,167b,174a), **eri** (13d,21c,146d), **Eri** (18c)

- EI **dei** (68d), **fei** (16a,185b), **hei** (65a), **lei** (65b,74c), **rei** (89b,121c), **Rei** (18d), **Vei** (91d), **Wei** (30b,162b)

EK - **eke** (14c,117c)

E - K **elk** (22c,90d,178a)

- EK **lek** (65c)

EL - **ela** (21c,53c,72b,76c,108b,174c), **elb** (85c), **eld** (10b,93c,110b, 165d), **ele** (48c), **elf** (54b,154b), **Eli** (18c,d,76c,96a,137a,185a), **elk** (22c,90d,178a), **ell** (10d,24b,32c,98a), **elm** (168c), **els** (140a), **elt** (87a,117c,139d), **Ely** (27c,50b)

E - L **eel** (36a,49c,57a,b,88a,102c,176c), **ell** (10d,24b,32c,98a)

- EL **bel** (64a,93c,168d,173b,183d), **Bel** (15b,68a,126d), **eel** (36a,49c, 57a,b,88a,102c,176c), **gel** (32d,73d,150a), **Hel** (68d,93c,172d), **mel** (77d), **pel** (55c,160d), **rel** (49b,173b), **sel** (62c,140b), **tel** (34a, b,122c), **zel** (40c)

EM - **eme** (38d,70a,140c,172b), **Ems** (125a,151c), **emu** (19b,58c,111d)

E - M **elm** (168c)

- EM **gem** (104b), **hem** (22a,36a,48b,52c,155a), **mem** (91c), **Sem** (107c), **Tem** (143a,159b)

EN - **Ena** (8c,126b), **end** (8b,67d,120a,125d,130a,166a), **ene** (35b,158b,c), **eng** (48a,146a) **ens** (17d,18a,51a,52d), **ent** (34d,158b,c)

E - N **ean** (17d,23b,88a), **een** (52a,139c,185d), **ein** (66b,c), **eon** (8a,37b,51d,116b), **ern** (19c,d,47b,54b,141a)

- EN **ben** (78c,81b,102c,115c), **Ben** (12d,77c,96a,106c,139d,140a), **den** (38b,44d,74b,130d,133c,140d), **een** (52a,139c,185d), **fen** (21c,97a,160a), **gen** (31d,76b), **hen** (19a,60c,114c,136c), **ken** (60b,87c,122b,172d), **men** (38c,116a,117b,170a), **Men** (94d), **pen** (36a,50a,80d,118b,126d,160a,185c), **sen** (190), **ten** (19a,26c,41c,42b), **wen** (40c,72a,110a,170c,177b), **yen** (33b,42d,93c,174a), **Zen** (24a)

EO - **eon** (8a,37b,51d,116b), **Eos** (14d,41a,68d)

E - O **ebo** (28b,110a), **edo** (162a), **Edo** (107a,166d), **ego** (51a,79a,142b), **eso** (34d,183b), **ETO** (184d), **exo** (122d)

- EO **geo** (34a,47d), **Leo** (36b,c,92d,186d), **Meo** (27b,80c), **neo** (34a,b,c,100d,106d,108c,122c,d,128c), **Reo** (26c)

EP - **epi** (56c,61c,d,111c,112d,122d,133c,153c,167b,174a)

E - P **e.s.p.** (147b)

- EP **cep** (63a), **hep** (52c), **kep** (139b), **nep** (27c,32d,56a,87c,184b), **pep** (50b,176b), **rep** (53b,d,131a,171c), **yep**, **Zep**

ER - **era** (8a,51a,116b,165d), **erd** (47d,119d,145c), **ere** (17d,150c), **erg** (50b,173b,184c), **eri** (13d,21c,146d), **Eri** (18c), **ern** (19c,d,47b,54b,141a), **err** (21a,43a,67d,100c,d,147a,148b,157b,168b,178a), **ers** (20a,176a), **ert** (140c,174a), **ery** (155d,158c,d)

E - R **ear** (14c,d,28c,63d,64a,73c,111b,116a,124b,137d,150d,153c), **eer** (9b,52a), **Eir** (69a,75a), **err** (21a,43a,67d,100c,d,147a,148b,157b,168b,178a), **Eur.** (36c)

- ER **aer** (8b,28d,34a,b,175a), **ber** (85c), **der** (13b,66b,d,164a), **eer** (9b,52a), **ger** (8d,36d,75c,124d), **her** (124b,c), **ier** (50a,158c), **Ker** (71b,95d), **Ler** (23d,28a,b,64b,106c,141a), **mer** (62c,141a), **ner** (137c), **o'er** (6b,112a), **per** (25c,122d,165b,176a), **ser** (80d,83b,d,116c,152d,180a), **ter** (34d,122d,165a), **xer** (34a), **zer** (188)

ES - **ESA** (8a), **ese** (35b,158c), **eso** (34d,183b), **esp** (147b), **ess** (39d,78a,91c,158c,184d), **est** (50a,61c,62a,79b,89c,158d,159c)

E - S **ees** (139c), **eis** (66c), **els** (140a), **Ems** (125a,151c), **ens** (17d,18a,51a,52d), **Eos** (14d,41a,68d), **ers** (20a,176a), **ess** (39d,78a,91c,158c,184d)

- ES **aes** (23c,89a,101c,132d,133a,b), **Bes** (68b,119c), **ces** (62b), **des** (13b,61a,62b,d), **ees** (139c), **Ges** (151b), **les** (13b,61a), **mes** (62b), **nes** (26b), **oes** (109a), **pes** (59d), **res** (80a,89d,91a,97c,164c), **ses** (61d), **yes** (7c,55a)

ET - **eta** (71a,84c,91c), **etc** (10b), **ete** (36c,62d,141c,159b), **eth** (91c,158d), **ETO** (184d)

E - T **eat** (37b,96b,135d,179b), **ect** (35a,122d,183b), **eft** (93b,107a,136c,169d), **elt** (87a,117c,139d), **ent** (34d,158b,c), **ert** (140c,174a), **est** (50a,62a,79b,89c,158d,159c)

- ET **aet** (89a,109d), **bet**, **cet** (62d,180b), **get** (44d,64b,109b,141d), **jet** (20b,35a,154c), **ket** (189), **let** (9a,76d,77c,116b,130a,158b,163a), **met** (28d), **net** (26c,32a,50d,53b,60d,99a,124a,142a,149b), **pet** (26d,37c,55a,59b,162d), **ret** (58b,95a,149c,155d), **set** (7b,11d,13a, 23c,32b,33c,37c,58a,73d,109b,118c,121c,142c,150a,186a), **Set** (52b, 68a,b,111d), **vet**, **wet** (40d,46a,101a,124a,127c,149c), **yet** (18b, 24d,64c,77c,80a,108c,156b,165b)

EU - **Eur.** (136c)

E - U **eau** (63a,178c), **ecu** (58a,144b,c), **emu** (19b,58c,111d)

- EU **feu** (55d,61c,88b), **heu** (8b,30c,52c), **jeu** (61d), **leu** (190), **meu** (153b), **peu** (62a), **Reu** (115d)

EV - **Eva** (157a,183c), **eve** (47a,131a,143a,165d,171c), **Eve** (183c)

- EV **dev** (42a,b), **lev** (33b) **rev**

EW - **ewe** (88a,143d)

- EW **dew** (41a), **few**, **hew** (40a), **Jew**, **lew** (190), **Lew** (96a), **mew** (25b, 27b,50a,55b,72c,74d,101b,141b,153b), **new** (11a,63c,88d,111c, 128c), **pew** (30d,52c,57d,120b,141c), **rew** (75c,140c,176b), **sew**, **yew** (36a,52a,b,145d,168c,d)

EX - **Exe** (43a), **exo** (122d)

- EX **Aex** (46d), **hex** (18c), **lex** (90b), **rex** (86c,96a), **sex**, **vex** (7c,10d, 44c,82c)

EY - **eye** (93d,111b,140d)

E - Y **Ely** (27c,50b), **ery** (155d,158c,d)

- EY **bey** (70b,170d), **dey** (8d,84a,114c,135a,139b,170d), **fey** (49c), **gey** (140a), **hey** (25c,52c), **key** (14c,82d,88b,117c,118c,150b,180c), **ley** (190), **Ney** (63b,97b,105d), **rey** (86c,152b), **sey** (120c), **wey** (173b)

- EZ **fez** (75a,162a), **gez** (188), **nez** (62b), **tez** (125c), **yez**

FA - **fac** (41c), **fad** (38b,108c,163a), **fag** (55a,166a), **fan** (43a,154b, 156b,182d), **far** (44c), **fas** (44d,89d,129d), **fat** (110a,124a), **fay** (32c,54b,154b), **Fay** (183c)

F - A **Fha** (8a), **fra** (23c,63c,101d,123b,129d)

- FA **MFA** (42a)

F - B **fib** (162a), **fob** (29b,59b,113b,178c), **fub** (29b,119d)

F - C **fac** (41c)

F - D **fad** (38b,108c,163a), **fed**, **fid** (16b,54d,118a,167b), **fod** (188)

FE - **fed**, **fee** (29a,58a,70d,166a,d), **fei** (16a,185b), **fen** (21c,97a,160a), **feu** (55d,61c,88b), **few**, **fey** (49c), **fez** (75a,162a)

F - E **fee** (29a,58a,70d,166a,d), **fie** (52c,59d), **foe** (111a)

- FE **ife** (22c,75d)

- FF **off** (6b,15c,44c,76a)

F - G **fag** (55a,166a), **fig**, **fog** (109b), **fug** (129a)

FH - **FHA** (8a)

F - H **foh** (52c)

FI - **fib** (162a), **fid** (16b,54d,118a,167b), **fie** (52c,59d), **fig**, **fin** (86a), **fir** (16a,36a,52a,168c,d,169a), **fit** (7a,11d,51b,75a,114a,123a, 124c,126a,153a,157c,159a), **fix** (7b,10a,13a,14c,43a,c,141d,165c)

F – I **fei** (16a,185b)

FL – **flo, flu, fly** (58c,81b,163b,178d)

F – L **Ful** (158b)

– FL **AFL** (173a)

F – N **fan** (43a,154b,156b,182d), **fen** (21c,97a,160a), **fin** (86a), **Fon** (40b), **fun**

FO – **fob** (29b,59b,113b,178c), **fod** (188), **foe** (111a), **fog** (109b), **foh** (52c), **Fon** (40b), **foo** (42c), **fop** (38a,40d,46d), **for** (123d,163a,166c), **fot** (188), **fou** (139a), **fox** (134a)

F – O **Flo, foo** (42c), **fro** (15b)

– FO **Ufo** (59a)

F – P **fop** (38a,40d,46d)

FR – **fra** (23c,63c,101d,123b,129d), **fro** (15b), **fry** (57d)

F – R **far** (44c), **fir** (16a,36a,52a,168c,d,169a), **for** (123d,163a,166c), **fur**

– FR **Afr.** (36c)

F – S **fas** (44d,89d,129d)

F – T **fat** (110a,124a), **fit** (7a,11d,51b,75a,114a,123a,124c,126a, 153a,157c,159a), **fot** (188), **fut** (188)

– FT **aft** (14a,15b,17d,128b,167d), **eft** (93b,107a,136c,169d), **oft** (63c)

FU – **fub** (29b,119d), **fug** (129a), **Ful** (158b), **fun, fur, fut** (188)

F – U **feu** (55d,61c,88b), **flu, fou** (139a)

F – W **few**

F – X **fix** (7b,10a,13a,14c,43a,c,141d,165c), **fox** (134a)

F – Y **fay** (32c,54b,154b), **Fay** (183c), **fey** (49c), **fly** (58c,81b,163b,178d), **fry** (57d)

F – Z **fez** (75a,162a)

GA – **gab** (29b,78a,116c,122a,161c,183a), **gad** (58c,100a,127d,132b, 153c,154b,178a), **Gad** (84a,186d), **gaf** (12b), **gag** (146c,183a), **gaj** (190), **gal, gam** (76b,176d,180c), **Gan** (132d), **gap** (11b,23a,29b, 76c,110d,128a), **gar** (57b,c,d,106b), **gas** (10b,29b,59a,116d,161c), **gat** (28d,72c,131a), **gau** (66d,67a), **gav** (72d), **gaw** (140c), **gay, Gay** (17d), **gaz** (188,190)

G – A **goa** (65d,104b,126c), **Goa** (121c), **gra** (59b,94b,160c)

– GA **aga** (35a,39a,48b,102d,103a,b,111c,166b,170d,171a)

– GB **KGB** (135d)

G – B **gab** (29b,78a,116c,122a,161c,183a), **Geb** (47d), **gib** (17b,38b,95d, 166d,179d), **gob** (97b,136c)

G – D **gad** (58c,100a,b,127d,132b,153c,154b,178a), **Gad** (84a,186d), **ged** (140a), **Ged** (100a), **gid** (143d), **god** (42a), **God** (84d)

GE – **Geb** (47d), **Ged** (100a,140a), **gee** (35a,91c,100a,131c,139c,162c), **Geg** (8c), **gel** (32d,73d,150a), **gem** (104b), **gen** (31d,76b), **geo** (34a, 47d), **ger** (8d,36d,75c,124d), **Ges** (151b), **get** (44d,64b,109b,141d), **gey** (140a), **gez** (188)

G – E **gee** (35a,91c,100a,131c,139c,162c), **gie** (139c,140a), **gue** (176c)

– GE **age** (51d,66a,92a,97c,98c,116b,141c)

G – F **gaf** (12b)

G - G **gag** (146c,183a), **Geg** (8c), **gig** (26d,28d,57c,105b,127a,144c,153a, 171d), **gog** (95b)

- GG **egg** (32d,80b,81c,112c,174a)

GH - **ghi** (24d)

- GH **ugh** (52c)

GI - **gib** (17b,38b,95d,166d,179d), **gid** (143d), **gie** (139c,140a), **gig** (26d,28d,57c,105b,127a,144c,153a,171d), **gin** (37c,92d,139a,142a, 149b), **gip** (29b,160c), **git** (101a)

G - I **ghi** (24d), **goi** (107c), **gri** (75c,78b)

G - J **gaj** (190)

G - L **gal**, **gel** (32d,73d,150a), **gul** (134a)

G - M **gam** (76b,176d,180c), **gem** (104b), **gum** (7b,53c,80b,130c,156b), **gym** (154a)

GN - **gnu** (11a,181d)

G - N **gan** (132d), **gen** (31d,76b), **gin** (37c,92d,139a,142a,149b), **gon** (188), **gun** (56d,131a,146a)

GO - **goa** (65d,104b,126c), **Goa** (121c), **gob** (97b,136c), **god** (42a), **God** (84d), **gog** (95b), **goi** (107c), **gon** (188), **goo** (156b), **Gor** (81a), **got**, **goy** (107c), **goz** (190)

G - O **geo** (34a,47d), **goo** (156b)

- GO **ago** (25a,69d,114d,147a), **ego** (51a,79a,142b)

G - P **gap** (11b,23a,29b,76c,110d,128a), **gip** (29b,160c), **gup** (70a), **gyp** (29b,42a,160c)

GR - **gra** (59b,94b,160c), **gri** (75c,78b), **grr** (52c), **gry** (78b)

G - R **gar** (57b,c,d,106b), **ger** (8d,36d,75c,124d), **Gor** (81a), **grr** (52c), **gur** (159a)

G - S **gas** (10b,29b,59a,116d,161c), **Ges** (151b), **Gus** (96a)

G - T **gat** (28d,72c,131a), **get** (44d,64b,109b,141d), **git** (101a), **got**, **gut** (114d,130a)

GU - **gue** (176c), **gul** (134a), **gum** (7b,53c,80b,130c,156b), **gun** (56d, 131a,146a), **gup** (70a), **gur** (159a), **Gus** (96a), **gut** (114d,130a), **guy** (55b,131b,155d), **Guy** (96a), **guz** (188)

G - U **gau** (66d,67a), **gnu** (11a,181d)

- GU **ngu** (188

G - V **gav** (72d)

G - W **gaw** (140c)

GY - **gym** (154a), **gyp** (29b,42a,160c)

G - Y **gay**, **Gay** (17d), **gey** (140a), **goy** (107c), **gry** (78b), **guy** (55b,131b, 155d), **Guy** (96a)

G - Z **gaz** (188,190), **gez** (188), **goz** (190), **guz** (188)

HA - **had**, **hae** (139c), **hag** (140a,183a), **hah** (52c), **hai** (55c), **hak** (46d), **Hal** (69d), **ham** (98a,144b), **Ham** (18d,107c), **Han** (16c,30b,185b), **hao** (189) **hap** (17d,28d), **har** (139c), **has**, **hat** (74d), **Hat** (183d), **haw** (35a,52c,74d,91a,155a,162c), **hay** (52c,55c,165d)

H - A **Hea** (15b), **hia** (114b), **hoa** (39b)

- HA **aha** (52c,55c,159c), **cha** (162b,c), **dha** (99c), **FHA** (8a), **Kha** (88d, 106b), **sha** (110c,143d,144a,c,174c,181c)

H - B **hob** (40c,56d,100c,124b,167a,180c), **hub** (28b,118b,180c)

H - C **hic** (52c,90a,164c)

H - D **had, hid, hod** (23b,32d,102d,141a)

HE - **Hea** (15b), **Heh** (191), **hei** (65a), **Hel** (68d,93c,172d), **hem** (22a,36a, 48b,52c,155a), **hen** (19a,60c,114c,136c), **hep** (52c), **her** (124b,c), **heu** (8b,30c,52c), **hew** (40a), **hex** (18c), **hey** (25c,52c)

H - E **hae** (139c), **hie** (79a,153b), **hoe** (39c), **hue** (33c,143b)

- HE **che** (145d), **rhe** (59a), **she** (124b), **She** (73a), **the** (13b)

H - G **hag** (140a,183a), **hog** (45b,117c,160c), **hug** (32c,49d)

H - H **hah** (52c), **Heh** (191), **Hoh** (80d), **hsh** (79c), **huh** (52c)

HI - **hia** (114b), **hic** (52c,90a,164c), **hid, hie** (79a,153b), **him** (124b), **hin** (189), **hip** (52c,54b,85b,133c,134a), **hir** (76a), **his** (124c), **hit** (32d,157c,158a)

H - I **hai** (55c), **hei** (65a), **hoi** (52c,74b,185b), **hui** (14a,30b,56d,114c)

- HI **Ahi** (32c,147d), **chi** (91c), **Chi** (69c), **ghi** (24d), **ihi** (57c,156b), **phi** (91c)

H - K **hak** (46d)

H - L **Hal** (69d), **Hel** (68d,93c,172d)

H - M **ham** (98a,144b), **Ham** (18d,107c), **hem** (22a,36a,48b,52c,155a), **him** (124b), **hum** (24d,46b,150d)

- HM **ohm** (49b,67a,173b)

H - N **Han** (16c,30b,185b), **hen** (19a,60c,114c,136c), **hin** (189), **Hun** (16c,21d,174b)

HO - **hoa** (39b), **hob** (40c,56d,100c,124b,167a,180c), **hod** (23b,32d,102d, 141a), **hoe** (39c), **hog** (45b,117c,160c), **Hoh** (80d), **hoi** (52c,74b, 185b), **hop** (40b), **Hor** (103d), **hot** (10c,176c), **how, hoy** (16c,52c)

H - O **hao** (189)

- HO **cho** (188), **mho** (49b,173b), **oho** (52c), **Rho** (71b,91c), **sho** (188), **tho** (52a), **Tho** (167a), **who** (129c)

H - P **hap** (17d,28d), **hep** (52c), **hip** (52c,54b,85b,133c,134a), **hop** (40b), **hup** (35a), **hyp**

H - R **har** (139c), **her** (124b,c), **hir** (76a), **Hor** (103d), **Hur** (91d)

- HR **ihr** (66d)

HS - **hsh** (79c)

H - S **has, his** (124c)

H - T **hat** (74d), **Hat** (183d), **hit** (32d,157c,158a), **hot** (10c,176c), **hut** (143c)

HU - **hub** (28b,118b,180c), **hue** (33c,143b,) **hug** (32c,49d), **huh** (52c), **hui** (14a,30b,56d,114c), **hum** (24d,46b,150d), **Hun** (16c,21d,174b), **hup** (35a), **Hur** (91d), **hut** (143c)

H - U **heu** (8b,30c,52c)

- HU **ahu** (24c,41d,65d,103d,120d), **dhu** (40b), **Dhu** (28a,87d), **phu** (38c), **Shu** (30b,127a)

H - W **haw** (35a,52c,74d,91a,155a,162c), **hew** (40a), **how**

H - X **hex** (18c)

HY - **hyp**

H - Y **hay** (52c,55c,165d), **hey** (25c,52c), **hoy** (16c,52c)

- HY **shy** (16d,99d,128c,160c,165d,175a), **thy**, **why** (52c)

IA - **ial** (158b), **Ian** (85b,96a,139d), **iao** (78a,96c,178d)

I - A **iba** (117a), **Ida** (103d,183c), **Ila** (16b), **ILA** (173a), **ina** (158c), **Ina** (183c), **Ira** (18c,d,41a,68c,82c,96a,164a,178a,c), **Ita** (51b,71d, 94d,95d,106b,117a), **ITA** (173a), **iva** (76a,97b,127b,185b) **iwa** (63c), **iya** (95b,108d,111c)

- IA **dia** (122b,d,152a,165b), **hia** (114b), **Lia** (82b), **mia** (83c), **pia** (13b, 22d,48a,120d), **ria** (38c,51d,81b,152a,b), **Sia** (80c), **tia** (151d), **via** (132a,133a,b,179a)

IB - **iba** (117a), **Ibo** (107a,180b)

- IB **bib**, **dib** (21b,43b,c,120d,140a), **fib** (162a), **gib** (17b,38b,95d,166d, 179d), **jib** (38b,136b,146a), **mib** (8d,96c), **nib** (17b,19d,115d), **rib** (37c,85b,90c,98a,144d,159d,172a), **sib** (86b,129c,139d,147b)

IC - **ice** (30a,36d,42d,63d), **ich** (66c), **ici** (61d), **Ici** (9b), **ics** (158d), **icy** (65d)

- IC **hic** (52c,90a,164c), **pic** (188), **sic** (90a,165b,168b), **tic** (104d,153a, 171c,d)

ID - **Ida** (103d,183c), **ide** (40c,57a,b,d,158b), **Ido** (13c,81d,88c,173c)

I - D **Ind** (80c)

- ID **aid** (14a,15b,64c,75d,158b), **bid** (35a,82a,109d,111b,174c), **Cid** (151c,d), **did**, **fid** (16b,54d,118a,167b), **gid** (143d), **hid**, **kid** (67d, 85b,90d,186a), **lid** (167b), **mid** (9d,28b,73b), **nid** (72a,106b,c,116d), **oid** (158c), **rid** (32a,44a,60d), **Sid** (96a)

IE - **ier** (50a,158c)

I - E **ice** (30a,36d,42d,63d), **Ide** (40c,57a,b,d,158b), **ife** (22c,75d), **Ike** (123a), **ile** (62a,63b,158c), **ine** (29c,158b,c), **Ine** (10c,137d,180b), **ire** (10c,30c,52b,64c,125a,130b,185a), **ise** (40d,158c,d), **Ise** (78a, 84c), **ite** (59b,81a,105d,130c,158b,c,d,161a), **ive** (158c)

- IE **cie** (61b,63b), **die** (27b,54a,65a,155a,167a), **fie** (52c,59d), **gie** (139c,140a), **hie** (79a,153b), **lie** (53a,69d,162a), **nie** (53c), **pie** (42d,85d,95b,114d,171b,172a), **rie** (28c,70d,97d), **sie** (46c,66d, 139b,140b,146b), **tie** (10a,14c,38b,45d,51a,88d,109b,127c,138b, 170b), **vie** (36c,157c,170c)

IF - **ife** (22c,75d)

- IF **Lif** (107d), **rif** (188), **Sif** (164d), **vif** (62a), **Zif** (102a)

I - G **ing** (114b,d,148d,158c,d,175c), **Ing** (10c,115b)

- IG **big**, **cig**, **dig** (52b), **fig**, **gig** (26d,28d,57c,105b,127a,144c, 153a,171d), **jig** (40b,d), **mig** (8d,96c,145b), **Mig** (118d), **nig** (33b, 40a,46a), **pig** (27a,45b,99a,151b,160c), **rig** (51b,112a), **tig** (46b), **wig** (73b), **zig** (84a)

IH - **ihi** (57c,156b), **ihr** (66d)

I - H **ich** (66c), **ish** (158b), **Ith** (10a,28a,82b,99d)

I - I **ici** (61d), **Ici** (9b), **ihi** (57c,156b), **ini** (158d), **iri** (18a,d,75a)

- II **dii** (68d), **oii** (105c), **rii** (157b,175b)

IJ - **Ijo** (107a)

IK - **Ike** (123a)

I - K **ilk** (31d,54c,86b,136d,139c,140b), **ink** (20b,40c), **irk** (10d)

- IK **aik** (139d), **pik** (188)

IL - **ila** (16b), **ILA** (173a), **ile** (62a,63b,158c), **ilk** (31d,54c,86b,136d, 139c,140b), **ill** (43d,121a,173a,c,d), **ILO** (184c), **ils** (62b,d,164b)

I - L **ial** (158b), **ill** (43d,121a,173a,c,d)

- IL **ail** (170a), **kil** (82b), **lil** (72d), **mil** (80b,110c,164d,182d), **Mil** (10a), **nil** (108c), **oil** (11a,71a), **pil** (34b), **sil** (30c,185c,d), **til** (142d)

IM - **imp** (42b,127d,174a), **imu** (15d)

I - M **ism** (45a,79b,161c)

- IM **aim** (42d,43d,67d,109b,125d,157c), **Bim** (16c), **dim** (47a,48b,54a, 74d,94d,109b), **him** (124b), **Jim** (96a), **Kim** (86d), **lim** (21a), **mim** (12b), **nim** (96d,155d), **rim** (22a,48b,96d,116b,124b,166a,180c), **Sim** (96b), **Tim** (43b), **vim** (50b,176b)

IN - **ina** (158c), **Ina** (183c), **Ind** (80c), **ine** (29c,158b,c), **Ine** (10c, 137d,180b), **ing** (114b,d,158c,d,175c) **Ing** (10c,115b), **ini** (158d), **ink** (20b,40c), **inn** (72b,73b,78c,132b,150a,161c,162b,179a), **Inn** (41a), **Ino** (14b,25b), **ins** (164d), **INS** (107a,182d)

I - N **ian** (85b,96a,139d), **inn** (72b,73b,78c,132b,150a,161c,162b,179a), **Inn** (41a), **ion** (11c,29a,49b,101b,114c,158c)

- IN **ain** (18d,91c,110c,124b,140a,154b,180a), **bin** (22c,59a,78a,128c, 156d), **din** (31c,130b,174a), **ein** (66b,c), **fin** (86a), **gin** (37c,92d, 139a,142a,149b), **hin** (189), **jin** (42b,153c), **kin** (30b,81c,129d) **Kin** (30b), **lin** (140c,168c,178d), **Lin** (115d,186c), **Min** (29d,68b, 113c), **nin** (107d), **pin** (45d,54d,141d,147d), **rin** (33b,142b), **sin** (91c,140b,147a,168b,176a), **Sin** (102b), **tin** (36c,99a,b,108b,155a, 179c), **vin** (63a,182b), **win** (7a,17b,64b,123b), **yin** (140a), **Yin** (30b, 143c,185b)

IO - **ion** (11c,29a,101b,114c,158c), **ior** (50a,158c), **ios** (74d), **IOU** (124b)

I - O **iao** (78a,96c,178d), **Ibo** (107a,180b), **Ido** (13c,81d,88c,173c), **Ijo** (107a), **ILO** (184c), **Ino** (14b,25b), **iso** (34a,122c,d), **Ito** (84a,c, 186d), **iyo** (7d,176b)

- IO **CIO** (173a), **mio** (152c), **rio** (33a,131d,132a,152c,157b), **Rio** (23a), **tio** (152d), **Zio** (147d,163d)

I - P **imp** (42b,127d,174a)

- IP **dip** (26a,79d,117c,138c), **gip** (29b,160c), **hip** (52c,54b,85b,133c, 134a), **kip** (17c,72d,76c,189), **lip** (48b,58b,80a,131c), **nip** (20c, 29b,45d,46a,b,115c,118a), **pip** (11d,44a,121d,142a,154a), **Pip** (43b), **rip** (87b,130a,162c), **Rip** (178b), **sip** (46b,79d,104a,162b), **tip** (26b,d,50a,70d,77b,78a,120a,165d), **yip** (16c), **zip** (24b,50b, 176b)

IR - **Ira** (18c,d,41a,68c,82c,96a,164a,178a,c), **ire** (10c,30c,52b,64c,

125a,130b,185a), **Iri** (18a,d,75a), **irk** (10d)

I - R **ier** (50a,158c), **ihr** (66d), **ior** (50a,158c)

- IR **air** (11c,12c,42b,44c,53a,96b,98c,99d,125b,170c), **Eir** (69a,75a), **fir** (16a,36a,52a,168c,d,169a), **hir** (76a), **mir** (29d,135c,d,166c,176b), **pir** (103a,b,136c), **sir** (163b,166b), **tir** (61d,62c,87a,145b), **vir** (89c)

IS - **ise** (40d,158c,d), **Ise** (78a,84c), **-ish** (158b), **ism** (45a,79b,161c), **iso** (34a,122c,d), **ist** (7b,34b,43a,59b,66c,158c,d)

I - S **ics** (158d), **ils** (62b,d,164b), **ins** (164d), **INS** (107a,182d), **ios** (74d), **its** (124c)

- IS **bis** (50a,90a,102c,130b,171c), **cis** (34c,122c), **dis** (122b,d), **Dis** (68b,73a,119d,172d,174b), **eis** (66c), **his** (124c), **lis** (54b, 58b,60c,62a,92b), **Lis** (47a), **mis** (122b,c,d,185c), **nis** (23d,67d, 68a,87c), **Nis** (19d), **ris** (131d), **sis** (67b,129c), **tis**, **vis** (59d,89b,d, 90b,176b), **wis** (79d,164c)

IT - **Ita** (51b,71d,94d,95d,106b,117a), **ITA** (173a), **ite** (59b,81a,105d, 130c,158b,c,d,161a), **Ite** (130c), **Ith** (10a,28a,82b,99d), **Ito** (84a, c,186d), **its** (124c)

I - T **ist** (7b,34b,43a,59b,66c,158b,c,d)

- IT **ait** (82d,132a), **bit** (46a,86b,114c,167a,b,171c,180d), **cit** (81a, 167d), **dit** (62b,d,120a,159d), **fit** (7a,11d,51b,75a,114a,123a,124c, 126a,153a,157c,159a), **git** (101a), **hit** (32d,157c,158a), **kit** (112a, 176c), **Kit** (96a,183d), **lit**, **mit** (56c,66d,183b), **nit** (48d), **pit** (52b, 142a,164a,168a), **rit** (148c,140b,153d), **sit** (98c,116a,121c,130c, 142d), **tit** (19c,130d), **uit** (47a,111d,151a), **wit** (78d,85b,177b)

I - U **imu** (15d), **I.O.U.** (124b)

- IU **piu** (102c), **Tiu** (7c,68c,147d,163d,166c,170c), **Ziu** (147d,163d)

IV - **iva** (76a,97b,127b,185b), **ive** (158c), **ivy** (32b,38c,176b)

- IV **div** (42b,139b), **Liv** (93b)

IW - **iwa** (63c)

- IW **Tiw** (68c,147d,163d)

- IX **Aix** (46b), **dix** (118b), **Dix** (60b), **fix** (7b,10a,13a,14c,43a,c,141d, 165c), **mix** (156b), **nix** (23d,108c,178d), **pix** (31a,51d,175d), **six** (26c), **vix** (89d,138b)

IY - **iya** (95b,108d,111c), **iyo** (7d,176b)

I - Y **icy** (65d), **ivy** (32b,38c,176b)

- IZ **biz**, **viz** (105b)

JA - **jab** (120b,125c) **jag** (124d,148a) **Jah** (84d), **jam** (123a,156d,165c), **Jap**, **jar** (31d,70d,143b), **Jat** (80d,125c), **jaw** (97d,138c), **jay** (19b, 91c)

J - B **jab** (120b,125c), **jib** (38b,136b,146a), **job** (30d,184c), **Job** (96a)

JE - **jet** (20b,35a,154c), **jeu** (61d), **Jew**

J - E **Joe** (96a)

J - G **jag** (124d,148a), **jig** (40b,d), **jog** (82c,85c,170a), **jug** (118c,123d)

J - H **Jah** (84d)

JI - **jib** (38b,136b,146a), **jig** (40b,d), **Jim** (96a), **jin** (42b,153c)

- JI **tji** (189), **uji** (146d)

J – M **jam** (123a,156d,165c), **Jim** (96a), **jum** (39c)

J – N **jin** (42b,153c)

JO – **job** (30d,184c), **Job** (96a), **Joe** (96a), **jog** (82c,85c,170a), **jot** (82a, 114c,166c,180d), **jow** (188), **joy**

– JO **djo** (188), **ljo** (107a)

J – P **Jap**

J – R **jar** (31d,70d,143b), **Jur** (107b)

J – S **jus** (61d,90b)

J – T **Jat** (80d,125c), **jet** (20b,35a,154c), **jot** (82a,114c,166c,180d), **jut** (53a,124a)

JU – **jug** (118c,123d), **jum** (39c), **Jur** (107b), **jus** (61d,90b), **jut** (53a,124a)

J – U **jeu** (61d)

J – W **jaw** (97d,138c), **Jew**, **jow** (188)

J – Y **jay** (19b,91c), **joy**

KA – **kab** (75c), **kae** (84a,140b), **kaf** (12b), **Kaf** (104a), **kai** (59c), **Kai** (14d,84c), **kan** (93a), **kas** (32c,47a), **kat** (105d), **kay** (82d), **Kay** (13b,134b)

K – A **kea** (114a,b), **Kha** (88d,106b), **koa** (74c), **Kra** (11b,91d), **Kua** (95c)

– KA **aka** (176b), **Aka** (13d,88b,c), **oka** (170c,184a,189)

K – B **kab** (75c), **Keb** (47d), **KGB** (135d), **kob** (11a)

K – D **ked** (140b,144a), **kid** (67d,85b,90d,186a)

KE – **kea** (114a,b), **Keb** (47d), **ked** (140b,144a), **kef** (12a,46c,75d,88c), **keg** (27a,105b), **ken** (60b,87c,122b,172d), **kep** (139b), **Ker** (71b, 95d), **ket** (189) **key** (14c,82d,88b,117c,118c,150b,180c)

K – E **kae** (84a,140b)

– KE **ake** (60a,107a), **eke** (14c,117c), **Ike** (123a), **oke** (189)

K – F **kaf** (12b), **Kaf** (104a), **kef** (12a,46c,75d,88c)

KG – **KGB** (135d)

K – G **keg** (27a,105b)

KH – **Kha** (88d,106b)

– KH **akh** (153d)

KI – **kid** (67d,85b,90d,186a), **kil** (82b), **Kim** (86d), **kin** (30b,81c,129d), **Kin** (30b), **kip** (17c,72d,76c,189), **kit** (112a,176c), **Kit** (96a,183d)

K – I **kai** (59c), **Kai** (14d,84c), **koi** (26d), **kri** (75c,96d), **Kri** (75c), **Kui** (86a,88c,146a)

– KI **ski** (149c)

K – L **kil** (82b), **Kol** (18b), **kyl** (76d,79b)

K – M **Kim** (86d)

K – N **kan** (93a), **ken** (60b,87c,122b), **kin** (30b,81c), **Kin** (30b)

KO – **koa** (74c), **kob** (11a), **koi** (26d), **Kol** (18b), **kop** (76d), **kor** (75c), **Kos** (77c,82d), **kou** (169a)

– KO **ako** (189), **TKO** (22c)

K – P **kep** (139b), **kip** (17c,72d,76c,189), **kop** (76d), **kup** (188)

KR - **Kra** (11b,91d), **kri** (75c,96d), **Kru** (91d)

K - R **Ker** (71b,95d), **kor** (75c)

K - S **kas** (32c,47a), **Kos** (77c,82d)

K - T **kat** (105d), **ket** (189), **kit** (112a,176c), **Kit** (96a,183d)

KU - **Kua** (95c), **Kui** (86a,88c,146a), **kup** (188)

K - U **kou** (169a), **Kru** (91d)

- KU **aku** (57c,176a)

KY - **kyl** (76d,79b)

K - Y **kay** (82d), **Kay** (13b,134b), **key** (14c,82d,88b,117c,118c,150b, 180c)

- KY **sky** (56d)

LA - **lab**, **lac** (53c,99d,130c,135b,174d), **lad** (22c,25b,55b,157c,186a), **lag** (93c,155d), **Lai** (24c,d,88c), **lai** (98b,161b), **lak** (38a), **lam** (51b, 58b,93d,164d,178a), **lan** (37b,d,160b), **Lao** (80d,88c,146a,161b), **lap** (31b,37d,59b,127a,131d,153d,167d), **lar** (24c,51d,67a,78d,95d, 101d,171b), **las** (13b,151d) **lat** (24a,33d,106b,118a), **lav** (72d), **law** (26b,33a,40a,48c,60b,85d,91a,111b,134d,155d), **lax** (93d,130a), **lay** (16a,25c,80a,98b,107d,141d,150b), **Laz** (27d)

L - A **lea** (56a,97d,114d,185b), **Lea** (22d), **Lia** (82b), **loa** (7d,53c,97d,184d)

- LA **ala** (6d,13a,15c,61a,133d,182c,d), **Ala.** (151b), **ela** (21c,53c,72b, 76c,108b,174c), **Ila** (16b), **ILA** (173a), **ola** (113b), **ula** (72c,158c)

L - B **lab**, **LLB** (42a), **lob** (15d,23b,94c,100b,163a,172d)

- LB **alb** (65b,176a), **elb** (85c), **LLB** (42a)

LC - **LCI** (21b)

L - C **lac** (53c,99d,130c,135b,174d)

L - D **lad** (22c,25b,55b,157c,186a), **led**, **lid** (167b), **LLD** (42a), **lud** (100a), **Lud** (23c,144b)

- LD **eld** (10b,93c,110b,165d), **LLD** (42a), **old** (8a,71a,77c,123c,175b)

LE - **lea** (56a,97d,114d,185b), **Lea** (22d), **led**, **lee** (74b,144b), **Lee** (9c, 31c,96a), **leg** (37d,92b,141d,159d,169c), **lei** (65b,74c), **lek** (65c), **Leo** (36b,c,92d,186d), **Ler** (23d,28a,b,64b,106c,141a), **les** (13b, 61a), **let** (9a,76d,77c,116b,130a,158b,163a), **leu** (190), **lev** (33b), **lew** (190), **Lew** (96a), **lex** (90b), **ley** (190)

L - E **lee** (74b,144b), **Lee** (9c,31c,96a), **lie** (53a,69d,162a), **loe** (139d), **lue** (146b), **lye** (8d,27d,93b)

- LE **ale** (17c,18c,50c,55d,92d,104c), **cle** (158d), **ele** (48c), **ile** (62a,63b, 158c), **ole** (24b,29b,113b,152a,158b,d), **ule** (23a,27d,134c,158c, 168d)

L - F **Lif** (107d), **lof** (188)

- LF **Alf** (96a), **elf** (54b,154b)

L - G **lag** (93c,155d), **leg** (37d,92b,141d,159d,169c), **log** (64a,128d), **lug** (27a,45d,47b,73c,136b), **Lug** (28b)

LI - **Lia** (82b), **lid** (167b), **lie** (53a,69d,162a), **Lif** (107d), **lil** (72d), **lim** (21a), **lin** (92c,140c,168c,178d), **Lin** (115d,186c), **lip** (48b,58b,80a, 131c), **lis** (54b,58b,60c,62a,92b), **Lis** (47a), **lit**, **Liv** (93b)

L - I **lai** (98b,161b), **Lai** (24c,d,88c), **LCI** (21b), **lei** (65b,74c), **loi** (62a)

- LI **Ali** (7b,12a,25c,48b,55a,60c,92d,101a,103a,164a,166b,170d), **Eli** (18c,d,76c,96a,137a,185a)

L - K **lak** (38a), **lek** (65c), **Lok** (15d,68b)

- LK **alk** (171b), **elk** (22c,90d,178a), **ilk** (31d,54c,86b,136d,139c,140b)

LL - **LLB** (42a), **LLD** (42a)

L - L **lil** (72d)

- LL **all** (35c,118a,126d,181a), **ell** (10d,24b,32c,98a), **ill** (43d,121a,173a, c,d), **Ull** (7c,68c,146b,164d)

L - M **lam** (51b,58b,93d,164d,178a), **lim** (21a), **lum** (30a)

- LM **elm** (168c), **olm** (48c), **ulm** (49c), **Ulm** (40d)

L - N **lan** (37b,d,160b), **lin** (140c,168c,178d), **Lin** (115d,186c), **Lon** (86c, 96a), **lyn** (140c,178d)

LO - **loa** (7d,53c,97d,184d), **lob** (15d,23b,94c,100b,163a,172d), **loe** (139d), **lof** (188), **log** (64a,128d), **loi** (62a), **Lok** (15d,68b), **Lon** (86c, 96a), **loo** (65a), **lop** (30c,40a,46b,143a), **los** (13b,151d), **lot** (24b, 28d,55a,65d,114a,119c,143c,150d,168a), **Lot** (6b,73d), **Lou** (96a, 183d), **low** (16c,149d), **loy** (121c,148b,151c,167a)

L - O **Lao** (80d,88c,146a,161b), **Leo** (36b,c,92d,186d), **loo** (65a), **Luo** (107b), **Lwo** (107b)

- LO **Flo, ILO** (184c), **ulo** (34b,80d)

L - P **lap** (31b,37d,59b,127a,131d,153d,167d), **lip** (48b,58b,80a,131c), **lop** (30c,40a,46b,143a)

- LP **alp** (24b,103d,115c)

L - R **lar** (24c,51d,67a,78d,95d,101d,171b), **Ler** (23d,28a,28b,64b,106c, 141a), **Lur** (116c)

LS - **Lst** (21a,b,88b)

L - S **las** (13b,151d), **les** (13b,61a), **lis** (54b,58b,60c,62a,92b), **Lis** (47a), **los** (13b,151d), **lys** (58b,92b)

- LS **als** (66d,163d), **els** (140a), **ils** (62b,d,164b)

L - T **lat** (24a,33d,106b,118a), **let** (9a,76d,77c,116b,130a,158b,163a), **lit**, **lot** (24b,28d,55a,65d,114a,119c,143c,150d,168a), **Lot** (6b,73d), **Lst** (21a,b,88b), **lut** (189)

- LT **alt** (66c76c,109c), **elt** (87a,117c,139d), **Olt** (41a)

LU - **lud** (100a), **Lud** (23c,144b), **lue** (146b), **lug** (27a,45d,47b,73c,136b), **Lug** (28b), **lum** (30a), **Luo** (107b), **Lur** (116c), **lut** (189), **lux** (79d)

L - U **leu** (190), **Lou** (96a,183d)

- LU **flu, ulu** (87a)

L - V **lav** (72d), **lev** (33b), **Liv** (93b)

LW - **Lwo** (107b)

L - W **law** (26b,33a,40a,48c,60b,85d,91a,111b,134d,155d), **lew** (190), **Lew** (96a), **low** (16c,149d)

L - X **lax** (93d, 130a), **lex** (90b), **lux** (79d)

LY - **lye** (8d,27d,93b), **lyn** (140c,178d), **lys** (58b,92b)

L - Y **lay** (98b,107d,141d,150b), **ley** (190), **loy** (121c,148b,151c,167a)

- LY **aly** (95d), **Ely** (27c,50b), **fly** (58c,81b,163b,178d), **ply** (59b,90b, 118d,164b,171c,174a,181b,184c), **sly** (13b,38b,64c,81b,132c)

L - Z **Laz** (27d)

MA - **maa** (97d,143d), **Mab** (54b,126b,183d), **Mac** (96a,140b,150b), **mad** (10c,82b), **Mae** (183c), **mag** (73b,95b,166c), **Mag** (183d), **Mah** (10b, 57c,102b), **mai** (62a), **mal** (34a,b,44a,52b,62c,122b), **Mal** (94b), **Mam** (192), **man** (29c,60c,64c,65a,142d,161d), **mao** (115b), **Mao** (30b), **map** (27a,29b,54a,98d,160a), **mar** (40b,44a,79a,d,81a,140d), **Mar** (93d), **mas** (34b,55b,119a), **mat** (46d,50d,94d,117c,161d), **Mat** (96a), **mau** (170c,188), **maw** (38b,d,72c,111a,121a,142a,156c), **Max** (96a), **may** (74d), **May** (183c)

M - A **maa** (97d,143d), **MFA** (42a), **mia** (83c), **mna** (71d,179d), **moa** (19b), **Mya** (31c)

- MA **ama** (26a,28d,31a,35b,39c,95b,108d,111c,117b,182c), **oma** (158c,d, 170c), **sma** (140b,148d), **Uma** (43a,69b,153d)

M - B **Mab** (54b,126b,183d), **mib** (8d,96c), **mob** (39a,127a,165b)

M - C **Mac** (96a,140b,150b)

M - D **mad** (10c,82b), **mid** (9d,28b,73b), **Mod** (138d), **mud** (6c)

ME - **mee** (169a), **Meg** (8c,183d), **mel** (77d), **mem** (91c), **men** (38c,116a, 117b,170a), **Men** (94d), **Meo** (27b,80c), **mer** (62c,141a), **mes** (62b), **met** (28d), **meu** (153b), **mew** (25b,27b,50a,55b,72c,74d,101b,141b, 153b)

M - E **Mae** (183c), **mee** (169a), **Mme.** (166b), **Moe** (96a)

- ME **ame** (37a,62d,131b), **eme** (38d,70a,140c,172b), **Mme.** (166b), **ume** (11d)

MF - **MFA** (42a)

M - G **mag** (73b,95b,166c), **Mag** (183d), **Meg** (8c,183d), **mig** (8d,96c, 145b), **Mig** (118d), **mug** (46b,54a,65a)

MH - **mho** (49b,173b)

M - H **Mah** (10b,57c,102b)

MI - **mia** (83c), **mib** (8d,96c), **mid** (9d,28b,73b), **mig** (8d,96c,145b), **Mig** (118d), **mil** (80b,110c,164d,182d), **Mil** (10a,82b), **mim** (12b), **Min** (29d,68b,113c), **mio** (152c), **mir** (29d,135c,d,166c,176b), **mis** (122b,c,d,185c), **mit** (56c,66d,183b), **mix** (156b)

M - I **mai** (62a), **Moi** (80d)

- MI **ami** (61d)

M - L **mal** (34a,b,44a,52b,62c,122b), **Mal** (94b), **mel** (77d), **mil** (80b,110c, 164d,182d), **Mil** (10a,82b), **mol** (58b,70c), **mul** (188)

MM - **Mme.** (166b)

M - M **Mam** (192), **mem** (91c), **mim** (12b), **mom**, **mum** (30d,95a,146c)

MN - **mna** (71d,179d)

M - N **man** (29c,60c,64c,65a,142d,161d), **men** (38c,116a,117b,170a), **Men** (94d), **Min** (29d,68b,113c), **mon** (15d,84b) **Mon** (24c), **mun** (157b)

MO - **moa** (19b), **mob** (39a,127a,165b), **Mod** (138d), **Moe** (96a), **Moi** (80d), **mol** (58b,70c), **mom**, **mon** (15d,84b), **Mon** (24c), **moo** (94b), **mop** (160a), **mos** (59b), **mot** (126d,130a,137d,183b), **mow** (32b,40a)

M - O **mao** (115b), **Mao** (30b), **Meo** (27b,80c), **mho** (49b,173b), **mio** (152c), **moo** (94b), **Mro** (88c)

- MO **amo** (79a,89c), **omo** (34d)

M - P **map** (27a,29b,54a,98d,160a), **mop** (160a)

- MP **amp** (49b,173b), **imp** (42b,127d,174a)

MR - **Mro** (88c), **Mrs.** (166b), **Mru** (80d,88c)

M - R **mar** (40b,44a,79a,d,81a,140d), **Mar** (93d), **mer** (62c,141a), **mir** (29d, 135c,d,166c,176b), **mur** (63a,177d)

M - S **mas** (34b,55b,119a), **mes** (62b), **mis** (122b,c,d,185c), **mos** (59b), **Mrs.** (166b), **Mus** (104a,132c)

- MS **Ems** (125a,151c)

M - T **mat** (46d,50d,94d,117c,161d), **Mat** (96a), **met** (28d), **mit** (56c,66d, 183b), **mot** (126d,130a,137d,183b), **mut** (39c), **Mut** (9b,127a)

- MT **amt** (37d,40d,108a,163c)

MU - **mud** (6c), **mug** (46b,54a,65a), **mul** (188), **mum** (30d,95a,146c), **mun** (157b), **mur** (63a,177d), **Mus** (104a,132c), **mut** (39c), **Mut** (9b,127a), **muy** (152d,175d)

M - U **mau** (170c,188), **meu** (153b), **Mru** (80d,88c)

- MU **emu** (19b,58c,111d), **imu** (15d), **SMU** (40b), **umu** (112a)

M - W **maw** (38b,d,72c,111a,121a,142a,156c), **mew** (25b,27b,50a,55b,72c, 74d,101b,141b,153b), **mow** (32b,40a)

M - X **Max** (96a), **mix** (156b)

MY - **Mya** (31c)

M - Y **may** (74d), **May** (183c), **muy** (152d,175d)

- MY **amy** (63c), **Amy** (8c,94b,183c)

NA - **nab** (13b,26c,27b,142a), **nae** (139d), **nag** (73d,78b,138c,184d), **nak** (156b), **Nan** (183c), **nap** (65a,117d,146b,148a), **nar** (139d), **nas** (74a, 89c,178b), **nat** (7a,24c,d,106a), **nay** (42b,106b)

N - A **NEA** (162c), **noa** (35b,124a,161a), **NRA** (8a,20d)

- NA **ana** (10b,33c,60d,93a,98c,122b,d,140d,142b), **Ana** (28a,68d,100c), **Ena** (8c,126b), **ina** (158c), **Ina** (183c), **mna** (71d,179d), **Ona** (26b, 64a), **sna** (105b,140b,143d,144a,149c,181c,d), **Una** (54a,153b, 170c,183c)

N - B **nab** (13b,26c,27b,142a), **neb** (17b,19a,d,115d), **nib** (17b,19d,115d), **nob** (38c,74d,84a,149d) **nub** (67b,94d,95c,118c,124d)

N - D **Ned** (96a), **nid** (72a,106c,116d), **nod** (17c,46c), **Nod** (18d,25b)

- ND **and** (36a), **end** (8b,67d,120a,125d,130a,166a), **Ind** (80c), **und** (66b)

NE - **N.E.A.** (162c), **neb** (17b,19a,d,115d), **Ned** (96a), **nee** (19d,22b,25c, 60b,95c), **nef** (32b,144c,d), **neo** (34a,b,c,100d,106d,108c,122c,d, 128c), **nep** (27c,32d,56a,87c,184b), **ner** (137c), **nes** (26b), **net** (26c, 32a,50d,53b,60d,99a,124a,142a,149b), **new** (11a,63c,88d,111c, 128c, **Ney** (63b,97b,105d), **nez** (62b)

N - E **nae** (139d), **nee** (19d,22b,25c,60b,95c), **nie** (53c,66c), **NNE** (35b), **nye** (72a,116d), **Nye** (9c,18b)

- NE **ane** (61c,140a,158b), **ene** (35b,158b,c), **ine** (29c,158b,c), **Ine** (10c, 137d,180b), **NNE** (35b), **one** (79a,b,80b,d,124b,147a,148d,173a,c),

une (13b,61a,62b,95c)

N - F **nef** (32b,144c,d)

NG - **ngu** (188)

N- G **nag** (73d,78b,138c,184d), **nig** (33b,40a,46a), **nog** (20c,46a,48d,54d,100b,115d,118a)

- NG **eng** (48a,146a), **ing** (114b,d,148d,158c,d,175c), **Ing** (10c,115b)

N - H **nth** (42a)

NI - **nib** (17b,19d,115d), **nid** (72a,106c,116d), **nie** (53c,66c), **nig** (33b,40a,46a), **nil** (108c), **nim** (96d,155d), **nin** (107d), **nip** (20c,29b,45d,46a,b,115c,118a), **nis** (23d,67d,68a,87c), **Nis** (19d), **nit** (48d), **nix** (23d,108c,178d)

- NI **ani** (19b,d,20b,39b), **ini** (158d), **oni** (11b), **uni** (34c,118d,122c), **Uni** (51d)

N - K **nak** (156b)

- NK **ink** (20b,40c)

N - L **nil** (108c), **nul** (108c,177a)

N - M **nim** (96d,155d), **nom** (62b,125a), **Nym** (54c,76a)

NN - **NNE** (35b), **NNW** (35b)

N - N **Nan** (183c), **nin** (107d), **non** (34c,62b,89c,106b,122c,147a), **nun** (24c,91c,117d,147b), **Nun** (29a,85c)

- NN **Ann** (183c), **inn** (72b,73b,78c,150a,161c,162b,179a), **Inn** (41a)

NO - **noa** (35b,124a,161a), **nob** (38c,74d,84a,149d), **nod** (17c,46c,148a), **Nod** (18d,25b), **nog** (20c,46a,48d,54d,100b,115d,118a), **nom** (62b,125a), **non** (34c,62b,89c,106b,122c,147a), **noo** (108c,139d), **nor** (10b,36a,37b,92b), **nos** (62b,90a,179a), **not** (78b,106b), **now** (60b,79d), **Nox** (69b)

N - O **neo** (34a,b,c,100d,106d,108c,122c,d,128c), **noo** (108c,139d)

- NO **ano** (19d,20b,34d,122d,174a), **Ino** (14b,25b), **ono** (34a), **Ono** (18d,118d), **uno** (83c,151d)

N - P **nap** (65a,117d,146b,148a), **nep** (27c,32d,56a,87c,184b), **nip** (20c,29b,45d,46a,b,115c,118a)

NR - **NRA** (8a,20d)

N - R **nar** (139d), **ner** (137c), **nor** (10b,36a,37b,92b), **nur** (67d)

N - S **nas** (74a,89c,178b), **nes** (26b), **nis** (23d,67d,87c), **Nis** (19d), **nos** (62b,90a,179a)

- NS **Ans** (92a), **ens** (17d,18a,51a,52d), **ins** (164d), **INS** (107a,182d), **ons** (38c), **uns** (66d,174c)

NT - **nth** (42a)

N - T **nat** (7a,24c,d,106a), **net** (26c,32a,50b,53d,60d,99a,124a,142a,149b), **nit** (48d), **not** (78b,106b), **nut** (24c,32d,38b,54d,64a,65d,86b,141c,165a), **Nut** (69a)

- NT **ant** (49d,60b,81b,118c), **ent** (34d,158b,c), **TNT** (53a)

NU - **nub** (67b,94d,95c,118c,124d), **nul** (108c,177a), **nun** (24c,91c,117d,147b), **Nun** (29a,85c,129d), **nur** (67d), **nut** (24c,32d,38b,54d,64a,65d,86b,141c,165a), **Nut** (69a)

N - U **ngu** (188)

- NU **Anu** (15b,28a,68a,d,75b,88c,147d), **gnu** (11a,181d), **Unu** (24d)

N - W **new** (11a,63c,88d,111c,128c), **NNW** (35b), **now** (60b,79d)

- NW **NNW** (35b), **WNW** (35b)

N - X **nix** (23d,108c,178d), **Nox** (69b), **Nyx** (69b)

NY - **nye** (72a,116d), **Nye** (9c,18b), **Nym** (54c,76a), **Nyx** (69b)

N - Y **nay** (42b,106b), **Ney** (63b,97b,105d)

- NY **any** (14b,150b), **ony** (139a), **sny** (18a,39d,43d,87a,119a,144d,145a, 165d,176a)

N - Z **nez** (62b)

OA - **oaf** (22a,45b,146d,157d,185d), **oak** (73d,168c,169a), **oar** (20b,124c, 134b), **oat** (15a,28b,70b,144b)

O - A **oca** (48c,112c,116d,133d,170c,184a), **oda** (74a,170d), **oka** (170c, 184a,189), **ola** (113b) **oma** (158c,d,170c), **Ona** (26b,64a), **OPA** (8a), **ora** (10c,40d,41b,45b,83a,c,101c,104a,122d,123d), **ova** (48d), **oxa** (29c)

- OA **boa** (36c,55b,106a,125d,138b,142d,149a), **goa** (65d,104b,126c), **Goa** (121c), **hoa** (39b), **koa** (74c), **loa** (7d,53c,184d), **Loa** (97d), **moa** (19b), **noa** (35b,124a,161a), **poa** (20d,70d,97d), **roa** (23d,87a), **toa** (17c,178b), **Zoa** (20b)

OB - **obe** (31d,87d,150d), **obi** (55d,67b,84c,137b,150d)

O - B **orb** (50a,53c,67d,153b)

- OB **bob** (57c,115d), **Bob** (96a), **cob** (28c,78b,95d,160b,177d), **fob** (29b, 59b,113b,178c), **gob** (97b,136c), **hob** (40c,56d,100c,124b,167a, 180c), **job** (30d,184c), **Job** (96a), **kob** (11a), **lob** (15d,23b,94c,100b, 163a,172d), **mob** (39a,127a,165b), **nob** (38c,74d,84a,149d), **pob** (121b,129b,139c), **rob** (119d,155d), **Rob** (96a), **sob** (39b,179d)

OC - **oca** (48c,112c,116d,133d,170c,184a), **och** (8b), **ock** (189), **oct** (34a, 122c)

O - C **orc** (28c,70c,180b)

- OC **Doc** (143a), **roc** (19c,53b,54a,147a), **soc** (44c,85d)

OD - **oda** (74a,170d), **odd** (46b,53a,109b,157a,172d,173c), **ode** (26b,79c, 94d,118a,119d,120a,150b), **Odo** (181d), **ods** (109a)

O - D **odd** (46b,53a,109b,157a,172d,173c), **oid** (158c), **old** (8a,71a,77c, 123c,175b), **Ord** (25b,60b)

- OD **cod** (57b,c), **dod** (11a,32a,43b,140c), **fod** (188), **god** (42a), **God** (84d), **hod** (23b,32d,102d,141a), **Mod** (138d), **nod** (17c,46c), **Nod** (18d,25b), **pod** (76b,78d,91b,141b,180c), **rod** (6a,72d,88b,131a, 154d,156a,160a), **sod** (160b,170d), **tod** (24d,60c,83d), **Vod** (16a)

OE - **o'er** (6b,112a), **oes** (109a)

O - E **obe** (31d,87d,150d), **ode** (26b,79c,94d,118a,119d,120a,150b), **oke** (189), **ole** (24b,29b,113b,152a,158b,d), **one** (79a,b,80d,124b,147a, 148d,173a,c), **ope** (172b,173c), **ore** (39a,99b,108a,115b,141c,151a, 160b), **ose** (102a,146d,158b,c,d,159a), **owe, ote** (158d), **oye** (139c)

- OE **coe** (143d), **Coe** (33c), **doe** (41d,55b,127a), **foe** (111a), **hoe** (39c), **Joe** (96a), **loe** (139d), **Moe** (96a), **poe** (114b), **Poe** (9c,d,128a, 172a), **roe** (27d,41d,48d,57b,76d,95b,157b), **soe** (170c,184a), **toe** (43c,69d,148a,156a), **voe** (17a,81b), **woe** (25b), **Zoe** (36b,183c)

OF -	**off** (6b,15c,44c,76a), **oft** (63c)
O - F	**oaf** (22a,45b,146d,157d,185d), **off** (6b,15c,44c,76a), **orf** (57b,185c), **ouf** (52c)
- OF	**lof** (188)
- OG	**bog** (97a,160a), **cog** (33a,65d,163b,167b,180c), **dog** (10b,45b,59b), **fog** (109b), **gog** (95b), **hog** (45b,117c,160c), **jog** (82c,85c,170a), **log** (64a,128d), **nog** (20c,46a,48d,54d,100b,115d,118a), **sog** (149c), **tog** (46a), **vog** (189)
OH -	**ohm** (49b,67a,173b), **oho** (52c)
O - H	**och** (8b)
- OH	**boh** (24c), **doh** (113b), **foh** (52c), **Hoh** (80d), **poh** (52c), **soh** (52c, 72d,) **zoh** (13d,186b)
OI -	**oid** (158c), **oii** (105c), **oil** (11a,71a)
O - I	**obi** (55d,67b,84c,137b,150d), **oii** (105c), **oni** (11b), **ori** (34a), **ovi** (34a)
- OI	**goi** (107c), **hoi** (52c,74b,185b), **koi** (26d), **loi** (62a), **Moi** (80d), **poi** (44a,59c,74c,117a,162a,164b), **roi** (55c,62a,133d), **toi** (62b,d,63a), **Toi** (18d), **yoi** (52c,79a)
OK -	**oka** (170c,184a,189), **oke** (189)
O - K	**oak** (73d,168c,169a), **ock** (189), **ork** (180b), **ouk** (140c)
- OK	**Bok** (9c), **Lok** (15d,68b), **Rok** (87c), **sok** (188), **yok** (10c,185a)
OL -	**ola** (113b), **old** (8a,71a,77c,123c,175b), **ole** (24b,29b,113b,152a, 158b,d), **olm** (48c), **Olt** (41a)
O - L	**oil** (11a,71a), **owl**
- OL	**col** (103d,114c), **Kol** (18b), **mol** (58b,70c), **sol** (108b), **Sol** (117b, 159b), **tol** (137b), **vol** (155a,182d)
OM -	**oma** (158c,d,170c), **omo** (34d)
O - M	**ohm** (49b,67a,173b), **olm** (48c)
- OM	**com** (122d), **dom** (121c,166b,c), **Dom** (94b), **mom**, **nom** (62b,125a), **pom** (45a,148d), **rom** (72d), **tom** (95d), **Tom** (96b,157a), **yom** (41a)
ON -	**Ona** (26b,64a), **one** (79a,b,80b,d,124b,147a,148d,173a,c), **oni** (11b), **ono** (34a), **Ono** (18d,118d), **ons** (38c) **ony** (139a)
O - N	**own** (6d)
- ON	**bon** (30a,61d,86b,88c), **Bon** (84b), **con** (7d,29b,83c,116d,157d), **don** (151d,166c), **Don** (96a), **eon** (8a,37b,51d,116b), **Fon** (40b), **gon** (188), **ion** (11c,29a,49b,101b,114c,158c), **Lon** (86c,96a), **mon** (15d,84b), **Mon** (24c), **non** (34c,62b,89c,106b,122c,147a), **ron** (152c), **Ron** (86c,88a), **son** (42d,75d), **ton** (158d,167d,179d), **von** (66d,67a), **won**, **yon** (44c,112a,164d)
OO -	**oop** (139a), **oot** (140a)
O - O	**Odo** (181d), **oho** (52c), **omo** (34d), **ono** (34a), **Ono** (18d,118d), **oro** (34c,122c,152a), **Oro** (161b), **oto** (34a) **Oto** (147b)
- OO	**boo**, **coo** (19b), **Coo** (82d), **foo** (42c), **goo** (156b), **loo** (65a), **moo** (94b), **noo** (108c,139d), **roo** (140a), **soo** (127d,140b,151b), **Soo** (137c), **too** (18b,102c), **woo**, **zoo** (181b)
OP -	**OPA** (8a), **ope** (172b,173c), **Ops** (28c,69a,b,74a,137c), **opt** (30c)

O - P **oop** (139a), **orp** (140c,179d)

- OP **cop** (36a,120c,126d,153c,155d), **dop** (39c,43b), **fop** (38a,40d,46d), **hop** (40b), **kop** (76d), **lop** (30c,40a,46b,143a), **mop** (160a), **oop** (139a), **pop** (52d,53a,130b,149d), **sop** (23b,35d,149c,155d), **top** (38c,52b,118b,123d,160a,174a,186b), **wop**

OR - **ora** (10c,40d,41b,45b,83a,c,101c,104a,122d,123d), **orb** (50a,53c, 67d,153b), **orc** (28c,70c,180b), **Ord** (25b,60b), **ore** (39a,99b,108a, 115b,141c,151a,160b), **orf** (57b,185c), **ori** (34a), **ork** (180b), **oro** (34c,122c,152a), **Oro** (161b), **orp** (140c,179d), **orr** (77c), **ort** (59b, 90d,91a,102c,129b,140d,180a,184d), **ory** (36c)

O - R **oar** (20b,124c,134b), **oer** (6b,112a), **orr** (77c), **our** (124c)

- OR **Bor** (120c), **cor** (36c,75b,155b), **dor** (17d,24b,32b,46b,47a,81b,85d), **for** (123d,163a,166c), **Gor** (81a), **Hor** (103d), **ior** (50a,158c), **kor** (75c), **nor** (10b,36a,37b,92b), **por** (152a), **tor** (38b,76d,85d,115c, 124b,132b,c), **Vor** (69a)

OS - **ose** (102a,146d,158b,c,d,159a), **ost** (15d,86b)

O - S **ods** (109a), **oes** (109a), **ons** (38c), **Ops** (28c,69a,b,74a,137c), **ous** (158b)

- OS **Bos** (27c), **cos** (91d,132d), **dos** (45d,61a,97a,181b), **Eos** (14d,41a, 68d), **ios** (74d), **Kos** (77c,82d), **los** (13b,151d), **mos** (59b), **nos** (62b, 90a,179a), **ros** (37b), **Ros** (138a,174d), **SOS**

OT - **ote** (158d), **oto** (34a), **Oto** (147b)

O - T **oat** (15a,28b,70b,144b), **oct** (34a,122c), **oft** (63c), **Olt** (41a), **oot** (140a), **opt** (30c), **ort** (59b,90d,91a,102c,129b,140d,180a,184d), **ost** (15d,86b), **out** (6b,14b,60b,69d,80a,108b,185c)

- OT **bot** (59a,88d), **cot** (129b,148b), **dot** (45d,97a,104d,105a,116b,153a, 162d), **fot** (188), **got**, **hot** (10c,176c), **jot** (82a,114c,166c,180d), **lot** (24b,28d,55a,65d,114a,119c,143c,150d,168a), **Lot** (6b,73d), **mot** (126d,130a,137d,183b), **not** (78b,106b), **oot** (140a), **pot** (120b, 145b,154d,175d), **rot** (22b,134c,143d,153d), **sot** (46c,167b,c), **tot** (186a), **Vot** (56d)

OU - **ouf** (52c), **ouk** (140c), **our** (124c), **ous** (158b), **out** (6b,14b,60b,69d, 80a,108b,185c)

- OU **fou** (139a), **IOU** (124b), **kou** (169a), **Lou** (96a,183d), **sou** (63b), **you**

OV - **ova** (48d), **ovi** (34a)

OW - **owe**, **owl**, **own** (6d)

- OW **bow** (11c,21b,39d,60a,107c,109a,125a,144d,158a), **cow** (22c,45b, 81d), **dow** (17d,87a,88d,175d), **how**, **jow** (188), **low** (16c,149d), **mow** (32b,40a), **now** (60b,79d), **pow**, **row** (44c,56b,92c,109a,126b, 127d,165c), **sow** (45b,117c,119a,138b,160c), **tow** (45d,58b,75d, 125b), **vow** (119c,150a), **wow** (52c,158a), **yow** (52c)

OX - **oxa** (29c)

- OX **box** (36a,c,128c,145d,152d), **cox** (156a), **fox** (134a), **Nox** (69b), **pox** (44a), **vox** (90a,177a)

OY - **oye** (139c)

O - Y **ony** (139a), **ory** (36c)

- OY **boy** (142d,157c), **coy** (16d), **goy** (107c), **hoy** (16c,52c), **joy**, **loy** (121c,148b,151c,167a), **Roy**, **soy** (17b,137c,74d), **toy** (169d)

- OZ **Boz** (43b,115d), **coz**, **goz** (190)

PA - **pab** (139c), **pac** (73b,94c,100d), **pad** (39d,59c,76c,157d,161a,168b), **pah** (52c,60b,106d), **pal** (35b,38d), **pam** (26c,65a,87a,105b), **pan** (34a,61a,104a,175d), **Pan** (56a,68a,b,76b,120c,135b,161a,184a), **pap** (59c), **par** (15a,51a,b,c,69d,107c,135b,155a), **pas** (40d,156a), **pat** (11d,116d,159a,161d,167c), **Pat** (96a), **Pau** (48c,76a,130c), **paw** (32d,59c,73c), **pax** (89d,115b), **pay** (35b,128c,130a,d,177b)

P - A **pea** (32d,91b,142a,175a), **pia** (13b,22d,48a,120d), **poa** (20d,70d,97d), **pta** (6a), **pua** (74c,76a)

- PA **apa** (23a,177d), **OPA** (8a), **spa** (75b,100b,130c,154b,178d)

P - B **pab** (139c), **pob** (121b,129b,139c)

P - C **pac** (73b,94c,100d), **pic** (188)

P - D **pad** (39d,59c,76c,157d,161a,168b), **ped** (16d,34b), **pod** (76b,78d,91b,141b,180c), **pud** (59d,73c,115a)

PE - **pea** (32d,91b,142a,175a), **ped** (16d,34b), **pee** (91c), **peg** (38c,46b,54d,98a,118a,184c), **pel** (55c,160d), **pen** (36a,50a,80d,118b,126d,160a,185c), **pep** (50b,176b), **per** (25c,122d,165b,176a), **pes** (59d), **pet** (26d,37c,55a,59b,162d), **peu** (62a), **pew** (30d,52c,57d,120b,141c)

P - E **pee** (91c), **pie** (42d,85d,95b,114d,171b,172a), **poe** (114b), **Poe** (9c,d,128a,172a), **pre** (17d,122b,c), **pue** (52c), **Pye** (50d,55a)

- PE **ape** (36d,79d,100a,101d,146d), **ope** (172b,173c)

P - G **peg** (38c,46b,54d,98a,118a,184c), **pig** (27a,45b,99a,151b,160c), **pug** (45a,101a,108a,148d)

PH - **phi** (91c), **phu** (38c)

P - H **pah** (52c,60b,106d), **poh** (52c)

PI - **pia** (13b,22d,48a,120d), **pic** (188), **pie** (42d,85d,95b,114d,171b,172a), **pig** (27a,45b,99a,151b,160c), **pik** (188), **pil** (34b), **pin** (45d,54d,141d,147d), **pip** (11d,44a,121d,142a,154a), **Pip** (43b), **pir** (103a,b,136c), **pit** (52b,142a,164a,168a) **piu** (102c), **pix** (31a,51d,175d)

P - I **phi** (91c), **poi** (44a,59c,74c,117a,162a,164b), **psi** (91c)

- PI **api** (34a,76d), **epi** (56c,61c,d,111c,112d,122d,133c,153c,167b,174a), **UPI** (107a,182d)

P - K **pik** (188)

PL - **ply** (59b,90b,118d,164b,171c,174a,181b,184c)

P - L **pal** (35b,38d), **pel** (55c,160d), **pil** (34b), **pul** (190), **Pul** (14a)

P - M **pam** (26b,65a,87a,105b), **pom** (45a,148d)

P - N **pan** (34a,61a,104a,175d), **Pan** (56a,68a,b,76b,120c,135b,161a,184a), **pen** (36a,50a,80d,118b,126d,160a,185c), **pin** (45d,54d,141d,147d), **pun** (119c)

PO - **poa** (20d,70d,97d), **pob** (121b,129b,139c), **pod** (76b,78d,91b,141b,180c), **poe** (114b), **Poe** (9c,d,128a,172a), **poh** (52c), **poi** (44a,59c,74c,117a,162a,164b), **pom** (45a,148d), **pop** (52d,53a,130b,149d), **por** (152a), **pot** (120b,145b,154d,175d), **pow**, **pox** (44a)

P - O **pro** (59d,126d), **Pwo** (88c)

- PO **apo** (122b), **Apo** (177c)

P - P **pap** (59c), **pep** (50b,176b), **pip** (11d,44a,121d,154a), **Pip** (43b), **pop** (52d,53a,130b,149d), **pup** (141b,148d,185d)

PR - **pre** (17d,122b,c), **pro** (59d,126d), **pry** (52b,91d,98b,123d)

P - R **par** (15a,51a,b,c,69d,107c,135b,155a), **per** (25c,122d,165b,176a), **pir** (103a,b,136c), **por** (152a), **pur**, **pyr** (92a,b,122c,173b)

PS - **psi** (91c), **pst** (25c,126d,146c)

P - S **pas** (40d,156a), **pes** (59d), **pus**

- PS **Ops** (28c,69a,b,74a,137c)

PT - **Pta** (6a)

P - T **pat** (11d,116d,159a,161d,167c), **Pat** (96a), **pet** (26d,37c,55a,59b, 162d), **pit** (52b,142a,164a,168a), **pot** (120b,145b,154d,175d), **pst** (25c,126d,146c), **put** (65a,69d,90b)

- PT **apt** (11d,23b,32b,58a,80b,92b,114d,116d,124b,159a), **opt** (30c)

PU - **pua** (74c,76a), **pud** (59d,73c,115a), **pue** (52c), **pug** (45a,101a,108a, 148d), **pul** (190), **Pul** (14a), **pun** (119c), **pup** (141b,148d,185d), **pur**, **pus**, **put** (65a,69d,90b), **puy** (61d)

P - U **Pau** (48c,76a,130c), **peu** (62a), **phu** (38c), **piu** (102c)

PW - **Pwo** (88c)

P - W **paw** (32d,59c,73c), **pew** (30d,52c,57d,120b,141c), **pow**

P - X **pax** (89d,115b), **pix** (31a,51d,175d), **pox** (44a), **pyx** (31a,51d,175d)

PY - **Pye** (50d,55a), **pyr** (92a,b,122c,173b), **pyx** (31a,51d,175d)

P - Y **pay** (35b,128c,130a,d,177b), **ply** (59b,90b,118d,164b,171c,174a, 181b,184c), **pry** (52b,91d,98b,123d), **puy** (61d)

- PY **spy** (44a,51c,52b,141d)

QA - **Qaf** (104a)

Q - A **qua** (13c,80a,89c,147a)

Q - E **que** (62d)

Q - F **Qaf** (104a)

Q - I **qui** (62d)

Q - O **quo** (188)

QU - **qua** (13c,80a,89c,147a), **que** (62d), **qui** (62d), **quo** (188)

RA - **rab** (17c,75c,85b,102d,162c,166b), **Rab** (45a), **rad** (50b,138d,173b), **rae** (136b,138d,140b), **Rae** (183c), **rag** (59b,77c,100c,133c,161a), **rah** (29b), **rai** (188), **raj** (129c), **ram** (17a,45b,50b,79c,112b,121d, 143d,157d), **Ram** (36b), **ran** (73d), **Ran** (7c,107d,141a,163d), **rap** (90d,110a,147c,157c), **ras** (6c,26b,48b,51d,53d,61c,75a,111c,123c, 166b), **rat** (16a,42d,73b,132c), **raw** (20c,39a,105d,173d), **ray** (38a, 49a,57b,58b,147b), **Ray** (96a)

R - A **rea** (9c,171a), **ria** (38c,51d,81b,152a,b), **roa** (23d,87a), **rua** (118c), **Rua** (16b)

- RA **ara** (33a,114a,116a,118b,163d), **Ara** (9b,18c,36b,c,68d,69b,c,85a, 95a,175b), **dra** (188), **era** (8a,51a,116b,165d), **fra** (23c,63c,101d, 123b,129d), **gra** (59b,94b,160c), **Ira** (18c,d,41a,68c,82c,96a,164a, 178a,c), **Kra** (11b,91d), **NRA** (8a,20d), **ora** (10c,40d,41b,45b,83a,c,

101c,104a,122d,123d), **tra** (33b)

R - B **rab** (17c,75c,85b,102d,162c,166b), **Rab** (45a), **reb** (35d,75c,85b, 162c,166b), **rib** (37c,85b,90c,98a,144d,159d,172a), **rob** (119d, 155d), **Rob** (96a), **rub** (6b,24d,28c,43c,120c,179b)

- RB **orb** (50a,53c,67d,153b)

R - C **roc** (19c,53b,54a,147a)

- RC **arc** (31b,39d,92a,126a,127c,142a), **orc** (28c,70c,180b)

R - D **rad** (50b,138d,173b), **red** (33c,38d,59a,127b,134c,135b), **Red** (151b), **rid** (32a,44a,60d), **rod** (6a,72d,88b,131a,154d,156a,160a), **rud** (26d,57b)

- RD **erd** (47d,119d,145c), **Ord** (25b,60b), **urd** (17b,184b), **Urd** (68d,107d)

RE - **rea** (9c,171a), **reb** (35d,75c,85b,162c,166b), **red** (33c,38d,59a,127b, 134c,135b), **Red** (151b), **ree** (12c,50a,80c,134d,137a,140b,144a, 146b), **Ree** (25a), **ref, reh** (8d), **rei** (89b,121c), **Rei** (18d), **rel** (49b, 173b), **Reo** (26c), **rep** (53b,d,131a,171c), **res** (80a,89d,91a,97c), **ret** (58b,95a,149c,155d), **Reu** (115d), **rev, rew** (75c,140c,176b), **rex** (86c,96a), **rey** (86c,152b)

R - E **rae** (136b,138d,140b), **Rae** (183c), **ree** (12c,50a,80c,134d,137a, 140b,144a,146b), **Ree** (25a), **rhe** (59a,173b), **rie** (28c,70d,97d), **roe** (27d,41d,48d,57b,76d,95b,157b), **rue** (76a,b,129c,150d,183a), **rye** (28b,70b,72d,92d)

- RE **are** (51a,88b,98a,99b,110c,166c,175c), **ere** (17d,150c), **ire** (10c, 52b,30c,64c,125a,130b,185a), **ore** (39a,99b,108a,115b,141c,151a, 160b), **pre** (17d,122b,c), **tre** (37b,83c,122d,165a,167d), **ure** (40a, 139d,155d,158b,d), **Ure** (138d,185d)

R - F **ref, rif** (188)

- RF **orf** (57b,185c)

R - G **rag** (59b,77c,100c,133c,161a), **rig** (51b,112a), **rug**

- RG **erg** (50b,173b,184c)

RH - **rhe** (59a,173b), **rho** (71b,91c)

R - H **rah** (29b), **reh** (8d)

RI - **ria** (38c, 51d, 81b, 152a, b), **rib** (37c, 85b, 90c, 98a, 144d, 159d,172a), **rid** (32a,44a,60d), **rie** (28c,70d,97d), **rif** (188), **rig** (51b, 112a), **rii** (157b,175b), **rim** (22a,48b,96d),116b,124b,166a,180c), **rin** (33b,142b), **rio** (33a,131d,132a,152c,157b), **Rio** (23a), **rip** (87b, 130a,162c), **Rip** (178b), **ris** (131d), **rit** (140b,148c,153d)

R - I **rai** (188), **rei** (89b,121c), **Rei** (18d), **rii** (157b,175b), **roi** (55c,62a, 133d)

- RI **Ari** (18d), **eri** (13d,21c,146d), **Eri** (18c), **gri** (75c,78b), **Iri** (18a,d, 75a), **kri** (75c,96d), **ori** (34a), **sri** (60c,77b,166c), **Sri** (17c), **tri** (122d,169d), **Uri** (162d)

R - J **raj** (129c)

R - K **Rok** (87c)

- RK **ark** (21a,29d,38a,58b,60d,175d), **irk** (10d), **ork** (180b)

R - L **rel** (49b,173b)

R - M **ram** (17a,45b,50b,79c,112b,121d,143d,157d), **Ram** (36b), **rim** (22a,

48b,96d,116b,124b,166a,180c), **rom** (72d), **rum** (8c,92d)

- RM **arm** (22d,60c,81b,92b,124b,161b)

R - N **ran** (73d), **Ran** (7c,107d,141a,163d), **rin** (33b),142b), **ron** (152c), **Ron** (86c,88a), **run** (10d,23c,58d,110d,148d,153b,154b,167d)

- RN **arn** (8c,139a), **ern** (19c,d,47b,54b,141a), **urn** (36c,174d)

RO - **roa** (23d,87a), **rob** (119d,155d), **Rob** (96a), **roc** (19c,53b,54a,147a), **rod** (6a,72d,88b,131a,154d,156a,160a), **roe** (27d,41d,48d,57b,76d, 95b,157b), **roi** (55c,62a,133d), **Rok** (87c), **rom** (72d), **ron** (152c), **Ron** (86c,88a), **roo** (140a), **ros** (37b), **Ros** (138a,174d), **rot** (22b, 134c,143d,153d), **row** (44a,56b,92c,109a,126b,127d,165c), **Roy**

R - O **Reo** (26c), **rho** (71b,91c), **rio** (33a,131d,132a,152c,157b), **Rio** (23a), **roo** (140a)

- RO **Aro** (107a,111c), **cro** (104c,115b,180a), **fro** (15b), **Mro** (88c), **oro** (34c,122c,152a), **Oro** (161b), **pro** (59d,126d), **S.R.O.** (6a,164a), **Uro** (192)

R - P **rap** (90d,110a,147c,157c), **rep** (53b,d,131a,171c), **rip** (87b, 130a,162c), **Rip** (178b)

- RP **orp** (140c,179d)

R - R **rur** (132b)

- RR **err** (21a,43a,67d,100c,d,147a,148b,157b,168b,178a), **grr** (52c), **orr** (77c)

R - S **ras** (6c,26b,48b,51d,53d,61c,75a,111c,123c,166b), **res** (80a,89d, 91a,97c,164c), **ris** (131d), **ros** (37b), **Ros** (138a,174d), **rus** (89b), **Rus** (138a)

- RS **ars** (13b,89a), **Ars** (112c), **ers** (20a,176a), **Mrs.** (166b)

R - T **rat** (16a,42d,73b,132c), **ret** (58b,95a,149c,155d), **rit** (140b,148c, 153d), **rot** (22b,134c,143d,153d), **rut** (73a)

- RT **art** (22d,38b,39c,43b,56c,124a,162c,181d), **ert** (140c,174a), **ort** (59b,90d,91a,102c,129b,140d,180a,184d)

RU - **rua** (118c), **Rua** (16b), **rub** (6b,24d,28c,43c,120c,179b), **rud** (26d, 57b), **rue** (76a,b,129c,150d,183a), **rug**, **rum** (8c,92d), **run** (10d,23c, 58d,110d,148d,153b,154b,167d), **rur** (132b), **rus** (89b), **Rus** (138a), **rut** (73a), **rux** (154a,184d)

R - U **Reu** (115d)

- RU **aru** (80c,82b), **Aru** (82d), **cru** (63a,176c), **Kru** (91d), **Mru** (80d,88c), **Uru** (192)

R - V **rev**

R - W **raw** (20c,39a,105d,173d), **rew** (75c,140c,176b), **row** (44c,56b,92c, 109a,126b,127d,165c)

R - X **rex** (86c,96a), **rux** (154a,184d)

RY - **rye** (28b,70b,72d,92d)

R - Y **ray** (38a,49a,57b,58b,147b), **Ray** (96a), **rey** (86c,152b), **Roy**

- RY **cry** (25c,124a,145c,179d), **dry** (46d,85a,137c,164c), **ery** (155d,158c, d), **fry** (57d), **gry** (78b), **ory** (36c), **pry** (52b,91d,98b,123d), **try** (7c, 10d,14c,50a,51c,130a), **wry** (13d)

SA - **saa** (98a), **sac** (15d,121d), **Sac** (80c), **sad** (29c,42c,94c,98c,104a,

150d,173a), **sae** (140b,149c), **sag** (46b), **sah** (188), **sai** (101d), **saj** (48a,169a), **sak** (37c), **Sak** (88c), **sal** (29c,48a,136d,149d,152d, 169a,183a), **Sal** (183d), **Sam** (96a,162a), **san** (91c), **San** (24d), **sao** (141b), **Sao** (113c), **sap** (45d,52d,85c,169b,176d,179a), **sar** (57d), **sat** (13d), **saw** (7a,11b,40c,54c,97d,125a,137d,167a), **sax** (40c,148a,167a), **say** (131c,174c,177a)

S - A **saa** (98a), **sea** (19a,52d,58c,112c,178d), **sha** (110c,143d,144a,c, 174c,181c), **sia** (80c), **sma** (140b,148d), **sna** (105b,140b,143d,144a, 149c,181c,d), **spa** (75b,100b,130c,154b,178d), **sta** (13c,91b,104d, 105a), **sua** (89d),

- SA **Asa** (6a,18c,71a,84d,86d,164c), **ESA** (8a)

S - B **Seb** (47d), **sib** (86b,129c,139d,147b), **sob** (39b,179d), **sub** (90a, 122d,172c)

S - C **sac** (15d,121d), **Sac** (80c), **sec** (46c,182c), **sic** (90a,165b,168b), **soc** (44c,85d)

- SC **BSC** (42a)

S - D **sad** (29c,42c,94c,98c,104a,150d,173a), **sed** (89a), **Sid** (96a), **sod** (160b,170d), **sud** (59a)

SE - **sea** (19a,52d,58c,112c,178d), **Seb** (47d), **sec** (46c,182c), **sed** (89a), **see** (20a,43c,44a,51c,53c,93d,109b,113c,116a,176d,178c,183b), **sel** (62c,140b), **Sem** (107c), **sen** (190) **ser** (80d,83b,d,116c, 152d,180a), **ses** (61d), **set** (7b,11d,13a,23c,32b,33c,37c,58a,73d, 109b,118c,121c,142c,150a,186a), **Set** (52b,68a,b,111d), **sew**, **sex**, **sey** (120c)

S - E **sae** (140b,149c), **see** (20a,43c,44a,51c,53c,109b,113c,116a,176d, 178c,183b), **she** (124b), **She** (73a), **sie** (46c,66d,139b,140b,146b), **soe** (170c,184a), **SSE** (35b), **ste** (62c,136c), **sue** (119c), **Sue** (63a, 178a,183d), **sye** (40c,46c,139b,141a,167a)

- SE **ase** (51a,139a), **Ase** (79b,115d), **ese** (35b,158c), **ise** (40d,158c,d), **Ise** (78a,84c), **ose** (102a,146d,158b,c,d,159a), **SSE** (35b), **use** (7b, 47a,49d,64c,109b,168b,c,181b)

S - F **Sif** (164d)

S - G **sag** (46b), **sog** (149c)

SH - **sha** (110c,143d,144a,c,174c,181c), **she** (124b), **She** (73a), **sho** (188), **Shu** (30b,127a), **shy** (16d,99d,128c,160c,165d,175a)

S - H **sah** (188), **soh** (52c,72d)

- SH **ash** (24d,33c,49c,73d,134b,168c,169a), **hsh** (79c), **ish** (158b), **ush**

SI - **Sia** (80c), **sib** (86b,129c,139d,147b), **sic** (90a,165b,168b), **Sid** (96a), **sie** (46c,66d,139b,140b,146b), **Sif** (164d), **sil** (30c,185c,d), **Sim** (96b), **sin** (91c,140b,147a,168b,176a), **Sin** (102b), **sip** (46b,79d, 104a,162b), **sir** (87a,163b,166b), **sis** (67b,129c), **sit** (98c,116a,121c, 130c,142d), **six** (26c)

S - I **sai** (101d), **Sia** (80c), **ski** (149c), **sri** (60c,77b,166c), **Sri** (17c), **sui** (30b)

- SI **asi** (137a), **psi** (91c)

S - J **saj** (48a,169a)

SK - **ski** (149c), **sky** (56d)

S - K **sak** (37c), **Sak** (88c), **sok** (188), **Suk** (107b)

- SK **ask** (38b,82a,126c)

SL - **sly** (13b,38b,64c,81b,132c)

S - L **sal** (29c,48a,136d,149d,152d,169a,183a), **Sal** (183d), **sel** (62c, 140b), **sil** (30c,185c,d), **sol** (108b), **Sol** (117b,159b)

SM - **sma** (140b,148d), **SMU** (40b)

S - M **Sam** (96a,162a), **Sem** (107c), **Sim** (96b), **sum** (8a,123a,167c)

- SM **ism** (45a,79b,161c)

SN - **sna** (105b,140b,143d,144a,149c,181c), **sny** (18a,39d,43d,87a,119a, 144d,145a,165d,176a)

S - N **san** (91c), **San** (24d), **sen** (190), **sin** (91c,140b,147a,168b,176a), **Sin** (102b), **son** (42d,75d), **sun** (75d,111a,117b,155b), **syn** (122d,183b)

SO - **sob** (39b,179d), **soc** (44c,85d), **sod** (160b,170d), **soe** (170c,184a), **sog** (149c), **soh** (52c,72d), **sok** (188), **sol** (108b) **Sol** (117b,159b), **son** (42d,75d), **soo** (127d,140b,151b), **Soo** (137c), **sop** (23b,35d, 149c,155d), **SOS**, **sot** (46c,167b,c), **sou** (63b), **sow** (45b,117c,119a, 138b,160c), **soy** (17b,137c,174d)

S - O **sao** (141b), **Sao** (113c), **sho** (188), **soo** (127d,140b,151b), **Soo** (137c), **S.R.O.** (6a,164a)

- SO **Aso** (84c), **DSO** (99d), **eso** (34d,183b), **iso** (34a,122c,d)

SP - **spa** (75b,100b,130c,154b,178d), **spy** (44a,51c,52b,141d)

S - P **sap** (45d,52d,85c,169b,176d,179a), **sip** (46b,79d,104a,162b), **sop** (23b,35d,149c,155d), **sup** (46b,104a,162b)

- SP **asp** (7b,32b,149a,174a,176c), **e.s.p.** (147b)

S - Q **suq** (22a,97a)

SR - **sri** (60c,77b,166c), **Sri** (17c), **S.R.O.** (6a,164a)

S - R **sar** (57d), **ser** (80d,83b,d,116c,152d,180a), **sir** (87a,163b,166b), **sur** (34a,62b,d,104b,151a,152d,174a)

SS - **SSE** (35b), **ssu** (189), **SSW** (35b)

S - S **ses** (61d), **sis** (67b,129c), **SOS**, **sus** (117c), **Sus** (160c,181b)

- SS **ass** (17b,20c,45b,c,59c,110c,112b,146d,157d), **ess** (39d,78a,91c, 158c,184d)

ST - **sta** (13c,91b,104d,105a), **ste** (62c,136c), **sty** (50a,53c)

S - T **sat** (13d), **set** (7b,11d,13a,23c,32b,33c,37c,58a,73d,109b,118c, 121c,142c,150a,186a), **Set** (52b,68a,b,111d), **sit** (98c,116a,121c, 130c,142d), **sot** (46c,167b,c)

- ST **est** (50a,61c,62a,79b,89c,158d,159c), **ist** (7b,34b,43a,59b,66c,158b, c,d), **LST** (21a,88b), **ost** (15d,86b), **pst** (25c,126d,146c), **tst** (81d, 126d)

SU - **sua** (89d), **sub** (90a,122d,172c), **sud** (59a), **sue** (119c), **Sue** (63a, 178a,183d), **Sui** (30b), **Suk** (107b), **sum** (8a,123a,167c), **sun** (75d, 111a,117b,155b), **sup** (46b,104a,162b), **suq** (22a,97a), **sur** (34a,62b, d,104b,151a,152d,174a), **sus** (117c), **Sus** (160c,181b)

S - U **Shu** (30b,127a), **SMU** (40b), **sou** (63b), **ssu** (189)

- SU **ssu** (189)

S - W **saw** (7a,11b,40c,54c,97d,125a,137d,167a), **sew**, **sow** (45b,117c, 119a,138b,160c), **SSW** (35b)

- SW **SSW** (35b), **WSW** (35b)

S - X **sax** (40c,148a,167a), **sex**, **six** (26c)

SY - **sye** (40c,46c,139b,141a,167a), **syn** (122d,183b)

S - Y **say** (131c,174c,177a), **sey** (120c), **shy** (16d,99d,128c,160c,165d, 175a), **sky** (56d), **sly** (13b,38b,64c,81b,132c), **sny** (18a,39d,43d,87a, 119a,144d,145a,165d,176a), **soy** (17b,137c,174d), **spy** (44a,51c, 52b,141d), **sty** (50a,53c)

TA - **taa** (112d), **tab** (29b,39c,58b,86a,128d,145a), **tac** (34d,130a), **tad** (22c,174a,186a), **tae** (138d,140c,166c,d), **tag** (45a,54c,65a,87b, 144a), **tai** (84b,111c,121b), **Tai** (80d), **taj** (75a,97d), **tal** (40c,77a, 113b), **tam** (74d), **tan** (23d,33c,46a,72d,90d), **tao** (10d,131c, 170b), **Tao** (117a), **tap** (55a,114d,153c), **tar** (8c,68a,94d,111c,118c, 136a,c,176d), **tat** (43b,48c,72d,87c), **Tat** (82a), **tau** (71b,91c,136c, 161a), **tav** (91c), **taw** (90d,91c,96c,d,145b,161d), **tax** (13a,14a,80a, 91d)

T - A **taa** (112d), **tea** (13d,18c,79c,81a,145d,149c,159d), **tia** (151d), **toa** (17c,178b), **tra** (33b), **tua** (117a)

- TA **ata** (58d,97d,158d,160c,173d), **Ata** (79c,80d,94d,95d,100a,106b, 117a), **eta** (71a,84c,91c), **Ita** (51b,71d,94d,95d,106b,117a), **ITA** (173a), **Pta** (6a), **sta** (13c,91b,104d,105a), **uta** (53c,84d,93b,147c, 150b)

T - B **tab** (29b,39c,58b,86a,128d,145a), **tub** (21a,27a,36c,174d)

TC - **tch** (52c), **tck** (52c)

T - C **tac** (34d,130a), **tec** (43a), **tic** (104d,153a,171c,d)

- TC **etc** (10b)

T - D **tad** (174a,186a), **ted** (74d,138b,154b), **Ted** (96b), **tod** (24d,60c,83d)

TE - **tea** (13d,18c,79c,81a,145d,149c,159d), **tec** (43a), **ted** (74d,138b, 154b), **Ted** (96b), **tee** (39d,52b,69d,91c,112d,115d,118b,172a), **teg** (45a,54b,143d,144a,171d), **tel** (34a,b,122c), **Tem** (143a,159b), **ten** (19a,26c,41c,42b), **ter** (34d,122d,165a), **tez** (125c)

T - E **tae** (138d,140c,166c,d), **tee** (39d,52b,69d,91c,112d,115d,118b, 172a), **the** (13b), **tie** (10a,14c,38b,45d,51a,88d,109b,127c,138b, 170b), **toe** (43c,69d,148a,156a), **tre** (37b,83c,122d,165a,167d), **tue** (114b), **tye** (28c,134a)

- TE **ate** (81a,108c,158c,174c), **Ate** (20c,68b,d,69a,b,116c,186b), **ete** (36c,62d,141c,159b), **ite** (59b,81a,105d,130c,158b,c,d,161a), **ote** (158d), **ste** (62c,136c), **Ute** (145c,180b)

T - G **tag** (45a,54c,65a,87b,144a), **teg** (45a,54b,143d,144a,171d), **tig** (46b), **tog** (46a), **tug** (45d,125b), **tyg** (46b)

TH - **the** (13b), **tho** (52a), **Tho** (167a), **thy**

T - H **tch** (52c)

- TH **eth** (91c,158d), **Ith** (10a,28a,82b,99d), **nth** (42a)

TI - **tia** (151d), **tic** (104d,153a,171c,d), **tie** (10a,14c,38b,45d, 51a,88d,109b,127c,138b,170b), **tig** (46b), **til** (142d), **Tim** (43b), **tin** (36c,99a,b,108b,155a,179c), **tio** (152d), **tip** (26b,d,50a,70d,77b,78a,

120a,165d), **tir** (61d,62c,145b), **tis, tit** (19c,130d), **Tiu** (7c,68c, 147d,163d,166c,170c), **Tiw** (68c,147d,163d)

T - I **tai** (84b,111c,121b), **Tai** (80d), **tji** (189), **toi** (62b,d,63a), **Toi** (18d), **tri** (122d,169d), **tui** (47c,114b,117a), **Twi** (69c)

- TI **ati** (106d,107a), **Ati** (45d,106b,113c,117a)

TJ - **tji** (189)

T - J **taj** (75a,97d)

TK - **TKO** (22c)

T - K **tck** (52c)

T - L **tal** (40c,77a,113b), **tel** (34a,b,122c), **til** (142d), **tol** (137b)

T - M **tam** (74d), **Tem** (143a,159b), **Tim** (43b), **tom** (95d), **Tom** (96b, 157a), **tum** (26d), **Tum** (143a,159b)

TN - **TNT** (53a)

T - N **tan** (23d,33c,46a,72d,90d), **ten** (19a,26c,41c,42b), **tin** (36c,99a,b, 108b,155a,179c), **ton** (158d,167d,179d), **tun** (23b,27a,182b)

TO - **toa** (17c,178b), **tod** (24d,60c,83d), **toe** (43c,69d,148a,156a), **tog** (46a), **toi** (62b,d,63a), **Toi** (18d), **tol** (137b), **tom** (95d), **Tom** (96b, 157a), **ton** (158d,167d,179d), **too** (18b,102c), **top** (38c,52b,118b, 123d,160a,174a,186b), **tor** (38b,76d,85d,115c,124b,132b,c), **tot** (186a), **tow** (45d,58b,75d,125b), **toy** (169d)

T - O **tao** (10d,131c,170b), **Tao** (117a), **tho** (52a), **Tho** (167a), **tio** (152d), **TKO** (22c), **too** (18b,102c), **two** (26c,37d,80a,93a)

- TO **ETO** (184d), **Ito** (84a,c,186d), **oto** (34a), **Oto** (147b)

T - P **tap** (55a,114d,153c), **tip** (26b,d,50a,70d,77b,78a,120a,165d), **top** (38c,52b,118b,123d,160a,174a,186b), **tup** (115a,117d,127d,143d)

TR - **tra** (33b), **tre** (37b,83c,122d,165a,167d), **tri** (122d,169d), **try** (7c, 10d,14c,50a,51c,130a)

T - R **tar** (8c,68a,94d,111c,118c,136a,c,176d), **ter** (34d,122d,165a), **tir** (61d,62c,145b), **tor** (38b,76d,85d,115c,124b,132b,c), **tur** (14d,27c, 68a,79b,117d,174c), **tyr** (7c,68c,147d,163d,170c,178a)

TS - **tst** (81d,126d)

T - S **tis**

- TS **its** (124c)

T - T **tat** (43b,48c,72d,87c), **Tat** (82a), **tit** (19c,130d), **TNT** (53a), **tot** (186a), **tst** (81d,126d), **tut** (52c)

- TT **att** (146a)

TU - **tua** (117a), **tub** (21a,27a,36c,174d), **tue** (114b), **tug** (45d,125b), **tui** (47c,114b,117a), **tum** (26d), **Tum** (143a,159b), **tun** (23b,27a, 182b), **tup** (115a,117d,127d,143d), **tur** (14d,27c,68a,79b,117d, 174c), **tut** (52c)

T - U **tau** (71b,91c,136c,161a), **Tiu** (7c,68c,147d,163d,166c,170c)

- TU **utu** (35b,137c), **Utu** (96c,107a,159b)

T - V **tav** (91c)

TW - **Twi** (69c), **two** (26c,37d,80a,93a)

T - W **taw** (90d,91c,96c,d,145b,161d), **Tiw** (68c,147d,163d), **tow** (45d, 58b,75d,125b)

T - X **tax** (13a,14a,80a,91d)

TY - **tye** (28c,134a), **tyg** (46b), **Tyr** (7c,68c,109c,147d,163d,170c,178a)

T - Y **thy, toy** (169d), **try** (7c,10d,14c,50a,51c,130a)

- TY **sty** (50a,53c)

T - Z **tez** (125c)

U - A **Uca** (56a), **ula** (72c,158c), **Uma** (43a,69b,153d), **Una** (54a,153b, 170c,183c), **uta** (53c,84d,93b,147c,150b), **uva** (64a,70c)

- UA **dua** (122d), **Kua** (95c), **pua** (74c,76a), **qua** (13c,80a,89c,147a), **rua** (118c), **Rua** (16b), **sua** (89d), **tua** (117a)

UB - **ube** (185b), **ubi** (90a,180d,185b)

- UB **bub** (22c), **cub** (92d,185d), **dub** (25c,46a,c,87a,105b,121a,140a), **fub** (29b,119d), **hub** (28b,118b,180c), **nub** (67b,94d,95c,118c 124d), **rub** (6b,24d,28c,43c,120c,179b), **sub** (90a,122d,172c), **tub** (21a,27a,36c,174d)

UC - **Uca** (56a)

- UC **duc** (61c)

UD - **Udi** (108a), **udo** (28a,30c,48c,84b,c,d,136c,149d)

U - D **und** (66b), **urd** (17b,184b), **Urd** (68d,107d)

- UD **bud** (22c), **cud** (126c,135a), **dud** (21c,54a), **lud** (100a), **Lud** (23c, 144b), **mud** (6c), **pud** (59d,73c,115a), **rud** (26d,57b), **sud** (59a)

U - E **ube** (185b), **ule** (23a,27d,134c,158c,168d), **ume** (11d), **une** (13b, 61a,62b,95c), **ure** (40a,139d,155d,158b,d), **Ure** (138d,185d), **use** (7b,47a,49d,64c,109b,168b,c,181b), **Ute** (145c,180b), **uve** (185b)

- UE **cue** (7a,27b,92c,117d,124b,132c,146c,159a), **due** (7b,115b,124c), **gue** (176c), **hue** (33c,143b), **lue** (146b), **pue** (52c), **que** (62d), **rue** (76a,b,129c,150d,183a), **sue** (119c), **Sue** (63a,178a,183d), **tue** (114b)

UF - **ufo** (59a)

- UF **ouf** (52c)

UG - **ugh** (52c)

- UG **bug** (24b,66b,81b), **dug, fug** (129a), **hug** (32c,49d), **jug** (118c, 123d), **lug** (27a,45d,47b,73c,136b), **Lug** (28b), **mug** (46b,54a,65a), **pug** (45a,101a,108a,148d), **rug, tug** (45d,125b), **vug** (28a,66a)

U - H **ugh** (52c), **ush**

- UH **auh** (52c), **huh** (52c)

UI - **uit** (47a,111d,151a)

U - I **ubi** (90a,180d,185b), **Udi** (108a), **uji** (146d), **uni** (34c,118d,122c), **Uni** (51d), **UPI** (107a,182d), **Uri** (162d), **uvi** (185b)

- UI **dui** (46d), **hui** (14a,30b,56d,114c), **Kui** (86a,88c,146a), **qui** (62d), **Sui** (30b), **tui** (47c,114b,117a)

UJ - **uji** (146d)

- UK **auk** (19b), **ouk** (140c), **Suk** (107b)

UL - **ula** (72c,158c), **ule** (23a,27d,134c,158c,168d), **Ull** (7c,68c,146b, 164d), **ulm** (49c), **Ulm** (40d), **ulo** (34b,80d), **ulu** (87a)

U - L **Ull** (7c,68c,146b,164d)

- UL **Bul** (25d,102a), **Ful** (158b), **gul** (134a), **mul** (188), **nul** (108c,177a), **pul** (190), **Pul** (14a)

UM - **Uma** (43a,69b,153d), **ume** (11d), **umu** (112a)

U - M **ulm** (49c), **Ulm** (40d)

- UM **aum** (189), **bum** (21b), **cum** (159b), **dum** (45c,67b,113a), **gum** (7b, 53c,80b,130c,156b), **hum** (24d,46b,150d), **Jum** (39c), **lum** (30a), **mum** (30d,95a,146c), **rum** (8c,92d), **sum** (8a,123a,167c), **tum** (26d), **Tum** (143a,159b)

UN - **Una** (54a,153b,170c,183c), **und** (66b), **une** (13b,61a,62b,95c), **uni** (34c,118d,122c), **Uni** (51d), **uno** (83c,151d), **uns** (66d,174c), **Unu** (24d)

U - N **urn** (36c,174d)

- UN **bun** (25b,73b), **dun** (19a,39d,46d,71a,97d,115b,160b), **fun**, **gun** (56d,131a,146a), **Hun** (16c,21d,174b), **mun** (157b), **nun** (24c,91c, 117d,129d,147b), **Nun** (29a,85c), **pun** (119c), **run** (10d,23c,58d, 110d,148d,153b,154b,167d), **sun** (75d,111a,117b,155b), **tun** (23b, 27a,182b), **wun** (24c), **Yun** (88d)

U - O **udo** (28a,30c,48c,84b,c,d,136c,149d), **ufo** (59a), **ulo** (34b,80d), **uno** (83c,151d), **Uro** (192)

- UO **duo** (46d,113a,171d), **Luo** (107b), **quo** (188)

UP - **UPI** (107a,182d)

- UP **cup** (46b,69d,118b,170a), **gup** (70a), **hup** (35a), **kup** (188), **pup** (141b,148d,185d), **sup** (46b,104a,162b), **tup** (115a,117d,127d, 143d)

- UQ **suq** (22a,97a)

UR - **urd** (17b,184b), **Urd** (68d,107d), **ure** (40a,139d,155d,158b,d), **Ure** (138d,185d), **Uri** (162d), **urn** (36c,174d), **Uro** (192), **Uru** (192)

- UR **bur** (123b), **cur** (101d), **dur** (95c), **Eur.** (36c), **fur**, **gur** (159a), **Hur** (91d), **Jur** (107b), **Lur** (116c), **mur** (63a,177d), **nur** (67d), **our** (124c), **pur**, **rur** (132b), **sur** (34a,62b,d,104b,151a,152d,174a), **tur** (14d,27c,68a,79b,117d,174c)

US - **use** (7b,47a,49d,64c,109b,168b,c,181b), **ush**

U - S **uns** (66d,174c)

-US **aus** (66c), **Aus** (98b), **bus** (125b,168b), **Gus** (96a), **jus** (61d,90b), **Mus** (104a,132c), **ous** (158b), **pus**, **rus** (89b,138a), **sus** (117c), **Sus** (160c,181b)

UT - **uta** (53a,84d,93b,147c,150b), **Ute** (145c,180b), **utu** (35b, 137c), **Utu** (96c,107a,159b)

U - T **uit** (47a,111d,151a)

- UT **aut** (34d,89d), **but** (36a,52b,156b,173c), **cut** (30c,32b,145c), **fut** (188), **gut** (114d,130a), **hut** (143c), **jut** (53a,124a), **lut** (189), **mut** (39c), **Mut** (9b,127a), **nut** (24c,32d,38b,54d,64a,65d,86b,141c, 165a), **Nut** (69a), **out** (6b,14b,60b,69d,80a,108b,185c), **put** (65a, 69d,90b), **rut** (73a), **tut** (52c)

U - U **ulu** (87a), **umu** (112a), **Unu** (24d), **Uru** (192), **utu** (35b,137c), **Utu** (96c,107a,159b)

UV - **uva** (64a,70c), **uve** (185b), **uvi** (185b)

- UX **aux** (6d,61a), **dux** (31d,64a,90c), **lux** (79d), **rux** (154a,184d)

- UY **buy**, **guy** (55b,131b,155d), **Guy** (96a), **muy** (152d,175d), **puy** (61d)

- UZ **guz** (188)

VA - **Vac** (153b), **vae** (176b), **vag** (174b,178a), **Vai** (91d), **van** (7b,59d, 60a,63d,90c), **vas** (46d,89d,119c,133b,175d), **vat** (31b,36c,163a, 170c), **vau** (91c)

V - A **via** (132a,133a,b,179a)

- VA **ava** (78d,86a,116a,120d,139a,167b), **Ava** (24c), **Eva** (157a,183c), **iva** (76a,97b,127b,185b), **ova** (48d), **uva** (64a,70c)

V - C **Vac** (153b)

V - D **Vod** (16a)

VE - **vee** (58a,91c,106a), **Vei** (91d), **vet**, **vex** (7c,10d,44c,82c)

V - E **vae** (176b), **vee** (58a,91c,106a), **vie** (36c,157c,170c), **voe** (17a,81b)

- VE **ave** (54c,71d,73a,122a,134a,136d), **eve** (47a,131a,143a,165d,171c), **Eve** (183c), **ive** (158c), **uve** (185b)

V - F **vif** (62a)

V - G **vag** (174b,178a), **vog** (189), **vug** (28a,66a)

VI - **via** (132a,133a,b,179a), **vie** (36c,157c,170c), **vif** (62a), **vim** (50b, 176b), **vin** (63a,182b), **vir** (89c), **vis** (59d,89b,d,90b,176b), **vix**, (89d,138b), **viz** (105b)

V - I **Vai** (91d), **Vei** (91d)

- VI **ovi** (34a), **uvi** (185b)

V - L **vol** (155a,182d)

V - M **vim** (50b,176b)

V - N **van** (7b,59d,60a,63d,90c), **vin** (63a,182b), **von** (66d,67a)

VO - **Vod** (16a), **voe** (17a,81b), **vog** (189), **vol** (155a,182d), **von** (66d, 67a), **Vor** (68d), **Vot** (56d), **vow** (119c,150a), **vox** (90a,177a)

V - R **vir** (89c), **Vor** (68d)

V - S **vas** (46d,89d,119c,133b,175d), **vis** (59d,89b,d,90b,176b)

V - T **vat** (31b,36c,163a,170c), **vet**, **Vot** (56d)

VU - **vug** (28a,66a)

V - U **Vau** (91c)

V - W **vow** (119c,150a)

V - X **vex** (7c,10d,44c,82c), **vix** (89d,138b), **vox** (90a,177a)

V - Z **viz** (105b)

- VY **ivy** (32b,38c,176b)

WA - **wad** (94d,97b,109c,112b,149d), **wag** (85b,104a,183a), **wah** (113c), **wan** (113a), **war** (157c), **was** (166c,175c), **Was** (24d), **wat** (73d, 140d,163a,180b), **waw** (12b,91c), **wax** (28b,72a,80b,120c), **way** (37d,96b,134b,164d)

W - A **Wea** (192)

- WA **awa** (100a,139a), **iwa** (63c)

W - B **web** (50d,70a,98c,99a,106c,149b)

W - D **wad** (94d,97b,109c,112b,149d), **wed** (97a,173c)

WE - **Wea** (192), **web** (50d,70a,98c,99a,106c,149b), **wed** (97a,173c), **wee** (52c,100c,148c), **Wei** (30b,162b), **wen** (40c,72a,110a,170c,177b), **wet** (40d,46a,101a,124a,127c,149c), **wey** (173b)

W - E **wee** (52c,100c,148c), **woe** (25b), **wye** (91c)

- WE **awe** (81d,100a,130d,175b,182b), **ewe** (88a,143d), **owe**

W - G **wag** (85b,104a,183a), **wig** (73b)

WH - **who** (129c), **why** (52c)

W - H **wah** (113c)

WI - **wig** (73b), **win** (7a,17b,64b,123b), **wis** (79d,164c), **wit** (78d,85b, 177b)

W - I **Wei** (30b,162b)

- WI **Twi** (69c)

- WL **awl** (145b,167a), **owl**

- WM **cwm** (31b,37b,103d)

WN - **WNW** (35b)

W - N **wan** (113a), **wen** (40c,72a,110a,170c,177b), **win** (7a,17b,64b,123b), **won**, **wun** (24c) **wyn** (110a)

- WN **awn** (12c,17b,140a), **own** (6d)

WO - **woe** (25b), **won**, **woo**, **wop**, **wow** (52c,158a)

W - O **who** (129c), **woo**

- WO **Lwo** (107b), **Pwo** (88c), **two** (26c,37d,80a,93a)

W - P **wop**

WR - **wry** (13d)

W - R **war** (157c)

WS - **WSW** (35b)

W - S **was** (166c,175c), **Was** (24d), **wis** (79d,164c)

W - T **wat** (73d,140d,163a,180b), **wet** (40d,46a,101a,124a,127c), **wit** (78d,85b,177b)

WU - **wun** (24c)

W - W **waw** (12b,91c), **WNW** (35b), **wow** (52c,158a), **WSW** (35b)

W - X **wax** (28b,72a,80b,120c)

WY - **wye** (91c), **wyn** (110a)

W - Y **way** (37d,96b,134b,164d), **wey** (173b), **why** (52c), **wry** (13d)

XA - **xat** (167c)

- XA **oxa** (29c)

XE - **xer** (34a)

- XE **axe** (30c,40c,167a), **Exe** (43a)

- XO **exo** (122d)

X - R **xer** (34a)

X - T **xat** (167c)

YA - **yah** (52c), **yak** (112c,161d,165b), **yam** (48c,121d,160b,170c), **Yao** (30a,c,104b), **yap** (16c,29b,122a), **yar** (72a), **Yau** (30c), **yaw** (43a, 155d)

Y - A **yea** (7c,175c)

- YA **aya** (77b,166b), **Aya** (143c), **iya** (95b,108d,111c), **Mya** (31c)

YE - **yea** (7c,175c), **yen** (33b,42d,93c,174a), **yep**, **yes** (7c,55a), **yet** (18b, 24d,64c,77c,80a,108c,156b,165b), **yew** (36a,52a,b,145d,168c,d) **yez**

- YE **aye** (7c,9b,55a,60a), **bye** (38c,141d), **dye** (33c,154d), **eye** (93d, 111b,140d), **lye** (8d,27d,93b), **nye** (72a,116d), **Nye** (9c,18b), **oye** (139c), **Pye** (50d,55a), **rye** (28b,70b,72d), **sye** (40c,46c,139b,141a, 167a), **tye** (28c,134a), **wye** (91c)

- YG **tyg** (46b)

Y - H **yah** (52c)

YI - **yin** (140a), **Yin** (30b,143c,185b), **yip** (16c)

Y - I **yoi** (52c,79a)

Y - K **yak** (112c,161d,165b), **yok** (10c,185a)

- YL **kyl** (76d,79b)

Y - M **yam** (48c,121d,160d,170c), **yom** (41a)

- YM **gym** (154a), **Nym** (54c,76a)

Y - N **yen** (33b,42d,93c,174a), **yin** (140a), **Yin** (30b,143c,185b), **yon** (44c,112a,164d), **Yun** (88d)

- YN **lyn** (140c,178d), **syn** (122d,183b), **wyn** (110a)

YO - **yoi** (52c,79a), **yok** (10c,185a), **yom** (41a), **yon** (44c,112a,164d), **you**, **yow** (52c)

Y - O **Yao** (30a,c,104b)

- YO **iyo** (7d,176b)

Y - P **yap** (16c,29b,122a), **yep**, **yip** (16c)

- YP **cyp** (169d), **gyp** (29b,42a,160c), **hyp**

Y - R **yar** (72a)

- YR **pyr** (92a,b,122c,173b), **Tyr** (7c,68c,109c,147d,163d,170c,178a)

Y - S **yes** (7c,55a)

- YS **lys** (58b,92b)

Y - T **yet** (18b,24d,64c,77c,80a,108c,156b,165b)

YU - **Yun** (88d)

Y - U **Yau** (30c), **you**

- YU **ayu** (160c)

Y - W **yaw** (43a,155d), **yew** (36a,52a,b,145d,168c,d), **yow** (52c)

- YX **Nyx** (69b), **pyx** (31a,51d,75d)

Y - Z **yez**

ZA - **zac** (27c), **zag** (84a), **zak** (188), **Zal** (135d), **Zan** (186b), **zar** (188), **zat** (148a), **zax** (148a)

Z - A **zea** (95c), **Zoa** (20b)

Z - C **zac** (27c)

Z - D **zed** (91c)

ZE - **zea** (95c), **zed** (91c), **zee** (81b,91c), **zel** (40c), **Zen** (24a), **Zep**, **zer** (188)

Z - E **zee** (81b,91c), **Zoe** (36b,183c)

Z - F **Zif** (102a)

Z - G **zag** (84a), **zig** (84a)

Z - H **zoh** (13d,186b)

ZI - **Zif** (102a), **zig** (84a), **Zio** (147d,163d), **zip** (24b,50b,176b), **Ziu** (147d,163d)

Z - K **zak** (188)

Z - L **Zal** (135d), **zel** (40c)

Z - N **Zan** (186b), **Zen** (24a)

ZO - **zoa** (20b), **Zoe** (36b,183c), **zoh** (13d,186b), **zoo** (181b)

Z - O **Zio** (147d,163d), **zoo** (181b)

- ZO **azo** (107c)

Z - P **Zep, zip** (24b,50b,176b)

Z - R **zar** (188), **zer** (188)

Z - T **zat** (148a)

Z - U **Ziu** (147d,163d)

Z - X **zax** (148a)

FOUR-LETTER WORDS

AA - - **Aalu** (6b,48d), **Aani** (45a,48d), **Aare, Aaru** (6b,48d)

- AA - **baal** (142b), **baas** (97c), **caam** (93d), **Faam** (111a), **gaal** (23b,174d), **Haab** (97d), **haaf** (57d), **haak** (57b,178a), **haar** (139c), **kaan** (93d, 116c), **kaat** (105d), **laap** (51d,91b,141d), **maal** (188), **ma'am** (95a, 166b), **maar** (177a), **Maas** (132a), **Maat** (69a,b,85d), **Naab, naam** (44c), **Naam** (105b), **paal** (188), **paar** (28c,137a), **raab** (32d), **raad** (14a,49b,151a,165b), **Raad** (151a), **raas** (91b), **Saad** (12b), **saah** (188), **saal** (66c,73b), **Saan** (24d), **Saar** (63b,102d,132a), **Taal** (7d, 88c,151a), **taar** (12b), **Waac, waag** (71d,101d)

- - AA **blaa, chaa** (162b), **draa** (188)

A - - A **Abba** (20a,55a,161c), **Abfa** (76b), **Abia** (18d,137a), **abra** (26b), **Abra, acca** (53b,d), **acta** (41d,123d,128d,164c), **adda** (147d), **Adda** (68c,119d,157a,182a), **aera** (8a), **Aeta** (94d,100a,106b,117a), **Afra** (183c), **agha** (35a,171a), **agla** (7a), **agra** (26d,34d), **Agra** (161b), **agua** (152d,166c,178c), **Aida** (110d,175c), **Aira** (70d), **Akha** (86a,c), **akia** (74c), **Akka** (125d), **akra** (176a), **Akra** (191), **akua** (120d), **alba** (98b,181a), **Alba** (151d), **Alca** (14c,128b), **alda** (152b), **Alda** (110d,150c), **Alea** (14b,31c,167d), **alfa** (70d), **alga** (141b,c), **alia** (89d), **alla** (6d), **alma** (40d,53d,146d,147a), **Alma** 38d, 183c), **alta** (89c,152d), **Alva** (151d), **Alya** (155b,c), **amba** (161a), **amia** (22c,170d), **amla** (48a,161d,168c,169a), **amma** (6a), **amra** (77c), **anba** (36d), **anda** (23a,168c), **anna** (190), **Anna** (110c,166d, 183c), **anoa** (28a,60a,112c,181c), **ansa** (73c,93d,137c), **anta** (83d, 117c,d,121a), **Anta** (164a), **apia** (121b), **aqua** (90a,178c), **arba** (135d,171a), **arca** (9a,22c,29d,115a,130a), **Arca** (101b), **area** (37d, 38a,44c,53a,93b,110d,127d,138c,168a,186d), **aria** (8b,98c,150a,c, 170c), **arna** (24a,181b), **Aroa** (175b), **arpa** (83b), **arra** (47d,52c,82b),

Arta (72b), **Arya** (80d), **asea** (39b,177c), **Asha** (191), **Asia** (48a), **asta** (188), **Asta** (107a,164c), **Atka** (11a), **atma** (150d), **atta** (58d, 90c,97d,160c,173d), **Atta** (94d,95d,100a,106b,117a), **atua** (120d), **Auca** (192), **aula** (66c,73b), **aura** (44c,49c,66a,96b,158a,170d, 177c), **Ausa, Azha** (155b)

AB - - **abas** (61c), **Abba** (20a,55a,161c), **abbe** (32b,63b,123b), **Abby** (183d), **ABC's** (57a), **abed** (130c), **Abel** (7a,25b), **abet** (8b,15b,50a, 59b,75d,81c,141d,159d), **Abfa** (76b), **Abia** (18d,137a), **Abib** (102 a,b), **Abie** (96b,107a), **abir** (129a), **able** (26b,35b,126a,147c), **ably** (147c), **aboo** (17a), **Abot** (100c), **Abou** (48b,55a), **abox** (22d), **abra** (26b), **Abra, abri** (61c,62c,144b), **Absi** (191), **abut** (22a, 167c)

- AB - **baba** (108d,120c,166c,171a), **babe, Babi** (116c), **babu** (77a), **baby, caba** (184c), **Faba, gabe** (162a), **gabi** (162a), **gaby** (59c,146d), **haba** (151d), **habe** (191), **Maba** (103a,168d), **mabi** (58d), **nabk** (30d, 164d), **nabo** (117a), **Nabu** (68c,183d), **Raba, rabi** (38d,74a), **Rabi** (14b,117b), **saba** (56a,117a), **Saba** (143d), **sabe, tabi** (84c, 149d), **tabu** (59d,111d), **Wabi** (192)

- - AB **Ahab** (18c,26c,85b,86d,100d,116a,180b), **Arab** (30a,78b,c,106a, 107c,157b,160c,185d), **blab** (162b), **brab** (113b), **chab** (184a), **crab** (39b,144b,181b), **doab** (157c), **drab** (23d,29c,33d,46d,53b,d), **duab** (157c), **frab** (138c), **grab** (105b,142a,149b), **Haab** (97d), **Joab** (41a), **knab** (107a), **Moab** (18d,85a,86d,94a), **Naab, raab** (32d), **scab** (80b, 107d,157c), **slab** (148b), **snab** (23c,139a), **stab** (14c,87a,117c), **swab** (102b)

A - - B **Abib** (102a,b), **Adib** (155b), **Agib** (12a,42d), **Ahab** (18c,26c,85b, 86d,100d,116a,180b), **Arab** (30a,78b,c,106a,107c,157b,160c,185d)

AC - - **acca** (53b,d), **Acer** (96c), **ache** (79a,112d,185b), **acht** (66c), **achy, acid** (151a,162a), **Acis** (64b), **acle** (13d,82c,115d), **acme** (39c,115c, 186b), **acne** (147c), **acon** (62c,140d), **acor** (6d), **acre** (39b,56a,88b), **Acre, acta** (41d,123d,128d,164c), **acth** (13b), **acto** (152b), **Acts, actu** (7a,89a), **acus** (89d,118a), **acyl** (6d)

- A C - **Bach** (35c), **back** (75d,76d,159d), **Caca** (67a), **caco** (73b), **dace** (57a,b), **each, face** (159d,176c), **fact** (7a,128b), **hack** (40a,77c, 184d), **jaca** (84a), **jack** (26c,58a,127c), **Jack** (96b), **jacu** (19a,151b), **lace** (58b,179c), **lack** (178a), **lact** (34c), **lacy, mace** (49d,108d,153b, 154d,161a,178a), **mack, nach, paca** (132c,154a), **pace** (64b,98a, 153b,156a,170b,177d), **pack** (24b,140d), **paco** (9b,146d), **pacs** (94c), **pact** (8a), **raca** (19a,59c,130b,184d), **race** (116a,153b,154b, 169c), **rack** (32c,64b), **racy** (153b), **sack** (43d,118a,119d,182b), **saco** (189), **tace** (13a,155d), **tack** (28d,37d,54d), **tact** (43c,d,116a), **Vach** (153b), **Waco, Zach** (96b)

- - AC **utac** (22d), **Waac**

A - - C **aesc** (12d,64d), **alec** (10a,57c,d,76c,137c), **amic** (9d), **avec** (63a, 183a)

AD - - **adad** (52c,56a), **Adad** (68c,157a,182a), **Adah** (25b,51b), **Adam** (26b,96a,111c) **adan** (102d), **Adar** (85c,102a), **adat** (90b,95d), **adda** (147d), **Adda** (68c,119d,157a,182a), **Addu** (68c,157a,182a), **Addy** (183d), **aden** (34b), **Aden, Ader** (18d), **Ades** (73a), **Adib** (155b), **adit** (51a,100a,114d), **admi** (65d), **ador** (153b), **adry** (164c), **adze** (40c,167a)

-AD- **Badb** (82b), **bade, cade** (25c,27a,76c,85d,116d), **Cade** (50c), **cadi** (12a,103a,171a), **cady** (69d), **Dada** (13b,63a,157d), **dado** (41c,111c, 115c,177d), **Eads** (23b,24b,50b,82a), **fade** (181d,183b), **fado** (121c), **fady, gade, hade** (66a,148c,173c), **hadj** (98b,118a), **jade** (33c,65d,71d,166a), **jadu** (95a), **jady, kada** (188), **kade** (144a), **kadi** (103a,171a), **Kadu** (191), **lade** (24c,26d,43c,93b,100a,132a,139d, 161b,178d), **Ladd** (143c), **lady, made, Madi** (174a), **mado** (14d,57a, 170b), **padi** (131b), **rada** (135c,172a), **rade** (138d), **sadd** (33a,40b, 58c,107b), **sade** (91d), **sadh** (77a), **sado** (26d,84d), **sadr** (94a), **Sadr** (155b), **vade** (42c,67d,89b), **wadd** (109c), **wade, wadi** (46c,106a, 109a,128a,132a), **wady** (109a,128a,132a)

--AD **adad** (52c,56a), **Adad** (68c,157a,182a), **arad** (13a,c,84a), **bead** (17a, 122a,146b), **brad** (54d,67c,105b), **Chad** (158b), **clad** (46a,82a), **dead, diad** (113a), **duad** (113a,171d), **dyad** (113a), **ecad** (73a, 119b), **egad** (100a,109a), **Fuad** (54d), **glad** (85c), **goad** (80b,154b), **grad** (28b), **head** (29d), **Ibad** (191), **Irad** (18d), **Joad** (50c), **lead** (35d,43d,72b,74d,81a), **load** (24c,26d,161b), **mead** (46a,78a,97d, 99b), **Mead** (78a), **orad** (104a), **Phad** (155b), **quad** (33c,172a), **raad** (14a,49b,151a,165b), **read** (116d,157d), **road** (37d,164d), **Saad** (12b), **scad** (31a,57a,78b,88d,137c), **shad** (27d,57a,b,c), **spad** (105b), **Spad** (118d), **stad** (151b,167d,176b), **swad** (94d), **toad** (10a, 17a,63d,126d), **udad** (143d,144a,181c), **woad** (20d,47c)

A--D **abed** (130c), **acid** (151a,162a), **adad** (52c,56a), **Adad** (68c,157a, 182a), **aged** (110a), **alod** (51c,55d,88a,124c), **amid** (9d,50a), **apod** (59d), **arad** (13a,c,84a), **arid** (46c,85a), **Arnd** (67a), **Arod** (86c), **avid** (47b,71a,186b)

AE-- **aera** (8a), **aeri** (34a), **aero** (8b,34a,b,58c,59a), **aery** (47b,51d,106c), **aesc** (12d,64d), **Aeta** (94d,95d,100a,106b,117a)

-AE- **Caen, daer** (22b), **daez, faex** (46a), **Gaea** (47d,69a), **Gael** (28a,96c, 138d), **haec** (90a,164c), **haem** (122b), **Jael** (147b), **laet** (60d), **nael** (189), **saer** (163a), **tael** (91d,179d), **waeg** (19b,72c,87a), **waer** (40b)

--AE **alae** (182d), **blae** (93b), **brae** (76d,139a,c,140b,148c), **Irae** (43c), **koae** (74b), **quae** (176b), **spae** (139c)

A--E **Aare, abbe** (32b,63b,123b), **Abie** (96b,107a), **able** (26b,35b,126a, 147c), **ache** (79a,112d,185b), **acle** (13d,82c,115d), **acme** (39c,115c, 186b), **acne** (147c), **acre** (39b,56a,88b), **Acre, adze** (40c,167a), **agee** (13d,15c,38d), **ague** (30a,55d,95c,137b), **aide** (7b,14a,75d), **aile** (62b,63a,182c,d), **aine** (49b,62c,142c), **aire** (82c), **Aire, ajee** (15c,139a), **akee** (168c), **alae** (182d), **albe** (133a)
alee (15c,75d,144b,157a,182a), **Alle** (14c), **alme** (40d,147a), **aloe** (7d,20a,76a,b,92b,98b,119b,158b,167a,183d), **amie** (61d), **ance** (158b,c,d), **Ande** (193), **ange** (61a), **Anne** (50c,84a,143b,183c), **ante** (87a,89a,115b,120b,122b,125d,154d), **a-one** (52b,167b), **apse** (9b, 20a,31a,128c,130a,142b,175a), **arme** (63a,179b), **Arne** (35c,50c, 134d), **asse** (25a,60d,74a), **atle** (136d,161d,169b), **Aude, auge** (123c,132b), **aune** (188), **axle** (153c,180c)

AF-- **afar** (44c), **Afar** (6c), **afer** (48a,182b), **affy** (18b), **Afra** (183c)

-AF- **baff** (69d), **baft** (14a,53b), **cafe, daff** (125d), **daft** (59c), **gaff** (57c, d,152d,153a), **haft** (76d), **Kafa** (6c), **raff** (75b), **raft** (27b,33c,58c, 75b), **safe** (141d,157d,174d), **Safi** (191), **Taft** (29d), **Wafd** (49a), **waft** (20d,58c)

- - AF **deaf**, **goaf** (104b), **Graf** (37c,66b,67a,107c,186b), **haaf** (57d), **heaf** (144a), **leaf** (55c,73c,119b), **loaf** (79b,94b), **neaf** (58a,73c), **Olaf** (108a,176b), **Piaf** (63c), **Wraf**

A - - F **alef** (91c), **alif** (12b), **arif** (127d), **atef** (39a,48d), **Azof** (20b,135d)

AG - - **Agag** (18c,86c,137a), **agal** (17c,36d), **Agao** (6c,73c), **agar** (7d,28c, 39c,103c,141c), **Agau** (73c), **Agaz** (193), **aged** (110a), **agee** (13d, 15c,38d), **ager** (47c,56a,89b,c,131d,133b), **agha** (35a,171a), **Agib** (12a,42d), **agio** (52c,60a,101c,123a), **Agis** (86d), **agla** (7a), **agni** (88a,89c), **Agni** (56d,68b), **agog** (47b,52c,86b), **agon** (12c,36c,41b, 55d,71b), **agra** (26d,34d), **Agra** (161b), **agri** (89b), **agro** (149d), **agua** (152d,166c,178c), **ague** (30a,55d,95c,137b)

- AG - **baga** (171b), **bago** (13d), **cage** (36a), **cagy** (178b), **dagg** (118c), **dagh** (76d), **Dago**, **gage** (28d,98a,119c,d), **gagl** (160b), **hagg**, **hagi** (84b), **lago** (54b,111d,143c), **Jaga** (191), **jagg**, **kago** (113a), **kagu** (106c), **lago** (83b,152b), **mage** (95b), **magg** (95b), **Magh** (102a), **magi** (123c), **Magi** (95b,116c,183a), **naga** (13d,33a,55b,127c), **Naga** (24c,77a,88c,176d), **Nagy** (78d), **Paga** (117a), **page** (51b,59b, 142d,159b), **raga** (56d,105a), **rage** (10c,30c,157a,161d), **ragi** (28b), **saga** (79b,91a,138a,157a,161b,c,168a), **Saga**, **sage** (13a,90d,100c, 141c,145c,180b,183a), **sago** (54c,59b,113b,125b,155c), **sagy**, **vagi** (38b), **wage** (27a,115b), **yage** (23a)

- - AG **Agag** (18c,86c,137a), **brag** (21a,175a), **coag** (45d,118a,163b), **crag** (132c), **drag** (74a,125b), **flag** (16b,50d,82b,88c,115a,155a), **knag** (115d,139c), **krag** (131c), **peag** (144a,178a), **quag** (21c,102c), **shag** (73b,105b,161d,166d), **skag** (7d,46d), **slag** (46c,99a,138c,148d, 177a), **snag** (11b,27b,35c,87c,124b,166a), **stag** (65a,98d), **swag** (22a,156c), **waag** (71d,101d)

A - - G **Agag** (18c,86c,137a), **agog** (47b,52c,86b), **ajog**, **areg** (116a,137a)

AH - - **Ahab** (18c,26c,85b,86d,100d,116a,180b), **Ahaz** (86d), **ahem**, **Ahet** (49a,102a), **ahey** (52c), **Ahir** (27b), **Ahom** (88c), **ahoy** (106a), **ahum**

- AH - **bahi** (60c), **baho** (122a), **baht** (146a), **haha** (55c,159c), **kaha** (123d), **kahu** (14d), **maha** (28c,88c,136d), **mahr** (103a), **Oahu**, **paha** (67b), **pahi** (21b,26a), **paho** (122a), **Rahu** (42b,48b), **saha**, **sahh** (188), **Saho** (6c), **sahu** (153d), **taha** (179b), **tahr** (68a,76d)

- - AH **Adah** (25b,51b), **Amah** (95b,108d,111c), **arah** (52c), **ayah** (108d), **blah**, **drah** (188), **Elah** (18c,86d), **Etah** (51c,71d), **eyah** (95b,108d, 111c), **Ivah** (18d), **kyah** (19a), **Leah** (19a,84a,87b,183c), **Noah** (88a, 99b), **odah** (170d), **opah** (23b,57a,b,86d), **prah** (21b,26a,95c,d), **Ptah** (48d,98c), **saah** (188), **seah** (188), **shah** (116c), **Utah** (180b), **yeah**

A - - H **acth** (13b), **Adah** (25b,51b), **aich** (9a), **Alph** (132a), **amah** (95b, 108d,111c), **ankh** (38d,162b), **arah** (52c), **arch** (29d,38b,39d,123d, 132c), **ayah** (108d)

AI - - **aich** (9a), **Aida** (110d, 175c), **aide** (7b,14a,75d), **aile** (62b,63a,182c, d), **aine** (49b,62c,142c), **Aino** (84a,c), **aint**, **Ainu** (84a,c), **aipi** (27a), **Aira** (70d), **aire** (82c), **Aire**, **airs** (123b), **airy** (177a,176d)

- AI - **bail** (43c), **bain** (61a), **bait** (15d,51a,94d,167b), **caid** (35a,151d, 152b), **cain** (169c), **Cain** (6a,7a,50d,88a,104c,143a), **Dail** (49a, 82b, c), **dain** (188), **dais** (119b), **fail**, **fain** (42d,67c,183b), **fair** (17a,55d),

fait (6d,61b), **Gaia** (47d,69a), **gail** (23b,174d), **Gall** (183d), **gain** (7a, b,124a,181d), **gait** (96b,179a), **haik** (57b,65b,108a), **hail** (6d,15a, 71d), **hair** (56b,164d), **jail** (123d), **Jain** (77b), **kaid** (29d,66a), **kaif** (88c), **kaik** (96c), **kail** (18c,22a.25a,79b), **Kain, kair, laic** (32b,90b, 107d,124a,141d), **laid, lain, lair** (37c,42b), **Lais** (17c), **lait** (62a), **Maia** (76b,109a,153b,155b,177c), **maid** (45b.142d), **mail** (12d,99b, 121c), **maim** (43d,81a,105c), **main** (29d,35d,123d), **mais** (61b), **Naia** (33a), **naid** (63c), **naif** (74b,105d). **naik, nail** (31d,54d,141d,161d, 173a), **naio** (107a,168c), **Nair** (45d), **nais** (63c,132a), **paid** (129c), **pail, pain** (7c), **pair** (22d,37d,85b,171d), **pais** (37d), **qaid** (35a), **raia** (107d), **Raia** (147b), **raid** (59d,80c), **raik** (188,189), **rail** (16b,19b,c, 37a,97b,138c,150c,177b), **rain** (121d,162d), **raip** (36d), **rais** (26c, 29d,75a,103b), **Rais** (106b), **saic** (86b,91d,175d), **said** (174c), **Said** (42d,101a,121b), **sail** (144c,185a), **sain** (20c,38d,48a), **sair** (140b, 150d), **sais** (48d,71d), **tail** (11d,27d,59b,143b), **tain** (166a), **tair** (68a,76d), **tait** (14d), **vail** (94b,124a,174b), **vain** (81a), **vair** (64c, 154c), **waif** (157b), **wail** (39b,88a), **wain** (177b), **Wain, wait** (26d, 42b,92c,155d,162a), **zaim** (170d), **zain** (41a)

- - AI **alai** (171a), **Alai** (135c), **anai** (163b,181a), **chai** (72d), **goai** (106d, 168c), **ngai** (48a,159c), **peai** (98b), **quai** (88b,117c,180c), **Thai** (146a)

A - - I **Aani** (45a,48d), **abri** (61c,62c,144b), **Absi** (191), **admi** (65d), **aeri** (34a), **agni** (88a,89c), **Agni** (56d,68b), **agri** (89b), **aipi** (27a), **alai** (171a), **Alai** (135c), **Albi** (58a), **alii** (74c,134c), **ambi** (34a,122c), **amli** (48a,161d,168c,169a), **ammi** (98c), **amoi** (62a), **anai** (163b, 181a), **Andi** (27d), **anti** (7d,111a,122b), **Anti** (193), **apii** (74c), **arni** (24a,181b), **arui** (11b,143d,144a,181c), **asci** (154a), **assi** (77d), **Asti** 83d,'182b), **Atli** (14c,72b,79a,107d), **Atri, auri** (34a)

AJ - - **ajar** (110c), **Ajax** (71b,162d), **ajee** (15c,139a), **ajog**

- AJ - **baju** (84a), **caja** (152a), **caji** (180b), **gajo** (107c), **haje** (33a,48d), **maja** (151c), **Maja** (153b), **majo, Naja** (33a), **pajo** (122a), **raja** (77a, 123c), **Raja, tajo** (152a,d), **yaje** (23a)

AK - - **Akal** (56d), **Akan** (191), **akee** (168c), **akey** (189), **Akha** (86a,c), **akia** (74c), **Akim** (135d,191), **akin** (8b,92b,129c), **Akka** (125d), **akov** (189), **akra** (176a), **Akra** (191), **akua** (120d)

- AK - **baka** (52b), **bake** (139a), **baku** (26d,157b,168c), **cake, caky, fake** (123a,143c), **faky, hake** (57a,b), **hakh** (46d), **hako** (115b), **haku** (86d), **jake** (40d), **Jake** (96b), **jako** (71a), **kaka** (114b), **kaki** (84c, 106d), **lake** (117d), **lakh** (110c), **laky, make** (35b,36d,54a,123a) **maki** (91b), **mako** (18a,19a,20d,143c,168c,182c), **Maku** (192), **oaks** (154d), **oaky, rake** (41b,44c,134b,140d), **Saka** (10a), **sake** (84b,125d), **saki** (39c,84b,102a), **take, takt** (105a,163a), **Taku** (80c), **taky, waka** (26a), **wake** (134b,168a), **wakf** (103a), **waky, Yaka** (191), **Yaki** (193)

- - AK **Anak** (67a), **asak** (13d,168c,169a), **beak** (19a), **coak** (45d,118a, 163b), **dhak** (48a,169a), **Dyak** (22b), **feak** (39d,171c), **fiak** (11a), **haak** (57b,178a), **Irak** (99a,d), **kiak** (51c), **kyak** (51c), **leak** (110c), **peak** (9a,38c,159b,186b), **siak** (72d), **soak** (46c,137c), **teak** (41a, 48a,168c), **weak** (55b)

A - - K **amok** (18b,63c), **Anak** (67a), **asak** (13d,168c,169a), **asok** (13d), **Atik** (155b)

AL - - **alae** (182d), **alai** (171a), **Alai** (135c), **alan** (45a,79a,183), **Alan, alar** (15c,145c,182d), **alas** (52c,136b,183b), **alat** (136d), **alay** (96c), **alba** (98b,181a), **Alba** (151d), **albe** (133a), **Albi** (58a), **albo** (34d,181a), **Alca** (14c,128b), **alco** (45b), **alda** (152b), **Alda** (110d, 150c), **Alea** (14b,31c,167d), **alec** (10a,57c,d,76c,137c), **alee** (15c, 75d,144b,157a,182a), **alef** (91c), **alem** (98b,155a,170d,171a), **alen** (40d,138a), **alfa** (70d), **alga** (141b,c), **Algy** (96b), **alia** (89d), **alif** (12b), **alii** (74c,134c), **alim** (103b,162c), **alin** (188), **alit** (44b,143a), **Alix** (183c), **alky, alla** (6d), **Alle** (14c), **allo** (34c), **ally** (14a,35c,d, 173c), **alma** (40d,53d,146d,147a), **Alma** (38d,183c), **alme** (40d, 147a), **alms** (29a), **alod** (51c,55d,88a,124c), **aloe** (7d,20a,76a,b,92b, 98b,119b,158b,167a,183d) **alop** (13d,46b,93d), **alow** (18a,172c), **Alph** (132a), **Alps** (85d), **also** (10b,18b,80a), **alta** (89c,152d), **alto** (152b,176c,177a), **alum** (14a,45c), **Alur** (191), **Alva** (151d), **Alya** (155b,c), **Alys** (183c)

- AL - **Aalu** (6b,48d), **Bala** (26c,66a), **bald** (16c), **bale** (24b,74a), **bali, Bali, balk** (118c,146a,156d), **ball, balm** (110a,172c), **Balt** (93a), **balu** (104b,159a,181d), **cale** (72d), **calf, calk** (78c,109a,141c,178d), **call** (145c,159b,176d), **calm** (8d,11d,112b,118d,126c,d,172b,173d), **calo** (72d), **calp** (92b), **calx** (23c,75c,112c), **dale** (43c,128a,174b), **dali** (168c,169b), **fala** (129b), **fall** (46b,141c), **falx** (133b), **gala** (55d), **Gala** (191), **gale** (181d), **gali** (6c), **gall** (19a,28c,29b,82c,160c, 176a), **galt, hala** (112b), **hale** (125b), **Hale** (9d,131a), **half** (101a), **hall** (37b,114d), **halm, halo** (14d,31b,92a,107b,131d), **Hals** (47a), **halt** (13b,28a,38d,156d), **lalu** (48d), **kala** (19a), **kale** (22a,25a, 119b,175a), **kali** (26d,67c,136d,167a), **Kali** (147b), **kalo** (162a), **lala** (129b), **lalo** (16b,34d,153a), **Lalo** (35c), **mala** (89b,c,90a,94b, 97d,109d,185c), **male** (154d), **Male** (45d), **mali** (27b), **mall** (95d,124b,143b), **malm** (32a,92b), **malo** (23a,74c,152a), **malt** (17c), **Nala** (77a), **pala** (189), **Pala** (88b), **pale** (113a,117c,178a), **pali** (122b), **Pali** (23d,24a,137b,175a), **pall** (32d,81b,112a), **palm** (59b, 168c,169b), **palo** (152c), **palp** (11a,55b,58b,167c), **paly** (194), **rale** (7c,23a,29d,41b), **ralo** (188), **sala** (152a,b,c), **Sala** (50c), **sale** (14c,61c,62b,c,168b), **salp** (109c,148d), **salt** (35d,105b,123a,136c, 141c,149d), **tala** (16d,113a,168c,d), **talc** (28d,63b,99c,100b,122a, 149c), **tale** (91a,185b), **tali** (189), **talk, tall** (118d), **vale** (54c,128a, 174b), **Vale** (7c,109c), **vali** (171a,176a), **Vali** (7c,109c), **wale** (70b, 131b,157c,163d,179a,180a,c,d), **wali** (171a), **walk, wall, Walt** (96b), **Yale** (173c), **yali** (171a)

- - AL **agal** (17c,36d), **Akal** (56d), **Aral** (135d), **aval** (70c), **axal** (120b), **Baal** (142b), **beal** (139d), **bual** (182c), **coal** (49c,64a), **cral, deal** (11d,16c,36c,44c,81a,168b), **dhal** (12b), **dial** (25c), **dual** (45c,171d), **eral** (51a), **etal** (89a), **foal** (78c), **gaal** (23b,174d), **geal** (47d,163c), **goal** (8b,109b,120b,125d), **heal, ical** (158c), **keal** (25a), **kral, leal** (54b,94c,139d), **maal** (188), **meal** (72a,130b), **Neal, odal** (48a,88b, 112c), **opal** (20a,65d,67b,82b) **oral** (114a,153d,174c,175c), **oval** (48d,49c,127a), **paal** (188), **peal** (131c,d), **pyal** (175c), **real** (7a), **rial** (190), **ryal** (110a,190), **saal** (66c,73b), **seal** (10c,d,54d,64c,96a, 118b,128a), **sial** (112a), **Taal** (7d,88c,151a), **teal** (19b,20d,46c,d), **udal** (76b,88b,131c), **unal** (147a), **ural, Ural** (135c), **uval** (70c), **veal, vial** (148c), **weal** (124d,157c,180c,d), **zeal** (12c,55d)

A - - L **Abel** (7a,25b), **acyl** (6d), **agal** (17c,36d), **Akal** (56d), **amil** (45a,48a,

185c), **amyl** (155c), **anil** (47c,80d,180b), **Aoul** (191), **Aral** (135d), **aril** (142a), **aval** (70c), **axal** (120b), **axil** (10c), **azul** (151d)

AM - - **amah** (95b,108d,111c), **amar** (189), **amba** (161a), **ambi** (34a,122c), **ambo** (125b,128b), **amen** (14a,80b,94a,137a,149c,175c,184b), **Amen** (86d,127d,159b,164a), **amer** (61b), **Ames** (9c,82a), **Amex** (184d), **amia** (22c,170d), **amic** (9d), **amid** (9d,50a), **amie** (61d), **amil** (45a,48a,185c), **amin** (9d), **amir** (7c,12a,103a,b,123c,170d), **amit** (94a), **amla** (48a,161d,168c,169a), **amli** (48a,161d,168c,169a), **amma** (6a), **ammi** (98c), **ammo** (9d), **ammu** (9d), **amoi** (62a), **amok** (18b,63c), **Amon** (86d,96d,127d,159b,164a), **amor** (152b), **Amor** (39c,68b), **Amos** (96a,144b), **Amoy** (88c), **amra** (77c), **Amun** (86d,127d,159b,164a), **amyl** (155c)

- AM - **came** (182b), **Came** (192), **camp** (163b), **dama** (65d,152b), **dame** (67b,87c,166b), **damn**, **damp** (101a), **Fama** (135a), **fame** (130a), **famn** (188), **Gama** (121c), **game** (64d,154a), **gamp** (172a), **hami** (78a), **iamb** (59c), **jama** (103b), **jamb** (12d,45c,118a,146b,174a), **jami** (103b), **Kama** (56d), **kame** (67b,139b), **kami** (68a,84b), **Kami** (88c,107c,144c), **lama** (23d,24a,91d,165b), **Lamb** (49c), **lame** (38d, 43d,73b), **lamp** (92a,94c), **mama**, **Mama** (116d), **mamo** (19a,d,74b), **Nama** (78c), **name** (8a,11b,d,25c,46c,107c,130b,157d,163b,166b), **Rama** (77a,80b,176d), **rame** (22d), **rami** (22d), **ramp** (65a,80b, 127b,148b), **sama** (105c,169d), **same** (44d,79b), **samh** (56b), **samp** (70b,77d,121b), **Tama** (192), **tame** (45a,b,66a), **Tame**, **tamp** (46b, 112b,121d,127d), **vamp** (80a,145a), **Yama** (57a,68a), **Zama** (73d, 141d)

- - AM **Adam** (26b,96a,111c), **anam** (159a,168c), **Anam**, **Aram** (18d,50c, 105c,144b,161c), **Azam** (166c), **beam**, **Bram** (96a), **caam** (93d), **cham** (20a,29d), **Cham** (8c), **clam** (20b,101b), **cram** (157d), **dram** (46b,110c,121d,148c), **edam** (29c), **Elam** (18d,37d,82a,116c,144b), **enam** (70c,77a), **Enam** (85c), **exam**, **Faam** (111a), **flam** (169c), **foam** (63d,154b), **gram** (29d,99b,148d,160d,180a), **Gram**, **Guam**, **imam** (25c,102d,103a), **klam** (189), **Liam** (181d), **loam** (47d,150a), **lyam** (139a), **ma'am** (95a,166b), **miam** (14d), **naam** (44c,105b), **ogam** (82b,c), **olam** (51a,d,75c,81a), **pram** (15a), **ream** (18c,37d, 50d,113d,171c), **roam** (178a), **seam** (85b,d,160a,176d,185a), **sham** (41c,55b,60d,80a,123a,b,146d), **Siam** (163d,181a), **slam** (180d, 182d), **swam**, **team** (38c,72a,113a), **Tiam**, **tram** (170a), **Ulam** (67b), **wham** (157c)

A - - M **Adam** (26b,96a,111c), **ahem**, **Ahom** (88c), **ahum**, **Akim** (135d,191), **alem** (98b,155a,170d,171a), **alim** (103b,162c), **alum** (14a,45c), **anam** (159a,168c), **Anam**, **Anim** (18d), **Aram** (18d,50c,105c,144b, 161c), **arum** (13a,39b,58d,92b,155c), **Arum** (66a), **asem** (9a,49a, 69c), **Asom** (18d), **atom** (101c,114c,180d), **Atum** (143a,159b), **Azam** (166c)

AN - - **anai** (163b,181a), **Anak** (67a), **anam** (159a,168c), **anan** (49a,159a, 180c), **Anas** (46c,d), **Anat** (138c,147d), **Anax** (43c,120c), **anay** (72b,163b,181a), **anba** (36d), **ance** (158b,c,d), **ancy** (158c), **anda** (23a,168c), **Ande** (193), **Andi** (27d), **Andy** (96b), **Aner** (18d,96b), **anes** (110c,140a), **anet** (43c), **anew** (7c), **ange** (61a), **ango** (171a), **anil** (47c,80d,180b), **Anim** (18d), **anis** (55c), **ankh** (38d,162b), **anna** (190), **Anna** (110c,166d,183c), **Anne** (50c,84a,143b,183c),

anoa (28a,60a,112c,181c), **anon** (7d,14d,79d,80b,123a,145c,150c, 164a), **ansa** (73c,93d,137c), **anse** (61d), **ansu** (11d), **anta** (83d, 117c,d,121a), **Anta** (164a), **ante** (87a,89a,115b,120b,122b,125d, 154d), **anti** (7d,111a,122b), **Anti** (193), **anzu** (11d)

- AN - **Aani** (45a,48d), **Bana** (67a), **banc** (61a,85c), **band** (72a,157c), **bane** (74a,106b,120b,139a), **bang** (75d,105d,148a), **bani** (190), **bank** (18a,58c), **bans, bant** (43c), **Cana** (57a,64b,100c), **cane** (17b, 128a,156a,159a,177d), **Cane, cang** (184a), **cano** (152a), **cant** (28d, 81b,84d,90c,109b,136c,165d,166a), **Dana** (28a,96a,171d), **Dane** (85d,107d,138a), **dang, dank** (40b,101a), **dans** (62a), **Danu** (28a), **fana, fane** (30d,137a,162d), **fang** (167b), **Fano** (51d,96b,113c,d), **gane** (185b), **gang** (38c), **Gano** (132d), **hand** (60c,114c,115d,184c), **hang** (160a), **hank** (147c), **Hano** (125b), **Hans** (66d,96a), **hant** (67a), **jane** (190), **Jane** (183c), **Jann** (102d), **kana** (84d), **Kane** (74c), **k'ang** (30a), **Kano** (84c,177d), **kant** (28d), **Kant** (67a), **lana** (58a,66a,90a,184b), **land** (44a,163c), **lane** (134b,157b), **lank** (148b,164b), **lanx** (133a,b), **mana** (30a,120d,122a,159c), **mand** (28b), **mane, mani** (115c), **mann** (189), **Mann** (9c,48c,185c), **mano** (71d,73d,74b,83b), **Mans** (30a), **Manu** (10a,76d,77a,b), **Manx** (27b, 28a,82d), **many** (108d), **nana** (118b), **Nana** (15c,105d,116d,186d), **nane** (139d), **Pana, pane** (113c,155a,b), **pang** (165b), **Pani** (120c), **pank** (189), **pant, rana** (77a,123c), **Rana** (63d), **rand** (16d,22a, 131b,145a,b), **Rand** (69c), **rang, rani** (72d,77b,123c,127c), **rank** (31d,55d,70b,92c,94d,157d), **rann** (175c), **rant** (41c,127b,128a, 161d), **sana** (56a,166d), **Sana** (185d), **sand** (71d,146c), **sane** (128a), **sang, sank, sano** (152b), **sans** (63a,183b), **tana** (159a), **Tana** (87d), **Tane** (120d), **tang** (30b,58b,186b), **tanh** (97c), **tank** (175a,d), **Tano** (192), **uang** (131a), **vane** (179b,182a), **vang** (72d,134a,140b), **Vans** (107d), **wand** (120b,132c,156a), **wane** (41c,43c), **wang** (189), **want** (41b,42d,87b,106b,122a), **wany, Yana** (192,193), **yang** (30b,70a), **yank, Yank, zany** (24a,32d,59c)

- - AN **adan** (102d), **Akan** (191), **alan** (45a,79a,183c), **Alan** (96a), **anan** (49a,159a,180c), **Aran** (18c,48c,64d,82d,174c), **Awan** (191), **azan** (102d), **bean** (91b,142a,175a), **bran** (23c,39a,72a,79c,70b), **Bran** (23c,50c), **chan** (26c,130c), **clan** (169c), **Coan** (37b), **cran** (160c), **cyan, dean** (33c,109d), **dhan** (124c), **dian** (46c,130d,170b), **Dian** (68d,69a,c,102b), **duan** (64b), **elan** (12c,41a,50d,62a,153c,177a, 186b), **Eoan** (41a,85b), **Evan** (96a), **Ewan, flan** (39d,40a,114d), **gean** (29c), **Goan, gran, guan** (151b), **Iban** (47c), **Iran** (6a,48c, 116b), **Ivan** (40c,85b,96a), **jean** (37c), **Jean** (183c), **Joan** (183c), **juan** (113a), **Juan** (96a), **kaan** (93d,116c), **khan** (7c,26c,81b,93d, 116c,123c,130c,166c), **kran** (190), **kuan** (30b,c), **Kuan, kwan** (30b), **lean** (128a,148b,152d,164b,166a), **loan, mean** (15a,42b, 146c,156b), **mian** (97c,147b,166b), **moan, ngan, oban** (190), **Olan** (115c), **Oman** (159a), **Onan** (18c,85c), **Oran, oxan, pean** (65c), **plan** (99b,124a,138b), **quan** (190), **roan** (78b,c,114c,128d,144a, 181a), **Saan** (24d), **Sean** (85b,96a), **Shan** (13c,80d,88c,101d), **scan** (52b,93d,98a,116d,128b,c,140d), **span** (23b,107b,113a,128b,162c), **Svan** (27d), **swan** (19b,33a) **tean** (140c167a), **than** (35b), **tran** (7a), **tuan** (95d,147b,166c), **ulan** (27d,88a), **uran** (101d), **Uran, uzan** (189), **wean** (8d,42d), **yean** (88a), **yuan** (190), **Yuan** (30b,101d)

A - - N **acon** (62c,140d), **adan** (102d), **aden** (34b), **Aden, agon** (12c,36c, 41b,55d,71b), **Akan** (191), **akin** (8b,92b,129c), **alan** (45a,79a, 183c), **Alan** (96a), **alen** (40d,138a), **alin** (188), **amen** (14a, 80b,94a,137a,149c,175c,184b), **Amen** (86d,127d,159b,164a), **amin** (9d), **Amon** (86d,96b,127d,159b,164a), **Amun** (86d,127d, 159b,164a), **anan** (49a,159a,180c), **anon** (7d,14d,79d,80b,123a, 145c,150c,164a), **Aran** (18c,48c,64d,82d,174c), **Asin** (102a), **aten** (150a,159b), **aton** (150a,159b), **Avon** (143b), **Awan** (191) **axon** (106c,153c), **ayin** (91c), **azan** (102d), **azon** (127b)

AO - - **aone** (52b,167b), **Aoul** (191)

- AO - **faon** (33c,55a), **gaol** (123d), **Gaol** (164a), **Gaon** (85b), **jaob, Laos** (80d,129c), **naos** (28a,71c,137a,163a), **Naos** (155b), **paon** (115b), **Taos** (192), **Yaou** (30c)

- - AO **Agao** (6c,73c), **dhao** (24c), **grao** (189), **guao** (168c,169b), **Miao** (30a,b), **omao** (165b), **prao** (21b,26a,95c,d), **tiao**

A - - O **aboo** (17c), **acto** (152b), **aero** (8b,34a,b,58c,59a), **Agao** (6c,73c), **agio** (52c,60a,101c,123a), **agro** (149d), **Aino** (84a,c), **albo** (34d, 181a), **alco** (45b), **allo** (34c), **also** (10b,18b,80a), **alto** (152b,176c, 177a), **ambo** (125b,128b), **ammo** (9d), **ango** (171a), **apio** (125b), **areo** (34c), **Argo** (12c,36b,c), **Arno** (27a), **aroo** (80c,82b), **arro** (52c), **arto** (34a), **asno** (151d), **Ateo** (120d), **atmo** (34d,174d), **auto** (34d)

AP - - **Apap** (102a), **apar** (12d), **aper** (32d), **Apet** (97c), **apex** (39c,76c, 115c,118b,159b,166a,167b), **apia** (121b), **apii** (74c), **apio** (125b), **Apis** (17c,24b,49a,125a,136a), **apod** (59d), **apse** (9b,20a,31a,128c, 130a,142b,175a), **Apsu** (29a), **Apus** (36b,c)

- AP - **capa** (152a,166d), **cape** (75a,96c,124b,161a), **caph** (91c), **capp** (27a), **gape** (185b), **gapo** (60a), **gapy, Hapi** (66a,107b,136a), **hapu** (106d), **jape** (85a,b), **kapa** (74b), **kaph** (91d), **kapp, Lapp** (108a), **mapo** (68a,148d), **napa** (25c,67d,90d), **Napa** (182c), **nape** (15b, 108c,d), **napu** (29d,80d), **papa, pape** (19b,113a), **rapt** (6c,27a,50d), **sapa** (70c), **sapo** (149c,166d), **tapa** (16c,32c,53b,56a,74b,104b,112b, 113d,120d), **tape** (16a,19a,128d), **tapu, wapp** (54b,133d,145d), **yapa** (113b), **Yapp** (22a)

- - AP **Apap** (102a), **atap** (113b), **chap** (55b), **clap** (58b), **drap** (61b,c, 62a), **flap** (17b,59a,104a,118d,161a,182d), **frap** (45d,165c), **heap** (117d), **knap** (76d,107a,139b,159b,166a,170c,185b), **laap** (51d,91b, 141d), **leap** (26c), **neap** (165c,167a,177b), **plap** (54b), **reap** (7a,40a, 74a), **shap, slap** (24a,128c,148c), **snap** (23a,36d,38b,48b,54d,56c, 58c,149d), **soap, swap** (168a), **trap** (27b,67b,132b,149b), **wrap** (32b,51a)

A - - P **alop** (13d,46b,93d), **Apap** (102a), **asop** (180b), **atap** (113b), **atip** (14b,166a), **atop** (112a,174a)

AQ - - **aqua** (90a,178c)

- AQ - **waqf** (103a)

- - AQ **Iraq** (99a,d)

AR - - **Arab** (30a,78b,c,106a,107c,157b,160c,185d), **arad** (13a,c,84a), **arah** (52c), **Aral** (135d), **Aram** (18d,50c,105c,144b,161c), **Aran** (18c, 48c,64d,82d,174c), **arar** (137a,168c), **Aras, arba** (135d,171a), **arca**

(9a,22c,29d,115a,130a), **Arca** (101b), **arch** (29d,38b,39d,123d, 132c), **area** (37d,38a,44c,53a,93b,110d,127d,138c,168a,186d), **areg** (116a,137a), **areo** (34c), **Ares** (49b,51b,68c,76a,97a,105c,110b, 178a,186d), **aret** (128c), **Argo** (12c,36b,c), **aria** (8b,98c,150a,c, 170c), **arid** (46c,85a), **arif** (127d), **aril** (142a), **aris** (101b), **arme** (63a,179b), **arms, army** (78c), **arna** (24a,181b), **Arnd** (67a), **Arne** (35c,50c,134d), **arni** (24a,181b), **Arno** (27a), **arn't, Aroa** (175b), **Arod** (86c), **aroo** (80c,82b), **arow** (92c,158b), **arpa** (83b), **arra** (47d,52c,82b), **arro** (52c), **Arta** (72b), **arto** (34a), **arts** (138c), **arty, arui** (11b,143d,144a,181c), **arum** (13a,39b,58d,92b,155c), **Arum** (66a), **Arya** (80d)

- AR - **Aare, Aaru** (6b,48d), **bara** (188), **barb** (20b,57d,78b,117d,120a,b, 124b), **bard** (12d,120a), **bare** (43d,157c), **bari** (79c), **Bari** (37c,83d), **bark** (115c), **barm** (185b), **barn** (156d), **baro** (71a,122c), **barr** (49b), **Bart** (96b), **baru** (168c), **cara** (83a), **Cara** (48b,183c), **card** (33d, 114d), **care** (11b,14c,35d,150a,184d), **cark** (26d,184d), **carl** (115c, 135d), **Carl** (96a), **carn** (156c), **caro** (83a,183d), **carp** (27d,38d, 40c,55a,56c,57a), **carr** (120d,140a), **cart** (171d,175a,177b), **Dara** (18d), **Dard, dare** (28d,41b,42a,74d,175b), **Dare** (57a), **dari** (38a, 70b), **dark** (47a,67d,109b,160b), **darn** (130b), **darr** (163c), **dart** (13b,88a,100c,120b,153a,160c), **Dart** (100c), **earl** (107c), **earn** (42d,64b,99a), **fard** (112d), **fare** (43c,59b,67d,123b), **farl** (138c, 140b), **farm** (165d), **faro** (65a), **gara** (190), **garb** (32c,46a), **gare** (61b,c,62c,127c,184b), **Garm** (178c), **garn** (67d,185b), **Garo** (88c), **Harb** (191), **hard** (109b), **hare** (91b,132c), **hark** (92d), **harl** (16b,56b, 59a), **harm** (40b,81a), **harp** (105a,129a), **hart** (41d,154d), **jarl** (40d, 107d), **kara** (132a), **Kari** (14d), **Karl** (96a), **karn** (156c), **karo** (106d), **Lara** (25c), **lard** (54d,61a,71a,110a), **lari** (78a,101c), **Lari** (72c), **lark** (19a,63d,177b), **larp** (51d), **Lars** (51d,121b), **mara** (114d), **Mara** (24a,d,105b,107b), **marc** (70c), **Marc** (96a), **mare** (78b,108b), **mari** (16a,61d), **mark, Mark** (52a,96a,146b,155a), **marl** (32a,42c, 55d), **maro** (144d), **Mars** (68c,118d,119a,178a), **mart** (49d,97a), **Mart** (96b,183d), **maru** (84c,144d), **Mary** (50c,126b,183c), **nard** (13a, 97c,102b,110a,153c), **Nare** (93c), **nark** (81a,156d), **nary** (108b), **oary, para** (134c,170d), **Para** (18a,51d), **parc** (62b,112c), **pard** (27b, 91b), **pare** (115c,129a), **pari** (34a,180a), **park, parr** (136d,147c), **pars** (89d), **part** (44d,60d,121c,159c), **paru** (57a), **rara** (119a), **rare** (138b,164b,172b,173d), **Sara** (24d,183c), **sard** (26d,28d,65d,111a, 142b,156d), **Sarg** (96d,125c), **sari** (48b,65b,77b), **Sark** (28d), **Sart** (82b, 103b, 170d), **tara** (22a, 55c, 113a, 168c), **Tara** (82b,c,138b), **tare** (9a,18d,41a,176a,179d), **tari** (47d,69a), **tarn** (87d,103d,120d), **taro** (13c,48c,49b,64b,112b,120a,133d,155c,170a, c), **tarp** (26b,178d), **tart** (114d), **vara** (151d), **vare** (179b), **vari** (34d,91b,134d,174d), **vary** (28d,43c), **ward** (31c,55c,86b), **ware** (27d,35a), **warf, warm** (7c,75b,163b), **warn** (7b), **warp** (36c,165a, 171c), **wart** (124d), **wary** (27d,176b), **yard** (152d), **yare** (96b,124b, 128b), **yark** (22c), **yarl** (40d,107d), **yarn** (154b,161b,184b), **yarr** (72a), **Yaru** (48d), **zarf** (39c,155a), **zarp** (120c)

- - AR **Adar** (85c,102a), **afar** (44c), **Afar** (6c), **agar** (7d,28c,39c,103c,141c), **ajar** (110c), **alar** (15c,145c,182d), **amar** (189), **apar** (12d), **arar** (137a,168c), **asar** (67b), **atar** (58d,116b,134a), **Avar** (27d,108a), **bear** (27a,50b,113c,155a), **Bhar** (191), **boar** (77c,117c,160c,181c),

char (24d,138c,170b), **czar** (42d,49d,60b,135c), **dear, Dhar, duar, Edar** (18d), **fear** (113c,155a), **gear** (32c,112a,167b), **gnar** (72a), **guar** (46c,59d), **haar** (139c), **hear** (75b,c,92d), **hoar** (63d,71a, 181a), **inar** (65b), **Isar** (41a,104c,132a), **Iyar** (102b), **izar** (65b, 103b,155b), **joar** (100a), **juar** (100a), **khar** (189), **knar** (87c,134b), **kuar** (102a), **kyar** (33a), **lear** (139d), **Lear** (37a,143b, **liar** (98d), **maar** (177a), **near** (11d,32c,107b), **omar** (103b), **Omar** (48c,51b, 163b), **osar** (51b,67b,131b), **paar** (28c), **pear** (64a), **rear** (15b,23a, b,24a,51b,76d,127c), **roar** (145c) **Saar** (63b,102d,132a), **scar** (31a, 184d), **sear** (23d,27d,72d,138c), **soar** (59a), **spar** (22c,24c,64b, 97b,100b,144d), **star** (14a,21c,94c,100c), **taar** (12b), **tear** (67c, 87b,130a), **thar** (68a,76d), **tiar** (39a,75a,121a), **tsar** (42d,49d, 60b,135c), **tzar** (42d,49d,60b,135c), **usar** (8d,16c), **wear** (50b), **year, Zoar**

A - - R **Abir** (129a), **Acer** (96c), **acor** (6d), **Adar** (85c,102a), **Ader** (18d), **ador** (153b), **afar** (44c), **Afar** (6c), **afer** (48a,182b), **agar** (7d,28c, 39c,103c,141c), **ager** (47c,56a,89b,c,131d,133b), **Ahir** (27b), **ajar** (110c), **alar** (15c,145c,182d), **Alur** (191), **amar** (189), **amer** (61b), **amir** (7c,12a,103a,b,123c,170d), **amor** (152b), **Amor** (39c,68b), **Aner** (18d,96b), **apar** (12d), **aper** (32d), **arar** (137a,168c), **asar** (67b), **Aser** (84a), **Askr** (107d), **asor** (75c,105a), **Asur** (68c), **atar** (58d,116b,134a), **Ater** (18c), **Auer** (79a), **Avar** (27d,108a), **aver** (7c,14a,15c,41c,95c,140d,155c,160b,184c)

AS - - **asak** (13d,168c,169a), **asar** (67b), **asci** (154a), **asea** (39b,177c), **asem** (9a,49a,69c), **Aser** (84a), **Asha** (191), **ashy** (113a,178a), **Asia** (48a), **Asin** (102a), **Askr** (107d), **asno** (151d), **asok** (13d), **Asom** (18d), **asop** (180b), **asor** (75c,105a), **asse** (25a,60d,74a), **assi** (77d), **asta** (188), **Asta** (107a,164c), **Asti** (83d,182b), **Asur** (68c)

- AS - **base** (6a,43b,44b,51c,60c,79b,94b,122b), **bash, bask** (94d), **bass** (57b,c,177a), **bast** (16c,56a,117b,184a), **Bast** (27b), **casa** (152b), **case** (22c,36c,81c,91a,108c), **cash** (101c), **cask, Caso** (82d), **cass** (140c,177a), **Cass** (147a), **cast** (165b,167c), **dash** (125c,162d), **dasi** (77a), **ease** (7c,8d,35a,100d,129d,130b,c,150c), **East** (111b), **easy** (54a,146d,149d,172b), **fash** (140c,176a), **fass** (189), **fast** (56d, 126c,141d,160c,173a,d), **gash** (40a), **gasp** (113c), **hase** (74d), **hash, hasp** (31d,54d,153c), **hast, jass** (160d), **kasa** (48a), **kasi** (116b), **kasm** (189), **lash** (58c,87b,165c,180d), **Lasi** (191), **lass** (95b, **last** (36c,50b,145a,174c), **masa** (37a), **mash** (39b,156c), **mask** (44a,45c), **mass** (8a,24b,35b,142d), **mast** (17c,108d,120b,144d,152d), **masu** (57a,84c), **nase** (26b,75a,124b), **Nash** (9c), **nasi** (34c,108a,115a), **Nast** (9c,27a), **oast** (15d,86b,112a), **pasa** (46a,127c,152c), **pasi** (94b), **pass** (110b,155c), **past** (25c,69d,165d), **rasa** (51c), **rase** (42b, d,91d), **rash** (75a), **rasp** (56b,70d,140d), **sasa** (55c), **sash** (18a,45c, 67b,182b), **sass, tash** (154d), **task** (156b), **Tass** (107a,135d,151b), **vasa** (46d,114a,160b,175d), **Vasa, vase, vast** (78d,79d), **vasu** (106c), **Vasu** (176d), **wash, wasp, wast**

- - AS **abas** (61c), **alas** (52c,136b,183b), **Anas** (46c,d), **Aras, baas** (97c), **bias** (43b,123a), **blas** (6c,49c), **Blas** (67b), **bras** (61a), **Dyas** (66a), **ELAS** (71c), **eyas** (106c,173a), **gras** (78b), **Idas** (27b,71c), **Iras** (11b,32a), **khas** (153a), **kras** (76d), **kvas** (135c), **Lias** (66a), **Lyas** (66a), **Maas** (132a), **mias** (111a), **Nias** (82d), **oras** (40d), **quas**

(135c), **upas** (84d,120b,168c,d), **Usas** (68d), **utas** (49a,109c), **Xmas, yeas** (177c), **Zoas** (20b)

A - - S **abas** (61c), **ABC's** (57a), **Acis** (64b), **Acts, acus** (89d, 118a), **Ades** (73a), **Agis** (86d), **Aias, Airs** (123b), **alas** (52c,136b,183b), **alms** (29a), **Alps** (85d), **Alys** (183c), **Ames** (9c,82a), **Amos** (96a,144b), **Anas** (46c,d), **Anes** (110c,140a), **anis** (55c), **Apis** (17c,24b,49a, 125a,136a), **Apus** (36b,c), **Aras, Ares** (49b,51b,68c,76a,97a,105c, 110b,178a,186d), **aris** (101b), **arms, arts** (138c), **ates** (160c), **atis** (76d,102a), **Aves** (19d), **Avis** (89a,183c), **avus** (89b), **axis** (28b, 41d,77c,153c), **ayes** (177c)

AT - - **atap** (113b), **atar** (58d,116b,134a), **atef** (39a,48d), **aten** (150a, 159b), **Ateo** (120d), **Ater** (18c), **ates** (160c), **Atik** (155b), **atip** (14b,166a), **atis** (76d,102a), **Atka** (11a), **atle** (136d,161d,169b), **Atli** (14c,72b,79a,107d), **atma** (150d), **atmo** (34d,174d), **Atmu** (143a,159b), **atom** (101c,114c,180d), **aton** (150a,159b), **atop** (112a, 174a), **Atri, atry** (141b), **atta** (58d,90c,97d,160c,173d), **Atta** (94d, 95d,100a,106b,117a), **Attu, atua** (120d), **Atum** (143a,159b)

- AT - **bata** (30a,142d), **bate** (43c,91b,100d), **bath, Bath** (50d,151c), **batt** (37c), **batz** (190), **cata** (122c), **cate** (165c), **Cato** (132d,133b), **data** (54a), **date** (64a,153a), **dato** (95c,102c,117a), **datu** (95c,102c, 117a), **eats, fate** (42d,52a,87a,94a), **gata** (143c), **gate** (51a,121b), **Gath** (117a), **hate** (6a,43a), **hath, Hati** (48d), **jati** (27b), **jato** (173b), **Kate** (143c,183d), **kath** (14a), **Katy** (183d), **lata** (85d,95d), **late** (128c), **lath** (157c), **latu** (190), **mate** (18c,35b,41d,113a,154a,162c), **math** (77a), **Matt, maty** (80c), **Nata** (15c,47c), **Nate** (22b), **Nath** (155c), **Nato** (6a,8d), **natr** (189), **Natt** (107b), **oath** (119c,150a), **pata** (32c,160d), **pate** (39a,74d), **path** (132a,134b), **pato** (46d), **patu** (179b), **rata** (29d,56b,89d,96c,106d,120c,168c), **rate** (11d,14a,31d, 36b,51d,52a,70b,85c,112b,123b,127d,128a,138c,143a,174b), **rath** (29a,76d,162d), **rati** (189), **rats, sate** (32d,52c,67d,70d,137c,159d), **sati, Sati** (49a,126b,147b), **tate** (183a), **tatt** (87c), **tatu** (12d), **Tatu, Wate** (141a), **watt, Watt** (82a,173b,177c), **yate** (51d,168c), **yati** (76d), **zati** (21d)

- - AT **adat** (90b,95d), **alat** (136d), **Anat** (138c,147d), **beat** (58c,87b,131a, 164d,165b,180d), **bhat** (80c), **blat** (25b), **boat** (27b,106a), **brat, chat** (9b,19c,161c), **coat** (160a), **doat** (17a,94b,112a,165d), **drat** (100a), **Duat** (172d), **erat** (89c), **etat** (62d), **feat** (7a,52d), **fiat** (35a, 41d,48c,111b,137a), **Fiat** (83c), **flat** (41b,124b,173a), **frat, geat** (77d,101a), **Geat** (138a), **ghat** (32d,88b,103d,132a), **gnat** (59a, 81b,99c), **goat** (135a), **heat, ikat** (53b,159a), **kaat** (105d), **khat** (105d), **kyat** (189), **Maat** (69a,b,85d), **meat** (59b), **moat** (44d), **neat** (165c,169d), **peat** (64a,175a), **piat** (11a), **plat** (22d,96c,114a,119c, 133d), **pyat** (95b), **scat** (26b,67a,d,126c,169c), **seat** (98c,156b), **shat** (87d), **skat** (181b), **Skat** (155b), **slat** (58b,89a,117c,184a), **spat** (112c,126b,134b), **stat** (72d), **swat** (15d,20d,32d,157c), **Swat** (103a), **that** (42b,124b,129c), **what** (129c)

A - - T **abet** (8b,15b,50a,59b,75d,81c,141d,159d), **Abot** (100c), **abut** (22a, 167c), **acht** (66c), **adat** (90b,95d), **adit** (51a,100a,114d), **Ahet** (49a,102a), **aint, alat** (136d), **alit** (44b,143a), **amit** (94a), **Anat** (138c,147d), **anet** (43c), **Apet** (97c), **aret** (128c), **arn't, aunt** (129c)

AU - - **Auca** (192), **Aude, Auer** (79a), **auge** (123c,132b), **aula** (66c,73b),

aulu (74c,168c), **aune** (188), **aunt** (129c), **aura** (44c,49c,66a,96b, 158a,170d,177c), **auri** (34a), **Ausa**, **ausu** (168c,180b), **auto** (34d), **auza** (168c,180b)

- AU - **baud** (162d), **baul** (18b), **Baum** (9c,112c), **cauk** (139b), **caul** (16d, 74d), **caur** (139a), **daub** (148d), **dauk** (95c), **Daur** (139b), **dauw** (24c), **eaux** (178c), **faun** (56a,68b,137c,161a,184a), **gaub** (116c), **gaud** (169d), **gaue** (67a), **Gaul** (10a,60d,63c), **gaup**, **gaur** (112c, 181c), **gaus** (67d), **gaut** (88b,103d,132a), **haul** (27b,45d), **jaun** (113a), **kaun** (93d), **laud** (122a), **laun** (146b), **maud** (53d,136d, 143c), **Maud** (181a,183c), **Maui** (120d), **maul** (73c), **maun** (139d), **naut** (141b), **Paul** (96a), **paun** (18b), **paut** (140a), **Sauk** (192), **saul** (48a,168c), **Saul** (18c,86d,115a), **saum** (189), **taun** (188), **taut** (163b,165c), **Vaux** (63b), **yaup**

- - AU **Agau** (73c), **beau**, **Diau** (192), **Drau**, **Esau** (82c,84a,128c), **frau** (181b), **miau** (27b,99b), **prau** (21b,26a,95c,d), **sgau** (88c), **unau** (148c,171d), **whau** (107a,168c)

A - - U **Aalu** (6b,48d), **Aaru** (6b,48d), **Abou** (48b,55a), **actu** (7a,89a), **Addu** (68c,157a,182a), **Agau** (73c), **Ainu** (84a,84c), **ammu** (9d), **ansu** (11d), **anzu** (11d), **Apsu** (29a), **Atmu** (143a,159b), **Attu**, **aulu** (74c,168c), **ausu** (168c,180b), **auzu** (168c,180b)

AV - - **aval** (70c), **Avar** (27d,108a), **avec** (63a,183a), **aver** (7c,14a,15c,41c, 95c,140d,155c,160b,184c), **Aves** (19d), **avid** (47b,71a,186b), **avis** (89a), **Avis** (183c), **Avon** (143b), **avow** (6d,36a,41c,112c), **avus** (89b)

- AV - **bave** (61d,146c), **cava** (116a,175b), **cave** (27d), **cavy** (72b,120d, 132c,157b), **Dave** (96b), **Davy** (96b,136b), **eave** (133c), **favi** (138a, 165d), **gave**, **have**, **Java** (33a), **Jave** (84d), **kava** (18c,116a), **Kavi** (84d), **lava** (101c,132b,151a,177a), **lave** (16d,178b), **nave** (30d,31a, 78d,114b,180c), **navy** (33c,58b), **pave** (85a), **pavo** (115b), **Pavo** (36b,c), **pavy** (115b), **rave** (41c,157a,161d), **ravi**, **Ravi** (16b), **save** (52b,110c,123a,173c), **Tave** (183d), **Tavy** (183d), **wave** (19a, 59a,111c,131d,160c,172d), **wavy** (147b,172d), **yava**

- - AV **Muav** (66a), **Slav** (13c,40c,48b,52a,120b,135b)

A - - V **akov** (189), **Azov** (20b,135d)

AW - - **Awan** (191), **away** (6b,69d,76a,109d,111d), **awry** (13d,38d,171c)

- AW - **bawl**, **bawn** (181a), **cawk** (133c), **dawk** (95c), **dawm** (190), **dawn** (14d,41b), **fawn** (33c), **gawd** (169c), **gawk** (146d), **gawp**, **hawk** (19c, 115c), **jawy**, **kawa** (18c,116a), **Kawi** (84d), **kawn** (93d), **lawn** (20a, 37c,53b,92c), **pawa** (189), **pawl** (43a,95a), **pawn** (29c,119c), **sawk** (188), **sawn**, **tawa** (106d,168c), **yawl** (136b,171d,175d), **yawn**, **yawp**

- - AW **chaw** (97c), **claw** (29c,105b,161d,173a), **craw** (38d,72c,156c), **dhaw** (125a), **draw** (42c,53a,92b,117c,121c,167d), **flaw**, **gnaw** (20a,107a, 178b), **miaw** (27b,99b), **shaw** (164b), **Shaw** (50c,53b), **slaw**, **thaw**

A - - W **alow** (18a,172c), **anew** (7c), **arow** (92c,158b), **avow** (6d,36a,41c, 112c)

AX - - **axal** (120b), **axil** (10c), **axis** (28b,41d,77c,153c), **axle** (153c,180c), **axon** (106c,153c)

- AX - **saxe** (20d,33c), **taxi** (13a,125b), **taxo** (13a), **waxy** (119c,149d)

- - AX Ajax (71b,162d), Anax (43c,120c), coax (180c), Crax (19b,39d), flax, hoax (41c,122a), Odax (132c), Olax (52b)

A - - X abox (22d), Ajax (71b,162d), Alix (183c), Amex (184d), Anax (43d,120c), apex (39c,76c,115c,118b,159b,166a,167b),

AY - - ayah (108d), ayes (177c), ayin (91c)

- AY - baya (179b), Baya (191), cayo, Daye (123d), days, hayz, kayo (87c), maya (179b), Maya (23d,186c), Mayo (193), raya (19b,23c,76d, 107d), saya (117a), Vayu (68c,182a), ways, yaya (113c,168c)

- - AY alay (96c), anay (72b), away (6b,69d,76a,109d,111d), blay (57d), bray, chay (48a,128d), Clay (9d), dray (27a,154c,177b), esay, flay (147c,157c), fray (56b,60d), gray (33c,77c), Gray (50c), okay (8d), olay (113b), piay (98b), play (63d,154a), pray (18b,51a,159d), quay (88b,117c,180c), ruay (189), shay (110c), slay, stay (72d, 124c,130a,134a,162a), sway (104a)

A - - Y Abby (183d), ably (147c), achy, Addy (183d), adry, (164c), aery (47b,51d,106c), affy (18b), ahey (52c), ahoy (106a), airy (176d, 177a), akey (189), alay (96c), Algy (96b), alky, ally (14a,35c,d, 173c), Amoy (88c), anay (72b,163b,181a), ancy (158c), Andy (96b), army, arty, ashy (113a,178a), atry (141b), away (6b,69d,76a,109d, 111d), awry (13d,38d,171c)

AZ - - Azam (166c), azan (102d), Azha (155b), Azof (20b,135d), azon (127b), Azov (20b,135d), azul (151d)

- AZ - caza, cazi (103a), cazy (103a), Daza (191), daze (157d), dazy, faze (43d), Gaza (117a), gaze, gazi, gazy, haze (100c,174d), hazy (174b), jazz, Kazi (103a), kazy (103a), laze (79b), Laze (191), Lazi (191), lazo (88d,128b,133d), lazy, maze (87b,157d), naze (26b, 124b), Nazi, raze (42b,d,91d), razz (131b), vaza (114a)

- - AZ Agaz (193), Ahaz (86d), Boaz (135d)

A - - Z Agaz (193), Ahaz (86d)

BA - - Baal (142b), baas (97c), baba (108d,120c,166c,171a), babe, Babi (116c), babu (77a), baby, Bach (35c), back (75d,76d,159d), Badb (82b), bade, baff (69d), baft (14a,53b), baga (171b), bago (13d), bahi (60c), baho (122a), baht (146a), bail (43c), bain (61a), bait (15d,51a,94d,167b), baju (84a), baka (52b), bake (139a), baku (26d,157b,168c), Bala (26c,66a), bald (16c), bale (24b,74a), balk (118c,146a,156d), ball, balm (110a,172c), Balt (93a), balu (104b, 159a,181d), Bana (67a), banc (61a,85c), band (72a,157c), bane (74a,106b,120b,139a), bang (75d,105d,148a), bani (190), bank (18a,58c), bans, bant (43c), bara (188), barb (20b,57d,78b,117d, 120a,b,124b), bard (12d,120a), bare (43d,157c), bari (37c,79c), Bari (83d), bark (115c), barm (185b), barn (156d), baro (71a,122c), barr (49b), Bart (96b), baru (168c), base (6a,43b,44b,51c,60c,79b,94b, 122b), bash, bask (94d), bass (57b,c,177a), bast (16c,56a,117b, 184a), Bast (27b), bata (30a,142d), bate (43c,91b,100d), bath, Bath (50d,151c), batt (37c), batz (190), baud (162d), baul (18b), Baum (9c,112c), bave (61d,146c), bawl, bawn (181a), baya (179b), Baya (191)

- BA - abas (61c), Ibad (191), Iban (47c), oban (190)

- - BA Abba (20a,55a,161c), alba (98a,181a), Alba (151d), amba (161a),

69c,186b), **imbe** (37a,56a,133d), **jibe** (8a,33b,35d,37b,42c,100d, 138c,144c,149b), **jube** (28d), **kibe, Kobe** (78a), **lobe** (90c,134b), **lube** (110a), **ribe** (139a), **robe** (65b), **rube** (37d,135d,185d), **Rube** (96b), **sabe, tobe** (7d,137b), **tube** (118b,158a)

B - - E **babe, bade, bake** (139a), **bale** (24b,74a), **bane** (74a,106b,120b, 139a), **bare** (43d,157c), **base** (6a,43b,44b,51c,60c,79b,94b,122b), **bate** (43c,91b,100d), **bave** (61d,146c), **Bede** (48c,50c,101d,175b), **bene** (18a,83c,90a,106d,122a,180a), **bete** (61a,107c), **bice** (20d, 117d), **Bice** (27b), **bide** (47c,50b,130a,158b), **bike, bile** (30c), **bine** (145b,156a,171c,176b), **bise** (182a), **bite** (29d,156b), **bize** (182a), **blae** (93b), **blue** (33c,98c,102c,150d,173a), **boce** (23b,52a,57b), **bode** (14c,60a,110b,121b), **bole** (31d,32a,169b), **bone, bore** (14c, 25b,46a,116a,165c,179b), **bose** (163c), **brae** (76d,139a,c,140b, 148c), **bree** (139a), **Brie** (29c), **Bube** (180b), **bure** (61b), **byee** (189), **byre** (38a)

- BF - **Abfa** (76b)

B - - F **baff** (69d), **beef, biff, buff** (134c,161d)

B - - G **bang** (75d,105d,148a), **beng** (43a), **berg** (79b), **bing, bong, borg** (40d), **brag** (21a,175a), **brig** (72b,106a,144d), **bung** (119d,156d), **burg** (22b,73c)

BH - - **Bhar** (191), **bhat** (80c), **bhel** (126d), **Bhil** (191), **b'hoy** (134b), **bhut** (67a)

- - BH **Cobh** (37a)

B - - H **Bach** (35c), **bash, bath, Bath** (50d,151c), **beth** (91c), **Beth** (8c, 183d), **bikh** (120b), **binh** (189), **bish** (120b), **blah, booh** (52c), **bosh, both, bruh** (95a), **bukh** (122a), **bush**

BI - - **bias** (43b,123a), **bibb** (97c,146b), **bibi** (87d), **bice** (20d,117d), **Bice** (27b), **bide** (47c,50b,130a,158b,162a,177b), **bien** (63a,140c,179a, 180a), **bier** (33b,66b), **biff, biga** (171d), **bija** (168c), **bike, bikh** (120b), **bile** (30c), **bilk** (29b,41c,42a), **bill** (17b,147a), **Bill** (96b), **bilo** (131b), **bina** (77a), **bind** (33b,165c), **bine** (145b,156a,171c, 176b), **bing, binh** (189), **Bini** (191), **binn** (22c), **bino** (113b,117a), **biod** (59d,79c), **bion** (117b), **bios** (92a), **bird, birl** (93c,131a,153c), **birn** (31d,139a), **birr** (180d), **bisa** (11a), **bise** (182a), **bish** (120b), **bisk** (120b,151a), **bite** (29d,156b), **biti** (20b), **bito** (7d,57d,168c), **bitt** (54d,175c), **biur** (35a), **biwa** (93d,168c), **Bixa** (145d), **bize** (182a), **bizz**

- BI - **Abia** (18d,137a), **Abib** (102a,b), **Abie** (96b,107a), **abir** (129a), **ibid** (80a,117a,137a), **ibis** (48d,49a,177b), **ibit** (117a), **obia** (55d), **obit** (41b,64c), **Ubii** (191)

- - BI **Albi** (58a), **ambi** (34a,122c), **Babi** (116c), **bibi** (87d), **Bubi** (180b), **cubi** (188), **gabi** (162a), **gobi, Gobi** (42d), **kobi** (84b), **mabi** (58d), **rabi** (38d,74a), **Rabi** (14b,117b), **sebi** (34b), **tabi** (84c,149d), **Tybi** (102a), **Wabi** (192), **Yobi**

B - - I **Babi** (116c), **bahi** (60c), **Bali, bani** (190), **bari** (79c), **Bari** (37c, 83d), **Beli** (23c), **beni** (116a,142d), **Beni** (191), **bibi** (87d), **Bini** (191), **biti** (20b), **Boii** (191), **Boni** (63b), **Bori** (110d,150c), **Bubi** (180b), **Bugi** (191), **buri** (56b)

- - BK **nabk** (30d,164d), **nubk** (30d,164d), **Sobk** (38d)

B - - K **back** (75d,76d,159d), **balk** (118c,146a,156d), **bank** (18a,58c), **bark** (115c), **bask** (94d), **beak** (19a), **beck** (107c), **bilk** (29b,41c,42a), **bisk** (120b,151a), **bock** (17c,90d,144a), **bonk** (190), **book**, **bosk** (164b), **bowk** (155d), **buck**, **bukk** (122a), **bulk** (97b), **bunk**, **busk** (17b,37b,55d,161b)

BL - - **blaa**, **blab** (162b), **blae** (93b), **blah**, **blas** (6c,49c), **Blas** (67b), **blat** (25b), **blay** (57d), **bleb** (20c,23d,67c), **bled**, **blet** (64a), **bleu** (61b), **blew**, **blob**, **bloc** (173a), **blot**, **blow**, **blub**, **blue** (33c,98c,102c,150d, 173a), **blup**, **blur**, **blut** (66b)

- BL - **able** (26b,35b,126a,147c), **ably** (147c)

B - - L **baal** (142b), **bail** (43c), **ball**, **baul** (18b), **bawl**, **beal** (139d), **bell** (24c,39d), **Bell** (162d), **bhel** (126d), **Bhil** (191), **bill** (17b,147a), **Bill** (96b), **birl** (93c,131a,153c), **boil**, **boll** (119b,d), **bool** (39d), **bowl**, **bual** (182c), **buhl** (81a), **bull** (113c), **burl** (87c,169a)

B - - M **balm** (110a,172c), **barm** (185b), **Baum** (9c,112c), **beam**, **berm** (25d, 90d,145c), **boom** (152d), **Bram** (96a), **brim**

B - - N **bain** (61a), **barn** (156d), **bawn** (181a), **bean** (91b,142a,175a), **been** (149a), **behn** (137d), **Bern** (160d), **bien** (63a,140c,179a,180a), **binn** (22c), **bion** (117b), **birn** (31d,139a), **Bonn** (17d), **boon** (18b,20c, 55a), **born**, **bran** (23c,39a,70b,72a,79c), **Bran** (23c,50c), **bren** (72d, 95a), **brin** (32c,54c,146c), **bunn** (25b), **burn**

BO - - **boar** (77c,117c,160c,181c), **boat** (27b,106a), **Boaz** (135d), **boba** (29d,) **bobo** (112c,168c), **boca** (152b,c), **boce** (23b,52a,57b), **bock** (17c,90d,144a), **Bodb** (82b), **bode** (14c,60a,110b,121b), **Bodo** (88c), **body** (72a), **Boer** (151a), **boga** (57d,180b), **bogo** (117a,168c), **Bogo** (191), **bogy** (153a), **boho** (117a,179d), **Bohr** (14b,40d,138c), **Boii** (191), **boil**, **bois** (62b,63a,183d), **bojo** (117a), **boko** (52b), **bola** (16a, 179b), **bold** (41a), **bole** (31d,32a,169b), **boll** (119b,d), **bolo** (87a, 179b), **bolt** (13b,54d,58b,132d,160a), **boma** (7d), **bomb** (144a), **bona** (89d), **Bona** (183c), **bond** (92a,101c,141d,143b,159d,165c), **bone**, **bong**, **Boni** (63b), **bonk** (190), **Bonn** (17d), **bony** (147c), **Bony** (96b), **boob** (146d), **booh** (52c), **book**, **bool** (39d), **boom** (152d), **boon** (18b,20c,55a), **boor** (47a,135d,172c), **boot** (128d), **bora** (181d, 182b), **bord** (100b), **bore** (14c,25b,46a,116a,165c,179b), **borg** (40d), **Bori** (110d,150c), **born**, **boro** (154b), **Boro** (193), **Bors** (70b,134b), **bort** (43b), **Bort** (134b), **bosa** (12a), **Bosc** (115c), **bose** (163c), **bosh**, **bosk** (164b), **boss** (49d,157d), **bota** (189), **both**, **Boto** (192), **bott** (32a,88d), **bout** (36c), **bouw** (188), **bowk** (155d), **bowl**, **boxy**, **boza** (12a), **bozo** (55b)

- BO - **aboo** (17a), **Abot** (100c), **Abou** (48b,55a), **abox** (22d), **eboe** (28b, 110a,168c,169b), **Eboe**, **ebon** (20b), **oboe** (74b,104d,105a,182a, 184a), **obol** (29b,110a)

- - BO **albo** (34d,181a), **ambo** (125b,128b), **bobo** (112c,168c), **bubo** (112c), **Egbo** (141d), **Gobo** (84d), **hobo** (168a,174b), **jobo** (77c), **lobo** (165d,183c), **nabo** (117a), **Nebo** (68c,102d,103d,183a), **umbo** (22b), **zobo** (186b)

B - - O **bago** (13d), **baho** (122a), **baro** (71a,122c), **beno** (113b,117a), **bilo** (131b), **bino** (113b,117a), **bito** (7d,52d,168c), **bobo** (112c,168c), **Bodo** (88c), **bogo** (117a,168c), **Bogo** (191), **boho** (117a,179d), **bojo** (117a), **boko** (52b), **bolo** (87a,179b), **boro** (154b), **Boro** (193), **Boto**

(192), **bozo** (55b), **broo** (139a), **bubo** (112c), **Bufo** (166c), **Buto** (142d), **buyo** (18b), **bygo** (114c)

B - - P **blup, bump**

BR - - **brab** (113b), **brad** (54d,67c,105b), **brae** (76d,139a,c,140b,148c), **brag** (21a,175a), **Bram** (96a), **bran** (23c,39a,70b,72a,79c), **Bran** (23c,50c), **bras** (61a), **brat, bray, brea** (100b), **bred** (23c,48c,127c), **bree** (139a), **bren** (72d,95a), **Brer** (172b), **Bres, brew** (35d), **brey** (194), **Brie** (29c), **brig** (72b,106a,144d), **brim, brin** (32c,54c,146c), **brit** (76c), **brob** (153c), **broo** (139a), **brow, bruh** (95a), **brut** (182c), **Brut** (23c)

- BR - **abra** (26b), **Abra, abri** (61c,62c,144b), **Ebro** (132a), **obra** (152d, 184c)

B - - R **barr** (49b), **bear** (27a,50b,113c,155a), **beer** (18c), **Bhar** (191), **bier** (33b,66b), **birr** (180d), **biur** (35a), **blur, boar** (77c,117c,160c,181c), **Boer** (151a), **Bohr** (14b,40d,138c), **boor** (47a,135d,172c), **Brer** (172b), **buhr** (180d), **burr** (123b)

- BS - **Absi** (191)

- - BS **dibs** (70c), **Lubs** (94c), **nibs** (116c), **nobs** (38c,87a)

B - - S **baas** (97c), **bans, bass** (57b,c,177a), **bees** (185b), **Bess** (76c,183d), **bias** (43b,123a), **bios** (92a), **blas** (6c,49c), **Blas** (67b), **bois** (62b, 63a,183d), **Bors** (70b,134b), **boss** (49d,157d), **bras** (61a), **Bres, buss** (87a,148c)

- - BT **debt** (91d,109b)

B - - T **baft** (14a,53b), **baht** (146a), **bait** (15d,51a,94d,167b), **Bait** (93a), **bant** (43c), **Bart** (96b), **bast** (16c,56a,117b,184a), **Bast** (27b), **batt** (37c), **beat** (58c,87b,131a,164d,165b,180d), **beet** (175a), **belt** (16a, 31a), **bent** (80b), **Bert** (96b), **best** (41d,159c,160a), **bhat** (80c), **bhut** (67a), **bitt** (54d,175c), **blat** (25b), **blet** (64a), **blot, blut** (66b), **boat** (27b,106a), **bolt** (13b,54d,58b,132d,160a), **boot** (128d), **bort** (43b), **Bort** (134b), **bott** (32a,88d), **bout** (36c), **brat, brit** (76c), **brut** (182c), **Brut** (23c), **bult** (76d), **bunt** (15d,180c), **bust, butt** (27a,77b,127d,162a,182b)

BU - - **bual** (182c), **buba** (170a), **Bube** (180b), **Bubi** (180b), **bubo** (112c), **buck, buda** (83d), **buff** (134c,161d), **Bufo** (166c), **Bugi** (191), **buhl** (81a), **buhr** (180d), **bukh** (122a), **bukk** (122a), **bulb** (37a,172c), **bulk** (97b), **bull** (113c), **bult** (76d), **bump, buna** (161c), **bund** (49c,66c,90c), **bung** (119d,156d), **bunk, bunn** (25b), **bunt** (15d, 180c), **buoy** (28d,58c), **bura** (182b), **bure** (61b), **burg** (22b,73c), **buri** (56b), **burl** (87c,169a), **burn, burr** (123b), **bury** (81d), **bush, busk** (17b,37b,55d,161b), **buss** (87a,148c), **bust, busy, Buto** (142d), **butt** (27a,77b,127d,162a,182b), **buxy** (115b), **buyo** (18b) **buzz**

- BU - **abut** (22a,167c), **ebur** (89c)

- - BU **babu** (77a), **kobu** (84b), **Nabu** (68c,183a), **tabu** (59d,111d), **Tibu** (191), **zebu** (22d,80d,112c)

B - - U **babu** (77a), **baju** (84a), **baku** (26d,157b,168c), **balu** (104b,159a, 181d), **baru** (168c), **beau, benu** (49a), **bleu** (61b)

B - - W **blew, blow, bouw** (188), **brew** (35d), **brow**

BY - - **byee,** (189), **bygo** (114c), **Byrd** (9c,120b), **byre** (38a)

- - BY **Abby** (183d), **baby, doby** (159b,c), **gaby** (59c,146d), **goby** (57d), **kiby** (29a), **ruby** (20a,65d,179c), **toby** (8c,85c,104b), **Toby** (96b, 125c)

B - - Y **baby, bevy** (38a,58c), **b'hoy** (134b), **blay** (57d), **body** (72a), **bogy** (153a), **bony** (147c), **Bony** (96b), **boxy, bray, brey** (194), **buoy** (28d,58c), **bury** (81d), **busy, buxy** (115b)

B - - Z **batz** (190), **bizz, Boaz** (135d), **buzz**

CA - - **caam** (93d), **caba** (184c), **Caca** (67a), **caco** (73b), **cade** (25c,27a,76c, 85d,116d), **Cade** (50c), **cadi** (12a,103a,171a), **cady** (69d), **Caen, cafe, cage** (36a), **cagy** (178b), **caid** (35a,151d,152b), **cain** (169c), **Cain** (6a,7a,50d,88a,104c,143a), **caja** (152a), **caji** (180b), **cake, caky, cale** (72d), **calf, calk** (78c,109a,141c,178d), **call** (145c,159b, 176d), **calm** (8d,11d,112b,118d,126c,d,172b,173d), **calo** (72d), **calp** (92b), **calx** (23c,75c,112c), **came** (182b), **Came** (192), **camp** (163b), **Cana** (57a,64b,100c), **cane** (17b,128a,156a,159a,177d), **Cane, cang** (184a), **cano** (152a), **cant** (28d,81b,84d,90c,109b,136c,165d,166a), **capa** (152a,166d), **cape** (75a,96c,124b,161a), **caph** (91c), **Capp** (27a), **cara** (83a), **Cara** (48b,183c), **card** (33d,114d), **care** (11b, 14c,35d,150a,184d), **cark** (26d,184d), **carl** (115c,135d), **Carl** (96a), **carn** (156c), **caro** (83a), **Caro** (183d), **carp** (27d,38d,40c,55a,56c, 57a), **carr** (120d,140a), **cart** (171d,175a,177b), **casa** (152b), **case** (22c,36c,81c,91a,108c), **cash** (101c), **cask, Caso** (82d) **cass** (140c, 177a), **Cass** (147a), **cast** (165b,167c), **cata** (122c), **cate** (165c), **Cato** (132d,133b), **Catt** (9d), **cauk** (139b), **caul** (16d,74d), **caup, caur** (139a), **cava** (116a,175b), **cave** (27d), **cavy** (72b,120d,132c, 157b), **cawk** (133c), **cayo, caza, cazi** (103a), **cazy** (103a)

- CA - **ecad** (73a,119b), **ical** (158c), **scab** (80b,107d,157c), **scad** (31a,57a, 78b,88d,137c), **scan** (52b,93d,98a,116d,128b,c,140d), **scar** (31a, 184d), **scat** (26b,67a,d,126c,169c)

- - CA **acca** (53b,d), **Alca** (14c,128b), **arca** (9a,22c,29d,115a,130a), **Arca** (101b), **Auca** (192), **boca** (152b,c), **Caca** (67a), **coca** (29d,33a,105d, 113a), **cuca** (33a,105d), **deca** (34d,122d), **Ecca** (66a), **esca** (11c, 44a,70c), **Inca** (14b,30a), **jaca** (84a), **juca** (27a), **mica** (82c,100b, 146c), **onca** (189), **orca** (86b), **paca** (132c,154a), **peca** (190), **pica** (66b,95b,172c), **puca** (68a), **raca** (19a,59c,130b,184d), **Teca** (192), **unca** (49a), **Ynca** (193), **yuca** (27a)

C - - A **caba** (184c), **Caca** (67a), **caja** (152a), **Cana** (57a,64b,100c), **capa** (152a,166d), **cara** (83a), **Cara** (48b,183c), **casa** (152b), **cata** (122c), **cava** (116a,175b), **caza, ceba** (169b), **cela** (62d), **cena** (88d,133a), **cepa** (110c), **cera** (152d,161d,179a), **chaa** (162b), **chia** (136d), **cima** (83b,c), **Civa** (56d), **coca** (29d,33a,105d,113a), **coda** (32c,35d,55d, 56c), **coja** (103b,166b), **cola** (25b,108d,149d,168c), **coma** (91c, 157d,170c,172b), **copa** (88b,113c), **cora** (65d), **Cora** (42b,69c,80c, 116b,124d,172b,183c), **cota** (117a), **coxa** (77b), **crea** (92c,151d), **cuba** (189), **Cuba** (180b), **cuca** (33a,105d), **Cuna** (193), **cura** (152c), **cuya** (39b), **cyma** (101a,b)

C - - B **chab** (184a), **chib** (167a), **chob** (23c), **chub** (40c,154c), **club** (39c), **Cobb** (9c), **comb** (38c), **crab** (39b,144b,181b), **crib** (96b,120d), **curb** (130c,146b)

- CC - **acca** (53b,d), **Ecca** (66a), **ecce** (17d,89a,c)

C - - C **chic** (148d), **circ** (31a), **cric** (131c), **croc** (13a,74a)

C - - D **caid** (35a,151d,152b), **card** (33d,114d), **Chad** (158b), **chid**, **Chud** (191), **clad** (46a,82a), **clod** (22a,45b,157d), **coed**, **cold** (65d), **cond** (156a), **cord** (39b,131a), **curd** (99d)

CE - - **ceba** (169b), **cede** (67b,70c,129d,160a,168b,185d), **ceil** (92c,112a), **cela** (62d), **cell** (39b), **celt** (30c,123a,156c,167b,179b), **Celt** (10a, 180a,b), **cena** (88d,133a), **cene** (34c), **cens** (115b), **cent** (36d), **cepa** (110c), **cepe** (48c), **cera** (152d,161d,179a), **cere** (19a,114b,149d, 179a), **cern** (41c), **cero** (57b,c,d,180b), **cess** (91d,94c,162b), **cest** (18a,67b), **cete** (180b,c), **ceto** (34a), **Ceyx** (73b)

- CE - **Acer** (96c), **icer**

- - CE **ance** (158b,c,d), **bice** (20d,117d), **Bice** (27b), **boce** (23b,52a,57b), **dace** (57a,b), **dice** (65a), **duce** (29d), **ecce** (17d,89a,c), **ence** (158c), **esce** (158d), **face** (159d,176c), **lace** (58b,179c), **luce** (58c,117d), **Luce** (7b,35a), **mace** (49d,108d,153b,154d,161a,178a), **mice**, **nice** (54d,119c,130c), **Nice** (98c), **once** (60b,79b), **pace** (64b,98a,153b, 156a,170b,177d), **pice** (190), **puce** (33c,d,52a), **race** (116a,153b, 154b), **Rice** (46a), **sice** (71d,147b), **syce** (71d), **tace** (13a,155d), **tice** (9a,38c,51a,185d), **vice** (31d,158a), **voce** (83c,177a)

C - - E **cade** (25c,27a,76c,85d,116d), **Cade** (50c), **cafe**, **cage** (36a), **cake**, **cale** (72d), **came** (182b), **Came** (192), **cane** (17b,128a,156a,159a, 177d), **Cane**, **cape** (75a,96c,124b,161a), **care** (11b,14c,35d,150a, 184d), **case** (22c,36c,81c,91a,108c), **cate** (165c), **cave** (27d), **cede** (67b,70c,129d,160a,168b,185d), **cene** (34c), **cepe** (48c), **cere** (19a, 114b,149d,179a), **cete** (180b,c), **chee** (189), **cine** (104b,152c), **cise** (147b), **cite** (15a,98d,126d,159b), **cive** (110c), **clee** (19a,129a), **Cloe** (183c), **clue**, **code** (21c,31a,40c,161c), **coke** (32d,64a), **cole** (25a), **Cole**, **come**, **cone** (66b,150a,157c), **cope** (12b,26b,36c,65b, 157d,176a), **core** (28b,51c,75b,81b), **cose** (29b), **cote** (19b,143d, 144a,b), **cove** (17a,73d,107d), **coze** (29b), **Cree** (192), **cube** (66b, 150a), **cuke** (39b), **cure** (123b,d), **cute** (39c), **cyke** (40c), **cyme** (58d, 69c)

C - - F **calf**, **chef**, **clef** (104d,105a), **coif** (73a), **cuff** (148a), **cuif** (139a,d, 140c)

C - - G **cang** (184a), **chug** (53a), **clog** (30c,145b), **coag** (45d,118a,163b), **crag** (132c), **crig** (20d)

CH - - **chaa** (162b), **chab** (184a), **Chad** (158b), **chai** (72d), **cham** (20a,29d), **Cham** (8c) **chan** (26c,130c), **chap** (55b), **char** (24d,138c,170b), **chat** (9b,19c,161c), **chaw** (97c), **chay** (48a,128d), **chee** (189), **chef**, **chek** (59c), **Chen** (149b), **cher** (61b), **chew** (97c), **chez** (14b,61a), **chia** (136d), **chib** (167a), **chic** (148d), **chid**, **ch'ih** (188), **chil**, **chin**, **Chin** (30b), **chip** (69d), **chir** (29b,116d), **chit** (67b,98c,108b,116c, 177c), **chiv** (87a), **chob** (23c), **chol** (118d), **Chol** (192), **chop** (98a), **chor** (164b), **chou** (61b), **Chou** (30b), **chow** (45a), **choy** (48a,128d), **chub** (40c,154c), **Chud** (191), **chug** (53a), **chum** (38d), **Chun** (30c), **chut!**

- CH - **ache** (79a,112d,185b), **acht** (66c), **achy**, **echo** (130b,d), **Echo** (105d), **icho** (67b), **ichu** (10b,70d), **ocha** (189), **tcha** (162c), **tche** (13d,30b, 105a), **tchi**, **Tchi**, **tchu**

- - CH **aich** (9a), **arch** (29d,38b,39d,123d,132c), **bach**, **Bach** (35c), **each**, **etch**, **Foch** (63b), **hoch** (52c,66c), **Hoch**, **inch**, **itch**, **Koch** (66d), **lech** (102b), **loch** (88a,139d), **much**, **nach**, **ouch**, **rich**, **Roch** (136c), **sech** (97c), **such** (146d), **Tech**, **Vach** (153b), **Zach** (96b)

C - - H **caph** (91c), **Caph**, **cash** (101c), **ch'ih** (188), **Cobh** (37a), **cosh** (35a, 97c), **cush** (101c), **Cush** (51d,73c)

CI - - **cima** (83b,c), **cine** (104b,152c), **cinq** (61d), **cion** (42d,70b,145b, 148b,154b,156a), **cipo** (91d), **circ** (31a), **cirl** (24c), **cise** (147b), **cist** (22c,29d,156c), **cite** (15a,98d,126d,159b), **cito** (89d,126c), **cits**, **city**, **Civa** (56d), **cive** (110c)

- CI - **acid** (151a,162a), **Acis** (64b), **Scio**

- - CI **asci** (154a), **deci** (163b), **foci** (28b), **fuci** (132c), **loci** (66b,118c), **Pici** (19c,184a), **unci** (31d)

C - - I **cadi** (12a,103a,171a), **Cadi**, **caji** (180b), **cazi** (103a), **chai** (72d), **coli**, **Coni**, **Cori** (138c), **cubi** (188)

- - CK **back** (75d,76d,159d), **beck** (107c), **bock** (17c,90d,144a), **buck**, **cock** (19a,29a,55a,133d,136d,161d,174b), **deck** (13b,41c, 144d), **dick** (43a,55b), **Dick** (96b), **dock** (40a,117c,144d,179d), **duck** (26b,53b,179c), **hack** (40a,77c,184d), **heck** (100a), **hick** (185d), **hock** (91a,115b,182b,c), **huck** (167d), **jack** (26c,58a,127c), **Jack** (96b), **jock** (96b), **Jock**, **juck** (114c), **kick**, **lack** (178a), **lick** **lock** (54d), **luck** (28d), **mack**, **mick** (82c), **mock** (131b,162b), **muck**, **neck** (83a), **nick** (30c,108b), **nock** (13b,108b), **pack** (24b,140d), **peck** (24d), **pick**, **puck** (44b,68a,77c,100c), **Puck** (99d,143b), **rack** (32c,64b), **reck** (26d,75c), **rick** (74d,117d), **rock** (160b), **ruck** (39a, 185a), **sack** (43d,118a,119d,182b), **seck** (173d), **sick**, **sock** (157c, 182a), **suck**, **tack** (28d,37d,54d), **teck** (128b), **tick** (12b,20d,97c), **tock** (7d,19b), **tuck** (156b), **wick**

C - - K **calk** (78c,109a,141c,178d), **cark** (26d,184d), **cask**, **cauk** (139b), **cawk** (133c), **chek** (59c), **coak** (45d,118a,163b), **cock** (19a,29a, 55a,133d,136d), **conk** (41c,108a,156d,157c), **cook** (137b), **cork** (119d), **cusk** (57b)

CL - - **clad** (46a,82a), **clam** (20b,101b), **clan** (169c), **clap** (58b), **claw** (29c, 105b,161d,173a), **clay**, **Clay** (9d), **clee** (19a,129a), **clef** (104d,105a), **clem** (56b,158b), **Cleo** (126b), **clew** (16a,33a,77b,136b,164d), **Clim** (12b), **Clio** (104d), **clip** (54d,143d), **clod** (22a,45b,157d), **Cloe** (183c), **clog** (30c,145b), **clop**, **clot** (32d,94d), **clou** (62b), **clow** (58c,148c), **cloy** (61b,137c,159d), **club** (39c), **clue**, **Clym** (12b)

- CL - **acle** (13d,82c,115d)

C - - L **call** (145c,159b,176d), **carl** (115c,135d), **Carl** (96a), **caul** (16d,74d), **ceil** (92c,112a), **cell** (39b), **chil**, **chol** (118d), **Chol** (192), **cirl** (24c), **coal** (49c,64a), **coel** (39b), **coil** (39d,171c,185a), **cool** (25c,107d), **cowl** (101d), **cral**, **cull** (117c), **curl** (38d,73b,93b,131d)

- CM - **acme** (39c,115c,186b)

C - - M **caam** (93d), **calm** (8d,11d,112b,118d,126c,d,172b), **cham** (20a,29d), **Cham** (8c), **chum** (38d), **clam** (20b,101b), **clem** (56b,158b), **Clim** (12b), **Clym** (12b), **coom** (32d,150c,178d), **corm** (24b,38d,156a), **cram** (157d), **Crom**, **culm** (11a,32d,70d,145a,156a)

CN - - **Cnut** (40d,50c)

-CN- **acne** (147c)

C--N **Caen, cain** (169c), **Cain** (6a,7a,50d,88a,104c,143a), **carn** (156c), **cern** (41c), **chan** (26c,130c), **Chen** (149b), **chin, Chin** (30b), **Chun** (30c), **cion** (42d,70b,145b,148b,154b,156a), **clan** (169c), **Coan** (37b), **coin** (19b,37a,100c,101c,179d), **conn** (43d,156a), **coon** (121c), **corn** (39d,95c,123a), **coyn** (37a), **cran** (160c), **crin** (146c), **cyan**

CO-- **coag** (45d,118a,163b), **coak** (45d,118a,163b), **coal** (49c,64a), **Coan** (37b), **coat** (160a), **coax** (180c), **Cobb** (9c), **Cobh** (37a), **coca** (29d, 33a,105d,113a), **cock** (19a,29a,55a,133d,136d,161d,174b), **coco,** (113a), **coda** (32c,35d,56c), **code** (21c,31a,40c,161c), **codo** (188), **coed, coel** (39b), **coho** (136d), **coif** (73a), **coil** (39d,171c,185a), **coin** (19b,37a,100c,101c,179d), **coir** (33a,37a,56a,133d), **Coix** (70d,85b), **coja** (103b,166b), **coke** (32d,64a), **coky, cola** (25b,108d,149d,168c), **cold** (65d), **cole** (25a), **Cole, coli, colp** (28a,148b), **colt** (78c,131a, 185d,186b), **Colt, coly** (104a), **coma** (91c,157d,170c,172b), **comb** (38c), **come, Como, cond** (156a), **cone** (66b,150a,157c), **Coni, conk** (41c,108a,156d,157c), **conn** (43d,156a), **cony** (127a), **cook** (137b), **cool** (25c,107d), **coom** (32d,150c,178d), **coon** (121c), **coop, Coos,** (192), **coot** (19b,46d,72b,138d,141a,146d,157d), **copa** (88b,113c), **cope** (12b,26b,36c,65b,157d,176a), **copt** (48d), **copy, cora** (65d), **Cora** (42b,69c,80c,116b,124d,172b,183c), **cord** (39b,139a), **core** (28b,51c,75b,81b), **Cori** (138c), **cork** (119d), **corm** (24b,38d,156a), **corn** (39d,95c,123a), **cose** (29b), **cosh** (35a,97c), **coso** (152c), **coss** (98a), **cost** (29a), **cosy** (149c), **cota** (117a), **cote** (19b,143d,144a,b), **coto** (16c,90b), **Coty** (63c), **coup** (20d,97c,157b,c,162d), **cous** (38a), **cove** (17a,73d,107d), **cowl** (101d), **coxa** (77b) **coyn** (37a), **coyo** (15a,30c), **coze** (29b), **cozy** (149c)

-CO- **acon** (62c,140d), **acor** (6d), **icon** (79d,92b,136a), **scob** (42a), **scon** (162c), **scop** (120a), **scot** (14a,162b), **Scot** (64b,132c), **scow** (21a, 58b)

--CO **alco** (45b), **caco** (73b), **coco** (113a), **Duco, fico** (169d), **loco** (38b, 119b,120b), **mico** (97a), **paco** (9b,146d), **peco** (162b), **pico** (65a, 152c), **poco** (83b,93a), **saco** (189), **soco** (22d), **Teco** (192), **toco** (19b,167c), **unco** (140c), **Waco**

C--O **caco** (73b), **calo** (72d), **cano** (152a), **caro** (83a), **Caro** (183d), **Caso** (82d), **Cato** (132d,133b), **cayo, cero** (57b,c,d,180b), **ceto** (34a), **cipo** (91d), **cito** (89d,126c), **Cleo** (126b), **Clio** (104d), **coco,** (113a), **codo** (188), **coho** (136d), **Como, coso** (152d), **coto** (16c,90b), **coyo** (15a,30c)

C--P **calp** (92b), **camp** (163b), **Capp** (27a), **carp** (27d,38d,40c,55a,56c, 57a), **caup, chap** (55b), **chip** (69d), **chop** (98a), **clap** (58b), **clip** (54d,143d), **clop, colp** (28a,148b), **coop, coup** (20d,97c,157b,c, 162d), **crop** (38b), **cusp** (38c,78b,119a,120a,b)

C--Q **cinq** (61d)

CR-- **crab** (39b,144b,181b), **crag** (132c), **cral, cram** (157d), **cran** (160c), **craw** (38d,72c,156c), **Crax** (19b,39d), **crea** (92c,151d), **Cree** (192), **crew** (72a,106a), **Crex** (37a), **crib** (96b,120d), **cric** (131c), **crig** (20d), **crin** (146c), **cris** (40b,95d), **croc** (13a,74a), **Crom, crop** (38b), **crow** (19a), **crus** (91a,143c), **crux** (39a,151b)

-CR- **acre** (39b,56a,88b), **Acre, ecru** (17d,23d,172b), **ocra** (72c,175a)

C--R **carr** (120d,140a), **caur** (139a), **char** (24d,138c,170b), **cher** (61b), **chir** (29b,116d), **chor** (164b), **coir** (33a,37a,56a,133d), **cuir** (45c,62a), **curr** (104c), **Czar** (42d,49d,60b,135c)

--CS **ABC's** (57a), **pacs** (94c)

C--S **cass** (140c,177a), **Cass** (147a), **cens** (115b), **cess** (91d,94c,162b), **cits, Coos** (192), **coss** (98a), **cous** (38a), **cris** (40b,95d), **crus** (91a, 143c), **cuss**

-CT- **acta** (41d,123d,128d,164c), **acth** (13b), **acto** (152b), **Acts, actu** (7a, 89a), **ecto** (34c,122d), **octa** (122c), **octo** (34a,89b,122c)

--CT **duct** (170c), **fact** (7a,128b), **lact** (34c), **pact** (8a), **Pict** (23c,47d), **rect** (117b), **sect** (42b,54a,114c), **tact** (43c,d,116a)

C--T **cant** (28d,81b,84d,90c,109b,136c,165d,166a), **cart** (171d,175a, 177b), **cast** (165b,167c), **Catt** (9d), **celt** (30c,82c,123a,156c,167b, 179b), **Celt** (10a,180a,b), **cent** (36d), **cest** (18a,67b), **chat** (9b,19c, 161c), **chit** (67b,98c,108b,116c,177c), **chut!, cist** (22c,29d,156c), **clot** (32d,94d), **coat** (160a), **colt** (78c,131a,185d,186b), **Colt** (131a), **coot** (19b,46d,72b,138d,141a,146d,157d), **Copt** (48d), **cost** (29a), **cult** (141d,161c), **curt** (145b,c), **cyst**

CU-- **cuba** (189), **Cuba** (180b), **cube** (66b,150a), **cubi** (188), **cuca** (33a, 105d), **cuff** (148a), **cuif** (139a,d,140c), **cuir** (45c,62a), **cuke** (39b), **cull** (117c), **culm** (11a,32d,70d,145a,156a), **cult** (141d,161c), **Cuna** (193), **cura** (152c), **curb** (130c,146b), **curd** (99d), **cure** (123b), **curl** (38d,73b,93b,131d), **curr** (104c), **curt** (145b,c), **cush** (101c), **Cush** (51d,73c), **cusk** (57b), **cusp** (38c,78b,119a,120a,b), **cuss, cute** (39c), **cuvy** (141a), **cuya** (39b)

-CU- **acus** (89d,118a), **scud** (32c,126c,135b,160c), **scum** (129b), **scup** (57a,121b), **scur** (78b), **scut** (145c,161b)

--CU **jacu** (19a,151b), **jocu** (45b,57a)

C--U **chou** (61b), **Chou** (30b), **clou** (62b)

C--V **chiv** (87a)

C--W **chaw** (97c), **chew** (97c), **chow** (45a), **claw** (29c,105b,161d,173a), **clew** (16a,33a,77b,136b,164d), **clow** (58c,148c), **craw** (38d,72c, 156c), **crew** (72a,106a), **crow** (19a)

C--X **calx** (23c,75c,112c), **Ceyx** (73b), **coax** (180c), **Coix** (70d,85b), **Crax** (19b,39d), **Crex** (37a), **crux** (39a,151b)

CY-- **cyan, cyke** (40c), **cyma** (101a,b), **cyme** (58d,69c), **cyst**

-CY- **acyl** (6d)

--CY **ancy** (158c), **lacy, Lucy** (183c), **racy** (153b)

C--Y **cady** (69d), **cagy** (178b), **caky, cavy** (72b,120d,132c,157b), **cazy** (103a), **chay** (48a,128d), **choy** (48a,128d), **city, clay, Clay** (9d), **cloy** (61b,137c,159d), **coky, coly** (104a), **cony** (127a), **copy, cosy** (149c), **Coty** (63c), **cozy** (149c), **cuvy** (141a)

CZ-- **czar** (42d,49d,60b,135c)

C--Z **chez** (14b,61a)

DA-- **dace** (57a,b), **Dada** (13b,63a,157d), **dado** (41c,111c,115c, 177d), **daer** (22b), **daez, daff** (125d), **daft** (59c), **dagg** (118c), **dagh**

(76d), **Dago, Dail** (49a,82b,c), **dain** (188), **dais** (119b), **dale** (43c, 128a,174b), **dali** (168c,169b), **dama** (65d,152b), **dame** (67b,87c, 166b), **damn, damp** (101a), **Dana** (28a,96a,171d), **Dane** (85d,107d, 138a), **dang, dank** (40b,101a), **dans** (62a), **Danu** (28a), **Dara** (18d), **Dard, dare** (28d,41b,42a,74d,175b), **Dare** (57a), **dari** (38a,70b), **dark** (47a,67d,109b,160b), **darn** (130b), **darr** (163c), **dart** (13b,88a, 100c,120b,153a,160c), **dash** (125c,162d), **dasi** (77a), **data** (54a), **date** (64a,153a), **dato** (95c,102c,117a), **datu** (95c,102c,117a), **daub** (148d), **dauk** (95c), **Daur** (139b), **dauw** (24c), **Dave** (96b), **Davy** (96b,136b), **dawk** (95c), **dawm** (190), **dawn** (14d,41b), **Daye** (123d), **days, Daza** (191), **daze** (157d), **dazy**

- DA - **adad** (52c,56a), **Adad** (68c,157a,182a), **Adah** (25b,51b), **Adam** (26b,96a,111c), **adan** (102d), **Adar** (85c,102a), **adat** (90b,95d), **Edam** (29c), **Edar** (18d), **Idas** (27b,71c), **odah** (170d), **odal** (48a,88b,112c), **Odax** (132c), **udad** (143d,144a,181c), **udal** (76b, 88b,131c)

- - DA **adda** (147d), **Adda** (68c,119d), **Aida** (110d,175c), **aida** (152b), **Alda** (110d,150c), **anda** (23a,168c), **Beda** (101d), **Buda** (83d), **coda** (32c,35d,56c), **Dada** (13b,63a,157d), **Edda** (76b,79b,107d), **Erda** (23d,41a,47d,68d,69a,131d,177b), **Juda, kada** (188), **Leda** (27b, 75d,120c,153a,171d,186b), **Lida** (183c), **meda** (110a), **nuda** (39b), **peda** (114d,144b), **rada** (135c,172a), **Roda** (107b), **sida** (37a, 126c,170a), **soda** (19a,149d,181a), **Teda** (191), **Toda** (45d,76d), **Veda** (77a,b), **Vida** (183c)

D - - A **Dada** (13b,63a,157d), **dama** (65d,152b), **Dana** (28a,96a,171d), **Dara** (18d), **data** (54a), **Daza** (191), **deca** (34d,122d), **depa** (188), **dera** (34c), **deva** (23d,42a,b,56d,77a), **dewa, dika** (23a), **Disa** (111a), **dita** (117a), **diva** (110d,123c), **dola** (189), **dona** (83d,121c,151d), **dopa** (117d), **dora** (70b), **Dora** (36d,41a,43b), **dosa** (74b), **doxa** (48b), **draa** (188), **Duma** (135c), **dura** (153c), **dyna** (34c)

- - DB **Badb** (82b), **Bodb** (82b), **Medb**

D - - B **daub** (148d), **dieb** (84a), **doab** (157c), **doob** (18b), **doub** (18b), **drab** (23d,29c,33d,46d,53b,d), **drib** (46b), **drub** (17b,39c), **duab** (157c), **dubb** (161c), **dumb** (153b)

D - - C **disc** (31b), **douc** (101d)

DD - - **DDSC** (42a)

- DD - **adda** (147a), **Adda** (68c,119d,157a,182a), **Addu** (68c,157a,182a), **Addy** (183d), **Edda** (76b,79b), **eddo** (162a), **eddy** (37d, 39d,160d, 180d), **odds** (28d,172d)

- - DD **dodd** (139c,140c), **gedd** (140a), **Ladd** (143c), **ludd** (23c), **mudd** (188), **Nudd** (23c), **Redd** (153a), **Ridd** (94a), **rodd** (38d), **rudd** (26d, 57a,b), **sadd** (33a,40b,58c,107b), **sudd** (40b,58c,107b), **wadd** (109c)

D - - D **dard, dead, deed** (7a,52d,91a,166c,168b), **diad** (113a), **dord** (42c), **dowd** (143b), **duad** (113a,171d), **dyad** (113a)

DE - - **dead, deaf, deal** (11d,16c,36c,44c,81a,168b), **dean** (33c,109d), **dear, debt** (91d,109b), **deca** (34d,122d), **deci** (163b), **deck** (13b, 41c,144d), **dedo** (188), **deed** (7a,52d,91a,166c,168b), **deem** (36b, 85c,164c), **deep** (124a), **deer** (28c,135a,154d) **defi** (61b), **deft** (147c), **defy** (28d), **degu** (132c), **deil** (139b), **dein** (66d), **dele** (26a, 49c,51b,53a,110b,123d,124c,130a,145c,161b), **dell** (43c,174b),

deme (71b,c,167d), **demi** (34b,122c), **demo** (122d), **demy** (113d), **dene** (137a), **Dene** (192), **dens** (90a,167b), **dent** (42c,77d), **deny** (36d,43d,129b), **depa** (188), **dera** (34c), **dere** (74a,79c), **derm** (147c,158d), **desi** (85d), **desk, deul** (77b), **deus** (68a,89b), **Deva** (23d,42a,b,56d,77a), **Devi** (147b,153b), **dewa, dewy** (101a)

- DE - **aden** (34b), **Aden, Ader** (18d), **Ades** (73a), **edel** (66c), **Eden** (6b,50d, 107c,113d,123c), **Eder, EDES** (71c), **idea** (54c,108c,124a,164d), **idee** (61d), **idem** (89d,164a), **Iden** (76a), **ideo** (34b,d), **ides** (41a, b,133a), **odea** (105a,164a), **odel** (48a,112c), **Oder** (132a)

- - DE **aide** (7b,14a,75d), **Ande** (193), **Aude, bade, Bede** (48c,50c,101d, 175b), **bide** (47c,50b,130a,158b,162a), **bode** (14c,60a,110b,121b), **cade** (25c,27a,76c,85d,116d), **Cade** (50c), **cede** (67b,70c,129d, 160a,168b,185d), **code** (21c,31a,40c,161c), **Dode** (96b), **dude** (40d), **eide** (119c), **fade** (181d,183b), **fide, gade, Gide** (63a), **hade** (66a, 148c,173c), **hide** (53a), **hyde** (188), **Hyde** (45a), **inde, jade** (33c, 65d,71d,166a), **Jude** (11c,96a), **kade** (144a), **lade** (24c,26d,43c,93b, 100a,132a,139d,161b,178d), **lode** (42c,99a,111b,175b), **made, Mede** (10a,b,13c), **mide** (110a), **mode** (54d,96b,157d,179a), **nide** (23c,72a,106c,116d), **node** (35c,85b,87c,94d,120a,124d,160c), **nude** (16c), **onde** (63a,178d), **rede** (37c,81d,138d), **ride** (46b,85c), **rode** (46c), **rude** (134b,172b), **sade** (91d), **side** (13d,22a,b,54a,58a,89a, 161b), **tide** (39d,75d,109c,141c,159d), **Tide, tode** (80a,148a), **unde** (179a), **urde** (86b), **vade** (42c,67d,89b), **vide** (89d,126a,142a), **wade, wide** (133d)

D - - E **dace** (57a,b), **dale** (43c,128a,174b), **dame** (67b,87c,166b), **Dane** (85d,107d,138a), **dare** (28d,41b,42a,74d,175b), **Dare** (57a), **date** (64a,153a), **Dave** (96b), **Daye** (123d), **daze** (157d), **dele** (26a,49c, 51b,53a,110b,123d,124c,130a,145c,161b), **deme** (71b,c,167d), **dene** (137a), **Dene** (192), **dere** (74a,79c), **dice** (65a), **dike** (49c, 91d), **Dike** (78a), **dime, dine, dire** (45d,55a,104a,163c), **dite** (150b), **dive** (42b,74b,119d), **dobe** (159b,c,172b), **Dode** (96b), **doge** (95b), **dole** (44c,118c,121c,129d), **Dole** (74c), **dome** (39c,133c,155d), **done, dope** (46c,105d), **dore** (61d,67b,69d,117d), **Dore** (50d,63a,b), **dose** (123a), **dote** (17a,90b,94b,97a,112a,139d,165d), **dove** (19a, 117d), **doze** (148a), **dree** (139b,140c,158b,172c), **duce** (29d), **dude** (40d), **duff** (125b), **duke** (107c), **dune** (137a), **dupe** (27c,41c, 72c,160c), **duse** (83c), **dyke** (49c,91d), **dyne** (59d)

D - - F **daff** (125d), **deaf, doff** (130a,161b), **duff** (125b)

- DG - **edge** (22a,96d,131c,143c,146b), **edgy** (106c)

D - - G **dagg** (118c), **dang, ding** (130b), **Doeg** (137c), **dong, drag** (74a, 125b), **dreg, drug** (105d)

DH - - **dhak** (48a,169a), **dhal** (12b), **dhan** (124c), **dhao** (24c), **Dhar, dhaw** (125a), **dhow** (88d,111c,175d)

- - DH **sadh** (77a), **Sadh, yodh** (91d)

D - - H **dagh** (76d), **Dagh, dash** (125c,162d), **dish, doth, drah** (188)

DI - - **diad** (113a), **dial** (25c), **dian** (46c,130d,170b), **Dian** (68d,69a,c, 102b), **Diau** (192), **dibs** (70c), **dice** (65a), **dick** (43a,55b), **Dick** (96b), **dido** (11b,26c,65a,122a), **Dido** (27a,172c), **dieb** (84a), **diem** (89b,116a), **dier, dies** (41b,89b), **diet** (14a,54c,84c,91b,176a), **Dieu** (61d), **dika** (23a), **dike** (49c,91d), **Dike** (78a), **dill** (13a,117c), **dilo**

(120d,168c), **dime, dine, ding** (130b), **dino** (34b), **dint** (48c,59d, 122a), **Dion** (96a,152a), **dipt, dire** (45d,55a,104a,163c), **dirk** (40b), **dirt, Disa** (111a), **disc** (31b), **dish, disk** (31b), **diss** (98b), **dita** (117a), **dite** (150b), **diva** (110d,123c), **dive** (42b,74b,119d), **divi, dixi**

- DI - **Adib** (155b, **adit** (51a,100a,114d), **edit** (20d,49d,123a,129a,131a), **idic** (79b), **idio** (34b,c), **odic** (79c,120a), **Odin** (7c,29d,63c,68c,175d, 183b), **odio** (83b), **udic** (108a)

- - DI **Andi** (27d), **cadi** (12a,103a), **kadi** (103a,171a), **Lodi** (105d), **ludi** (133b), **Madi** (174a), **medi** (34c), **Midi** (151b), **nidi** (106c), **nodi** (35c,87c), **padi** (131b), **pedi** (34b), **rodi** (98c), **sidi** (103b), **wadi** (46c,106a,109a,128a,132a)

D - - I **dali** (168c,169b), **dari** (38a,70b), **dasi** (77a), **deci** (163b), **defi** (61b), **demi** (34b,122c), **desi** (85d), **Devi** (147b,153b), **divi, dixi, doni** (21a,28c,168a), **drei** (66d,165a)

- DJ - **Idjo** (191)

- - DJ **hadj** (98b,118a)

D - - K **dank** (40b,101a), **dark** (47a,67d,109b,160b), **dauk** (95c), **dawk** (95c), **deck** (13b,41c,144d), **desk, dhak** (48a,169a), **dick** (43a,55b), **Dick** (96b), **dirk** (40b), **disk** (31b), **dock** (40a,117c,144d,179d), **dook** (184a), **duck** (26b,53b,179c), **dunk** (43c,79d), **dusk** (171c), **Dyak** (22b)

- DL - **idle** (174b,c,178c), **idly**

D - - L **Dail** (49a,82b,c), **deal** (11d,16c,36c,44c,81a,168b), **deil** (139b), **dell** (43c,174b), **deul** (77b), **dhal** (12b), **dial** (25c), **dill** (13a,117c), **doll** (125c), **dowl, dual** (45c,171d), **duel, dull** (21a,32c,173a), **Dull** (94b)

- DM - **admi** (65d)

D - - M **dawm** (190), **deem** (36b,85c,164c), **derm** (147c,158d), **diem** (89b, 116a), **doom** (42d,55a,134d), **dorm, doum** (168c), **dram** (46b,110c, 121d,148c), **drum** (105a), **duim** (188)

- DN - **Edna** (183c)

D - - N **dain** (188), **darn, damn, dawn** (14d,41b), **dean** (33c,109d), **dein** (66d), **dhan** (124c), **dian** (46c,130d,170b), **Dian** (68d,69a,c,102b), **Dion** (96a,152a), **Domn** (135a), **doon** (140b,168c), **dorn** (164d), **down** (149d), **duan** (64b)

DO - - **doab** (157c), **doat** (17a,94b,112a,165d), **dobe** (159b,c,172b), **doby** (159b,c), **dock** (40a,117c,144d,179d), **dodd** (139c,140c), **Dode** (96b), **dodo** (19b), **Doeg** (137c), **doer** (8a,116b), **does, doff** (130a,161b), **doge** (95b,175b), **dogy** (46d,103c), **doit** (47a,169d,180d), **Doko** (191), **dola** (189), **dole** (44c,118c,121c,129d), **Dole** (74c), **doli, doll** (125c), **dolt** (20c,59c,157d), **dome** (39c,133c,155d), **Domn** (135a), **domy, dona** (83d,121c,151d), **done, dong, doni** (21a,28c, 168a), **don't, doob** (18b), **dook** (184a), **doom** (42d,55a,134d), **doon** (140b,168c), **door** (51a,121b), **dopa** (117d), **dope** (46c,105d), **dopp** (43c), **dora** (70b), **Dora** (36d,41a,43b,183c,d), **dord** (42c), **dore** (61d,67b,69d,117d), **Dore** (50d,63a,b), **dorm, dorn** (164d), **dorp** (73c,176b), **dorr** (32b), **dory** (21b,58b,144c), **dosa** (74b), **dose** (123a), **doss** (17c), **dost, dote** (17a,90b,94b,97a,112a,139d,165d),

doth, Doto (141b), **doty** (43d), **doub** (18b), **douc** (101d), **doum** (168c), **dour** (67d,159a), **dove** (19a,117d), **dowd** (143b), **dowl, down** (149d), **doxa** (48b), **doxy** (129d), **doze** (148a), **dozy**

- DO - **ador** (153b), **Edom** (18c,51b,79b,82c,84a), **idol** (48c,54c,55a,75b, 79d,112d,130b,184d), **odor** (138b,156a)

- - DO **Bodo** (88c), **codo** (188), **dado** (41c,111c,115c,177d), **dedo** (188), **dido** (11b,26c,65a,122a), **Dido** (27a,172c), **dodo** (19b), **eddo** (162a), **endo** (34d,122d,183b), **fado** (121c), **Jodo** (113d), **judo** (84b,85c, 142b), **Lido** (83d,175b), **ludo** (65a,112b), **mado** (14d,57a,170b), **ordo** (22a,30d,122a,171a), **pedo** (34b), **redo** (165c), **sado** (26d, 84d), **todo** (22b,24d,35b,64c,156b), **undo** (11a,93d), **Yedo** (166d)

D - - O **dado** (41c,111c,115c,177d), **Dago, dato** (95c,102c,117a), **dedo** (188), **demo** (122d), **dhao** (24c), **dido** (11b,26c,65a,122a), **Dido** (27a,172c), **dilo** (120d,168c), **dino** (34b), **dodo** (19b), **Doko** (191), **Doto** (141b), **Duco, duro** (190)

D - - P **damp** (101a), **deep** (124a), **dopp** (43c), **dorp** (73c,176b), **drap** (61b, c,62a), **drip, drop** (43d,54b,100b,114c,168b), **dump**

DR - - **draa** (188), **drab** (23d,29c,33d,46d,53b,d), **drag** (74a,125b), **drah** (188), **dram** (46b,110c,121d,148c), **drap** (61b,c,62a), **drat** (100a), **Drau, draw** (42c,53a,92b,117c,121c,167d), **dray** (27a,154c,177b), **dree** (139b,140c,158b,172c), **dreg, drei** (66d,165a), **drew, drey** (154c), **drib** (46b), **Drin, drip, drop** (43d,54b,100b,114c,168b), **drub** (17b,39c), **drug** (105d), **drum** (105a), **drun** (132b)

- DR - **adry** (164c)

- - DR **sadr** (94a), **Sadr** (155b)

D - - R **daer** (22b), **darr** (163c), **Daur** (139b), **dear, deer** (28c,135a,154d), **Dhar, dier, doer** (8a,116b), **door** (51a,121b), **dorr** (32b), **dour** (67d, 159a), **duar, Duhr** (155b), **durr** (70b), **dyer**

- DS - **DDSC** (42a)

- - DS **duds** (32c,166d), **Eads** (23b,24b,50b,82a), **odds** (28d,172d), **suds** (59a)

D - - S **dais** (119b), **dans** (62a), **days, dens** (90a,167b), **deus** (68a,89b), **dibs** (70c), **dies** (41b,89b), **diss** (98b), **does, doss** (17c), **duds** (32c,166d), **Duns, Dyas** (66a)

D - - T **daft** (59c), **dart** (13b,88a,100c,120b,153a,160c), **debt** (91d,109b), **deft** (147c), **dent** (42c,77d), **diet** (14a,54c,84c,91b,176a), **dint** (48c,59d,122a), **dipt, dirt, doat** (17a,94b,112a,165d), **doit** (47a, 169d,180d), **dolt** (20c,59c,157d), **don't, dost, drat** (100a), **Duat** (172d), **duct** (170c), **duet** (104d,171d), **duit** (190), **Duit** (192), **dunt, dust**

DU - - **duab** (157c), **duad** (113a,171d), **dual** (45c,171d), **duan** (64b), **duar, Duat** (172d), **dubb** (161c), **duce** (29d), **duck** (26b,53b,179c), **Duco, duct** (170c), **dude** (40d), **duds** (32c,166d), **duel, duet** (104d,171d), **duff** (125b), **Dufy** (63a), **Duhr** (155b), **duim** (188), **duit** (190), **Duit** (192), **duke** (107c), **duku** (95d,168c), **dull** (21a,32c,173a), **Dull** (94b), **Duma** (135c), **dumb** (153b), **dump, dune** (137a), **dunk** (43c, 79d), **Duns, dunt, dupe** (27c,41c,72c,160c), **dura** (153c), **duro** (190), **durr** (70b), **duse** (83c), **dusk** (171c), **dust, duty** (109b,162b)

- DU - **idun** (107d), **odum** (168c,180a)

- - DU **Addu** (68c,157a,182a), **Jadu** (95a), **Kadu** (191), **kudu** (11a), **ordu** (170d), **pudu** (41d), **Urdu** (77b), **widu** (102d), **wudu** (102d)

D - - U **Danu** (28a), **datu** (95c,102c,117a), **degu** (132c), **Diau** (192), **Dieu** (61d), **Drau,** **duku** (95d,168c)

D - - W **dauw** (24c), **dhaw** (125a), **dhow** (88d,111c,175d), **draw** (42c,53a, 92b,117c,121c,167d), **drew**

DY - - **dyad** (113a), **Dyak** (22b), **Dyas** (66a), **dyer,** **dyke** (49c,91d), **dyna** (34c), **dyne** (59d,173b)

- DY - **idyl** (114d), **Idyo** (191), **odyl** (59d,79c)

- - DY **Addy** (183d), **Andy** (96b), **body** (72a), **cady** (69d), **eddy** (37d,39d, 160d,180d), **fady,** **jady,** **Judy** (125c,183d), **lady,** **sidy** (123b), **tidy** (106a,111b), **tody** (19b,d,59a,166a), **undy** (179a), **urdy** (86b), **wady** (109a,128a,132a)

D - - Y **Davy** (96b,136b), **dazy,** **defy** (28d), **demy** (113d), **deny** (36d,43d, 129b), **dewy** (101a), **doby** (159b,c), **dogy** (46d,103c), **domy,** **dory** (21b,58b,144c), **doty** (43d), **doxy** (129d), **dozy,** **dray** (27a,154c, 177b), **drey** (154c), **Dufy** (63a), **duty** (109b,162b)

- DZ - **adze** (40c,167a), **Idzo** (191)

- - DZ **Lodz**

D - - Z **Daez**

EA - - **each,** **Eads** (23b,24b,50b,82a), **eard** (139b), **earl** (107c,166b), **earn** (42d,64b,99a), **ease** (7c,8d,35a,100d,129d,130b,c,150c), **east,** **East** (111b), **easy** (54a,146d,149d,172b) **eats,** **eaux** (178c), **eave** (133c),

- EA - **bead** (17a,122a,146b), **beak** (19a), **beal** (139d), **beam,** **bean** (91b, 142a,175a), **bear** (27a,50b,113c,155a), **beat** (58c,87b,131a,164d, 165b,180d), **beau,** **dead,** **deaf,** **deal** (11d,16c,36c,44c,81a,168b), **dean** (33c,109d), **dear,** **feak** (39d,171c), **fear** (113c,155a), **feat** (7a, 52d), **geal** (47d,163c), **gean** (29c), **gear** (32c,112a,167b), **geat** (77d, 101a), **Geat** (138a), **head** (29d), **heaf** (144a), **heal,** **heap** (117d), **hear** (75b,c,92d), **heat,** **jean** (37c), **Jean** (183c), **keal** (25a), **lead** (35d,43d,72b,74d,81a), **leaf** (55c,73c,119b), **Leah** (19a,84a,87b, 183c), **leak** (110c), **leal** (54b,94c,139d), **lean** (128a,148b,152d, 164b,166a), **leap** (26c), **lear** (139d), **Lear** (37a,143b), **mead** (46a, 78a,97d,99b), **Mead** (78a), **meal** (72a,130b), **mean** (15a,42b,146c, 156b), **meat** (59b), **neaf** (58a,73c), **Neal,** **neap** (165c,167a,177b), **near** (11d,32c,107b), **neat** (165c,169d), **peag** (144a,178a), **peai** (98b), **peak** (9a,38c,159b,186b), **peal** (131c,d), **pean** (64c,150b), **pear** (64a), **peat** (64a,175a), **read** (116d,157d), **real** (7a), **ream** (18c,37d,50d,113d,171c), **reap** (7a,40a,74a), **rear** (15b,23a,b,24a, 51b,76d,127c), **seah** (188), **seal** (10c,d,54d,64c,96a,118b,128a), **seam** (85b,d,160a,176d,185a), **Sean** (85b,96a), **sear** (23d,27d,72d, 138c), **seat** (98c,156b), **teak** (41a,48a,168c), **teal** (19b,20d,46c,d), **team** (38c,72a,113a), **tean** (140c,167a), **tear** (67c,87b,130a), **veal,** **weak** (55b), **weal** (124d,157c,180c,d), **wean** (8d,42d), **wear** (50b), **yeah,** **Yean** (88a), **year,** **yeas** (177c), **zeal** (12c,55d)

- - EA **Alea** (14b,31c,167d), **area** (37d,38a,44c,53a,93b,110d,127d, 138c,168a,186d), **asea** (39b,177c), **brea** (100b), **crea** (92c,151d), **evea** (82a), **Evea** (95a), **flea** (81b), **Frea,** **Gaea** (47d,69a), **idea** (54c, 108c,124a,164d), **Itea** (145d,160c,181d), **odea** (105a,164a), **olea**

(170b), **Olea** (110b), **Otea** (71a,82d), **oxea** (153d), **plea** (51a,52d, 122a,130b), **rhea** (37a,56a,111d,133d), **Rhea** (19b,68d,87c,103c, 186b), **shea** (25a,168c,d), **Thea** (162c), **uvea** (53c,82b)

E - - A **Ecca** (66a), **Edda** (76b,79b,107d,136b), **Edna** (183c), **Egba** (191), **Ekka** (26d), **Elba** (105d), **Elia** (88a,115d), **ella** (152c, 158c), **Ella** (183c), **Elsa** (70a,93c,110d,177b,183c), **Emma** (183c), **Enna** (146a), **epha** (75c), **Erda** (23d,41a,47d,68d,69a,131d,177b), **eria** (13d,146d), **Erma** (183c), **Erua** (103c), **esca** (11c,44a,70c), **esta** (152d,164c), **etna** (75b,153c,157a,175d,177a,c), **Etta** (183c), **evea** (82a,95a), **eyra** (181d), **ezba** (188), **Ezra** (96a)

EB - - **Eben** (96a), **Eber** (51a,75c,99d), **Ebro** (132a), **eboe** (28b,110a,168c, 169b), **Eboe, ebon** (20b), **ebur** (89c)

- EB - **ceba** (169b), **debt** (91d,109b), **Hebe** (39c,69c,186b), **Nebo** (68c, 102d,103d,183a), **peba** (12d), **Peba** (193), **Reba** (18d,86c,144a), **Seba** (18c,39d), **sebi** (34b), **ueba** (188), **zebu** (22d,80d,112c)

- - EB **bleb** (20c,23d,67c), **dieb** (84a), **pleb** (10d,35b,180b), **Sleb** (12a), **sweb** (160d), **theb** (188)

EC - - **ecad** (73a,119b), **Ecca** (66a), **ecce** (17d,89a,c), **echo** (130b,d), **Echo** (105d), **ecru** (17d,23d,172b), **ecto** (34c,122d)

- EC - **beck** (107c), **deca** (34d,122d), **deci** (163b), **deck** (13b,41c,144d), **heck** (100a), **lech** (102b), **neck** (83a), **peca** (190), **peck** (24d), **peco** (162b), **reck** (26d,75c), **rect** (117b), **sech** (97c), **seck** (173d), **sect** (42b,54a,114c), **teca, Teca** (192), **Tech, teck** (128b), **Teco** (192)

- - EC **alec** (10a,57c,d,76c), **Alec** (137a), **avec** (63a,183a), **haec** (90a, 164c), **spec**

E - - C **epic** (76b,120a), **eric** (115b), **Eric** (71d,96a,107d,138a,164a,176b), **eruc** (37a,56a)

ED - - **Edam** (29c), **Edar** (18d), **Edda** (76b,79b,107d,136b), **eddo** (162a), **eddy** (37d,39d,160d,180d), **edel** (66c), **Eden** (6b,50d,107c,113d, 123c), **Eder, Edes** (71c), **edge** (22a,96d,131c,143c,146b), **edgy** (106c), **edit** (20d,49d,123a,129a,131a), **Edna** (183c), **Edom** (18c, 51b,79b,82c,84a)

- ED - **Beda** (101d), **Bede** (48c,50c,101d,175b), **cede** (67b,70c,129d,160a, 168b,185d), **dedo** (188), **gedd** (140a), **Leda** (27b,75d,120c,153a, 171d,186b), **meda** (110a), **Medb, Mede** (10a,b,13c), **medi** (34c), **peda** (114d,144b), **pedi** (34b), **pedo** (34b), **redd** (153a), **rede** (37c, 81d,138d), **redo** (165c), **Teda** (191), **Veda** (77a,b), **Yedo** (166d)

- - ED **abed** (130c), **aged** (110a), **bled, bred** (23c,48c,127c), **coed, deed** (7a,52d,91a,166c,168b), **feed** (108c), **fled, Fred** (96b), **gled** (19a, 52a,87a), **heed** (14c,75b,109b), **hued, lied** (66d,150b), **meed** (128c, 131a), **Moed** (100c), **need** (42b,52d,87b,122a,178a), **Obed** (135d), **pied** (96c,103c,114b,117c,154a,174d), **reed** (16a,70d,97b,105a, 111b,118b,144b), **Reed** (163a), **roed, seed** (70b,111c,112c,119a, 151b,154a), **shed** (27a,90c,101b,144b), **sled** (40a), **sned** (93d,125a, 140a), **sped, syed** (103b), **tied, toed, used** (6d,73a), **weed**

E - - D **eard** (139b), **ecad** (73a,119b), **egad** (100a,109a), **eild** (138d,140a), **elod** (49b,59d,79c), **emyd** (163c,167c), **Enid** (13b,25d,66b,163a, 183c)

EE - - **eely** (185a), **eery** (172b,180a)

-EE- **beef, been** (149a), **beer** (18c), **bees** (185b), **beet** (175a), **deed** (7a, 52d,166c,168b), **deem** (36b,85c,164c), **deep** (124a), **deer** (28c, 135a,154d), **feed** (108c), **feel** (72a,142c), **fees** (128c), **Geez** (6c, 51d), **heed** (14c,75b,109b), **heel, Heep** (41a,43b), **heer** (47a,184b, 185b), **jeel, jeep, jeer** (138c,162b), **keef** (75d), **keek** (154c), **keel** (128d,134d,144c,d), **keen** (15a,88a,177b), **keep** (123a,130d), **keet** (72b), **leek** (58b,76a,110c,177d), **leer** (9d,58a,67c,93d,112a,148c), **lees** (46a,142a), **leet** (26a,38a,139d), **meed** (128c,131a), **meek** (93d,99d), **meer, meet** (11d,13d,36a,50a,81d,142d), **need** (42b, 52d,87b,122a,178a), **neem** (96d,168c,169a), **neep** (140c,171b), **neer** (14b,86b,108b), **peek** (93d), **peel** (53a,114a), **peen** (73c), **peep** (93d,115c), **peer** (51a,107c), **peet** (64a), **reed** (16a,70d,97b,105a, 111b,118b,144b), **Reed** (163a), **reef** (129a,137a,145a), **reek** (49d, 53c,64a,148d,149a), **reel** (21b,40b,d,153c,154a,c,d,180d), **reem** (18d), **seed** (70b,111c,112c,119a,151b,154a), **seek** (141c), **seel** (20c,32c,143b), **seem** (11c), **seen, seep** (110c,116a,154b), **seer** (60a,124c,150c), **teel** (142d), **teem** (6b,121d), **teen** (139b,c,140b, 158d), **teer** (25b,69d), **Tees** (108a), **veer** (28d,144c,171b), **weed week, weel** (16d,57d,140d,180d), **weep** (39b,88a,104a), **weet** (19d)

--EE **agee** (13d,15c,38d), **ajee** (15c,139a), **akee** (168c), **alee** (15c,75d, 144b,157a,182a), **bree** (139a), **byee** (189), **chee** (189), **clee** (19a, 129a), **Cree** (192), **dree** (139b,140c,158b,172c), **epee** (55c,160d), **flee, free** (44a,70d,131b), **ghee** (24d), **glee** (99a,150b), **idee** (61d), **inee** (120b), **Klee** (113a), **knee** (85b), **ogee** (40c,101a,b,120b), **pree** (139d), **Rhee** (87c), **shee** (82b), **skee** (149c), **slee** (140b,148c), **smee** (19b,46c,d,118b,119d,141b,181b), **Smee** (116d), **snee** (40a, b,43d,87a), **Spee** (66d,70b), **thee** (124b), **tree** (11d,37a,66a,184b), **twee, tyee** (29d), **usee, whee**

E--E **ease** (7c,8d,35a,100d,129d,130b,c,150c), **eave** (133c), **eboe** (28b, 110a,168c,169b), **Eboe, ecce** (17d,89a,c), **edge** (22a,96d,131c, 143c,146b), **elde** (119c), **eine** (66c), **Eire** (82b), **Elbe** (108a), **elle** (62b,c), **else** (18b,79b,111d), **ence** (158c), **enne** (34c), **ense** (139b, 158c), **ente** (70b,151d), **epee** (55c,160d), **Erie** (82c,87d), **erne** (19c, d,47b,54b,141a) **Erse** (28a,64b,82b), **esce** (158d), **esne** (10c,45b, 142c,148a,164d), **esse** (7a,18a,52d,89a,90a,159a,166c), **este** (152b, d,164c), **Este** (55c,83c,112d), **etre** (61a,c,62d,166c), **ette** (158a,c,d), **euge** (180a), **evoe** (15b,130d,181c), **eyre** (23c,31b,85c), **Eyre**

EF-- **Efik** (191)

-EF- **defi** (61b), **deft** (147c), **defy** (28d), **heft** (179d), **Heft, jefe** (152a), **jeff** (133d), **left** (42c), **reft** (32a,42c,44d,167b), **teff** (6c), **weft** (39a,165a,184b)

--EF **alef** (91c), **atef** (39a,48d), **beef, chef, clef** (104d,105a), **elef** (91c), **fief** (55d), **keef** (75d), **kief** (75d), **lief** (181d), **reef** (129a,137a, 145a), **tref** (172b)

E--F **elef** (91c), **Enif** (155b)

EG-- **egad** (100a,109a), **Egba** (191), **Egbo** (141d), **Eger** (49a), **eggs** (112a), **eggy** (185d), **Egil** (107d), **egis** (14b,d,115a,124d,144b,154a,161a), **egol** (11b)

-EG- **bega** (188), **degu** (132c), **hegh, mega** (34b,c), **pega** (57a,130a, 158b), **Pegu** (24c,102a,127d), **sego** (24b,25a,92b,174c), **tegg** (143d,

171d), **vega** (110d,152c), **Vega** (155b), **Wega** (155b), **Wegg** (111d), **yegg** (24c)

- - EG **areg** (116a,137a), **Areg**, **Doeg** (137c), **dreg**, **Gheg** (8c), **skeg** (7d, 86a,144d,157d,184a), **sneg** (139b), **waeg** (19b,72c,87a)

EH - - **eheu** (52c)

- EH - **behn** (137d), **Hehe** (191), **jehu** (46b), **Jehu** (18c), **lehr** (67c,112a), **peho** (19b,102c,106d), **sehr** (66d), **tehr** (27c,68a)

- - EH **okeh** (8d,37b)

E - - H **each**, **Elah** (18c,86d), **Esth** (16a,51d), **Etah** (51c,71d), **etch**, **eyah** (95b,108d,111c)

EI - - **eide** (119c), **eild** (138d,140a), **eine** (66c) **Eire** (82b)

- EI - **Beid** (155b), **ceil** (92c,112a), **deil** (139b), **dein** (66d), **feis** (82b), **gein** (67d), **heii** (74b), **hein** (52c,61c), **heir**, **keif** (75d), **keir** (20c, 174d), **Leif** (107d), **Leir**, **mein** (30b), **nein** (66c), **meio** (188), **Neil** (96a), **reim** (112c), **rein** (29b,130c), **reis** (26c,29d,75a,103b), **seid** (103b), **Seid** (42d,101a,171a), **Seik** (77b), **Seim** (120c), **sein** (146c), **seip** (110c), **Seir** (51b,94a,103d), **seis** (147b,152c), **seit** (189), **Teig** (96a), **teil** (92b,c,168c), **veil** (74d,76c), **vein** (20d,157b), **weir** (40b,57d), **zein**

- - EI **drei** (66d,165a), **kuei** (44a), **kwei** (44a), **Omei** (24a), **quei** (189), **vlei** (38c,160a)

E - - I **Ekoi** (191), **Enki** (15b), **equi** (122d), **etui** (27a,29b,62c,106b,148d, 166d,174b)

EJ - - **ejoo** (55b,168c)

- EJ - **Beja** (6c,191), **Nejd**, **reja** (152b), **Sejm** (120c), **teju** (151b)

EK - - **Ekka** (26d), **Ekoi** (191)

- EK - **beka** (189), **feke**, **Peke** (45a,148d), **Reki** (16a), **weka** (58c,106d, 107a,127b), **weki** (55c), **Zeke** (96b)

- - EK **chek** (59c), **esek** (18d), **hoek** (39d), **keek** (154c), **leek** (58b,76a, 110c,177d), **meek** (93d,99d), **peek** (93d,115c), **reek** (49d,53c, 64a,148d,149a), **seek** (141c), **trek** (85c,93c,99d,168b)

E - - K **Efik** (191), **esek** (18d)

EL - - **Elah** (18c,86d), **Elam** (18d,37d,82a,116c,144b), **elan** (12c,41a,50d, 62a,153c,177a,186b), **ELAS** (71c), **Elba** (105d), **Elbe** (108a), **elef** (91c), **Elia** (88a,115d), **Elis** (22c,37d,71b,107c), **ella** (152c,158c, **Ella** (183c), **elle** (62b,c), **elmy**, **elod** (49b,59d,79c), **Elon** (18c,51b, 108a), **Elsa** (70a,93c,110d,177b,183c), **else** (18b,79b,111d), **Elul** (102b)

- EL - **bela** (12a), **Bela** (18b,48c,78d), **Beli** (23c), **bell** (24c,39d), **Bell** (162d), **belt** (16a,31a), **cela** (62d), **cell** (39b), **celt** (30c,82c,123a, 156c,167b,179b), **Celt** (10a,180a,b), **dele** (26a,49c,51b,53a,110b, 123d,124c,130a,145c,161b), **dell** (43c,174b), **eely** (185a), **fell** (40a, 58b,76c,115d,147d), **fels** (190), **felt**, **geld** (162b), **gelt** (101c), **Hela** (93c), **held**, **helm** (144d,165d), **help** (14a), **kela** (189), **keld** (154b), **kelp** (82a,141c), **Kelt** (180b), **Lely** (47a), **mele** (74b,150b), **melt**, **Nell** (110a,183d), **pela** (30c), **Pele** (69c,74c), **pelf** (131b), **pelo** (83b), **pelt** (53a), **pelu** (30a,106d,168c), **rely** (16b,170b), **self** (48d,80d), **sell** (97a,115c,175b), **tela** (22d,98c,121b,166a,179c), **tele** (34b,

122c), **teli** (94b), **tell** (105d,129c,154b), **Tell** (160d), **vela** (98c 136b,149d), **Vela** (36b,c), **veld** (151a), **velo** (175b), **weld** (47c,85b, 173c), **Welf** (67a), **welk** (65c,96d,141b), **well, welt** (36d,131b, 145a,b,177b,d), **yell** (145c), **yelp, yelt** (151b)

- - EL **Abel** (7a,25b), **bhel** (126d), **coel** (39b), **duel, edel** (66c), **esel** (66b), **ezel** (47a,85d), **feel** (72a,142c), **fuel** (65c), **Gael** (28a,96c,138d), **goel** (15a,75c), **heel, Jael** (147b), **jeel, Joel** (96a), **keel** (128d,134d, 144c,d), **kiel** (128d,134d), **Kiel** (25d), **koel** (19a,b,39b), **nael** (189), **noel** (26d,150b), **Noel** (30d,96a), **odel** (48a,112c), **Orel, peel** (53a, 114a), **reel** (21b,40b,d,153c,154a,c,d,180d), **Riel** (129a), **ryel** (190), **seel** (20c,32c,143b), **tael** (91d,179d), **teel** (142d), **tuel, weel** (16d, 57d,140d,180d), **wiel** (140d,180d)

E - - L **earl** (107c), **edel** (66c), **Egil** (107d), **egol** (11b), **Elul** (102b), **Emil** (96a), **enol** (29c,158b), **eral** (51a), **esel** (66b), **etal** (89a), **evil** (79c, 95d,147a,181a,185c), **ezel** (47a,85d)

EM - - **Emer** (39b,183c), **emeu** (111d), **Emil** (96a), **Emim** (67a,100d), **emir** (12a,103a,b,123c,134d,135a,171a), **emit** (43d,49a,53c,58d,83a, 142c), **Emma** (183c), **emyd** (163c,167c), **Emys** (167c,171b)

- EM - **bema** (28d,31a,114b,119b,125b,137a), **deme** (71b,c,167d), **demi** (34b,122c), **demo** (122d), **demy** (113d), **feme** (181b), **hemi** (122c), **hemo** (34a,122b), **hemp** (26a,37a,56a,133d), **kemp** (139b), **memo** (108b), **Nema** (34d,48c,134b,164d,176c), **nemo** (34b), **Nemo** (56a, 85c), **Remi** (10b), **Rems, seme** (45c,138b,151b,154b,155c,157b), **semi** (34b,80b,122c,d), **tema** (12a,164a), **Tema, xema** (72c), **Xema** (12c), **zeme** (55d,161b,180b), **zemi** (55d,161b,180b)

- - EM **ahem, alem** (98b,155a,170d,171a), **asem** (9a,49a,69c), **clem** (56b, 158b), **deem** (36b,85c,164c), **diem** (89b,116a), **haem** (122b), **idem** (89d,164a), **item** (6d,13b,42d,51a,90d,92d,107a,113d,114c), **Khem** (113c), **neem** (96d,168c,169a), **poem** (51a), **reem** (18d), **riem** (76c, 112c,157c,164d), **seem** (11c), **Shem** (107c), **stem** (29b,125a,154d, 155a,156d), **teem** (6b,121d), **them** (124b)

E - - M **edam** (29c), **Edom** (18c,51b,79b,82c,84a), **Elam** (18d,37d,82a,116c, 144b), **Emim** (67a,100d), **enam** (70c,77a), **Enam** (85c), **etym** (133d), **exam**

EN - - **enam** (70c,77a,85c), **ence** (158c), **endo** (34d,122d,183b), **Enid** (13b,25d,66b,163a,183c), **Enif** (155b), **enin** (20d), **Enki** (15b), **Enna** (146a), **enne** (34c), **enol** (29c,158b), **Enon** (18c,d), **Enos** (7a,18d,52a, 70c,96a,143a), **enow** (50d,123a,158b), **ense** (139b,158c), **enso** (34d,183b), **ente** (70b,151d), **ento** (34b,d,183b), **envy** (41b), **Enyo** (12c,69c,178a), **Enzu** (102b)

- EN - **bena** (176a), **bend** (39d,171b), **bene** (18a,83c,90a,106d,122a, 180a), **beng** (43a), **beni** (116a,142d), **Beni** (191), **beno** (113b,117a), **bent** (80b), **benu** (49a), **cena** (88d,133a), **cene** (34c), **cens** (115b), **cent** (36d), **dene** (137a), **Dene** (192), **dens** (90a,167b), **dent** (42c, 77d), **deny** (36d,43d,129b), **fend** (114b,178b), **gena** (29b), **gene** (54a,76b), **Gene** (96b), **gens** (42d,132d), **gent, genu** (6b,18a,87a, 89c), **hens** (121d), **Jena** (105d,165b), **keno, Kent** (90d), **lena** (56d), **Lena** (36b), **lend** (6d,79d), **lene** (36b,149a,172b), **leno** (37c, 53b), **lens** (67c,95b,111a,129b,162d), **lent** (54d), **Lent** (115d,141c), **mend** (130b), **mene** (19a,73d,108d,185c), **Ment** (54b,164a), **menu**

(19a,27a), **Menu**, **nene** (19b,74c), **pend**, **pene**, **pent** (36a), **rena** (25b,132c), **rend** (32a,159c,162c,185a), **Reni** (83d), **Reno**, **rent** (58a,91b,138b,153d,162c,167c), **send** (42c,44b,95c,121c,130a, 144c,168b), **senn** (76b), **Sens** (63b), **sent**, **tend** (26d,80b,93d,100a), **tene** (34d,131b), **teng** (188), **tent** (26b,115a), **vena** (90a,175a), **vend** (97a,115c,142b), **Vend** (10b,148a), **vent** (8b,11b,110d,112a), **wend** (67d,123d), **Wend** (10b,148a), **went** (42c), **xeno** (34d), **yeni** (19b,161d), **Zend**, **Zeno** (71b), **zenu** (143d)

- - EN **aden** (34b), **Aden**, **alen** (40d,138a), **amen** (14a,80b,94a,137a,149c, 175c,184b), **Amen** (86d,127d,164a), **aten** (150a,159b), **been** (149a), **bien** (63a,140c,179a,180a), **bren** (72d,95a), **Caen**, **Chen** (149b), **Eben** (96a), **Eden** (6b,50d,107c,113d,123c), **even** (51a,58b,79d,91d, 149a,173a), **glen** (43c), **hien** (30b), **hoen** (189), **Iden** (76a), **Iren** (127c), **Iten** (192), **keen** (15a,88a,177b), **lien** (65c,91a,124c), **mien** (11c,17b,26d,44c,96b), **omen** (14c,59d,60a,121c,123a,146b), **open** (26a,60d,81a,109b,112c,125b,172b,173c), **oven** (15d,78c,86b), **Owen** (96a,183c), **oxen** (10c), **peen** (73c), **pien** (13b), **rien** (62b), **seen**, **Shen** (68a), **sken** (164a), **sten** (72c,95a), **teen** (139b,c,140b, 158d), **then**, **tien** (147d), **T-men** (168b), **when** (180d), **wren** (19b,c), **Wren** (50b)

E - - N **earn** (42d,64b,99a), **Eben** (96a), **ebon** (20b), **Eden** (6b,50d,107c, 113d,123c), **elan** (12c,41a,50d,62a,153c,177a,186b), **Elon** (18c, 51b), **enin** (20d), **Enon** (18c,d), **Eoan** (41a,85b), **Eoin** (85b), **Erin** (82b), **Eton** (33b,50c,84a), **Evan** (96a), **even** (51a,58b,79d,91d, 149a,173a), **Ewan**

EO - - **Eoan** (41a,85b), **Eoin** (85b)

- EO - **feod** (55d), **Leon** (96a), **meou**, **meow**, **neon** (65c), **peon** (28c,59c, 99c), **Teos** (82a)

- - EO **areo** (34c), **Ateo** (120d), **Cleo** (126b), **ideo** (34b,d,164d), **oleo** (34c), **skeo** (57d)

E - - O **Ebro** (132a), **echo** (130b,d), **Echo** (105d), **ecto** (34c,122d), **eddo** (162a), **Egbo** (141d), **ejoo** (55b,168c), **endo** (34d,122d,183b), **enso** (34d,183b), **ento** (34b,d,183b), **Enyo** (12c,69c,178a), **ergo** (164b)

EP - - **epee** (55c,160d), **epha** (75c), **epic** (76b,120a), **epos** (51a,76b,120a)

- EP - **cepa** (110c), **cepe** (48c), **depa** (188), **kepi** (99d), **kept**, **Nepa** (106b, 178c), **pepo** (39b,64a,70a,98c,125c,154c), **repp** (53b,131a), **seps** (93b,142d), **sept** (31d,82b,143a,149c), **Sept** (45b), **Veps** (191), **wept**

- - EP **deep** (124a), **Heep** (41a,43b), **jeep**, **keep** (123a,130d), **neep** (140c, 171b), **peep** (93d,115c), **prep** (138b), **seep** (110c,116a,154b), **skep** (16d,17c,77c), **step** (70b,112b,177b,d), **weep** (39b,88a,104a)

EQ - - **equi** (122d)

ER - - **eral** (51a), **erat** (89c), **Erda** (23d,41a,47d,68d,69a,131d,177b), **erer** (17d,150c), **ergo** (164b), **eria** (13d,146d), **eric** (115b), **Eric** (71d, 96a,107d,138a,164a,176b), **Erie** (82c,87d), **Erin** (82b), **Eris** (12c, 68d,109c), **Erma** (183c), **erne** (19c,d,47b,54b,141a), **Eros** (11c, 39c,68b,97c,182d), **Erse** (28a,64b,82b), **erst** (60b), **Erua** (103c), **eruc** (37a,56a), **eryx** (137a)

- ER - **aera** (8a), **aeri** (34a), **aero** (8b,34a,b,58c,59a), **aery** (47b,51d,106c), **Bera** (86d), **berg** (79b), **berm** (25d,90d,145c), **Bern** (160d), **Bert**

(96b), **cera** (152d,161d,179a), **cere** (19a,114b,149d,179a), **cern** (41c), **cero** (57b,c,d, 180b), **dera** (34c), **dere** (74a,79c), **derm** 147c,158d), **eery** (172b,180a), **fern** (142a), **feru** (37a,56a,133d), **gerb** (56d,143d), **Gerd** (63c), **Gere** (183c), **Geri** (183c), **germ** (17d, 99c,134d), **Hera** (69c,85d,110b,126b,186b,d), **herb** (58b,158b), **herd** (39a,46c,72a), **here, herl** (16b,59a), **hero** (42b,124d,137b), **Hero** (90c), **Herr** (66c), **hers** (124c), **jerk** (153a), **kerb** (146b), **kere** (75c,128b), **kerf** (40a,108b), **keri** (75c,128b), **kern** (59c,172a), **Kern** (132b), **Kerr, Lero** (82d), **lerp** (51d,141d), **mere** (16c,22b, 62a,78b,87d,96c,110c,120d,146d,148b), **merl** (20b), **mero** (72a), **Meru** (77a,103d), **Nera** (165b), **Neri, Nero** (8a,126d,133a,172c), **Pera** (60a), **pere** (61c,63b), **peri** (54b,116b,c,122b), **perk** (84d, 93a), **perm** (49b,97d), **pern** (78a), **pero** (152a), **pert** (80a,93a,137c, 154b), **Peru, qere** (75c), **qeri** (75c), **sera** (11b,20d,59a,83a,180d), **Serb** (15d,148a,186c), **sere** (24d,46a,46c,138c,183b), **Sere** (158b), **serf** (21d,148a), **seri** (18b), **Seri** (192), **sero** (34d,88d,164b,178d), **Sert** (151d), **tera** (23d,84c), **term** (92b,105b,142b,166b), **tern** (19b, 32d,72c,94a,138c,141a,160a), **terp** (12b,123a), **vera** (140c,151b, 175c), **Vera** (183c), **verb** (7a,114b,184b), **verd** (71d), **veri** (28b), **vert** (71d,166a,171b), **very** (149c), **were** (139b), **werf** (54d), **weri** (15c,27c), **wert, zero** (31a,84c,108c), **Zero** (118d)

- - ER **Acer** (96c) **Ader** (18d), **afer** (48a,182b), **ager** (47c,56a,89b,c,131d, 133b), **amer** (61b), **aner** (18d,96b), **aper** (32d), **Aser** (84a), **Ater** (18c), **Auer** (79a), **aver** (7c,14a,15c,41c,95c,140d,155c,160b, 184c), **beer** (18c), **bier** (33b,66b), **Boer** (151a), **Brer** (172b), **cher** (61b), **daer** (22b), **deer** (28c,135a,154d), **dier, doer** (8a,116b), **dyer, Eber** (51a,75c,99d), **Eder, Eger** (49a), **Emer** (39b,183c), **erer** (17d, 150c), **eser, euer** (66d), **ever** (9b,14b,80b), **ewer** (84c,85c,118c, 181b), **eyer, gier** (47b), **goer, heer** (47a, 184b, 185b), **hier** (63a, 185d), **Hler** (141a), **hoer, icer, Imer, Iser** (49a), **iter** (22d,76c,85c, 89c,114d,132a,b,133a,b), **jeer** (138c,162b), **kier** (20c,174d), **leer** (9d,58a,67c,93d,112a,148c), **meer, neer** (14b,86b,108b), **Oder** (132a), **omer** (51a,75c), **oner** (20d,53a,75c,162d,173a,d), **oser** (61b), **over** (6b,38c,80a,114d,130a), **oxer** (55c), **oyer** (38a,75b,119c), **peer** (51a,93d,107c), **pier** (23a,88b,180c), **rier** (180b), **roer** (72d), **ruer, saer** (163a), **seer** (60a,124c,150c), **sher** (65d,165c), **sier** (57a,118b), **ster** (158c,d), **suer** (124d), **teer** (25b,69d), **tier** (118a,134b), **tyer, uber** (66b), **user** (49d), **veer** (28d,144c,171b), **vier** (66c), **waer** (40b), **Ymer** (67a,131c), **Yser**

E - - R **Eber** (51a,75c,99d), **ebur** (89c), **Edar** (18d), **Eder, Eger** (49a), **Emer** (39b,183c,), **emir** (12a,103a,b,123c,171a), **erer** (17d,150c), **eser, euer** (66d), **ever** (9b,14b,80b), **ewer** (84d,85c,118c,181b), **eyer**

ES - - **Esau** (82c,84a,128c), **Esay, esca** (11c,44a,70c), **esce** (158d), **esek** (18d), **esel** (66b), **eser, esne** (10c,45b,142c,148a,164d), **Esop** (53b, 54a), **esox** (57b), **espy** (44a,142a), **esse** (7a,18a,52d,89a,90a,159a, 166c), **esta** (152d,164c), **este** (152b,d,164c), **Este** (55c,83c,d,112d), **Esth** (16a,51d), **Esus**

- ES - **aesc** (12d,64d), **Besa** (68b,119c), **Bess** (76c,183d), **best** (41d,159c, 160a), **cess** (91d,94c,162b), **cest** (18a,67b), **desi** (85d), **desk, euer** (66d), **fess** (23c,51b), **fest, gest** (7c,41d,52d,133c), **hest** (35a), **jess** (157a), **jest** (169c), **Jesu, less** (100c,108b,141d), **lest** (59d,163d),

mesa (49b,76d,119b,161a), **mese** (71c), **mesh** (50d,106c), **mess** (22b,44b,77c,85d,104b,165c,173d), **ness** (26b,75a,124b), **nest** (38b, 74b,130d,149c,160b), **oese** (15d,119c), **pesa** (190), **peso** (99c), **pest** (108c,116b,118d,170a), **rese** (127b), **resh** (91d), **rest** (15d,91b, 104d,105a,115a,b,130a,b,161b), **sesi** (20b,57a,149b), **sess** (149c, 162b), **Tesa** (80c), **Tess** (73d,164c,183d), **test** (26a,51c,144a,169c, 170c), **vest** (32c,177b), **West** (9c,50b,109b), **Yeso** (72d), **zest** (55d, 72d)

- - ES **Ades** (73a), **Ames** (9c,82a), **anes** (110c,140a), **Ares** (49b,51b,68c, 76a,97a,105c,110b,178a,186d), **ates** (160c), **Aves** (19d), **bees** (185b), **Bres**, **dies** (41b,89b), **does**, **EDES** (71c), **fees** (128c), **Ghes** (193), **gres** (156d), **ides** (41a,b,133a), **Ives** (9c,90b), **lees** (46a, 142a), **ones** (116a), **oyes** (38a,39b,75b), **pres** (62b), **spes**, **Spes** (69a,78a), **Tees** (108a), **tres** (19a,52b,63a,152d,165a,175c), **uses** (18a), **wies** (185a)

E - - S **Eads** (23b,24b,50b,82a), **eats**, **EDES** (71c), **eggs** (112a), **egis** (14b, d,115a,124d,144b,154a,161a), **ELAS** (71c), **Elis** (22c,37d,71b, 107c), **Emys** (167c,171b), **Enns**, **Enos** (7a,18d,52a,70c,96a,143a), **epos** (51a,76b,120a), **Eris** (12c,68d,109c), **Eros** (11c,39c,68b,97c, 182d), **Esus**, **etes** (177c), **eyas** (106c,173a)

ET - - **Etah** (51c,71d), **etal** (89a), **etat** (62d), **etch**, **etes** (177c), **etna** (75b, 153c,157a,175d,177a,c), **Eton** (33b,50c,84a), **etre** (61a,c,62d,166c), **Etta** (183c), **ette** (158a,c,d), **etui** (27a,29b,62c,106b,148d,166d, 174b), **etym** (133d)

- ET - **Aeta** (94d,95d,100a,106b,117a), **beta** (71a,91c,141d), **bete** (61a,107c), **beth** (91c), **Beth** (8c,183d), **cete** (180b,c), **ceto** (34a), **fete** (55d,129b), **geta** (84b,145a), **gett** (44d), **Heth** (77c), **jete** (16a), **Jeth** (102a), **keta** (45a), **Keta**, **Ketu** (48b), **lete**, **Leti** (82d), **Leto** (11c), **Lett** (16a,90a,93a), **meta** (132d,133a), **Meta**, **mete** (9a, 11d,22b,44c,45b,98a,121c), **nete** (71c,108b,163d), **neti** (164a), **nett**, **pete** (136b), **Pete** (96b), **peto** (57a,177b), **Peto** (76a), **rete** (106c,119c), **seta** (23b,27c,73a,b,123b,153c), **seth** (98d), **Seth** (7a, 52b,68a,b,96a,98d), **seti** (34a), **Seti** (116d), **sett** (115a,156d), **tete** (61d,73b,74d), **teth** (91d), **veta** (104a), **veto** (94a,124a), **Veto**, **weta** (93c), **yeta** (84c), **zeta** (71b,91c)

- - ET **abet** (8b,15b,50a,59b,75d,81c,141d,159d), **Ahet** (49a,102a), **anet** (43c), **Apet** (97c), **aret** (128c), **beet** (175a), **blet** (64a), **diet** (14a, 54c,84c,91b,176a), **duet** (104d,171d), **evet** (48d,107a,136c,169d), **fret** (28c,35b,111c,184d), **keet** (72b), **khet** (188), **laet** (60d), **leet** (26a,38a), **meet** (11d,13d,36a,50a,81d,142d), **oket** (189), **peet** (64a), **piet** (29b,95b), **plet** (135d), **poet** (49b), **pret** (188), **pyet** (95b), **spet** (16c,57a,142c), **stet** (91b,123d,124c), **suet** (54d), **tret** (9a,178b,179d), **voet** (188), **weet** (19d), **whet** (143c,156b)

E - - T **east**, **East** (111b), **edit** (20d,49d,123a,129a,131a), **emit** (43d,49a, 53c,58d,83a,142c), **erat** (89c), **erst** (60b), **etat** (62d), **evet** (48d, 107a,136c,169d), **exit** (114d), **eyot** (82d)

EU - - **euer** (66d), **euge** (180a)

- EU - **deul** (77b), **deus** (68a,89b), **feud** (55d,126b,175b), **Geum** (76b), **jeux** (61d), **meum** (27a,89c), **Meum**, **neue** (66c), **peur** (61c), **Zeus** (135a)

- - EU **bleu** (61b), **Dieu** (61d), **eheu** (52c), **emeu** (111d), **lieu** (118c,155d)

E - - U **ecru** (17d,23d,172b), **eheu** (52c), **emeu** (111d), **Enzu** (102b), **Esau** (82c,84a,128c)

EV - - **Evan** (96a), **even** (51a,58b,79d,91d,149a,173a), **evea** (82a,95a), **ever** (9b,14b,80b), **evet** (48d,107a,136c,169d), **evil** (79c,95d,147a, 181a,185c), **evoe** (15b,130d,181c)

- EV - **bevy** (38a,58c), **Deva** (23d,42a,b,56d,77a), **Devi** (147b,153b), **hevi** (111d), **Leve** (62a), **Levi** (84a,90c), **levo** (91a), **levy** (14a, 162b), **Neva** (91b,132a), **neve** (56d,67c,70c,149b), **peva** (12d), **pevy** (91d,94c), **reve** (61c,104d), **revs** (131a), **seve** (63a,182c)

- - EV **Kiev**, **Stev** (155b)

EW - - **Ewan**, **ewer** (84d,85c,118c,181b), **ewry** (133c)

- EW - **dewa**, **dewy** (101a), **hewn**, **mewl** (180d), **mews** (154c), **news** (165c), **newt** (48d,136c,169d), **sewn**, **Tewa** (193)

- - EW **anew** (7c), **blew**, **brew** (35d), **chew** (97c), **clew** (16a,33a,77b,136b, 164d), **crew** (72a,106a), **drew**, **flew**, **grew**, **knew**, **Llew** (40c), **phew** (52c), **plew** (17c), **shew** (44c), **skew** (148a,160c,171c), **slew** (160a), **smew** (19b,46d,99a,137d), **spew** (35a,49a), **stew** (21c,44b,184d), **thew** (104c), **view** (93d,138b), **whew**

E - - W **enow** (50d,123a,158b)

EX - - **exam**, **exit** (114d)

- EX - **next** (106a), **sext** (26b,111b,147b), **text** (21c,140d)

- - EX **Amex** (184d), **apex** (39c,76c,115c,118b,159b,166a,167b), **Crex** (37a), **faex** (46a), **flex** (18a), **ibex** (67d,68a), **ilex** (77d), **obex** (22d), **plex** (60b), **spex**, **Ulex** (153c)

E - - X **eaux** (178c), **eryx** (137a), **esox** (57b)

EY - - **eyah** (95b,108d,111c), **eyas** (106c,173a), **eyer**, **eyey** (74b), **eyot** (82d), **eyra** (181d), **eyre** (23c,31b,85c), **Eyre**, **eyry** (47b,106c)

- EY - **Ceyx** (73b), **teyl** (92b,c,168c)

- - EY **ahey** (52c), **akey** (189), **brey** (194), **drey** (154c), **eyey** (74b), **fley** (63d), **Frey** (7c,68b,124d), **grey** (33c), **hoey** (114c), **joey** (86a,185d), **Joey** (96b,109c), **obey** (35c,75c), **prey** (119d,176a), **roey** (103d), **skey** (185d), **sley** (179b), **Spey**, **they** (124b), **trey** (26c,165a), **Urey** (14b,107c,138c), **whey** (100a)

E - - Y **easy** (54a), **eddy** (37d,39d,160d,180d), **edgy** (106c), **eely** (185a), **eery** (172b,180a), **eggy** (185d), **elmy**, **envy** (41b), **esay**, **espy** (44a, 142a), **ewry** (133c), **eyey** (74b), **eyry** (47b,106c)

EZ - - **ezba** (188), **ezel** (47a,85d), **Ezra** (96a)

- - EZ **chez** (14b,61a), **daez**, **Geez** (6c,51d), **Inez** (45c,183c), **juez** (152b), **knez** (123c), **oyez** (38a,39b,75b)

FA - - **Faam** (111a), **Faba**, **face** (159d,176c), **fact** (7a,128b), **fade** (181d, 183b), **fado** (121c), **fady**, **faex** (46a), **fail**, **fain** (42d,67c,183b), **fair** (17a,55d), **fait** (6d,61b), **fake** (123a,143c), **faky**, **fala** (129b), **fall** (46b,141c), **falx** (133b), **Fama** (135a), **fame** (130a), **famn** (188), **fana**, **fane** (30d,137a,162d), **fang** (167b), **fano** (51d,96b,113c,d), **faon** (33c,55a), **fard** (112d) **fare** (43c,59b,67d,123b), **farl** (138c, 140b), **farm** (165d), **faro** (65a), **fash** (140c,176a), **fass** (189), **fast** (56d,126c,141d,160c,173a,d), **fate** (42d,52a,87a,94a), **faun** (56a,

68b,137c,161a,184a), **favi** (138a,165d), **fawn** (33c), **faze** (43d)

- FA - **afar** (44c), **Afar** (6c)

- - FA **Abfa** (76b), **alfa** (70d), **gufa** (21b,99a), **Kafa** (6c), **kufa** (21b,99a), **Offa** (163d), **sofa** (44d), **tufa** (121b,177a), **Urfa** (99a)

F - - A **Faba, fala** (129b), **Fama** (135a), **fana, flea** (81b), **fora** (133a), **Frea, Fria, fuga**

F - - B **flub** (22b), **frab** (138c), **frib** (43d)

F - - C **fisc** (52c,134c), **floc** (149a)

- - FD **Wafd** (49a)

F - - D **fard** (112d), **feed** (108c), **fend** (114b,178b), **feod** (55d), **feud** (55d, 126b,175b), **find** (44a), **fled, fold, fond** (7c,94b), **food** (109a,176b), **ford** (177b), **foud** (54d,144b), **Fred** (96b), **Fuad** (54d), **fund** (6d, 101c,130c), **fyrd** (110a)

FE - - **feak** (39d,171c), **fear** (113c,155a), **feat** (7a,52d), **feed** (108c), **feel** (72a,142c), **fees** (128c), **feis** (82b), **feke, fell** (40a,58b,76c,115d, 147d), **fels** (190), **felt, feme** (181b), **fend** (114b,178b), **feod** (55d), **fern** (142a), **feru** (37a,56a,133d), **fess** (23c,51b), **fest, fete** (55d, 129b), **feud** (55d,126b,175b)

- FE - **afer** (48a,182b)

- - FE **cafe, fife** (59a,105a), **jefe** (152a), **life** (19a,177a), **nife** (37a), **orfe** (57a,b,185c), **rife** (6b,c,39d,123b), **safe** (141d,157d,174d), **wife** (154a)

F - - E **face** (159d,176c), **fade** (181d,183b), **fake** (123a,143c), **fame** (130a), **fane** (30d,137a,162d), **fare** (43c,59b,67d,123b), **fate** (42d,52a,87a, 94a), **faze** (43d), **feke, feme** (181b), **fete** (55d,129b), **fide, fife** (59a,105a), **fike** (139c), **file** (13a,127d), **fine** (49b,50a,104b,115d, 159a), **fire** (13a,43d,44b), **five flee, floe** (79b), **flue** (8b,30a), **fore** (63d,174b), **free** (44a,70d,131b), **froe** (32a,167a,179d), **fume** (129a, 149a,157a), **fuse** (98c), **fute** (51c), **fuze** (98c), **fyke** (15d)

- FF - **affy** (18b), **offa, Offa** (163d), **offs** (38c)

- - FF **baff** (69d), **biff, buff** (134c,161d), **cuff** (148a), **daff** (125d), **doff** 130a,161b), **duff** (125b), **gaff** (57c,d,152d,153a), **goff** (32d), **guff, huff** (58a), **jeff** (133d), **Jeff, jiff** (101c), **kiff** (88c), **koff** (47a), **luff** (136b), **miff** (44c), **moff** (53b,146c), **muff, piff** (24b), **puff** (180d), **raff** (75b), **riff** (131d), **Riff** (18b,102c), **ruff** (19b,33b,63d, 137a), **teff** (6c), **tiff** (126b), **toff** (40d), **tuff** (121b,177a)

F - - F **fief** (55d)

F - - G **fang** (167b), **flag** (16b,50d,82b,88c,115a,155a), **flog** (180d), **Fong** (40b), **frog** (10a,17a,126d), **Fung** (191)

F - - H **fash** (140c,176a), **fish, Foch** (63b)

FI - - **fiat** (35a,41d,48c,111b,137a), **Fiat** (83c), **fico** (169d), **fide, fief** (55d), **fife** (59a,105a), **fike** (139c), **file** (13a,127d), **fili, fill** (109b), **film** (164b), **filo, fils** (62d,150b), **find** (44a), **fine** (49b,50a,104b, 115d,159a), **fink** (19a,56c,157c), **Finn** (107d), **Fiot** (191), **fire** (13a,43d,44b), **firm** (154c,173d), **firn** (67c,70c,106c,149b), **fisc** (52c,134c), **fish, fisk** (24d,52c,134c), **fist** (80c), **five**

- FI - **Efik** (191), **ifil** (117a,168c)

- - FI **defi** (61b), **Safi** (191), **sufi** (103a,116c)

F - - I **favi** (138a,165d), **fili**, **foci** (28b), **fuci** (132c), **fuji** (84b), **Fuji** (84d)

F - - J **Funj**

F - - K **feak** (39d,171c), **fink** (19a,56c,157c), **fisk** (24d,52c,134c), **flak** (11a), **folk** (116a,169c), **fork**, **fulk** (173a), **funk** (63d,113c)

FL - - **flag** (16b,50d,82b,88c,115a,155a), **flak** (11a), **flam** (169c), **flan** (39d,40a,114d), **flap** (17b,59a,104a,118d,161a,182d), **flat** (41b, 124b,173a), **flaw**, **flax**, **flay** (147c,157c), **flea** (81b), **fled**, **flee**, **flew**, **flex** (18a), **fley** (63d), **flip** (167c), **flit** (41a), **flix**, **floc** (149a), **floe** (79b), **flog** (180d), **flop** (54a), **flot** (173a), **flow** (157b), **flub** (22b), **flue** (8b,30a), **flux** (28d,58d)

F - - L **fail**, **fall** (46b,141c), **farl** (138c,140b), **feel** (72a,142c), **fell** (40a, 58b,76c,115d,147d), **fill** (109b), **foal** (78c), **foil** (15d,55c,165b), **fool** (24a,41c,47a,146d), **foul** (173a), **fowl**, **fuel** (65c), **full** (7b, 130b), **furl** (132d)

F - - M **Faam** (111a), **farm** (165d), **film** (164b), **firm** (154c,173d), **flam** (169c), **foam** (63d,154b), **form** (54d,143c), **frim** (58d), **from**

F - - N **fain** (42d,67c,183b), **famn** (188), **faon** (33c,55a), **faun** (56a,68b, 137c,161a,184a), **fawn** (33c), **fern** (142a), **Finn** (107d), **firn** (67c, 70c,106c,149b), **flan** (39d,40a,114d), **fohn** (182b)

FO - - **foal** (78c), **foam** (63d,154b), **Foch** (63b), **foci** (28b), **fogy**, **fohn** (182b), **foil** (15d,55c,165b), **fold**, **folk** (116a,169c), **fond** (7c,94b), **Fong** (40b), **fono** (137a), **fons** (60c), **font** (16b,171d,172a), **food** (109a,176b), **fool** (24a,41c,47a,146d), **foot** (115a), **fora** (133a), **ford** (177b), **fore** (63d,174b), **fork**, **form** (54d,143c), **fort** (63d, 157d), **foss** (44d,100d), **foud** (54d,144b), **foul** (173a), **four** (26c), **fowl**, **foxy** (38b,39c,181d)

- - FO **Bufo** (166c)

F - - O **fado** (121c), **fano** (51d,96b,113c,d), **faro** (65a), **fico** (169d), **filo**, **fono** (137a)

F - - P **flap** (17b,59a,104a,118d,161a,182d), **flip** (167c), **flop** (54a), **frap** (45d,165c)

FR - - **frab** (138c), **frap** (45d,165c), **frat**, **frau** (181b), **fray** (56b,60d), **Frea**, **Fred** (96b), **free** (44a,70d,131b), **fret** (28c,35b,111c,184d), **Frey** (7c,68b,124d), **Fria**, **frib** (43d), **frim** (58d), **frit** (64c,67c), **friz** (39d), **froe** (32a,167a,179d), **frog** (10a,17a,126d), **from**, **frot** (28c), **frow** (47a,167a)

- FR - **Afra** (183c)

F - - R **fair** (17a,55d), **fear** (113c,155a), **four** (26c)

- - FS **offs** (38c)

F - - S **fass** (189), **fees** (128c), **feis** (82b), **fels** (190), **fess** (23c,51b), **fils** (62d,150b), **fons** (60c), **foss** (44d,100d), **fuss** (22b,35b)

- - FT **baft** (14a,53b), **daft** (59c), **deft** (147c), **gift** (123a), **haft** (76d), **heft** (179d), **Heft**, **left** (42c), **lift** (49b), **loft** (14c,69d,104b,178b), **raft** (27b,33c,58c,75b), **reft** (32a,42c,44d,167b), **rift** (30c,32a,58a, 110d), **sift** (140d,142c,146b), **soft** (48b,95d,99d,163a), **Taft** (29d), **tuft** (24b,32d,38c), **waft** (20d,58c), **weft** (39a,165a,184b), **yuft** (135c)

F - - T **fact** (7a,128b), **fait** (6d,61b), **fast** (56d,126c,141d,160c,173a,d), **feat** (7a,52d), **felt**, **fest**, **Fiat** (83c), **fiat** (35a,41d,48c,111b,137a), **Fiot** (191), **fist** (80c), **flat** (41b,124b,173a), **flit** (41a), **flot** (173a), **font** (16b,171d,172a), **foot** (115a), **fort** (63d,157d), **frat**, **fret** (28c, 35b,111c,184d), **frit** (64c,67c), **frot** (28c), **fust** (105c,143b)

FU - - **Fuad** (54d), **fuci** (132c), **fuel** (65c), **fuga**, **fugu** (84b), **fuji** (84b), **Fuji** (84d), **fulk** (173a), **full** (7b,130b), **fume** (129a,149a,157a), **fumy**, **fund** (6d,101c,130c), **Fung** (191), **funk** (63d,113c), **furl** (132d), **fury** (157a), **fuse** (98c), **fuss** (22b,35b), **fust** (105c,143b), **fute** (51c), **fuze** (98c), **fuzz** (45d)

F - - U **feru** (37a,56a,133d), **frau** (181b), **fugu** (84b)

F - - W **flaw**, **flew**, **flow** (157b), **frow** (47a,167a)

F - - X **faex** (46a), **falx** (133b), **flax**, **flex** (18a), **flix**, **flux** (28d,58d)

FY - - **fyke** (15d), **fyrd** (110a)

- - FY **affy** (18b), **defy** (28d), **Dufy** (63a)

F - - Y **fady**, **faky**, **flay** (147c,157c), **fley** (63d), **fogy**, **foxy** (38b,39c,181d), **fray** (56b,60d), **Frey** (7c,68b,124d), **fumy**, **fury** (157a)

F - - Z **friz** (39d), **fuzz** (45d)

GA - - **gaal** (23b,174d), **gabe** (162a), **gabi** (162a), **gaby** (59c,146d), **gade** **Gaea** (47d,69a), **Gael** (28a,96c,138d), **gaff** (57c,d,152d,153a), **gage** (28d,98a,119c,d), **gagl** (160b), **Gaia** (47d,69a), **gail** (23b, 174d), **Gail** (183d), **gain** (7a,b,124a,181d), **gait** (96b,179a), **gajo** (107c), **gala** (55d), **Gala** (191), **gale** (181d), **gali** (6c), **gall** (19a, 28c,29b,82c,160c,176a), **galt**, **Gama** (121c), **game** (64d,154a), **gamp** (172a), **gane** (185b), **gang** (38c), **Gano** (132d), **gaol** (123d), **Gaol** (164a), **Gaon** (85b), **gape** (185b), **gapo** (60a), **gapy**, **gara** (190), **garb** (32c,46a), **gare** (61b,c,62c,127c,184b), **Garm** (178c), **garn** (67d,185b), **Garo** (88c), **Gary**, **gash** (40a), **gasp** (113c), **gata** (143c), **gate** (51a,121b), **Gath** (117a), **gaub** (116c), **gaud** (169d), **gaue** (67a), **Gaul** (10a,60d,63c), **gaup**, **gaur** (112c,181c), **gaus** (67a), **gaut** (88b,103d,132a), **gave**, **gawd** (169c), **gawk** (146d), **gawp**, **Gaza** (117a), **gaze**, **gazi**, **gazy**

- GA - **Agag** (18c,86c,137a), **agal** (17c,36d), **Agao** (6c,73c), **agar** (7d,28c, 39c,103c,141c), **Agau** (73c), **Agaz** (193), **egad** (100a,109a), **ngai** (48a,159c), **ngan**, **ogam** (82b,c), **Sgau** (88c)

- - GA **alga** (141b,c), **baga** (171b), **bega** (188), **biga** (171d), **boga** (57d, 180b), **fuga**, **giga** (56a,105a), **goga** (24a), **hoga** (144b), **inga** (145d, 170a), **Jaga** (191), **juga** (27a), **mega** (34b,c), **muga**, **naga** (13d, 33a,55b,127c), **Naga** (24c,77a,88c,176d), **Olga** (135c,183c), **paga** (117a), **pega** (57a,130a,158b), **raga** (56d,105a), **riga** (118b), **ruga** (59b,185a), **saga** (79b,91a,138a,157a,161b,c,168a), **Saga**, **soga** (70d,152b), **Soga** (191), **toga** (132d,133a,b), **vega** (152c), **Vega** (155b), **Wega** (155b), **yoga** (10b,13c,77a), **Yuga** (76d), **zyga** (134b)

G - - A **Gaea** (47d,69a), **Gaia** (47d,69a), **gala** (55d), **Gala** (191), **Gama** (121c), **gara** (190), **gata** (143c), **Gaza** (117a), **gena** (29b), **geta** (84b, 145a), **giga** (56a, 105a), **gila** (93b), **Gita**, **Gjoa** (144d), **glia** (106c), **goga** (24a), **gola** (27b,40c,70c,157a), **Goma** (191), **Gona** (106d), **gora** (81c), **Goya** (151d), **gufa** (21b,99a),

Guha (191), **gula** (90a,101a,165b), **guna** (106a,137b)

-GB- **Egba** (191), **Egbo** (141d)

G--B **garb** (32c,46a), **gaub** (116c), **gerb** (56d,143d), **glib** (58d,149a,177c), **glub**, **grab** (105b,142a,149b), **grub** (88d), **guib** (11a)

G--D **gaud** (169d), **gawd** (169c), **gedd** (140a), **geld** (162b), **Gerd** (63c), **gild** (14a,49c,69c,98b), **gird** (32c,50a,123a,160a), **glad** (85c), **gled** (19a,52a,87a), **goad** (80b,154b), **gold**, **Gond**, **good**, **grad** (28b), **grid** (17a,70d,119b,156d)

GE-- **geal** (47d,163c), **gean** (29c), **gear** (32c,112a,167b), **geat** (77d,101a), **Geat** (138a), **gedd** (140a), **Geez** (6c,51d), **gein** (67d), **geld** (162b), **gelt** (101c), **gena** (29b), **gene** (54a,76b), **Gene** (96b), **gens** (42d, 132d), **gent**, **genu** (6b,18a,87a,89c), **gerb** (56d,143d), **Gerd** (63c), **Gere** (183c), **Geri** (183c), **germ** (17d,99c,134d), **gest** (7c,41d,52d, 133c), **geta** (84b,145a), **gett** (44d), **Geum** (76b)

-GE- **aged** (110a), **agee** (13d,15c,38d), **ager** (47c,56a,89b,c,131d,133b), **Eger** (49a), **ogee** (101a,b,120b)

--GE **ange** (61a), **auge** (123c,132b), **cage** (36a), **doge** (95b,175b), **edge** (22a,96d,131c,143c,146b), **euge** (180a), **gage** (28d,98a,119c,d), **huge**, **Inge** (24d,67d,117c,119c), **kuge** (84c), **loge** (164a), **luge** (148a), **mage** (95b), **page** (51b,59b,142d,159b), **rage** (10c,30c,157a, 161d), **sage** (13a,90d,100c,141c,145c,180b,183a), **tige** (118a), **urge** (42d,46b,79d,80a,b,81c,124a,150a), **wage** (27a,115b), **yage** (23a)

G--E **gabe** (162a), **gade**, **gage** (28d,98a,119c,d), **gale** (181d), **game** (64d, 154a), **gane** (185b), **gape** (185b), **gare** (61b,c,62c,127c, 184b), **gate** (51a,121b), **gaue** (67a), **gave**, **gaze**, **gene** (54a,76b), **Gene** (96b), **ghee** (24d), **gibe** (8a,42c,84d,100d,138c,144c,149b), **Gide** (63a), **gime** (77d), **gite** (62a,118d), **give** (79d,123a), **glee** (99a, 150b), **glue** (7b,156a), **gone** (6b,15c,42c,44c,114d), **gore** (115d, 117c,154c,169c), **guze** (128d), **gybe** (144c), **gyle** (23b,174d), **gyne** (34b,55b,183c), **gyre** (31b,171b), **gyve** (55d,143b)

G--F **gaff** (57c,d,152d,153a), **goaf** (104b), **goff** (32d), **golf** (154a), **goof**, **Graf** (37c,66b,67a,107c,186b), **guff**, **gulf** (6c)

-GG- **eggs** (112a), **eggy** (185d)

--GG **dagg** (118c), **hagg**, **hogg** (144a), **jagg**, **magg** (95b), **migg** (96c), **nogg** (48d), **tegg** (143d,171d), **vugg** (28a,66a,132b), **Wegg** (111d), **wigg**, **yegg** (24c)

G--G **gang** (38c), **Gheg** (8c), **glug**, **gong**, **grig** (38c,70d,93a), **grog** (92d, 153d)

GH-- **ghat** (32d,88b,103d,132a), **ghee** (24d), **Gheg** (8c), **Ghes** (193), **ghor** (174b), **ghos** (30b), **Ghuz** (171a)

-GH- **agha** (35a,171a)

--GH **dagh** (76d), **hegh**, **high**, **Hugh** (96a), **Lugh** (28b), **Magh** (102a), **nigh** (106a), **ough**, **pugh**, **sigh**, **vugh** (28a,66a,136b), **yogh** (10c, 185a)

G--H **gash** (40a), **Gath** (117a), **gish** (102c), **gosh**, **Goth** (16c), **gush** (35a, 154c)

GI-- **gibe** (8a,42c,84d,100d,138c,144c,149b), **Gide** (63a), **gier** (47b),

gift (123a), **giga** (56a,105a), **gila** (93b), **gild** (14a,49c,69c,98b), **gill** (22d), **gilo** (48a), **gilt** (69c,77c,151b,185d), **gime** (77d), **gimp** (169d), **gink** (48b), **gird** (32c,50a,123a,160a), **girl**, **giro** (38c,83c, 167c), **girt** (50a), **gish** (102c), **gist** (95c,118c), **Gita**, **gite** (62a, 118d), **give** (79d,123a)

- GI - **Agib** (12a,42d), **agio** (52c,60a,101c,123a), **Agis** (86d), **Egil** (107d), **egis** (14b,d,115a,124d,144b,154a,161a)

- - GI **Bugi** (191), **hagi** (84b), **jogi** (76d), **magi** (123c), **Magi** (95b,116c, 183a), **ragi** (28b), **sugi** (84b), **vagi** (38b), **yogi** (76d)

G - - I **gabi** (162a), **gali** (6c), **gazi**, **Geri** (183c), **goai** (106d,168c), **gobi**, **Gobi** (42d), **goli** (105c), **Guti**, **gyri** (22d,131b)

GJ - - **Gjoa** (144d)

G - - J **gunj** (70c)

G - - K **gawk** (146d), **gink** (48b), **gowk** (146d)

GL - - **glad** (85c), **gled** (19a,52a,87a), **glee** (99a,150b), **glen** (43c), **glia** (106c), **glib** (58d,149a,177c), **glim**, **glis** (45c), **glom** (155d,160d, 178c), **glow** (144c), **glub**, **glue** (7b,156a), **glug**, **glum** (102c,159a), **glut** (52c,70a,137c,159d)

- GL - **agla** (7a), **iglu** (51c,149b), **ogle** (9d,53c,91a,93d,148c)

- - GL **gagl** (160b)

G - - L **gaal** (23b,174d), **Gael** (28a,96c,138d), **gagl** (160b), **gail** (23b,174d), **Gail** (183d), **gall** (19a,28c,29b,82c,160c,176a), **gaol** (123d), **Gaol** (164a), **Gaul** (10a,60d,63c), **geal** (47d,163c), **gill** (22d), **girl**, **goal** (8b,109b,120b,125d), **goel** (15a,75c), **Goll**, **goul** (102a), **gowl** (102a, 140d,185b), **gull** (32d,41c,42a,72c,99b,141a)

G - - M **Garm** (178c), **germ** (99c,134d), **Geum** (76b), **glim**, **glom** (155d, 160d,178c), **glum** (102c,159a), **gram** (29d,99b,148d,160d,180a), **Gram**, **grim** (156a), **grum** (102c), **Guam**

GN - - **gnar** (72a), **gnat** (59a,81b,99c), **gnaw** (20a,107a,178b)

- GN - **agni** (88a,89c), **Agni** (56d,68b)

- - GN **sign** (121c,146c)

G - - N **gain** (7a,b,124a,181d), **Gaon** (85b), **garn** (67d,185b), **gean** (29c), **gein** (67d), **glen** (43c), **Goan**, **goon** (157c,163c), **gown**, **gran**, **grin**, **guan** (151b), **Gwyn** (40c,50b)

GO - - **goad** (80b,154b), **goaf** (104b), **goai** (106d,168c), **goal** (8b,109b, 120b,125d), **Goan**, **goat** (135a), **gobi**, **Gobi** (42d), **gobo** (84d), **goby** (57d), **goel** (15a,75c), **goer**, **goff** (32d), **goga** (24a), **gogo** (16b,24a, 149c), **Gogo** (191), **gola** (27b,40c,70c,157a), **gold**, **golf** (154a) **goli** (105c), **Goll**, **Golo** (191), **Goma** (191), **Gona** (106d), **Gond**, **gone** (6b,15c,42c,44c,114d), **gong**, **good**, **goof**, **goon** (157c,163c), **Goop** (107d), **goor**, **gora** (81c), **gore** (115d,117c,154c,169c), **gory**, **gosh**, **Goth** (16c,163d), **goul** (102a), **gour** (112c,181c), **gout**, **gowk** (146d), **gowl** (102a,140d,185b), **gown**, **Goya** (151d)

- GO - **agog** (47b,52c,86b), **agon** (12c,36c,41b,55d),71b), **egol** (11b), **Igor** (135d), **Ogor** (170d)

- - GO **ango** (171a), **Argo** (12c,36b,c), **bago** (13d), **bogo** (117a, 168c), **Bogo** (191), **bygo** (114c), **Dago**, **ergo** (164b), **gogo** (16b,24a,

149c), **Gogo** (191), **Hugo** (63a,96a), **Iago** (54b,111d,143c), **kago** (113a), **lago** (83b,152b), **mogo** (74b), **Pogo** (121c), **sago** (54c, 59b,113b,125b,155c), **sego** (24b,25a,92b,174c), **upgo** (13c), **zogo** (136a)

G - - O **gajo** (107c), **Gajo, Gano** (132d), **gapo** (60a), **Garo** (88c), **gilo** (48a), **giro** (38c,83c,167c), **gobo** (84d), **gogo** (16b,24a,149c), **Gogo** (191), **Golo** (191), **grao** (189), **guao** (168c,169b), **Gulo** (183c), **gyro** (34d)

- GP - **Ogpu** (135d)

G - - P **gamp** (172a), **gasp** (113c), **gaup, gawp, gimp** (169d), **Goop** (107d), **gulp** (46a,79d,160a), **Gump** (43b), **grip** (159a)

GR - - **grab** (105b,142a,149b), **grad** (28b), **Graf** (37c,66b,67a,107c,186b), **gram** (29d,99b,148d,160d,180a), **grao** (189), **gras** (78b), **gray** (33c, 77c), **Gray** (50c), **gres** (156d), **grew, grey** (33c), **grid** (17a,70d, 119b,156d), **grig** (38c,70d,93a), **grim** (156a), **grin, grip** (159a), **gris** (61d), **grit** (137a,b), **grog** (92d,153d), **gros** (47a,53d,146c), **Gros** (63a), **grot** (27d), **grow** (154b), **grub** (43c,88d), **grum** (102c), **Grus** (36b,c,38b)

- GR - **agra** (26d,34d), **Agra** (161b), **agri** (89b), **agro** (149d), **ogre** (67a, 102a)

G - - R **gaur** (112c,181c), **gear** (32c,167b), **Ghor** (174b), **gier** (47b), **gnar** (72a), **goer, goor, gour** (112c,181c) **guar** (46c,59d), **guhr** (47d)

- - GS **eggs** (112a), **togs** (32c)

G - - S **gaus** (67a), **gens** (42d,132d), **Gens, Ghes** (193), **ghos** (30b), **glis** (45c), **Glis, gras** (78b), **gres** (156d), **gris** (61d), **gros** (47a,53d,146c), **Gros** (63a), **Grus** (36b,c,38b), **gyps, Gyps** (71d)

- - GT **togt** (77c), **Vogt**

G - - T **gait** (96b,179a), **galt, gaut** (88b,103d,132a), **geat** (77d,101a), **Geat** (138a), **gelt** (101c), **gent, gest** (7c,41d,52d,133c), **gett** (44d), **ghat** (32d,88b,103d,132a), **gift** (123a), **gilt** (69c,77c,151b), **girt** (50a), **gist** (95c,118c), **glut** (52c,70a,137c,159d), **gnat** (59a,81b,99c), **goat** (135a), **grit** (137a,b), **grot** (27d), **gust**

GU - - **Guam, guan** (151b), **guao** (168c,169b), **guar** (46c,59d), **gufa** (21b, 99a), **guff, gugu, Guha** (191), **guhr** (47d), **guib** (11a), **gula** (90a, 101a,165b), **gulf** (6c), **gull** (32d,41c,42a,72c,99b,141a), **Gulo** (183c), **gulp** (46a,79d,160a), **Gump** (43b), **guna** (106a,137b), **gunj** (70c), **guru** (77b), **gush** (35a,154c), **gust, Guti, guze** (128d)

- GU - **agua** (152d,166c,178c), **ague** (30a,55d,95c), **ogum** (82b)

- - GU **degu** (132c), **fugu** (84b), **gugu, kagu** (106c), **Pegu** (24c,102a,127d)

G - - U **genu** (6b,18a,87a,89c), **gugu, guru** (77b)

GW - - **Gwyn** (40c,50b)

G - - W **glow** (144c), **gnaw** (20a,107a,178b), **grew, grow** (154b)

GY - - **gybe** (144c), **gyle** (23b,174d), **gyne** (34b,55b,183c), **gyps, Gyps** (71d), **gyre** (31b,171b), **gyri** (22d,131b), **gyro** (34d), **gyve** (55d, 143b)

- - GY **algy, Algy** (96b), **bogy** (153a), **cagy** (178b), **dogy** (46d,103c), **edgy** (106c), **eggy** (185d), **fogy, logy** (46d), **Nagy** (78d), **orgy** (26d,130d, 137c), **pogy** (57a,88a,98d,103c), **sagy**

G - - Y **gaby** (59c,146d), **Gaby, gapy, Gary, gazy, goby** (57d), **gory, gray** (33c,77c), **Gray** (50c), **grey** (33c)

G - - Z **Geez** (6c,51d), **Ghuz** (171a)

HA - - **Haab** (97d), **haaf** (57d), **haak** (57b,178a), **haar** (139c), **haba** (151d), **Habe** (191), **hack** (40a,77c,184d) **hade** (66a,148c,173c), **hadj** (98b,118a), **haec** (90a,164c), **haem** (122b), **haft** (76d), **hagg, hagi** (84b), **haha** (55c,159c), **haik** (57b,65b,108a), **hail** (6d,15a,71d), **hair** (56b,164d), **haje** (33a,48d), **hake** (57a,b), **hakh** (46d), **hako** (115b), **haku** (86d), **hala** (112b), **hale** (125b), **Hale** (9d,131a), **half** (101a), **hall** (37b,114d), **halm, halo** (14d,31b,92a,107b,131d), **Hals** (47a), **halt** (13b,28a,38d,156d), **hami** (78a), **hand** (60c,114c,115d,184c), **hang** (160a), **hank** (147c), **Hano** (125b), **Hans** (66d,96a), **hant** (67a), **Hapi** (66a,107b,136a), **hapu** (106d), **Harb** (191), **hard** (109b), **hare** (91b,132c), **hark** (92d), **harl** (16b,56b,59a), **harm** (40b,81a), **harp** (105a,129a), **hart** (41d,154d), **hase** (74d) **hash, hasp** (31d, 54d,153c), **hast, hate** (6a,43a), **hath, Hati** (48d), **haul** (27b,45d), **have, hawk** (19c,115c), **hayz, haze** (100c,174d), **hazy** (174b)

- HA - **Ahab** (18c,26c,85b,86d,100d,116a,180b), **Ahaz** (86d), **Bhar** (191), **bhat** (80c), **chaa** (162b), **chab** (184a), **Chad** (158b), **chai** (72d), **cham** (20a,29d), **Cham** (8c), **chan** (26c,130c), **chap** (55b), **char** (24d,26c, 170b), **chat** (9b,19c,161c), **chaw** (97c), chay (48a,128d), **dhak** (48a, 169a), **dhal** (12b), **dhan** (124c), **dhao** (24c), **Dhar, dhaw** (125a), **ghat** (32d,88b,103d,132a), **khan** (7c,26c,81b,93d,116c,123c,130c, 166c), **khar** (189), **khas** (153a), **khat** (105d), **Phad** (155b), **shad** (27d,57a,b,c), **shag** (73b,105b,161d,166d), **shah** (116c), **sham** (41c, 55b,60d,80a,123a,b,146d), **Shan** (13c,80d,88c,101d), **shap, shat** (87d), **shaw** (164b), **Shaw** (50c,53b), **shay** (110c), **Thai** (146a), **than** (35b), **thar** (68a,76d), **that** (42b,124b,129c), **thaw, wham** (157c), **what** (129c), **whau** (107a,168c)

- - HA **agha** (35a,171a), **Akha** (86a,c), **Asha** (191), **Azha** (155b), **epha** (75c), **Guha** (191), **haha** (55c,159c), **Isha** (174a), **kaha** (123d), **maha** (28c,88c,136d), **moha** (42b,83d), **ocha** (189), **paha** (67b), **poha** (74c), **saha, taha** (179b), **tcha** (162c), **Usha** (16a,150c),

H - - A **haba** (151d), **Haba, haha** (55c,159c), **hala** (112b), **Hela** (93c), **Hera** (69c,85d,110b,126b,186b,d), **hila** (53c), **Hima** (191), **hoga** (144b), **hoja** (166b), **hola** (74c,152b), **hora** (22a,40b), **Hova** (95a), **Hoya** (14d), **Hsia** (30b,47c), **huia** (19a,106d), **hula** (74b), **Hupa** (192), **hura** (20a,137a), **Hura, Hyla** (10a,166d,169b)

H - - B **Haab** (97d), **Harb** (191), **herb** (58b,158b), **hobb** (124b), **hubb** (118b)

H - - C **haec** (90a,164c)

H - - D **hand** (60c,114c,115d,184c), **hard** (109b), **head** (29d), **heed** (14c, 75b,109b), **held, herd** (39a,46c,72a), **Hild, hind** (15b,41d,45a), **hold** (95c,124c,130d), **hood** (38a,74d), **hued**

HE - - **head** (29d), **heaf** (144a), **heal, heap** (117d), **hear** (75b,c,92d), **heat, Hebe** (39c,69c,186b), **heck** (100a), **heed** (14c,75b,109b), **heel, Heep** (41a,43b), **heer** (47a,184b,185b), **heft** (179d), **Heft, hegh, Hehe** (191), **heil** (74b), **hein** (52c,61c), **heir, Hela** (93c), **held, helm** (144d,165d), **help** (14a), **hemi** (122c), **hemo** (34a,122b), **hemp** (26a, 37a,56a,133d), **hens** (121d), **Hera** (69c,85d,110b),126b,186b,d), **herb** (58b,158b), **herd** (39a,46c,72a), **here, herl** (16b,59a), **hero**

(42b,124d,137b), **Hero** (90c), **Herr** (66c), **hers** (124c), **hest** (35a), **Heth** (77c), **hevi** (111d), **hewn**

-HE- **ahem, Ahet** (49a,102a), **ahey** (52c), **bhel** (126d), **chee** (189), **chef, chek** (59c), **Chen** (149b), **cher** (61b), **chew** (97c), **chez** (14b,61a), **eheu** (52c), **ghee** (24d), **Gheg** (8c), **Ghes** (193), **Hehe** (191), **Khem** (113c), **khet** (188), **phew** (52c), **rhea** (37a,56a,111d), **Rhea** (19b,68d, 87c,103c,186b), **Rhee** (87c), **shea** (25a,168c,d), **shed** (27a,90c,101b, 144b), **shee** (82b), **Shem** (107c), **Shen** (68a), **sher** (65d,165c), **shew** (44c), **Thea** (162c), **theb** (188), **thee** (124b), **them** (124b), **then, thew** (104c), **they** (124b), **whee, when** (180d), **whet** (143c,156b), **whew, whey** (100a)

--HE **ache** (79a,112d,185b), **Hehe** (191), **Hohe** (192), **tche** (13d,30b,105a)

H--E **Habe** (191), **hade** (66a,148c,173c), **haje** (33a,48d), **hake** (57a,b), **hale** (125b), **Hale** (9d,131a), **hare** (91b,132c), **hase** (74d), **hate** (6a, 43a), **have, haze** (100c,174d), **Hebe** (39c,69c,186b), **Hehe** (191), **here, hide** (53a), **hike, hipe** (185a), **hire** (49d,50b,91b,130a), **hive** (17c), **Hohe** (192), **hole** (6c,11b,110d,118c,147a), **home, hone** (110a,143c,180d), **hope** (13d,52d), **hose** (156c), **hove** (92a,157d), **howe** (77d), **Howe** (17a,82a), **huge, hule** (23a,134c), **Hume** (50c), **huse** (180c), **hyde** (188), **Hyde** (45a), **hyke, hyle** (97c), **hype** (185a)

H--F **haaf** (57d), **half** (101a), **heaf** (144a), **hoof** (173a), **huff** (58a)

H--G **hagg, hang** (160a), **hing** (13c), **hogg** (144a), **hong** (30b), **hung**

--HH **sahh** (188)

H--H **hakh** (46d), **hash, hath, hegh, Heth** (77c), **high, hish, hoch,** (52c, 66c), **Hoch, hoth, Hoth** (20c), **Hugh** (96a), **hunh?, hush** (17b,146c)

HI-- **hick** (185d), **hide** (53a), **hien** (30b), **hier** (63a,185d), **high, hike, hiku** (57a,106d,138a), **hila** (53c), **Hild, hill, hilo** (74c), **hilt** (73c), **Hima** (191), **hind** (15b,41d,45a), **hing** (13c), **hino** (106d,168c), **hint** (9a,39c,159a), **hipe** (185a), **hire** (49d,50b,91b,130a), **hiro, hish, hiss** (146a), **hist** (25c,93d), **hive** (17c)

-HI- **Ahir** (27b), **Bhil** (191), **chia** (136d), **chib** (167a), **chic** (148d), **chid, ch'ih** (188), **chil, chin, Chin** (30b), **chip** (69d), **chir** (29b,116d), **chit** (67b,98c,108b,116c,177c), **chiv** (87a), **jhil, ohia** (74c,168c), **Ohio, Phil** (96b), **phit** (24b), **phiz** (54a), **Rhin, shih** (189), **Shik** (171a), **shim** (91d,144c,162a,179d), **shin** (91a,d,140b,143c), **ship, shir** (36d, 65d,165c), **thin** (43b,c,148b), **this** (42b,124b), **Whig, whim** (26c, 54c,108c), **whin** (64c,70a,132b,181d), **whip** (58c,88d), **whir** (25c, 181a), **whit** (166c), **whiz** (25c)

--HI **bahi** (60c), **Bahi, pahi** (21b,26a), **tchi, Tchi, tshi, Tshi** (69c)

H--I **hagi** (84b), **hami** (78a), **Hapi** (66a,107b,136a), **Hati** (48d), **heli** (74b), **hemi** (122c), **hevi** (111d), **Holi** (77a), **hopi** (33c), **Hopi** (12c, 102c,125b), **hoti**

H--J **hadj** (98b,118a)

H--K **haak** (57b,178a), **hack** (40a,77c,184d), **haik** (57b,65b,108a), **hank** (147c), **hark** (92d), **hawk** (19c,115c), **heck** (100a), **hick** (185d), **hock** (91a,115b,182b,c), **hoek** (39d), **honk** (70a), **hook** (27b,39d), **howk** (139b), **huck** (167d), **hulk** (144d,173d), **hunk, husk** (53a,78d, 142a)

HL-- **Hler** (141a)

- - HL **buhl** (81a), **kohl** (53c), **kuhl** (53c)

H - - L **hail** (6d,15a,71d), **hall** (37b,114d), **harl** (16b 56b,59a), **haul** (27b, 45d), **heal, heel, herl** (16b,59a), **hill, howl** (39b), **hull** (141d,142a, 144c,d), **hurl** (167c)

H - - M **haem** (122b), **halm, harm** (40b,81a), **helm** (144d,165d), **holm** (77d, 82d,109a)

- HN - **ohne** (66d,183b)

- - HN **behn** (137d), **fohn** (182b), **John** (11c,96a,121a,186b)

H - - N **hein** (52c,61c), **hewn, hien** (30b), **hoen** (189), **hoon** (190), **horn** (11a, 105a,170b,182a), **hymn** (150c)

HO - - **hoar** (63d,71a,181a), **hoax** (41c,122a), **hobb** (124b), **hobo** (168a, 174b), **hoch** (52c,66c), **hock** (91a,115b,182b,c), **hoek** (39d), **hoen** (189), **hoer, hoey** (114c), **hoga** (144b), **hogg** (144a), **Hohe** (192), **hoja** (166b), **hoju** (84b), **hola** (74c,152b), **hold** (95c,124c,130d), **hole** (6c,11b,110d,118c,147a), **Holi** (77a), **holm** (77d,82d,109a), **holt** (36d,119b,184b), **holy, home, homo** (122d), **homy** (38b), **hone** (110a,143c,180d), **hong** (30b), **honk** (70a), **hood** (38a,74d), **hoof** (173a), **hook** (27b,39d), **hoon** (190), **hoop** (181b), **hoot** (112c), **hope** (13d,52d), **hopi** (33c), **Hopi** (12c,102c,125b), **hops** (17c), **hora** (22a, 40b), **horn** (11a,105a,170b,182a), **hors** (62b), **hose** (156c), **host** (13a,51d,104c), **Hoth** (20c), **hoti, hour, Hova** (95a), **hove** (92a, 157d), **howe** (77d), **Howe** (17a,82a), **howk** (139b), **howl** (39b), **Hoya** (14d)

- HO - **Ahom** (88c), **ahoy** (106a), **b'hoy** (134b), **chob** (23c), **chol** (118d), **Chol** (192), **chop** (98a), **chor** (164b), **chou** (61b), **Chou** (30b), **chow** (45a), **choy** (48a,128d), **dhow** (88d,111c,175d), **Ghor** (174b), **ghos** (30b), **khot**, **mhor** (180b), **ohoy** (106a), **phon** (94a), **phoo, phos, phot** (173b), **rhob** (64a,85c), **Shoa** (6c), **shod, shoe** (166a), **shoo** (46b,67a,138b), **shop, shoq** (169a), **shor** (136d), **Shor** (162b), **shot** (9d,43d,90c,174d), **shou** (41d), **show** (42b,44c,96b), **thob** (128a), **Thor** (7c,68c,99c,100c,109c,165b), **Thos** (84a,181c), **thou** (124b), **whoa** (156d), **whom** (42b), **whoo**

- - HO **baho** (122a), **boho** (117a,179d), **coho** (136d), **echo** (130b,d), **Echo** (105d), **icho** (67b), **kiho** (82a), **moho** (19a,78a), **otho** (133a), **paho** (122a), **peho** (19b,102c,106d), **Saho** (6c), **soho!, Soho** (93c), **toho** (79a)

H - - O **hako** (115b), **halo** (14d,31b,92a,107b,131d), **Hano** (125b), **hemo** (34a,122b), **hero** (42b,124d,137b), **Hero** (90c), **hilo** (74c), **hino** (106d,168c), **hiro, hobo** (168a,174b), **homo** (168a,174b), **Hugo** (63a,96a), **huso** (180c), **hypo** (117b)

H - - P **harp** (105a,129a), **hasp** (31d,54d,153c), **heap** (117d), **Heep** (41a, 43b), **help** (14a), **hemp** (26a,37a,56a,133d), **hoop** (181b), **hump** (124d)

- HR - **Shri** (17c,166c)

- - HR **Bohr** (14b,40d,138c), **buhr** (180d), **Duhr** (155b), **guhr** (47d), **lehr** (67c,112a), **mahr** (103a), **mohr** (65d), **rohr** (72d), **Ruhr, sehr** (66d), **tahr** (68a,76d), **tehr** (27c,68a)

H - - R **haar** (139c), **hair** (56b,164d), **hear** (75b,c,92d), **heer** (47a,184b, 185b), **heir, Herr** (66c), **hier** (63a,185d), **Hier** (141a), **hoar** (63d,

	71a,181a), hoer, hour
HS - -	**Hsia** (30b,47c)
H - - S	**Hals** (47a), **Hans** (66d,96a), **hens** (121d), **hers** (124c), **hiss** (146a), **hops** (17c), **hors** (62b), **hyps**
- - HT	**acht** (66c), **baht** (146a)
H - - T	**haft** (76d), **halt** (13b,28a,38d,156d), **hant** (67a), **hart** (41d,154d), **hast, heat, heft** (179d), **Heft, hest** (35a), **hilt** (73c), **hint** (9a,39c, 159a), **hist** (25c,93d), **holt** (36d,119b,184b), **hoot** (112c), **host** (13a, 51d,104c), **hunt** (141c), **hurt**
HU - -	**hubb** (118b), **huck** (167d), **hued, huff** (58a), **huge, Hugh** (96a), **Hugo** (63a,96a), **huia** (19a,106d), **hula** (74b), **hule** (23a,134c), **hulk** (144d,173d), **hull** (141d,142a,144c,d), **hulu** (55b), **Hume** (50c), **hump** (124d), **hung, hunh?, hunk, hunt** (141c), **Hupa** (192), **hura** (20a,137a), **Hura, hurl** (167c), **hurt, huse** (180c), **hush** (17b,146c), **husk** (53a,78d,142a), **huso** (180c), **huzz**
- HU -	**ahum, bhut** (67a), **chub** (40c,154c), **Chud** (191), **chug** (53a), **chum,** (38d), **Chun** (30c), **chut!, Ghuz** (171a), **jhum, Phud** (110b), **phut** (24b), **Phut** (110b), **rhum** (8c), **Rhus** (159a), **shul** (161a), **shun** (15a, 51b,52a), **shut, thud, thug** (65a), **thus** (149c), **whun** (64c,70a)
- - HU	**ichu** (10b,70d), **jehu** (46b), **Jehu** (18c), **kahu** (14d), **Oahu, Rahu** (42b,48b), **sahu** (153d), **tchu**
H - - U	**haku** (86d), **hapu** (106d), **hiku** (57a,106d,138a), **hoju** (84b), **hulu** (55b)
- HV -	**IHVH** (159d), **JHVH** (159d), **YHVH** (159d)
- HW -	**JHWH** (159d), **YHWH** (159d)
H - - X	**hoax** (41c,122c)
HY - -	**hyde** (188), **Hyde** (45a), **hyke, Hyla** (10a,166d,169b), **hyle** (97c), **hymn** (150c), **hype** (185a), **hypo** (117b), **hyps**
- HY -	**whyo** (59d,65a)
- - HY	**achy, ashy** (113a,178a)
H - - Y	**hazy** (174b), **hoey** (114c), **holy, homy** (38b)
H - - Z	**Hayz, huzz**
IA - -	**Iago** (54b,111d,143c), **Ialu** (48d), **Iamb** (59c)
- IA -	**bias** (43b,123a), **diad** (113a), **dial** (25c), **dian** (46c,130d,170b), **Dian** (68d,69a,c,102b), **Diau** (192), **fiat** (35a,41d,48c,111b,137a), **Fiat** (83c), **kiak** (51c), **Liam** (181d), **liar** (98d), **Lias** (66a), **miam** (14d), **mian** (97c,147b,166b), **Miao** (30a,b), **mias** (111a), **Mias, miau** (27b,99b), **miaw** (27b,99b), **Nias** (82d), **Piaf** (63c), **piat** (11a), **piay** (98b), **rial** (190), **siak** (72d), **sial** (112a), **Siam** (163d,181a), **Tiam, tiao, tiar** (39a,75a,121a), **vial** (148c)
- - IA	**Abia** (18d,137a), **akia** (74c), **amia** (22c,170d), **apia** (121b), **aria** (8b,98c,150a,c), **Asia** (48a), **chia** (136d), **Elia** (88a,115d), **eria** (13d, 146d), **Fria, Gaia** (47d,69a), **glia** (106c), **Hsia** (30b,47c), **huia** (19a, 106d), **ilia** (21d,77b,115d), **inia** (9b,109b), **Inia** (28c,45b), **ixia** (37a), **Maia** (76b,109a,153b,155b,177c), **Naia** (33a), **obia** (55d), **ohia** (74c, 168c), **okia** (190), **raia** (107d), **Raia** (147b), **Soia, tsia** (162c), **Uria** (14c,16d)

I - - A **idea** (54c,108c,124a,164d), **ijma** (103b), **ikra** (27d), **Ilia** (21d,77b, 115d), **Inca** (14b,30a), **inga** (145d), **inia** (9b,109b), **Inia** (28c,45b), **Inka** (193), **Iola, Iona** (28a,82d), **iota** (71a,85c,91c,114c,166c,176a, 180d), **Iowa** (193), **Irra** (68c,178a), **isba** (135c), **Isha** (174a), **Itea** (145d,160c,181d), **Itza** (192), **ixia** (37a)

IB - - **Ibad** (191), **Iban** (47c), **ibex** (67d,68a), **ibid** (80a,117a,137a), **ibis** (48d,49a,177b), **ibit** (117a)

- IB - **bibb** (97c,146b), **bibi** (87d), **dibs** (70c), **gibe** (8a,42c,84d,100d,138c, 144c,149b), **jibb, jibe** (8a,33b,35d,37b,42c,100d,138c,144c,149b), **kibe, kiby** (29a), **nibs** (116c), **ribe** (139a), **Tibu** (191)

- - IB **Abib** (102a,b), **Adib** (155b), **Agib** (12a,42d), **chib** (167a), **crib** (96b, 120d), **drib** (46b), **frib** (43d), **glib** (58d,149a,177c), **guib** (11a), **snib** (54d,93c), **stib** (19b,47a,137a)

I - - B **iamb** (59c)

IC - - **ical** (158c), **icer, icho** (67b), **ichu** (10b,70d), **icon** (79d,92b,136a)

- IC - **aich** (9a), **bice** (20d,117d), **Bice** (27b), **dice** (65a), **dick** (43a,55b), **Dick** (96b), **fico** (169d), **hick** (185d), **kick, lick, mica** (82c,100b, 146c), **mice, mick** (82c), **mico** (97a), **nice** (54d,119c,130c), **Nice** (98c), **nick** (30c,108b), **pica** (66b,95b,172c), **pice** (190), **Pici** (19c, 184a), **pick, pico** (65a,152c), **Pict** (23c,47d), **rice, Rice** (46a), **rich, rick** (74d,117d,154d), **sice** (71d,147b), **sick, tice** (9a,38c,51a,185d), **tick** (12b,20d,97c), **vice** (31d,158a), **wick**

- - IC **amic** (9d), **chic** (148d) **cric** (131c), **epic** (76b,120a), **eric** (115b), **Eric** (71d,96a,107d,138a,164a,176b), **idic** (79b), **laic** (32b,90b,107d, 124a,141d), **odic** (79c,120a), **olic** (158b), **otic** (14c,d,47b), **saic** (86b, 91d,175d), **Udic** (108a), **Uvic** (70c)

I - - C **idic** (79b)

ID - - **Idas** (27b,71c), **idea** (54c,108c,124a,164d), **idee** (61d), **idem** (89d, 164a), **Iden** (76a), **ideo** (34b,d,164d), **ides** (41a,b,133a), **idic** (79b), **idio** (34b,c), **Idjo** (191), **idle** (174b,c,178c), **idly, idol** (48c,54c,55a 75b,79d,112d,130b,184d), **Idun** (107d), **idyl** (114d), **Idyo** (191), **Idzo** (191)

- ID - **Aida** (110d,175c), **aide** (7b,14a,75d), **bide** (47c,50b,130a,158b, 162a,177b), **dido** (11b,26c,65a,122a), **Dido** (27a,172c), **eide** (119c), **fide, Gide** (63a) **hide** (53a), **Lida** (183c), **Lido** (83d,175b), **mide** (110a), **Midi** (151b), **nide** (23c,72a,106c,116d), **nidi** (106c), **Ridd** (94a), **ride** (46b,85c), **sida** (37a,126c,170a), **side** (13d,22a,b,54a, 58a,89a,161b), **sidi** (103b,166b), **sidy** (123b), **tide** (39d,75d,109c, 141c,159d), **tidy** (106a,111b), **Vida** (183c), **vide** (89d,126a,142a), **wide** (133d), **widu** (102d)

- - ID **acid** (151a,162a), **amid** (9d,50a), **arid** (46c,85a), **avid** (47b,71a, 186b), **Beid** (155b), **caid** (35a,151d,152b), **chid, Enid** (13b,25d,66b, 163a,183c), **grid** (17a,70d,119b,156d), **ibid** (80a,117a,137a), **imid** (29c), **irid** (38d,67c), **kaid** (29d,66a), **laid, maid** (45b,142d), **naid** (63c), **olid** (55d,60c,148d,157d), **ooid** (48d), **Ovid** (132d,133b), **oxid** (112c), **paid** (129c), **qaid** (35a), **quid** (39b,166d), **raid** (59d,80c), **said** (174c), **Said** (42d,101a,121b), **seid** (103b), **Seid** (42d,101a, 171a), **skid** (148b), **slid, uvid** (101a), **void** (11a,49d,108d), **zoid**

I - - D **Ibad** (191), **ibid** (80a,117a,137a), **imid** (29c), **Irad** (18d), **irid** (38d, 67c)

- IE - **bien** (63a,140c,179a,180a), **bier** (33b,66b), **dieb** (84a), **diem** (89b, 116a), **dier**, **dies** (41b,89b), **diet** (14a,54c,84c,91b,176a), **Dieu** (61d), **fief** (55d), **gier** (47b), **hien** (30b), **hier** (63a,185d), **kief** (75d), **kiel** (128d,134d), **Kiel** (25d), **kier** (20c,174d), **Kiev**, **lied** (66d,150b), **lief** (181d), **lien** (65c,91a,124c), **lieu** (118c,155d), **mien** (11c,17b, 26d,44c,96b), **pied** (96c,103c,114b,117c,154a,174d), **pien** (13b), **pier** (23a,88b,180c), **piet** (29b,95b), **Riel** (129a), **riem** (76c,112c, 157c,164d), **rien** (62b), **rier** (180b), **sier** (57a,118b), **tied**, **tien** (147d), **tier** (118a,134b), **vier** (66c), **view** (93d,138b), **wiel** (140d, 180d), **wies** (185a)

- - IE **Abie** (96b,107a), **Amie** (61d), **Brie** (29c), **Erie** (82c,87d), **Okie** (99d), **Opie** (50c), **plie** (32c,59b), **soie** (62c), **unie** (173a)

I - - E **idee** (61d), **idle** (174b,c,178c), **ille** (89b,d,163d), **imbe** (37a,56a, 133d), **inde**, **inee** (120b), **Inge** (24d,67d,117c,119c), **inre** (35d,80a), **Iole** (52a,76b,123c), **Ione** (24b,88d,94d), **ipse** (44d,89c), **Irae** (43c), **isle** (8b,53c,81d,82d,86b,88a), **ixle** (56a)

IF - - **ifil** (117a,168c)

- IF - **biff**, **fife** (59a,105a), **gift** (123a), **jiff** (101c), **kiff** (88c), **life** (19a,177a), **lift** (49b), **miff** (44c), **nife** (37a), **piff** (24b), **rife** (6b,c, 39d,123b), **riff** (131d), **Riff** (18b,102c), **rift** (30c,32a,58a,110d), **sift** (140d,142c,146b), **tiff** (126b), **wife** (154a)

- - IF **alif** (12b), **arif** (127d), **coif** (73a), **cuif** (139a,d,140c), **Enif** (155b), **kaif** (88c), **keif** (75d), **Leif** (107d), **luif**, **naif** (74b,105d), **waif** (157b)

IG - - **iglu** (51c,149b), **Igor** (135d)

- IG - **biga** (171d), **giga** (56a,105a), **high**, **migg** (96c), **nigh** (106a), **riga** (118b), **Riga**, **sigh**, **sign** (121c,146c), **tige** (118a), **wigg**

- - IG **brig** (72b,106a,144d), **crig** (20d), **grig** (38c,70d,93a), **prig** (112a, 116c), **snig** (45d), **swig** (46a,72c), **Teig** (96a), **trig** (106a,148d,154b, 169d), **twig**, **Whig**

I - - G **ilog** (132a,161b)

IH - - **IHVH** (159d)

- IH - **kiho** (82a)

- - IH **ch'ih** (188), **shih** (189)

I - - H **IHVH** (159d), **inch**, **itch**, **Ivah** (18d)

II - - **iiwi** (19a,74b)

- II - **liin** (188), **Riis** (9d)

- - II **alii** (74c,134c), **apii** (74c), **Boii** (191), **heli** (74b), **Ubii** (191)

I - - I **iiwi** (19a,74b), **immi** (189), **impi** (86a), **Inti** (159b), **Ioni** (192)

IJ - - **ijma** (103b)

- IJ - **bija** (168c), **Ilja** (57a,90d,173a)

IK - - **ikat** (53b,159a), **ikmo** (18b), **ikon** (79d,136a), **ikra** (27d)

- IK - **bike**, **bikh** (120b), **dika** (23a), **dike** (49c,91d), **Dike** (78a), **fike** (139c), **hike**, **hiku** (57a,106d,138a), **kiki** (27b), **kiku** (30d), **like** (13c,37d,146d), **mike**, **Mike** (96b), **Nike** (69c,100c,182d), **pika** (93a,128a,132c), **pike** (57a,b,76c,120b,153a), **piki** (95c), **piky**,

rikk (49a), **sika** (41d,84b), **Sikh** (77b), **tike** (29d), **Tiki** (120c)

- - IK **Atik** (155b), **Efik** (191), **haik** (57b,65b,108a), **kaik** (96c), **naik, raik** (188,189), **Seik** (77b), **Shik** (171a)

I - - K **Irak** (99a,d), **irok** (55b)

IL - - **ilex** (77d), **ilia** (21d,77b,115d), **ille** (89b,d,163d), **ills** (170a), **ilog** (132a,161b), **ilot** (82d), **Ilus** (88d,170b)

- IL - **aile** (62b,63a,182c,d), **bile** (30c), **bilk** (29b,41c,42a), **bill** (17b,147a), **Bill, bilo** (131b), **dill** (13a,117c), **dilo** (120d,168c), **eild** (138d,140a), **file** (13a,127d), **fili, fill** (109b), **film** (164b), **filo, fils** (62d,150b), **gila** (93b), **gild** (14a,49c,69c,98b), **gill** (22d), **gilo** (48a), **gilt** (69c,77c,151b,185d), **hila** (53c), **Hild, hill, hilo** (74c), **hilt** (73c), **Jill** (183d), **jilt, kile** (189), **kill** (38c), **kiln** (15d,112a), **kilo** (99b, 122d), **kilt, Lila** (183c), **lill** (15d,118a), **lilt** (93a,131a,147a), **lily, mila** (188), **mild** (32a,66a), **mile** (64c), **milk, mill** (126c), **milo** (70b, 87c,150d), **Milo, milt** (153d), **nile** (33c,71d), **Nile** (106b), **nill** (173d), **oily** (110b,172c), **pile** (45d,75b,117c), **pili** (34b,108d), **pill, pily, rile** (10c,d,82c,125a,156b,176a), **rill** (23c,102b,132a,148d,157b), **rily** (176a), **silk** (53b,179c), **sill** (45c,76c,165a,182b), **silo** (59a, 156d), **silt** (104b), **tile** (31d,56d,72b,95b,133c,163c), **till** (39c,101c, 173d), **tilt** (26b,d,166a), **vila** (54b), **vile** (16c,56c), **vili** (54b), **Vili** (109c), **vill** (176b), **vily** (54b), **wild** (38b,173d), **wile** (13b,41c,157b, 169c), **wilk** (65c,96d,141b), **will** (18b,43a,163c,177c), **wilt** (46b), **wily** (13b,38b,39c)

- - IL **amil** (45a,48a,185c), **anil** (47c,80d,180b), **aril** (142a), **axil** (10c), **bail** (43c), **Bhil** (191), **boil, ceil** (92c,112a), **chil, coil** (39d,171c, 185a), **Dail** (49a,82b,c), **deil** (139b), **Egil** (107d), **Emil** (96a), **evil** (79c,95d,147a,181a,185c), **fail, foil** (15d,55c,165b), **gail** (23b, 174d), **Gail** (183d), **hail** (6d,15a,71d), **ifil** (117a,168c), **ipil** (117a, 168c,169a), **Ixil** (192), **jail** (123d), **jhil, kail** (8c,22a,25a,79b), **mail** (12d,99b,121c), **moil** (46c,184c), **nail** (31d,54d,141d,161d,173a), **Neil** (96a), **noil** (87c,178b), **pail Phil** (96b), **rail** (16b,19b,c,37a,97b, 138c,150c,177b), **roil** (44c,104b,156b,170d,176a), **sail** (144c,185a), **skil** (57a), **soil** (154d,159a,163c), **tail** (11d,27d,59b,143b), **teil** (92b, c,168c), **toil** (46c,184c), **vail** (94b,124a,174b), **veil** (74d,76c), **wail** (39b,88a), **ypil** (117a,168c)

I - - L **ical** (158c), **idol** (48c,54c,55a,75b,79d,112d,130b,184d), **idyl** (114d), **ifil** (117a,168c), **ipil** (117a,168c,169a), **itol** (158b), **Ixil** (192)

IM - - **imam** (25c,102d,103a), **imbe** (37a,56a,133d), **Imer, imid** (29c), **immi** (189), **impi** (86a)

- IM - **cima** (83b,c), **dime, gime** (77d), **gimp** (169d), **Hima** (191), **lima** (17b,152b,174d), **Lima** (31b), **limb** (12d,22d), **lime** (25b,27d,31b, 33c,102d,168c), **limn** (45d,121c), **limp** (58a,81a,177d), **limu** (141c), **limy** (176d), **mima** (185d), **mime** (24a,71b,85a,100a), **Mime** (131d, 148d), **mimi** (14d), **Mimi** (87b,110d,125b,183d), **nimb** (31b, 73b,92a,107b,131d), **oime** (8b), **pima** (37c), **Pima** (192), **rima** (23a,30c,32a,58a,110d), **rime** (30c,36a,58a,63d,77c), **rimu** (79d,106d,129a,168c), **rimy** (63d), **sima** (132b) **sime** (101d), **Simi** (82d), **simp** (59c,146d), **time** (47a,131a), **Yima** (84a,116b,c), **Zimb** (6c)

--IM **Anim** (18d), **Akim** (135d,191), **alim** (103b,162c), **brim**, **Clim** (12b), **duim** (188), **Emim** (67a,100d), **frim** (58d), **glim**, **grim** (156a), **maim** (43d,81a,105c), **prim** (156b), **Seim** (120c), **shim** (91d,144c,162a, 179d), **skim** (67c), **slim** (148b,160a), **swim** (58c), **trim** (40a,106a, 154b,160a,165c,169d), **urim** (18d,23a,110a), **whim** (26c,54c,108c), **zaim** (170d)

I--M **idem** (89d,164a), **imam** (25c,102d,103a), **item** (6d,13b,42d,51a, 90d,92d,107a,113d,114c)

IN-- **inar** (65b), **Inca** (14b,30a), **inch**, **inde**, **inee** (120b), **Inez** (45c,183c), **inga** (145d,170a), **Inge** (24d,67d,117c,119c), **inia** (9b,109b), **Inia** (28c,45b), **Inka** (193), **inky** (20b), **inly**, **inre** (35d,80a), **inro** (84b,c, 106c), **Inti** (159b), **into** (123a,183b)

-IN- **aine** (49b,62c), **Aine** (142c), **Aino** (84a,c), **aint**, **Ainu** (84a,c), **bina** (77a), **bind** (33b,165c), **bine** (145b,156a,171c,176b), **bing**, **binh** (189), **Bini** (191), **binn** (22c), **bino** (113b,117a), **cine** (104b, 152c), **cinq** (61d), **dine**, **ding** (130b), **dino** (34b), **dint** (48c,59d, 122a), **fine** (49b,50a,104b,115d,159a), **fink** (19a,56c,157c), **Finn** (107d), **gink** (48b), **hind** (15b,41d,45a), **hing** (13c), **hino** (106d, 168c), **hint** (9a,39c,159a), **jink**, **jinn** (42b,103b,153c), **jinx** (78a), **kina** (126d), **kind** (150d,153a,174d), **kine** (38a,112c), **king** (26c, 29c), **kink** (38b,171c), **kino** (27c,34c,47c,72c,98b,161d,168c), **lina** (188), **Lina** (183d), **line** (12b,22b,36d,38a,126c,134b,157b,158b, 162d,175c), **ling** (24c,57a,b,75b,178c), **link** (36a,81d,85b), **Linn** (120d,140a,c,168c,178d), **lino**, **lint** (46a,58d), **liny** (157b), **Linz** (40d), **mina** (10b,70b,71d), **Mina** (23a,183d), **mind** (75c,81d,93d, 109b), **mine** (69c,79d,111b,124c), **Ming** (30b,c), **mink** (176d), **mino** (84c), **mint** (13a,33b,58b,76a), **minx** (116c), **miny**, **nina** (152a), **Nina** (26c,33d,68d,183d), **nine** (26c,104d), **nino** (152a), **pina** (35d,118b), **pine** (36a,52a,88c,93c,168c,d,169a), **ping**, **pink** (26d,33c,60c,138a), **pino** (152c), **pint** (67b), **piny**, **rind** (53a, 115c), **Rind** (109c,174b), **rine** (44d,75d,135c), **ring** (50a), **rink** (147c,154a), **sina** (46c), **Sina** (102d,103d), **Sind**, **sine** (64c,66b,90a, 97c,126a,163b,169d,183b), **sing** (26d,178a), **sinh** (97c), **sink** (41c, 43c,46b,158a), **sino** (34a), **Tina** (183d), **tind** (86b), **tine** (11b,124b, 167b), **ting** (166a), **Ting** (30c), **Tino** (136d), **tint** (33c,d,114d), **tiny** (100c,148c), **vina** (77a,105a), **vine** (32b), **vino** (92d,182b), **vint** (26c,182c), **viny**, **wind** (33b,39d,171c,185a), **wine**, **wing** (10d,58c, 59a,118b,d), **wink** (107a), **winy** (176c), **Xina** (183d), **zinc** (21a), **zing**

--IN **akin** (8b,92b,129c), **alin** (188), **amin** (9d), **Asin** (102a), **ayin** (91c), **bain** (61a), **brin** (32c,54c,146c), **cain** (169c), **Cain** (6a,7a,50d,88a, 104c,143c), **chin**, **Chin** (30b), **coin** (19b,37a,100c,101c,179d), **crin** (146c), **dain** (188), **dein** (66d), **Drin**, **enin** (20d), **Eoin** (85b), **Erin** (82b), **fain** (42d,67c,183b), **gain** (7a,b,124a), **gein** (67d), **grin**, **hein** (52c,61c), **Jain** (77b), **join** (36a,173c), **Kain**, **lain**, **liin** (188), **loin** (98a), **main** (29d,35d,123d), **mein** (30b), **nein** (66c), **Odin** (7c, 29d,63c,68c,175d,183b), **pain** (7c), **rain** (121d,162d), **rein** (130c), **Rhin**, **ruin** (42d), **sain** (20c,38d,48a), **sein** (146c), **shin** (91a,d,140b, 143c), **skin** (53a,76c,115c,d), **spin** (131a,180d), **tain** (166a), **thin** (43b,c,148b), **trin** (169d), **Tsin** (30b), **twin** (45c,171d), **vain** (81a), **vein** (20d,157b), **wain** (177b), **Wain**, **whin** (64c,70a,132b,181d),

zain (41a), **zein**

I - - N **Iban** (47c), **icon** (79d,92b,136a), **Iden** (76a), **Idun** (107d), **ikon** (79d,136a), **Iran** (6a,48c,116b), **Iren** (127c), **iron** (55c,d,69d,81a, 97b,143b,149a,173d,179c), **Iten** (192), **Ivan** (40c,85b,96a)

IO - - **Iola**, **Iole** (52a,76b,123c), **Iona** (28a,82d), **Ione** (24b,88d,94d), **Ioni** (192), **iota** (71a,85c,91c,114c,166c,176a,180d), **Iowa** (193)

- IO - **biod** (79c,59d), **bion** (117b), **bios** (92a), **cion** (42d,70b,145b,148b, 154b,156a), **Dion** (96a,152a), **Fiot** (191), **lion** (55b,86c), **niog** (33a,168c), **niou** (188), **pion** (43c,52b), **piot** (95b), **riot** (44c, 111d,170c,173d), **siol** (82c), **sion** (125c,158c), **Sion** (75b,c,83a,157d), **tion** (158b), **Tiou** (192), **viol** (105a), **Zion** (75b,c,83a,157d)

- - IO **agio** (52c,60a,101c,123a), **apio** (125b), **Clio** (104d), **idio** (34b,c), **meio** (188), **moio** (188), **naio** (107a,168c), **noio** (107c,163c), **odio** (83b), **Ohio**, **olio** (44b,77c,98c,100d,121d), **Scio**, **skio** (57d), **trio** (104d,165a,169c), **Unio** (105c)

I - - O **Iago** (54b,111d,143c), **icho** (67b), **ideo** (34b,d,164d), **idio** (34b,c), **Idjo** (191), **Idyo** (191), **Idzo** (191) **ikmo** (18b) **inro** (84b,c,106c), **into** (123a), **ipso** (89c), **itmo** (18b)

IP - - **ipil** (117a,168c,169a), **ipse** (44d,89c), **ipso** (89c)

- IP - **aipi** (27a), **cipo** (91d), **dipt**, **hipe** (185a), **kipp**, **lipa** (54d), **nipa** (14b, 46b,48a,164a,168c), **pipa** (159d) **pipe** (105a,180d,182a), **pipi** (106d, 119d), **pipy** (145d), **ripa** (16b,131d), **ripe** (58a,97c,98c), **Sipe** (101a, 110c,140b), **tipe** (168b), **tipi** (181b), **wipe**, **Xipe** (15c), **Zipa** (29d), **zipp**, **Zips** (40c)

- - IP **atip** (14b,166a), **chip** (69d), **clip** (54d,143d), **drip**, **flip** (167c), **grip** (159a), **knip** (115c), **quip** (183a,b), **raip** (36d), **seip** (110c), **ship**, **skip** (110b,114c,147c), **slip** (67c,119a), **snip** (32b,40a), **trip** (85c), **whip** (58c,88d)

I - - Q **Iraq** (99a,d)

IR - - **Irad** (18d), **Irae** (43c), **Irak** (99a,d), **Iran** (6a,48c,116b), **Iraq** (99a,d), **Iras** (11b,32a), **Iren** (127c), **irid** (38d,67c), **iris** (53c,58a,111c), **Iris** (127c), **Irma** (96d), **irok** (55b), **iron** (55c,d,69d,81a,97b,143b,149a, 173d,179c), **Irra** (68c,178a), **irus** (109d)

- IR - **Aira** (70d), **aire** (82c), **Aire**, **airs** (123b), **airy** (176d,177a), **bird**, **birl** (93c,131a,153c), **birn** (31d,139a), **birr** (180d), **cirl** (24c), **circ** (31a), **dire** (45d,55a,104a,163c), **dirk** (40b), **dirt**, **Eire** (82b), **fire** (13a,43d,44b), **firm** (154c,173d), **firn** (67c,70c,106c,149b), **gird** (32c,50a,123a,160a), **girl**, **giro** (38c,83c,167c), **girt** (50a), **hire** (49d,50b,91b,130a), **hiro**, **kiri** (86a,87c,115a,168c), **kirk** (31a,139b), **lira** (28b,79a,170d), **lire** (62c), **Mira** (155b,174d), **mire** (21c,104b), **mirk** (41a,67d), **miro** (19a,106d,184a), **Miro** (113a, 151d), **miry**, **pirn** (21b,129a,179b), **Piro** (192), **pirr** (181a), **rire** (62a), **sire** (17d,55a,59d,124a,163b,166b), **siri** (18b), **tire** (15a,22a, 52d,55a,179b,180d), **tiro** (9b,17d,108c), **Vira** (191), **vire** (11a,13b), **wire**, **wiry** (147a,167c), **zira** (188)

- - IR **Abir** (129a), **Ahir** (27b), **amir** (7c,12a,103a,b,123c,170d), **chir** (29b,116d), **coir** (33a,37a,56a,133d), **cuir** (45c,62a), **emir** (12a, 103a,b,123c,134d,135a,171a), **fair** (17a,55d), **hair** (56b,164d), **heir**, **kair**, **keir** (20c,174d), **koir** (33a), **lair** (37c,42b), **Leir**, **loir** (45c),

Loir, Muir (8b,142c), Nair (45d), noir (61b,134b), pair (22d,37d, 85b,171d), sair (140b,150d), Seir (51b,94a,103d), shir (36d,65d, 165c), skir, soir (61c), spir (97c), stir (8a,13a,35b,78d,100d), tair (68a,76d), vair (64c,154c), weir (40b,57d), whir (25c,181a), Ymir (67a,131c)

I - - R icer, Igor (135d), Imer, inar (65b), Isar (41a,104c,132a), Iser (49a), iter (22d,76c,85c,89c,114d,132a,b,133a,b), Iyar (102b), izar (65b,103b), Izar (155b)

IS - - Isar (41a,104c,132a), isba (135c), Iser (49a), Isha (174a), Isis (68d, 78c,111d), isle (8b,53c,81d,82d,86b,88a), ismy (45a)

- IS - bisa (11a), bise (182a), bish (120b), bisk (120b,151a), cise (147b), cist (22c,29d,156c), Disa (111a), disc (31b), dish, disk (31b), diss (98b), fisc (52c,134c), fish, fisk (24d,52c,134c), fist (80c), gish (102c), gist (95c,118c), hish, hiss (146a), hist (25c,93d), kish (16d,70c), Kish (137c), kiss (148c), kist (29d,58a,139b), Lisa (183d), lisp (153b), liss (54b,58b,60c,129d,140a), list (26d,27b, 75b,83d,134a,138b,165d), mise (8a,10a,70c), miss, mist (46b,59b, 59b,174d), Nish (19d), nisi (90a,173c), Oise, Pisa (90c), pise (127d), pish (36c,107d), pisk (9c,19b), piso (189), pist (25c), rise (49d,80b,155a), Rise (110d,150c), risk (74d), risp (99a), Riss (66a), sise (62c,147b), sish (79b), sisi (121b), sist (139b), visa (114d), vise (31d,77d,114d), viss (189), wise (136b), wish (42d), wisp (148c), wist (87c)

- - IS acis (64b), Agis (86d), anis (55c), Apis (17c,24b,49a,125a,136a), aris (101b), atis (76d,102a), avis (89a), Avis (183c), axis (28b, 41d,77c,153c), bois (62b,63a,183d), Bois, cris (40b,95d), dais (119b), egis (14b,d,115a,124d,144b,154a,161a), Elis (22c,37d, 71b,107c), Eris (12c,68d,109c), feis (82b), glis (45c), gris (61d), ibis (48d,49a,177b), iris (53c,58a,111c), Iris (127c), kris (40b,95d), Isis (68d,78c,111d), itis (158c), Lais (17c), Lois (165d,183c), mais (61b), nais (63c,132a), Otis (9c,d,24d,82a,111a), Ovis (143d), pais (37d), rais (26c,29d,75a,103b), Rais (106b), reis (26c,29d,75a, 103b), Riis (9d), sais (48d,71d), seis (147b,152c), this (42b,124b), tris (122d), unis (91b), Upis (13b)

I - - S ibis (48d,49a,177b), Ibis, Idas (27b,71c), ides (41a,b,133a), ills (170a), Ilus (88d,170b), Iras (11b,32a), iris (53c,58a,111c), Iris (127c), Irus (109d), Isis (68d,78c,111d), Itys (163b), Ives (9c,90b)

IT - - itch, Itea (145d,160c,181d), item (6d,13b,42d,51a,90d,92d,107a, 113d,114c), Iten (192), iter (22d,76c,85c,89c,114d,132a,b,133a,b), itis (158c), itmo (18b), itol (158b), Itys (163b), Itza (192)

- IT - bite (29d,156b), biti (20b), bito (7d,57d,168c), bitt (54d,175c), cite (15a,98d,126d,159b), cito (89d,126c), cits, city, dita (117a), dite (150b), Gita, gite (62a,118d), jiti, kite (19c,49a,74c,d), kith (63c), lite (158c,d), lith (34d,156c), liti (60d) litz (127b), mite (12b,81b,82a,114a,c,148c,d,181b), mitt (56c), mitu (39d), mity, nito (55c), pita (9c,28b,56a,83a), pith (37a,51c,67b,95c,97a, 119b,126d), pitt (50d), Pitt (155d), pito (9c,28b,83a), pity (35b), rita, Rita (37b,78d,183c), rite (93a,131d), Sita (127d), site (93b), sito (34b), titi (20d,102a,145d,168d,181b), Tito (186c), vita (89c, 92a), vite (62b), viti (176b), with (10b)

- - IT **adit** (51a,100a,114d), **alit** (44b,143a), **amit** (94a), **bait** (15d,51a, 94d,167b), **brit** (76c), **chit** (67b,98c,108b,116c,177c), **doit** (47a, 169d,180d), **duit** (190), **Duit** (192), **edit** (20d,49d,123a,129a,131a), **emit** (43d,49a,53c,58d,83a,142c), **exit** (114d), **fait** (6d,61b), **flit** (41a), **frit** (64c,67c), **gait** (96b,179a), **grit** (137a,b), **ibit** (117a), **knit** (173c,179b), **lait** (62a), **nuit** (62b), **obit** (41b,64c), **omit** (49c, 52c,106b,114c,147d), **phit** (24b), **quit** (90d,130c), **seit** (189), **skit** (145c), **slit** (40a), **spit** (120a,132b,c), **suit** (38a,58a,91a,112a,119c, 137c), **tait** (14d), **trit** (34d,164c), **twit** (162b,c), **unit** (101c,110c, 147a), **wait** (26d,42b,92c,155d,162a), **whit** (166c), **writ** (91a), **Yuit** (51c)

I - - T **ibit** (117a), **ikat** (53b,159a), **ilot** (82d)

- IU - **biur** (35a), **Niue** (137d), **Pius** (121a)

I - - U **lalu** (48d), **ichu** (10b,70d), **iglu** (51c,149b)

IV - - **Ivah** (18d), **Ivan** (40c,85b,96a), **Ives** (9c,90b)

- IV - **Civa** (56d), **cive** (110c), **diva** (110d,123c), **dive** (42b,74b,119d), **divi**, **five**, **give** (79d,123a), **hive** (17c), **jiva** (77a), **jive** (160c), **kiva** (28c,125b), **kive** (174d), **kivu** (170c), **live** (47c), **Livy** (132d,133a), **rive** (32a,153d), **siva** (67a,120d), **Siva** (56d,77a), **sive** (146a), **viva** (93d), **vive** (93d), **vivo** (93a), **wive** (97a)

- - IV **chiv** (87a), **skiv** (151b)

- IW - **Biwa** (93d,168c), **iiwi** (19a,74b), **kiwi** (11d,19a,58c)

IX - - **ixia** (37a), **Ixil** (192), **ixle** (56a)

- IX - **Bixa** (145d), **dixi**, **Mixe** (192), **mixy**, **pixy** (154b)

- - IX **Alix** (183c), **Coix** (70d,85b), **flix**, **noix** (67c)

IY - - **Iyar** (102b)

- IY - **kiyi** (185d)

I - - Y **idly**, **inky** (20b), **inly**, **ismy** (45a)

IZ - - **izar** (65b,103b), **Izar** (155b)

- IZ - **bize** (182a), **bizz**, **size**, **sizy** (176d), **sizz**, **tiza** (172a), **zizz** (181a)

- - IZ **friz** (39d), **phiz** (54a), **swiz** (160c), **whiz** (25c)

I - - Z **Inez** (45c,183c)

JA - - **jaca** (84a), **jack** (26c,58a,127c), **Jack** (96b), **jacu** (19a,151b), **jade** (33c,65d,71d,166a), **jadu** (95a), **jady**, **Jael** (147b), **Jaga** (191), **jagg**, **jail** (123d), **Jain** (77b), **jake** (40d), **Jake** (96b), **jako** (71a), **jama** (103b), **jamb** (12d,45c,118a,146b,174a), **jami** (103b), **jane** (190), **Jane** (183c), **jann** (102d), **jaob**, **jape** (85a,b), **jarl** (40d,107d), **jass** (160d), **jati** (27b), **jato** (173b), **jaun** (113a), **Java** (33a), **Jave** (84d), **jawy**, **jazz**

- JA - **ajar** (110c), **Ajax** (71b,162d)

- - JA **Beja** (6c,191), **bija** (168c), **caja** (152a), **coja** (103b,166b), **hoja** (166b), **lija** (57a,90d,173a), **maja** (151c), **Maja** (153b), **Naja** (33a), **puja** (77a), **raja** (77a,123c), **reja** (152b), **soja** (151b)

J - - A **jaca** (84a), **Jaca**, **Jaga** (191), **jama** (103b), **Java** (33a), **Jena** (105d, 165b), **jiva** (77a), **jota** (151c), **Jova** (193), **juba** (106b), **juca** (27a), **Juda**, **juga** (27a), **jula**, **jura**, **Juza** (155b)

J - - B **jamb** (12d,45c,118a,146b,174a), **jaob**, **jibb**, **Joab** (41a)

- - JD **Nejd**

J - - D **Joad** (50c)

JE - - **jean** (37c), **Jean** (183c), **jeel, jeep, jeer** (138c,162b), **jefe** (152a), **jeff** (133d), **Jeff, jehu** (46b), **Jehu** (18c), **Jena** (105d,165b), **jerk** (153a), **jess** (157a), **jest** (169c), **Jesu, jete** (16a), **Jeth** (102a), **jeux** (61d)

- JE - **ajee** (15c,139a)

- - JE **haje** (33a,48d), **yaje** (23a)

J - - E **jade** (33c,65d,71d,166a), **jake** (40d), **Jake** (96b), **jane** (190), **Jane** (183c), **jape** (85a,b), **Jave** (84d), **jefe** (152a), **jete** (16a), **jibe** (8a, 33b,35d,37b,42c,100d,138c,144c,149b), **jive** (160c), **joke** (183a), **jole** (29b), **Jose** (96a), **Jove** (85d), **jube** (28d), **Jude** (11c,96a), **juke** (114c), **Jule** (183d), **June** (183c), **jupe** (62b,84a), **jure** (90b), **jute** (37a,48a,56a,133d,136a), **Jute**

J - - F **jeff** (133d), **Jeff, jiff** (101c)

J - - G **jagg, joug** (138d), **Jung** (125a)

JH - - **Jhil, jhum, JHVH** (159d), **JHWH** (159d)

J - - H **Jeth** (102a), **josh** (85b), **JHVH** (159d), **JHWH** (159d)

JI - - **jibb, jibe** (8a,33b,35d,37b,42c,100d,138c,144c,149b), **jiff** (101c), **Jill** (183d), **jilt, jink, jinn** (42b,103b,153c), **jinx** (78a), **jiti, jiva** (77a), **jive** (160c)

- - JI **caji** (180b), **Caji, fuji** (84b), **Fuji** (84d), **koji** (185b), **suji** (180c)

J - - I **jami** (103b), **jati** (27b), **Jati, jiti, jogi** (76d), **joli** (62b), **joti**

J - - K **jack** (26c,58a,127c), **Jack** (96b), **jerk** (153a), **jink, jock, Jock** (96b), **jonk, juck** (114c), **junk** (30a,134c)

J - - L **Jael** (147b), **jail** (123d), **jarl** (40d,107d), **jeel, jhil, Jill** (183d), **Joel** (96a), **jowl** (29b)

- JM - **ijma** (103b)

- - JM **Sejm** (120c)

J - - M **jhum, joom** (39c)

J - - N **Jain** (77b), **jann, Jann** (102d), **jaun** (113a), **jean** (37c), **Jean** (183c), **jinn** (42b,103b,153c), **Joan** (183c), **John** (11c,96a,121a,186b), **join** (36a,173c), **juan** (113a), **Juan** (96a)

JO - - **Joab** (41a), **Joad** (50c), **Joan** (183c), **joar** (100a), **jobo** (77c), **jock, Jock** (96b), **jocu** (45b,57a), **Jodo** (113d), **Joel** (96a), **joey** (86a, 185d), **Joey** (96b,109c), **jogi** (76d), **John** (11c,96a,121a,186b), **join** (36a,173c), **joke** (183a), **joky, jole** (29b), **joli** (62b), **jolt** (143b), **jonk, joom** (39c), **Jose** (96a), **josh** (85b), **joss** (30b), **Josy** (183d), **jota** (151c), **joti, joug** (138d), **Jova** (193), **Jove** (85d), **jowl** 29b), **Jozy**

- JO - **ajog, ejoo** (55b,168c), **Gjoa** (144d)

- - JO **bojo** (117a), **gajo** (107c), **Idjo** (191), **majo, mojo** (177c), **pajo** (122a, **rojo** (129a,152c), **tajo** (152a,d)

J - - O **jako** (71a), **Jako, jato** (173b), **jobo** (77c), **Jodo** (113d), **judo** (84b, 85c,142b), **Juno** (69c,85d,100c,126b)

J - - P **jeep, jump**

J - - R **jeer** (162b), **joar** (100a), **juar** (100a)

J - - S **jass** (160d), **jess** (157a), **joss** (30b)

J - - T **jest** (169c), **jilt**, **jolt** (143b), **just** (51b,54b)

JU - - **juan** (113a), **Juan** (96a), **juar** (100a), **juba** (106b), **jube** (28d), **juca** (27a), **juck** (114c), **Juda**, **Jude** (11c,96a), **judo** (84b,85c,142b), **Judy** (125c,183d), **juez** (152b), **juga** (27a), **juju** (29b,55d), **juke** (114c), **jula**, **Jule** (183d), **jump**, **June** (183c), **Jung** (125a), **junk** (30a,134c), **Juno** (69c,85d,100c,126b), **jupe** (62b,84a), **jura**, **Jura**, **jure** (90b), **jury** (38a), **just** (51b,54b), **jute** (37a,48a,56a,133d, 136a), **Jute**, **Juza** (155b)

- - JU **baju** (84a), **hoju** (84b), **juju** (29b,55d), **teju** (151b)

J - - U **jacu** (19a,151b), **jadu** (95), **jehu** (46b), **Jehu** (18c), **Jesu**, **jocu** (45b,57a), **juju** (29b,55d)

J - - X **jeux** (61d), **jinx** (78a), **jynx** (78a), **Jynx** (184a)

JY - - **jynx** (78a), **Jynx** (184a)

J - - Y **jady**, **jawy**, **joey** (86a,185d), **Joey** (96b,109c), **joky**, **Josy** (183d), **Jozy**, **Judy** (125c,183d), **July**, **jury** (38a)

J - - Z **jazz**, **juez** (152b)

KA - - **kaan** (93d,116c), **kaat** (105d), **kada** (188), **kade** (144a), **kadi** (103a, 171a), **Kadu** (191), **Kafa** (6c), **kago** (113a), **kagu** (106c), **kaha** (123d), **kahu** (14d), **kaid** (29d,66a), **kaif** (88c) **kaik** (96c), **kail** (18c, 22a,25a,79b), **Kain**, **kair**, **kaka** (114b), **kaki** (84c,106d), **kala** (19a), **kale** (22a,25a,119b,175a), **kali** (26d,67c,136d,167a), **Kali** (147b), **kalo** (162a), **Kama** (56d), **kame** (67b,139b), **Kami** (68a,84b,88c, 107c,144c), **kana** (84d), **Kane** (74c), **k'ang** (30a), **Kano** (84c,177d), **kant** (28d), **Kant** (67a), **kapa** (74b), **kaph** (91d), **Kapp**, **Kara** (132a), **Kari** (14d), **Karl** (96a), **karn** (156c), **karo** (106d), **kasa** (48a), **kasi** 116b), **kasm** (189), **Kate** (143c,183d), **kath** (14a), **Katy** (183d), **kaun** (93d), **kava** (18c,116a), **Kavi** (84d), **kawa** (18c,116a), **Kawi** (84d), **kawn** (93d), **kayo** (87c), **kazi** (103a), **kazy** (103a)

- KA - **Akal** (56d), **Akan** (191), **ikat** (53b,159a), **okay** (8d), **skag** (7d, 46d), **skat** (181b), **Skat** (155b)

- - KA **Akka** (125d), **Atka** (11a), **baka** (52b), **beka** (189), **dika** (23a), **Ekka** (26d), **Inka** (193), **kaka** (114b), **loka** (173c,184c), **pika** (93a, 128a,132c), **puka** (107a,168c), **roka** (95a,168c,d), **Saka** (10a), **sika** (41d,84b), **soka** (20c), **waka** (26a), **weka** (58c,106d,107a,127b), **Yaka** (191)

K - - A **kada** (188), **Kafa** (6c), **kaha** (123d), **kaka** (114b), **kala** (19a), **Kama** (56d), **kana** (84d), **kapa** (74b), **kara** (132a), **kasa** (48a), **kava** (18c 116a), **kawa** (18c,116a), **kela** (189), **keta** (45a), **kina** (126d), **kiva** (28c,125b), **koba** (11a), **kola** (25b,84a,108d), **Kola** (135b,c,d), **kona** (74c), **kora** (19a,178c), **kota** (117a), **Kota** (45d), **kuba** (26d,189), **kufa** (21b,99a), **kula** (189), **kusa**

K - - B **kerb** (146b), **knab** (107a), **knob** (73c,107c,124d), **knub** (178b).

K - - D **kaid** (29d,66a), **keld** (154b), **kind** (150d,153a,174d), **Kurd** (48b, 82a)

KE - - **keal** (25a), **keef** (75d), **keek** (154c), **keel** (128d,134d,144c,d), **keen** (15a,88a,177b), **keep** (123a,130d), **keet** (72b), **keif** (75d), **keir**

(20c,174d), **kela** (189), **keld** (154b), **kelp** (82a,141c), **Kelt** (180b), **kemp** (139b), **keno**, **Kent** (90d), **kepi** (99d), **kept**, **kerb** (146b), **kere** (75c,128b), **kerf** (40a,108b), **keri** (75c,128b), **kern** (59c,172a), **Kern** (132b), **Kerr**, **keta** (45a), **Ketu** (48b)

- KE - **akee** (168c), **akey** (189), **okeh** (8d,37b), **oket** (189), **skee** (149c), **skeg** (7d,86a,144d,157d,184a), **sken** (164a), **skeo** (57d), **skep** (16d,17c,77c), **skew** (148a,160c,171b,c), **skey** (185d)

- - KE **bake** (139a), **bike**, **cake**, **coke** (32d,64a), **cuke** (39b), **cyke** (40c), **dike** (49c,91d), **Dike** (78a), **duke** (107c), **dyke** (49c,91d), **fake** (123a,143c), **feke**, **fike** (139c), **fyke** (15d), **hake** (57a,b), **hike**, **hyke!**, **jake** (40d), **Jake** (96b), **joke** (183a), **juke** (114c), **lake** (117d), **like** (13c,37d,146d), **Loke** (15d,68b), **luke**, **Luke** (52a, 96a), **make** (35b,36d,54a,123a), **mike**, **Mike** (96b), **moke** (45c, 157d), **Nike** (69c,100c,182d), **Peke** (45a,148d), **pike** (57a,b,76c, 120b,153a), **poke** (108c), **rake** (41b,44c,134b,140d), **roke** (174d, 175b), **sake** (84b,125d), **soke** (44c,85d), **syke** (194), **take**, **tike** (29d), **tuke** (26b,53b), **tyke** (29d), **wake** (134b,168a), **woke**, **yoke** (85b,92d,173c), **Zeke** (96b)

K - - E **kade** (144a), **kale** (22a,25a,119b,175a), **kame** (67b,139b), **Kane** (74c), **Kate** (143c,183d), **kere** (75c,128b), **kibe** **kile** (189), **kine** (38a,112c), **kite** (19c,49a,74c,d), **kive** (174d), **Klee** (113a), **knee** (85b), **koae** (74b), **Kobe** (78a), **Kome** (71d), **kore** (107b) **Kore** (29a, 42b,116b,124d), **kuge** (84c), **Kure** (84c), **kyle** (57a,139c)

- - KF **wakf** (103a), **wukf** (103a)

K - - F **kaif** (88c), **keef** (75d), **keif** (75d), **kerf** (40a,108b), **kief** (75d), **kiff** (88c), **koff** (47a)

K - - G **k'ang** (30a), **king** (26c,29c), **knag** (115d,139c), **krag** (131c), **kung** (125b)

KH - - **khan** (7c,26c,81b,93d,116c,123c,130c,166c), **khar** (189), **khas** (153a), **khat** (105d), **Khem** (113c), **khet** (188), **khot**

- KH - **Akha** (86a,c)

- - KH **ankh** (38d,162b), **bikh** (120b), **bukh** (122a), **hakh** (46d), **lakh** (110c), **rukh** (53b,54a), **Sikh** (77b)

K - - H **kaph** (91d), **kath** (14a), **kish** (16d,70c), **Kish** (137c), **kith** (63c), **Koch** (66d), **koph** (91d), **Kush**, **kyah** (19a)

KI - - **kiak** (51c), **kibe**, **kiby** (29a), **kick**, **kief** (75d), **kiel** (128d,134d), **Kiel** (25d), **kier** (20c,174d), **Kiev**, **kiff** (88c), **kiho** (82a), **kiki** (27b), **kiku** (30d), **kile** (189), **kill** (38c), **kiln** (15d,112a), **kilo** (99b,122d), **kilt**, **kina** (126d), **kind** (150d,153a,174d), **kine** (38a,112c), **king** (26c,29c), **kink** (38b,171c), **kino** (27c,34c,47c,72c,98b,161d,168c), **kipp**, **kiri** (86a,87c,115a,168c), **kirk** (31a,139b), **kish** (16d,70c), **Kish** (137c), **kiss** (148c), **kist** (29d,58a,139b), **kite** (19c,49a,74c,d), **kith** (63c), **kiva** (28c,125b), **kive** (174d), **kivu** (170c), **kiwi** (11d, 19a,58c), **kiyi** (185d)

- KI - **akia** (74c), **Akim** (135d,191), **akin** (8b,92b,129c), **okia** (190), **Okie** (99d), **skid** (148b), **skil** (57a), **skim** (67c), **skin** (53a,76c,115c, d), **skio** (57d), **skip** (110b,114c,147c), **skir**, **skit** (145c), **skiv** (151b)

- - KI **Enki** (15b), **kaki** (84c,106d), **kiki** (27b), **Kuki** (191), **Loki** (7c,15d, 68b), **maki** (91b), **moki** (127b), **piki** (95c), **Reki** (16a), **saki** (39c,

84b,102a), **Tiki** (120c), **weki** (55c), **yaki** (193)

K - - I **kadi** (103a,171a), **kaki** (84c,106d), **kali** (26d,67c,136d,167a), **Kali** (147b), **Kami** (68a,84b,88c,107c,144c), **Kari** (14d), **kasi** (116b), **Kavi** (84d), **Kawi** (84d), **kazi** (103a), **kepi** (99d), **keri** (75c,128b), **kiki** (27b), **kiri** (86a,87c,115a,168c), **kiwi** (11d,19a,58c), **kiyi** (185d), **kobi** (84b), **koji** (185b), **Koli** (27b), **Komi** (191), **kopi** (107a, 168c), **Kopi** (172a), **kori** (7d,77a), **kuei** (44a), **Kuki** (191), **Kuli** (27b), **Kuri** (191), **kwei** (44a)

- KK - **Akka** (125d), **Ekka** (26d)

- - KK **bukk** (122a), **rikk** (49a)

K - - K **kaik** (96c), **kiak** (51c), **keek** (154c), **kick**, **kink** (38b,171c), **kirk** (31a,139b), **konk** (41c), **kunk** (188), **kurk** (31a,139b), **kyak** (51c)

KL - - **klam** (189), **Klee** (113a), **klom** (189), **klop** (150d)

K - - L **kail** (18c,22a,25a,79b), **Karl** (96a), **keal** (25a), **keel** (128d,134d, 144c,d), **kiel** (128d,134d), **Kiel** (25d), **kill** (38c), **koel** (19a,b,39b), **kohl** (53c), **kral**, **kuhl** (53c)

- KM - **ikmo** (18b)

K - - M **kasm** (189), **Khem** (113c), **klam** (189), **klom** (189)

KN - - **Knab** (107a), **knag** (115d,139c), **knap** (76d,107a,139b,159b,166a, 170c,185b), **knar** (87c,134b), **knee** (85b), **knew**, **knez** (123c), **knip** (115c), **knit** (173c,179b), **knob** (73c,107c,124d), **knop** (124b,170c, 185b), **knor** (87c), **knot** (43c,99d,107c,124d,137b), **knub** (178b), **knur** (67d,87c,107c), **knut**, **Knut** (40d,50c,96a)

K - - N **kaan** (93d,116c), **Kain**, **karn** (156c), **kaun** (93d), **kawn** (93d), **keen** (15a,88a,177b), **kern** (172a), **Kern** (132b), **khan** (7c,26c,81b,93d, 116c,123c,130c,166c), **kiln** (15d,112a), **kran** (190), **kuan** (30b), **Kuan** (30c), **kwan** (30b)

KO - - **koae** (74b), **koba** (11a), **Kobe** (78a), **kobi** (84b), **kobu** (84b), **Koch** (66d), **koel** (19a,b,39b), **koff** (47a), **kohl** (53c), **koir** (33a), **koji** (185b), **koko** (106d,114b), **Koko** (93d,186c), **koku** (189), **kola** (25b,84a,108d,168c), **Kola** (135b,c,d), **Koli** (27b), **kolo** (59b,135c), **Kome** (71d), **Komi** (191), **kona** (74c), **konk** (41c), **koop** (16c), **koph** (91d), **kopi** (107a,168c), **Kopi** (172a), **kora** (19a,178c), **Kora**, **kore** (107b), **Kore** (29a,42b,116b,124d), **kori** (7d,77a), **koso** (6c,80d), **Koso** (192,193), **koss** (188), **kota** (117a), **Kota** (45d), **koto** (84b), **kozo** (113d,168c)

- KO - **akov** (189), **Ekoi** (191), **ikon** (79d,136a)

- - KO **boko** (52b), **Doko** (191), **hako** (115b), **jako** (71a), **koko** (106d,114b), **Koko** (93d,186c), **mako** (18a,19a,20d,143c,168c,182c), **moko** (96c), **toko** (30c)

K - - O **kago** (113a), **kalo** (162a), **Kano** (84c,177d), **karo** (106d), **kayo** (87c), **keno**, **kiho** (82a), **kilo** (99b,122d), **kino** (27c,34c,47c,72c, 98b,161d,168c), **koko** (106d,114b), **Koko** (93d,186c), **kolo** (59b, 135c), **koso** (6c,80d), **Koso** (192,193), **koto** (84b), **kozo** (113d,168c), **Kroo** (191)

K - - P **Kapp**, **keep** (123a,130d), **kelp** '82a,141c), **kemp** (139b), **kipp**, **klop** (150d), **knap** (76d,107a,139b.159b,166a,170c,185b), **knip** (115c), **knop** (124b,170c,185b), **koop** (16c)

KR - - **krag** (131c), **kral**, **kran** (190), **kras** (76d), **kris** (40b,95d), **Kroo** (191)

- KR - **akra** (176a), **Akra** (191), **ikra** (27d), **okra** (72c,175a), **okro** (72c, 175a)

- - KR **Askr** (107d)

K - - R **kair**, **keir** (20c,174d), **Kerr**, **khar** (189), **kier** (20c,174d), **knar** (87c,134b), **knor** (87c), **knur** (67d,87c,107c), **koir** (33a), **Kuar** (102a), **kyar** (33a)

- - KS **oaks** (154d)

K - - S **khas** (153a), **kiss** (148c), **koss** (188), **kras** (76d), **kris** (40b,95d), **kvas** (135c)

- - KT **takt** (105a,163a)

K - - T **kaat** (105d), **kant** (28d), **Kant** (67a), **keet** (72b), **Kelt** (180b), **Kent** (90d), **kept**, **khat** (105d), **khet** (188), **khot**, **kilt**, **kist** (29d,58a, 139b), **knit** (173c,179b), **knot** (43c,99d,107c,124d,137b), **knut**, **Knut** (40d,50c,96a), **kyat** (189)

KU - - **Kuan** (30c), **kuan** (30b), **Kuar** (102a), **kuba** (26d,189), **kudu** (11a), **kuei** (44a), **kufa** (21b,99a), **kuge** (84c), **kuhl** (53c), **Kuki** (191), **kuku** (19a,106d), **kula** (189), **Kuli** (27b), **kung** (125b), **kunk** (188), **Kurd** (48b,82a), **Kure** (84c), **Kuri** (191), **kurk** (31a,139b), **kusa**, **Kush**

- KU - **akua** (120d), **skua** (19b,72c,84a,141a)

- - KU **baku** (26d,157b,168c), **duku** (95d,168c), **ḥaku** (86d), **hiku** (57a, 106d,138a), **kiku** (30d), **koku** (189), **kuku** (19a,106d), **Maku** (192), **poku** (11a), **puku** (11a), **Suku** (191), **Taku** (80c)

K - - U **Kadu** (191), **kagu** (106c), **kahu** (14d), **Ketu** (48b), **kiku** (30d), **kivu** (170c), **kobu** (84b), **koku** (189), **kudu** (11a), **kuku** (19a,106d)

KV - - **kvas** (135c)

- KV - **NKVD** (135d)

K - - V **Kiev**

KW - - **kwan** (30b), **kwei** (44a)

K - - W **knew**, **know**

KY - - **kyah** (19a), **kyak** (51c), **kyar** (33a), **kyat** (189), **kyle** (57a,139c)

- KY - **Skye** (163c), **skyr** (21d,151a), **skyt** (138c,140b)

- - KY **alky**, **caky**, **coky**, **faky**, **inky** (20b), **joky**, **laky**, **oaky**, **piky**, **poky** (148c), **taky**, **waky**

K - - Y **Katy** (183d), **kazy** (103a), **kiby** (29a)

K - - Z **knez** (123c)

LA - - **laap** (51d,91b,141d), **lace** (58b,179c), **lack** (178a), **lact** (34c), **lacy**, **Ladd** (143c), **lade** (24c,26d,43c,93b,100a,132a,139d,161b,178d), **lady**, **laet** (60d), **lago** (83b,152b), **laic** (32b,90b,107d,124a,141d), **laid**, **lain**, **lair** (37c,42b), **Lais** (17c), **lait** (62a), **lake** (117d), **lakh** (110c), **laky**, **lala** (129b), **lalo** (16b,34d,153a), **Lalo** (35c), **lama** (23d,24a,91d,165b), **lamb**, **Lamb** (49c), **lame** (38d,43d,73b), **lamp** (92a,94c), **lana** (58a,66a,90a,184b), **land** (44a,163c), **lane** (134b, 157b), **lank** (148b,164b), **lant**, **lanx** (133a,b), **Laos** (80d,129c), **Lapp** (108a), **Lara** (25c), **lard** (54d,61a,71a,110a), **lari** (78a,101c),

Lari (72c), **lark** (19a,63d,177b), **larp** (51d), **Lars** (51d,121b), **lash** (58c,87b,165c,180d), **Lasi** (191), **lass** (95b), **last** (36c,50b,145a, 174c), **lata** (85d,95d), **late** (128c), **lath** (157c), **latu** (190), **laud** (122a), **laun** (146b), **lava** (101c,132b,151a,177a), **lave** (16d,178b), **lawn** (20a,37c,53b,92c), **laze** (79b), **Laze** (191), **Lazi** (191), **lazo** (88d,128b,133d), **lazy**

- LA - **alae** (182d), **alai** (171a), **Alai** (135c), **alan** (45a,79a,183c), **Alan**, **alar** (15c,145c,182d), **alas** (52c,136b,183b), **alat** (136d), **alay** (5c), **blaa**, **blab** (162b), **blae** (93b), **blah**, **blas** (6c,49c), **Blas** (17b), **blat** (25b), **blay** (57d), **clad** (46a,82a), **clam** (20b,101b), **clan** (169c), **clap** (58b), **claw** (29c,105b,161d,173a), **Clay** (9d), **Elah** (18c,86d), **elan** (12c,41a,50d,62a,153c,177a,186b), **Elam** (18d,37d, 82a,116c,144b), **ELAS** (71c), **flag** (16b,50d,82b,88c,115a,155a), **flak** (11a), **flam** (169c), **flan** (39d,40a,114d), **flap** (17b,59a,104a, 118d,161a,182d), **flat** (41b,124b,173a), **flaw**, **flax**, **flay** (147c,157c), **glad** (85c), **klam** (189), **Olaf** (108a,176b), **olam** (51a,d,75c,81a), **Olan** (115c), **Olax** (52b), **olay** (113b), **plan** (99b,124a,138b), **plap** (54b), **plat** (22b,96c,114a,119c,133d), **play** (63d,154a), **slab** (148b), **slag** (46c,99a,138c,148d,177a), **slam** (180d,182d), **slap** (24a,128c, 148c), **slat** (58b,89a,117c,184a), **Slav** (13c,40c,48b,52a,120b,135b), **slaw**, **slay**, **Ulam** (67b), **ulan** (27d,88a)

- - LA **agla** (7a), **alla** (6d), **amla** (48a,161d,168c,169a), **aula** (66c,73b), **Bala** (26c,66a), **bela** (12a), **Bela** (18b,48c,78d), **bola** (16a,179b), **cela** (62d), **cola** (25b,108d,149d,168c), **dola** (189), **ella** (152c, 158c), **Ella** (183c), **fala** (129b), **gala** (55d), **Gala** (191), **gila** (93b), **gola** (27b,40c,70c,157a), **gula** (90a,101a,165b), **hala** (112b), **Hela** (93c), **hila** (53c), **hola** (74c,152b), **hula** (74b), **Hyla** (10a,166d, 169b), **lola**, **jula**, **kala** (19a), **kela** (189), **kola** (25b,84a,108d,168c), **Kola** (135b,c,d), **kula** (189), **lala** (129b), **Lila** (183c), **Lola** (27d,97b), **mala** (89c,90a,94b,97d,109d,185c), **mela** (34a,129d), **mila** (188), **Mola** (159c), **Nala** (77a), **Nola**, **olla** (36d,44b,84d,113b,121d, 151d,152c,181b), **pala** (189), **Pala** (88b), **pela** (30c), **Pola**, **pyla** (22d), **sala** (50c,152a,b,c), **Sala** (50c), **sola** (9a,48a,74b,118c, 154a,167b), **Sula** (65a), **tala** (16d,113a,168c,d), **tela** (22d,98c, 121b,166a,179c), **tola** (48a,80d,180a), **Tola** (85b), **tula** (9a), **Tula**, **upla**, **vela** (98c,136b,149d), **Vela** (36b,c), **vila** (54b), **vola** (89d), **Zola** (63a)

L - - A **lala** (129b), **lama** (23d,24a,91d,165b), **lana** (58a,66a,90a,184b), **Lara** (25c), **lata** (85d,95d), **lava** (101c,132b,151a,177a), **Leda** (27b, 75d,120c,153a,171d,186b), **lena** (56d), **Lena** (36b), **Lida** (183c), **lija** (57a,90d,173a), **Lila** (183c), **lima** (17b,152b,174d), **Lima** (31b), **lina** (188), **Lina** (183d), **lipa** (54d), **lira** (28b,79a,170d), **Lisa** (183d), **loka** (173c,184c), **Lola** (27d,97b), **loma** (58b,63d), **lora** (146b,149b, 151c,169b), **Lora** (183c), **lota** (24c,121d,178d), **Lota**, **lowa** (19a), **Luba** (191), **luna** (103c), **Luna** (102b), **lura** (22d,82a), **lyra**, **Lyra** (36b,74a)

- LB - **alba** (98b,181a), **Alba** (151d), **albe** (133a), **Albi** (58a), **albo** (34d, 181a), **Elba** (105d), **Elbe** (108a)

- - LB **bulb** (37a,172c)

L - - B **lamb**, **Lamb** (49c), **limb** (12d,22d), **lobb** (23b,94c,163a)

- LC - **Alca** (14c,128b), **alco** (45b)

- - LC **talc** (28d,63b,99c,100b,122a,149c)

L - - C **laic** (32b,90b,107d,124a,141d)

- LD - **Alda** (110d,150c), **alda** (152b)

- - LD **bald** (16c), **bold** (41a), **cold** (65d), **eild** (138d,140a), **fold, geld** (162b), **gild** (14a,49c,69c,98b), **gold, held, Hild, hold** (95c,124c, 130d), **Keld** (154b), **meld** (26a,41c,99a,118b), **mild** (32a,66a), **mold** (54d,143c), **sold, suld** (188), **told** (129c), **veld** (151a), **weld** (47c, 85b,173c), **wild** (38b,173d), **wold** (47c,60a,118d,174a,184a)

L - - D **Ladd** (143c), **laid, land** (44a,163c), **lard** (54d,61a,71a,110a), **laud** (122a), **lead** (35d,43d,72b,74d,81a), **lend** (6d,79d), **lied** (66d,150b), **load** (24c,26d,161b), **lood** (189) **lord** (107c), **loud** (156a), **Ludd** (23c)

LE - - **lead** (35d,43d,72b,74d,81a), **leaf** (55c,73c,119b), **Leah** (19a,84a, 87b,183c), **leak** (110c), **leal** (54b,94c,139d), **lean** (128a,148b,152d, 164b,166a), **leap** (26c), **lear** (139d), **Lear** (37a,143b), **lech** 102b), **Leda** (27b,75d,120c,153a,171d,186b), **leek** (58b,76a,110c,177d), **leer** (9d,58a,67c,93d,112a,148c), **lees** (46a,142a), **leet** (26a, 38a,139d), **left** (42c), **lehr** (67c,112a) **Leif** (107d), **Leir, Lely** (47a), **lena** (56d), **Lena** (36b), **lend** (6d,79d), **lene** (36b,149a, 172b), **leno** (37c,53b), **lens** (67c,95b,111a,129b,162d), **lent** (54d), **Lent** (115d,141c), **Leon** (96a), **Lero** (82d), **lerp** (51d,141d), **less** (100c,108b,141d), **lest** (59d,163d), **lete, Leti** (82d), **Leto** (11c), **Lett** (16a,90a,93a), **leve** (62a), **Levi** (84a,90c), **levo** (91a), **levy** (14a, 162b)

- LE - **Alea** (14b,31c,167d), **alec** (10a,57c,d,76c,137c), **alee** (15c,75d, 144b,157a,182a), **alef** (91c), **alem** (98b,155a,170d,171a), **alen** (40d, 138a), **bleb** (20c,23d,67c), **bled, blet** (64a), **bleu** (61b), **blew, clee** (19a,129a), **clef** (104d,105a), **clem** (56b,158b), **clew** (16a,33a,77b, 136b,164d), **elef** (91c), **flea** (81b), **fled, flee, flew, flex** (18a), **fley** (63d), **gled** (19a,52a,87a), **glee** (99a,150b), **glen** (43c), **Hler** (141a), **ilex** (77d), **Klee** (113a), **Lleu** (40c), **Llew** (40c), **olea** (170b), **Olea** (110b), **oleo** (34c), **plea** (51a,52d,122a,130b), **pleb** (10d,35b,180b), **plet** (135d), **plew** (17c), **plex** (60b), **Sleb** (12a), **sled** (40a), **slee** (140b,148c), **slew** (160a), **sley** (179b), **Ulex** (153c), **vlei** (38c, 160a), **vley** (160a)

- - LE **able** (26b,35b,126a,147c), **acle** (13d,82c,115d), **aile** (62b,63a,182c, d), **Alle** (14c), **atle** (136d,161d,169b), **axle** (153c,180c), **bale** (24b, 74a), **bile** (30c), **bole** (31d,32a,169b), **cale** (72d), **cole** (25a), **Cole, dale** (43c,128a,174b), **dele** (26a,49c,51b,53a,110b,123d,124c,130a, 145c,161b), **dole** (44c,118c,121c,129d), **Dole** (74c), **elle** (62b,c), **file** (13a,127d), **gale** (181d), **gyle** (23b,174d), **hale** (125b), **Hale** (9d,131a), **hole** (6c,11b,110d,118c,147a), **hule** (23a,134c), **hyle** (97c), **idle** (174b,c,178c), **ille** (89b,d,163d), **lole** (52a,76b,123c), **isle** (8b,53c,81d,82d,86b,88a), **ixle** (56a), **jole** (29b), **Jule** (183d), **kale** (22a,25a,119b,175a), **kile** (189), **kyle** (57a,139c), **male** (154d), **Male** (45d), **mele** (74b,150b), **mile** (64c), **mole** (19d,23a,24d,85a, 117c,155c), **Mole** (88c), **mule** (45b,148b,153c,180b), **nile** (33c, 71d), **Nile** (106b), **ogle** (9d,53c,91a,93d,148c), **orle** (17b,56b,76a, 144b,177a), **pale** (113a,117c,178a), **Pele** (69c,74c), **pile** (45d,75b, 117c), **pole** (132c,143b,177b,184a), **Pole** (52a), **pule** (180d), **pyle** (34b), **Pyle** (9c,178a), **rale** (7c,23a,29d,41b), **rile** (10c,d,82c,125a,

156b,176a), **role** (114b), **rule** (11b,26b,90b), **sale** (14c,61c,62b,c, 168b), **sole** (52c,57a,b,58b,d,110c,115d,150a), **tale** (91a,185b), **tele** (34b,122c), **tile** (31d,56d,72b,95b,133c,163c), **tole** (9a,51a,99b, 163a), **tule** (24b,27c), **vale** (54c,128a,174b), **Vale** (7c,109c), **vile** (16c,56c), **vole** (97d,104a), **wale** (70b,131b,157c,163d,179a,180a, c,d), **wile** (13b,41c,157b,169c), **Yale** (173c), **Yule** (30d)

L - - E **lace** (58b,179c), **lade** (24c,26d,43c,93b,100a,132a,139d,161b), 178d), **lake** (117d), **lame** (38d,43d,73b), **lane** (134b,157b), **late** (128c), **lave** (16d,178b), **laze** (79b), **Laze** (191), **lene**(36b,149a, 172b), **lete, leve** (62a), **life** (19a,177a), **like** (13c,37d,146d), **lime** (25b,27d,31b,33c,102d,168c), **line** (12b,22b,36d,38a,126c,134b, 157b,158b,162d,175c), **lire** (62c), **lite** (158c,d), **live** (47c), **lobe** (90c,134b), **lode** (42c,99a,111b,175b), **loge** (164a), **Loke** (15d,68b), **Lome, lone** (150a), **lope** (48b,64b,d), **lore** (77c,87c,90d,151c,183a), **lose** (60a,100c), **lote** (24c,94a), **love** (163a), **lube** (110a), **luce** (58c,117d), **Luce** (7b,35a), **luge** (148a), **luke, Luke** (52a,96a), **lune** (38c,73b,74d), **lupe** (19a,64a), **lure** (41c,51a,54b,163a), **lute** (11c, 28b,84d,105a,131d), **luxe** (61c,62d,159c), **lyre** (11c,81c,105a,111c), **lyse**

- LF - **alfa** (70d)

- - LF **calf, golf** (154a), **gulf** (6c), **half** (101a), **pelf** (22a,56c,131b), **self** (48d,80d), **Welf** (67a), **wolf**

L - - F **leaf** (55c,73c,119b), **Leif** (107d), **lief** (181d), **loaf** (49b,94b), **loof** (144c,153d), **luff** (136b), **luif**

- LG - **alga** (141b,c), **Algy** (96b), **Olga** (135c,183c)

L - - G **ling** (24c,57a,b,75b,178c), **long** (38b,185b), **lung, lurg** (96d,141b, 184d)

L - - H **lakh** (110c), **lash** (58c,87b,165c,180d), **lath** (157c), **Leah** (19a,84a, 87b,183c), **lech** (102b), **lith** (34d,156c), **loch** (88a,139d), **losh** (178b), **loth** (15a,173d), **Lugh** (28b), **lush** (94d)

LI - - **Liam** (181d), **liar** (98d), **Lias** (66a), **lick, Lida** (183c), **Lido** (83d, 175b), **lied** (66d,150b), **lief** (181d), **lien** (65c,91a,124c), **lieu** (118c, 155d), **life** (19a,177a), **lift** (49b), **liin** (188), **lija** (57a,90d,173a), **like** (13c,37d,146d), **Lila** (183c), **lill** (15d,118a), **lilt** (93a,131a, 147a), **lily, lima** (17b,152b,174d), **Lima** (31b), **limb** (12d,22d), **lime** (25b,27d,31b,33c,102d,168c), **limn** (45d,121c), **limp** (58a,81a,177d), **limu** (141c), **limy** (176d), **lina** (188), **Lina** (183d), **line** (12b,22b,36d,38a,126c,134b,157b,158b,162d,175c), **ling** (24c,57a,b,75b,178c), **link** (36a,81d,85b), **linn** (120d,140a,c, 168c,178d), **lino, lint** (46a,58d), **liny** (157b), **Linz** (40d), **lion** (55b, 86c), **lipa** (54d), **lira** (28b,79a,170d), **lire** (62c), **Lisa** (183d), **lisp** 153b), **liss** (54b,58b,60c,129d,140a), **list** (26d,27b,75b,83d,134a, 138b,165d), **lite** (158c,d), **lith** (34d,156c), **liti** (60d), **litz** (127b), **live** (47c), **Livy** (132d,133a)

- LI - **alia** (89d), **alif** (12b), **alii** (74c,134c), **alim** (103b,162c) **alin** (188), **alit** (44b,143a), **Alix** (183c), **Clim** (12b), **Clio** (104d), **clip** (54d, 143d), **Elia** (88a,115d), **Elis** (22c,37d,71b,107c), **flip** (167c), **flit** (41a), **flix, glia** (106c), **glib** (58d,149a,177c), **glim, glis** (45c), **ilia** (21d,77b,115d), **ille** (89b,d), **olic** (158b), **olid** (55d,60c,148d,157d), **olio** (44b,77c,98c,100d,121d), **plie** (32c,59b), **slid, slim** (148b,

160a), **slip** (67c,119a), **slit** (40a)

- - LI **amli** (48a,161d,168c,169a), **Atli** (14c,72b,79a,107d), **Bali**, **Beli** (23c), **coli**, **dali** (168c,169b), **doli**, **fili**, **gali** (6c), **goli** (105c), **Holi** (77a), **joli** (62b), **kali** (26d,67c,136d,167a), **Kali** (147b), **Koli** (27b, **Kuli** (27b), **mali** (27b), **pali** (122b), **Pali** (23d,24a,137b,175a), **pili** (34b,108d), **puli** (45a,78d), **soli** (12c,110c), **tali** (189), **teli** (94b), **vali** (171a,176a), **Vali** (7c,109c), **vili** (54b), **Vili** (109c), **wali** (171a), **yali** (171a)

L - - I **Lari** (72c), **lari** (78a,101c), **Lasi** (191), **Lazi** (191), **Leti** (82d), **Levi** (84a,90c), **liti** (60d), **loci** (66b,118c), **Lodi** (105d), **Loki** (7c,15d, 68b), **lori** (91b), **Loti** (63a,176a), **ludi** (133b), **Luri** (191)

- LK - **alky**

- - LK **balk** (118c,146a,156d), **bilk** (29b,41c,42a), **bulk** (97b), **calk** (78c, 109a,141c,178d), **folk** (116a,169c), **fulk** (173a), **hulk** (144d,173d), **milk**, **mulk** (60d), **polk** (37c), **pulk** (37c,88d), **silk** (53b,179c), **sulk** (159a), **talk**, **volk** (66c,105d,116a), **Volk**, **walk**, **welk** (65c,96d, 141b), **yolk**

L - - K **lack** (178a), **lank** (148b,164b), **lark** (19a,63d,177b), **leak** (110c), **leek** (58b,76a,110c,177d), **lick**, **link** (36a,81d,85b), **lock** (54d), **lonk** (143d), **look** (11c,53c,142a), **luck** (28d), **lurk** (92a, 147d)

LL - - **llyn** (120d,140a), **Lleu** (40c), **Llew** (40c)

- LL - **alla** (6d), **Alle** (14c), **allo** (34c), **ally** (14a,35c,d,173c), **ella** (152c, 158c), **Ella** (183c), **elle** (62b,c), **ille** (89b,d,163d), **ills** (170a), **olla** (36d,44b,84d,113b,121d,151d,152c,181b), **ullo** (6a,144a), **Ullr** (146b,164d)

- - LL **ball**, **bell** (24c,39d), **Bell** (162d), **bill** (17b,147a), **Bill** (96b), **boll** (119b,d), **bull** (113c), **call** (145c,159b,176d), **cell** (39b), **cull** (117c), **dell** (43c,174b), **dill** (13a,117c), **doll** (125c), **dull** (21a,32c,173a), **Dull** (94b), **fall** (46b,141c), **fell** (40a,58b,76c,115d,147d), **fill** (109b), **full** (7b,130b), **gall** (19a,28c,29b,82c,160c,176a), **gill** (22d), **Goll**, **gull** (32d,41c,42a,72c,99b,141a), **hall** (37b,114d), **hill**, **hull** (141d,142a,144c,d), **Jill** (183d), **kill** (38c), **lill** (15d,118a), **loll** (94b,128c), **lull** (126d,150c), **mall** (95d,124b,143b), **mill** (126c), **moll**, **Moll** (183d), **mull** (53b,135a,164c), **Nell** (110a,183d), **nill** (173d), **Noll** (96b,110b), **null** (108c,177a), **pall** (32d,81b,112a), **pill**, **poll** (74d,160a,177c), **pull** (45d,167d), **rill** (23c,102b,132a,148d, 157b), **roll** (134a,160b), **rull** (170b), **sell** (97a,115c,175b), **sill** (45c, 76c,165a,182b), **tall** (118d), **tell** (105d,129c,154b), **Tell** (160d), **till** (39c,101c,173d), **toll** (131c), **vill** (176b), **wall**, **well**, **will** (18b,43a, 163c,177c), **yell** (145c)

L - - L **leal** (54b,94c,139d), **lill** (15d,118a), **loll** (94b,128c), **lull** (25c,126d,150c)

- LM - **alma** (40d,53d,146d,147a), **Alma** (38d,183c), **alme** (40d,147a), **alms** (29a), **elmy**, **ulme** (49c)

- - LM **balm** (110a,172c), **calm** (8d,11d,112b,118d,126c,d,172b,173d), **culm** (11a,32d,70d,145a,156a), **film** (164b), **halm**, **helm** (144d, 165d), **holm** (77d,82d,109a), **malm** (32a,92b), **palm** (59b,168a,169b)

L - - M **Liam** (181d), **loam** (47d), **loom** (11c,146b,179b), **lyam** (139a)

- LN - **ulna** (21d,39b)

- - LN **kiln** (15d,112a), **vuln** (184d)

L - - N **Lain, laun** (146b), **lawn** (20a,37c,53b,92c), **lean** (128a,148b,152d, 164b,166a), **Leon** (96a), **lien** (65c,91a,124c), **liin** (188), **limn** (45d, 121c), **linn** (120d,140a,c,168c,178d), **lion** (55b,86c), **llyn** (120d, 140a), **loan, loin** (40a,98a), **loon** (19a,b,c,157d,179c), **lorn** (42d, 60b), **loun** (19a,b), **lown** (157d)

LO - - **load** (24c,26d,161b), **loaf** (79b,94b), **loam** (47d,150a), **loan, lobb** (23b,94c,163a), **lobe** (90c,134b), **lobo** (165d,183c), **loch** (88a,139d), **loci** (66b,118c), **lock** (54d), **loco** (38b,119b,120b), **lode** (42c,99a, 111b,175b), **Lodi** (105d), **Lodz, loft** (14c,69d,104b,178b), **loge** (164a), **logy** (46d), **loin** (40a,98a), **loir** (45c), **Loir, Lois** (165d,183c), **loka** (173c,184c), **Loke** (7c,15d,68b), **Loki** (7c,15d,68b), **Lola** (27d, 97b), **loll** (94b,128c), **Lolo** (27d,30a), **loma** (58b,63d), **Lome, lone** (150a), **long** (38b,185b), **Lonk** (143d), **lood** (189), **loof** (144c,153d) **look** (11c,53c,142a), **loom** (11c,146b,179b), **loon** (19a,b,c,157d, 179c), **loop** (31b,107d), **Loos, loot** (22a,118a,119d,136a,153d), **lope** (48b,64b,d), **lora** (146b,149b,151c,169b), **Lora** (183c), **lord** (107c), **lore** (77c,87c,90d,151c,183a), **lori** (91b), **lorn** (42d,60b), **loro** (19a,114b), **lory** (19a,114a), **lose** (60a,100c), **losh** (178b), **loss** (42c,123d,178b), **lost, lota** (24c,121d,178d), **lote** (24c,94a), **loth** (15a,173d), **Loti** (63a,176a), **loto** (65a,121d,178d), **lots, loud** (156a), **loun** (19a,b), **loup** (61d,62a,90c,139d), **Loup** (193), **lour** (13d,63d), **lout** (15c,22a,24b,45b,109a,157d), **love** (163a), **lowa** (19a), **lown** (157d), **lowp** (90c,139d)

- LO - **alod** (51c,55d,88a,124c), **aloe** (7d,20a,76a,b,92b,98b,119b,158b, 167a,183d), **alop** (13d,46b,93d), **alow** (18a,172c), **blob, bloc** (173a), **blot, blow, clod** (22a,45b,157d), **Cloe** (183c), **clog** (30c,145b), **clop, clot** (32d,94d), **clou** (62b), **clow** (58c,148c), **cloy** (61b,137c, 159d), **elod** (49b,59d,79c), **Elon** (18c,51b,108a), **floc** (149a), **floe** (79b), **flog** (180d), **flop** (54a), **flot** (173a), **flow** (157b), **glom** (155d, 160d,178c), **glow** (144c), **ilog** (132a,161b), **ilot** (82d), **klom** (189), **klop** (150d), **Olor** (160a,b), **plod** (170b), **plop** (54b), **plot** (25a,36b, 118d,138b), **plow** (39c,165d), **ploy** (43c), **slob** (173d), **sloe** (14a,20b, 64a,119d,181c), **slog** (157c,170b,177d), **sloo** (160a), **slop, slot** (10d, 11b,41d,110d,167d,168a,181b), **slow** (43c)

- - LO **allo** (34c), **bilo** (131b), **bolo** (87a), **calo** (72d), **dilo** (120d,168c), **filo, gilo** (48a), **Golo** (191), **Gulo** (183c), **halo** (14d,31b,92a), **hilo** (74c), **kalo** (162a), **kilo** (99b,122d), **kolo** (59b,135c), **lalo** (16b,34d), **Lalo** (35c), **Lolo** (27d,30a), **malo** (23a,74c,152a), **milo** (70b,87c), **Milo, nolo** (42a), **orlo** (56b,119c), **Oslo, palo** (152c), **pelo** (83b), **polo** (154a), **Polo** (175b), **ralo** (188), **silo** (59a), **solo** (12c,89a,110c), **ullo** (6a,144a), **velo** (175b)

L - - O **lago** (83b,152b), **lalo** (16b,34d), **Lalo** (35c), **lazo** (88d,128b,133d), **leno** (37c,53b), **Lero** (82d), **Leto** (11c), **levo** (91a), **Lido** (83d,175b), **lino, lobo** (165d,183c), **loco** (38b,119b,120b), **Lolo** (27d,30a), **loro** (19a,114b), **loto** (65a,121d), **ludo** (65a,112b)

- LP - **Alph** (132a), **Alps** (85d), **olpe** (90d,182c)

- - LP **calp** (92b), **colp** (28a,148b), **gulp** (46a,79d,160a), **help** (14a), **kelp** (82a,141c), **palp** (11a,55b,58b,167c), **pulp, salp** (148d), **yelp**

L - - P **laap** (51d,91b,141d), **lamp** (92a,94c), **Lapp** (108a), **larp** (51d), **leap** (26c), **lerp** (51d,141d), **limp** (58a,81a,177d), **lisp** (153b), **loop** (31b,107d), **loup** (61d,62a,90c,139d), **Loup** (193), **lowp** (90c,139d), **lump** (45a,160c)

- - LR **Ullr** (146b,164d)

L - - R **lair** (37c,42b), **lear** (139d), **Lear** (37a,143b), **leer** (9d,58a,67c,93d, 112a,148c), **lehr** (67c,112a), **Leir, liar** (98d), **loir** (45c), **Loir, lour** (13d,63d)

- LS - **also** (10b,18b,80a), **Elsa** (70a,93c,110d,177b,183c), **else** (18b,79b, 111d)

- - LS **fels** (190), **fils** (62d,150b), **Hals** (47a), **ills** (170a)

L - - S **Lais** (17c), **Laos** (80d,129c), **Lars** (51d,121b), **lass** (95b), **lees** (46a, 142a), **lens** (95b,111a,129b,162d), **less** (100c,108b,141d), **Lias** (66a), **liss** (54b,58b,60c,129d,140a) **Lois** (165d,183c), **Loos, loss** (42c,123d,178b), **lots, Lubs** (94c), **Lyas** (66a)

- LT - **alta** (89c,152d), **alto** (152b,176c,177a)

- - LT **Balt** (93a), **belt** (16a,31a), **bolt** (13b,54d,58b,132d,160a), **bult** (76d), **celt** (30c,82c,123a,156c,167b,179b), **Celt** (10a,180a,b), **colt** (78c,131a,185d,186b), **Colt, cult** (141d,161c), **dolt** (20c,59c,157d), **felt, galt, gelt** (101c), **gilt** (69c,77c,151d,185d), **halt** (13b,28a,38d, 156d), **hilt** (73c), **holt** (36d,119b,184b), **jilt, jolt** (143b), **Kelt** (180b), **kilt, lilt** (93a,131a,147a), **malt** (17c), **melt, milt** (153d), **molt** (27a, 143d) **pelt** (53a), **salt** (35d,105b,123a,136c,141c,149d), **silt** (104b, 142a), **tilt** (26b,d,166a), **tolt, volt** (49b,78c), **Walt** (96b), **welt** (36d,131b,145a,b,177b,d), **wilt** (46b), **yelt** (151b)

L - - T **lact** (34c), **laet** (60d), **lait** (62a), **lant, last** (36c,50b,145a,174c), **leet** (26a,38a,139d), **left** (42c), **lent** (54d), **Lent** (115d,141c), **lest** (59d, 163d), **Lett** (16a,90a,93a), **lift** (49b), **lilt** (93a,131a,147a), **lint** (46a, 58d), **list** (26d,27b,75b,83d,134a,138b,165d), **loft** (14c,69d,104b, 178b), **loot** (22a,118a,119d,136a,153d), **lost, lout** (15c,22a,24b,45b, 109a,157d), **lust** (41b)

LU - - **Luba** (191), **lube** (110a), **Lubs** (94c), **luce** (58c,117d), **Luce** (7b,35a), **luck** (28d), **lucy, Lucy** (183c), **Ludd** (23c), **ludi** (133b), **ludo** (65a, 112b), **luff** (136b), **luge** (148a), **Lugh** (28b), **luif, luke, Luke** (52a, 96a), **lull** (25c,126d,150c), **lulu** (19a,57b,112c), **Lulu** (183d), **lump** (45a,160c), **luna** (103c), **Luna** (102b), **lune** (38c,73b,74d), **lung, luny** (38b), **lupe** (19a,64a), **lura** (22d,82a), **lure** (41c,51a,54b,163a), **lurg** (96d,141b,184d), **Luri** (191), **lurk** (92a,147d), **lush** (94d), **lust** (41b), **lute** (11c,28b,84d,105a,131d), **luxe** (61c,62d,159c)

- LU - **alum** (14a,45c), **Alur** (191), **blub, blue** (33c,98c,102c,150d,173a), **blup, blur, blut** (66b), **club** (39c), **clue, Elul** (102b), **flub** (22b), **flue** (8b,30a), **flux** (28d,58d), **glub, glue** (7b,156a), **glug, glum** (102c, 159a), **glut** (52c,70a,137c,159d), **Ilus** (88d,170b), **plug** (156d,184d), **plum, plup, plus** (10b,102c) **slub** (171c), **slue** (97b,148b,160a), **slug** (46b,99b,157c), **slum, slur** (44b,124c,148b,168a), **ulua** (57a,74c), **Ulua** (141b)

- - LU **Aalu** (6b,48d), **aulu** (74c,168c), **balu** (104b,159a,181d), **hulu** (55b), **lalu** (48d), **iglu** (51c,149b), **lulu** (19a,57b,112c), **Lulu** (183d), **pelu** (30a,106d,168c), **pulu** (74c), **Sulu** (102c), **tolu** (16a), **Tulu** (45d), **zulu** (171d,175d), **Zulu** (86a)

L - - U **latu** (190), **lieu** (118c,155d), **limu** (141c), **Lleu** (40c), **lulu** (19a,57b, 112c), **Lulu** (183d)

- LV - **Alva** (151d), **Ulva** (141b)

LW - - **Lwow**

L - - W **Llew** (40c), **Lwow**

- - LX **calx** (23c,75c,112c), **falx** (133b)

L - - X **lanx** (133a,b), **lynx** (26c,181d), **Lynx** (36b)

LY - - **lyam** (139a), **Lyas** (66a), **lynx** (26c,181d), **Lynx** (36b), **Lyra** (36b, 74a), **lyre** (11c,81c,105a,111c), **lyse**

- LY - **Alya** (155b,c), **Alys** (183c), **Clym** (12b), **Ilyn** (120d,140a)

- - LY **ably** (147c), **ally** (14a,35c,d,173c), **coly** (104a), **eely** (185a), **holy, idly, inly, July, Lely** (47a), **lily, moly** (76a,181c), **oily** (110b, 172c), **only** (24d,52c,98d,147a,150a), **Orly** (8b), **paly** (194), **pily, poly** (34c,76b), **puly, rely** (16b,170b), **rily** (176a), **ugly, vily** (54b), **wily** (13b,38b,39c)

L - - Y **Lacy, lady, laky, lazy, Lely** (47a), **levy** (14a,162b, **lily, limy** (176d), **liny** (157b), **livy** (132d,133a), **logy** (46d), **lory** (19a,114a), **lucy, Lucy** (183c), **luny** (38b)

L - - Z **Linz** (40d), **litz** (127b), **Lodz**

MA - - **maal** (188), **ma'am** (95a,166b), **maar** (177a), **Maas** (132a), **Maat** (69a,b,85d), **Maba** (103a,168d), **mabi** (58d), **mace** (49d,108d,153b, 154d,161a,178a), **mack, made, Madi** (174a), **mado** (14d,57a,170b), **mage** (95b), **magg** (95b), **Magh** (102a), **magi** (123c), **Magi** (95b, 116c,183a), **maha** (28c,88c,136d), **mahr** (103a), **Maia** (76b,109a, 153b,155b,177c), **maid** (45b,142d), **mail** (12d,99b,121c), **maim** (43d,81a,105c), **main** (29d,35d,123d), **mais** (61b), **maja** (151c), **Maja** (153b), **majo, make** (35b,36d,54a,123a), **maki** (91b), **mako** (18a,19a,20d,143c,168c,182c), **Maku** (192), **mala** (89b,c,90a,94b, 97d,109d,185c), **male** (154d), **Male** (45d), **mali** (27b), **mall** (95d, 124b,143b), **malm** (32a,92b), **malo** (23a,74c,152a), **malt** (17c), **mama, Mama** (116d), **mamo** (19a,74b), **mana** (30a,120d,122a, 159c), **mand** (28b), **mane, mani** (115c), **mann** (189), **Mann** (9c, 48c,185c), **mano** (71d,73d,74b,83b), **Mans** (30a), **Manu** (10a,76d, 77a,b), **Manx** (27b,28a,82d), **many** (108d), **mapo** (68a,148d), **mara** (114d), **Mara** (24a,d,105b,107b), **marc** (70c), **Marc** (96a) **mare** (78b), **Mare** (108b), **mari** (61d), **Mari** (16a), **mark** (146b,155a), **Mark** (52a, 96a), **marl** (32a,42c,55d), **maro** (144d), **Mars** (68c,118d,119a,129a, 178a), **mart** (49d,97a), **Mart** (96b,183d), **maru** (84c,144d), **Mary** (50c,126b,183c), **masa** (37a), **mash** (39b,156c), **mask** (44a,45c), **mass** (8a,24b,35b,142d), **mast** (17c,108d,120b,144d,152d), **masu** (57a,84c), **mate** (18c,35b,41d,113a,154a,162c), **math** (77a), **Matt, maty** (80c), **maud** (53d,71a,136d,143c), **Maud** (181a,183c), **Maui** (120d), **maul** (73c,96b), **maun** (139d), **maya** (77a,179b), **Maya** (23d, 186c), **Mayo** (193), **maze** (87b,157d)

- MA - **amah** (95b,108d,111c), **amar** (189), **imam** (25c,102d,103a), **Oman** (159a), **omao** (165b), **omar** (103b), **Omar** (48c,51b,116c,163b), **Xmas**

- - MA **alma** (40d,53d,146d,147a), **Alma** (38d,183c), **amma** (6a), **atma** (150d), **bema** (28d,31a,114b,119b,125b,137a), **boma** (7d),

cima (83b,c), **coma** (91c,157d,170c,172b), **cyma** (101a,b), **dama** (65d,152b), **Duma** (135c), **Emma** (183c), **Erma** (183c), **Fama** (135a), **Gama** (121c), **Goma** (191), **Hima** (191), **ijma** (103b), **Irma** (96d), **jama** (103b), **Kama** (56d), **lama** (23d,24a,91d,165b), **lima** (17b,152b,174d), **Lima** (31b), **loma** (58b,63d), **mama, Mama** (116d), **mima** (185d), **Nama** (78c), **Nema** (34d,48c,134b,164d,176c), **Numa** (133a), **pima** (37c), **Pima** (192), **puma** (27b,37c,55b,103d), **Rama** (77a,80b,176d), **rima** (23a,30c,32a,58a,110d), **Roma** (83c,d), **sama** (105c,169d), **sima** (132b), **soma** (10c,21c,34a,48a,81d,136b), **Tama** (192), **tema** (12a,164a), **Toma** (191), **xema** (72c), **Xema** (12c), **Yama** (57a,68a), **Yima** (84a,116b,c), **Yuma, Zama** (73d, 141d)

M - - A **Maba** (103a,168d), **maha** (28c,88c,136d), **Maia** (76b,109a,153b, 155b,177c), **maja** (151c), **Maja** (153b), **mala** (89b,c,90a,94b,97d, 109d,185c), **mama, Mama** (116d), **mana** (30a,120d,122a,159c), **mara** (114d), **Mara** (24a,d,105b,107b), **masa** (37a), **maya** (77a, 179b), **Maya** (23d,186c), **meda** (110a), **mega** (34b,c), **mela** (34a, 129d), **mesa** (49b,76d,119b,161a), **meta** (132d,133a), **Meta, mica** (82c,100b,146c), **mila** (188), **mima** (185d), **mina** (10b,70b,71d, 179d), **Mina** (23a,183d), **mira** (174d), **Mira** (155b), **moha** (42b, 83d), **Mola** (159c), **mona** (72b,101d), **mora** (42b,65a,72b,83d,99b, 153a,161a), **mota** (103a), **moxa** (27d,30c), **muga, mura** (84d), **Mura** (192), **Musa** (16a), **muta** (28d,103a), **myna** (19a,c,70b), **Myra** (10a, 31b,183c), **myxa** (168c,169a)

- MB - **amba** (161a), **ambi** (34a,122c), **ambo** (125b,128b), **imbe** (37a,56a, 133d), **umbo** (22b)

- - MB **bomb** (144a), **comb** (38c), **dumb** (153b), **iamb** (59c), **jamb** (12d, 45c,118a,146b,174a), **lamb, Lamb** (49c), **limb** (12d,22d), **nimb** (31b,73b,92a,107b,131d), **numb, rumb** (120b), **tomb, Zimb** (6c)

M - - B **medb, Moab** (18d,85a,86d,94a)

M - - C **marc** (70c), **Marc** (96a)

M - - D **maid** (45b,142d), **mand** (28b), **maud** (53d,71a,136d,143c), **Maud** (181a,183c), **mead** (46a,78a,97d,99b), **Mead** (78a), **meed** (128c, 131a), **meld** (26a,41c,99a,118b), **mend** (130b), **mild** (32a,66a), **mind** (75c,81d,93d,109b), **Moed** (100c), **mold** (54d,143c), **mood** (44c), **mudd** (188), **mund** (124d)

ME - - **mead** (46a,78a,97d,99b), **Mead** (78a), **meal** (72a,130b), **mean** (15a, 42b,146c,156b), **meat** (59b), **meda** (110a), **Medb, Mede** (10a,b,13c), **medi** (34c), **meed** (128c,131a), **meek** (93d,99d), **meer, meet** (11d, 13d,36a,50a,81d,142d), **mega** (34b,c), **mein** (30b), **meio** (188), **mela** (34a,129d), **meld** (26a,41c,99a,118b), **mele** (74b,150b), **melt, memo** (108b), **mend** (130b), **mene** (19a,73d,108d,185c), **Ment** (54b,164a), **menu** (19a,27a), **Menu, meou, meow, mere** (16c,22b, 62a,78b,87d,96c,110c,120d,146d,148b), **merl** (20b), **mero** (72a), **Meru** (77a,103d), **mesa** (49b,76d,119b,161a), **mese** (71c), **mesh** (50d,106c), **mess** (22b,44b,77c,85d,104b,165c,173d), **meta** (132d, 133a), **Meta, mete** (9a,11d,22b,44c,45b,98a,121c), **meum** (27a, 89c), **Meum, mewl** (180d), **mews** (154c)

- ME - **amen** (14a,80b,94a,137a,149c,175c,184b), **Amen** (86d,127d,159b, 164a), **amer** (61b), **Ames** (9c,82a), **Amex** (184d), **Emer** (39b,183c),

emeu (111d), **Imer, Omei** (24a), **omen** (14c,59d,60a,121c,123a, 146b), **omer** (51a,75c), **smee** (19b,46c,d,118b,119d,141b,181b), **Smee** (116d), **smew** (19b,46d,99a,137d), **T-men** (168b), **Ymer** (67a, 131c)

- - ME **acme** (39c,115c,186b), **alme** (40d), **arme** (63a,179b), **came** (182b), **Came** (192), **come, cyme** (58d,69c), **dame** (67b,87c,166b), **deme** (71b,c,167d), **dime, dome** (39c,133c,155d), **fame** (130a) **feme** (181b), **fume** (129a,149a,157a), **game** (64d,154a), **gime** (77d), **home, Hume** (50c), **kame** (67b,139b), **Kome** (71d), **lame** (38d,43d, 73b), **lime** (25b,27d,31b,102d,168c), **Lome, mime** (24a,71b,85a, 100a), **Mime** (131d,148d), **name** (8a,11b,d,25c,46c,107c,130b,157d, 163b,166b), **nome** (71c,163b), **Nome, oime** (8b), **pome** (11d), **Pume** (137b,175b,185b), **rame** (22d), **rime** (30c,36a,58a,63d,77c), **Rome** (31c,51d), **ryme** (178d), **same** (44d,79b), **seme** (45c,138b,151b, 154b,155c,157b), **sime** (101d), **some** (114b,121c,126a), **tame** (45a, 66a), **Tame, time** (47a,131a), **tome** (21d,177c), **ulme** (49c), **zeme** (55d,161b,180b), **zyme** (55c)

M - - E **mace** (49d,108d,153b,154d,161a,178a), **made, mage** (95b), **make** (35b,36d,54a,123a), **male** (154d), **Male** (45d), **mane, mare** (78b), **Mare** (108b), **mate** (18c,35b,41d,113a,154a,162c), **maze** (87b, 157d), **Mede** (10a,b,13c), **mele** (74b,150b), **mene** (19a,73d,108d, 185c), **mere** (16c,22b,62a,78b,87d,96c,110c,120d,146d,148b), **mese** (71c), **mete** (9a,11d,22b,44c,45b,98a,121c), **mice, mide** (110a), **mike, Mike** (96b), **mile** (64c), **mime** (24a,71b,85a,100a), **Mime** (131d,148d), **mine** (69c,79d,111b,124c), **mire** (21c,104b), **mise** (8a, 10a,70c), **mite** (12b,81b,82a,114a,c,148c,d,181b), **Mixe** (192), **mode** (54d,96b,157d,179a), **moke** (45c,157d), **mole** (19d,23a,24d,85a, 117c,155c), **Mole** (88c), **mope** (92d,159a), **more** (71a), **More** (50b), **Mose** (96b), **mote** (114c,153a), **moue** (61d,62b), **move, mule** (45b, 148b,153c,180b), **mure** (177d), **muse** (65b,93d,120d,164c), **Muse** (68d), **mute** (146c,153b)

M - - F **miff** (44c), **moff** (53b,146c), **muff**

M - - G **magg** (95b), **migg** (96c), **Ming** (30b,c), **morg** (188), **mung** (70d)

MH - - **mhor** (180b)

- - MH **samh** (56b)

M - - H **Magh** (102a), **mash** (39b,156c), **math** (77a), **mesh** (50d,106c), **moth, Moth** (112d), **much, mush** (97d), **muth** (188), **myth** (8b,91a)

MI - - **miam** (14d), **mian** (97c,147b,166b), **Miao** (30a,b), **mias** (111a), **miau** (27b,99b), **miaw** (27b,99b), **mica** (82c,100b,146c), **mice, mick** (82c), **mico** (97a), **mide** (110a), **Midi** (151b), **mien** (11c, 17b,26d,44c,96b), **miff** (44c), **migg** (96c), **mike, Mike** (96b), **mila** (188), **mild** (32a,66a), **mile** (64c), **milk, mill** (126c), **milo** (70b,87c, 150d), **Milo, milt** (153d), **mima** (185d), **mime** (24a,71b,85a,100a), **Mime** (131d,148d), **mimi** (14d), **Mimi** (87b,110d,125b,183d), **mina** (10b,70b,71d,179d), **Mina** (23a,183d), **mind** (75c,81d,93d,109b), **mine** (69c,79d,111b,124c), **ming** (30b,c), **mink** (176d), **mino** (84c), **mint** (13a,33b,58b,76a), **minx** (116c), **miny, Mira** (155b,174d), **mire** (21c,104b), **mirk** (41a,67d), **miro** (19a,106d,184a), **Miro** (113a, 151d), **miry, mise** (8a,10a,70c), **miss, mist** (46b,59b,174d), **mite** (12b,81b,82a,114a,c,148c,d,181b), **mitt** (56c), **mitu** (39d), **mity, Mixe** (192), **mixy**

-MI- **amia** (22c,170d), **amic** (9d), **amid** (9d,50a), **amie** (61d), **amil** (45a, 48a,185c), **amin** (9d), **amir** (7c,12a,103a,b,123c,170d), **amit** (94a), **Emil** (96a), **Emim** (67a,100d), **emir** (12a,103a,b,123c,134d,135a, 171a), **emit** (43d,49a,53c,58d,83a,142c), **imid** (29c), **omit** (49c, 52c,106b,114c,147d)

--MI **admi** (65d), **ammi** (98c), **demi** (34b,122c), **hami** (78a), **hemi** (122c), **immi** (189), **jami** (103b), **kami** (68a,84b), **Kami** (88c,107c,144c), **Komi** (191), **mimi** (14d), **Mimi** (87b,110d,125b,183d), **rami** (22d), **Remi** (10b), **romi** (72d), **semi** (34b,80b,122c,d), **Simi** (82d), **zemi** (55d,161b,180b)

M--I **Mabi** (58d), **Madi** (174a), **magi** (123c), **Magi** (95b,116c,183a), **maki** (91b), **mali** (27b), **mani** (115c), **mari** (61d), **Mari** (16a), **Maui** (120d), **medi** (34c), **Midi** (151b), **mimi** (14d), **Mimi** (87b,110d,125b,183d), **moki** (127b), **Moki**

M--J **munj** (70d)

M--K **Mack**, **mark** (146b,155a), **Mark** (52a,96a), **mask** (44a,45c), **meek** (93d,99d), **mick** (82c), **milk**, **mink** (176d), **mirk** (41a,67d), **mock** (131b,162b), **monk** (28b,63c,129d), **mosk** (97b,103b), **muck**, **mulk** (60d), **murk** (41a,67d), **musk** (116b)

-ML- **amla** (48a,161d,168c,169a), **amli** (48a,161d,168c,169a)

M--L **maal** (188), **mail** (12d,99b,121c), **mall** (95d,124b,143b), **marl** (32a, 42c,55d), **maul** (73c,96b), **meal** (72a,130b), **merl** (20b), **mewl** (180d), **mill** (126c), **moil** (46c,184c), **moll**, **Moll** (183d), **mull** (53b, 135a,164c)

-MM- **amma** (6a), **ammi** (98c), **ammo** (9d), **ammu** (9d), **Emma** (183c), **immi** (189)

M--M **ma'am** (95a,166b), **maim** (43d,81a,105c), **malm** (32a,92b), **meum** (27a,89c), **Meum**, **miam** (14d)

-MN- **omni** (34a)

--MN **damn**, **Domn** (135a), **famn** (188), **hymn** (150c), **limn** (45d,121c)

M--N **main** (29d,35d,123d), **mann** (189), **Mann** (9c,48c,185c), **maun** (139d), **mean** (15a,42b,146c,156b), **mein** (30b), **mian** (97c,147b, 166b), **mien** (11c,17b,26d,44c,96b), **moan**, **moon** (40b,132c,137c), **morn**, **mown**

MO-- **Moab** (18d,85a,86d,94a), **moan**, **moat** (44d), **mock** (131b,162b), **mode** (54d,96b,157d,179a), **Moed** (100c), **moff** (53b,146c), **mogo** (74b), **moha** (42b,83d), **moho** (19a,78a), **mohr** (65d), **moil** (46c, 184c), **moio** (188), **mojo** (177c), **moke** (45c,157d), **moki** (127b), **moko** (96c), **Mola** (159c), **mold** (54d,143c), **mole** (19d,23a,24d,85a, 117c,155c), **Mole** (88c), **moll**, **Moll** (183d), **molt** (27a,143d), **moly** (76a,181c), **mona** (72b,101d), **monk** (28b,63c,129d), **mono** (34c, 78d,122d,147a), **Mono** (193), **mons** (89c), **Mons** (184d), **mont** (62b), **mood** (44c), **moon** (40b,132c,137c), **moor** (10a,75b,137b,141d, 178b), **Moor** (102c,d,111d), **moot** (41b,44c), **mope** (92d,159a), **mora** (42b,65a,72b,83d,99b,153a,161a), **more** (71a), **More** (50b), **morg** (188), **morn**, **moro** (19a,56c), **Moro** (100a,103a,117a,159a), **Mors** (41b), **mort** (41b,47a,78b,136d), **Mose** (96b), **mosk** (97b,103b), **moss** (91d,104c,114a,170c), **most**, **mosy** (67d), **mota** (103a), **mote** (114c,153a), **moth**, **Moth** (112d), **moto** (104b), **moue** (61d,62b),

move, **mown**, **moxa** (27d,30c), **Moxo** (192), **mozo** (152b)

-MO- **amoi** (62a), **amok** (18b,63c), **Amon** (86d,96b,127d,159b,164a), **amor** (152b), **Amor** (39c,68b), **Amos** (96a,144b), **Amoy** (88c)

--MO **ammo** (9d), **atmo** (34d,174d), **Como**, **demo** (122d), **hemo** (34a, 122b), **homo** (122d), **ikmo** (18b), **itmo** (18b), **mamo** (19a,b,74b), **memo** (108b), **nemo** (34b), **Nemo** (56a,85c), **Pomo** (192), **Sumo**

M--O **mado** (14d,57a,170b), **majo**, **mako** (18a,19a,20d,143c,168c,182c), **malo** (23a,74c,152a), **mamo** (19a,74b), **mano** (71d,73d,74b,83b), **mapo** (68a,148d), **maro** (144d), **Mayo** (193), **meio** (188), **memo** (108b), **mero** (72a), **Miao** (30a,b), **mico** (97a), **milo** (70b,87c, 150d), **Milo**, **mino** (84c), **miro** (19a,106d,184a), **Miro** (113a,151d), **mogo**, (74b), **moho** (19a,78a), **moio** (188), **mojo** (177c), **moko** (96c), **mono** (34c,78d,122d,147a), **Mono** (193), **moro** (19a,56c), **Moro** (100a,103a,117a,159a), **moto** (104b), **Moxo** (192), **mozo** (152b), **Muso** (192), **Muzo** (192), **myxo**

-MP- **impi** (86a), **umph**

--MP **bump**, **camp** (163b), **damp** (101a), **dump**, **gamp** (172a), **gimp** (169d), **Gump** (43b), **hemp** (26a,37a,56a,133d), **hump** (124d), **jump**, **kemp** (139b), **lamp** (92a,94c), **limp** (58a,81a,177d), **lump** (45a, 160c), **mump** (29b,153d), **pomp** (111d,112d), **pump**, **ramp** (65a, 80b,127b,148b), **romp** (63d), **rump**, **samp** (70b,77d,121b), **simp** (59c,146d), **sump** (28c,45d,100b), **tamp** (46b,112b,121d), **tump** (60a,76d,103d), **tymp** (20c), **vamp** (80a,145a)

M--P **mump** (29b,153d)

-MR- **amra** (77c), **Omri** (18c,86d)

M--R **maar** (177a), **mahr** (103a), **meer**, **mhor** (180b), **mohr** (65d), **moor** (10a,75b,137b,141d,178b), **Moor** (102c,d,111d), **Muir** (8b, 142c), **murr** (72b,128b)

-MS- **Omsk**

--MS **alms** (29a), **arms**, **Rems**

M--S **Maas** (132a), **Mais** (61b), **Mans** (30a), **Mars** (68c,118d,119a,129a, 178a), **mass** (8a,24b,35b,142d), **mess** (22b,44b,77c,85d,104b,165c, 173d), **mews** (154c), **mias** (111a), **miss**, **mons** (89c), **Mons** (184d), **Mors** (41b), **moss** (91d,104c,114a,170c), **muss** (135b,173d)

M--T **Maat** (69a,b,85d), **malt** (17c), **mart** (49d,97a), **Mart** (96b,183d), **mast** (17c,108d,120b,144d,152d), **Matt**, **meat** (59b), **meet** (11d,13d,36a,50a,81d,142d), **melt**, **Ment** (54b,164a), **milt** (153d), **mint** (13a,33b,58b,76a), **mist** (46b,59b,174d), **mitt** (56c), **moat** (44d), **molt** (27a,143d), **mont** (62b), **moot** (41b,44c), **mort** (41b,47a, 78b,136d), **most**, **must** (70c,101a,106d,157d,182c), **mutt** (39c, 101d), **myst** (71c,123b)

MU-- **Muav** (66a), **much**, **muck**, **mudd** (188), **muff**, **muga**, **Muir** (8b, 142c), **mule** (45b,148b,153c,180b), **mulk** (60d), **mull** (53b,135a, 164c), **mump** (29b,153d), **mund** (124d), **mung** (70d), **munj** (70d), **mura** (84d), **Mura** (192), **mure** (177d), **murk** (41a,67d), **murr** (72b, 128b), **Musa** (16a), **muse** (65b,93d,120d,164c), **Muse** (68d), **mush** (97d), **musk** (116b), **Muso** (192), **muss** (135b,173d), **must** (70c,101a, 106d,157d,182c), **muta** (28d,103a), **mute** (146c,153b), **muth** (188), **mutt** (39c,101d), **Muzo** (192)

- MU - **Amun** (86d,127d,159b,164a), **smug, smur** (32c,46b,100c), **smut** (32d,44a,119a,150c)

- - MU **ammu** (9d), **Atmu** (143a,159b), **limu** (141c), **rimu** (79d, 106d,129a, 168c)

M - - U **Maku** (192), **Manu** (10a,76d,77a,b), **maru** (84c,144d), **masu** (57a, 84c), **menu** (19a,27a), **Menu, meou, Meru** (77a,103d), **miau** (99b), **mitu** (39d), **Mitu**

M - - V **Muav** (66a)

M - - W **meow, miaw** (27b,99b)

M - - X **Manx** (27b,28a,82d), **minx** (116c)

MY - - **myna** (19a,c,70b), **Myra** (10a,31b,183c), **myst** (71c,123b), **myth** (8b,91a), **myxa** (168c,169a), **myxo**

- MY - **amyl** (155c), **emyd** (163c,167c), **Emys** (167c,171b)

- - MY **army** (78c), **demy** (113d), **domy, elmy, fumy, homy** (38b), **ismy** (45a), **limy** (176d), **rimy** (63d)

M - - Y **many** (108d), **Mary** (50c,126b,183c), **maty** (80c), **miny, miry, mity, mixy, moly** (76a,181c), **mosy** (67d)

NA - - **Naab, naam** (44c,150b), **nabk** (30d,164d), **nabo** (117a), **Nabu** (68c, 183a), **nach, nael** (189), **naga** (13d,33a,55b,127c), **Naga** (24c,77a, 88c,176d), **Nagy** (78d), **Naia** (33a), **naid** (63c), **naif** (74b,105d), **naik, nail** (31d,54d,141d,161d,173a), **naio** (107a,168c), **Nair** (45d), **nais** (63c,132a), **Naja** (33a), **Nala** (77a), **Nama** (78c), **name** (8a, 11b,25c,46c,107c,130b,157d,163b,166b), **nana** (118b), **Nana** (15c, 105d,116d,186d), **nane** (139d), **naos** (28a,71c,137a,163a), **Naos** (155b), **napa** (25c,67d,90d), **Napa** (182c), **nape** (15b,108c,d), **napu** (29d,80d), **nard** (13a,97c,102b,110a,153c), **Nare** (93c), **nark** (81a, 156d), **nary** (108b), **nase** (26b,75a,124b), **Nash** (9c), **nasi** (34c,108a, 115a), **Nast** (9c,27a), **nata** (47c), **Nata** (15c), **Nate** (22b), **Nath** (155c), **Nato** (6a,8d), **natr** (189), **Natt** (107b), **naut** (141b), **nave** (30d,31a,78d,114b,180c), **navy** (33c,58b), **naze** (26b,124b), **Nazi**

- NA - **anai** (163b,181a), **Anak** (67a), **anam** (159a,168c), **Anam, anan** (49a,159a,180c), **Anas** (46c,d), **Anat** (138c,147d), **Anax** (43c, 120c) **anay** (72b,163b,181a), **enam** (70c,77a), **Enam** (85c), **gnar** (72a), **gnat** (59a,81b,99c), **gnaw** (20a,107a,178b), **inar** (65b), **knab** (107a), **knag** (139c), **knap** (76d,107a,139b,159b,166a,170c,185b), **knar** (87c,134b), **Onan** (18c,85c), **snab** (23c,139a), **snag** (11b, 27b,35c,87c,124b,166a), **snap** (23a,36d,38b,48b,54d,56c,58c,149d), **unal** (147a), **unau** (148c,171d)

- - NA **anna** (190), **Anna** (110c,166d), **arna** (24a,181b), **Bana** (67a), **bena** (176a), **bina** (77a), **bona** (89d), **Bona** (183c), **buna** (161c), **Cana** (57a,64b,100c), **cena** (88d,133a), **Cuna** (193), **Dana** (28a,96a, 171d), **dona** (83d,121c,151d), **dyna** (34c), **Edna** (183c), **Enna** (146a), **etna** (75b,153c,157a,175d,177a,c), **fana, gena** (29b), **Gona** (106d), **guna** (106a,137b), **Iona** (28a,82d), **Jena** (105d,165b), **kana** (84d), **kina** (126d), **kona** (74c), **lana** (58a,66a,90a,184b), **lena** (56d), **Lena** (36b), **lina** (188), **Lina** (183d), **luna** (103c), **Luna** (102b), **mana** (30a,120d,122a,159c), **mina** (10b,70b,71d,179d), **Mina** (23a, 183d), **mona** (72b,101d), **myna** (19a,c,70b), **nana** (118b), **Nana** (15c,105d,116d,186d), **nina** (152a), **Nina** (26c,33d,68d,183d),

nona (89b,107b), **Nona** (69a,114a,183c), **orna** (169d,182c), **Pana, pina** (35d,118b), **puna** (10b,33b,104a,119b,182a), **rana** (77a,123c), **Rana** (63d), **rena** (132c), **sana** (56a,166d), **Sana** (185d), **sina** (46c), **Sina** (102d,103d), **tana** (159a), **Tana** (87d), **Tina** (183d), **tuna** (57a, b,123b,170d), **ulna** (21d,39b), **urna** (133a), **vena** (90a,175a), **vina** (77a,105a), **Xina** (183d), **Yana** (192,193), **zona** (144c,186d)

N - - A **naga** (13d,33a,55b,127c), **Naga** (24c,77a,88c,176d), **Naia** (33a), **Naja** (33a), **Nala** (77a), **Nama** (78c), **nana** (118b), **Nana** (15c,105d, 116d,186d), **napa** (25c,67d,90d), **Napa** (182c), **nata** (47c), **Nata** (15c), **nema** (34d,48c,134b,164d,176c), **Nepa** (106b,178c), **Nera** (165b), **Neva** (91b,132a), **Nina** (26c,33d,68d,183d), **nipa** (14b, 46b,48a,164a,168c), **Nola, nona** (89b,107b), **Nona** (69a,114a,183c), **Nora** (79b,107a,164c,183c), **nota** (15c,89c), **nova** (20c,106d,155c, 174d), **noxa, Nuba** (108c), **Nuda** (39b), **Numa** (133a)

- NB - **anba** (36d)

N - - B **Naab, nimb** (31b,73b,92a,107b,131d), **numb**

- NC - **ance** (158b,c,d), **ancy** (158c), **ence** (158c), **Inca** (14b,30a), **inch, onca** (189), **once** (60b,79b), **unca** (49a), **unci** (31d), **unco** (140c), **Ynca** (193)

- - NC **banc** (61a,85c), **zinc** (21a)

- ND - **anda** (23a,168c), **Ande** (193), **Andi** (27d), **Andy** (96b), **endo** (34d, 122d,183b), **inde, onde** (63a,178d), **unde** (179a), **undo** (11a,93d), **undy** (179a)

- - ND **Arnd** (67a), **band** (72a,157c), **bend** (39d,171b), **bind** (33b,165c), **bond** (92a,101c,141d,143b,159d,165c), **bund** (49c,66c,90c), **cond** (156a), **fend** (114b,178b), **find** (44a), **fond** (7c,94b), **fund** (6d,101c, 130c), **Gond, hand** (60c,114c,115d,184c), **hind** (15b,41d,45a), **kind** (150d,153a,174d), **land** (44a,163c), **lend** (6d,79d), **mand** (28b), **mend** (130b), **mind** (75c,81d,93d,109b), **mund** (124d), **pend, pond, pund** (189), **rand** (16d,22a,131b,145a,b), **Rand** (69c), **rend** (32a, 159c,162c,185a), **rind** (53a,115c), **Rind** (109c,174b), **rynd** (100a), **sand** (71d,146c), **send** (42c,44b,95c,121c,130a,144c,168b), **Sind, tend** (26d,80b,93a,100a), **tind** (86b), **tund** (121d), **vend** (97a,115c, 142b), **Vend** (10b,148a), **wand** (120b,132c,156a), **wend** (67d,123d), **Wend** (10b,148a), **wind** (33b,39d,171c,185a), **yond** (164d), **Zend**

N - - D **naid** (63c), **nard** (13a,97c,102b,110a,153c), **need** (42b,52d,87b, 122a,178a), **Nejd, NKVD** (135d), **Nudd** (23c)

NE - - **neaf** (58a,73c), **Neal, neap** (165c,167a,177b), **near** (11d,32c,107b), **neat** (165c,169d), **Nebo** (68c,102d,103d,183a), **neck** (83a), **need** (42b,52d,87b,122a,178a), **neem** (96d,168c,169a), **neep** (140c, 171b), **neer** (14b,86b,108b), **Neil** (96a), **nein** (66c), **Nejd, Nell** (110a, 183d), **nema** (34d,48c,134b,164d,176c), **nemo** (34b), **Nemo** (56a,85c), **nene** (19b,74c), **neon** (65c), **Nepa** (106b,178c), **Nera** (165b), **Neri, Nero** (8a,126d,133a,150b,172c), **ness** (26b,75a,124b), **nest** (38b,74b,130d,149c,160b), **nete** (71c,108b,163d), **neti** (164a), **nett, neue** (66c), **Neva** (91b,132a), **neve** (56d,67c,70c,149b), **news** (165c), **newt** (48d),136c,169d), **next** (106a)

- NE - **Aner** (18d,96b), **anes** (110c,140a), **anet** (43c), **anew** (7c), **inee** (120b), **Inez** (45c,183c), **knee** (85b), **knew, knez** (123c), **oner** (20d, 53a,75c,162d,173a,d), **ones** (116a), **sned** (93d,125a,140a), **snee**

(40a,43d,87a), **sneg** (139b)

- - NE **acne** (147c), **aine** (49b,62c,142c), **Anne** (50c,84a,143b,183c), **a-one** (52b,167b), **Arne** (35c,50c,134d), **aune** (188), **bane** (74a,106b,120b, 139a), **bene** (18a,83c,90a,106d,122a,180a), **bine** (145b,156a,171c, 176b), **bone, cane** (17b,128a,156a,159a,177d), **Cane, cene** (34c), **cine** (104b,152c), **cone** (66b,150a,157c), **Dane** (85d,107d,138a), **dene** (137a), **Dene** (192), **dine, done, dune** (137a), **dyne** (59d,173b), **eine** (66c), **enne** (34c), **erne** (19c,d,47b,54b,141a), **esne** (10c, 45b,142c,148a,164d), **fane** (30d,137a,162d), **fine** (49b,50a,104b, 115d,159a), **gane** (185b), **gene** (54a), **Gene** (96b), **gone** (6b,15c,42c, 44c,114d), **gyne** (34b,55b,183c), **hone** (110a,143c,180d), **Ione** (24b,88d,94d), **jane** (190), **Jane** (183c), **June** (183c), **kane** (74c), **kine** (38a,112c), **lane** (134b,157b), **lene** (36b,149a,172b), **line** (12b, 22b,36d,38a,126c,134b,157b,158b,162d,175c), **lone** (150a), **lune** (38c,73b,74d), **mane, mine** (69c,79d,111b,124c), **mene** (19a,73d, 108d,185c), **nene** (19b,74c), **nine** (26c,104d), **none** (108b), **ohne** (66d,183b), **orne** (169d,182c), **Orne** (25b), **pane** (113c,155a,b), **pene, pine** (36a,52a,88c,93c,168c,d,169a), **pone** (37a,85b), **rine** (44d,75d, 135c), **rone** (127c,164b), **rune** (9b,67a,94a,95a,105c,107d,120a, 141d,163d), **sane** (128a), **sine** (64c,66b,90a,97c,126a,163b,169d, 183b), **syne** (140b,147a), **Tane** (120d), **tene** (34d,131b), **tine** (11b, 124b,167b), **tone** (6c,118c,150d), **tune** (8b,12c,98c), **tyne, Tyne** (108a), **vane** (179b,182a), **vine** (32b), **wane** (41c,43c), **wine, zone** (44c,50a,160a)

N - - E **name** (8a,11b,d,25c,46c,107c,130b,157d,163b), **nane** (139d), **nape** (15b,108c,d), **Nare** (93c), **nase** (26b,75a,124b), **Nate** (22b), **nave** (30d,31a,78d,114b,180c), **naze** (26b,124b), **nene** (19b,74c), **nete** (71c,108b,163d), **neue** (66c), **neve** (56d,67c,70c,149b), **nice** (54d, 119c,130c), **Nice** (98c), **nide** (23c,72a,106c,116d), **nife** (37a), **Nike** (69c,100c,182d), **nile** (33c,71d), **Nile** (106b), **nine** (26c,104d), **Niue** (137d), **node** (35c,85b,87c,94d,120a,124d,160c), **nome** (71c,163b), **Nome, none** (108b), **Nore** (163d), **nose** (118d,125a,149b), **note** (98c,109b,124b,128d,130a,177c), **nove** (83b), **noze** (75a), **nude** (16c,172d), **Nupe** (191)

N - - F **naif** (74b,105d), **neaf** (58a,73c)

NG - - **ngai** (48a,159c), **ngan**

- NG - **ange** (61a), **ango** (171a), **inga** (145d,170a), **Inge** (24d,67d,117c 119c)

- - NG **bang** (75d,105d,148a), **beng** (43a), **bing, bong, bung** (119d,156d), **cang** (184a), **dang, ding** (130b), **dong, fang** (167b), **Fong** (40b), **Fung** (191), **gang** (38c), **gong, hang** (160a), **hing** (13c), **hong** (30b), **hung, Jung** (125a), **k'ang** (30a), **king** (26c,29c), **kung** (125b), **ling** (24c,57a,b,75b,178c), **long** (38b), **lung, Ming** (30b,c), **mung** (70d), **pang** (165b), **ping, pong, pung** (22c,148b), **Qung** (191), **rang, ring** (50a), **Rong** (88c), **rung** (28c,39a), **sang, sing** (26d,178a), **song** (12c,170c), **sung, Sung** (30b), **tang** (30b,58b,186b), **teng** (188), **ting** (166a), **Ting** (30c), **tong** (30a,c), **tung** (110a,168c), **uang** (131a), **vang** (72d,134a,140b), **wang** (189), **wing** (10d,58c,59a, 118b,d), **wong** (56a), **yang** (30b,70a), **zing**

N - - G **niog** (33a,168c), **nogg** (48d)

- - NH **binh** (189), **hunh?**, **sinh** (97c), **tanh** (97c)

N - - H **Nach**, **Nash** (9c), **Nath** (155c), **nigh** (106a), **Nish** (19d), **Noah** (88a, 99b)

NI - - **Nias** (82d), **nibs** (116c), **nice** (54d,119c,130c), **Nice** (98c), **nick** (30c,108b), **nide** (23c,72a,106c,116d), **nidi** (106c), **nife** (37a), **nigh** (106a), **Nike** (69c,100c,182d), **nile** (33c,71d), **Nile** (106b), **nill** (173d), **nimb** (31b,73b,92a,107b,131d), **nina** (152a), **Nina** (26c, 33d,68d,183d), **nine** (26c,104d), **nino** (152a), **niog** (33a,168c), **niou** (188), **nipa** (14b,46b,48a,164a,168c), **Nish** (19d), **nisi** (90a, 173c), **nito** (55c), **Niue** (137d)

- NI - **anil** (47c,80d,180b), **Anim** (18d), **anis** (55c), **Enid** (13b,25d,66b, 163a,183c), **Enif** (155b), **enin** (20d), **inia** (9b,109b), **Inia** (28c,45b), **knip** (115c), **knit** (173c,179b), **snib** (54d,93c), **snig** (45d), **snip** (32b,40a), **unie** (173a), **Unio** (105c), **unis** (91b), **unit** (101c,110c, 147a)

- - NI **Aani** (45a,48d), **agni** (88a,89c), **Agni** (56d,68b), **arni** (24a,181b), **bani** (190), **beni** (116a,142d), **Beni** (191), **Bini** (191), **Boni** (63b), **Coni**, **doni** (21a,28c,168a), **loni** (192), **mani** (115c), **omni** (34a), **Pani** (120c), **rani** (72d,77b,123c,127c), **Reni** (83d), **yeni** (19b,161d), **Zuni** (125b)

N - - I **nasi** (34c,108a,115a), **Nazi**, **Neri**, **neti** (164a), **ngai** (48a,159c), **nidi** (106c), **nisi** (90a,173c), **nodi** (35c,87c), **nori** (8c,141c)

- - NJ **Funj**, **gunj** (70c), **munj** (70d)

NK - - **NKVD** (135d)

- NK - **ankh** (38d,162b), **Enki** (15b), **Inka** (193), **inky** (20b)

- - NK **bank** (18a,58c), **bonk** (190), **bunk**, **conk** (41c,108a,156d,157c), **dank** (40b,101a), **dunk** (43c,79d), **fink** (19a,56c,157c), **funk** (63d, 113c), **gink** (48b), **hank** (147c), **honk** (70a), **hunk**, **jink**, **jonk**, **junk** (30a,134c), **kink** (38b,171c), **konk** (41c), **kunk** (188), **lank** (148b, 164b), **link** (36a,81d,85b), **lonk** (143d), **mink** (176d), **monk** (28b, 63c,129d), **pank** (189), **pink** (26d,33c,60c,138a), **punk** (9b,166a, 167c), **rank** (31d,55d,70b,92c,94d,157d), **rink** (147c,154a), **sank**, **sink** (41c,43c,46b,158a), **sunk**, **tank** (175a,d), **tonk** (173c), **wink** (107a), **yank**, **Yank**

N - - K **nabk** (30d,164d), **naik**, **nark** (81a,156d), **neck** (83a), **nick** (30c, 108b), **nock** (13b,108b), **nook** (37a,130d), **nubk** (30d,164d)

- NL - **inly**, **only** (24d,52c,98d,147a,150a)

N - - L **nael** (189), **nail** (31d,54d,141d,161d,173a), **Neal**, **Neil** (96a), **Nell** (110a,183d), **nill** (173d), **noel** (26d,150b) **Noel** (30d,96a), **noil** (87c, 178b), **Noll** (96b,110b), **noyl** (87c), **null** (108c,177a), **nurl** (33b,87c)

N - - M **naam** (44c,105b), **Naam**, **neem** (96d,168c,169a), **norm** (15a,115a, 128a,155a)

- NN - **Anna** (110c,166d,183c), **anna** (190), **Anne** (50c,84a,143b,183c), **Enna** (146a), **enne** (34c), **Enns**

- - NN **binn** (22c), **Bonn** (17d), **bunn** (25b), **conn** (43d,156a), **Finn** (107d), **Jann** (102d), **jinn** (42b,103b,153c), **linn** (120d,140a,c,168c,178d), **mann** (189), **Mann** (9c,48c,185c), **rann** (175c), **senn** (76b), **sunn** (56a), **wynn** (165d)

N - - N **nein** (66c), **neon** (65c), **ngan**, **noon**, **Norn** (69a,163d,174b), **noun** (114b,158a)

NO - - **Noah** (88a,99b), **nobs** (38c,87a), **nock** (13b,108b), **node** (35c,85b, 87c,94d,120a,124d,160c), **nodi** (35c,87c), **noel** (26d,150b), **Noel** (30d,96a), **noes** (177c), **nogg** (48d), **noil** (87c,178b), **noio** (107c, 163c), **noir** (61b,134b), **noix** (67c), **Nola**, **Noll** (96b,110b), **nolo** (42a), **nome** (71c,163b), **Nome**, **nona** (89b,107b), **Nona** (69a,114a, 183c), **none** (108b), **nono** (83b), **nook** (37a,130d), **noon**, **Nora** (79b, 107a,164c,183c), **Nore** (163d), **nori** (8c,141c), **norm** (15a,115a, 128a,155a), **Norn** (69a,163d,174b), **nose** (118d,125a,149b), **Nosu** (27d), **nosy**, **nota** (15c,89c), **note** (98c,109b,124b,128d,130a,177c), **Nott** (107b), **noun** (114b,158a), **noup** (124b), **nous** (81d,100a, 128b), **nova** (20c,106d,155c,174d), **nove** (83b), **nowt** (106a,139a), **nowy** (194), **noxa**, **noyl** (87c), **noze** (75a)

- NO - **anoa** (28a,60a,112c,181c), **anon** (7d,14d,79d,80b,123a,145c,150c, 164a), **enol** (29c,158b), **Enon** (18c,d), **Enos** (7a,18d,52a,70c,96a, 143a), **enow** (50d,123a,158b), **knob** (73c), **knop** (124b,170c,185b), **knor** (87c), **knot** (43c,99d,107c,124d,137b), **know**, **snob** (159c), **snod** (169d), **snow**

- - NO **Aino** (84a,c), **Arno** (27a), **asno** (151d), **beno** (113b,117a), **cano** (152a), **dino** (34b), **fano** (51d,96b,113c,d), **fono** (137a), **Gano** (132d), **Hano** (125b), **hino** (106d,168c), **Juno** (69c,85d,100c,126b), **Kano** (84c,177d), **keno** (161d,168c), **kino** (27c,34c,47c,72c,98b), **leno** (37c,53b), **lino**, **mano** (71d,73d,74b,83b), **mino** (84c), **mono** 34c,78d,122d,147a), **Mono** (193), **nino** (152a), **nono** (83b), **pino** (152c), **puno** (182a), **Reno**, **sano** (152b), **sino** (34a), **Tano** (192), **Tino** (136d), **tuno** (28b,168c), **vino** (92d,182b), **xeno** (34d), **Zeno** (71b)

N - - O **nabo** (117a), **naio** (107a,168c), **Nato** (6a,8d), **Nebo** (68c,102d,103d, 183a), **nemo** (34b), **Nemo** (56a,85c), **Nero** (8a,126d,133a,150b, 172c), **nino** (152a), **nito** (55c), **noio** (107c,163c), **nolo** (42a), **nono** (83b)

N - - P **neap** (165c,167a,177b), **neep** (140c,171b), **noup** (124b)

- - NQ **cinq** (61d)

- NR - **inre** (35d,80a), **inro** (84b,c,106c)

N - - R **Nair** (45d), **natr** (189), **near** (11d,32c,107b), **neer** (14b,86b,108b), **noir** (61b,134b), **nurr** (67d)

- NS - **ansa** (73c,93d,137c), **anse** (61d), **ansu** (11d), **ense** (139b,158c), **enso** 34d,183b)

- - NS **bans**, **cens** (115b), **dans** (62a), **dens** (90a,167b), **Duns**, **Enns**, **fons** (60c), **gens** (42d,132d), **Hans** (66d,96a), **hens** (121d), **lens** (67c, 95b,111a,129b,162d), **Mans** (30a), **mons** (89c), **Mons** (184d), **oons** (100a,186d), **Pons** (13d,63c,110d,150c), **sans** (63a,183b), **Sens** (63b), **sons** (98d,109d), **Vans** (107d)

N - - S **nais** (63c,132a), **naos** (28a,71c,137a,163a), **Naos** (155b), **ness** (26b, 75a,124b), **news** (165c), **Nias** (82d), **nibs** (116c), **nobs** (38c,87a), **noes** (177c), **nous** (81d,100a,128b)

- NT - **anta** (83d,117c,d,121a), **Anta** (164a), **ante** (87a,89a,115b,120b, 122b,125d,154d), **anti** (7d,111a,122b), **Anti** (193), **ente** (70b,151d),

ento (34b,d,183b), **Inti** (159b), **into** (123a,183b), **onto** (76a,174a), **unto** (166c), **untz** (189)

- - NT **aint, arn't, aunt** (129c), **bant** (43c), **bent** (80b), **bunt** (15d,180c), **cant** (28d,81b,84d,90c,109b,136c,165d,166a), **cent** (36d), **dent** (42c,77d), **dint** (48c,59d,122a), **dont, dunt, font** (16b,171d,172a), **gent, hant** (67a), **hint** (9a,39c,159a), **hunt** (141c), **kant** (28d), **Kant** (67a), **Kent** (90d), **lant, lent** (54d), **Lent** (115d,141c), **lint** (46a,58d), **Ment** (54b,164a), **mint** (13a,33b,58b,76a), **mont** (62b), **oont** (25d), **pant, pent** (36a), **pint** (67b), **pont** (55d,61b), **punt** (21a,58b), **rant** (41c,127b,128a,161d), **rent** (58a,77c,91b,138b, 153d,162c,167c), **runt** (47a,172d), **sent, tent** (26b,115a), **tint** (33c, d,114d), **vent** (8b,11b,110d,112a), **vint** (26c,182c), **want** (41b, (38b,74b,106b,122a), **went** (42c), **wont** (6d,40a,73a,174c)

N - - T **Nast** (9c,27a), **Natt** (107b), **naut** (141b), **neat** (165c,169d), **nest** (38b,74b,130d,149c,160b), **nett, newt** (48d,136c,169d), **next** (106a), **Nott** (107b), **nowt** (106a,139a), **nuit** (62b)

NU - - **Nuba** (108c), **nubk** (30d,164d), **nuda** (39b), **Nudd** (23c), **nude** (16c, 172d), **nuit** (62b), **null** (108c,177a), **Numa** (133a), **numb, Nupe** (191), **nurl** (33b,87c), **nurr** (67d)

- NU - **Cnut** (40d,50c), **knub** (178b), **knur** (67d,87c,107c), **knut, Knut** (40d,50c,96a), **onus** (24c,93b,109b), **snub** (128c,148b), **snug** (35a, 38b,165c), **Snug** (99d), **snup** (149b)

- - NU **Ainu** (84a,c), **benu** (49a), **Danu** (28a), **genu** (6b,18a,87a,89c), **Manu** (10a,76d,77a,b), **menu** (19a,27a), **Menu, tunu** (28b), **zenu** (143d)

N - - U **Nabu** (68c,183a), **napu** (29d,80d), **niou** (188), **Nosu** (27d)

- NV - **envy** (41b)

- - NX **jinx** (78a), **jynx** (78a), **Jynx** (184a), **lanx** (133a,b), **lynx** (26c,181d), **Lynx** (36b), **Manx** (27b,28a,82d), **minx** (116c), **Yunx** (184a)

N - - X **noix** (67c)

- NY - **Enyo** (12c,69c,178a), **onym** (162c), **onyx** (25d,28d,65d,142b), **Pnyx** (71c)

- - NY **bony** (147c), **Bony** (96b), **cony** (127a), **deny** (36d,43d,129b), **liny** (157b), **luny** (38b), **many** (108d), **miny, piny, pony, puny** (55b, 179a), **tiny** (100c,148c), **tony, Tony** (96b), **tuny, viny, wany, winy** (176c), **zany** (24a,32d,59c)

N - - Y **Nagy** (78d), **nary** (108b), **navy** (33c,58b), **nosy, nowy** (194)

- NZ - **anzu** (11d), **Enzu** (102b), **onza** (189), **unze** (189)

- - NZ **Linz** (40d)

OA - - **Oahu, oaks** (154d), **oaky, oary, oast** (15d,86b,112a), **oath** (119c, 150a)

- OA - **boar** (77c,117c,160c,181c), **boat** (27b,106a), **Boaz** (135d), **coag** (45d,118a,163b), **coak** (45d,118a,163b), **coal** (49c,64a), **Coan** (37b), **coat** (160a), **coax** (180c), **doab** (157c), **doat** (17a,94b,112a,165d), **Eoan** (41a,85b), **foal** (78c), **foam** (63d,154b), **goad** (80b,154b), **goaf** (104b), **goai** (106d,168c), **goal** (8b,109b,120b,125d), **Goan, goat** (135a), **hoar** (63d,71a,181a), **hoax** (41c,122a), **Joab** (41a), **Joad** (50c), **Joan** (183c), **joar** (100a), **koae** (74b), **load** (24c,26d,161b), **loaf** (79b,94b), **loam** (47d,150a), **loan, Moab** (18d,85a,86d,94a),

moan, moat (44d), **Noah** (88a,99b), **road** (37d,164d), **roam** (178a), **roan** (78b,c,114c,128d,144a,181a), **roar** (145c), **soak** (46c,137c), **soap, soar** (59a), **toad** (10a,17a,63d,126d), **woad** (20d,47c), **Zoar, Zoas** (20b)

- - OA **anoa** (28a,60a,112c,181c), **Aroa** (175b), **Gjoa** (144d), **pooa** (76a, 125b), **proa** (21b,26a,95c,d), **Shoa** (6c) **stoa** (33c,121a,c), **tooa** (17c), **whoa** (156d)

O - - A **obia** (55d), **obra** (152d,184c), **ocha** (189), **ocra** (72c,175a), **octa** (122c), **odea** (105d,164a), **Offa** (163d), **ohia** (74c,168c), **okia** (190), **okra** (72c,175a), **olea** (170b), **Olea** (110b), **Olga** (135c,183c), **olla** (36d,44b,84d,113b,121d,151d,152c,181b), **onca** (189), **onza** (189), **orca** (86b), **orna** (169d,182c), **orra** (139c,d,140a), **ossa** (21d), **Ossa** (103d,110b,164b), **Otea** (71a,82d), **otra** (152c), **oxea** (153d)

OB - - **oban** (190), **Obed** (135d), **obex** (22d), **obey** (35c,75c), **obia** (55d), **obit** (41b,64c), **oboe** (74b,104d,105a,182a,184a), **obol** (29b,110a), **obra** (152d,184c)

- OB - **boba** (29d), **bobo** (112c,168c), **Cobb** (9c), **Cobh** (37a), **dobe** (159b, c,172b), **doby** (159b,c), **gobi, Gobi** (42d), **gobo** (84d), **goby** (57d), **hobb** (124b), **hobo** (168a,174b), **jobo** (77c), **Koba** (11a), **Kobe** (78a), **kobi** (84b), **kobu** (84b), **lobb** (23b,94c,163a), **lobe** (90c, 134b), **lobo** (165d,183c), **nobs** (38c,87a), **robe** (65b), **Sobk** (38d), **Toba** (80c), **tobe** (7d,137b), **toby** (8c,85c,104b), **Toby** (96b,125c), **Yobi, zobo** (186b)

- - OB **blob, boob** (146d), **brob** (153c), **chob** (23c), **doob** (18b), **jaob, knob** (73c,107c,124d), **rhob** (64a,85c), **scob** (42a), **slob** (173d), **snob** (159c), **swob** (102b), **thob** (128a)

OC - - **ocha** (189), **ocra** (72c,175a), **octa** (122c), **octo** (34a,89b,122c)

- OC - **boca** (152b,c), **boce** (23b,52a,57b), **bock** (17c,90d,144a), **coca** (29d, 33a,105d,113a), **cock** (19a,29a,55a,133d,136d,161d,174b), **coco, dock** (40a,117c,144d,179d), **Foch** (63b), **foci** (28b), **hoch** (52c, 66c), **hock** (91a,115b,182b,c), **jock, Jock** (96b), **jocu** (45b,57a), **Koch** (66d), **loch** (88a,139d), **loci** (66b,118c), **lock** (54d), **loco** (38b, 119b,120b), **mock** (131b,162b), **nock** (13b,108b), **poco** (83b,93a), **Roch** (136c), **rock** (160b), **sock** (157c,182a), **soco** (22d), **tock** (7d, 19b), **toco** (19b,167c), **voce** (83c,177a)

- - OC **bloc** (173a), **croc** (13a,74a), **floc** (149a)

O - - C **odic** (79c,120a), **olic** (158b), **otic** (14c,d,47b)

OD - - **odah** (170d), **odal** (48a,88b,112c), **Odax** (132c), **odds** (28d,172d), **Odea** (105a,164a), **odel** (48a,112c), **Oder** (132a), **odic** (79c,120a), **Odin** (7c,29d,63c,68c,175d,183b), **odio** (83b), **odor** (138b,156a), **odum** (168c,180a), **odyl** (59d,79c)

- OD - **Bodb** (82b), **bode** (14c,60a,110b,121b), **Bodo** (88c), **body** (72a), **coda** (32c,35d,56c), **code** (21c,31a,40c,161c), **codo** (188), **dodd** (139c,140c), **Dode** (96b), **dodo** (19b), **Jodo** (113d), **lode** (42c,99a,111b,175b), **Lodi** (105d), **Lodz, mode** (54d,96b,157d, 179a), **node** (35c,85b,87c,94d,120a,124d,160c), **nodi** (35c,87c), **Roda** (107b), **rodd** (38d), **rode** (46c), **rodi** (98c), **soda** (19a,149d, 181a), **Toda** (45d,76d), **tode** (80a,148a), **todo** (22b,24d,35b,64c, 156b), **tody** (19b,d,59a,166a), **yodh** (91d)

- - OD **alod** (51c,55d,88a,124c), **apod** (59d), **Arod** (86c), **biod** (59d,79c),

clod (22a,45b,157d), **elod** (49b,59d,79c), **feod** (55d), **food** (109a, 176b), **good, hood** (38a,74d), **lood** (189), **mood** (44c), **plod** (170b, 177d), **pood** (189), **prod** (67d,80b,106b,120b), **quod** (123d), **rood** (38d,39a,88b), **shod, snod** (169d), **stod** (40d,67d), **trod, wood**

O - - D **obed** (135d), **olid** (55d,60c,148d,157d), **ooid** (48d), **oord** (190), **orad** (104a), **Ovid** (132d,133b), **oxid** (112c)

OE - - **oese** (15d,119c)

- OE - **Boer** (151a), **coed, coel** (39b), **Doeg** (137c), **doer** (8a,116b), **does, goel** (15a,75c), **goer, hoek** (39d), **hoen** (189), **hoer, hoey** (114c), **Joel** (96a), **joey** (86a,185d), **Joey** (96b,109c), **koel** (19a,b,39b), **Moed** (100c), **noel** (26d,150b), **Noel** (30d,96a), **noes** (177c), **poem** (51a), **poet** (49b), **roed, roer** (72d), **roey** (103d), **toed, voet** (188)

- - OE **aloe** (7d,20a,76a,b,92b,98b,119b,158b,167a,183d), **Cloe** (183c), **eboe** (28b,110a,168c,169b), **evoe** (15b,130d,181c), **floe** (79b), **froe** (32a,167a,179d), **oboe** (74b,104d,105a,182a,184a), **Otoe** (147b), **shoe** (166a), **sloe** (14a,20b,64a,119d,181c)

O - - E **oboe** (74b,104d,105a,182a,184a), **oese** (15d,119c), **ogee** (40c,101a, b,120b), **ogle** (9d,53c,91a,93d,148c), **ogre** (67a,102a), **ohne** (66d, 183b), **Oime** (8b), **Oise, Okie** (99d), **olpe** (90d,182c), **once** (60b, 79b), **onde** (63a,178d), **ooze** (53c,104b,116a), **orfe** (57a,b,185c), **orle** (17b,56b,76a,144b,177a), **orne** (169d,182c), **Orne** (25b), **oste** (21d,83b), **Otoe** (147b), **Ouse** (132a,185d), **owse**

OF - - **Offa** (163d), **offs** (38c)

- OF - **doff** (130a,161b), **goff** (32d), **koff** (47a), **loft** (14c,69d,104b, 178b), **moff** (53b,146c), **sofa** (44d), **soft** (48b,95d,99d,163a), **toff** (40d)

- - OF **Azof** (20b,135d), **goof, hoof** (173a), **loof** (144c,153d), **poof, roof** (78d), **stof** (135c), **woof** (39a,163d,165a,179d)

O - - F **Olaf** (108a,176b)

OG - - **ogam** (82b,c), **ogee** (40c,101a,b,120b), **ogle** (9d,53c,91a,93d,148c), **Ogor** (170d), **Ogpu** (135d), **ogre** (67a,102a), **ogum** (82b)

- OG - **boga** (57d,180b), **bogo** (117a,168c), **Bogo** (191), **bogy** (153a), **doge** (95b,175b), **dogy** (46d,103c), **fogy, goga** (24a), **gogo** (16b,24a, 149c), **Gogo** (191), **hoga** (144b), **hogg** (144a), **jogi** (76d), **loge** (164a), **logy** (46d), **mogo** (74b), **nogg** (48d), **Pogo** (121c), **pogy** (57a,88a,98d,103c), **soga** (70d,152b), **Soga** (191), **toga** (132d,133a, b), **togs** (32c), **togt** (77c), **Vogt, yoga** (10b,13c,77a), **yogh** (10c, 185a), **yogi** (76d), **zogo** (136a)

- - OG **agog** (47b,52c,86b), **ajog, clog** (30c,145b), **flog** (180d), **frog** (10a, 17a,126d), **grog** (92d,153d), **ilog** (132a, 161b), **niog** (33a,168c), **slog** (157c,170b,177d), **stog** (155a), **voog** (28a,66a,132b)

OH - - **ohia** (74c,168c), **Ohio, ohne** (66d,183b), **ohoy** (106a)

- OH - **boho** (117a,179d), **Bohr** (14b,40d,138c), **coho** (136d), **fohn** (182b), **Hohe** (192), **John** (11c,96a,121a,186b), **kohl** (53c), **moha** (42b,83d), **moho** (19a,78a), **mohr** (65d), **poha** (74c), **rohr** (72d), **soho!, Soho** (93c), **toho** (79a)

- - OH **booh** (52c), **pooh** (22b,107d)

O - - H **oath** (119c,150a), **odah** (170d), **okeh** (8d,37b), **opah** (23b,57a,b, 86d), **ouch!, ough**

OI - - **oily** (110b,172c), **oime** (8b), **Oise**

- OI - **Boii** (191), **boil, bois** (62b,63a,183d), **coif** (73a), **coil** (39d,171c, 185a), **coin** (19b,37a,100c,101c,179d), **coir** (33a,37a,56a,133d), **Coix** (70d,85b), **doit** (47a,169d,180d), **Eoin** (85b), **foil** (15d,55c, 165b), **join** (36a,173c), **koir** (33a), **loin** (40a,98a), **loir** (45c), **Loir, Lois** (165d,183c), **moil** (46c,184c), **moio** (188), **noil** (87c,178b), **noio** (107c,163c), **noir** (61b,134b), **noix** (67c), **ooid** (48d), **roil** (44c, 104b,156b,170d,176a), **Soia, soie** (62c), **soil** (154d,159a,163c), **soir** (61c), **toil** (46c,184c), **void** (11a,49d,108d,174b), **zoid**

- - OI **amoi** (62a), **Ekoi** (191)

O - - I **Omei** (24a), **omni** (34a), **Omri** (18c,86d)

- OJ - **bojo** (117a), **coja** (103b,166b), **hoja** (166b), **hoju** (84b), **koji** (185b), **mojo** (177c), **rojo** (129a,152c), **soja** (151b)

OK - - **okay** (8d), **okeh** (8d,37b), **oket** (189), **okia** (190), **Okie** (99d), **okra** (72c,175a), **okro** (72c,175a)

- OK - **boko** (52b), **coke** (32d,64a), **coky, Doko** (191), **joke** (183a), **joky, koko** (106d,114b), **Koko** (93d,186c), **koku** (189), **loka** (173c,184c), **Loke** (15d,68b), **Loki** (7c,15d,68b), **moke** (45c,157d), **moki** (127b), **Moki, moko** (96c), **poke** (108c), **poku** (11a), **poky** (148c), **roka** (95a,168c,d), **roke** (174d,175b), **soka** (20c), **soke** (44c,85d), **toko** (30c), **woke, yoke** (85b,92d,173c)

- - OK **amok** (18b,63c), **asok** (13d), **book, cook** (137b), **dook** (184a), **hook** (27b,39d), **irok** (55b), **look** (11c,53c,142a), **nook** (37a,130d), **pook** (68a), **rook** (19b,29c,39a), **sook** (22a,25c,97a), **took**

O - - K **Omsk**

OL - - **Olaf** (108a,176b), **olam** (51a,d,75c,81a), **Olan** (115c), **Olax** (52b), **olay** (113b), **Olea** (110b,170b), **oleo** (34c), **Olga** (135c,183c), **olic** (158b), **olid** (55d,60c,148d,157d), **olio** (44b,77c,98c,100d,121d), **olla** (36d,44b,84d,113b,121d,151d,152c,181b), **Olor** (160a,b), **olpe** (90d,182c)

- OL - **bola** (16a), **bold** (41a), **bole** (31d,32a,169b), **boll** (119b,d), **bolo** (87a,179b), **bolt** (13b,54d,58b,132d,160a), **cola** (25b,108d,149d, 168c), **cold** (65d), **cole** (25a), **Cole, coli, colp** (28a,148b), **colt** (78c, 131a,185d,186b), **Colt, coly** (104a), **dola** (189), **dole** (44c,118c, 121c,129d), **Dole** (74c), **doli, doll** (125c), **dolt** (20c,59c,157d), **fold folk** (116a,169c), **gola** (27b,40c,70c,157a), **gold, golf** (154a), **goli** (105c), **Goll, Golo** (191), **hola** (74c,152b), **hold** (95c,124c,130d), **hole** (6c,11b,110d,118c,147a), **Holi** (77a), **holm** (77d,82d,109a), **holt** (36d,119b,184b), **holy, lola, lole** (52a,76b,123c), **jole** (29b), **joli** (62b), **jolt** (143b), **kola** (25b,84a,108d,168c), **Kola** (135b,c,d), **Koli** (27b), **kolo** (59b,135c), **Lola** (27d,97b), **loll** (94b,128c), **Lolo** (27d,30a), **Mola** (159c), **mold** (54d,143c), **mole** (19d,23a,24d,85a, 117c,155c), **Mole** (88c), **moll, Moll** (183d), **molt** (27a,143d), **moly** (76a,181c), **Nola, Noll** (96b,110b), **nolo** (42a), **Pola, pole** (132c,143b,177b,184a), **Pole** (52a), **polk** (37c), **poll** (74d,160a, 177c), **polo** (154a), **Polo** (175b), **poly** (34c,76b), **role** (114b), **roll** (134a,160b), **sola** (9a,48a,74b,118c,154a,167b), **sold, sole** (52c, 57a,b,58b,d,110c,115d,150a), **soli** (12c,110c), **solo** (12c,89a,110c), **tola** (48a,80d), **Tola** (85b,180a), **told** (129c), **tole** (9a,51a,99b,163a), **toll** (131c), **tolt, tolu** (16a), **vola** (89d,150a), **vole** (97d,104a,148a,

149b), **volk** (66c,105d,116a,184c), **Volk, volt** (49b,78c,173b), **wold** (47c,60a,118d,174a,184a), **wolf, yolk, Zola** (63a)

- - OL **bool** (39d), **chol** (118d), **Chol** (192), **cool** (25c,107d), **egol** (11b), **enol** (29c,158b), **fool** (24a,41c,47a,146d), **gaol** (123d), **Gaol** (164a), **idol** (48c,54c,55a,75b,79d,112d,130b,184d), **itol** (158b), **obol** (29b, 110a), **pool** (65a,119d,120d), **siol** (82c), **tool** (27c), **viol** (105a), **wool** (58b,179c)

O - - L **obol** (29b,110a), **odal** (48a,88b,112c), **odel** (48a,112c), **odyl** (59d, 79c), **opal** (20a,65d,67b,82b), **oral** (114a,153d,174c,175c), **Orel, oval** (48d,49c), **oxyl** (112c)

OM - - **Oman** (159a), **omao** (165b), **omar** (103b), **Omar** (48c,51b,116c, 163b), **Omei** (24a), **omen** (14c,59d,60a,121c,123a,146b), **omer** (51a,75c), **omit** (49c,52c,106b,114c,147d), **omni** (34a), **Omri** (18c, 86d), **Omsk**

- OM - **boma** (7d), **bomb** (144a), **coma** (91c,157d,170c,172b), **comb** (38c), **come, Como, dome** (39c,133c,155d), **Domn** (135a), **domy, Goma** (191), **home, homo** (122d), **homy** (38b), **Kome** (71d), **Komi** (191), **loma** (58b,63d), **Lome, nome** (71c,163b), **Nome, pome** (11d), **Pomo** (192), **pomp** (111d,112d), **Roma** (83c,d), **Rome** (31c,51d), **romi** (72d), **romp** (63d), **soma** (10c,21c,34a,48a,81d,136b), **some** (114b, 121c,126a), **Toma** (191), **tomb, tome** (21d,177c)

- - OM **Ahom** (88c), **asom** (18d), **atom** (101c,114c,180d), **boom** (152d), **coom** (32d,150c,178d), **Crom, doom** (42d,55a,134d), **Edom** (18c, 51b,79b,82c,84a), **from, glom** (155d,160d,178c), **joom** (39c), **klom** (189), **loom** (11c,146b,179b), **room** (28d), **stom** (34c), **toom** (139b), **whom** (42b), **zoom**

O - - M **odum** (168c,180a), **ogam** (82b,c), **ogum** (82b), **olam** (51a,d,75c, 81a), **onym** (162c), **ovum** (48d)

ON - - **Onan** (18c,85c), **onca** (189), **once** (60b,79b), **onde** (63a,178d), **oner** (20d,53a,75c,162d,173a,d), **ones** (116a), **only** (24d,52c,98d, 147a,150a), **onto** (76a,174a), **onus** (24c,93b,109b), **onym** (162c), **onyx** (25d,28d,65d,142b), **onza** (189)

- ON - **a-one** (52b,167b), **bona** (89d), **Bona** (183c), **bond** (92a,101c,141d, 143b,159d,165c), **bone, bong, Boni** (63b), **bonk** (190), **Bonn** (17d), **bony** (147c), **Bony** (96b), **cond** (156a), **cone** (66b,150a,157c), **Coni, conk** (41c,108a,156d,157c), **conn** (43d,156a), **cony** (127a), **dona** (83d,121c,151d), **done, dong, doni** (21a,28c,168a), **don't, fond** (7c,94b), **Fong** (40b), **fono** (137a), **fons** (60c), **font** (16b,171d,172a), **Gona** (106d), **Gond, gone** (6b,15c,42c,44c,114d), **gong, hone** (110a, 143c,180d), **hong** (30b), **honk** (70a), **Iona** (28a,82d), **Ione** (24b, 88d,94d), **Ioni** (192), **jonk, kona** (74c), **konk** (41c), **lone** (150a), **long** (38b,185b), **lonk** (143d), **mona** (72b,101d), **monk** (28b,63c, 129d), **mono** (34c,78d,122d,147a), **Mono** (193), **mons** (89c), **Mons** (184d), **mont** (62b), **nona** (89b,107b), **Nona** (69a,183c), **none** (108b), **nono** (83b), **oons** (100a,186d), **oont** (25d), **pond, pone** (37a,85b), **pong, Pons** (13d,63c,110d,150c), **pont** (55d,61b), **pony, rone** (127c,164b), **Rong** (88c), **song** (12c,170c), **sons** (98d,109d), **tone** (6c,118c), **tong** (30a,c), **tonk** (173c), **tony, Tony** (96b), **wong** (56a), **wont** (6d,40a,73a), **yond** (164d), **zona** (144c,186d), **zone** (44c,50a,160a)

- - ON **acon** (62c,140d), **agon** (12c,36c,41b,55d,71b), **Amon** (86d,96b, 127d,159b,164a), **anon** (7d,14d,79d,80b,123a,145c,150c,164a), **aton** (150a,159b), **Avon** (143b), **axon** (106c,153c), **azon** (127b), **bion** (117b), **boon** (18b,20c,55a), **cion** (42d,70b,145b,148b,154b, 156a), **coon** (121c), **Dion** (96a,152a), **doon** (140b,168c), **ebon** (20b), **Elon** (18c,51b,108a), **Enon** (18c,d), **Eton** (33b,50c,84a), **faon** (33c, 55a), **Gaon** (85b), **goon** (157c,163c), **hoon** (190), **icon** (79d,92b, 136a), **ikon** (79d,136a), **iron** (55c,d,69d,81a,97b,143b,149a,173d, 179c), **Leon** (96a), **lion** (55b,86c), **loon** (19a,b,c,157d,179c), **moon** (40b,132c,137c), **neon** (65c), **paon** (115b), **peon** (28c,59c,99c), **phon** (94a), **pion** (43c,52b), **poon** (97c), **roon** (41a,168b), **scon** (162c), **sion** (125c,158c), **Sion** (75b,c,83a,157d), **soon** (123a), **tion** (158b), **toon** (80c,95b,168c), **tron** (180a), **upon** (6b), **woon** (24c), **Zion** (75b,c,83a,157d) **zoon** (43a)

O - - N **oban** (190), **Odin** (7c,29d,63c,68c,175d,183b), **Olan** (115c), **Oman** (159a), **omen** (14c,59d,60a,121c,123a,146b), **onan** (18c), **Onan** (85c), **open** (26a,60d,81a,109b,112c,125b,172b,173c), **Oran, oven** (15d,78c,86b), **Owen** (96a,183c), **oxan** (65c), **oxen** (10c)

OO - - **ooid** (48d), **oons** (100a,186d), **oont** (25d), **oord** (190), **ooze** (53c, 104b,116a), **oozy** (148b)

- OO - **boob** (146d), **booh** (52c), **book, bool** (39d), **boom** (152d), **boon** (18b,20c,55a), **boor** (47a,135d,172c), **boot** (128d), **cook** (137b), **cool** (25c,107d), **coom** (32d,150c,178d), **coon** (121c), **coop, Coos** (192), **coot** (19b,46d,72b,138d,141a,146d,157d), **doob** (18b), **dook** (184a), **doom** (42d,55a,134d), **doon** (140b,168c), **door** (51a,121b), **food** (109a,176b), **fool** (24a,41c,47a,146d), **foot** (115a), **good, goof, goon** (157c,163c), **Goop** (107d), **goor, hood** (38a,74d), **hoof** (173a), **hook** (27b,39d), **hoon** (190), **hoop** (181b), **hoot** (112c), **joom** (39c), **koop** (16c), **lood** (189), **loof** (144c,153d), **look** (11c,53c,142a), **loom** (11c,146b,179b), **loon** (19a,b,c,157d,179c), **loop** (31b,107d), **Loos, loot** (22a,118a,119d,153d), **mood** (44c), **moon** (40b,132c, 137c), **moor** (10a,75b,137b,141d,178b), **Moor** (102c,d,111d), **moot** (41b,44c), **nook** (37a,130d), **noon, pooa** (76a,125b), **pood** (189), **poof, pooh** (22b,107d), **pook** (68a), **pool** (65a,119d,120d), **poon** (97c), **poop** (41c), **poor** (33a), **poot!, rood** (38d,39a,88b), **roof** (78d), **rook** (19b,29c,39a), **room** (28d), **roon** (41a,168b), **root** (53a), **Roos** (67a), **sook** (22a,25c,97a), **soon** (123a,145c), **soot** (20b, 26c,88a), **tooa** (17c), **took, tool** (27c), **toom** (139b), **toon** (80c, 95b,168c), **toot, voog** (28a,66a,132b), **wood, woof** (39a,163d, 165a,179d), **wool** (58b,179c), **woon** (24c), **yoop, zoon** (43a)

- - OO **aboo** (17a), **aroo** (80c,82b), **broo** (139a), **ejoo** (55b,168c), **Kroo** (191), **phoo, shoo** (46b,67a,138b), **sloo** (160a), **whoo**

O - - O **octo** (34a,89b,122c), **odio** (83b), **Ohio, okro** (72c,175a), **oleo** (34c), **olio** (44b,77c,98c,100d,121d), **omao** (165b), **onto** (76a,174a), **ordo** (22a,30d,122a,171a), **orlo** (56b,119c), **Oslo, otho** (133a), **otro** (151d), **otto** (58d,116b,134a), **Otto** (14c,66d,67a,96a)

OP - - **opah** (23b,57a,b,86d), **opal** (20a,65d,67b,82b), **open** (26a,60d, 81a,109b,112c,125b,172b,173c), **Opie** (50c), **opus** (35c,105a,184c)

- OP - **copa** (88b,113c), **cope** (12b,26b,36c,65b,157d,176a), **Copt** (48d),

copy, **dopa** (117d), **dope** (46c,105d), **dopp** (43c), **hope** (13d,52d), **hopi** (33c), **Hopi** (12c,102c,125b), **hops** (17c), **koph** (91d), **kopi** (107a,168c), **Kopi** (172a), **lope** (48b,64b,d), **mope** (92d,159a), **pope** (20a,30d,31c,120d), **qoph** (91d), **rope** (36d,88d,128b), **ropy** (157c, 176d), **soph**, **Sopt** (45b), **tope** (24a,46b,57a,143c,151a), **toph** (75c), **topi** (37a,75a,118c), **tops** (159c)

- - OP **alop** (13d,46b,93d), **asop** (180b), **atop** (112a,174a), **chop** (98a), **clop**, **coop**, **crop** (38b), **drop** (43d,54b,100b,114c,168b), **Esop** (53b,54a), **flop** (54a), **Goop** (107d), **hoop** (181b), **klop** (150d), **knop** (124b,170c,185b), **koop** (16c), **loop** (31b,107d), **plop** (54b), **poop** (41c), **prop** (159d), **scop** (120a), **shop**, **slop**, **stop** (73b,111b), **swop** (168a), **trop** (62d,167a), **yoop**

- - OQ **shoq** (169a)

OR - - **orad** (104a), **oral** (114a,153d,174c,175c), **Oran**, **oras** (40d), **orca** (86b), **ordo** (22a,30d,122a,171a), **ordu** (170d), **Orel**, **orfe** (57a,b, 185c), **orgy** (26d,130d,137c), **orle** (17b,56b,76a,144b,177a), **orlo** (56b,119c), **Orly** (8b), **orna** (169d,182c), **orne** (169d,182c), **Orne** (25b), **orra** (139c,d,140a), **orts** (60d), **oryx** (11a)

- OR - **bora** (181d,182b), **bord** (100b), **bore** (14c,25b,46a,116a,165c, 179b), **borg** (40d), **Bori** (110d,150c), **born**, **boro** (154b), **Boro** (193), **Bors** (70b,134b), **bort** (43b), **Bort** (134b), **cora** (65d), **Cora** (42b, 69c,80c,116b,124d,172b,183c), **cord** (39b,131a), **core** (28b,51c, 75b,81b), **cork** (119d), **Cori** (138c), **corm** (24b,38d,156a), **corn** (39d,95c,123a), **dora** (70b), **Dora** (36d,41a,43b,183c,d), **dord** (42c), **dore** (61d,67b,69d,117d), **Dore** (50d,63a,b), **dorm**, **dorn** (164d), **dorp** (73c,176b), **dorr** (32b), **dory** (21b,58b,144c), **fora** (133a), **ford** (177b), **fore** (63d,174b), **fork**, **form** (54d,143c), **fort** (63d,157d), **gora** (81c), **gore** (115d,117c,154c,169c), **gory**, **hora** (22a,40b), **horn** (11a,105a,170b,182a), **hors** (62b), **kora** (178c), **Kora**, **kore** (107b), **Kore** (29a,42b,116b,124d), **kori** (7d,77a), **lora** (146b,149b,151c,169b), **Lora** (183c), **lord** (107c), **lore** (77c,87c, 90d,151c,183a), **lori** (91b), **lorn** (42d,60b), **loro** (19a,114b), **lory** (19a,114a), **mora** (42b,65a,72b,83d,99b,153a,161a), **more** (71a), **More** (50b), **morg** (188), **morn**, **moro** (19a,56c), **Moro** (100a,103a, 117a,159a), **Mors** (41b), **mort** (41b,47a,78b,136d), **Nora** (79b, 107a,164c,183c), **Nore** (163d), **nori** (8c,141c), **norm** (15a,115a, 128a,155a), **Norn** (69a,163d,174b), **oord** (190), **pore** (59d,110d, 111c,120d,157d), **pork**, **Poro** (141d), **port** (73d,136b,140c,170c,d, 182b,c), **Rori** (16b), **sora** (19b,c,127b), **sorb** (11d,103d,134b,142d), **Sorb** (148a,180a), **sore** (23d,142c), **sori** (55c,64a), **sorn** (139a,d), **sors** (44d,89b), **sort** (31d,39c,70b,86b,153a), **sory** (176d), **tora** (11a,44d,74a,75c,85c,90b,102d,115d), **tore**, **tori** (101b), **torn** (130a), **toro** (38a,107a,152a,168c), **torp** (54c), **tort** (31c,91a,185c), **Tory** (23c,36b,94c,172a), **word** (124b,165c), **wore**, **work** (64c,76b), **worm**, **worn** (143b), **wort** (76a,95d,121d), **yore** (10b,69d,93c,110b, 165d), **york** (38c), **York** (50b,c)

- - OR **acor** (6d), **ador** (153b), **amor** (152b), **Amor** (39c,68b), **asor** (75c, 105a), **boor** (47a,135d,172c), **chor** (164b), **door** (51a,121b), **Ghor** (174b), **goor**, **Igor** (135d), **knor** (87c), **mhor** (180b), **moor** (10a, 75b,137b,141d,178b), **Moor** (102c,d,111d), **odor** (138b,156a), **Ogor** (170b), **Olor** (160a,b), **poor** (33a), **shor** (136d), **Shor** (162b), **Thor**

(7c,68c,99c,100c,109c,165b), **utor** (90a,166c)

O - - R **Oder** (132a), **odor** (138b,156a), **Ogor** (170d), **Olor** (160a,b), **omar** (103b), **Omar** (48c,51b,116c), **omer** (51a,75c), **oner** (20d,53a,75c, 162d,173a,d), **osar** (51b,67b,131b), **oser** (61b), **over** (6b,38c,80a, 114d), **oxer** (55c), **oyer** (38a,75b,119c)

OS - - **osar** (51b,67b,131b), **oser** (61b), **Oslo, ossa** (21d) **Ossa** (103d,110b, 164b), **oste** (21d,83b)

- OS - **bosa** (12a), **Bosa, Bosc** (115c), **bose** (163c), **bosh, bosk** (164b), **boss** (49d,157d), **cosh** (35a,97c), **cose** (29b), **coso** (152c), **coss** (98a), **cost** (29a), **cosy** (149c), **dosa** (74b), **dose** (123a), **doss** (17c), **dost, foss** (44d,100d), **gosh, hose** (156c), **host** (13a,51d,104c), **Jose** (96a), **josh** (85b), **joss** (30b), **Josy** (183d), **koso** (6c,80d), **Koso** (192,193), **koss** (188), **lose** (60a,100c), **losh** (178b), **loss** (42c,123d, 178b), **lost, Mose** (96b), **mosk** (97b,103b), **moss** (91d,104c,114a, 170c), **most, mosy** (67d), **nose** (118d,125a,149b), **Nosu** (27d), **nosy, pose** (14c,15d), **posh** (49b,148c), **post** (89a,95c,155d), **Rosa** (58d, 134a,145d,183c), **rose** (33c), **Rose** (6a,50c,183c), **ross** (16c,161d), **Ross** (50c), **rosy** (21a,111a), **sosh** (81d), **soso** (99c,114c,166d), **tosh** (106a), **Tosk** (8c), **toss** (24a,132d, **Xosa** (86a)

- - OS **Amos** (96a,144b), **bios** (92a), **Coos** (192), **Enos** (7a,18d,52a,70c, 96a,143a), **epos** (51a,76b,120a), **Eros** (11c,39c,68b,97c,182d), **ghos** (30b), **gros** (47a,53d,146c), **Gros** (63a), **Laos** (80d,129c), **Loos, naos** (28a,71c,137a,163a), **Naos** (155b), **phos, Taos** (192), **Teos** (82a), **Thos** (84a,181c)

O - - S **oaks** (154d), **odds** (28d,172d), **offs** (38c), **ones** (116a), **onus** (24c, 93b,109b), **oons** (100a,186d), **opus** (35c,105a,184c), **oras** (40d), **orts** (60d), **Otis** (9c,d,24d,82a,111a), **Otus** (67a), **ours** (124c), **Ovis** (143d), **oyes** (38a,39b,75b)

OT - - **Otea** (71a,82d), **Otho** (133a), **otic** (14c,d,47b), **Otis** (9c,d,24d,82a, 111a), **Otoe** (147b), **otra** (152c), **otro** (151d), **otto** (58d,116b,134a), **Otto** (14c,66d,67a,96a), **Otus** (67a)

- OT - **bota** (189), **both, Boto** (192), **bott** (32a,88d), **cota** (117a), **cote** (19b,143d,144a,b), **coto** (16c,90b), **Coty** (63c), **dote** (17a,90b,94b, 97a,112a,139d,165d), **doth, Doto** (141b), **doty** (43d), **Goth** (16c, 163d), **Hoth** (20c), **hoti, iota** (71a,85c,91c,114c,166c,176a,180d), **jota** (151c), **joti, kota** (117a), **Kota** (45d), **koto** (84b), **lota** (24c, 121d,178d), **loth** (15a,173d), **lote** (24c,94a), **Loti** (63a,176a), **loto** (65a,121d,178d), **lots, mota** (103a), **mote** (114c,153a), **moth, Moth** (112d), **moto** (104b), **nota** (15c,89c), **note** (98c,109b,124b, 128d,130a,177c), **Nott** (107b), **pott** (113d), **rota** (27c,30d,38a,79a, 92d,133a,134a,b,180c), **rote** (130b,134b,143a,159d), **roti** (62c), **rotl** (103b,111c), **roto** (30a,122d,127b,152c,171b), **sote** (150c), **tota** (71d), **tote** (27a,73c), **toto** (8d,15a,34d,89a,181a), **toty** (87b), **vota** (133b), **vote** (60b), **Vote** (56d), **Voth** (191), **Voto** (192), **Wote** (191)

- - OT **Abot** (100c), **blot, boot** (128d), **clot** (32d,94d), **coot** (19b,46d,72b, 138d,141a,146d,157d), **eyot** (82d), **Fiot** (191), **flot** (173a), **foot** (115a), **frot** (28c), **grot** (27d), **hoot** (112c), **ilot** (82d), **khot, knot** (43c,99d,107c,124d,137b), **loot** (22a,118a,119d,136a,153d), **moot** (41b,44c), **phot** (173b), **piot** (95b), **plot** (25a,36b,118d,138b), **poot!, riot** (44c,111d,170c,173d), **root** (53a), **ryot** (115c), **scot** (14a,

162b), **Scot** (64b,132c), **shot** (9d,43d,90c,174d), **slot** (10d,11b,41d, 110d,167d,168a,181b), **soot** (20b,26c,88a), **spot** (93b,118c,154d, 162a), **stot** (154d,155d,157d,179b,186a), **swot, toot, trot** (85b, 93d,112d)

O - - T **oast** (15d,86b,112a), **obit** (41b,64c), **oket** (189), **omit** (49c,52c, 106b,114c,147d), **oont** (25d), **oust** (44c,49a,52b,125d)

OU - - **ouch!, ough!, ours** (124c), **Ouse** (132a,185d), **oust** (44c,49a,52b, 125d)

- OU - **Aoul** (191), **bout** (36c), **bouw** (188), **coup** (20d,97c,157b,c,162d), **cous** (38a), **doub** (18b), **douc** (101d), **doum** (168c), **dour** (67d, 159a), **foud** (54d,144b), **foul** (173a), **four** (26c), **goul** (102a), **gour** (112c,181c), **gout, hour, joug** (138d), **loud** (156a), **loun** (19a,b), **loup** (61d,62a,90c,139d), **Loup** (193), **lour** (13d,63d), **lout** (15c, 22a,24b,45b,109a,157d), **moue** (61d,62b), **noun** (114b,158a), **noup** (124b), **nous** (81d,100a,128b), **pouf, poul** (190), **pour** (162d), **pous** (188), **pout** (159a), **roud** (57a,b), **roue** (41b,44c,127c,134b), **roup** (44a,121d), **rout** (41d,44b,46b), **souf** (146b), **souk** (22a,97a), **soul** (10d,125a,153c,176d), **soup, sour, sous** (62d,172c), **toug** (171a), **toup** (95d), **tour** (31b,85c), **tout** (61a,127a), **youp** (185d), **your** (124c)

- - OU **Abou** (48b,55a), **chou** (61b), **Chou** (30b), **clou** (62b), **meou, niou** (188), **shou** (41d), **thou** (124b), **Tiou** (192), **Yaou** (30c)

O - - U **Oahu, Ogpu** (135d), **ordu** (170d)

OV - - **oval** (48d,49c,127a), **oven** (15d,78c,86b), **over** (6b,38c,80a,114d, 130a), **Ovid** (132d,133b), **Ovis** (143d), **ovum** (48d)

- OV - **cove** (17a,73d,107d), **dove** (19a,117d), **Hova** (95a), **hove** (92a, 157d), **Jova** (193), **Jove** (85d), **love** (163a), **move, nova** (20c,106d, 155c,174d), **nove** (83b), **rove** (127d,132b,178a), **wove, Xova** (193)

- - OV **akov** (189), **Azov** (20b)

OW - - **Owen** (96a,183c), **owse**

- OW - **bowk** (155d), **bowl, cowl** (101d), **dowd** (143b), **dowl, down** (149d), **fowl, gowk** (146d), **gowl** (102a,140d,185b), **gown, howe** (77d), **Howe** (17a,82a), **howl** (39b), **howk** (139b), **Iowa** (193), **jowl** (29b), **lowa** (19a), **lown** (157d), **lowp** (90c,139d), **mown, nowt** (106a,139a), **nowy** (194), **powe, rowy** (157b), **town** (73c), **towy** (58b), **yowl, yowt** (139c)

- - OW **alow** (18a,172c), **arow** (92c,158b), **avow** (6d,36a,41c,112c), **blow, brow, chow** (45a), **clow** (58c,148c), **crow** (19a), **dhow** (88d,111c, 175d), **enow** (50d,123a,158b), **flow** (157b), **frow** (47a,167a), **glow** (144c), **grow** (154b), **know, Lwow, meow, plow** (39c,165d), **prow** (21b,22c,144d,156a), **scow** (21a,58b), **show** (42b,44c,96b), **slow** (43c), **snow, stow** (112b), **swow** (100a), **trow** (18a,21a,159d,164c, 170b)

OX - - **oxan** (65c), **oxea** (153d), **oxen** (10c), **oxer** (55c), **oxid** (112c), **oxyl** (112c)

- OX - **boxy, coxa** (77b), **doxa** (48b), **doxy** (129d), **foxy** (38b,39c,181d), **moxa** (27d,30c), **Moxo** (192), **noxa, Roxy** (183d), **toxa** (153d)

- - OX **abox** (22d), **esox** (57b)

O - - X **obex** (22d), **Odax** (132c), **Olax** (52b), **onyx** (25d,28d,65d,142b),

oryx (11a)

OY - - **oyer** (38a,75b,119c), **oyes** (38a,39b,75b), **oyez** (38a,39b,75b)

- OY - **coyn** (37a), **coyo** (15a,30c), **Goya** (151d), **Hoya** (14d), **noyl** (87c), **soya** (151b)

- - OY **ahoy** (106a), **Amoy** (88c), **b'hoy** (134b), **buoy** (28d,58c), **choy** (48a,128d), **cloy** (61b,137c,159d), **ohoy** (106a), **ploy** (43c), **troy** (161c,180a), **Troy**

O - - Y **oaky**, **oary**, **obey** (35c,75c), **ohoy** (106a), **oily** (110b,172c), **okay** (8d), **olay** (113b), **only** (24d,52c,98d,147a,150a), **oozy** (148b), **orgy** (26d,130d,137c), **Orly** (8b)

- OZ - **boza** (12a), **bozo** (55b), **coze** (29b), **cozy** (149c), **doze** (148a), **dozy**, **Jozy**, **kozo** (113d,168c), **mozo** (152b), **noze** (75a), **ooze** (53c, 104b,116a), **oozy** (148b)

O - - Z **oyez** (38a,39b,75b)

PA - - **paal** (188), **paar** (28c), **paca** (132c,154a), **pace** (64b,98a,153b,156a, 170b,177d), **pack** (24b,140d), **paco** (9b,146d), **pacs** (94c), **pact** (8a), **padi** (131b), **paga** (117a), **page** (51b,59b,142d,159b), **paha** (67b), **pahi** (21b,26a), **paho** (122a), **paid** (129c), **pail**, **pain** (7c), **pair** (22d,37d,85b,171d), **pais** (37d), **pajo** (122a), **pala** (189), **Pala** (88b), **pale** (113a,117c,178a), **pali** (122b), **Pali** (23d,24a,137b,175a), **pall** (32d,81b,112a), **palm** (59b,168c,169b), **palo** (152c), **palp** (11a,55b, 58b,167c), **paly** (194), **Pana**, **pane** (113c,155a,b), **pang** (165b), **Pani** (120c), **pank** (189), **pant**, **paon** (115b), **papa**, **pape** (19b,113a), **para** (134c,170d), **Para** (18a,51d), **parc** (62b,112c), **pard** (27b, 91b), **pare** (115c,129a), **pari** (34a,180a), **park**, **parr** (136d,137a, 147c), **pars** (89d), **part** (44d,60d,121c,159c), **paru** (57a), **pasa** (46a,127c,152c), **pasi** (94b), **pass** (110b,155c), **past** (25c,69d,165d), **pata** (32c,160d), **pate** (39a,74d), **path** (132a,134b), **pato** (46d), **patu** (179b), **paul**, **Paul** (96a), **paun** (18b), **paut** (140a), **pave** (85a), **pavo** (115b), **Pavo** (36b,c), **pavy** (115b), **pawa** (189), **pawl** (43a, 95a), **pawn** (29c,119c)

- PA - **Apap** (102a), **apar** (12d), **opah** (23b,57a,b,86d), **opal** (20a,65d,67b, 82b), **spad** (105b), **Spad** (118d), **spae** (139c), **span** (23b,107b,113a, 128b,162c), **spar** (22c,24c,64b,97b,100b,144d), **spat** (112c,126b, 134b), **upas** (84d,120b,168c,d)

- - PA **arpa** (83b), **capa** (152a,166d), **cepa** (110c), **copa** (88b,113c), **depa** (188), **dopa** (117d), **Hupa** (192), **kapa** (74b), **lipa** (54d), **napa** (25c, 67d,90d), **Napa** (182c), **Nepa**, 106b,178c), **nipa** (14b,46b,48a,164a, 168c), **papa**, **pipa** (159d), **pupa** (30d,81b,c), **ripa** (16b,131d), **ropa** (152a), **rupa** (60b), **sapa** (70c), **supa** (168c), **tapa** (16c,32c,53b, 56a,74b,104b,112b,113d,120d), **yapa** (113b), **Zipa** (29d)

P - - A **paca** (132c,154a), **paga** (117a), **paha** (67b), **pala** (189), **Pala** (88b), **Pana**, **papa**, **para** (134c,170d), **Para** (18a,51d), **pasa** (46a, 127c,152c), **pata** (32c,160d), **pawa** (189), **peba** (12d), **Peba** (193), **peca** (190), **peda** (114d,144b), **pega** (57a,130a), **pela** (30c), **Pera** (60a), **pesa** (190), **peva** (12d), **pica** (66b,95b,172c), **pika** (93a,128a, 132c), **pima** (37c), **Pima** (192), **pina** (35d,118b), **pipa** (159d), **Pisa** (90c), **pita** (9c,28b,56a,83a), **plea** (51a,52d,122a,130b), **poha** (74c), **pola**, **pooa** (76a,125b), **proa** (21b,26a,95c,d), **puca** (68a),

puja (77a), **puka** (107a,168c), **puma** (27b,37c,55b,103d), **puna** (10b,33b,104a,119b,182a), **pupa** (30d,81b,c), **Puya** (118b), **pyla** (22d)

P - - B **pleb** (10d,35b,180b)

P - - C **parc** (62b,112c)

P - - D **paid** (129c), **pard** (27b,91b), **pend, Phad** (155b), **Phud** (110b), **pied** (96c,103c,114b,117c,154a,174d), **plod** (170b,177d), **pond, pood** (189), **prod** (67d,80b,106b,120b), **pund** (189), **puud** (189)

PE - - **peag** (144a,178a), **peai** (98b), **peak** (9a,38c,159b,186b), **peal** (131c,d), **pean** (64c,150b), **pear** (64a), **peat** (64a,175a), **peba** (12d), **Peba** (193), **peca** (190), **peck** (24d), **peco** (162b), **peda** (114d,144b), **pedi** (34b), **pedo** (34b), **peek** (93d,115c), **peel** (53a,114a), **peen** (73c), **peep** (93d,115c), **peer** (51a,93d,107c), **peet** (64a), **pega** (57a,130a,158b), **Pegu** (24c,102a,127d), **peho** (19b,102c,106d), **Peke** (45a,148d), **pela** (30c), **Pele** (69c,74c), **pelf** (22a,56c,131b), **pelo** (83b), **pelt** (53a), **pelu** (30a,106d,168c), **pend, pene, pent** (36a), **peon** (28c,59c,99c), **pepo** (39b,64a,70a,98c,125c,154c), **Pera** (60a), **pere** (61c,63b), **peri** (54b,116b,c,122b), **perk** (84d,93a), **perm** (49b,97d), **pern** (78a), **pero** (152a), **pert** (80a,93a,137c,154b), **Peru, pesa** (190), **peso** (99c), **pest** (108c,116b,118d,170a), **pete** (136b), **Pete** (96b), **peto** (57a,177b), **Peto** (76a), **peur** (61c), **peva** (12d), **pevy** (91d,94c)

- PE - **aper** (32d), **Apet** (97c), **apex** (39c,76c,115c,118b,159b,166a,167b), **epee** (55c,160d), **open** (26a,60d,81a,109b,112c,125b,172b,173c), **spec, sped, Spee** (66d,70b), **spes, Spes** (69a,78a), **spet** (16c,57a, 142c), **spew** (35a,49a), **spex, Spey**

- - PE **cape** (75a,96c,124b,161a), **cepe** (48c), **cope** (12b,26b,36c,65b,157d, 176a), **dope** (46c,105d), **dupe** (27c,41c,72c,160c), **gape** (185b), **hipe** (185a), **hope** (13d), **hype** (185a), **jape** (85a,b), **jupe** (62b, 84a), **lope** (48b,64b,d), **lupe** (19a,64a), **mope** (92d), **nape** (15b,108c,d), **Nupe** (191), **olpe** (90d), **pape** (19b,113a), **pipe** (105a,180d,182a), **pope** (20a,30d,31c,120d), **ripe** (58a,97c,98c), **rope** (36d,88d,128b), **rype** (19b,125a), **sipe** (101a,110c,140b), **supe** (53a,154d), **sype** (110c), **tape** (16a,19a,128d), **tipe** (168b), **tope** (24a,46b,57a,143c, 151a), **type** (31d,115a,155a), **wipe, Xipe** (15c)

P - - E **pace** (64b,98a,153b,156a,170b,177d), **page** (51b,59b,142d,159b), **pale** (113a,117c,178a), **pane** (113c,155a,b), **pape** (19b,113a), **pare** (115c,129a), **pate** (39a,74d), **pave** (85a), **Peke** (45a,148d), **Pele** (69c,74c), **pene, pere** (61c,63b), **pete** (136b), **Pete** (96b), **pice** (190), **pike** (57a,b,76c,120b,153a), **pile** (45d,75b,117c), **pine** (36a, 52a,88c,93c,168c,d,169a), **pipe** (105a,180d,182a), **pise** (127d), **plie** (32c,59b), **poke** (108c), **pole** (132c,143b,177b,184a), **Pole** (52a), **pome** (11d), **pone** (37a,85b), **pope** (20a,30d,31c, 120d), **pore** (59d,110d,111c,120d,157d), **pose** (14c,15d), **powe, pree** (139d), **puce** (33c,d,52a), **pule** (180d), **pume** (137b), **Pume** (175b,185b), **pure** (29b,172b,173c), **pyle** (34b), **Pyle** (9c,178a), **pyre** (64c)

P - - F **pelf** (22a,56c,131b), **Piat** (63c), **piff** (24b), **poor, pouf, puff** (180d)

- PG - **upgo** (13c)

P - - G **pang** (165b), **peag** (144a,178a), **ping, plug** (156d,184d), **pong,**

prig (112a,116c), **pung** (22c,148b)

PH - - **Phad** (155b), **phew** (52c), **Phil** (96b), **phit** (24b), **phiz** (54a), **phon** (94a), **phoo, phos, phot** (173b), **Phud** (110b), **phut** (24b), **Phut** (110b)

- PH - **epha** (75c)

- - PH **Alph** (132a), **caph** (91c), **kaph** (91d), **koph** (91d), **qoph** (91d), **soph, toph** (75c), **umph**

P - - H **path** (132a,134b), **pish** (36c,107d), **pith** (37a,51c,67b,95c,97a, 119b,126d), **pooh** (22b,107d), **posh** (49b,148c), **prah** (21b, 26a,95c,d), **Ptah** (48d,98c), **pugh!, push** (145c)

PI - - **Piaf** (63c), **piat** (11a), **piay** (98b), **pica** (66b,95b,172c), **pice** (190), **Pici** (19c,184a), **pick, pico** (65a,152c), **Pict** (23c,47d), **pied** (96c, 103c,114b,117c,154a,174d), **pien** (13b), **pier** (23a,88b,180c), **piet** (29b,95b), **piff** (24b), **pika** (93a,128a,132c), **pike** (57a,b,76c,120b, 153a), **piki** (95c), **piky, pile** (45d,75b,117c), **pili** (34b,108d), **pill, pily, pima** (37c), **Pima** (192), **pina** (35d,118b), **pine** (36a,52a,88c, 93c,168c,d,169a), **ping, pink** (26d,33c,60c,138a), **pino** (152c), **pint** (67b), **piny, pion** (43c,52b), **piot** (95b), **pipa** (159d), **pipe** (105a, 180d,182a), **pipi** (106d,119d), **pipy** (145d), **pirn** (21b,129a,179b), **Piro** (192), **pirr** (181a), **Pisa** (90c), **pise** (127d), **pish** (36c,107d), **pisk** (9c, 19b), **piso** (189), **pist** (25c), **pita** (9c,28b,56a,83a), **pith** (37a, 51c,67b,95c,97a,119b,126d), **pito** (9c,28b,83a), **Pitt** (50d,155d), **pity** (35b), **Pius** (121a), **pixy** (154b)

- PI - **apia** (121b), **apii** (74c), **apio** (125b), **Apis** (17c,24b,49a,125a,136a), **epic** (76b,120a), **ipil** (117a,168c,169a), **Opie** (50c), **spin** (131a, 180d), **spir** (97c), **spit** (120a,132b,c), **Upis** (13b), **ypil** (117a,168c)

- - PI **aipi** (27a), **Hapi** (66a,107b,136a), **Hopi** (12c,102c,125b), **hopi** (33c), **impi** (86a), **kepi** (99d), **kopi** (107a,168c), **Kopi** (172a), **pipi** (106d,119d), **tipi** (181b), **topi** (37a,75a,118c), **Tupi** (192)

P - - I **padi** (131b), **pahi** (21b,26a), **pali** (122b), **Pali,** (23d,24a,137b,175a), **Pani** (120c), **pari** (34a,180a), **pasi** (94b), **peai** (98b), **pedi** (34b), **peri** (54b,116b,c,122b), **Pici** (19c,184a), **piki** (95c), **pili** (34b, 108d), **pipi** (106d,119d), **puli** (45a,78d), **puri** (80d)

P - - K **pack** (24b,140d), **pank** (189), **park, peak** (9a,38c,159b,186b), **peck** (24d), **peek** (93d,115c), **perk** (84d,93a), **pick, pink** (26d,33c,60c, 138a), **pisk** (9c,19b), **polk** (37c), **pook** (68a), **pork, puck** (44b,68a, 77c,100c), **Puck** (99d,143b), **pulk** (37c,88d), **punk** (9b,166a,167c)

PL - - **plan** (99b,124a,138b), **plap** (54b), **plat** (22d,96c,114a,119c,133d), **play** (63d,154a), **plea** (51a,52d,122a,130b), **pleb** (10d,35b,180b), **plet** (135d), **plew** (17c), **plex** (60b), **plie** (32c,59b), **plod** (170b, 177d), **plop** (54b), **plot** (25a,36b,118d,138b), **plow** (39c,165d), **ploy** (43c), **plug** (156d,184d), **plum, plup, plus** (10b,102c)

- PL - **upla**

P - - L **paal** (188), **pail, pall** (32d,81b,112a), **paul, Paul** (96a), **pawl** (43a, 95a), **peal** (131c,d), **peel** (53a,114a), **Phil** (96b), **pill, poll** (74d, 160a,177c), **pool** (65a,119d,120d), **poul** (190), **pull** (45d,167d), **purl** (87c,104c), **pyal** (175c)

P - - M **palm** (59b,168c,169b), **perm** (49b,97d), **plum, poem** (51a), **pram** (15a), **prim** (156b)

PN - - **Pnyx** (71c)

P - - N **pain** (7c), **paon** (115b), **paun** (18b), **pawn** (29c,119c), **pean** (64c, 150b), **peen** (73c), **peon** (28c,59c,99c), **pern** (78a), **phon** (94a), **pien** (13b), **pion** (43c,52b), **pirn** (21b,129a,179b), **plan** (99b,124a, 138b), **poon** (97c)

PO - - **poco** (83b,93a), **poem** (51a), **poet** (49b), **Pogo** (121c), **pogy** (57a, 88a,98d,103c), **poha** (74c), **poke** (108c), **poku** (11a), **poky** (148c), **pola, pole** (132c,143b,177b,184a), **Pole** (52a), **polk** (37c), **poll** (74d,160a,177c), **polo** (154a), **Polo** (175b), **poly** (34c,76b), **pome** (11d), **Pomo** (192), **pomp** (111d,112d), **pond, pone** (37a,85b), **pong, Pons** (13d,63c,110d,150c), **pont**,(55d,61b), **pony, pooa** (76a,125b), **pood** (189), **poof, pooh** (22b,107d), **pook** (68a), **pool** (65a,119d, 120d), **poon** (97c), **poop** (41c), **poor** (33a), **poot!, pope** (20a,30d, 31c,120d), **pore** (59d,110d,111c,120d,157d), **pork, Poro** (141d), **port** (73d,136b,140c,170c,d,182b,c), **pose** (14c,15d), **posh** (49b, 148c), **post** (89a,95c,155d), **pott** (113d), **pouf, poul** (190), **pour** (162d), **pous** (188), **pout** (159a), **powe**

- PO - **apod** (59d), **epos** (51a,76b,120a), **spot** (93b,118c,154d,162a), **upon** (6b)

- - PO **cipo** (91d), **gapo** (60a), **hypo** (117b), **mapo** (68a,148d), **pepo** (39b, 64a,70a,98c,125c,154c), **sapo** (149c,166d), **typo** (35c,51b)

P - - O **paco** (9b,146d), **paho** (122a), **pajo** (122a), **palo** (152c), **pato** (46d), **pavo** (115b), **Pavo** (36b,c), **peco** (162b), **pedo** (34b), **peho** (19b, 102c,106d), **pelo** (83b), **pepo** (39b,64a,70a,98c,125c,154c), **pero** (152a), **peso** (99c), **peto** (57a,177b), **Peto** (76a), **phoo, pico** (65a, 152c), **pino** (152c), **Piro** (192), **piso** (189), **pito** (9c,28b,83a), **poco** (83b,93a), **Pogo** (121c), **polo** (154a), **Polo** (175b), **Pomo** (192), **Poro** (141d), **prao** (21b,26a,95c,d), **puno** (182a), **pyro**

- - PP **Capp** (27a), **dopp** (43c), **kapp, kipp, Lapp** (108a), **repp** (53b,131a), **typp** (185b), **wapp** (54b,133d,145d), **Yapp** (22a), **zipp**

P - - P **palp** (11a,55b,58b), **peep** (93d,115c), **plap** (54b), **p'op** (54b), **plup, pomp** (111d,112d), **poop** (41c), **prep** (138b), **prop** (159d), **pulp, pump**

PR - - **prah** (21b,26a,95c,d), **pram** (15a), **prao** (21b,26a,95c,d), **prau** (21b, 26a,95c,d), **pray** (18b,51a,159d), **pree** (139d), **prep** (138b), **pres** (62b), **pret** (188), **prey** (119d,176a), **prig** (112a,116c), **prim** (156b), **proa** (21b,26a,95c,d), **prod** (67d,80b,106b,120b), **prop** (159d), **prow** (21b,22c,144d,156a), **prut!, Prut** (41a)

- PR - **spry** (7a,107b)

P - - R **paar** (28c), **pair** (22d,37d,85b,171d), **parr** (136d,137a,147c), **pear** (64a), **peer** (51a,93d,107c), **peur** (61c), **pier** (23a,88b,180c), **pirr** (181a), **poor** (33a), **pour** (162d), **purr** (104c)

- PS - **apse** (9b,20a,31a,128c,130a,142b,175a), **Apsu** (29a), **ipse** (44d, 89c), **ipso** (89c)

- - PS **Alps** (85d), **gyps, Gyps** (71d), **hops** (17c), **hyps, seps** (93b,142d), **tops** (159c), **Veps** (191), **Zips** (40c)

P - - S **pacs** (94c), **pais** (37d), **pars** (89d), **pass** (110b,155c), **phos, Pius** (121a), **plus** (10b,102c), **Pons** (13d,63c,110d,150c), **pous** (188), **pres** (62b), **puss**

PT - - **Ptah** (48d,98c)

- - PT **Copt** (48d), **dipt, kept, rapt** (6c,27a,50d), **sept** (31d,82b,143a,149c), **Sept** (45b), **Sopt** (45b), **wept**

P - - T **pact** (8a), **pant, part** (44d,60d,121c,159c), **past** (25c,69d,165d), **paut** (140a), **peat** (64a,175a), **peet** (64a), **pelt** (53a), **pent** (36a), **pert** (80a,93a,137c,154b), **pest** (108c,116b,118d,170a), **phit** (24b), **phot** (173b), **phut** (24b), **Phut** (110b), **piat** (11a), **Pict** (23c, 47d), **piet** (29b,95b), **pint** (67b), **piot** (95b), **pist** (25c), **Pitt** (50d, 155d), **plat** (22d,96c,114a,119c,133d), **plet** (135d), **plot** (25a,36b, 118d,138b), **poet** (49b), **pont** (55d,61b), **poot!, port** (73d,136b, 140c,170c,d,182b,c), **post** (89a,95c,155d), **pott** (113d), **pout** (159a), **pret** (188), **prut!, Prut** (41a), **punt** (21a,58b), **putt** (69d), **pyat** (95b), **pyet** (95b)

PU - - **puca** (68a), **puce** (33c,d,52a), **puck** (44b,68a,77c,100c), **Puck** (99d,143b), **pudu** (41d), **puff** (180d), **pugh!, puja** (77a), **puka** (107a,168c), **puku** (11a), **pule** (180d), **puli** (45a,78d), **pulk** (37c, 88d), **pull** (45d,167d), **pulp, pulu** (74c), **puly, puma** (27b,37c,55b, 103d), **pume** (137b), **Pume** (175b,185b), **pump, puna** (10b,33b, 104a,119b,182a), **pund** (189), **pung** (22c,148b), **punk** (9b,166a, 167c), **puno** (182a), **punt** (21a,58b), **puny** (55b,179a), **pupa** (30d, 81b,c), **pure** (29b,172b,173c), **puri** (80d), **purl** (87c,104c), **purr** (104c), **Puru** (192), **push** (145c), **puss, putt** (69d), **puud** (189), **puxy, Puya** (118b)

- PU - **Apus** (36b,c), **opus** (35c,105a,184c), **spud** (121d,151c), **spun, spur** (10d,67d,167d,168a,181b), **sput** (21c)

- - PU **hapu** (106d), **napu** (29d,80d), **Ogpu** (135d), **tapu**

P - - U **paru** (57a), **patu** (179b), **Pegu** (24c,102a,127d), **pelu** (30a,106d, 168c), **Peru, poku** (11a), **prau** (21b,26a,95c,d), **pudu** (41d), **puku** (11a), **pulu** (74c), **Puru** (192)

P - - W **phew** (52c), **plew** (17c), **plow** (39c,165d), **prow** (21b,22c,144d, 156a)

P - - X **plex** (60b), **Pnyx** (71c)

PY - - **pyal** (175c), **pyat** (95b), **pyet** (95b), **pyla** (22d), **pyle** (34b), **Pyle** (9c,178a), **pyre** (64c), **pyro**

- - PY **copy, espy** (44a,142a), **gapy, pipy** (145d), **ropy** (157c,176d), **typy**

P - - Y **paly** (194), **pavy** (115b), **pevy** (91d,94c), **piay** (98b), **piky, pily, piny, pipy** (145d), **pity** (35b), **pixy** (154b), **play** (63d,154a), **ploy** (43c), **pogy** (57a,88a,98d,103c), **poky** (148c), **poly** (34c,76b), **pony, pray** (18b,51a,159d), **prey** (119d,176a), **puly, puny** (55b,179a), **puxy**

P - - Z **phiz** (54a)

QA - - **Qaid** (35a)

Q - - D **Qaid** (35a), **quad** (33c,172a), **quid** (39b,166d), **quod** (123d)

QE - - **qere** (75c), **qeri** (75c)

Q - - E **qere** (75c), **quae** (176b)

- - QF **waqf** (103a)

Q - - G **quag** (21c,102c), **Qung** (191)

Q - - H **qoph** (91d)

Q - - I **qeri** (75c), **quai** (88b,117c,180c), **quei** (189)

Q - - N **quan** (190)

QO - - **qoph** (91d)

Q - - P **quip** (183a,b)

Q - - S **quas** (135c)

Q - - T **quit** (90d,130c)

QU - - **quad** (33c,172a), **quae** (176b), **quag** (21c,102c), **quai** (88b,117c, 180c), **quan** (190), **quas** (135c), **quay** (88b,117c,180c), **quei** (189), **quid** (39b,166d), **quip** (183a,b), **quit** (90d,130c), **quiz, Qung** (191), **quod** (123d)

- QU - **aqua** (90a,178c), **equi** (122d)

Q - - Y **quay** (88b,117c,180c)

Q - - Z **quiz**

RA - - **raab** (32d), **raad** (14a,49b,151a,165b), **raas** (91b), **Raba, rabi** (38d, 74a), **Rabi** (14b,117b), **raca** (19a,59c,130b,184d), **race** (116a,153b, 154b,169c), **rack** (32c,64b), **racy** (153b), **rada** (135c,172a), **rade** (138d), **raff** (75b), **raft** (27b,33c,58c,75b), **raga** (56d,105a), **rage** (10c,30c,157a,161d), **ragi** (28b), **Rahu** (42b,48b), **Raia** (107d,147b), **raid** (59d,80c), **raik** (188,189), **rail** (16b,19b,c,37a,97b,138c,150c, 177b), **rain** (121d,162d), **raip** (36d), **rais** (26c,29d,75a,103b), **Rais** (106b), **raja** (77a,123c), **rake** (41b,44c,134b,140d), **rale** (7c,23a, 29d,41b), **ralo** (188), **Rama** (77a,80b,176d), **rame** (22d), **rami** (22d), **ramp** (65a,80b,127b,148b), **rana** (77a,123c), **Rana** (63d), **rand** (16d,22a,131b,145a,b), **Rand** (69c), **rang, rani** (72d,77b,123c,127c), **rank** (31d,55d,70b,92c,94d,157d), **rann** (175c), **rant** (41c,127b, 128a,161d), **rapt** (6c,27a,50d), **rara** (119a), **rare** (138b,164b,172b, 173d), **rasa** (51c), **rase** (42b,91d), **rash** (75a), **rasp** (56b,70d,140d), **rata** (29d,56b,89d,96c,106d,120c,168c), **rate** (11d,14a,31d,36b,51d, 52a,70b,85c,112b,123b,127d,128a,138c,143a,174b), **rath** (29a, 76d,162d), **rati** (189), **rats, rave**,(41c,157a,161d), **ravi** (61b), **Ravi** (16b), **raya** (19b,23c,76d,107d), **raze** (42b,91d) **razz** (131b)

- RA - **Arab** (30a,78b,c,106a,107c,157b,160c,185d), **arad** (13a,c,84a), **arah** (52c), **Aral** (135d), **Aram** (18d,50c,105c,144b,161c), **Aran** (18c,48c,64d,82d,174c), **arar** (137a,168c), **Aras, brab** (113b), **brad** (54d,67c,105b), **brae** (76d,139a,c,140b,148c), **brag** (21a,175a), **Bram** (96a), **bran** (23c,39a,70b,72a,79c), **Bran** (23c,50c), **bras** (61a), **brat, bray, crab** (39b,144b,181b), **crag** (132c), **cral, cram** (157d), **cran** (160c), **craw** (38d,72c,156c), **Crax** (19b,39d), **draa, drab** (23d,29c,33d,46d,53d), **drag** (74a,125b), **drah** (188), **dram** (46b,110c,121d,148c), **drap** (61b,c,62a), **drat** (100a), **Drau, draw** (42c,53a,92b,117c,121c,167d), **dray** (27a,154c), **eral** (51a), **erat** (89c), **frab** (138c), **frap** (45d,165c), **frat, frau** (181b), **fray** (56b,60d), **grab** (105b,142a,149b), **grad** (28b), **Graf** (37c,66b,67a, 107c,186b), **gram** (29d,99b,148d,160d,180a), **grao** (189), **gras** (78b), **gray** (33c,77c), **Gray** (50c), **Irad** (18d), **Irae** (43c), **Irak** (99a,d), **Iran** (6a,48c,116b), **Iraq** (99a,d), **Iras** (11b,32a), **krag** (131c), **kral, kran** (190), **kras** (76d), **orad** (104a), **oral** (114a,153d, 174c,175c), **Oran, oras** (40d), **prah** (21b,26a,95c,d), **pram** (15a), **prao** (21b,26a,95c,d), **prau** (21b,26a,95c,d), **pray** (18b,51a,159d), **tram** (170a), **tran** (7a), **trap** (27b,67b,132b,149b), **tray** (128c,136d,

142d,143c), **ural, Ural** (135c), **uran** (101d), **Wraf, wrap** (32b,51a)

- - RA **abra** (26b), **Abra, aera** (8a), **Afra** (183c), **agra** (26d,34d), **Agra** (161b), **Aira** (70d), **akra** (176a), **Akra** (191), **amra** (77c), **arra** (47d, 52c,82b), **aura** (44c,49c,66a,96b,158a,170d,177c), **bara** (188), **Bera** (86d), **bora** (181d,182b), **bura** (182b), **cara** (83a), **Cara** (48b, 183c), **cora** (65d), **Cora** (42b,69c,80c,116b,124d,172b,183c), **cura** (152c), **Dara** (18d), **dera** (34c), **dora** (70b), **Dora** (36d,41a,43b, 183c,d), **dura** (153c), **eyra** (181d), **Ezra** (96a), **fora** (133a), **gara** (190), **gora** (81c), **Hera** (69c,85d,110b,126b,186b,d), **hora** (22a,40b), **hura** (20a,137a), **Hura, ikra** (27d), **Irra** (68c, 178a), **jura, Jura, Kara** (132a), **kora** (19a,178c), **Kora, Lara** (25c), **lira** (28b,79a,170d), **lora** (146b,149b,151c,169b), **Lora** (183c), **lura** (22d,82a), **Lyra** (36b,74a), **mara** (114d), **Mara** (24a,d,105b,107b), **mira** (174d), **Mira** (155b), **mora** (42b,65a,72b,83d,99b,153a,161a), **mura** (84d), **Mura** (192), **Myra** (10a,31b,183c), **Nera** (165b), **Nora** (79b,107a,164c,183c), **ocra** (72c,175a), **okra** (72c,175a), **orra** (139c,d,140a), **otra** (152c), **para** (134c,170d), **Para** (18a,51d), **Pera** (60a), **Sara** (24d,183c), **sera** (11b,20d,59a,83a,180d), **sora** (19b,c, 127b), **sura** (87c,113b,166d), **Syra, tara** (22a,55c,113a,168c), **Tara** (82b,c,138b), **tera** (23d,84c), **tora** (11a,44d,74a,75c,85c,90b,102d, 115d), **vara** (151d), **vera** (140c,151b,175c), **Vera** (183c) **Vira** (191), **zira** (188)

R - - A **Raba, raca** (19a,59c,130b,184d), **rada** (135c,172a), **raga** (56d,105a), **Raia** (107d,147b), **raja** (77a,123c), **Rama** (77a,176d), **rana** (77a,123c), **Rana** (63d), **rara** (119a), **rasa** (51c), **rata** (29d,56b,89d), 96c,106d,120c,168c), **raya** (19b,23c,76d,107d), **reba** (144a), **Reba** (18d,86c), **rede** (37c,81d), **reja** (152b), **rena** (25b,132c), **rhea** (37a, 56a,111d,133d), **Rhea** (19b,68d,87c,103c,186b), **riga** (118b), **Riga, rima** (23a,30c,32a,58a,110d), **ripa** (16b,131d), **rita, Rita** (37b, 78d,183c,), **Roda** (107b), **roka** (95a,168c,d), **Roma** (83c,d), **ropa** (152a), **Rosa** (58d,134a,145d,183c), **rota** (27c,30d,38a,79a,92d, 133a,134a,b,180c), **ruga** (59b,185a), **rupa** (60b), **rusa, Rusa** (41d, 136d), **Ruta** (76b,134d)

- RB - **arba** (135d,171a)

- - RB **barb** (20b,57d,78b,117d,120a,b,124b), **curb** (130c,146b), **garb** (32c,46a), **gerb** (56d,143d), **Harb** (191), **herb** (58b,158b), **kerb** (146b), **Serb** (15d,148a,186c), **sorb** (11d,103d,134b,142d), **Sorb** (148a,180a), **verb** (7a,114b,184b)

R - - B **raab** (32d), **rhob** (64a,85c), **rumb** (120b)

- RC - **arca** (9a,22c,29d,115a,130a), **Arca** (101b), **arch** (29d,38b,39d,123d, 132c), **orca** (86b)

- - RC **circ** (31a), **marc** (70c), **Marc** (96a), **parc** (62b,112c)

- RD - **Erda** (23d,41a,47d,68d,69a,131d,177b), **ordo** (22a,30d,122a,171a), **ordu** (170d), **urde** (86b), **Urdu** (77b), **urdy** (86b)

- - RD **bard** (12d,120a), **bird, bord** (100b), **Byrd** (9c,120b), **card** (33d,114d), **cord** (39b,131a), **curd** (99d), **Dard, dord** (42c), **eard** (139b), **fard** (112d), **ford** (177b), **fyrd** (110a), **Gerd** (63c), **gird** (32c,50a,123a,160a), **hard** (109b), **herd** (39a,46c,72a), **Kurd** (48b, 82a), **lard** (54d,61a,71a,110a), **lord** (107c), **nard** (13a,97c,102b, 110a,153c), **oord** (190), **pard** (27b,91b), **sard** (26d,28d,65d,111a),

142b,156d), **Sard, surd** (82c,177a), **verd** (71d), **ward** (31c,55c,86b), **word** (124b,165c), **Wurd, Wyrd** (107d), **yard** (152d)

R - - D **raad** (14a,49b,151a,165b), **Raad** (151a), **raid** (59d,80c), **rand** (16d, 22a,131b,145a,b), **Rand** (69c), **read** (116d,157d), **redd** (153a), **reed** (16a,70d,97b,105a,111b,118b,144b), **Reed** (163a), **rend** (32a,159c, 162c,185a), **Ridd** (94a), **rind** (53a,115c), **Rind** (109c,174b), **road** (37d,164d), **rodd** (38d), **roed, rood** (38d,39a,88b), **roud** (57a,b), **rudd** (26d,57a,b), **rynd** (100a)

RE - - **read** (116d,157d), **real** (7a), **ream** (18c,37d,50d,113d,171c), **reap** (7a,40a,74a), **rear** (15b,23a,b,24a,51b,76d,127c), **reba** (144a), **Reba** (18d,86c), **reck** (26d,75c), **rect** (117b), **redd** (153a), **rede** (37c, 81d,138d), **redo** (165c), **reed** (16a,70d,97b,105a,111b,118b,144b), **Reed** (163a), **reef** (129a,137a,145a), **reek** (49d,53c,64a,148d,149a), **reel** (21b,40b,d,153c,154a,c,d,180d), **reem** (18d), **reft** (32a,42c, 44d,167b), **reim** (112c), **rein** (29b,130c), **reis** (26c,29d,75a,103b), **reja** (152b), **Reki** (16a), **rely** (16b,170b), **Remi** (10b), **Rems, rena** (25b,132c), **rend** (32a,159c,162c,185a), **Reni** (83d), **Reno, rent** (58a,77c,91b,138b,153d,162c,167c), **repp** (53b,131a), **rese** (127b), **resh** (91d), **rest** (15d,91b,104d,105a,115a,b,130a,b,161b), **rete** (106c,119c), **reve** (61c,104d), **revs** (131a)

- RE - **area** (37d,38a,44c,53a,93b,110d,127d,138c,168a,186d), **areg** (116a, 137a), **areo** (34c), **Ares** (49b,51b,68c,76a,97a,105c,110b), **aret** (128c), **brea** (100b), **bred** (23c,48c,127c), **bree** (139a), **bren** (72d, 95a), **Brer** (172b), **Bres, brew** (35d), **brey** (194), **crea** (92c), **Cree** (192), **crew** (72a,106a), **Crex** (37a), **dree** (139b,140c,158b,172c), **drei** (66d,165a), **dreg, drew, drey** (154c), **erer,** (17d,150c), **Frea, Fred** (96b), **free** (44a,70d,131b), **fret** (28c,35b,111c,184d), **Frey** (7c, 68b,124d), **gres** (156d), **grew, grey** (33c), **Iren** (127c), **Orel, pree** (139d), **prep** (138b), **pres** (62b), **pret** (188), **prey** (119d), **tree** (11d, 37a,66a,184b), **tref** (172b), **trek** (85c,93c,99d,168b), **tres** (19a,52b, 63a,152d,165a,175c), **tret** (9a,178b,179d), **trey** (26c,165a), **Urey** (107c,138c), **wren** (19b,c), **Wren** (50b)

- - RE **Aare, acre** (39b,56a,88b), **Acre, aire** (82c), **Aire, bare** (43d,157c), **bore** (14c,25b,46a,116a,165c,179b), **bure** (61b), **byre** (38a), **care** (11b,14c,35d,150a,184d), **cere** (19a,149d,179a), **core** (28b,51c, 75b,81b), **cure** (123b), **dare** (28d,41b,42a,74d,175b), **Dare** (57a), **dere** (74a,79c), **dire** (45d,55a,104a,163c), **dore** (61d,67b,69d, 117d), **Dore** (50d,63a,b), **Eire** (82b), **etre** (61a,c,62d,166c), **eyre** (23c,31b,85c), **Eyre, fare** (43c,59b,67d,123b), **fire** (13a,43d, 44b), **fore** (63d,174b), **gare** (61b,c,62c,127c), **Gere** (183c), **gore** (115d,117c,154c,169c), **gyre** (31b,171b), **hare** (91b,132c), **here, hire** (49d,50b,91b,130a), **inre** (35d,80a), **jure** (90b), **kere** (75c, 128b), **kore** (107b), **Kore** (29a,42b,116b,124d), **Kure** (84c), **lire** (62c), **lore** (77c,87c,90d,151c,183a), **lure** (41c,51a,54b,163a), **lyre** (11c,81c,105a,111c), **mare** (78b), **Mare** (108b), **mere** (16c,22b,62a, 78b,87d,96c,110c,120d,146d,148b), **mire** (21c,104b), **more** (71a), **More** (50b), **mure** (177d), **Nare** (93c), **Nore** (163d), **ogre** (67a,102a), **pare** (115c,129a), **pere** (61c,63b), **pore** (59d,110d,111c,120d,157d), **pure** (29b,172b,173c), **pyre** (64c), **qere** (75c), **rare** (138b,164b, 172b,173d), **rire** (62a), **sere** (24d,46a,c,138c,183b), **Sere** (158b), **sire** (17d,55a,59d,124a,163b,166b), **sore** (23d,142c), **sure** (173d), **tare** (9a,18d,41a,176a,179d), **tire** (15a,22a,52d,55a,179b,180d),

tore, tyre (15a), **Tyre** (31b,90d,117b), **vare** (179b), **vire** (11a,13b), **ware** (27d,35a), **were** (139b), **wire, wore, yare** (96b,124b,128b), **yore** (10b,69d,93c,110b,165d)

R - - E **race** (116a,153b,154b,169c), **rade** (138d), **rage** (10c,30c,157a, 161d), **rake** (41b,44c,134b,140d), **rale** (7c,23a,29d,41b), **rame** (22d), **rare** (138b,164b,172b,173d), **rase** (42b,d,91d), **rate** 11d,14a,31d,36b,51d,52a,70b,85c,112b,123b,127d,128a,138c,143a, 174b), **rave** (41c,157a,161d), **raze** (42b,d,91d), **rede** (37c,81d,138d), **rese** (127b), **rete** (106c,119c), **reve** (61c,104d), **ribe** (139a), **Rice** (46a), **ride** (46b,85c),. **rife** (6b,c,39d,123b), **rile** (10c,d,82c,125a, 156b,176a), **rime** (30c,36a,58a,63d,77c), **rine** (44d,75d,135c), **ripe** (58a,97c,98c), **rire** (62a), **rise** (49d,80b,155a), **Rise** (110d,150c), **rite** (93a,131d), **rive** (32a,153d), **robe** (65b), **rode** (46c), **role** (114b), **Rome** (31c,51d), **rone** (127c,164b), **rope** (36d,88d,128b), **rose** (33c), **Rose** (6a,50c,183c), **rote** (130b,134b,143a,159d), **roue** (41b,44c,127c,134b), **rove** (127d,132b,178a), **rube** (37d,135d, 185d), **Rube** (96b), **rude** (134b,172b), **rule** (11b,26b,90b), **rune** (9b,67a,94a,95a,105c,107d,120a,141d,163d), **ruse** (13b,77c,157b, 169c), **rute** (188), **ryme** (178d), **rype** (19b,125a)

- RF - **orfe** (57a,b,185c), **Urfa** (99a)

- - RF **kerf** (40a,108b), **serf** (21d,148a), **surf** (23a), **turf** (115c,149d, 160b), **warf, werf** (54d), **zarf** (39c,155a)

R - - F **raff** (75b), **reef** (129a,137a,145a), **riff** (131d), **Riff** (18b,102c), **roof** (78d), **ruff** (19b,33b,63d,137a)

- RG - **Argo** (12c,36b,c), **ergo** (164b), **orgy** (26d,130d,137c), **urge** (42d, 46b,79d,80a,b,81c,124a,150a)

- - RG **berg** (79b), **borg** (40d), **burg** (22b,73c), **lurg** (96d,141b,184d), **morg** (188), **Sarg** (96d,125c)

R - - G **rang, ring** (50a), **Rong** (88c), **rung** (28c,39a)

RH - - **rhea** (37a,56a,111d,133d), **Rhea** (19b,68d,87c,103c,186b), **Rhee** (87c), **Rhin, rhob** (64a,85c), **rhum** (8c), **Rhus** (159a)

R - - H **rash** (75a), **rath** (29a,76d,162d), **resh** (91d), **rich, Roch** (136c), **rukh** (53b,54a), **rush, ruth** (35b,118c), **Ruth** (105b,183c)

RI - - **rial** (190), **ribe** (139a), **rice, Rice** (46a), **rich, rick** (74d,117d,154d), **Ridd** (94a), **ride** (46b,85c), **Riel** (129a), **riem** (76c,112c,157c,164d), **rien** (62b), **rier** (180b), **rife** (6b,c,39d,123b), **riff** (131d), **Riff** (18b, 102c), **rift** (30c,32a,58a,110d), **riga** (118b), **Riga, Riis** (9d), **rikk** (49a), **rile** (10c,d,82c,125a,156b,176a), **rill** (23c102b,132a,148d, 157b), **rily** (176a), **rima** (23a,30c,32a,58a,110d), **rime** (30c,36a,58a, 63d,77c), **rimu** (79d,106d,129a,168c), **rimy** (63d), **rind** (53a,115c), **Rind** (109c,174b), **rine** (44d,75d,135c), **ring** (50a), **rink** (147c, 154a), **riot** (44c,111d,170c,173d), **ripa** (16b,131d), **ripe** (58a,97c, 98c), **rire** (62a), **rise** (49d,80b,155a), **Rise** (110d,150c), **risk** (74d), **risp** (99a), **Riss** (66a), **rita, Rita** (37b,78d,183c), **rite** (93a,131d), **rive** (32a,153d)

- RI - **aria** (8b,98c,150a,c,170c), **arid** (46c,85a), **arif** (127d), **aril** (142a), **aris** (101b), **Brie** (29c), **brig** (72b,106a,144d), **brim, brin** (32c,54c,146c), **brit** (76c), **crib** (96b,120d), **cric** (131c), **crig** (20d), **crin** (146c), **cris** (40b,95d), **drib** (46b), **Drin, drip, eria** (13d,146d), **eric** (115b), **Eric** (71d,96a,107d,138a,164a,176b), **Erie** (82c,87d),

Erin (82b), Eris (12c,68d,109c), Fria, frib (43d), frim (58d), frit (64c,67c), friz (39d), grid (17a,70d,119b,156d), grig (38c,70d,93a), grim (156a), grin, grip (159a), gris (61d), grit (137a,b), irid (38d,67c), iris (53c,58a,111c) Iris (127c), kris (40b,95d), prig (112a,116c), prim (156b), trig (106a,148d,154b,169d), trim (40a,106a,154b,160a,165c,169d), trin (169d), trio (104d,165a,169c), trip (85c), tris (122d), trit (34d,164c), Uria (14c,16d), urim (18d,23a,110a), writ (91a)

- - RI abri (61c,62c,144b), aeri (34a), agri (89b), Atri, auri (34a), bari (37c,79c), Bari (83d), Bori (110d,150c), buri (56b), Cori (138c), dari (38a,70b), Geri (183c), gyri (22d,131b), kari (14d), keri (75c,128b), kiri (86a,87c,115a,168c), kori (7d,77a), Kuri (191), lari (78a,101c), Lari (72c), lori (91b), Luri (191), mari (61d), Mari (16a), Neri, nori (8c,141c), Omri (18c,86d), pari (34a,180a), peri (54b,116b,c,122b), puri (80d), qeri (75c), Rori (16b), sari (48b,65b,77b), seri (18b), Seri (192), Shri (17c,166c), siri (18b), sori (55c,64a), Tari (47d,69a), tori (101b), Turi (191), vari (34d,91b,134d,174d), veri (28b), weri (15c,27c)

R - - I rabi (38d,74a), Rabi (14b,117b), ragi (28b), rami (22d), rani (72d,77b,123c,127c), rati (189), ravi (61b), Ravi (16b), Reki (16a), Remi (10b), Reni (83d), rodi (98c), romi (72d), Rori (16b), roti (62c)

- - RK bark (115c), cark (26d,184d), cork (119d), dark (47a,67d,109b,160b), dirk (40b), fork, hark (92d), jerk (153a), kirk (31a,139b), kurk (31a,139b), lark (19a,63d), lurk (92a,147d), mark (146b,155a), Mark (52a,96a), mirk (41a,67d), murk (41a,67d), nark (81a,156d), park, perk (84d,93a), pork, Sark (28d), Turk (101d,102d,106a,111d), work (64c,76b), yark (22c), york (38c), York (50b,c)

R - - K rack (32c,64b), raik (188,189), rank (31d,55d,70b,92c,94d,157d), reck (26d,75c), reek (49d,53c,64a,148d,149a), rick (74d,117d,154d), rikk (49a), rink (147c,154a), risk (74d), rock (160b), rook (19b,29c,39a), ruck (39a,185a), rusk (23a)

- RL - orle (17b,56b,76a,144b,177a), orlo (56b,119c), Orly (8b)

- - RL birl (93c,131a,153c), burl (87c,169a), carl (115c,135d), Carl (96a), cirl (24c), curl (38d,73b,93b,131d), earl (107c), farl (138c,140b), furl (132d), girl, harl (16b,56b,59a), herl (16b,59a), hurl (167c), jarl (40d,107d), Karl (96a), marl (32a,42c,55d), merl (20b), nurl (33b,87c), purl (87c,104c), yarl (40d,107d)

R - - L rail (16b,19b,c,37a,97b,138c,150c,177b), real (7a), reel (21b,40b,d,153c,154a,c,d,180d), rial (190), Riel (129a), riil (23c,102b,132a,148d,157b), roil (44c,104b,156b,170d,176a), roll (134a,160b), rotl (103b,111c), rull (170b), ryal (110a,190), ryel (190)

- RM - arme (63a,179b), arms, army (78c), Erma (183c), Irma (96d)

- - RM barm (185b), berm (25d,90d,145c), corm (24b,38d,156a), derm (147c,158d), dorm, farm (165d), firm (154c,173d), form (54d,143c), Garm (178c), germ (17d,99c,134d), harm (40b,81a), norm (15a,115a,128a,155a), perm (49b,97d), term (92b,105b,142b,166b), turm (132d), warm (7c,75b,163b), worm, wurm (67c)

R - -M ream (18c,37d,50d,113d,171c), reem (18d), reim (112c), rhum (8c), riem (76c,112c,157c,164d), roam (178a), room (28d)

- RN - arna (24a,181b), Arnd (67a), Arne (35c,50c,134d), arni (24a,181b),

Arno (27a), **arn't**, **erne** (19c,d,47b,54b,141a), **orna** (169d,182c), **orne** (169d,182c), **Orne** (25b), **urna** (133a)

- - RN **barn** (156d), **Bern**, 160d), **birn** (31d), **born**, **burn**, **carn** (156c), **cern** (41c), **corn** (39d,95c,123a), **darn** (130b), **dorn** (164d), **earn** (42d, 64b,99a), **fern** (142a), **firn** (67c,70c,106c,149b), **garn** (67d,185b), **horn** (11a,105a,170b,182a), **karn** (156c), **kern** (59c,172a), **Kern** (132b), **lorn** (42d,60b), **morn**, **Norn** (69a,163d,174b), **pern** (78a), **pirn** (21b,129a,179b), **sorn** (139a,d), **tarn** (87d,103d,120d), **tern** (19b,32d,72c,94a,138c,141b,160a), **torn** (130a), **turn** (28d,131a, 175a), **warn** (7b), **worn** (143b), **yarn** (154b,161b,184b)

R - - N **rain** (121d,162d), **rann** (175c), **rein** (29b,130c), **Rhin**, **rien** (62b), **roan** (78b,c,114c,128d,144a,181a), **roon** (41a,168b), **ruin** (42d)

RO - - **road** (37d,164d), **roam** (178a), **roan** (78b,c,114c,128d,144a, 181a), **roar** (145c), **robe** (65b), **Roch** (136c), **rock** (160b), **Roda** (107b), **rodd** (38d), **rode** (46c), **rodi** (98c), **roed**, **roer** (72d), **roey** (103d), **rohr** (72d), **roil** (44c,104b,156b,170d,176a), **rojo** (129a, 152c), **roka** (95a,168c,d), **roke** (174d,175b), **role** (114b), **roll** (134a, 160b), **Roma** (83c), **Rome** (31c,51d), **romi** (72d), **romp** (63d), **rone** (127c, 164b), **Rong** (88c), **rood** (38d,39a,88b), **roof** (78d), **rook** (19b,29c,39a), **room** (28d), **roon** (41a,168b), **Roos** (67a), **root** (53a), **ropa** (152a), **rope** (36d,88d,128b), **ropy** (157c,176d), **Rori** (16b), **Rosa** (58d,134a,145d,183c), **rose** (33c), **Rose** (6a,50c,183c), **ross** (16c,161d), **Ross** (50c), **rosy** (21a,111a), **rota** (27c,30d,38a,79a,92d, 133a,134a,b,180c), **rote** (130b,134b,143a,159d), **roti** (62c), **rotl** (103b,111c), **roto** (30a,122d,127b,152c,171b), **roud** (57a,b), **roue** (41b,44c,127c,134b), **roup** (44a,121d), **rout** (41d,44b,46b), **rove** (127d,132b,178a), **rowy** (157b), **Roxy** (183d)

- RO - **Aroa** (175b), **Arod** (86c), **aroo** (80c,82b), **arow** (92c,158b), **brob** (153c), **broo** (139a), **brow**, **croc** (13a,74a), **Crom**, **crop** (38b), **crow** (19a), **drop** (43d,54b,100b,114c,168b), **Eros** (11c,39c,68b,97c,182d), **froe** (32a,167a,179d), **frog** (10a,17a,126d), **from**, **frot** (28c), **frow** (47a,167a), **grog** (92d,153d), **gros** (47a,53d), **Gros** (63a), **grot** (27d), **grow** (154b), **irok** (55b), **iron** (55c,d,69d,81a,97b,143b, 149a,173d,179c), **Kroo** (191), **proa** (21b,26a,95c,d), **prod** (67d,80b, 106b,120b), **prop** (159d), **prow** (21b,22c,144d,156a), **trod**, **tron** (140d,180a), **trop** (62d,167a), **trot** (85b,93d,112d), **trow** (18a,21a, 159d,164c,170b), **troy** (161c,180a)

- - RO **aero** (8b,34a,b,58c,59a), **agro** (149d), **arro** (52c), **baro** (71a,122c), **boro** (154b), **Boro** (193), **caro** (83a), **Caro** (183d), **cero** (57b,c,d, 180b), **duro** (190), **Ebro** (132a), **faro** (65a), **Garo** (88c), **giro** (38c, 167c), **gyro** (34d), **hero** (42b,124d,137b), **Hero** (90c), **hiro**, **inro** (84b,c,106c), **karo** (106d), **Lero** (82d), **loro** (19a,114b), **maro** (144d), **mero** (72a), **miro** (19a,106d,184a), **Miro** (113a,151d), **moro** (19a,56c), **Moro** (100a,103a,117a,159a), **Nero** (8a,126d,133a,150b, 172c), **okro** (72c,175a), **otro** (151d), **pero** (152a), **Piro** (192), **Poro** (141d), **pyro**, **sero** (34d,88d,164b,178d), **taro** (13c,48c,49b,64b, 112b,120a,133d,155c,170a,c), **tiro** (9b,17d,108c), **toro** (38a,107a, 152a,168c), **tyro** (9b,17d,108c), **zero** (31a,84c,108c), **Zero** (118d)

R - - O **ralo** (188), **redo** (165c), **Reno**, **rojo** (129a), **roto** (30a,122d,127b)

- RP - **arpa** (83b)

- - RP **carp** (27d,38d,40c,55a,56c,57a), **dorp** (73c,176b), **harp** (105a,129a),

larp (51d), **lerp** (51d,141d), **tarp** (26b,178d), **terp** (12b,123a), **torp** (54c), **turp**, **warp** (36c,165a,171c), **zarp** (120c)

R - - P **raip** (36d), **ramp** (65a,80b,127b,148b), **rasp** (56b,70d,140d), **reap** (7a,40a,74a), **repp** (53b,131a), **risp** (99a), **romp** (63d), **roup** (44a, 121d), **rump**

- RR - **arra** (47d,52c,82b), **arro** (52c), **Irra** (178a), **orra** (139c,d,140a)

- - RR **barr** (49b), **birr** (180d), **burr** (123b), **carr** (120d,140a), **curr** (104c), **darr** (163c), **dorr** (32b), **durr** (70b), **Herr** (66c), **Kerr**, **murr** (72b,128b), **nurr** (67d), **parr** (136d,137a,147c), **pirr** (181a), **purr** (104c), **turr** (24d,105a), **Tyrr** (68c,109c,163d,178a), **yarr** (72a)

R - - R **rear** (15b,23a,b,24a,51b,76d,127c), **rier** (180b), **roar** (145c), **roer** (72d), **rohr** (72d), **ruer**, **Ruhr**

- RS - **Erse** (28a,64b,82b), **erst** (60b), **Ursa** (17b,36b,43d)

- - RS **airs** (123b), **Bors** (70b,134b), **hers** (124c), **hors** (62b), **Lars** (51d, 121b), **Mars** (68c,118d,119a,129a,178a), **Mors** (41b), **ours** (124c), **pars** (89d), **sors** (44d,89b)

R - - S **raas** (91b), **rais** (26c,29d,75a,103b), **Rais** (106b), **rats**, **reis** (26c, 29d,75a,103b), **Rems**, **revs** (131a), **Rhus** (159a), **Riis** (9d), **Riss** (66a), **Roos** (67a), **ross** (16c,161d), **Ross** (50c), **Russ** (135b)

- RT - **Arta** (72b), **arto** (34a), **arts** (138c), **arty**, **orts** (60d), **Urth** (68d, 107d,163d)

- - RT **Bart** (96b), **Bert** (96b), **bort** (43b), **Bort** (134b), **cart** (171d,175a, 177b), **curt** (145b,c), **dart** (13b,88a,100c,120b,153a,160c), **dirt**, **fort** (63d,157d), **girt** (50a), **hart** (41d,154d), **hurt**, **mart** (49d,97a), **Mart** (96b,183d), **mort** (41b,47a,78b,136d), **part** (44d,60d,121c, 159c), **pert** (80a,93a,137c,154b), **port** (73d,136b,140c,170c,d,182b, c), **Sart** (82b,103b,170d), **Sert** (151d), **sort** (31d,39c,70b,86b,153a), **tart** (114d), **tort** (31c,91a,185c), **vert** (71d,166a,171b), **wart** (124d), **wert**, **wort** (76a,95d,121d), **yurt** (101d)

R - - T **raft** (27b,33c,58c,75b), **rant** (41c,127b,128a,161d), **rapt** (6c,27a, 50d), **rect** (117b), **reft** (32a,42c,44d,167b), **rent** (58a,77c,91b,138b, 153d,162c,167c), **rest** (15d,91b,104d,105a,115a,b,130a,b,161b), **rift** (30c,32a,58a,110d), **riot** (44c,111d,170c,173d), **root** (53a), **rout** (41d,44b,46b), **runt** (47a,172d), **rust** (37b,112c,119a), **ryot** (115c)

RU - - **ruay** (189), **rube** (37d,135d,185d), **Rube** (96b), **ruby** (20a,65d, 179c), **ruck** (39a,185a), **rudd** (26d,57a,b), **rude** (134b,172b), **ruer** **ruff** (19b,33b,63d,137a), **ruga** (59b,185a), **Ruhr**, **ruin** (42d), **rukh** (53b,54a), **rule** (11b,26b,90b), **rull** (170b), **rumb** (120b), **rump**, **rune** (9b,67a,94a,95a,105c,107d,120a,141d,163d), **rung** (28c,39a), **runt** (47a,172d), **rupa** (60b), **ruru** (19b,102c,106d), **rusa**, **Rusa** (41d, 136d), **ruse** (13b,77c,157b,169c), **rush**, **rusk** (23a), **Russ** (135b), **rust** (37b,112c,119a), **Ruta** (76b,134d), **rute** (188), **ruth** (35b,118c), **Ruth** (105b,183c)

- RU - **arui** (11b,143d,144a,181c), **arum** (13a,39b,58d,92b,155c), **Arum** (66a), **bruh** (95a), **brut** (182c), **Brut** (23c), **crus** (91a,143c), **crux** (39a,151b), **drub** (17b,39c) **drug** (105d), **drum** (105a), **drun** (132b), **erua** (103c), **eruc** (37a,56a), **grub** (43c,88d), **grum** (102c), **Grus** (36b,c,38b), **irus** (109d), **prut!**, **Prut** (41a), **true** (7a,8d,37b,54b, 94c,149c), **urus** (14d,53a,112c)

- - RU **Aaru** (6b,48d), **baru** (168c), **ecru** (17d,23d,172b), **feru** (37a,56a, 133d), **guru** (77b), **maru** (84c,144d), **Meru** (77a,103d), **paru** (57a), **Peru, Puru** (192), **ruru** (19b,102c,106d), **Yaru** (48d)

R - - U **Rahu** (42b,48b), **rimu** (79d,106d,129a,168c), **ruru** (19b,102c,106d)

- RV - **urva** (38b)

RY - - **ryal** (110a,190), **ryel** (190), **ryme** (178d), **rynd** (100a), **ryot** (115c), **rype** (19b,125a)

- RY - **Arya** (80d), **eryx** (137a), **oryx** (11a), **tryp** (114a)

- - RY **adry** (164c), **aery** (47b,51d,106c), **airy** (177a,176d), **atry** (141b), **awry** (13d,38d,171c), **bury** (81d), **dory** (21b,58b,144c), **eery** (172b, 180a), **ewry** (133c), **eyry** (47b,106c), **fury** (157a), **Gary, gory, jury** (38a), **lory** (19a,114a), **Mary** (50c,126b,183c), **miry, nary** (108b), **oary, sory** (176d), **spry** (7a,107b), **Tory** (23c,36b,94c,172a), **vary** (28d,43c), **very** (149c), **wary** (27d,176b), **wiry** (147a,167c)

R - - Y **racy** (153b), **rely** (16b,170b), **rily** (176a), **rimy** (63d), **roey** (103d), **ropy** (157c,176d), **rosy** (21a,111a), **rowy** (157b), **Roxy** (183d), **ruay** (189), **ruby** (20a,65d,179c)

R - - Z **razz** (131b)

SA - - **Saad** (12b), **saah** (188), **saal** (66c,73b), **Saan** (24d), **Saar** (63b,102d, 132a), **saba** (56a,117a), **Saba** (143d), **sabe, sack** (43d,118a,119d, 182b), **saco** (189), **sadd** (33a,40b,58c,107b), **sade** (91d), **sadh** (77a), **sado** (26d,84d), **sadr** (94a), **Sadr** (155b), **saer** (163a), **safe** (141d,157d,174d), **Safi** (191), **saga** (79b,91a,138a,157a,161b,c, 168a), **Saga, sage** (13a,90d,100c,141c,145c,180b,183a), **sago** (54c, 59b,113b,125b,155c), **sagy, saha, sahh** (188), **Saho** (6c), **sahu** (153d), **saic** (86b,91d,175d), **said** (174c), **Said** (42d,101a,121b), **sail** (144c,185a), **sain** (20c,38d,48a), **sair** (140b,150d), **sais** (48d, 71d), **Saka** (10a), **sake** (84b,125d), **saki** (39c,84b,102a), **sala** (152a, b,c), **Sala** (50c), **sale** (14c,61c,62b,c,168b), **salp** (109c,148d), **salt** (35d,105b,123a,136c,141c,149d), **sama** (105c,169d), **same** (44d, 79b), **samh** (56b), **samp** (70b,77d,121b), **sana** (56a,166d), **Sana** (185d), **sand** (71d,146c), **sane** (128a), **sang, sank, sano** (152b), **sans** (63a,183b), **sapa** (70c), **sapo** (149c,166d), **Sara** (24d,183c), **sard** (26d,28d,65d,111a,142b,156d), **Sard, Sarg** (96d,125c), **sari** (48b,65b,77b), **Sark** (28d), **Sart** (82b,103b,170d), **sasa** (55c), **sash** (18a,45c,67b,182b), **sass, sate** (32d,52c,67d,70d,137c,159d), **sati, Sati** (49a,126b,147b), **Sauk** (192), **saul** (48a,168c), **Saul** (18c,86d, 115a), **saum** (189), **save** (52b,110c,123a,173c), **sawk** (188), **sawn saxe** (20d,33c), **saya** (117a)

- SA - **asak** (13d,168c,169a), **asar** (67b), **Esau** (82c,84a,128c), **Esay, Isar** (41a,104c,132a), **osar** (51b,67b,131b), **tsar** (42d,49d,60b,135c), **usar** (8d,16c), **Usas** (68d)

- - SA **ansa** (73c,93d,137c), **Ausa, Besa** (68b,119c), **bisa** (11a), **bosa** (12a), **casa** (152b), **Disa** (111a), **dosa** (74b), **Elsa** (70a,93c,110d, 177b,183c), **kasa** (48a), **kusa, Lisa** (183d), **masa** (37a), **mesa** (49b, 76d,119b,161a), **Musa** (16a), **ossa** (21d), **Ossa** (103d,110b,164b), **pasa** (46a,127c,152c), **pesa** (190), **Pisa** (90c), **rasa** (51c), **Rosa** (58d,134a,145d,183c), **rusa, Rusa** (41d,136d), **sasa** (55c), **Susa** (49a), **Tesa** (80c), **Ursa** (17b,36b,43d), **vasa** (46d,114a,160b,175d), **Vasa, visa** (114d), **Xosa** (86a)

S - - A **saba** (56a,117a), **Saba** (143d), **saga** (79b,91a,138a,157a,161b,c, 168a), **saha, Saka** (10a), **sala** (152a,b,c), **Sala** (50c), **sama** (105c, 169d), **sana** (56a,166d), **Sana** (185d), **sapa** (70c), **Sara** (24d,183c), **sasa** (55c), **saya** (117a), **Seba** (18c,39d), **sera** (11b,20d,59a,83a, 180d), **seta** (23b,27c,73a,b,123b,153c), **shea** (25a,168c,d), **Shoa** (6c), **sida** (37a,126c,170a), **sika** (41d,84b), **sima** (132b), **sina** (46c), **Sina** (102d,103d), **Sita** (127d), **siva** (67a,120d), **Siva** (56d,77a), **skua** (19b,72c,84a,141a), **soda** (19a,149d,181a), **sofa** (44d), **soga** (70d,152b), **Soga** (191), **Soia, soja** (151b), **soka** (20c), **sola** (9a,48a, 74b,118c,154a,167b), **soma** (10c,21c,34a,48a,81d,136b), **sora** (19b, c,127b), **soya** (151b), **stoa** (33c,121a,c), **Sula** (65a), **supa** (168c), **sura** (87c,113b,166d), **Susa** (49a), **Syra**

- SB - **isba** (135c)

S - - B **scab** (80b,107d,157c), **scob** (42a), **Serb** (15d,148a,186c), **slab** (148b), **Sleb** (12a), **slob** (173d), **slub** (171c), **snab** (23c,139a), **snib** (54d,93c), **snob** (159c), **snub** (128c,148b), **sorb** (11d,103d,134b, 142d), **Sorb** (148a,180a), **stab** (14c,87a,117c), **stib** (19b,47a,137a), **stub** (156c), **swab** (102b), **sweb** (160d), **swob** (102b)

SC - - **scab** (80b,107d,157c), **scad** (31a,57a,78b,88d,137c), **scan** (52b,93d, 98a,116d,128b,c,140d), **scar** (31a,184d), **scat** (26b,67a,d,126c, 169c), **Scio, scob** (42a), **scon** (162c), **scop** (120a), **scot** (14a,162b), **Scot** (64b,132c), **scow** (21a,58b), **scud** (32c,126c,135b,160c), **scum** (129b), **scup** (57a,121b), **scur** (78b), **scut** (145c,161b)

- SC - **asci** (154a), **esca** (11c,44a,70c), **esce** (158d)

- - SC **aesc** (12d,64d), **Bosc** (115c), **DDSC** (42a), **disc** (31b), **fisc** (52c,134c)

S - - C **saic** (86b,91d,175d), **spec**

S - - D **Saad** (12b), **sadd** (33a,40b,58c,107b), **said** (174c), **Said** (42d,101a, 121b), **sand** (71d,146c), **sard** (26d,28d,65d,111a,142b,156d), **Sard, scad** (31a,57a,78b,137c), **scud** (32c,126c,135b,160c), **seed** (70b, 111c,112c,119a,151b,154a), **seid** (103b), **Seid** 42d,101a, 171a), **send** (42c,44b,95c,121c,130a,144c,168b), **shad** (27d,57a, b,c), **shed** (27a,90c,101b,144b), **shod, Sind, skid** (148b), **sled** (40a), **slid, sned** (93d,125a), **snod** (169d), **sold, spad** (105b), **Spad** (118d), **sped, spud** (121d,151c), **stad** (151b,167d,176b), **stod** (40d,67d), **stud** (22b,25a,42d,54d,111c,143a,174a), **sudd** (40b,58c,107b), **suld** (188), **surd** (82c,177a), **swad** (94d), **syed** (103b), **syud** (103b)

SE - - **seah** (188), **seal** (10c,d,54d,64c,96a,118b,128a), **seam** (85b,d,160a, 176d,185a), **Sean** (85b,96a), **sear** (23d,27d,72d,138c), **seat** (98c, 156b), **Seba** (18c,39d), **sebi** (34b), **sech** (97c), **seck** (173d), **sect** (42b,54a,114c), **seed** (70b,111c,112c,119a,151b,154a), **seek** (141c), **seel** (20c,32c,143b), **seem** (11c), **seen, seep** (110c,116a, 154b), **seer** (60a,124c,150c), **sego** (24b.25a,92b,174c), **sehr** (66d), **seid** (103b), **Seid** (42d,101a,171a), **Seik** (77b), **Seim** (120c), **sein** (146c), **seip** (110c), **Seir** (51b,94a,103d), **seis** (147b,152c), **seit** (189), **Sejm** (120c), **self** (48d,80d), **sell** (97a,115c,175b), **seme** (45c, 138b,151b,154b,155c,157b), **semi** (34b,80b,122c,d), **send** (42c, 44b,95c,121c,130a,144c,168b), **senn** (76b), **Sens** (63b), **sent, seps,** (93b,142d), **sept** (31d,82b,143a,149c), **Sept** (45b), **sera** (11b,20d, 59a,83a,180d), **Serb** (15d,148a,186c), **sere** (24d,46a,c,138c.183b), **Sere** (158b), **serf** (21d,148a), **seri** (18b), **Seri** (192), **sero** (34d,88d,

164b,178d), **Sert** (151d), **sesi** (20b,57a,149b), **sess** (149c,162b), **seta** (23b,27c,73a,b,123b,153c), **seth** (98d), **Seth** (7a,52b,68a,b,96a, 98d), **seti** (34a), **Seti** (116d), **sett** (115a,156d), **seve** (63a,182c), **sewn, sext** (26b,111b,147b)

- SE - **asea** (39b,177c), **asem** (9a,49a,69c), **Aser** (84a), **esek** (18d), **esel** (66b), **eser, Iser** (49a), **oser** (61b), **used** (6d,73a), **usee, user** (49d), **uses** (18a), **yser**

- - SE **anse** (61d), **apse** (9b,20a,31a,128c,130a,142b,175a), **asse** (25a, 60d,74a), **base** (6a,43b,44b,51c,60c,79b,94b,122b), **bise** (182a), **bose** (163c), **case** (22c,36c,81c,91a,108c), **cise** (147b), **cose** (29b), **dose** (123a), **duse** (83c), **ease** (7c,8d,35a,100d,129d,130b,c,150c), **else** (18b,79b,111d), **ense** (139b,158c), **Erse** (28a,64b,82b), **esse** (7a,18a,52d,89a,90a,159a,166c), **fuse** (98c), **hase** (74d), **hose** (156c), **huse** (180c), **ipse** (44d,89c), **Jose** (96a), **lose** (60a,100c), **lyse, mese** (71c), **mise** (8a,10a,70c), **Mose** (96b), **muse** (65b,93d, 120d,164c), **Muse** (68d), **nase** (26b,75a,124b), **nose** (118d,125a, 149b), **oese** (15d,119c), **Oise, Ouse** (132a,185d), **owse, pise** (127d), **pose** (14c,15d), **rase** (42b,d,91d), **rese** (127b), **rise** (49d,80b,155a), **Rise** (110d,150c), **rose** (33c), **Rose** (6a,50c,183c), **ruse** (13b,77c, 157b,169c), **sise** (62c,147b), **vase, vise** (31d,77d,114d), **wise** (136b)

S - - E **sabe, sade** (91d), **safe** (141d,157d,174d), **sage** (13a,90d,100c,141c, 145c,180b,183a), **sake** (84b,125d), **sale** (14c,61c,62b,c,168b), **same** (44d,79b), **sane** (128a), **sate** (32d,52c,67d,70d,137c,159d), **save** (52b,110c,123a,173c), **saxe** (20d,33c), **seme** (45c,138b,151b,154b, 155c,157b), **sere** (24d,46a,c,138c,183b), **Sere** (158b), **seve** (63a, 182c), **shee** (82b), **shoe** (166a), **sice** (71d,147b), **side** (13d,22a,b, 54a,58a,89a,161b), **sime** (101d), **sine** (64c,66b,90a,97c,126a,163b, 169d,183b), **sipe** (101a,110c,140b), **sire** (17d,55a,59d,124a,163b, 166b), **sise** (62c,147b), **site** (93b), **sive** (146a), **size, skee** (149c), **Skye** (163c), **slee** (140b,148c), **sloe** (14a,20b,64a,119d,181c), **slue** (97b,148b,160a), **smee** (19b,46c,d,118b,119d,141b,181b), **Smee** (116d), **snee** (40a,b,43d,87a), **soie** (62c), **soke** (44c,85d), **sole** (52c, 57a,b,58b,d,110c,115d,150a), **some** (114b,121c,126a), **sore** (23d, 142c), **sote** (150c), **spae** (139c), **Spee** (66d,70b), **supe** (53a,154d), **sure** (173d), **syce** (71d), **syke** (194), **syne** (140b,147a), **sype** (110c)

S - - F **self** (48d,80d), **serf** (21d,148a), **souf** (146b), **stof** (135c), **surf** (23a)

SG - - **Sgau** (88c)

S - - G **sang, Sarg** (96d,125c), **shag** (73b,105b,161d,166d), **sing** (26d,178a), **skag** (7d,46d), **skeg** (7d,86a,144d,157d,184a), **slag** (46c,99a,138c, 148d,177a), **slog** (157c,170b,177d), **slug** (46b,99b,157c), **smug, snag** (11b,27b,35c,87c,124b,166a), **sneg** (139b), **snig** (45d), **snug** (35a,38b,165c), **Snug** (99d), **song** (12c,170c), **stag** (65a,98d), **stog** (155a), **sung, Sung** (30b), **swag** (22a,156c), **swig** (46a,72c)

SH - - **shad** (27d,57a,b,c), **shag** (73b,105b,161d,166d), **shah** (116c), **sham** (41c,55b,60d,80a,123a,b,146d), **Shan** (13c,80d,88c,101d), **shap, shat** (87d), **shaw** (164b), **Shaw** (50c,53b), **shay** (110c), **shea** (25a, 168c,d), **shed** (27a,90c,101b,144b), **shee** (82b), **Shem** (107c), **Shen** (68a), **sher** (65d,165c), **shet, shew** (44c), **shih** (189), **Shik** (171a), **shim** (91d,144c,162a,179d), **shin** (91a,d,140b,143c), **ship, shir** (36d, 65d,165c), **Shoa** (6c), **shod, shoe** (166a), **shoo** (46b,67a,138b), **shop, shoq** (169a), **shor** (136d), **Shor** (162b), **shot** (9d,43d,90c,174d), **shou**

(41d), **show** (42b,44c,96b), **Shri** (17c,166c), **shul** (161a), **shun** (15a, 51b,52a), **shut**

- SH - **Asha** (191), **ashy** (113a,178a), **Isha** (174a), **Tshi** (69c), **Usha** (16a, 150c)

- - SH **bash**, **bish** (120b), **bosh**, **bush**, **cash** (101c), **cosh** (35a,97c), **cush** (101c), **Cush** (51d,73c), **dash** (125c,162d), **dish**, **fash** (140c,176a), **fish**, **gash** (40a), **gish** (102c), **gosh**, **gush** (35a,154c), **hash**, **hish**, **hush** (17b,146c), **josh** (85b), **kish** (16d,70c), **Kish** (137c), **Kush** **lash** (58c,87b,165c,180d), **losh** (178b), **lush** (94d), **mash** (39b, 156c), **mesh** (50d,106c), **mush** (97d), **Nash** (9c), **Nish** (19d), **pish** (36c,107d), **posh** (49b,148c), **push** (145c), **rash** (75a), **resh** (91d), **rush**, **sash** (18a,45c,67b,182b), **sish** (79b), **sosh** (81d), **tash** (154d), **tosh** (106a), **tush** (167b), **wash**, **wish** (42d)

S - - H **saah** (188), **sadh** (77a), **sahh** (188), **samh** (56b), **sash** (18a,45c,67b, 182b), **seah** (188), **sech** (97c), **seth** (98d), **Seth** (7a,52b,68a,b,96a, 98d), **shah** (116c), **shih** (189), **sigh**, **Sikh** (77b), **sinh** (97c), **sish** (79b), **soph**, **sosh** (81d), **such** (146d)

SI - - **siak** (72d), **sial** (112a), **Siam** (163d,181a), **sice** (71d,147b), **sick**, **sida** (37a,126c,170a), **side** (13d,22a,b,54a,58a,89a,161b), **sidi** (103b, 166b), **sidy** (123b), **sier** (57a,118b), **sift** (140d,142c,146b), **sigh**, **sign** (121c,146c), **sika** (41d,84b), **Sikh** (77b), **silk** (53b,179c), **sill** (45c,76c,165a,182b), **silo** (59a,156d), **silt** (104b,142a), **sima** (132b), **sime** (101d), **Simi** (82d), **simp** (59c,146d), **sina** (46c), **Sina** (102d, 103d), **Sind**, **sine** (64c,66b,90a,97a,126a,163b,169d,183b), **sing** (26d,178a), **sinh** (97c), **sink** (41c,43c,46b,158a) **sino** (34a), **siol** (82c), **sion** (125c,158c), **Sion** (75b,c,83a,157d), **sipe** (101a,110c, 140b), **sire** (17d,55a,59d,124a,163b,166b), **siri** (18b), **sise** (62c, 147b), **sish** (79b), **sisi** (121b), **siss**, **sist** (139b), **Sita** (127d), **site** (93b), **sito** (34b), **siva** (67a,120d), **Siva** (56d,77a), **Sive** (146a), **size**, **sizy** (176d), **sizz**

- SI - **Asia** (48a), **Asin** (102a), **Hsia** (30b,47c), **Isis** (68d,78c,111d), **tsia** (162c), **Tsin** (30b)

- - SI **Absi** (191), **assi** (77d), **dasi** (77a), **desi** (85d), **kasi** (116b), **Lasi** (191), **nasi** (34c,108a,115a), **nisi** (90a,173c), **pasi** (94b), **sesi** (20b,57a), **sisi** (121b), **susi** (53b,d)

S - - I **Safi** (191), **saki** (39c,84b,102a), **sari** (48b,65b,77b), **sati**, **Sati** (49a, 126b,147b), **sebi** (34b), **semi** (34b,80b,122c,d), **seri** (18b), **Seri** (192), **sesi** (20b,57a,149b), **seti** (34a), **Seti** (116d), **Shri** (17c,166c), **sidi** (103b,166b), **Simi** (82d), **siri** (18b), **sisi** (121b), **soli** (12c,110c), **sori** (55c,64a), **sufi** (103a,116c), **sugi** (84b), **suji** (180c), **susi** (53b,d)

SK - - **skag** (7d,46d), **skat** (181b), **Skat** (155b), **skee** (149c), **skeg** (7d,86a, 144d,157d,184a), **sken** (164a), **skeo** (57d), **skep** (16d,17c,77c), **skew** (148a,160c,171b,c), **skey** (185d), **skid** (148b), **skil** (57a), **skim** (67c), **skin** (53a,76c,115c,d), **skio** (57d), **skip** (110b,114c,147c), **skir**, **skit** (145c), **skiv** (151b), **skua** (19b,72c,84a,141a), **Skye** (163c), **skyr** (21d,151a), **skyt** (138c,140b)

- SK - **Askr** (107d)

- - SK **bask** (94d), **bisk** (120b,151a), **bosk** (164b), **busk** (17b,37b,55d, 161b), **cask**, **cusk** (57b), **desk**, **disk** (31b), **dusk** (171c), **fisk** (24d,52c,134c), **husk** (53a,78d,142a), **mask** (44a,45c), **mosk** (97b,

103b), **musk** (116b), **Omsk, pisk** (9c,19b), **risk** (74d), **rusk** (23a), **task** (156b), **Tosk** (8c), **tusk** (167b)

S - - K **sack** (43d,118a,119d,182b), **sank, Sark** (28d), **Sauk** (192), **sawk** (188), **seck** (173d), **seek** (141c), **Seik** (77b), **Shik** (171a), **siak** (72d), **sick, silk** (53b,179c), **sink** (41c,43c,46b,158a), **soak** (46c,137c), **Sobk** (38d), **sock** (157c,182a), **sook** (22a,25c,97a), **souk** (22a,97a), **suck, sulk** (159a), **sunk**

SL - - **slab** (148b), **slag** (46c,99a,138c,148d,177a), **slam** (180d,182d), **slap** (24a,128c,148c), **slat** (58b,89a,117c,184a), **Slav** (13c,40c,48b,52a, 120b,135b), **slaw, slay, Sleb** (12a), **sled** (40a), **slee** (140b,148c), **slew** (160a), **sley** (179b), **slid, slim** (148b,160a), **slip** (67c,119a), **slit** (40a), **slob** (173d), **sloe** (14a,20b,64a,119d,181c), **slog** (157c,170b, 177d), **sloo** (160a), **slop, slot** (10d,11b,41d,110d,167d,168a,181b), **slow** (43c), **slub** (171c), **slue** (97b,148b,160a), **slug** (46b,99b,157c), **slum, slur** (44b,124c,148b,168a)

- SL - **isle** (8b,53c,81d,82d,86b,88a), **Oslo**

S - - L **saal** (66c,73b), **sail** (144c,185a), **saul** (48a,168c), **Saul** (18c,86d, 115a), **seal** (10c,d,54d,64c,96a,118b,128a), **seel** (20c,32c,143b), **sell** (97a,115c,175b), **shul** (161a), **sial** (112a), **sill** (45c,76c,165a, 182b) **siol** (82c), **skil** (57a), **soil** (154d,159a,163c), **soul** (10d,125a, 153c,176d)

SM - - **smee** (19b,46c,d,118b,119d,141b,181b), **Smee** (116d), **smew** (19b, 46d,99a,137d), **smug, smur** (32c,46b,100c), **smut** (32d,44a,119a, 150c)

- SM - **ismy** (45a)

- - SM **kasm** (189)

S - - M **saum** (189), **scum** (129b), **seam** (85b,d,160a,176d,185a), **seem** (11c), **Seim** (120c), **Sejm** (120c), **sham** (41c,55b,60d,80a,123a,b, 146d), **Shem** (107c), **shim** (91d,144c,162a,179d), **Siam** (163d,181a), **skim** (67c), **slam** (180d,182d), **slim** (148b,160a), **slum, stem** (29b, 125a,154d,155a,156d), **stom** (34c), **stum** (70c,105c,131a,173a), **swam, swim** (58c), **swum**

SN - - **snab** (23c,139a), **snag** (11b,27b,35c,87c,124b,166a), **snap** (23a, 36d,38b,48b,54d,56c,58c,149d), **sned** (93d,125a,140a), **snee** (40a, b,43d,87a), **sneg** (139b), **snib** (54d,93c), **snig** (45d), **snip** (32b, 40a), **snob** (159c), **snod** (169d), **snow, snub** (128c,148b), **snug** (35a,38b,165c), **Snug** (99d), **snup** (149b)

- SN - **asno** (151d), **esne** (10c,45b,142c,148a,164d)

S - - N **Saan** (24d), **sain** (20c,38d,48a), **sawn, scan** (52b,93d,98a,116d, 128b,c,140d), **scon** (162c), **Sean** (85b,96a), **seen, sein** (146c), **senn** (76b), **sewn, Shan** (13c,80d,88c,101d), **Shen** (68a), **shin** (91a,d,140b, 143c), **shun** (15a,51b,52a), **sign** (121c,146c), **sion** (125c,158c), **Sion** (75b,c,83a,157d), **sken** (164a), **skin** (53a,76c,115c,d), **soon** (123a, 145c), **sorn** (139a,d), **span** (23b,107b,113a,128b,162c), **spin** (131a, 180d), **spun, sten** (72c,95a), **stun** (145a,157d), **sunn** (56a), **Svan** (27d), **swan** (19b,33a)

SO - - **soak** (46c,137c), **soap, soar** (59a), **Sobk** (38d), **sock** (157c,182a), **soco** (22d), **soda** (19a,149d,181a), **sofa** (44d), **soft** (48b,95d,99d, 163a), **soga** (70d,152b), **Soga** (191), **soho!, Soho** (93c), **Soia, soie**

(62c), **soil** (154d,159a,163c), **soir** (61c), **soja** (151b), **soka** (20c), **soke** (44c,85d), **sola** (9a,48a,74b,118c,154a,167b), **sold**, **sole** (52c,57a,b, 58b,d,110c,115d,150a), **soli** (12c,110c), **solo** (12c,89a,110c), **soma** (10c,21c,34a,48a,81d,136b), **some** (114b,121c,126a), **song** (12c, 170c), **sons** (98d,109d), **sook** (22a,25c,97a), **soon** (123a,145c), **soot** (20b,26c,88a), **soph**, **Sopt** (45b), **sora** (19b,c,127b), **sorb** (11d,103d, 134b,142d), **Sorb** (148a,180a), **sore** (23d,142c), **sori** (55c,64a), **sorn** (139a,d), **sors** (44d,89b), **sort** (31d,39c,70b,86b,153a), **sory** (176d), **sosh** (81d), **soso** (99c,114c,166d), **sote** (150c), **souf** (146b), **souk** (22a,97a), **soul** (10d,125a,153c,176d), **soup**, **sour**, **sous** (62d,172c), **soya** (151b)

- SO - **asok** (13d), **asom** (18d), **asop** (180b), **asor** (75c,105a), **Esop** (53b, 54a), **esox** (57b)

- - SO **also** (10b,18b,80a), **Caso** (82d), **coso** (152c), **enso** (34d,183b), **huso** (180c), **ipso** (89c), **koso** (6c,80d), **Koso** (192,193), **Muso** (192), **peso** (99c), **piso** (189), **soso** (99c,114c,166d), **yeso** (72d)

S - - O **saco** (189), **sado** (26d,84d), **sago** (54c,59b,113b,125b,155c), **Saho** (6c), **sano** (152b), **sapo** (149c,166d), **Scio**, **sego** (24b,25a,92b,174c), **sero** (34d,88d,164b,178d), **shoo** (46b,67a,138b), **silo** (59a,156d), **sino** (34a), **sito** (34b), **skeo** (57d), **skio** (57d), **sloo** (160a), **soco** (22d), **soho!**, **Soho** (93c), **solo** (12c,89a,110c), **soso** (99c,114c,166d), **Sumo**

SP - - **spad** (105b), **Spad** (118d), **spae** (139c), **span** (23b,107b,113a,128b, 162c), **spar** (22c,24c,64b,97b,100b,144d), **spat** (112c,126b,134b), **spec**, **sped**, **Spee** (66d,70b), **spes**, **Spes** (69a,78a), **spet** (16c,57a, 142c), **spew** (35a,49a), **spex**, **spey**, **spin** (131a,180d), **spir** (97c), **spit** (120a,132b,c), **spot** (93b,118c,154d,162a), **spry** (7a,107b), **spud** (121d,151c), **spun**, **spur** (10d,67d,167d,168a,181b), **sput** (21c)

- SP - **espy** (44a,142a)

- - SP **cusp** (38c,78b,119a,120a,b), **gasp** (113c), **hasp** (31d,54d,153c), **lisp** (153b), **rasp** (56b,70d,140d), **risp** (99a), **wasp**, **wisp** (24b,148c)

S - - P **salp** (109c,148d), **samp** (70b,77d,121b), **scop** (120a), **scup** (57a, 121b), **seep** (110c,116a,154b), **seip** (110c), **shap**, **ship**, **shop**, **simp** (59c,146d), **skep** (16d,17c,77c), **skip** (110b,114c,147c), **slap** (24a, 128c,148c), **slip** (67c,119a), **slop**, **snap** (23a,36d,38b,48b,54d,56c, 58c,149d), **snip** (32b,40a), **snup** (149b), **soap**, **soup**, **step** (70b,112b, 177b,d), **stop** (73b,111b), **sump** (28c,45d,100b), **swap** (168a), **swop** (168a)

S - - Q **shoq** (169a)

S - - R **Saar** (63b,102d,132a), **sadr** (94a), **Sadr** (155b), **saer** (163a), **sair** (140b,150d), **scar** (31a,184d), **scur** (78b), **sear** (23d,27d,72d,138c), **seer** (60a,124c,150c), **sehr** (66d), **Seir** (51b,94a,103d), **sher** (65d, 165c), **shir** (36d,65d,165c), **shor** (136d), **Shor** (162b), **sier** (57a, 118b), **skir**, **skyr** (21d,151a), **slur** (44b,124c,148b,168a), **smur** (32c,46b,100c), **soar** (59a), **soir** (61c), **sour**, **spar** (22c,24c,64b,97b, 100b,144d), **spir** (97c), **spur** (10d,67d,167d,168a,181b), **star** (14a, 21c,94c,100c), **ster** (158c,d), **stir** (8a,13a,35b,78d,100d,104a), **suer** (124d)

- SS - **asse** (25a,60d,74a), **assi** (77d), **esse** (7a,18a,52d,89a,90a,159a, 166c), **ossa** (21d), **Ossa** (103d,110b,164b)

- - SS **bass** (57b,c,177a), **Bess** (76c,183d), **boss** (49d,157d), **buss** (87a, 148c), **cass** (140c,177a), **Cass** (147a), **cess** (91d,94c,162b), **coss** (98a), **cuss, diss** (98b), **doss** (17c), **fass** (189), **fess** (23c,51b), **foss** (44d,100d), **fuss** (22b,35b), **hiss** (146a), **jass** (160d), **jess** (157a), **joss** (30b), **kiss** (148c), **koss** (188), **lass** (95b), **less** (100c,108b,141d), **liss** (54b,58b,60c,129d,140a), **loss** (42c,123d,178b), **mass** (8a,24b, 35b,142d), **mess** (22b,44b,77c,85d,104b,165c,173d), **miss, moss** (91d,104c,114a,170c), **muss** (135b,173d), **ness** (26b,75a,124b), **pass** (110b,155c), **puss, Riss** (66a), **ross** (16c,161d), **Ross** (50c), **Russ** (135b), **sass, sess** (149c,162b), **siss, Tass** (107a,135d,151b), **Tess** (73d,164c,183d), **toss** (24a,132d), **viss** (189)

S - - S **sais** (48d,71d), **sans** (63a,183b), **sass, seis** (147b,152c), **sens** (63b), **seps** (93b,142d), **sess** (149c,162b), **siss, sons** (98d,109d), **sors** (44d, 89b), **sous** (62d,172c), **spes, Spes** (69a,78a), **suds** (59a)

ST - - **stab** (14c,87a,117c), **stad** (151b,167d,176b), **stag** (65a,98d), **star** (14a,21c,94c,100c), **stat** (72d), **stay** (72d,124c,130a,134a,162a), **stem** (29b,125a,154d,155a,156d), **sten** (72c,95a), **step** (70b,112b, 177b,d), **ster** (158c,d), **stet** (91b,123d,124c), **stev** (155b), **stew** (21c,44b,184d), **stib** (19b,47a,137a), **stir** (8a,13a,35b,78d,100d, 104a), **stoa** (33c,121a,c), **stod** (40d,67d), **stof** (135c), **stog** (155a), **stom** (34c), **stop** (73b,111b), **stot** (154d,155d,157d,179b,186a), **stow** (112b), **stub** (156c), **stud** (22b,25a,42d,54d,111c,143a,174a), **stum** (70c,105c,131a,173a), **stun** (145a,157d), **Styx** (29b,73a,105c)

- ST - **asta** (188), **Asta** (107a,164c), **Asti** (83d,182b), **esta** (152d,164c), **este** (152b,d,164c), **Este** (55c,83c,d,112d), **Esth** (16a,51d), **oste** (21d,83b)

- - ST **bast** (16c,56a,117b,184a), **Bast** (27b), **best** (41d,159c,160a), **bust, cast** (165b,167c), **cest** (18a,67b), **dost, dust, east, East** (111b), **erst** (60b), **fast** (56d,126c,141d,160c,173a,d), **fest, fist** (80c), **fust** (105c,143b), **gest** (7c,41d,52d,133c), **gist** (95c,118c), **gust, hast, hest** (35a), **hist** (25c,93d), **host** (13a,51d,104c), **jest** (169c), **just** (51b,54b), **kist** (29d,58a,139b), **last** (36c,50b,145a,174c), **lest** (59d, 163d), **list** (26d,27b,75b,83d,134a,138b,165d), **lost, lust** (41b), **mast** (17c,108d,120b,144d,152d), **mist** (46b,59b,174d), **most, must** (70c,101a,106d,157d,182c), **myst** (71c,123b), **Nast** (9c,27a), **nest** (38b,74b,130d,149c,160b), **oast** (15d,86b,112a), **oust** (44c, 49a,52b,125d), **past** (25c,69d,165d), **pest** (108c,116b,118d,170a), **pist** (25c), **post** (89a,95c,155d), **rest** (15d,91b,104d,105a,115a,b, 130a,b,161b), **rust** (37b,112c,119a), **sist** (139b), **test** (26a,51c,144a, 169c,170c), **vast** (78d,79d), **vest** (32c,177b), **wast, west, West** (9c, 50b,109b), **wist** (87c), **zest** (55d,72d)

S - - T **salt** (35d,105b,123a,136c,141c,149d), **Sart** (82b,103b,170d), **scat** (26b,67a,d,126c,169c), **scot** (14a,162b), **Scot** (64b,132c), **scut** (145c,161b), **seat** (98c,156b), **sect** (42b,54a,114c), **seit** (189), **sent, sept** (31d,82b,143a,149c), **Sept** (45b), **Sert** (151d), **sett** (115a,156d), **sext** (26b,111b,147b), **shat** (87d), **shot** (9d,43d,90c, 174d), **shut, sift** (140d,142c,146b), **silt** (104b,142a), **skat** (181b), **Skat** (155b), **skit** (145c), **skyt** (138c,140b), **slat** (58b,89a,117c, 184a), **slit** (40a), **slot** (10d,11b,41d,110d,167d,168a,181b), **smut** (32d,44a,119a,150c), **soft** (48b,95d,99d,163a), **soot** (20b,26c,88a), **Sopt** (45b), **sort** (31d,39c,70b,86b,153a), **spat** (112c,126b,134b),

spet (16c,57a,142c), **spit** (120a,132b,c), **spot** (93b,118c,154d,162a), **sput** (21c), **stat** (72d), **stet** (91b,123d,124c), **stot** (154d,155d,157d, 179b,186a), **suet** (54d), **suit** (38a,58a,91a,112a,119c,137c), **swat** (15d,20d,32d,157c), **Swat** (103a), **swot**

SU - - **such** (146d), **suck**, **sudd** (40b,58c,107b), **suds** (59a), **suer** (124d), **suet** (54d), **sufi** (103a,116c), **sugi** (84b), **suit** (38a,58a,91a,112a, 119c,137c), **suji** (180c), **Suku** (191), **Sula** (65a), **suld** (188), **sulk** (159a), **Sulu** (102c), **Sumo**, **sump** (28c,45d,100b), **sung**, **Sung** (30b), **sunk**, **sunn** (56a), **supa** (168c), **supe** (53a,154d), **sura** (87c,113b, 166d), **surd** (82c,177a), **sure** (173d), **surf** (23a), **Susa** (49a), **susi** (53b,d), **susu** (20c), **Susu** (191), **Susy** (183d)

- SU - **Asur** (68c), **Esus**, **tsun** (30b), **Usun** (191)

- - SU **ansu** (11d), **Apsu** (29a), **ausu** (168c,180b), **Jesu**, **masu** (57a,84c), **Nosu** (27d), **susu** (20c), **Susu** (191), **vasu** (106c), **Vasu** (176d)

S - - U **sahu** (153d), **Sgau** (88c), **shou** (41d), **Suku** (191), **Sulu** (102c), **susu** 20c), **Susu** (191)

SV - - **Svan** (27d)

S - - V **skiv** (151b), **Slav** (13c,40c,48b,52a,120b,135b), **stev** (155b)

SW - - **swab** (102b), **swad** (94d), **swag** (22a,156c), **swam**, **swan** (19b,33a), **swap** (168a), **swat** (15d,20d,32d,157c), **Swat** (103a), **sway** (104a), **sweb** (160d), **swig** (46a,72c), **swim** (58c), **swiz** (160c), **swob** (102b), **swop** (168a), **swot**, **swow** (100a), **swum**

S - - W **scow** (21a,58b), **shaw** (164b), **Shaw** (50c,53b), **shew** (44c), **show** (42b,44c,96b), **skew** (148a,160c,171b,c), **slaw**, **slew** (160a), **slow** (43c), **smew** (19b,46d,99a,137d), **snow**, **spew** (35a,49a), **stew** (21c, 44b,184d), **stow** (112b), **swow** (100a)

S - - X **spex**, **Styx** (29b,73a,105c)

SY - - **syce** (71d), **syed** (103b), **syke** (194), **syne** (140b,147a), **sype** (110c), **Syra**, **syud** (103b)

- - SY **busy**, **cosy** (149c), **easy** (54a,146d,149d,172b), **Josy** (183d), **mosy** (67d), **nosy**, **rosy** (21a,111a), **Susy** (183d)

S - - Y **sagy**, **shay** (110c), **sidy** (123b), **sizy** (176d), **skey** (185d), **slay**, **sley** (179b), **sory** (176d), **Spey**, **spry** (7a,107b), **stay** (72d,124c,130a, 134a), **Susy** (183d), **sway** (104a)

S - - Z **sizz**, **swiz** (160c)

TA - - **Taal** (7d,88c,151a), **taar** (12b), **tabi** (84c,149d), **tabu** (59d,111d), **tace** (13a,155d), **tack** (28d,37d,54d), **tact** (43c,d,116a), **tael** (91d, 179d), **Taft** (29d), **taha** (179b), **tahr** (68a,76d), **tail** (11d,27d,59b, 143b), **tain** (166a), **tair** (68a,76d), **tait** (14d), **tajo** (152a,d), **take**, **takt** (105a,163a), **Taku** (80c), **taky**, **tala** (16d,113a,168c,d), **talc** (28d,63b,99c,100b,122a,149c), **tale** (91a,185b), **tali** (189), **talk**, **tall** (118d), **Tama** (192), **tame** (45a,b,66a), **Tame**, **tamp** (46b,112b, 121d,127d), **tana** (159a), **Tana** (87d), **Tane** (120d), **tang** (30b,58b, 186b), **tanh** (97c), **tank** (175a,d), **Tano** (192), **Taos** (192), **tapa** (16c, 32c,53b,56a,74b,104b,112b,113d,120d), **tape** (16a,19a,128d), **tapu**, **tara** (22a,55c,113a,168c), **Tara** (82b,c,138b), **tare** (9a,18d,41a, 176a,179d), **Tari** (47d,69a), **tarn** (87d,103d,120d), **taro** (13c,48c, 49b,64b,112b,120a,133d,155c,170a,c), **tarp** (26b,178d), **tart** (114d), **tash** (154d), **task** (156b), **Tass** (107a,135d,151b), **tate** (183a), **tatt**

(87c), **tatu** (12d), **Tatu, taun** (188), **taut** (163b,165c), **Tave** (183d), **Tavy** (183d), **tawa** (106d,168c), **taxi** (13a,125b), **taxo** (13a)

- TA - **atap** (113b), **atar** (58d,116b,134a), **Etah** (71d,51c), **etal** (89a), **etat** (62d), **Ptah** (48d,98c), **stab** (14c,87a,117c), **stad** (151b,167d,176b), **stag** (65a,98d), **star** (14a,21c,94c,100c), **stat** (72d), **stay** (72d,124c, 130a,134a,162a), **utac** (22d), **Utah** (180b), **utas** (49a,109c)

- - TA **acta** (41d,123d,128d,164c), **Aeta** (94d,95d,100a,106b,117a), **alta** (89c,152d), **anta** (83d,117c,d,121a), **Anta** (164a), **Arta** (72b), **asta** (188), **Asta** (107a,164c), **atta** (58d,90c,97d,160c,173d), **Atta** (94d,95d,100a,106b,117a), **bata** (30a,142d), **beta** (71a, 91c,141d), **bota** (189), **cata** (122c), **cota** (117a), **data** (54a), **dita** (117a), **esta** (152d,164c), **Etta** (183c), **gata** (143c), **geta** (84b,145a), **Gita, iota** (71a,85c,91c,114c,166c,176a,180d), **jota** (151c), **keta** (45a), **kota** (117a), **Kota** (45d), **lata** (85d, 95d), **lota** (24c,121d,178d), **Lota meta** (132d,133a), **Meta, mota** (103a), **muta** (28d,103a), **nata** (47c), **Nata** (15c), **nota** (15c, 89c), **octa** (122c), **pata** (32c,160d), **pita** (9c,28b,56a,83a), **rata** (29d,56b,89d,96c,106d,120c,168c), **rita, Rita** (37b,78d,183c), **rota** (27c,30d,38a,79a,92d,133a,134a,b,180c), **Ruta** (76b,134d), **seta** (23b,27c,73a,b,123b,153c), **Sita** (127d), **tota** (71d), **veta** (104a), **vita** (89c,92a), **vota** (133b), **weta** (93c), **yeta** (84c), **zeta** (71b,91c)

T - - A **taha** (179b), **tala** (16d,113a,168c,d), **Tama** (192), **tana** (159a), **Tana** (87d), **tapa** (16c,32c,53b,56a,74b,104b,112b,113d,120d), **tara** (22a, 55c,113a,168c), **Tara** (82b,c,138b), **tawa** (106d,168c), **tcha** (162c), **teca, Teca** (192), **Teda** (191), **tela** (22d,98c,121b,166a,179c), **tema** (12a,164a), **Tema, tera** (23d,84c), **tesa** (80c), **Tewa** (193), **Thea** (162c), **Tina** (183d), **tiza** (172a), **Toba** (80c), **Toda** (45d,76d), **toga** (132d,133a,b), **tola** (48a,80d,180a), **Tola** (85b), **Toma** (191), **tooa** (17c), **tora** (11a,44d,74a,75c,85c,90b,102d,115d), **tota** (71d), **toxa** (153d), **tsia** (162c), **tuba** (105a,137d), **tufa** (121b,177a), **tula** (9a), **Tula, tuna** (57a,b,123b), **tuza** (119d)

T - - B **theb** (188), **thob** (128a), **tomb**

TC - - **tcha** (162c), **tche** (13d,30b,105a), **tchi, Tchi, tchu**

- TC - **etch, itch**

T - - C **talc** (28d,63b,99c,100b,122a,149c)

T - - D **tend** (26d,80b,93d,100a), **thud, tied, tind** (86b), **toad** (10a,17a, 63d,126d), **toed, told** (129c), **trod, tund** (121d)

TE - - **teak** (41a,48a,168c), **teal** (19b,20d,46c,d), **team** (38c,72a,113a), **tean** (140c,167a), **tear** (67c,87b,130a), **teca, Teca** (192), **Tech, teck** (128b), **Teco** (192), **Teda** (191), **teel** (142d), **teem** (6b,121d), **teen** (139b,c,140b,158d), **teer** (25b,69d), **Tees** (108a), **teff** (6c), **tegg** (143d,171d), **tehr** (27c,68a), **Teig** (96a), **teil** (92b,c,168c), **teju** (151b), **tela** (22d,98c,121b,166a,179c), **tele** (34b,122c), **teli** (94b), **tell** (105d,129c,154b), **Tell** (160d), **tema** (12a,164a), **Tema, tend** (26d,80b,93d,100a) **tene** (34d,131b), **teng** (188), **tent** (26b), 115a), **Teos** (82a), **tera** (23d,84c), **term** (92b,105b,142b,166b), **tern** (19b,32d,72c,94a,138c,141a,160a), **terp** (12b,123a), **tesa** (80c), **Tess** (73d,164c,183d), **test** (26a,51c,144a,169c,170c), **tete** (61d,73b,74d), **teth** (91d), **Tewa** (193), **text** (21c,140d), **teyl** (92b, c,168c)

-TE- **atef** (39a,48d), **aten** (150a,159b), **Ateo** (120d), **Ater** (18c), **ates** (160c), **Itea** (145d,160c,181d), **item** (6d,13b,42d,51a,90d,92d,107a, 113d,114c), **Iten** (192), **iter** (22d,76c,85c,89c,114d,132a,b,133a,b), **Otea** (71a,82d), **stem** (29b,125a,154d,155a,156d), **sten** (72c,95a), **step** (70b,112b,177b,d), **ster** (158c,d), **stet** (91b,123d,124c), **stev** (155b), **stew** (21c,44b,184d)

--TE **ante** (87a,89a,115b,120b,122b,125d,154d), **bate** (43c,91b,100d), **bete** (61a,107c), **bite** (29d,156b), **cate** (165c), **cete** (180b,c), **cite** (15a,98d,126d,159b), **cote** (19b,143d,144a,b), **cute** (39c), **date** (64a,153a), **dite** (150b), **dote** (17a,90b,94b,97a,112a,139d,165d), **ente** (70b,151d), **este** (152b,d,164c), **Este** (55c,83c,d,112d), **ette** (158a,c,d), **fate** (42d,52a,87a,94a), **fete** (55d,129b), **fute** (51c), **gate** (51a,121b), **gite** (62a,118d), **hate** (6a,43a), **jete** (16a), **jute** (37a,48a,56a,133d,136a), **Jute, Kate** (143c,183d), **kite** (19c,49a, 74c,d), **late** (128c), **lete, lite** (158c,d), **lote** (24c,94a), **lute** (11c,28b, 84d,105a,131d), **mate** (18c,35b,41d,113a,154a,162c), **mete** (9a, 11d,22b,44c,45b,98a,121c), **mite** (12b,81b,82a,114a,c,148c,d,181b), **mote** (114c,153a), **mute** (146c,153b), **Nate** (22b), **nete** (71c,108b, 163d), **note** (98c,109b,124b,128d,130a,177c), **oste** (21d,83b), **pate** (39a,74d), **pete** (136b), **Pete, rate** (11d,14a,31d,36b,51d,52a,70b, 85c,112b,123b,127d,128a,138c,143a,174b), **rete** (106c,119c), **rite** (93a,131d), **rote** (130b,134b,143a,159d), **rute** (188), **sate** (32d,52c, 67d,70d,137c,159d), **site** (93b), **sote** (150c), **tate** (183a), **tete** (61d, 73b,74d), **tote** (27a,73c), **tute** (171b), **vite** (62b), **vote** (60b), **Vote** (56d), **Wate** (141a), **Wote** (191), **yate** (51d,168c)

T--E **tace** (13a,155d), **take, tale** (91a,185b), **tame** (45a,b,66a), **Tame, Tane** (120d), **tape** (16a,19a,128d), **tare** (9a,18d,41a,176a,179d), **tate** (183a), **Tave** (183d), **tche** (13d,30b,105a), **tele** (34b,122c), **tene** (34d,131b), **tete** (61d,73b,74d), **thee** (124b), **tice** (9a,38c,51a, 185d), **tide** (39d,75d,109c,141c,159d), **tige** (118a), **tike** (29d), **tile** (31d,56d,72b,95b,133c,163c), **time** (47a,131a), **tine** (11b,124b, 167b), **tipe** (168b), **tire** (15a,22a,52d,55a,179b,180d), **tobe** (7d, 137b), **tode** (80a,148a), **tole** (9a,51a,99b,163a), **tome** (21d,177c), **tone** (6c,118c,150d), **tope** (24a,46b,57a,143c,151a), **tore, tote** (27a, 73c), **tree** (11d,37a,66a,184b), **true** (7a,8d,37b,54b,94c,149c), **tube** (118b,158a), **tuke** (26b,53b), **tule** (24b,27c), **tune** (8b,12c, 98c), **tute** (171b), **twee, tyee** (29d), **tyke** (29d), **tyne, Tyne** (108a), **type** (31d,115a,155a), **tyre** (15a), **Tyre** (31b,90d,117b)

T--F **teff** (6c), **tiff** (126b), **toff** (40d), **tref** (172b), **tuff** (121b,177a), **turf** (115c,149d,160b)

T--G **tang** (30b,58b,186b), **tegg** (143d,171d), **Teig** (96a), **teng** (188), **thug** (65a), **ting** (166a), **Ting** (30c), **tong** (30a,c,), **toug** (171a), **trig** (106a,148d,154b,169d), **tung** (110a,168c), **twig**

TH-- **Thai** (146a), **than** (35b), **thar** (68a,76d), **that** (42b,124b,129c), **thaw, Thea** (162c), **theb** (188), **thee** (124b), **them** (124b), **then, thew** (104c), **they** (124b), **thin** (43b,c,148b), **this** (42b,124b), **thob** (128a), **Thor** (7c,68c,99c,100c,109c,165b), **Thos** (84a,181c), **thou** (124b), **thud, thug** (65a), **thus** (149c)

-TH- **Otho** (133a)

--TH **acth** (13b), **bath, Bath** (50d,151c), **beth** (91c), **Beth** (8c,183d), **both, doth, Esth** (16a,51d), **Gath** (117a), **Goth** (16c,163d), **hath,**

Heth (77c), **Hoth** (20c), **Jeth** (102a), **kath** (14a), **kith** (63c), **lath** (157c), **lith** (34d,156c), **loth** (15a,173d), **math** (77a), **moth, Moth** (112d), **muth** (188), **myth** (8b,91a), **Nath** (155c), **oath** (119c,150a), **path** (132a,134b), **pith** (37a,51c,67b,95c,97a,119b,126d), **rath** (76d,162d), **ruth** (35b,118c), **Ruth** (105b,183c), **seth** (98d), **Seth** (7a,52b,68a,b,96a,98d), **teth** (91d), **Urth** (68d,107d,163d), **Voth** (191), **with** (10b)

T - - H **tanh** (97c), **tash** (154d), **Tech, teth** (91d), **toph** (75c), **tosh** (106a), **tush** (167b)

TI - - **Tiam, tiao, tiar** (39a,75a,121a), **Tibu** (191), **tice** (9a,38c,51a,185d), **tick** (12b,20d,97c), **tide** (39d,75d,109c,141c,159d), **tidy** (106a, 111b), **tied, tien** (147d), **tier** (118a,134b), **tiff** (126b), **tige** (118a), **tike** (29d), **Tiki** (120c), **tile** (31d,56d,72b,95b,133c,163c), **till** (39c, 101c,173d), **tilt** (26b,d,166a), **time** (47a,131a), **Tina** (183d), **tind** (86b), **tine** (11b,124b,167b), **ting** (166a), **Ting** (30c), **Tino** (136d), **tint** (33c,d,114d), **tiny** (100c,148c), **tion** (158b), **Tiou** (192), **tipe** (168b), **tipi** (181b), **tire** (15a,22a,52d,55a,179b,180d), **tiro** (9b,17d, 108c), **titi** (20d,102a,145d,168d,181b), **Tito** (186c), **tiza** (172a)

- TI - **Atik** (155b), **atip** (14b,166a), **atis** (76d,102a), **itis** (158c), **otic** (14c, d,47b), **Otis** (9c,d,24d,82a,111a), **stib** (19b,47a,137a), **stir** (8a, 13a,35b,78d,100d,104a)

- - TI **anti** (7d,111a,122b), **Anti** (193), **Asti** (83d,182b), **biti** (20b), **Guti, Hati** (48d), **hoti, Inti** (159b), **jati** (27b), **jiti, joti, Leti** (82d), **liti** (60d), **Loti** (63a,176a), **neti** (164a), **rati** (189), **roti** (62c), **sati, Sati** (49a,126b,147b), **seti** (34a), **Seti** (116d), **titi** (20d,102a,145d,168d, 181b), **viti** (176b), **yati** (76d), **zati** (21d)

T - - I **tabi** (84c,149d) **tali** (189), **Tari** (47d,69a), **taxi** (13a,125b), **tchi, Tchi, teli** (94b), **Thai** (146a), **Tiki** (120c), **tipi** (181b), **titi** (20d,102a, 145d,168d,181b), **topi** (37a,75a,118c), **tori** (101b), **tshi, Tshi** (69c), **Tupi** (192), **Turi** (191), **tuwi** (117a,168c), **Tybi** (102a)

- TK - **Atka** (11a)

T - - K **tack** (28d,37d,54d), **talk, tank** (175a,d), **task** (156b), **teak** (41a, 48a,168c), **teck** (128b), **tick** (12b,20d,97c), **tock** (7d,19b),**tonk** (173c), **took, Tosk** (8c), **trek** (85c,93c,99d,168b), **tuck** (156b), **Turk** (101d,102d,106a,111d), **tusk** (167b)

- TL - **atle** (136d,161d,169b), **Atli** (14c,72b,79a,107d)

- - TL **rotl** (103b,111c)

T - - L **Taal** (7d,88c,151a), **tael** (91d,179d), **tail** (11d,27d,59b,143b), **tall** (118d), **teal** (19b,20d,46c,d), **teel** (142d), **teil** (92b,c,168c), **tell** (105d,129c,154b), **Tell** (160d), **teyl** (92b,c,168c), **till** (39c,101c, 173d), **toil** (46c,184c), **toll** (131c), **tool** (27c), **tuel**

TM - - **T-men** (168b)

- TM - **atma** (150d), **atmo** (34d,174d), **Atmu** (143a,159b), **itmo** (18b)

T - - M **team** (38c,72a,113a), **teem** (6b), **term** (92b,105b,142b,166b), **them** (124b), **tiam, toom** (139b), **tram** (170a), **trim** (40a,106a,154b, 160a,165c,169d), **turm** (132d)

- TN - **etna** (75b,153c,157a,175d,177a,c)

T - - N **tain** (166a), **tarn** (87d,103d,120d), **taun** (188), **tean** (140c,167a), **teen** (139b,c,140b,158d), **tern** (19b,32d,72c,94a,138c,141a,160a),

than (35b), **then, thin** (43b,c,148b), **tien** (147d), **tion** (158b), **T-men** (168b), **toon** (80c,95b,168c), **torn** (130a), **town** (73c), **tran** (7a), **trin** (169d), **tron** (140d,180a), **Tsin** (30b), **tsun** (30b), **tuan** (95d,147b,166c), **turn** (28d,131a,175a), **twin** (45c,171d)

TO - - **toad** (10a,17a,63d,126d), **Toba** (80c), **tobe** (7d,137b), **toby** (8c, 85c,104b), **Toby** (96b,125c), **tock** (7d,19b), **toco** (19b,167c), **Toda** (45d,76d), **tode** (80a,148a), **todo** (22b,24d,35b,64c,156b), **tody** (19b,d,59a,166a), **toed, toff** (40d), **toga** (132d,133a,b), **togs** (32c), **togt** (77c), **toho** (79a), **toil** (46c,184c), **toko** (30c), **tola** (48a,80d,180a), **Tola** (85b), **told** (129c), **tole** (9a,51a,99b,163a), **toll** (131c), **tolt, tolu** (16a), **Toma** (191), **tomb, tome** (21d,177c), **tone** (6c,118c,150d), **tong** (30a,c), **tonk** (173c), **tony, Tony** (96b), **tooa** (17c), **took, tool** (27c), **toom** (139b), **toon** (80c,95b,168c), **toot, tope** (24a,46b,57a,143c,151a), **toph** (75c), **topi** (37a,75a, 118c), **tops** (159c), **tora** (11a,44d,74a,75c,85c,90b,102d,115d), **tore, tori** (101b), **torn** (130a), **toro** (38a,107a,152a,168c), **torp** (54c), **tort** (31c,91a,185c), **Tory** (23c,36b,94c,172a), **tosh** (106a), **Tosk** (8c), **toss** (24a,132d), **tota** (71d), **tote** (27a,73c), **toto** (8d,15a,34d, 89a,181a), **toty** (87b), **toug** (171a), **toup** (95d), **tour** (31b,85c), **tout** (61a,127a), **town** (73c), **towy** (58b), **toxa** (153d)

- TO - **atom** (101c,114c,180d), **aton** (150a,159b), **atop** (112a,174a), **Eton** (33b,50c,84a), **itol** (158b), **Otoe** (147b), **stoa** (33c,121a,c), **stod** (40d,67d), **stof** (135c), **stog** (155a), **stom** (34c), **stop** (73b,111b), **stot** (154d,155d,157d,179b,186a), **stow** (112b), **utor** (90a,166c)

- - TO **acto** (152b), **alto** (152b,176c), **auto** (34d), **bito** (7d,57d,168c), **Boto** (192), **Buto** (142d), **Cato** (132d,133b), **ceto** (34a), **cito** (89d,126c), **coto** (16c,90b), **dato** (95c,102c,117a), **Doto** (141b), **ecto** (34c,122d), **ento** (34b,d), **into** (123a,183b) **jato** (173b), **koto** (84b), **Leto** (11c), **loto** (65a,121d,178d), **moto** (104b), **Nato** (6a,8d), **nito** (55c), **octo** (34a,89b,122c), **onto** (76a,174a), **otto** (58d,116b,134a), **Otto** (14c,66d,67a,96a), **pato** (46d), **peto** (57a,177b), **Peto** (76a), **pito** (9c,28b,83a), **roto** (30a,122d,127b,152c,171b), **sito** (34b), **Tito** (186c), **toto** (8d,15a,34d,89a,181a), **Tyto** (16c), **unto** (166c), **veto** (94a,124a), **Veto, Voto** (192)

T - - O **tajo** (152a,d), **Tano** (192), **taro** (13c,48c,49b,64b,112b,120a,133d, 155c,170a,c), **taxo** (13a), **Teco** (192), **tiao, Tino** (136d), **tiro** (9b, 17d,108c), **Tito** (186c), **toco** (19b,167c), **todo** (22b,24d,35b,64c, 156b), **toho** (79a), **toko** (30c), **toro** (38a,107a,152a,168c), **toto** (8d,15a,34d,89a,181a), **trio** (104d,165a,169c), **tuno** (28b,168c), **typo** (35c,51b,123d), **tyro** (9b,17d,108c), **Tyto** (16c)

T - - P **tamp** (46b,112b,121d,127d), **tarp** (26b,178d), **terp** (12b,123a), **torp** (54c), **toup** (95d), **trap** (27b,67b,132b,149b), **trip** (85c), **trop** (62d,167a), **tryp** (114a), **tump** (60a,76d,103d), **turp, tymp** (20c), **typp** (185b)

TR - - **tram** (170a), **tran** (7a), **trap** (27b,67b,132b149b), **tray** (128c, 136d,142d,143c), **tree** (11d,37a,66a,184b), **tref** (172b), **trek** (85c, 93c,99d,168b), **tres** (19a,52b,63a,152d,165a,175c), **tret** (9a,178b, 179d), **trey** (26c,165a), **trig** (106a,148d,154b,169d), **trim** (40a,106a,154b,160a,165c,169d), **trin** (169d), **trio** (104d,165a, 169c), **trip** (85c), **tris** (122d), **trit** (34d,164c), **trod, tron** (140d, 180a), **trop** (62d,167a), **trot** (85b,93d,112d), **trow** (18a,21a,159d,

164c,170b), **troy** (161c,180a), **Troy, true** (7a,8d,37b,54b,94c,149c), **tryp** (114a)

- TR - **Atri, atry** (141b), **etre** (61a,c,62d,166c)

- - TR **natr** (189)

T - - R **taar** (12b), **tahr** (68a,76d), **tair** (68a,76d), **tear** (67c,87b,130a), **teer** (25b,69d), **tehr** (27c,68a), **thar** (68a,76d), **Thor** (7c,68c,99c, 100c,109c,165b), **tiar** (39a,75a,121a), **tier** (118a,134b), **tour** (31b, 85c), **tsar** (42d,49d,60b,135c), **turr** (24d,105a), **tyer, Tyrr** (68c, 109c,163d,178a), **tzar** (42d,49d,60b,135c)

TS - - **tsar** (42d,49d,60b,135c), **tshi, Tshi** (69c), **tsia** (162c), **Tsin** (30b), **tsun** (30b)

- - TS **Acts, arts** (138c), **cits, eats, lots, orts** (60d), **rats**

T - - S **Taos** (192), **Tass** (107a,135d,151b), **Tees** (108a), **Teos** (82a), **Tess** (73d,164c,183d), **this** (42b,124b), **Thos** (84a,181c), **thus** (149c), **togs** (32c), **tops** (159c), **toss** (24a,132d), **tres** (19a,52b,63a,152d,165a, 175c), **tris** (122d)

- TT - **atta** (58d,90c,97d,160c,173d), **Atta** (94d,95d,100a,106b,117a), **Attu, Etta** (183c), **ette** (158a,c,d), **otto** (58d,116b,134a), **Otto** (14c,66d,67a,96a)

- - TT **batt** (37c), **bitt** (54d,175c), **bott** (32a,88d), **butt** (27a,77b,127d, 162a,182b), **Catt** (9d), **gett** (44d), **Lett** (16a,90a,93a), **Matt, mitt** (56c), **mutt** (39c,101d), **Natt** (107b), **nett, Nott** (107b), **Pitt** (50d,155d), **pott** (113d), **putt** (69d), **sett** (115a,156d), **tatt** (87c), **watt** (173b,177c), **Watt** (82a)

T - - T **tact** (43c,d,116a), **Taft** (29d), **tait** (14d), **takt** (105a,163a), **tart** (114d), **tatt** (87c), **taut** (163b,165c), **tent** (26b,115a), **test** (26a, 51c,144a,169c,170c), **text** (21c,140d), **that** (42b,124b,129c), **tilt** (26b,d,166a), **tint** (33c,d,114d), **todt** (66b), **tolt, toot, tort** (31c,91a,185c), **tout** (61a,127a), **tret** (9a,178b,179d), **trit** (34d,164c), **trot** (85b,93d,112d), **tuft** (24b,32d,38c), **twit** (162b,c)

TU - - **tuan** (95d,147b,166c), **tuba** (105a,137d), **tube** (118b,158a), **tuck** (156b), **tuel, tufa** (121b,177a), **tuff** (121b,177a), **tuft** (24b,32d, 38c), **tuke** (26b,53b), **tula** (9a), **Tula, tule** (24b,27c), **Tulu** (45d), **tump** (60a,76d,103d), **tuna** (57a,b,123b,170d), **tund** (121d), **tune** (8b,12c,98c), **tung** (110a,168c), **tuno** (28b,168c), **tunu** (28b), **tuny, Tupi** (192), **turf** (115c,149d,160b), **Turi** (191), **Turk** (101d,102d, 106a,111d), **turm** (132d), **turn** (28d,131a,175a), **turp, turr** (24d, 105a), **tush** (167b), **tusk** (167b), **tute** (171b), **tutu** (16a,106d,147d), **tuwi** (117a,168c), **tuza** (119d)

- TU - **atua** (120d), **Atum** (143a,159b), **etui** (27a,29b,62c,106b,148d, 166d,174b), **Otus** (67a), **stub** (156c), **stud** (22b,25a,42d,54d,111c, 143a,174a), **stum** (70c,105c,131a,173a), **stun** (145a,157d), **Utug** (159b), **utum** (19b,112c)

- - TU **actu** (7a,89a), **Attu, datu** (95c,102c,117a), **Ketu** (48b), **latu** (190), **mitu** (39d), **patu** (179b), **tatu** (12d), **Tatu, tutu** (16a,106d,147d), **yutu** (19b,166a)

T - - U **tabu** (59d,111d), **Taku** (80c), **tapu, tatu** (12d), **Tatu, tchu, teju** (151b), **thou** (124b), **Tibu** (191), **Tiou** (192), **tolu** (16a), **Tulu** (45d), **tunu** (28b), **tutu** (16a,106d,147d)

TW - - **twee**, **twig**, **twin** (45c,171d), **twit** (162b,c)

T - - W **thaw**, **thew** (104c), **trow** (18a,21a,159d,164c,170b)

TY - - **Tybi** (102a), **tyee** (29d), **tyer**, **tyke** (29d), **tymp** (20c), **tyne**, **Tyne** (108a), **type** (31d,115a,155a), **typo** (35c,51b,123d), **typp** (185b), **typy**, **tyre** (15a), **Tyre** (31b,90d,117b), **tyro** (9b,17d,108c), **Tyrr** (68c,109c,163d,178a), **Tyto** (16c)

- TY - **etym** (133d), **Itys** (163b), **Styx** (29b,73a,105c)

- - TY **arty**, **city**, **Coty** (63c), **doty** (43d), **duty** (109b,162b), **Katy** (183d), **maty** (80c), **mity**, **pity** (35b), **toty** (87b)

T - - Y **taky**, **Tavy** (183d), **they** (124b), **tidy** (106a,111b), **tiny** (100c,148c), **toby** (8c,85c,104b), **Toby** (96b,125c), **tody** (19b,d,59a,166a), **tony**, **Tony** (96b), **tory**, **Tory** (23c,36b,94c,172a), **toty** (87b), **towy** (58b), **tray** (128c,136d,142d,143c), **trey** (26c,165a), **troy** (161c,180a), **Troy**, **tuny**, **typy**

TZ - - **tzar** (42d,49d,60b,135c)

- TZ - **Itza** (192)

- - TZ **batz** (190), **litz** (127b), **untz** (189)

UA - - **uang** (131a)

- UA - **bual** (182c), **duab** (157c), **duad** (171d), **dual** (45c,171d), **duan** (64b), **duar**, **Duat** (172d), **Fuad** (54d), **Guam**, **guan** (151b), **guao** (168c,169b), **guar** (46c,59d), **juan** (113a), **Juan** (96a), **juar** (100a), **kuan** (30b), **Kuan** (30c), **Kuar** (102a), **Muav** (66a), **quad** (33c,172a), **quae** (176b), **quag** (21c,102c), **quai** (88b,117c,180c), **quan** (190), **quas** (135c), **quay** (88b,117c,180c), **ruay** (189), **tuan** (95d,147b, 166c), **yuan** (190), **Yuan** (30b,101d)

- - UA **agua** (152d,166c,178c), **akua** (120d), **aqua** (90a,178c), **atua** (120d), **Erua** (103c), **skua** (19b,72c,84a,141a), **ulua** (57a,74c), **Ulua** (141b)

U - - A **ueba** (188), **ulna** (21d,39b), **ulua** (57a,74c), **Ulua** (141b), **Ulva** (141b), **unca** (49a), **upla**, **Urfa** (99a), **Uria** (14c,16d), **urna** (133a), **Ursa** (17b,36b,43d), **urva** (38b), **Usha** (16a,150c), **uvea** (53c,82b)

UB - - **uber** (66b), **Ubii** (191)

- UB - **buba** (170a), **Bube** (180b), **Bubi** (180b), **Bubo** (112c), **cuba** (189), **Cuba** (180b), **cube** (66b,150a), **cubi** (188), **dubb** (161c), **hubb** (118b), **juba** (106b), **jube** (28d), **kuba** (26d,189), **Luba** (191), **lube** (110a), **Lubs** (94c), **Nuba** (108c), **nubk** (30d,164d), **rube** (37d, 135d,185d), **Rube** (96b), **ruby** (20a,65d,179c), **tuba** (105a,137d), **tube** (118b,158a)

- - UB **blub**, **chub** (40c,154c), **club** (39c), **daub** (148d), **doub** (189), **drub** (17b,39c), **flub** (22b), **gaub** (116c), **glub**, **grub** (43c,88d), **knub** (178b), **slub** (171c), **snub** (128c,148b), **stub** (156c)

- UC - **Auca** (192), **buck**, **cuca** (33a,105d), **duce** (29d), **duck** (26b,53b, 179c), **Duco**, **duct** (170c), **fuci** (132c), **huck** (167d), **juca** (27a), **juck** (114c), **luce** (58c,117d), **Luce** (7b,35a), **luck** (28d), **lucy**, **Lucy** (183c), **much**, **muck**, **ouch!**, **puca** (68a), **puce** (33c,d,52a), **puck** (44b,68a,77c,100c), **Puck** (99d,143b), **ruck** (39a,185a), **such** (146d), **suck**, **tuck** (156b), **yuca** (27a)

- - UC **douc** (101d), **eruc** (37a,56a)

U - - C **Udic** (108a), **Utac** (22d)

UD- - **udad** (143d,144a,181c), **udal** (76b,88b,131c), **Udic** (108a)

-UD- **Aude, buda** (83d), **Buda, dude** (40d), **duds** (32c,166d), **Juda, Jude** (11c,96a), **judo** (84b,85c,142b), **Judy** (125c,183d), **kudu** (11a), **Ludd** (23c), **ludi** (133b), **ludo** (65a,112b), **mudd** (188), **nuda** (39b), **Nudd** (23c), **nude** (16c,172d), **pudu** (41d), **rudd** (26d,57a,b), **rude** (134b,172b), **sudd** (40b,58c,107b), **suds** (59a), **wudu** (102d)

- -UD **baud** (162d), **Chud** (191), **feud** (55d,126b,175b), **foud** (54d,144b), **gaud** (169d), **laud** (122a), **loud** (156a), **maud** (53d,71a,136d,143c), **Maud** (181a,183c), **Phud** (110b), **puud** (189), **roud** (57a,b), **scud** (32c,126c,135b,160c), **spud** (121d,151c), **stud** (22b,25a,42d,54d,111c,143a,174a), **syud** (103b), **thud**

U- -D **udad** (143d,144a,181c), **used** (6d,73a), **uvid** (101a)

UE- - **ueba** (188)

-UE- **Auer** (79a), **duel, duet** (104d,171d), **euer** (66d), **fuel** (65c), **hued, juez** (152b), **kuei** (44a), **quei** (189), **ruer, suer** (124d), **suet** (54d), **tuel**

- -UE **ague** (30a,55d,95c), **blue** (33c,98c,102c,150d,173a), **clue, flue** (8b,30a), **gaue** (67a), **glue** (7b,156a), **moue** (61d,62b), **neue** (66c), **Niue** (137d), **roue** (41b,44c,127c,134b), **slue** (97b,148b,160a), **true** (7a,8d,37b,54b,94c,149c)

U- -E **ulme** (49c), **unde** (179a), **unie** (173a), **unze** (189), **urde** (86b), **urge** (42d,46b,79d,80a,b,81c,150a), **usee**

-UF- **buff** (134c,161d), **Bufo** (166c), **cuff** (148a), **duff** (125b), **Dufy** (63a), **gufa** (21b,99a), **guff, huff** (58a), **kufa** (21b,99a), **luff** (136b), **muff, puff,** (180d), **ruff** (19b,33b,63d,137a), **sufi** (103a,116c), **tufa** (121b,177a), **tuff** (121b,177a), **tuft** (24b,32d,38c), **yuft** (135c)

- -UF **pouf, souf** (146b)

UG- - **ugly**

-UG- **auge** (123c,132b), **Bugi** (191), **euge** (180a), **fuga, fugu** (84b), **gugu, huge, Hugh** (96a), **Hugo** (63a,96a), **juga** (27a), **kuge** (84c), **luge** (148a), **Lugh** (28b), **muga, ough, pugh, ruga** (59b,185a), **sugi** (84b), **vugg** (28a,66a,132b), **vugh** (28a,66a,132b), **Yuga** (76d)

- -UG **chug** (53a), **drug** (105d), **glug, joug** (138d), **plug** (156d,184d), **slug** (46b,99b,157c), **smug, snug** (35a,38b,165c), **Snug** (99d), **thug** (65a), **toug** (171a), **Utug** (159b)

U- -G **uang** (131a), **Utug** (159b)

-UH- **buhl** (81a), **buhr** (180d), **Duhr** (155b), **Guha** (191), **guhr** (47d), **kuhl** (53c), **Ruhr**

- -UH **bruh** (95a)

U- -H **umph, Urth** (68d,107d,163d), **Utah** (180b)

-UI- **cuif** (139a,d,140c), **cuir** (45c,62a), **duim** (188), **duit** (190), **Duit** (192), **guib** (11a), **huia** (19a,106d), **luif, Muir** (8b,142c), **nuit** (62b), **quid** (39b,166d), **quip** (183a,b), **quit** (90d,130c), **quiz, ruin** (42d), **suit** (38a,58a,91a,112a,119c,137c), **Yuit** (51c)

- -UI **arui** (11b,143d,144a,181c), **equi** (122d), **etui** (27a,29b,62c,106b,148d,166d,174b), **Maui** (120d)

U - - I **Ubii** (191), **unci** (31d)

- UJ - **fuji** (84b), **Fuji** (84d), **juju** (29b,55d), **puja** (77a), **suji** (180c)

- UK - **bukh** (122a), **bukk** (122a), **cuke** (39b), **duke** (107c), **duku** (95d, 168c), **juke** (114c), **Kuki** (191), **kuku** (19a,106d), **luke, Luke** (52a,96a), **puka** (107a,168c), **puku** (11a), **rukh** (53b,54a), **Suku** (191), **tuke** (26b,53b), **wukf** (103a)

- - UK **cauk** (139b), **dauk** (95c), **Sauk** (192), **souk** (22a,97a)

UL - - **Ulam** (67b), **ulan** (27d,88a), **Ulex** (153c), **ullo** (6a,144a), **Ullr** (146b,164d), **ulme** (49c), **ulna** (21d,39b), **ulua** (57a,74c), **Ulua** (141b), **Ulva** (141b)

- UL - **aula** (66c,73b), **aulu** (74c,168c), **bulb** 37a,172c), **bulk** (97b), **bull** (113c), **bult** (76d), **cull** (117c), **culm** (11a,32d,70d,145a,156a), **cult** (141d,161c), **dull** (21a,32c,173a), **Dull** (94b), **fulk** (173a), **full** (7b, 130b), **gula** (90a,101a,165b), **gulf** (6c), **gull** (32d,41c,42a,72c,99b, 141a), **Gulo** (183c), **gulp** (46a,79d,160a), **hula** (74b) **hule,** (23a, 134c), **hulk** (144d,173d), **hull** (141d,142a,144c,d), **hulu** (55b), **jula, Jule** (183d), **July, kula** (189), **Kuli** (27b), **lull** (25c,126d,150c), **lulu** (19a,57b,112c), **Lulu** (183d), **mule** (45b,148b,153c,180b), **mulk** (60d), **mull** (53b,135a,164c), **null** (108c,177a), **pule** (180d), **pulk** (37c,88d), **puli** (45a,78d), **pull** (45d,167d), **pulp, pulu** (74c), **puly, rule** (11b,26b,90b), **rull** (170b), **Sula** (65a), **suld** (188), **sulk** (159a), **Sulu** (102c), **tula** (9a), **Tula, tule** (24b,27c), **Tulu** (45d), **vuln** (184d), **Yule** (30d), **zulu** (171d,175d), **Zulu** (86a)

- - UL **Aoul** (191), **azul** (151d), **baul** (18b), **caul** (16d,74d), **deul** (77b), **Elul** (102b), **foul** (173a), **Gaul** (10a,60d,63c), **goul** (102a), **haul** (27b,45d), **maul** (73c,96b), **paul, Paul** (96a), **poul** (190), **saul** (48a, 168c), **Saul** (18c,86d,115a), **shul** (161a), **soul** (10d,125a,153c, 176d)

U - - L **udal** (76b,88b,131c), **unal** (147a), **Ural** (135c), **uval** (70c)

UM - - **umbo** (22b), **umph**

- UM - **bump, Duma** (135c), **dumb** (153b), **dump, fume** (129a,149a,157a), **fumy, Gump** (43b), **Hume** (50c), **hump** (124d), **jump, lump** (45a, 160c), **mump** (29b,153d), **Numa** (133a), **numb, puma** (27b,37c,55b, 103d), **Pume** (137b,175b,185b), **pump, rumb** (120b), **rump, Sumo, sump** (28c,45d), **tump** (60a,76d,103d), **Yuma**

- - UM **ahum, alum** (14a,45c), **arum** (13a,39b,58d,92b,155c), **Arum** (66a), **Atum** (143a,159b), **Baum** (9c,112c), **chum** (38d), **doum** (168c), **drum** (105a), **Geum** (76b), **glum** (102c,159a), **grum** (102c), **jhum, meum** (27a,89c), **Meum, odum** (168c,180a), **ogum** (82b), **ovum** (48d), **plum, rhum** (8c), **saum** (189), **scum** (129b), **slum, stum** (70c,105c,131a,173a), **swum, Ulam** (67b), **utum** (19b,112c)

U - - M **urim** (18d,23a,110a), **utum** (19b,112c)

UN - - **unal** (147a), **unau** (148c,171d), **unca** (49a), **unci** (31d), **unco** (140c), **unde** (179a), **undo** (11a,93d), **undy** (179a), **unie** (173a), **Unio** (105c), **unis** (91b), **unit** (101c,110c,147a), **unto** (166c), **untz** (189), **unze** (189)

- UN - **aune** (188), **aunt** (129c), **buna** (161c), **bund** (49c,66c,90c), **bung** (119d,156d), **bunk, bunn** (25b), **bunt** (15d,180c), **Cuna** (193), **dune** (137a), **dunk** (43c,79d), **Duns, dunt, fund** (6d,101c,130c), **Fung**

(191), **Funj, funk** (63d,113c), **guna** (106a,137b), **gunj** (70c), **hung, hunh?, hunk, hunt** (141c), **June** (183c), **Jung** (125a), **junk** (30a, 134c), **Juno** (69c,85d,100c,126b), **kung** (125b), **kunk** (188), **luna** 103c), **Luna** (102b), **lune** (38c,73b,74d), **lung, luny** (38b), **mund** (124d), **mung** (70d), **munj** (70d), **paun** (18b), **puna** (10b,33b,104a, 119b,182a), **pund** (189), **pung** (22c,148b), **punk** (9b,166a,167c), **puno** (182a), **punt** (21a,58b), **puny** (55b,179a), **Qung** (191), **rune** (9b,67a,94a,105c,107d,120a,141d,163d), **rung** (28c,39a), **runt** (47a172d), **sung, Sung** (30b), **sunk, sunn** (56a), **tuna** (57a,b,123b, 170d), **tund** (121d), **tune** (8b,12c,98c), **tung** (110a,168c), **tuno** (28b,168c), **tunu** (28b), **tuny, Yunx** (184a), **Zuni** (125b)

- - UN **Amun** (86d,127d,159b,164a), **Chun** (30c), **drun** (132b), **faun** (56a, 68b,137c,161a,184a), **Idun** (107d), **jaun** (113a), **kaun** (93d), **laun** (146b), **loun** (19a,b), **maun** (139d), **noun** (114b,158a), **paun** (18b), **shun** (15a,51b,52a), **spun, stun** (145a,157d), **taun** (188), **tsun** (30b), **Usun** (191), **whun** (64c,70a)

U - - N **ulan** (27d,88a), **upon** (6b), **uran** (101d), **Usun** (191), **uzan** (189)

- UO - **buoy** (28d,58c), **quod** (123d)

U - - O **ullo** (6a,144a), **umbo** (22b), **unco** (140c), **undo** (11a,93d), **Unio** (105c), **unto** (166c), **upgo** (13c)

UP - - **upas** (84d,120b,168c,d), **upgo** (13c), **Upis** (13b), **upla, upon** (6b)

- UP - **dupe** (27c,41c,72c,160c), **Hupa** (192), **jupe** (62b,84a), **lupe** (19a, 64a), **Nupe** (191), **pupa** (30d,81b,c), **rupa** (60b), **supa** (168c), **supe** (53a,154d), **Tupi** (192)

- - UP **blup, caup, coup** (20d,97c,157b,c,162d), **gaup, loup** (61d,62a,90c, 139d), **Loup** (193), **noup** (124b), **plup, roup** (44a,121d), **scup** (57a, 121b), **snup** (149b), **soup, toup** (95d), **yaup, youp** (185d)

UR - - **Ural** (135c), **uran** (101d), **urde** (86b), **Urdu** (77b), **urdy** (86b), **Urey** (17b,36b,43d), **Urth** (68d,107d,163d), **urus** (14d,53a,112c), **urva** 150a), **Uria** (14c,16d), **urim** (18d,23a,110a), **urna** (133a), **Ursa** (17b,36b,43d), **Urth** (68d,107d,163d), **urus** (14d,53a,112c), **urva** (38b)

- UR - **aura** (44c,49c,66a,96b,158a,170d,177c), **auri** (34a), **bura** (182b), **bure** (61b), **burg** (22b,73c), **buri** (56b), **burl** (87c,169a), **burn, burr** (123b), **bury** (81d), **cura** (152c), **curb** (130c,146b), **curd** (99d), **cure** (123b), **curl** (38d,73b,131d), **curr** (104c), **curt** (145b,c), **dura** (153c), **duro** (190), **durr** (70b), **furl** (132d), **fury** (157a), **guru** (77b), **hura** (20a,137a), **Hura, hurl** (167c), **hurt, jura, Jura, jure** (90b), **jury** (38a), **Kurd** (48b,82a), **Kure** (84c), **Kuri** (191), **kurk** (31a,139b), **lura** (22d,82a), **lure** (41c,51a,54b,163a), **lurg** (96d,141b,184d), **Luri** (191), **lurk** (92a,147d), **mura** (84d), **Mura** (192), **mure** (177d), **murk** (41a,67d), **murr** (72b,128b), **nurl** (33b,87c), **nurr** (67d), **ours** (124c), **pure** (29b,172b,173c), **puri** (80d), **purl** (87c,104c), **purr** (104c), **Puru** (192), **ruru** (19b,102c,106d), **sura** (87c,113b,166d), **surd** (82c,177a), **sure** (173d), **surf** (23a), **turf** (115c,149d,160b), **Turi** (191), **Turk** (101d,102d,106a,111d), **turm** (132d), **turn** (28d, 131a,175a), **turp, turr** (24d,105a), **Wurd, wurm** (67c), **yurt** (101d)

- - UR **Alur** (191), **Asur** (68c), **biur** (35a), **blur, caur** (139a), **Daur** (139b), **dour** (67d,159a), **ebur** (89c), **four** (26c), **gaur** (112c,181c), **gour** (112c,181c), **hour, knur** (67d,87c,107c), **lour** (13d,63d), **peur** (61c),

pour (162d), **scur** (78b), **slur** (44b,124c,148b,168a), **smur** (32c,46b, 100c), **sour, spur** (10d,67d,167d,168a,181b), **tour** (31b,85c), **your** (124c)

U - - R **uber** (66b), **Ullr** (146b,164d), **usar** (8d,16c), **user** (49d), **utor** (90a, 166c)

US - - **usar** (8d,16c), **Usas** (68d), **used** (6d,73a), **usee, user** (49d), **uses** (18a), **Usha** (16a,150c), **Usun** (191)

- US - **Ausa, ausu** (168c,180b), **bush, busk** (17b,37b,55d,161b), **buss** (87a,148c), **bust, busy, cush** (101c), **Cush** (51d,73c), **cusk** (57b), **cusp** (38c,78b,119a,120a,b), **cuss, duse** (83c), **dusk** (171c), **dust, fuse** (98c), **fuss** (22b,35b), **fust** (105c,143b), **gush** (35a,154c), **gust, huse** (180c), **hush** (17b,146c), **husk** (53a,78d,142a), **huso** (180c), **just** (51b,54b), **kusa, Kush, lush** (94d), **lust** (41b), **Musa** (16a), **muse** (65b,93d,120d,164c), **Muse** (68d), **mush** (97d), **musk** (116b), **Muso** (192), **muss** (135b,173d), **must** (70c,101a,106d,157d,182c), **Ouse** (132a,185d), **oust** (44c,49a,52b,125d), **push,** (145c) **puss, rusa, Rusa** (41d,136d), **ruse** (13b,77c,157b,169c), **rush, rusk** (23a), **Russ** (135b), **rust** (37b,112c,119a), **Susa** (49a), **susi** (53b,d), **susu** (20c), **Susu** (191), **Susy** (183d), **tush** (167b), **tusk** (167b),

- - US **acus** (89d,118a), **Apus** (36b,c), **avus** (89b), **cous** (38a), **crus** (91a, 143c), **deus** (68a,89b), **Esus, gaus** (67a), **Grus** (36b,c,38b), **Ilus** (88d,170b), **irus** (109d), **nous** (81d,100a,128b), **onus** (24c,93b,109b), **opus** (35c,105a,184c), **Otus** (67a), **Pius** (121a), **plus** (10b, 102c), **pous** (188), **Rhus** (159a), **sous** (62d,172c), **thus** (149c), **urus** (14d,53a,112c), **Zeus** (135a)

U - - S **unis** (91b), **upas** (84d,120b,168c,d), **Upis** (13b), **urus** (14d,53a, 112c), **uses** (18a), **Usas** (68d), **utas** (49a,109c)

UT - - **utac** (22d), **Utah** (180b), **utas** (49a,109c), **utor** (90a,166c), **Utug** (159b), **utum** (19b,112c)

- UT - **auto** (34d), **Buto** (142d), **butt** (27a,77b,127d,162a,182b), **cute** (39c), **duty** (109b,162b), **fute** (51c), **Guti, jute** (37a,48a,56a,133d, 136a), **Jute, lute** (11c,28b,84d,105a,131d), **muta** (28d,103a), **mute** (146c,153b), **muth** (188), **mutt** (39c,101d), **putt** (69d), **Ruta** (76b, 134d), **rute** (188), **ruth** (35b,118c), **Ruth** (105b,183c), **tute** (171b), **tutu** (16a,106d,147d), **yutu** (19b,166a)

- - UT **abut** (22a,167c), **bhut** (67a), **blut** (66b), **bout** (36c), **brut** (182c), **Brut** (23c), **chut!, Cnut** (40d,50c), **gaut** (88b,103d,132a), **glut** (52c,70a,137c,159d), **gout, knut, Knut** (40d,50c,96a), **lout** (15c, 22a,24b,45b,109a,157d), **naut** (141b), **paut** (140a), **phut** (24b), **Phut** (110b), **pout** (159a), **prut!, Prut** (41a), **rout** (41d,44b,46b), **scut** (145c,161b), **shut, smut** (32d,44a,119a,150c), **sput** (21c), **taut** (163b,165c), **tout** (61a,127a)

U - - T **unit** (101c,110c,147a)

- UU - **puud** (189)

U - - U **unau** (148c,171d), **Urdu** (77b)

UV - - **uval** (70c), **uvea** (53c,82b), **uvic** (70c), **uvid** (101a)

- UV - **cuvy** (141a)

- UW - **tuwi** (117a,168c)

- - UW **bouw** (188), **dauw** (24c)

- UX - **buxy** (115b), **luxe** (61c,62d,159c), **puxy**

- - UX **crux** (39a,151b), **eaux** (178c), **flux** (28d,58d), **jeux** (61d), **Vaux** (63b)

U - - X **Ulex** (153c)

- UY - **buyo** (18b), **cuya** (39b), **Puya** (118b)

U - - Y **ugly, undy** (179a), **urdy** (86b), **Urey** (14b,107c,138c)

UZ - - **uzan** (189)

- UZ - **auzu** (168c,180b), **buzz, fuze** (98c), **fuzz** (45d), **guze** (128d), **huzz, Juza** (155b), **Muzo** (192), **tuza** (119d), **wuzu** (102d), **zuza** (189)

- - UZ **Ghuz** (171a)

U - - Z **untz** (189)

VA - - **Vach** (153b), **vade** (42c,67d,89b), **vagi** (38b), **vail** (94b,124a,174b), **vain** (81a), **vair** (64c,154c), **vale** (54c,128a,174b), **Vale** (7c,109c), **vali** (171a,176a), **Vali** (7c,109c), **vamp** (80a,145a), **vane** (179b, 182a), **vang** (72d,134a,140b), **Vans** (107d), **vara** (151d), **vare** 179b), **vari** (34d,91b,134d,174d), **vary** (28d,43c), **vasa** (46d,114a, 160b,175d), **Vasa, vase, vast** (78d,79d), **vasu** (106c), **Vasu** (176d), **Vaux** (63b), **Vayu** (68c,182a), **vaza** (114a)

- VA - **aval** (70c), **Avar** (27d,108a), **Evan** (96a), **Ivah** (18d), **Ivan** (40c, 85b,96a), **kvas** (135c), **oval** (48d,49c,127a), **Svan** (27d), **uval** (70c)

- - VA **Alva** (151d), **cava** (116a,175b), **Civa** (56d), **deva** (23d,42a,42b, 56d,77a), **diva** (100d,123c), **Hova** (95a), **Java** (33a), **jiva** (77a), **Jova** (193), **kava** (18c,116a), **kiva** (28c,125b), **lava** (101c,151a, 177a), **Neva** (91b,132a), **nova** (20c,106d,155c,174d), **peva** (12d), **siva** (67a), **Siva** (56d,77a), **Ulva** (141b), **urva** (38b), **viva** (93d), **Xova** (193), **yava**

V - - A **vara** (151d), **vasa** (46d,114a,160b,175d), **Vasa, vaza** (114a), **Veda** (77a,b), **vega** (110d,152c), **Vega** (155b), **vela** (98c,136b,149d), **Vela** (36b,c), **vena** (90a,175a), **vera** (140c,151b,175c), **Vera** (183c), **veta** (104a), **Vida** (183c), **vila** (54b), **vina** (77a,105a), **Vira** (191), **visa** (114d), **vita** (89c,92a), **viva** (93d), **vola** (89d,150a), **vota** (133b)

V - - B **verb** (7a,114b,184b)

- - VD **NKVD** (135d)

V - - D **veld** (151a), **vend** (97a,115c,142b), **Vend** (10b,148a), **verd** (71d), **void** (11a,49d,108d,174b)

VE - - **veal, Veda** (77a,b), **veer** (28d,144c,171b), **vega** (110d,152c), **Vega** (155b), **veil** (74d,76c), **vein** (20d,157b), **vela** (98c,136b,149d), **Vela** (36b,c), **veld** (151a), **velo** (175b), **vena** (90a,175a), **vend** (97a, 115c,142b), **Vend** (10b,148a), **vent** (8b,11b,110d,112a), **Veps** (191), **vera** (140c,151b,175c), **Vera** (183c), **verb** (7a,114b,184b), **verd** (71d), **veri** (28b), **vert** (71d,166a,171b), **very** (149c), **vest** (32c, 177b), **veta** (104a), **veto** (94a,124a), **Veto**

- VE - **avec** (63a,183a), **aver** (7c,14a,15c,41c,95c,140d,155c,160b,184c), **Aves** (19d), **evea** (82a,95a), **even** (51a,58b,79d,91d,149a,173a), **ever** (9b,14b,80b), **evet** (48d,107a,136c,169d), **Ives** (9c,90b), **oven** (15d,78c,86b), **over** (6b,38c,80a,114d,130a), **uvea** (53c,82b)

- - VE **bave** (61d,146c), **cave** (27d), **cive** (110c), **cove** (17a,73d,107d),

Dave (96b), **dive** (42b,74b,119d), **dove** (19a,117d), **eave** (133c), **five, gave, give** (79d,123a), **gyve** (55d,143b), **have** (92a), **hive** (17c), **hove** (92a), **Jave** (84d), **jive** (160c), **jove** (85d), **kive** (174d), **lave** (16d,178b), **leve** (62a), **live** (47c), **love** (163a), **move, nave** (30d,31a,78d,114b,180c), **neve** (56d,67c,70c,149b), **nove** (83b), **pave** (85a), **rave** (41c,157a,161d), **reve** (61c,104d), **rive** (32a,153d), **rove** (127d,132b,178a), **save** (52b,110c,123a,173c), **seve** (63a, 182c), **sive** (146a), **Tave** (183d), **vive** (93d), **wave** (19a,59a,111c, 131d,160c,172d), **wive** (97a), **wove**

V - - E **vade** (42c,67d,89b), **vale** (54c,128a,174b), **Vale** (7c,109c), **vane** (179b,182a), **vare** (179b), **vase, vice** (31d,158a), **vide** (89d,126a, 142a), **vile** (16c,56c), **vine** (32b), **vire** (11a,13b), **vise** (31d,77d, 114d), **vite** (62b), **vive** (93d), **voce** (83c,177a), **vole** (97d,104a, 148a,149b), **vote** (60b), **Vote** (56d)

V - - G **vang** (72d,134a,140b), **voog** (28a,66a,132b), **vugg** (28a,66a,132b)

- - VH **IHVH** (159d), **JHVH** (159d), **YHVH** (159d)

V - - H **Vach** (153b), **Voth** (191), **vugh** (28a,66a,132b)

VI - - **vial** (148c), **vice** (31d,158a), **Vida** (183c), **vide** (89d,126a,142a), **vier** (66c), **view** (93d,138b), **vila** (54b), **vile** (16c,56c), **vili** (54b), **Vili** (109c), **vill** (176b), **vily** (54b), **vina** (77a,105a), **vine** (32b), **vino** (92d,182b), **vint** (26c,182c), **viny, viol** (105a), **Vira** (191), **vire** (11a,13b), **visa** (114d), **vise** (31d,77d,114d), **viss** (189), **vita** (89c, 92a), **vite** (62b), **viti** (176b), **viva** (93d), **vive** (93d), **vivo** (93a)

- VI - **avid** (47b,71a,186b), **avis** (89a), **Avis** (183c), **evil** (79c,95d,147a, 181a,185c), **Ovid** (132d,133b), **Ovis** (143d), **uvic** (70c), **uvid** (101a)

- - VI **Devi** (147b,153b), **divi, favi** (138a,165d), **hevi** (111d), **Kavi** (84d), **Levi** (84a,90c), **ravi** (61b), **Ravi** (16b)

V - - I **vagi** (38b), **vali** (171a,176a), **Vali** (7c,109c), **vari** (34d,91b,134d, 174d), **veri** (28b), **vili** (54b), **Vili** (109c), **viti** (176b), **vlei** (38c,160a)

V - - K **volk** (66c,105d,116a,184c)

VL - - **vlei** (38c,160a), **vley** (160a)

V - - L **vail** (94b,124a,174b), **veal, veil,** (74d,76c), **vial** (148c), **vill** (176b), **viol** (105a)

V - - N **vain** (81a), **vein** (20d,157b), **vuln** (184d)

VO - - **voce** (83c,177a), **voet** (188), **Vogt, void** (11a,49d,108d,174b), **vola** (89d,150a), **vole** (97d,104a,148a,149b), **volk** (66c,105d,116a,184c), **volt** (49b,78c,173b), **voog** (28a,66a,132b), **vota** (133b), **vote** (60b), **Vote** (56d), **Voth** (191), **Voto** (192)

- VO - **Avon** (143b), **Avow** (6d,36a,41c,112c), **evoe** (15b,130d,181c)

- - VO **levo** (91a), **pavo** (115b), **Pavo** (36b,c), **vivo** (93a)

V - - O **velo** (175b), **veto** (94a,124a), **Veto, vino** (92d,182b), **vivo** (93a), **Voto** (192)

V - - P **vamp** (80a,145a)

V - - R **vair** (64c,154c), **veer** (28d,144c,171b), **vier** (66c)

- - VS **revs** (131a)

V - - S **Vans** (107d), **Veps** (191), **viss** (189)

V - - T **vast** (78d,79d), **vent** (8b,11b,110d,112a), **vert** (71d,166a,171b),

	vest (32c,177b), **vint** (26c,182c), **voet** (188), **Vogt, volt** (49b,78c, 173b)
VU - -	**vugg** (28a,66a,132b), **vugh** (28a,66a,132b), **vuln** (184d)
- VU -	**avus** (89b), **ovum** (48d)
- - VU	**kivu** (170c)
V - - U	**vasu** (106c), **Vasu** (176d), **Vayu** (68c,182a)
V - - W	**view** (93d,138b)
V - - X	**Vaux** (63b)
- - VY	**bevy** (38a,58c), **cavy** (72b,120d,132c,157b), **cuvy** (141a), **Davy** (96b,136b), **envy** (41b), **levy** (14a,162b), **Livy** (132d,133a), **navy** (33c,58b), **pavy** (115b), **pevy** (91d,94c), **Tavy** (183d), **wavy** (147b, 172d)
V - - Y	**vary** (28d,43c), **very** (149c), **vily** (54b), **viny, vley** (160a)
WA - -	**Waac, waag** (71d,101d), **Wabi** (192), **Waco, wadd** (109c), **wade, wadi** (46c,106a,109a,128a,132a), **wady** (109a,128a,132a), **waeg** (19b,72c,87a), **waer** (40b), **Wafd** (49a), **waft** (20d,58c), **wage** (27a, 115b), **waif** (157b), **wail** (39b,88a), **wain** (177b), **Wain, wait** (26d, 42b,92c,155d,162a), **waka** (26a), **wake** (134b,168a), **wakf** (103a), **waky, wale** (70b,131b,157c,163d,179a,180a,c,d), **wali** (171a), **walk, wall, Walt** (96b), **wand** (120b,132c,156a), **wane** (41c,43c), **wang** (189), **want** (41b,42d,87b,106b,122a), **wany, wapp** (54b,133d, 145d), **waqf** (103a), **ward** (31c,55c,86b), **ware** (27d,35a), **warf, warm** (7c,75b,163b), **warn** (7b), **warp** (36c,165a,171c), **wart** (124d), **wary** (27d,176b), **wash, wasp, wast, Wate** (141a), **watt** (173b, 177c), **Watt** (82a), **wave** (19a,59a,111c,131d,160c,172d), **wavy** (147b,172d), **waxy** (119c,149d), **ways**
- WA -	**Awan** (191), **away** (6b,69d,76a,109d,111d), **Ewan, kwan** (30b), **swab** (102b), **swad** (94d), **swag** (22a,156c), **swam, swan** (19b,33a), **swap** (168a), **swat** (15d,20d,32d,157c), **Swat** (103a), **sway** (104a)
- - WA	**biwa** (93d,168c), **dewa, lowa** (193), **kawa** (18c,116a), **lowa** (19a), **pawa** (189), **tawa** (160d,168c), **Tewa** (193)
W - - A	**waka** (26a), **Wega** (155b), **weka** (58c,106d,107a,127b), **weta** (93c), **whoa** (156d)
W - - C	**Waac**
- - WD	**dowd** (143b), **gawd** (169c)
W - - D	**wadd** (109c), **Wafd** (49a), **wand** (120b,132c,156a), **ward** (31c,55c, 86b), **week, weld** (47c,85b,173c), **wend** (67d,123d), **Wend** (10b, 148a), **wild** (38b,173d), **wind** (33b,39d,171c,185a), **woad** (20d,47c), **wold** (47c,60a,118d,174a,184a), **wood, word** (124b,165c), **Wurd, Wyrd** (107d)
WE - -	**weak** (55b), **weal** (124d,157c,180c,d), **wean** (8d,42d), **wear** (50b), **weed, week, weel** (16d,57d,140d,180d), **weep** (39b,88a,104a), **weet** (19d), **weft** (39a,165a,184b), **Wega** (155b), **Wegg** (111d), **weir** (40b,57d), **weka** (58c,106d,107a,127b), **weki** (55c), **weld** (47c,85b, 173c), **Welf** (67a), **welk** (65c,96d,141b), **well welt** (36d,131b,145a, b,177b,d), **wend** (67d,123d), **Wend** (10b,148a), **went** (42c), **wept, were** (139b), **werf** (54d), **weri** (15c,27c), **wert, west, West** (9c,50b, 109b), **weta** (93c)

-WE- **ewer** (84d,85c,118c,181b), **kwei** (44a), **Owen** (96a,183c), **sweb** (160d), **twee**

--WE **howe** (77d), **Howe** (17a,82a), **powe**

W--E **wade**, **wage** (27a,115b), **wake** (134b,168a), **wale** (70b,131b,157c, 163d,179a,180a,c,d), **wane** (41c,43c), **ware** (27d,35a), **Wate** (141a), **wave** (19a,59a,111c,131d,160c,172d), **were** (139b), **whee**, **wide** (133d), **wife** (154a), **wile** (13b,41c,157b,169c), **wine**, **wipe**, **wire**, **wise** (136b), **wive** (97a), **woke**, **wore**, **Wote** (191), **wove**

W--F **waif** (157b), **wakf** (103a), **waqf** (103a), **warf**, **Welf** (67a), **werf** (54d), **wolf**, **woof** (39a,163d,165a,179d), **Wraf**, **wukf** (103a)

W--G **waag** (71d,101d), **waeg** (19b,72c,87a), **wang** (189), **Wegg** (111d), **Whig** **wigg**, **wing** (10d,58c,59a,118b,d), **wong** (56a)

WH-- **wham** (157c), **what** (129c), **whau** (107a,168c), **whee!**, **when** (180d), **whet** (143c,156b), **whew**, **whey** (100a), **Whig**, **whim** (26c, 54c,108c), **whin** (64c,70a,132b,181d), **whip** (58c,88d), **whir** (25c, 181a), **whit** (166c), **whiz** (25c), **whoa** (156d), **whom** (42b), **whoo!**, **whun** (64c,70a), **whyo** (59d,65a)

--WH **JHWH** (159d), **YHWH** (159c)

W--H **wash**, **wish** (42d), **with** (10b)

WI-- **wick**, **wide** (133d), **widu** (102d), **wiel** (140d,180d), **wies** (185a), **wife** (154a), **wigg**, **wild** (38b,173d), **wile** (13b,41c,157b,169c), **wilk** (65c,96d,141b), **will** (18b,43a,163c,177c), **wilt** (46b), **wily** (13b,38b,39c), **wind** (33b,39d,171c,185a), **wine**, **wing** (10d,58c, 59a,118b,d), **wink** (107a), **winy** (176c), **wipe**, **wire**, **wiry** (147a, 167c), **wise** (136b), **wish** (42d), **wisp** (24b,148c), **wist** (87c), **with** (10b), **wive** (97a)

-WI- **swig** (46a,72c), **swim** (58c), **swiz** (160c), **twig**, **twin** (45c,171d), **twit** (162b,c)

--WI **iiwi** (19a,74b), **Kawi** (84d), **kiwi** (11d,19a,58c), **tuwi** (117a,168c)

W--I **Wabi** (192), **wadi** (46c,106a,109a,128a,132a), **wali** (171a), **weki** (55c), **weri** (15c,27c)

--WK **bowk** (155d), **cawk** (133c), **dawk** (95c), **gawk** (146d), **gowk** (146d), **hawk** (19c,115c), **sawk** (188)

W--K **walk**, **weak** (55b), **week**, **welk** (65c,96d,141b), **wick**, **wilk** (65c, 96d,141b), **wink** (107a), **work** (64c,76b)

--WL **bawl**, **bowl**, **cowl** (101d), **dowl**, **fowl**, **gowl** (102a,140d,185b), **howl** (39b), **jowl** (29b), **mewl** (180d), **pawl** (43a,95a), **yawl** (136b,171d, 175d), **yowl**

W--L **wail** (39b,88a), **wall**, **weal** (124d,157c,180c,d), **weel** (16d,57d,140d, 180d), **well**, **wiel** (140d,180d), **will** (18b,43a,163c,177c), **wool** (58b, 179c)

--WM **dawm** (190)

W--M **warm** (7c,75b,163b), **wham** (157c), **whim** (26c,54c,108c), **whom** (42b), **worm**, **wurm** (67c),

--WN **bawn** (181a), **dawn** (14d,41b), **down** (149d), **fawn** (33c), **gown**, **hewn**, **kawn** (93d), **lawn** (20a,37c,53b,92c), **lown** (157d), **mown**, **pawn** (29c,119c), **sawn**, **sewn**, **town** (73c), **yawn**

W--N **wain** (177b), **Wain**, **warn** (7b), **wean** (8d,42d), **when** (180d), **whin**

	(64c,70a,132b,181d), **whun** (64c,70a), **woon** (24c), **worn** (143b), **wren** (19b,c), **Wren** (50b), **wynn** (165d)
WO - -	**woad** (20d,47c), **woke**, **wold** (47c,60a,118d,174a,184a), **wolf**, **wong** (56a), **wont** (6d,40a,73a,174c), **wood woof** (39a,163d,165a, 179d), **wool** (58b,179c), **woon** (24c), **word** (124b,165c), **wore**, **work** (64c,76b), **worm**, **worn** (143b), **wort** (76a,95d,121d), **Wote** (191), **wove**
- WO -	**Lwow**, **swob** (102b), **swop** (168a), **swot**, **swow** (100a)
W - - O	**Waco**, **whoo**, **whyo** (59d,65a)
- - WP	**gawp**, **lowp** (90c,139d), **yawp**
W - - P	**wapp** (54b,133d,145d), **warp** (36c,165a,171c), **wasp**, **weep** (39b, 88a,104a), **whip** (58c,88d), **wisp** (24b,148c), **wrap** (32b,51a)
WR - -	**Wraf**, **wrap** (32b,51a), **wren** (19b,c), **Wren** (50b), **writ** (91a)
- WR -	**awry** (13d,38d,171c), **ewry** (133c)
W - - R	**waer** (40b), **wear** (50b), **weir** (40b,57d), **whir** (25c,181a)
- WS -	**owse**
- - WS	**mews** (154c), **news** (165c)
W - - S	**ways**, **wies** (185a)
- - WT	**newt** (48d,136c,169d), **nowt** (106a,139a), **yowt** (139c)
W - - T	**waft** (20d,58c), **wait** (26d,42b,92c,155d,162a), **Walt** (96b), **want** (41b,42d,87b,106b,122a), **wart** (124d), **wast**, **watt** (173b,177c), **Watt** (82a), **weet** (19d), **weft** (39a,165a,184b), **welt** (36d,131b, 145a,b,177b,d), **went** (42c), **wept**, **wert**, **west**, **West** (9c,50b,109b), **what** (129c), **whet** (143c,156b), **whit** (166c), **wilt** (46b), **wist** (87c), **wont** (6d,40a,73a,174c), **wort** (76a,95d,121d), **writ** (91a)
WU - -	**wudu** (102d), **wukf** (103a), **Wurd**, **wurm** (67c), **wuzu** (102d)
- WU -	**swum**
W - - U	**whau** (107a,168c), **widu** (102d), **wudu** (102d), **wuzu** (102d)
W - - W	**whew!**
WY - -	**wynn** (165d), **Wyrd** (107d)
- WY -	**Gwyn** (40c,50b)
- - WY	**dewy** (101a), **jawy**, **nowy** (194), **rowy** (157b), **towy** (58b)
W - - Y	**wady** (109a,128a,132a), **waky**, **wany**, **wary** (27d,176b), **wavy** (147b,172d), **waxy** (119c,149d), **whey** (100a), **wily** (13b,38b,39c), **winy** (176c), **wiry** (147a,167c)
W - - Z	**whiz** (25c)
- XA -	**axal** (120b), **exam**, **oxan** (65c)
- - XA	**Bixa** (145d), **coxa** (77b), **doxa** (48b), **moxa** (27d,30c), **myxa** (168c, 169a), **noxa**, **toxa** (153d)
X - - A	**xema** (72c), **Xema** (12c), **Xina** (183d), **Xosa** (86a), **Xova** (193)
XE - -	**xema** (72c), **Xema** (12c), **xeno** (34d)
- XE -	**oxea** (153d), **oxen** (10c), **oxer** (55c)
- - XE	**luxe** (61c,62d,159c), **Mixe** (192), **saxe** (20d,33c)
X - - E	**Xipe** (15c)
XI - -	**Xina** (183d), **Xipe** (15c)

- XI - **axil** (10c), **axis** (28b,41d,77c,153c), **exit** (114d), **ixia** (37a), **Ixil** (192), **oxid** (112c)

- - XI **dixi**, **taxi** (13a,125b)

- XL - **axle** (153c,180c), **ixle** (56a)

XM - - **Xmas**

XO - - **Xosa** (86a), **Xova** (193)

- XO - **axon** (106c,153c)

- - XO **Moxo** (192), **myxo**, **taxo** (13a)

X - - O **xeno** (34d), **xylo** (35a,183d)

X - - S **Xmas**

- - XT **next** (106a), **sext** (26b,111b,147b), **text** (21c,140d)

XY - - **xylo** (35a,183d)

- XY - **oxyl** (112c)

- - XY **boxy**, **buxy** (115b), **doxy** (129d), **foxy** (38b,39c,181d), **mixy**, **pixy** (154b), **puxy**, **Roxy** (183d), **waxy** (119c,149d)

YA - - **yage** (23a), **yaje** (23a), **Yaka** (191), **Yaki** (193), **Yale** (173c), **yali** (171a), **Yama** (57a,68a), **Yana** (192,193), **yang** (30b,70a), **yank**, **Yank**, **Yaou** (30c), **yapa** (113b), **Yapp** (22a), **yard** (152d), **yare** (96b,124b,128b), **yark** (22c), **yarl** (40d,107d), **yarn** (154b,161b, 184b), **yarr** (72a), **Yaru** (48d), **yate** (51d,168c), **yati** (76d), **yaup**, **yava**, **yawl** (136b,171d,175d), **yawn**, **yawp**, **yaya** (113c,168c)

- YA - **ayah** (108d), **cyan**, **dyad** (113a), **Dyak** (22b), **Dyas** (66a), **eyah** (95b, 108d,111c), **eyas** (106c,173a), **Iyar** (102b), **kyah** (19a), **kyak** (51c), **kyar** (33a), **kyat** (189), **lyam** (139a), **Lyas** (66a), **pyal** (175c), **pyat** (95b), **ryal** (110a,190)

- - YA **Alya** (155b,c), **Arya** (80d), **baya** (179b), **Baya** (191), **cuya** (39b), **Goya** (151d), **Hoya** (14d), **maya** (77a,179b), **Maya** (23d,186c), **Puya** (118b), **raya** (19b,23c,76d,107d), **saya** (117a), **soya** (151b), **yaya** (113c,168c)

Y - - A **Yaka** (191), **Yama** (57a,68a), **Yana** (192,193), **yapa** (113b), **yava**, **yaya** (113c,168c), **yeta** (84c), **Yima** (84a,116b,c), **Ynca** (193), **yoga** (10b,13c,77a), **yuca** (27a), **Yuga** (76d), **Yuma**

- YB - **gybe** (144c), **Tybi** (102a)

- YC - **syce** (71d)

- YD - **hyde** (188), **Hyde** (45a)

- - YD **emyd** (163c,167c)

Y - - D **yard** (152d), **yond** (164d)

YE - - **yeah**, **yean** (88a), **year**, **yeas** (177c), **Yedo** (166d), **yegg** (24c), **yell** (145c), **yelp**, **yelt** (151b), **yeni** (19b,161d), **yeso** (72d), **yeta** (84c)

- YE - **ayes** (177c), **byee** (189), **dyer**, **eyer**, **eyey** (74b), **oyer** (38a,75b, 119c), **oyes** (38a,39b,75b), **oyez** (38a,39b,75b), **pyet** (95b), **ryel** (190), **syed** (103b), **tyee** (29d), **tyer**

- - YE **Daye** (123d), **Skye** (163c)

Y - - E **yage** (23a), **yaje** (23a), **Yale** (173c), **yare** (96b,124b,128b), **yate** (51d,168c), **yoke** (85b,92d,173c), **yore** (10b,69d,93c,110b,165d), **Yule** (30d)

- YG -	**bygo** (114c), **zyga** (134b)
Y - - G	**yang** (30b,70a), **yegg** (24c)
YH - -	**YHVH** (159d), **YHWH** (159d)
Y - - H	**yeah**, **YHVH** (159d), **YHWH** (159d), **yodh** (91d), **yogh** (10c,185a)
YI - -	**Yima** (84a,116b,c)
- YI -	**ayin** (91c)
- - YI	**kiyi** (185d)
Y - - I	**Yaki** (193), **yali** (171a), **yati** (76d), **yeni** (19b,161d), **Yobi**, **yogi** (76d)
- YK -	**cyke** (40c), **dyke** (49c,91d), **fyke** (15d), **hyke!**, **syke** (194), **tyke** (29d)
Y - - K	**yank**, **Yank**, **yark** (22c), **yolk**, **york** (38c), **York** (50b,c)
- YL -	**gyle** (23b,174d), **Hyla** (10a,166d,169b), **hyle** (97c), **kyle** (57a, 139c), **pyla** (22d), **pyle** (34b), **Pyle** (9c,178a), **Xylo** (35a,183d)
- - YL	**acyl** (6d), **amyl** (155c), **idyl** (114d), **noyl** (87c), **odyl** (59d,79c), **oxyl** (112c), **teyl** (92b,c,168c)
Y - - L	**yarl** (40d,107d), **yawl** (136b,171d,175d), **yell** (145c), **yowl**, **ypil** (117a,168c)
YM - -	**Ymer** (67a,131c), **Ymir** (67a,131c)
- YM -	**cyma** (101a,b), **cyme** (58d,69c), **hymn** (150c), **ryme** (178d), **tymp** (20c), **zyme** (55c)
- - YM	**clym** (12b), **etym** (133d), **onym** (162c)
YN - -	**Ynca** (193)
- YN -	**dyna** (34c), **dyne** (59d,173b), **gyne** (34b,55b,183c), **jynx** (78a), **Jynx** (184a), **lynx** (26c,181d), **Lynx** (36b), **myna** (19a,c,70b), **rynd** (100a), **syne** (140b,147a), **tyne**, **Tyne** (108a), **wynn** (165d)
- - YN	**coyn** (37a), **Gwyn** (40c,50b), **llyn** (120d,140a)
Y - - N	**yarn** (154b,161b,184b), **yawn**, **yean** (88a), **yuan** (190), **Yuan** (30b, 101d)
YO - -	**Yobi**, **yodh** (91d), **yoga** (10b,13c,77a), **yogh** (10c,185a), **yogi** (76d), **yoke** (85b,92d,173c), **yolk**, **yond** (164d), **yoop**, **yore** (10b,69d,93c, 110b,165d), **york** (38c), **York** (50b,c), **youp** (185d), **your** (124c), **yowl**, **yowt** (139c)
- YO -	**eyot** (82d), **ryot** (115c)
- - YO	**buyo** (18b), **cayo**, **coyo** (15a,30c), **Enyo** (12c,69c,178a), **Idyo** (191), **kayo** (87c), **Mayo** (193), **whyo** (59d,65a)
Y - - O	**Yedo** (166d), **yeso** (72d)
YP - -	**ypil** (117a,168c)
- YP -	**gyps**, **Gyps** (71d), **hype** (185a), **hypo** (117b), **hyps**, **rype** (19b,125a), **sype** (110c), **type** (31d,115a,155a), **typo** (35c,51b), **typp** (185b), **typy**
- - YP	**tryp** (114a)
Y - - P	**Yapp** (22a), **yaup**, **yawp**, **yelp**, **yoop**, **youp** (185d)
- YR -	**Byrd** (9c,120b), **byre** (38a), **eyra** (181d), **eyre** (23c,31b,85c), **Eyre**, **eyry** (47b,106c), **fyrd** (110a), **gyre** (31b,171b), **gyri** (22d,

131b), **gyro** (34d), **Lyra** (36b,74a), **lyre** (11c,81c,105a,111c), **Myra** (10a,31b,183c), **pyre** (64c), **pyro**, **Syra**, **tyre** (15a), **Tyre** (31b,90d, 117b), **tyro** (9b,17d,108c), **Tyrr** (68c,109c,163d,178a), **Wyrd** (107d)

- - YR **skyr** (21d,151a)

Y - - R **yarr** (72a), **year**, **Ymer** (67a,131c), **Ymir** (67a,131c), **your** (124c), **Yser**

YS - - **Yser**

- YS - **cyst**, **lyse**, **myst** (71c,123b)

- - YS **Alys** (183c), **Emys** (167c,171b), **days**, **Itys** (163b), **ways**

Y - - S **yeas** (177c)

- YT - **myth** (8b,91a), **Tyto** (16c)

- - YT **skyt** (138c,140b)

Y - - T **yelt** (151b), **yowt** (139c), **yuft** (135c), **Yuit** (51c), **yurt** (101d)

YU - - **yuan** (190), **Yuan** (30b,101d), **yuca** (27a), **yuft** (135c), **Yuga** (76d), **Yuit** (51c), **Yule** (30d), **Yuma**, **Yunx** (184a), **yurt** (101d), **yutu** (19b,166a)

- YU - **syud** (103b)

- - YU **Vayu** (68c,182a)

Y - - U **Yaou** (30c), **Yaru** (48d), **yutu** (19b,166a)

- YV - **gyve** (55d,143b)

- YX - **myxa** (168c,169a), **myxo**

- - YX **Ceyx** (73b), **eryx** (137a), **onyx** (25d,28d,65d,142b), **oryx** (11a), **Pnyx** (71c), **Styx** (29b,73a,105c)

Y - - X **Yunx** (184a)

- - YZ **hayz**

ZA - - **Zach** (96b), **zaim** (170d), **zain** (41a), **Zama** (73d,141d), **zany** (24a, 32d,59c), **zarf** (39c,155a), **zarp** (120c), **zati** (21d)

- ZA - **Azam** (166c), **azan** (102d), **czar** (42d,49d,60b,135c), **izar** (65b, 103b), **Izar** (155b), **tzar** (42d,49d,60b,135c), **Uzan** (189)

- - ZA **boza** (12a), **caza**, **Daza** (191), **Gaza** (117a), **Itza** (192), **Juza** (155b), **onza** (189), **tiza** (172a), **tuza** (119d), **vaza** (114a), **zuza** (189)

Z - - A **Zama** (73d,141d), **zeta** (71b,91c), **Zipa** (29d), **zira** (188), **Zola** (63a), **zona** (144c,186d), **zuza** (189), **zyga** (134b)

- ZB - **ezba** (188)

Z - - B **Zimb** (6c)

Z - - C **zinc** (21a)

Z - - D **Zend**, **zoid**

ZE - - **zeal** (12c,55d), **zebu** (22d,80d,112c), **zein**, **Zeke** (96b), **zeme** (55d,161b,180b), **zemi** (55d,161b,180b), **Zend**, **Zeno** (71b), **zenu** (143d), **zero** (31a,84c,108c), **Zero** (118d), **zest** (55d,72d), **zeta** (71b,91c), **Zeus** (135a)

- ZE - **ezel** (47a,85d)

- - ZE **adze** (40c,167a), **bize** (182a), **coze** (29b), **daze** (157d), **doze** (148a), **faze** (43d), **fuze** (98c), **gaze**, **guze** (128d), **haze** (100c,174d), **laze** (79b), **Laze** (191), **maze** (87b,157d), **naze** (26b,124b), **noze** (75a), ooze (53c,104b,116a), raze (42b,d,91d), size, unze (189)

Z - - E Zeke (96b), zeme (55d,161b,180b), zone (44c,50a,160a), zyme (55c)

Z - - F zarf (39c,155a)

Z - - G zing

- ZH - Azha (155b)

Z - - H Zach (96b)

ZI - - Zimb (6c), zinc (21a), zing, Zion (75b,c,83a,157d), Zipa (29d), zipp, Zips (40c), zira (188), zizz (181a)

- - ZI cazi (103a), gazi, kazi (103a), Lazi (191), Nazi

Z - - I zati (21d), zemi (55d,161b,180b), Zuni (125b)

Z - - L zeal (12c,55d)

Z - - M zaim (170d), zoom

Z - - N zain (41a), zein, Zion (75b,c,83a,157d), zoon (43a)

ZO - - Zoar, Zoas (20b), zobo (186b), zodi, zogo (136a), zoid, Zola (63a), zona (144c,186d), zone (44c,50a,160a), zoom, zoon (43a)

- ZO - Azof (20b,135d), azon (127b), Azov (20b,135d), mozo (152b), Muzo (192)

- - ZO bozo (55b), Idzo (191), kozo (113d,168c), lazo (88d,128b,133d)

Z - - O Zeno (71b), zero (31a,84c,108c), Zero (118d), zobo (186b), zogo (136a)

Z - - P zarp (120c), zipp

- ZR - Ezra (96a)

Z - - R Zoar

Z - - S Zeus (135a), Zips (40c), Zoas (20b)

Z - - T zest (55d,72d)

ZU - - zulu (171d,175d), Zulu (86a), Zuni (125b), zuza (189)

- ZU - azul (151d)

- - ZU anzu (11d), auzu (168c,180b), Enzu (102b), wuzu (102d)

Z - - U zebu (22d,80d,112c), zenu (143d), zulu (171d,175d), Zulu (86a)

ZY - - zyga (134b), zyme (55c)

- - ZY cazy (103a), cozy (149c), dazy, dozy, gazy, hazy (174b), Jozy, kazy (103a), lazy, oozy (148b), sizy (176d)

Z - - Y zany (24a,32d,59c)

- - ZZ bizz, buzz, fuzz (45d), huzz, jazz, razz (131b), sizz, zizz (181a)

Z - - Z zizz (181a)